Music in
European Capitals

Antonio Bucchi inv.   Wagner sc. Venezia C.P.E.S.

Europa mia tra l'altre tue sorelle   *Perche il mondo ha da dir tutte son belle,*

Quanto piu sai superba ergi la testa; L'EUROPA   *Ma in ogni età la mia Regina è questa.*

FUR 3·11

Music in European Capitals

The Galant Style

1720–1780

Daniel Heartz

W · W · NORTON & COMPANY

NEW YORK   LONDON

For information about permission to reproduce selections from this book, write to
Permissions, W. W. Norton & Company, Inc., 500 Fifth Avenue, New York, NY 10110

Manufacturing by Maple-Vail Book Manufacturing Group
Book design by Margaret M. Wagner
Production manager: Julia Druskin

Library of Congress Cataloging-in-Publication Data

Heartz, Daniel.
Music in European capitals : the galant style, 1720–1780 / Daniel Heartz.—1st ed.
p. cm.
Includes bibliographical references (p.   ) and index.
ISBN 0-393-05080-7
1. Music—Europe—18th century—History and criticism. I. Title.
ML240.3 .H43 2003
780' .9'032—dc21

2002015693

W. W. Norton & Company, Inc., 500 Fifth Avenue, New York, N.Y. 10110
www.wwnorton.com

W. W. Norton & Company Ltd., Castle House, 75/76 Wells Street, London W1T 3QT

1 2 3 4 5 6 7 8 9 0

For
CLAIRE BROOK

in memory of
BARRY S. BROOK

Contents

List of Illustrations

FRONTISPIECE. Antonio Zucchi. *L'Europa*, engraved by Joseph Wagner.

Figures

Credits

Fig. 9.9: Budenheim, Germany, Collection of Dr. Gerhard Christmann. Fig. 6.5: Copenhagen, Statens museum for Kunst, SMK Foto. Figs. 1.4, 4.1, 4.8: Dresden, Staatliche Kunstsammlungen. Fig. 2.10: Florence, Collection of Alan Curtis. Hamburg, Hamburger Kunsthalle. Photographer: Elke Walford, Hamburg. Fig. 1.8: Hartford, Wadsworth Atheneum. Figs. 5.8, 5.9, 5.15: Mannheim, Reiss Museum. Fig. 2.7: Naples, Conservatorio di Musica S. Pietro Magella. Fig. 1.5: New York, Collection of Janos Scholz. Fig. 6.7: New York Metropolitan Museum of Art. Fig. 7.8: Paris, Cliché Bibliothêque nationale de France. Fig 2.2: Rohrau, Austria, Graf Harrach'sche Familiensammlung A-2471 Schloss Rohrau. NO. Fig. 8.7: Kungl Biblioteket. Sverignes nationalbibliotek.

List of Color Plates

Following page 264

Preface

I BEGAN work on this volume in 1975 then set it aside during the 1980s in order to write its companion, *Haydn, Mozart and the Viennese School 1740–1780*, which was published in 1995. Returning to work on the earlier project I found the original chapters of some use but rewrote them almost entirely. Not only had research uncovered much new evidence during the intervening years, but also my ideas had changed about how to situate the galant style in the history of eighteenth-century music. This style became for me a crucial element that moved the tonal art ahead and led the way to its next phase.

The book required an expansion of viewpoint beyond musicology's traditional fixation on Bach and Handel. It invited a rethinking from the point of view of eighteenth-century values. We cannot pretend to escape the intellectual heritage of the last two centuries, but let us at least attempt to understand the *settecento* on its own terms. I propose for a start to restore honor to the concept "artificial" by invoking its primary meaning: "made by art or artifice as a substitute for nature." The castrato's art provides a fine example. Schiller referred to preceding times (in *Die Räuber*, 1782) as "the century of the castrato," and he knew whereof he spoke.

Charles Burney, the lodestar of this volume, was a city man, one who late in life decried Wordsworth's paeans to rural solitude as inimical to civil society. The countryside held no romance for Burney, nor did it for his hero Metastasio, the poet he admired the most. The latter wrote a rich trove of letters to his dear "twin" Farinelli that Burney translated and published. After two decades of singing in Spain, where he amassed a fortune and rose to the status of a prime minister,

Farinelli retired to a luxurious villa in Bologna. Burney visited him there in 1770, an occasion the Englishman treasured and recorded in delightful detail. In a letter to Farinelli dated Vienna, 30 November 1768, Metastasio cautioned the singer to avoid "the autumnal exhalations, and the poisonous vapours of a great part of our country." Life was more healthy and pleasant within walls: "the air of paved cities is much less impregnated with this poison, not only from the exhalations of the earth being impeded, but from the numerous and constant fires, as well as the motions of the inhabitants, which agitate and correct the air." In other letters the poet wrote disparagingly, "I hardly know a nettle from a thistle" and said he greatly preferred rococo art to anything produced by antiquity.

Today's gladiators of ideological correctness would consider Metastasio ecologically challenged, shockingly insensitive to eternal aesthetic values. Yet his way of thinking had potent allies. Boucher, *premier peintre du roi*, complained that nature was "too green, and badly lit." He made up for these perceived imperfections by using pastel shades and painting stage scenery that, necessarily, had dimmer, more flattering lighting. The great naturalist Bouffon, who created the Jardin des Plantes in Paris and published an *Histoire naturelle* in forty-four volumes, was repelled by nature in the raw and determined to shape it more to his liking: "Brute Nature is hideous and dying; I, and I alone, can render her pleasant and living." Giving pleasure!—here is a notion central to the new meanings lent the term *galant* by the eighteenth century.

The era was little swayed by nationalism. It was, above all, cosmopolitan. Cities came into their own and often outshone courts. Even in decidedly autocratic Vienna, Metastasio made a point of describing in his letters what pleased the city, not just the court, for example, in relating the success of his *Didone abbadonata* as set to music by Jommelli (letter of 13 December 1749).

From the book's very beginnings I decided to concentrate on capital cities. One of my earliest and most astute critics, the late Barry Brook, disputed me on this point, saying I should encompass all France, not just Paris (and presumably all of Italy and all of Germany as well). It might have been possible three generations ago, I countered, but was no longer feasible, at least not for me. In order to consolidate my smaller canvas I have even excluded some of the largest and most bustling cities. Commercial capitals such as Hamburg and Amsterdam are absent because, bereft of opera, they lacked the prime driving force of musical modernity. The choice of capitals was based not on political or historic importance, but on which cities were most important in the creation and diffusion of new music. Once these were selected, the major task was to mediate between the conflicting claims of geography, chronology, and musical topics.

Enlightenment is a concept associated with the era's intellectual history. Its meaning varied in different places; generally it signified a quest for knowledge and more openness to the world at large. Enlightenment imagery, like that of the

Freemasons, often depicted the arts and sciences, with some reference to the "life-giving orb of day" (the sun) or to our planet. The sun beams its rays on a scene of industry in the seal of the American Academy of Arts and Sciences, granted its charter by the Legislature of Massachusetts on 4 May 1780, its aim being "to cultivate every art and science which may tend to advance the interest, honor, dignity, and happiness of a free, independent, and virtuous people." The academy's alphabetical list of charter members began with the names of John and Samuel Adams.

The frontispiece of this volume, Antonio Zucchi's *L'Europa*, evokes the arts and sciences as well as showing a globe of the world. Its image first came into my possession as an unsigned painting for which I have my colleague Alan Curtis to thank (he traded it for a rare image of Handel I owned). I urged him to find the engraving made from the painting, the shadowy existence of which was known to us only by a few clues. One day while walking in Padua's center he saw Wagner's engraving of Zucchi's painting in a shop window and acquired it for me. I can never thank Alan enough for what he has meant to this book as a scholar, performer, and advisor. I am indebted to him also for his droll caricature of Jommelli by Ghezzi reproduced here (Figure 2.10 on p. 146). Ghezzi ends his inscription stating that he made the effigy for Metastasio. Metastasio must have sent it to Farinelli in Madrid, Alan points out, because it landed in the Spanish royal collection, before it went as a spoils of war to the duke of Wellington, whence it eventually came on the market. Thus do three of my major figures—poet, composer, and singer—convene in one story.

Assembling a picture collection with which to illustrate the book has been one of my most pleasant pastimes over the long course of its gestation and has occupied me scarcely less than collecting the pertinent music and works written about it. Vernet's sweeping view of the Bay of Naples and Mount Vesuvius (book jacket) first came to me in the form of a postcard from Claire Brook announcing that she agreed to accept an award in my stead for *Haydn, Mozart and the Viennese School*. I interpreted her choice as an admonition to get busy and finish this book, like Aeneas being warned, "On to Italy!"

Another pleasant task remains, and that is to thank those who have offered help and advice over the years. If I forget some it is not for lack of gratitude but due to the span of time involved, which clouds my memory. Among the earliest readers, besides the aforementioned, was Bruce Alan Brown, who contributed his expertise on the eighteenth century even as a graduate student assistant when the first chapters were being sketched. Bruce has never since then ceased to answer questions, send requested materials, and give sound advice. Colin Slim, whose treasured friendship goes back to our graduate student days together, has also answered urgent requests for material (when something was missing from the libraries here it could usually be found slumbering on some shelf in southern California). I have had the benefit of help from many foremost scholars in their special fields of study: Marita McClymonds on Jommelli and Kathleen Hansell on Noverre; the Mannheim experts Paul Corneilson and Eugene K. Wolf; John Rice on Italian opera; Sven Hansell on Hasse; Dale Monson on Pergolesi; Charles Carroll on Philidor; David Charlton on Grétry; Elisabeth LeGuin on Boccherini; and David Fuller on keyboard music.

The burden of transforming my typed pages into technologically viable copy fell upon the ever-resourceful Robert Fallon, who offered many useful criticisms during the process. Michael Zwiebach engraved the musical examples and offered further help as the author of a doctoral dissertation on the comic operas of Paisiello. Cartographer Cherri Northon drew the map that opens Chapter 5. The Music Library and the staff on the Berkeley campus were unfailingly helpful. I am indebted to the Research Committee of the University Senate for many grants-in-aid and also to the Guggenheim Foundation for two fellowships, all in pursuit of the same goal.

The Brooks never wavered in their support from the project's outset. Barry returned the chapters I sent him richly annotated with suggestions for improvement. Claire's keen knowledge of the eighteenth century and experience as an editor combined to set me going and keep me on course. The book's text finally reached the publisher at a time of transition and change of command in the music office. The outgoing and incoming editors agreed to recall Claire to editing duty if she could be persuaded once again. Fortunately for me, she accepted the challenge. My dedication of the book renders thanks the best way an author can.

Daniel Heartz
Berkeley, California
April 2002

Music in
European Capitals

1

Prologue: Three Rococo Idylls

Watteau, *Galant* Cynosure

THE new style of music that emerged early in the eighteenth century sounded against a background of marked changes in culture and society. In order to explore these changes I have chosen to begin by presenting individuals of diverse callings: an artist (Watteau), a poet (Metastasio), a singer (Farinelli), and a historian (Burney). Composers will come later, with few exceptions, in the chapters that follow.

Several general concepts compete for lending a name to the period 1720–80. The main ones are Enlightenment, a philosophical movement; rococo, from art history; and the galant style, from music history. Choosing the last as the subtitle of the book was not done without giving the others serious consideration. All three are intertwined throughout.

Rococo style originated as a light, arabesque kind of decoration in late-seventeenth-century France. It spread widely during the first half of the eighteenth century. Art historians have extended it, sometimes with reluctance, to include much French art of the period, beginning with Watteau. An Italian equivalent flourished especially among Venetian artists. Neoclassical art, with its straight lines and geometrical shapes, gradually supplanted curvilinear caprices by the 1760s, although the charms of the rococo style lingered longer in some quarters.

Enlightenment is best understood in its literal, etymological sense as a movement spreading light to the intellect. It celebrated the power of knowledge in liberating the human spirit. Wide currency was first given to the term through the French *lumières* and later by Immanuel Kant's definition of the German *Aufklärung*. Readers particularly interested in this current will find many references to it in the Index.

The term *galant* has a complex of meanings. Its general sense is explored by way of Watteau in the two opening sections; the third section then leads eventually to its ramifications for music.

A New Art of Visual Enchantment

Antoine Watteau sprang from artisan stock at Valenciennes on the French-Flemish border. Born in 1684, he left for Paris at age eighteen and became an apprentice to a painter of stage sets for opera. He painted several pictures that reflect the warfare in Flanders during the early years of the century. They show soldiers in arms straggling along against a dreary landscape or resting. Even these military pictures look theatrical, as do his depictions of country festivals, with music and dancing. Soon he began to cultivate two kinds of subject that became specialties: depictions of actors or stage works in the course of performance, and idyllic garden scenes with lovers disporting in couples, a social phenomenon that had long been called *fêtes galantes*.

Watteau won second place in the Prix de Rome competition of 1709, and in 1712 became an associate of the Académie des Beaux-Arts. He never went to Italy but became successful nevertheless. His depictions of *fêtes galantes* were so much in demand that he made nearly fifty of them in a few years around 1715. In order to become a full member of the Académie he was required to submit a reception painting, normally on an assigned historical or biblical subject. Years went by and he did not submit the piece, despite being allowed to choose his own subject and receiving annual reminders of the requirement. In January 1717 he was given a deadline of six months, and finally, eight months later, the secretary of the Académie recorded the arrival of his canvas *Le pèlerinage à l'isle de Cithère*, then crossed out the title and replaced it with *Une feste galante*. Watteau was received as an academician but not as a history painter, the highest category. Rather, he was acknowledged as the master of "a special, novel kind of genre."[1]

Fêtes galantes had pictorial ancestors as far back as the Garden of Love in the Middle Ages, often associated with the epic poem *Roman de la Rose*. Watteau's particular ancestors in the genre belonged to the seventeenth-century Flemish school, above all Peter Paul Rubens, whose ample female forms and gorgeous colorings were well known in Paris from the Marie de Médicis cycle at the Luxem-

---

[1]Donald Posner, *Antoine Watteau* (London, 1984), p. 194.

bourg Palace. Watteau made sketches of the Rubenesque ladies but put them on a slimming diet for his purposes and made them much more refined. Perhaps no painting of the eighteenth century is better known or more often reproduced than his *Pilgrimage to Cythera*, either in his original version, which has always remained in Paris, or in the version he painted a few years later, which is now in Berlin. It is in many ways the painting that launched an era. He made a smaller picture that excerpted two central figures from his conception, a painting now lost and known only from an engraving entitled *Bon Voyage* (Figure 1.1). A kneeling lover gently invites his lady, demure and elegant, to join the couples in the background embarking on a voyage of love, beckoned by cupids in flight and billowing sails. The lovers carry staves that betoken their pilgrim state, and one staff lies on the ground before the main couple. These pilgrims' staves are hardly to be differentiated from the crooks of shepherds and shepherdesses, the whole convention being pastoral. Nor is Watteau's Cythera, the fabled island of Venus, to be differentiated in its archaizing, pastoral significance from another remote and primitive part of Greece, the Arcadia of the poets.

FIGURE 1.1. Antoine Watteau, *Bon voyage*, ca. 1717. Anonymous print after a lost painting.

These ethereal pictures appeared at a time when many longed for some relief from the seemingly interminable rule of Louis XIV, a once brilliant reign that ended in sanctimony and a dull sameness of routine. Under the Regency of Philip of Orleans (1715–23), the atmosphere of imposing grandeur dissipated. Compared to the grandiose deeds of the recent past, a simpler style of life seemed preferable. The life of shepherds and shepherdesses was of course no more achievable than was an escape to the simple joys of a bucolic past in Arcadia. Yet it is no coincidence that smaller and more comfortable apartments, even in grand palaces, became the fashion. The tone was set during the Regency not by Versailles, but by Paris. Smaller apartments required smaller pictures, and many of Watteau's are very small. Even his largest are small in comparison with the enormous history paintings of previous reigns, which often covered entire walls. The miniature was in great honor (not that it had ever fallen totally out of fashion).

Watteau's drawings and paintings were so highly prized that many of them were subsequently engraved by other artists. Even his single figures were engraved from drawings and sold well. Such is the case with his signature form: a woman seen from the back, seated on the grass. She appears in several of his larger compositions and represents the ultimate in nonchalance (Figure 1.2). Sinuosity, the most defining element of rococo decorative style, attains an eloquence here that is the very opposite of grandiloquence. Charm, dignity, and impeccable bearing are conveyed, as well as intimacy, all this without so much as a look at the lady's full countenance. In her rippling and flowing gown Watteau has caught an essence of feminine grace.

Particularly influential were the engravings of Watteau's small, oval paintings of the four seasons, which were quite as path breaking in the visual arts as was Antonio Vivaldi's contemporary *Four Seasons* in music.

FIGURE 1.2. Antoine Watteau. Seated female figure from the back.

Whereas the painter Nicolas Poussin had interpreted the seasons in terms of four grandiose biblical scenes, Watteau chose pagan antiquity, depicted by nearly naked, fetching young models representing the Roman deities Flora (spring), Ceres (summer), and Bacchus (autumn). Even Winter, warming himself at a fire with attending youths, is scantily clad. A certain informality in Watteau's art may explain why his patrons came not from the high nobility or the court but mainly from townspeople.[2]

Actors, singers, and instrument players were always highly favored by Watteau as subjects for his drawings and paintings. One of his early pictures shows the departure from Paris of the Italian comedians in 1697 after they had been dismissed by Louis XIV, an event that the artist could not have witnessed in person.[3] They walk along a street with despairing gestures and are easily recognized as several of the commedia dell'arte characters that remained Watteau's favorites: Harlequin with his slapstick at his side, bending low before the leading lady (*première amoureuse*); Scaramouche in his black costume with white neck ruff; Pulcinella with his fat stomach; Mezzetin in his striped outfit; and Pierrot in his loose white suit and hat, bowing low on the ground before an order posted on the wall that begins in large letters"DE PAR LE ROY"(i.e., the order that sent them packing).

In 1716 the regent summoned from Italy a troupe of comedians under the direction of Luigi Riccoboni to take the place of the troupe that had departed in disgrace two decades earlier. They arrived within a few months and took up residence, eventually, in the refurbished Hôtel de Bourgogne. Watteau made a small painting depicting the new troupe in a night scene, its twelve actors stretched across the stage in a row, as if for singing the final vaudeville. It was engraved in the same size and direction as the original (without the reversal usual to the process) and given the title *L'Amour au Théâtre Italien*; a verse was also added (Figure 1.3). The principal figures are the mature man with a torch wearing the striped costume of Mezzetin, obviously Riccoboni himself, and the Pierrot in his baggy suit, who strums a guitar. Between them is a Harlequin, his right arm akimbo in a typical gesture, and a little moon-faced creature who has been identified as a Scapin. To the right of them an aged and white-haired Pantaloon is bent over his cane, in front of a Scaramouche in black with white neck ruff. To the left of them are the two principal females, the diminuitive Sylvia holding a mask, and the taller Flaminia, next to whom is the stooping figure of the Doctor; behind him are three secondary figures, two of whom are professional singers. There is evi-

[2]Katie Scott, *The Rococo Interior. Decoration and Social Spaces in Early Eighteenth-Century Paris* (New Haven and London, 1995), pp. 153–54.

[3]The engraving after Watteau's lost painting is reproduced often in the literature on the artist. For two paintings of the event by earlier artists see Pierre-Louis Duchartre, *La commedia dell'arte et ses enfants* (Paris, 1955), p. 25.

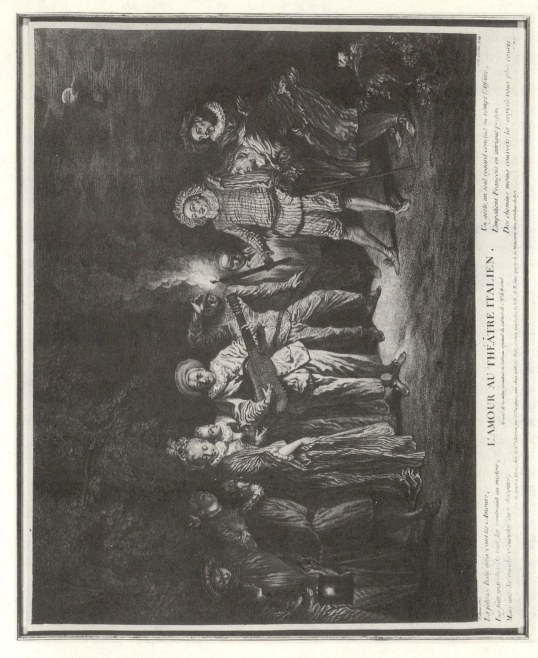

FIGURE 1.3. Antoine Watteau. Italian comedians, engraved by C. N. Cochin.

The young François Boucher, already superbly talented, was commissioned to make many of the engravings, a number matched only by his fellow student Laurent Cars. Boucher received the honor of engraving the frontispiece, a portrait of Watteau showing the master in informal dress with unkempt hair straggling down and clutching a portfolio of his drawings. The verse, added by one C. Moraine, does more justice to the subject than many that were added to engravings.

Watteau, par la Nature, orné d'heureux talents	Watteau, adorned by Nature with happy talents,
Fut tres reconnoissant des dons, qu'il reçut d'elle:	was very grateful for the gifts he received from her:
Jamais une autre main ne la peignit plus belle,	never did another hand paint her so beautifully,
Et ne la sçut montrer sous des traits si galants.	or know how to show her under such *galant* traits.

Thus, while Watteau's taste was styled "new," his traits were called "galant."

Having seen to the engraving of all the drawings by Watteau that he could gather, Jullienne set about the even more ambitious task of having all the master's paintings engraved. Once again he marshaled the best graphic artists in Paris and produced as a result *L'oeuvre d'Antoine Watteau*. Long in preparation, it was announced in 1734 and published in two large volumes in 1735.[9] No artist of the time had a greater diffusion in print. Later artists lived with these images. They could scarcely escape them.

Jean-Baptiste Siméon Chardin, born in 1699, admired Watteau and learned from his art, but sought a different vision. Where Watteau was often narrative in his pictures, Chardin eschewed narration. Watteau made copies after Flemish and Italian masters. Chardin did not. To find his own path Chardin renounced *galant* subjects altogether. Even where Chardin comes closest to Watteau, as in his early paintings of ladies taking tea or sealing a letter, his models look like country cousins to the elegant female customers in Gersaint's shop, Watteau's valedictory.[10]

Boucher, four years younger than Chardin, was technically more deft and climbed higher in official status, becoming Royal Painter. Like Watteau he could do everything in art superbly and easily. He has been called "Watteau's great posthumous pupil."[11] Yet to a critic like Denis Diderot he lacked Chardin's truth to

[9]Emile Dacier and Albert Vuaflart, *Jean de Jullienne et les graveurs de Watteau au XVIIIᵉ siècle*, 4 vols. (Paris, 1921–29).

[10]Colin B. Bailey, "Anglo-Saxon Attitudes: Recent Writings on Chardin," in *Chardin*, ed. Pierre Rosenberg (New York, 2000), pp. 77–97; 90.

[11]Michael Levy, *Painting and Sculpture in France, 1700–1789* (New Haven and London, 1992), p. 161.

dence aplenty to match these roles with the actual roster of twelve individual performers who made up the new Italian troupe.[4]

The return of the Italian comedians may be seen as a kind of revenge on the regent's part to make up for their dismissal under Louis XIV. Watteau's last full-scale painting, the amazing shop sign for his friend and dealer Edme Gersaint, contains a detail that is relevant here. In the lower left corner of the painting a shop assistant is putting a portrait of Louis XIV in a box, as if for shipping, and as if it were now his turn to be sent packing. This could be read, wrote one imaginative critic, as a "declaration of love to the grand Italian comedy that has finally returned to Paris: a sigh of freedom."[5]

Watteau's preoccupation with the stage emerges not only in his depictions of performers. Some of his *fêtes galantes,* seemingly so full of fantasy that they are divorced from any reality, have been related to actual stage works. Even the most famous, the epochal *Pilgrimage to Cythera,* may have parallels with theater. Three stage works were created by different poets on this same subject in the years between 1714 and 1716, which indicates that the topic was in great vogue just before Watteau painted his masterwork.[6] The painting in its turn inspired further theatrical scenes, by Pierre Marivaux among others. The idea of using celebrated pieces of visual art as a wellspring for stage works was very common at the time in Paris.[7]

The early death of Watteau in July 1721 at age thirty-seven had the effect of making his works all the more prized. Some of his admirers organized to perpetuate and diffuse his pictures by means of engravings. Jean de Jullienne, a collector and friend who was a wealthy merchant, later ennobled, took the lead by having the engraving of Watteau's drawings published in two volumes under the title *Figures de différentes caractères* (1726–28). He prefaced the work by writing, "They belong to a new taste; they have graces that are so closely connected to the author's spirit that they can be considered inimitable."[8]

[4]It is laid out in detail in Daniel Heartz, "Watteau's Italian Comedians," *Eighteenth-Century Studies* 22 (1988–89): 156–81.

[5]Giovanni Macchia, "I fantasmi dell'opera: il mito teatrale di Watteau," in *I fantasmi dell'opera* (Milan, 1971), pp. 1–36; 36. "E la scena in cui il ritratto del Re Sole è li pronto per essere incasato dal ragazzo nella bottega di Gersaint può essere letta anche come una dichiarazione d'amore alla grande commedia italiana ritornata finalmente a Parigi: un sospiro di libertà." The essay was reprinted, translated into French, without acknowledgement of the Italian original, in *Antoine Watteau (1684–1721): le peintre, son temps et sa légende,* ed. François Moureau and Margaret Morgan Grasselli (Paris and Geneva, 1987), pp. 187–96.

[6]Robert Tomlinson, *La fête galante: Watteau et Marivaux* (Geneva, 1981), pp. 129–33. The poets were Fuzelier (1713), Letellier (1714), and Charpentier (1715).

[7] Daniel Heartz, "Opéra-Comique and the Théâtre Italien from Watteau to Fragonard," in *Music in the Classic Period: Essays in Honor of Barry S. Brook,* ed. Allan W. Atlas (New York, 1985), pp. 69–84.

[8]Marianne Roland Michel, "Watteau et les *Figures de différents caractères,*" in *Antoine Watteau (1684–1721),* pp. 117–27; 117.

nature. If Boucher was by inspiration (not direct study) a first-generation disciple of Watteau, Jean-Baptiste Greuze and Jean Honoré Fragonard were second-generation followers. Fragonard, born in 1732, brought *fêtes galantes* to their ultimate visual fantasy. Greuze, seven years older, was preferred by Diderot for instilling morality by means of pictorial narrations of everyday life among common people. These artists shared a desire to capture momentary and fleeting visions, to a degree that was new in the arts.[12]

European Vogue

Watteau, although untraveled, became a European phenomenon. His art attracted admirers everywhere, but nowhere did it snare more adherents and exert more fascination than among Venetian artists. In return, Watteau showed an interest in Venetian art, and even in Venetian subjects. One of his greatest *fêtes galantes* is known, after the engraving made from his painting, as *Fêtes vénitiennes* (Plate I). Everything Watteau had to offer is present here in superlative degree: music, dancing, gorgeous costumes, couples in conversation, an importunate lover, and a voluptuous statue (a reclining female nude whose hair, like that of Mélisande, keeps flowing down and seems to dissolve into a silvery stream). There is another symbol of lust in the ram's head on the large vase. All is set in a sylvan glade of ethereal beauty. An impeccable sense of form guides Watteau to highlight his three main figures, the man at left by a shaft of sky above, his lady by the vase, the bagpiper by the statue.

Something special and personal attaches to this vision of an earthly paradise. It contains at least two portraits that have been identified. The portly man in exotic costume, exerting himself as a dancer, resembles Watteau's friend and patron Nicolas Vleughels, with whom he lived for about a year from the end of 1718 to late 1719. Of Flemish descent, Vleughels would have been about fifty years old at the time. Watteau liked to dress his subjects in theatrical costumes, and Vleughels provides a good example. With his baggy trousers, long sash, cloak, and turban, he looks vaguely Turkish, as if he might have just stepped off a ship from the Levant. There is another theatrical costume on view: that on the man dressed in green seated under the statue, wearing a fool's cap on his head. The beautiful dancing lady in blue has eluded identification so far. Not so the bagpipe player, who animates the dance with his drones and squeelings. He, according to good evidence, represents a self-portrait of the artist.[13]

Art historians have puzzled over what, specifically, led to giving the picture a

[12]As argued persuasively by Thomas M. Kavanaugh in *Esthetics of the Moment: Literature and Art in the French Enlightenment* (Philadelphia, 1996). Kavanaugh champions Roger de Piles, the art critic most attuned to the dynamics of the moment, at the expense of Jean-Baptiste Dubos, the defender of mimesis.
[13]Michael Levy, *Rococo to Revolution* (London, 1966), pp. 74–78.

Venetian title (there is no accompanying verse). A sylvan glade hardly suggests the Queen of the Adriatic. Had they paid more attention to the dance, which is, after all, the featured event, they would have found a clue. Vleughels in fact wears the costume of a Venetian gondolier of that day. The same loose knickers down to the knees, sash around the waist, cloak, and turbanlike hat are seen on the dancing gondoliers depicted by engravings in Gregorio Lambranzi's *Neue und Curieuse Theatrialische Tantz-Schul,* printed in Nuremberg in 1716; moreover, the pose, with hands behind back and left foot forward, corresponds to depictions of the forlana in Lambranzi and other sources.[14] The forlana is a vigorous wooing dance in which the man tries to impress the lady with his steps. Its main melody was handed down orally over many generations. In other words it could claim status as a folk song. The dance itself was the closest thing Venice had to a national emblem in this realm. It was a folk dance, closely identified with gondoliers. By choosing to have a country instrument like the bagpipe accompany the dance, Watteau injects an earthy, popular tone even in the midst of so much elegance and "high art."

The title given Watteau's picture was also that of the most successful work in the genre of opéra-ballet, *Les fêtes vénitiennes,* by the poet Antoine Danchet and composer André Campra, first staged at the Opéra in 1713 and rarely absent from the boards for sixty years thereafter. It was Campra, with the poet Antoine Houdar de La Motte, who inaugurated this light genre of music and dance with *L'Europe galante* in 1697. Epochal in importance, like Watteau's paintings, *L'Europe galante* gave Campra the opportunity to introduce a dance melody, "La Forlana," that matches in cadential structure the traditional forlana of the gondoliers.[15]

Although Watteau did not visit Italy he communed extensively with Italian art. Among his drawings are several copies he made of works of Venetian landscape artists of the sixteenth century that he found in Parisian collections. As a colorist, an admirer of Rubens, he was naturally partial to Venetian painting of the great century, when Venice boasted such titans as Giovanni Bellini, Giorgione, Paolo Veronese, Titian, and Tintoretto.[16] These Renaissance painters were not matched in brilliance of coloring by other Venetians until the eighteenth century, when several artists rejected *seicento* hyperbole and tenebrism, lightened their palettes, and began displaying a range of bright hues and limpid forms inspired by the *cinquecento* masters, especially Veronese. They were led by the Riccis, Sebastiano and his nephew Marco, and included Giovanni Antonio Pellegrini and Giambattista Pittoni. Pellegrini was married to the sister of the age's greatest pas-

---

[14] Daniel Heartz, "A Venetian Dancing Master Teaches the Forlana: Lambranzi's *Balli Teatrali, Journal of Musicology* 17 (1999): 136–51, plates III, IV, and V.

[15] Ibid., p. 147, example 2.

[16] Posner, *Antoine Watteau,* p. 167, suggests that Watteau alludes to Veronese in "Les plaisirs du bal" by the figure of a negro servant leaning over the balustrade.

tel portraitist, Rosalba Carriera of Venice. Watteau did not need to visit these artists. They came to him.

Exchanges between Watteau and the leading Venetian artists began around 1715. His patron Pierre Crozat, a financier who lived in luxury on the rue de Richelieu and at his chateau at Montmorency, had earlier begun corresponding with Rosalba Carriera. In 1716, as the Riccis were returning from London to Venice, they stopped in Paris, where Crozat guided them to Watteau's studio. Sebastiano Ricci did Watteau the honor of copying several of his drawings. At Crozat's urging Carriera herself came to Paris along with her sister and Pellegrini. She stayed with Crozat from April 1719 until March 1720. This was a pilgrimage of another sort, and its main object was Watteau. They met, got along famously, and portrayed each other. She was received as a member of the Royal Academy on 26 October 1720. Watteau also sketched Pittoni's portrait in a drawing that ended up in the possession of another Venetian artist, Antonio Maria Zanetti the elder, to whom it was once ascribed.[17] Zanetti himself joined the band of Venetian guests of Crozat in 1720.

The Riccis died in Venice, Marco in 1730 and Sebastiano in 1734. Their place on the international scene was taken by a trio of famous history painters, Jacopo Amigoni, Giovanni Battista Piazzetta, and, greatest of all, Giovanni Battista Tiepolo. Piazzetta remained in Venice, but Amigoni and Tiepolo traveled widely, fulfilling commissions on a grand scale all over Europe. Besides these commanding figures, two Venetian specialists in view painting were in demand everywhere, Antonio Canaletto and his nephew Bernardo Bellotto. Staying at home in Venice were two other artists of endearing charms, Francesco Guardi and the genre painter Pietro Longhi. Not since the Renaissance had Venice been able to boast such a pleiade of artistic genius.

Tiepolo was Europe's premier painter. To what extent he was an artist of the rococo is an issue with which experts still grapple.[18] All agree that he was as theatrically inspired as was Watteau, indeed, that he was even more seduced by the world of opera.

Amigoni had a career that included long stays in Germany, England, and Spain, where he died in 1752. His close connection with Carlo Broschi Farinelli may have begun when they were both in London during the 1730s. Together they visited Paris in 1736. Amigoni was captivated by Watteau's paintings and their

---

[17] *Watteau, 1684-1721*, ed. Pierre Rosenberg (Paris, 1984), p. 52. The drawing in red chalk is inscribed "Pittoni a Parigi, Broccantor da Quadri, Pittore, ed. Amico del Zanetti." It is reproduced in *Caricature di Anton Maria Zanetti*, ed. Alessandro Bettagno and Giuseppe Fiocco (Venice, 1969), figure 175.
[18] Svetlana Alpers and Michael Baxandall, *Tiepolo and the Pictorial Intelligence* (New Haven and London, 1994), pp. 143–53. They refer to *Armida and Rinaldo* (our Plate VII) as being set "in a splendid rococo escutcheon of yellow stuff" (pp. 151–52).

engravings in Jullienne's published collections. When he returned to Venice in
1739 his disciples included a young painter from Paris, Charles-Joseph Flipart,
and a Swiss graphic artist, Joseph Wagner, with whom he later opened a print
shop of the highest quality, first in London, then in Venice.[19] Wagner engraved
many paintings of Amigoni and Flipart, and also of Amigoni's Venetian student,
Antonio Zucchi, whose *Europa* is illustrated in the frontispiece.

L'Europa by Zucchi follows the fashion of depicting the four continents in
terms of human activities. The most imposing examples of this style are Tiepolo's
fresco paintings in the grand staircase of the bishop's palace at Würzburg. Zucchi's picture is composed like one of Watteau's small-sized *fêtes galantes* and even
employs the pyramid shape often seen there. The statue of Minerva (goddess of
wisdom, the arts, and war) presiding on high is appropriate to the demonstration
below of the arts and sciences, of which painting, sculpture, geography, music,
and architecture are signaled. A man with his arm on a globe looks particularly
relaxed, calipers in one hand, a book in the other. An elegant gentleman holds a
cane in one hand and gestures with the other. The rather languid-looking women
amuse themselves with a lute and a fan. Unclear is the significance of the man on
horseback riding off in the background, following a footman. Perhaps he signals
European travel and communication in the context of the praises sung in the
verse below. In the foreground some earth flows over into the poem's space
below, breaking the rectangular frame (a detail not found in the painting).

Europa mia tra l'altre tue sorelle	Europe mine, among your sisters
Quanto piu sai superba ergi la testa;	How proudly you raise your head;
Perche il mondo ha da dir tutte son belle	The world must declare all are beautiful
Ma in ogni età la mia Regina è questa.	But in every age my Queen is this one.

Europe's assurance was at a high point in the middle of the eighteenth century, intermittent wars, plagues, and famines notwithstanding. A great natural
disaster such as the Lisbon earthquake of 1755 hardly shook the general confidence and sense of pride, an attitude of smugness that Voltaire satirized with
deadly shafts of wit in his *Candide* (1759). A more gentle satirist, Laurence Sterne,
put the case for optimism as well as it could be put in his *Sentimental Journey*

[19]Leslie Griffen Hennessey, "Notes on the Formation of Giuseppe Wagner's Bella Maniera and his Venetian
Printshop," *Ateneo Veneto* 178 (1990): 211–28. Her convincing arguments about the influence of Watteau on
Amigoni and Wagner have been extended to include his influence on Tiepolo, in Leslie Griffen Hennessey,
"French *conversation*—and Venetian *poesia:* Giambattista Tiepolo's *Finding of Moses*," *Apollo* (September
1994): 33–39.

through France and Italy. He admired the French for being so smitten with sentiment and courtesy that they deferred to women in almost everything save the
running of the country (had he known how much that was done by Madame de
Pompadour when she ruled the heart of Louis XV he might have qualified even
this statement). Journeys of discovery were broadening, Sterne maintained,
though the home country (England) was already very enlightened."It is an age so
full of light, that there is scarce a country or corner of Europe whose beams are
not crossed and interchanged with others—Knowledge in most of its branches,
and in most affairs, is like music in an Italian street, whereof those may partake,
who pay nothing."[20] Literacy rates soared. In northern France they nearly doubled
in the course of a century.[21] The human race seemed perfectible, or at least susceptible to improvement.

Europe and Enlightenment became somewhat synonymous. One central
publishing event contributed more than any other to the spread of enlightened
ideals. The *Encyclopédie,* short for *Encyclopédie ou Dictionnaire raisonné des sciences,
des arts et des métiers,* came out under the editorship of Diderot in twenty folio volumes between 1751 and 1772. Charles Burney was one of the first subscribers.
Thumbing through the pages of these ponderous tomes today the reader must
marvel still at Diderot's heroic achievement in carrying the work to completion.

The project began when a bookseller asked Diderot to translate the *Cyclope-
dia* of Ephraim Chambers into French. Almost at once he envisioned a new compendium of universal knowledge, based on the latest scientific discoveries and
philosophical thought. Concerned as he was with practical consequences and values, he did not neglect crafts or performing arts, which enter alongside the most
erudite theories and speculations. He enlisted the help of his nation's foremost
thinkers and writers, and appointed as coeditor Jean le Rond d'Alembert, a distinguished mathematician. A compendium of new ideas such as this was bound
to incur the enmity of many in political and ecclesiastical authority. More than
once these enemies succeeded in stopping the great project. A particularly severe
crisis shook the whole enterprise after volume seven was published in 1757: a
court-ordered seizure discouraged the contributors and caused many of them,
including D'Alembert, to desert.

Diderot persisted, shouldering the burden of writing much of the work himself and seeing the monumental edifice through to the end. One powerful figure
at court who stood behind him was Madame de Pompadour, mistress of Louis XV.
She was a great patron of the arts, which she knew intimately, being herself gifted
as a poet, musician, and visual artist. Many portraits of her emphasize these gifts

---

[20]Laurence Sterne, *A Sentimental Journey through France and Italy* (London, 1768). I cite the edition by Graham Petrie for Penguin Books (1967), p. 36.
[21]John McManners, *Church and Society in Eighteenth-Century France,* 2 vols. (Oxford, 1998), 1: 193.

and interests, no doubt by her precise command. One, in particular, confirms her support of Diderot.

Maurice Quentin de La Tour, known as the prince of pastel painters, came, like Watteau, from the north. He was born at Saint Quentin in 1704 of an artisanal family, traveled to Paris for instruction as early as age fifteen, and was known to the circle around Watteau.[22] Received by the Académie Royale de Peinture et de Sculpture in 1737, after he painted a striking portrait of Voltaire, he quickly became famous for the pictures he exhibited annually at the Salon in the Louvre. Pastel remained his preferred medium and the portrait his genre, in which respects he was the greatest successor to Rosalba Carriera. By royal command he painted many intimate portraits of the king, the queen, their children, and their grandchildren. Madame de Pompadour commissioned from him the full-length portrait of her that created a stir at the Salon of 1755 (see Plate II). Gorgeously gowned, but wearing not a single piece of jewelry, she holds a large musical score. A guitar leans against the sofa in the background. Spilling off the table is an engraving signed "Pompadour sculpsit" (her art teacher was Boucher). Carefully arrayed on the table are several bound volumes the spines of which read PASTOR FIDO (by Guarini), HENRIADE (by Voltaire), and ESPRIT DES LOIS (by Montesquieu)—an indication of her openness and breadth of interests. Standing aloof to the right, flanked by a globe of the world, is a tall volume: ENCYCLOPEDIE TOM IV. It sent a message to Diderot's opponents that could not be missed, the more so given the Salon's placement of the portrait on a special easel set apart by a balustrade.[23] La Tour's refinement in every detail, virtuosity in the service of clarity, penetration to the core of the individual's personality, all done with breathtaking grace and lightness, make him a worthy heir of Carriera and of Watteau.

The *Galant* Style

What is in a word? The term in question has a long and complex history. Randle Cotgrave compiled and published the first important French-English dictionary in London in 1611.[24] It represents a milestone in lexicography, the richest such collection of its time by far. Cotgrave defined *Gallant homme* as "A gallant, goodlie; noble, worthie, vertuous; also a subtill, wise, craftie, cunning, wylie, fellow." He followed this term with *Gallanterie*, "Gallantnesse, worthinesse, brauerie stoutness, frankenesse of humour; also a knavish pranke." Thus there was also a pejorative shade to the word's main meaning, a suggestion of *Till Eulenspiegels lustige Streiche*. Cotgrave also defined the verb *Galler*, "to gall, fret, itch; to rub, scrape,

[22]Christine Debrie and Xavier Salmon, *Maurice-Quentin de La Tour Prince des pastellistes* (Paris, 2000), p. 12.
[23]Ibid., p. 110.
[24]Randle Cotgrave, *A Dictionairie of the French and English Tongues* (London, 1611). Reproduced in facsimile from the first edition by the University of South Carolina Press (Columbia, 1950).

scrub, claw, scratch where it itcheth; also, to be verie iocund, or full of glee; to intertaine with varietie of sport, game or glee." He did not offer a definition of the adjective *gallant* per se. In his day the word had a double consonant in the middle, as it still does in English today. The chief meaning of *gallant* in modern English, "brave, high-spirited, or chivalrous," remains within the compass of the old French term. The main meaning of *galant* in modern French ("attentive to ladies, pleasing, elegant") was unknown to Cotgrave. It evolved in the course of the seventeenth century and by the eighteenth had eclipsed the older French meanings. Modernization also reduced the double consonant to a single *l*.

Voltaire wrote the articles "Galant" and "Galanterie" in the *Encyclopédie*. In the first he wrote "Etre galant, en général, c'est chercher à plaire par les soins agréables et par les empressements flatteurs." He puts a finer point on who was attempting to please whom in defining the second, "Galanterie": "C'est dans les hommes une attention marquée à dire aux femmes, d'une manière fine et delicate, des choses qui leur plaisent." Thus for Voltaire and in French civilization generally the terms were bound to a verbal culture. Even *fêtes galantes* were at first verbal, having to do either with text or with conversation, before they became supremely visual with Watteau.[25] Verbal allusion remains in Louis-Gabriel Guillemain's *Quatuors ou conversations galantes* (1743). The opéra-ballet, beginning with *L'Europe galante*, became a species of *fêtes galantes* at once textual, visual, and musical. In attempting to define this new genre the dance historian Louis de Cahusac harked back to Watteau and emphasized his grace, color, and moderation as opposed to the works of grandiose scale that preceded him, exemplified by those of Philippe Quinault and Jean Baptiste Lully.

> The opera conceived by Quinault is composed of one central dramatic action over the course of five acts. It is a vast concept, such as that of Raphael and Michelangelo. The spectacle recreated by La Motte is composed of several different acts, each representing a single action and including *divertissements* of song and dance. These are pretty Watteaus, piquant miniatures that demand precision of design, grace of brushstroke and brilliance of colour.[26]

L'Europe galante consists of four different acts, united only by the theme of amatory stratagems, as employed in France, Italy, Spain, and Turkey. Jean-Philippe Rameau's *Les Indes galantes* (1735) caps the genre of opéra-ballet, extending the amatory intrigues to the wide world beyond Europe.

German critics of the eighteenth century extended these terms to wider cul-

[25] Mary Vidal, *Watteau's Painted Conversations* (New Haven and London, 1992).
[26] Louis de Cahusac, *La danse ancienne et moderne*, 3 vols. (The Hague, 1754; facsimile, Geneva, 1971), 3: 108. Cited in the translation of James R. Anthony, *French Baroque Music from Beaujoyeulx to Rameau*, rev. ed. (New York, 1978), p. 132.

tural purposes and specifically to music. At first they borrowed the term *galant* to convey verbal usage, analogous with its main meaning in contemporary France. Thus C. F. Hunold (Menantes) entitled his 1702 manual for self-instruction *Die allerneuste Manier höflich und galant zu schreiben*. Note that "Manier" was also borrowed from French (but not so recently). Johann Gottfried von Herder and other writers of the later eighteenth century denounced manuals like this as effeminate and corrupting of the German language. Johann Mattheson of Hamburg was one of the main offenders too, judging by the number of foreign words in the title of his first publication, which was also a manual for self-instruction. He emphasized the borrowed words by putting them in Roman type (here they appear in italics), as if proud of their number: "Das neu-eröffnete *Orchestre,* oder *Universelle* und gründliche Anleitung wie ein *Galant homme* einen vollkommenen Begriff von der Hoheit und Würde der edlen *Music* erlangen, seinen *Gout* darnach formieren, die *Terminos technicos* verstehen und geschicklich von dieser vortrefflichen Wissenschaft *raisonnieren* möge" (The newly-inaugurated orchestra or universal and fundamental guide showing how the galant man may acquire a perfect notion of the majesty and worth of the noble art of music, may form his taste therefrom, understand the technical terms, and reason with skill about this splendid science). Mattheson's "Galant homme" was a man (or woman) of fashion who was instructed enough in music to make judgments as to what was pleasing to the ears. "Galanterie" he employed in more than one musical sense. He used it to mean tasteful ornamentation of melodies and also as a generic title of short keyboard pieces, for which he preferred the clavichord to the harpsichord because its dynamic nuances brought it closer to the voice. "Galanteries" in the sense of small dances or songs were also current in French harpsichord music.

Mattheson apparently originated the term *style galant* in music. In *Das forschende Orchestre* of 1721 he speaks of a lighter kind of music being in "einem galanten Stylo" (p. 352). Elsewhere he enumerates eleven composers whom the "galant homme" was bound to find "the most famous and most galant composers in Europe" (p. 276): Giovanni Bononcini, Antonio Caldara, Giovanni Maria Capelli, Francesco Gasparini, George Frideric Handel, Reinhard Keiser, Antonio Lotti, Benedetto Marcello, Alessandro Scarlatti, Georg Philipp Telemann, and Antonio Vivaldi. What these composers have in common is that they were all living practitioners of Italian opera around 1720. Almost all were based in or connected with either Hamburg or Venice. In applying this adjectival use of "galant" to composers, Mattheson identified music of the most up-to-date kind, that of the Hamburg opera led by his master Keiser. Of the many German music critics who came after Mattheson, none denied that what they called *galant* music originated in the Italian theater. Thus an original French term with mainly societal and conversational connotations was adapted by German critics for musical purposes, often to mean no more than "modern" and very often "Italian modern."

Galant will henceforth shed its italics or quotations marks in this book and become one of those foreign terms adapted to present purposes as if it were English, because it occurs so often, like prima donna, primo uomo, maestro di cappella, vice maestro di cappella, and a few others. Its meanings differ slightly as generation succeeds generation in the course of the eighteenth century. Yet it never means anything less than elegant, new, and fashionable.[27]

Johann Scheibe in his periodical *Der critische Musikus* (1737–40) argued that the new style was greatly preferable to the old. He had moved from Leipzig to Hamburg and become a partisan of Telemann's direct and lusty musical strains. He praised Johann Sebastian Bach but also reproached him for being excessively complex, lacking in natural qualities, and allowing too much artifice to obscure the beauties in his music. Scheibe also charged that Bach erred by demanding that singers and players be able to execute everything that came to his fingers as a keyboard player. Scheibe was reprimanded by Bach's friends for writing this, but the charge does not fail to hit its mark.

Carl Philipp Emanuel Bach throughout his *Versuch über die wahre Art das Clavier zu spielen* (1753) distinguished between the learned and galant styles, and several other Berlin writers on music agreed with him. The dichotomy reached a final codification with Heinrich Koch, who contrasted the galant or free style, appropriate to the theater and to chamber music, with the strict or learned style, associated with church music. The galant style, he wrote, was distinguished from the strict style

1. through many elaborations of the melody, and divisions of the principal melodic tones, through more obvious breaks and pauses in the melody, and through more changes in the rhythmic elements, and especially in the lining up of melodic figures that do not have a close relationship with each other, etc.
2. through a less interwoven harmony
3. through the fact that the remaining voices simply serve to accompany the main voice and do not take part in the expression of the sentiment of the piece, etc.[28]

In characterizing the galant style as "lining up of melodic figures" not closely related, Koch describes the opposite of baroque *Fortspinnung,* achieved by motivic repetition and development. Disparate melodic snippets or themes in the newer style hang together by some subtler musical logic, what Leopold Mozart called "the thread" (*il filo*). Galant, not at first a technical term in music, became one, so that it is preferable to terms borrowed from other arts.

---

[27] The principal study in English remains David A. Sheldon, "The Galant Style Revisited and Re-evaluated," *Acta Musicologica* 47 (1975): 240–70. It is supplemented by David A. Sheldon, "The Concept *Galant* in the 18th Century," *Journal of Musicological Research* 9 (1989): 89–108.

[28] Heinrich Koch, *Musikalisches Lexikon* (Frankfort, 1802), translated in Leonard G. Ratner, *Classic Music: Expression, Form, and Style* (New York, 1980), p. 23.

Daniel Gottlob Türk also codified the galant style by placing it in opposition to the strict style. His discussion of dissonance treatment in the newer manner remains valuable.

> In the free or galant style the composer does not always follow the grammatical rules so strictly. He allows, for example, certain dissonances to enter unprepared; he transfers their resolutions to other voices, or omits the resolutions altogether. He gives to dissonances a longer duration than to the following consonances, something which does not take place in the strict style. Moreover, he modulates excessively, allows various kinds of embellishments, and adds diverse passing tones. In short, he composes more for the ear, and if I might say so, appears less as a learned composer.[29]

The freedoms described are abundantly evident in the keyboard sonatas of Carl Philipp Emanuel Bach, Türk's idol and primary model as a music theorist.

Eighteenth-century critics of music did not go so far as to talk about the galant style in terms of French music. Their successors two centuries later had no such compunctions. It would have seemed natural for them to have lighted upon Campra's more familiar style of music for opéra-ballet, compared as we have seen by one observer to Watteau's pictures. Shy about vocal music, they lit instead upon a lighter keyboard style adopted by François Couperin le Grand, especially in the last two books of his *Pièces de clavecin*, twenty-seven *ordres* or suites that were published in four volumes dated 1713, 1717, 1722, and 1730. These pieces were said to represent a first or early phase of the galant style.[30]

Couperin did in fact travel some distance from the weighty allemandes of his first books. "L'Auguste," as he titles the initial allemande of the first book, well illustrates his starting point, and the reference can be to none other than the most august monarch of all, Louis XIV. Book 3 marks a decisive turn to simpler, easier pieces, with somewhat less ornamentation and more sensuous and amorous content (i.e., an increase in galant subjects). Pastorals, theatrical pantomimes, and character pieces largely displace what remained of the old dance suite, which was already disappearing in the second book. "Les lis naissans" (Nascent lilies or *fleurs de lys*) begins Book 3 and must refer to the boy king, Louis XV. It is followed at the beginning of the next *ordre* by "Le rossignol-en-amour." Couperin's amorous

[29]Daniel Gottlob Türk, *Anweisung zum Generalbassspielen*, a revision of his *Kurze Anweisung zum Generalbassspielen* (Leipzig and Halle, 1791), as translated by David A. Sheldon, "Exchange, Anticipation, and Ellipsis: Analytical Definitions of the *Galant* Style," in *Music East and West: Essays in Honor of Walter Kaufmann*, ed. Thomas Noblitt (New York, 1981), pp. 225–41. In his *Clavierschule* (Leipzig and Halle, 1789), p. 405, Türk says, "in the free (galant) way of writing the composer . . . allows himself bold turns of phrase that even go against the rules of modulation."

[30]Ernst Bücken, "Der galante Stil: eine Skizze seiner Entwicklung," *Zeitschrift zur Musikwissenschaft* 6 (1923–24), 418–30. Hugo Riemann had earlier defined "Style galant" in terms of French keyboard music in the various editions of his *Musik-Lexikon;* see Wilhelm Seidel, "Style galant," in *Die Musik in Geschichte und Gegenwart*, ed. Ludwig Finscher, 2nd ed. (Kassel and Stuttgart, 1994–).

nightingale is the instrument's singing treble voice, which enchants us with its simple, stepwise melody and its use of an accelerating trill in the repetition of the concluding part, a trill prophetic of the birds represented in the "Scene by the brook" movement of Beethoven's Pastoral Symphony. Before this *14e ordre* in D/d is over, there is a sound of change ringing in "Le carillon de Cythère," perhaps an allusion to the lures of Watteau's imagined realm of Venus, an erotic deflection of the normal role of bells summoning worshipers to church.

Couperin refined his intricate textures to a simple flow in eighth notes for "Le dodo ou l'Amour au berceau," which follows "La régente ou La Minerve" at the beginning of the *15e ordre.* The melody of the refrain uses only the four conjunct tones above the tonic (Example 1.1). It begins on the second half of the measure in cut time, gavottelike, and continues like many a dance by falling into a regular period, 4 + 4, and an **a a'** shape, a tentative close in mm. 3–4 being replaced by a stronger close in mm. 7–8. The movement is that of a lullaby, says the tempo direction, and *dodo* is the colloquial word for sleep used with children in French.

EXAMPLE 1.1. *Couperin, Rondeau, "Le dodo, ou l'Amour au berceau"*

Could anything be more simple or bewitching? The tenor range of the harpsichord is magically warm and soothing, like an ensemble of three cellos. Unusual also is the nontonic beginning, a rich-sounding dominant chord in third inversion on its way to resolution in the chord of I⁶. Cupid in the cradle sounds not only lulling but seductive.

"Le dodo" has ramifications beyond those of salon music. Its refrain parallels the melody of an earlier air for carillon, "L'angélus," and led subsequently to a texted nursery song, "Do, do, l'enfant do."[31] Its simplicity and clarity helped to achieve the status of a folk song.

---

[31]Henri Davenson, *Le livre des chansons ou introduction à la connaissance de la chanson populaire française* (Neuchâtel, 1962), p. 496.

Couperin's pieces depicting natural phenomena or sounds from everyday life (e.g. "Le réveil-matin" [The alarm clock]) are charming. Those portraying individuals are even more original.[32] They took in not only the striding gait of majesty and high estate but also the traits of more modestly situated people, perhaps some of his own acquaintances among them. These portraits in tone are related to the vogue for literary portraits that swept society in France during the reign of the Sun King, which were gathered in the *Receuil de pièces galantes en prose et en vers des plus beaux esprits du temps,* reprinted fourteen times between 1663 and 1748.[33]

The portraits in music by Couperin set a fashion followed by several other French composers. A notable non-French follower was Emanuel Bach, who portrayed both people and states of mind in short harpsichord pieces with French titles.[34] Johann Georg Sulzer, in his encyclopedic work on the fine arts, noted the connection in an article entitled "Painting in Music" (Mahlerei): "many dance melodies are essentially depictions of character. Couperin as well as a few other French composers, have depicted quite specific characteristics of individual men. And after him, C. P. E. Bach has published some short keyboard pieces that express quite strikingly the various characteristics of his friends and acquaintances."[35] Sulzer does not explain how it is possible to convey traits of character in tones, but his reference to dance melodies hints that a clue may be sought in qualities of motion, that is, in the rhythmic as well as the melodic. Another German writer on music of the late eighteenth century, Wilhelm Heinse, claimed in his novel *Hildegard von Hohenthal* that "there is a person presented in every melody, or a particular being whose life advances in motion with time."[36]

Galant portraits in music aside, Couperin showed how it was possible to continue the great tradition while speaking a simpler language. There is a revealing portrait of the composer painted by André Bouys, well known from its fine 1735

[32]Jean-Baptiste Dubos, *Réflexions critiques sur la poésie, la peintre et la musique* (Paris, 1719), allowed that music could imitate not only natural sounds but also human nature. Charles Batteux took this idea further in *Les beaux-arts réduits à un même principe* (Paris, 1746). Excerpts from both treatises are translated in *Music and Aesthetics in the Eighteenth and Early-Nineteenth Centuries,* ed. Peter le Huray and James Day (Cambridge, 1981).

[33]David Fuller, "Of Portraits, 'Sappho' and Couperin: Titles and Characters in French Instrumental Music of the High Baroque," *Music and Letters* 78 (1997): 149–74; 162, n. 60. I am indebted to the author for friendly advice on many matters over a long period.

[34]Darrell M. Berg, "C. P. E. Bach's Character Pieces and his Friendship Circle," *C. P. E. Bach Studies,* ed. Stephen L. Clark (Oxford, 1988), pp. 1–32.

[35]Johann Georg Sulzer, *Allgemeine Theorie der schönen Künste,* 4 vols. (Leipzig, 1771–74), 3: 356–57, translated in Thomas Christensen, *Aesthetics and the Art of Musical Composition in the German Enlightenment: Selected Writings of Johann Georg Sulzer and Heinrich Christoph Koch,* ed. Nancy Kovaleff Baker and Thomas Christensen (Cambridge, 1995), p. 89.

[36]"Bey jeder Melodie ist Darstellung von einer Person, oder eines besonderen Wesen, dessen Leben in Bewegung mit der Zeit fortrücket," Wilhelm Heinse, *Sämtliche Werke,* 5: 249, cited after Sylvie Le Moël, *Le corps et le vêtement: Écrire et penser la musique au siècle des Lumières: Wilhelm Heinse* (Paris, 1996), p. 176.

engraving by a member of the Flipart dynasty.[37] With a no-nonsense gaze on his plain face, he appears in elegant dress, a model of grace. His hand rests upon the notated score of a *pièce de clavecin* from his *2ᵉ ordre*, "Les idées heureuses," as if to say, "This is who I am." No long tresses for him. Like a modern gentleman of his day, he wears a short wig.

Galant style, the concept as defined above by Koch and exemplified throughout this book, came about independently of French models. Adumbrated by Archangelo Corelli, the Bononcinis, and others who sought to simplify Italian baroque style, it flowered in the 1720s at Naples, whence it spread widely, dominating music for much of the century and defining it as a musical-historical epoch. Elsewhere I have identified the Italian operatic current as the mainstream and referred to French achievements as a kind of counterpoint, another antidote to the stiffness of the older style.[38] Every French generation beginning with Couperin went further with regard to assimilating Italian modern style. What resulted ultimately was an international style that merged French and Italian currents, along with German ones.

Two cadences became so frequent in eighteenth-century music in the galant style that they can be used to identify it (Example 1.2ab). The first and the most common is often found in minuets and became known as a *cadence galante.* In its simple harmonic form it was nothing other than the common I - IV (or ii$^{6}_{5}$) - V - I ending, often decorated with a characteristic descent in the treble melody. The second is an elaboration of the first, with the bass rising by step from the first to the fifth degree, and the treble descending. Earlier I referred to this pattern as "the Hasse cadence," but I now call it "the wedge cadence" because Johann Adolf Hasse made less use of it than did certain of his followers, especially Carl Heinrich Graun.[39] The term *minuet* (or *menuet*, the French original, *minuetto* or *menuetto* in Italian) approached synonymy with the term *galant*.

EXAMPLE 1.2. *Cadences*

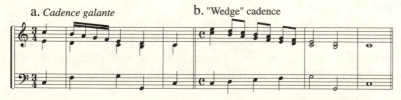

37It is reproduced in the article "Couperin" by David Fuller in *The New Grove Dictionary of Music and Musicians*, ed. Stanley Sadie, 20 vols. (London, 1980), referred to subsequently throughout this book as *New Grove.*

38Daniel Heartz, "Approaching a History of 18th-Century Music," *Current Musicology* 4 (1969): 92–95.

39Daniel Heartz, *Haydn, Mozart and the Viennese School, 1740–1780* (New York, 1995), the companion volume that will be cited throughout this book as *Haydn, Mozart.*

Two Sirens: Farinelli and Metastasio

A New Art of Poetic Enchantment

One lyric poet made such a mark on the period that it could be called simply the age of Metastasio. A child of modest circumstances, like many of the century's greatest figures, Pietro Metastasio nevertheless became the most celebrated Italian poet of his time and its premier librettist. His father, Felice Trapassi, was a papal soldier and ran a small grocery in Rome when Pietro was born, on 3 January 1698. Fortunately the child had a powerful and generous godfather in the person of Cardinal Pietro Ottoboni, who looked after his early education. In 1708 he passed under the tutelage of Gian Vincenzo Gravina, a distinguished jurist, classical scholar, and pillar of the Arcadian Academy in its early years. Gravina adopted the lad and supervised his studies of the classics. By 1712 young Pietro had written an entire verse play, *Giustino,* in imitation of ancient tragedy. A year later Gravina transformed his Italian name (*trapassare* means to pass from one state to another) into a Greek equivalent, Metastasio.

The Arcadian Academy was founded at Rome in 1690 in honor of the late Queen Christina of Sweden, the paragon convert who had presided over an earlier academy in Rome dedicated to the purification of Italian literature. A pupil of René Descartes and correspondent of Pierre Corneille, she was an international figure with close ties to Paris. Her influence and the political power of France combined to enhance the sway of French dramatists such as Corneille and Jean Baptiste Racine in Italy. These models, in addition to those of antiquity, were sought as a remedy against the excesses and exaggerations of the previous period, especially the poet Giovanni Battista Marino and the so-called *Marinismo*. Still held in honor were the greatest figures of earlier Italian poetry, mainly Dante, Petrarch, Ariosto, and Tasso, who preceded what was perceived as the bombast and vulgarity of the baroque *seicento*. They were cited as well in warding off French critical attacks on Italian literature.

Pastoral simplicity, as implied by the name Arcadia, was to be the main defense against Marinism. Each academy member took a pastoral name upon admittance. Colonies of Arcadia soon spread from Rome to other cities, creating a "republic of letters" and lending some cultural unity to a land that had none in a political sense.

Metastasio arrived on the scene as the Arcadian movement was gathering momentum. He took minor orders at Rome in 1714, an action quite expected of a budding scholar. Gravina lived to see his ward publish a collection of his writings (including *Giustino*) entitled *Poesie di Pietro Metastasio* in 1717. Gravina then died, leaving his heir a small sum. Having studied jurisprudence among other things, Metastasio entered a law office in Naples to further secure his finances.

His fame as a poet grew. He was admitted to the Arcadian Academy Aletino at Naples under the name Artino Corasio. He is said to have sung as a reception piece his famous *canzonetta* "Già riede primavera," which has been called "the first voicing of his new poetry."[40] It begins as follows:

Già riede primavera	Spring already smiles
col suo fiorito aspetto;	with its flowered aspect,
già il grato zeffiretto	and welcome breezes already
scherza fra l'erbe e i fior.	play among the grass and flowers.
Tornan le fronde agli alberi,	The leaves return to the trees,
l'erbette al prato tornano;	grass returns to the meadow;
sol non ritorna a me	but what does not return to me
la pace del mio cor.	is the peace of my heart.

Metastasio's many soft vowels and liquid consonants, as well as his short lines, are very favorable to musical setting. Intelligibility upon singing is favored too by the small vocabulary to which he restricted himself. The poem, a landmark in 1720, was still treasured three generations later, when Giovanni Paisiello chose to set it in his *Barbiere di Siviglia*. He used the first stanza and added another four lines to suit his purpose.

In Naples, Metastasio sought and won lucrative commissions to write librettos for several celebratory works during the early 1720s. These included the *azione teatrale Endimione*, and two others, *Gli orti esperidi* and *Angelica et Medoro*. They brought him together with the composer Nicola Porpora and with Carlo Broschi Farinelli, Porpora's star pupil. Marianna Benti Bulgarelli ("La Romanina") sang the part of Venus in *Gli orti esperidi*, and there is some evidence to suggest that, although married, she was the poet's personal Venus.

The court theater at Naples, then the San Bartolomeo, called upon Metastasio to rework an old libretto, *Siface*. The result, with music by Francesco Feo, was successfully performed in 1723, leading to a commission for an original *dramma per musica*, *Didone abbandonata*, with La Romanina in the title part and music by Domenico Sarro, in 1724. It brought acclaim especially to the poet, who would, like Aeneas, forsake the leading lady of the drama for greener pastures. Demands upon the librettist poured in from Rome and Venice, as well as from Naples, prompting him to create in quick succession the series of epochal *drammi* culminating with *Artaserse* (1730), which was eventually set to music no fewer than ninety times.

Apostolo Zeno of Venice, a classical scholar and somewhat reluctant opera poet, had already regularized the libretto before Metastasio. He purged what remained of comic actors and action (they returned in the form of comic inter-

---

[40]Luigi Russo, *I classici italiani*, 3 vols. (Florence, 1957), 2: 801.

mezzi between the acts of the serious drama). He settled on the three-act division, reduced the number of arias, and placed them mainly at the ends of scenes,
followed by the singer's exit. It was Zeno who "threw off the yoke of seventeenth-
century bad taste," wrote one of his contemporaries.[41] He also imposed regular
verse on the aria, dismissing the polymetry that was frequent in earlier years. All
these changes were being made in the early eighteenth century by a number of
librettists, but Zeno was the most distinguished among them. From 1719 to 1729
Zeno occupied the post of Caesarean poet in Vienna, where he intensified his glo-
rification of the heroic virtues. In 1729, having recommended Metastasio as his
successor, he retired to Venice, devoted his efforts to the scholarly pursuits that
interested him most, and wrote no more librettos, although he continued to supply oratorio texts to the imperial court.

The new libretto was subject to many additional rules. Giuseppe Baretti codified these in a review of Metastasio's *Opere drammatiche* (Venice, 1757–60) in his
periodical *La frusta letteraria.*[42] *Frusta* means "scourge" and Baretti did indeed
scourge most of his contemporary writers, particularly the Arcadian poets, yet he
placed Metastasio on a plateau and declared him unequalled. He praised three
virtues above all—clarity, precision, and an incomparable facility for versifying—
then added, "Metastasio is so sweet, so intensely sweet and extremely galant
[galantissimo] in expressing amorous feelings, that in many of his dramas he is
able to touch all the most remote fibres of the heart and move one to tears." There
is no mention of Zeno by Baretti, but the comparison, though unspoken, is nevertheless clear. Political virtue, which Zeno lauded, especially in his role as imperial poet, was played down, although not eliminated, by Metastasio, who played
up amorous intrigue—in a word, the galant.

Carlo Goldoni, the reformer of Italian spoken comedy, also a librettist and
member of Arcadia, sings the praises of both Zeno and Metastasio in his memoirs. As a child (he was born in 1707) Goldoni dreamed of leaving his native
Venice for Rome so that he could study with Gravina and become another Metastasio. After failing with a serious libretto for Milan, *Amalasunta,* he decided to seek
help when trying another for Venice in 1736:

> I chose for my judge and counsel Apostolo Zeno, then returned from Vienna, where he
> was replaced by Metastasio. Italy owes to these two illustrious authors the reform of

[41]Quoted by Robert Freeman, *Opera without Drama: Currents of Change in Italian Opera, 1675–1725* (Ann
Arbor, Mich., 1981), p. 65.
[42]Giuseppe Baretti, *La frusta letteraria,* ed. L. Piccioni, 2 vols. (Bari, 1932), 1: 60–67. The review appeared in
the third number of the first year, dated 1 November 1763. The "rules" prohibited two arias in a row for the
same singer or two successive arias sharing the same affect. They recommended larger arias as act endings,
a duet or trio for the leading singers, and inclusion of one obbligato recitative followed by a bustling aria
["un recitativo romoroso seguito da un' aria di trambusto"]. Baretti claims that Metastasio was the author
of these "rules," but this gives insufficient credit to Zeno.

the opera. Before them one saw in musical spectacles gods and devils, machines and the marvelous. Zeno was the first to believe that tragedy could be represented in lyric verses without degrading it, and could be sung without weakening it. He executed his project in a manner most satisfactory to the public, and most glorious for him and for his country. One sees in his operas heroes such as they were, or at least such as historians represented them, the characters vigorously sustained, and his plans always well conducted, the episodes always linked in unity with the action. His style was masculine, robust, and the words of his arias were well adapted to the music of his time.[43]

With due reservations about Goldoni's dismissal of earlier opera, his main point stands. Zeno constructed the taut edifice of the new heroic libretto, concentrating on a rational structure, with diminished reliance upon visual effects. His successor embellished the structure with beauties of all kinds.

Metastasio brought to a peak that perfection of which lyric tragedy was capable. His style is pure and elegant, his verses flowing and harmonious. An admirable clarity in the sentiment, an apparent facility that hid the painful work of precision, a touching energy in the language of the passions, his portraits, his tableaux, his smiling descriptions, his sweet morale, his insinuating philosophy, his analyses of the human heart, his learning, applied sparingly, and with art, his arias, or better said his incomparable madrigals, sometimes in the taste of Pindar, sometimes in that of Anacreon, all these, I say, have rendered him worthy of admiration and have merited him the immortal crown conferred by Italians, which foreigners as well have not refused to grant him.

FIGURE 1.4. Rosalba Carriera. Portrait of Pietro Metastasio.

Goldoni concluded with another comparison, saying that Metastasio imitated Racine in his style, and Zeno imitated Corneille in his vigor. Their genius was a reflection of their characters, he maintains, Metastasio being sweet, polished, and agreeable in society, and Zeno serious, profound, and instructive. Rosalba Carriera at the height of her fame captured the young Metastasio's image during her visit to Vienna in 1730 (Figure 1.4).

The intense labor with which Metastasio reached exactness in verbal expression

[43]Carlo Goldoni, *Tutte le opere,* ed. G. Ortolani, 14 vols. (Milan, 1935–52), 1: 187.

("le pénible travail de la précision") struck others besides Goldoni. Giacomo Casanova visited Vienna in 1752 and, armed with a letter of introduction from the poet Giovanni Ambrogio Migliavacca of Dresden, presented himself to Metastasio. "I asked him if his beautiful lines cost him much effort, and he at once showed me four or five pages filled with erasures due to his trying to bring fourteen lines to perfection. He assured me that he had never been able to compose more lines than that in a day."[44] Metastasio confirmed Casanova's suspicion that the lines which seemed most effortless to amateurs cost him the most labor. When asked which of his operas he liked the best, he named *Attilio Regolo,* a choice confirmed by Hasse. One other point elicited by Casanova deserves attention: "On the subject of his ariettas, he said that he had never written one of them without setting it to music himself, but that he usually did not show his music to anyone." Metastasio too had studied music with Porpora and could sing his own verses. Their appropriateness to musical setting, their concision and extreme beauty with regard to verbal sounds all played a part in making him the *magister magistrorum* that composers of the time proclaimed him to be.[45] Perhaps no poet has been more sensitive to combining within short verses a variety of sounds, while balancing consonance, assonance, and meter to a supreme degree.

Genial verses generated, or could generate, great music. Jean-Jacques Rousseau, in the article "Génie" of his *Dictionnaire de musique,* rises to a peak of enthusiasm when counselling young musicians where to look for inspiration.

> Do you wish to know if some spark of this devouring fire animates you? Run, fly to Naples and listen to the masterpieces of Leo, Durante, Jommelli, and Pergolesi. If your eyes fill with tears, and you feel your heart palpitate, if shudders agitate you and oppression suffocates your transports, take up Metastasio and go to work. His genius will warm yours and you will create after his example. That is what genius is about.[46]

Raniero de' Calzabigi, a writer and librettist who was no friend to Metastasio in his later years, wrote something similar a decade before Rousseau's paean to the imperial poet: "From the majesty, energy, and brilliant images of Metastasio's poetry come the force, variety, and beauty of our music, in my opinion. The harmony of his verses even at a simple reading impresses itself at once on the spirit of our composers, providing them all those musical splendors that demand admiration and respect from enlightened souls."[47] Antonio Eximeno y Pujades went

[44]Giacomo Casanova, Chevalier de Seingalt, *History of My Life,* trans. Willard R. Trask, 12 vols. in 6 (New York, 1966–68; reprint 1997), 3: 221.

[45]Daniel Heartz, "Metastasio, 'maestro dei maestri di cappella dramatici,'" in *Metastasio e il mondo musicale,* ed. Maria Teresa Muraro (Florence, 1986), pp. 315–38.

[46]Original language cited ibid., p. 318. Durante was a poor choice in this context.

[47]Raniero de Calzabigi, "Dissertazione sulle poesie drammatiche del Sig. Abate Pietro Metastasio," in *Poesie . . . del Signor Metastasio,* ed. Calzabigi, 3 vols. (Paris, 1755–57), 1: 188. Original in Heartz, "Metastasio," pp. 316–17.

one step beyond these claims, saying that the poet inspired not only all the greatest composers of the age but the greatest singers as well.

> Metastasio placed composers in the position that Horace demands of poets in order to create with taste. . . . In fact with his dramas, Vinci, Pergolesi, Leo, Perez, Hasse, Galuppi, Jommelli, Piccinni, Sacchini, Anfossi, and others carried the music of this century to its fulfillment, which is the expression of the most tender affects and the most violent passions of the human heart. Metastasio's sweetness of expression was also the cause of forming that divine school of singers, now beginning to decline, according to the taste of which sang Raaff, Farinelli, Caffarelli, Gizziello, Guarduci, Mazzanti, and Guadagni.[48]

It can be no coincidence that Eximeno lined up these particular singers. They were all male, and all castrati, with the exception of Anton Raaff, a high tenor. Suspicions arise as to the relationship between Metastasio's muse and the taste for high voices, particularly those of castrati, that so dominated the epoch.

The waning of the Metastasian ideal was gradual but perceptible by 1770. Niccolò Jommelli complained about the lack of new dramas from the master— they had nearly ceased in the 1760s. Writing to his librettist Gaetano Martinelli in Lisbon, Jommelli bemoaned the fact: "I love, venerate, kneel before, adore Metastasio and all his works, but I wish that he too, adapting himself to the fashion, would make something new, which all the world desires as well."[49] Jommelli's wishes were not fulfilled.

Metastasio himself complained in 1754 that he no longer had the inspiration of great singers to goad him on, which makes it seem as if the interaction of poet and vocalists was both mutual and circular. The Viennese court could be parsimonious when it came to hiring the very best actor-singers, and such was the case in the mid-1750s.

> I am threatened with a new opera for our court. The worst of it is, that there is no proper preparation for it. The making a dress without knowing who is to wear it [di far abiti, senza conoscere chi devrò portarli] is the business of a Jew: I do not know, nor ought I absolutely to make it. We have no singers in the service of the court, no one at least upon whom we can venture to found a character. And those which can be had from other countries, however ordinary their talents, ought to be engaged some years before they are wanted.[50]

[48]Antonio Eximeno y Pujades, *Dell'Origine e delle regole della Musica, colla storia del suo progresso, decadenza, e rinnovazione* (Rome, 1774), p. 442. Original in Heartz, "Metastasio," p. 319.

[49]Letter dated Naples, 14 November 1769, original in Marita P. McClymonds, *Niccolò Jommelli: The Last Years* (Ann Arbor, Mich., 1980), pp. 487–88.

[50]Letter to Farinelli dated Vienna, 4 February 1754, in Charles Burney, ed., *Memoirs of the Life and Writings of the Abate Metastasio,* 3 vols. (London, 1796; reprint 1971), 2: 115. Burney and Metastasio both understood "Jew" in this usage as meaning no more than tradesman. Burney's translations are cited throughout the present volume by the date the letter was written.

As a clothes designer and tailor for the human voice, Metastasio felt it beneath his dignity as imperial poet to make raiments that could be worn by anyone. When he was still in Italy he had the greatest singers of the age with which to work. But this can hardly be said of even his first decade in Vienna, the 1730s, when he wrote several of his most famous librettos. The wars of the 1740s and 1750s put a further crimp in Viennese court opera by reducing the available funds.

Singers and singing played a considerable part in the creation of Metastasio's lyric poetry, according to his own testimony. Singers also stamped particular roles with their own vocal personalities, carrying them from place to place. Giovanni Carestini, one of the finest castrati, was highly prized in the primo uomo role of Timante in *Demofoonte*, although he did not create it at the premiere (Vienna, 1733, music by Caldara).[51] In one of the poet's superb metaphor arias (Act I, Scene 4), Timante, afflicted by a sea of troubles, expresses his lost hopes of salvation.

Sperai vicino il lido,	The shore, I hoped, was near
Credei calmato il vento;	the wind, I believed, was calmed,
Ma transportar mi sento	then I felt myself transported
Fra le tempeste ancor;	once again amidst the storms;
E da uno scoglio infido	And from one hostile cliff
Mentre salvar mi voglio,	trying to save myself,
Urto in un altro scoglio	I was dashed against another
Del primo assai peggior.	Even worse than the first.

Hopes gradually betrayed can be rendered in music by passing from serenity to its opposite. Not by chance does the third line, where the modulation to a second key would normally take place, offer a handy verb of motion. Caldara grasped none of these possibilities and by choosing to use the minor mode made a setting that was rejected by later composers as a model (if they knew it), and probably by the poet as well, who complained about Caldara's melodic gifts.[52]

Two settings that Carestini sang, Christoph Gluck's for Milan in 1743 and Hasse's for Dresden in 1748, show a certain similarity (Example 1.3ab). Gluck sets the first line as a stately rise through the triad to the high tonic, then descent to the fifth, deployed in a leisurely four-measure phrase. The second line, taken twice, reaffirms the key but brings slightly unsettling three-measure phrases. The third line, a brief two measures in *Allegro,* explodes up to E, accomplishing the modulation on the word "sento," and confirms it with an athletic descent for the fourth line. Gluck's setting typifies the shock he can administer by simple musi-

[51]Klaus Hortschansky, "Die Rolle des Sängers im Drama Metastasios: Giovanni Carestini als Timante im *Demofoonte,*" in *Metastasio e il mondo musicale,* pp. 207–34.
[52]*Haydn, Mozart,* p. 136.

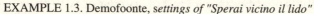

EXAMPLE 1.3. Demofoonte, *settings of "Sperai vicino il lido"*

cal means such as the phrase contractions and melodic ambitus. Metastasio disapproved of Gluck's music because it called too much attention to the composer at the expense of the poet, and because his vocal lines often were rather instrumental, as demonstrated by m. 13. Hasse begins with the calmness of repeated tones, allowing the voice to rest on G while the bass and harmony change underneath. For "calmato" in line 2 he uses the paired eighth notes with which he characteristically painted lapping waves. Repeating the second line the voice becomes more active, which is achieved by the octave leap in syncopated rhythm. The overall rhythm is still calm compared to Gluck's because of the short and symmetrical phrase lengths. For the third line Hasse too resorts to a fast tempo, and moreover to the same rise up to the high third then modulation to G. For the fourth line he reaches the same goal as Gluck, but smoothly, without acrobatics, which helps to explain why Hasse was Metastasio's favorite composer. For all their dissimilarities the setting of the third line in each is very close. It is unlikely that Hasse knew the earlier setting by Gluck until Carestini demonstrated to him how well it suited his voice. If this were the case, the singer became a kind of co-creator with the poet and composer.[53]

Gluck later blamed Italian singers for carrying their favorite music from opera to opera. In a letter to the issue of the *Mercure de France* dated November 1776 he defended himself against charges made by Nicolas Étienne Framery in the same publication two months earlier. Framery claimed that Gluck wrote passages for the castrato Giuseppe Millico similar to those of Antonio Sacchini in the aria "Se cerca, se dice," written for a pasticcio version of Metastasio's *L'Olimpiade* at London in 1773. Gluck pointed out that his relevant pieces for Millico had been printed before 1773. He also took the occasion to defend Sacchini.

> M. Framery is unaware that a composer of Italian opera is very often forced to make accommodation with the caprice and the voice of a singer, and that it is M. Millico who obliged M. Sacchini to insert these phrases in his aria. M. Gluck himself reproached his friend Millico for this. . . . M. Sacchini, genius that he is, and full of beautiful ideas, has no need to pillage others, but he was accommodating enough toward the singer to borrow these passages in which Millico believed he shone the most.[54]

Gluck went on to say that Sacchini's long-established reputation could be diminished by French parodies of his Italian operas if proper melodic and prosodic styles of the two languages were not respected.

The advice Rousseau gave would-be composers in search of inspiration was to take up Metastasio and read. Paisiello used this stratagem as a teacher, telling a young pupil that the poet would be much more use than he was. One young composer who overcame his creative block only by reading Metastasio was André-Ernest-Modeste Grétry, according to his memoirs. Diderot advised keyboard composers in search of musical ideas to consult Metastasio's arias.[55] These unrelated cases offer only a few of the many testimonials to the power and range of the Italian poet, who held his century in thrall. A siren singer he certainly was, truly the twin of Farinelli.

THE PEERLESS SINGER

Carlo Broschi Farinelli was born at Andria in Apulia on 24 January 1705. His father is said to have been a minor official in that Adriatic province of the Kingdom of

[53]A parallel case has been made for the castrato Ferdinando Tenducci, whose music in the title role of settings by Paisello (Rome, carnival 1772) and by Galuppi (Venice, May 1772) of Cigna-Santi's *Motezuma* is remarkably similar. See Dale E. Monson, "Galuppi, Tenducci, and *Motezuma*: A Commentary on the History and Musical Style of Opera Seria after 1750, *Galuppiana 1985. Studi e Ricerche*, ed. Maria Teresa Muraro and Franco Rossi (Florence, 1986), pp. 279–300.

[54]*Querelle des Gluckistes et des Piccinnistes,* ed. François Lesure, 2 vols. (Geneva, 1984), 1: 100–101.

[55]Letter to Charles Burney dated 10 October 1771, cited by Robert M. Isherwood, "The Third War of the Musical Enlightenment," *Studies in Eighteenth-Century Culture* 4 (1975): 223–45; 229 and n. 15.

Naples. He was also said to have been the first music instructor of Carlo and his brother Riccardo, born in 1701. Their early lives are poorly documented. By about age ten Carlo was in Naples studying singing with Porpora, as were two other castrati later renowned, Antonio Uberti ("Porporino") and Gaetano Majorano ("Caffarelli"). It was the practice for young singers to take a patron's or teacher's name as a soubriquet, and possibly Carlo adopted his stage name from the Neapolitan family, Farina. He became the most famous singer of the time. Burney went even further, describing him in his Italian tour journal as "the greatest musician of this century, and perhaps of all ages and countries."[56]

Farinelli's debut before the public came in 1720 at the same event at which Metastasio offered his first libretto, the serenata *Angelica e Medoro,* with music by Porpora. Singer and poet regarded this as an omen and proclaimed themselves "twins."[57] They remained friendly until the end, both dying in 1782, and always used this affectionate term in addressing each other during their long correspondence. Farinelli's part as Tirsi in *Angelica* was only a minor one but he soon worked his way up, singing major female roles in the Roman carnivals of 1722, 1723, and 1724 in the Teatro Alibert; the operas had been composed by Porpora, Antonio Pollarolo, Luca Antonio Predieri, and Leonardo Vinci. He received further vocal instruction from the famous alto castrato Antonio Bernacchi of Bologna, who was himself a pupil of Francesco Pistocchi, the most eminent castrato of the previous generation. In 1725 at Naples he sang opposite Vittoria Tesi in the serenata *Antonio e Cleopatra* with music by Hasse, who, along with Vinci, became his favorite composer.

The pantheon of great singers who graced the eighteenth century was erected as one of the four huge engraved plates devoted to musicians and published by the Studio Rainaldi at Florence between 1801 and 1807 (Figure 1.5). Farinelli is honored with the middle position in the uppermost medallion, where he is flanked on the left by La Tesi and his teacher Bernacchi; on the right by Marianna Benti Bulgarelli, Metastasio's mistress, who had sung with him in Porpora's serenatas of the early 1720s; and on the far right, by Pistocchi. The engravers, Luigi Scotti and Antonio Fedi, or whoever planned and assembled the images, knew what they were doing when they placed Farinelli in this position, surrounded by singers or teachers who were connected to him, as if defining his artistic lineage. A laurel wreath placed above drapes itself mainly over his head. The images themselves were collected from various portraits, or simply invented for the purpose. They often lack veracity or individuality, yet in many cases they are the only surviving depictions of these musicians. Coming after Eximeno's list of great

[56]Charles Burney, *The Present State of Music in France and Italy* (London, 1771). Facsimile edition by Broude Brothers (New York, 1969). Hereafter in this book cited only by author's name or as *Italian Tour.*
[57]Daniel Heartz, "Farinelli and Metastasio, Rival Twins of Public Favour," *Early Music* 12 (1984): 358–66.

FIGURE 1.5. Luigi Scotti and Antonio Fedi. *Italian Singers*, detail.

singers, consisting entirely of castrati except for one tenor, it cannot surprise that, a generation later, the castrati still dominate. Nevertheless there are several women on the detail from the larger plate reproduced in our illustration, and several tenors: Anton Raaff (extreme right), Angelo Amorevoli, Gregorio Babbi, Matteo Babbini, Domenico Mombelli, and Giuseppe Tibaldi. The day for so honoring low male voices had not yet arrived in Italy.

Farinelli was a handsome man according to most portraits offering his likeness, which make a point of depicting him full face, not in profile. The earliest to survive is a caricature by Pierleone Ghezzi which is signed and dated (Figure 1.6). It reads: "Farinello Napolitano famoso cantore di soprano che canto nel Teatro Alibert dell Anno 1724, fatto da me Pierleone Ghezzi a di 2 Marzo 1724" (Farinello of Naples, famous soprano singer who sang in the Alibert Theater in the year 1724, done by me, Pierleone Ghezzi on 2 March 1724.) Farinelli sang two prima donna roles during this season in Rome, Berenice in Vinci's *Farnace,* and Salonice in Predieri's *Scipione.* Both are set in ancient times, but this could scarcely be guessed from the singer's costume. He looks every bit a lady of fashion from the 1720s, alluringly gotten up in a gown with furbellows, feathers in his hair and fan in hand. Ghezzi gives his countenance a weak chin and protruding upper lip, exaggerated for comic effect no doubt, but also present in the drawings of other caricaturists who depicted him in profile.[58]

In his memoirs Johann Joachim Quantz provided the best description of Farinelli's singing in the 1720s. He heard the singer in several cities. His detailed account refers to an opera he witnessed at Parma in 1726.

Farinelli had a penetrating, full, rich, bright, and even soprano voice, the range of which extended from A below middle C to D above the staff. A few years later it added a few tones at the bottom without sacrificing any at the top. In many operas one aria, usually an *adagio,*

FIGURE 1.6. Pierleone Ghezzi. Caricature of Farinelli, 1724.

[58]Daniel Heartz, "Farinelli Revisited," *Early Music* 18 (1990): 430–43. See the caricature by Anton Maria Zanetti of the singer as Arbace in Metastasio's *Catone in Utica,* set by Leo for the Venetian carnival of 1729, p. 431.

was written for him in the contralto range, while the others were in the soprano range. His intonation was pure, his *trillo* beautiful, his chest unusually strong in protracting tones. His throat was very flexible, so that he could produce the largest intervals quickly and with the greatest ease and certainty. Broken passages, as well as all the other runs, provided no difficulty for him, and he was very prolific in his use of the optional ornaments of an *adagio*. The fire of his youth, his great talent, the universal applause and his ready throat guaranteed that he was at times too spendthrift of his abilities. His appearance was advantageous for the stage but acting he did not take greatly to heart [die Action aber ging ihm nicht sehr von Herzen].[59]

The last remark suggests that he may have been a "stand and deliver" type of singer rather than one gifted in histrionics. It may also help explain why Farinelli retired so early from the public stage to the comforts of being a royal chamber singer: he may not have enjoyed the hurly-burly of life in the theater.

The great variety of styles mastered by Farinelli went from vocal acrobatics throughout his entire range to the perfection of *adagio* singing in his deep contralto. Hasse cultivated the latter in the aria "Per questo dolce amplesso," which Farinelli sang as Arbace in Metastasio's *Artaserse* at Venice in 1730.[60] Farinelli told Burney in 1770 that this was one of the arias he repeated nightly for the melancholic Philip V of Spain, from his arrival in 1737 to the king's death in 1746. Another thing the singer purportedly told Burney was that he went to Vienna three times and was advised there by his imperial majesty Charles VI that he should cultivate a simple and direct way of singing rather than showing off his great vocal agility. The advice "made him change his style altogether," says Burney, quoting what he was told. This makes little sense because composers continued to cultivate both styles when clothing his voice. In his *History* Burney becomes more specific and says that Farinelli visited Vienna in 1724, 1728, and 1731. Librettos printed in Vienna at those times make no mention of his name. While it is true that most Viennese librettos omitted singers' names, there is still some anomaly here. The only Vienna visit on record is Lent 1732, when he sang in two oratorios by Caldara.[61]

Efforts to lure Farinelli to London began as early as 1729. In a letter Handel's librettist Paolo Rolli wrote to Senesino (Francesco Bernardi) on 4 February 1729 he reports the news from Venice that "all throng to the theatre at which Farinelli is singing, and that the theatre where you and Faustina are singing is nearly

---

[59]Friedrich Wilhelm Marpurg, *Historisch-kritische Beyträge zur Aufnahme der Musik*, 5 vols. (Berlin, 1754–78), 1: 228.

[60]See figures 4.2–4.3 for the aria from *The Favourite Song in the Opera Call's Artaxerxes by Sigᵣ. Hasse* printed by John Walsh in London (1734).

[61]Robert S. Freeman, "Farinelli and his Repertory," *Studies in Renaissance and Baroque Music in Honor of Arthur Mendel*, ed. Robert L. Marshall (Kassel, 1974), pp. 301–30; 328.

FIGURE 1.7. Jacopo Amigoni. Portrait of Farinelli, engraved by J. Wagner, 1735.

empty."[62] The impressario John Jacob Heidegger and Handel both failed to persuade Farinelli to join a troupe of singers recruited for London. Only in 1734 did the singer relent and agree to join another troupe recruited by his old teacher Porpora and set up as a rival to Handel as the Opera of the Nobility, sponsored by the Prince of Wales. Rolli, having joined the new troupe, wrote to a friend two weeks after Farinelli's debut expressing amazement, the more remarkable because of Rolli's generally caustic tone.

Farinelli was a revelation to me, for I realized that till I had heard him I had heard only a small part of what human song can achieve, whereas I now conceive that I have heard all there is to hear. He has, besides, the most agreeable and clever manners, hence I take the greatest pleasure in his company and acquaintance. He has made me a present which I much desired and which will help me pass many pleasant hours, directing my thoughts to our country's fame and that of our common master [Gravina], which perhaps we two alone have further increased in poetical honour; the present I mean is the works and verses of the Abate Metastasio, to whom, please, remember me.[63]

Rolli overestimated his own talents here by putting himself on a par with Metastasio.

Jacopo Amigoni preceded Farinelli to London in 1730 and became one of its most fashionable portrait painters.[64] The first of his portraits of Farinelli was an oval painting engraved by Joseph Wagner, bearing the date 1735 (Figure 1.7). The inscription conveys some of the excitement of the moment.

[62]Otto Erich Deutsch, *Handel: A Documentary Biography* (London, 1955), p. 237.
[63]Letter to the diplomat Giuseppe Riva in Vienna, dated London, 9 November 1734, ibid., p. 374.
[64]Amigoni painted three portraits of Frederick, Prince of Wales, in 1735. One, in a short wig, is reproduced in Christopher Lloyd, *The Quest for Albion: Monarchy and the Patronage of British Painting* (London, 1998), p. 49.

Partenope il produsse, e le Sirene	Naples produced him and all the Sirens
Tutte fur vinte al paragon del Canto:	Were defeated contesting him in song:
Fama il guida sulle Britanne Scene,	Fame guides him to the stages of Britain,
E furon Nomi suoi Prodigio e Incanto.	And his names were ever Prodigy and Enchantment.

Farinelli is depicted without a wig, or with a very short one, a new fashion in the 1730s that separated the young and fashionable from the "old wigs" like Handel, who continued to favor long tresses down to the shoulders. A striking feature of Farinelli's countenance, evident in several portraits, is his widely spaced eyes, enhanced by prominent eyebrows. One of Amigoni's last and greatest portraits, painted at Madrid in 1750, was of Farinelli, depicted looking still very much like the thirty-year-old idol in London in 1735 (Plate III).

Farinelli made his debut at the Opera of the Nobility in an *Artaserse* that was mostly by Hasse, with additions by the singer's brother Riccardo Broschi. Etiquette demanded that he also be presented at court before the royal family. On this occasion Princess Anne offered to accompany him, asking that he sing two arias of Handel at sight. This Farinelli did with some difficulty, he told Burney in 1770, because he was unfamiliar with Handel's style. The princess was a pupil of Handel and remained devoted to his music, promoting it on the Continent after she married Prince William of Orange. She tried to interest her cousin Frederick of Prussia (the crown prince later known as "the Great") in Handel's music and received for her pains the opinion from him that "Handel's great days are over, his inspiration is exhausted and his taste behind the fashion."[65]

The stay of Farinelli in London is relatively well documented thanks to all the work that has been done on Handel. It was an unparalleled success. Even so, the singer decided to test the waters in another great capital, Paris. In mid-1736 he crossed the Channel and sang for new audiences at Versailles and other residences of the high nobility. Louis XV rewarded him with a royal portrait embroidered with diamonds and a golden snuffbox. These and other presents were deemed insufficient to make him stay or return, and perhaps they no more than matched the lavish gifts showered upon the singer in London, so entertainingly satirized by Hogarth in the second plate of *The Rake's Progress*.[66] He was back in London for a third and final season at the Opera of the Nobility in 1736–37, one that was less successful than the first two. There were several cancellations of

[65]Letter dated Rheinsberg, 19 October 1737, in Deutsch, *Handel,* p. 441.
[66]Heartz, "Farinelli Revisited," 438–39.

scheduled performances in May and June of 1737 caused by what was announced as the singer's indisposition. Farinelli bade farewell to England with a recitative and aria expressing his thanks. He wrote the music himself. It was published in 1737 on four folio sheets under the title of *Ossequioso Ringraziamento per Le cortessime Grazie ricevute nella Britannica Gloriosa Nazione dall'umilissimo et obbligatissimo Servo Carlo Broschi Farinello. Musica del Medesimo.*[67] He contemplated returning to London but never did.

The Spanish court began negotiations with Farinelli while he was still in London. When he arrived in Madrid he was given an immense annual salary and many perquisites. He had few duties at first, mainly private recitals for the king and queen, Philip V and Elizabeth Farnese. As the years went on he took on more responsibilities, some of a kind that had more to do with governing: importation of a herd of horses from Hungary, rechanneling of the river Tagus, and master of the revels. Philip V died in 1746 and under his successor, Fernando VI, Farinelli was given the task of redesigning the royal opera house and directing the production of several works, some of which Metastasio revised specifically for Madrid. *Nitteti* (1756) the poet wrote afresh for Farinelli, who had it set by Nicola Conforto. Other composers whose works figured in the operatic revival under Farinelli's direction were Hasse, Baldassare Galuppi, and Jommelli.

Farinelli was knighted with the order of Calatrava in 1750 and commissioned Amigoni's two late portraits of him (one including Metastasio) bedecked with the order's cross.[68] A solo portrait depicts him in a moment of relaxation, his left hand clutching a piece of music, an amorous aria from Metastasio's *Zenobia* as set to music by Gaetano Latilla (see Plate III).[69] His right hand strokes a little dog behind which are shown some pleasure barges on the river Tagus at Aranjuez, which recall a marine entertainment he staged there for the court.[70] He did sing in some of the operas under his direction, as is clear from his correspondence with Metastasio. No costume designs survive for any of them, unfortunately. To get an idea of the costumer's art at its most lavish during the midcentury, it is necessary to turn to the figure of a castrato contemporary with Farinelli, Carlo Scalzi.

CASTRATI ON STAGE

The Arcadian reform of the serious libretto, completed by Zeno and Metastasio, reduced the scenic splendors of seventeenth-century opera. Theater engineers and machinists found less work as a result, although they still remained busy in

---

[67]The beginning of the aria is transcribed ibid., p. 437.
[68]Leslie Griffin Hennessey, "Friends Serving Itinerant Muses: Jacopo Amigoni and Farinelli in Europe," *Italian Culture in Northern Europe in the Eighteenth Century,* ed. Shearer West (Cambridge, 1999), pp. 20–45; 38.
[69]Heartz, "Farinelli and Metastasio," p. 365, gives a detail of the painting and a transcription.
[70]C. M. Borrero, *Fiestas reales en el reinato de Fernando VI* (Madrid, 1972).

festival operas celebrating special events. The scenic brilliance lacking in regular opera was compensated by the greater luxury bestowed upon costumes for the principal singers. Pier Jacopo Martello seemed to take account of this change in his satirical treatise *Della tragedia antica et moderna* of 1715.[71] The librettist, "whether he likes it or not, shall write bad musical tragedies; yet tragedies they shall be, for they would not provide the opportunity to display the royal garments that glitter in the Impresario's wardrobe if they imitated lesser characters than Kings and Demigods." Kings were impersonated especially by castrati, who mimicked regal bearing to a tee. Martello took this into account: "Let the castratos be chosen not only for the nimble and excellent voices but for their presence. . . . Let the costumes be bejeweled and embroidered with sham gold and silver, and cut for the most part in the royal fashion." Ideally, the poet and composer should be the same person, and this was achieved, says Martello, by the famous castrato Pistocchi.

Carlo Scalzi was born around 1700 in Genoa. According to printed librettos he began appearing in female roles at Rome in 1718. He then graduated to secondary male roles in Venice and other cities of northern Italy. By the mid-1720s he was singing primo uomo in all the great theaters. Metastasio declared him incomparable, referring to the role of Arbace in *Artaserse.*[72]

Scalzi was the object of a truly regal portrait painted by Charles-Joseph Flipart (Figure 1.8). Flipart, the youngest of a Parisian family of artists, had apprenticed in Venice under Amigoni, whom he followed to Spain. A piece of music to which the singer points is headed "Sign. Scalzi Atto 3^{zo} Arbace" and the text is that of a substitute aria for Arbace derived from the duet in Act III of Metastasio's *Artaserse.*

Vivrò se vuoi cosi	I shall live at thy command
Ma in pegno di mia fide	But in pledge of my faith
Vorei spirarti ai piedi	I would expire at thy feet,
Vorei morir per te.[73]	I wish to die for thee.

The notes, though difficult to read, are not faked, as in so many portraits with music. They make sense and present a charming melody with bass in 3/4 time and the key of A, disposed in three-measure phrases with the shape **a b b'**, in other

[71]Piero Weiss, "Pier Jacopo Martello on Opera (1715): An Annotated Translation," *Musical Quarterly* 66 (1980): 378–403.

[72]Daniel Heartz, "Portrait of a Primo Uomo: Carlo Scalzi in Venice ca. 1740," *Musikalische Ikonographie,* ed. Harald Heckmann, Monika Holl, and Hans Joachim Marx (Hamburger Jahrbuch für Musikwissenschaft 12) (Laaber, 1994): 133–45; 137.

[73]The fourth line is supplied from the setting of this aria in Christian Bach's *Artaserse* (Turin, 1761).

FIGURE 1.8. Charles-Joseph Flipart. Portrait of Carlo Scalzi.

words, a statement followed by what is called a galant extension.[74] From Amigoni the young artist could have learned the importance of incorporating real music in a musician's portrait. The setting cannot be identified with any composer. It may be by the singer himself, in which case it would agree with several portraits of Farinelli that include music.

Scalzi's costume, including the bejeweled hat with plume on the table, reaches the acme of sumptuousness, overtopping all other rococo portraits of musicians in this regard. His flairing jacket, stiffened with whalebone like a woman's panier, is gorgeously embroidered in gold upon a light blue ground; the sash he wears over his shoulder, as if it were some great royal order, is silver-embroidered on a darker blue.[75] A long train flowing from his back to the floor is an off-white embroidered with more gold. The costume, in sum, is "cut in the royal

[74]Heartz, "Portrait of a Primo Uomo: Carlo Scalzi," p. 140, gives a transcription.
[75]For a reproduction in color see *The Oxford Illustrated History of Opera*, ed. Roger Parker (Oxford, 1994), facing p. 65.

fashion" as Martello recommended, and the pose is haughty enough to suit a ruler. The portrait cannot be identified with any particular role. Rather it seems to be intended to sum up the singer's career, which came to an end with retirement to a life of ease in his native Genoa following the 1739 season, when he played two title roles in Rome.

During the second half of the eighteenth century great castrato voices began to wane in number, a decline noted by Eximeno in his remarks on Metastasio's role in making them flourish in the first place. The number of castrati in general diminished. Economics offers a better explanation than Eximeno's for both the flourishing and the decline.[76] The times were very bad in seventeenth-century Italy, as they were indeed throughout most of Europe. An Italian family with more than one young son, even if fairly well placed in the societal hierarchy, looked to the church as a place to send younger males. Some became priests or monks. Those showing musical talents could be castrated with a hope of finding a place for them in church choirs, at the least. Very few of them made it onto the opera stage and fewer still became a Scalzi or a Farinelli, but hopes remained high. A wave of economic recovery began to spread in Italy during the second quarter of the eighteenth century. No longer was it deemed moral to mutilate children on the basis of desperate hopes. The practice became an embarrassment and excuses had to be found, such as a riding accident, as was the case with the early biographers of Farinelli. An eminent author was drawn to the general subject.

Montesquieu, (Charles-Louis de Secondat), born of nobility near Bordeaux in 1689, won early fame with his *Lettres persanes* (1721), stinging critiques of society and religion, both Moslem and Christian. In 1728, newly elected to the Académie Française, he set out on a three-year journey that took him all over Europe, ending with eighteen months in London. He kept a journal that shows his concern with various modes of government, filled with humane observations and planting seeds for his masterpiece, *L'esprit des lois* (1748), a pillar of enlightened thought. He also took interest in music, especially Italian opera. Like several other French writers, he was fascinated by castrati.

In early 1729 Montesquieu was in Florence, then Rome, where he attended comedies in the smaller Teatro Capranica and serious operas in the larger Teatro delle Dame.

> At Rome, women do not mount the stage. In their place are castrati dressed as women. That has a very bad effect on morals, because nothing I know of inspires Romans so much to *l'amour philosophique....* During my time at Rome, in the Capran-

---

[76]John Rosselli, "The Castrati as a Professional Group and a Social Phenomenon, 1550–1850," *Acta Musicologica* 60 (1988): 143–79. See also John Rosselli, *Singers of Italian Opera: The History of a Profession* (Cambridge, 1992).

ica theater, there were two little eunuchs, Mariotti and Chiostra, dressed as women, who were the most beautiful creatures I ever saw in my life, and who would have inspired the taste of Gomorrah in people whose tastes were the least depraved in this respect. A young Englishman, believing one of them was a woman, became madly in love and entertained this passion for more than a month.[77]

Some female sopranos did indeed pose as castrati in order to gain the stage. One of them enchanted Casanova, who minutely describes in his memoirs how he investigated the case.[78] Mariotti and Chiostra were both men. Montesquieu did not make them up in order to enhance his story (as Casanova sometimes did). They sang female parts in January 1729 at the Capranica in *La Costanza*, a *commedia per musica* by Bernardo Saddumene with roles divided between Tuscan and Neapolitan dialects, set to music by Giovanni Fischietti. A month later followed *La Somiglianza*, a comedy without Neapolitan roles, by Saddumene and Fischetti, in which the same two castrati sang. No music survives. Chiostra quickly disappeared from printed librettos, but Mariotti went on to a career singing on stage as late as 1741 in Berlin.

Montesquieu made a few more remarks on singers in the same passage, and on opera in general. "I did not hear Faustina sing, nor Senesino, but only Turcotti at Florence, and at Rome Farfallino and Scalzi."[79] Once again he was accurate. Maria Turcotti sang a seria role at Florence in early January 1729. The castrati Farfallino and Scalzi both sang at the Teatro delle Dame during the Roman carnival of 1729, the works being two *drammi* by Metastasio, Pietro Auletta's *Ezio* and Vinci's *Semiramide riconosciuta*. The singers whose names were thought worthy of mention by Montesquieu were all sopranos: two women and five castrati, a ratio roughly equivalent to the attention and the salaries both types commanded.

Montesquieu's general comments are few but choice.

There are three theaters at Rome, the grand one called Alibert [delle Dame], Capranica and La Pace, which is a small theater. They are always full. That is where the abbés go to study their theology, where the whole populace gathers down to the last bourgeois, all crazy about music—the shoemaker and tailor are connoisseurs. The decorations greatly please the Romans. They have poor dances, of which they are enchanted. Lacking a true idea of the dance, they confuse it with jumping, and who jumps the highest pleases them the most.

Some other visitors concurred about the dancing. That opera attracted various classes of society is confirmed by several other sources.

---

[77]Charles Louis de Montesquieu, *Oeuvres complètes*, 2 vols. (Paris, 1949), 1: 679.
[78]Casanova, *History of My Life*, 2: 3–30.
[79]Montesquieu, *Oeuvres complètes*, 1: 679.

Baron Karl Ludwig Pöllnitz, Prussian adventurer, attended the same Roman carnival as Montesquieu and made several observations on the Teatro delle Dame.[80] He found it very grand, but so large that voices were lost. Although its seven ranks of boxes were imposing, the individual boxes were so small that the interior, he wrote, resembled a chicken coop. The scenery changed too slowly for him. While the costumes of the three principals were splendid, those of the other singers he pronounced horrible. Good voices and good music gratified him, but not the dancing, upon which he came down severely: "Les danses ne peuvent se regarder; vous ne sauriez vous imaginer rien de plus affreux." Passionately fond of Italian music though he was, the unchanging stage picture of six actors, with no machines, no chorus, and no dances except in the entr'actes, finally became boring: "Il me parait qu'un tel opéra meriteroit mieux le nom de Concert." Other detractors would say much the same, complaining that what should be a grand spectacle was only a concert in costume. Pöllnitz differed markedly with Montesquieu on the subject of castrati. He found ridiculous not only their playing the roles of women, but also their representation of heroes from myth and ancient history.

Casanova, the century's most infamous adventurer, wrote his life's story at unprecedented length, sparing no sexual details, however lubricious. Born in Venice in 1725 to parents who were actors, he was educated at Padua for an ecclesiastical career. Scandals put an early end to his religious vocation. Given a choice of exile he picked Constantinople, then thought an exotic, far-away capital. Back in Venice by 1746 he was reduced to playing violin in the orchestra of the San Samuele theater in order to earn a living. Many of his affairs involved opera singers and dancers, and his sexual gratifications were not confined to the female gender. He was in many ways an ideal commentator on sexual confusions projected by castrati, particularly when they were playing women's roles on the stage.

Like Montesquieu, Casanova was captivated by the feminine charms on display in the Teatro delle Dame during a Roman carnival. In his case the castrato who impressed all Rome, and whose charms overwhelmed him, took his name from a protector, Cardinal Borghese. He was Tommaso Borghesi, who created the principal female role of La Cecchina in the century's most successful comic opera, Goldoni's *La buona figliuola,* set to music by Niccolò Piccinni and first performed at the Teatro delle Dame on 6 February 1760. Casanova cared little about music, which he considered beneath his dignity as the "Chevalier de Seingalt," a title he invented—like Voltaire and many others of the time, he promoted himself to the nobility. Infuriatingly, he never deigns to cite operas or composers by name. His commentary is incisive, on the other hand, about the castrato *en femme* on stage, the social havoc this caused, and the reasons why he believed the system should be altered.[81]

---

[80]*Lettres du baron de Pöllnitz,* 3 vols. (London, 1747), 2: 231, cited after Giulio Roberti, "La musica in Italia nel secolo XVIII secondo le impressioni di viaggiatori stranieri," *Rivista Musical Italiana* 7 (1900): 698–729; 707.

Burney and the Grand Tour

Cosmopolitan figures like Sterne and Montesquieu were emblematic of their times. Travel became more widespread during the eighteenth century. It attracted not only the privileged classes, which had long enjoyed its pleasures, but also persons of relatively modest means and status.[82] Rich or promising young men north of the Alps were increasingly expected to round off their educations with a tour of Italy, mainly in order to inspect the art and architecture of the Renaissance and the remains of antiquity (Figure 1.9). A few young ladies were sent to the same finishing school. Touring became an institution, a travel business that required scholarly advisors and tutors. Gradually improving conditions affected transportation, lodging, and nurture. Many of the genteel tourists were required by parents to write letters home demonstrating their edification. Many also kept journals and diaries. Some tourists of lesser standing wrote travel guides for commercial gain, and publishers made profits from them, before the market became saturated. The written material that survives is vast and has become a field of study in its own right. Introducing individuals to a culture other than their own has been seen as one aspect of the Enlightenment.[83]

FIGURE 1.9. A coach-and-four. Frontispiece from *La vera guida per chi viaggi in Italia,* 1775.

By and large peaceful conditions prevailed in Italy after the Treaty of Utrecht (1713), ending the War of the Spanish Succession. Exceptions were the mid-1730s (War of the Polish Succes-

---

[81]Casanova, *History of My Life,* 7: 250–52.
[82]Jeremy Black, *The Grand Tour in the Eighteenth Century* (New York, 1992).
[83]Robert Shackleton, "Travel and the Enlightenment: Naples as a Specimen," *Essays on the Age of Enlightenment in Honor of Ira O. Wade,* ed. Jean Macary (Geneva, 1977), pp. 281–91.

sion) and intermittent outbreaks during the 1740s (War of the Austrian Succession or Silesian Wars). In all these conflicts the peninsula was a battleground for France, Spain, and Austria (which had several possessions in Italy). The century's most violent conflict before the upheavals of the 1790s was the Seven Years War (1756–63), but it scarcely affected Italy because in it France and Austria were allied, as they remained until 1792, and Spain was little involved.

Music and musical interest has determined my selection of tourist-writers. They range from a young practicing musician, Johann Joachim Quantz, who exemplifies the artisan class, to an aristocrat madly in love with music and Italy, the jurist Charles de Brosses; from famous travelers to little-known *mélomanes* and professional travel writers. They pave the way that leads to Charles Burney, who makes them all seem preludial in comparison, and without whom the present book could not have been written.

Casanova was among the century's most restless travelers and most entertaining storytellers. Although only a background to his amatory adventures, his verbal portraits of Venice are memorable, as are those of Rome and Naples. Gambling and shady financial deals, some verging on outright swindles, made and lost him fortunes time and again, insuring that he was not long welcome wherever he resided. He first saw Paris in 1750 and found it "enchanting."[84] Later he called it "the city of cities" (8: 3). The court at Versailles impressed him but not as much as another in 1752: "I saw at Dresden the most brilliant court in Europe, and the arts which flourished at it" (3: 218). What he witnessed there was the triumph of Italian opera under Hasse. Dresden lost its luster after being partly destroyed by Frederick the Great. It was succeeded by a smaller capital, Stuttgart, which Casanova visited in 1760: "At this period the most brilliant court in Europe was that of the Duke of Württemberg" (6: 66). Stuttgart's opera seria under Jommelli had in fact replaced Dresden's as the finest in Germany. In the course of his travels Casanova visited every capital discussed in this book.

QUANTZ RECALLS THE 1720S

One of the most informative sources on new music of the 1720s is Quantz, later the favorite flautist and teacher of Frederick the Great. He wrote his autobiography in 1754 at the request of Friedrich Wilhelm Marpurg, who printed it in the first volume of an extensive collection of documents.[85] Born in 1697 in a village near Merseburg in the Electorate of Hanover, Quantz arose from lowly begin-

[84]Casanova, *History of My Life*, 3: 215.
[85]Marpurg, *Historisch-Kritische Beyträge*, 5 vols. (Berlin, 1754–78): 1: 197–250; reproduced in facsimile in Willi Kahl, *Selbstbiographien deutscher Musiker des XVIII. Jahrhunderts* (Cologne, 1958), pp. 104–57; translated in Paul Nettl, *Forgotten Musicians* (New York, 1951), pp. 280–319. The translations here are mine. They will be identified only by page numbers in the original. Hereafter in this book, Quantz's autobiography is quoted without further ascription except to the author's name.

nings to become a town musician and eventually a Saxon court musician. Wanderlust emerged early in his life. Freed from duties in Dresden during the summer of 1717, he used his holiday to journey through upper and lower Silesia, Moravia, and Austria to Vienna, where he took some lessons in counterpoint from Jan Dismas Zelenka, returning to Dresden in October. The following year he was appointed to the Polish capella of Augustus the Strong, king of Poland and elector of Saxony. His duties involved making many journeys back and forth between Dresden and Warsaw. By 1719 he had switched from oboe to flute. In 1722 one of his patrons recommended him to the king for a subvention that would allow him to travel to Italy for further study. The request was granted but put in effect somewhat later.

The coronation of Emperor Charles VI as king of Bohemia took place at Prague in July 1723 and attracted spectators from all parts. Several of the leading musicians of the Dresden court were in attendance. Quantz was among them and provided a firsthand account of the music, the high point of which was performance of the opera *Costanza e Fortezza* by Johann Joseph Fux, imperial Oberkapellmeister.

> The opera was performed outdoors by 100 singers and 200 instrumentalists. It was written more in the church style than theatrically, but made a magnificent effect. Concertizing and linking of the violins with one another in the ritornellos, although consisting of movements that might appear stiff and dry on paper, mostly made, with so numerous a band, an excellent effect, indeed a much better one than would have a more galant melody ornamented with many small figures and quick notes [ein galanterer, und mit vielen kleinen Figuren, und geschwinden Noten gezierter Gesang]. (p. 216)

Quantz uses this comparative form of the term *galant* immediately again in trying to explain what he meant.

> It goes without saying that a more galant song for the instruments, admittedly better in a smaller locale and with fewer players, would be impossible to perform with appropriate ensemble here, especially being executed by so many musicians who were unused to playing with each other. The broad space also militated against clarity in performing figures that consisted of small and quick notes. The truth of this observation convinced me on many occasions, including at Dresden, where the otherwise rather dry overtures by Lully, when played by a full orchestra, make a better effect than do many more pleasant and galant overtures by other famous composers, works that, in a chamber, unquestionably receive preference. The many choruses in the Prague opera served at the same time for ballets, in the French manner. (p. 216)

Because the forces were so large it was necessary for Kapellmeister Caldara to give the beat (presumably with a scroll as in large-scale church music). "Old Fux himself was present but on account of his gout (the emperor had him carried from Vienna to Prague in a sedan-chair) had the pleasure of hearing this unusually splendid rendition of his work while seated near the emperor." There followed a description of individual singers and players. While in Prague Quantz also heard Giuseppe Tartini and praised his beautiful tone and strong technique.

Not long after returning to Dresden Quantz was invited to Würzburg, whose bishop offered him a position as flautist. He refused, perhaps on account of the promised sojourn in Italy in Saxon service, which soon came to pass.

Quantz's long-desired goal of an *Italienreise* began in the spring of 1724. He traveled with a diplomat in the king's service who was leaving to take up an ambassador's post in Rome. They went by way of Augsburg, Innsbruck, Mantua, Modena, Bologna, Loreto, and Ancona. Leaving Dresden on 23 May, they arrived on 11 July in Rome, where the young musician took up residence in the embassy. He promptly set about hearing everything he could in Rome's innumerable churches and cloisters. Oddly enough his first musical recollection is of a novelty from the world of opera.

> The newest thing to my ears was the so-called Lombard taste, totally unknown to me, that Vivaldi had shortly before introduced in one of his operas at Rome. The inhabitants would listen to almost nothing but what was similar to this taste. It gave me trouble at first to find any pleasure therein to go along with the fashion. Other than this the taste seemed to be the same which I noted in good Italian operas a few years earlier, performed by good Italian singers, in 1719 at Dresden and in 1723 at Prague. (p. 223)

Exhausted by running around Rome from church to church, Quantz became ill. When he recovered he sought out the aged Francesco Gasparini for lessons in composition. These occupied six months, into early 1725, by which time the master was satisfied he had nothing more to teach his pupil, who was full of praise for the instruction.

Quantz had little to say about the composers and performers he heard in Rome. He named only Giuseppe Pitoni of the papal chapel ("artful, but bizarre and bold") and Pietro Paolo Bencini ("less artful, but natural and pleasing"). Only three singers did he think worth naming, plus the violinist Francesco Montanari and the cellist Giovanni Batista Costanzi ("neither very strong composers"). Of greater interest is his third instrumentalist "Memo Scarlatti," whom he describes as "the old Neapolitan Alessandro Scarlatti's son, who was also then in Rome, a galant keyboard player in the manner of the time who was in Portuguese service, and who later went over to Spanish service, to which he still belongs." This can only mean Domenico Scarlatti, and Quantz was right about his employments.

There was no opera in Rome during 1725 because it was a Jubilee year, so Quantz left for Naples. He attended the San Bartolomeo theater and heard

Domenico Sarro's *Tito Sempronio Gracco,* the carnival opera of early 1725, pronouncing it to be "almost in Vinci's taste." For the first of several times he heard Farinelli, described as "approaching ever nearer his famous perfection." The other singers he mentioned were the celebrated Anna Maria Strada del Pò, later a principal soprano for Handel in London, and Vittoria Tesi, "gifted by nature with a masculinely strong contralto voice." He had heard La Tesi earlier at Dresden in 1719 and described in some detail the changes in her voice since then.

Naples meant to Quantz not only opera of the first class, but composers as well, chief of whom was Alessandro Scarlatti. He met Hasse, another young German destined for fame, who was studying counterpoint with Scarlatti. They became good friends and shared the same dwelling. Quantz asked Hasse to introduce him to the reluctant Scarlatti, who was disposed against wind instruments, saying they were always out of tune. Hasse persisted until his master agreed to meet and hear Quantz.

> Scarlatti let me hear him on the harpsichord, which he knew how to play in a learned manner, although he possessed less fluency in performing than his son [ob er gleich nicht so viel Fertigkeit der Ausführung besass, als sein Sohn]. He accompanied me on it in a solo. I had the luck of winning his favor, even to the extent that he composed a few flute solos for me. He introduced me at various distinguished houses and he even wanted to procure for me an attractive position in Portuguese service, which I thought best to decline. . . . He was not only one of the greatest contrapuntists of his time but also one of the most prolific composers who ever lived. (pp. 228–29)

Quantz made his way so rapidly as a flautist that he was invited to perform in concerts honoring the prince of Liechtenstein, alongside Hasse, Farinelli, Tesi, and Francischello (Francesco Alborea), the great cellist. At these events he made the personal acquaintance of Farinelli and won his friendship.

The Scarlattis, father and son, come into focus through Quantz's description: one plays in a learned manner, the other is a galant player. Just so does Fux's opera illustrate a generational dichotomy. Learned and more in a church style than a theatrical one, it eschewed galant melodies with rapid and intricate ornaments. Rapidity and intricately embellished melody were perhaps one factor that made Domenico's playing galant whereas his father in comparison exhibited less fluency at the keyboard. Fux and Alessandro Scarlatti, exact contemporaries, represented the peaks of the generation born around 1660, the distinguished elders who were in their sixties during the 1720s. Held in the greatest respect for their immense accomplishments and learning, they were nevertheless not the models for galant melody that young Hasse and Quantz were seeking. In this respect, Italian singers and violinists of their own generation provided major inspiration.

Quantz returned to Rome in time to hear the famous *Miserere* by Gregorio Allegri sung in the papal chapel on Good Friday, 1725. He received and refused further offers of lucrative positions. Permission was granted him to travel more widely in Italy. In October he visited Florence, where he heard operas and praised some of the instrumentalists, notably the theorbo player Domenico Palafuti. Subsequently he heard operas at Livorno, Bologna, and Ferrara. He arrived in Venice for carnival 1726 and stayed three months. His musical experiences are recounted in part below. In May he traveled to Reggio and Parma in order to hear operas. He heard Farinelli again at Parma and described his vocal prowess in great detail, along with that of Carestini. He had received permission from the Saxon embassy in Rome to visit France, and so he began the slow journey north, visiting Milan and Turin, where he met the violinist Jean-Marie Leclair, who was studying with Giovanni Battista Somis.

He crossed the Mount Senis pass in June 1726 and traveled via Geneva and Lyon to Paris, where he arrived on 15 August. He disliked most features of French opera, the style of which was already known to him. He particularly disliked French singing and singers, as might be expected from his Italian orientation. French instrumentalists came off better, and he named several good violinists and flautists, with special praise for Michel Blavet, who befriended him. He preferred French church music to French opera and had a good word for the Concert Spirituel, but regretted that it was more popular than the Concert Italien. French music would not get better, he predicted, until the prejudice against foreign music was overcome. When he wrote this in 1754 the transformation was well underway.

Summoned back to Dresden in early 1727, he made so bold as to travel to London without permission. There he admired Handel's *Admeto* and heard Faustina Bordoni and Francesca Cuzzoni, whose respective powers he described at length. He returned home via Holland, Hannover, and Brunswick, reaching Dresden on 23 July. In sum, he accomplished a typical Grand Tour of the time, even though he was only a lowly musician.

BROSSES IN ITALY, 1739–40

Charles de Brosses was born at Dijon in 1709 to a prominent legal family (noblesse de robe). He became president of the *Parlement* of Burgundy and the author of several eminent scholarly works (in 1750 he was the first to publish a description of the excavations at Herculaneum). In June 1739 he set out for Italy. Traveling with some friends he reached Genoa by sea and made his way across the peninsula from Milan to Padua and Venice. Then he headed south, visiting Bologna, Florence, and Rome, where he arrived in October 1739. After visiting Naples he returned to Rome for the winter. He took a different route north along the Adriatic Sea and reached Milan and Turin by April 1740. During the trip he sent long letters about Italy to his friends at home. After he returned to Dijon, he revised his letters, added further essays, and polished the whole as a gift he made to his friends, who received it not only as a practical guide to travel but as a source of wit and delectation. Brosses never intended to publish his letters, an action he considered unbecoming to his dignity as a high magistrate. Writing for himself and his friends, he could be candid on all subjects, even the Catholic Church, the Italian manifestations of which mostly appalled him. Only after his death were his "Lettres familières d'Italie" published (in 1799). They scandalized most nineteenth-century readers by their complete freedom of expression, but not Stendahl, who called Brosses "the most charming because he did not write for publication by press."[86]

Brosses devoted his longest essays to Rome and Naples, with substantial sections on their music. "Naples is the sole Italian city that seems truly a capital. . . . Everything contributes to give it that vibrant and animated character possessed by Paris and London, and which is not found at all in Rome" (1: 394). Nevertheless Venice struck him as so special in its physical situation that he named it the second city of Europe after Paris (1: 187). Greatly interested in visual art, he compiled long, annotated lists of what was to be seen. To him, Italy's glorious past far outweighed its diminished present: "The only painters of great reputation still remaining in Italy are Solimena in Naples, Trevisani in Rome, and Canaletto in Venice" (1: 399). (Batoni in Rome would have been a better choice than Trevisani, and Tiepolo had not yet left Venice.)

Rome impressed Brosses mainly by its monuments of the past. The city's social and economic conditions he deplored. "Imagine a people of whom one quarter are priests, one quarter statues, a third quarter scarcely work, and the fourth quarter do nothing whatsoever. The city has no agriculture, no commerce, and no industries, although situated in the middle of a fertile countryside on a navigable river" (2: 9). In sum, he regarded Rome as a lazy and corrupt sycophancy living off the rest of Catholic Christendom. In music, he said, it lived off the Neapolitan composers, of whom he named several (2: 313). His description of serious opera in the main Roman theaters is detailed, beginning with the papal proscription of female singers and the complete confusion of genders.

> The sexes are greatly mixed in opera. At Naples la Baratti [Teresa Baratta] plays men's roles. Here in Rome women are not permitted on the stage. Propriety forbids it and allows only pretty little boys dressed as girls and (may God pardon me) I strongly believe that, given the universal passion for *filles de théâtre*, fornication is not lessened thereby. Sometimes these disguised beauties are not so small. Marianini, six foot in

---

[86]*Lettres d'Italie du Président de Brosses,* ed. Frédéric d'Agay, 2 vols. (Paris, 1986), 1: 34. This edition, with copious notes and indices, is based on all surviving sources and supersedes earlier editions. It is cited throughout the present book only by volume and page number. It adduces new evidence to show that the redaction of the letters was completed by the early 1740s, not in 1755 as claimed by Claude Palisca, "'Baroque' as a Music-Critical Term," *French Musical Thought, 1600–1800,"* ed. Georgia Cowart (Ann Arbor, Mich., 1989), pp. 7–21; 13.

> height, plays the role of a woman on the stage of the Argentina, making her the most
> sizable princess I shall ever see. (2: 296)

Long comparisons with French opera elucidate production, libretto structure, staging, scenery, and audience behavior. What Brosses praised most were Italian opera orchestras, particularly their gradual transition from *pianissimo* to *fortissimo* and back, which he recommended as a model that ought to be followed in France (2: 308).

Brosses was a modernist in his musical tastes, as is evident from his espousal of the new *crescendo-diminuendo* orchestral dynamics. At Naples, where he missed no opportunities to hear music, he witnessed the revival of Sarro's *Partenope* (1722) at the recently opened San Carlo theater. He was disappointed. "La composition n'en était pas bonne. Sarri est un musicien savant mais sec et triste" (1: 400). Yet he praised the performance, especially the leading roles sung by Senesino and Teresa Baratta, in spite of Sarro's "learned, but dry and sad" musical style. What pleased him most in Naples was Leonardo Leo's *La finta Frascatana*, a *commedia per musica* performed in the smaller Teatro Fiorentini. "What invention, what harmony, what excellent musical drollery! I shall bring this opera back to France! . . . but will it be understood?" Clearly Brosses was ahead of musical advances in his own country with respect to recognizing the attainments of the Neapolitans.

> Naples is the capital of the musical world. In its several conservatories of music were raised most of the students who became famous composers: Scarlatti, Leo, Vinci, the true god of music, Rinaldo [da Capua] and my charming Pergolesi. All these artists occupied themselves only with vocal music. Instrumental music has its reign in Lombardy. (1: 401)

The various violinists appraised by Brosses will find mention later in Chapter 3. His high regard for Hasse, whom he rightly considered a Neapolitan by adoption, finds place in Chapter 4.

Many French travelers besides Charles de Brosses set down their reactions to music in Italy. One of the best informed was Madame Du Boccage, author of a published *Lettres d'Italie* that Goldoni praised in his memoirs.[87] She arrived in the spring of 1757 and followed an itinerary that took her from Turin to Venice, Bologna, Florence, Rome, and Naples. Commenting on the excellent comic opera witnessed at Florence, she said it was more novel than serious opera, hence more à la mode in Italy (3: 195). The carnival season in early 1758 found her at Rome,

---

[87]Marie-Anne Le Page, dame Fiquet Du Boccage, *Recueil des oeuvres,* 3 vols. (Lyons, 1762). The Italian letters conclude the third volume. They deserve a modern edition.

where she wanted to listen to the serious operas in the theaters, but politeness required that she receive visitors in her box and converse with them as did everyone else (3: 331). She was not offended by the boys playing women's roles as singers and dancers, saying in fact that they were very convincing. She was amazed that silence reigned only during the ballets: "Dans ce spectacle le silence ne regne que quand il n'y a rien à attendre" (3: 331). She confessed that Metastasian dramas, although often very interesting to read, ceased being so when sung. The tedium of long recitatives and excessively long arias made her remember some of the superior features of French opera, which she otherwise disdained for its monotonous singing. If only the two genres could be amalgamated, something more listenable might be created: "on pourrait de l'un et l'autre Opéra en former un plus propre à se faire écouter" (3: 333). Hers was not the only expression of this desire, so prophetic of the operatic reforms about to flower, notably in Parma, which she visited during her return to France in May 1758.

The Italian tour of Madame Du Boccage overlapped with the beginning of the Seven Years War (1756–63). English tourists were less fortunate than French in reaching Italy during this period because their country was at war with France and Austria. Once the Peace of Paris went into effect in early 1763 the floodgates to an English influx opened. Prominent visitors to Italy who wrote their impressions included David Garrick, James Boswell, and Edward Gibbon. Published guides were composed by Samual Sharp and Tobias Smollett, drawing refutation from an Italian author in London, Giuseppe Baretti, all forming an interlude that leads directly to Burney's Italian tour.

Travelers in the 1760s and 1770s

Garrick, the eminent actor and theater director, was Burney's patron and one of his closest friends. The Garrick family were Huguenots from Bordeaux who left France after the revocation in 1685 of the Edict of Nantes (1598) that granted Protestants some religious liberties. Born in England in 1717, young David captured the London stage as soon as he appeared on it and dominated the theatrical scene by the 1750s. In 1746 he married a ballet dancer from Vienna, Eva Maria Weigel, a protegée of Gluck. Garrick trained many actors, and even tamed some opera singers, notably Gaetano Guadagni. He reformed the stage in ways that influenced his musical collaborators, including Burney and Gluck.[88]

Garrick and his wife set out for the Continent in September 1763. He was already well known in Paris from an earlier trip.[89] On his return he was admired

---

[88]Daniel Heartz, "From Garrick to Gluck: The Reform of Theatre and Opera in the Mid-18th Century," *Proceedings of the Royal Musical Association* 94 (1967–68): 11–27.
[89]*The Diary of David Garrick being a record of his memorable trip to Paris in 1751*, ed. R. C. Alexander (New York, 1928).

even more and celebrated in particular by Melchior Grimm, Diderot, and the *philosophes*.[90] His travel goal was Italy. Burney had given him a list of music to be purchased there, asking for a report on "the present state of Music in Italy."[91] This shows that Burney had already on his mind in 1763 not only his own Italian tour of 1770 but also the title under which his recounting of it would eventually be published. Garrick sent a report to Burney from Naples, dated 5 February 1764. He found nothing to his liking aside from "the Climate, Situation and Curiosities." The people, low- and high-born alike, he compared to so many Harlequins, Scaramouches, and Pantaloons, summing them up as "worthless." Of the San Carlo, he wrote, "The Theatre is a Most Magnificent one." What he encountered on its stage, a revival of Tommaso Traetta's *Didone abbandonata* created at Milan a year earlier as a vehicle for Caterina Gabrielli, won from him no praise.

> Now for a little Musick—to speak of it in general here, I think the taste is very bad—it is all execution without Simplicity or Pathos—I have heard the famous Gabrielli, who has indeed astonishing powers, great Compass of voice, & great flexibility, but she is always the same, & tho you are highly transported at first with her, yet wanting that nice feeling of ye passions, (without which every thing in ye dramatic way will cease to Entertain), she cannot give that variety, & that peculiar Pleasure which alone can support the tediousness of an Opera—in short the Musick vocal & instrumental has lost its Nature, and it is all dancing ye slack rope, and tumbling thro' ye hoop.[92]

So severe an indictment of the Neapolitan operatic stage would have discouraged most travelers, but not Burney, convinced as he was of its excellence. Garrick called it "ill conducted & the Gabrielli, who is ye only Performer of Consequence is so whimsical, that she scarcely Endeavours to Sing once in three times." He wrote further, "I have lately heard an Excellent Hauboy, & Fabio the Violin, but they are not worth coming to Italy for—*You* will get little by such a Journey & I protest to you that I felt more at y^e *first Air* of *Rousseau,* than at all ye Operas I heard at Turin, Genoa, Leghorn, Rome, & Naples." The reference is to Rousseau's *Le devin du village,* which Garrick produced two years later in an English translation by Burney. True to his French heritage, even in music, Garrick rated Italian brio beneath the simple, pathetic, and natural, which he apparently heard in "J'ai perdu mon serviteur." Only one musical event pleased him in Naples, the singing of Caffarelli at the ceremony of an aristocrat's daughter taking the veil: "the first

---

[90]Frank A. Hedgcock, *A Cosmopolitan Actor: David Garrick and His French Friends* (London, 1912).
[91]Roger Lonsdale, *Dr. Charles Burney* (Oxford, 1965), p. 61.
[92]*Memoirs of Dr. Burney, 1726–1769,* ed. Slava Klima, Garry Bowers, and Kerry S. Grant (Lincoln, Neb., 1988), fragment 102, pp. 154–55.

part was sung by yᵉ famous Caffarelli, who tho Old has pleas'd me more than all yᵉ Singers I have yet heard—He *touch'd* Me, & it was yᵉ first time I had been touch'd since I came to Italy."

Young James Boswell had quite a different reaction to the operas he witnessed in Italy. On his return home through France he described in his diary a musical entertainment he experienced in the theater at Marseilles on 21 December 1765.

> The French squeaking and grimaces were insufferable to a man just come from the operas of Italy. O Italy! Land of felicity! True seat of all elegant delight! My mind shall ever soothe itself with the image of thy charms. Thy divine music has harmonized my soul. That nature, that sweet simplicity, that easy grace which has pleased me so often in thy theatres, shall never fade from my memory.[93]

Burney would have fully agreed. Boswell was twenty-five at the time and a musician of sorts (he sang and played the flute with gusto). He later considered publishing an account of his travels. His idol Samuel Johnson dissuaded him with this advice, given in 1778: "Most modern travellers in Europe who have published their travels, have been laughed at: I would not have you added to the number. The world is now not contented to be merely entertained by a traveller's narration; they want to learn something."[94]

Garrick dismissed the production of *Didone* in Naples as "ill conducted." This belies other reports of magnificent processions, battles, and conflagrations on the stage of the San Carlo. The occasion was certainly grand, as the printed libretto proclaimed, being the birthday of Carlos IV, king of Spain, who as king of Naples (1734–59) had had the San Carlo built. Many anomalies point to the theater's slipping as a center of opera. Not only was the *Didone* a year old, but its composer was not present—the libretto specifies "diretta dal signor D. Pasqual Cafaro." There was even a kind of *lèse majesté* in the very fact that a kingdom borrowed an old opera from a dukedom like Milan (and one possessed by the Habsburgs at that). What Garrick said about the cast was true. Aside from Gabrielli they were little-known singers, without the great names expected at Naples. Possibly she insisted upon mediocre co-singers as part of her hiring contract. If so, there could be no more telling evidence of the theater's decline.

The Garricks followed what had become the classic Grand Tour for Londoners: Channel crossing, a stop in Paris of some length, descent to Italy by one route, return by another, another stay in Paris, then home.[95] The span of their travels,

---

[93]*Boswell on the Grand Tour: Italy, Corsica, and France, 1765–1766,* ed. Frank Brady and Frederick A. Pottle (London, 1953), p. 254. For Boswell on music at the Mannheim court, see the Appendix.

[94]Lonsdale, *Burney,* p. 99.

[95]Black, *The Grand Tour in the Eighteenth Century,* p. xi.

nearly two years, was also typical. Having departed in the fall of 1763, they returned in the spring of 1765.

Giuseppe Baretti wrote what might be called an antidote to mid-eighteenth-century travel guides, particularly those by antipathetic English Protestants. He was born in Turin in 1719 and raised speaking both French and Italian. He settled in London in 1751. There he made a name for himself by publishing a *Dictionary and Grammar of the Italian Language* (1760), followed by the *Manners and Customs of Italy*.[96] This work repudiates point by point Samuel Sharp's *Letters from Italy* (London, 1766) and also attacks Smollett's more solid travel book published in London the same year.[97] Laurence Sterne satirized Smollett as the "learned Smelfungus" in his wonderful *Sentimental Journey through France and Italy* (1768).

Baretti rarely uses the term *country* or *nation* for Italy and takes care to explain that his native land was separated into many parts, divided not only by political rule but also by dialects so different that they could scarcely be understood from region to region. Yet Italy as a whole, he maintained, rivaled England in wealth.

> But if Italy is near so rich as England, how does it happen, that the English nation is so renowned all over the world for its power, which is the natural consequence of its riches, and how does it happen, that the Italian makes no figure at all either in Europe or anywhere else? To this question I cannot give answer, until I see all Italy, or even the greater part of it, under a single government, either free or slavish, no matter which; and until then, Mr. Sharp is very welcome to call the few frigates and gallies of the Pope and King of Naples "Lilliputian fleets" . . . [and to write] a thousand such impertinences no less nauseous to read than to relate.[98]

"Slavish" was a common expression of the time referring to despotic states such as Prussia, as opposed to governments that allowed some political freedoms.

Italians did not lag behind in all fields according to Baretti. In music they dominated Europe. "Music is more the growth of Italy than any other part of Europe" (1: 296). He gave Metastasio the main credit for putting Italian composers in the position of achieving musical preeminence.

> The elegance, liveliness, and rapidity of Metastasio's diction are not to be paralleled, and his numbers are enchanting. His airs, duo's, and choruses run into music with such surprising facility, and our composers have but little trouble in cloathing them with harmony; so that it is chiefly to him, that they owe that honour of musical pre-

[96]Joseph Baretti, *An Account of the Manners and Customs of Italy with Observations on the Mistakes of Some Travellers*, 2 vols. (London, 1768).
[97]Tobias Smollett, *Travels through France and Italy*, ed. Frank Felsenstein (Oxford, 1979), p. 427, n. 3.
[98]Baretti, *An Account of the Manners*, 2: 215–16.

eminence which they have incontestably enjoyed throughout Europe for these many years. (1: 179)

Baretti had no tolerance, on the other hand, for opera buffa, which he called a "mongrel composition." He preferred spoken comedy, and his favorite author was not Goldoni, whom he accused of using too many gallicisms, but Carlo Gozzi.

In answer to complaints by the travel writers that Italians were noisy and inattentive at concerts and operas, he replied that music was little regarded in Italy because there was so much of it heard everywhere. On the other hand there were situations, he said, in which Italians remained silent, for instance, a serenade by moonlight on the water in Venice. With this point he ended his first volume.

Baretti gave Italian lessons to Londoners of fashion, just as Burney gave music lessons to the same. The two shared a similar status and were on friendly terms with each other. Baretti's *Manners and Customs* was one of several stimuli to Burney's first tour and the publication of his report of it. Baretti offered criticism of Burney's text before it was published. In his preface Burney stated that travel writers had covered everything about Italy except its music, which they scarcely touched.

> And this is still the more unaccountable, as no one of the liberal arts is at present so much cultivated, and encouraged, nor can the Italians now boast a superiority over the rest of Europe in any of them so much as in music; for few of their painters, sculptors, architects, historians, poets, or philosophers of the present age, as in some centuries past, so greatly surpass their contemporaries on this side of the Alps, as to excite much curiosity to visit or converse with them.

Baretti objected to this statement, but Burney stood his ground and retained it.[99] "Music still *lives* in Italy," he wrote, "while most of the other arts only speak a *dead language.*" Baretti also criticized Burney's claim that Italian audiences paid little attention in the theater, to which Burney responded, "You asked why you should be attentive: let me in my turn ask you why you should go to a theatre to talk when you would be less disturbed at home."[100]

Baretti was a member of the circle that gathered at the home of the wealthy Mrs. Hester Thrale (later Piozzi), who in 1789 published her own travel book.[101]

---

[99]Kerry S. Grant, *Dr. Burney as Critic and Historian of Music* (Ann Arbor, Mich., 1983), p. 71.

[100]Ibid., p. 320, n. 78.

[101]Hester Lynch Piozzi, *Observations and Reflections Made in the Course of a Journey Through France, Italy, and Germany,* ed. Herbert Barrows (Ann Arbor, Mich., 1967). Visiting the private rooms of the recently deceased King Frederick II at Sans Souci, Piozzi took note of what books and pictures he kept close by: "The first were chiefly works of Voltaire and Metastasio—the last were small landscapes of Albano and Watteau" (p. 403).

The eminences of this gathering, besides Boswell and Garrick, were Edmund Burke, Samuel Johnson, Joshua Reynolds, and later Burney, who became a replacement for Baretti. Quarrels between Mrs. Thrale and Baretti led to his exit in 1776; she called him "the ferocious Italian," one who was "insolent and breathing defiance against all Mankind," and still worse.[102] French and English travel writers had mentioned the propensity of Italians, when slighted or enraged, to murder their enemies, a claim Baretti protested as a gross exaggeration. In 1769, one year after having chastized Sharp and Smollett in print, he was assaulted on a London street by a person he slew instantly with a knife. Arraigned and brought to trial for murder, he was acquitted with the help of Dr. Johnson, who testified to his good reputation.

Charles Burney was born in Shrewsbury, Shropshire, on 7 April 1726. His early life as an organist included a period of apprenticeship to Thomas Arne in London. He worked mostly in provincial towns until he settled in London for good in 1760, where he cultivated an extensive clientele of pupils as a fashionable teacher of music. His aspirations to visit Italy and to write a history of music were apparent already in his twenties. He first visited Paris in 1764, having accompanied two of his daughters there where they were put in school. He returned to fetch one of them in 1765. The visits allowed him to sample the musical offerings of the French metropolis and also to visit libraries in search of material. These were only a foretaste of the serious venture he planned next. In preparation he took the degrees of Mus.B. and Mus.D. at Oxford in June 1769. Arming himself with letters of recommendation to various English diplomats in France and Italy formed another part of the preparation. His London friends were also generous with their recommendations. Baretti, Felice Giardini, and Vincenzo Martinelli wrote for him to various persons in Italy. Garrick did the same to his learned French friends. An undated letter from Garrick to Jean Baptiste Suard in Paris survives, giving an idea of the process.

> My dear Suard,
> I will not attempt to excuse myself to you for the liberty I take in presenting to you my friend, Dr. Burney, and in recommending him to your friendship, for he is a very amiable, honest, and clever man. He is doctor of music, and although the degree of doctor does not always imply great talents, the honour and genius of his profession are none the less happily united in the person of this gentleman, my friend. You need only to know him to love and esteem him. He has undertaken to write a History of Music, and his conscience would upbraid him if he did not seek to make his work as complete as possible. His journey into France and Italy has no other aim.

[102]Lonsdale, *Burney,* p. 230.

> Great is the expectation of his friends; and he considers it his duty to write a book worthy of their esteem and his own reputation. He could desire nothing more than that.[103]

The solidarity of Burney's friends in standing behind him during the many years of what proved to be a gruelling task was amply rewarded in the end. Burney set off for Paris on 8 June 1770 and reached it in time to attend the Concert Spirituel on 14 June, the feast of Corpus Christi. He met Suard, Abbé François Arnaud, and Jean Monnet, impresario and former director of the Opéra-Comique. Rousseau and Diderot were in the country but Burney would meet both on his return to Paris. On his way to Italy he visited Voltaire in Ferney near Geneva. He reached Milan by 16 July. His remarks on its music are reproduced in Chapter 3, as are many of his reactions to music in Venice, which he visited in August. In Bologna he ran across the Mozarts, visited the retired Farinelli, and paid homage to the learned Padre Martini, himself engaged in a monumental history of music. The two scholars quickly became friends. They corresponded often until Martini's death in 1784. Florence, Rome, and Naples were his next stops, and what he wrote about them has provided rich fare for the present volume's second chapter. At Naples he met and characterized two of the greatest living Italian composers, Jommelli and Niccolò Piccinni.

The idea of publishing a book about his tour in anticipation of the history may have been on Burney's mind all along. He confessed it openly in a letter of mid-October sent to Garrick from Naples: "As my general history must be a work of time, I intend publishing, as soon as I get home, in a pamphlet, or small volume, an account of the present state of music in France and Italy, in which I shall describe, according to my judgment and feelings, the merits of the several compositions and performers I have heard in travelling through those countries."[104] After a harrowing return through Italy he reached Paris on 8 December and was with his family in London by Christmas Eve.

Burney on tour filled his notebooks with observations on art and architecture plus many other things that interested him in France and Italy besides music. His friends at home persuaded him that these had been so thoroughly described in published travel books that he should omit all but the portions on music, and he did. The rejected materials are of great interest even so, partly because of Burney's lively style of narration. They have been reintegrated in one of the major modern editions by conflating the manuscript versions with the printed ones.[105]

---

[103]Hedgcock, *David Garrick*, pp. 330–31.
[104]Lonsdale, *Burney*, p. 98.
[105]*Dr. Burney's Musical Tours in Europe*, ed. Percy A. Scholes, 2 vols. (London, 1959). One of Burney's friends, Samuel Crisp, argued against the others, saying that the "miscellaneous observations had entertained him far more than the musical" (1: xxx).

By early May 1771 the book about the Italian tour had made its appearance. It earned the author many praises from diverse quarters, and the more serious reviews that followed (surreptitiously arranged by Burney himself and assigned to his friends) consecrated his triumph with the public. The edition was sold out by 1773. A second, corrected edition was published in short order (Figure 1.10). Meanwhile Burney had completed his second major tour.

Burney once again meticulously prepared his trip with recommendations, both from authorities to British ministers and consuls, and from his friends and acquaintances to those who could be useful to him. He had a German translation of the plan for his history prepared to show abroad. Crossing the Channel on 6 July 1772 he made stops in Antwerp and Brussels, visiting libraries to consult rare materials. In Germany he was shocked by the poor conditions for travel and by the poverty of the common people in contrast with the profligacy of the petty courts and of the aristocrats in general. At Mannheim he studied the famous orchestra but met none of its members. Midsummer was not the most auspicious time for a visit. He found the court at its summer retreat in Schwetzingen and was greatly entertained by the ballet and comic opera, *La contadina in corte:* "The music was com-

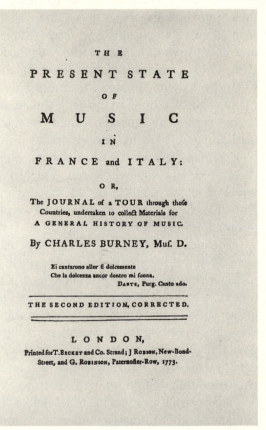

THE

PRESENT STATE

OF

MUSIC

IN

FRANCE and ITALY:

OR,

The JOURNAL of a TOUR through those
Countries, undertaken to collect Materials for
A GENERAL HISTORY OF MUSIC.

By CHARLES BURNEY, Muf. D.

Ei cantarono allor fi dolcemente
Che la dolcezza ancor dentro mi fuona.
DANTE, Purg. Canto 2do.

THE SECOND EDITION, CORRECTED.

LONDON,

Printed for T. BECKET and Co. Strand; J ROBSON, New-Bond-
Street, and G. ROBINSON, Paternofter-Row, 1773.

FIGURE 1.10. Title page of Burney's *Italian Tour*.

posed by Signor Sacchini, and was full of that clearness, grace, and elegant simplicity, which characterise the productions of that author."[106] In Württemberg, likewise, the court was at its summer retreat. There was not much music to be heard, but Burney did learn about the great days of Stuttgart's musical past by

[106]Charles Burney, *The Present State of Music in Germany, The Netherlands, and United Provinces*, 2nd ed. (London, 1775). Facsimile edition by Broude Brothers (New York, 1969). Hereafter in this book quoted only by author's name or as *German Tour*.

conversing with Christian Friedrich Daniel Schubart, court organist. Burney, who could not speak German, questioned him in Italian and he answered in Latin. In Munich, which Burney reached on 16 August, he was fortunate to be taken under the wing of the British envoy, Louis Devisme, who gained him admittance to the elector's rich musical library and to the elector himself, as well as to his sister, the electress dowager of Saxony, Maria Antonia Walpurgis, a noted composer and patron of music.

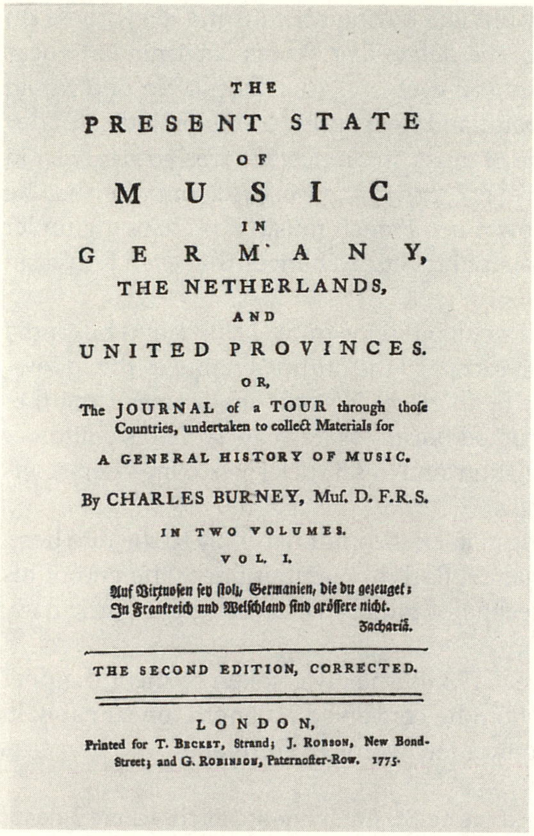

In Vienna, the chief goal of his trip, he had even greater good fortune: he was presented by Lord Stormont, the British ambassador, to Gluck and to his idol, the notoriously reclusive Metastasio. He met a kind reception as well from his musical idol Hasse. His two weeks passed quickly between interviews and visits to libraries. Leaving Vienna on 13 September he visited Prague, then Dresden, Leipzig, and Berlin. His reactions provide ample material for our Chapter 4. On 9 October he arrived in Hamburg and met at length with Emanuel Bach. He returned home by way of the Low Countries, reaching London in early November.

Profiting from his earlier experiences, Burney took care to record his trip in a journal, which was close to what he published on his return. This time he gave the public his nonmusical as well as musical observations, with the result that the work was twice as long and required two volumes. After publication in 1773, the frankness of his comments shocked some Germans, including the editors in Hamburg who undertook to translate his work into German. He made the mistake of including a remark that made them furious: "If innate genius exists, Germany certainly is not the seat of it; though it must be allowed to be that of perseverance and application." The irony is that these words were not even his own, but were written to him in a letter from Louis Devisme, which Burney quotes without attri-

THE

PRESENT STATE

OF

MUSIC

IN

GERMANY,

THE NETHERLANDS,

AND

UNITED PROVINCES.

OR,

The JOURNAL of a TOUR through those
Countries, undertaken to collect Materials for

A GENERAL HISTORY OF MUSIC.

By CHARLES BURNEY, Muſ. D. F.R.S.

IN TWO VOLUMES.

VOL. I.

Auf Virtuosen ſey ſtolz, Germanien, die du gezeuget;
In Frankreich und Welſchland ſind größere nicht.
Zachariä.

THE SECOND EDITION, CORRECTED.

LONDON,

Printed for T. BECKET, Strand; J. ROBSON, New Bond-
Street; and G. ROBINSON, Paternoſter-Row. 1775.

FIGURE 1.11. Title page of Burney's *German Tour*.

bution.[107] Perhaps to soften the blow of this opinion he quoted the poet Zachariä on his title page: "Germans, be proud of the virtuosos you have born; no greater are found in France and Italy." A second edition followed the first two years later, with printing errors corrected and a few other emendations made, but no retraction of the injurious statement (Figure 1.11). In the fourth volume of his *History of Music,* published in 1789, Burney retracted the claim and apologized for it.[108]

Burney's reports on the musical life of his own time remain invaluable. For the purposes of the present volume they are like having an ear- and eyewitness on the spot. As he wrote in the preface of the *Italian Tour,* "I was determined to hear with my *own* ears, and to see with my *own* eyes . . . " (his italics). No one would claim that Burney was without his blind and deaf spots, or his prejudices. They worked especially to the disadvantage of music in France. He was so steadfast in adhering to Rousseau's positions in the *Lettre sur la musique française* that he closed his ears and mind, ignoring how much French music was changing under the impetus of his beloved Italian masters and Gluck, changes that even Rousseau himself admitted late in his life.

The tours continued to inform Burney's opinions in his *History* and beyond. I quote them without further ascription except to the author's name in the following chapters, while specifying merely by the term *History* what comes from that source. The two major works that occupied Burney's late years were his edition of Metastasio's letters in English translation and his articles on composers contributed to Abraham Rees's *Cyclopaedia.*[109]

A sample of Burney's travel writing at its best comes naturally to the fore here. I select his description of visiting Emanuel Bach in Hamburg near the end of his second tour. Their remarks on the decline of music in Hamburg are particularly insightful.

On Saturday morning, 10 October 1773, Burney was taken to meet the poet Friedrich Gottlieb Klopstock, with whom he conversed at length, presumably in French, for Burney could still speak only a few words of German.

> After this visit, M. Bach accompanied me to St. Catherine's church, where I heard some very good music, of his composition, very ill performed, and to a congregation wholly inattentive. This man was certainly born to write for great performers, and for a refined audience; but he now seems to be out of his element. There is a fluctuation

[107]Lonsdale, *Burney,* pp. 124–35; Grant, *Dr. Burney as Critic,* pp. 80–81.
[108]Charles Burney, *A General History of Music from the Earliest Ages to the Present Period,* 4 vols. (London, 1776–89). Re-edition with critical and historical notes by Frank Mercer, 2 vols. (New York, 1957), 2: 963.
[109]*Memoirs of the Life and Writings of the Abate Metastasio,* ed. Charles Burney, 3 vols. (London, 1786). *The Cyclopaedia; or Universal Dictionary of Arts, Sciences, and Literature,* ed. Abraham Rees, 45 vols. (London, 1802–1819). Burney's articles take the place of a biographical dictionary of musicians he long contemplated.

in the arts of every city and country where they are cultivated, and this is not a bright period for music at Hamburg.

Burney continues, switching to direct quotation of his interlocutor, although these cannot be Bach's exact words because of the language barrier.

> At church, and in the way home, we had a conversation, which was extremely inter-esting to me: he told me, that if he was in a place, where his composition could be well executed, and well heard, he should certainly kill himself, by exertions to please. "But adieu music!" now, he says, "these are good people for society, and I enjoy more tranquillity and independence here, than at a court; after I was fifty, I gave the thing up, and said let us eat and drink, for to-morrow we die! and I am now reconciled to my situation; except indeed, when I meet with men of taste and discernment, who deserve better music than we can give them here. Then I blush for myself and my good friends, the Hamburgers."

Once published, Bach's words on his fellow citizens caused him to be embar-rassed. He asked that the final sentence about blushing be deleted; Burney acqui-esced, striking it in the second edition.[110]

The old Hanseatic city of Hamburg, earlier a center of German opera, retained little of its former musical glory, except in the person of Bach himself. Its artistic decline worked on Burney's mind, as is evident from a passage late in the *History* that argued the low status of commercial cities, in comparison with great capitals.

> If Sebastian Bach and his admirable son Emanuel, instead of being musical-directors in commercial cities, had been fortunately employed to compose for the stage and public of great capitals, such as Naples, Paris, or London, and for performers of the first class, they would doubtless have simplified their style more to the level of their judges: the one would have sacrificed all unmeaning art and contrivance, and the other been less fantastical and *recherché*, and both, by writing in a style more popular, and generally intelligible and pleasing, would have extended their fame, and been indisputably the greatest musicians of the present century.

In short, Burney clung to an ideal of Italian opera in the mouths of the greatest singers as the summit of all eighteenth-century music. Only the great capitals could afford as much. Paris comes as a surprise in this context, because Burney generally dismissed its singers out of hand, if not the Italian composers who

[110]Grant, *Dr. Burney as Critic,* p. 91.

worked for the Opéra. The discrepancy can be explained. Burney later admitted that the observation was not his but came from Carl Friedrich Abel.[111] There was of course one Bach who did write operas with success for all three "great capitals" mentioned: Abel's friend Johann Christian.

/ / /

A postscript follows about some of Burney's contemporaries on the Continent who wrote about music. A few deserve an introduction here because they figure repeatedly in the following chapters. The most distinguished were Giovanni Battista Martini of Bologna, a revered music teacher; the Parisian aristocrat and essayist Jean-Benjamin de la Borde; Daniel Schubart, Swabian organist and critic; and the Saxon lexicographer Ernst Ludwig Gerber.

Padre Martini, as he was known to all the world of music, brought out three volumes of his *Storia della musica* before he died in 1784, but they did not go beyond antiquity in subject matter. His main importance to his own time, besides teaching countless students, was as a collector of books and portraits, and as a clearinghouse for information. Scholars and practical musicians alike wrote him often and received prompt replies to their queries.[112]

La Borde used his privileged position in society to several worthy purposes, composing music, collecting it, and writing the four hefty volumes of his essay on ancient and modern music.[113] The third volume is devoted to modern composers and benefited particularly from his travels in Italy during 1773–74, which took him as far as Naples. Burney appropriated material from him as he saw fit, almost always acknowledging its source.

Schubart excelled as a keyboard player and as a critic of music in Germany. He provided Burney with a wealth of information when they met at Stuttgart in 1772. Although his own travels were confined to southern Germany he formed opinions about music elsewhere and set them down at length in a work written during the 1780s, which is identified throughout this book as his *Ideen*.[114] He derived much from Burney and other printed sources.

Gerber began with the idea of enlarging Johann Gottfried Walther's *Musikalisches Lexikon* (Leipzig, 1732). (There is a lovely parallel in that Diderot began with the idea of updating an earlier reference work and created the *Encyclopédie*, the century's greatest publishing feat.) Gerber was an organist and

[111]*Memoirs . . . Metastasio,* 3: 309.

[112]Anne Schnoebelen, *Padre Martini's Collection of Letters* (New York, 1979).

[113]Jean-Benjamin La Borde, *Essai sur la musique ancienne et moderne,* 4 vols. (Paris, 1780; reprint 1972).

[114]Christian Friedrich Daniel Schubart, *Ideen zu einer Ästhetik der Tonkunst,* ed. Ludwig Schubart [his son] (Vienna, 1806). Facsimile edition annotated by Fritz and Margrit Kaiser (Hildesheim, 1969).

lawyer. His two-volume biographical dictionary profited greatly from his reading of Burney and La Borde.[115] Its amplified revision two decades later doubled the size of the original.[116]

The keenest observer of eighteenth-century music was its greatest composer—Wolfgang Amadeus Mozart. I cite his letters, as in *Haydn, Mozart,* only by their date, from the complete modern edition.[117] The translations are my own, like all translations throughout the book unless indicated otherwise. As in the parallel volume, I have left some simple passages in French untranslated.

[115]Ernst Ludwig Gerber, *Historisch-biographisches Lexikon der Tonkünstler,* 2 vols. (Leipzig, 1790; reprint 1966).
[116]Ernst Ludwig Gerber, *Neues historisch-biographisches Lexikon der Tonkünstler,* 4 vols. (Leipzig, 1812–14; reprint 1966). Gerber's manuscript supplements are edited by Othmar Wessely in *Ernst Ludwig Gerber: Ergänzungen—Berichtungen—Nachträge* (Graz, 1969).
[117]*Mozart: Briefe und Aufzeichungen. Gesamtausgabe,* ed. Wilhelm A. Bauer, Otto Erich Deutsch, and Joseph Heinz Eibl, 7 vols. (Kassel, 1962–75).

2

Naples

N APLES was the capital of a country that achieved royal status in the twelfth century when Norman conquerors united the entire south of Italy with the island of
Sicily. It was known as the Kingdom of Naples, or alternatively as the Kingdom
of the Two Sicilies (the two did not always remain united). After its conquest by
several other powers Spain took possession in 1503 and it was ruled by Spanish
viceroys until 1707, when it was taken over by the Habsburgs. In 1734 Charles
Bourbon, son of Philip V of Spain, took back the kingdom and ruled it personally
as Charles III until 1759, when he succeeded to the Spanish throne. His son, who
inherited the Kingdom of Naples and had a long reign as Ferdinand IV, was
forced into exile on Sicily by the French in 1806, but came back to Naples after the
restoration of 1815 for another ten years.

The vast kingdom stretched over nearly half of the Italian peninsula as well
as Sicily. A topographical survey of it was made in the last ten years of the eighteenth century. The publisher Zanoni brought it out in 1801 under the title *Regno
di Napoli,* a map of the kingdom incised on thirty-one huge plates by the royal
engraver Giuseppe Guerra (Figure 2.1). Our detail from plate 14 shows the capital, the famous bay, and the volcanic district called Phlegraean Fields to the west
of it (Mount Vesuvius, not shown, is to the east). Of particular note to the north are
the city of Aversa, where Niccolò Jommelli was born in 1714, and the coastal town
of Pozzuoli to the southwest, where Giovanni Battista Pergolesi died in 1736.

Although the kingdom was poor and lacking in industries, Naples itself was

FIGURE 2.1. Naples and environs from Guerra's *Regno di Napoli.*

one of the largest cities of Western civilization, with a population during the eighteenth century estimated near 400,000 (twice that of Venice, and four times that of Rome). Only Paris exceeded this number at the time. Stendhal, visiting Naples in 1811–12, thought it approached Paris in other ways, praising the opera, balls, social gatherings, concerts, theaters and antiquities: "Naples," he later wrote, "alone among Italian cities, has the true makings of a capital; the rest are but glorified provincial towns."[1]

Scores of churches dotted Naples, serving its teeming populace. These, as well as other religious institutions, provided employment for many of the musicians trained at the conservatories, which would not have otherwise flourished to such an extent. This economic reasoning does not fully explain the individual striving for excellence passed on from teachers to pupils that marked several generations of musicians.

Conservatories

The conservatories were founded at various times during the sixteenth century as orphanages that offered boys a religious and classical education. By the first half of the seventeenth century they had begun to emphasize instruction in music, preparing students with aptitude for the possibility of becoming professional musicians. Besides the many churches large and small, there were several religious confraternities and monastic orders, all requiring music in one form or another, as did the city and the court, to all of which the conservatories provided groups of young musicians for hire. The number of paying students they enrolled in addition to orphans bore witness to the efficacy of their musical training.

There were four conservatories in Naples during the first part of the eighteenth century: Santa Maria di Loreto, Santa Maria della Pietà dei Turchini, San Onofrio a Capuana, and Poveri di Gesù Cristo. The last, which came under the jurisdiction of the archbishop of Naples, was suppressed in 1743 when it was converted to a seminary. The other three were run by layman boards of governors who were responsible to the crown. San Onofrio was joined with Santa Maria di Loreto in 1797 and further consolidated with the Turchini in 1806, when by decree of the new ruler, Joseph Bonaparte, the single remaining conservatory became the Real Collegio di Musica, an all-professional music school that was not an orphanage and no longer stressed religious and general education.

The first music masters in the conservatories were priests, but this gradually

---

[1]R. Burr Litchfeld, "Naples under the Bourbons: An Historical Overview," in *The Golden Age of Naples: Art and Civilization Under the Bourbons 1734–1805*, 2 vols. (Detroit and Chicago, 1981), 1: 1–14; 1.

changed as some of the best professional musicians in Naples took up teaching in addition to other duties. Francesco Provenzale, born in Naples ca. 1626, became a leading opera composer of his native city by the 1650s. In 1663 he was named primo maestro di cappella of the Loreto conservatory, and two years later maestro di cappella of the city of Naples. In 1675 he left the Loreto in order to take charge of music at the Turchini, where he taught until his retirement in 1701. The opera composer Pietro Andrea Ziani, born in Venice, settled in Naples by 1677 and became maestro di cappella of the court; he taught at the San Onofrio conservatory. At his death in 1684 it was expected that Provenzale would be named in his place. The position went instead to the twenty-three-year-old Alessandro Scarlatti, a native of Palermo, and thus a subject of the crown, not a foreigner. Scarlatti also held an appointment as first music master of the Loreto conservatory for a brief time in 1689. The governors fired him because he overstayed a leave he was granted to go to Rome, where his music was much in demand. Scarlatti wrote many operas for Naples during his first court appointment (1684–1702). During his second, from 1709 until his death in 1725, he wrote fewer operas, accepted no conservatory positions, but attracted private students, the most famous of whom was Johann Adolf Hasse from Germany. Scarlatti's case shows that, although the conservatories wanted famous composers, they were not always willing to tolerate celebrities who were derelict in their teaching duties. Even the highly respected Provenzale gave cause for concern, prompting the governors of the Loreto to stipulate on 24 February 1669 that he and the violin teacher were to be reported when they failed to show up to give their lessons.[2]

By the early years of the eighteenth century the conservatories were producing musicians native to the kingdom who would go on to take the major positions that the city and court had to offer. Following are some admittedly unfamiliar names of composers who played an important part in the history of music in Naples. Francesco Mancini, born in 1672, was educated from 1688 at the Turchini, where he studied with Provenzale. He eventually became vice maestro of the court under Scarlatti and maestro on Scarlatti's death. In a painting by Nicola Rossi dated 1732 it is presumably Mancini (right rear) who beats time with a raised scroll for a group of singers and players from the royal chapel (Figure 2.2). The court, under Count Harrach, viceroy, was on a pilgrimage to the Madonna of Pedigrotta. Mancini directed music at the Loreto conservatory from 1720 to 1735 (Table 2.1). His major rival was Domenico Sarro (or Sarri), born in 1679 and trained at the San Onofrio conservatory. Sarro's first sacred opera was performed in 1702 by one of the religious confraternities. He was appointed vice maestro at

[2]Michael F. Robinson, *Naples and Neapolitan Opera* (Oxford, 1972), p. 14.

the court in 1704, dismissed in 1707, and regained this post in 1725. He became maestro on Mancini's death in 1737 and remained so until his own death in 1744.

Slightly younger than these two figures were a group of musicians from the conservatories who went on to European fame and fortune. Giuseppe Porsile, born in Naples in 1680, emerged from the Conservatorio dei Poveri di Gesù Cristo. After a stay in Spain he went in 1713 to Vienna, where he eventually rose to the highest position in the court's musical hierarchy. Nicola Porpora was born in Naples on 17 August 1686, the third son of a local bookseller, who paid for his musical education at the Poveri di Gesù Cristo for three years starting in 1699, after which he went tuition free, which means that he became a pupil-teacher who instructed younger students. His long and successful career as an opera composer began with an *Agrippina* commissioned for performance in the royal palace on 4 November 1708. In 1721 he became first music master at San Onofrio, and without doubt the most famous of all singing teachers, from whose private classes emerged both Carlo Broschi Farinelli and Caffarelli (Gaetano Majorano). After many trips to the major capitals, he returned to Naples as music master of

FIGURE 2.2. Nicola Rossi. The royal chapel visits Santa Maria di Pedigrotta, 1732, detail.

court musician and music teacher of Queen Maria Carolina. When he assumed the highest post, maestro of the royal chapel, in 1771, he ceased writing operas. Cafaro, it has been claimed, was one of the essential links between the generation of Leo and Durante and that of Domenico Cimarosa and Paisiello.

Continuity was a conspicuous feature of musical life in Naples. Often a conservatory student would eventually rise to the highest music posts of the same institution. The will to preserve tradition and achieve continuity is manifest in the minutes of the Loreto's board of governors. By deliberations of 15 May 1761 the board decided to appoint as first and second masters of music Gallo and Sacchini.

> Our decision has been influenced both by the needs of the Conservatory and by the fact that the said maestri di cappella have been students of the same and have given proof of their ability and honesty, the first having been student of the celebrated, late maestro di cappella D. Francesco Mancini and the second pupil of the famous maestro di cappella D. Francesco Durante, whose names must always be esteemed and remembered throughout our Conservatory.[3]

Rather typically, the lackluster Gallo remained in the position until the end of his life in 1777, while the brilliant Sacchini was soon gone. Born in Florence in 1730, Sacchini was taken to Naples by his father at age four and entered the Loreto at age ten, where he studied singing with Gennaro Manna, violin with Nicola Fiorenza, and the organ, harpsichord, and composition with Durante. Within a few months of being appointed, Sacchini applied for and received leave to go to Venice to write operas. Instead of returning to Naples he went on to an international career that ended with triumphs in both London and Paris.

The detailed minutes of the Loreto do not always paint a rosy picture of the students and teachers. Nicola Logroscino, born in 1698, entered with his younger brother Pietro in 1714; they were both expelled "for bad traits of character" in 1727. Pietro was readmitted but Nicola was not. The Nicola Fiorenza who was Sacchini's violin teacher and an esteemed composer of concertos and symphonies was warned repeatedly by the governors because of complaints by the boys that he threatened them with physical abuse and actually beat them. He was dismissed as incorrigible in 1762.

The Loreto ran into increasing financial trouble after 1760, partly because of unscrupulous accountants, but also because of unrest among the students. Yet it still attracted some of the best young talent, such as Niccolò Zingarelli, born in 1752 and entered at age seven. Domenico Cimarosa was his fellow pupil, born in 1749 and entered in 1761. Zingarelli eventually became music director of the sole

[3]Michael F. Robinson, "The Governors' Minutes of the Conservatory S. Maria di Loreto, Naples," *Research Chronicle of the Royal Musical Association* 10 (1972): 38–39.

surviving conservatory in the early nineteenth century. In 1822 he taught composition to young Vincenzo Bellini, while attempting to ward off the influence of Gioachino Rossini and promulgate the Neapolitan vocal tradition. There can be few examples clearer than this why "Neapolitan School" is justified as a concept. It expresses the reality of how and where, for several generations, a large and cohesive group of musicians were trained.

Inequities of treatment between the orphans and the paying students (called *convittore*) caused dissension at the Loreto and presumably at other conservatories as well. Up to 1758 the paying students received an entire loaf of bread and a carafe of wine each day, while the orphans received no wine and only six rolls.[4] What particularly displeased the poor orphans was that they were required to take part in all musical activities for which the conservatory was contracted, such as funerals, parades, and other civic functions, while the paying students did not have to participate. In 1758 the governors resolved to raise the enrollment fees to 40 ducats a year for subjects of the kingdom and 45 ducats for foreigners, and to treat these *convittore* exactly as they treated the orphans, but there is no evidence that they were in fact able to equalize the privileges and duties between the two bodies of students.

A great famine hit the kingdom between 1764 and 1767, and the situation was made worse in Naples itself by an outbreak of the plague. These unfortunate events coincided with the financial difficulties caused by embezzlements at the Loreto. By 22 July 1772 the number of pupils was down from an average of 150 to only 82. Piccinni told Burney in 1770 that there were 200, but he was misinformed or perhaps was simply recalling better times during the 1750s.

Inflation made it more difficult for the conservatory to keep up its standards, and during the 1770s there was a kind of revolt by the paying students, who refused to remit their fees. Fourteen of them even lodged a complaint by writing to the king and signing their names. They were subsequently punished. With income from performances dwindling along with the number of students and the Loreto's old buildings in serious need of repair, the situation steadily grew worse. The combined San Onofrio–Loreto students, paying and nonpaying, who passed into the Turchini on 31 December 1806 numbered only 46.

Part of the blame for the decline of music in conservatories and the decline of the conservatories themselves has been placed on political interference and lack of support from the crown.[5] In the early years of Ferdinand's reign, power was concentrated in the hands of the first minister, Marquis Tanucci, who had little use

---

[4]Robinson, "The Governors' Minutes," pp. 52–53. All students received regular meals besides these private rations.
[5]Ibid., pp. 69–72.

for music or the traditions of the conservatories. A social reformer, he was apparently behind the royal decree that put students in the sciences in the Loreto, plus masters to teach them, thereby reducing the role of music.

Burney arrived in Naples on 16 October 1770 bearing a letter of introduction to Piccinni from his friend Felice Giardini in London. He was courteously received by the composer, to whom he addressed a number of questions about the conservatories. The answers did not always match the facts, as we have seen in relation to the number of students at the Loreto. According to Piccinni it was the duty of the primo maestro to oversee and correct the students' compositions and of the secondo maestro to teach singing and give lessons; but this was only one possible division of duties. On Wednesday, the last day of October, Burney paid a visit to the San Onofrio, having previously heard its students sing at the Franciscan's church. He was guided there by a young Englishman, Mr. Oliver, who had studied there for four years.

> This morning I went with young Oliver to his Conservatorio of St. Onofrio, and visited all the rooms where the boys practice, sleep, and eat. On the first flight of stairs was a trumpeter, screaming upon his instruments till he was ready to burst; on the second was a french-horn, bellowing in the same manner. In the common practicing room there was a *Dutch concert,* consisting of seven or eight harpsichords, more than as many violins, and several voices, all performing different things, and in different keys: other boys were writing in the same room; but it being holiday time, many were absent who usually study and practice there together.
>
> The jumbling them all together in this manner may be convenient for the house, and may teach the boys to attend to their own parts with firmness, whatever else may be going forward at the same time; it may likewise give them force, by obliging them to play loud in order to hear themselves; but in the midst of such jargon, and continued dissonance, it is wholly impossible to give any kind of polish or finishing to their performance; hence the slovenly coarseness so remarkable in their public exhibitions; and the total want of taste, neatness, and expression in all these musicians, till they have acquired them elsewhere.

Burney's surprise was the greater because he had entered Naples expecting it to be the veritable musical paradise on earth: "What lover of music could be in the place which had produced the two Scarlattis, Vinci, Leo, Pergolesi, Porpora, Farinelli, Jomelli, Traetta, Sacchini, and innumerable others of the first eminence among composers and performers, both vocal and instrumental, without the most sanguine expectations?"

Pursuing his inspection of the San Onofrio, Burney observed that some boys also slept in the main practice room.

> The beds, which are in the same room, serve for seats to the harpsichords and other instruments. Out of thirty or forty boys who were practicing, I could discover but two

that were playing the same piece: some of those who were practicing on the violin seemed to have a great deal of hand [i.e., dexterity]. The violoncellos practice in another room: and the flutes, hautbois, and other wind instruments, in a third, except the trumpets and horns, which are obliged to fag, either on the stairs, or on the top of the house.

There are in this college sixteen young *castrati,* and these lye upstairs, by themselves, in warmer apartments than the other boys, for fear of colds, which might not only render their delicate voices unfit for exercise at present, but hazard the entire loss of them for ever.

Burney concluded his observations by citing the schedule students observed.

The only vacation in these schools in the whole year, is in autumn, and that for a few days only: during the winter, the boys rise two hours before it is light, from which time they continue their exercise, an hour and a half at dinner excepted, till eight o'clock at night; and this constant perseverance, for a number of years, with genius and good teaching, must produce great musicians.

Does his final hopeful remark sound a note of irony?

Michael Kelly, Mozart's future tenor, went from Dublin to Naples as a youth to study in 1779. He sought out Fedele Fenaroli of the Loreto for a singing teacher and wrote in his memoirs that communal practice prevailed there as well. Like Piccinni he overestimated the numbers studying at the Loreto, possibly because they counted day students who were not enrolled.

He [Fenaroli] took me to see his Conservatorio, in which there were between three and four hundred boys; they studied composition, singing, and to play on all instruments. There were several rooms, but in the great school-room, into which I was introduced, there were some singing, others playing upon the violin, hautboy, clarionet, horn, trumpet, etc. etc. each different music, and in different keys. The noise was horrible; and in the midst of this terrific Babel, the boy who studied composition was expected to perform his task, and harmonize a melody given him by his master. I left the place in disgust, and swore to myself never to become an inmate of it.[6]

To Michael Kelly's good fortune, Fenaroli took a liking to him, accepted him as a student, and offered him a small apartment in his own house and access to his table. Kelly became a member of the conservatory but was exempt from all obligatory duties, including the requirement to wear the school uniform, described by Burney as white with a black sash.

There were smaller rooms at the Loreto for practice and teaching, as revealed

[6]Michael Kelly, *Reminiscences of Michael Kelly of the King's Theatre and Theatre Royal Drury Lane,* 2 vols. (London, 1826; reprint 1968), 1: 42–43.

by the minutes of the board of governors for 27 February 1772. Misbehavior by the senior boys, as perceived by the board, caused these rooms to be declared off limits.

> Serious consideration has been given to the fact that although—for the boys' sake— permission was granted to the first, second, and third [junior] maestri di cappella, first violinist, and first oboist, to stay in the rooms where the masters from outside customarily give their lessons, so that they could study and look to their compositions in quiet and without disturbance, nevertheless experience has shown that they have turned their time there to other use, namely, to confer with other boys on the pretext of giving lessons in their capacity of sotto maestri, or mastricelli. . . . It has been decided for the present that the said rooms are to be used solely by the masters from outside for their classes and that when the classes are finished the rooms are to be locked and the keys consigned to the rector or vicerector. . . .[7]

The overall picture that emerges from the Loreto board is that the governors contributed as much as any other factor to the institution's long decline by their capricious and inconsistent policies.

Contributing as well was the mediocrity of the maestri during the last third of the century. The greatest composers no longer taught in the conservatories. Piccinni held the position of second organist at court from 1771, but his salary was docked during his frequent leaves of absence.[8] Piccinni was famous enough to live mostly from his commissions, and live quite well, moreover, as Burney observed in 1770. The music master of the San Onofrio, where Piccinni had studied under Durante, was then the undistinguished composer Carlo Cotumacci, who claimed he was a student of Alessandro Scarlatti in 1719 and who showed Burney the lessons he had received from the great composer.

One of Burney's triumphs in Naples was to corner his idol Jommelli just as this master, returned from many years abroad, was preparing a serious opera, his fourth setting of Metastasio's *Demofoonte* for the fourth of November 1770 gala, celebrating the name day of Charles, former king of Naples. Burney considered Jommelli among the greatest living Italian opera composers, along with Galuppi, Piccinni, and Sacchini. Jommelli received Burney "very politely" in spite of being so busy at the Teatro San Carlo. When asked about the conservatories, he told his visitor that they "were now at a low ebb, though formerly so fruitful in great men." Jommelli did no conservatory teaching after his student days in Naples.

[7]Robinson, "The Governors' Minutes," p. 84.
[8]Hanns-Bertold Dietz, "A Chronology of Maestri and Organisti at the Cappella Reale in Naples, 1745–1800," *JAMS* 25 (1972): 379–406; 392–93.

Vinci

Leonardo Vinci was born ca. 1696 in the hill town of Strongoli in Calabria, near the Gulf of Taranto. He entered the Conservatorio dei Poveri di Gesù Cristo on 14 November 1708 as a *convittore* at an annual fee of 26 ducats. Burney in his *History* relates that Vinci ran away from the conservatory "on account of a quarrel with Porpora." Whether this anecdote is true or not, Porpora, ten years older, was a *maestrocello* in the same school when Vinci arrived and known from subsequent incidents to have been unusually quarrelsome. By 1711 Porpora had left the conservatory and Vinci was exempted from paying the annual fee, meaning he had become a *maestrocello* himself. After mastering counterpoint Vinci would have gone on to write sacred music, cantatas, and the like for his fellow students to perform, but none of these compositions survives, even as recorded mentions. He left the conservatory around 1718 and was appointed to the service of the prince of Sansevero, a powerful member of an old Neapolitan family. Vinci's principal task was the musical education of the prince's young nephew and heir.[9]

COMMEDIA PER MUSICA

Vinci made a name for himself first in comic opera. Comic scenes had been a part of serious opera in Naples as they were elsewhere in the late seventeenth and early eighteenth centuries, and as at Venice they eventually came to be called intermezzi.[10] What was so singular at Naples was the emergence of full-length operatic comedies in three acts with a cast of several characters, most of which were wholly or partly sung in Neapolitan dialect. Their history is connected with a particular theater, located in the Via de' Fiorentini, a few blocks north of the royal palace, and called Teatro de' Fiorentini. In 1709 a new and flexible theater management determined to compete against the serious operas in the nearby and larger Teatro San Bartolomeo, with a more local variety of entertainment. There emerged as a result *Patrò Calienno de la Costa* with a libretto in Neapolitan dialect attributed to Nicolò Corvo. Two others followed under the nom de plume Agasippo Mercotellis. Another poet, Aniello Piscopo, contributed three dialect comedies to the Fiorentini between 1717 and 1719. Other poets who soon followed with libretti were Bernardo Saddumene, Gennaro Federico, Pietro Trinchera, and Antonio Palomba.[11] The success of these comic operas eventually led the Fiorentini to stop trying to rival the San Bartolomeo in serious opera.

[9]Ulisse Prota-Giurleo, "Leonardo Vinci," *Convegno musicale* 2 (1965): 3–11.

[10]Robinson, *Naples and Neapolitan Opera*, pp. 178–89.

[11]The major study of this literary phenomenon remains Michele Scherillo, *L'opera buffa napoletana durante il settecento. Storia letteraria*, 2nd enlarged ed. (Milan, 1916).

The composer of *Patrò Calienno* was Antonio Orefice, who had written a heroic opera *Il Maurizio* for the San Bartolomeo in 1708. Music for neither opera survives, as is the case with almost all his comic and serious works, several written in collaboration with other composers. As a further token of its flexibility the Fiorentini offered a season of operatic comedies in the Tuscan language in 1718–19, all on texts by Francesco Tullio. Orefice set his *Il gemino amore* (music lost) and Francesco Feo his *La forza della virtù* (music lost). Alessandro Scarlatti set his *Il trionfo dell'onore,* a masterpiece of a score that alone should ensure the Fiorentini and its impresario a place in operatic history.

Scarlatti, the most revered figure in Neapolitan music, held the highest musical post in the kingdom, maestro di cappella of its court. His long career had produced several dozen operas for Naples, Rome, Venice, and other cities, but nothing quite like the comedy he wrote for the Fiorentini. In it the comic characters were Rosina, a servant, and her basso buffo counterpart. They were integrated with the other more serious roles, and not isolated as they would be in an intermezzo given as entr'acte to a *dramma per musica*. Rosina sings a hesitant aria to her suitor in which she cannot quite bring herself to declare her positive reaction to his advances (Example 2.1). The cut of her delightfully unpretentious little melody is periodic, that is to say, made up of balanced units: the second measure answers the first, the fourth echoes the third, which is later mimicked by the violins. On a larger scale the whole first phrase, with its harmonic motion from I to V (mm. 1–8), is answered melodically and harmonically by the second (mm. 8–15), which returns the compliment, as it were, by reversing the progression, V - I. Following this a little codetta invoking the minor mode reinforces the hesitancies and doubts already expressed.

In this particular aria, melodic and harmonic considerations control the discourse, as they do preponderantly in the most adventurous of Scarlatti's colleagues among the young Neapolitan composers, whom he may well be copying, for his usual manner is more intricate and contrapuntal. In the lightness and regularity of this new style we have no difficulty in recognizing kinships with Mozart (who uses a similar melodic beginning, quite by accident, for the chorus that ends Act III of *Le nozze di Figaro*) or with Haydn, notably in the spirit of repartee. The coyness with which Scarlatti's tune "gets stuck" in mm. 3–4, and the expressive use of long silences that create dramatic suspense through incomplete melodic and harmonic motion, also suggest Haydn. Often the violins double the voice or parody its wavering seconds (mm. 6–7) on the way to the first cadence. In this same parodistic vein the violins seem to mock every downward turn of the voice in mm. 11–12—a fourfold statement of the same upbeat figure!—with a saucy little upward motion, a three-note slide that is picked up by the voice in the following minor-mode extension. The three-note slide will become one of the trademarks of Neapolitan composers and remain so for decades. Scarlatti here seems almost

EXAMPLE 2.1. *Alessandro Scarlatti*, Il trionfo dell'onore, *Aria*

too sophisticated and refined for a popular audience, and his public perhaps reacted the same way because he wrote less and less for the theater in his last decade, the final opera being *La Griselda* (1721), a *dramma per musica* for Rome, four years before he died.

Vinci found ways to be less highbrow than Scarlatti. His first comedy for the Fiorentini came immediately after the "Tuscan" season of 1718, when the management decided to return to operas in the local dialect. It was *Lo cecato fausto* on a libretto by Piscopo, first given in April 1719 with enthusiastic reception in the local press; the music is lost. Another sign of success is that Vinci followed it up with another opera of the same kind as soon as the following July. Five more followed in regular succession until *Li zite 'n galera* on a libretto by Saddumene, staged on 3 January 1722, Vinci's first comic opera to have survived as a complete score. This notice appeared in the official journal dated 6 January 1722: "Saturday for the first time was staged in the Teatro de' Fiorentini the opera in music in Neapolitan dialect entitled *Li zite 'n galera . . .* the music, an excellent success, composed by the celebrated maestro di cappella Leonardo Vinci."[12]

Li zite 'n galera (The lovers on the galley) survives as an autograph score dated 20 November 1721. The premiere took place on 3 January 1722, which gives a rough idea of how much rehearsal time was allowed at the Fiorentini. Its plot is the usual farrago of crossed lovers, disguises, and mix-ups, sorted out at the end when the galley captain Federico (the only role sung in Tuscan) allows his daughter to have her way.[13]

The first act opens with a song for Ciccariello, a boisterous servant-barber (sung by a woman) who says he wishes to nibble on the foot of his mistress, Sister Annella, and give her a start (Example 2.2). A lilting *Canzonetta* in 12/8 meter with dotted rhythm, it is of a type that Johann Mattheson, in treatises of 1713 and 1739, equated with Neapolitan and Sicilian popular singing. The orchestra, consisting of strings only, enters playing a short introductory ritornello in unisons and octaves, outlining the tonic triad in strongly etched dotted rhythm, with syncopations. When the voice enters it ignores the dotted rhythms but accentuates the syncopations by lengthening the weak final syllables of "deventare" and "sorecillo," an exaggeration of the iambic short-long phrase ending that was also characteristic of Neapolitan popular music. A bare fifth relieves the monody for an instant, as the ritornello figure sounds on the dominant, overlapping the voice. At its second entrance the voice, upon repeating the words "la sia Annella," introduces a further touch of local color, the flat supertonic or Neapolitan sixth, B♭. Moreover, it makes a charming musical pun whereby becoming a very small ani-

[12]Thomas Griffin, *Musical References in the Gazzetta di Napoli 1681–1725* (Berkeley, 1993), no. 455, p. 100.
[13]There is a synopsis in Kurt Sven Markstrom, "The Operas of Leonardo Vinci Napoletano" (Ph.D. diss., University of Toronto, 1993), pp. 16–17.

EXAMPLE 2.2. *Vinci*, Li zite 'n galera, Canzonetta

mal, a mouse ("sorecillo"), is translated into the smallest musical interval, a minor second above and below the tonic, and precisely at the mention of the object of this transformation—Sister Annella. The pun is so potent and timeless that Mozart was not loathe to use the same when he constricted Papageno's melodic line to minor seconds at the words "Oh I would I were a mouse" in the first-act finale of *Die Zauberflöte.*

Li zite is not totally lacking in the musical ostentation then thought appropriate to heroic opera. Federico sings a coloratura aria with trumpets and oboes, "Or più non mi fa guerra." Otherwise the arias are quite plain, without melismatic extensions and with minimal orchestral accompaniments. In the second act, when Ciccariello pretends to be sick in order to escape a beating from his master, he sings in such a lively and straightforward manner as to belie the prevarication he embroiders (in a case like this music has the choice of painting either the truth or the fiction) (Example 2.3). The periodic cut of the melody, combined with short

EXAMPLE 2.3. *Vinci*, Li zite 'n galera, *Aria*

two-bar phrases separated by rests to match the *quinarii* lines of the text, results in a catchy melody typical of Vinci. Selection of an evasive move toward IV preceding the falsehood of "having a fever" ("ch'aggio la fevra") seems so simple but sounds so right. The three-note slides at the beginning of mm. 2 and 4 recall the slides used by Scarlatti in Example 2.1. In this slight three-part texture the violins double the voice continuously, and not just occasionally, as in Scarlatti, which helps to project the voice and keep it on pitch (the singers at the Fiorentini tended to be younger and less gifted than their more famous and highly paid colleagues in serious opera). Worthy of note are the modal inflections (flat third and flat seventh degrees) and the momentary dipping towards the minor mode in mm. 5–6, a typically Neapolitan trait that was also present in Example 2.1. Vinci's directness offered audiences and singers alike exactly what they wanted and needed. From minimal musical means Vinci extracted maximum theatrical effects.

Vinci often chooses 3/8 time in a rapid meter for comic effect, as in an aria for the elderly Meneca, a woman's role sung by the tenor Simone de Falco (Example 2.4). She is introduced by a ritornello in which the strings play mostly in unisons and octaves, *presto* and staccato, producing a result that has been compared with the chattering of an angry and toothless old hag. Perhaps she tried a dance step to this lively introduction, with a kick to match the violins' leap up to high C in mm. 9 and 11. The cadential repetition, rapid tempo, staccato articulation, melodic leaps, and mainly *unisono* texture are all earmarks of the comic style that would profit Pergolesi and other followers of Vinci.

EXAMPLE 2.4. *Vinci*, Li zite 'n galera, *Meneca's aria, ritornello*

In Act II of *Li zite* Ciccariello is asked to feign a love duet with one of the other characters such as might be sung by the warblers in a serious opera. He obliges by affecting an earnest tone and employing the key of A, particularly associated with love duets in Italian opera (and in Mozart). Even before ending the first phrase Vinci resorts to rapid repetition of the words "fa pazzia" (drives one crazy), a lapse into patter that effectively deflates the proffered endearments and earnest tone of the opening with hilarious effect. Parody of the situations and styles associated with serious opera was a mainstay of all types of comic opera, and Vinci was a master at it, partly because he commanded both serious and comic genres. Unlike those of Vinci's serious operas, the libretto of *Li zite* offered several ensembles. The quintet that ended Act I has its own form, corresponding to the drama, and thus containing the seeds of what will eventually bloom as the buffo finale. By way of contrast, the quartet in Scarlatti's *Il trionfo dell'onore* is cast like an aria and has the usual repetition, da capo.

Scarlatti never wrote anything in so popular a style as Vinci consistently employs in *Li zite.* He eschewed outright street songs in the vein of Ciccariello's opening *Canzonetta.* The tone of broad farce that prevails throughout *Li zite* (for which literary critics have reproved Saddumene) sets it far apart from Scarlatti's occasional touches of sophisticated comedy, confined usually to a couple of roles, as in *Il trionfo dell'onore.* It should hardly come as a surprise that Neapolitans preferred Vinci to the urbane, elderly master.

The popular nature of operatic entertainments at the Fiorentini did not mean it was shunned by the court, especially during the vice-regency of the Habsburgs (1707–34) and the reign of Ferdinand IV. The report in the *Avvisi di Napoli* of 6 January 1722 is specific on this point and mentions other aspects of the production.

On Saturday the *opera in musica* in Neapolitan dialect entitled *Li zite 'n galera* was put on stage for the first time at the Teatro Fiorentini, attaining the summit of satisfaction of the most excellent Viceregents who went there to listen to it with almost all the nobility. The present contractor procured pleasure through the charming costumes, the variety of the spectacle to be seen, and not least of all the music, an excellent success, composed by the celebrated *maestro di cappella* Leonardo Vinci.[14]

Li zite was so successful it was revived at the Teatro della Pace in late 1724 because, as the reprinted libretto stated, "it created so much madness when given at the Fiorentini."[15] Parts of the work (including our examples 2.3 and 2.4) were retained in performance as late as the midcentury. Few Neapolitan composers wrote music that remained current for so long a time.

DRAMMA PER MUSICA

Success at the Fiorentini opened the way for Vinci to compose serious operas for the Teatro San Bartolomeo. After *Li zite*'s triumph in early 1722 Vinci received the signal honor of a commission to compose the opera for St. Charles Day, 4 November 1722. Normally this honor would have gone to one of the court composers, who were Scarlatti, Mancini, and Sarro. Of the three, Scarlatti had retired from the stage and Mancini had only sporadic success in composing operas, but Sarro was at the height of his powers and quite favored by the public. Why he was not chosen over Vinci is not easily explained. (Sarro did compose Silvio Stampiglia's *Partenope* for the same season of the San Bartolomeo, with premiere on 16 December.) The official notice declared that Vinci's opera, *Publio Cornelio Scipione,* won universal applause and went on to sing the praises of the cast, headed by Battista Pacini in the title role and Faustina Bordoni, prima donna. For another gala occasion the following year, the birthday of Emperor Charles VI on 1 October, Vinci was chosen again, resulting in his setting of *Silla dittatore.* Both *Scipione* and *Silla* were revised librettos from earlier Venetian works. With Vinci's next opera he received a libretto, *Farnace,* specifically written for him by the Venetian librettist Antonio Maria Lucchini. It was his first commission outside Naples and came from the Teatro Alibert in Rome.

In *Farnace* the primo uomo was the castrato Domenico Gizzi, and the prima donna Farinelli, singing in his first Vinci opera. *Farnace*'s success added to the demand for Vinci's compositions. In his *History* Burney wrote, "so great was the success of this drama, that he was called upon to furnish at least one opera a year till 1730, when he composed two." The second opera of the carnival season at

[14]Ibid., p. 29, no. 31 (original), p. 15 (partial translation). The contractor, or impresario, was Bernardino Bottone.

[15]Scherillo, *L'opera buffa napoletana,* p. 151, no. 3.

Rome was a setting of an old Zeno libretto, *Scipione,* by the Bolognese composer Luca Antonio Predieri. A dispatch from Rome dated 25 February 1724 appearing four days later in Naples says it displeased the public because of the poor quality of the libretto, which was without incident ("senz' accidenti"); Vinci's *Farnace* was revived in its place, winning renewed applause for Farinelli and Gizzi.[16] Thus it must be as Berenice in Vinci's *Farnace* that Ghezzi caricatured Farinelli on 2 March 1724 (see Figure 1.6 on p. 35).

Vivaldi was in Rome at the same time as Vinci, writing operas for the rival Teatro Capranica. His *Giustino,* composed on a reworked libretto from 1683, was the second opera for the same carnival season of 1724 (the first was a pasticcio in which he composed only the second act). *Giustino* may have been as successful as *Farnace,* but it was Vinci, not Vivaldi, who was called back to Rome to write several subsequent operas.[17] Ghezzi made caricatures of both composers.

When Vinci returned to Naples in April 1724 he was kept busy composing sacred works and a new *commedia per musica, La mogliera fedele,* to inaugurate the Teatro della Pace. Once again he was asked to compose the opera celebrating the emperor's birthday on 1 October which was *Eraclea,* given at the San Bartolomeo with Vittoria Tesi in the title role. In this case the libretto was by the aged imperial court poet Stampiglia, who had settled into retirement in Naples. He extensively revised his 1700 libretto, first set by Scarlatti, specifically for Vinci. The regular pair of buffo singers at the San Bartolomeo were on leave in Venice and so the entr'actes consisted not of comic intermezzi but of ballets.

A modern historian of Vinci's operas was able to make some broad comparisons between Scarlatti's and Vinci's setting of *Eraclea,* with insights that also throw light on Handel's relationship to earlier operas.

> It is indicative of the radical changes in contemporary Italian music that, although Stampiglia's libretto from 1700 could be revived for performance in 1724, albeit with extensive changes, Scarlatti's music could not—this in spite of the fact that both men were living in Naples at the time. Not only was Scarlatti's music not revived, but Vinci's score shows absolutely no parallels with Scarlatti's—Vinci composed his *Eraclea* as if Scarlatti's had never existed. This contrasts with Handel who, when setting an old libretto, sometimes made use of the original score as a source of thematic material, the most obvious example being the Stampiglia/Bononcini *Serse* of 1684. This does not merely reflect the individual compositional practices of two composers, but also two very different aesthetic perspectives. Handel, whose style grows out of

[16]Markstrom, "The Operas of Leonardo Vinci," p. 58.
[17]Comparing the two operas an expert wrote: "[Vinci's] music is ahead of Vivaldi's in the terse and powerful text setting, if not in the use of the instruments." Reinhard Strohm, "Vivaldi's Career as an Opera Composer," in *Antonio Vivaldi: Teatro musicale, cultura e società,* ed. Lorenzo Bianconi and Giovanni Morelli, 2 vols. (Florence, 1982) 2: 11–63; 50.

the turn-of-the century cosmopolitan style, was free to draw inspiration from this rich musical source at any point in his career, whereas Vinci, whose style grows out of the radical hothouse environment of fashion-conscious Naples and Rome, seems continually striving to be as innovative and modern as possible.[18]

It is no wonder that Vinci's music attained even more renown the following year, 1725. In Rome the theaters remained closed because of the Holy Year. By late 1724, Venice called Vinci, who came at the invitation of the main opera house, San Giovanni Grisostomo (Vivaldi worked for the less esteemed Teatro Sant'Angelo). As Burney put it, "In 1725 the Venetian theatre first heard the natural, clear, and dramatic strains of Leonardo Vinci, in his two operas of *Ifigenia in Aulide* and *La Rosmira fidele.*" Both operas featured Faustina Bordoni in the title role, and having sung for Vinci in Naples she may have played a role in securing for him the commissions from her native Venice.

The libretto of *Ifigenia* was by a Venetian nobleman, Benedetto Pasqualigo, first set by Giuseppe Maria Orlandini for the same theater in 1719 and revised for Vinci. A complete score for this five-act opera has not been located, but the individual arias do survive in keyboard score. Some of the arpeggio writing in the accompaniment is concerto-like and may show Vinci's attempt to profit from Vivaldi.[19] The second opera was revised from a 1699 libretto by Stampiglia. To save time and effort on the part of Faustina, Vinci borrowed the recitatives from an earlier setting of the libretto by Sarro, in which she had sung. Carlo Scalzi sang the role of Arsace.

As a result of his success in Venice, the court of Parma, ruled by Duke Francesco Farnese, invited Vinci and most of his Venetian cast to visit in the spring of 1725. There Vinci composed Stampiglia's *Il trionfo di Camilla,* first set by Giovanni Bononcini in 1696. Carlo Innocenzo Frugoni, at this time young and inexperienced, revised the old libretto and subsequently wrote sonnets in praise of both Scalzi and Faustina for their performances. Little survives of the music from the opera. Reliance on old librettos or nonprofessional writers like Pasqualigo shows how much need there was for a great poet to emerge who could match the "natural, clear, and dramatic strains" of Vinci.

DIDONE ABBANDONATA

After Scarlatti died on 22 October 1725, Mancini regained the post of maestro of the court music, from which he was demoted in 1708, and Sarro again became vice maestro. Vinci was appointed pro vice maestro, meaning he would succeed Sarro if he outlived him. In the latter part of 1725 Vinci was busy composing three

---

[18]Markstrom, "The Operas of Leonardo Vinci," pp. 74–75. The musical examples from Vinci's *Eraclea* following this overview certainly bear out the author's claims.
[19]Ibid., p. 85.

operas, *Astianatte* for the San Bartolomeo (premiere in December 1725), *Didone abbandonata* for the Roman Teatro Alibert, reopened under new management as the Teatro delle Dame (premiere in January 1726) and *Siroe, re di Persia* for the San Giovanni Grisostomo theater in Venice (premiere in February 1726).

Sarro had made the first setting of Metastasio's *Didone* for the San Bartolomeo, a version first staged in February 1724. The title role was sung by soprano Marianna Bulgarelli. Nicolo Grimaldi ("Nicolini"), the veteran alto castrato, created the part of Enea, and Antonia Merichi played the Moorish King Jarba. Bulgarelli could not sing Didone in Vinci's version for Rome because of the papal stricture against women on the stage, but she is thought to have coached the young castrato Giacinto Fontana ("Farfallino") in this role, which had been specifically tailored by the poet to display her great abilities as an actress. Metastasio revised his libretto carefully for Rome, making major changes in the second act. The opera, his first full-scale tragic drama, caused a sensation.

In Metastasio's telling of the tale, Didone is doomed from the beginning, although she does not know it, by Enea's resolve to quit Carthage and sail on to Italy. Of all the characters, only she approaches being honest and straightforward. When King Jarba demands her hand in marriage and threatens violent consequences if refused, she rises from her throne and sings her first aria.

Son regina e sono amante,	I am both queen and lover,
e l'impero io sola voglia	And I wish to rule alone
del mio soglio e del mio cor.	Over my realm and my heart.

Metastasio's clarity and force inspired Vinci to simplify and clarify his music even further. After a forceful ritornello for strings of 28 mm. establishes the key and the meter, Didone begins with the simple rise of a third, sounding regal indeed, and then descends in a three-note slide, the ultimate in musical fashion of the time (Example 2.5). The next two measures present more slides plus a *cadence galante*, and are repeated, lending the initial statement the **a b b** shape destined for such favor in mid- and late-eighteenth-century music. Then Vinci uses the drooping slide motif as a turn around tonic C, three times in succession, which sounds a kind of obstinate determination that suits perfectly what Didone is expressing in words and in action. Her steadfastness also emerges in the pedals she later holds against the descending tenths in the strings.

Desperate to persuade her lover not to leave, Didone gradually unravels as a character. In Act II she tries to make him jealous by accepting Jarba's offer of marriage (her only act of deceit). This ruse fails, increasing her anger and chagrin, and also that of Jarba when she tells him the truth. To begin Act III Jarba challenges Enea to a duel. Enea is victorious but spares Jarba's life so as to increase his own glory. The aria he sings at this point, "Vivi, superbi e regno" (deleted by Metastasio from later editions of the libretto), is in the same key (C) and meter as "Son

EXAMPLE 2.5. *Vinci*, Didone abbandonata, *Aria*

Regina,"but the music is more complex in its phrase construction, in keeping with the character of the wily Trojan visitor.

Didone sings no arias in Act III but manages to dominate it almost completely. Vinci relies on a colorful palette of arioso and recitative, both simple and obbligato, for her—the others are confined to simple recitative. In her first soliloquy she imagines that her misfortunes will become the stuff of legend and tragic dramas. In another scene she curses Enea, wishing him a horrible journey. To this her sister Selena responds that she too loved Enea and was a rival for his love, to the queen's great distress. Jarba, repulsed again and more firmly than ever, sets fire to Carthage and storms it with his army. Didone finally has no one left but her confidant, Osmida, who also leaves, scandalized, after Didone inveighs against the gods. The final scene begins.

Ah, che disi, infelici! A qual eccesso	Ah, what sayest thou, wretch! To what excess
mi trasse il mio furore!	does my fury lead me!
Oh dio, cresce l'orrore!	Oh God, the horror swells! Wherever I look
mi ven la morte e lo spavento in faccia:	Death and terror stare me in the face
trema la reggia e di cader minaccia.	The palace trembles and threatens to fall.
Selene, Osmida, ah! tutti,	Selene, Osmida, ah! all,
tutti cedeste alla mia sorte infida:	all flee at my treacherous fate:
non v'è chi mi soccorra o chi m'uscida.	There is no one to aid or to kill me.
Vado . . . Ma dove? Oh Dio!	I go . . . but where? Oh God!
Resto . . . Ma poi . . . Che fo?	I stay . . . but then . . . what to do?
Dunque morir dovrò	Must I die therefore
senza trovar pietà?	without finding pity?
E v'è tanta viltà nel petto mio?	And is there so much baseness in my breast?
No, no, si mora; e l'infedele Enea	No, no, I die; and may the faithless
abbia nel mio destino	Enea find in my destiny
un augurio funesto al suo camino.	an ill omen for his voyage.
Precipiti Cartago,	Fall Carthage,
arda la reggia, e sia	burn royal palace, and may
il cenere de lei la tomba mia.	your cinders be my tomb.
	(She leaps into the flames.)

Metastasio planned this climax with an opportunity for a lyrical moment of contrast in the middle, where a quatrain is set off in the text. Sarro had understood this and set the quatrain of indecision to a minor-mode arioso over a throbbing string accompaniment in 3/4 time.[20] His harmonies are rich but not fully in

[20]Robinson, *Naples and Neapolitan Opera*, illustrates Sarro's arioso, pp. 80–81.

control as to how they succeed each other, with the result that his arioso sounds somewhat haphazard, more like the *seicento* past than like Vinci. Effective, on the other hand, is his choice of a Neapolitan sixth chord at the key word "morir." In his setting Vinci did much more with less (Example 2.6). At first his strings accompany in slow chords (what Rousseau calls "récitatif accompagné"), but then they become agitated and necessarily measured exactly, with falling scales to paint the trembling and falling palace (what Rousseau calls "récitatif obligé").[21]

Didone's tragic monologue was one of the pieces that made Vinci's fame. In 1755 it was still so much alive in the memories of musicians that Francesco Algarotti in his *Saggio sopra l'opera in musica* could propose it as a model of how to handle recitative reinforced by the orchestra: "Virgil himself would have been pleased to hear a composition so lively and so terrible" (i.e., capable of inspiring terror). The legendary status of the composer as reformer was already well underway before Algarotti, as the final section on Vinci below will demonstrate.

The exact nature of Vinci's duties as pro vice maestro is unclear, but evidently he was confined almost entirely to the well-traveled operatic circuit of Rome–Naples, although his music was greatly in demand throughout the world of Italian opera. He did go to Parma to compose a wedding opera, *Medo,* on a libretto by Carlo Innocenzo Frugoni, in May 1728. Political considerations probably played a role here, as the Habsburgs set great store on their alliance with the strategically located duchy of Parma. When Vinci returned from Parma to Naples in 1728 he was asked to serve as interim maestro of his old conservatory (dei Poveri), replacing his teacher Gaetano Greco, who had died. He was paid 44 ducats for several months of service and for some books of music that he provided.[22] He was repaid in another sense by teaching a brilliant pupil, Pergolesi, destined to become his artistic successor.

ARTASERSE

In the final lustrum of Vinci's short life he composed regularly on commission from the Teatro delle Dame in Rome (carnival season) and from the San Bartolomeo (fall season). His greatest works were the operas for Rome in collaboration with Metastasio, whose favorite composer he became. Vinci made the first setting of the poet's *Catone in Utica* (1728), *Semiramide riconosciuta,* and finally both *Alessandro nell'Indie* and *Artaserse* (1730). *Catone in Utica,* ranked highly for its stylistic consistency, was modeled to some extent on *Didone* in that the title

---

[21]Robinson (ibid., p. 78) muddles the question of recitative categories by referring to Rousseau's articles on "récitatif accompagné" and "recitatif mesuré" but omitting altogether Rousseau's long and crucial article on "récitatif obligé." He admits even so that, normally, recitative elaborately punctuated by orchestral interjections was called "recitativo obbligato."

[22]Markstrom, "The Operas of Leonardo Vinci," p. 237.

EXAMPLE 2.6. *Vinci*, Didone abbandonata, *final scene*

role is given impassioned obbligato recitatives in Act III but no arias, and goes to his death at the end. The final collaboration brought forth in *Artaserse* an opera that put the seal of genius on both poet and composer.[23] Almost all Italian operas were works of a single season, meant to be replaced the following season. Yet Vinci's setting became the closest thing to a classic in its genre, holding the stage for many years in revivals. As for the poem, more composers set it than any other libretto in history (the only rivals being some of the others among the most frequently set dramas by Metastasio). Charles de Brosses made this reflection on the

[23]Robert Burns Meikle, "Leonardo Vinci's *Artaserse:* An Edition, with an editorial and critical commentary" (Ph.D. diss., Cornell University, 1970).

demand in Italy for operatic novelty, so unlike the situation in Paris at the time: "People do not want to see an opera, ballet, stage-decor or singer they have already seen in another season, unless it is some excellent opera by Vinci or some very famous voice" (2: 292). Brosses also claimed that he knew all the arias from Vinci's *Artaserse* by heart from hearing them sung in concerts.

One aria in *Artaserse* particularly singled out for praise was the climactic monologue ending Act I. Arbace, forsaken in turn by father, sister, king, and lover, is left to bewail his fate, an innocent victim accused of murder who cannot reveal the identity of the real culprit (his father). Metastasio acquitted himself with one of his most moving metaphor arias to convey the hero's state, which he compares with an imminent nautical disaster.

Vo solcando un mar crudele	I go plowing a cruel sea
Senza vele,	Without a sail
E senza sarte:	And without rigging:
Freme l'onda, il ciel s'imbruna	The waves boil, the sky darkens,
Cresce il vento, e manca l'arte;	The wind increases, and I lack skill;
E il voler della fortuna	And the will of fortune
Son costretto a seguitar.	I am constrained to follow.
Infelice! in questo stato	Unhappy man! in this state
Son da tutti abandonato:	Am I abandoned by all:
Meco sola e l'innocenza,	With me is only my innocence,
Che mi porta a naufragar.	Which carries me toward shipwreck.

Unhappy the poets who came after Metastasio and tried to imitate this aria! They included Mozart's Abbé Gianbattista Varesco in his shipwreck aria for *Idomeneo*.[24]

Vinci chose the key of D, in which the strings are so brilliant, and adds to them, unusually for him, pairs of oboes and horns, in a broadly conceived and flowing *Andante* in cut time (Example 2.7). Giovanni Carestini was the primo uomo who first had to sing those difficult trilled whole notes ascending in an implied crescendo to the high A of his voice; at the revival in Rome a year later Arbace was sung by Carlo Scalzi.

When Grétry as a young man of nineteen arrived in Rome to study music in 1760, his teachers were still in awe of Vinci's *Artaserse*. In his memoirs written late in life Grétry disagreed, at least in part. He cited the melody of Semira's aria "Torna innocente, e poi / T'ascolterò se vuoi" (Return innocent and then I shall listen to you if you wish), apparently from memory, with several mistakes. He dismissed Vinci's setting for not conveying the anger of Arbace's sister and for being a gigue air, "a gay dance air suitable to express the anger of Pulcinella." What he failed to recognize was that Vinci seized upon the single word "innocent" for his affect, not the complete sentence, as Grétry himself would have done. With the shipwreck aria he found no fault.

How far removed is "Torna innocente" from "Vo solcando" by the same composer. In the latter, the melody, and above all the accompaniments, agree entirely with the words. This is the first *tableau* that was made in music, the first beam of light in the direction of the truth. The Romans entered into a delirium when they heard, for the

[24]Daniel Heartz, *Mozart's Operas*, ed. Thomas Baumann (Berkeley, 1990), pp. 22–23.

EXAMPLE 2.7. *Vinci, Artaserse, Aria*

first time, this sublime reunion of sounds with the proper expression of the words. Vinci was thus the first inspired one, according to what the old Roman teachers told me, and, as creative artist, he merited the statue that has been erected to him in the [artistic] pantheon. If the genius of Vinci was the first to feel that sounds could paint the heart's agitation in terms of the diverse movements of a storm-tossed vessel, the aria "Torna innocente," which I just cited, proves that he did not understand that melody has as much power as harmony, and more power even. . . . Pergolesi was born and the truth became known.[25]

"Vo solcando" inspired a great tone painting from Vinci. The syncopated agitations of the violins in mm. 28–29 suggest choppy seas, and the building up in the voice to high A beginning in the same spot and ending with the plunge down an octave could be compared with the building up of a huge wave that suddenly comes crashing down. Following this the *subito piano* with half-note suspended dissonances in the second violins as the voice sinks down to the low tonic in whole notes imitates gathering darkness. For the increasing winds Vinci resorts to his familiar tattoo of rapid notes following longer ones in the violins while the voice wavers back and forth on a few tones, and with more syncopations. The half-cadence in the new key of A as the voice descends by step at "e manca l'arte" (mm. 43–45) perhaps sounds familiar because Pergolesi duplicated it exactly in the first half-cadence on the dominant in Serpina's aria "Stizzoso" from *La serva padrona* (see Example 4.16b on p. 397).

Artaserse gained immortality for Vinci, according to Gerber in the second edition of his *Lexikon der Tonkünstler* (1812–14). Besides the aria "Vo solcando," Gerber cited the third-act duet "Tu vuoi ch'io viva, o cara," sung by Arbace and his beloved Mandane, saying "one will always admire them and find them to be models of their type."[26] According to one critic writing in 1754, Vinci's *Artaserse* "passed for the most beautiful Italian opera, just as Lully's *Armide* is the masterpiece of French music."[27]

The first run of *Artaserse* in Rome was cut short by the death of Pope Benedict XIII on 21 February 1730, which caused all the theaters to be closed. Returning to Naples, Vinci had but a few months to live himself. He died in late May 1730, suddenly, and probably from poison.[28] On hearing about the successful revival of *Artaserse* at Rome from La Romanina, Metastasio wrote from Vienna on

---

[25]André Modeste Grétry, *Mémoires, ou essais sur la musique,* 3 vols. (Paris, 1797; reprint New York, 1971), 1: 422–24. Volume 1 came out in a first edition of 1789 in Paris. Markstrom, in "The Operas of Leonardo Vinci," pp. 287–88, reads Grétry too literally when he suggests that a statue was erected to Vinci in the Pantheon of Rome. He also errs in saying that Duni was Grétry's teacher in Rome. Duni went to Paris in 1757 and remained there. In his article "Vinci" in *The New Grove Dictionary of Opera*, ed. Stanley Sadie (London, 1992), Markstrom unaccountably assigns the two *Artaserse* arias discussed by Grétry to *Semiramide*.

[26]Ernst Ludwig Gerber, *Neues historisch-biographisches Lexikon der Tonkünstler*, 4 vols. (Leipzig, 1812–14; reprint 1966), S.V. "Vinci."

[27]Anonymous, "Reflexions d'un patriote sur l'opera françois, et sur l'opera italien," in *La Querelle des Bouffons*, ed. Denise Launay, 2 vols. (Geneva, 1973), 2: 2057. Fétis attributed the pamphlet to a certain Rochement, Swiss merchant.

[28]Markstrom, "The Operas of Leonardo Vinci," pp. 316–19, sifts all the evidence and cautiously concludes that the early stories about Vinci's poisoning can be neither proved nor disproved. In *Historisch-biographisches Lexikon der Tonkünsler* (Leipzig, 1792), Gerber states unequivocally that Vinci was poisoned because of envy and jealousy on the part of other composers.

7 July 1731 asking her to thank all the performers in his name, "particularly the incomparable Scalzi, and Farfallino, who I salute and embrace. Poor Vinci! Now that merit will be known, which during his life, was blasted by his enemies." Who were these enemies?

Vinci's troubles with Porpora went back to his days as a conservatory pupil in Naples, as we have seen. The rivalry became more heated with each Vinci success. They were often rivals in the most direct sense of having concurrent productions on the stage in the same city. In Venice during the carnival of 1726 Popora's *Siface* and Vinci's *Siroe* were sharing the stage of the San Giovanni Grisostomo theater. Quantz was there and wrote in his autobiography that "both composers were present, but the latter opera was more acclaimed than the former." Porpora's *Siface* was revived at the Capranica theater in Rome in February 1730 at the same time that Vinci's *Artaserse* was being performed in the Teatro delle Dame. Marpurg tells a long anecdote about how Vinci planned to disrupt Porpora's dress rehearsal and how one of Vinci's singers, the alto castrato Gaetano Berenstadt, whom Porpora had maligned, actually did disrupt it by blowing enough snuff toward the stage while hidden in one of the boxes to cause the actors a fit of sneezing.[29] Metastasio later warned La Romanina after Porpora had caused a scandal in Rome: "In sum, where Porpora mixes in disgrace enters by necessity. For goodness sake keep from ever having the slightest thing to do with him."[30]

Sarro, Vinci's superior in the court music, was another potent rival. As Vinci's star continued to ascend, Sarro's waned. In his autobiography Quantz implies that Sarro tried to rival Vinci by copying his style. The first opera he heard in Naples was Sarro's *Tito Sempronio Gracco* in early 1725, which he called "almost in the style of Vinci." Sarro wrote no operas after his *Siroe* for the San Bartolomeo in 1727 until Vinci died three years later, and then he wrote but few. In 1739 Sarro's *La Partenope* of 1722 was revived in the new San Carlo theater; Charles de Brosses was on hand and expressed his disappointment (1: 400). It also displeased King Charles III, which was a more serious matter. The minister who was responsible for the revival made what excuse he could, saying, "The composer Sarro has always been a most celebrated man. It is true however that he flourished in a bygone age."[31]

THE VINCI LEGEND

One of the greatest Italian architects and stage designers, Filippo Juvarra, honored Vinci with the design for a sepulchral monument. Juvarra, born in Messina in

---

[29]Friedrich Wilhelm Marpurg, *Kritische Briefe über die Tonkunst,* 2 vols. (Berlin, 1760–64; reprint 1973), 1: 225–27.

[30]"In somma, dove si mischia Porpora entra per necessità la disgrazia. Guardatevi per carità di non aver mai il minimo affare in sua compagnia." Letter of 21 June 1731, in Pietro Metastasio, *Tutte le opere,* ed. Bruno Brunelli, 5 vols. (Milan, 1943–44), 1: 329. This language is unusally blunt for Metastasio—so blunt, in fact, that the pious Burney omitted these two sentences from the English translation.

[31]Michael F. Robinson, "Sarro," in *The New Grove Dictionary of Opera.*

1678, was trained in Rome and worked there as a stage designer with several composers until 1714, when he entered the service of Duke Victor Amadeus II of Savoy, who by the Treaty of Utrecht had just received Sicily and the royal title that went with it. As principal architect in Turin, Juvarra began an ambitious program of construction in an attempt to make a truly royal capital out of the city. The king exchanged Sicily with Austria for Sardinia in 1720 and henceforth became the king of Sardinia. His son succeeded him in 1730 as Charles Emmanuel III and ruled until 1773. Charles allied himself with Spain and France against Austria in an attempt to drive the Austrians out of Italy in the War of Polish Succession. In bloody battles of 1734 around the city of Parma, Savoy lost most of its military leaders. Juvarra began his *Memorie sepolcri dell'homine più insigne di questo secolo conosciuto da Me* (Memorial tombs of the most famous men of this century known to me) as a set of *tombeaux* to honor the fallen generals. But before he died in 1736 he expanded the collection of drawings to include many artists, including his teacher Carlo Fontana, plus five composers. The five were Andrea Fiorè, maestro di cappella of the Turin court until his death in 1732; Archangelo Corelli, who died in Rome in 1713 and who, like Juvarra, was patronized by Cardinal Pietro Ottoboni and lived under his roof in the Palazzo Cancelleria; Francesco Gasparini, who died in Rome in 1727; Carlo Francesco Pollarolo, who died in Venice in 1722; and Vinci,

FIGURE 2.3. Filippo Juvarra. Tombeau of Vinci, 1729.

described as a "famous master of theatrical music, dead in Naples in 1729 [*sic*]" (Figure 2.3).[32]

It is difficult to say where Juvarra might have encountered Vinci in person because the architect was kept in Turin by his grand building schemes during the 1720s. And perhaps the two did not actually meet, contrary to the case of the other famous men Juvarra honored. It may have sufficed that Vinci's fame was so great by the time of this death in 1730 that Juvarra merely selected him as the greatest opera composer of his time. The odd thing is that, as stage designer for Cardinal Ottoboni in Rome, the architect had often worked directly with Scarlatti, whom he did not deign to include among his musical honorees. One would like to believe that, in honoring Vinci, Juvarra was recognizing the most daring mod-

[32]Oscar Mischiati, "Un memoria sepolcrale di Filippo Juvarra per Arcangelo Corelli," *Nuovi studi corelliani*, ed. Giulia Giachin (Florence, 1978), pp. 105–10.

ernist in music as a kindred soul representing in music what he himself represented in architecture and stage design.

Vinci turns up often on lists of musicians who modernized opera, or reformed
melody or taste. His legend spread particularly among French visitors, who were
more prone to setting down music criticism in writing than were Italians. Brosses
paid homage to "Vinci and his disciple Pergolesi" after his visit to Rome and
Naples in 1739–40. Rousseau, who spent a year in the French legation to Venice
in 1745–46, wrote in his *Lettre sur la musique française* (1753) in denunciation of
the old harmonists. They were not really musicians at all, he averred. The first to
make real music were Corelli, Bononcini, Vinci, and Pergolesi. This is an apt
sequence for his way of thinking, because well before Vinci's time, both Corelli
and Bononcini had led the way to simplifying harmonic complexities in favor of
lighter textures supporting short-breathed lyric melodies. Corelli's Rome, that is,
the Rome of the Arcadian Academy, was in the forefront of attempts to escape the
inflated pomposity of *seicento* poetry. In the article "Opéra" in his *Dictionnaire de
musique* (1768), Rousseau credited Zeno and Metastasio, the two main librettists
to emerge from the Arcadian Academy, for encouraging "a music as full of nobility and dignity as it was of enthusiasm and fire," thereby forcing composers "to
give expression to heroes and to the language of the human heart." These composers, he continued, "the Vincis, Leos, and Pergolesis, disdaining the servile imitation of their predecessors, started seeking a new path, opened it on the wings
of genius, and reached the goal almost with the first steps." Mattei cited Pergolesi
as an indispensable precursor of Jommelli but then he went on to recall that Vinci
was "the first reformer of taste, who in his serious operas *Didone, Artaserse, and
Catone* preceded Pergolesi."[33]

Vinci's name remained prominent in the polemics surrounding the Parisian
quarrel between Gluckists and Piccinnistes in the 1770s. Already in 1765, without
naming Vinci, Chastellux defined the musical period as the essence of Italian
melodic superiority.[34] Jean-François Marmontel, chief spokesman for Piccinni and
the Italian faction, went further. In his *Essai sur les révolutions de la musique en
France*, printed twice in 1777 and reprinted with critical annotation in G. M.
Leblond's edition of *Mémoires pour servir à l'histoire de la révolution dans la musique
par M. Le Chevalier Gluck* in 1781, Marmontel named Vinci as the composer who
perfected periodic melody.

> Melody without expression is a small thing; expression without melody is something,
> but not enough. Expression and melody, both to the highest degree, where they can
> soar together: there is music's problem. It remains to be seen who will give us a solu-
> tion to this problem. The Italians searched for it: they began like us. Their music at the

[33]Saverio Mattei, *Memorie per servire alla vita Metastasio ed Elogio di N. Jommelli* (Colle, 1785), p. 74.
[34]François-Jean Chastellux, *Essai sur l'union de la poésie et de la musique* (The Hague and Paris, 1765; reprint
Geneva, 1970), pp. 17–20.

time of Lully was the same as his. They worked at giving it more force and expression. But the true moment of glory was when Vinci for the first time traced the circle of periodic song, of that song which, in a pure, elegant and sustained design, presented to the ear, as the period did to the spirit, the development of a thought completely rendered. It was then that the great mystery of melody was revealed.[35]

One of Gluck's champions contested Marmontel's claims for Vinci, as well as those of Prince Beloselski, who maintained that Vinci achieved the same heights in tragic ideas, the same warmth, the same fluency of styles as Corneille, saying, "It might perhaps be very embarrassing to apply them [these words] to an aria from *Artaserse* or *Didone.*"[36]

Burney sided with Marmontel, and thus it is not surprising that he would combine what he learned from touring Italy, where Vinci was still revered, with his partisan views as to the superiority of Italian melody, fanned by the vehement critical debates in Paris. In his *History* (1789) Burney takes up Leo and Porpora before Vinci but he leaves no doubt as to the historical role of the last.

> The vocal compositions of Vinci form an æra in dramatic music, as he was the first among his countrymen, who, since the invention of recitative by Jacopo Peri, in 1600, seems to have occasioned any considerable revolution in musical drama. The airs in the first operas were few and simple; but as singing improved, and orchestras became more crowded, the voice-parts were more laboured, and the accompaniments more complicated. In process of time, however, poetry seems to have suffered as much as ever from the pedantry of musicians, who forgetting that the true characteristic of dramatic Music is clearness; and that sound being the vehicle of poetry and the colouring of passion, the instant the business of the drama is forgotten, and the words are unintelligible, Music is so totally separated from poetry, that it becomes merely instrumental; and the voice-part may as well be performed by a flute or a violin, in the orchestra, as by one of the characters of the piece, on the stage. Vinci seems to have been the first opera composer who saw this absurdity, and, without degrading his art, rendered it the friend, though not the slave to poetry, by simplifying and polishing melody, and calling the attention of the audience chiefly to the voice-part, by disentangling it from fugue, complication, and laboured contrivance.

This paean to Vinci is followed a few paragraphs later by a short mention of Sarro: "He was one of the early reformers, who, like Vinci, simplified harmony, and polished melody in his production for the stage," and a longer passage devoted to Hasse: "He poured the elegant and simple manner of Vinci in his vocal composi-

[35]Leblond's 1781 version with annotations is reprinted in facsimile in *La Querelle des Gluckistes et des Piccinnistes,* ed. François Lesure, 2 vols. (Geneva, 1984), 1: 153–93; 169.
[36]Jean-Baptiste Suard, in *The Collected Correspondence and Papers of Christoph Willibald Gluck,* ed. Hedwig and E. H. Müller von Asow (London, 1962), p. 154.

tions, and as he long survived this first reformer of lyric melody, he frequently surpassed him in grace and expression." Mattei spoke of Vinci as a "reformer of taste," but he meant the same thing as Burney's "reformer of lyric melody."

The claims that Burney, Marmontel, and others made for Vinci's priority have been put to the test recently in the first comprehensive study of all surviving works by the master.[37] Particularly telling are the author's many comparisons between Vinci and Handel, who had a penchant for parodying or adapting Vinci's works for the London stage. More to the point here, he measured them against the prescriptions formulated by the late eighteenth-century theorist Heinrich Christoph Koch, who codified the rules of periodic composition. Koch's stricture that each line or couplet of an aria text be set to a single melodic fragment or phrase fits Vinci's normal practice in the da capo arias of his serious operas. Summing up the situation with all necessary caution, the author concludes:

> Vinci's da capo arias are probably the first large body of music by a single composer upon which Koch's principles of Classical periodicity can be consistently applied, thereby demonstrating a direct link between Vinci and the late eighteenth-century Classical style. Moreover, the binary organization of the first section of Vinci's da capo arias closely approximates the so-called sonata form of the late eighteenth century. The only ingredient missing is the development, which was later created by omitting the da capo and splicing the modulatory second section between the two halves of the first section.[38] [Koch does not use the term *classical*.]

Koch also describes the accompanied melody with static bass in both three-part textures most favored by Vinci: (1) first violin colla parte, second violin in parallel thirds and sixths; viola col basso; (2) violins in unison; viola in parallel sixths and thirds; basso (favored particularly for ritornello sections). These are the textural means by which Vinci repeatedly simplified and polished melody, "calling the attention of the audience chiefly to the voice-part," as Burney claimed.

Pergolesi

Few great composers have captured the imagination and sympathy of music lovers as completely as has Pergolesi. Small in person, sickly, and deformed, he was born on 4 January 1710 in Jesi, a small city near Ancona on the Adriatic, in the province of Marche. He died of tuberculosis at twenty-six. In his few years of activity,

[37] Markstrom, "The Operas of Leonardo Vinci," chapter 11, "Towards the Classical Style," pp. 328–45.
[38] Ibid., p. 336. In a note to his statement Markstrom credits Marita McClymonds for demonstrating this sonata-like abbreviation of the da capo aria in Jommelli.

scarcely five as a composer, he created masterpieces in several genres, and some of his works had a profound impact on his contemporaries and followers.

Unlike almost all the musicians trained at Naples, Pergolesi was from outside the kingdom, a "foreigner" from one of the church states ruled from Rome by the pope. His first training was at the hands of musicians connected with the cathedral of Jesi, and he must have distinguished himself early in order to be sent away for study sometime before the age of fourteen, probably by Marchese Pianetti, a military architect who had served the Austrian cause in Italy and was thus in a good position to gain entrance for a protégé in Habsburg-ruled Naples.[39] The young musician's name first appears as "Jesi" in July 1725 on the rolls of the Conservatorio dei Poveri di Gesù Cristo, where the teachers of composition were Greco (until 1728), Vinci for several months succeeding him, and then Durante. "Jesi" was still a soprano at age fifteen in the summer of 1725, and this evidence, combined with two other documents showing that he received treatment in the form of medicinal baths and special transportation to one of the conservatory's public performances, has led to suspicions that Pergolesi was a castrato.[40] If so, he did not pursue this route to fame. By 1729 his musical instrument was not the voice but the violin, and as violinist he was a leader ("capoparanzo") to one of the small bands sent out of the conservatory to earn money.

The first compositions by Pergolesi to survive are probably some school exercises, "Solfeggi, a due e tre voci," showing that the doctrine of the old mensurations (Proportio sequialtera, Proportio tripla, Proportio dupla, etc.) were still being taught.[41] An early cantata, "Questo è il piano," is dated 24 April 1731, representing the last stage of conservatory training before Pergolesi left the Poveri di Gesù Cristo. It consists of a prelude, aria, recitative, and aria, in which the music shows the Vinci-like building of larger units by repetition of small phrase parts.

In the summer of 1731 Pergolesi's *dramma sacro, Guglielmo d'Aquitania,* commissioned by the Oratorians, whose church faced the Poveri conservatory, was performed by students in the courtyard of the San Agnello monastery. Every August it was the practice to perform such pieces composed by students who were near or at the end of their training. Leo's public career began the same way, as did Durante's. Pergolesi's oratorio was apparently successful because it was copied and revised for further performances. Especially delightful are the comic scenes, dominated by a Capitano figure. In the final aria for him the music imi-

[39]Francesco Degrada, "Pergolesi, il marchese Pianetti e il Conservatorio di S. Maria di Loreto. Su alcune relazioni tra Jesi e Napoli nel primo Settecento," *Studi Pergolesiani* 2 (1988): 20–48. The principal biography is a manuscript *Elogio* by Sigismondo, printed in Francesco Degrada, "Giuseppe Sigismondo, il marchese di Villarosa e la biografio di Pergolesi," *Studi Pergolesiani* 3 (1999): 251–77; 264–69.

[40]Francesco Degrada, Roberto De Simone, Dario Della Porta, and Gianni Race, *Pergolesi* (Naples, 1986), pp. 72, 97–98.

[41]Helmuth Hucke, "Die neapolitanische Tradition in der Oper," *Report of the Eighth Congress of the International Musicological Society, New York, 1961,* ed. Jan Larue, 2 vols. (Kassel, 1961), 1: 253–77; 257.

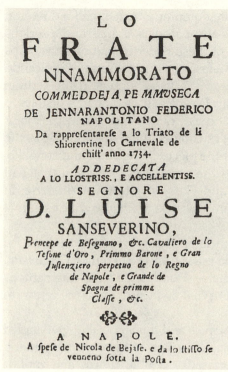

FIGURE 2.4. Title page of Pergolesi's *Lo frate 'nnamorato.*

tates the tolling of church bells and the scourging of the flagellant, set by the young composer in a fashion to indicate to the singer exactly how he should act on the stage. A music so suggestive of gesture already shows a mastery of the buffo style and a gift for the theatrically effective.[42]

Another sign of the oratorio's success was the commission Pergolesi received from the San Bartolomeo for a serious opera, the first of the 1732 carnival season. He composed *Salustia* on a libretto adapted from *Alessandro Severo* by Zeno. The work was planned around Nicolini, its primo uomo.[43] As the opera went into rehearsal Nicolini became ill. He died on 1 January 1732 and was replaced by a young castrato called from Rome, Gioacchino Conti, alias Ghizziello, who had a lower voice (and presumably different vocal abilities). Hurried revisions were in order. No reports survive on the opera's reception, but it was probably not very favorable. The premiere could not have taken place much before the middle of January, and already on 2 February the second opera of the season, Mancini's setting of *Alessandro nell'Indie,* was brought to the stage.

Pergolesi's next opera was a *commedia musicale* for the Fiorentini, *Lo frate 'nnamorato* on a libretto by Gennaro Federico, a Neapolitan lawyer and leading writer of comic texts. The opera had its premiere on 27 September 1732 and was a brilliant success. Many repeat performances were given and in 1734 Pergolesi revised the work to suit a new cast (Figure 2.4). The first vocal number is a *Canzona a due* in 12/8 vein, a lilting Siciliana in d sung by the two maidservants in turn, and reminiscent of the similar type of street song that opened "Vinci's *Li Zite* (Example 2.2). It is followed by another *Canzona,* "Pupillette," sung by Don Pietro in 3/8 time and marked "Tempo di Minuetto." There are several short lyric songs in the minuet rhythm with iambs favored by Vinci in the course of the opera. Many ensembles enliven the work, including a comic duet of exchanged insults

[42]Helmuth Hucke, "Pergolesi in der Musikgeschichte," *Studi Pergolesiani* 2 (1988): 7–19; 10–11.
[43]Dennis Libby, "The Singers of Pergolesi's *Salustia,*" *Studi Pergolesiani* 3 (1999): 173–81.

ending the first act, an expansive trio and final quintet in Act II, and a duet and short *Coro finale* ending the opera. There are also parodies of arias in the serious style, especially in the role of Nena. In one of these Federico parodies the shipwreck aria sung by Arbace ending Act I of Metastasio's *Artaserse* as "Vo solcando il mar d'amore." Pergolesi adds a solo flute to the usual strings in the setting. Oboes and horns are also added occasionally. Pergolesi uses many excursions to the minor mode in those numbers, the great majority of which are in the major mode. Surprising nevertheless is the number of choices of the minor mode as the main tonality— no fewer than six —some of the pieces being short and songlike, others long, resembling seria arias. Perhaps the pendulum of fashion that had reached one extreme in 1730 with Vinci's and Hasse's settings of *Artaserse*, in which the minor-mode aria all but disappeared, was beginning to shift back to a more varied tonal tapestry.

Vinci often introduced a minor-mode phrase, with augmented-sixth chord for special color, in the context of a major-mode piece.[44] In Don Pietro's *Canzonetta*, Pergolesi deploys about as much minor as major (Example 2.8). His augmented-sixth chord in m. 16 is arrived at with ease but quit awkwardly, and the return to major in the next measure is rather jolting.

In late 1732 there were earthquakes in Naples and the archbishop persuaded the regent to close the theaters during carnival as a sign of the city's atonement. Pergolesi is reported to have composed a mass for double chorus and various psalms to celebrate the feast of Saint Emidius, the protector against earthquakes, but this mass is not believed to be the same as his surviving Mass in D, which dates from 1731 or 1732. His *Missa S. Emidio* or Mass in F was probably first performed on 31 December 1733, and again the following May in Rome, where it evoked an enthusiastic response (and whence it became known also as his *Missa Romana*).[45]

Pergolesi's ties with the regime soon to be replaced are evident in his appointment in 1732 as maestro di capella to Prince Colonna Stigliano, equerry to the last Austrian vice-regent in Naples. They are apparent as well in his commission from the San Bartolomeo to celebrate the birthday of the empress in Vienna, Elisabeth Christine, on 28 August 1733. The ban on theatrical performances was lifted with this occasion and there resulted the composer's setting of Francesco Silvani's libretto *La fede tradita* (also known as *Ricimero*), first performed on 5 September 1733 under the title *Il prigionero superbo*. Circumstances were unusual in that economies forced the impresario to stage the work with a smaller than usual cast

[44]For an example from *Artaserse* see *Report of the Tenth Congress, Ljubljana of the International Musicological Society,* ed. Dragotin Cvetko (Kassel, 1970), pp. 191–92.
[45]Helmuth Hucke, "Pergolesi's *Missa S. Emidio,*" in *Music in the Classic Period: Essays in Honor of Barry S. Brook,* ed. Allan W. Atlas (New York, 1985), pp. 99–116. An early version of the work dates from 1731, argues Allan W. Atlas, "On the Date of Pergolesi's Mass in F," *Studi Pergolesiani* 3 (1999): 201–9.

EXAMPLE 2.8. *Pergolesi*, Lo frate 'nnamorato, *Canzonetta of Don Pietro*

of six, no primo uomo, and a contralto prima donna. Considering these restrictions Pergolesi delivered what is notably more expert and coherent than the disjointed *Salustia,* his first commission from the big theater. In part the reason may be not only his increasing maturity but the sentimentality of this drama as opposed to the stiffness and pathos of his first serious libretto. The orchestration is richer and more varied, with some prominent uses of mottolike accompanimental figures as unifying devices. The fate of *Prigionero* was nevertheless like that of most serious operas of the time: no diffusion and no revivals. Its intermezzo, on the other hand, was destined to become the most famous of all specimens of its genre.

LA SERVA PADRONA

Federico and Pergolesi created this most famous intermezzo for the buffa pair of Gioacchino Corrado and Laura Monti. The basso buffo Corrado had long been a mainstay at the San Bartolomeo and had sung under Vinci. Federico can scarcely be praised too highly for his part. He created a cogent, witty text that provided Pergolesi with one colorful action after another.

   With only two singing characters, plus a mute, Federico contrived a retelling of an old comic plot that had been around for centuries. An impertinent maidservant dupes her lecherous and elderly master into marrying her, and thus becomes "the Maid as Mistress." Old Uberto appears first. He complains that three things will be the death of him: waiting for someone who fails to appear; staying in bed without sleeping; and serving in vain an object of affection. Federico manages to say what took here a long English sentence in four pithy lines:

> Aspettare, e non venire
> Stare a letto, e non dormire,
> Ben servire, e non gradire
> Son tre cose da morire.

This short verse gives Pergolesi all he needs. Its point comes only with the last word, epigram fashion, which is always a good construction for musical purposes. The exaggerated seriousness of that "morire" with regard to the preceding recital of mundane annoyances will be further exaggerated by the music.

After a brief orchestral introduction in B♭ Uberto sings in unison with all the strings—the simplest possible texture and a frequent characteristic of the buffo style, as are the wide melodic leaps. At the words "son tre cose" the texture becomes two-part, with the bass line providing dissonant suspensions to Uberto. "Morire" brings forth an absurd sort of chromatic grovelling in the lowest register of his voice—a parody of the kind of tonal painting with which such an affective word might be treated in serious opera. This chromatic passage in unison serves to make the modulation to the dominant. Pergolesi then repeats the text, jumbling the order of the words and using new melodic materials, ending over a dominant pedal. He starts through the text a third time as tonic B♭ returns definitively. This is no routine reprise, as the material is all newly invented except for the precadential chromatics of "morire." Such spontaneity of invention is truly delightful. Everything is said in a scant 48 measures. The formal handling, while very free, is assured and shapely, with a melodic climax coming near the end as the voice climbs up to high F while repeating "cose" (stated three times, and with the additional pun, possible in Italian, that "cose" (things) can also be made to sound like "cos'è?" (what is the matter?).

The beginning of the following recitative reveals the cause of Uberto's grumpy complaint: he has been waiting three hours for his morning cup of chocolate. One can almost see the veteran Corrado as Uberto, his nightcap askew and his bed dishevelled, and a great singer-actor he must have been to inspire Federico's portrait in words and Pergolesi's portrait in gesture-laden rhythms and tones. He is a silly old fool, unable to command respect in his own household, but a master still capable of dismissing his servants. He calls for Serpina ("little snake") and begins a dialogue with his manservant, Vespone, who cannot answer back because he is mute.

Serpina enters and arrogantly asserts her will while beating Vespone. She demands respect, she says. Uberto reproaches her for her pretensions and launches into a second piece, "Sempre in contrasti con te si sta," this one in the key of F and again in fast common time. In it he not only berates her but makes asides to Vespone, asking his opinion, which of course cannot be given. The main point of this rapid patter song is made vividly in the line where Uberto claims he knows not where he is at, whether up or down, here or there, yes or no, giving Pergolesi graphic possibilities that he will realize fully (Example 2.9). The piece has a separate middle section in the minor mode, near the beginning of which there is an absurdly long melisma on "piangere" ("to weep"), again parodistic, after which the first part returns, da capo.

Following Uberto's two pieces in flat keys, Serpina's aria in the key of A sounds very bright and sprightly, contributing in a subtle way to her musical portrait. It is also more subtle than Uberto's music in the way her air proceeds by contrasting three-measure phrases (beginning) with four-measure ones (continuation) (Example 2.10). She tells Uberto that being peevish will no longer do him any good; she commands him to remain silent ("star cheto e non parlare"). Her musical language is a little smoother than his but still contains octave leaps. Certain traits in the accompaniment are the composer's trademarks and have been heard already in the first two numbers. Thus the little *forte* punctuation between phrases in mm. 3 and 6 corresponds to the similar bustling movement between the tonic and a neighbor tone in Uberto's first piece, and the upbeat figure moving to the third above and back in mm. 7 and 8 can be found in Uberto's second number. Of course these same figures occur sporadically in Vinci, but it is Pergolesi who puts his personal stamp upon them. Serpina's aria is a full-scale piece with da capo return, like Uberto's second number.

After another altercation in recitative, the concluding duet of the first intermezzo quickly ensues, the famous "Lo conosco." It is full of action between a cleverly pursuing Serpina bent upon marriage and a reluctant and doltish Uberto dodging the issue. This masterpiece repays the closest study.[46] The give and take between the two characters comes alive through a continually evolving and changing musical commentary using several short motifs, including a rising third that passes from major to minor. The way in which Pergolesi is able to capture minute nuances in the text and paint them in tones accounts in large part for the encomiums bestowed upon him by Grétry and others. Pergolesi provides here a culminating example of how the short, self-contained fragments pioneered by Vinci become, within a large and freely organized tonal span, compellingly dramatic. As one specialist writes:

> Pergolesi can invent fragments which will point up both Serpina's vivaciousness, mock dejection, girlish *hauteur* and tongue-in-cheek seductiveness, and Uberto's rotund

---

[46]It is given in full in *The Historical Anthology of Music,* ed. Archibald T. Davison and Willi Apel, 2 vols. (Cambridge, Mass., 1950), 2, no. 287.

EXAMPLE 2.9. *Pergolesi*, La serva padrona, *Aria*

EXAMPLE 2.10. *Pergolesi*, La serva padrona, *Aria*

ostentation, fearful asides and dissembling show of off-handedness; and he can advance the action during the course of the duet (for at the end Uberto is much more deeply ensnared than he was at the beginning), all without sacrificing musical coherence.[47]

The duet is in an ample binary form, 115 measures in common time with no large-scale repeats. Its dramatization of tonic and dominant, together with their satellites, plays an important part in making the conflict between the two characters vivid. It would be impossible to overestimate the historical importance of pieces like this for the future of comic opera. The seeds of the buffo finale, soon to be invented by Goldoni and his composers of the midcentury, are already present in Federico and Pergolesi.

The second intermezzo begins with Vespone masquerading as a soldier come to marry Serpina. Uberto is taken in at once by the disguise, as people always are in opera. Serpina sings a pathetic farewell to Uberto, asking him to think of her with kindness one day. Federico provides a text that incorporates three separate voices: Serpina addressing Uberto, her quoting what he will say one day, and the real Serpina observing in an aside how her act is working on him. Add Uberto as a fourth voice, as it were, since he must act in accordance with her responses and observations, shedding a tear perhaps, or dabbing his eyes with a handkerchief.

A Serpina penserete	You will think of Serpina
Qualche volta e qualche dì	Sometimes and some day
E direte "ah! poverina,	And you will say "poor lass!
Cara un tempo ella mi fu."	She was once dear to me."
(Ei mi par che già pian piano	(It seems to me that little by little
S'incomincia a intenerir.)	He is already beginning to soften.)

For this Pergolesi writes the first slow music of the work, with rising triads in first inversion lending an idyllic tone to "penserete" (Example 2.11). The modulation is accomplished swiftly with the E♮ introduced for "direte," leading to the expressive interval of a falling diminished fifth for "ah! poverina" over the even more expressive harmony of an augmented-sixth chord. This very same melodic fall and harmonic accompaniment will resound throughout the century in the mouths of poor distressed damsels, most famously of all perhaps as Barbarina closes her lament for the lost pin, beginning the last act of *Le nozze di Figaro* with the identical Phrygian cadence, note for note. Serpina, unlike Barbarina, goes on to make a cadence in the dominant key, F. Then she launches into her aside, *sotto voce*, for

[47]Robert Meikle, "Leonardo Vinci's *Artaserse*: An Edition, with an Editorial and Critical Commentary," 2 vols. (Ph.D. diss., Cornell University, 1970), 1: 520–21. For another assessment of the duet's historic significance see Robinson, *Naples and Neapolitan Opera*, pp. 226–27. In his article "Duo" in *Dictionnaire de musique* (1767), Rousseau singled out "Lo conosco" as "un modèle de Chant agréable, d'unité de Mélodie, d'Harmonie simple, brillante & pure, d'accent, de dialogue & de goût."

EXAMPLE 2.11. *Pergolesi*, La serva padrona, *Aria*

which Pergolesi provides a scherzolike, fleet-footed *Allegro* in 3/8, in utmost contrast with the lumbering *Larghetto* in common time. Up the scale she climbs, coming down with iambic accents that give spice to the words, rendered still spicier by the trailing suspensions in the bass that make dissonances on the first beats. From these two contrasting sections Pergolesi fashioned a tableau that ends with Uberto pressing Serpina's hand.

Serpina leaves the stage to Uberto in the following recitative, which turns

obbligato as he confronts his momentous decision. His aria in E$\flat$ follows. He is caught in a dilemma, he says, but it does not sound very serious because of his rapid declamation in patter. This changes when he hears a certain voice within that warns him to think of his own welfare. A parody of serious opera is again at stake, in this case the dread decrees of specters and oracles, often sung to long-held tones as here and emphasizing the perfect intervals. The third act of the main opera, following this intermezzo, opened with just such a piece, in the same serious key of E$\flat$, which was often reserved for deep and other-wordly reflections and the appearance of ghosts (i.e., in the so-called *ombra* aria).

There remained in the second intermezzo but the unmasking of Vespone and the reconciliation of Uberto and Serpina, sealed in their final love duet in rapid 3/8 time in A, the same key as her initial piece. With this the little drama (intermezzo) within the drama is over. The last duet, although perfect in every respect, was often replaced by another in D, borrowed from the intermezzo *La contadina astuta*, often attributed to Hasse, except for the duet in question. It comes from *Flaminio*, Pergolesi's last *commedia per musica* (1735). This piece is noteworthy for the way in which voice and orchestra mimic the sound of the male and female heartbeats, a happy invention that subsequent composers were only too glad to copy.

The other authentic Pergolesi intermezzo to survive is *Livietta e Tracollo* of the following year on a libretto attributed to Tommaso Mariani, sung by the same comic pair of Corrado and Monti. The text is a clumsy hodge-podge of disguises and pranks. Pergolesi's fine music could accomplish only so much with this text, which is greatly inferior to Federico's sparkling *Serva padrona.*

A NEW REGIME

The war raging in the north between Spain and Austria for the duchy of Parma in 1734 had its southern counterpart in the turmoil attending the conquest of the Kingdom of Naples by Charles Bourbon, the eighteen-year-old second son of the king of Spain. Nobles and artists alike who had been adherents of the Habsburgs had reason to fear reprisals, and many wisely betook themselves to Rome until the issue was settled and the time of troubles over. Pergolesi's patron, the prince of Stigliano, had withdrawn to Rome, as had another of his patrons, Duke Carafa Maddaloni. The latter ordered a performance of a mass by the composer, given under Pergolesi's direction in the Roman church of San Lorenzo in Lucina on the feast of Saint John Nepomuk (16 May—the saint was a Bohemian canonized in 1729 at Habsburg insistence). This is now believed to be one of the versions of Pergolesi's superb *Missa Romana,* a Kyrie and Gloria in F also known as the *Missa San Eumidia.* Meanwhile Charles had entered Naples with Spanish troops and the high Habsburg officials had fled. Duke Carafa Maddaloni was politic enough to be able to return to Naples in June 1734, and Pergolesi probably was among the many in his entourage. The duke was fortunate that his uncle, Lelio Carafa, marquis d'Arienzo, was among the friends and advisors of the young Bourbon prince.

The San Bartolomeo reopened under Salvatore Narmicola's management with Leonardo Leo's *Il castello d'Atlante* on 4 July 1734. In September Lelio Carafa became the theater's supervisor under King Charles. Pergolesi received a commission to set Metastasio's *Adriano in Siria* in order to celebrate the birthday of the king's mother, Elizabeth Farnese, queen of Spain, on 25 October 1734. Thus both Leo and Pergolesi ended up being supported by the winning side. To their cello-playing patron, Duke Carafa Maddaloni, we owe Leo's cello concertos and Pergolesi's cello sonata. When the patrons survive in spite of political turmoil, art can only benefit.

A splendid cast was at Pergolesi's disposal for *Adriano in Siria,* headed by Maria Turcotti, prima donna, and primo uomo Caffarelli, who had made his Neapolitan debut in Leo's opera.[48] In order to show off Caffarelli's abilities in the role of Farnaspe drastic alterations were made in the libretto, so that he could sing arias at the end of both Act I and Act II. Metastasio's fine libretto was less than two years old, having been first set by Antonio Caldara in Vienna to celebrate the

[48]Pergolesi, *Adriano in Siria,* ed. Dale E. Monson (Pergolesi Complete Works, no. 1) (New York, 1986). Caffarelli is listed as "virt. della R. cap. di Napoli" for the first time in the original printed libretto.

name day of Emperor Charles VI on 4 November 1732. Only ten of Metastasio's twenty-seven arias were retained, to which ten completely new aria texts were added, along with a new duet. So many changes naturally required many adjustments to the recitatives as well. Pergolesi took particular care to make Caffarelli's arias, all of which are on new texts, extensive and colorful. His "Lieto così tal volta" to end Act I is graced with a concertante oboe solo, and his "Torbido in volta e nero" to end Act II offers coloratura and is scored for double orchestra (the composer reused this piece with text intact in *L'Olimpiade* for Rome in early 1735). In spite of all cares taken, *Adriano* was not a success. Impresario Salvatore Narmicola reported in 1735 to the marquis d'Arienzo that Pergolesi, though esteemed as a musician, had failed to please with this opera. His name was not included on a list of those composers who could be called on for further commissions from the San Bartolomeo. Thus one avenue for the composer, who was by this time listed as royal organist, had been closed.

L'OLIMPIADE

The favorable reception of Pergolesi's Mass in F at Rome in 1734 led to his being commissioned to write an opera for the Tordinona theater, to be performed as the first carnival opera in early 1735. Unlike *Adriano* for Naples, the casting did not include any luminaries of the first order among the singers. Pergolesi wrote the work in the fall of 1734 while still in Naples and reused or reworked five arias from *Adriano,* as well as the outer movements of its overture. For some reason the performances did not begin until mid-January, perhaps because he had to make further revisions. Unfortunately the theaters were closed a few days later because of the death of Maria Sobieska, wife of the Stuart pretender to the English throne. They reopened on 23 January but closed again for Candlemas, 1–2 February. On 5 February the second carnival opera, *Demofoonte,* set by Vincenzo Ciampi, began its run, replacing Pergolesi's *L'Olimpiade.* Egidio Duni told Grétry and others that the Roman public was hostile to Pergolesi and his opera, but this may be an exaggerated reaction to the circumstances that initially limited its number of performances. Many manuscript copies were made of *L'Olimpiade,* unlike Pergolesi's other serious operas, which testified that the work was appreciated from the time of its original production, and long after.

Metastasio reached the height of his powers when writing the libretto, first set by Caldara in Vienna two years earlier. In *Adriano in Siria* the poet celebrated imperial magnanimity. In *L'Olimpiade* he sang the double theme most congenial to him, that celebrating youthful love and friendship, enhanced in this case by a setting that evoked the Olympic games of ancient Greece. The robust Megacle loves and is loved by Aristea, daughter of King Clistene. Megacle has promised to enter the games and win the prize under the name of his best friend Licida, who once saved his life. Licida is loved by the maid Argene, but currently estranged from him she enters the action under the disguise of a shepherdess, Licori. To introduce her in Act I, Scene 4, the set changed to a sparsely wooded countryside at the foot of a mountain, with a rustic bridge and view of the city of Olimpia in the distance. Metastasio wanted a pastoral chorus here to sing his poem "Oh care selve, oh cara felice libertà!" The Tordinona had no chorus, so Pergolesi set the text as a short song for Argene in 12/8 dotted rhythm and in the key of G. By the end of Act I Megacle has learned that the prize he has promised to win for Licida is the hand of his beloved Aristea. Confused but resolved to keep the promise to his friend, he takes leave of Aristea in a splendid duet. In Act II he wins the prize as "Licida" and departs in despair. He attempts suicide by drowning but is rescued by a fisherman. Eventually Clistene discovers that Licida is none other than his own son, thus brother to Aristea. Megacle and Aristea are happily reunited, as are Licida and Argene.[49]

The duet that ends Act I is an example of music inspired by and wedded to great lyrics. Megacle says farewell to Aristea and asks her to remember him in her happy days to come ("Ne' giorni tuoi felice / Ricordati di me"). She answers with two rhyming lines asking why he says such a thing ("Perchè cosi mi dici, / Anima mia, perchè?"). Then they exchange one line apiece before singing together for the first time. The poet is as much composer of the piece as the composer himself in a case like this, because he sets up the structure. Pergolesi responded with a sensuous *Larghetto amoroso* in common time and in the key of A, well established in Neapolitan operas as the place for two sopranos to sing glorious duets about love and the pangs it causes upon parting. In the article "Duo" in his *Dictionnaire de musique,* Rousseau quotes the entirety of Metastasio's text and tells his readers to search out Pergolesi's setting in order to see "how this foremost musician of his time, and of ours, set it to music."

Even more famous than the duet is the breathtakingly beautiful aria that Megacle sings in the middle of Act II, "Se cerca, se dice." The games are over and, learning that Licida has won her hand, Aristea faints. Megacle tells Licida what to say to her when she revives.

Se cerca, se dice:	If she asks and says:
"L'amico dov'è?	"Where is the friend?
L'amico infelice"	The unhappy friend"
rispondi, "mori."	Tell her, "He died."
Ah! no, sì gran duolo	Ah! do not give her such
non darle per me:	Great pain on my account:
rispondi, ma solo:	Respond but this alone:
"Piangendo partì."	"He departed weeping."

[49]For a sensitive critique of the poetry and Pergolesi's setting, see Reinhard Strohm, *Die italienische Oper im 18. Jahrhundert* (Wilhelmshaven, 1979), pp. 212–23.

Che abisso di pene	What an abyss of pain
lasciare il suo bene,	It is to leave one's love,
lasciarelo per sempre,	Leave her forever,
lasciarlo così! (*parte*)	And leave her in this state! (*exit*)

The poem thwarts da capo repetition because of the *crescendo* of suffering in the third stanza. Thus Metastasio himself, at least here, helped to free musicians from one of the "tyrannies" he had done so much to enforce. Pergolesi sets it as a large through-composed binary form using the third stanza in the middle, and again as a *Presto* coda at the end. He chose the key of c, *Larghetto* in 2/4, with three-note overlapping motifs between the string accompaniment and the voice, which plunges in before the orchestra can sound a tone. This must have had a startling effect on his audience, so used to the orchestral ritornello at the beginning (Example 2.12). In order to paint musically the contradiction the text expresses at the beginning of the second stanza he abruptly leaves the relative major, E♭, for a key that turns out to be the minor dominant, g. To extract the maximum expressiveness out of the cadence in mm. 18–20, he precedes it with the Neapolitan sixth chord under "weeping," makes it deceptive to VI, and intensifies the repetition with inverted dotted figures ("sobs") in the voice.

Pergolesi's "Se cerca, se dice" was loved so much it was still sung up and down the Italian peninsula during the early nineteenth century according to Stendhal, and included in countless collections. Critics did not cease to marvel at it. Chastellux (1765) considered the text a model of how to express opposing sentiments in the same poem and he singled out Pergolesi's setting as incomparable for making the words so touching.[50] Yet Pergolesi's initial strategy of overlapping voice and accompaniment in three-note groups was already present in Caldara's less expressive setting of two years earlier.[51] Composers subsequent to Pergolesi who set the text were often haunted by one or more features of his setting, which was perhaps inevitable. Leo (1743) wrote what sounds like a gloss or variation on the music of his deceased friend.[52] He set the question "dov'è?" to the same music as Serpina's "poverina" (Example 2.11). Galuppi (1747) transformed Pergolesi's setting into a more concentrated form. Cimarosa (1784) began his version very differently, with a triadic descent and fioraturas in the key of C, as if trying to escape the tradition. But by the time he reached "Ah no, sì gran duolo" he fell back on Pergolesi. Both settings were favorite concert arias, and

---

[50]François Jean marquis de Chastellux, *Essai sur l'union de la poésie et de la musique* (The Hague and Paris, 1765; reprint Geneva, 1970), pp. 51–52.

[51]For Caldara's beginning, see *Haydn, Mozart*, p. 506.

[52]For the opening of Leo's setting, an *Agitato* in the key of f, see Robinson, *Naples and Neapolitan Opera*, example 12, p. 130.

EXAMPLE 2.12. *Pergolesi*, L'Olimpiade, *Aria*

one critic of the early nineteenth century even complained about Cimarosa's plagiarism.[53]

---

[53]Robinson (ibid.) quotes the beginning of Cimarosa's setting as example 13, p. 131. He does not go as far as the passage that is parallel with Pergolesi, which was noticed in *Correspondance des amateurs musiciens* (Paris, 1803), issue of 5 February.

The sinfonia to *L'Olimpiade* borrowed the one from *Adriano*, in its outer movements, and can be viewed as the composer's most important and widely dispersed legacy to the genre. It was also used to precede Pergolesi's *Guglielmo d'Aquitania* in a 1742 revival.[54] The first movement is an *Allegro assai* in common time and in D that begins with hammerstroke unisons and a celebration of the tonic triad, climbing higher and higher, until the violins burst into sixteenth-note runs carrying them all the way up to high D. This will become a formula in subsequent decades, represented at its best by Jommelli and Johann Stamitz, but in 1735 it must have sounded nothing short of electrifying. In texture and sonority Pergolesi anticipates midcentury norms here, while his formal elaboration remains rudimentary and without a hint of any secondary thematic idea in the dominant. He reinforces the texture with oboes, horns, and trumpets (in some copies) that play slow I - V - I fanfares in the tonic, against a running counterpoint in quick notes. The same fanfares in the dominant as a middle section are followed by a few transitional measures and then the return of the fanfares in the tonic, and finally the initial rise to high D is repeated. From high D the strings tumble down the triad in unison to low G♯, on which they pause, resolution coming with the next movement, in 3/4 and in the key of d, the main melodic content is a series of drooping melodic sighs in inverted dotted rhythm or "sobs" such as have just been remarked in a vocal line. Since this is the one movement of the sinfonia Pergolesi wrote anew for *L'Olimpiade,* it can be assumed that he found this figure particularly appropriate to the extreme sensibility and frequent tears of this particular drama. The middle movement reaches a cadence on d, which is then turned into a cheerful minuet (not called such) in D, in 3/8 time, the preferred meter of Italians for their minuets. The piece is in binary form with repeats and is graced by the natural instruments playing their fanfarelike calls where appropriate, which are particularly full sounding at the terminal *cadence galante.*

For sheer brio this sinfonia had hardly any peers. It enjoyed an independent existence aside from the three works by Pergolesi to which it was attached. As late as 1762 the Breitkopf thematic catalogue offered it as a string symphony, albeit under the name of Sammartini, an error rectified in the first supplement of 1766. Thus the operatic sinfonia not only nourished the repertory of the later concert symphony, but also traveled along in that repertory as if indistinguishable from it.

After Rome, Pergolesi returned again to Naples. His last stage work was the composition of Federico's *Flaminio* for the Teatro Nuovo in the fall of 1735. The setting is a villa near Naples belonging to a young widow, Giustina, who is being visited by a rich Neapolitan, Polidoro, and his sister Agata. After the usual complications, all ends happily as Giustina and her lover Flaminio are joined, as are Agata and her suitor Ferdinando, and the servant pair of Checca and Vastiano (the

---

[54]Marvin E. Paymer, "The Pergolesi Overtures: Problems and Perplexities," *Studi Pergolesiani* 2 (1988): 78–88.

last three use Neapolitan dialect). Polidoro is an older Pantaloon type and the center of much of the buffoonery. He initiates the action by singing a lilting siciliana type of song in 12/8 time and in d, "Mentre l'erbetta," to the accompaniment of a chitarrino (a popular instrument like a small guitar that much intrigued Burney on his visit to Naples in 1770). As might be guessed, Polidoro was smitten by the charming Giustina. Opinions differ as to the worth of Federico's libretto. One critic dismissed it as "sentimental," saying "it testifies to the decline of Neapolitan comedy under the influence of Metastasian opera."[55] Another praised it for the same quality, saying "the sentimentalism, melancholy and lyrical pathos of Giustina and Flaminio . . . make this work a predecessor of Galuppi's sentimental comedies."[56]

Flaminio was revived at Naples in 1737 and 1749. The latter revival could have been experienced by young Piccinni when he was a student and perhaps had some role in his eventual setting (for Rome in 1760) of the sentimental opera par excellence, Goldoni's *La buona figliuola*. Igor Stravinsky used three numbers from *Flaminio* in his ballet *Pulcinella* (1919). It was appropriate, then, that another revival, at Venice in 1982, celebrated Stravinsky's one-hundredth birthday.

Very little instrumental music ascribed to Pergolesi has passed the tests of authenticity. One such is the Sinfonia in F for solo cello and continuo written for Duke Caraffa Maddaloni. "Sonata" would be the usual name to designate a solo piece in the four-movement sequence of slow-fast-slow-fast. Pergolesi, even more than Leo in his cello concertos for the same patron, makes the most of the singing qualities of the solo instrument, especially in the third movement, an *Adagio* in the key of d that shares a few melodic turns with the composer's setting of "Se cerca, se dice" in *L'Olimpiade* (Example 2.12). A different aspect of his operatic language informs the final *Presto,* which is another of the pieces Stravinsky chose to use in *Pulcinella* (Example 2.13). The opening three-measure phrase is worthy of the irate Uberto. It is followed by a soft echo that has an oddly comical effect, as if of timidity after bluster. Use of the same three-note slides, up and down, in a long descending sequence, with perfectly square phrasing, carries the art of building melodies out of small melodic fragments to an extreme that, like most extremes, is humorous. An extension via the tonic minor, a trait very characteristic of Pergolesi's arias, lends color and drama to the second half of the movement. Buffo traits in instrumental music show up consistently in fast movements, while the pathetic arias of serious opera make their mark more readily upon slow movements.

---

[55]Helmuth Hucke, "Pergolesi," in *New Grove.*
[56]Gordana Lazarevich, "Flaminio," in *The New Grove Dictionary of Opera.* A better choice would have been "Goldoni's sentimental comedies."

EXAMPLE 2.13. *Pergolesi, Sinfonia for Violoncello, IV*

STABAT MATER

According to Pergolesi's first biographer, the marquis of Villarosa, an aristocratic brotherhood of Our Lady of Sorrows commissioned the composer to make a setting of the famous medieval sequence relating Christ's death on the cross through the eyes of Mary.[57] It was the practice of this confraternity to celebrate every Friday in March with a performance of the *Stabat mater* at religious services in the church of San Luigi di Palazzo or in San Ferdinando across from the palace. Alessandro Scarlatti's *Stabat mater* for solo soprano, solo alto, and strings was written on commission for this purpose, and Pergolesi's setting was intended to replace that of the older master with music in a more modern style. Villarosa says the commission was given to Pergolesi in late 1735, but that he was unable to fulfill it until his last days spent at the coastal spa of Pozzuoli west of Naples, where he was cared for at the Franciscan monastery that was under the patronage of the Carafa Maddaloni family, who founded it. There is a poetic congruence here in that the medieval poem, although no longer believed to be by Jacapone da Todi, who died in 1306, is thought to be of thirteenth-century Franciscan origin.

During his final illness (from tuberculosis) the young composer was unable to complete a commissioned wedding cantata. The perfection of the *Stabat mater* argues that the work must have been all but finished before this time. That Pergolesi kept his autograph with him until shortly before his death on 16 March 1736 betokens his personal piety.

Pergolesi was confined to using the same small forces as Scarlatti, although he added a viola part to the two violins and bass employed by Scarlatti in the earlier work. Setting the octosyllabic verses for only two voices, without chorus to add variety, was a challenge to both composers, as was the lugubrious and repetitive nature of the verses themselves. Lenten economy was at least served by the small forces. The brethren had but to hire two castrati and a few string players from one of the conservatories. Women's voices would have been out of place.

---

[57]Carlantonio de Rosa, marquis of Villarosa, *Lettera biografica intorno alla patria ed alla vita di G. B. Pergolesi* (Naples, 1831), cited after Pergolesi, *Stabat mater,* ed. Helmut Hucke (Wiesbaden, 1987), Preface.

One should imagine the work sung by the powerful, nonvibrato voices of a male soprano and a male alto, as it would have been in Naples at the time.[58]

The secret of Pergolesi's success in this, his most famous work of all, lies in the variety of styles he commands and the contrasts he achieves from movement to movement by tonal, textural, and rhythmic means. His tonal plan is masterly and somewhat symmetrical, as may be seen from Table 2.2. He anchors the work firmly in the key of f, to which he returns in the middle and at the end. Note also

TABLE 2.2 *Stabat mater*

No.	1	2	3	4	5	6
	f	c	g	$E^\flat$	c	f
	duet	soprano solo	duet	alto solo	duet	soprano solo
	Grave **C**	Andante amoroso 3/8	Larghetto **C**	Allegro 2/4	Largo **C** Allegro 6/8	A tempo giusto **C**

No.	7	8	9	10	11	12
	c	g	$E^\flat$	g	$B^\flat$	f
	alto solo	duet	duet	alto solo	duet	duet
	Andantino 3/8	Allegro **¢**	A tempo giusto **C**	Largo **C**	Allegro **C**	Largo assai Presto **¢**

that No. 6, the medial piece in f, inaugurates a sequence of tonalities the same as in the first half: f - c - g - $E^\flat$. The dual realm of g - $E^\flat$ is in fact as weighty and important as is f. The weightiest piece of all is the fugue *à 3* in No. 8, followed by the *Largo* in dotted rhythm, like a French overture, in No. 10; both of these pieces are in the key of g, surrounding the most lyrical outpouring of the duet No. 9 in $E^\flat$. The mysterious alliance of g and $E^\flat$ in music did not await the rise of the Viennese school in the 1740s. It is a legacy of Naples.

Pergolesi makes smooth tonal connections between numbers by moving only to keys that are close and related either by the interval of a fourth or a third. The contrasts between pieces are sharp, on the other hand, because of the range of styles used. No. 1 is a very polished Corellian trio sonata in texture, two imitative voices over a walking bass. Rousseau declared this the most perfect piece that ever issued from a composer's pen. Its successor seems intentionally jerky

[58]Perhaps the closest sonority to this possible today was achieved in the recording of 1983 directed by countertenor René Jacobs, in which he sings alto to the boy soprano Sebastian Hennig (Harmonia Mundi France 1901119). They follow Pergolesi's tempo markings exactly and perform the work in 37 minutes and 20 seconds.

because of its iambic rhythm in the treble, contradicted by trochees in the bass (Example 2.14). Latin is flexible enough so that the treble could have been set in trochees as well as iambs. Besides the conflict between bass and treble there is the sudden accent on the last and weak measure of the four-measure phrase, then the startling repetition of the whole phrase one whole tone lower. Mattheson presents a similar melody, in that it is in minor and dominated by iambs, as a typical specimen of Neapolitan or Sicilian singing or playing (Example 2.15).[59] Here the text is a love song, warning us to pay more attention to the *amoroso* Pergolesi attached to the *Andante.* Mattheson says in addition about his example that "the iamb's characteristic peculiarity is a moderate liveliness, not flighty or running; the true Sicilian style has something very tender and nobly simple about it." This suggests that Pergolesi was giving his audience something they would recognize as local, and related to folk song, with his stream of iambs. As far as his sudden accents are concerned, perhaps he was alluding to the last line of his text: "Her groaning spirit / Mournful and grief-stricken / Seemed as if pierced by a sword."

Pergolesi does not paint the images of death and mourning as often as his text brings them up, but he does not avoid doing so at opportune moments. The actual moment when Mary sees her dear son, abandoned, die on the cross, is one of these, and this is the medial piece in f, No. 6 (Example 2.16). The inverted dotted rhythms at the beginning are sobs in the language of opera seria (cf. Example 2.12 from *L'Olimpiade,* m. 25). Also from serious opera and its laments is the chromatic descent of a fourth in the bass at "morientem"—the very image of death in the tonal language and consecrated not only by generations of operatic laments but from settings of "Crucifixus . . . passus et sepultus est" from the Credo of the mass. As Christ literally "gives up the ghost" the harmonic rhythm slows and the voice can utter only one syllable at a time of "e - mi - sit," separated by rests, a treatment of the word followed by Traetta and Haydn in their respective settings of the *Stabat mater.*

No. 6 in f restarts the tonal cycle we have observed. Its successor, No. 7 in c has more than tonality in common with No. 2. It is another solo number, there for soprano, here for alto. Moreover, it brings back 3/8 meter, a similar tempo, *Andantino,* and still more telling the iambic rhythms, now cloaked as two sixteenth notes followed by a quarter note. This text begins "Eja mater fons amoris" (Oh Mother, source of love) and continues with the personal plea to be allowed to mourn with her. Evident is the connection in Pergolesi's mind between a love song that might

---

[59] Johann Mattheson, *Der vollkommene Capellmeister* (Hamburg, 1739); facsimile reprint, ed. Margarete Reimann (Kassel, 1954), p. 165. Handel made delightful use of the same rhythm for a rather serious text, the penultimate number of *Solomon* (1748), a duet for King Solomon and the Queen of Sheba, "Ev'ry joy that wisdom knows / May'st thou pious monarch share," setting the first line to trochees and the second to iambs.

EXAMPLE 2.14. *Pergolesi*, Stabat Mater, *Aria (No. 2)*

EXAMPLE 2.15. *Mattheson*, Der vollkommene Capellmeister *(1739), Neapolitan song*

EXAMPLE 2.16. *Pergolesi*, Stabat Mater, *Aria (No. 6)*

have come from the streets of Naples and the overflowing love in Mary's heart. Padre Martini was not so wrong when he complained that pieces like these were of too popular a nature, too close to comic opera, for their serious words. He merely misread a Neapolitan cultural tradition, and he was not the first nor last rationalist from northern Italy to do so.

The impressive fugue in g of No. 8 may owe some of its majesty to the text's image of Christ as Lord and God, or to the newly found zeal of the individual penitent ("Make my heart burn / In loving Christ the Lord / That I may find grace with Him"). Certainly this piece should have pleased even a Padre Martini. But did he notice that in the orchestral postlude Pergolesi introduced a brief, jagged figure in the violins, of upward-moving minor seconds in a descending chain? This figure too is associated with death on the cross and finds use in more than one setting of the "Crucifixus" of the mass. Mozart, for example, uses it accordingly in his *Coronation* Mass, K.317 (1779) and also as the "Duol" motif of his opera *Idomeneo* (1780–81).

Most criticized of all, perhaps, has been Pergolesi's cheerful setting of the penultimate number, the duet in B♭, No. 11. Of his need for the key of B♭ to get from g to the terminal key of f there can be no question. He has built the entire piece as a succession of closely related keys. The text once again concerns Christ's death and the day of judgment, but the main message is that of the penitent's redemption, which will be achieved through the intercession of Mary. It is true that the music is so light and buoyant it could easily be absorbed in *La serva padrona*. Like many love duets it even has the two voices exchanging long-held notes. Its syncopated main idea ends with a three-tone slide, than which nothing could be more Neapolitan. As musical contrast this is a welcome change to what comes before and after, and Pergolesi's sense of the *chiaroscuro* of the whole remains unassailable.

The final number ruminates on the penitent's own death. Its text is simple: "Quando corpus morietur / Fac ut animae donetur / Paradisi gloria. / Amen" (When my body dies / Grant that my soul receives / The glory of paradise. / Amen). Pergolesi returns to the lugubrious *Largo* of the first number and an imitative duet texture, but this one is much simpler, with close overlapping between the two voices. For the final Amen there is a return to the fugue in No. 8, also greatly shortened and simplified. This may be a sign that Pergolesi had difficulty in finishing the piece, but it cannot be adjudged insufficient as an ending because it lacks the weight of No. 8.[60]

Recorded commentary on Pergolesi's *Stabat mater* would fill a book of modest length in its own right. Musicians who came later proclaimed that they would have given anything to have written it themselves.[61] Nowhere was there a more devoted following than in France. Several critics took to calling Pergolesi a great painter, by which they meant that his tonal canvasses were pictorially suggestive to an uncommon degree. One such assessment must suffice here. In his *Traité du Melo-drame* (1772) Laurent Garcin wrote: "I regard Pergolesi as the first of all the moderns in his art. He invented and perfected the art of painting with music. His *Stabat mater* is a continuous picture" (un tableau continuel). It is ironic that there survives no portrait of this painter-musician that is regarded as authentic, except for the caricatures by Pierleone Ghezzi at Rome in 1734.[62]

---

[60]As claimed by Alfred Einstein in his Eulenberg edition of the work (1927). Einstein sees evidence of haste in the autograph, especially in the handwriting of the last number, which might be used as evidence to confirm that Pergolesi held off finishing the work altogether until he himself was close to the state of the penitent of the text, hoping only in the glory of paradise. There is a rival to the *Stabat mater* for the distinction of being the last piece completed by the master, his setting of the Marian antiphon "Salve regina" for soprano and strings. Its closing moments achieve a poignancy that is no less touching. They consist of a direct plea for mercy to Mary.

[61]Degrada et al., *Pergolesi*, pp. 151–61. Two composers quoted to this effect are Donizetti and Halévy.

[62]Pierlugi Petrobelli, "Pergolesi and Ghezzi Revisited," in *Music in the Classic Era*, pp. 213–20.

Teatro San Carlo

Naples had been outdone by Rome in building large theaters. Paradoxically, the papal city lacked the consistent court support for opera found in Naples. In a system that normally elected only old men to the papal throne, their reigns did not last as long as those of kings, and it was always a possibility that one of them might turn puritanical enough to ban theater altogether. It was in Rome, nevertheless, that the architect Carlo Fontana, teacher of Juvarra, pioneered the elliptical horseshoe shape of auditorium that became the norm for all big opera houses. He did this in remodeling the Tordinona theater in 1696. Within a year Pope Innocent XII ordered the theaters closed. He allowed the Capranica theater to reopen in 1698, but then it remained shut to the public until 1711. A distinctive and small private theater was designed by Juvarra for the music-loving Cardinal Ottoboni in his residence, the Palazzo della Cancellaria, in 1709. Juvarra also renovated Prince Capranica's theater in 1713. Another milestone was the erection of the Teatro Alibert in 1716–17, which was enlarged and improved in 1720 by Francesco Galli-Bibiena to include six tiers of thirty boxes each. Vying with this theater in grandeur was the Teatro Argentina, owned by the Sforza-Cesarini family, and constructed in 1731, with six tiers of thirty-one boxes each. It was the main model for the new theater in Naples that opened in 1737, "Il real Teatro di San Carlo," proudly named for the young sovereign's onomastic saint.

An overall idea of what the San Carlo's interior might have looked like on a gala night is best conveyed by a depiction of the Teatro Argentina. The latter was the setting for an event in 1747 that led Giovanni Paolo Pannini to paint its glories on a large canvas (Plate IV). Since it was a ceremonial event, and presumably restricted only to those who were invited, the sixth and highest tier of boxes, where the lowest economic level of the public audience would have found seats at a regular operatic spectacle, was not used. Pannini shows it blocked off by a material that relates to his depiction of the ceiling. At ground level in front of a large audience sit some twenty cardinals in special chairs representing the papal court. Off to the right of them is a bewigged gentleman surrounded by two other figures. On what was normally the operatic stage an orchestra, chorus, and vocal soloists are deployed, in the midst of fleecy clouds, backed by an impressive and templelike stage set, its columns adorned with garlands and gigantic human figures. Surmounting the stage, held aloft by two angels, is an escutcheon bearing the triple *fleur-de-lys* on a blue background identifying the French royal family. At the bottom of this spectacle, where the orchestra would normally be stationed for an opera, are two large female figures joining hands and presiding over cascades that represent the Seine and Elba rivers. Being celebrated in a serenata by the poet Flaminio Scarcelli set to music (lost) by Jommelli, is the wedding of the dauphin, son of Louis XV, to the princess royal of Saxony (her father, Elector Augustus II, was King Augustus III of Poland). Pannini's painting was long thought to represent a celebration in Rome for the birth of the same dauphin in 1729, at which Metastasio's *La contesa dei Numi*, set to music by Vinci, was performed in the courtyard of a palace inhabited by Cardinal Polignac.[63] In 1729 the Teatro Argentina had yet to be constructed.

The royal advisors in charge of erecting the new theater in Naples had plans and profiles of the Teatro Argentina brought from Rome for study. They also had, from Verona, the plans of the Teatro Filarmonica, which was built by Francesco Galli-Bibiena between 1715 and 1729, and inaugurated in 1732 with Vivaldi's setting of *La fida ninfa* by local poet Scipione Maffei.[64] This theater had five tiers of boxes, with twenty-eight in each row, and took so long to build because it was elaborately sculpted in wood in the late baroque style of architecture (it burned down in 1749).[65] Charles III was not about to wait several years for his new royal theater. Like the Argentina, it would have a relatively plain interior and would be constructed in a remarkably short time. It was ready to open in October 1737. There were six tiers of twenty-eight boxes each, besides the lavish royal box in the middle of the second and third tiers. Total capacity was 2,400 places, 600 of them in the orchestra. Several engravings survive depicting the elevation and plan of the original interior (Figures 2.5–6).

Charles III was determined to have the most impressive opera house that could be built quickly, not because he was interested in music but because he understood the symbolism involved and the prestige. He also wanted to please his new wife Maria Amalia of Saxony, who did love music.[66] The theater was to stand adjacent to his palace and be connected with it, unlike the rectangular-shaped San Bartolomeo, a few blocks away, which was pulled down. The real star of the San Carlo was the imposing royal box, whether the king was present or not. It must have occurred to some, and perhaps possibly to the king, that the superb new theater was a fitting tribute to the widespread triumph of opera created by composers and performed by singers who had been trained in Naples.

The San Carlo, built on plans by the architect Giovanni Medrano, was carried out by Angelo Carasale so quickly that some of the workmanship was flawed, and

[63]This incorrect identification still persists in the article "Rome" in *New Grove* and *The New Grove Dictionary of Opera*. For the correct data see Roger Savage, "A Dynastic Marriage Celebrated," *Early Music* 36 (1998): 632–35.

[64]Franco Mancini, *Il Teatro di San Carlo 1737–1987*, vol. 2: *La storia, la struttura* (Naples, 1987), p. 9. The cost of building was estimated at 100,000 ducats, of which a third was to be paid by the king and the rest of the sum raised by selling boxes.

[65]For an illustration of the interior, see the article "Verona" in *New Grove*.

[66]Hanns-Bertold Dietz, "The Dresden-Naples Connection, 1737–1763: Charles of Bourbon, Maria Amalia of Saxony, and Johann Adolf Hasse," *International Journal of Musicology* 5 (1996): 95–130; 98–99.

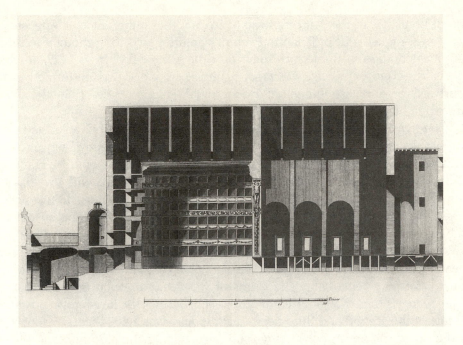

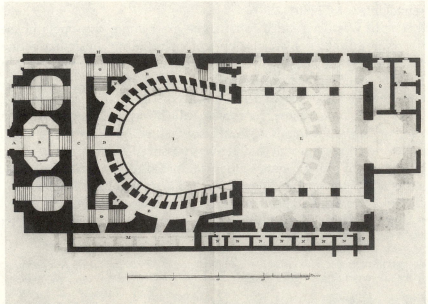

FIGURES 2.5–6. Elevation and floor plan of the Teatro San Carlo.

the acoustics proved to be poor. In 1742 Giovanni Maria Galli-Bibiena was called upon to solve the acoustic problem, while there were numerous attempts to improve the interior decoration. Contemporary with the theater and a rival to it was the grand Teatro Regio erected in that other royal capital, Turin, a theater originally planned by Juvarra, among others, with five tiers of boxes and a capacity of 2,500. A distinction is made between the two great theaters in that, while both adopted the horseshoe shape for the interiors, the Regio was in the form of a truncated oval, the San Carlo in the form of a bell. The Regio opened soon after the San Carlo. Its earliest state is recorded in the painting by Pietro Domenico Olivero showing the orchestral players, part of the parterre and boxes, and the whole of the stage, with a performance in 1740 of *Arsace* by Francesco Feo.[67] The ambassador of the king of Sardinia to Naples wrote to his sovereign in Turin a few years after the opening of the San Carlo, "I have seen the vast royal theater, which has not succeeded moreover in its proportions and in good taste as much as your majesty's theater, also with respect to the ornamentation."[68] Nevertheless, the San Carlo became one of the wonders of Italy that had to be seen on the Grand Tour. A long procession of visitors described its features. Most were impressed with its size, décor, and comforts, if not with its sounds. One visitor in 1765 complained about the tremendous tumult made by the spectators, adding that only the ballets seemed to quiet the audience, who had come to see but not to hear the opera.[69] Burney made a distinction between occasions when the king was present and those when he was not, but found the audience too noisy even when he was there.

The vastness of the San Carlo created both problems and possibilities. Its auditorium was perhaps twice the size of the San Bartolomeo's. Singers even in that age of great voices must have trembled at the thought that they might not be heard in so large a space. Metastasio complained to Princess di Belmonte in Naples that the tenor Anton Raaff would be inadequate in the title role of *Attilio Regolo* in the San Carlo. (The poet's apprehensions stemmed from observing Raaff act and sing under Jommelli in the Viennese Burgtheater in 1749.)

> This drama cannot succeed unless the audience really takes the main character to its heart, and our dear Raaff is physically incapable of sustaining such a weight. There are many reasons for me saying so, all based on experience. . . . Furthermore that huge volume of air in the Teatro San Carlo will swallow up all the inimitable graces and the

[67]The painting has often been reproduced, among other places in a fuzzy but colored picture in Hellmuth Christian Wolff, *Oper: Szene und Darstellung von 1600 bis 1900* (Leipzig, 1968), book jacket and illustration 83.
[68]Mancini, *Il Teatro di San Carlo*, p. 11.
[69]Samuel Sharp, *Letters from Italy, describing the customs and manners of that country* (London, 1766), pp. 84–85. For other reactions see Robinson, *Naples and Neapolitan Opera*, pp. 7–11.

extraordinary agility which make this singer so admirable when he performs in a room; he has come up against this difficulty in theaters that are less than a third the size of this one, thus one cannot hope he will have better luck here.[70]

Yet Raaff apparently did succeed; at least he was given further roles. It probably helped that Jommelli's *Attilio* score of 1753 was drastically revised by Nicola Sala so as to make Raaff shine, by cutting the other roles severely and adapting arias especially for him, including one that took the place of the final chorus.[71] This raises the question of how the art of composition or means of performance might have changed in order to take advantage of the spacious new theater.

Leo

Leonardo Leo was born on 5 August 1694 at San Vito dei Normanni in Apulia, a small hill town near Brindisi. In 1709 he went to Naples and became a pupil of Nicola Fago at the Turchini conservatory. His first *dramma sacro, Santa Chiara*, was performed at the conservatory in early 1712 and marked his emergence into public life as a composer. There soon followed a performance at the viceroy's palace and an appointment as supernumerary royal organist. Leo advanced steadily to the top of the musical hierarchy in the court chapel. He became first organist upon Scarlatti's death in 1725, pro vice maestro when Vinci died in 1731, vice maestro when Mancini died in 1737, and finally maestro with the death of Sarro on 25 January 1744. He held this post only nine months, until his own death on 31 October 1744. In addition Leo had become master of San Onofrio conservatory in 1739 and two years later of the Turchini conservatory.

As an opera composer Leo began in rather sporadic fashion. His setting of Domenico Lalli's *Pisistrato* for the San Bartolomeo in 1714 was not followed by another opera for this house until 1720. During the 1720s Leo was renowned enough to receive commissions from Rome and Venice, but he wrote little in the way of serious opera for Naples. Compare this with Vinci's output, or Hasse's seven operas in six years for the San Bartolomeo (1725–31). Only with the death of Vinci in 1730 and Hasse's departure from Naples the same year did the field open wide for Leo. Also to be taken into consideration is that Pergolesi failed to please in Naples with his serious operas. These considerations help explain how Leo became the leading composer of serious opera in Naples, but not until the 1730s. Although older than Vinci, Hasse, and Pergolesi he became in a certain artistic sense their successor. His solid craftsmanship and many sacred compositions also placed him in the succession of Alessandro Scarlatti.

---

[70]Letter of 1 December 1760, in Metastasio, *Tutte le opere,* 4: 172–73.
[71]Pierluigi Petrobelli, "The Italian Years of Anton Raaff," *Mozart-Jahrbuch 1773/74,* pp. 233–243; 239.

One of Leo's most admirable rivals as composer and teacher was Francesco Feo, who was born in Naples in 1691 and educated at the Turchini conservatory, where his fellow students included Leo and Giuseppe de Majo. Feo's career was almost exactly parallel to Leo's, with a first opera for the San Bartolomeo in 1713, followed by a *dramma sacro* on the martyrdom of Saint Catherine. His first and only *commedia per musica* came in 1719. He taught for sixteen years at the San Onofrio conservatory, where his pupils included Jommelli and Gaetano Latilla. Leo replaced him in 1739 when Feo replaced Durante as primo maestro of the Conservatorio dei Poveri di Gesù Cristo. When this conservatory was abolished in 1743, Feo retired from teaching except for taking some private pupils, but he continued to be active as a composer of sacred music. He had composed his last opera, *Arsace,* on a libretto by Antonio Salvi, for the Teatro Regio in Turin in 1740. As an opera composer Feo was eclipsed by Vinci, Hasse, and Leo.

Leo himself must have labored to remain true to his ideals in an age that vaunted Vinci's popular and accessible style. Vinci's *Artaserse* was revived at the San Carlo in 1738 and 1743. In Leo's late opera *L'Andromaca* for the San Carlo in 1743, the libretto gave Pirro an aria, "Son regnante e son gueriero," that suggested Didone's "Son regina, e son amante." Leo began his setting as if he would ignore Vinci's famous aria for Didone, making a broad triadic statement in gavotte rhythm (Example 2.17). He continued by repeating the little three-note snap down to the tonic, which cannot be other than an homage to Vinci (cf. Example 2.5).

Leo requested and received permission to travel to Rome in 1726, where he composed G. G. Alborghetti's *Il Cid* for the Teatro Capranica (first performance on 10 February 1727) and to Venice in 1727, where he composed Domenico Lalli's

EXAMPLE 2.17. *Leo*, L'Andromaca, *Aria*

Argene for the San Giovanni Gristostomo theater (first performance on 17 January 1728); in the latter case he was given a leave of three months with proviso that he return in time for Lent.[72] A year later the same Venetian theater commissioned from him a setting of Metastasio's *Catone in Utica* for the carnival of 1729. Apparently the records of the royal chapel in Naples do not contain a request for a leave

---

[72]Francesco Cotticelli and Paologiovanni Maione, *Le Istituzioni musicali a Napoli durante il Viceregno Austriaco (1707–1734). Materiali inediti sulla Real Cappella ed il Teatro di San Bartolomeo* (Naples, 1993), pp. 84–85.

of absence in this case, and it is possible that Leo, contrary to the custom, fulfilled the commission from afar. Metastasio says that Leo answered requests by sending his scores.[73] How would the poet know this long after he left Italy for good? He may be referring to this very occasion, the Venetian carnival of 1729.

Vinci made the first setting of *Catone* in 1728 for Rome, where audiences were displeased with the suicide and death on stage assigned to the title role. For Venice Metastasio changed this ending so that Cato's death is merely reported, not shown. If Leo was in Venice he could not have been altogether happy with how he was treated. Farinelli was making his Venetian debut in the role of Arbace, the primo uomo. Two of his stunning arias were not by Leo at all, nor written on Metastasio's verse. They were from Vinci's *Medo* (Parma, 1728) and must have suited Farinelli particularly well because he often introduced them into his roles.[74] This could mean that he did not trust Leo to do as well by him as Vinci had, or that Leo was not there in person to take the measure of that fabulous voice as it sounded in early 1729 (he must have heard it often earlier, in Naples). Nicolini sang the title role in Venice. Handel arranged Leo's setting as a pasticcio for the King's Theatre in the Haymarket in November 1732, padding it with additional arias by Hasse, Porpora, Vinci, and Vivaldi.[75] He may well have made his choice on the basis of what the singers most desired to sing.

A look at the long list of Leo's operas will reveal that he often collaborated with other composers. Thus his setting of Metastasio's *Demofoonte* for the San Bartolomeo in early 1735 was shared with his two superiors in the court music, Mancini and Sarro. Giuseppe Sellitto supplied the comic intermezzo *Drusilla e Strabone*. Sarro wrote the first act, Mancini the second, and Leo the third. Three years later Leo incorporated his act in a setting entirely his own.

Metastasio wrote *Demofoonte* in 1733, following *L'Olimpiade,* and the first setting was made by Caldara to celebrate Saint Charles day in Vienna. It is the one opera by Metastasio that Hasse did not set. Perhaps he found it too full of pathos. The climax of long suffering comes in Act III. Timante regards his son as the issue of an incestuous liaison with Dircea, whom he (wrongly) believes to be his sister; he is moved by tenderness and terror alike at the sight of the child:

Misero pargoletto,	Unfortunate youth,
Il tuo destin non sai.	Your fate you know not.
Ah! non gli dite mai	Ah! never reveal
Qual era il genitor.	Who your father was.

[73]Letter of 12 November 1749 to Farinelli, quoted in Daniel Heartz, "Metastasio, 'Maestro dei Maestri di Cappella Drammatici,' " in *Metastasio e il mondo musicale,* ed. Maria Teresa Muraro (Florence, 1986), pp. 315–38; 331.

[74]Reinhard Strohm, *Italienischen Opernarien des frühen Settecento (1720–1730),* 2 vols. (Cologne, 1976), 2: 232.

[75]Leo, Hasse, Porpora, et al., *Catone,* arranged by George Frideric Handel, ed. Howard Mayer Brown (Italian Opera 1640–1770, vol. 71) (New York, 1983).

Leo turns Timante's pathetic entreaty into a somber plaint in the key of f (Example 2.18). By expressive distortions, prolonging the first syllable of "Misero" and the words "Il" and "Ah!", Leo works up to a melodic climax on high G♭, which becomes a dissonant minor ninth and is then reinterpreted as part of a diminished chord prior to the cadence. (Note also the unprepared minor ninth in the soprano at "destin.") Other features of note are the seventh chord in m. 27, the typically Neapolitan three-note slides on the repetition of the word "genitor,"

FIGURE 2.7. Anonymous portrait of Leonardo Leo.

the deceptive cadence used to stretch out the phrase, the slow-moving harmonic bass, with many repeated notes, and the dramatic use of rests. From this excerpt it is clear that Leo favored a richer harmonic language than Vinci; also that he took chances by writing in a more sophisticated musical style. The danger was that his finesse would be lost upon a big audience in a large theater.

Leo was equally famous for his church music and other works on sacred subjects. Aside from two examples of the *dramma sacro* written in 1712 and 1713 as he was emerging from conservatory training, he wrote several oratorios, the most celebrated being on two librettos of the 1730s by Metastasio, *La morte d'Abel* and *Sant'Elena al Calvario*. In the first Eve sings a lament for her two sons, "Miseri figli miei!", which has many of the same expressive traits as "Misero pargoletto," including stretching of the first syllable.[76] The second must have been a favorite of the composer. A bound score of it is depicted in a late portrait of the composer (Figure 2.7). Oratorio as much as opera was for Leo an opportunity to mix the new, lighter periodic style (the Vinci-Pergolesi inheritance) with the solid and more contrapuntal manner (the Scarlatti inheritance). As one expert has put it: "This mixture is seen at times in the combination of clearly balanced phrases together with a relatively complex texture and rich harmonic vocabulary, and at other times in simple texture and harmony but melodic lines developed through a sequential, spinning out process."[77] Several

[76]Howard E. Smither, *A History of the Oratorio,* vol. 3: *The Oratorio in the Classical Era* (Chapel Hill, N.C., 1987), example III-3, p. 95. The author devotes a penetrating discussion to Leo's *La morte d'Abel* as a whole, pp. 87–98.
[77]Ibid., p. 70.

EXAMPLE 2.18. *Leo*, Demofoonte, *Aria*

eighteenth-century commentators appreciated Leo in the same light. Leo introduced the practice of using boys from the conservatories to sing operatic choruses. It had to be abandoned around 1780 because the quality and quantity of conservatory students had fallen to the point where they could not meet even minimal choral standards.

During the last seven years of Leo's life he wrote several operas for the San Carlo and the Teatro Regio in Turin. If there were changes in compositional style effected by the mere fact of larger auditoriums they ought to show up in Leo's late works. That Leo achieved a European renown only with his latest works would seem to argue that, indeed, there were marked changes in his style after 1737.

For the carnival of 1739 in the Teatro Regio, Turin, Leo made a setting of Metastasio's *Il Ciro riconosciuto* that was a decided success. He was invited to write the main opera for the following carnival in Turin. On 5 November 1739 he requested four months of leave in order to go to Turin and Milan "to compose and accompany two operas," which request was granted.[78] There resulted his settings of Metastasio's *Achille in Sciro* (Turin, 1740) and of Zeno's *Scipione nelle Spagne* (Milan, 1740).

The composer and critic Johann Friedrich Reichardt singled out an aria from Leo's *Ciro riconosciuto*, praising it for its grand and strikingly bold melody.[79] The aria is sung in Act II, Scene 5, by the tyrant Astiage, who is confronted by the son he condemned to death many years earlier as a threat to his throne, and who he believed dead.

Non so: con dolce moto	I know not with what sweet motion
Il cor mi trema in petto;	The heart trembles in my breast;
Sento un affetto ignoto	I feel an unknown sensation
Che intenerir mi fa.	That makes me soften.
Come si chiama, oh Dio,	What is the name, oh God,
Questo soave affetto?	Of this sweet passion?
(Ah, se non fosse mio,	(Ah, if it were not my own,
Lo crederei pietà.)	I should believe it pity.)

Once again the language is of the simplest a poet could choose, but filled with rich possibilities for music, such as the verbs "tremble" and "soften," or the adjectives "unknown," and "sweet." Caldara took little advantage of these possibilities when he made the first setting for Vienna in 1736. Leo planned his music around them.

Reichardt's commentary accompanied a reduced score of the aria's **A¹** and **A²** sections published in his *Musikalisches Kunstmagazin* of 1782 (Figures 2.8–9).

---

[78]Cotticelli and Maione, *Le Istituzioni musicali a Napoli*, p. 86.

[79]For Reichardt's commentary see Hellmuth Christian Wolff, "Italian Opera 1700–1750," in *Opera and Church Music 1630–1750*, ed. Anthony Lewis and Nigel Fortune (*The New Oxford History of Music*, vol. 5) (London, 1975), pp. 73–168; 110–11.

FIGURES 2.8–9. Aria from Leo's *Ciro riconosciuto* transcribed by Reichardt.

40

Leo chooses a slow triple meter and the key of F. The accompanying strings begin with a short ritornello of six measures, *mezzo voce* for the first three, then *forte, piano, forte* for the outburst of sixteenth notes and half-cadence. The "dolce moto" he sets to the sweet sounds of the subdominant in 6/4 position, while "trema" is anticipated and followed by the burst of sixteenth-note agitation. Then once again the soothing subdominant harmony, leading to a half-cadence. An "unknown sensation" lends itself perfectly to the modulatory process which occurs next. The possibilities of depicting "softening" at "intenerir" are manifold. Leo does more than just sound the flat third, with which many Italian composers would have been content. (The Italian word for "flat," *bemolle,* is more evocative than its English equivalent because *bemolle* means "soft" or "pliant," also "effeminate.") The bass line has been rising by half step since the beginning of the modulation. It continues with the movement from G to A♭, a deceptive cadence, for the arrival of the verb "fa." The augmented chord in the previous measure offers an example of the kind of harmony that earned Rameau Burney's condemnation. An augmented-sixth chord leads back to the dominant, and before Leo is ready to pause he has used four flattened degrees. In the **A²** section he recomposes nearly everything, though departing from the same materials. Three-note slides are prominent, and there is an opportunity for an improvised cadenza, prepared by a *forte* chromatic rise in the bass. The **B** section (not shown in the illustration) Leo sets simply in the minor mode. What is perhaps the most striking feature of the music is his ability to spin long melodic lines at this slow tempo by avoiding cadences. He showed that it was possible to set Metastasio in a musical style that was new and yet appropriate to the sense and economy of the poetry. The dignified and elegiac result he achieved was particularly important for Jommelli and his generation.

In line with the broad cantabile arias of Leo's last years is his late *Salve regina* in F. It has none of the pathos that Pergolesi lent his famous setting of the same prayer, but rather a serene and joyful confidence, like a blithe benediction (Example 2.19a–c). The typically Neapolitan sweetness, with emphasis on the tonal relaxation provided by the subdominant chord, is deployed with a breadth of periodic melody that pointed beyond Leo's time, to the graceful and sometimes equally simple melodic arches of Piccinni. Probably close in time is the very different music of his famous eight-part *Miserere* of 1739, said to have been written in rivalry with Francesco Durante and long held up as a model of the strict style. Tradition has it that Leo was a more severe advocate of the old contrapuntal virtues than even Durante, which may or may not be true. It is safe to say, on the other hand, that only an opera composer like Leo could have written the *Salve regina* in F, not a harmonist-contrapuntist like Durante who shunned writing operas.

Comic opera proved as congenial to Leo as it was to Vinci and Pergolesi. He took up the *commedia musicale* that was flourishing at the Fiorentini in 1723–24, just as Vinci was quitting the field and moving exclusively to serious opera. Not much survives from Leo's early comic works, but they must have been successful because the composer kept supplying works in the genre with regularity to the small theaters. In 1739 he wrote his most famous one on a fine libretto by Federico for the Teatro Nuovo, *Amor vuol sofferenza*. The composer was busy revising the opera as *La finta Frascatana* when he died in 1744 and, thus revised, it made its way to Rome and points further north.

Amor vuol sofferenza opens with an impressive sinfonia in D in three movements, the opening *Allegro di molto* of which has the expected violinistic flourishes up to high D as well as a contrasting second theme in minor. The comedy preserves Neapolitan dialect for the lower-class characters, the *parti buffi;* the *parti serie* sing in Tuscan. Fazio, the main character, hails from Lucca and is a parody of the noble lover as found in serious opera. He cannot utter more than a few words

EXAMPLE 2.19. *Leo,* Salve regina *in F*

without saying "Cioè" (that is to say). Audiences loved the character as created by the veteran bass Gioacchino Corrado, Pergolesi's Uberto, to the extent that the opera was nicknamed "Il Cioè."[80] It was also called "Frascatana" after Eugenia, the deserted maidservant of the plot. Fazio's rival was played by another bass who served in the royal chapel, Girolamo Piani, who received the choice dialect role of Mosca, meaning "fly," or better, "gadfly." Leo introduced a characteristic buzzing motion in the voice and strings in Mosca's first aria, which he then used again in the orchestra alone during the trio that ends Act I (Example 2.20ab). This ensemble is an unusual piece in which two other characters respond with various animal noises to match Mosca and his buzzing.

Federico deserves much credit for Leo's comic masterpiece. The sparring between the fatuous nobleman from Lucca and the simple but crafty son of Naples comes to a head in the last act with this exchange:

Fazio:	Io son galantuomo	I am a gentleman, *un galant homme*
Mosca:	E io so figlio	And I am the son of my own actions
	all'azesune meje	[i.e., I am what I am]

Smoldering beneath the surface of such exchanges is the age-old rivalry between north and south in Italy. Distinctions of class also emerge, in this case the rich fool versus the shrewd peasant. Needless to say, the latter wins the contest.

The encomiums of Charles de Brosses for *Amor vuol sofferenza* are cited earlier in Chapter 1. Brosses ranked Leo with Vinci and Hasse as the composers who were most highly regarded in Italy, those who had superseded Scarlatti, Sarro, and Porpora. He commented specifically: "Leo has an uncommon genius; he is good at creating pictures, his harmony is very pure, and his melodies have an agreeable and delicate curve, full of refined imagination" (2: 315).

Leo continued to be praised long after his death. Abbé de Saint-Non says that Piccinni, who claimed Leo as his mentor, made this evaluation of his expressive range:

> Leonardo Leo surpassed all his Masters, and one can even say that, having combined all genres, he is regarded as the greatest Painter in his art that Italy has ever seen. A learned Composer as well as a pleasant Singer, he succeeded in the great and terrible and excelled also in conveying the most gentle and tender sentiments. His "Misero Pargoletto" in Metastasio's *Demofoonte* will always be regarded as a model of Cantabile and expressiveness.[81]

[80]Graham Hood Hardie, "Leonardo Leo (1694–1744) and His Comic Operas *Amor vuol sofferenza* and *Alidoro*" (Ph.D. diss., Cornell University, 1973), p. 162. Hardie reproduces Fazio's splendid first aria in its entirety, pp. 111–25.

[81]Jean-Chrétien de Saint-Non, *Voyage pittoresque ou description des royaumes de Naples et de Sicile,* 5 vols. (Paris, 1781–86), cited after Graham Hardie, "Leonardo Leo," p. 22.

EXAMPLE 2.20. *Leo*, Amor vuol sofferenza, *"Mosca's motif"*

a. Aria, Act I, Scene 10

b. Ensemble, Act I

La Borde in his *Essai* (1780) had similar praises for Leo, noting that "noble pathos is always predominant in his composition."[82]

Reichardt looked back at Leo's career from the vantage point of 1792 with an unusual amount of historical consciousness.

> Leo, for the observer, historian of art, and artist, is the most important composer of this century. No one affected his century so broadly and diversely as he has. In his works are to be found all the forms that composers have employed since, and still employ. The old ones he beautifies and perfects, and to their company adds innu-

---

[82]Jean-Benjamin La Borde, *Essai sur la musique ancienne et moderne*, 4 vols. (Paris, 1780; reprint 1972).

merable new ones. Grand opera in Italy has to this day nothing in which the ground forms did not repose in his works.[83]

Reichardt went on to discuss some of Leo's specific contributions, which included, he claimed, the Rondo aria. Leo's role certainly was central to the Neapolitan School. He was the only master who was considered worthy of being Scarlatti's successor, and he became a model for the generation that followed him, including Jommelli, Piccinni, Leo's Viennese pupil Giuseppe Bonno, and that Neapolitan by adoption, Johann Christian Bach. Stefano Arteaga specifically linked Scarlatti and Leo as the first masters to lend arias the combination of graceful melody and brilliant accompaniments.[84]

Even in the early nineteenth century Leo's reputation stood high, as this evaluation by Count Orloff shows.

> This composer was eminently useful to the progress of his art in all things. He perfected the recitative, and the *cantabile,* ensemble pieces and accompaniments. What Alessandro Scarlatti began, Leo continued; that which Sarro and Porpora could only sketch, he knew how to finish. Through him the melody was released more and more from those elements that were foreign to the workings of its power; it emerged always pure in his beautiful compositions. Without taking anything away from expression, he gave melody its greatest charm, which is to please by the delightful alliance of grace and truth. His style was always elevated without affectation, expressive without extravagance, and grand without being inflated.[85]

Not until the meteoric rise to prominence of Rossini and his music were Leo and most other Neapolitan masters consigned to oblivion.

An anonymous artist painted a touching oil portrait of Leo, perhaps on the occasion of his elevation to be first master of the royal chapel in early 1744 (see Figure 2.7 on p. 133). It shows a sensitive and proud mien, a lack of ostentation in the simple hairdress, without wig (one of the most telling indications of how people wished to appear to the world was their choice of wig, or whether to be bewigged at all). The pose and costume befit high office. Leo's right hand holds a quill, resting on a page of music inscribed *Olimpiade,* propped up by three tomes bearing the names of works by which he apparently wished to be remembered: *ANDROMACA; [SA]NTA ELENA; DEMOFOONTE.* The page of music beneath is from his *Miserere.*

[83]Johann Friedrich Reichardt, *Musikalisches Monatschrift,* Viertes Stück (October 1792). Reprinted in Gerber, *Neues Lexikon.*
[84]Stefano Arteaga, *Le rivoluzioni del teatro musicale italiana dalla sua origine fino al presente,* rev. 2nd ed. (Venice, 1785), pp. 20–21.
[85]Comte Grégoire Orloff, *Essai sur l'Histoire de la Musique en Italie* (Paris, 1822), p. 277.

Jommelli

The son of a prosperous cloth merchant, Niccolò Jommelli was born on 10 September 1714 in Aversa, ten miles north of Naples. After some instruction in the cathedral of his native city he was sent in 1725 as a *convittore* to the San Onofrio conservatory, where he was taught by Prota and Feo; in 1728 he transferred to the Turchini conservatory and was taught by Nicola Fago, among others. Jommelli grew to maturity in a Naples that witnessed within a few years the collective brilliance of Vinci, Pergolesi, Hasse, and Leo, the last three being of particular importance to him as models. He was born in the same year as two other giants of European music, Gluck and Emanuel Bach.

Saverio Mattei, a lawyer and poet in Naples who befriended Jommelli, wrote about the composer's last years in his *Saggio di poesie latine, ed italiane* (Naples, 1774), an obituary notice that Burney translated in his *History*; Mattei wrote about the entire career in his *Elogio di Jommelli,* which was coupled with his memoir on Metastasio's life and works (1785). Mattei claims that Jommelli first went to the Poveri conservatory, but this seems to be an error. He says that the young composer won attention in 1736 with a cantata performed in the house of Leo's pupil Signora Barbapiccola. From this encounter Leo predicted that Jommelli would soon win the admiration of all Europe.

> In 1737, when music was in its most flourishing state, and when Jommelli was twenty-three he wrote his first opera, *L'Errore amoroso,* for the Teatro nuovo of Naples, under the protection of Marchese del Vasto Avalos, of whom he was the maestro di cappella according to the libretto. The reception accorded this music was incredible, and the approval of the famous Leo played a great role in protecting the young composer from envy. Jommelli had won the friendship of this master and cultivated it continually, to the extent that he passed for a student of Leo's notwithstanding that in truth he had studied with Canon Muzzillo in Aversa, then in Naples under Fago, and then under Prota, and Feo. But it cannot be denied that, not being content with his other fine teachers, he sought to learn from Leo the grand and the sublime in music. According to those who know, Jommelli made a searching study of Leo's scores, and often reclothed the master's designs in better shades of color [ha rivestito di miglio colorito gli stessi disegni del suo direttore].[86]

Leo went several times to hear the opera of his protégé in the Teatro Nuovo and proclaimed that his prediction would soon come true.

The success of Jommelli's first comic opera is demonstrated as well by a com-

---

[86]Mattei, *Elogio di N. Jommelli*, p. 75.

mission to write another one, *Odoardo,* the following year for the Fiorentini theater. Both works are lost except for a few arias. The earliest comic work by Jommelli to survive in its entirety is the intermezzo *Don Chichibio* (Rome, Teatro delle
Valle, 1742). Apparent from this score is the nearness not only to Leo but also to
Pergolesi, for example, in the use of the "su e giu" figure from *La serva padrona.*

Jommelli was probably occupied with the composition of sacred music at this
nascent part of his career, but nothing in his vast oeuvre of liturgical music and
oratorios can be securely dated so early.[87] His first commission for an opera seria
came from Rome, where he soon found a wealthy patron in the person of Cardinal Alessandro Albani. *Ricimero rè di Goti* on a libretto by Zeno adapted by Pietro
Pariati had its premiere at the Teatro Argentina on 16 January 1740.

The score of *Ricimero* is replete with those "heavy" characteristics that Jommelli is supposed to have acquired in Germany after he went there in the 1750s:
complicated orchestral accompaniments, some textures in four real parts, and
rather fussily ornamented vocal lines. Charles de Brosses was in Rome at the time
Ricimero was produced. He singled out for praise the composer's use of obbligato
recitative: "the force of the declamation, the variety of the harmony, and the sublimity of the accompaniment created a sense of drama greater than the best
French recitative or the most beautiful Italian melody" (2: 307). Hasse had earlier
excelled in his obbligato recitatives, for instance, with a particularly famous one in
his setting of *Artaserse* for Venice (1730) sung by Nicolini as Artabano, "Eccomi al
fine in liberta."[88] It may well have been this manner of motivically unified but
free-flowing and agitated orchestral outbursts in support of intermittent vocal
declamation that Jommelli learned from Hasse.

After the two operas for Rome, Jommelli was called to Bologna to write his
first setting of Metastasio's *Ezio* for the Teatro Malvezzi (premiere on 29 April
1741). In Bologna he met Padre Martini, who became a lifelong friend and correspondent. He also took some lessons with him and became a member of the
Accademia Filarmonica.

Venice was the next city to call on Jommelli's talents. He composed a setting
of Zeno's *Merope* to inaugurate the Venetian carnival season of 1741–42 in the San
Giovanni Grisostomo theater (premiere on 26 December 1741). He returned a
year later in the same function with a setting of Silvani's *Semiramide,* having
meanwhile composed three operas for Turin and Bologna. For all Jommelli's professed devotion to the works of Metastasio, it seems odd that there are so few

---

[87]Wolfgang Hochstein, *Die Kirchenmusik von Niccolò Jommelli (1714–1774)*, 2 vols. (Hildesheim, 1984).
[88]The entire recitative and beginning of the following aria is reproduced in Daniel Heartz, "Hasse, Galuppi,
and Metastasio," in *Venezia e il Melodramma nel Settecento,* ed. Maria Teresa Muraro (Florence, 1978), example 1, pp. 313–22.

libretti by the Caesarean poet chosen by the composer (or chosen for him) at this time. Did he perhaps favor older librettos, as did Handel, because they allowed more spectacle? Zeno's *Merope,* one of the poet's best, went back to 1712. As staged in Venice thirty years later the opera incorporated a major addition: "its first and second acts are linked with an unusual scene including chorus, obbligato recitative, ballet and pantomime, depicting war games, foreshadowing in startling fashion the French-inspired operas to come [in Jommelli's later career]."[89] Incursions of ballet like this were indeed unusual; the dancers normally performed independent pieces between the acts of the opera. Transforming these entr'acte entertainments into something imbedded in the drama implies innovation from both the choreographer, who in this case was Gaetano Grossatesta, and the composer, and perhaps the theater poet as well.

Zeno retired from the stage in 1729, when Metastasio succeeded him in Vienna, as we have seen. The latter was at the zenith of his fame around 1740, and it may have been more tempting to adventurous spirits to tamper in massive ways with the librettos of his predecessor than to upset the delicate balance achieved by Metastasio in his best librettos, which had reached near-canonical status by midcentury.

Jommelli's successes in Venice in the first half of the 1740s coincided with two Venetian operas by Gluck in 1742 and 1744; the two composers almost certainly met there. No later than 1745, and perhaps earlier, Jommelli, on the strength of a recommendation by Hasse, was appointed director of the Ospedale degli Incurabile, one of the four conservatories for orphan girls in Venice. The first works he composed that can be securely tied to this post are a Kyrie-Gloria Mass in F for high voices and a setting of Metastasio's oratorio *Gioas re de Giuda,* both dating from 1745.[90]

Local musicians in Venice could scarcely have been pleased that yet another composer from Naples had won one of the city's major positions. Neapolitan or Neapolitan-trained composers began to prevail in Venetian opera houses in the 1720s. After both Hasse and Jommelli were appointed to conservatory positions it seemed as if the outsiders would take over the city's musical life altogether. This did not happen, although the influx of Neapolitans continued. Jommelli himself must have been frequently absent from Venice because of the many operatic commissions he fulfilled elsewhere.

It was perhaps as early as 1747 that Jommelli gave up his post in Venice. He was in Naples and Rome for several operas from 1747 to 1749. His cantata celebrating the wedding of the dauphin in the Teatro Argentina is dated 9 February 1747. In Rome he became *maestro coadiutore* to the papal chapel, that is, vice maestro di cappella, but in reality the director of music at Saint Peter's basilica,

[89]Marita P. McClymonds, "Jommelli," in *The New Grove Dictionary of Opera.*
[90]Hochstein, *Die Kirchenmusik von Niccolò Jommelli,* 1: 24–27.

because the maestro di cappella, Pietro Paolo Bencini, was too aged and infirm to carry out his duties in leading the Cappella Giulia. Cardinals Albani and Benedict secured this post for Jommelli, as well as his nomination to the Accademia di Santa Cecilia. Formal installation in the new post took place on 20 April 1749. In the three years between 1750 and 1753 the composer wrote the bulk of his sacred music, a long list of hymns, psalm settings, antiphons, and the like, but no masses, for the papal chapel in Rome.[91] Ghezzi made several caricatures of Jommelli showing him to be formidable in face and figure, as in the one reproduced here that mentions his appointment to Saint Peter's (Figure 2.10).

Sigᵣ Jomella Maestro di Musica Napoletano

FIGURE 2.10. Pierleone Ghezzi. Caricature of Niccolò Jommelli.

Soon after Jommelli's formal appointment in Rome he embarked on a major voyage. Crossing the Alps for the first time, the composer made his way to Vienna in order to fulfill operatic commissions arranged by his patron Cardinal Albani. At last he was able to meet the poet so idolized by all the world of opera, whose *Achille in Scrio* he set for the Burgtheater (premiere on 30 August 1749), followed by Jommelli's second version of the poet's *Didone abbandonata* (premiere on 8 December 1749). Metastasio's initial reaction was positive. He proclaimed the composer to possess "all the grace, invention and fecundity of Vinci," as well as the harmonic science of the Saxon, meaning Hasse, which shows that the poet's tastes in music had not changed since he left Italy. Once Metastasio got a better knowledge of Jommelli's music he became quite disapproving, as he was likewise of Galuppi's and Gluck's; in the end he trusted only Hasse to keep the faith, that is, to keep music subordinate to his poetry. A comparison of the final scene of Vinci's *Didone* (Example 2.6) with Jommelli's setting for Vienna shows that the latter was far more expansive with regard to the role of music and more symphonic in nature.

---

[91]The impressive output is summarized by Hochstein's table 1, *Die Kirchenmusik von Niccolò Jommelli*, 1: 38–41.

LA PASSIONE DI GESÙ CRISTO

At the peak of his fame in Rome, Jommelli was commissioned by Cardinal Henry Benedict, Duke of York and grandson of King James II of England, to set Metastasio's first oratorio text, *La Passione di Nostro Signore Gesù Cristo.* The work was later printed by Bremner in score in London.[92] It is one of the rare vocal works listed nearly complete in the Breitkopf thematic catalogue, in Supplement II of 1767 (Figure 2.11). The poem is written for four soloists, Peter (tenor), John (contralto), Joseph of Arimathea (bass), and Mary Magdalen (soprano). They sing a dozen arias and one duet, interspersed with recitatives. There is no action as such. Peter, filled with remorse for betraying his master, encounters the others, who narrate the crucifixion and aftermath. The oratorio ends as they gather at the tomb. Moralizing choruses close the two parts of the work and a third chorus early in Part I reacts to Peter's guilt by extending the blame to all mankind.

From the first moments of the orchestral sinfonia it is obvious that this work is special to its composer, and deeply felt. He chooses the key of $E^\flat$ and introduces it in a slow chordal passage, using dotted rhythm in common time, suggestive of a model in the French overture. The following *Allegro moderato* does nothing to dispel the link when it begins with imitations between the two violin parts. The slow chordal music returns to mark the end of the section in the dominant (where the double bar and repeat sign would be were they present) and at the equivalent spot after tonic $E^\flat$ has been restored and confirmed. A short final *Allegro* in 3/8 concludes the overture. Horns and oboes lend color to the orchestra. Remarkable about the slow introduction and its emphasis on the subdominant is its prophetic anticipation of another overture in $E^\flat$, that to *Die Zauberflöte.* Mattei in his *Elogio* (1785) calls the sinfonia "worthy of study for being so well adapted to its subject, and often imitated [by other composers] but never surpassed."

Metastasio began with twenty-four lines of recitative for Peter, leading to his first aria; Jommelli continues on with the key of the overture in an obbligato recitative that is so elaborate it stretches out the lines of the text by orchestral interruptions or anticipations until they reach a duration of nearly five minutes—as long as many arias by other composers. The words seem to become secondary to the music with this amount of orchestral commentary, which was disapproved in principle by Metastasio, as we know from his letter to Hasse about setting *Attilio Regolo.* It could be argued that Jommelli's arias had become so long by 1750 that lengthening the recitatives seems only fitting. Peter's first aria, in da capo form like almost all the others, is close to ten minutes in duration.

[92]Bremner's handsome printed score of ca. 1765 serves as the text for the reprinting of the work in volume 18 of *The Italian Oratorio 1650–1800,* ed. Joyce L. Johnson and Howard E. Smither. It includes a list of subscribers to the original London edition that shows many names from the high nobility as well as that of Charles Burney.

FIGURE 2.11. Detail from Breit-kopf's *Thematic Catalogue,* Supplement II, 1767.

Jommelli himself lamented Metastasio's short and word-economical aria texts.[93] They did not suit his long musical phrases and sections. The poet's lin-guistic parsimony and perfection achieved ideal union with the mostly short

[93]Letter of 14 November 1769.

phrases of Vinci and others close to his style. Jommelli was forced to repeat words and whole lines over and over in order to clothe his generous store of musical ideas. In at least one aria of *La Passione*, the one sung by John near the end of the second part, Jommelli does simplify his complex style so as to take flight from the poet's simple grandeur and sublimity. The poem is one of the master's greatest and most famous.[94]

Dovunque il guardo giro,	Wherever my glance strays,
immenso Dio ti vedo:	I see Thee, immense God;
nell'opre tue t'ammiro	in Thy works I admire Thee,
ti riconosco in me oh Dio.	in myself I recognize Thee.
La terra, il mar	The earth, the ocean,
le sfere parlan del tuo potere:	the planets speak of Thy power;
tu sei per tutto	Thou art present in all
e noi tutti viviamo in te.	And we all live in Thee.

Jommelli chooses the key of E, used nowhere else in the work, and discards his usually nervous rhythms for a simple string of quarter notes in slow 3/4 time, beginning with a canonic imitation (No. 13 in Breitkopf's list). With minute control of all his materials he expands this even-toned and arching song to become a temple of perfect proportions, a unified outpouring of about twelve minutes that matches the visionary exaltation of the poem. As closing material he introduces tones 1–4–3. The motif plays a role throughout the entire oratorio, figuring as it does at the beginning of the first aria and of the last chorus as well as in other incipits (cf. Nos. 1, 7, 11, and 16 in Breitkopf's thematic list).

Another aria in which Jommelli catches just the right musical accent for the words is Mary Magdalen's "Vorrei dirti il mio dolore" (I wish to tell you my sadness), in which she can scarcely bring words to her lips (Breitkopf's No. 3). Here the composer also chooses a simple word setting, interspersed with rests that convey a gasping for breath. Admirable too is the four-part fugue for the first chorus, "Quanto costa il tuo delitto" (How much your crime costs), sung to Peter (Breitkopf's No. 2). In working a well-known fugue subject, one expressive of grief, Jommelli shows both good judgment and a command of strict counterpoint. After a cadence in the initial key of g, he introduces without transition a chordal section in E♭ before bringing back the fugue in g. The expressive key contrast, associated particularly with later Viennese composers, is as prominent here as it is in Pergolesi's *Stabat mater.*

If Jommelli errs sometimes, it is through overrichness of detail. He is the composer to whom a Habsburg emperor could have justifiably complained "too many

---

[94]René Jacobs sings it complete in 12 minutes and 20 seconds. Any doubts about the greatness of Jommelli will vanish upon listening to his powerful and serene performance, recorded in 1984 under the direction of Arturo Sacchetti, in a shortened version of the oratorio (Accord 49544).

notes!" In one case he sins outright by committing a basic flaw in text setting. Peter's first aria contains the line "tutto disciolto in lacrime" (all dissolved in tears). Jommelli, before setting the last word as an entity, places a long melisma of several measures on its first syllable: "tutto disciolto in la———etc." The keen and mischievous listener might well interpret this as a musical pun meaning all dissolves in the key of A, a mirthful possibility that completely destroys the affect intended. Jommelli told Mattei that he learned from Metastasio that a composer must set an entire word before excerpting any syllable for coloratura. It is difficult to believe that Jommelli failed to learn this lesson before 1749. But in point of fact the oratorio dates from early 1749, and his trip to Vienna and meeting with Metastasio from later the same year. The lapse in Peter's aria is so prominent, coming in the very first aria, that it could well be the direct cause of Metastasio's scolding.

In terms of tonality Jommelli has obviously attempted to give some kind of unity to the whole by ending both Part I and Part II with choruses in E♭, the key of the overture (Nos. 9 and 16 in Breitkopf's list). An odd thing about the first of these two choruses is that he concludes not on the tonic but on the dominant, repeating the final word "pensaci" (think about it), intended as direct plea to the audience to meditate on Christ's sacrifice. The open ending in this case provides an invitation. In some places a sermon was given between the two parts of a Lenten oratorio. At the very least the repeated chords of B♭ provide a bridge to Part II, which begins with an obbligato recitative in E♭.

Obbligato recitative was such a powerful weapon of the Italian opera composer that Metastasio wanted it used only rarely. Some critics thought otherwise, notably the anonymous author who claimed that Italian composers were too parsimonious with this potent resource.[95] Jommelli was exempt from any such claim. No composer made more of a specialty of the device than Jommelli, and he used it from his early works throughout his career. The ever-perceptive Diderot included mention of an obbligato recitative by Jommelli in his satirical masterpiece, *Le neveu de Rameau.* When the nephew is demonstrating an entire modern opera by every manner of sound and gesture, he slips imperceptibly into the performance of a nonoperatic piece.

> In singing a fragment of the *Lamentations* by Jommelli he repeated it with precision and an incredible truth and warmth. That beautiful obbligato recitative where the prophet paints the desolation of Jerusalem, he watered with a torrent of tears that made the same flow from every eye. Everything was there, the delicate cantabile and the force of expression, the sadness. He insisted on those parts where the musician particularly showed himself to be a great master. If he left the voice part momentar-

---

[95] *Lettre sur le mechanisme de l'opéra italien* (1756). See *Haydn, Mozart*, p. 160.

ily it was in order to take an instrumental part, which he left suddenly upon rejoining the vocal line, binding one to the other in a manner so as to preserve the connections, and the unity of the whole. He stole our souls away and held them suspended in a way so singular that I have never experienced the like.

Only one of the several surviving *Lamentations* by Jommelli has such an obbligato recitative, and it is his setting of "Jod. Manum suam misit" for Holy Thursday at Saint Peter's, thought to date from 1751.[96]

The orchestral sinfonia is another genre to which Jommelli made decisive contributions. Initially, he continued the advances made by Pergolesi and Leo. The "favorite" Sinfonia in D of the former, used as the overture to three different works with only slight changes, exerted a particular fascination for the young composer. Its first movement, with wind fanfares and violin scales running up to high D, served as a model for the opening movement of the sinfonia preceding Jommelli's *Ricimero* (1740), and the emulation included the ordering of the instruments on the score pages.[97] By this same criterion Leo became an even more important model for Jommelli in his next opera, *Astianatte* (1742), the sinfonia of which begins with a fast movement in common time and in D, with another rise up to high D in the violins (Example 2.21). The soft echoes of one measure stretch the process out and imply a long crescendo up to the arrival of the dominant in root position at the beginning of m. 14. The similarity to Leo is most apparent when Jommelli introduces a contrasting theme in the minor, with reduced orchestration, thin texture, and soft dynamics (mm. 20–26), similar to the parallel spot in the first movement of Leo's overture to *Emira* (1735). In general, Leo was fond of writing canonic themes in descending thirds, as Jommelli does here. Moreover, a very similar second theme in minor occurs in Leo's sinfonia to his *commedia per musica L'Alidoro* (1740), a resemblance that removes any doubts about the indebtedness of one master to the other. This helps explain what Mattei says about Jommelli's studying Leo's scores and clothing their designs "in better colors." Jommelli's careful and idiomatic treatment of oboes, horns, trumpets, and violins illustrates the point.

By the mid-1740s Jommelli was going beyond Leo's model in the opening movements of his overtures in length, in momentum, in the long dynamic building up through two octaves, and in the telling use of soft contrasting passages as second themes. The *crescendo* appears in perfected form in the culminating masterpiece of his Roman period, his setting of Metastasio's *Attilio Regolo* (1753). Here

[96]Hochstein, *Die Kirchenmusik von Niccolò Jommelli*, 2: 201, no. 11. See also Marita P. McClymonds and Walter Rex, "Ce beau récitatif obligé de Jommelli," *Diderot Studies* 22 (1986), 63–77.
[97]Heinrich Hell, *Die neapolitanische Opernsinfonie in der ersten Hälfte des 18. Jahrhunderts* (Tutzing, 1971), pp. 307–11.

EXAMPLE 2.21. *Jommelli*, Astianatte, *Sinfonia, I*

he specifies *crescendo* and gives the violins an unimpeded sweep up two octaves to high D in the first movement of the sinfonia (Example 2.22). The consequences of these hair-raising effects were wide and especially evident in the most mature symphonies of Stamitz.

Jommelli's success at Vienna in 1749 brought him an international reputation, soon followed by offers of well-paid posts elsewhere. By midcentury Vienna had

become such an advanced center of Italian opera that Jommelli's talents as a composer and director had to vie in quick succession with those of Hasse, Galuppi, and Gluck. They were not found wanting. From all contemporary accounts, Jommelli was one of the most demanding orchestra leaders of the century. Galuppi was famous for the discipline he exacted, as was Hasse, but only Gluck, besides Jommelli, seems to have commanded as much fear as respect. Jommelli's overwhelming physical presence when leading an ensemble, stressed in many contemporary accounts, forced singers and players alike to do their best and do his bidding. Early symphonists from the Viennese sphere such as Christoph Georg Wagenseil and Carl Ditters von Dittersdorf were awed by the musician and leader, as well as by his music. The latter mentions in his memoirs that at his debut in 1751 as concertmaster of the palace orchestra of Prince Hildburghausen the symphony they performed was one by Jommelli.

The first part of Jommelli's career, which is all that concerns us here, ended when he left to take up his post at Stuttgart in 1753. The formal contract was signed on 1 January 1754. He composed *Attilio Regolo* for the Roman carnival of 1753 (first performance in the Teatro delle Dame on 8 January 1753). Metastasio's libretto, first set by Hasse at Dresden in 1750, is the one that the poet himself declared his best. He valued it so highly because of its grandly heroic conclusion as Regolo bids farewell to family and to Rome—grander even, and more elevated in style because of the circumstances, than the last moments of *Didone.* Regolo

EXAMPLE 2.22. *Jommelli*, Attilio Regolo, *Sinfonia, I*

takes leave of his daughter near the end of Act III with a touching aria that he begins without instrumental ritornello (Example 2.23). He continues with a beautiful vocal line that is mostly independent of the wavering sixteenth-note accompaniments in the violins (as if underscoring the character's independence in choosing banishment over dishonor). In an operatic tradition in which the singer is mostly supported by the first violins, such independence could well have caused problems in performance. One professional singer judged this very aria to be too overloaded with detail in the voice part.[98] It is true that, after a touching simple beginning, Jommelli becomes concerned with writing in ornamental

[98]Pierluigi Petrobelli, "Un cantante fischiate e le appoggiature di mezza battuta: Cronaca teatrale e prassi esecutiva ala meta del '700," in *Studies in Renaissance and Baroque Music in Honor of Arthur Mendel*, ed. Robert L. Marshall (Kassel, 1974), pp. 363–76. The singer supposedly hissed at during his singing of this aria was the soprano castrato Ventura Rocchetti, according to a gossipy letter to Padre Martini from the tenor Giuseppe Tibaldi, who may not be the most trustworthy witness since he was singing at the same time in a rival opera produced in the Teatro Argentina.

EXAMPLE 2.23. *Jommelli*, Attilio Regolo, *Aria*

details such as most composers would have left to the improvising skill of the individual singer.

Jommelli's finest moment in *Attilio Regolo* coincided with Metastasio's, as the hero bids Rome and its inhabitants farewell and asks that the final leave-taking be worthy of them: "Romani, addio. Siano i congedi estremi degni di noi." Jommelli sets the partially rhymed speech of nineteen lines in a noble obbligato recitative with elaborate symphonic interjections that prefigure those in many later operas, including the final monologue in Mozart's *Idomeneo*. Burney claimed that Regolo's farewell was so affecting that it was encored in the pasticcio version given in London the following year, the only case he knew in which a recitative was accorded such public favor. The parallel was not missed between Regolo and the composer, who was also leaving Rome.

Piccinni

Niccolò Piccinni led a generation of composers born around 1730 that included Pasquale Anfossi and Traetta (1727), Pietro Guglielmi and Giacomo Insanguiné (1728), Fedele Fenaroli and Sacchini (1730), and Francesco de Majo (1732). Piccinni himself was born in Bari on 16 January 1728. The earliest article on the composer (in La Borde's *Essai*, 1780) was written by Pierre Louis Ginguené, who later wrote the principal biography.[99] In May 1742 Piccinni entered the San Onofrio conservatory, where he studied with Leo, then with Durante. He remained attached to his school in later years, even returning to act in spoken comedies during carnival.

During 1754, as Jommelli formally took up his post in Stuttgart, Piccinni began a successful series of comic operas with Neapolitan dialect roles for the Fiorentini and Nuovo theaters. Then in 1756 he wrote his first opera for the San Carlo, a setting of Metastasio's *Zenobia*, followed a year later by a setting of Metastasio's *Nitteti* to celebrate the name day of King Charles, 4 November 1757. With these important commissions it became clear that Piccinni was moving into the forefront of Neapolitan composers, replacing the defunct Leo and the departed Jommelli. Tommaso Traetta began writing comic operas a few years earlier and composed a royal name day opera, *Farnace,* for the San Carlo as early as 1751. But Traetta left Naples for a series of commissions from northern cities after 1756 and did not return. Piccinni had no major rivals among Neapolitan composers for the favor of opera goers in Rome and Naples until the emergence of Anfossi and Paisiello.

Before Piccinni's triumph in the comic theaters the principal opera composers, aside from Vinci, Pergolesi, Leo, and Jommelli, were Gaetano Latilla, born in Bari on 12 January 1711; Nicola Logroscino, born in Bitonto and baptized on 22 October 1698; Gioacchino Cocchi, born ca. 1720; Domenico Fischietti, born ca. 1725; and Vincenzo Ciampi, whose date and place of birth are uncertain. Another was Pietro Auletta, best known for his setting of Palomba's *La maestra* of 1747. The most important of these composers was Latilla, who was a pupil at the Loreto conservatory and began writing comedies for the Fiorentini in 1732. His best-known comedies are his 1737 setting of Federico's *Gismondo* (alias *La finta cameriera,* alias *Don Colascione*) and of Giovanni Barlocci's *Madama Ciana* for Rome in 1738. These two works, along with *La commedia in commedia* (Rome, 1737) and *La libertà nociva* (Rome, 1740) by Rinaldo da Capua, formed the basis

[99]Pierre Louis Ginguené, *Notice sur la vie et les ouvrages de Nicolas Piccinni* (Paris, 1800–1801).

of a comic repertory that traveled throughout Italy and beyond in the 1740s and early 1750s.[100] Latilla was Piccinni's uncle.

Defenders of the Neapolitan *commedia musicale* in dialect, or partly in dialect, maintained that the local speech was more musical than Tuscan; in a history of the dialect Abate Galiani wrote:

> If any doubts remained about the singular and distinct attributes accorded to the dialect's musicality, we call to witness the many illustrious composers still living which it produced. All, including Piccinni, Paisiello, Sacchini, Anfossi, Guglielmi, Latilla, Monopoli [Insanguine], and Cimarosa, insist that Neapolitan is as superior to Italian for singing as Italian is to French.[101]

Peculiar, but not outlandish, is the notion that writing for the voice in dialect formed these composers, an idea parallel and supplementary to the more general concept that they comprised a school by virtue of their conservatory training in Naples. It remained true that opera in Neapolitan dialect was not exportable, unless revised. To a man, all these composers sought and received commissions to write operas for other cities, using the Tuscan language.

LA BUONA FIGLIUOLA

By 1760 Piccinni had written more than a dozen operas, including his first setting of Metastasio's *Alessandro nell'Indie* for the Teatro Argentina in Rome, given during the carnival season of 1758. When he wrote again for Rome two years later, the Teatro delle Dame allowed the second carnival opera to be a comedy instead of the usual opera seria. It was not even a new libretto, but its author, the Venetian Carlo Goldoni, had by this time long since become not only Italy's most successful playwright, but also its premier author of comic librettos. He called his *La buona figliuola,* or *La Cecchina* as it was often titled, a *dramma giocoso.* Duni made the first setting of it in 1756–57 for Parma, where Goldoni was a guest. In his memoirs (1787) Goldoni says that Duni's setting was not as successful as it might have been because the Parmesan court did not get the best comic actor-singers. What he says next makes it appear that the composer chose the libretto, which would have been something of an anomaly for a still relatively young composer: "*La Bonne Fille* fut plus heureuse entre les mains de M. Piccini qui, étant chargés

---

[100]Barbara Dobbs Mackenzie, "The Creation of a Genre: Comic Opera's Dissemination in Italy in the 1740s" (Ph.D. diss., University of Michigan, 1993). See also Piero Weiss, "La diffusione del repertorio operistico nell'Italia del Settecento: il caso dell'opera buffa," *Civiltà teatrale e Settecento emiliano,* ed. Susi Davoli (Bologna, 1985), pp. 241–56.

[101]Ferdinando Galiani, *Del dialetto napoletane,* 2 vols. (Naples, 1779), 1: 1. Cited after Andrea della Corte, *Piccinni: settecento italiano* (Bari, 1928), p. 9.

quelques années après d'un opéra-comique pour Rome, préféra ce vieux drame à tous les nouveaux qu'on lui avait proposé."[102]

Jommelli, returned from Stuttgart to Italy for a visit in 1760, heard one of the performances of the new comedy in Rome, which prompted him to laud the composer in public: "questo é inventore!" (this man is a creator!).[103] *La buona figliuola* became the opera of the decade. None was performed more times or in more places. Piccinni's reputation, in consequence, soared above that of all others.

Goldoni derived *La buona figliuola* from Samuel Richardson's *Pamela* (1740), on which he had previously based a play, as had Voltaire.[104] The current of *sensibilité* running so strongly in England and France (with Pierre Claude Nivelle de La Chausée, Abbé Prévost, and Pierre Marivaux, as well as Voltaire) found a new home in Italian opera by way of Goldoni. To the credit of Piccinni, he seized at once upon the libretto's fine mixture of pathos and comedy, ensuring that the heroine, an orphaned girl against whom nearly all the characters turn, becomes a believable object of pity. Ginguené relates that the opera was composed in eighteen days, Piccinni being in total isolation except for two copyists. The overture in three movements is nothing special, and in general Piccinni's overtures do not come up to Jommelli's. The older composer, on the other hand, probably could not have found so simple and direct a means by which to introduce Cecchina in her first song. Alone in her garden she muses on the pleasure morning brings of gazing on roses competing with jasmine (Example 2.24). The way her voice joins the violin line after it starts lends her character an informality that has been aptly described as giving us the illusion of "slipping invisible into the privacy of Cecchina's thoughts."[105] We can also tell by the tune's melodic sighs that she is in love. At the measures marked *forte* the violins become independent of her vocal line, initiating the modulation to the dominant. Like an ordinary song, more than an aria, the piece has an **A B A** form. An opening air like this, without a preceding recitative, and folklike in its simplicity, had a long pedigree in the Neapolitan *commedia musicale.*

Goldoni next brings on Mengotto, a peasant who protests his love for Cecchina—his is a basso buffo role and he sings a song in two strophes to her. She cannot love him in turn because she is secretly in love with another, the Marchese, who arrives next and commands her to love him. Exit Cecchina hurriedly in a fluster of embarrassment. Sandrina, another servant, next appears complaining of her hard lot (she carries two baskets of fruit on her shoulders). Piccinni sets her song "Poverina, tutto il dì / Faticar deggio così!" (Poor me, all day I have to work like this) in the key of g, and we feel sympathy for her too. This

[102]Carlo Goldini, *Tutte le opere*, ed. Giuseppe Ortolani, 14 vols. (Milan, 1935–46), 1:378.
[103]Ginguené, *Notice sur la vie et les ouvrages de Nicolas Piccinni*, p. 16.
[104]William C. Holmes, "Pamela Transformed," *Musical Quarterly* 38 (1952): 581–94.
[105]Mary Hunter, "Pamela: The Offspring of Richardson's Heroine in Eighteenth-Century Opera," *Mosaic* 18 (1985): 61–77; 63.

EXAMPLE 2.24. *Piccinni*, La buona figliuola, *Cavatina*

could be considered a mistake, for she will soon turn into a mean little creature who, together with the other maidservant, Paoluccia, torments Cecchina. But she has reason to turn sour, having believed the Marchese had eyes for her, only to learn from his confiding in her that he loves Cecchina. Besides, Sandrina will eventually marry the good Mengotto, so she needs to be seen in a sympathetic light somewhere. When the Marchese's haughty sister Lucinda gets wind of his love for a commoner she raises a row, as does her lover the Cavalier Armidoro— these are both seria parts. The Marchesa dismisses Cecchina from her service.

Dismayed and weeping, Cecchina sings "Una povera ragazza, / Padre e Madre che non hà" (A poor girl who has neither father nor mother). Piccinni sets this to a tune in lilting 6/8 time that approaches folk song in its simple structure (Example 2.25). The first violins initially sing the tune high up while the seconds have an insistent rustling figure in quick notes that lends the music a serialike quality, then they join her at pitch. Landing on a modal degree, the supertonic, for the second chord, anticipates a fashion that will persist in opera all the way to Bellini's "Casta Diva" in *Norma* and beyond. The tritones to which Cecchina sings "Si maltratta si strapazza" (So mistreated, so abused) are identical to those sung by Serpina at "Ah! poverina" in *La serva padrona* (Example 2.11).

Goldoni has so deftly shaded both the comic and serious elements in this opera that Piccinni was able to achieve a great variety of musical effects. The chattering servant girls are unforgettable. Characterization of the blustering German soldier Tagliaferro, who eventually saves the day by revealing that Cecchina is noble-born, is masterly and thrilling. Tagliaferro's German-Italian dialect may seem somewhat exotic now, but in Goldoni's day Italy was full of itinerant military men from the Habsburg empire. The seria characters rage and burn in displays of high dudgeon. But it was Cecchina's music that made this opera so epochal. Piccinni himself is said to have praised the variety and originality offered by the work. Ginguené in his biography sang the praises in particular of "les pleintes douces et touchantes de Cecchina."

Johann Adam Hiller astutely pointed out in 1768 that the pair of seria characters in Italian comic operas, and the slightly more demanding level of singing technique required by their roles, characterized the latest stage works, following in the wake of *La buona figliuola*.

> Now Piccinni dominates the comic stage and seems, through the great quantity of his operas, to be nearly exhausting the possibilities of innovation in that department. Not so simple melodically as Pergolesi, less comical than Galuppi or Cocchi, he seems more inclined to be naive and tender. He has pieces as touching as we might hope to hear in a serious opera, at least in one by an Italian. Lest it should be thought that the serious opera is quite forgotten, the Italians now never fail to introduce in their comic operas a pair of serious characters who would prompt as much yawning as the others do laughter, were it not that their somewhat better style of singing attracts a modicum of attention.[106]

By 1768 Piccinni had in fact composed more than sixty operas. Many were still to come.

Burney in his *History* claims that *La buona figliuola* "had a success that no

---

[106]Johann Adam Hiller, *Wöchentliche Nachrichten und Anmerkungen die Musik betreffend,* 5 vols. (22 August 1768), 3: no. 8; translated by Piero Weiss in *Music in the Western World: A History in Documents,* ed. Piero Weiss and Richard Taruskin (New York, 1984), p. 282.

EXAMPLE 2.25. *Piccinni*, La buona figliuola, *Aria*

musical drama could boast before. It was no sooner heard at Rome than copies were multiplied, and there was no musical theater in Europe where this burletta was not frequently performed, in some language or other, during many years." London heard it in English in 1767, with spoken dialogue instead of recitative, in a production at Covent Garden that purported to be the "first attempt of bringing an entire Italian musical composition on the English stage, by applying our language to the harmony of their most eminent composer."[107]

Ginguené claimed that a newer type of duet had replaced the old da capo form advocated by Rousseau and exemplified by Pergolesi's duet in *L'Olimpiade*. In the newer type there were two tempos, a slower one for the initial expression of gentle sentiments followed by a faster, energetic one, without reverting to the initial tempo. Here we have the ancestor of the sentimental rondo in two tempos that was allowed only to the prima donna or primo uomo in Italian operas, a vogue that spread in the 1770s and peaked in the 1780s.

> It was M. Piccinni who first dared depart from the beaten paths of the past, and who hazarded at first some arias, and then duets in this form that was so favorable to expression. The success of this novelty, which he employed, I believe in his first setting of *Olimpiade,* at Rome in 1760 or 1761, engaged other masters to adopt it. Every opera lover has his duet "Ne' giorni tuoi felice," and can compare it with those composed earlier by Pergolesi, Jommelli, and Galuppi. They will see in M. Piccinni not only a new form but a new style, one rescued from the remains of pedantry and scholasticism from which the others were still not free. Let them compare then the same duet in the same opera as set by Sacchini, Anfossi, and many other masters. They will recognize the same *marche* for which Piccinni provided the model.[108]

Piccinni set his first *L'Olimpiade* for the Teatro delle Dame during the Roman carnival of 1761, his second for Rome in 1768, revived at Naples in 1774.

BURNEY AT THE OPERA

Burney encountered recent operas by Piccinni during his Italian journey of 1770. On 3 September in Florence he reports:

> I went to the little theatre *di via Santa Maria,* to hear the comic opera of *La Pescatrice,* composed by Signor Piccini. There are but four characters in this drama, two of which were represented by Signora Giovanna Baglioni, and her sister Costanza, whom I had heard at Milan; the other two were Signor Paolo Bonaveri, a good tenor, and Signor Constantino Ghigi. Costanza Baglioni appeared here to much greater advantage than

---

[107]Holmes, "Pamela Transformed," p. 591.
[108]Pierre Louis Ginguené, "Duo," in *Encyclopédie méthodique: musique,* ed. N. E. Framery and P. L. Ginguené, vol. 1 (Paris, 1791).

at Milan, where the theatre is of such a size as to require the lungs of a Stentor to fill it. She sung very well; her voice is clear, and always in tune, her shake open and perfect, and her taste and expression left nothing to wish in the songs she had to sing. She was extremely applauded; the house was very much crowded, the band was good, and the music worthy of Signor Piccini; full of that fire and fancy which characterise all the productions of that ingenious and original composer.

Three days later Burney praised the same cast in another opera in two acts by Piccinni, *Le donne vendicate,* and noted that each act was followed by *balli pantomimi* that were almost as long as the acts of the opera.

In Naples itself Burney was not so pleased with the singing and he regretted the lack of dances at the Fiorentini theater. In 1741 King Charles banished comic intermezzi as entr'actes in the San Carlo, substituting ballets, and at the same time forbade dancing to the smaller theaters, which he never attended. His principal musical interest was in ballet, not opera. His third son succeeded him when he was eight years old and took the name of King Ferdinand IV when he came of age in 1767; he married Archduchess Maria Carolina of Austria in 1768. This pair did not shun the smaller theaters in Naples; thus it seems strange that the old ban against dancing was not lifted. Like her mother, Maria Theresa, Maria Carolina was strong-willed and succeeded in creating her own faction at court. By 1776 she forced the first minister, Bernardo Tenucci, into retirement.

Burney betook himself to the theater the very first night he was in Naples.

I arrived here about five o'clock in the evening, on Tuesday, October 16, and at night went to the *Teatro de' Fiorentini,* to hear the comic opera of [Lorenzi's] *Gelosia per Gelosia,* set to music by Signor Piccini. This theatre is as small as Mr. Foote's in London, but higher, as there are five rows of boxes in it. Notwithstanding the court was at Portici, and a great number of families were at their *Villeggiatura's,* or country-houses, so great is the reputation of Signor Piccini, that every part of the house was crowded. Indeed this opera had nothing else but the merit and reputation of the composer to support it, as both the drama and singing were bad.

Burney goes on to praise the comic acting of one Signor Casaccia, which excited gales of laughter, then concludes: "The airs of this burletta are full of pretty passages, and, in general, most ingeniously accompanied: there was no dancing, so that the acts, of which there were three, seemed rather long."

Two nights later Burney went to the Teatro Nuovo, where he witnessed a comic opera by a potent younger rival of Piccinni, the thirty-year-old Paisiello.

This house is not only less than the *Fiorentini,* but is older and more dirty. The way to it, for carriages, is through streets very narrow, and inconvenient. This burletta was called *Le Trame per Amore,* and set by Signor Giovanni Paisiello, *Maestro di Capella Napolitano.* The singing was but indifferent; there were nine characters in the piece, and yet not one good voice among them; however, the music pleased me very much; it was full of fire and fancy, the ritornels abounding in new passages, and the vocal parts in elegant and simple melodies, such as might be remembered and carried away after the first hearing, or be performed in private by a small band, or even without any other instrument than a harpsichord.

This thought leads him to a comparison with Piccinni's scoring, which he found heavier.

Indeed Piccini is accused of employing instruments to such excess, that in Italy no copist will transcribe one of his operas without being paid a sequin more than for one by any other composer. But in burlettas he has generally bad voices to write for, and is obliged to produce all his effects with instruments; and, indeed, this kind of drama usually abounds with brawls and *squabbles,* which it is necessary to enforce with the orchestra.

He means here the long and noisy buffo finales, by this time entrenched in Naples, as everywhere else. He continued on Paisiello:

The overture to the burletta of tonight, consisting of one movement only, was quite comic, and contained a perpetual succession of pleasant passages. There was no dancing, which made it necessary to spin the acts out to a rather tiresome length. The airs were much applauded, though it was the fourteenth representation of the opera. The author was engaged to compose for Turin, at the next carnival, for which place he set out while I was at Naples. The performance began about a quarter before eight, and continued till past eleven o'clock.

Burney's observations are invaluable because their like can be found almost nowhere else.

Burney correctly surmised that Piccinni and Paisiello had entered into a contest for supremacy with the Neapolitan public. On Monday, 21 October, he was back in the Teatro Nuovo for another performance of the latter's comedy.

It pleased me full as much now as before, and in the same places. The overture still seemed comic and original, the airs far from common, though in general plain and simple. If this composer has any fault, it is in repeating passages too often, even to five or six times, which is like driving a nail into a plaistered wall; two or three strokes fix it better than more, for after that number, it either grows loose, or recoils; thus an energy is often given by reiterated strokes on the tympanum; but too often repeated, they not only cease to make any further impression, but seem to obliterate those already made. I still think this opera too long for want of the *intermezzi* of dancing.

Here he adds a note saying he was informed only later that dancing was prohibited in any theater at Naples except the San Carlo.

Three days later, on 24 October, Burney returned to the Fiorentini theater and made a direct comparison.

> I went again this evening to Piccini's opera, but was too late for the overture; the house was very full, and the music pleased me more than the first time. The airs are not so familiar as those in Paisiello's opera, yet there is much better writing in them; and there are some accompanied recitatives, in the ritornels of which, though several different parts are going on at the same time, there is clearness, and, if it may be so called, a *transparency*, which is wonderful. The singing, as I observed before, is wretched.

Thus the palm for writing more correctly and keeping distinct various voices in the part writing went to Piccinni. But were these necessarily virtues with the general public of opera goers? Piccinni's years in Naples were drawing to a close, and Paisiello's melodic gift of seeming "familiarities" had something to do with the decision of the older composer to move on.

GALIANI'S LETTERS

Taking up the tale where Burney left off was the erudite Abate Ferdinando Galiani, born in 1728, the same year as Piccinni. He was secretary to the Neapolitan legation in Paris during the 1760s, when he formed numerous friendships with the *philosophes* and particularly with Madame Louise d'Epinay, novelist, mistress of Melchior Grimm, and coeditor with him of the *Correspondance littéraire*. Galiani was also the author of learned treatises on the Neapolitan economy, such as *Della moneta* (1751) and *Dialogues sur le commerce de blés* (1770). He was called back to Naples in 1769. Around 1770 he began a campaign to promote Piccinni's interests in letters to Madame d'Epinay. He wrote her on 15 June 1771: "He [Piccinni] has attained the summit of perfection in art. . . . Believe me, this opera of Piccinni is something of which you have no idea, it is so superior to everything you have ever heard."[109] The allusion must be to *La donna di bell'umore* given at the Fiorentini in May 1771. Madame d'Epinay replied asking for a copy of the opera in question, to which he replied, somewhat coyly,

> Not until you know Neapolitan, without which you would not understand a word, or appreciate any of the beauty. It would be impossible for you to understand from this masterpiece the heights to which Piccinni has pushed our comic opera. Have no fear that his Neapolitan operas will travel to France. This has never happened; they do not even travel as far as Rome. You will have his comic operas in Italian, such as *Buona figliuola*, but none of his Neapolitan ones. To convince you I shall send one or two pieces with an explanation in Italian or French, and you will see that it is necessary to come to Naples to hear this.

---

[109]*Correspondance inédite de l'Abbé Ferdinando Galiani* (Paris, 1818), cited after Della Corte, *Piccinni: settecento italiano*, p. 68. Subsequent citations are from his pp. 68–74.

Neapolitan comic opera did travel to Rome, but revised as to the roles in dialect.

By letter of 13 May 1772 Galiani informed Madame d'Epinay that the arias she requested from the grand opera [San Carlo] of that season could not be sent because they were so detestable.

> On the other hand we have excellent comic operas, two by Piccinni and two by Paisiello. Those by the latter are superior even to those by the former, who is starting to grow old. There is no way of sending you anything of Paisiello, because it is too Neapolitan; I send you thus an aria of Piccinni that could have been placed as well in a serious as in a comic opera.

From this it sounds as if Galiani's admiration for Piccinni was waning because of Paisiello's greater comic verve. In the spring of 1772 Piccinni composed the *farsa Gli amanti dispersi* for the Fiorentini theater, while Paisiello was represented at the Nuovo by a setting of Francesco Cerlone's *commedia musicale, La Dardané.*

Piccinni had another challenger in the person of Anfossi, who, although a year older, emerged as an opera composer about a decade later. Anfossi studied composition, with Piccinni and Sacchini, only after years of playing the violin in one of the smaller Neapolitan theaters. Piccinni helped him to get commissions to write operas. There was a sudden craze among the notoriously fickle Roman public for Anfossi after 1773, and once Piccinni found himself hissed by a cabal, or so he told Ginguené. Anfossi's setting of *La finta giardiniera* for Rome did have a public success during the Roman carnival of 1774 and it traveled to several other cities, including Vienna. Mozart's incomparably finer setting of the same libretto followed in early 1775.

In 1774 Piccinni regained favor with his second setting of *Alessandro nell'Indie* for the San Carlo to celebrate the king's birthday on 12 January. Critics praised it as his best and most mature serious opera. Galiani wrote to Madame d'Epinay on 15 February 1774: "Piccinni has just given to our grand theater an opera that surpasses everything heard up to this time as to good music. Gluck's *Orfeo,* given at the same time at court, was furiously eclipsed by it." The Gluck-Piccinni controversy of the late 1770s in Paris may have begun right here. In fact *Orfeo ed Euridice* pleased at court, as one could have expected from the tastes of its Austrian queen, Maria Carolina. *Orfeo* was repeated the following November at the San Carlo.[110]

Particularly acclaimed in Piccinni's *Alessandro* was the duet for Poro (Gasparo Pacchierotti) and Cleofide (Anna Lucia De Amicis) ending Act I, "Se mai turbo il tuo riposo." The piece is in A and in three tempos, getting progressively faster, with no da capo. Each singer begins with simple, affecting music but soon bursts

[110]Both productions were padded with music by other composers. See Robinson, *Naples and Neapolitan Opera,* pp. 66–68.

into elaborate coloratura, which the two also sing together in thirds. Vocal display of this showy kind exposes the enormous gulf then existing between opera seria and tragédie-lyrique. In early 1774 Piccinni was approached by La Borde with an invitation to Paris. Galiani even wrote Madame d'Epinay on 14 May 1774 announcing the composer's departure.

> Piccinni will leave us, without blame, in order to go to you. He is worthy of knowing you personally. His wife sings very prettily. It is said that M. de La Borde on his return from Italy, spoke of him with Madame la contese Du Bary, and she is the one who engaged him to come, with conditions very lucrative to him; he decided to do so. Everyone is upset about his departure, but no one offered ten cents to make him stay.

It may be recalled that Piccinni had held the minor court post of second organist since 1771, and that he was not fully paid for it during his absences, which were frequent. What Galiani did not know was that Louis XV died on 10 May 1774, which led to the rapid banishment of his last mistress, Madame Du Barry. The Neapolitan ambassador to Paris persisted in furthering Piccinni's appointment, and permission to leave Naples was sought in 1775 and again in 1776. It finally came on 9 November 1776. The royal ordinance stipulated one year's leave of absence with pay, but with deduction of two ducats for payment to his substitute, Paolo Orgitano.[111] On 2 November 1776 Galiani wrote d'Epinay: "We shall send you Piccinni in two weeks, along with his wife, a good, amiable, and sweet person who sings perfectly and who will please you. As for him, he is a kind of Duni: his conversation does not come up to his compositions, but he is a very honest man and I strongly recommend him to you." They began their long arduous trip to Paris on 16 November 1776 and arrived on 31 December.

Why did Piccinni leave Naples for Paris? This is a question actually posed in a furious letter written by Gluck on 15 January 1777. Piccinni's modern biographer offers two simple but adequate answers: because he had begun to lose public favor to Paisiello; and because he needed more money in order to support his large family.[112] The Opéra wanted an Italian composer to pit against Gluck, to which desire the court, including Gluck's former pupil, Queen Marie Antoinette, acquiesced. Doubts arise as to whether Piccinni was the best choice for the task. Jommelli, had he lived, would have exerted more force in mastering the situation. Traetta had much more experience than Piccinni in meeting the demands of French-style grand opera. Galiani believed that Paisiello would have been a better choice. Sacchini, then enjoying success in London, would have been an excellent choice, as he later proved to be.

---

[111]Dietz, "A Chronology of Maestri and Organisti," p. 395.
[112]Della Corte, *Piccinni*, p. 85.

Galiani, relegated to the position of being a far-distant observer of the celebrated quarrel between *Gluckistes* and *Piccinnistes,* fretted about the honor of the Neapolitan School, and whether Piccinni was energetic enough to sustain it. When he learned that Grétry had not paid Piccinni the honor of a visit, he wrote in a letter of 30 November 1777 to Marmontel: "What did Piccinni do to this *Liégois?*[113] One answer, leaving aside Grétry's devotion to Gluck's works for the Opéra, is that Grétry was treated coldly as a student in Rome when he first went to see Piccinni, according to an anecdote from Grétry's memoirs. In addition to writing his grand operas for Paris, Piccinni took charge of a season of opera buffa, directing a troupe of Italians at the Opéra in 1778–79. Besides his own works he directed performances of comic operas by Anfossi, Paisiello, Sacchini, and Traetta. The experiment was a failure and was not repeated. Galiani fumed at this in a letter to a friend dated Naples, 7 November 1778, which led him to another comparison.

> Paisiello is infinitely stronger than Piccinni in counterpoint; thus he is sure to succeed, aiding his nature with the art. Yet there are pieces produced by nature alone that come from Piccinni, pieces that neither Paisiello nor anyone else will ever equal. The duet in *Buona figliuola* and the duet in *Alessandro* and a certain quintet in a Neapolitan comedy entitled *I viaggiatori* [1775] are three pieces that will never be surpassed. But these pieces are rare, as you say. Piccinni is not always sure to succeed. Paisiello is so strong in music that he can draw advantage from everything.[114]

FIGURE 2.12. Anonymous portrait of Niccolò Piccinni.

That Piccinni was weaker in counterpoint than Paisiello is doubtful and goes directly counter to Burney's reaction that the former's opera of 1770 was distinguished by "better writing."

In disposition Piccinni was a mild-mannered person, in physique short and thin, quite the opposite of Jommelli and Gluck, who were large, of fiery temperament, and legendary for their dictatorial ways with orchestras and singers. An

[113]Cited by Della Corte, ibid., p. 87, n. 1.
[114]Ibid., p. 92, n. 3.

anonymous engraved portrait perhaps does justice to his fine features (Figure 2.12). Burney gave his readers what was then called a "character" of the composer upon their first meeting on 18 October 1770.

> This morning I visited Signor Piccini, and had the pleasure of a long conversation with him. He seems to live in a reputable way, has a good house, and many servants and attendants about him. He is not more than four or five and forty; looks well, has a very animated countenance, and is a polite and agreeable little man, though rather grave in his manner for a Neapolitan possessed of so much fire and genius. His family is rather numerous; one of his sons is a student in the university of Padua. After reading a letter which Mr. Giardini was so obliging as to give me to him, he told me that he should be extremely glad if he could be of any use either to me or to my work.

Piccinni then answered Burney's questions about the conservatories of Naples, as we saw earlier. If he lacked the extroversion that Burney expected him to possess, he was nonetheless a patient and generous guide to the musical lore of Naples.

3

Venice

Tributaries, Rivals, Polity

*T*HE polar attraction of Naples as a musical center was matched in Italy during the eighteenth century only by Venice. Although the Most Serene Republic was at the end of a centuries-old economic and territorial decline, one that would come to an ignominious conclusion with its collapse at the approach of Napoleon's troops in 1797, the final century was one of its most brilliant, at least in the visual and musical arts. Venice's far-flung possessions in the eastern Mediterranean, along with its maritime trade, had long been lost, but there remained the solid block of territory on the mainland that stretched from the Adriatic to the Alps, and westward into Lombardy as far as Brescia, Bergamo, and Crema, three cities conquered in the fifteenth century (Figure 3.1). The three states across the top of this 1768 map are Savoy-Piedmont, imperial Lombardy, and Venice.

Venice's provinces amounted to more than just a hinterland that paid taxes. The upper Po valley was particularly rich in music history. Crema, Brescia, and Bergamo, along with Cremona, were the site of epochal changes connected with the rise of the violin and its perfection by the greatest makers. Vivaldi's forebears lived for generations in Brescia; only in 1665 did they move to Venice. Besides Vivaldi, père Brescia produced Biagio Marini, the Pollarolo family, Vincenzo Pallavicini, Benedetto Vinaccesi, and Ferdinando Bertoni. Bergamo was the birthplace of Giovanni Legrenzi, Pietro Locatelli, Antonio Lolli, and Gaetano

Donizetti. From Crema came Francesco Cavalli. Giuseppe Tartini was born in Pirano on the Istrian peninsula and resided for most of his life in Padua, where Giovanni Platti and Giuseppe Paganelli were born. Tartini's connections with the capital city were strong and manifold, as was the case with all those individual subjects of the Venetian Republic just mentioned.

The last century of Venice's independence encompassed a resurgence in the visual arts and music that has been compared with the glories achieved during the sixteenth century. Continuity of tradition favored this final sunset burst during the *settecento*. Relatively peaceful and plague-free times allowed Venice to become a mecca for wealthy tourists second to none. These visitors not only kept the art market afloat with their purchases and commissions, they also helped maintain Venice as the European capital of musical performance, especially of opera and instrumental music. Another part in Venetian eminence was played by the simultaneous decline in musical importance of three rival cities that had been leading centers during the seventeenth century: Rome, Florence, and Bologna.

Rome and Naples had long enjoyed a cultural and political symbiosis, the former city prevailing in music up until about 1720, when the latter became preeminent. The last era of Rome's greatness in music was due to Cardinal Pietro Ottoboni, patron of Arcangelo Corelli and a host of other musicians. In this environment Locatelli matured from age 15 to 27. Largely forgotten Roman composers such as the Bencinis, Girolomo Chiti, and Pompeo Canniciari were among those who provided the city's major churches with music. The long-lived Giuseppe Pitoni (born in 1657 and died in 1743) was renowned as a teacher and contrapuntist. Others who followed him at Rome included Giovanni Battista Costanzi, who taught Luigi Boccherini for several months in 1757, and Giovanni Battista Casali, with whom Grétry studied counterpoint for two years in the early 1760s. Given the great wealth and power of the papal city, it is odd that many more young musicians destined for fame did not emerge from its innumerable churches and collegiate institutions. The massive amount of sacred music produced in Rome had little export value, while the city's operatic life depended mainly upon imports, mostly from Naples, but also from Venice (Vivaldi, Galuppi, and Bertoni).

Florence slipped into mediocrity as a musical center under the last Medici grand duke, Gian Gastone, who ruled from 1723 until his death in 1737. A consortium of noblemen ran the opera, which depended heavily on Venetian and Neapolitan composers, whose works were often altered for local performance by the prolific maestro di cappella of the court, Giuseppe Maria Orlandini, who was born in Florence in 1675 and died there in 1760. Conditions did not improve under the next grand duke, Francis of Lorraine. He made only one visit to Florence, early in a reign lasting from 1737 to 1765. As Francis I, ruler of the Holy Roman Empire and consort of Maria Theresa, he had more than enough to do in

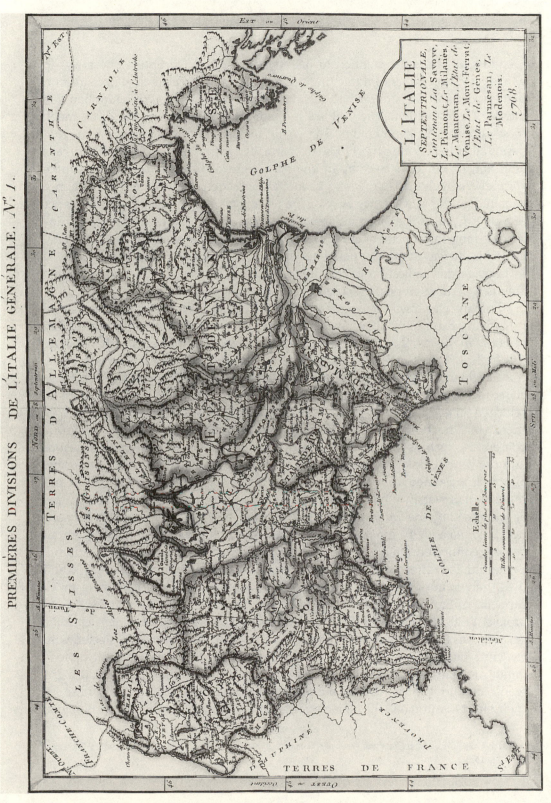

FIGURE 3.1. Northern Italian states in 1768. Map from *Cosmographie Universelle*, 1770.

Vienna and paid little attention to Tuscany. If anything, Florentine opera was in worse condition under him than in the previous reign, because final decisions on matters of financial support had to come from Vienna instead of being handled locally.[1] Carlo Goldoni practiced law in Tuscany during the 1740s and has much to say about it in his memoirs. The vogue for his plays and comic operas that swept all of Italy during the 1750s was particularly strong in Florence, which calls attention to the absence there of any playwright or librettist of commensurate stature. When Grand Duke Pietro Leopoldo succeeded his father in 1765 Florence acquired a ruler in residence once again. During his reign, which lasted a quarter of a century, he took a direct interest in the court music and restored some of Florence's long-lost operatic glory. His favorite composer was Tommaso Traetta. Raised as he was at the Viennese court, he was also partial to Gluck and received in homage the dedication of the printed score to *Alceste* (1769). Efforts to gain Traetta a permanent post in Florence did not succeed.

Bologna was briefly one of Italy's most important centers of music because of its thriving band of violinists and composers associated with the basilica of San Petronio in the last third of the seventeenth century. They played a path-breaking role in the emergence of the concerto grosso and solo concerto. By the turn of the century financial restrictions caused San Petronio to lose many of its best musicians, including the outstanding violinist-composer Giuseppe Torelli, although he returned for a few years after touring northern Europe. With Torelli's death in 1709 there were no Bolognese luminaries left comparable to the brilliant violinist-composers, such as Vivaldi, Tartini, and Locatelli, who were emerging in Venice and the Veneto. Bologna was one of the papal states, actually ruled from Rome, although it claimed to be self-governed by a local senate. Because of its old and renowned university it had long been a center of learning, even musical learning, as witnessed by the founding of a chair of music in 1450. To this academic tradition Bologna added a reputation as a leading center for the training of singers, an activity connected mainly with the contraltos Francesco Pistocchi and Antonio Bernacchi. The latter settled in Bologna after his stage career was over in 1736 and died there twenty years later. The long-lived Giacomo Antonio Perti, maestro di cappella of San Petronio for sixty years and an active composer at least until around 1720, also died in 1756. Pier Francesco Tosi's *Opinioni de' cantori antichi e moderni* was first published in Bologna in 1723. Like many things connected with the city's musical life, it looked backward rather than forward. The Galli-Bibiena family of theatrical architects and engineers came from Bologna. By the mid-eighteenth century the younger members were reaping more blame than praise for their efforts. Antonio Galli-Bibiena designed the Teatro Communale in Bologna,

---

[1] William C. Holmes, *Opera Observed: Views of a Florentine Impresario in the Early Eighteenth Century* (Chicago, 1993), p. 158.

which was built from 1755 to 1757, then, due to financial difficulties, waited several years for its opening (in 1763, with Gluck's *Il trionfo di Clelia*). Bologna was also the permanent abode of the learned Padre Martini, who instructed Jommelli, Bertoni, and Christian Bach among many others. A more potent musical rival to Venice than Bologna was Milan, which is discussed below in connection with Giovanni Battista Sammartini.

Venice reigned supreme over all *settecento* Italy in the visual arts. In the field of drama Goldoni reclaimed a leading role for Venice with his comedies. No Venetian composer attained quite such a dominant position on the stage as Goldoni, but Vivaldi and Galuppi often gave their best efforts in the attempt. As to its concert and operatic life, Venice retained and even enhanced the primacy it had achieved earlier. The musical efflorescence of the four *ospedali grandi* of Venice, an eighteenth-century phenomenon, assured the superiority of Venetian concerts and secured the means to hire as music directors the most eminent composers, many of them born or trained in Naples.

Visitors to Venice in the last decades of the republic have left many impressions of the city in the form of letters and diaries. Few fail to mention the extent of music making they observed. The canals offered floating serenades that prompted Charles de Brosses to write, "Not a single evening goes by without a concert somewhere. The people run along the canal to hear it. . . . You cannot imagine how crazy the city is about this art" (1: 242). Burney came thirty years after Brosses and made a surmise as to why there was so much music in Venice: being water bound, the citizens lacked the usual outlets for physical exercise.

> Many circumstances concur to render music in Venice better, and more general than elsewhere. The Venetians have few amusements but what the theatres afford; walking, riding, and all field-sports, are by the situation of their city denied them. This, in some degree, accounts for music being so much, and in so costly a manner, cultivated by them; the number too of theatres, in all of which the Gondoliers have admission gratis, may account for the superior manner in which they sing compared with people of the same class elsewhere. And in private families, into which the girls of the Conservatorios marry, it is natural to suppose that good taste and a love for music are introduced.

Burney may exaggerate as to the number of theaters still operating in 1770. He was told that "during the last Carnival, there were seven opera-houses open at once in Venice, three serious, and four comic, besides four play-houses, and these were crowded every night." Printed librettos do not bear out these numbers. They show only the San Benedetto offering opera seria, while opera buffa was staged at the San Cassiano and San Moisé.

Politics present a less rosy picture than Venetian cultural life. Venice was a sacral state ruled by a small oligarchy of ancient noble families, headed by the doge, whom they elected, just as the College of Cardinals elected the pope. Their system of government went back to early medieval times and derived from the Byzantine Empire, whose ruler was head of both state and church. The basilica of San Marco was the doge's personal chapel as well as the state church. This arrangement was bound to collide with the claims of the Vatican to supremacy, and collide the two often did over the centuries. Yet Venice retained its position as a distinct church state partly beyond the jurisdiction of the pope to the very end of the republic. Not that papal authority went unrepresented in Venice, for there was a cathedral, San Pietro di Castello, whose bishop, appointed by the pope, held the title of patriarch. As far as the history of music is concerned, the cathedral meant little, but the basilica of San Marco was at the very center of European music from the sixteenth century through several generations. Burney's first remarks upon the city take cognizance of its long musical history and other claims to superior status.

> The church of St. Marc has had a constant supply of able masters, from Adriano [Willaert], Zarlino's predecessor, to Galuppi, its present worthy composer. Venice has likewise been one of the first cities in Europe that has cultivated the musical drama or opera: and in the graver stile, it has been honoured with a Lotti and a Marcello. Add to these advantages the *conservatorios* established here, and the songs of the *Gondolieri*, or Watermen, which are so celebrated, that every musical collector of taste in Europe is well furnished with them, and it will appear that my expectations were not ill grounded.

Forerunners of Galuppi as maestri di capella or organists of San Marco that Burney might also have mentioned include the Gabrieli, Andrea and his nephew Giovanni, Claudio Merulo, Monteverdi, Cavalli, and Legrenzi.[2]

San Marco was governed by a body of procurators. It adjoined the ducal palace at the very heart of the city (unlike the cathedral, which was remote from the center). The choir of the basilica grew to include thirty-six members by the end of the seventeenth century, at the head of which was the maestro di cappella and the vice maestro. Orchestral forces witnessed a similar growth, beginning with a mainly wind ensemble but becoming dominated by stringed instruments during Legrenzi's tenure as maestro (1685–90). One of the main functions of the orchestra as a body independent of the voices was to provide an epistle sonata or concerto during the celebration of mass. The practice was required on certain feast days.[3] Full orchestra played on the feasts of San Pietro Orseolo (14 January), the Annunciation (25 March), Easter, San Marco (25 April), San Antonio da Padua (12

---

[2]Eleanor Selfridge-Field, *Venetian Instrumental Music from Gabrielli to Vivaldi* (Oxford, 1975), pp. 292–96.
[3]Ibid., pp. 18–25.

June), the Assumption (15 August), Christmas Eve, Christmas Day, the coronation of a doge, and its anniversaries. A number of feasts, including Pentecost, required only half orchestra. During a cappella masses on the following feast days the orchestra was required to perform after the reading of the Epistle: Epiphany (6 January), Purification of the Blessed Virgin Mary (2 February), Sant'Isidro (16 April), apparition of San Marco (25 June), All Saints (1 November), and Corpus Christi. The feast of the Ascension, celebrated forty days after Easter, required all the musical forces of the basilica to accompany the doge as he sallied forth on the Bucintoro annually in order to wed Venice once again to the sea.

The state church employed in all some eighty musicians during the last years of the republic. Individual choristers could work up to a maximum salary of 100 ducats per annum. Orchestral musicians, about the same in number as the chorus, earned much less. The maestro di capella received 400 ducats annually. From 1701 to 1732 the maestro was Antonio Biffi, and from 1736–1740 the renowned Antonio Lotti, teacher of Galuppi. In 1720 the well-traveled violinist and prolific composer Carlo Tessarini earned only 15 ducats a year in the orchestra of San Marco. A glamorous solo player, on the other hand, such as Francesco Veracini, earned this much and more for playing violin solos at the masses on Christmas Eve and Christmas Day in 1711. He returned in the same capacity a year later, and in 1713 he was listed as an attraction in Coronelli's guide to Venice. Two principal organists were employed by the basilica plus auxiliary organists for special occasions.[4]

At nonfestive daily services a small complement of singers without instruments sufficed. They sang mostly from the *bigonzo* (literally, the "tub"), an octagonal enclosed dais, which flanked the choir screen on each side. The elderly Antonio Canaletto made a superb drawing in 1766 of the singers in the *bigonzo* to the right of the choir screen (Figure 3.2). A similar octagonal structure can still be seen in Santa Sophia at Istanbul.

From the surviving evidence it has been possible to deduce by brilliant detective work the answers to several questions about the nature of musical performance at mass and vespers in the basilica.[5] Lists were compiled to instruct the musicians on their precise duties and posted in the sacristy. Then in 1761 a single large printed folio incorporated all the information.[6]

Regular employment at the state church was sought by the musicians of Venice as a matter of prestige, but for most it did not provide a living wage, nor were many hours of service demanded. Hence the widespread practice of work-

[4]On their duties see Michael Talbot, *Benedetto Vinaccesi: A Musician in Brescia and Venice in the Age of Corelli* (Oxford, 1994), pp. 97–99.

[5]James H. Moore, *Vespers at St. Mark's: Music of Alessandro Grandi, Giovanni Rouetta and Francesco Cavalli*, 2 vols. (Ann Arbor, Mich., 1981), 1: 181–85.

[6]Ibid., 1: 302–7.

FIGURE 3.2. Antonio Canaletto. Singers in the basilica of San Marco, 1767.

ing at the same time for other churches, for the opera and playhouses, and most notably for the *ospedali*, which were also state institutions of a sort, each in its own individual and complicated way.

The *Ospedali*

The four *ospedali grandi* famous for their music were charitable institutions with origins that went back to the sixteenth century or earlier. The Pio Ospedale della Pietà was founded in 1346. This orphanage took in all abandoned infants, had them baptized, and branded them with a "P" before sending them out to wet nurses throughout the Veneto. At first the responsibility for rearing male children was taken over by a Franciscan monastery, while that for rearing females remained the charge of a women's sodality under the direction of a prioress. Financial legacies from 1475 enabled the institution to occupy its present site on the Riva degli Schiavoni. Only later did the specialization in music by female children come about.

The Ospedale di San Lazaro e dei Mendicanti had origins even earlier. Its special function was as a hospice for beggars and for the indigent in general. In the late sixteenth century it moved into a splendid new building on the northern shore of Venice's main island, the newly developed Fondamente Nuove (see Figure 3.9 on p. 261). It could hold four hundred adults and a hundred children and was constructed in the form of double monasteries, with the men's wing on the lagoon and the women's wing on its southern side, separated by a chapel in the middle.

Nearby was the Ospedale di Santa Maria dei Derelitti, adjoining the church of San Giovanni e Paolo, also known as the Ospedaletto. It accepted orphans who had lost both parents and boys of poor families who indentured themselves to serve in the Venetian navy, plus a number of aged or infirm persons.

The Ospedale degl'Incurabili was founded by members of some of Venice's oldest and richest families, hence it had a social cachet somewhat above its three sister institutions, even though its main purpose, originally, was to harbor the victims of such "incurable" diseases as leprosy and syphilis. Like the Mendicanti, it was constructed as a *monasterium duplex* surrounding a common chapel, and it was located on the Fondamente delle Zattere on the Canale della Giudecca, near the Chiesa dello Santo Spirito. Unlike the other three *ospedale grande*, which still remain as hospitals or charitable institutions in Venice today, the Incurabili was almost completely demolished in 1821. Its facade on the water remains.[7]

Music only gradually came to play a major role in the life of the *ospedali*, which were run like monastic institutions, although they were neither monasteries nor nunneries. A prioress assured the direction of the women's section, first at the Incurabili, then at the others.[8] It is still not clear when or why women were chosen for advanced training in music. Possibly the choice was another way of contravening the authority of the pope, who forbade female musicians to perform in public worship services, a ban effective at least in Rome and the church states. For whatever reasons, young men from the poorer classes who had good voices often got to exercise them as gondoliers, who provided the city with its main means of transportation. Young women from the lower social strata, if they were fortunate and had musical gifts, could hope to be trained for the *cori* of the *ospedali*. These were so successful by the end of the seventeenth century that some of the daughters of the aristocracy also took music lessons there, as well as

[7]See the illustrations of plans and elevations reproduced by Sven Hansell, "Sacred Music at the *Incurabili* in Venice at the Time of J. A. Hasse," *JAMS* 23 (1970): 282–301, 505–21; 518–20.
[8]Jane L. Baldauf-Berdes, *Women Musicians of Venice: Musical Foundations, 1525–1855* (Oxford, 1996), pp. 53–54.

paying students from Venice and elsewhere. By 1700 at the latest the female choirs were fully established as concert-giving organizations, open to the public as such, albeit the choir was hidden from view by grillwork and screens to preserve decorum. In 1698 a Russian visitor to Venice, Count Piotr Tolstoy, claimed that people came from all parts of the world to be refreshed by the angelic singing of the cloistered women, and above all, those at the Incurabili.[9]

One of the most intriguing descriptions of the *ospedali* was made by the English traveler Edward Wright, who visited Venice in the early 1720s. He cites a very high number of souls for the Pietà, but this would have included all the infants farmed out to wet nurses throughout the Veneto.

> Those put into the Pietà are generally Bastards. There are a prodigious number of Children taken care of in this Hospital: they say they amount sometimes to at least six thousand; and that before the Erection of this Charity, Multitudes us'd to be found which had been thrown into the Canals of the City. Every *Sunday* and *Holiday* there is a performance of Musick in the Chapels of these Hospitals, Vocal and Instrumental, perform'd by the young Women of the Place: who are set in a Gallery above, and (tho' not profess'd) are hid from any distinct View of those below, by a Lattice of Iron-work. The Organ-parts, as well as those of other Instruments, are all perform'd by the young Women. They have an Eunuch for their Master, and he composes their Musick. Their Performance is surprisingly good; and many excellent Voices are among them: and there is something still more amusing in that their Persons are conceal'd from View.[10]

The eunuch in question who composed music for the Pietà is sometimes taken to be Vivaldi, but the dates are wrong for him since he was mainly in Mantua from 1718 to 1720. In 1719 the authorities of the Pietà finally got around to replacing Francesco Gasparini as *maestro di coro* by appointing Carlo Luigi Pietro Grua, recruited from distant Düsseldorf. Librettos refer to Grua as a Florentine and he sang contralto in the Hofkapelle at the Saxon court in 1691, which leaves open the possibility that he was in fact a castrato or, as Wright says, "an Eunuch."

Instrumental music was confined at first to the organ. In the course of the seventeenth century various other instruments were added to the all-women ensembles, until the *cori* were finally able to field full-fledged symphonic bands.[11] In his letters about Venice of 1739 Charles de Brosses explained:

> The transcendent music is that of the ospedali. There are four of these, made up of illegitimate and orphaned girls and those whose parents are not in a position to raise

[9]Walter Kolneder, *Antonio Vivaldi,* trans. B. Hopkins (Berkeley and Los Angeles, 1970), pp. 10–11.

[10]Edward Wright, *Some Observations Made in Travelling through France, Italy . . . in the Years 1720, 1721 and 1722,* 2 vols. (London, 1730), 1: 79.

[11]Baldauf-Berdes, *Women Musicians of Venice,* pp. 169–71.

them. They are brought up at the expense of the state and trained solely to excel in music. They sing like angels and play the violin, the flute, the organ, the oboe, the cello, and the bassoon. . . . They are cloistered like nuns. . . . About forty girls take part in each concert. (1: 243)

Teachers of stringed and woodwind instruments were hired from outside the *ospedali,* with supplementary instruction given by older members of the *cori.* The *cori* came to resemble modern conservatories of music. Alms from the public concerts and numerous bequests helped them expand, and state support was constant.

Financial success led to the hiring of music directors from outside Venice. One of the first and most distinguished was Giovanni Legrenzi, who worked for the Mendicanti before becoming the maestro di cappella of San Marco in 1682. Legrenzi was not quite the outsider he has been made out to be. As a native of Bergamo he was a subject of the Most Serene Republic. A true outsider was appointed music director by the Pietà in 1701, Francesco Gasparini, a Tuscan who was born in 1661 and came to Venice after successes in the opera houses of Rome and Naples. He accepted a stipend of quite modest size, 200 ducats annually, for directing the Pietà. His major income came from a string of successful operas written for the Venetian theaters, mainly the San Cassiano, from 1702 to 1711. He engaged Vivaldi as violin master of the Pietà and presided over one of its finest periods.

Prominent composers and teachers such as Gasparini not only brought new glory to music at the *ospedadi,* they encouraged even patrician families to send young women for musical instruction. Such was the case with one of the best and most famous sopranos from Venice, Faustina Bordoni, born in 1697. Under the patronage of the Marcellos, she studied as a paying student from an early age at the Pietà. By the age of seventeen, Faustina was already embarked on an international operatic career, and in 1730 she married Hasse. Rosalba Carriera depicted her youthful charms in a pastel portrait from 1724 (Plate V).

The influx of Neapolitans brought singers as well as composers.[12] It spread from the opera houses of Venice to the *ospedali.* Nicola Porpora led the way, becoming master of the Incurabili in 1726, a position he retained until 1733 and occupied again in 1737–38. As the most reputed of singing teachers, Porpora was always in demand, and he returned to Venice to serve as master of the Pietà in 1742–44 and of the Derelitti in 1744–47. Hasse had a long connection with the Incurabili, beginning as a consultant from ca. 1727 to 1733 and serving many times in this capacity or as master. In the mid-1740s, besides Porpora and Hasse in Venice, there was young Niccolò Jommelli, as described in the previous chap-

---

[12]Sylvie Mamy, *Les grands castrats napolitains à Venise au XVIIIe siècle* (Liège, 1994).

ter. One of the most remarkable successions of Neapolitan composers was that at the Derelitti, which began with Traetta in 1766, included his substitutes Antonio Sacchini and Pasquale Anfossi, and concluded with Domenico Cimarosa. Not all the directors from Naples won approval. Gennaro d'Alessandro ("Alessandro Gennaro Napolitano" in the records of the Pietà) was dismissed in May 1740 for lack of diligence. An overview of music directors at the *ospedali* during the eighteenth century is offered by Table 3.1.

TABLE 3.1. *Maestri di Coro* at the *Ospedali* of Venice during the Eighteenth Century*

Ospedali			
della Pietà	**degli Incurabili**	**dei Mendicante**	**dei Derelitti [Ospidaletto]**
Gasparini 1701–13	C. F. Pollarolo 1696–1722	Biffi 1700–30	Vinaccesi 1694–1715
Vivaldi 1703–†			
Grua 1719–26	Lotti 1722–25?		A. Pollarolo 1716–30
Porta 1726–37	Porpora 1726–33, 1737–38	Saratelli 1732–39	Cordans 1733–34
d'Alessandro 1739–40	Hasse 1736, 1738–39	Galuppi 1740–51	A. Pollarolo 1738–43
Porpora 1742–44	Carcani 1739–44		Porpora 1743–47
Bernasconi 1746–52	Jommelli 1745–47		Pampani 1747–66
	Ciampi 1747–48		
	Runcher 1748–54		
Latilla 1753–66	Cocchi 1754–56	Bertoni 1752–97	
	G. Scarlatti 1757–60		
	Ciampi 1760–62		
	Galuppi 1762–65		
Sarti 1766–67	Brusa 1765–68		Traetta 1766–79
Furlanetto 1768–1817	Galuppi 1768–76		Sacchini 1768–72‡
			Anfossi 1773–77‡
			Cimarosa 1782–84

*Dates, in some cases approximate or conjectural, mostly follow Elsie Arnold's appendix I "Ospedali Musicians," in Jane L. Baldauf-Berdes, *Women Musicians of Venice,* rev. ed. (Oxford, 1996).
†Vivaldi was designated *maestro di violino* or *maestro di concerto* at the Pietà for various periods up to 1738.
‡Substitute for the absent Traetta.

The instrumental music performed at the concerts of the *ospedali* was the focus of praise by some visitors to Venice. Pöllnitz claimed in his memoirs that the *cori* were equal to the best court orchestras in Europe, and that Anna Maria, the concert mistress at the Derelitti, was nothing less than the best violinist he ever heard.[13] Brosses confirms this judgment by saying that Chiaretta of the Pietà would be the best in Europe were it not for Anna Maria of the Derelitti (1: 244). Vivaldi wrote solo concertos for both of them.[14]

Music and performance remained at a high level during the 1740s, achieved under the direction of Porpora at the Pietà and Derelitti, of Jommelli at the Incurabili, and of that genial Venetian composer then emerging, Baldassare Galuppi, at the Mendicanti. One of the witnesses to this efflorescence was the young Jean-Jacques Rousseau, who was in Venice from the summer of 1743 to September 1744 as private secretary to the French ambassador, M. de Montaigu. In his *Confessions* Rousseau speaks of enjoying the opera at the San Giovanni Grisostomo theater in spite of "la longuer du spectacle." His true delight was found elsewhere.

> A music in my opinion quite superior to the operas, and which had not its like in Italy nor in the rest of the world, was that of the *scuole*, which are charitable houses established to educate young women without means, whom the republic then endows either for marriage or for the convent. Among the talents cultivated in these young ladies music comes first. Every Sunday at the churches of each of the four *scuole* during Vespers are performed motets for chorus and orchestra composed and directed by the greatest Italian masters, performed on screened platforms by girls the oldest of whom is no more than twenty. Nothing surpasses the voluptuous, touching qualities of this music; the richness of artistry, the exquisite taste of the singing, the beauty of the voices, the justness of the execution, —all combine in these delicious concerts to produce an impression, assuredly out of place, but irresistible to the human heart.[15]

An esthete raised in Calvinist Geneva naturally would find such music out of place in a church.

Rousseau's reaction had much to do with his own yearning for female voluptuousness. He admired the beautiful daughters of M. Leblond, the French consul, but dared not cast his eyes in their direction, nor, out of fear, toward Venice's famed courtesans. He resorted to fantasies about the angelic female voices. With his friend Carrio, secretary to the Spanish embassy, he never missed going to vespers at the Mendicanti.

> And we were not the only ones. The church was always full of music lovers: even the actors of the opera came in order to learn from the true taste of these excellent models. What riled me were the cursed screens which allowed only the sounds to pass, and hid from me those angels whose beauty was equal to their voices. I spoke of

[13]Karl Ludwig von Pöllnitz, *Lettres: Nouveaux mémoires contenant l'histoire de sa vie et la relation de ses premieres Voyages,* 4 vols. (Liège, 1734), 4: 113, cited after Baldauf-Berdes, *Women Musicians of Venice,* p. 205.
[14]Baldauf-Berdes, *Women Musicians of Venice,* pp. 199–200.
[15]Jean-Jacques Rousseau, *Les confessions,* Seconde Partie, Livre Septième. I translate from the edition of Garnier Frères (Paris, 1964), pp. 371–72.

nothing else. One day as I was carrying on about this with M. Leblond he told me, "If you are curious to see the young ladies that is easily arranged as I am one of the administrators of their house and I wish you to meet them." I gave him no peace until he kept his word. In entering the parlor which contained the beauties so greatly desired I felt a shudder of love such as I had never experienced before. M. Leblond presented to me one after the other those famous singers, whose voices and names were all that I knew. "Come Sophie." She was horrible. "Come Cattina." She was lame. "Come Bettina." Smallpox had disfigured her. Scarcely one was without some notable defect. The executioner laughed at my cruel surprise. Two or three alone appeared passable to me: they sang only in the choruses.

A generation later Burney was offered the same privilege of going to the source. His reactions, less amusingly told (or invented) than Rousseau's, reveal more.

An odd sidelight on the preceding tale concerns one of Leblond's daughters who sought acceptance as an outside student at the Mendicante. An administrator of the house the consul may have been, but his daughter was refused by the governors, apparently for lack of sufficient musical ability.[16] This points to a high degree of selectivity even for entrance to the training provided by the *cori.*

Rousseau's experiences with the invisible performers at the Mendicanti serve to emphasize a point of difference between the Neapolitan and Venetian music schools. Both put on concerts that brought in revenue. In Naples the boys were ambulatory and often sent out in bands under contract to perform at some civic or private function, such as weddings and funerals. The young ladies of the Venetian *cori* were restricted to the churches of their charitable institutions and rarely performed elsewhere except on occasions of state. The visit of the Russian crown prince and his wife to Venice in 1782 was one such occasion, at which players and singers from the *ospedali* appeared in a large hall arranged in long rows in three tiers along one of the walls, as captured in a well-known oil painting by Francesco Guardi.[17]

Burney subscribed to the notion of that time that only males could be trained in composition. In fact he seems to have rejected training in instrumental performance for females in his proposal of 1774 to set up a music school. He foresaw two divisions, one for girls "chiefly in singing," and the other for boys "who have talents for composition and for the performing on different instruments." His plans reflect the Neapolitan model and called for a course of study lasting seven

[16]Baldauf-Berdes, *Women Musicians of Venice,* p. 117, n. 62.

[17]Denis and Elsie Arnold, "Russians in Venice: The Visit of the 'Conti del Nord' in 1782," in *Slavonic and Western Music: Essays for Gerald Abraham,* eds. M. H. Brown and R. J. Wiley (Oxford, 1985), pp. 123–30. Guardi's painting is known as *Concerto di dame nella Sala di Filarmonici.* According to Hans Dörge, *Musik in Venedig* (Wilhelmshaven, 1991), p. 198, the hall was in the Procuratoria on the west side of the Piazza San Marco facing the basilica, a building torn down along with the Sansovino church of San Geminiano in 1807 when Napolean had the piazza rebuilt.

years, with the trainees leaving by age 21. He proposed to finance the school by having the boys go out "singly or in Bands, for Musical Performance in Churches, for Oratorios, and Public and Private Concerts; as well as to attend Persons of Rank into the Country, at a settled and stated price."[18] The scheme came to naught. Paris took the lead in this area with the founding of the Ecole Royale de Chant in 1783, intended as "une école dans le goût des conservatoires d'Italie."

At midcentury there was some dimming of the *ospedali*'s luster, to judge by the renown of their directors. Jommelli and Porpora left Venice for good, being replaced at the Incurabili and Derelitti, respectively, by the relatively obscure figures of Giovanni Battista Runcher, a native of Dresden trained at Naples, and Antonio Gaetano Pampani of Modena. Galuppi left Venice to fulfill operatic commissions at London and Vienna during the 1740s while retaining directorship of music at the Mendicante. In 1748 he became maestro di cappella at the basilica and at the same time launched an epochal series of comic operas, mainly in collaboration with Goldoni. The governors of the Mendicanti by 1751 judged him insufficiently attentive to his duties there and severed their ties. He was replaced by his assistant Ferdinando Bertoni.

Naming the musical director of one of the *ospedali* was a matter of state in Venice, as appears from the correspondence of Hasse. Lord Venier, procurator of the republic, asked Hasse's opinion about a replacement for the deceased Giovanni Brusa, a priest who was Galuppi's substitute as *maestro di coro* at the Incurabili from 1765 to 1768. Hasse's letter to Venier is not extant, but it is paraphrased in his letter from Vienna of four days later, dated 15 June 1768, to his Venetian friend Abbé Gian Maria Ortes.

> If I had another Carcani or Jommelli on hand, both of whom have done so much honor to my choice, I would have associated myself with the glory and singular satisfaction of being able, on this occasion to suggest a third. . . . But since I have been away from Italy for almost three years, and do not, for this reason have sufficient knowledge of the composers who are in vogue today . . . I actually do not know who possesses all the necessary prerequisites for [the direction of] that group of performers. Trajetta would be superb, but he is at the Ospedaletto. As for Sarti, I would have nominated him had I known four days ago that he is no longer at the Pietà. I have seen here a well-written piece of his music, from which evidence I believe that he knows his métier very well. . . . My opinion is that he should be chosen unless the Most Eminent Governors of the pious place prefer to take back Carcani or to choose one of the better among the Neapolitan youth, and particularly among those who are graduating from the school of the late Durante, which has produced many good students.[19]

---

[18]Charles Burney, *Sketch of a Plan for a Public Music School* (London, 1774).
[19]Sven Hostrup Hansell, "Sacred Music at the *Incurabili* in Venice at the time of J. A. Hasse," *JAMS* 23 (1970): 282–83. I have further abbreviated his abbreviated translation.

Events overtook both Venier and Hasse, who was evidently looked up to as the sage and arbiter of modern music. Galuppi returned from Russia in mid-1768 and was reappointed to his post by the Incurabili. When Hasse learned this, he responded with the warm praise and generosity that was characteristic of his relations with other composers.

> As for Buranello, either because I thought he was still in Moscow, or because I did not think that the post could be combined with the position that this excellent composer occupies at the Cathedral of Saint Mark, it is certain that he never crossed my mind when I wrote the Lord Procurator Venier; otherwise I would have suggested him before all others. But as it is, the Lord Governors have chosen him by themselves, and they surely could not have done better.[20]

Galuppi's last term of office at the Incurabili corresponded with its finest period.

Burney arrived in Venice in August 1770 when the four *ospedali* were giving concert after concert, making up for the lack of opera at this season. He went first to the Pietà on the evening of Saturday, 4 August, and heard a concert under its music director, Bonaventura Furlanetto, a priest. "The composition and performance which I heard to-night did not exceed mediocrity; among the singers I could discover no remarkable fine voice, nor performer possessed of great taste. However, the instruments finished with a symphony, the first movement of which, in point of spirit, was well written and well executed." After visiting various churches on Sunday morning, including the basilica, he went to the famed afternoon vesper service at the Mendicanti, directed by Bertoni.

> Upon the whole, the compositions had some pretty passages, mixed with others that were not very new. The subjects of the fugues and choruses were trite, and but slightly put together. The girls here I thought accompanied the voices better than at the *Pietà*: as the choruses are wholly made up of female voices, they are never in more than three parts, often only in two: but these, when reinforced by the instruments, have such an effect, that the full complement to the chords is not missed, and the melody is much more sensible and marked, by being less charged with harmony. In these hospitals many of the girls sing in the countertenor as low as A and G, which enables them always to keep below the *soprano* and *mezzo soprano.*

From the Mendicante it was but a few steps to the Derelitti around the corner. Here Burney found the music more to his liking.

> From hence I went to the *Ospedaletto,* of which Signor Sacchini is the master, and was indeed very much pleased by the composition of part of the famous hymn *Salve*

---

[20]Letter of 13 August 1768 from Hasse to Ortes, translated in Hansell, "Sacred Music at the *Incurabili.*"

Regina, which was singing when I entered the church; it was new, spirited, and full of ingenious contrivances for the instruments, which always *said* something interesting without disturbing the voice. Upon the whole, there seemed to be as much genius in this composition as in any I had heard since my arrival in Italy. The performers here too are all orphan girls; one of them, *la Ferrarese,* sung very well, and had a very extraordinary compass of voice, as she was able to reach highest E of our harpsichords, upon which she could dwell a considerable time, in a fair, natural voice.

On the next day, Burney was fortunate to see a procession of the doge from the basilica to San Giovanni e Paolo, followed by a mass in four parts accompanied only by organ, a composition by Lotti that evoked Burney's praise. He was approached by Gaetano Latilla, who advised him to go to hear the music at the Incurabili, under the direction of Galuppi. This he did the same day, Monday, 6 August.

> Unluckily when I arrived there, the performance was begun; however, I had only lost the overture and part of the first air. The words are taken from three or four of the Psalms in Latin, from the hymn *Salve Regina,* and one of the Canticles put into Latin verse, and in dialogue. I knew not whether I was most delighted with the composition, or with the execution; both were admirable. . . .This music, which was of the higher sort of theatric stile, was not mixed with the church service, and the audience sat the whole time, as at a concert; and, indeed, this might be called a *concerto spirituale,* with great propriety.

On his way to Italy, Burney was in Paris for the feast of Corpus Christi and in attendance at the Concert Spirituel in the Tuileries Palace. He had few good impressions from it, and his use of the equivalent Italian term here, qualified by "with great propriety," sounds a note of ironic contrast.

Upon several return trips to the *ospedali* and the major churches Burney heard nothing that changed his initial impressions. He respected the music heard in the basilica under Galuppi but he adored the more modern style allowed the same composer at his *ospedale.* "At present, the great abilities of Signor Galuppi are conspicuous in the performances at the *Incurabili,* which is, in point of music, singing, and orchestra, in my opinion, superior to the rest. Next to that, the *Ospedaletto* takes place of the other two; so that the *Pietà* seems to enjoy the reputation of being the best school, not for what it *does now,* but for what it *has done* heretofore." He went one more time to marvel at the music and performance level at the Incurabili.

Burney found an apt name for the *ospedali* of Venice when he called them "these admirable musical seminaries." He remains the best witness, by both ear and eye, of an extraordinary musical flowering achieved by women. The heights to which they rose, he claimed, exceeded the level of music making anywhere else in Italy.

Vivaldi

PRIEST, VIOLINIST, AND MUSICAL GENIUS

Antonio Vivaldi was born in Venice on 4 March 1678, the same day on which an earthquake shook the city. The midwife who presided at his birth took the precaution of baptizing him at once, because his life was in danger; official baptism followed on 6 May. Late in life the composer complained of a debilitating infirmity of the chest that sounds like bronchial asthma. The dank conditions prevailing in the city of canals and lagoons could only have worsened his ailment.

The Vivaldi family resided in the district of San Martino, near the Arsenale. Antonio was the first of six children to arrive. His father, Giovanni Battista, was called Rossi on account of his red hair. He was a violinist at San Marco and presumably the main teacher of his eldest son, who was hired as an extra violinist there for Christmas 1696.[21] It has been recently confirmed that Antonio was a fellow student with the violinist Giovanni Battista Somis in Turin during 1700–1701 and again in 1703.[22] Several kinds of evidence show that Antonio was trained only as a violinist and did not undergo the vocal and keyboard training thought necessary to form a maestro di cappella.

In September 1693, at age fifteen and a half, young Antonio took the first step towards the priesthood, being tonsured (the minimum age for which was 12); then in 1703 he was ordained a priest (the minimum age for which was 25). Within a year or so of his ordination he stopped saying mass, contrary to his vows, an infraction that would eventually come back to hurt him. He would later claim ill health as the reason. The pity was that he failed to get a formal dispensation from his bishop at the time.

Besides his ordination, something of which the Vivaldi family was undoubtedly proud, the year 1703 saw his first recorded connections with the Pietà, where he became *maestro di violino;* it was possibly the year of his first publication as well. In 1704 his salary from the Pietà was advanced to 100 ducats per annum after he took on the teaching of additional stringed instruments. In 1705 Giuseppe Sala of Venice published as his Op. 1 a set of twelve trio sonatas dedicated to a Venetian nobleman from Brescia (a first edition may go back to 1703). These are competent, interesting, but not particularly original *sonate da camera* on the Corellian model. Op. 2, a set of sonatas for violin and basso continuo, followed in 1709, dedicated to Frederick IV, king of Denmark and Norway, who visited Venice in late 1708 and attended a concert under Vivaldi's direction at the Pietà. In the dedication Vivaldi exceeded the usual self-abasement of the genre,

---

[21]Michael Talbot, *Vivaldi* (New York, 1993), pp. 165–66.
[22]Michael Talbot, *The Sacred Vocal Music of Antonio Vivaldi* (Florence, 1995), p. 49.

saying that he was not worthy to kiss the lowest stair leading to his royal patron's throne.

Vivaldi's Op. 3 was the epochal collection of concertos entitled *L'estro armonico* that appeared in 1711. It established the composer's name throughout Europe and was printed not in Venice, where the music printers no longer satisfied him, but in Amsterdam, engraved and sold by Estienne Roger, whom Vivaldi praises in the preface. He dedicated the collection to the music-loving grand prince of Tuscany, Ferdinand de' Medici. The electrifying effects of Vivaldi's sharply etched rhythms and forceful ritornellos of many parts proved so attractive to J. S. Bach that he made arrangements of them for keyboard and, eventually, lightly disguised imitations. In his memoirs Quantz tells how he encountered the concertos at the age of seventeen in 1714 at Pirna in Saxony, on his way to Dresden. "At that time I first saw violin concertos by Vivaldi. As a then completely new species of musical pieces, they made more than a slight impression on me. I did not fail to collect a considerable assortment of them. In later times the splendid ritornellos of Vivaldi provided me with good models." They provided models for many others as well, to the point that Vivaldi swept away memories of important predecessors, such as Torelli, and overshadowed the concertos of his leading Venetian contemporaries, such as Tomaso Albinoni.

L'estro armonico represents the first harvest of Vivaldi's experiments with the fine orchestra and soloists of the Pietà, which were his to command in the same sense that Haydn later commanded the forces of his Esterházy band. Some of the violin solos were meant for Vivaldi himself to play, while others were intended for his lady pupils, several of whom became celebrated violinists themselves. Concertos like this were heard at both mass and vespers in the *ospedali*.[23]

Vivaldi's increasing renown became manifest in a number of ways. The Philippine order (or Oratorians) at Brescia in 1712 commissioned him to make a setting of the *Stabat mater*, one of his first pieces of sacred vocal music. This is another instance showing that his family's ancestral ties with Brescia continued. In 1713 Vivaldi appeared by name, along with his father, in a tourist guide for strangers visiting Venice, where he is described as one of the city's best violinists. In this same year he began to compose sacred vocal music extensively. Gasparini, the excellent *maestro di coro* of the Pietà, fell ill and was given a six-month leave of absence in 1713 (he went to Rome and never returned). Vivaldi remained *maestro di concerto* of the Pietà (as he styled himself on the title page of his Op. 2) but took over duties that belonged to the *maestro di coro*, composing such impressive works as the famous Gloria in D (RV 489). At the same time Vivaldi blossomed into a composer of opera. By the time he was thirty-five he seemed to be making

[23]Denis Arnold, "Music at the *Ospedali,*" *Journal of the Royal Musical Association* 113 (1988), 156–67; 161. Names on part music sometimes identify individual performers.

up for his lack of training as a maestro di cappella by the practical experience of composing. He also brazenly made up for some deficiencies by borrowing music from others, as is the case with the "Amen" fugue in *stile antico* that ends the Gloria in D.[24]

OPERAS

Gasparini was the leading composer of operas in Venice during his twelve-year residency from 1701 to 1713. In this respect he replaced Carlo Francesco Pollarolo, who was the dominant figure in Venetian opera during the 1690s. Gasparini wrote two dozen operas for Venice, all but the first for the Teatro San Cassiano. His departure paved the way not only for Vivaldi's plunge into sacred vocal music, but also for his decision to enter the sometimes lucrative and always frantic world of opera. His first foray was not in Venice but in one of the main cities of the terra firma.

Vivaldi began his operatic career with *Ottone in Villa* on a libretto of Domenico Lalli for Vicenza in 1713. It was followed by a series of operas for the Teatro Sant'Angelo in Venice, begun in 1714. He also wrote for the Teatro San Moisé, but never for Venice's main opera house, the San Giovanni Grisostomo. Gasparini had made the first settings of several librettos by Zeno. Vivaldi did set a few librettos by Zeno, but he never made a first setting of anything by the poet. It is misleading to claim that he collaborated with Zeno and Metastasio.[25] From what we know of his churlish personality it seems likely that he would have gone out of his way to avoid meeting two such men of the world as the learned Zeno, who left Venice for Vienna in 1719, or the fastidious Metastasio, who followed Zeno to Vienna ten years later.

Vivaldi went into the theater because it was where the most money was to be made. For the rest of his life he was involved with operatic productions, either as composer or impresario. Together with his father he ran the Sant'Angelo theater for a time around 1715, and again later. They also managed the San Moisé theater off and on. Besides composing arias or whole operas for his theaters Vivaldi also functioned as orchestra leader and violin soloist. One of the attractions his shows provided to the public was hearing the red priest ("il prete rosso") as a virtuoso violinist playing fantastic and brilliant solos on his instrument. A visitor to Venice from Germany recorded direct impressions of such an event in his diary.

Johann Friedrich Armand von Uffenbach was a law student from a wealthy bourgeois family in Frankfurt who collected the latest music and delighted in performing it on his violin. He already owned music by Vivaldi when, as a student at

---

[24]Talbot, *The Sacred Vocal Music of Antonio Vivaldi,* p. 165: "this type of writing evidently did not come naturally to him and gave rise to many borrowings from other composers."
[25]Eleanor Selfridge-Field, *Venetian Instrumental Music,* p. 222.

Strasbourg in 1712, he presented pieces by Pepusch, Vivaldi, and Telemann to the local "Statt musicis" and got them performed.[26] In Venice on holiday for the carnival of 1714–15, he went to the opera at the San Giovanni e Paolo theater, where he apparently saw the *favola pastorale* of *Marsia deluso* by Count Agostino Piovene set to music by Carlo Pollarolo. He marveled at the size and elegance of the hall, the magnificence of the decors, the lavishness of the spectacle, and the hordes of people on stage along with artificial camels and elephants plus live horses (rarely seen outside the theater in Venice). He praised the strength of the orchestra and the voices, especially that of Senesino, but excoriated the behavior of some people in the loges, who, under the freedom of carnival masks and the season, threw objects at and spat upon people in the parterre, where he was seated. A gob of spit struck the libretto he was holding. This "beastly custom" was confined to Venice.[27]

Uffenbach went next to Vivaldi's Teatro Sant'Angelo. It offered two operas in the carnival season of 1715, Antonio Salvi's *Lucio Papirio* as set by Luca Antonio Predieri and *Nerone fatto Cesare* by Matteo Norris, a pasticcio to which Vivaldi contributed twelve arias and which cleared the censor on 12 February 1715. Vivaldi signed the dedication in the libretto of the first to Count Kollowrat of Prague, perhaps inducing Uffenbach to believe he composed the whole opera.

> Venice, 4 February 1715. I remained [at the masked ball in the *ridotto*] until it was time to go to the opera, then went with some friends to the Sant'Angelo, which is smaller and less elegant than the other theater described above, but the *entrepreneur* of this one was the famous Vivaldi, who also composed the opera, which was really good [richt artig] and a fine spectacle as well. The machines were not so costly as in the other theater, and the orchestra not so large, but well worth hearing nevertheless. . . . Towards the end Vivaldi played an admirable solo in accompanying an aria, to which he added in conclusion a fantasy that quite alarmed me, for I doubt that its like was ever done before or will ever be done again: he came within a hairsbreadth of the bridge, leaving no room for the bow. He did this on all four strings while playing fugues at incredible speed. He astonished everyone with this, but to say it pleased me I cannot do, for it was not as agreeable to listen to as it was cunningly contrived. The singers were incomparable, and not inferior to those at the grand opera, especially the female ones, among whom the so-called Fabbri excelled in musical art and charm, in addition to which she was beautiful to behold, at least on the stage.[28]

Anna Maria Fabbri sang Sabina in *Lucio Papirio* and Nerone in the second opera. Uffenbach returned to the same theater for another performance on 19 February,

[26]Eberhard Preussner, *Die musikalischen Reisen des Herrn von Uffenbach* (Kassel and Basel, 1949), p. 23.
[27]Joseph Baretti, *An Account of the Manners and Customs of Italy* (London, 1768), pp. 58–59.
[28]Preussner, *Die musikalsschen Reisen des Herrn von Uffenbach*, pp. 67–68.

but this he liked less, complaining about a stylistic mishmash of French, Spanish, and Persian costumes; "to my misfortune Vivaldi himself played only a very small solo air on his violin." He went a third time to the Sant'Angelo on 4 March. *Nerone fatto Cesare* was revived during the following carnival season at Brescia.

Vivaldi became acquainted with Uffenbach, who wrote a revealing portrait of the composer in his diary.

> Wednesday, 6 March 1715. After dinner Vivaldi the famous composer and violinist came to me as I had repeatedly left word at his house requesting him to do so. I had spoken to him about certain concerti grossi that I wished to have from him and placed an order for them, accompanied by several bottles of wine since he belongs to the musical clan. He let me hear his very difficult and altogether inimitable fantasy playing on the violin which made me marvel all the more at his cleverness close up, and I clearly saw that, while he played extra difficult and colorful things, he played them without any charming or cantabile manner.

> Saturday, 9 March 1715. In the afternoon Vivaldi came and brought me 10 concerti grossi as ordered. He said he composed some of them expressly for me and he wished to teach me how to play them on the spot so that I could hear them better; we made a start today and he wants to come to see me from time to time for further lessons.[29]

Uffenbach does not say how much he paid the master. Further lessons were unlikely, because the young German planned to go to Rome for Holy Week. He and his companion, a young man named Tardieu from Geneva, left Venice on 12 March.

Vivaldi wrote and staged several operas for the Sant'Angelo or San Moisé theaters between 1715 and 1720. His setting of *La verità in cimento* by Palazzi and Lalli for the Sant'Angelo in the autumn of 1720 is thought to be one stimulus for Benedetto Marcello's witty satire *Il teatro all moda,* licensed by the censor in the same month of October 1720 as this opera. An anagram of A. Vivaldi ("Aldiviva") appears as the printer's name beneath the vignette on the title page (Figure 3.3). Pictured is a common rowboat ("peata") such as was used to transport goods on the canals. In the prow is a bear in a jacket and full-bottomed wig carrying a flag, standing guard over what appear to be a keg of wine and other victuals. The reference may be to the bear ("orso") who was the impresario of the San Moisé, Giovanni Orsato. By analogy the man in the hat doing the rowing may represent the impresario of the Sant'Angelo. There is no mistaking the figure steering the bark with one foot to the rudder, the other raised as if in a dance. He bears the wings of an angel, a priest's hat, and plays the violin. In other words, it was Vivaldi

---

[29]Ibid., p. 71.

who led the dance, who steered the fortunes of the Sant'Angelo. Marcello's comedy of allusions begins with the title itself.

> The Theater à la mode or a sure and easy method for composing Italian operas well and executing them in music according to the modern manner. In which is given useful and necessary directions to poets, composers of music, singers of the one and the other sex, impresarios, instrumentalists, engineers, scene painters, buffo parts, tailors, pages, extras, prompters, copyists, patrons, and the mothers of lady virtuosi, and other persons belonging to the theater. Dedicated by the author of the book to the compositor of the same. Printed in the BORGHI of BELSANIA by ALDIVIVA LICANTE; at the sign of the bear in PEATA. And is sold in the STRADA of the CORALLO at the PORTA of the palace of ORLANDO. And will be reprinted every year with new additions.

FIGURE 3.3. Title page of Marcello's *Teatro alla moda*, 1720.

The names capitalized were all meant to be recognized by the public. Belisani, Borghi, Corali, Orlandi, Strada, and Cantelli (in anagram as "Licante") were all singers at the Sant'Angelo or San Moisé. "Orlando" could also refer to Giuseppe Orlandini, composer of *Paride* for the San Giovanni Grisostomo, carnival of 1720. "Porta," meaning "gate," surely refers to Giovanni Porta, composer of *Teodorico* for the same theater in the autumn of 1720.

Marcello spared no one in his verbal satire, but Vivaldi appears to have been the main target. Who else could be the butt of the witticism about the *maestro de' concerto* who improvises an enormous cadenza that he carefully prepared ahead of time? The composer of operas is instructed to compose arias with pizzicato strings and exotic instruments such as the tromba marina and Jew's harp ("piomè"). Vivaldi liked to use odd instruments as concertante accompaniments in arias, as in his superb oratorio *Juditha triumphans devicta Holofernis barbarie* for the Pietà in 1716, and doubtless in the opera houses as well, not to mention in his hundreds of concertos. All composers of the time, including Handel, were fond of unison orchestral accompaniments, another object of satire, but surely no one was more identified with them and by them than Vivaldi. Even Vivaldi's excesses of dedicatory humility, as we saw above in his Op. 2, bring a stinging retort from Marcello. Dedications should be concluded, he says, by words of abasement such as "the author kissing the fleabites on the legs of His Excellency's dog as an act of deepest respect." As satire of courtly groveling the passage matches in scorn one in Swift's *Gulliver's Travels* (1726): "his Majesty would please to appoint a day and hour, when it would be his gracious pleasure that I might have the honour to lick the dust before his footstool" (part III, chapter 9).

The barely literate composer and his singers suffer no worse at Marcello's hands than does the uneducated and greedy theater poet. "Should the modern poet discover that a singer enunciates poorly he must not correct him because if the defect were remedied and the singer were to enunciate clearly, sales of the libretto might be hurt." It has been argued that Marcello's satire hit home so hard that Vivaldi ceased to write operas for Venice for five years.[30]

Vivaldi's residence in Mantua from 1718 to 1720 brought him into what was perhaps the first of his several connections with the empire. The Marquisat of Mantua was governed for the Habsburgs by Prince Philip of Hessen-Darmstadt, a noted patron of music. Porpora was Prince Philip's (nonresident) maestro di cappella. Vivaldi called himself the prince's *maestro di cappella da camera* and he retained this odd title after leaving Mantua. In 1721 Vivaldi wrote the pastoral opera *La Silvia* for the Regio Ducal Teatro in Milan, to celebrate the birthday of the Empress Elisabeth on 28 August.

After Mantua, Vivaldi's life was mainly itinerant, like those of the Neapolitan masters of opera with whom he now competed for commissions. He may have lived continuously at Rome between 1723 and 1725, where his operatic career reached one of its peaks with his setting of Pariati's *Giustino* for the Teatro Capranica in the carnival season of 1724.[31] Quantz reached Rome in the same year and claimed in his autobiography that Vivaldi had made the Lombard style of inverted dotted rhythms newly fashionable there. This may be true, but the trait was in wide use earlier in Naples and elsewhere.

Vivaldi began writing operas for Venice again in the fall of 1725. By this time he was committed to promoting the career of Anna Giraud (or Girò), a former student of his at the Pietà who sometimes lived with him, causing tongues to wag. She was of Mantuan descent. As a soprano she apparently had more tech-

[30]Reinhard Strohm, *Essays on Handel and Italian Opera* (Cambridge, 1985), p. 48. See also Eleanor Selfridge-Field, "Marcello, Sant'Angelo, and *Il teatro alla moda*," in *Antonio Vivaldi: teatro musicale, cultura e società,* ed. Lorenzo Bianconi and Giovanni Morelli (Florence, 1982), pp. 533–46.
[31]Antonio Vivaldi, *Giustino,* ed. Reinhard Strohm (Venice, 1991), Commentary, p. 9.

nique than voice. Abbé Conti wrote Madame de Caylus reporting on Vivaldi's opera at the Sant'Angelo for the carnival of 1727 (*Farnace*): "La musique est de Vivaldi; elle est très variée dans le sublime et dans le tendre; son elève y fait des merveilles quoyque sa voix ne soit pas des plus belles."[32]

In 1730 Vivaldi visited Prague, accompanied by his aged father, Anna Giraud, and possibly her sister Paolina, whom Vivaldi claimed was his nurse. Antonio Denzio's operatic troupe had been playing Italian works in the theater of Franz Anton Count von Sporck since 1724. *Farnace* was repeated with success in Prague under the composer's direction, followed by a new opera, Vivaldi's *Argippo*. Gluck was then a young student in Prague and surely would have tried to hear the famous Vivaldi play. Denzio was a Venetian and a tenor who had sung the role of Artabano in Vivaldi's *La constanza trionfante degl'amori degl'odi* (1716). Vivaldi also took sacred music with him to Prague. Its subsequent spread throughout Bohemia was probably in consequence of this trip. In light of the encouragement that Emperor Charles VI is said to have given the composer in 1728, the Vivaldi party may have visited Vienna as well as Prague.

Vivaldi's next important engagement was composing Scipione Maffei's libretto of *La fida ninfa* for the festive opening of the Teatro Filarmonico in Verona on 6 January 1732.[33] Vivaldi was Verona's second choice, the first being Orlandini. Giraud did not take a part but she remained active. She is reported as participating in the concert on 26 August 1739 at the palace of the Spanish ambassador to Venice celebrating the wedding of the infante Philip. At this event Vivaldi directed from the harpsichord.

In October 1736 Vivaldi proposed to Marquis Guido Bentivoglio of Ferrara that he produce operas for the next carnival season there. He intended to organize his company in Venice around the indispensable Anna Giraud and offered two of his older operas especially adapted for the purpose. Ferrara wanted music by Hasse rather than by Vivaldi, so the latter agreed to arrange Hasse's *Demetrio* for his troupe: "I have decided to compose all the recitatives afresh and to provide the singers with a great many of my arias," wrote Vivaldi on 24 November 1736. By adapting his music to the *Demetrio* libretto he seemed to be trying to get around the stated preference of the Ferrarese gentlemen for Hasse. After *Demetrio* he was asked to arrange Hasse's *Alessandro nell'Indie*. Many problems arose with individual performers, dancers as well as singers. Negotiations dragged on through 1737 and became focused on producing a season for the carnival of 1738. Vivaldi proposed to arrive in Ferrara in time to open the new season on 26 December 1737.

---

[32] Remo Giazotto, *Vivaldi* (Milan, 1965), p. 191.

[33] For a study of the theater architecture and stage sets see Maria Teresa Muraro and Elena Povoledo, "Le Scene della *Fida Ninfa*: Maffei, Vivaldi e Francesco Bibiena," *Vivaldi Veneziano Europeo*, ed. Francesco Degrada (Florence, 1980), pp. 235–52, especially plates 1–5.

At this point the Cardinal of Ferrara, Tommaso Ruffo, stepped in and forbad Vivaldi from entering the city because of his liaison with Anna Giraud and because the composer-impresario, still a priest, refused to say mass. This led to the famous, mainly autobiographical letter, in which Vivaldi tries to justify his behavior and that of the Giraud sisters. It is dated 16 November 1737.

The apostolic nunzio to Venice summoned Vivaldi to his palace and ordered him in the name of Cardinal Ruffo not to go to Ferrara. On the subject of the Giraud sisters Vivaldi wrote: "For fourteen years we have traveled together to many cities of Europe, and everywhere their honesty was admired, even in Ferrara. Every week they make their devotions, as sworn witnesses can testify." This can have done but little to assuage the irate cardinal. On the subject of saying mass Vivaldi is somewhat more persuasive.

> I have not said Mass for 25 years and I shall never do so, not because I am forbidden to do so, as Your Excellency can inform himself, but by my own choice, and because I have been afflicted since birth by an illness. Right after being ordained I said Mass for a year and a little more, then I had to desist because I was forced to leave the altar three times without finishing the Mass on account of my illness. For this reason I remain almost always at my house and only go about in a gondola or a coach, because I cannot walk on account of an illness or narrowness in my chest. No gentlemen summon me to their dwelling, not even our Prince, because they all know about my defect. Immediately after the midday meal I can go out, but never on foot. This is the reason that I do not celebrate Mass. I was in Rome for three carnival seasons writing operas, as Your Excellency knows, and I never said Mass; I played the violin in the theater and it is known that even His Holiness wanted to hear me play, and that I received many compliments. I was called to Vienna where I did not say Mass. I was three years in the service of the very pious Prince of Darmstadt: I was there with the ladies who were always looked upon by His Highness with utmost benevolence; also there I never said Mass. My journeys are always very costly because I have to make them with four or five people to assist me.[34]

The letter goes on in the same vein and includes the statement, "I have been a maestro at the Pietà for thirty years and never with any scandal."

Without Vivaldi's presence in Ferrara the operas went badly, for which Vivaldi blamed local incompetents who had the gall to tamper with his recitatives. An acrimonious lawsuit ensued between Vivaldi and the scene painter Antonio Mauro, on whom the composer had attempted to shift financial responsibilities for the Ferrara contracts. More than just money was at stake. Vivaldi's reputation in Italy began to plummet. In May 1740 he began his final trip across the Alps. Anna Giraud probably accompanied him (she sang at Graz in his *Catone in*

---

[34]Giazotto, *Vivaldi*, pp. 308–9.

Utica in the fall of 1740). Emperor Charles VI, upon whose support Vivaldi was banking, died suddenly on 20 October 1740. Vivaldi followed him to the grave, a pauper's grave in his case, in Vienna, on 28 July 1741.

An eyewitness account of Vivaldi at his worktable is provided in the well-known vignettes found in Goldoni's Italian memoirs (1761) and his French ones (1787). More credence should be given to the first. As he tells it, the scene takes on some of the vivacity for which his plays are famous. The year was 1735 and Michele Grimani sent the young poet to Vivaldi in order to revise Zeno's *Griselda* for performance at the San Samuele.

> That year, for the Ascension opera, the composer was the priest Vivaldi, known as the red priest because of his hair, and sometimes referred to as Rossi, so that people thought that was his surname. This most famous violinist, this man famous for his sonatas, especially for those known as the Four Seasons, also composed operas; and although the real connoisseurs say that he was faulty in counterpoint and did not write basses as he should, he made the parts sing and his operas were mostly successful. That year the role of the prima donna was to be taken by Signora Annina Girò, or Giraud, who was commonly called Annina of the red priest, because she was Vivaldi's pupil. She did not have a beautiful voice, nor was she a great musician, but she was pretty and attractive; she acted well (a rare thing in those days) and had protectors: one needs nothing more to deserve the role of prima donna.[35]

Goldoni did as he was bidden, substituting an action aria for a cantabile one that did not suit Giraud. He wrote it on the spot without hesitation, to the composer's amazement. "When Vivaldi finished reading the poem he threw his breviary down, got up, embraced me, ran to the door and called Signora Annina." Vivaldi was not always incapable of movement, it appears. An earlier anecdote is told about Johann Georg Pisendel, one of Vivaldi's pupils in 1716, who, with Vivaldi, walked rapidly across the Piazza San Marco in order to escape police surveillance.[36]

One wonders who the connoisseurs were who informed Goldoni that Vivaldi lacked contrapuntal skill and that his basses were not what they should be. Goldoni seems to answer this complaint himself by saying that even so Vivaldi made the parts sing ("faceva cantar bene le parti") and for the most part his operas pleased. Mattheson maintained that "Vivaldi, although not a singer, knew how to write idiomatically for the voice."[37] Tartini, one of Vivaldi's main rivals as a

---

[35]Preface to volume 13 of the *Commedie* published by Pasquali (Venice, 1761), in *Tutte le opere di Carlo Goldoni*, ed. Giuseppe Ortonlani, 14 vols. (Milan, 1935–56), 1: 721. The opera has been elucidated by two superior studies: John W. Hill, "Vivaldi's *Griselda*," *JAMS* 31 (1978): 53–82, and Eric Cross, *Vivaldi's Late Operas* (Ann Arbor, Mich., 1981), chapter 4. Both argue in favor of the work's dramatic integrity.
[36]Johann Adam Hiller, *Lebensbeschreibungen berühmter Musikgelehrten* (Leipzig, 1784), p. 184.
[37]Johann Mattheson, *Der vollkommene Capellmeister* (Hamburg, 1739), p. 205.

violinist, teacher, and instrumental composer, thought differently. He told Brosses that Vivaldi lacked cantabile, that he treated the human throat too much like the fingerboard of a violin.

As an opera composer Vivaldi had strengths as well as weaknesses. In *La fida ninfa,* for example, a work in which he presumably took care to do his best since the occasion of opening the Verona theater in 1732 was an auspicious one, he serves his two bass singers well with blustery arias worthy of Handel. He fares less well with more delicate emotions. He missed an opportunity for splendid vocal effects in the pastoral duet for two contraltos in Act I. The piece never takes wing, much less soars, with the result that it sounds like a rather wooden trio sonata. Even the most pathetic and touching piece, "Amor mio," an $E^\flat$ love-death aria in the second act, bogs down into harmonic sequences at one point, followed by a passage in which the voice is made to sing a particularly ungainly leaping figure. Faustina Bordoni told Burney that she often found Handel's cantilena "rude"— had she ever sung Vivaldi she would have found it ruder still.

La fida ninfa includes many lovely melodic ideas, but few pieces that are not marred at some point by mechanical sequential treatment. Why should this trait disturb us less in Vivaldi's instrumental music than in his arias? Perhaps because we are kept busy in the former reveling in the kaleidoscopic play of instrumental timbres, sonorities, and textures. Vivaldi does not lack many of the modish turns of phrase of the day. The three-note rhythmic snaps of Neapolitan music, used sparingly in *Giustino,* abound in *La fida ninfa* to the point of becoming a mannerism. During his last decade Vivaldi was obviously trying to update his style in order to keep up with evolving tastes.[38] He had tried and failed to make the Venetian style of opera prevail with *Giustino* for Rome in 1724.

CONCERTOS

Vivaldi is responsible for making the solo concerto in three movements, fast–slow–fast, the most important instrumental genre of the time. There can be no doubt that he shaped the ritornello form of concerto that came to dominate the field. As to its beginnings, Quantz offers credible testimony that earlier there was nothing so powerful or influential as the strength and clarity of Vivaldi's ritornello structures. A legacy this potent had consequences for the entire century. By the sheer force of his musical personality Vivaldi propelled Locatelli and Tartini into slightly different paths. His impact could be likened to Rameau's on French music in this regard. Rameau was only five years younger than Vivaldi.

[38]Talbot, *The Sacred Vocal Music of Antonio Vivaldi,* pp. 235–37, makes a telling comparison between Vivaldi's early "Magnificat" setting and one made in 1739, the first rich in rhythmic complexity and motivic *Fortspinnung,* the second pieced together out of complementary little units and employing a more limited harmonic vocabulary.

One of Vivaldi's innovations was his frequent reduction of the bass to a mere drumlike function, marking the pulse and repeating the same few tones. He favored this device especially for the slow middle movements of his concertos. A fine example is the *Largo* of the Chamber Concerto in D, RV 94, which begins like the *Largo* of "Winter" in *The Four Seasons* (Example 3.1).

Vivaldi dedicated the concertos of his Op. 9, *La Cetra* (published by Le Cène in Amsterdam in 1727) to Emperor Charles VI. It may be this publication that

EXAMPLE 3.1. *Vivaldi, Chamber Concerto in D (RV 94), II*

resulted in his being "called to Vienna," as he puts it in a later letter. In any case the composer was said to be warmly received by the emperor on a visit to the imperial port city of Trieste in 1728. Abbé Conti wrote Madame de Caylus in a letter of 19 September 1728 that "the emperor gave a lot of money to Vivaldi along with a chain and gold medal, and also ennobled him."[39] The last cannot be true, for when he later enumerated all his distinctions Vivaldi omitted saying anything about being ennobled, an honor he surely would have included. Conti continued, "the emperor had a long talk with Vivaldi about music and they say that in fifteen days he spoke to him more than to his ministers in two years. . . . His taste for music is very developed." The famously taciturn emperor was indeed partial to music and musicians and was a gifted composer and keyboard performer himself. It should be added that this whole report is rather suspect and cannot be confirmed.

Vivaldi's concertos, especially those in printed collections, provided a rich store of nourishment for other composers. In the Op. 8 of 1724 there is a Concerto in d, No. 7, that begins with an expressive ritornello in which the bass leaps up a sixth, making the treble a dissonant suspension in need of resolution (Example 3.2). Vivaldi's freedom in treating dissonances is particularly evident at the beginning of the second measure. When the bass resolves its dissonant suspension on the second eighth note, the middle voice has leaped up to make a dissonance with the resolution, and the dissonances do not clear to a consonance lasting one beat until the last beat of the measure. Vivaldi's harmonic richness is also apparent, as in the fourth measure where an unexpected Neapolitan sixth chord gives way to a diminished chord on the way to the dominant. Gluck used something very close to Vivaldi's opening in his *Telemaco* (1764).[40] He then reused it at the beginning of his first opera for Paris, *Iphigénie en Aulide* (1774).

Violinists should bless Vivaldi for enriching the literature of the concerto for solo violin and strings with over two hundred works.[41] Cellists, bassoonists, oboists, and flautists, among others, also have him to thank for a rich legacy of solo concertos. The repertory for solo oboe is further enriched by two sets of twelve concertos for one or two oboes by Tomaso Albinoni published in Amsterdam in 1715 and 1722. Vivaldi's flute concertos are among the earliest in Italy, where the flute was regarded as somewhat foreign, perhaps because of French predominance in flute making and playing. The flute was also considered more appropriate to secular than to sacred music. Pope Benedict XIV in his encyclical

[39]Michael Talbot, "Vivaldi and the Empire," *Informazioni e studi vivaldiani* 8 (1987): 31–50; 39. Talbot has been unable to locate any court documents confirming Conti's claims, and the emperor's personal diary makes no mention of Vivaldi.

[40]Exemplified in *Haydn, Mozart*, p. 216.

[41]Chappell White, *From Vivaldi to Viotti: A History of the Early Classical Violin Concerto* (Philadelphia, 1992), p. 21.

EXAMPLE 3.2. *Vivaldi, Concerto in d, Op. 8 No. 7 (RV 242), I*

Annus qui of 1749 banned flutes from church music but allowed oboes (trombones were allowed but not horns and trumpets). Vivaldi became very partial to the flute in the late 1720s, not only composing or arranging the flute concertos of his Op. 10 but also using the instrument in his sacred music. Venice may have lost to Naples the absolute priority in the field of opera it enjoyed up to about 1720, but Vivaldi and Albinoni insured that Venice remained the unrivaled capital of the concerto.

In his *Versuch einer Anweisung die Flöte traversiere zu spielen* of 1752 Quantz made an elaborate comparison between Vivaldi and Tartini in which neither of them comes off very well.

> The first [Vivaldi] was lively and rich in invention, and supplied almost half the world with his concertos. Although Torelli, and after him Corelli, had made a start in this genre of music, this violinist, together with Albinoni, gave it a better form, and produced good models in it. And in this way he also achieved general credit, just as Corelli had with his twelve solos [Op. 5]. But finally, as a result of excessive daily composing, and especially after he had begun to write theatrical vocal pieces, he sank into frivolity and eccentricity both in composition and performance; in consequence his last concertos did not gain as much approbation as his first. It is said that he is one of those who invented the so-called Lombardic style. . . . Whatever the case may be, because of his character this change in his manner of thinking in his last years almost completely deprived the above-mentioned celebrated violinist of good taste in both performance and composition.[42]

According to his autobiography Quantz was warmly enthusiastic upon encountering Vivaldi's concertos in 1714 and took them for his models. Then he encountered Vivaldi as an opera composer at Rome in 1724. In his *Versuch* Quantz speaks for the Berlin establishment of the 1740s, with which Vivaldi was no longer in favor.

Vivaldi's legacy to the concert symphony was considerable as well. Aside from his vivacious and colorful operatic overtures in three movements, he left a body

---

[42]Johann Joachim Quantz, *On Playing the Flute*, a complete translation with an introduction and notes by Edward R. Reilly (New York, 1966), pp. 323–24. Quantz could not have heard Vivaldi play the violin in person after 1724 because their paths did not cross again.

of works for string orchestra without soloists called either sinfonia, *concerto a quat-tro,* or *concerto ripieno.*[43] These truly symphonic essays are in three movements, fast–slow–fast, and often begin with hammerstroke chords with multiple stops for the violins. Sammartini and Locatelli may have both profited from them in their own contributions to the genre.

THE FOUR SEASONS

Vivaldi dedicated his Op. 8 concertos, published in Amsterdam in 1724 as *Il cimento dell'armonia e dell'inventione,* to Count Venceslas von Morzin. This collection houses the most famous of all the composer's works, *The Four Seasons.* Vivaldi refers to them in the preface so as to suggest that they were written for Morzin some years earlier in a shorter form:"Your Illustrious Grace will find the Four Seasons, already long since under the indulgent and generous eye of Your Grace, but may you believe me that I took pride in publishing them, because they are in any case the same, but enlarged apart from the Sonnets, with detailed explanation of everything in them and I am sure they will seem new to you." In his salutation Vivaldi speaks of the "many years in which I have had the great good fortune to serve your Illustrious Grace as Maestro di Musica in Italy." More surprising still, he speaks of "the great understanding for music possessed by your Illustrious Grace and the high standard of your brilliant virtuoso orchestra." Not even kings and emperors traveled to Italy accompanied by their orchestras. Did Vivaldi visit Count Morzin in Vienna or Prague? Of such a trip nothing is known, but his words suggest that sometime even before 1720 he may have made his first foray across the Alps to the Habsburg realms.

Before the famous *Four Seasons* there were certainly many instrumental works with programmatic content. None was to have the sweeping success of these four concertos. From the preface already quoted we know that the cycle had a long gestation and that the poems appended to explain and describe each of the seasons came later, after the concertos were originally conceived. Description by literary means of what the music has already painted seems in itself an epochal departure. It foreshadows Berlioz a century later, making up stories to spell out his originally nonverbal fantasies in tone, as he admits in the case of the *Symphonie fantastique,* the verbal descriptions of which he kept revising.

---

[43]The terms are interchangeable according to Cesare Fertonani, *La musica strumentale di Antonio Vivaldi* (Florence, 1998), p. 513. Marc Pincherle, *Antonio Vivaldi et la musique instrumentale,* 2 vols. (Paris, 1948), 1: 186–204, discusses at length the composer's possible role in the evolution of the sinfonia. Six sinfonias for strings formerly preserved at Darmstadt and attributed to Albinoni are spurious works, as demonstrated by Michael Talbot, *Tomaso Albinoni: The Venetian Composer and His World* (Oxford, 1990), pp. 253–55. Two other composers who contributed to the early concert symphony were Giuseppe Matteo Alberti, with *XII Sinfonie a quattro* (Amsterdam, 1725), and Andrea Zani, with *Sei sinfonie di camera e altretanti concerti da chiesa: À quattro stromenti* (Casalmaggiore, 1729).

The poems are rather clumsy sonnets, perhaps written by Vivaldi himself, but certainly by a Venetian.[44] They were printed along with the parts as an intended enhancement. The first is entitled "Sonetto dimonstrativo sopra il Concerto Intitolato La Primavera del Sig.re D. Antonio Vivaldi," literally, an illustrative sonnet written upon the Concerto entitled "Spring." It divides into the traditional form of two quatrains followed by two tercets:

A	Giunt'è la Primavera e festosetti	Spring has come, and gaily
B	La salutan Gl'Augei con lieto canto,	the birds greet her with joyous song,
C	E i fonti allo spirar dé'Zeffiretti	and fountains that to zephyr's breath
	Con dolce mormoio scorrono intanto:	plash on with sweet murmurings.
D	Vengon' coprendo l'aer di nero amanto	Suddenly, covering the sky with black,
	E Lampi, e tuoni ad annuntiarla eletti	Lightning and thunder disturb them
E	Indi tacendo questi, gl'Augelletti;	While the little birds cease,
	Tornan' di nuovo al lor canoro incanto:	Then resume their charming strains;
F	E quindi sul fiorito ameno prato	Meanwhile on the lovely flowered plain
	Al caro mormorio di fronde e piante	to the sweet rustling of leafy plants
	Dorme'l Caprar col fido can'à lato.	sleeps the goatherd aside his trusty hound.
G	Di pastoral Zampogna al suon festante	To the bagpipe's festive sounds
	Danzan Ninfe e Pastor nel tetto amato	nymphs and shepherds dance under the lovely skies
	Di primavera all'apparir brillante.	of springtime in all its glory.

Vivaldi cued the text into the instrumental parts rather freely, changing the order here and there, as may be seen from the first page of the Violino Primo (Figure 3.4). There are actually two sets of verbal cues, the captions that occur at the large letters A, B, C, and D, and then quotes from the poem, which look as if they were added later.

The choice of E major for spring was a happy one. Its sonority had been a favorite for expressing astonishment as far back as the sixteenth-century Italian madrigal and should be heard in the mind's ear with reference to neutral C major

---

[44]Paul Everett, *Vivaldi: The Four Seasons and other concertos, Op. 8* (Cambridge, 1996), p. 70. The author proposes *L'allegro* and *Il penseroso*, two complementary poems by John Milton, as distant ancestors of Vivaldi's poems, pp. 77–80.

FIGURE 3.4. Vivaldi. "La Primavera," violino primo part.

in order to assume its proper color value. The *Allegro* begins with an upbeat and the repeated third degree. Also typical are the motoric regularity and the terraced dynamics. The solo violin enters on a single tone, the fifth degree, repeated at first in quarter notes, then in eighth notes, representing the singing of the birds, which gets more elaborate with the trilled offbeats in the next line and reaches up to the high tonic for the final trills. At letter C, after a short restatement of the opening, the strings drop to a *piano* level and intone a little wavering figure in sixteenth notes that outlines thirds by conjunct motion, up and down. This represents the murmuring of wind and wave. A short section of the tutti ritornello on the dominant then leads (at letter D) to very rapid repeated notes on low B, representing thunder ("Tuoni"), followed by vigorous scales representing lightning ("Lampi"). Note that the poem inverts their order to lightning and thunder.

Orchestral painting like this was common enough in opera, where the depiction of natural phenomena was required in simile arias and in elaborate recitatives of the obbligato type. Vivaldi, as an opera composer himself, was well acquainted with the arsenal of pictorial effects then in use. He certainly did not invent them, although he may have done more than anyone else, by means of *The Four Seasons,* to diffuse them. The history of such stereotyped figures stretches over many generations. Mozart was but one in a long line of composers to use the same "murmuring Zephyr" figure, as he did among other places in the Terzetto "Soave sia il vento" near the beginning of *Così fan tutte.* Even the key of E major had a specific connection with gentle breezes and placid seas for Mozart.

The second movement of "La Primavera," a *Largo* in the relative minor, is entitled "Il capraro che dorme" (The Sleeping Goatherd). Vivaldi writes a long-breathed elegiac melody for the solo violin while the orchestral strings, minus cellos and basses, maintain an incessant "murmuring" motion, related to that in the first movement but in dotted rhythm. There is indeed a dreamlike quality to this exquisite air for solo violin—a vision of Arcadian felicity worthy of Metastasio (even if the poem is not) or of Watteau. Like those great artists Vivaldi is very much a part of the new century, and he is never greater than here. His slow movement as a whole has a clarity of shape, with reprise of the main idea after modulation to the dominant, that is more similar to an aria than it is to the equivalent slow movements of Corelli, which are often only a transitional section, not a full-fledged movement in the eighteenth-century sense.[45] The final cadence is full and

---

[45]David Burrows, "Style in Culture: Vivaldi, Zeno and Ricci," *Journal of Interdisciplinary History* 4 (1973–74): 1–23, shows that the trend in Zeno to "fewer and longer arias per libretto is analogous to Vivaldi's trend toward fewer and longer movements with fewer and longer sections within movements" (p. 7). He shows further that Marco Ricci's landscapes join Vivaldi's concertos and Zeno's librettos "to confirm a single trend toward simplifying, sharpening distinctions, and standardizing" (p. 19).

sonorous: I - IV - V^7 - I$^6_4$ - V^7 - I. There are no added suspensions, the usual inheritance of the concerto from its ecclesiastical past.

E major returns with the final *Allegro*, a kind of contredanse in 2/4, with drone
bass to paint the rustic bagpipe, also evoked in the poem. "La primavera" has
pleased legions of listeners who did not know exactly what was being painted,
proving that its program, while providing an added bonus, is not indispensable.

Vivaldi never surpassed these program concertos. While he was sometimes
negligent in polishing his works, he left no detail of the *Seasons* that was not polished to a high degree. In 1754, when Charles Henri de Blainville published his
L'esprit de l'art musical, he declared these concertos unsurpassed of their kind,
while placing Vivaldi's works as a whole in the category of the "sonabile" composers, who were inferior to the "cantabile" ones, but superior, according to him,
to the somnolent old Corelli style, which he labeled "harmonico."

Across the Channel there were harsher words about Vivaldi. Francesco Geminiani, Corelli's pupil, in his *Art of Playing on the Violin* (London, 1751), pointedly
announced that there would be no imitations of birds and other phenomena that
rather "belong to the Professors of Legerdemain and Posture-masters than to the
Art of Musick." A year later, Charles Avison, Geminiani's pupil, published an essay
in which he vaunts "the chaste and faultless Corelli" and praises Geminiani as the
greatest composer of instrumental music. Vivaldi he consigns to the composers
without abilities or discernment: "Of the first and lowest Class, are Vivaldi, Tessarini, [Giuseppe Matteo] Alberti, and Locatelli, whose Compositions being
equally deffective in various Harmony and true Invention, are only a fit Amusement for Children; nor indeed for these, if ever they be intended to be led to just
Taste in Music."[46] Avison would not likely have been so bold in his condemnation
had it not been endorsed by Geminiani.

At least one critic took issue with Avison's judgments, first by doubting his
qualifications for making them. In an anonymously printed response to Avison,
written by William Hayes of Oxford, Tessarini is called a mere copier of Vivaldi,
while Vivaldi himself is described as rambling and inclined to cheapen his happy
gifts, but capable nevertheless of writing a good fugue, an instance of which is
cited the one in Concerto 11 of Op. 3 (Example 3.3).[47] Hayes picked a good example, and since Avison was mainly interested in fugues, the point hits home. Not
even Bach found anything to change in this magnificent fugue when transcribing
it for organ (BWV 596).

Vivaldi's career has been discussed in some detail here because it presents a
test case of the extent to which an individual of genial powers could challenge the

---

[46]Charles Avison, *An Essay on Musical Expression* (London, 1752), p. 42.
[47]William Hayes, *Remarks on Mr. Avison's Essay on Musical Expression* (London, 1753), cited after Pincherle,
Vivaldi, p. 243.

EXAMPLE 3.3. *Vivaldi, Concerto in d, Op. 3 No. 11 (RV 565), II*

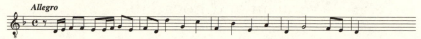

rigid systems of church and state at that time. The answer depends on which authorities were involved. Venice, a rigorously policed autocratic state with severe censorship restrictions, run by a small number of nobles bent upon self-preservation, even by the most repressive means, gave its distinguished son little trouble, no matter how far the rumormongers went in defaming him. The papacy showed an equally permissive latitude to one of its own, at least in the 1720s, when Vivaldi was at the height of his fame. Even the ultra-Catholic Emperor Charles VI apparently looked upon the genius with favor. A single and rather backward church-state, Ferrara, under the aegis of its narrow-minded cardinal, called Vivaldi to account, and thus began his slide into financial ruin and personal humiliation. Later in the century the career of Lorenzo da Ponte offers a parallel case of an individual who raised himself up from a lower-class background via the priesthood, then failed to live up to the requirements of his holy vows. How much we should have lost had either one not become what he did become!

Charles de Brosses in his letter of 29 August 1739 offers the last portrait in words that we have taken from the life of the famous (and by this time infamous) violinist-composer.

> Vivaldi has made himself one of my close friends in order to sell me some concertos at a very high price. In this he partly succeeded, as did I in my intention, which was to hear him play and have good musical recreation often. He is a *vecchio* with a prodigious fury for composing. I have heard him boast of composing a concerto, with all its parts, quicker than a copyist could write them down. I found, to my great astonishment, that he is not as well regarded as he deserves in this country, where everything has to be modish, where his works have been heard for too long, and where last year's music is no longer profitable. Today the man celebrated is the famous Saxon [Hasse]. (1: 242–43)

Vivaldi was only sixty-two, but Venice had been hearing him for nearly forty years in one capacity or another. It was tired of his brusque and energetic musical style. His strong and readily identifiable personality in music only hastened Vivaldi's fall from fashion.

Veracini and Locatelli

The violin from its beginnings in the sixteenth century was associated with northern Italy, where the greatest violin makers flourished. They also made superb
lower instruments of the violin family, but it was the violin and its virtuosi who
captured the most attention during the eighteenth century, just as did sopranos,
especially castrati, among singers. The era was partial to high treble sounds, a
preference that spread from Italy with the traveling virtuosi, vocal and instrumental. One of the four engraved plates with multiple portraits of musicians from
the Studio Rainaldi in Florence at the beginning of the nineteenth century was
entitled *Professori celebri di Suono*, which could be interpreted to mean celebrated
instrumental performers. It includes thirty-four portraits. They are almost all violinists and with few exceptions all Italians. The upper portion of the huge plate is
reproduced as Figure 3.5. The top medallion honors Somis, Locatelli, and Geminiani. Tartini figures to the left of the next row across, which is continued by his
pupil Domenico Ferrari, Lolli, Wilhelm Cramer of Mannheim, and Felice Giardini,
above whom Veracini looks out of step with his long wig. Above the beak-nosed
Tartini, and partially obscured by him, is his most famous French pupil, André-
Noël Pagin. Overlapping Tartini below him are Gaetano Pugnani and Carlo
Chiabrano. The bottom row contains Giovanni Battista Viotti, Janovick (i.e., Giovanni Mane Giornovichi), Pietro Nardini, and Galeotti, presumably Salvatore the
violinist and not Stefano the cellist. *Settecento* Italy did not lack for famous cellists,
such as Francesco Aborea, alias Francischello, Giovanni Battista Costanzi, and
Antonio Vandini, not to mention Luigi Boccherini, none of whom appears. On the
complete plate the only instrument represented besides the violin is the harp, in
the persons of the Bohemian-born Jean-Baptiste Krumpholtz and his wife,
Madame Krumpholtz, the only woman performer in the whole assemblage. Italian wind players, of whom the most famous were the Besozzis, are lacking altogether, and Vivaldi is forgotten.

Traveling virtuosi of the violin were not a new phenomenon in the eighteenth
century. Torelli, to mention only one, made some of the same rounds in central
Europe as the Italian solo violinists who came after him, but he was honored as
much or more for composition as for his playing. Francesco Veracini, born in Florence in 1690, provides an example of the more typically modern phenomenon of
a pampered virtuoso traveling from place to place as a star performer. His appearances as a soloist at San Marco at the Christmas masses of 1711 and 1712 have
already been mentioned. On his subsequent tours in Germany he is known to
have played, besides his own music, pieces from the *Invenzioni da camera* (1712)
by Francesco Bonporti.

Veracini seemed ideally suited to providing Venice with the superior solo per-

FIGURE 3.5. Luigi Scotti and Antonio Fedi. *Professori celebri di Suono,* detail.

former on the violin for whom the public clamored. (Vivaldi's multifarious activities as teacher, orchestra leader, impresario, and opera composer limited his solo performances, and in spite of his technical wizardry on the violin he did not necessarily please everyone, as we have seen.) Yet Venice could not or would not offer Veracini enough financial rewards to keep him. In 1714 he pursued his career in London, appearing as a soloist between the acts of operas at the royal theater. By July 1716 he was back in Venice, whence he dedicated a manuscript of twelve "Sonate a Violino, o Flauto solo e Basso" to the prince elector of Saxony, who opened the way to his being hired at a high salary in Dresden for several years.[48]

Veracini's 1716 sonatas made relatively modest demands on the solo player, in keeping with their dual destination for flute or violin, and this framework imposed a certain simplicity and directness on the composer that were in tune with his closeness to Corelli but not with the wildness and extravagance of his personality, which would emerge in his later works. These sonatas are neither of the church nor chamber variety, having four movements (slow–fast–slow–fast) as in the former, but no fugues, and having dancelike movements as in the latter. They are melodious and homophonic. What dissonances do occur are treated freely, a leading tone being resolved, for instance, in an octave above or below (for which Johann Heinichen provided justification when describing the theatrical style in his treatises of 1711 and 1728).

With their short and symmetrical phrases, their freedom from harmonic sequences and *Fortspinnung,* Veracini's sonatas clearly belong to the galant style. Quantz in his *Versuch* defined the style in several ways, one being that a galant melody always forms more consonances than dissonances with the bass, which is another way of saying that the linear sonority formed by suspensions was less important than the vertical sonorities of treble supported by bass, well illustrated by Veracini. It is not surprising that Burney considered the young Veracini to be an innovator.

The older Veracini got, the more he renounced his early orientation, as can be seen in the progressive stages of his published sonatas for violin and bass. His Op. 1 in 1721, written in Dresden and also dedicated to the electoral prince, draws closer to Corelli in many ways, including a division into church and chamber sonatas, the former offering fugues in three parts akin to Corelli's Op. 5. In the Op. 2 sonatas of 1744, "texture and form are even more complicated and the whole style more original than in the earlier sonatas."[49] They are dedicated once again to the

[48]The definitive study is John Walter Hill, "The Life and Works of Francesco Maria Veracini," 4 vols. (Ph.D. diss., Harvard University, 1972) (UM 74–16, 720, which includes a biographical supplement of 1974).

[49]John Walter Hill, "The Anti-Galant Attitude of F. M. Veracini," *Studies in Musicology in Honor of Otto E. Albrecht,* ed. John Walter Hill (Kassel, 1980), pp. 158–96; 178. The author cleverly brings together the composer's long quest for the contrapuntal virtues of his boyhood training with the verbal expression of them from his late years, his manuscript treatise "Il trionfo della pratica musicale."

same prince, by this time king of Poland. The composer's path was at least consistent, leading to his last set, the manuscript "Dissertation on Corelli Sonatas," in which he rewrote the older master's Op. 5 so as to make it more contrapuntal.

Veracini spent his later years in London, where he wrote four operas between 1736 and 1744, and in Florence, where he occupied some minor church posts while continuing to perform as a violin soloist. Brosses heard him in Florence in 1739 and wrote that "his playing is just, noble, knowledgeable, and precise, but a little lacking in grace" (1: 307). Burney, who heard him also, wrote in the *History* that "by travelling all over Europe he formed a style of playing peculiar to himself." Burney also wrote that "the peculiarities of his performance were his bowhand, his shake, his learned arpeggios, and a tone so loud and clear, that it could be distinctly heard through the most numerous band of a church or theater." At the advanced age of seventy-five, Veracini was still performing. He played for young Archduke Leopold, newly installed as grand duke of Tuscany, in the fall of 1765. He died three years later.

Veracini and Locatelli were paired in a report written to Padre Martini in 1764: "Signor Locatelli of Bergamo came from the celebrated school of the most divine Corelli, and was, with the Florentine Veracini (still living), the most excellent violinist and composer for violin; he was also a great collector of theoretical works, books and paintings."[50] Locatelli went to Rome in late 1711, probably hoping to study with Corelli, but he was too late to have received much if any personal instruction from the master, who suffered a long decline during his last year and died in January 1713. Nevertheless, Locatelli profited from the experience in the sense that he took Corelli's violin compositions as his lifelong model, as did Veracini, Geminiani, Tartini, and many others. Veracini has also been called a Corelli pupil in the more usual sense, without any greater factual foundation.

Locatelli was playing violin in Bergamo's main church already as a boy.[51] By age fourteen in 1710 he was paid as much as the adult violinists there. In 1711 he applied for leave to go to Rome in order to improve himself in his profession. Permission was granted and he left in September 1711. In all likelihood Locatelli studied with Corelli's rival, Giuseppe Valentini, whom he mentions having accompanied on a trip in a letter of 17 March 1714 to his father.[52] He became a

[50]Letter dated Florence, 7 October 1764, written by the court musician Domenico Palafuti. Mario Fabbri, "Una nuova fonte per la conoscenza di Giovanni Platti e del suo 'Miserere'," *Chigiana* 24 (1967): 181–202; 189. There is nothing in this document about Locatelli's being a student of Veracini, contrary to what John Walter Hill has claimed.

[51]Paola Palermo, "La musica nella Basilica di Santa Maria Maggiore a Bergamo all'epoca dell' infanzia di Locatelli," in *Intorno a Locatelli: Studi in occasione del tricentenario della nascità di Pietro Antonio Locatelli (1695–1764)*, ed. Albert Dunning, 2 vols. (Lucca, 1995), 2: 653–748.

[52]Albert Dunning, *Pietro Antonio Locatelli: Der Virtuose und seine Welt*, 2 vols. (Buren, 1981), 1: 48–49. Dunning does not explore Locatelli's possible debt to the attractive violin sonatas Valentini published as *Allettamenti per camera*, Op. 8 (Rome, 1714).

part of the circle of Cardinal Pietro Ottoboni, who lived magnificently in the Cancelleria palace, which had its own church, San Lorenzo in Damaso, and its own theater. Ottoboni's Monday evening musical academies counted as Rome's finest. Locatelli flourished as both violinist and composer in these luxurious surroundings for several years, remaining in Rome until 1723. They are thought to have provided the milieu for his first set of concertos, published by Roger in Amsterdam in 1721 as *XII concerti grossi a 4 e a 5,* for two violins, one or two violas, and bass. The collection ranks as a very distinguished Op. 1.

In 1725 Locatelli was appointed *virtuoso di camera* by Prince Philip, regent of Mantua and Vivaldi's patron. Around the same time he was giving concerts in Venice. These eventually turned into his concertos Op. 3, printed at Amsterdam in 1733 as *L'arte del violino.* In his dedication of the print to a Venetian patrician, Girolamo Michiel Lini, the composer speaks of performing the works in Venice "with a skilled orchestra of unparalleled size." Lini was also a native of Bergamo, one who had earned a prodigious fortune in the spice trade and who could well afford to provide the composer with a fine orchestra.

The lure of the northern courts worked upon Locatelli as it had earlier on the haughty Veracini. In June 1727 Locatelli was in Munich being paid for having performed before the elector Carl Albert. In the following year he made various stops in Frankfurt, Dresden, Kassel, and Berlin. At the court of Kassel, it is claimed, took place an encounter with Jean-Marie Leclair, during which they both played solos.[53] Then in 1729 Locatelli reached Amsterdam, where his music had first been published eight years earlier. Perhaps it was the active music publishing business there that made him decide to stay. He became a close friend and collaborator of the publisher La Cène. Although he had no official position, he was able to make a good living in the Dutch metropolis by giving house concerts, teaching amateurs, editing, and dealing in the sale of his own music. Dedications to some of his rich pupils also brought rewards. He was one of the first freelance artists to succeed, and his personality must have won over the frugal and industrious Dutch by similar traits they could admire. In his house on the Prinsengracht, one of the three main canals of Amsterdam, he left behind a magnificent collection of books, pictures, and musical instruments. Once settled in Amsterdam he gave up concert tours and performed only in private, not in public.

Locatelli kept aloof from other professional musicians. "He won't admit a Professed Musician into his Concert; and he never will Play anywhere but with Gentlemen," wrote young Benjamin Tate from Amsterdam in a long letter describing Locatelli, dated 11 April 1741.[54] If this be true an exception was apparently made in the case of Leclair, who was contracted to spend part of each year in Holland serv-

[53]Ibid., 1: 118–19.
[54]Ibid., 1: 204–5.

ing a wealthy patron between 1740 and 1743. Leclair's necrologist claims that the French master profited greatly from hearing Locatelli play when he was in Holland.

Locatelli remained in touch with European-wide currents of musical life while in Holland. As a publisher's corrector he saw through the press some of the grander works of his elders, including Corelli, Vivaldi, Geminiani, and Handel. The continued popularity of their sonatas testifies to the widespread respect for the solid workmanship of the older style, even while newer currents were coming to the fore. Locatelli also saw through the press the latest works of several composers whose music was closer to his own: Hasse, Tartini, Tessarini, Giovanni Battista Ferradini, and Sammartini.

The new in music also came to Holland in the form of touring Italian singers. In his correspondence with Padre Martini (obligatory, it seems, for all expatriate Italian musicians of stature), Locatelli reported his favorable impression of the tenor Giuseppe Tibaldi, who appeared at Amsterdam in 1754, much as Tartini had conveyed his enthusiasm for Anton Raaff's singing in a letter to Martini a few years earlier. Locatelli's reputation as a virtuoso violinist grew to the point that it brought musicians to Amsterdam to hear him. An English visitor in 1741, Thomas Dampier, conjectured that, because he played with so much fury, he must wear out a dozen violins a year. Locatelli's artistic sphere extended to the Concert Spirituel at Paris, where his works were played, even if he did not appear there himself as soloist.

Like so many other instrumental composers of the early eighteenth century, Locatelli began writing under the shadow of the great Corelli and only gradually emerged from it. In his Op. 1 (1721), a set of twelve concerti grossi that were reedited in 1729, the inspiration of Corelli's Op. 6 is evident. The order as to church and chamber type is arranged exactly as in the model: eight church sonatas, followed by four suites. As in Corelli also, the eighth concerto represents a high point, with beautiful pastoral effects appropriate to its function as a "concerto fatto per la notte di Natale." Locatelli departed from the model, even so, by expanding the Corellian trio-concertino to a quartet including viola, a step already suggested by Georg Muffat in 1701, and subsequently adopted by Geminiani, Vivaldi (Op. 12, 1732), and Tartini. Locatelli was more adventurous than Corelli in his choice of keys, especially on the flat side, which posed more difficulties for stringed instruments. The fugal style coexists in these works alongside those of a more homophonic cast. Only the sixth concerto has the three movements typical of the solo concerto, and in it the first violin is notably favored; the other concertos have four or more movements.[55] Locatelli figured his basses quite thoroughly, as did

---

[55]Eugene K. Wolf, "I Concerti Grossi dell' Opera I (1721) di Pietro Antonio Locatelli e le origini della Sinfonia," *Intorno a Locatelli* (1995), 2: 1169–93, argues that concertos Nos. 1, 7, and 9 are forebears of the concert symphony.

Veracini, a fact that bears witness to their mutual awareness of the needs of musical amateurs in the northern countries. The practice in Italy, on the other hand, was more casual, and is summed up in Vivaldi's obscenely scornful remark upon adding a few figures "per i coglioni."

Music for the dilettante comes especially to the fore in the flute sonatas with basso continuo that Locatelli published himself in 1732 and dedicated to a very wealthy young man, one of his pupils and presumably a flautist. The elegant title page with its several type fonts calls attention mostly to the illustrious "Signor," mentions the composer's origins, "da Bergamo," as Locatelli never ceased doing, and is personally signed in order to guarantee

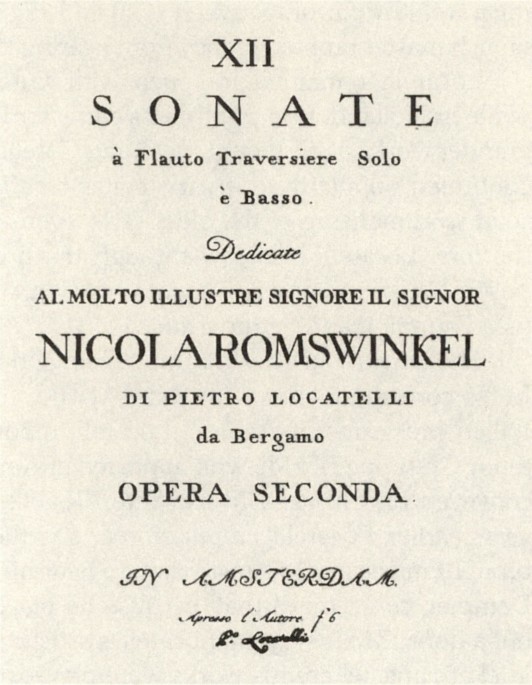

XII

S O N A T E

à Flauto Traversiere Solo

è Basso.

Dedicate

AL MOLTO ILLUSTRE SIGNORE IL SIGNOR

NICOLA ROMSWINKEL

DI PIETRO LOCATELLI

da Bergamo

OPERA SECONDA.

IN AMSTERDAM.

FIGURE 3.6. Title page of Locatelli's Sonatas, Op. 2.

authenticity (Figure 3.6). Some of these sonatas follow the four-movement pattern of slow–fast–slow–fast; others exhibit a variety of three-movement plans. Locatelli favors for first movements a florid lyric outpouring such as the *Andante* in common time that opens Sonata No. 9 in E (Example 3.4). The refined and delicate melody begins with two clichés of the galant style, the three-note slide and Lombard snap. Corelli is still the model, yet there is not so much a typically Corellian "walking bass" moving constantly by step, but quite often a "standing still" bass marking time by repeated tones, although not so frugal as some of Vivaldi's drum basses. The bass is still suspended occasionally, as in the case of the A resolving to G♯ in m. 2, but most of the time it offers harmonic support rather than contrapuntal interest. As to choice of keys among movements Locatelli sometimes surprises. Sonata No. 7 in A has for its third movement a *Largo* in F, a Siciliano-like movement in 12/8 that captures a pastoral mood (Example 3.5). Tartini was so fond of this lilting tune that he used it over and over. The suavity lent to it by the long subdominant harmony over a tonic pedal is also reminiscent of Hasse.

Locatelli's most important compositions, not surprisingly, were for solo violin, both in the sonata and in the concerto, to which Veracini had made but negligible contributions. His most famous publication was undoubtedly his *L'arte del violino* (Op. 3, 1733), a set of twelve concertos for violin and orchestra. In form the

EXAMPLE 3.4. *Locatelli, Sonata in E, Op. 2 No. 9, I*

EXAMPLE 3.5. *Locatelli, Sonata in A, Op. 2 No. 7, II*

concertos follow Vivaldi, but the tendency to make the solo part more cantabile brings them closer to Tartini. The first and third movements include elaborate cadenzas called "Capricci" that make extreme technical demands on the soloist. Locatelli does not hesitate to require hand positions up to the fourteenth. Yet Geminiani in his treatise (1761) states that the usual upper limit for a good player was an octave lower. Locatelli also included easier cadenzas as alternatives, in keeping with the mainly didactic basis of this as well as his other publications. Even so, the high writing for the solo violin is exceptional, and not just in the Capricci. Quite typically, the soloist was called upon to repeat ritornello material an octave higher than the orchestral violins, an act of bravura that sums up the impression these concertos make as a whole. Burney's friend and Italian tutor Vincenzo Martinelli probably had Locatelli in mind when he took violinists to task in his *Lettere familiari e critiche* (London, 1758) for being unvocal and using "very high sounds in their ungrateful and vain bravura passages." This accords with Burney's unjust dismissal of Locatelli's music in the *History* as exciting "more surprise than pleasure."

With the twelve sonatas for solo violin and continuo, published in 1737 as Op. 6 but probably stretching over several years in the composition, Locatelli put his stamp upon the galant chamber sonata. Of fugue or serious contrapuntal elaboration there is no longer a hint. The new genre consists, typically, of three movements all in the same key: an initial *Andante* (or slow to moderate movement), a vigorous *Allegro* (which with Locatelli is often quite concerto-like in rhythm and virtuosity), and a concluding minuet or other dance type. This sequence, endorsed by Johann Adolph Scheibe (1745) and Quantz (1752), quickly became that of an entire generation. Peculiar to Locatelli are the virtuosic variations he liked to write upon the final dance air, giving this movement a weight equal to that of the others. His first two movements both adopt an expanded bipartite dance form, with repeat signs after both halves. The expansion comes in the second part, in which Locatelli often has a clear reprise in the tonic, after modulations initiated by stating the main material in the dominant (in the major mode).

Four of the twelve sonatas are in minor, and the first of these ends in major. The collection, dedicated to a wealthy Italian merchant residing in Amsterdam, offers an up-to-date companion worthy of Corelli's Op. 5 sonatas. It displays all the latest melodic fashions—Lombard snaps, offbeat patterns, triplets (especially to conclude a melodic period), and sighing appoggiatura figures. This whole gallery of modish turns of phrase goes together with frequent passages in thirds and other double stops, arpeggiated chords over a wide span, and some of the same high writing that marked his concertos. The keys venture as far afield as B major. For all that is novel, tuneful, and idiomatic in these sonatas, Locatelli has still not been able to get away from a rather routine use of harmonic sequences, especially in the second parts of the *Andante* and *Allegro* movements. But then, even Tartini suffered the same limitation until late in his life, and Veracini gave up trying to find a solution early in his.

In his Op. 4 of 1735, published by La Cène and entitled *VI Introduttioni teatrali et VI concerti*, Locatelli begins with six three-movement works on the fast–moderate–fast model of the Neapolitan opera sinfonia. All are in major and do not go beyond two accidentals (D is used twice). In texture these overtures remain concerti grossi for strings without winds and have concertino and ripieno parts. They are not sufficiently diverse and seem to have been composed all at once. In musical substance they are close to Vivaldi's more flamboyant sinfonie. This exuberance in the opening fast movements begins to wear thin for lack of variety. All are in common time, without repeat signs; after the big cadence on V they move in formulaic ways by harmonic sequences to a cadence on iii (four times) or vi (twice) followed by a short reprise. The second movements are in the parallel minor except for No. 3, which is in the subdominant key. The third movements are all fast dances in 3/8 time, in rounded binary form with repeat signs. Presumably the overtures made good openers for Locatelli's house concerts, but were they also used as theatrical "introductions," that is, overtures? Amsterdam, strangely enough for a great and wealthy capital of banking, trade, and industry, had no operatic life to speak of until later, but it did enjoy a lively tradition of spoken plays, principally in the century-old Schouwburg on the Keizergracht, near which the composer lived when he first settled in Amsterdam. The leading painter of the city, Cornelis Troost, who drew and engraved Locatelli's portrait (for *L'arte del violino*) also worked for this theater as a scene painter. Perhaps the small theater orchestra there used these overtures.

Locatelli occasionally invoked extramusical associations in some of his works, although he published nothing so explicit as Vivaldi's program concertos. The last concerto of Op. 7 (1741) is subtitled "Pianto d'Arianna." It goes so far as to introduce some striking examples of instrumental recitative for the solo violin, as well as a series of slow laments. The final dirge pushes as far afield as $e^\flat$, with wonderfully muted effect upon the strings, and ends with a series of halting syncopated chords and a final dominant seventh of which the dissonant member is resolved in the octave below. No doubt intended to evoke tears quite as much as the lamenting Ariannas of the operatic stage, this finale bears comparison in the lachrymal vein with Pergolesi's *Stabat mater*. The sequence of several movements interrupted by solo recitatives urges us to imagine a program in line with the subtitle, even if one is not specified. The heroine is of course represented by the solo violin, and, taken to another level, the solo was initially or ideally played by the composer himself. That leads to further reveries about unhappy loves and tragic abandonments.

We have moved into the sphere of emotional suggestion by literary allusion. D'Alembert propounded exactly this as a way to free instrumental music and make it meaningful in his *De la liberté de la musique* (1759), with a specific reference to Tartini's *Didone abbandonata* sonata. The "Pianto d'Arianna" came close to being Locatelli's swan song. It was followed only by a set mixing solo violin sonatas and trio sonatas, published as Op. 8 in 1744. A later set of concertos supposedly published as Op. 9 in 1762 has never been found. Having said what he had to say to the world, and having left it a legacy of violinistic legerdemain still unsurpassed, Locatelli fell silent. His life ended placidly at Amsterdam in 1764.

Locatelli's music remained current throughout the eighteenth century. Young Ditters formed his hand on the violin sonatas of Locatelli, he tells us in his memoirs, and he recommended their study to all young violinists. (The engraved collection he owned was perhaps Op. 6.) On the other hand, he was told by his teacher that the pieces of Locatelli and Tartini "are well enough for practice, but not for show; besides that they are too well known here [Vienna]."[56] Instead he was counseled to play the concertos and sonatas of the Tartini pupil Domenico Ferrari, which he did. But Locatelli was played in public at the Concert Spirituel (by Ferrari among other violinists).

Publishers in London and Paris judged that the market for Locatelli could absorb their pirated editions of his Amsterdam publications. His reputation was high in France but low in England, as we saw from Avison's scathing remarks ranking him with Vivaldi, Tessarini, and Alberti. Robert Price, one of the band of Englishmen who heard Locatelli in 1741, reported the difficulties he encountered among his countrymen in attempting to promote the composer's concertos.

> They cannot bear anything but Handel, Corelli and Geminiani, which they are eternally playing over and over again at all their concerts. I was at a concert at Lord Brooke's where Carbonelli played the first fiddle; Tate brought with him some concertos of Locatelli without solo parts, which are extremely easy, but because there were some passages out of the common road, they looked upon them as the most extravagant things in the world and not to be played at sight. Tate and I are of a concert of gentlemen performers where Festing plays the first fiddle, we tried to bring in some of Locatelli's musick there, but when we mentioned it to Festing he looked as if he had been condemned to be hanged.[57]

Locatelli stood as little chance as Vivaldi in a society whose ideas of musical propriety were dictated by Geminiani. The price of this musical insularity was exacted in the mediocre level of midcentury English composers of instrumental music. Paris, on the other hand, was the capital of a country avid for new musical experiences and embracing, even while protesting, the newest currents from Italy.

French critics around midcentury claimed that the pair of Locatelli and Tartini had quite dethroned the old style of composition. Thus in the *Jugement de l'orchestre de l'opera* (1753), one of the antimodern pamphlets of the Querelle des Bouffons, the author protested that the French had been the first to admire Corelli and Vivaldi and several others, "but at present in Italy, following the example of the innovators of the Queen's corner [the proponents of Pergolesi and opera

[56]Carl Ditters, *The Autobiography of Karl von Dittersdorf, Dictated to His Son*, trans. A. D. Coleridge (London, 1896; reprint 1970), p. 40.

[57]Letter of 19 December 1741 to Lord Haddington, quoted by Dunning, *Pietro Antonio Locatelli*, 1: 279.

buffa] one treats their music as being old-fashioned, and has abandoned them for the Tartinis, the Locatellis, who offer only bizarre difficulties." Grimm cited Tartini approvingly in 1753. Diderot joined the fray in his master satire *Le neveu de Rameau,* where he has the nephew go through all the grimaces of a performer playing a violin sonata—not one by Corelli or Vivaldi, to be sure, nor Handel either. The nephew "embroiders with his voice an *Allegro* by Locatelli while his right hand imitates the movement of the bow and his left and his fingers seem to promenade up and down the length of the neck . . . as you have sometimes seen at the Concert Spirituel when Ferrari or Chiabrano, or some other virtuoso goes into the same convulsions." A proposed identification of the actual piece as the Sonata in E of Op. 6 has been made.[58] In any case modern style, as far as violin music was concerned, began for Diderot with Locatelli and Tartini, who are named in tandem at the end of *Le neveu de Rameau,* along with a host of Neapolitan opera composers from Vinci to Traetta. A visual satire of Caffarelli by an anonymous French artist brings together Locatelli and Tartini, as well as the oboe player Giuseppe Sammartini, cellist Salvatore Lanzetti, and, at the harpsichord, Domenico Scarlatti (Figure 3.7).

De ces grands Maîtres d'Italie
Le Concert seroit fort joli,
Si le Chat que l'on voit icy
N'y vouloit Chanter sa partie

CONCERT
ITALIEN.
6 Le Chat de Cafarelli, chantant
une Parodie Italienne

De deux cœurs que ta chaîne lie
C'est ainsy, petit Dieu d'Amour,
Que quelque Animal chaque jour
Vient troubler la douce harmonie

1. Scarlatti
2. Tartini.
3. Martini.
4. Locatelli
5. Lanzetti.

FIGURE 3.7. Anonymous satire of Italian musicians in concert.

[58]Daniel Heartz, "Locatelli and the Pantomime of the Violinist in *Le Neveu Rameau,*" *Diderot Studies* 27 (1998): 115–27.

Tartini

Giuseppe Tartini, born on 8 April 1692, was three years older than Locatelli, whom he probably never met. Destined for the priesthood by his parents, he became a violinist against their wishes. During 1708–9 he enrolled as a student of law at Padua, the university town where he chose to spend most of his life. His major occupation while a law student was fencing, even though he wore the clerical garb of minor orders. In 1710 he was so imprudent as to marry an indigent young woman of the town. He was obliged to flee, leaving his wife. He found refuge in the convent of Saint Francis in Assisi for three years, but when his protector there died he had to earn his keep as an orchestral violinist in the theater at Ancona (1714). The following year he returned to the Veneto, where he was reunited with his wife. During 1717–18 he was primo violino in Fano.[59]

In music Tartini was mostly self-taught. His violin technique was formed partly in emulation of other virtuosi, if we may believe the story of his encounter with Veracini at Venice in 1716. He quickly became an admired virtuoso in his own right, enjoying wide support among Venetian patricians. The result was his appointment in 1721 as "Sonator singolare" and "Primo Violino, e Capo di Concerto" at the Paduan basilica of San Antonio, at an annual salary of 150 fiorini. He was hired, in other words, both as violin soloist, the first such at Padua, and as orchestra leader. His contract allowed him freedom to give concerts elsewhere, another token of the esteem he enjoyed. He attended the coronation of Emperor Charles VI at Prague in 1723 and remained in Bohemia in the service of Count Kinsky until 1726, when his precarious health dictated a return to Italy. From this point on he rarely quitted Padua except to go to nearby Venice, turning down lucrative offers from Paris, London, and Amsterdam.

Padua's university, whose students had included Bembo, Galileo, and Tasso, was one of the oldest (founded in 1222) and most distinguished in Italy. Unlike most Italian universities Padua welcomed Protestant students, a defiance of Rome scarcely possible except in the Veneto, and it was one of few universities in Europe to admit Jews as well as grant them degrees.[60] In this respect it was matched by the openness of contemporary Dutch universities. Padua was the first university to grant a degree to a woman (in 1678—it helped, of course, that she was a Cornaro,

---

[59]Pierluigi Petrobelli, *Giuseppe Tartini: Le fonti biografiche* (Venice, 1968), is the source of this capsule history. Claudio Bellinati, "Contributo alla biografia padovana di Giuseppe Tartini con nuovi documenti," in *Tartini: Il tempo e le opere*, ed. Andrea Bombi and Maria Nevilla Massaro (Bologna, 1994), pp. 23–35, adds details on the marriage, which was not, as some have maintained, clandestine.

[60]*Universities in Early Modern Europe 1500–1800*, ed. Hilde de Ridder-Symeons, vol. 2: *A History of the University in Europe* (Cambridge, 1996), pp. 295–96.

a family that sired doges). There is a curious parallel here: both Locatelli and Tartini chose to settle on islands of relative toleration in what was then a sea of bigotry.

Tartini attracted students from all over Europe to study violin with him (and theory and composition as well). Thus he became known as the "maestro delle Nazioni." From a letter he wrote to Padre Martini (18 September 1739) we can gather an idea of what his students had to pay and what they received in return. Martini had enquired on behalf of a young scholar. Tartini replied: "the expenses for his board (not in my house, as I do not care to take pupils in my home but in the house of my assistant), would be fifty *paoli* a month, because living is costlier in Padua than in Venice; as for my own honorarium, it will be two *zecchini* a month for solo violin alone; if he wishes counterpoint also, my fee will be three *zecchini*." One part of the instruction, and not the least, must have been listening to Tartini play at the Santo (as the shrine of Saint Anthony was familiarly called). This place of pilgrimage, with its hordes of visitors, allowed thousands to become acquainted with Tartini's music and playing over the years. Irrespective of one's religion, hearing the master at the Santo became a necessary part of the Grand Tour.

Brosses stayed an extra day (31 August 1739) in Padua on his way from Venice to Bologna, so that he could meet Tartini and hear him play.

> He passes commonly for Italy's prime violinist. It was a day well spent. I never heard better as to the extreme neatness of the sounds, of which not even the softest was lost, and for the perfect intonation. His playing is in the genre of Leclair, and has little brilliance to it; the justness of his touch is his forte. In all other respects Anna Maria of the Ospedaletto wins out over him, but he is unequalled for good spirit. As a lad he was not intended for the music profession. He saw himself reduced to it after being abandoned by his parents for making a stupid marriage while he was studying at the University of Padua. Polished and pleasant, he is without pride and without caprice. He reasons like an angel and without partiality on the different merits of French and Italian music. I was at least as satisfied with his conversation as with his playing. I was no less content with the excellent playing of the Abbé Vandini who was with him. (1: 250)

Antonio Vandini, one of the best cellists of the century, often played together with Tartini and apparently accompanied him on the cello during this private audience. A Franciscan friar born in Bologna who had served as cellist in the cathedral of Bergamo, he was appointed first cellist at the Santo in 1721 and remained active until his death some time after 1771. Tartini's two cello concertos are probably written for him, and Vivaldi's cello concertos may also have been written for Vandini, who taught at the Pietà in 1721–22.

Burney arrived in Italy too late to meet Tartini, who died on 26 February 1770 and had been relieved of his duties as leading violinist of the Santo five years earlier. Burney did hear Vandini and remarked that he played in the old-fashioned way by holding the bow under the hand, as did all the Italian cellists he encountered. He also said that Vandini played *"a parlare,* that is, in such a manner as to make his instrument speak." Pietro Nardini, Tartini's favorite pupil, kept his master's style of violin playing alive for Burney's generation.

Tartini's contribution to the violin literature is vast. Playing regularly for the same patrons year after year, he was under obligation to refine and diversify his music as much as possible, which was not the case with Veracini and Locatelli. His manuscripts show signs of constant revision over a long period, so that it is often impossible to speak of a "definitive version." This is particularly true of the solo sonatas, with or without continuo bass, of which there are approximately two hundred. They received additional or alternative movements, and alternative ways of ornamenting the same movements. Few bodies of music present such a bewildering array of choices to be made.[61]

Most of Tartini's music was written during the second quarter of the century, after which time he became increasingly concerned with theoretical speculation. He began as a follower of Corelli with respect to the sonata, and of Vivaldi with respect to the solo concerto. Some early concertos, preserved in Vienna, may date from his sojourn in Bohemia. They betray a kinship to Vivaldi in their ritornello structure, rather blatant harmonic sequences, and use of the solo sections as transitions (mostly nonthematic in figuration) to the tuttis. Tartini soon found his own path by reducing the tuttis in length and importance and by enhancing the singing quality of the solo part. La Cène at Amsterdam published three collections containing solo violin concertos of Tartini between 1728 and 1730, and another was brought out by Witvogel in 1754, quickly establishing the composer as a leader in the field.[62]

The soloist is much more prominent in Tartini's concertos than in violin concertos by others. Tartini put some of his thoughts about bowing in a 1760 letter to a pupil in the Mendicanti.[63] Robert Bremner, a disciple of Geminiani, translated the famous letter into English and published it in 1769. In a treatise of his own Bremner had this to say about the Tartinian manner of concertos.

> Tartini, perhaps from a supposition that a lady was not qualified to be the leader of a band capable of producing the great effects of harmony, thought it best to confine his

---

[61]See Paul Brainard, *Le sonate per violino di Giuseppe Tartini: Catalogo tematico* (Accademia Tartiniana di Padova, Le Opere di Giuseppe Tartini, III, 2) (Padua, 1975). This publication represents a revised and translated version of the catalogue in Brainard's dissertation, "Die Violinsonaten Giuseppe Tartinis" (Göttingen, 1959), which has been used to furnish the main basis for discussing Tartini's music here, along with Brainard's subsequent articles. For a catalogue of Tartini's concertos see Minos Dounias, *Die Violinkonzerte Giuseppe Tartinis als Ausdruck einer Künstler persönlichkeit und einer Kulturepoche* (Wolfenbüttel and Berlin, 1935).

[62]On Tartini's method of composing in the early concertos see George W. Thomson, "I primi concerti di Giuseppe Tartini: Fonti, abbozzi e revisioni," in *Tartini: Il tempo e l'opera,* pp. 347–62.

[63]*Lettera a Maddalena Lombardini,* first published in 1770 after Tartini's death. The original text along with contemporary English, French, and German translations is to be found in Erwin R. Jacobi's edition of Tartini's *Traité des agrements de la musique* (Celle, 1961), pp. 127–39.

instructions to those powers of the bow, necessary for the execution of his own solos and concertos, or others in the same style; in which the entertainment depends chiefly, if not entirely, upon the principal performer; for he, together with his auditors, consider the symphonies [i.e., ritornellos] in the concertos in no other light than as introductions, respites, and conclusions to his performance; and, therefore, he seldom joins in them, excepting to mark time; nor are the accompaniments to his solos regarded farther than as distant attendants; but that orchestra, on whose united powers the entertainment of the audience depends, will require a more spirited leader than this letter, however excellent in its way, can instruct.[64]

Bremner, like so many others in London, remained faithful to Geminiani and the concerto grosso.

The inroads of the galant style that are apparent in Tartini's concertos in the 1720s make their appearance in his sonatas somewhat later, for example, in some short song- and dancelike closing movements of the six sonatas published without permission by Witvogel in 1732. These rather plain movements were perhaps intended to provide the basis for improvised variations, as the addition of some model variations to two finales suggests. The unauthorized appearance of the Witvogel sonatas spurred Tartini to complete a set of twelve more serious sonatas for a rival publisher, La Cène, as is known from a letter he wrote to Padre Martini on 31 March 1731: "I have been occupied—and still am—in the writing of twelve sonatas for publication, not out of any desire of mine, but forced into it by a bad turn done me by a Dutch printer [Witvogel, whose edition must have already appeared, or been planned]."

What Tartini wrote and played in his own circle was not necessarily what he wished to be known by in the expanding European circle that was opened up by the big publishers. The twelve sonatas brought the composer seventy-two *zecchini* and fifty printed copies gratis. But that was not his concern, he intimates. Tartini wanted to be known as a follower of Corelli. The first six of the set are church sonatas in the slow–fast–slow–fast pattern (although the second slow movement is reduced to a few transitional measures, *pro forma,* and even this vestigial remnant disappears in the fourth sonata). Old-fashioned traits, such as the hemiola cadences in the finale of the first sonata, abound. The first two movements of these church sonatas are of the seamless contrapuntal sort, without repeats. Fugal writing prevails in all of the second movements and some of the finales. The last six sonatas of the set are of the chamber variety, disposed as slow–fast–fast movements, all being in bipartite form with repeats and with weighty finales, unlike those in the Witvogel set. Only the last sonata offers a minuet finale with variations. This impressive and consciously learned set was reedited several times during the eighteenth century in London and Paris.

[64]Gwilym Beechey, "Robert Bremner and his *Thoughts on the Performance of Concert Music," Musical Quarterly* 69 (1983): 244–52.

Tartini's sonatas following his Op. 1 brought him into the closest stylistic intersection with Locatelli. History repeated itself in that an unauthorized Op. 2 (six sonatas published by La Cène in 1743) was followed by an official set of twelve, corrected by the composer (published by Cleton in Rome in 1745). All fugal pretensions are laid aside in these works. The galant type of sonata has triumphed, and the composer reaches a new intensity of expression with his cantabile melodies. Unlike Locatelli, Tartini opts for the finale in a large bipartite form, often coming close to sonata form, instead of the short dance or air expanded by variations. The jolly finale from the last sonata of the Cleton set shows Tartini at his best. In it he draws a long movement—at once intense and playful, as Haydn would later be in his finales—from a minimum of melodic material, in this case the rising and falling second. Tartini's Op. 2, along with Locatelli's Op. 6, represents the high point of the galant violin sonata with basso continuo.

A further evolution in Tartini's style is represented by the "piccole sonate" commissioned in 1749 by Algarotti, in his function as chamberlain to the Prussian court. Tartini wrote on 24 February 1750 upon sending them, "The small sonatas are notated with a bass part for the sake of convention, but I play them without the bass, and this is my true intention." The pieces are diminutive not only in texture, but also in technical demands and in the proportions of the movements—dainty morsels well suited to grace the rococo salons of Sans Souci. An expert summarized their significance, saying: "Tartini's venture into unaccompanied violin writing embodies the homophonic, harmonically simplified, metrically regular, and melodically 'singable' style demanded by mid-century musical aesthetics, of which Tartini's own theoretical works show him to be an avid exponent."[65] Indeed, Tartini moved far towards the near monophony practiced and preached by Jean-Jacques Rousseau, and it can be no coincidence that they both exalted simple folk songs and related folk dances as repositories of "le naturel." The two men may well have met when Rousseau was in Venice during 1743–44. With Tartini, the cult of sensibility gained its central musical representative.

Tartini's most important legacy was to the violin concerto and includes well over a hundred works.[66] They stretch from early works like D. 89, which survives in a Dresden manuscript dated 1724 and was printed by La Cène in 1728, to late works that may belong to the 1750s or even later. Such a late work is the Concerto in D (D. 39). Its first movement begins with an idea that has both "bold" and "timid" components, nicely balanced, within the same theme (Example 3.6a). The timid component, marked "dolce," is echoed in slightly varied form, extending the

[65]Paul Brainard, "Tartini and the Sonata for Unaccompanied Violin," *JAMS* 14 (1961): 383–93.
[66]Minos Dounias, *Die Violinkonzerte Giuseppe Tartinis als Ausdruck einer Künstlerpersönlichkeit und einer Kulturpoche, Thematisches Verzeichnis* (Wolfbüttel and Berlin, 1935; reprint 1966), lists 125 concertos.

four-measure phrase to six measures. Tartini chooses to draw almost the entire first movement out of the dolce component, to the neglect of the more heroic figure of the opening. In fact the very opening returns only twice, once when the soloist begins (the second exposition, still in the tonic), and once when the soloist inaugurates the second half, after a tutti close in the dominant, by stating the full theme beginning on A. Aside from the first theme, the rule of the four-measure module is absolute from the beginning of the movement to its end. Another forward-looking feature is a clear second theme, stated first by the solo in the dominant, picked up later as the tutti close on the dominant, and heard again in e minor in the development and twice again after the tonic is restored, first by the solo and finally by the tutti. The interaction of ritornello structure with expanded bipartite form has progressed to a point here that is closer to Mozart than it is to Vivaldi.

Tartini's lyricism in the solo part challenges verbal description. One tiny detail of treatment, of an almost Mozartean subtlety, must suffice (Example 3.6b). When the violin solo first plays the main theme, the IV_4^6 harmony is replaced by V^6, which makes the B a dissonant appoggiatura and twice as expressive.

One of Tartini's formal innovations was to place repeat signs surrounding the beginning sections of the first movement, either from the very opening or from the solo entrance as here, through the modulation and confirmation of the new

EXAMPLE 3.6. *Tartini, Violin Concerto in D (D. 39), I*

key. He saved himself some labor thereby, shortened the middle ritornello, and brought the concerto's form closer to the expanded binary form with repeat signs characteristic of many symphonies.

It is typical of Tartini to unite an entire work by some motivic recurrences, especially between *Allegro* movements. This concerto is no exception. After an *Andante* cantabile in A, the final *Allegro* starts with a theme that plays upon the falling second from B to A, then from G to F♯ after an initial rise to high D. The sense of cyclic return lent by this motivic correspondence enhances further an experience made memorable by striking melodic ideas, beautiful string sonorities, and Tartini's perfect sense of form.

Tartini's famed cantabile, both as composer and player, is at the crux of his significance to the new in eighteenth-century music. Others may have approached Tartini in this respect, but Blainville, in his *Esprit de l'art musical* of 1754, ultimately placed Locatelli in the category of the "sonabile" composers, along with Vivaldi, while maintaining that "the sole glory of the cantabile was Tartini's." Quantz, on the other hand, took an opposite view: "Tartini has little sense of good singing style," and furthermore, "his compositions are almost nothing but dry, common, simple ideas, better suited to comic than to serious music." The key to this emphatic rejection is in its last clause. Quantz, like other North Germans, was committed in theory to the separation of comic and serious opera, and to the proposition that only the latter was worthy of emulation. He could not accept Tartini's rather loose and natural way of stringing together beautiful idiomatic passages and snippets of lyric melody, or his predilection for short, songlike phrases with many repetitions, as opposed to the long melodic arch. Tartini's freedom in treating his material seemed to Quantz like license, a departure from common models, an infraction of the rules. The mixture of comic and serious so pilloried by Berlin critics even in the greatest masters was one of the main forces in music that allowed it to move beyond the stratifications of the earlier eighteenth century. Quantz expressed a minority opinion about Tartini. Critical assessment at large is well summed up by John Mainwaring in *Memoirs of the Late George Frederic Handel* (London, 1760): "All his [Tartini's] melody is so truly vocal in style and character, that those parts of it which do not exceed the compass and powers of a voice, one would almost imagine were intended to be sung. . . . And all the Italians were so strongly sensible of this, that in speaking of his manner of playing, they often made use of the following expression, *non suona, canta sul violino.*"

The cantabile of Tartini is identified with a certain strain in his music that can best be called sentimental. Tartini spoke to his contemporaries in an especially emotion-filled way; "He spoke to the soul," as Blainville put it, and wrote music that "was more sentiment and language, than sound and harmony" (D'Alembert). Tartini's intellectual circle at Venice and Padua counted, besides Algarotti, the archaeologist Giovanni Rinaldo Carli, whose treatise, dedicated to Tartini in 1743, amounted to a summary of the old humanist position on what music could and should evoke. Published as *Osservazione sulla musica antica e moderna* (Venice, 1744), it inveighed against the insignificant arabesques of counterpoint and proposed instead the antique ideal of the *sentimentale,* roughly translatable as the transmitting of a state of the soul from composer to auditor. In a reedition many years later, Carli took credit for convincing Tartini of the path to be followed.

Tartini's reliance upon poetry would have pleased Plato himself. Algarotti claimed that Tartini awakened his muse by reading the verses of Petrarch, then inventing a melody.[67] In fact, Tartini must have preferred reading Metastasio. One of his necrologists maintained that Metastasio was the composer's sole source of inspiration. Many movements in Tartini's sonatas and concertos bear inscriptions from Metastasian arias, predominantly slow movements. Sometimes the mottos or textual incipits are spelled out in letters; in other sources (those designed for more public use) Tartini took the precaution of disguising his inspiration by a system of ciphers. If Tartini's instrumental melodies sounded as if they were songs conveying words to many of his contemporaries, it was because he often conceived them as just that.

Tartini sometimes went beyond just hinting at the expressive content of a movement with his verbal inscriptions and framed his instrumental melody to the text alluded to, as if he were writing an aria. The Concerto in C (D. 14) is a late work that will provide an example. It begins with a *Presto* theme, falling into antecedent and consequent halves; emphasis is on the subdominant and on the same melodic fall from the sixth to the fifth degree (intensified by trilling) found in the previous example. The following movement, marked *Andante,* is in the relative minor and scored for solo violin throughout, accompanied only by the first and second stands of orchestral violins, with no continuo. This is a frequent choice of scoring for Tartini's slow movements in concertos, which represents a further reduction than that seen in Vivaldi.

The *Andante* carries a motto, "Per pietà, bell'idol mio." These words come from the beginning of an aria sung by Artaserse in Act I, Scene 5, of Metastasio's justly acclaimed master libretto of the same name, which was first heard at Venice during the carnival of 1730, as set by Hasse. The first quatrain follows:

Per pietà, bell'idol mio	For pity's sake, my love,
Non mi dir, ch'io son ingrato	Tell me not that I'm ungrateful:
Infelice, e sventurato	Unhappy and wretched
Abbastanza il Ciel mi fa.	Enough has Heaven made me.

[67]In an addition made to the 1764 edition of his *Saggio sopra l'opera in music* that is possibly the work of his chosen literary executors, according to Ivano Cavallini, "Genio, Imitazione, Stile sentimentale e patetico. Gianrinaldo Carli et Tartini: Le Prospettive della Critica tartiniana nella seconda Metà del Settecento," in *Tartini: Il tempo e l'opera,* pp. 229–46; 241.

Typically for Metastasio the lines are septisyllabic, rhymed a b b' c, the first three ending with an unaccented syllable (which is not counted), the fourth ending with an accented syllable. Translated into music, this scheme calls for three weak cadences and a final strong one. This is close to what Tartini provides (Example 3.7). If the first line is repeated, as is frequently the case with aria settings, it fits quite well under mm. 1–8. Lines two and three, with their matching rhymes, fit well with the next two four-measure phrases, which are roughly equivalent except that the second is higher—not inappropriately to the heightening of verbal tension in line three. The last two four-measure segments could then accommodate the fourth line and its repetition; both end with the necessary accented cadence for the final word "fa."

EXAMPLE 3.7. *Tartini, Violin Concerto in C (D. 14), II*

A fine sense of musical climax is achieved by expressive harmonies, particularly the diminished-seventh chord outlined in m. 17, followed by the Neapolitan sixth chord (in the new key of e) and the augmented sixth chord, corresponding with the melodic climax of high E at the beginning of the last segment. Ornamentation increases the sense of climax. It is handled with much delicacy, increasing gradually from the completely undecorated beginning to the cascading passages with trills prior to the deceptive cadence in m. 20 and to the final cadence. The careful marshalling of expressive means, whether ornamental, harmonic, or melodic, marks the inspired choices of the master composer. If, in addition, we imagine the *Andante* played by a master violinist like Tartini, it is possible to begin to understand the ravishing effect he had upon his contemporaries.

Tartini's vocally conceived airs are not literally meant to be sung. They ascend out of vocal range, for one thing, as Mainwaring noted. They are best understood as a kind of personality transferal, as Tartini casting himself momentarily in the persona of one of the great singers of the time. His reverence for their art was unbounded. He was responsible for luring to Padua the young castrato Gaetano Guadagni in 1746. In a letter of 2 July 1751 he wrote to Padre Martini about the tenor Anton Raaff, a prize pupil of Bernacchi:

We have here in the person of Signor Antonio Raaff two angelic comforts blended into one: virtue and consummate musicianship. Here he is not only loved, he is adored and doted upon. . . . I have heard him in the Santo where he sang his evening prayers. I declare to you sincerely that I have never heard such singing in my life. God be praised that men with such a gift have been created, and may the professor who taught him be praised also. . . . And I have thanked God and thank Him still that I live and as a consequence I have been convinced that the true art of singing . . . has not been forgotten, but has been restored in its perfection through this worthy man, whose musical values cannot be separated from his moral ones, for he possesses both in the highest degree.

The earnest side of Tartini's personality, so evident here, was later to degenerate into mysticism. In 1751, when Raaff was in his prime, the composer was also at his creative pinnacle.

Tartini had the advantage of coming to maturity when the vocal art was still at a very high level. From singers he learned that intense and pathetic cantabile which penetrates his work and is one of his main legacies to violin music. He learned from them even in such matters as ornamentation, or gracing, to use the proper eighteenth-century term. Instrumental performers were not loath to borrow ideas from singers at that time, or from each other. Ditters admits in his memoirs to adopting his *Adagio* in a violin concerto after the singing of the castrato Pasquale Potenza, whom he heard at Bologna.

It is clear from this that singers had an immense effect upon instrumental performance (that is to say, the great singers of serious opera, to which the castrati were mostly confined). And slow movements were the domain where this influence was exerted to the maximum. Instrumental players had always taken the greatest singers as their models, and nothing new can be claimed for the eighteenth century in this respect. Novel, nevertheless, was the coming to prominence around 1720 of a generation of singers whose inspiring effects upon the art of music in general may have been without parallel. Tartini profited from their inspiration almost as much as if he had been an opera composer himself. Therein lies the main reason for his superiority over other violinist-composers.

Tartini's place in history is secure on the basis of his violin music. His contributions to music theory were neither as original nor as mathematically sound as he believed them to be, and their skeptical reception did much to sour his last years. (He believed the Devil responsible for hindering acceptance.) It was as a violinist-composer, and a teacher of other violinists, that Tartini left his most enduring mark upon the century. By 1736 Algarotti had already praised his instrumental music for going beyond Corelli, and in his *Saggio sopra l'opera in musica* of 1754 he proclaimed Tartini's playing one of the three singular and most perfect things in the world. He called his compositions an incomparable blend of variety and unity.

Tartini became something of a cult, especially in France, and it was a French violinist who propagated the fictitious legend of the "Devil's Trill Sonata." The best appreciation of Tartini's meaning for eighteenth-century music is the *Eloge de Tartini* written by Pierre Louis Ginguené in the article "Concerto" for the *Encyclopédie méthodique* (Paris, 1791). Ginguené praised Tartini for having revolutionized the concerto, as well as violin playing.

> Noble and expressive melodies, learned but natural traits, designed upon a harmony that is song-like, motifs followed through with infinite art, but without the air of slavery and pedanticism that even Corelli, more occupied with counterpoint than with melody, did not always avoid; nothing negligent, nothing affected, nothing in low style; ceremony without inflatedness in his first *Allegro*, in his *Adagio* a touching and pathetic expression, melodies to which it is impossible not to attach a meaning and in which one is scarcely aware that words are lacking; and finally his brilliant and varied *Presto*, light without being insignificant, gay without being extravagant—such are, in general, the character and the form that Tartini knew how to give his concertos.

Ginguené rated Tartini even higher than Johann Stamitz in a subsequent part of his article on the concerto, conceding only that the latter might have more force and majesty in his tuttis, while maintaining that he lacked Tartini's naturalness in the solo parts. The numerous manuscripts of Tartini's works preserved in France testify further to the special place he occupied there—but as a composer, not as a theorist. "Incomparable Tartini," as Algarotti called him, was indeed a violinist-composer without peer.

Sammartini of Milan and the Symphony

What Tartini was to the violin concerto, Giovanni Battista Sammartini of Milan became to the concert symphony. The careers of the two men were parallel in some ways. Sammartini also attracted a band of students, although small in comparison with that of the Paduan master. He was also a violinist, even if not a great virtuoso. Brosses rated him a better violin player than the renowned Somis, who presided over music at the neighboring court of Turin. Like Tartini, Sammartini preferred to stay in one place. To accomplish what he did there was no need to travel. Lombardy was a great center of violin making; moreover, amateur string players were nowhere more abundant. Pierre-Jean Grosely, in his *Observations sur l'Italie* (1765), recounts that he found a decided taste for music in the towns of Lombardy: "Tout le monde y joue du violon, avec tous le harpégemens et tous les démanchemens" (Everyone plays the violin here, with all the arpeggiations and all the positions shifts). In this fertile soil for music making the concert symphony flowered.

    Sammartini was born in 1700 or 1701 and lived to be 74. He was the son of a French oboe player, Alexis Saint-Martin, and his early training came at the hands of his father or those of his older brother Giuseppe, born in 1695. Both brothers are listed as oboists in the opera orchestra of the main theater, the Regio Ducal Teatro, in 1720. Thus they were at the center of musical life in Milan from early days on, and in the same capacity as their father had been. Giovanni Battista became a good organist as well, which skill was essential for the several church posts he accumulated at Milan. He was a prolific composer in all genres. His strong point was neither the concerto, although he wrote many, nor opera, to which he also bent his talents, but instrumental ensemble and orchestral music. He left some seventy or eighty symphonies and over two hundred ensemble sonatas. The early Haydn biographer Giuseppe Carpani maintained that Sammartini was a better instrumental than vocal composer, but then went on to claim that Sammartini's sacred music anticipated Haydn's in adopting a symphonic approach and creating a style at once brilliant and dignified. The author of *Le Haydine* (1812) deserves at least some credence, having grown up in Milan during Sammartini's day; he himself served as a link between the two masters.

Brosses arrived in Milan during July 1739 after first visiting Genoa, where he witnessed mass in the doge's chapel "sung by bad castrato voices to a rather poor music except for the choruses and ritornellos." In Milan, by contrast, he marveled at "the admirable symphonies and choruses that cannot be too highly praised; in the church music the large organ and horns [as well as strings] accompany the voices and make an effect much better than I would have expected" (1: 140). Turin, in spite of being a royal court, does not fare well in musical comparisons with Milan. On his return to France in 1740 Brosses visited Turin and was disappointed with a violin concerto performed by Somis at mass in the royal chapel. Young Rousseau spent a year there in 1728–29. At first he was impressed by the daily morning service in the court chapel, then bored by its unchanging pomp and ceremony. The ever-polite Burney was surprisingly candid in his impressions of the same. Pugnani, a pupil of Somis, led the orchestra by this time and played the solo part in a violin concerto on 14 July 1770.

> I need say nothing of the performance of Signor Pugnani, his talents being too well known in England to require it. I shall only observe, that he did not appear to exert himself: and it is not to be wondered at, as neither his Sardinian majesty nor any one of the numerous royal family, seem at present, to pay much attention to music. . . . There is now a gloomy sameness at this court, in the daily repetition of state parade and prayer, which renders Turin a dull residence to strangers except during the carnival.

Burney, passing through Turin on his way to Milan in midsummer, did not witness the carnival in person. What he refers to is opera in the great royal theater during carnival season, which was supported by the court as lavishly as any in Italy.

The duchy of Lombardy was a fief of the Habsburgs throughout most of the eighteenth century, and its musical life reflected this. The large opera house built at Milan in 1717 was subject to remote control from Vienna, a factor that brought several Austrian and Bohemian composers, including Mozart, commissions to write for it. Local talents were not scarce, the greatest in the operatic field being Giovanni Battista Lampugnani, who lived from 1706 to 1781. But Milan imported much more than it exported in the domain of opera throughout the eighteenth century. Leonardo Leo was in Milan and Turin for several productions in 1739–40, and other Neapolitan composers were also well represented. The first Goldoni-Galuppi successes in comic opera around 1750 were eagerly taken up by the Milanese public. Gluck, Christian Bach, Sarti, and Salieri were among the major composers to come to Milan for a time and win either employment, commissions, or both. During the 1770s the court theater in Milan, like its Viennese counterpart, became a battleground for the two great exponents of dramatic ballet, Gasparo Angiolini and Jean-Georges Noverre. By this time Milan had emerged as a leading center of the Enlightenment, with close ties to developments at Paris. Literary figures such as the Verri brothers, Cesare Beccaria, and Giuseppe Parini were in the thick of the controversies raging on many matters, including ballet and opera. Milan was thus a lively artistic center, notwithstanding its foreign yoke (and partly because of it). Sammartini was a friend of Parini, and like him a member of the Accademia dei Trasformati, along with Verri and Beccaria. His life was not untouched, consequently, by the intellectual ferment at Milan.

Sammartini's symphonies survive from as early as the 1730s. The earliest symphonic movements that can be dated are those that were incorporated into the composer's first complete opera, *Memet,* given at Lodi (near Milan) in 1732.[68] The overture to the same opera survives and it is similar in outline to most other Italian opera overtures of the time: a fast and relatively long first movement in some approximation of sonata form; a contrasting slow movement in minor; return to the major for a minuet finale. Already present is Sammartini's characteristic rhythmic drive, which is unflagging throughout the opening *Presto* in 6/8. Also typical are the arpeggiated figures of the violins, which play in unison throughout, the exception being a soft passage after the modulation to the dominant, where they play mostly in thirds. Chromatic inflections lend a lyric sweetness to the passage, which has inklings of a contrasted second theme, although it is really derived from a descending arpeggio figure near the beginning. The violins then resume their unison playing, *forte,* intoning an upward arpeggio in sixteenth notes that sounds like the inversion of the previously heard arpeggio figure, leading to a cadence. On the diagram, in Table 3.2, in which four-measure segments are marked off, **A** stands for the first theme, **B** for the incipient sec-

[68]*The Symphonies of G. B. Sammartini,* ed. Bathia Churgin, vol. 1: *The Early Symphonies* (Harvard Publications in Music, 2) (Cambridge, Mass., 1968), pp. 207–13.

ondary theme, and **C** for the vigorous closing idea. The wavy line in the key category indicates tonal instability with transitional function.

TABLE 3.2. Sammartini: Opening Movement, *Presto*, from Overture to *Memet* (1732)

Bar:	1	8	16	24	32	40	48	56
Theme:	‖: **A**		**B**	**C** ‖: (A) (C)		**A**	**B** (A)	**C** :‖
Key:	I ———		∿∿ V	———	V ∿∿	I		

[Reprise]

Sammartini's sense of metrical regularity on the large scale emerges clearly here. He brings in the first transition passage in m. 8, the lyric interlude in m. 16, the closing affirmation four measures later. In the proto-development after the double bar, beginning on the dominant with an arpeggio figure slightly related to some of the material in A, and passing through various secondary dominants, the music occupies twelve measures, arranged 4 + 4 + 4. Only after the reprise does the symmetry break down, when Sammartini eliminates the transitional material and brings in a variant of B (with deviation to the minor for its second half) in m. 45, then three and a half measures of material related to A, before closing with C. The bipartite dance form underlying this adumbration of sonata form is still perceptible. Its expansion in the second part to accommodate both development and recapitulation puts no strain upon the overriding musical fact that I - V is answered by V - I. Everything is closely related motivically, but that does not prevent the emergence of a subsidiary theme, created by changes in dynamic, textural, and melodic nuance.

The second movement of the *Memet* overture brings in the tonic minor to succeed A major. It is written in four-part texture, with the first violins getting all the melodic interest, the other parts being restricted to repeated eighth notes in accompaniment, which the basses do pizzicato. Unusual with respect to most other Italian overtures of the time is the choice of an expanded binary form, with repeat signs in the middle, as in the first movement. The glories of some later slow movements have yet to be glimpsed in this routine and rather plodding *Andante*. With the final *Presto, ma non tanto* in 3/4 the composer invokes the *menuetto galante* to which he would remain faithful to the end of his days. It is written as an orchestral trio, with violins in unison, as in most of the first movement, and is led to a nice melodic climax toward the end of the second part. Milanese minuets tended toward ample proportions and this one is no exception. When Mozart was in Italy for the first time in 1770 he commented upon the case: "The minuets in Milan, in fact the Italian minuets generally, have plenty of notes, are played slowly and have several measures, e.g., the first part has sixteen, the second twenty or twenty-four" (letter of 20 March 1770). He could have been describing the movement in question. It was Sammartini, more than anyone else, who shaped the Milanese tradition.

An early concert symphony by Sammartini parallels his *Memet* overture to such an extent that it must date from around the same period.[69] The key is the same, and its first movement is a *Vivace* in 3/8. Reason for the choice of 3/8 rather than 6/8 becomes apparent immediately when the first four-measure phrase is followed by one of only three measures (which would have led to phrase displacement in 6/8). The same textural disposition of violins in unison, plus violas and basses, prevails. There is no hint of an independent second theme, the energetic opening figure merely being stated in slightly varied form in the dominant. Following the double bar there is a longer excursionary passage than in the corresponding passage of the *Memet* overture. The proportions of the whole and the main keys traversed are as shown in Table 3.3.

TABLE 3.3. Sammartini, Opening Movement, Presto, Symphony in A

Measures:	‖: 1	-	35 ‖: 36	-	76 77	-	102 :‖
Keys:	A		E	E ⌒ C ⌒	a | A		A

The equivalent of the development stretches to a length nearly equal to that of the prima parte, making the seconda parte almost twice as long. To generalize from these two first movements is hazardous but necessary: the operatic overture tends toward overt symmetries and clearly perceptible shapes, including thematic dualism; the concert symphony plays with metric irregularities and indulges in an expansive developmental preparation for the reprise. The slow movement of the symphony, marked *Largo sempre piano,* is in a minor and 2/4 time, like that in the overture. It is slightly more expressive by virtue of its descending chromatic tetrachords in the first violin part, which reigns supreme over the four-part texture. The main key returns with the triumphant minuet finale, which offers a veritable catalogue of galant mannerisms, with its dotted rhythms alternating with triplets and its *cadence galante* marking the end of the first half. An interesting sidelight on this symphony is that it was chosen for performance at Amsterdam in 1738 to celebrate the centenary of the Schouwburg alongside a work by Vivaldi. The choice is not surprising. Sammartini's first movement is propelled by a rhythmic drive not unlike that in a Vivaldian concerto. His second and third movements complete the cycle in exemplary fashion. The piece is truly symphonic in sonority. Sammartini was clearly thinking in orchestral terms here, with doubling of the parts suitable to fill a large hall. We know from the listing of the festival orchestra in 1738 that the forces employed on that occasion were considerable; they

---

[69]Ibid., no. 16.

included a string ensemble of nineteen players: seven first violins, five seconds, three violas, two cellos, and two basses (doubled by two bassoons).[70]

Sammartini gradually abandoned the trio symphony, but it survived even so, as a favorite of Johann Stamitz, François-Joseph Gossec, and other early symphonists who came after Sammartini and followed his lead. A fine example of the string writing *à 4* that he came to prefer is afforded by an early symphony in D.[71] The unison opening is concerto-like and quite inventive (Example 3.8). It consists of a descending triad repeated in diminution, then double diminution, after which

EXAMPLE 3.8. *Sammartini, Symphony in D (J-C 14), I*

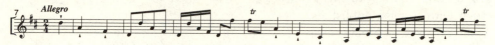

the four parts separate in order to sound the half-cadence. The process is repeated then from dominant to tonic, producing a perfectly regular eight-measure phrase, 4 + 4. Periodic themes like this, common enough in dance music, are not found very often as openings to symphonies prior to Sammartini. Within the overall symmetry there is considerable rhythmic ambiguity. One tends to hear an octave descent through the triad in even notes as a group of three, arriving at the tonic and the strong beat simultaneously. A grouping in three can also be carried through over the two diminutions, but the cadence with its two quarter notes puts a stop to the triple groupings. In other words the phrase can be perceived as 3 + 3 + 2 beats. In Sammartini's time the temptation to hear the initial figure as a triple grouping would have been greater because this triadic descent was often used to begin the great orchestral chaconnes in 3/4 that served to conclude the acts of operas and ballets in the French tradition. Son of a French oboe player that he was, Sammartini must have been aware of such associations. Even if he were not of French descent he would have known. French dances and dance music prevailed in the opera houses of Italy when the ballet appeared, to such an extent that many musicians must have been surprised and delighted by Sammartini's chaconne-like beginning.

No element of music fascinated Sammartini as much as the infinite possibilities of rhythm. And nowhere did he achieve finer results than in this symphony, for which he wrote a last movement to match the subtlety of the first, abandoning for once his usual minuet. His final *Presto* in 2/4 imitates the octaves of the posthorn, which lends it an added poetic meaning. By repeating and recombin-

[70]Marc Pincherle, *Antonio Vivaldi et la musique instrumentale,* 2 vols. (Paris, 1948), 1: facsimile facing p. 25.
[71]Newell Jenkins and Bathia Churgin, *Thematic Catalogue of the Works of Giovanni Battista Sammartini* (Cambridge, Mass., 1976), no. 14.

ing a few very simple figures over and over, the composer works up to a climax of great kinetic force.

Even more successful than Sammartini's symphonies, from a commercial point of view, were his chamber sonatas, else he would not have written so many. The great music publishers of northern Europe were eager—sometimes overeager— to attach the name of "St. Martini" to works of this kind, and they busily pirated each other's prints. Through his brother Giuseppe, who established himself in London, Sammartini was in touch with English publishers. A set of six trio sonatas was brought out by John Simpson in 1744 (Figure 3.8). A glance at this music is enough to show that the "principal composer in Milan," as he is called on the handsome and informative title page, adopted a more gracious and easy manner in his chamber music than in his symphonies. There is a semblance of imitation left as a heritage of the old trio sonata, but much of the time the second violin merely accompanies the first in thirds and sixths, or is in dialogue with it, as is the case with the arpeggios of the *Allegros*. The bass jogs along

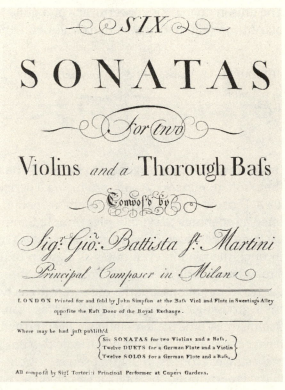

FIGURE 3.8. Title page of Sammartini's trio sonatas (London, 1744).

iterating long strings of tonic or dominant tones in support. Of contrapuntal interest there is rarely a hint. The form and style is that of the three-movement galant sonata discussed above in connection with Locatelli and Tartini.

A Sonata in E♭ from the 1744 set ends with a minuet that has the added attraction of offering a "Variatione" for the first violin—a lesson from Sammartini on how to ornament a strain upon repetition. The movement was well received, as is apparent from its transferral to another work. The French copyists who put together the enormous Blancheton collection in the 1740s tacked it onto the end of a three-movement Sammartini Symphony in G.[72] They transposed it, variation

[72]*The Early Symphonies*, ed. Churgin, no. 13.

and all, and added a viola part doubling the bass. As is evident from this instance, Sammartini's symphonies and sonatas are closest in their minuet movements. They are further apart in the fast movements in expanded binary form that open the symphonies (and some but not most sonatas). Fast sonata movements are less ambitious in design and proportion than the symphonies, especially with regard to the element of development. Less is made of the arrival of the tonic reprise.

The middle-period symphonies of Sammartini (ca. 1740–60) represent the high point of his art. They also form the most numerous group, far outnumbering the early and late symphonies, and they achieved the widest diffusion.[73] Copies and prints of them proliferated not only in England, France, and Germany, but also in the Austrian-Bohemian sphere, as one would expect from the political ties that bound Milan to Vienna. The same ties brought a young Bohemian composer to Milan in 1737, as a protégé of one of the nobles of the city. Christoph Gluck must have studied with Sammartini during his several years in Milan. There is no document to say he did, except his own music. The trio sonatas he published at London in 1746 are modeled on those of Sammartini. His direct borrowings from Sammartini's symphonies help date some of the latter. An example is the opening movement of Sammartini's Symphony in G (Jenkins-Churgin No. 44). It must date from no later than early 1747, because Gluck used it to open his *Nozze d'Ercole e d'Ebe,* an occasional opera for the royal marriages at Dresden in the summer of the same year.[74] Not unlikely, it dates from as early as 1744, after which time Gluck left Milan for London.

Sammartini's Symphony No. 44 begins with three ponderous chords, I - V⁷ - I, over which the violins intone a melodic figure in dotted rhythm, which produces the effect of an opening curtain. The first theme proper ensues. It consists of a slide up to the fifth degree, D, which is reiterated over a moving bass line, followed by attempts to arrive at a cadence that are undercut, the whole process then being repeated *piano.* When the cadence does arrive in m. 8, it coincides with a rising arpeggio figure in quick notes that starts the transition to the dominant, with continuing *forte* and *piano* alterations. As the harmony comes to rest on V/V a textural reduction occurs. The first violins, lightly accompanied, then sound a more lyrical two-note figure in Lombard snaps, which has very much the character of a second theme, even if arrival at the dominant is still a promise, not a fact.

When the dominant does arrive it brings less a sense of thematic identity than neutral ritornello-like bustling. The concerto had always exerted a considerable force upon Sammartini and it still does here. Further *piano-forte* contrasts stretch the bustling quick-note passages out until m. 32. The end of the first part

---

[73]Bathia Churgin, "The Symphonies of G. B. Sammartini" (Ph.D. diss., Harvard University, 1963), is the source of these data and much of the rest of our discussion on the composer's symphonies.
[74]Bathia Churgin, "Alterations in Gluck's Borrowings from Sammartini," *Studi Musicali* 9 (1980): 118–34.

comes with a deceptive cadence instead of the expected affirmation of the dominant. By thwarting tonal arrival here, Sammartini is only being consistent with the
tactical delays planted in his first theme. He places no double bar and repeat sign
at this spot, as he almost invariably did in the early symphonies. His practice has
moved nearer to the operatic overture in this respect. Leo's overtures from around
1740, when the Neapolitan master was in Milan, offer some likely models.

The development unfolds as a substantial segment of the movement, almost
equal in length to what precedes and follows it, which is not typical of the overture but does distinguish Sammartini's concert symphonies. The composer begins
by deploying the lyric second theme over a secondary dominant, V/ii. Interest is
not denied to the second violins, and even the violas occasionally get an independent part. Sammartini dissolves the end of the movement into a transition to
the slow movement. This effect, so beloved by Emanuel Bach, makes one wonder
at a possible connection between the two masters.

The slow movement of Sammartini's Symphony No. 44 is its finest. The
movement is in g and it begins as the first violins sing a cantabile melody in long-
breathed arches, filled with protracted sighings, against the murmuring of a
steady accompanimental figure in the second violins and pizzicato basses (Example 3.9). Texture and melody could have easily provided the initial inspiration for
Orfeo's obbligato recitative, "Che puro ciel!"—music that Gluck first wrote in one
of his Milanese operas and only later adapted to his masterpiece for Vienna. The
third movement restores the keynote with the customary minuet.

Symphony No. 44 does not lack cyclic unity. There are subtle references to the
first movement's opening curtain in the slow movement, and the concluding
minuet concentrates on the same three melodic tones initiating the symphony: G,
A, and B. After adapting the first movement with a few small modifications,
Gluck wrote his own slow movement and finale, paralleling Sammartini's. He
perhaps felt obliged to replace the older master's slow movement because it did
not come to a conclusion, but led to a return of the first movement (reprise
only) da capo. An operatic overture by function allowed limited scope for innovation or surprise. It received one hearing and little or no rehearsal. Sammartini
in his concert symphonies, on the other hand, allowed himself to be surprisingly
diverse and original. His Symphony No. 44 offers ample testimony. A contemporary theorist spelled out the same point when he wrote that the chamber symphony (as opposed to the church or theatrical symphony) allowed the most
freedom, because it had no function to fill and gave the composer's imagination
fullest rein.[75]

Sammartini achieved little renown in the rest of Italy, to judge from the

[75]Johann Adolph Scheibe, *Critischer Musikus* (Hamburg, 1745), p. 597. See Stefan Kunze, "Zur 'Theorie' der
Sinfonie im 18. Jahrhundert," in *Die Sinfonie im 18. Jahrhundert* (Laaber, 1993), pp. 256–57.

EXAMPLE 3.9. *Sammartini, Symphony in G (J-C 44), II*

scarcity of his works in peninsular libraries. The same is true of the little band of symphonists who gathered around him at Milan, including Lampugnani and Antonio Brioschi, two composers whose works were often attributed to Sammartini, and vice versa, and the lesser figures Giorgio Giulini, Ferdinando Galimberti, and Melchiorre Chiesa. What local conditions, we may ask, prompted the emergence of a school of symphony writers in a single Italian center? Relative to Sammartini himself, the symphonic achievements of his Milanese colleagues and disciples are sufficiently modest so that they can be regarded as satellite. The question then becomes more precise, but no less difficult. What conditions peculiar to Milan prompted Sammartini to become the main creator and foremost early exponent of the concert symphony? What was it about this vast and prosperous city, dominated by its sprawling Gothic cathedral, that made it at once a center of Italian symphonic writing and of the Italian Enlightenment?

The demands of Milanese church music could not have been much different than elsewhere, in spite of the special Ambrosian liturgy. Instrumental music accompanied the service here much as elsewhere. Sammartini selected several first movements from his symphonies as preludes to Lenten cantatas, and they were chosen, with appropriateness, mainly from among his most expressive symphonies in the minor mode. But the great body of his symphonies existed as a special repertory aside from the institution of the church, and unrelated to any other institution either, as far as is known. Private concerts were in vogue elsewhere, not just in Milan. If there was a musical factor that distinguished Milan from other Italian capitals, it was the abundance of amateur string players. Under Sammartini's guidance an *accademia filarmonica* was established in 1758 mainly for performing noblemen. "Martini's Concert at Milan" was famous enough to provide the setting for an amorous anecdote in Laurence Sterne's *Sentimental Journey through France and Italy* (1768).

The concert symphony arose mainly to fill the needs of nonprofessional music lovers. This is nowhere made more clear than in the correspondence of Sammartini's noble pupil, Giorgio Giulini. Sammartini received request after request for symphonic works from his peers, some of whom even tried to compose, although they could do no more than play the violin. One request specified that the symphonies be in G, "with easy separation of the instruments." It can be no coincidence that such an easy key for strings is also Sammartini's favorite. For all the violinistic arpeggios in his string writing, the works are rarely difficult to play or demanding with respect to high positions. Creation of a large body of good, up-to-date ensemble and orchestral music for dilettante hands to play can be understood as another facet of the spread of culture championed by Milanese Enlightenment.

When Burney reached Milan in July 1770, some thirty years after Charles de Brosses, he found Sammartini presiding over the music of several churches and doing so with great vigor, even though he was as old as the century. Burney wrote this under the date of 18 July:

> The second mass which I heard to-day was composed by Battista San Martini, and performed under his direction at the church of the Carmini; the symphonies were very ingenious, and full of the spirit and fire peculiar to that author. The instrumental

parts in his compositions are well written; he lets none of the performers be long idle; and the violins, especially, are never suffered to sleep. It might, however, sometimes be wished that he would please more if there were fewer notes, and fewer *allegros* in it: but the impetuosity of his genius impels him, in his vocal compositions, to run on in a succession of rapid movements, which in the end fatigue both the performer and the hearers. . . . San Martini is *Maestro di Capella* to half the churches in Milan, and the number of masses which he has composed is almost infinite; however his fire and invention still remain in their utmost vigour.

Without saying outright that Sammartini gave the violins too much busywork, Burney implies as much. He repented his other charge of too much fast music four days later.

> *Sunday, July 22.* This morning, after hearing the Ambrosian service in all its perfection, at the Duomo, I went to the Convent of *Santa Maria Maddalena;* I heard several motets performed by the nuns; it was their feast-day. The composition was by Signor B. S. Martini, who is *Maestro di Capella,* and teaches to sing at this convent. He made me ample amends for the want of slow movements in his mass on Friday, by an *adagio* in the motet of to-day, which was truly divine, and divinely sung by one of the sisters, accompanied, on the organ only, by another. It was by far the best singing, in every respect, that I had heard since my arrival in Italy, where there is so much, that one soon grows fastidious.

No music heard by Burney in Italy evoked such high praise until he reached Venice.

The European vogue of Sammartini was at its height between 1740 and 1760. It may be said to have begun with the collection of symphonies and trio sonatas that Le Clerc issued at Paris in 1742 for a price of 9 livres. Although Sammartini's music was still offered to the public for sale in the 1770s, he had long since yielded leadership to younger composers. He figured only a few times in the thematic catalogues that Breitkopf began bringing out in Leipzig in 1762. Like Tartini, he witnessed some of the musical trends after 1760, but more as a bystander than as a leader. Yet his violins in dialogue still provided a model for many Italian composers of the following generation, including Gaetano Brunetti and Boccherini. The continuous and flexible structure that is so characteristic of Sammartini reappears in Brunetti's symphonies.

Sammartini was also an important forerunner of the French and Austrian symphonists. The aged Haydn, as is well known, purportedly rejected the notion that his early symphonic style owed something to Sammartini. The vehemence of his protest, as related by Georg August Griesinger, should have made historians suspicious. Around 1750 there was hardly any model with more affinity to what Haydn would eventually accomplish in the symphony than Sammartini. Haydn also imbibed more than a few ideas from the Milanese master at second hand, through Gluck, whose operas of the 1760s impressed Haydn mightily. What provoked his reported remark that Sammartini was no more than a scribbler was a tale told about the Bohemian composer Josef Mysliveček. Summoned to Milan to write an opera in 1781, he chanced to hear some Sammartini performed, upon which he proclaimed, "Ho trovato lo padre dello stile di Josef Haydn" ("I have found the father of Joseph Haydn's style").[76] Such an oversimplified filiation Haydn was bound to reject. The history of musical style is infinitely more complex.

Sammartini played a major role at festive performances in Northern Italy. He organized concerts for the visit of Beatrice d'Este, wife of Milanese ruler Archduke Ferdinand, to Pavia and Cremona in 1765, events at which Boccherini played cello in the orchestra under Sammartini's direction. Five years earlier he took part in the concerts in honor of Princess Isabella of Parma, who was being fêted on her progress from Parma to Vienna to wed Crown Prince Joseph of Austria. She was the daughter of one of Sammartini's most important patrons, the infante Philip, duke of Parma, to whom the composer dedicated his fine set of six string trios in 1760 (later issued by Le Clerc in Paris as Op. 7). The concerts for Isabella brought him together with Christian Bach, who had been living mainly in Milan since 1755, while also traveling frequently to Bologna in order to study with Padre Martini.

Italy produced few composers of instrumental music after Tartini and Sammartini who attained their stature. Perhaps only Christian Bach and Boccherini rose to their eminence among Italian-trained instrumental composers, and they did so far from Italy. An ongoing diaspora of musical talent sapped some of the most genial from the peninsula. The lure of Paris for violinists was so strong that Viotti, Pugnani's best pupil, celebrated his greatest triumphs as a composer and performer in France.[77] Scholars have wrestled with the evident decline of Italian instrumental music and attempted to explain it. The usual thesis adduced is that opera came to absorb all or almost all Italian creative energy in music.[78] Rossini as a youth wrote such brilliant instrumental works he could well have revived the Italian symphony had he so chosen. His case seems to prove the point. Whatever the answer, there is no denying that, after Tartini and Sammartini, primacy in the violin concerto passed to Paris, and in the symphony to Mannheim and Vienna.

---

[76]*Haydn, Mozart*, p. 720.

[77]Chappell White, *From Vivaldi to Viotti: A History of the Early Classical Violin Concerto* (Philadelphia, 1992), pp. 329–31.

[78]Many viewpoints are gathered to this effect in Giacomo Fornari, "Del declino della musica strumentale in Italia nel settecento," in *Intorno a Locatelli*, ed. Dunning, 1: 241–74.

The Keyboard

Northern Italian superiority in the making of violins and related instruments extended also to the building of organs and stringed keyboard instruments. The Antegnati family of Brescia dominated organ building. Crucial to harpsichord building was an ample supply of fine hardwoods for the keys and fine softwoods (mainly cedar) for the soundboard and case. Typically, the Italian harpsichord was an elongated wing shape, with a thin inner case protected by a thick outer case. The most common disposition was a single manual and two sets of strings tuned in unison. Not much had changed in this regard since the sixteenth century, and many instruments from that era were still prized and playable two hundred years later. In the famous Verona portrait of 1770 Mozart is depicted playing a single-manual Venetian instrument of 1583.[79] The great length of many Italian harpsichords allowed them to sound particularly strong in the bass register, which rendered them ideal as continuo instruments for accompanying.

A major advance in keyboard building was due to the Paduan Bartolomeo Cristofori. From 1690 on he served Prince Ferdinand de' Medici and remained at the Florentine court after the prince's death in 1716. Cristofori was mainly a harpsichord builder, one with a strong experimental bent. Eventually one line of experimentation led to the invention of a system by which pivoted hammers struck the strings, allowing the player's fingers on the keys some control over dynamics according to the touch. Thus emerged the "gravicembalo col piano e forte," the ancestor of the modern piano. Cristofori's pianos adopted the same elongated wing shape as his harpsichords. Scipione Maffei published a pamphlet describing the invention in 1711 that was translated into German and widely diffused, attracting attention from the Saxon court organ builder, Gottfried Silbermann, who built several pianos after Cristofori's design.

Few instruments built by Cristofori survive, but the Metropolitan Museum in New York is fortunate to have a grand piano of his dated 1720. Although modified over time in order to increase its range, the instrument's structure has remained intact. "This piano's tone changes markedly from bass to treble; the bass is warm and reedy, the treble duller and short sustaining."[80] In other words it sounds rather similar to the classic Italian harpsichord. Despite its limitations the new instrument soon began to generate a literature of its own. In 1732 Lodovico Giustini di Pistoia published *XII Sonate da cimbalo di piano, e forte, detto volgarmente di martelletti* in Florence. Engraved keyboard music of any kind had become quite rare by the eighteenth century in Italy, so a collection specifically for fortepiano (as

[79]Daniel Heartz, *The Verona Portrait of Mozart and the Molto Allegro in G (KV 72a)* (Ala, 1995).
[80]Laurence Libin, "Keyboard Instruments," *Metropolitan Museum of Art Bulletin* (Summer 1989): 34–35.

early pianos will be called in this book) was indeed something special. The sonatas are more like suites and of only moderate musical interest. Giustini dedicated them to Prince Don Antonio, younger brother of King John V of Portugal. And herein lies a point of great interest. The prince, along with his niece Maria Barbara, were pupils of none other than Domenico Scarlatti, the genial son of Alessandro Scarlatti who entered royal Portuguese service in 1719 but probably did not go to Lisbon until 1723.[81]

Maria Barbara of Portugal married the infante Fernando of Spain and moved to Madrid in 1728, taking Scarlatti with her. She became queen of Spain in 1746 when her husband acceded to the throne as Fernando VI. The lists of instruments kept in her various royal residences show that, besides harpsichords, she owned several fortepianos: there is a good possibility that many of the hundreds of sonatas that Scarlatti wrote for his patroness were actually intended for the latter.[82] Farinelli, the other musical luminary in Madrid, had instruments of both kinds with him when he retired to a villa outside Bologna in 1760, as well as volumes of Scarlatti's sonatas bequeathed to him by Maria Barbara. His favorite instrument, says Burney, who visited him in 1770, was a fortepiano built in Florence in 1730.

In late 1738 or early 1739 Scarlatti had thirty *Essercizi per gravicembalo* engraved, not in Venice, as Burney believed, but in London. He dedicated these "exercises" (or *études,* as they might well be called) to King John V of Portugal, saying that the pieces were born under his auspices, which means, if taken literally, they were composed before Domenico left Lisbon for Spain in 1728. He mentions in a long and obsequious dedication his service to the infante Don Antonio as well as Maria Barbara, which confirms as much. The latter is praised for her mastery of singing, playing, and composing, which she exhibited to the astonishment and admiration of music masters and the delight of princes and monarchs. Reprints of the thirty pieces were made in London, Amsterdam, and Paris, the first under the aegis of Thomas Roseingrave, who added a musical introduction to his edition, *XLII Suites de pieces pour clavecin* (1739) as well as several additional pieces by Domenico and one by Alessandro Scarlatti.[83] This corpus was then pirated and reprinted often by Continental printers. Hundreds of other pieces by Domenico Scarlatti remained locked away in a few private manuscripts and did not become known to the public at large.

Scarlatti was relatively cut off from the rest of Europe in Spain and Portugal

---

[81]Ralph Kirkpatrick, *Domenico Scarlatti* (Princeton, N.J., 1953), pp. 72–73.

[82]For a translation of the list of keyboard instruments mentioned in Maria Barbara's will of 1756, see Joel Sheveloff, "Domenico Scarlatti: Tercentenary Frustrations (Part 2)," *Musical Quarterly* 72 (1986): 90–118. Further on the subject: David Sutherland, "Domenico Scarlatti and the Florentine piano," *Early Music* 23 (1995): 243–56, and John Henry van der Meer, "The Keyboard String Instruments at the Disposal of Domenico Scarlatti," *Galpin Society Journal* 50 (1997): 136–60.

[83]Malcolm Boyd, *Domenico Scarlatti—Master of Music* (London, 1986), pp. 158–89.

because "the Iberian countries remained closed and isolated societies until the end of the *ancien régime.*"[84] His father inspired a whole generation of Italian musicians by his example, including Domenico, who was born in Naples on 26 October 1685. Happenstance dictated a more modest role for the latter. Although remote from musical developments in Italy during most of his creative life, he did inspire a few Iberian disciples, notably Sebastian Albero and Antonio Soler. His career followed a pattern, moreover, elements of which recur in the cases of several other keyboard composers to be discussed: apprentice years spent in one or the other or both of the greatest Italian music centers, Naples and Venice; early connection with opera (of which Domenico wrote more than a dozen); emigration to serve a foreign court; role as teacher to a noble dilettante of great standing; publication outside Italy.

Scarlatti's influence on other Italian keyboard composers was minimal or nil, at least until the advent of Muzio Clementi, who encountered his works in London. At his most typical, Scarlatti clung in his sonatas to an older kind of binary form that was not rounded, and in which the greatest similarities occurred at the endings of both strains. His idiosyncratic chord clusters, with their suggestions of Spanish guitar music, defied Italian custom. He never adopted the three-movement sequence that gradually became the norm in Italy. Four-measure phrases occur quite often in his sonatas, but he rarely uses them to build symmetrical periods. One case in which he does occurs towards the end of the first strain of the late Sonata in C, K. 513, which is also called *Pastorale*, indicating its connection with Christmas pastorals and shepherds' droning pipes (Example 3.10). The phrasing is that of the galant extension, **A B B**, and claims have been made that he is quoting an actual popular song here.[85] Whatever its origin, the result, with its parallel thirds over static basses, corresponds to one of the favorite textures of Galuppi. Clear and often repeated IV - V - I cadences are another feature of Scarlatti's modern side. Less modern is the way he contracts and expands phrases in a seamless flow of sound that is more closely related to old-fashioned *Fortspinnung* than it is to the galant style.

The vogue of Scarlatti's sonatas in London was matched for a time in Paris, which saw even more prints and reprints of them. In 1760 Diderot visited the country house of Grimm and Madame d'Épinay, from which he reported hearing an excellent performance of a piece by Scarlatti, by a young lady "who played the harpsichord so lightly and knowingly as to astonish us."[86] About the same time Diderot wrote his novel *La religieuse* (it was too scandalous to be published). In it

---

[84]*Universities in Early Modern Europe 1500–1800*, ed. Hilde de Ridder-Symoens, vol. 2: *A History of the University in Europe*, (Cambridge, 1996), p. 424.

[85]It was identified as a Neapolitan Christmas song by Alessandro Longo, according to Boyd, *Domenico Scarlatti*, pp. 172–73.

[86]The letter, dated 15 September 1760, was written to Diderot's mistress Sophie Volland. It is quoted in Beatrice Durand-Sendrail, *La musique de Diderot: essai sur le hieroglyphe musicale* (Paris, 1994), p. 25.

EXAMPLE 3.10. *Domenico Scarlatti, Keyboard Sonata in C (K. 513)*

Sister Suzanne at her last convent is drawn into the cell of the mother superior and seated by force at the harpsichord, upon which she plays Couperin, Rameau, and Scarlatti. The older woman, one hand tight upon Suzanne's bared shoulder, meanwhile goes through the stages of sighs, heavy breathing, and orgasm.[87] Diderot leaves it to us to imagine a succession of pieces by the three composers that might correspond to these phases. We might think, for instance, of any number of sighing pieces by Couperin such as "Le Dodo" (Example 1.1 on p. 21), in which the two hands remain in close position, then of the more wide-open technique with skips demanded in a piece such as Rameau's "Les sauvages" (Example 6.1 on p. 622), capped by one of the typical Scarlatti sonatas in which massive chords in both treble and bass explode at the end of cascading arpeggios.

In 1756, a year before Scarlatti's death, the Nuremberg publisher Johann Ulrich Haffner began publishing a series of collections devoted to the keyboard sonatas of "celebrated Italian composers." He included in his second *Raccolta* the single movement in C that he attributed to Scarlatti, a piece now considered spurious, but distinct, nevertheless, from the multimovement sonatas of Giovanni Battista Pescetti, Giovanni Marco Rutini, Giuseppe Antonio Paganelli, Galuppi, and others that surround it.[88] This one-movement sonata abounds in rapid-broken octave scales in both hands and often-repeated cadences that are at least Scarlatti-like. The younger masters just mentioned provide the keyboard equivalent of what Tartini and Sammartini accomplished in violin music and the focus for the following discussion.

[87]Denis Diderot, *Oeuvres Romanesques*, ed. Henri Bénac (Paris, 1962), p. 340.
[88]*Raccolta musicale contenente VI sonate per il cembalo d'altretani celebre compositori italiani*, 5 vols. (Nuremberg, 1756–65). The first three volumes are reproduced in facsimile in *Raccolta musicale . . . a cura di G. U. Haffner* (Bologna, 1969). Haffner also published *VI sonate per cembalo* by Scarlatti in 1754. On the single sonata attributed to Scarlatti in the second collection see Kirkpatrick, *Domenico Scarlatti*, p. 426.

Published keyboard sonatas around 1730 by Azzolino Della Ciaja, Pietro San-
doni, and Francesco Durante offer a few intimations of things to come, but there
is no decisive breakthrough to a new style until the *Sonate per gravicembalo* by
Giovanni Battista Pescetti, printed in London in 1739 with a dedication to the
composer's pupil, Lady Boyle. Pescetti was a Venetian, born about 1704, two years
before Galuppi, with whom he was a co-disciple of Antonio Lotti. He made his
operatic debut as a composer at one of the smaller Venetian theaters in 1725 and
wrote much music for them subsequently, often in collaboration with Galuppi.
Between 1737 and 1744 he was producing operas at London. The nine sonatas
printed in 1739, together with a tenth that is an arrangement for keyboard of one
of his opera overtures, are mostly in three movements. They display a few retrospective features, such as quasi-fugues like those of Durante and Scarlatti, an
unusual reliance on minor keys, and some pompous French overture types of
movements. Several binary movements, on the other hand, have a clear return to
the initial theme and key midway in the second part, and the themes themselves
are often quite galant.

The last movement of Pescetti's first sonata is a minuet with variations and
offers one of the earliest occurrences of the "singing" right-hand melody over an
Alberti bass. Improvising variations on a theme, particularly on minuet-finales,
with ever-increasing rhythmic figuration under the melody would have led keyboard players to hit upon such an accompanimental figure had Alberti never
existed. Pescetti's minuet has good periodic structure, the motion from I to V being
answered symmetrically by V to I.

The Alberti bass is rare enough before 1740, except as an occasional or incidental configuration, that it can be used as a device for dating keyboard scores in
the absence of other evidence. This point is confirmed by the keyboard sonatas of
Benedetto Marcello, who died in 1739; effective in their use of long pedal harmonies, although rather deficient in variety of melodic inspiration, they include
no use of the Alberti bass.[89] Pescetti's sonatas exemplify what the younger Venetians had achieved by the 1730s, probably including the more genial Galuppi,
although none of his surviving sonatas for keyboard is datable so early as this.

Sonatas as good as Pescetti's were not easily found by publishers. In 1742
Padre Martini's *Sonate d'intavolatura per l'organo e il cembalo* were brought out in
Amsterdam by La Cène, a publishing venture in which both Tartini and Locatelli
were involved as intermediaries.[90] The sonatas were suites in the old contrapuntal style and dull. By way of contrast, Martini's *Sonate per l'organo et il cembalo*

[89]Benedetto Marcello, *Sonates pour clavecin*, ed. Luciano Sgrizzi and Lorenzo Bianconi (Paris, 1971) (*Le
pupitre* 28.) The sonatas circulated in manuscript. A printed edition, mentioned by Marcello's necrologist,
has never been found.

[90]Dunning, *Pietro Antonio Locatelli*, 1: 284–87.

(Bologna: Della Volpe, 1747) were written in a much more homophonic manner, and yet they too lack cantabile.[91]

Vincenzo Ciampi, born in Piacenza ca. 1719 and trained in Naples by Leo and Durante, was *maestro di coro* at the Incurabili when he was called to London in the fall of 1748. Unlike Pescetti and Galuppi, who preceded him at the King's Theatre, he was brought to put on Italian comic operas. He is most remembered for his collaboration with Goldoni on *Bertoldo* (Venice, 1748; London, 1754), a landmark in the evolution of the buffo finale and of opéra-comique, after which Favart constructed *Ninette à la cour* (Paris, 1755). In 1751 John Walsh published six *Sonate per cembalo composte da Vicenzo Ciampi,* works in two movements that show an idiomatic flair for the possibilities of the keyboard but rarely any of the tunefulness that mark the composer's comic operas. Ciampi returned to Venice in the second half of the 1750s, resumed his post at the Incurabili, and died in 1762.

Giovanni Platti came to the fore in 1742 when Haffner at Nuremberg published a collection with a long and informative title: *VI. Sonates pour le clavessin sur le goût italien. Dediées à Son Altesse Serenissime Marie Therese, Princesse d'Ottingue . . . composées par Jean Platti, musicien de la chambre de son Altesse Reverendissime le Prince Evèque de Bamberg et Wurtzbourg. Oeuvre premier.* Platti was born in Padua on 9 July 1697 and studied with Gasparini in Venice (perhaps with Vivaldi too). In 1722 he went to Würzburg along with other musicians from Venice, including Fortunato Chelleri. Although not an opera composer, he sang tenor, gave singing lessons, played several instruments, and was one of the mainstays of musical life at the Würzburg court, along with his wife, who was also a singer. In his dedication to Countess Ottingen he does not claim to have taught the lady, merely to have noticed, upon her visit to Würzburg, how the harpsichord drew the special attention of her "esprit éclairé." Enlightened spirit or not, she was presented with a collection of quite serious and sometimes rather old-fashioned sonatas. The composer, or more likely the publisher, vaunted that they were written "upon the Italian taste." In fact the sonatas conform to the old church sonata sequence, four movements arranged slow–fast–slow–fast. In one sonata, the third, dance movements fill out the sequence as in the old chamber sonata.

Binary form with both halves repeated prevails in Platti's sonatas except in the opening slow movements, which are mostly without a double bar in the middle. The movements remain all in the same key, with the exception of four third movements. The will to be Italian shows up in certain details within individual movements, such as the *Larghetto* of the second sonata, which is subtitled "Aria," or the "Siciliano" of the fifth sonata, in which the composer dutifully flaunts his

---

[91]Martini offered these first to La Cène, describing them in a letter of 1743 as "douze pièces de clavesin de la dernière façon." Dunning, *Pietro Antonio Locatelli,* 1: 288. See also Luigi Ferdinando Tagliavini, "Le sonate per organo e cembalo di Martini," in *Padre Martini: Musica e cultura nel settecento Europeo,* ed. Angelo Pompilo (Florence, 1987), pp. 295–303.

Neapolitan-sixth chord in the appropriate place, near the end of the second half. Platti's fast movements have been compared with those of Vivaldi, as well as with the Pergolesian buffo style. The *Allegro* finale of the second sonata shows affinities with both.[92] It opens with a passage in octaves that is quite concerto-like, while the closing passage approaches comic patter with its repeated cadential gestures, including a final diminution of rhythmic values (mimicking in reverse the augmentation of the opening).

Two-voiced texture prevails in Platti's keyboard music, but the harmony becomes rich and four-voiced on occasion, with some dramatic uses of diminished and augmented chords, which suggests the inspiration of serious opera, and particularly of obbligato recitative. Emanuel Bach employed similar effects in his first keyboard set, the "Prussian" sonatas, which by coincidence were brought out by another Nuremberg publisher the same year as Platti's first set. A second collection of six keyboard sonatas by Platti was issued by Haffner about four years later. They are more variable in plan, with a tendency towards the three-movement type preferred by Emanuel Bach, in which the slow movement is placed in the middle. Even though Platti was not German, his musical language deferred to the tastes of his patrons, and his artistic vision came closer to that of Bach than of Galuppi, who led the modern Italians as to keyboard composition. This is nowhere more clear than in the realm of the slow movement, in which Platti is richly expressive. Galuppi's sonatas have few slow movements. Platti never achieved the "singing *allegro*," which would indicate he lost touch with "le goût Italien" at some point. It is symptomatic that Haffner included none of Platti's music in his later anthologies, which were decidedly more galant in complexion. Platti did see some chamber music through Haffner's press, in addition to the two keyboard sets.

The Florentine court lutenist Domenico Palafuti wrote to Padre Martini in 1764 commemorating three masters recently deceased, Geminiani in 1762, Platti in 1763, and Locatelli in 1764.[93] Palafuti says he knew all three personally at different times. Locatelli and Geminiani were difficult of character, especially the latter, he says, who was not generous. He had much more to say about Platti, who gave Palafuti a score of his Psalm 1 "Miserere mei, Deus," set for four-part chorus and orchestra with oboes. This treasure was completed by the composer on his fortieth birthday, precisely the same day on which Gian Gastone, the last Medici prince, died (9 July 1737), the implication being that Platti was in Florence at the time. "A work noble in style, profound expression and unusual harmonic force,"

[92]*Historical Anthology of Music,* ed. Archibald T. Davison and Willi Apel, 2 vols. (Cambridge, Mass., 1950), 2: no. 284. Eighteen solo sonatas are edited in Fausto Torrefranca, *Giovanni Benedetto Platii e la sonata moderna* (Istitzioni e monumenti, new series, 2) (Milan, 1963).

[93]Fabbri, "Una nuova fonte per la conoscenza di Giovanni Platti," pp. 181–202.

says Palafuti. The Psalm is still extant and is indeed impressive; one chromatic descending progression for chorus in block chords with enharmonic changes bears a resemblance to the powerful setting of "Et in terra pax hominibus" in the key of b in Vivaldi's famous *Gloria* in D (R. 589).[94] Palafuti introduced Platti as "the Paduan master who studied in Venice with Gasparini and with good instrument teachers, who composed celebrated sonatas for the hammer *cembalo* that he got to know in Siena, as well as church music and chamber music." The keyboard reference must be to Cristofori's fortepiano, and the mention of Siena reinforces the idea that Platti visited Tuscany.

Domenico Alberti was the singer-cembalist *par excellence.* Already during the eighteenth century his name was attached to the ubiquitous accompanimental pattern of a broken triad by Georg Joseph Vogler, Schubart, and Gerber. Most of what we know about him comes from La Borde's *Essai sur la musique ancienne et moderne* (1780) and may stem from La Borde's visit to Venice in 1773.

> Venetian, amateur, he was a pupil of Biffi and Lotti. He went to Spain in the quality of a page to the Venetian ambassador. There he astonished the renowned Farinelli by the manner of his singing. . . . He then went with the Marquis [Giovanni] Molinari to Rome, where he perfected himself in singing and harpsichord playing. He set to music at Venice in 1737 *Endimione* a charming work of Metastasio, and subsequently *La galatea.* These two works are greatly esteemed because the composition is very agreeable and full of sentiment. All the professors remember him with enthusiasm: nothing could equal the graces of his singing; his improvising at the harpsichord (en préludant sur le clavecin) charmed large gatherings during entire nights. . . . He died very young and much regretted. He composed 36 sonatas.

Supposing that Alberti was born around 1710, he would have studied singing as a boy with Antonio Biffi, vice maestro of San Marco and *maestro di coro* of the Mendicanti, who died by 1733, and then counterpoint with Lotti, who died in 1740. Farinelli reached Spain in 1737. If Alberti did visit the Spanish court and astonish the great singer, he would have encountered Scarlatti there as well. Dating of *Endimione* is made more precise by an annotation on a surviving libretto of the work: "Serenata for four voices performed the evening of 24 September 1737 in a private house in the parish of San Felice in Venice by a company of merchants. . . . Music by Domenico Alberti, Venetian dilettante."[95]

Niccolo Pasquali, the violinist-composer, heard Alberti play in Italy before he left for London ca. 1743. At his premature death in Edinburgh at the age of thirty-nine in 1757, Pasquali left a treatise on performing, *The art of fingering the harpsi-*

---

[94]Fabbri (ibid.) quotes this passage in his note 80 on p. 201.
[95]Rome, Conservatorio (Allacci 288). A score survives in Modena. *La galatea* in Alberti's setting also survives in manuscripts at Brescia, Modena, and Paris.

chord. In it he criticizes Handel's keyboard fugues. To achieve as sustained and a cantabile quality on the instrument as possible he recommended a texture of no more than two parts. "Since I am on this Point, I cannot forbear taking Notice of *Dominico Alberti*'s lessons for Harpsichord, who played and understood the true Power of the instrument to the highest perfection."[96] Burney confirms in his *History* the impact that Alberti's music had even upon professionals. He inveighed against the old style of keyboard playing as "*notes, et rien que les notes*, till Jozzi, the singer, by his neat and elegant manner of executing the brilliant gracefull, and pleasing lessons of Alberti, rendered them objects of imitation." In another passage Burney expanded on Giuseppe Jozzi's role in the 1740s.

> At this time Jozzi, a castrato, and second singer at the opera, brought over Alberti's Lessons, which he played, printed, and sold, for his own, at a guinea each book; till detected by a gentleman coming from Venice, who had been personally acquainted with Alberti, and was in possession of a manuscript copy in his own hand writing; which, in order to expose the impudence and plagiarism of Jozzi, he gave to Walsh, who printed and sold the eight elegant and graceful lessons of the original composer, for six schillings. Jozzi, though not the author of these charming pieces, which were the first of a style that has been since too much imitated, but never equalled, had the merit of playing them with a neatness and precision that was truly admirable. The harpsichord having neither sostenuto nor expression, maintained its reputation by brilliant execution; and there was an accent, a spring, and smartness in Jozzi's touch, which I had then never heard.

John Walsh published without dedication *VIII Sonate per cembalo di Domenico Alberti* in London in 1748. The book had prodigious sales, says Burney, "the style being new, and so much more within the power of gentlemen and ladies to execute, than the rich and complicated pieces of Handel, and the wild and original legerdemain of Scarlatti." There were numerous reprints both in London and on the Continent, where the enterprising printers of Paris and Amsterdam did not fail in the usual piracies. Jozzi contributed pieces of his own in Alberti's style to this flourishing market. Pasquali took pains to distinguish the originals from their imitations.[97]

The customer who bought Walsh's collection found upon opening it the winsome *Andante* in Example 3.11. The repeated-note bass of the first measure shows

[96]Niccolo Pasquali, *The art of fingering the harpsichord* (Edinburgh, 1758; reprinted in 1760), p. 24. Modern edition edited by Davitt Moroney. Pasquali may be the "Pasqualino" whom Brosses ranked as a violinist with Veracini, and higher than Somis.

[97]Wilhelm Wörmann, "Die Klaviersonate Domenico Albertis," *Acta Musicologica* 27 (1955): 84–112. Barry Cooper, "Alberti and Jozzi: Another View," *Music Review* 39 (1978): 160–66, supports Pasquali's statement that the second movements of Walsh's Sonatas 1, 3, 4, 6, 8, and the entirety of Sonata 7 were by Jozzi.

EXAMPLE 3.11. *Domenico Alberti, Harpsichord Sonata No. 1, I*

that the composer had more than one kind of accompaniment. It supports a delicately spun cantilena, combining dotted rhythm and triplet figures. Alberti becomes more lyric still, especially in the rise of the soprano with chromatic inflections (m. 2), which is then repeated—a typical example of the galant extension. In fact all the essential qualities of galant keyboard music are present here. In his *Anweisung* of 1791 Daniel Gottlob Türk says that the galant composer works for the ear and uses chromatic inflections to lend his progressions a piquant flavor. This musical example qualifies both in the opening theme and in the succeeding transition to the dominant. The sonatas are all in two movements, an opening one in some approximation of sonata form, mostly in common time, followed by a slighter dance movement in the same key. Paired movements like this were common in the Italian keyboard sonata of the mid-eighteenth century, as were three-movement sequences like that of the galant chamber sonata.

The stylistic importance of Alberti, amply attested by Burney for London, is echoed by Diderot for Paris. In *Le neveu de Rameau,* sketched in the 1760s, the nephew mimes and sings keyboard sonatas by Alberti and Galuppi. In the *Leçons de clavecin et principes d'harmonie* (1771), printed under the name of Anton Bemetzrieder, but actually by Diderot, the principal subject is the musical education of the philosopher's brilliant daughter, Angélique, whose teacher was in fact a real-life Anton Bemetzrieder. She learns how to play a wide variety of keyboard literature, including "strong" and demanding music by Emanuel Bach, Johann Gottfried Müthel, and Johann Schobert. She confesses in the last resort that her favorite remains "Alberti, who must be played with delicacy and taste. . . . He will be my choice when, having become able to read anything at sight, I wish to bring something to perfection." If Diderot had had a son instead of a daughter being trained in music the preference expressed might have been different.

Several arias by Alberti were inserted into productions of *Demofoonte* and *Temistocle* at Bologna in 1744. A fine *ombra* aria of his, "Caro sposo, amato oggetto," figures in a Parisian miscellany containing pieces copied at Rome in the 1750s. Anton Raaff chose to sing a very sentimental little piece by Alberti to end Jommelli's *Attilio Regolo* as late as 1761 in Naples. Alberti died in Rome on 14 October 1746 according to his tombstone.

Giovanni Rutini signed his first set of keyboard sonatas at Prague in 1748 and dedicated them to a noble there. A Florentine born in 1723, Rutini was admitted in April 1739 to the Turchini conservatory in Naples, where he studied violin, harpsichord, and composition (with Leo). He finished his studies in 1744 and returned a few years later to Florence. Tuscany's imperial links provided an opening to the world beyond the Alps from which Rutini profited. Besides residing for a time at Prague, he visited Dresden, Berlin, and Saint Petersburg (1758–61), where he preceded Galuppi and composed an opera for the court. His later years were spent mainly in his native Florence. As a composer of keyboard sonatas he was almost as prolific as Galuppi. Unlike the Venetian master, he took care to see that his sonatas were published. One collection after another appeared over the years until a final Op. 18 was printed in 1793.

Rutini's first six sets of sonatas were brought out by Haffner at Nuremberg between 1748 and 1760.[98] They constitute the high point of his achievement. The Mozarts thought highly enough of Rutini to take some of his sonatas along on their first Italian tour, and Mozart later used one of his themes.[99] Rutini's Op. 1 No. 1, in D, begins with a *Largo* that has bold theatrical sweep. The second sonata includes instrumental recitatives. Flexible as to the number and order of movements, Rutini often uses modal contrast with good effect. For instance, he put a minor slow movement between two fast movements (Op. 1 No. 6). He added a trio in the relative minor to the minuet finale of Op. 2 No. 1, which also has a slow middle movement in the relative minor, and extended the minuet by two trios, one in the relative, the other in the tonic minor in Op. 5 No. 2.

While Rutini does not lack striking ideas, their force often seems to dissipate as he runs on. The wandering, rather indeterminate quality of much of his work is a consequence, and one that is not quite overcome by his resourcefulness in exploiting the harpsichord for all its idiomatic possibilities. The youthful fire and exuberance of his early works disappear little by little, as the publications multiply. In his later sonatas Rutini sought ever more simple means by which to woo the dilettante player. His Op. 7 of 1770 he sent to Metastasio in Vienna and received in reply an approbation he was only too happy to print as additional

[98]On the complicated bibliography of Rutini's sonatas and their modern editions see William S. Newman, *The Sonata in the Classic Era*, 3rd ed. (New York, 1983), 204–7. Newman argues convincingly that Rutini's sonatas decline in quality after Op. 6.

[99]The theme for variations of Mozart's Violin Sonata in G (K. 379) relates to the minuet of Rutini's Op. 10 No. 3 (1776) as shown by Giorgio Pestelli, "Mozart et Rutini," *Analecta Musicologica* 18 (1978): 291–307; 304–5.

advertisement: the venerable sage of Italian opera praised him for combining grace and charm with ease of execution.

Domenico Paradies, another cembalist-composer whose works were played in the Mozart circle, makes a stronger impression. The first edition of his set of twelve sonatas, frequently reprinted, came out in impressive circumstances in London in 1754. A sumptuous folio volume, it was entitled *Sonate di gravicembalo dedicate a sua Altezza Reale la Principessa Augusta da Pier Domenico Paradies Napoli-tano.* The dedicatee was no less than the Princess of Wales and mother of George III, from the Coburg-Gotha branch of the Saxon line. Paradies was responsible for her musical education, as is clear from the Italian dedication, one remarkably free of the usual fustian (fashions in dedications, as in wigs, bear watching). Paradies was born in Naples in 1707 and is said to have been a pupil of Porpora, but nothing specific is known of his education. He wrote stageworks for Lucca (1738) and Venice (1740) before settling in London, for which he wrote a *Fetonte* (1747). The opera was not a success, according to Burney, in spite of its lavish use of chorus and ballet (pointing to French models such as the *Phaeton* of Lully, which would serve Jommelli at Stuttgart a few years later). Paradies enjoyed his greatest success in England as a teacher of voice and harpsichord.

More than ordinary care was taken by Paradies to put together a set of sonatas with variety of character and balance of interest with respect to keys, meters, tempos, and styles. The result is a consistently fine collection. Each sonata consists of a pair of movements in the same key and mode, except Nos. 4 and 9, where the pairing is minor-major. The most frequent sequence, as with Alberti, is an expansive binary movement in duple meter, followed by a slighter dance movement in triple. If the first movement is in triple meter, Paradies resorts to a duple-meter finale. The exception is provided by Sonata No. 9, where both movements are duple, but sufficiently contrasted by mode, tempo, and style. As the collection progresses, the sonatas get a little more difficult, in line with their didactic function. By Sonata No. 6 in A, there are challenges even for the skilled player—Paradies was one of the composers whose keyboard music was set before young Mozart at London and Paris in order to test his sight-reading. Variety of style is achieved by taking several models. Sonata 5 in F begins like a two-part invention and ends both sections of the first movement with broken octaves marching down (right hand) and then up (left hand). As the difficulties increase it becomes apparent that Paradies was one of the rare Italian composers who did profit from the idiomatic techniques of Domenico Scarlatti. The hand crossings and *bariolage* in Sonata 11 testify to this, and so does some of the musical material in Sonata 10.[100] Sonata 9 in a minor begins with the rising arpeggio figure familiar from

[100]Newman, *Sonata in the Classic Era,* pp. 689–90, makes the case for a direct influence.

Scarlatti's well-known sonata in the same key (K. 119). The same sonata ends with a blithe rondo in A, the delicate *style brisé* of which is worthy of Couperin. It is as if the composer were showing how diverse he could be. There are other finales *en rondeau* in which the world of the *clavecinistes* seems close.

The big initial movements of Paradies often have secondary as well as primary themes of clear profile. In the reprise he usually cuts back to material just after but not including the opening theme. Compared with Alberti, Paradies has better control of long-range harmonic goals, along with a much greater variety of textures. It is not surprising that his sonatas were highly regarded by the Mozarts and by other keyboard specialists such as Clementi and Cramer. It is a pity Paradies did not write more. He retired to Italy around 1770, presumably with a royal pension, settled in Venice, and died there in 1791.

Giuseppe Paganelli was another opera composer *manqué* who subsequently turned to keyboard sonatas. The son of a wealthy merchant, he was born in 1710 in Padua, and studied with Giuseppe Saratelli in Venice. His operatic debut was at one of the smaller Venetian theaters in 1732. After this he held several posts in Germany, including cembalist to the Italian opera at Augsburg. Prince Frederick of Prussia wrote his sister in 1736 expressing contempt for Paganelli's arias and maintaining that the only good music in his operas was what he had stolen from Hasse, Vinci, and other Italian masters. Paganelli composed ensemble sonatas for flute and strings as well as keyboard sonatas. Typical of the latter is the collection called *Divertissement de la beau sex ou six sonatines*. The very title serves to point up the slight and ephemeral nature of so much galant keyboard music and also how much of it was written for or dedicated to lady amateurs. Gentlemen preferred to play the flute or a bowed stringed instrument. Paganelli's set consists of short and easy sonatas in two or three movements. They lack the structural solidity of Paradies' and do not quite attain the lyric breadth of Alberti's "singing *Allegro*." *Sonatines* they are indeed, and some of the movements are appropriately labeled *galante*. Most of these bagatelles were printed by Lotter at Augsburg as *XXX Ariae pro organo et cembalo* (1756) with a claim that they were well suited to liturgical use. Perhaps they were, in that the Catholic parts of southern Germany were then at the height of their entrancing adventure into rococo church building. Paganelli provided music that was as lighthearted as the cupid-angels in those airy constructs.

Haffner included Paganelli in his second anthology devoted to Italian masters, describing him as "Maestro di Camera di Sua Maestà Cattolica, etc. etc. in Madrid." Paganelli apparently succeeded Scarlatti at the Spanish court. He cuts a rather slight figure side by side with Pescetti, Galuppi, and Rutini, but he outshines some of Haffner's other "celebrated Italian composers." Haffner was not in the best situation to get much new Italian music. To convince composers to send him their keyboard sonatas, he promised six free printed copies in return. The economics of this arrangement could turn to the advantage of the composer, if he were clever in adding dedications of his own to wealthy friends and pupils. Haffner's Italian anthologies leave an impression that the overall quality achieved by the *cembalisti* was high, if uneven. They did much to insure that the gradual Italianization of music in central Europe became accelerated around 1760.

Galuppi

PREDECESSORS, TRAINING, EARLY SUCCESSES

Two famous composers who enjoyed high regard as teachers, Lotti and Gasparini, are said to have been taught by Giovanni Legrenzi during the 1680s when he was vice maestro then maestro at San Marco. Lotti was of Venetian descent, although he may have been born (1667) in Hanover where his father was Kapellmeister. Gasparini was born a year later near Lucca, came to Venice to study with Legrenzi by 1686, and was one of the most sought-after teachers in Venice during his years as *maestro di coro* at the Pietà (1701–13). His students included Domenico Scarlatti, sent from Naples by his father; Platti; Benedetto Marcello; and later, in Rome, Quantz. Gasparini also published an important treatise, *L'armonico pratico al cimbalo* (Venice, 1708). This manual on figured bass accompaniment at the keyboard is one of the primary sources of information on nonharmonic tones struck along with harmonic ones, including the *acciaccature* used so distinctively by Domenico Scarlatti. The list of Lotti's pupils is also long. They included Domenico Alberti, Pescetti, Saratelli, Benedetto Marcello, and, towering above all, Galuppi.

Benedetto Marcello and his older brother Alessandro were noblemen from an ancient patrician family. Benedetto, born in Venice in 1686, was trained in law and destined for important posts in the government of the republic. Both brothers were taught the violin by their father, a member of the Venetian senate. Both became accomplished authors and members of the Arcadian Academy. Both also became composers, but Benedetto went so far as to study singing and counterpoint with Gasparini, to the detriment of his formal studies, or so deemed his father. Benedetto's first musical publication was a set of twelve concertos in 1708. The mordant satire *Il teatro alla moda* followed in 1720. Then came his setting of fifty Psalms in the Italian translation by Girolomo Ascanio Giustiniani. He used a wide variety of means to sustain this monumental undertaking, solo and choral, homophonic and contrapuntal, traditional and modern, while claiming in the preface that he wished to be "varied, consistent, and severe in style" (di vario e insieme e grave stile). The Psalm settings were published between 1724 and 1727 at great expense in eight folio volumes, using the old moveable type—one of the last great feats of Venetian music printing. Out of the fifty, seven are for solo voice, twenty-one for two voices, sixteen for three, and only six for four voices.

An example from Psalm 8, for solo contralto and basso continuo, plus unison choral refrain, illustrates the simplest kind of setting (Example 3.12). The piece is an aria da capo in which the short middle part comes to rest on the relative minor. If listeners were unaware that the text praised the Lord's almighty name, they could hardly be blamed for thinking it sounded like a lusty tavern song. Marcello's severity with his muse may consist of choosing an old-fashioned continuo setting, but the effect is sumptuous in spite of the limitation of means. The well-written part for cello makes effective use of the instrument's low C and various pedal tones in a very euphonious ritornello that sets the dancelike piece in motion. The vocal melody is willfully simple. It has the modish three-note snaps so common with the Neapolitans and its perfectly square phrase (with galant extension of the second half) is built upon a two-measure rhythmic module repeated several times. The reduction to a single rhythm corresponds to the limitation of harmonic

EXAMPLE 3.12. *Benedetto Marcello, Psalm 8*

means: only I, IV, V and their respective dominants are used in the main section. A unison chorus serves to punctuate the form, which is crystal clear, by repeating phrases at the ends of sections. This is the radically simplified language of contemporaneous opera. A comparison with Vinci's aria (Example 2.5 on p. 90) of about the same date will show several similarities; their obvious debt to the minuet is mutual. It is also possible to recognize in Marcello's limpid cantilena the inspiration of his principal teacher, Antonio Lotti.

Marcello's Psalm settings became concert favorites and remained so throughout the century. Shortly after their publication, Algarotti wrote a passage in a letter to a friend that put Tartini and Marcello on a par for their innovations: "Who would have believed, a few years ago, that it was possible to add anything to vocal music after Scarlatti, or to instrumental music after Corelli? And yet Marcello and Tartini have shown that both the one and the other were capable of further development."[101] An interesting observation this, because it pinpoints the watershed between seventeenth-century accomplishments and those of the new century, which took a couple of decades or more to find its own musical personality.

Algarotti, a Venetian and proud of it (not yet ennobled, as he was to be later by Frederick II of Prussia), was vaunting two local composers at a time when music in Northern Italy was coming under the increasing domination of the Neapolitans. What Algarotti neglects to mention is as telling as what he says. Vivaldi is ignored, although his program concertos were even more influential than Marcello's works; but he did not inspire a cult of admirers as did Tartini. Hasse is also ignored, although he was undoubtedly the favorite of Venetian audiences at the time. He was, to be sure, a "foreigner"—a German become a Neapolitan. Also ignored is Lotti, who, from the time of his return to Venice in 1720 until his death two decades later, was the most widely respected musician and teacher the city could boast.

Lotti was the most prominent church musician in Venice since Legrenzi, whose successor he eventually became by working himself up the ladder of positions at San Marco until he was named primo maestro (on an interim basis in 1733, definitively in 1736). After his return from Dresden in 1720 he composed church music exclusively. His last years were devoted to writing a great quantity of masses, Psalm settings, and other service music, mostly a capella or with only organ accompaniment (i.e., with basso continuo) but some with strings as well. Besides commanding the old contrapuntal style Lotti had a flair for colorful har-

---

[101]Letter of 12 October 1735, written from Cirey, where Algarotti was staying as a protégé of Voltaire. See Pierluigi Petrobelli, "Tartini, Algarotti e la Corta di Dresda," *Analecta Musicologica* 2 (1965), pp. 72 ff. The context of Algarotti's remark is literary. He was sending a copy of Voltaire's *Jules César* with his letter, remarking that this play disproved the notion that it was impossible to go beyond the achievements of Corneille and Racine.

monies, and he deployed them even in his pieces à la Palestrina, as unaccompanied choral works were then often called. His most famous setting of the *Miserere* includes the phrase shown in Example 3.13. Use of the diminished and augmented chords, in particular, shows that Lotti, even though he may have forsaken the stage or been forsaken by it, did not put aside the more expressive harmonic means that had developed in opera for moments of high drama and passionate utterance. Among the Venetians he was the closest to Alessandro Scarlatti in style and technique. His opera *Porsenna* was revised and staged under Scarlatti himself at Naples in 1713. Like Scarlatti, Lotti became the highly regarded elder statesman of his musical world. The prime beneficiary of his legacy was Galuppi.

EXAMPLE 3.13. *Lotti*, Miserere

Born on 18 October 1706 on the little island of Burano, in the lagoon of Venice, Baldassare Galuppi became known as "il Buranello," the diminutive also having reference to his slight physical stature. As in the case of several others among the greatest eighteenth-century composers—Vivaldi, Gluck, Haydn, and Gossec spring to mind—he came from humble stock. Burano was a fishing village, and Galuppi's father was a barber who also played the violin. The young composer absorbed whatever training his father could give him and early became known as a good keyboard player. At the age of sixteen he composed a *favola pastorale* and succeeded in getting it put on the stage at Chioggia and Vicenza. The novelty of someone so young playing the maestro did not prevent the work from failing. Galuppi told his misfortune to Marcello, who scoffed at his temerity and extracted from him the promise that he would study for three years, without public appearances, under Lotti. Marcello paid for the lessons, which included organ study and counterpoint; thus he may be considered Galuppi's mentor, if not teacher. Toward the end of this strict training, Galuppi went with an itinerant troupe to Florence and served as cembalist to the opera orchestra in the Pergola theater. By 1727 he was back in Venice, where he relaunched his operatic career in collaboration with Pescetti. The long march had begun.

From 1728 to 1740 Galuppi wrote some ten serious operas for the Sant'Angelo theater (fall or carnival seasons) and four more for the San Samuele (spring or Ascension fair season). These brought him into the immediate proximity of Vivaldi, who had long dominated both stages and still composed operas for them. The two composers managed not to share the same season in the same theater, which must have taken some fancy footwork on both their parts. Presumably Vivaldi, still powerful, went out of his way to see that his works did not get staged in direct competition with those of his young rival.[102] They worked with some of the same librettists, but the musical results differed greatly. Vivaldi continued to rely mainly on his extroverted and highly rhythmic style, supported by colorful orchestration and violinistic virtuosity. Galuppi pared his music down to a simple Vinci-like style in which the violins usually doubled the voice. He won the day with the public. By the end of the 1730s his Venetian successes were confirmed by commissions to write operas on texts by Metastasio for Turin, Mantua, and Modena. Then in late 1740 his rise to the top was confirmed by an honor that Vivaldi never received, a commission for a carnival opera from Venice's main house, the San Giovanni Grisostomo. Here the greatest singers appeared, in operas hitherto supplied almost exclusively by Neapolitan composers. The opera was *Oronte, rè de' sciti* on a libretto by Carlo Goldoni. Galuppi's emergence as Venice's leading composer coincided with the demise of three musical luminaries around 1740: Lotti, Marcello, and Vivaldi.

SACRED MUSIC

Galuppi's first major appointment at Venice came in the summer of 1740. He was named *maestro di coro* at the Mendicanti.[103] The customary stipulations obtained: he was to lead the chorus and orchestra while composing music for the special religious occasions throughout the year. His first effort was an oratorio, *Sancta Maria Magdalena,* to honor the patron saint of the Mendicanti. Oratorios typically were performed at vespers service in two parts, separated by a sermon. Hardly had he begun his duties before he was petitioning for a leave to accept a lucrative

[102]Reinhard Wiesend, "Vivaldi e Galuppi: Rapporti biografici e stilistici," in *Antonio Vivaldi: Teatro musicale, cultura e società,* ed. Lorenzo Bianconi and Giovanni Morelli (Florence, 1982), pp. 233–55.
[103]Gastone Vio, "I maestri di coro dei Mendicanti e la Capella Marciana," in *Galuppiana,* ed. Maria Teresa Muraro and Franco Rossi (Florence, 1986), pp. 95–111.

offer from London. He was invited to become the main composer at the Haymarket Theatre, replacing Handel. Keeping the Mendicanti supplied with new music in his absence, he journeyed to England and put on operas there between December 1741 and early 1743. Returned home, he resumed all his duties at the Mendicanti and raised standards to the highest level. Rousseau became a regular visitor to this church (Figure 3.9). One of its young ladies was the recipient of the earliest surviving liturgical piece by Galuppi that can be dated. It is a *Salve regina* upon which the composer wrote "per la Signorina Buonafede, 1746." For soprano and strings, the piece begins with a short instrumental introduction followed by the solo in Example 3.14. Harmonic simplicity, with an emphasis on the subdominant, blithe cantilena, and slight texture—these are traits that have been encountered before, but nowhere with more grace.

The voice is doubled, typically, by the first violins, as in much operatic writing since Vinci. There is nothing, indeed, that would be out of place in the opera house, unless it is the ethereal delicacy. If a hint of churchly decorum remains, it is in the suspended dissonances at the end of the vocal excerpt. Galuppi approaches Hasse in this piece. The two had a long and friendly rivalry. Hasse was then music master (mostly in absentia) at the rival Incurabili.

Galuppi left over 200 masses, mass parts, and motets. These can often be distinguished as to destination, according to whether they have high voices (for one

FIGURE 3.9. Luca Carlevarijs. Ospedale dei Mendicanti.

EXAMPLE 3.14. *Galuppi*, Salve regina *in G*

of the *ospedlai*) or full vocal complement (for San Marco). The composer became vice maestro at the basilica in 1748 and maestro in 1762. He had resigned his post at the Mendicanti around 1752. When he returned from Russia in 1768 he accepted Hasse's old post at the Incurabili, at an annual salary of 400 ducats, as well as resuming his duties at San Marco. From this period come many a capella works as well as orchestrally accompanied ones. The former were especially connected with the Lenten season, when a little less splendor was reluctantly adopted—an aural equivalent to draping the statues and altarpieces. Galuppi's late works with orchestra often attain a directness of expression and rhythmic force that take him far beyond his earlier phase. An example is the beginning of his *Dixit Dominus,* which has descending parallel thirds in common with the previous example, but not much else.[104] Many of his liturgical pieces have fugal

[104]Galuppi wrote the piece in 1775 for the Incurabili, using two soprano and two alto parts, then he rewrote it for SATB for San Marco in 1781. Modern editions of both versions are available.

Amens or closing sections—opportunities for which his strict training under Lotti stood him in good stead. In this respect, as in every other, he towered over his fellow composers at Venice (as a giant among dwarfs, according to Burney's expression). Ferdinando Bertoni, his subordinate as organist at San Marco, was so unsure of his own skills, by way of contrast, that he introduced into his church music many borrowings from his teacher, Padre Martini.

Galuppi had few fixed duties as a church composer. He could and did perform other masters' music, especially Hasse's. Yet the great feasts of the church generally called his pen into action. The Venetian senate allowed him leave to go to Russia in 1766 on the one condition that he continue to supply a new mass for each Christmas Eve. During his last days of life on earth at the end of 1784 he managed to fulfill this obligation one final time. San Marco had seen one of its last days of glory three years earlier, when Pope Pius VI made a ceremonial visit. On 16 May 1781 Galuppi had conducted (from the organ) a *Te Deum* by Hasse that was accompanied by an orchestra of one hundred players. Two days later, as the pope entered the basilica in solemn procession, the chorus and orchestra performed Galuppi's *Ecce Sacerdos Magnus,* and then a complete mass of his composition. The same evening, in the ducal palace, his oratorio *Il ritorno di Tobia* was performed by seventy girls drawn from the four *ospedali.* It was repeated before an immense crowd on May 19. During this same spring the grand duke and duchess of Russia were in Venice and elaborate concerts were put on to entertain them. In the midst of all his other activities, Galuppi found time to make a present of six harpsichord sonatas to the grand duchess, a former pupil, for which he was well rewarded. Of private pupils there were many, including several harpsichord-playing daughters of wealthy Venetian families.

Burney's description of his meeting with Galuppi on 16 August 1770 is moving. The Neapolitan composer Gaetano Latilla, who had befriended Burney and was vice maestro at San Marco, escorted him to Galuppi's house and took part in the remarkable conversation that elicited from Galuppi this definition of good music: "vaghezza, chiarezza e buona modulazione" (charm, clarity and good harmony), which Burney found "admirable, and though short, very comprehensive." From this high point of his trip Burney went to Bologna and Florence. What impressed him most at Bologna was not the music but the personality of Padre Martini (whom Burney thought too learned in his writings) and that of Farinelli, who lived in a villa on the outskirts in luxurious retirement, an eloquent relic from the finest age of bel canto. Florence impressed Burney visually but hardly at all musically, and this mainly because of its past, not its present. Rome he regarded as even more of a mausoleum, a fit ground for his researches into old music but possessing little interest as to modern music. In general, Burney found Italian organs to be bad, and their players the same. Even though some pretense of keeping up the old contrapuntal style was made in Italian churches, it was not enough to win the respect of an Englishman who had grown up on Handel's music.

Sacred music in the modern symphonic style, to which Burney was entirely converted, impressed him only occasionally in Italy, and most powerfully at Venice, under Galuppi.

Opera Seria

Among northern Italians, Galuppi was the undisputed master of serious opera for the quarter century between about 1740 and 1765. Few of his earliest operas survive. They were confined to a single production for the most part, as was typical of the time, especially for a young composer. Only one score was necessary: the autograph from which the composer played at the first harpsichord. It typically remained with the theater that commissioned the opera, which helps explain why so few survive, theaters being notoriously prone to fire and destruction, and their libraries to neglect. Not until around 1750, when Galuppi's scores were in demand from several theaters at once, were enough copies of his scores made to insure that they frequently survived. An exception is furnished by his works for London and those directly after his return, which the publisher Walsh excerpted in the "favourite songs" kind of album he habitually printed. In Italy operatic music was hardly ever printed. It is thanks to the avidity for new Italian operas among the music-buying public in England that we have a representative selection of Galuppi's serious operas between 1741 and 1746: *Penelope, Scipione in Cartagine, Enrico, Sirbace, Antigona,* and *Il trionfo della continenza*.

Burney used these Walsh publications in his *History* when he was trying to reconstruct the Italian opera in London before his time. He says of the first London opera, *Penelope* (1741): "the genius of Galuppi was not yet matured; he now copied the hasty, light, and flimsy style which reigned in Italy at this time and which Handel's solidity and science had taught the English to despise." Burney is wrong here on at least two counts: Galuppi was brought to London precisely because Handel's "solidity and science" accounted for his failure with the public at the Italian opera; *Penelope* is on a par with the other operas in this series and shows all the characteristic features of its composer (*pace* Burney's irrepressible notion of progress). The deferential bows to Handel in Burney's *History* only show that the author was trying to ingratiate himself with George III, who doted upon the deceased master's music. What Burney really thought of Handel emerges in unguarded asides elsewhere: he had outgrown him to the point that his heart belonged almost totally to Metastasio and the more modern Italians like Galuppi.

Burney made amends to Galuppi a few sentences later in the *History* when speaking of *Scipione* (1742): "In this opera: *Di madre ai cari amplessi* is a fine cantabile air, in the *gran gusto;* the accompaniment, in *terzini* was his own or, at least new to us. Rinaldo da Capua and Terradellas had accompaniments of the same kind, about this time. Many of Galuppi's passages, indeed, have been made common by plagiarists; but at this time they were new." Concerning *Enrico,* which opened the London season on New Year 1743, Burney pursued the elusive question of Galuppi's innovations:"There are many pleasing and elegant movements in *Enrico;* and a gay air sung by Monticelli, beginning: *Son troppo vezzose,* was constantly encored at the Opera-house, and long remained in general favor. Indeed, many of the refinements in modern melody, and effects in dramatic Music, seem to originate from the genius of Galuppi at this period, at least in England."The last qualification rescues Burney's credibility as a historian of style; what he perceived as so modern belonged to a whole group of Neapolitans in addition to Galuppi; but Galuppi, it is true, was the main figure to carry the latest"refinements"to London. Burney's doubts as to priority were raised by finding similar passages in Porpora's *Temistocle,* the second opera of the 1743 season. In a note he commented that between the two composers they had invented pleasing chromatic alteration of the raised fifth, while referring his readers to the plates of musical examples entitled"Vocal Divisions and Refinements in Dramatic Music from 1740 to 1755." His first plate is reproduced as Figure 3.10. It commences with improvised divisions as performed by Giovanni Carestini, Moscovita, and Angelo Maria Monticelli, three leading singers.

The first three "refinements" are from Galuppi's *Enrico* and show, in turn, a chromatic passing tone that becomes an appoggiatura; an accompanimental figure in thirds labeled "shorthand"; and a melody that goes in parallel thirds throughout and in its second segment produces some very Mozartian-sounding appoggiatura thirds resolving upwards—correctly annotated by Burney, "These Passages were afterwards imitated by SACCHINI and others." What Burney selects to illustrate from *Sirbace* (April 1743), the last opera written during Galuppi's London sojourn, proves slightly less interesting. The first figure is quite common. The second shows the raised fifth, which then becomes an appoggiatura, giving way to triplet figures prior to the half-cadence. The next comes from the same aria and recurs repeatedly as a kind of motto—it has at once the old-fashioned polarity between the outer voices, as in Vinci, with one tritone giving way to another, and in conclusion a perfect example (probably explaining Burney's selection) of the *cadence galante.* The last example, labeled "close," includes the economy-style orchestration noted above ("shorthand") with a spacious and brilliant cadential formula, again very Mozartian, in which the major ninth chord over the dominant of the dominant prepares an effective tonal arrival. (Burney misattributes this excerpt, since it comes in reality from the end of the A^1 section of the aria in $B^\flat$ excerpted from *Enrico* in the second of the above illustrations.) The last score of Burney's plate is devoted to two examples by Lampugnani, who became Galuppi's successor at the Haymarket Theatre, and was his follower in an artistic sense, as well as his exact contemporary. The excerpts quoted seem banal, although vigorous, beside those of the Venetian master.

One item in these collections of which Burney should have taken note was

FIGURE 3.10. Burney. *History of Music,* vol. 4 (1789). Music examples.

the Quartet from *Sirbace.* It is an intensely serious piece in f, in which the primo uomo stands out against the other three singers in a dramatic confrontation. If claims were to be advanced that Galuppi overcame his "hasty, light, and flimsy" Italian style only after writing for London and experiencing the Handelian "solidity and science" admired by the English, this would be the piece to have chosen as an example.

One of the works by other composers that Galuppi put on when in London was a pasticcio made mostly from Pergolesi's *L'Olimpiade.* Burney comments that "the whole exquisite scene where *Se cerca se dice* occurs, was rendered so interesting by the manner in which it was acted as well as sung by Monticelli, that I have been assured by attentive hearers and good judges, that the union of poetry and Music, expression and gesture, seldom have had a more powerful effect on an English audience." The aria had a powerful effect on Galuppi as well. When he set *L'Olimpiade* as the first carnival opera at Milan in 1747, his "Se cerca se dice" borrowed some of its most affective features, melodic, rhythmic, and harmonic, from Pergolesi's setting. But music had not stood still during the time, little more than a decade, that separated the two settings. Going beyond Pergolesi, as well as standing on his shoulders, Galuppi introduced a certain concision, a direct and breathless mode of address that is far different from the frilly mannerisms of his *Salve regina* of the previous year. Moreover, he used an independent second theme that has stunning force of character. Set apart by orchestration and texture, as well as by melodic construction, it has no equivalent in Pergolesi's setting. An eighteenth-century commentator recognized this breakthrough on Galuppi's part for what it was. In 1778 Abbé Georg Joseph Vogler made a detailed comparison of Galuppi's "Se cerca" with the setting of the same aria by Anfossi in 1774; of Galuppi's second theme Vogler said in some wonderment that it must have provided a heavenly delight to the ears of that time, which were still somewhat rough, and he commented specifically on "the singing bass line, played by a tender, melancholy cello solo that runs through the whole compass of a sweet seventh-chord harmony."[105]

Galuppi's setting of *L'Olimpiade* was revived among other places at Mannheim (1749), Prague (1750), Naples (1750), again at Mannheim (1756), and perhaps as late as 1763 in Siena, an unusual life span for a serious opera at this time. The composer may have attended none of these productions, which is odd in that the maestro usually went along with his opera scores, supervising at least the first night's performance from the harpsichord. That Galuppi's scores were traveling without him is another testimony to his increasing international

[105]See Daniel Heartz, "Hasse, Galuppi, and Metastasio," in *Venezia e il melodramma nel settecento,* ed. Maria Teresa Murari, 2 vols. (Florence, 1978–81), 1: 309–39, for a facsimile of Vogler's reduction of the aria and further discussion.

celebrity. Repeated attempts to induce Galuppi to appear in person in Naples in order to preside over the production of one of his operas were foiled because the composer could not get the necessary permission from the procurators of San Marco. There must have been some reluctance on Galuppi's part about going to Naples, for he usually had little difficulty otherwise securing leaves when he wanted them. The revival of Leo's *Ciro riconosciuto* at the San Carlo in 1750 while negotiations were underway with Galuppi played some part in his refusal. Galuppi's decision propelled the authorities of the San Carlo into considering younger and relatively untested local composers. Thus did young Traetta get his first chance. Traetta was destined to replace Galuppi more than once. He collaborated with Goldoni on *Buovo d'Antona* (Venice, 1758). He succeeded Galuppi at Saint Petersburg in 1768; his final successes were comic operas at Venice a decade later.

Galuppi made a long journey in 1748–49 that his older biographers have mostly ignored. He was called to the court of Vienna. The moment was a crucial one for both court and composer. Maria Theresa, secure on her throne after the War of the Austrian Succession had threatened to depose her and dismember her states, made the Peace of Aix-la-Chapelle in May of 1748 a cause for special celebration. Reconstruction of an old ball house next to the palace was hastened, with the result that the Burgtheater, a permanent opera house disposed in the Italian style, was ready to celebrate the birthday of the empress on 14 May 1748. The event was also a political celebration of the peace. Metastasio's *Semiramide* was chosen, as it had been for the coronation four years earlier (in a setting probably by Hasse) and was set by Gluck. The second opera on the occasion was a comic one, *Il prottetore alla moda* (26 May 1748). Galuppi had a hand in this pasticcio, as did Wagenseil; it was based on an earlier work by Giuseppe Maria Buini (the interpenetration of Venetian and Viennese music at this time finds no better illustration). Galuppi himself was not in Vienna as early as May, but he was there for the composition and staging of two serious operas, *Demetrio* in the fall of 1748, and *Artaserse* for the following carnival, both on librettos by Metastasio. He received 200 ducats apiece for them, and in addition "a small sum with which to pay for his housing"; Gluck, by comparison, received a quite modest sum for his *Semiramide riconosciuta*.[106]

Gluck was thirty-five years of age, Galuppi forty-two. Something of the younger master's wildness (or vandalism, as it sounded to Metastasio) seems to have raised a spark in the established Venetian master. If Gluck reached a new

[106]412 gulden, 30 kreuzer (one ducat was worth four and a half gulden). These figures are given in Gustav Zechmeister, *Die Wiener Theater nächst der Burg und nächst dem Kärntnertor von 1747 bis 1776* (Theatergeschichte Oesterreichs, vol. 3, part 2) (Vienna, 1971), p. 206. On *Semiramide* see also Gerhard Croll, "Gluck's Debut am Burgtheater," *Oesterreichische Musik Zeitschrift* 31 (1976): 194–202.

peak in freewheeling dissonance treatment in his *Semiramide*—always with expressive intent, to be sure—so did Galuppi in his *Artaserse*. Mandane's first aria, "Conservati fedele," sung by Vittoria Tesi, already sets the tone with its extraordinary turn to the minor in the **A²** section and its many dissonances. The following aria sung by the hero Arbace (Monticelli), "Fra cento affanni e cento," is in E♭, a choice of key that promised exceptional expressiveness. The idea of multitude in the opening line of the text is projected by rapid sixteenth notes up and down in the violins, which produces quite a bustle in this *Allegro assai* in common time. Expressive dissonances abound in the voice part, especially ninths of various kinds. An initial G♭, which is neither approached nor quitted by the rules, recurs later as a melodic climax, an echappé resolution of a suspended minor ninth. The following aria of Artabano, "Se le Sponde del torbido lete," was sung by the tenor Domenico Panzacchi; in it Galuppi makes good use of a solo oboe against a somber string accompaniment that sometimes gets out of harmonic alignment, producing odd dissonances and lending the oboe great poignancy.

Opera lovers knew the libretto of *Artaserse* by heart. Imagine their surprise (and that of the imperial poet!) at Vienna when the four aria texts concluding Act I were conflated into a single dramatic ensemble, a quartet in which Arbace stands alone against his father (Artabano), ruler (Artaserse), and lover (Mandane). Little in opera previous to this time prepared the public for such a dramatic quartet. Of static or decorative ensembles there was no dearth, but pieces in which the stage action is written into the music, in which the music *becomes* the action, are exceedingly rare. Galuppi's earlier quartet in *Sirbace* showed the way and serves as a kind of preliminary study, but the *Artaserse* quartet, which is also in f, goes far beyond it in dramatizing the stage action. As Arbace is abandoned by one after the other, the emotional stakes continue to rise, along with the dissonance level, until the peak of suffering is reached, where one prolonged diminished chord resolves to another, and the hero is left alone to complete his chromatic wail.[107] The substantial **B** section introduces the relative major with a sweetness that is painful in its own way and serves as a perfect foil to enhance the return of the **A** section, da capo. After this **B** section, the repeated **A** fills the cup of bitterness to overflowing—the da capo form was never exploited with greater skill.

Vienna had called forth a breakthrough in dramatic music with Galuppi's *Artaserse* and the intensity it attained in a piece like the great quartet ending Act I. The reaction to it can readily be imagined, at least in one quarter. A scandalized Metastasio lashed out at Galuppi, just as he had at Gluck. In a letter of 27 December 1799 to Farinelli, he commented upon hearing that his "dear twin" was going to stage one of Galuppi's operas at Madrid:

---

[107]For musical excerpts and further discussion see Heartz, "Hasse, Galuppi, and Metastasio," in *Venezia e il melodramma*, ed. Muraro.

I wish you well with the music of Buranello, who from what I have heard will be a fine master for violins, for violoncellos, and for singers, but the worst possible collaborator for poets. When he writes he thinks as much about the words as you think of becoming a father; and if he did think about them more I doubt he would do better. He has a rich store of ideas but not all his own, nor always well put together. In sum, he is not my apostle.

Metastasio expected music to remain subservient to his words.

Galuppi had transgressed so far as to make people forget the words (not to mention combining the poet's verses at will). In so doing he joined a select company that included not only Gluck but Jommelli, who followed Galuppi to Vienna in the latter part of 1749. The deepening of all three masters' art in Vienna can be no coincidence. Rather than think primarily of an "operatic reform" beginning at Vienna in subsequent years, it makes more sense to lay the emphasis on the theatrical conditions that gave a composer full scope. An opera house run with both exacting disciplines (on the singers and players, as well as the audience) and great imagination made possible these breakthroughs around 1750. These conditions provided the impetus that led, step by step, to the advances of a decade later. It took even the wiser heads of Italy some time to realize that Vienna had preempted the best of Italian opera. As Pietro Verri wrote his brother incredulously in 1772 about the failure of Metastasio and his faithful apostle Hasse, compared with the Viennese achievements of Traetta and Gluck: "who would have believed that the fulcrum of the fine arts should become Vienna!"[108]

Local circumstances counted as much as the composer in moving serious opera along adventurous new paths. There is no better illustration of this than the fate of Galuppi's *Artaserse* when it traveled south of the Alps. A new opera house was erected at Padua and opened in June 1751. The civic authorities sought a new opera from Galuppi, but he could not oblige due to the pressure of other engagements. So they settled on his Viennese *Demetrio,* but then, hearing that it would be performed at the Ascension Fair in Venice, decided upon *Artaserse* instead. They sent to Vienna for the score—operas often remained the property of the theater that commissioned them, a practice documented with bitterness in the correspondence of both Jommelli and Mozart.

Padua had to make do without a new opera, but this did not prevent the city from lavishing money on the production, the singers, and the composer, who presided from the first harpsichord on opening night. He received 2,200 lire venete (equivalent to about 300 Austrian ducats), while Regina Mingotti and Gioacchino Conti ("Gizziello"), first singers, received over four times as much

[108]Paraphrased from the review by Kathleen and Sven Hansell of the modern edition of Hasse's *Ruggiero* (Milan, 1771), *JAMS* 29 (1976): 308–19.

apiece, and Anton Raaff, the tenor, received over twice as much. Galuppi did some recomposing for this new cast. He had to, because the great quartet was scrapped; in its place the principal singers reclaimed their arias. It was the same when the opera was revived at Venice in 1754 and 1761. What singers were constrained to do in the way of ensembles at the Habsburg court could be undone in the less regimented theaters of the peninsula. Yet the cast at Vienna had been just as stellar as that at Padua. Authoritarian Vienna allowed the upper hand to the composer, even at the expense of the vaunted singers' prerogatives.

A few years later, this time in Italy, Galuppi substituted an admirable trio, "In quel paterno amplesso," for the three arias ending the second act of Metastasio's *Adriano in Siria.* His first version of the libretto, for Turin in 1740, lacked the trio. The second version, including it, he wrote for Livorno in 1758, and there were further productions in Naples (1759), Venice (1760), Palermo (1761), and Udine (1763). Goldoni witnessed the opera in the San Salvatore theater, Venice, for which he was working then as a playwright. He included a description of it in a long wedding poem in Venetian dialect that dates from the same spring season of 1760.

> We entered the theater and our ears soon confirmed the wisdom of the choice. In fact when Buranello writes one can only bow and take off one's hat. Even the Sinfonia made our hearts beat faster. Never in my life have I enjoyed music so full of grace and spirit. . . . Open-mouthed until the end, I remained delighted and excited. And my guests, enlightened people, applauded and were quite pleased. . . . Listen to the trio. Oh what a trio! It is a sublime piece and reason enough by itself, I promise you, for attending the opera. Buranello, when flying high, is a very devil. This time he put all his skills into the work. As the trio finished the dancing began. Now, I thought, we can chat a bit. . . . As the second ballet ended the singers returned to the stage, and my box became quite still again as everyone listened, absorbed.[109]

This can serve as a corrective to Burney and others who maintained that the Italians were always chatting during the singing but strangely quiet during the dancing.

The trio is indeed an impressive act ending, an ensemble of grief and despair as all three principals face prison at the emperor's command. It begins with the orchestra softly playing a simple I - IV$^6_4$ - I - ii - V^7 progression, the chords moving slowly in a common-time *Andante*. Against the throbbing tonic pedal tones of the bass on the beat the violins have offbeat replies, while the violas and oboes, later the horns as well, sustain. The voices enter singly against this music upon its

---

[109]Carlo Goldoni, *Tutte le opere,* ed. Giuseppe Ortolani, 14 vols. (Milan, 1935–56), 8: 634–47, cited after Reinhard Wiesend, *Studien zur Opera Seria von Baldassare Galuppi,* 2 vols. (Tutzing, 1984) 1: 320–23. Wiesend's line-by-line translation into German of Goldoni's dialect poem was helpful, but I have tried to remain even closer to the original.

repetitions, first Osroa, then Farnaspe, fiancé of Osroa's daughter Emirena; during her entry the piece modulates to the dominant. All three sing together "Sento mancarmi il cor" (My heart begins to fail me) as the harmony returns to tonic F (Example 3.15). Perhaps Goldoni's ears thrilled to the suave sounds of V^7/IV going to IV with chromatic appoggiatura of the raised fifth in mm. 17–18 or to the accented, full vii^7 chord in m. 24, both progressions being repeated to enhance the effect. Breaking the word "mancarmi" with rests adds to the sobbing quality. After this cadence the *Andante* gives way to an extended *Allegro,* an agitated and often

EXAMPLE 3.15. *Galuppi,* Adriano in Siria, *Act II, Trio*

agonized litany of suffering humanity that ends the trio, there being no da capo return. Galuppi's mastery of dissonant ninths propels the piece forward as happened a decade earlier in his great quartet added to end the first act of *Artaserse*.

Goldoni concluded his remarks about Galupi's *Adriano* by describing its reception and offering a general assessment of the composer.

When the opera was over what a racket, what applause burst out for Buranello! Good music is such a joy and delight there exists no more beautiful diversion. But not all flowers combine to make a bouquet, for which an inspired master with brains is nec-

essary, one who goes deep, has taste, harmony, and knows how to tailor his music to the singers.[110]

Goldoni's metaphor of the bouquet is apt for opera seria. Each piece is like a flower, independent and often replaceable. The overall effect when all are gathered together requires a master's touch. Subduing Venetian maskers at an opera as Galuppi did was no easy task (Figure 3.11).

Galuppi continued to be in demand for serious operas at various courts and cities around Europe during the 1750s and 1760s. In his *Idomeneo* for the Roman carnival of 1756 he sought more continuity than was the rule with the genre, particularly in the last act, which includes an impressive *Marcia lugubre* in E♭. How receptive he was to the new reform current, given circumstances that were encouraging, is evident from his choice of *Ifigenia in Tauride* at Saint Petersburg in 1768, the very libretto that Marco Coltellini prepared for Traetta at Vienna in 1763. Galuppi's long experience with choral church music came to the fore at this time,

FIGURE 3.11. Maskers at the opera. From Giorgio Fossati, *Viaggi di Enrico Wanton*, 1749.

[110]The final lines of the original are: "Ma no bisogna far d'ogni erba un fasso, / Un Maestro ghe vol che abbia cervello. / Ghe vol el fondo, el gusto, e l'armonia, / E saver ben vestir la Compagnia."

when he was also writing unaccompanied choruses on Russian texts for the Orthodox liturgy. It was called upon again in connection with the long and moving choruses in *Ifigenia*.

After returning from Russia, Galuppi gradually withdrew from the field of opera. His last serious opera was *Motezuma* for the San Benedetto theater in 1772. The libretto was by Vittorio Amadeo Cigna-Santi, and, given Galuppi's venerable age and the esteem he enjoyed at Venice, its choice was probably his, and not one imposed on him by the impresario. Compared with Hasse in his later years, Galuppi was indeed no apostle of Metastasio. He had always collaborated with a great variety of librettists. Over a period of fifty years he composed some seventy serious operas.

Galuppi and Gluck were two of the best-remunerated composers of the century. Even at the start of his tenure at the Mendicanti, Galuppi received 350 ducats annually. His salary at San Marco was raised by the senate in 1780 from 400 to 600 ducats per annum, as a reward for excellent services. Along with this position went a house near the basilica, so he had no rent to pay. Every opera commission, and there were over a hundred, brought its considerable fee. In his last will Galuppi was able to leave his wife a considerable sum. From the son of a lowly barber, he had risen to become one of the wealthiest professional musicians anywhere. Musical genius did not always go unrewarded or poorly rewarded in those days, as we are likely to imagine from the desperate financial conditions in which Vivaldi and Mozart ended their lives. Galuppi's discipline with his musicians was strict, as several accounts testify, but this did not prevent the master from winning an esteem that bordered on devotion. His funeral took place in the large church of Santo Stefano in January 1785 at the expense of all the *professori di musica* of Venice and with the participation of the chief singers from the San Benedetto theater, the main opera house since the 1750s. The Latin ode commissioned by the musicians referred to the composer as "docte Galuppe." Bertoni succeeded as maestro at San Marco, but an era in Venetian music clearly passed with the demise of Galuppi.

GOLDONIAN OPERA BUFFA

Comic opera in northern Italy during the first half of the eighteenth century was sporadic and fell short of attaining the level of sustained interest with which poets and composers endowed the *commedia per musica* of Naples and Rome. Not until Goldoni consolidated the examples streaming from south to north with various local strains towards the middle of the century was there a continuous tradition reestablished in Venice, an epochal new genre that became known as opera buffa. Goldoni himself allowed the term *musica buffa* to comic intermezzos, typically in two acts for two or three singers. He reserved the term *opera buffa* for full-length comedies, usually in three acts and for several singers.[111] He also argued that adding a few seria elements gave opera buffa the variety of effects it needed. His usual name for this subtype of libretto was *drama giocoso*.

An earlier tradition of musical farce in Venice and the cities of the Po valley existed, best represented by the Bolognese librettist and composer Buini, who flourished mainly in the 1720s and also functioned as an impresario. His librettos often dealt with life in the theater, as in his successful "divertimento comico per musica" *Chi non fa non falla* (Bologna, 1729; Venice, 1732), the music of which has yet to be found. Another strain was represented by parodies of serious operas, such as Giuseppe Imer's *Il Trojano schernito* (Venice, San Samuele, 1743), a hilarious burlesque taking off Metastasio's sublime *Didone abbandonata,* with music by four different composers. Imer was the *capo comico* (director and lead actor) of a troupe of comedians for whom Goldoni wrote plays. This troupe staged Goldoni's first play, *Belisario,* in the fall of 1734 at the San Samuele, the success of which, claimed the author, marked the beginning of his reform of Italian theater.

Goldoni began his literary career scribbling intermezzo texts to go between the acts of Metastasian operas at the small town of Feltre in 1729–30. Throughout the 1730s he continued doing this hackwork. From these first dramatic strivings it is possible to catch a glimpse of the action finale in the making. It grew out of the traditional closing duet or trio. But restriction of the intermezzo to so few characters imposed a natural limit as to the amount of dramatic or musical composition that could be introduced. During the 1740s, the Neapolitan comic operas began to make their way north.[112] Goldoni, among other poets, was put to work revising and adapting the works to local tastes. This meant eliminating most of the dialect, or substituting for it, and also shortening the models. Musical revision was necessary as well, to a certain extent, and it fell largely to Galuppi.

One of the first Neapolitan comedies to reach Venice was Antonio Palomba's *Orazio,* another opera about opera. Pietro Auletta's original music was gradually diluted by that of several other composers, including Pergolesi. It was staged at Venice in early 1743. More successful still was the three-act comic opera *La finta cameriera* by Latilla, put on at Venice during the Ascension fair of 1743. Federico, author of *La serva padrona* and *Amor vuol sofferenza,* had written the libretto, which began life as *Gismondo* at Naples in 1737 and was revised the following year by Barlocci for Rome, where the title became *La finta cameriera.* The work also went under the title *Don Colascione,* after the main comic character (as at London in 1749). It was one of the works that was performed, albeit transmuted into a

[111]Daniel Heartz, "Goldoni, Opera Buffa, and Mozart's Advent in Vienna," in *Opera Buffa in Mozart's Vienna,* ed. Mary Hunter and James Webster (Cambridge, 1997), pp. 25–49.
[112]Barbara Dobbs Mackenzie, "The Creation of a Genre: Comic Opera's Dissemination in Italy in the 1740s" (Ph.D. diss., University of Michigan, 1993).

two-act intermezzo, during the memorable Paris season of 1752 that ignited the Querelle des Bouffons. From Paris it reached Germany. Latilla's original music underwent many changes in each of these metamorphoses, as local hands were employed to enhance it to suit particular conditions.

Exactly what was sung in *La finta cameriera* at Venice in 1743 cannot be known. The stir it created can be gathered, nevertheless, from one of the diarists of the time, Giovanni Zanetti, who recorded on 23 May 1743 that the Ascension-tide operas were Metastasio's *Ezio* set by Lampugnani for the San Samuele and "un' operetta bernesca" at the Sant'Angelo, *La finta cameriera*.[113] Of the first opera he found nothing to praise but the singing of Carestini. Speaking of the second he wrote: "the work was composed at Rome [an understandable mistake] and is passably beautiful [è bella mediocremente]; the actors are almost all from Bologna, and young, none of them having passed twenty-three." On the next day, May 24, he noted that the "opera ridicola" was beginning to please excessively, and great applause greeted certain duets set to music very skillfully. Five days later "l'opera burlesca" was still pleasing audiences, and on the last day of the month he wrote that "the opera bernesca was succeeding so well that the impresario, Angelo Mingotti, will earn 300 zecchini or more" (one sequin [zecchino] was worth slightly more than a ducat) and that "the musician who plays the role of Don Colascione [Francesco Baglioni] sends the public into gales of laughter."

Much is to be learned from Zanetti's remarks on how the two operas were received. The public flocked to Lampugnani's serious opera, which also earned well, in order to hear the solos of Carestini, one of the greatest castrati of the age. The young singers in the comic work pleased as much by their acting as their singing; certain ensembles are singled out. Zanetti calls Latilla's work alternatively an operetta, opera bernesca, opera ridicola, and opera burlesca, but not an opera buffa. This designation had not yet been commonly applied to a comic work of full length but was often used to designate comic roles, that is, "parti buffe." It was after the opera quarrels at Paris that "buffo" became such a popular term, and French critics seem to have been responsible also for coining the expression "opera seria," in opposition to "opera buffa."

Galuppi was returning from London in the spring of 1743, and whether he reached Venice in time to hear *La finta cameriera* or not, he must have heard talk of it. He had a hand in revising Latilla's three-act *Madama Ciana* for the San Cassian theater the following year, and Goldoni may have been involved as well. The libretto, originally written by Barlocci, is constructed around the exit aria, just as in Metastasio. There are twenty-three arias, a few less than might be expected in

---

[113]For the original document, see Daniel Heartz, "Vis Comica: Goldoni, Galuppi, and *L'Arcadia in Brenta* (Venice, 1749)," in *Venezia e il melodramma nel settecento*, ed. Maria Teresa Muraro, 2 vols. (Florence, 1978–81), 2: 33–69.

a serious opera of this time. For Venice, six substitute texts were required, and several scenes were deleted in their entirety—another case in which Neapolitan prolixity gave way to Venetian concision. The ensembles at the ends of the first two acts are no more developed than those in the contemporary intermezzo and employ only three singers at a time. Some clumsiness emerges in getting characters on and off the stage. Only stock scenery is required. The story turns on the pretensions of the minor nobility, a contemporary subject that is a potentially rich mine of parody, but treated here with a heavy hand. On the basis of books like this, it would have taken a seer's vision to predict a brilliant future for the genre.

Latilla apparently did not come to Venice himself until 1753, when he became *maestro di coro* at the Pietà. In 1762, when Galuppi was elevated from second to first master at San Marco, Latilla took his place. Relations between the two composers were cordial, as emerges from Burney's account of his visit in 1770. Galuppi's recommendation of Latilla would have been crucial in securing the Neapolitan composer his Venetian posts, just as his recommendation must have been necessary to make Traetta his successor at Saint Petersburg. Back in 1744, when Galuppi was getting into comic opera by working over Latilla's score, he could have had no inkling that the two would collaborate one day in directing music at the basilica.

Besides Latilla's comic operas, there were other Neapolitan works that were adapted for Venice at this time. Rinaldo da Capua's *La libertà nociva* (Venice, 1744) and his *L'ambizione delusa* (Venice, 1745) are thought to have passed through Galuppi's hands. In 1745 Galuppi assayed a comic opera of his own, *La forza d'amore,* on a libretto by an obscure local priest, for the carnival at the San Cassian. As with so much of the comic opera of this decade, the music is lost. The libretto survives. It shows no progress beyond *Madama Ciana* and, if anything, still less skill. Notably lacking is any hint of the action finale. Galuppi did not try an original comic work again for four years. Meanwhile, works as obscure as Antonio Palella's *Origille* and Natale Resta's *I tre cicisbei* were brought to the Venetian stage. Even Buini's *Chi non fà non falla* was revived, with Galuppi's help, and put on as *Il protettore alla moda* in 1747. With the return of Goldoni to Venice in 1748, after a lengthy sojourn practicing law in Tuscany, one of the ingredients to revivify comic opera was present. This same year saw the very successful staging at Venice of *Bertoldo, Bertoldino, e Cacasenno* by Vincenzo Ciampi. Revision of the work brought Galuppi and Goldoni together again, and from this encounter sprang the collaboration that has been compared to that between Gilbert and Sullivan.

L'Arcadia in Brenta for the Ascension fair of 1749 was the first collaboration between Galuppi and Goldoni on an original comic opera. Goldoni called his libretto a "dramma comico." For a setting he chose a country house along the Brenta river near Padua, a region to which many Venetians of means repaired during the summer. The plot, what little there is, turns upon the prodigality of Fabrizio, who has rented a country house and thrown it open to all comers, without having enough money to entertain them. He ruins himself in the attempt, just as Goldoni's own grandfather is reported to have done at the beginning of the dramatist's memoirs.

After a couple of arias inside Fabrizio's villa, the scene changes to a flower garden on the riverbank, as two pairs of guests join Fabrizio in an ensemble praising the lovely scene enhanced by songbirds and murmuring waters. Using text and music to comment on the stage scenery like this is one of Goldoni's favorite devices and represents an advance in Italian operatic dramaturgy (it is very frequent in French opera). Galuppi ably seconds his poet. He chooses a new and unexpected key, G following directly after F, and sounds a rustic melody in 6/8 with drones, first in the orchestra of strings and two horns, and then sung. More guests arrive: Lindora, a lady "of incredibly tiresome delicatesse" as Goldoni says in the preface to his libretto, and a bombastic count. These two characters, among Goldoni's most memorable, are welcomed simply and without affectation by their host. Every character gets an aria. Act I ends with an extensive sneezing trio in C, Fabrizio having given tobacco to the count and Lindora.

Act II of *Arcadia in Brenta* revolves around debates and country pastimes (hence the Arcadian reference), not excluding the usual stuff of aria texts: ruses, quarrels, protestations of love, reconciliations. For a climax, Goldoni has the guests plan and execute a masquerade as an after-dinner entertainment. Stock elements of the commedia dell'arte supply both plot and characters. Pantalon, a miserly old Venetian merchant as usual, has a daughter Diana, who is wooed by the noble Cintio. Diana's maidservant Columbine falls without ado for Pulcinella, the servant of Cintio. How to stage an operatic masquerade becomes the subject of an aria just prior to the masquerade itself, which opens with a dialogue in recitative between the pairs of lovers. Columbine then sings a hilarious aria about how lovemaking differs depending on social class, in which she mimics the sounds of her superiors ("Peno, moro, smanio, oh Dio!"). After some additional dialogue, the concerted finale begins.[114] The strains of a *Menuetto galante* in 3/8 sound forth very sweetly from the orchestra of strings and two horns. To these the lovers dance while singing endearments to each other, as the vocal texture expands gradually from one to four parts. Just as the cadence on the dominant is to arrive, and the lovers are about to embrace, the strings switch to a vigorous *martellato* figure in 4/4. Pantalon simultaneously arrives on the scene with a shout, literally breaking up the *cadence galante* of the lovers.

Outraged, Pantalon demands, "What are you doing? Embracing!" The strings

---

[114]It is transcribed in full in ibid.

take to trembling in sixteenth notes, conveying the fear that the old man strikes. There follow some maneuvers back and forth between Pantalon and the lovers, the music pushing first in one tonal direction then another, and going as far afield as E♭. No amount of pleading avails. Pantalon remains adamant and insists on cadencing on g, which threatens to end the scene on a sad note. Once more the lovers implore him, resorting to a long-held diminished chord *à 4,* a gesture which they then intensify by repeating it one tone higher. (Astonishment that Galuppi could have conceived such a passage in 1749 dwindles only upon recalling his use of diminished sevenths in the great quartet of *Artaserse,* written earlier the same year.) Such eloquent musical pleading finally disarms Pantalon, who yields with the charming remark, "After all, I'm Venetian," which he makes while resolving all the tension by returning the music to its original tonality, F. Dramatic resolution becomes inseparable from tonal resolution, or, to put it another way, the solution of the conflict becomes dramatically effective because it is projected by tonal means. General rejoicing and the celebration of F, over and over, are necessary to close the finale, in which all sing the praises of Pantalon, including the old man himself. Goldoni gave his composer the material with which to write a true action ensemble. Galuppi did not fail to take full advantage of it. Between the two of them, they had created the buffo finale.

Act III could not help but be an anticlimax after the theatrical and musical brilliance of the second-act finale. Even so, Goldoni managed to eke out arias for everyone. The opera ends with a little *coro* in D, the key of the opening sinfonia, as the merry company persuades Fabrizio to join them at a nearby villa that is better provided to entertain them. What this ending lacks in dramatic brio is supplied by bringing the pleasure boat, or *Burchiello,* as it was called, back onto the stage so that all the company could embark and make their exit—a touch of the famed Goldoni realism. The scene is drawn from contemporary life, using much local color, and that is one of its great attractions.

It took Galuppi and Goldoni several more operas to solve the third-act problem, which they did by saving at least a little of the action for the end and even allowing the last act to conclude with a short action finale, as happens, for instance, in *Il filosofo di campagna* (1754), the most successful of all their joint works. In the operas following *Arcadia in Brenta* Goldoni was wonderfully fertile in creating subjects from the world around him. *Il mondo della luna* (1750) makes fun of the craze for amateur astronomy. *Arcifanfano* (fall of 1749) assembles various social misfits and confines them on an island (hence the later French parody, *L'isle des foux*). *Le pescatrice* (1756) takes place in a fishing village. No fewer than fourteen comic operas emerged from the collaboration between 1749 and 1756. Many of them became immediately popular and reached production in several places, not only in Italy, but elsewhere.

Other composers eagerly sought new comic operas from Goldoni, or reset the ones originally destined for Galuppi. After 1756 there were only a few scattered libretti by Goldoni that were especially intended for Galuppi, the last coming in 1766. The Neapolitan Domenico Fischietti took Galuppi's place for a few years as Goldoni's main partner in Venice and they produced notably *Lo speziale* (1755), *La ritornata di Londra* (1756), *Il mercato di Malmantile* (1757), and *Il signor dottore* (1758). Fischietti followed Galuppi in a musical sense as well, adapting many of his traits and especially the finale technique. For the carnival of 1758–59 Traetta set Goldoni's fine libretto *Buovo d'Antona* based on a popular medieval romance.[115]

Not only other composers but other places and other ideals began to put a distance between Venice's leading musician and leading dramatist. Goldoni was hired by the court of Parma in 1756. At this Gallic-oriented center he first observed a troupe of French comedians and became very impressed with them, especially their playing of Molière. Here he became even more determined to achieve a similarly high literary quality in Italian spoken comedy, to become, in other words, Italy's Molière. He was so intent upon this goal in his memoirs as to belittle his own operatic activity, while exalting only his "legitimate" theater (an odd prejudice lies hidden in this expression). Goldoni's duties at Parma, paradoxically, were as a librettist, and he wrote for this court *La buona figliuola,* first set by Egidio Duni. Parma was a stepping-stone to the more lucrative possibilities of Paris, for Duni and Goldoni alike. After Goldoni's definitive removal to France in 1762 there were few librettos from his pen.

Among Goldoni's greatest virtues as a librettist are his sharp eye for the details of ordinary life, his gentle satire of contemporary foibles (such as astromania!) and, above all, his deft and light touch with dialogue. Complicated intrigues he avoided in favor of situation comedy. In spite of his disclaimers, he excelled as a librettist because he recognized and submitted to the requirements of music. Constructing the ensemble finale with elaborate stage action out of the earlier act-ending duets and trios of the intermezzo is but the most obvious example of this. Using text and music to establish mood, as upon a scene change, is another. Getting away from stock situations and language in aria texts, no easy task, provides a third. Galuppi was most likely to depart from the conventional form of the aria da capo when provided with a text that, either by shape or subject, suggested something new and different. His *Mondo della luna* opens with three cavatinas, little songs of folklike quality that replace the formal aria and are perfectly in place because Goldoni introduces the fiction of having the characters make music, one of his favorite devices. In a Venice saturated with music making on the canals, it

---

[115]The opera was chosen by the Fenice theater to commemorate the bicentenary of Goldoni's death in 1993 and given a splendid production under the musical direction of Alan Curtis.

was only natural (Figure 3.12). Galuppi gradually came to prefer the binary aria to the da capo in his comic operas, although not in his serious ones. The sum of these accomplishments was great and consequential for all comic opera.

The comic finale by itself represented a breakthrough in dramatic music that proved epochal. It added an element of continuity and fluidity in music that heretofore had been hardly possible, outside of the obbligato recitative. Defined as we have defined it—an ensemble of some length, in several sections, where different movements and different keys correspond to the ongoing stage action— the comic finale did not exist before Goldoni and Galuppi created it. The trio in Nicola Logroscino's *Il governatore* (Naples, 1747), which used to be lauded as an early example of the finale, has length but does not use keys in a drama-related way; it is not an action ensemble so much as an ensemble of perplexity, in which one situation prevails throughout—the text is repeated entire for the second half of the binary structure. Jommelli in his early comic works does not advance beyond Leo with respect to ensembles. Piccinni's supposed invention of the comic finale, once championed, has long since been disproved on chronological grounds.

FIGURE 3.12. Giovanni Maria de Pian. Serenade on a canal. From Carlo Goldoni, *Il bugiardo.*

A more credible rival to Galuppi who arrived at a similar finale technique around the same time was Rinaldo da Capua. In his *Gli impostori* for Modena in 1751, the first act ends with a quartet of 183 measures in two tempos, and the second with a sextet that has three contrasting sections corresponding to the stage action.[116] Most of the credit must still go to the (unknown) poet rather than to the composer. People at the time perceived what Goldoni offered composers in his finales as novel and exciting. Gasparo Gozzi, who was no friend of Goldoni's, reviewed *L'amore artigiano* (Venice, 1760, music by Latilla) and remarked, "It is by Doctor Goldoni, which is no matter for surprise, because it is full of those lively and fiery actions that the stage demands; and especially at the ends of the first and second acts. He can call himself the inventor of closing the act with this novel, speedy, and varied action."[117]

Abbé Vogler perceived the question of priority somewhat differently. Writing from a nonliterary perspective in the first volume of his *Betrachtungen der Mannheimer Tonschule* (1778), he concluded that "Galuppi was the author and inventor of comic opera and deserves an eternal monument from all comic theaters. Biting [i.e., sarcastic] traits, laughable personages, heated contrasts, variety in ensemble finales, with which the first part or act usually ends—in short, all those things called operetta or intermezzo among us—must look to Galuppi as their musical father." This testimony comes from a time when Galuppi's operas were still very much alive in people's ears and being performed in Germany, alongside those by younger Neapolitans like Piccinni, Anfossi, Guglielmi, and Paisiello. Vogler was quite aware of the music of the latter, and he knew it belonged to masters a good generation younger than Galuppi. When Gerber came to write his *Lexicon* (published in 1790–92) the Neapolitans had displaced Galuppi from the stage. With insufficient experience of Galuppi's music, Gerber claimed the invention of the comic finale for Piccinni, a historical impossibility. Ginguené, Piccinni's biographer, made the same mistake.

What Goldini and Galuppi owed the Neapolitan *commedia musicale* in creating Venetian opera buffa was great enough without including the buffo finale as well. The debt was paid back with ample interest by what the younger Neapolitans learned from the brilliant series of Venetian comedies that started with *Arcadia in Brenta*. The same story of borrowing and repayment applies to the relations between opera buffa and French comic opera. During the 1750s the creators of opéra-comique, chiefly Duni, François-André Philidor, and Pierre-Alexandre Monsigny, owed many debts to Italian models. By the 1760s the new genre at Paris had established itself so strongly that both texts and music began to provide models to the rest of Europe, even to Italy. Goldoni parodied the text of *Le roi et*

[116]Richard Bostian, "The Works of Rinaldo da Capua" (Ph.D. diss., University of North Carolina, 1961).
[117]Original text in Heartz, "Vis Comica."

le fermier (Sedaine–Monsigny, Paris, 1761) and turned it into *Il re alla caccia* for Galuppi (1763). A comparison of the two scores shows more clearly than anything else that by then the hour had struck for Galuppi as the leading composer of comic opera.

"BRAVE GALUPPI"

The great quartet in *Artaserse* and the comic finale of *Arcadia in Brenta,* both dating from 1749, demonstrate that Galuppi had mastered the ability to build dramatic intensification and to control its release as a part of the stage drama. Or to put it in slightly more abstract terms, he was able to make music the chief agent of the drama. To do this required perfect timing. Too little or too much of a musical idea, a tonal arrival too soon or too late, could weaken both music and drama. What raises Galuppi's art above that of so many of his contemporaries, in the instrumental as well as in the vocal sphere, was his unerring sense of proportion. He may not have contributed as much to the symphony as Sammartini—he did so through his operatic overtures and took little interest in the concert symphony per se. Yet the verve and direct appeal of his overtures assured them wide diffusion as concert symphonies. Goldoni singled out the overture in *Adriano in Siria* for praise as well as the trio. Outside the realm of the symphony and overture, a comparison between the two masters can be made on the basis of the works they contributed to the emerging medium of the string quartet.

Among Vivaldi's legacy of hundreds of concertos were a group of chamber pieces for various solo instruments that fell somewhere between the *sonata da camera* and the orchestral concerto. With their concertante dialogue and dramatic yet intimate tone, sometimes approaching that of conversation, these pieces are thought to have been the main forebears of the *concertini a quattro* or *concerto a quattro* cultivated by northern Italian composers around 1750. Sammartini wrote a set of concertini that is dated between 1750 and 1756.[118] They are filled with busywork for the strings but show little imagination either as to melodic ideas or their working out. A case could be made that Sammartini, like Vivaldi, did not always recognize the danger of "too much" with regard to small-scale literal repetitions. He was experimenting with an unfamiliar genre, to be sure, and deserves credit as a pioneer of the string quartet.

Galuppi's contributions are also experimental, and in some ways more retrospective, inasmuch as they sought to integrate fugal writing of the church sonata kind with more modern means in at least one movement of each of the seven three-movement works. The slow movement of the second *concerto a quattro* corresponds to the slow movement of the composer's overture to *Demetrio* (Vienna,

---

[118]Several examples from them are quoted in Ludwig Finscher, *Studien zur Geschichte des Streichquartetts,* vol. 1 (Kassel, 1974), pp. 327–41.

1748), which gives a hint as to the time, and perhaps the place, of composition. The set gets more interesting as it goes along, as if the composer were working out some task he set himself and was gradually finding the solution.[119] With the sixth quartet in B♭, each movement is consistently fine, and they all add up to a convincing cyclic whole. The opening *Grave sostenuto* is the most extensive and broadly arched anywhere in the set and does not fail to introduce such new-found melodic treasures as the chromatically raised fifth that Burney singled out as novel in Galuppi's arias of the early 1740s, as well as many minor shadings, and a final deceptive cadence in which an augmented sixth chord is substituted prior to the ultimate resolution. The mood of elegiac sadness sustained throughout this slow movement, as well as the delicate filigree work of the uppermost voices, bears comparison with the finest among Galuppi's harpsichord sonatas. The second movement is vigorous and fugal, and begins with the same falling fifth that inaugurated the first movement, but as a leap, not filled in as in the *Grave sostenuto.* From the intervals of the fugue subject, rearranged, Galuppi then derived the theme of the last movement, a jolly *Allegro* that truly caps the work (Example 3.16). The paired duets at the beginning of this finale have a teasing "we can do anything you can do" air about them. Strict periodicity prevails, with the four-measure unit as module (Sammartini typically preferred smaller and less regular modules in his quartets). As light in texture and playful as the beginning is, tension begins to accumulate with the *crescendo* passage, as the first violin works its way eventually up to a minor ninth, one of the composer's favorite melodic goals, and the viola keeps adding the leaping octave motif to the cello's pedal. The minor chords leading to the half-cadence seem to raise a question to be resolved. Will this piece turn in a grave or comic direction? The answer is blithely tossed off, using the leaping motif in a new way, with a hint of the mischievous.

Tonal arrival does not occur until the last of the four measures that this answer takes. The wit here is like that of an epigram. If, with a good joke, the timing of the punch line is all, Galuppi's in this case could not be better. Before us in this movement stands the master of comic opera. And therein lies the essential difference between Galuppi and Sammartini. The rapid passage in parallel thirds between the two violins, restating the cadence, belongs to Galuppi's buffo language and is not unlike some of the chattering that goes on in his comic finales. Both the closing idea and ultimate *tutti unisoni* are characteristically buffo in style. The degree to which the four parts carry on a conversation—not a learned one, but an amusing and chatty one, like some masked figures in a Venetian salon painted by Longhi—brings this music close to what Haydn would eventually

[119]Excerpts in Finscher, *Studien zur Geschichte des Streichquartetts*, pp. 318–26. The whole of Concerto a quattro No. 6 in B♭ is edited by Franco Piva (Florence, 1977).

EXAMPLE 3.16. *Galuppi, Concerto a quattro in B♭, III*

achieve in his string quartets. The voices in Sammartini's concertini, on the other hand, seem by comparison to come from an assembly in which Beccaria, Parini, and the Verri brothers or their like are weighing serious moral issues such as capital punishment.

The special gifts that Galuppi brought to instrumental music are nowhere more evident than in the voluminous repertory of his harpsichord sonatas, of which there are nearly a hundred. He surpassed all the *cembalisti* of his generation in variety and quality when writing for his own instrument. Where they tended to be discursive and formula bound, he is terse and cogent, saying neither too much nor too little with the material he proposes. Moreover, with him, one thought leads naturally to another, often imperceptibly, which may be what he had in mind by the "buona modulazione" part of his laconic definition of good music. The ultimate gift, the Mozartian thread of musical logic that defies explanation—*il filo*—he possessed in a degree superior to any of his Italian contemporaries. He did not seek to publish his keyboard works. The great bulk of them remained in manuscript. Unlike Rutini and most other composers, he did not have to depend upon dedications to eke out an existence. The chapelmaster of San Marco enjoyed a prestige and security that put him beyond groveling before wealthy patrons. His sonatas appeared infrequently in print, but they must have circulated widely even so. No less an authority than Emanuel Bach honored Galuppi for his keyboard playing and welcomed him into his home in Berlin when the Venetian master was on his way to Russia in 1765.

Galuppi's keyboard sonatas are usually in two or three movements, with a slight numerical edge going to the former. Like his Italian contemporaries he often ended the cycle with a *menuetto galante* in 3/8, using the slightest of textures. Yet there are some extraordinary pieces in the two collections published by Walsh at London in 1756 and 1759 as Opp. 1 and 2, pieces in which the complexion of the galant keyboard sonata is scarcely recognizable. The minor movements, in particular, contained in the Sonatas in e and d are lengthy studies exploring motivic development with such rhapsodic effect it is no wonder that they were called toccatas in some manuscripts.

A more typical sonata is the one in B$^\flat$ chosen for discussion here. It cannot be dated, in which respect it is like most of the composer's keyboard works. Its three movements, all in the same key, are marked *Allegro - Andante - Allegro*. The first is in cut time and begins with a rising arpeggio in the right hand and upbeat figure in eighths that starts in motion what will not finish until the piece is over. The left hand moves in longer note values, except when the right hand pauses, at which points the left takes up the eighth notes. These exchanges are not haphazard. They take place at important formal junctures such as the arrival of the dominant and with it simultaneously a broader and more lyric second theme. Thus textural change becomes a reinforcement of the melodic-harmonic structure, which it helps articulate. The proportions of the piece as a whole are typical of Galuppi's binary movements. The two halves are equivalent in length because economies are made in the reprise by shortening the first theme area. The second theme areas remain equal, as may be seen from the diagram in Table 3.4:

TABLE 3.4. Galuppi: Opening movement, Allegro, Sonata in B$^\flat$

			14			14	
Measure:	1	22	36	49	59	73
Theme:	‖: 1st theme	2nd theme	:‖: 1st	1st	2nd	:‖
Keys:	I	∿∿ V		V ∿∿ I	I	
				Reprise		

The slightly dry and exercise-like character of the opening *Allegro* provides a perfect foil for the heart of the sonata, an *Andante* that is anything but mechanical. It is the type of movement that gave rise to the phrase "singer-cembalist." For the right hand must sing its delicately ornamented melody with all the bel canto it can muster. The left merely accompanies in eighth notes throughout, providing a slow version of the two-note pattern that Burney called attention to as a novelty in Galuppi's arias of the 1740s (and labeled "shorthand") (Example 3.17). Confining himself drastically as to accompanimental figuration, Galuppi is all the more careful about doubling and spacing. Tonic B$^\flat$ in the bass becomes a dissonant suspension in the second half of m. 1, resolved at the beginning of m. 2, but taking longer to resolve at the beginning of the second four-measure phrase, a repetition of the first at the outset until it begins, ever so subtly, to move towards the dominant.

EXAMPLE 3.17. *Galuppi, Harpsichord Sonata in B♭, II*

Over the discreet harmonic underpinnings of the left hand's invariable eighth notes, the right hand is free to indulge in little rhythmic eddies, lingering here (the chromatically raised fifth as expressive appoggiatura in m. 3) and hurrying on there. This textural relationship of melody and accompaniment is particularly well suited to the Italian harpsichord, which typically had but one manual and two sets of eight-foot strings, meaning that there was no possibility of playing the accompaniment other than with the same registration as the melody. Galuppi has scaled the left-hand figuration down to good effect. A busier accompanimental figure (a rapid Alberti bass, for instance) would call overmuch attention to itself, to the detriment of what it is tempting to call the soprano soloist. The dominant of the dominant gives way to the dominant in m. 8. In the following measure, an ascent up the triad with melodic turns (from m. 3 and used again in m. 7) receives a novel answer, an even descent of parallel thirds drifting down through an octave, marked staccato. The new idea is not so idiomatic to the keyboard as the florid solos and arpeggiated figures, but it is clearly effective and could not be more Galuppian, nor more operatic in nature—as if a second soprano joined the first for an instant in an ensemble finale.

Three times the parallel thirds come floating down, starting a tone higher each time, as the harmony wavers back and forth over the pedal C. With the firm arrival of the new key in measure 12 the melody, once again solo, regains its activity, pushing rapidly up to the high C, in linear continuation of the previous rise, then down, with time for a lingering chromatic appoggiatura (like that in m. 3) to emphasize the subdominant of the new key, then an upward flourish pushing to the cadential area. The slowing to triplet motion over the tonic six-four chord prior to the cadence lends another exquisite touch. It is inevitably right and perfect, partly because Galuppi saved it for this climactic moment and did not squander it earlier, as so many lesser composers would have done. That it became a cliché to use triplet motion prior to the cadence in galant music all the way to Mozart does not detract from this instance. The trill over the dominant is likewise a fresh resource. A little closing figure repeats the cadence more rapidly and serves to wind the melody and bass down to a full stop.

The second half of the binary form makes the reverse modulation smoothly, with a maximum of concentration upon the main theme. It first appears, stretched out and over a minor harmony, with an effect that is quite development-like, as well as very poetic. The two-measure idea is repeated, starting a tone lower, but the progression veers off, just as a literal sequence seemed almost certain (and would have been certain in almost any other composer), so as to lead to E♭, the subdominant, via its dominant, which prepares the way for the dominant to lead in the reprise. If this reprise seems particularly satisfying and welcome, it is partly because it arrives as a cadence, IV - V - I, partly because the sheer lyric beauty of the main theme is all the more lustrous after the darkening and perturbance it has just passed through. The typical shortening of material takes place after the first theme is heard, by omitting the equivalent of mm. 3–6. The falling thirds return in the tonic in due course; we await them, too, which shows that this movement has a truly dualistic thematic basis. But they return at first in a different form, having by metamorphosis become descending sixths. No further alterations occur as the cadential area is readily accommodated to the tonic.

The prima parte and the seconda parte are identical in length. A scant twenty-eight measures suffice to encompass this little gem of lyric outpouring. It could have been made longer, but not better. All the elements of later sonata form are present and there is a perfect balance between the binary or bipartite structure and the ternary disposition of the main theme within it.

The sonata concludes with an *Allegro* in 6/8, a giguelike binary movement that resumes the *perpetuum mobile* character of the opening *Allegro*. It becomes even more brilliant in sonority, also more like Domenico Scarlatti, especially at the ends of the two sections. Technical difficulties increase, as when the descending thirds encountered in the *Andante* must now be performed rapidly. There is enough contrast in motion between the three movements to make up for their remaining in the same key. The cycle is successful as a whole without tonal contrast. With their emphasis on the kinetic, the bustling outer movements provide a perfect frame for the expressive and cantabile reverie of the *Andante*. If Galuppi did not invent the galant keyboard sonata—which, indeed, he may well have done—at least he brought it to its peak of perfection.

When Diderot in his *Neveu de Rameau* wished to conjure up the ultimate in violin playing, the reader may recall that he had Rameau's nephew do a pantomime of Locatelli. With regard to the keyboard it was a sonata by Galuppi or Alberti that the nephew mimed. The conjunction of these two names is an intriguing one and does great honor to the latter. Alberti's sonatas are indeed as modern as Galuppi's and were perhaps held in comparable esteem among the Italophile amateurs of music in Paris in the 1750s. What Alberti lacks is not striking melodic ideas—he too is a *cembalista-cantante*—but the skill to develop them, connect them, or order them in relationship to each other. In aural sensitivity to the harpsichord he was also not lacking, although no Italian after Domenico Scarlatti came close to Galuppi in this respect. In spite of the lack of evidence that can be dated, I suggest that Galuppi led the way here, as in so many other areas. He was, after all, from earliest youth first and foremost a harpsichordist. Credit for creating the galant harpsichord sonata belongs to the northern Italians in any case. It is a not-inconsiderable addition to the list of creative achievements brought to the fore in this chapter to be put alongside the virtuoso concerto for solo violin and orchestra, the concert symphony, the galant chamber sonata, the comic finale, and some early examples of the string quartet. If it can be maintained that the Neapolitans first formed the language of eighteenth-century modern style in their operas, it must also be admitted that the northern Italians were remarkably inventive in extending it to different uses and different media. The rest of Europe eagerly took up these latest gains as soon as they were made.

A century after Goldoni wrote a wedding poem in which he praises Galuppi, another poet mysteriously unearthed the by-then-forgotten master. Robert Browning filled his poem "A Toccata by Galuppi" with musical references that can indeed be related to the Venetian master: "Lesser [i.e., minor] thirds so plaintive"; "Sixths diminished"; "Dominant's persistence"; "Sigh on sigh"; "Suspensions, solutions"; "commiserating sevenths"; "An octave struck the answer." They can be related as well to countless other masters too. Still, there is a particular truth in two lines that touch upon the extent of the emotional world mastered by Il Buranello.

> Brave Galuppi! that was music!
> Good alike at grave and gay!

4

Dresden and Berlin

Saxony's Wettin Dynasty

WHILE the Habsburgs and Bourbons struggled for supremacy from one end of the Continent to the other, three ancient German dynasties vied for power in Central Europe: the Wittelsbachs, rulers of Bavaria and the Rhenish Palatinate; the Hohenzollerns, rulers of Brandenburg and Prussia; and the Wettins, rulers of Saxony. The Wettin family went back even further than the others, having obtained power in some Saxon lands as early as the tenth century. Its fortunes rose and fell over the years, as did those of Saxony, but it always remained a dominant force in German politics. Lacking the primogeniture principle of succession, Saxony was repeatedly divided between surviving sons of its rulers, which thus weakened its potential hegemony over the rest of Germany. Even so it was always the richest country within the Holy Roman Empire. In the sixteenth century it became the cradle of the Protestant Reformation. All the more ironic and astounding for this reason was the decision of the young elector Frederick Augustus ("the Strong") to convert to Catholicism after he acceded to the throne in 1694. His motives had to do more with politics than with religion. As a Catholic prince he could be elected king of Poland, which, in fact, he was in 1697. The title to one of Europe's oldest kingdoms brought him little benefit at first, for Poland was the main battleground of the Great Northern War that raged between Russia and Sweden from 1700 to 1721. The Swedes took Warsaw and Cracaw, which led the Polish magnates to dethrone Augustus and elect as their king one of their own, Stanislas Leszczyński. But after the defeat of Charles XII of Sweden by Russia at Poltava (1709), Augustus returned to Poland and drove out his rival. From this point on the elector-king devoted more and more resources toward enhancing his Saxon capital.

Frederick Augustus I of Saxony became Augustus II of Poland. His identically named son and successor also occupied both thrones. The former will be referred to here as Augustus, the latter as Frederick Augustus. The name "Frederick" will be reserved for Frederick II of Prussia, known as "the Great."

Their conversion to Catholicism brought the Wettins possibilities of intermarriage with other families of equal or superior rank, most especially of a marriage alliance with the Habsburgs. This came soon, during the second decade of the new century, as the son of Augustus wed Archduchess Maria Josepha, daughter of Emperor Joseph I. As Catholics their children could look forward to good marriages from the point of view of status. One child, Maria Amalia, married Charles Bourbon and became queen of Naples, later queen of Spain. Another, Maria Josepha, married the dauphin and gave birth to the future Louis XVI. A double marriage in 1747 united two more offspring with the Bavarian Wittelsbachs. Obviously the Saxon court had risen in status above the level permitted by the Protestant alliances of the previous century.

The leader of Saxony's immediate neighbor to the north, the elector of Brandenburg, was not about to suffer Augustus's elevation to king without a fight for similar advancement. The great elector, who ruled Brandenburg and Prussia from 1640 to 1688, had made his country into a stronger, better-run state. Although Protestant, he generally sided with Emperor Leopold I in political matters. His son Frederick plagued Leopold for a royal title, and in exchange for the promise of more military aid, sorely needed by the emperor, was granted the title "King in Prussia."[1] Frederick I crowned himself king while in Königsberg, Prussia, on 18 January 1701, with a display of enormous expense. He was a weak ruler compared to his father, one who loved ceremonial pomp and French culture.

The prospect of a Habsburg-Wettin marriage antedated the sudden death of Emperor Joseph I in 1711. Even earlier Augustus was planning to build a palace that would be worthy of the royal-imperial festivities. He sent his main architect, Daniel Pöppelmann, to France to study the latest trends in palace building. Pöppelmann also went to Vienna, where he was inspired particularly by buildings designed by Johann Lukas von Hildebrandt. Over several years there arose under Pöppelmann's direction the Zwinger Palace, an open and airy four-sided pavilion

[1]Prussia (i.e., the later East Prussia), like Poland, lay outside the empire, as did the kingdom of Hungary. Thus Leopold could grant this title and still insure that there remained only one kingdom within the empire, Bohemia, of which the Habsburgs were hereditary rulers.

adjacent to the old electoral residence, erected in the sixteenth century. The new garden structure was low and horizontal, like Versailles, in strong contrast to the lofty towers and gabled wings of the Renaissance palace. It made use of fountains, ponds, and arcades. An elaborate crownlike tower in the shape of an onion dome capped one entrance.[2]

Pöppelmann's Zwinger was but one of many building projects inaugurated by the elector, including the magnificent Augustus Bridge over the Elbe. The medieval Frauenkirche (where Heinrich Schütz was buried) began being replaced in 1726 by a great domed church designed by Georg Bähr on the model of Santa Maria della Salute in Venice. This new Frauenkirche, regarded as the zenith of Lutheran church architecture, was consecrated in 1734. Bernardo Bellotto painted his most famous cityscape of Dresden in 1748 (Figure 4.1). It shows the Frauenkirche in the distance, its dome looming over the middle of the Augustus

FIGURE 4.1. View of Dresden in 1748. Designed and engraved by Bernardo Bellotto.

[2]Hellmuth Christian Wolff, *Oper Szene und Darstellung von 1600 bis 1900* (Leipzig, 1968), pp. 104–5, illustrates the so-called Kronentor of the Zwinger side by side with a remarkably similar stage set by Giuseppe Galli-Bibiena intended for Antonio Lotti's *Ascanio* (Dresden, 1718).

Bridge across the Elbe. On the left, the long palace is that of the first minister, Count Heinrich von Brühl. To the right is the Catholic Hofkirche, begun on designs by Gaetano Chiaveri in 1738, with its high tower. Visible behind the Hofkirche in Bellotto's depiction is a wing of the old electoral palace and its tower.

EARLY OPERA

Dresden and Saxony had been in the vanguard of musical change throughout much of the seventeenth century, thanks largely to the greatness of Heinrich Schütz, whose services Elector Johann Georg I preempted from Moritz, landgrave of Hessen-Kassel in 1615. Schütz had studied in Venice, with Giovanni Gabrielli from 1610 to 1612. In 1627 the court was at Torgau on the Elbe to celebrate the wedding of the elector's daughter Sophia Eleonora to Landgrave Georg II of Hessen-Darmstadt. Schütz composed a pastoral tragicomedy for the occasion, *Dafne*, on a German text that Martin Opitz derived from the libretto Ottavio Rinuccini wrote for Jacopo Peri thirty years earlier. Schütz's music has been lost. *Dafne* is reckoned as the first opera produced in Germany. The following year Schütz requested permission to return to Italy so that he could study with Monteverdi. In his letter to the elector he mentioned that "everything has changed, and the music in use at princely banquets, comedies, ballets, and other such productions has markedly improved."[3]

For the next big electoral wedding, that of Prince Johann Georg and Magdalena of Brandenburg in 1638, Schütz wrote the music to an opera-ballet on the Orpheus myth, which is also lost. By the 1640s the electoral court music was suffering badly from the ravages of the Thirty Years War. The Peace of Westphalia in 1648 brought little initial relief because the war had so drained the state's finances that the court musicians went without pay most of the time. By the 1650s the crown prince began to improve the situation. He hired some young Italians, first Giovanni Bontempi, a castrato who had seen service in San Marco, Venice, then Vicenzo Albrici and Marco Peranda. Schütz welcomed the brilliant Bontempi as someone who could help him direct the court music. But in 1653, when the prince planned to alternate the two as directors of the Sunday service music, the aged composer complained that, as an old and not undeserving servant, he should not have to appear before the public on an equal footing with a man three times younger, "and castrated to boot."[4]

Elector Johann Georg II, who reigned from 1656 to 1680, was a strong supporter of the Italians and of Italian opera. In 1662 Bontempi wrote the text and music of *Il Paride*, which is considered a landmark in the triumph of Italian opera

[3]Joshua Rifkin, "Schütz," *New Grove.*
[4]Mary E. Frandson, "Allies in the Cause of Italian Music: Schütz, Prince Johann Georg III, and Musical Politics in Dresden," *Journal of the Royal Musical Association* 125 (2000): 1–40; 6.

in Germany. It anticipated by six years another landmark: Antonio Cesti's *Il pomo d'oro* for the imperial court in Vienna. Bontempi's *Dafne* (1671) and *Jupiter und Io* (1673), both in German, were probably written in collaboration with Peranda. In one of his literary works the multitalented Bontempi claimed that he switched to being a stage designer and master of the machines because the elector favored Albrici, and then Carlo Pallavicino, after his arrival in Dresden in 1667. The Venetian composer Pietro Andrea Ziani also worked in Dresden in 1666–67, the same year the new electoral theater was inaugurated.[5] During the elector's last decade, the 1670s, the Italians dominated the musical scene. Schütz died in 1672.

Elector Johann Georg III (reigned 1680–91) at first dismissed the Italians and promoted Schütz's pupil Christoph Bernhard to Kapellmeister. But this prince subsequently persuaded Pallavicino to return to Dresden. Italian opera also returned, and one of its luminaries was the prima donna Margarita Salicola. Johann Georg IV reigned less than three years before he died and was replaced by his younger brother. Augustus became a greater patron of the arts than even his most lavish predecessors. His tastes ran to French more than Italian culture. After his conversion to Catholicism he had the theater of 1667 transformed into a Catholic court chapel and built a new playhouse for his French players. His son, the crown prince, was more interested in Italian opera and it was his penchant that eventually won out in Dresden.

Dresden's musical eminence was gradually rebuilt with a series of brilliant court appointments. Jan Dismas Zelenka joined the orchestra as a bass player in 1710. In January 1712 the violinist Johann Georg Pisendel was appointed on the recommendation of concertmaster Jean Baptiste Volumier. Pisendel had the advantage of an excellent musical training at the court of Ansbach, where he was taught singing by Francesco Pistocchi and violin by Giuseppe Torelli. In 1715 Pisendel was selected to accompany Crown Prince Frederick to Paris along with Volumier, Kapellmeister Johann Christoph Schmidt, court organist Christian Petzold, and the oboist Christoph Richter. Pisendel and Richter are said to have particularly pleased the court of the duke of Lorraine in Lunéville by their performance.[6] The traveling musicians attending the prince were expected to polish their musical skills as well as provide entertainment. After they returned from Paris, they were sent next to Berlin, and then in 1716 to Venice, where the crown prince spent over a year beginning in April 1716. Zelenka was among those who made this trip. Pisendel profited from the Venetian stay by studying violin with Vivaldi.

---

[5]For an engraving of the interior, see the article "Dresden" in *New Grove*.
[6]Moritz Fürstenau, *Zur Geschichte der Musik und des Theaters am Hofe der Kurfürsten von Sachsen*, 2 vols. (Leipzig, 1861–62), 2: 85.

WEDDING FESTIVITIES

The goal of the journeys undertaken by the crown prince was Vienna, where his long-planned wedding with Archduchess Maria Josepha took place on 20 August 1719, following which they made a triumphal procession that took them to Dresden for the climax of the nuptial celebrations the following month. Once again, as with Schütz's *Dafne* of nearly a century earlier, a Saxon wedding took center stage in music history. All the Dresden court musicians were on hand to take part in the 1719 festivities, under the direction of Schmidt and Johann David Heinichen, both of whom held the title of Kapellmeister. Schmidt had been sent by the court to study in Italy in 1694. Heinichen came to Dresden in 1717 after several years in Venice, where he was a successful composer of opera and a friend of such leading figures as Gasparini, Lotti, and Vivaldi.

Quantz in his autobiography painted a picture of the Dresden court orchestra just before the wedding opera. As a boy Quantz was already an expert instrumentalist. His three main instruments were violin, oboe, and trumpet, undoubtedly the three most useful to a city musician such as he was in Merseburg. He also became acquainted with many other instruments and could play them. He took a position in a small town near Dresden in order to be close to the capital. From here he went to Pirna, where he first discovered Vivaldi's concertos.

> In March of the year 1716 I went to Dresden. Here I soon became aware that the mere playing of the notes as set down by the composer was far from being the greatest merit of a musician. The royal orchestra was already at that time in special favor. It distinguished itself from many other orchestras by its French evenness of performance [egale Art des Vortrags], introduced by the concertmaster at that time, Volumier. Under the direction of its next concertmaster, Herr Pisendel, who introduced a mixed style, it achieved a finesse of performance that I never heard surpassed in all my later travels. At that time it boasted of various famous instrumentalists such as: Pisendel and Veracini on the violin, Pantaleon Hebenstreit on the pantaleon, Sylvius Leopold Weiss, on the lute and theorbo, Richter on the oboe, [Pierre Gabriel] Buffardin on the transverse flute, not to speak of the good violoncellists, bassoonists, horn players, and bass violinists. Hearing these famous people I was greatly amazed, and my zeal for continuing musical studies was doubled. I wanted to prepare myself so that in time I too could become a tolerable member of this excellent company. (pp. 206–7)

Quantz was nineteen in 1716. He errs only by placing Francesco Veracini in Dresden a year before he actually arrived.

Antonio Lotti, first organist of San Marco in Venice, was invited to Dresden to compose the main wedding opera. He had to request permission to absent himself. Permission was granted on 22 July 1717—the signoria was not about to deny him an opportunity to enhance the musical fame of Venice at an imperial-royal wedding. Lotti was accompanied by his wife, the soprano Santa Stella, whom he had married that summer. In the party traveling from Venice to Dresden were also the famous alto castrato Senesino, the designer Alessandro Mauro, and the poet Antonio Maria Lucchini—in sum, the skeleton of an opera company, one that would be filled out by hiring other Italian singers. The orchestra was already in place and at their disposal.

Soon after their arrival, on 25 October 1717, the new troupe performed *Giove in Argo,* a *melodramma pastorale* by Lucchini set by Lotti, given on a provisional stage in the Redoutensaal of the old palace. It was revived in the great opera house next to the Zwinger built by Pöppelmann especially for this troupe and for the wedding festivities in 1719. In fact *Giove* opened the new house on 3 September 1719, because the wedding opera itself, *Teofane,* was not ready until ten days later. Lucchini and Lotti also wrote *Ascanio, ovvero Gli odi delusi dal sangue* given on the provisional stage in February 1718. Lucchini did not write the libretto for *Teofane.* Following a scandal involving a young lady he fled Dresden. Stefano Pallavicino, Carlo's son, who was Saxon court poet from 1687–95, returned in 1717 and was responsible for the libretto. After scouring medieval history he found an instance in which a German king, Otto II, wed an emperor's niece (a Byzantine emperor in this case). The story of Teofane and Ottone is thus an allegory of the wedding of Maria Josepha and Frederick Augustus.

King Augustus spent a truly royal sum on his new opera house next to the Zwinger, nearly 150,000 thalers. Unlike the opera house of 1667, which had a semicircular auditorium at the front of which sat the electoral family, Pöppelmann's theater was in the horseshoe shape favored in Italy, with the electoral-royal box one floor up in the rear, surmounted by an enormous crown.[7] Alessandro Mauro was responsible for the interior decoration of this theater, which was said to hold two thousand spectators. The three tiers of boxes were rather sparsely decorated, but the same was not true of the proscenium opening and the royal box, both held up by gigantic human figures, elaborately carved. The hall gives an impression of classical sobriety at war with baroque ostentation.

Visiting Dresden in the summer of 1719, besides a huge diplomatic corps, was a composer born in Halle, not far from electoral Saxony, but in fact ruled by the elector of Brandenburg. Handel was in Dresden in order to assess the singers for possible use in London.[8] Surely he missed none of the musical entertainments that were public. *Teofane* he probably witnessed in the splendid new theater. He took back with him a libretto of the opera and later had it adapted for his composition by Nicola Haym under the title *Ottone* (1723). Other composers present included Telemann and Quantz, who included these impressions in his autobiography.

---

[7]Both theater interiors are reproduced from contemporary depictions in the article "Dresden" in *The New Grove Dictionary of Opera,* ed. Stanley Sadie (London, 1992).

[8]Johannes Gress, "Händel in Dresden (1719)," *Händel-Jahrbuch 1963*: 135-49.

In the year 1719, after the nuptials of the Electoral Prince, various Italian operas, a pastoral play, two serenades, and a French divertissement were performed. The singers and dancers of the last consisted entirely of ladies and gentlemen of the court. Herr Schmidt, the Kapellmeister, declared himself the author of the music. For the Italian operas the most famous singers available had been hired from Italy. The music of the two operas *Gli odi delusi dal sangue* and *Teofane*, and the pastoral [*Giove in Argo*] was by maestro di cappella Lotti who had been especially commissioned for this. The rest of the music was by Heinichen. These were the first operas I heard in my life. Not only did they astound me, but they also gave me some idea of the then pure, but sensible, Italian taste [unvermischten, aber dabey vernünftigen Geschmacke], from which the Italians have since strayed too far, in my opinion. (p. 212)

Quantz went on to characterize the singers, Senesino, Matteo Berselli, Santa Stella, Vittoria Tesi, Margherita Durastanti, and a certain Frau Hesse, describing the first three in considerable vocal detail.

Lotti's *Teofane* was the artistic climax of the wedding celebrations and of the three years the composer and his little band of fellow Venetians spent in Dresden. Stefano Pallavicino, the poet, deserves a large share of the credit. His libretto has been praised in particular for the skillful way he integrated spectacle and ballet into the end of each of the three acts. Lotti's music has received more qualified approbation.

Lotti's immensely long score compares favorably with the operas of Bononcini, but suffers like them from excessive repetition and regularity of rhythm and phrase-length, two aspects in which Handel constantly outdistanced his contemporaries. It eschews the variety offered by cavatina, arioso, and accompanied recitative, but there are interesting points about the scoring. Corni di caccia play in the Italian overture and elsewhere; recorders are used quite extensively; Adelberto's "Lascia che nel suo viso" is an extended virtuoso piece with obbligato for archlute or mandoline.[9]

The player in this aria must have been none other than Silvius Leopold Weiss, who became the highest-paid instrumental virtuoso at the Dresden court.

Great care was taken in printing the librettos of *Giove in Argo, Teofane,* and the other celebratory works at Dresden in 1719. The text in Italian was accompanied on facing pages with a complete translation into French, the language preferred by the ruler.[10]

A typical sampling of Lotti's music for Dresden is offered by the final duet in *Teofane,* sung by Santa Stella Lotti in the title role and Senesino as Ottone (Exam-

---

[9]Winton Dean and John Merrill Knapp, *Handel's Operas 1704–1726* (Oxford, 1987), p. 421.

[10]*Giove in Argo* is reproduced in facsimile in Randell Holden, "The Six Extant Operas of Antonio Lotti (1667–1740)" (DMA thesis, University of Washington, 1970).

ple 4.1). Syncopations such as these were the height of fashion at the time and helped define the galant style, as did the simple homophonic texture and clear phrasing. The rather plain melody, with its small repetitions, is like many arias by Vinci, and perhaps illustrates what Quantz appreciated as Lotti's "pure but sensible taste." Another composer who appreciated Lotti was his pupil Galuppi, who often copied the opening texture of two violins in thirds in the high range. Note how the violins drop down an octave and merely double when the voices enter. A case has been made that Handel paid Lotti the compliment of copying features of this duet and other pieces from *Teofane* in his *Ottone*.[11]

EXAMPLE 4.1. *Lotti, Duet from* Teofane

---

[11]Fiona McLauchlan, "Lotti's *Teofane* (1719) and Handel's *Ottone* (1723): A Textual and Musical Study," *Music and Letters* 78 (1997): 349–90.

Aftermath

Handel may have also played the role of a provocateur who was partly responsible for the temporary end of Italian opera at Dresden. He had orders to engage singers for London during his stay in Dresden. At first he was unsuccessful. The castratos Senesino and Berselli extended their contracts for another year in Dresden beginning in October 1719. Senesino may have sought a means by which he could get out of his contract. If so, he found one. Quantz relates the story from first-hand experience, as he was serving at the time in the Polish capella as an oboist.

> After the nuptial celebrations Heinichen composed still another opera [*Flavio Crispo*, 1720] which was to be performed after the King's return from Poland. At the rehearsal, which took place at the royal palace in the presence of the music director, Baron von Mortax, the two singers, Senesino and Berselli, played a crude, virtuoso trick. They quarreled with Heinichen over an aria and charged this scholarly man who had spent seven years in Italy with making an error in setting the words. Senesino, who may have already had intentions of going to England, tore up Berselli's score and threw it at Heinichen's feet. This was reported to the King in Poland. In the meantime, Count von Wackerbart, who usually was a great patron of the Italians, had reconciled the Kapellmeister and the castrati to Heinichen's complete satisfaction in the presence of the most important members of the royal orchestra, such as Lotti, Schmidt, Pisendel, Weiss, etc. Meanwhile, a royal order came back commanding the dismissal of all the Italian singers. With this, opera for the present had an end. (p. 216)

Augustus, never a friend of Italian opera, was probably glad to have an excuse to unburden himself of its great expense. There is a slight contradiction in Quantz's tale even so, in that Lotti returned home to Venice in the fall of 1719, covered with honors and presents, including horses and a carriage.

Lotti's stay of three years left a mark on the entire musical scene in central Europe, not just on opera. Dlabač reported that between 1718 and 1720 Lotti visited Prague often and led not only his operas but also his oratorios to such applause that his compositions were often gladly performed later in the churches of the Czech metropolis.[12] As late as 1777 Michael Haydn led a performance of a gradual by Lotti that had been given to him in Vienna by Georg Reutter, the music winning the applause of Leopold Mozart (in his letters of 2 and 13 November 1777).

After Lotti's departure there were further signs of unruliness among the Dresden musicians, aside from the confrontation between Heinichen and the castrati. Silvius Weiss, the famous lutenist, saw his livelihood threatened when he

---

[12]Bohumír Jan Dlabač, "Lotti," in *Allgemeines historisches Künstler-Lexikon* (Prague, 1815).

was attacked by a French violinist named Petit, who attempted to bite off the top joint of his right thumb. On 13 August 1722 Veracini jumped to the ground from a third-story window, according to Mattheson, who ascribed the incident to a fit of madness brought on by too much immersion in music and alchemy. Veracini hinted darkly in his late treatise that there was a threat against his life inspired by jealousy, perhaps implying that this was on the part of Pisendel or Volumier, his supervisors. Veracini's years in Saxon service came to an end. He left and did not return. One other curious bit of information concerning the orchestra is that Pantaleon Hebenstreit became incapacitated by failing eyesight and had to stop playing his dulcimer-like invention, the pantaleon. This was such a favorite instrument of the court that a royal order came for Christoph Richter to learn the instrument and replace Hebenstreit, which he did after 1734.

Serious opera suffered a setback in Dresden with the departure of Senesino and company, but the king did not purge all Italians from his service. Stefano Pallavicino remained as court poet, and the troupe of Italian comedians under the direction of Tommaso Ristori also remained. Augustus appointed Ristori's son Giovanni composer to this troupe in 1717 and music director of the twelve-member Polish cappella.[13] The improvised comedies of the Ristori troupe undoubtedly required abundant music and dance in the normal course of events, just as did those of the better-known commedia dell'arte troupes in the Veneto, with which Carlo Goldoni grew up in the 1720s. With Pallavicino as poet and collaborator the younger Ristori went a step further, composing a comic opera *Calandro* given at Dresden in September 1726, followed a few months later by another, *Un pazzo ne fà cento, ovvero Don Chisciotte.* The Ristori troupe toured in both Poland and Russia. Their performance of *Calandro* in Moscow in 1731 figures as the first Italian opera staged in Russia. Only when Augustus died in 1733 was the troupe disbanded.

By the mid-1720s there were stirrings in Dresden that led to the hiring of new theatrical personnel from Italy and several young Italian singers, including the alto castrato Nicolo Pozzi. Then in 1728 the alto castrato Antonio Campioli, a veteran singer and teacher of singing whose career had begun as early as 1704, was sent to Venice to recruit and train singers for Dresden. Out of this foray emerged some young talents destined for success, such as the castratos Domenico Annibali and Venturo Rochetti, plus Anna Maria Negri, who were in Saxon service by 1730. The following year came Hasse and his new Venetian wife, Faustina Bordoni. Opera came to life again on the grandest scale with Hasse's *Cleofide*, staged in the Zwinger theater in September 1731. Faustina sang the title role. The other

[13]Curt Mengelberg, *Giovanni Alberto Ristori: Ein Beitrag zur Geschichte Italienischer Kunstherrschaft in Deutschland im 18. Jahrhunderts* (Leipzig, 1916), p. 3. The document is dated Warsaw, 11 February 1717, and names Ristori "Compositeur de la musique italienne" at an annual salary of 600 thalers.

parts were taken by Maria Catanea, Annibali, Rochetti, Campioli, and Pozzi. Of these Pozzi would remain in active service until 1742, Faustina, Annibali, and Rochetti until the 1750s.

One theme runs consistently through Saxon court music from the times of Schütz to those of Hasse. Each Wettin ruler looked mainly to Venice for musical sustenance and renewal along the most modern lines. Money was found to hire the best talent available. Dresden's musical eminence was more than just a matter of its having greater wealth than its neighboring courts in Germany. Musical sophistication and discriminating taste also contributed.

Hasse

EARLY YEARS

Johann Adolf Hasse was born at Bergedorf near Hamburg. His father Peter, who came from a long line of Lutheran church musicians, was organist of the Lutheran church in which Johann Adolf was baptized on 25 March 1699. Young Hasse studied voice in Hamburg for three years, from age fifteen, then joined the Hamburg opera company as a tenor in 1718. The following year he was appointed to a post at the court of Brunswick, where he sang in several operas, including the first of his own composition, *Antioco,* in the summer of 1721. With a court stipend he traveled to Italy and spent three *Wanderjahre* living intermittently in Venice, Bologna, Florence, and Rome. In 1724 he settled in Naples.[14]

Naples was also the destination of the peripatetic young Quantz at this time. They pooled their resources to mutual advantage, as Quantz recounted in his memoirs:

> Herr Hasse insisted that I share his dwelling. We became good friends. Up to this point he had no music performed publicly in Italy, but a prominent banker of Naples asked him to compose a Serenata for two persons, which he did during my stay with him. Farinelli and Tesi sang in it. Through this Serenata Hasse won so much applause that he was commissioned to compose the opera at the royal theater for [the following] May, and this opera opened the way to his future triumph. (p. 228)

The Serenata was *Romeo e Giulietta* by a minor poet, performed in September 1725 at the Carmignano villa outside Naples. The opera was *Il sesostrate* adapted by Angelo Caresale after Apostolo Zeno and Pietro Pariati, first performed on 13 May 1726. It was the first of seven successive serious operas Hasse composed for the main Neapolitan theater of San Bartolomeo.

---

[14]A portion of this section was printed earlier in honor of Hasse's three hundredth birthday: Daniel Heartz, "Hasse at the Crossroads: *Artaserse* (Venice, 1730), Dresden, and Vienna," *Opera Quarterly* 16 (2000): 24–33.

Hasse also caught the attention of the imperial family in Vienna, whose rule over the Kingdom of Naples had begun in 1707. The premiere of *Il sesostrate* coincided with the ninth birthday of Maria Theresa, heiress to the Habsburg throne, as trumpeted on the title page of the printed libretto. A revival on 28 August celebrating the birthday of her mother, Empress Elisabeth Christine of Brunswick, required a new libretto, or at least a new title page. In both Hasse bears the title of maestro di capella of the Duke of Brunswick, indicating that he was still receiving a subsidy from this quarter. He would have been rewarded as well by the vice regent, Cardinal Althann. In 1727 it was Hasse who was chosen to compose *Gerone, tiranno di Siracusa* to celebrate the name day of Empress Elisabeth on 19 November. In this libretto Hasse is shorn of his Brunswick title and becomes simply "il Sassone." The highest honor that could go to a musician in Naples was to compose an opera celebrating the name day of Emperor Charles VI on 4 November. The honor fell to Hasse in 1729, resulting in his setting of Francesco Silvani's *Tigrane,* in the libretto of which the composer is listed as "maestro sopranumerario" of the royal chapel. After Alessandro Scarlatti died in late October 1725 his subordinates Francesco Mancini, Francesco Feo, and Leonardo Leo moved up the chain a rung and filled all the official posts. Still, almost all of Hasse's works were sent in neat copies to Vienna, where many still survive.

Hasse's formation as a composer could well have included studying counterpoint with Scarlatti in 1725, as Quantz claimed, although it seems a little late for rudimentary studies. Hasse certainly undertook more advanced compositional study with the great master. He made copies of several arias from Scarlatti's last and best opera, *La Griselda,* in which he attempted to smooth out the phrasing and simplify the harmony.[15] The task could be one that Scarlatti assigned him or one that he entered on his own account. In either case he was under his teacher's guidance.

All Hasse's successes availed him little at the Neapolitan court, where the regular positions continued to go to local composers. His big chance came with the commission to compose the main carnival opera for 1730 for the San Giovanni Grisostomo theater in Venice. It is not unlikely that he had already visited Venice in 1727 or 1728, before moving there for good in November 1729. In the secret wedding contract of his marriage with Faustina Bordoni, dated 24 June 1730, he made it clear that he changed religion just before leaving Naples,

> in which he lived continuously for about six or seven years, and there, illuminated by God, embraced the [Roman] Catholic faith, disavowing in that [the Neapolitan] archbishop's court the errors of the Lutheran sect. He then gave up his residence in Naples

---

[15]Reinhard Strohm, "Hasse, Scarlatti, Rolli," *Analecta Musicologica* 15 (1975): 220–57. The author reproduces Scarlatti's originals alongside Hasse's recompositions.

and transferred his private household to Venice, where he has presently been living approximately six or seven months with the intention of residing permanently. In this city of Venice he has contracted the obligations of marriage.[16]

The conversion may have been divinely illuminated in more ways than one—perhaps by hopes of marrying a Catholic as fair and alluring as Faustina, perhaps by hopes of obtaining a high post at a Catholic court, or both. God works his illuminations at many levels. Conversions for the purposes of marriage were not unknown even in the highest ranks of society. Two young duchesses of the house of Brunswick abjured Lutheranism in order to advance their lot by marrying Habsburgs: Wilhelmina married the prince who became Emperor Joseph I in 1705; her sister Elisabeth married his younger brother, who became Emperor Charles VI in 1711. Hasse increased his chances in Vienna by marrying Faustina.

Faustina Bordoni made her public debut singing in Carlo Pollarolo's *Ariodante* at the San Giovanni Grisostomo in 1716. The libretto was dedicated to Crown Prince Frederick Augustus of Saxony, then twenty, who was almost certainly present and who later played a role in bringing her to Dresden. She sang widely throughout Italy during her first decade on the stage, including Venice, Bologna, and Florence, where Hasse certainly would not have missed seeing and hearing her. While Hasse was in Naples she was adding to her laurels in Munich, Vienna, and London. She was a particular favorite in Vienna, where she earned a salary of 12,500 florins between August 1725 and March 1726, singing in operas by Caldara, Fux, and others. She also sang in private houses and received rich rewards from the duke of Richelieu, the French ambassador, and the prince of Liechtenstein. Empress Elisabeth Christine showered her with favors and had her sing duets with Maria Theresa, the crown princess. Following Vienna, Faustina sang in London under Handel, earning astronomical fees. She returned to Italy in 1728 and again sang in several major centers. Her base of operations remained Venice, but she was at Turin for two operas during carnival season 1730 as Hasse was triumphing with his *Artaserse* in Venice. Then their paths crossed in the spring season of 1730 when she sang the title role in Hasse's *Dalisa* at the Teatro San Samuele in Venice.

Hasse was still listed as supernumerary member of the Neapolitan royal chapel in the libretto for *Artaserse.* In the libretto for *Dalisa* he sported an impressive new title: "primo maestro di cappella di sua maestà Augusto, rè di Polonia e Elettor di Sassonia." With the promise of such a position came the security needed to undertake marriage, which followed a month later in June.

The post of first Kapellmeister in Dresden had been vacant since Johann

---

[16]Sven Hostrup Hansell, "Sacred Music at the *Incurabili* in Venice at the time of J. A. Hasse," *JAMS* 23 (1970): 281–301, 505–21; 283–84.

Heinichen died in July 1729. A key figure in Hasse's appointment may have been Johann Ulrich von König, a librettist of the Hamburg opera and from 1720 to 1730 privy secretary and poet for court festivities in German to the elector. It was König who had recommended Hasse to the Hamburg opera in 1718, and then to the court of Brunswick.

No contract survives stipulating when or at what salary Hasse would later enter Saxon service. Possibly the contract went through a long stage of negotiating, because the Hasses made no move in the direction of Dresden. In August 1730 they visited Habsburg-ruled Milan to stage Hasse's *Arminio* with Faustina singing the role of Tusnelda, an occasion celebrating the birthday of Empress Elisabeth Christine on 28 August. Tacitus provided the story, and Antonio Salvi the libretto, which hailed Tusnelda as the faithful German wife who rescued her husband against all odds, a forerunner of Leonora/Fidelio, and thus a perfect choice with which to honor the emperor's German-born wife.

The fall of 1730 passed and still the Hasses remained in Venice. Faustina fulfilled her obligation to sing in two carnival operas at Turin in early 1731. Hasse was called to Vienna, where he set Zeno's oratorio *Daniello,* performed in the imperial court chapel in February 1731. Both Hasse and Faustina were obviously in high favor with the Viennese court. They may have been hoping for an offer there that would better what Dresden was offering, either because they would have been glad to accept it, or to use as further leverage with the Saxon court. With their nonarrival in the spring of 1731 the Saxon court began to suspect they were stalling. Hasse invoked as an excuse for their delayed arrival his affliction with gout, yet Hasse was only thirty-two at the time, a little young for severe gout, from which he admittedly did suffer later in life. The Hasses finally arrived in Dresden on 7 July 1731. The next day Faustina sang for King Augustus to his great satisfaction. A new era of Italian opera at the highest level was about to begin in Germany.

ARTASERSE

Pietro Metastasio visited Venice during the carnival of 1730, when he perhaps met Hasse for the first time. He was on his way to take up his post of imperial poet in succession to Apostolo Zeno in Vienna, from which he would never return. He was coming from Rome where the two most frequently set librettos of his entire oeuvre had just received their premieres in settings by Leonardo Vinci: *Alessandro nell'Indie* on 2 January 1730, and *Artaserse* on 4 February. Within two weeks of Vinci's *Artaserse*, Hasse's setting of the text, revised by Giovanni Boldini, opened in Venice. Domenico Lalli, manager of the San Giovanni Grisostomo theater, apparently told Boldini to enhance the roles of the three principal singers, Francesca Cuzzoni as Mandane, Farinelli as Arbace, and the Neapolitan contralto Nicolini as Artabano. The revisions gave Hasse the basis for the most successful arias he ever composed. If Metastasio was unhappy about this state of affairs he did not let on to his various correspondents, at least not in any letters that have been preserved. But how could he not have been peeved? Lalli had a second version of the libretto printed with the poet's unaltered text, to which the revised libretto made specific reference. Printing the entire libretto of *Artaserse* in its pristine form, it has been suggested, was the price that Metastasio exacted for Lalli to use it at all.[17]

Hasse was at a turning point of his career, just as was Metastasio. His setting of *Artaserse* marked the first of many contacts with the poet and his works. It was written at the same time as Vinci's version, and both settings can be considered as the poem's original musical garb. The enormous success of these works, both of which had an unparalleled number of revivals for serious Italian opera of the time, led to their becoming "the single most substantial tradition in eighteenth-century opera seria."[18]

Boldini introduced several kinds of changes in Metastasio's libretto. The most drastic was the replacement of the original ending of Act I, Arbace's great solo scene culminating with his shipwreck aria "Vo solcando un mar crudele." In its stead was a solo scene for the prima donna, Mandane, culminating with a pathetic aria, Cuzzoni's specialty. To comprehend this it must be remembered that in 1730 Cuzzoni was at the peak of her international career, while Farinelli, nearly a decade younger, was still climbing the ladder of fame. She was the greater star. Farinelli was compensated by being given some superb opportunities to shine elsewhere in the opera, including the new penultimate aria of Act I, "Se al labbro mio non credi." Hasse, writing his first opera for this demanding city, may have had little say about the revisions.[19]

Hasse's score gives the impression here and there that he knew Vinci's *Artaserse* and that he drove himself to greater heights because of its powerful beauties.[20] Toward the end of Act II Vinci's Mandane, sung by the castrato Farfallino (Giacinto Fontana, a great favorite with the Roman public) has an angry aria denouncing the guilty regicide Artabano for inculpating his innocent son Arbace. She tells him in no uncertain terms where to go: into the legendary Ircanian forest populated with monsters. Vinci makes the short lines spring to life in three phrases of three measures each, then applies the brakes, as it were, by a hemiola-like switch to three two-measure units (Example 4.2). The melody is admirable, as is the rhythmic drive. A literal sequence would have carried the

[17]Reinhard Strohm, *Dramma per Musica: Italian Opera Seria in the Eighteenth Century* (New Haven and London, 1997), p. 78.

[18]Ibid., p. 78.

[19]This is contrary to what I wrote assessing them in more detail in "Hasse, Galuppi and Metastasio," in *Venezia e il Melodramma nel Settecento,* ed. Maria Teresa Muraro (Florence, 1978), pp. 309–39.

[20]Reinhard Strohm points to their very similar settings of the aria "Amalo, e se al tuo sguardo," in *Italienische Opernarien des frühen Settecento (1720–1730),* 2 vols. (Analecta Musicologica 16) (Cologne, 1976), 2: 18.

melodic line up to high A in m. 14, but Vinci breaks the pattern with a descent of the dotted figure, then leaps to the high note in the next measure before descending into the cadence. The way Vinci achieves so much power using so few resources is uncanny! Mandane's portrait of the shifty Artabano here remains indelible. Hasse does nothing of the kind in setting this text, but he sets Artabano's aria in Act I disowning his son somewhat similarly (Example 4.3). Artabano attacks his aria without benefit of ritornello coming directly out of his recitative cadence, always a surprise because almost all other arias have ritornellos. Here there are four three-measure phrases before disruption by the two-measure cadential phrases.

One of the most moving scenes in *Artaserse* takes place in Act II when Arbace defers to his father, asks his forgiveness and his blessing, then goes off to his own death (as he imagines). Metastasio cleverly brings the whole drama together by having Arbace, in the aria text, enjoining his father not only to preserve himself, but to placate Arbace's beloved Mandane and to defend his sovereign (Artaserse). The second stanza opens a still wider horizon: a blessed death for the hero if by means of it he can save his country.

Arbace:

Oh temerario Arbace!	Oh foolhardy Arbace! Where
Dove trascorsi? A genitor! perdona:	Do you stray? Ah father! forgive:

EXAMPLE 4.2. *Vinci*, Artaserse, *Aria*

EXAMPLE 4.3. *Hasse*, Artaserse, *Aria*

Eccomi a piedi tuoi, Scusa i trasporti	Behold me at your feet, Pardon the outburst
D'un insano dolor. Tutto il mio sangue	Of an insane grief. May all my blood
Si versi pur, non me ne lagno; e in veci	Pour forth without complaint; instead
Di chiarmala tiranna,	Of calling tyrannical
Io bacio quella man, che mi condanna.	The hand that condemns me, I kiss it.

Artabace:

Basta, sorgi; pur troppo	Enough, rise, you have more
Ai ragion di lagnarti:	Than enough reasons to complain:
Ma sappi . . . (Oh Dio!)	But understand . . . (Oh God!)
Prendi un abbraccio e parti.	Accept an embrace and leave.

Arbace:

Per quel paterno amplesso,	Through this paternal embrace,
Per questo estremo addio,	This final farewell,
Conservami te stesso,	May you preserve yourself,
Placami l'idol mio,	Soothe my beloved,
Difendimi il mio Re.	And defend my king.
Vado a morir beato,	I go to die blessed,
Se della Persia il fato	If the fate of Persia
Tutto si sfoga in me.[21]	Is all vented in me.

Metastasio's aria text made a lovely summary of the opera up to this point, but it did not quite satisfy musical or other desiderata in Venice. Thus we have the spectacle of the minor Venetian poet giving a lesson to the major Roman one by squaring the first stanza to four lines and providing the favored "ah" sound in penultimate position where it can take melismatic writing or trills.

Per questo dolce amplesso,	Through this sweet embrace,
Per questo estremo addio,	Through this final farewell,
Serbami o Padre mio	Preserve, O father mine,
L'idolo amato.	The beloved idol.

Sol questo all'ombra mia	This alone to my soul
Pace e conforto sia	Will be a peace and comfort
Nel fier mio fato.	In my fierce destiny.

As to content, the revised aria dispenses with royalty as well as the kingdom of Persia. Could this betray a bias concerning monarchy in the Most Serene Republic?

The two texts are close enough in affect to make a comparison of the settings by Vinci and Hasse worth undertaking. Vinci chooses the key of G, perhaps

---

[21]These lines follow the edition of 1780, the last corrected by the poet himself. Pietro Metastasio, *Opere*, 12 vols. (Paris, 1780), 1: 76.

because it suits Giovanni Carestini's vocal range, given the melody he had in mind. Otherwise this key was rather neutral in affect, and not particularly well suited to the pathos of the text. After a ritornello of five bars Arbace enters, filling the entire rising octave from G to G with conjunct Lombard snaps, the same device said to have captivated the Roman public when first used there by Vivaldi (Example 4.4.). The half-cadence at the first "addio" returns at "Idol mio," this time reinforced by the violins in the upper octave. The cadence is bifocal, and Vinci makes you guess with the next two recurrences, for which he brings back "addio," exactly where the modulation occurs from G to D. By the next measure it becomes clear that it has occurred. The voice must make a precadential trill on the unfavorable "ee" sound of "il mio Rè," rendered somewhat more awkward by the elision with the last syllable of "difendimi." Vinci sets the even more pathos-laden second stanza by beginning in the tonic minor, g, but quickly leaves it in a rapid and perfunctory traversal of the text.

Hasse's setting for Venice in 1730 of the revised text was one of the numbers taken over in the London *Artaserse* during the 1734–35 season, in which both Farinelli and Cuzzoni repeated their roles. It figures in *The Favourite Songs in the Opera call'd Artaxerxes by Sig.^r Hasse* printed in an engraving by John Walsh (Figures 4.2–3).[22] Hasse chose a more rarefied key, E, clothing an *Adagio* in common time, as in Vinci's aria. He too uses Lombard rhythms, but more in the violins than in the voice part. He also deploys the ever-so-modish three-note snaps of the Neapolitans. Sometimes the violins accompany the voice in unison, as they do much of the time in Vinci's aria. Mostly they provide chord tones, so that the texture is predominantly three-part, in contrast to Vinci's predominantly two-part texture. Hasse thus places more store by the euphony of full triads, which gives his piece a more agreeable sound. His vocal writing is smooth, mostly conjunct, although with a surprising rapid arpeggio from low to high A on the first "idolo amato" (misprinted throughout as "gdolo amato"). The prolonged accent on the fourth beat of the next measure is a trait Hasse has in common with Vinci, who accented "placami" in the same way in his aria. Hasse's second "amato" gets only as far as the second syllable before indulging in a long melisma on the favored "ah" sound. Hasse's shorter text and more leisurely harmonic rhythms make for far more text repetition than in Vinci. For the second stanza Hasse chooses the subdominant, A, which projects a relaxation of tension. He takes his cue from "pace e conforto." All things considered, Hasse's aria is more cantabile than Vinci's and more moving. We can easily imagine Farinelli winning more applause in the theater with Hasse's suave setting of a mediocre text than did Carestini with Vinci's less suave setting of Metastasio's beautiful poem.

Metastasio ended his second act with a solo scene for Artabano. After a few lines, set by Vinci as simple recitative, Artabano concludes that if he could save

---

[22]A complete score of the piece is in Strohm, *Italienische Opernarien*, 2: 135–38.

EXAMPLE 4.4. *Vinci*, Artaserse, *Aria*

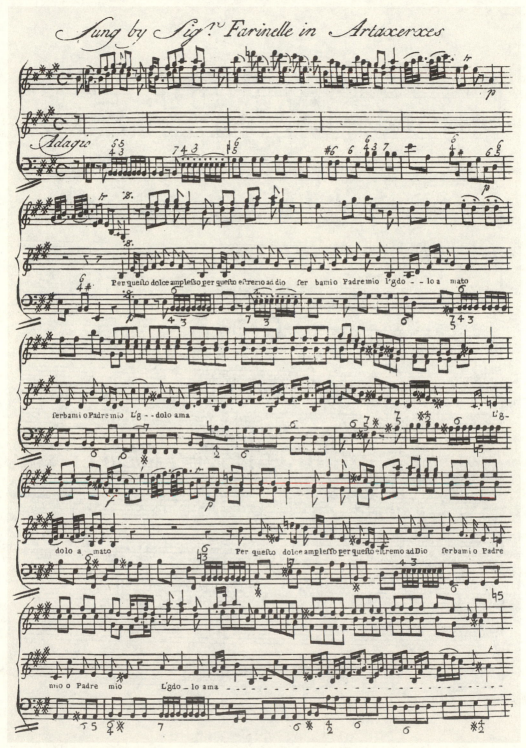

FIGURES 4.2–3. Hasse. Aria "Per questo dolce amplesso" from *Artaserse*.

himself he might be able to save his son, which leads to "Cosi stupisce e cade," a metaphor aria about the shepherd frightened by thunder and lightning. Something more bold was afoot in Venice for a finish to Act II. Artabano was to retain a solo scene with recitative and aria. But in place of the few lines of the original text, Boldini concocted a long recitation of the horrors the guilty father imagines. He hears the sobs of the innocent victim. He tries to stop the executioner, in vain. The head is cut off and falls to the ground. He tries to flee. In terror he hides from the ghost who hurries toward him. Then he realizes it was all a delirium. "If I save myself, dear Arbace will not fall oppressed," ends the recitative, with the only idea recognizable from Metastasio's original. My description omits about half of this phantasmagoria. Hasse sets it as an obbligato recitative almost from the beginning, fifty-eight measures in all, a powerful succession of different tempos, keys, and melodic-harmonic ideas, possibly the longest such piece attempted up to this time.[23] Sometimes the orchestra of strings reacts to the gruesome images, sometimes it anticipates them, and in the latter technique lay the groundwork for the German melodramas of Georg Benda and others of a later generation. Conjuring a ghost became one of the mainstays of serious operas in the so-called *ombra* scenes.

The substitute aria text for Artabano continues the same extravagant language as the preceding recitative. It maintains also the first person pronoun, avoiding the metaphorical crutch of Metastasio's fearful shepherd.

Pallido il sole, torbido il cielo	The sun pales, the sky darkens
Pena minaccia, morte prepara	Threatening trouble, and death.
Tutto mi spira rimorso e orror.	Everything fills me with remorse and horror.
Timor mi cinge di freddo gelo	Fear surrounds me with freezing cold,
Dolor mi rende la vita amara	Grief embitters my life and
Io stesso fremo contro il mio cor.	I shudder at my own heart.

Hasse's setting, sung by the veteran Nicolini, must have raised many a shudder in the theater. The key chosen, E♭, was reserved mostly for moments of sublime seriousness, appropriate for dying thoughts, or of love unto death, whether human or divine. Hasse sets up an agitation in sixteenth notes in the muted violins that murmur almost incessantly throughout the whole aria, an *Andante* in common time. There is nothing particularly original about a perpetual motion accompaniment in sixteenth notes; Vinci used it often.

"Pallido il sole" is another aria that was diffused by means of Walsh's *The Favourite Songs* in London, where the role was sung by Senesino (Nicolini died in 1732). It is reproduced from this source in its entirety (Figures 4.4–6). The main

---

[23]There is a complete score of the piece in Heartz, "Hasse, Galuppi and Metastasio," pp. 313–21.

FIGURES 4.4–6. Hasse. Aria "Pallido il sole" from *Artaserse*.

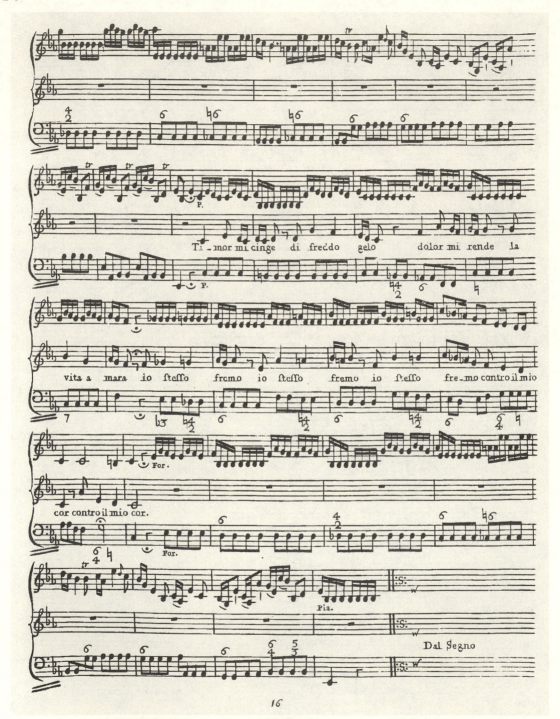

idea is a long wedge shape, the treble rising, mostly by diatonic steps, against the chromatic descent of the bass. Images of death, whether in sacred or secular music, had long elicited the descending chromatic fourth. Perhaps no one before Hasse had done it quite like this. On the first occurrence of the word "morte" he uses the most modern harmonic ploy in his arsenal, the augmented sixth chord. To make it more thrilling he repeats it directly, *forte.* In the following passage he resorts to the syncopations dear to Lotti, and still fashionable in Venice, and consequently in Dresden and London too. These lead to the cadence in the new key and the medial ritornello, marked *fortissimo,* which returns at once to the main key. Giving the voice the main idea in the secondary key is the usual procedure in arias here, but perhaps it would not have been satisfactory in vocal placement up a fifth or down a fourth. "Tutto mi spira" is again taken on the C that is the voice's highest tone, but this time the tone is the ninth of a very modern-sounding ninth chord. The concluding part of the aria is expansive in its celebration of the main key, twenty measures for the voice as against twelve in the first part.

Hasse is sure-handed and bold as well in setting the second stanza, which tends to be routinely handled by many composers of the time. He chooses the relative minor, c, then moves up a fourth, to f. The way he gets back to c involves a series of little wedge shapes, with a hair-raising chromatic rise in the violins and voice up to the climactic C, whence they tumble down an octave to the cadence. A long chromatic rising passage in the bass had played an important role in the beginning of the obbligato recitative preceding the aria, where agitated violin passages in sixteenth notes also obtrude, leaving no doubt that Hasse conceived recitative and aria together as one long stretch of thrilling musical drama. To enhance the reprise of the first stanza close to the end of the aria, he requires the mutes to be lifted (middle of the second page, "Si levano li Sordini la 2da Volta").

"Pallido il sole," although not written for Farinelli, became one of his show-pieces, as can be readily understood from its superb qualities. It is one of the handful of arias that he sang to the king of Spain night after night during his years in Madrid. Brosses regarded it as the most beautiful of all in his collection of several hundred arias. It made Hasse's reputation as did no other piece. Just so did the *Artaserse* of 1730, the gateway to his European renown, become his passport to Dresden and a position that allowed him to marry and contemplate raising a family.

CLEOFIDE

Dresden witnessed the beginning of a new era in its long operatic history with the arrival of Hasse and Faustina. Presumably it was Hasse in Venice in 1730 who singled out Metastasio's *Alessandro nell'Indie* as his vehicle of choice. He had it revised considerably by Michelangelo Boccardi of Turin in order to magnify the prima donna role of Cleofide, to be sung by Faustina, so that in the end it became very much her opera, and was thus appropriately renamed *Cleofide.* After the production in Dresden in September of 1731 the work remained the exclusive property of the Saxon court.

The title page of the libretto proclaims the magnificence of the event, "presented in the royal court theater by command of his sacred royal majesty Frederick Augustus" (Figure 4.7). Quite unusual is the printing of the composer's name in this place. Moreover, he is extolled as the "most famous Hasse, called il Sassone." More superlatives follow the name of the sovereign, described as "always great and most unconquerable." Those in the audience with long memories could ponder the king's humiliating retreat in 1706 after he unwisely made war on Sweden and was forced to abandon both Dresden and Warsaw to Swedish occupation. It was Russian intervention in the war that saved him and restored his territories, but this had the unfortunate consequence of giving Russia a sway over Polish affairs that was not relinquished. Augustus, named "the Strong" by posterity, was not "always great" in political terms, but he did make Dresden into a great cultural capital. He was also a great tactician in managing his Saxon subjects, who as Protestants resented his conversion. He brought them around step by step, avoiding antagonizing

FIGURE 4.7. Title page of the libretto to Hasse's *Cleofide* (Dresden, 1731).

them and guaranteeing the prerogatives of all Protestant institutions. Their loyalty to the Wettin dynasty eventually overcame their distaste for Rome.

Hasse could not have been entirely happy with the singers at his disposal. There was no tenor in the cast, although at least one was normal, and a role such as that of Alexander was often sung by a tenor (as happened in Handel's setting of the opera as *Poro* in 1730). Thus Hasse had to write for three sopranos and three contraltos. In Campioli he had a singer of no more than average abilities, less than was demanded by the primo uomo role of Poro. By 1731 Campioli was nearing the end of his career. After Dresden he worked briefly in London for Handel, who gave him little to sing. He was pensioned by Dresden in 1738 and returned to Italy. Hasse cut down the role of Poro so that he received only four relatively short arias, plus the joint pieces with the prima donna. Faustina/Cleofide, on the other hand, received six big arias, placed in the most strategic moments of the drama. Hasse helped out two of the other singers by making concertante use of the splendid Dresden orchestra. Pozzi as the treacherous general Timagene, a villain's role that Handel assigned to a bass, received a long metaphor aria about fishing in Act II, Scene 11, with two frolicking flutes (Quantz and Buffardin) playing solo parts much of the time. Another alto, Annibali as Alexander, sang an aria in Act III, Scene 6, about the wounded stag in the wood, "Cervo al bosco," in which a large share of the work went to solo horn and archlute (Silvius Weiss again). The horn part was in all probability written for Anton Hampel, born in Prague around 1710 and recruited by Hasse. Hampel was one of the greatest and most innovative hornists of the century. He served in the Dresden orchestra until his death in 1771. Annibali was still quite young in 1731, as were Rochetti in the role of the faithful Gandarte and Signora Catanea as Erissena, "sister of Poro and secretly in love with Alexander." The only singer of international renown in the cast was Faustina.

Metastasio held Cleofide off the stage at the beginning of the opera until the first scene change, from a littered battlefield to a "grove of cypress and palm trees with a little temple to Bacchus in the realm of Cleofide." Reserving the feminine element or the prima donna for a change of scene to something more pleasant or intimate works wonderfully on the stage. Lorenzo da Ponte profited from Metastasio's wisdom by withholding the Countess from *Le nozze di Figaro* until we see her in her own boudoir at the beginning of Act II and by having the scene change to a garden on the seashore for the first appearance of Fiordiligi and Dorabella in *Così fan tutte.* In *Cleofide* practicality or necessity dictated that Faustina should appear in the very first scene and dominate it by singing an aria, the long and intense complaint in the key of e minor, "Che sorte crudele." It is to be doubted if Metastasio would have allowed a cliché like "What a cruel fate" to begin any aria, much less such a prominent one. In any case Cleofide makes clear how much she suffers from the cruel treatment of her jealous lover, Poro. And the court got a chance to hear at once from the diva who was being paid more than the rest of the singers combined.

When Poro and Cleofide meet again in Hasse's Act I, Scene 8, the jealous suitor promises to mend his ways. In what amounts to a cavatina of three lines he sings an attractive melody in the key of D to these words.

Se mai più sarò geloso,	If ever again I become jealous,
Mi punisca il sacro Nume,	May I be punished by the sacred god
Che dell'India è domator.	Who has conquered India.

The reference is to the all-conquering Alexander, regarded for his feats as a divinity. Poro is in hiding and has not given up the fight. Cleofide fears for his life and resolves to save him by going to see Alexander. At this Poro quickly breaks his vow and becomes furiously jealous. She mocks him gently by singing as if in continuation of his cavatina, but in her key of G, an aria that declares her love.

Se mai turbo il tuo riposo, If ever I disturb your repose,
Se mi accendo ad altro lume, If another flame should ignite me,
Pace mai non abbia il cor. My heart would never find peace.

Foste sempre il mio bel Nume; You have always been my idol;
Sei tu solo il mio diletto; You alone are my delight;
E sarai l'ultimo affetto, And will be my last love,
Come fosti il primo Amor. Just as you were the first one.

The poet who wrote these simple but ingenious lines was Metastasio, and no one could match him at this kind of love lyric. Equally to his credit is the expert dramaturgy. Cleofide becomes one with Poro by taking up his verse form and filling it with different but related content. Hasse carried the point further by using the same melody for both. Handel differentiated the two in his *Poro* by giving them different melodies, although in the same triple meter.[24]

Poro is a character who is altogether too human in his weaknesses. The thought of his fiancée visiting the great Alexander drives him to a frenzy. He sings a vigorous aria in the bright key of A major about the power wielded by her two pretty eyes, "Se possono tanto / Due luci vezzose." It is one of the most memorable pieces in the opera, on the short side, like all of the pieces for Poro, but a high point musically. Hasse did not write it first for *Cleofide.* He borrowed it from his *Attalo* of 1728. In all, he borrowed nearly half the music in *Cleofide* from his earlier successes in Italy, music that would at least be new and unknown in Dresden. Perhaps there was a shortage of time that led him to do this, or perhaps it was his way of making sure that he put his best foot forward in his new position. He was not the kind of composer who needed extant music for inspiration. When he composed the libretto again in a form closer to Metastasio as *Alessandro nell'Indie* for Venice in 1736, he chose to write almost the entire opera anew.

In another genial stroke Metastasio closed Act I with a duet for the two principals that quotes Poro's vows and Cleofide's response. Now it is Cleofide who begins, repeating his words and, in Hasse's setting, the music of his vow in her key of G. Poro answers by quoting her response a fourth lower in his key of D, at the point in the piece where the dominant usually takes over. After various recriminations they sing together in faster music that eventually returns to tonic

[24]Graham Cummings, "Reminiscence and Recall in Three Early Settings of Metastasio's *Alessandro nell' Indie*," *Proceedings of the Royal Musical Association* 109 (1982–83): 80–104.

G. The music is full of contrasts, with rhetorical gestures in dotted rhythms at some words ("India" and "Infidel" for example) and a big deceptive cadence to flat VI before the end of the faster section. Hasse sets the **B** section to the same fast movement but in tonic minor, which allows the main sections to return in entirety, da capo. The return of text and music from the middle of the act in the final duet has a unifying effect.

The clever use of recurring material in Act I perhaps suggested to Hasse something similar in Act II, achieved by purely musical means without the help of text repetition. Poro and Cleofide meet again in Scene 6 of Act II. They become man and wife, then begin a prayer to the gods to protect their love. (The *Preghiera* will later become a frequent operatic feature.)

Sommi Dei, se giusti siete	Gods on high, if you are just,
Proteggete	Protect
Il bel desio	The noble longing
D'un amor cosi pudico;	Of a love so pure;
Proteggete . . .	Protect . . .

For his setting Hasse chooses the key of E, hitherto unused, and writes a calmly sensuous melody in parallel thirds, rising to the sixth degree and returning in a three-note downward slide (Example 4.5). The three small segments, each a measure long, add up to a model **a b b'**, the three-note slide upward on the first "sieti" mirrored by a downward slide on the next. This is a fine example of the galant extension. To perceive the sway Hasse achieved over Italian opera with such suave music as the prayer, one need look only at an instance in which Wagenseil duplicates Hasse's melody almost note for note in his *Ariodante* (Venice, 1745).[25]

EXAMPLE 4.5. *Hasse*, Cleofide, *Arioso a 2*

Alexander arrives suddenly, forcing the couple to break off their prayer. Poro resumes his disguise as Asbite. A piece of music lacking closure in an opera of some thirty numbers that all have full closure has the effect of suspending a sword

[25]"Dolce diletto mi scherza in petto," exemplified in *Haydn, Mozart*, p. 91.

above the characters' heads. The lingering effect of an unclosed E major is not even dissipated by Alexander's aria about punishing criminals, a furious piece in G and in 3/4 time during which the violins keep striking multiple-stop chords on G as if smiting a culprit. Alexander leaves the stage, having previously commanded Timagene to escort Cleofide to her castle but to imprison Asbite, who claimed he alone was responsible for setting a trap for Alexander. Cleofide next addresses Timagene and instructs him what to say should he find Poro. The strings begin an *Adagio* in E with a melody in thirds and sixths that sounds like the answer to the prayer begun but not ended (Example 4.6ab). The words are Metastasio's.

EXAMPLE 4.6. *Hasse*, Cleofide, *Aria*

Digli, chi'io son fedele;	Tell him that I am faithful;
Digli, ch'è il mio tesoro;	Tell him that he is my treasure;
Che m'ami, ch'io l'adoro;	And to love me, as I adore him,
Che non disperi ancor.	And that he should not despair.

The situation is ambiguous only in that Poro is standing right there, listening to this outpouring of affection from his beloved, but unrecognized by his captor Timagene. Hasse's aria is the slowest music in an opera that consists mostly of brisk, fast-moving pieces. It has an affinity with the *Adagio* in E he wrote in setting Arbace's farewell, "Per questo dolce amplesso," in *Artaserse*.[26] There the

---

[26]See Figures 4.2–3. There is a full transcription in Strohm, *Italienische Opernarien*, 2: 135–38.

melodic sighs climb upward from the first to the second measure. Here they fall down by step, one per measure. In the opening ritornello (Example 4.6a), they fall from the high tonic, E, in sigh after sigh, all the way to the second above the low tonic, F♯: 8 - 7, 6 - 5, 4 - 3, 3 - 2. Other touches characteristic of the composer are the accented high E in the first violins on the weak fourth beat of the third measure, protracted by a tie over the bar line, then falling rapidly down to 4 - 3 (making an expressive cross relation with the bass) to the half-cadence 3 - 2. For the vocal entry (Example 4.6b), Hasse removes the violinistic leaps and gives Faustina/Cleofide the smoothest possible cantilena, with no competition from the orchestra except when she rests. What was four measures in the ritornello shrinks to three. Repetition of the second line links this melody to the typical galant extension. Unusual, very original even, is the way Hasse lands on the subdominant in m. 11 coming right after the dominant.

The musical sigh has come into its own in this aria, where it seems to become the main event, an expression of longing that perfectly suits the words. If ever a single piece could be a criterion for the early galant style Cleofide's love song is it. Hasse's fame soared in consequence. It was this piece for which King Frederick set down in his own hand an intricately decorated version of **A** for the aria's reprise, da capo.[27] His intent was to teach the Berlin soprano castrato Porporino (Antonio Hubert) how to ornament a slow song. The Prussian king continued to honor even Hasse's early operas as unsurpassable monuments of good taste. He commanded *Cleofide* to be performed as late as 1777. Over two hundred years later, in 1987, the opera was revived in a brilliant recorded performance.[28]

Act III of *Cleofide* is not the anticlimax that all too frequently occurs in last acts of opera seria. Nor does it have as many fine pieces as the first two acts. Alexander's "Cervo al bosco" with solo horn and archlute has been mentioned. The regal status of Faustina/Cleofide is maintained to the very end. Believing her husband to be dead she prepares to immolate herself as is expected of widows in her society, but not before a solo scene in which she sings the longest aria in the opera, the lament "Perder l'amato bene" in the key of f (the text is not by Metastasio). Only after this, as she goes toward the funeral pyre, does Alexander intervene. Poro is brought in alive, a captive. The truth of their marriage comes out. Alexander forgives everyone (again) and the opera ends with choral rejoicing in D, complementing the fine Italian overture in D with which it began.[29]

[27]Friedrich II, *Auszierung zur Arie "Digli ch'io son fedele" von Johann Adolf Hasse*, facsimile ed. Wolfgang Goldhan (Wiesbaden, 1991). Emanuel Bach preserved this curiosity among his manuscripts.

[28]William Christie, director, *Cleofide*. Emma Kirkby sings the title role and the orchestra is the Cappella Coloniensis. Capriccio C27 193/96.

[29]This sinfonia is discussed and exemplified in Carl Mennicke, *Hasse und die Brüder Graun als Symphoniker* (Leipzig, 1906), pp. 157–60, 180–82, 186.

The nature of the Dresden appointment allowed Hasse the freedom to spend much of his time in Venice, where he also held official positions. He was not obligated to follow the court to Poland, although in the course of his long association with the electoral court he prepared scores for Warsaw. There were other impediments that delayed the flourishing of Hasse and Faustina in Dresden. In early 1733 Augustus died. Following the customary period of mourning the new ruler was anxious to resume full-scale opera seria under Hasse's direction, but he was also distracted by a challenger for the Polish throne, Stanislas Leszczyński, the same prince who had wrested the crown temporarily from his father. In the War of the Polish Succession (1733–35) France backed Stanislas, whose daughter was married to Louis XV. Russia and Austria backed Saxony and prevailed. By the Treaty of Vienna (5 October 1735) Frederick Augustus was confirmed king of Poland, Stanislas received the duchy of Lorraine for as long as he lived, and Francis of Lorraine was to be compensated with the grand duchy of Tuscany on the death of the last Medici.

Meanwhile Hasse worked intermittently in Dresden. In July 1734 he produced a revised version of his *Cajo Fabrizio.* The elector was in Poland most of the time until mid-1736; Hasse and Faustina enjoyed the opportunity to travel to Venice. They did not return to Dresden until early 1737. This time they remained for nearly two years, until the court left for Poland. Several operas were staged during this time. For the celebration accompanying the marriage of the elector's daughter, Maria Amalia, to Charles Bourbon in May 1738, the theater in the Zwinger was remodeled and redecorated. Pallavicino wrote a libretto, *Alfonso,* on a Spanish subject, appropriate to the Spanish-born Charles. Hasse set it for his usual cast: Faustina, Rochetti, Annibali, Negri, and Pozzi, plus one visitor, the tenor Francesco Ricci.

The Royal Chapel under Heinichen and Zelenka

Dresden's court chapel from 1708 to 1750 was the relatively modest-sized building on the Taschenberg next to the Residence that had been transformed from the court theater built in 1664–67. An engraving entitled *Vue interieure de la Chapelle Royale de Dresde* shows this handsome structure on the occasion of a *Te Deum* sung in 1719 to celebrate the royal-imperial wedding (Figure 4.8).[30] The auditorium of the theater, ringed by Corinthian columns, became the apse and transept of the church, while the large stage area became the nave, which was surrounded by one balcony. The engraving shows trumpets and drums hanging over the bal-

[30]Wolfgang Horn, *Die Dresdner Hofkirchenmusik, 1720–1745: Studien zu ihren Voraussetzungen und ihrem Repertoire* (Kassel, 1987), p. 9.

FIGURE 4.8. Raymond Le Plat. *Te Deum* in the Saxon court chapel, 1719.

cony but does not depict the court orchestra, which must have been placed at the back of the nave, whence the artist drew the scene. Quite unusual is the lack of architectural ostentation, except for the large crowns surmounting the pulpit and the altar. Surprisingly absent is the usual dependence of Catholic churches upon Italian baroque or so-called Jesuit style. The inspiration of Pöppelmann here was rather the French classical style of the late seventeenth century, and especially the court chapel at Versailles designed by François Mansart (begun in 1688). Besides the columns and pilasters with Corinthian capitals these two interiors have in common similar entablatures.

The chapel, consecrated and dedicated to the Holy Trinity in 1708, represented an impressive profession of faith on the part of the king, who had lost his Polish kingdom at the time. During the second decade of the century the chapel was allotted only meager musical resources by Augustus, who went out of his way to play down his conversion so as to placate his subjects in overwhelmingly Lutheran Saxony. As Catholic choirboys were scarcely to be found in the electorate, a group of several was imported from neighboring Bohemia. Jesuit priests helped fill out the chorus.

With the return of the crown prince after an absence of eight years and his wedding to Maria Josepha, everything changed. One reason for his long years away in France, Italy, and Austria was to keep Saxony unaware of his secret. He too had converted to Catholicism, but this was concealed until he reached Austria in 1717 and the negotiations for the marriage had begun. By this time the Habsburg alliance began to look more attractive even to Protestant Saxony. It certainly facilitated all the goings and comings between Dresden and Warsaw inasmuch as the shortest route between them lay through imperial Silesia.

The 1720s mark a high point in the music of the royal chapel, now assigned Heinichen as its Kapellmeister with Zelenka as his assistant, along with ample choral and orchestral forces. One of the strong features of Heinichen's masses were his colorful uses of the orchestra. But Zelenka, a masterly contrapuntist and worthy pupil of Fux, came more and more to the fore during the illnesses that preceded Heinichen's early death in July 1729. In 1723 Zelenka had the honor of composing a serenata for the coronation of Charles VI at Prague as king of Bohemia, the occasion for which Fux wrote the main opera. Among several Dresden musicians in Prague for the event was the young Franz Benda, who sang as a boy soprano in the royal chapel and claimed in his charming autobiography that he was one of Heinichen's favorite singers.[31]

Zelenka was never fully appreciated in Dresden. Hired as a contrabass player at a low salary in 1711, he seems to have been stigmatized as a perennial subaltern. On 31 January 1712 he petitioned for leave to travel to Italy and France in order to perfect himself "in the solid church style" and in "bon goust," respectively.[32] Some of his earliest works show that he was still inept at composition and needed further training, but unfortunately for him he was not hired as a composer. It may not be a coincidence that the crown prince was sojourning where Zelenka wanted to go. As a Bohemian and a Catholic, Zelenka would quite naturally yearn for the south, and perhaps he meant by Italy's "solid church style" the Palestrina style. His petition was turned down.

Not until late 1715 did Zelenka get permission to travel, and he did so mostly at his own expense. His journey took him not to France or Italy but to Vienna, where he studied with Fux and compiled a large collection of church compositions that saw subsequent use in Dresden. Whether he joined the crown prince in Venice in 1716, along with other court musicians, is uncertain. Four of his five brilliant compositions entitled *Capricci,* for instrumental ensemble, were put at the service of the crown prince in Vienna in 1717–18. By the beginning of 1719 Zelenka was back in Dresden as a contrabass player. More and more of the work of composing and directing performances of church music in the royal chapel fell

---

[31]Daniel Heartz, "Coming of Age in Bohemia: The Musical Apprenticeships of Benda and Gluck," *Journal of Musicology* 6 (1988): 510–27.

[32]Horn, *Die Dresdner Hofkirchenmusik*, p. 55, and Janice B. Stockigt, *Jan Dismas Zelenka: A Bohemian Musician at the Court of Dresden* (Oxford, 2000), p. 36.

on his shoulders in the 1720s but he was not compensated accordingly. Even when he was named church composer in 1735 he received only 800 thalers annually. Heinichen was hired at 1,200 thalers twenty years earlier (Hasse received 6,000 thalers a year).

Zelenka entered a phase rich in new compositions, precisely dated, that lasted from 1730 until 1734. In 1733 he petitioned unsuccessfully for the title of Kapellmeister, which he was in fact with regard to the court chapel. Hasse had authority over all the court music but contributed little to the chapel during the 1730s and 1740s, although he did take a hand with the traditional Lenten oratorios, which may or may not have been performed in the chapel. In 1734 Hasse composed the oratorio *Il cantico de' tre fanciulli.* In the absence of Hasse and the court during the next two Lenten seasons it was Zelenka who composed the oratorios *Gèsu al Calvario* (1735) and *I penitente al sepolcro del Redentore* (1736). When the court and Hasse returned in 1737, Zelenka again took a secondary position. He died in 1745. Ristori, whose relations to the court chapel remain unclear, died in 1753. Neither composer wrote much during his last years. After Zelenka the chapel music came under the direction of Tobias Butz, Michael Breunich, and Johann Georg Schürer.

The Hasse style of Italian opera made inroads even upon sacred music in Dresden. Zelenka, for instance, in his *Missa Eucharistica* of 1733, breaks the Christe into tiny little phrases with pauses and gives the violins Lombard snaps and three-note slides (Example 4.7). Perhaps this attempt to out-Hasse Hasse himself is related to Zelenka's petition for advancement of the same year. Whatever the case, Zelenka had an imitator of his Hasse style in the person of Johann Gottlob Harrer, as may be seen from the Christe of his Mass in A (Example 4.8). The composer of this dainty, chopped-up melody served from 1731 to 1750 as music master to Count Brühl, the virtual ruler of Saxony under Frederick Augustus. Harrer is mainly remembered in music history as the successor to Bach as Thomaskantor in Leipzig, whose authorities turned down Emanuel Bach among others in favor of Harrer (after receiving Brühl's recommendation, which was little short of a peremptory command).

Zelenka's achievement includes many masses and mass movements of a more serious and contrapuntal nature than the Christe just quoted. He may have pioneered the practice of unifying big sections of the mass, especially the long texts of the Gloria and Credo, with pregnant orchestral motives. He preceded Hasse in this technique and probably had an influence on his superior and successor in this respect.[33] It fell to Zelenka to compose the requiem mass for Elector Augustus in 1733 because Hasse was in Venice.

[33]Walther Müller, *Johann Adolf Hasse als Kirchenkomponist: Ein Beitrag zur Geschichte der Neapolitanischen Kirchenmusik* (Leipzig, 1910), pp. 60–63.

EXAMPLE 4.7. *Zelenka*, Missa Eucharista, *Christe eleison*

EXAMPLE 4.8. *Harrer, Mass in A, Christe eleison*

A Lutheran court chapel also existed in the Residence. It was the place where Schütz had worked and must have received some resources as long as the wife of Augustus, Christiane Eberhardine of Brandenburg-Bayreuth, remained a staunch Protestant, which she did until her death in 1727. Johann Christoph Gottsched wrote the Trauer-Ode set by Bach (BWV 198) commemorating her. The marriage contract of her only son, Crown Prince Frederick, specified that all his children by Maria Josepha be raised as Catholics. Maria Josepha gave birth to no fewer than fifteen. The first two sons died young but the third, Frederick Christian, lived to reign (briefly) and to father children. There was obvious need for more space for the growing family of the ruling pair in the Residence. It was found by transforming the Lutheran chapel into living quarters, as symbolically charged an act as can be imagined. The imperial marriage made it legal for anyone to make an open profession of faith to the Church of Rome, which had not been the case before 1719. Increasing numbers of Dresden's citizens apparently did just that. The musical rewards of attending the court's Catholic chapel must have lured some. By midcentury this chapel was replaced by the magnificent Catholic Court Church on the banks of the Elbe.

A leading Lutheran composer in Dresden at the time was Bach's eldest son, Wilhelm Friedemann, organist of the Sophienkirche from 1733 to 1747. He is thought to have written most of his keyboard sonatas while holding this post.[34] The Sophienkirche, across the square upon which the opera house next to the Zwinger fronted, was second in importance only to the Frauenkirche among Protestant temples. Father Bach came from Leipzig to perform on its fine Silbermann organ of 1720 in September 1731, when he also witnessed Hasse's *Cleofide*.

Hasse's Zenith

The return of Prince Frederick Christian from Italy in September 1740 was fêted with a new production of *Artaserse,* for which Hasse revised his Venetian opera of ten years earlier, writing nine new arias, five of them for Faustina as Mandane (originally sung by Cuzzoni). A month later the new Prussian king, Frederick II, invaded Austrian Silesia in an attempt to seize the province from Maria Theresa, also newly come to the throne. In spite of all the guarantees to respect Maria Theresa's rights, there were schemes for overthrowing her in several quarters, even in Dresden, where Maria Josepha still aspired to the Habsburg succession. Count Brühl made the fateful decision to join the war on Frederick's side, helping

---

[34]For a discussion of these intriguing works, see William S. Newman, *Sonata in the Classic Era*, 3rd ed. (New York, 1983), pp. 394–402.

Prussia to conquer Silesia and thereby begin its march to status as a great power, achieved mainly at the expense of Saxony/Poland.

In January 1742 King Frederick entered Dresden to negotiate a treaty that would give him control of Silesia. According to legend the talks were ended abruptly so that the king could attend a performance of *Lucio Papirio*.[35] He must have known Hasse's music earlier, if only by way of former Dresden musicians like the Grauns and Quantz, now in his service. But this was his first experience of a complete opera performed under Hasse's direction, and it marked his musical tastes for the rest of his life, leading to the production of a long series of the composer's operas in Berlin right up to 1786, the year Frederick died.

A high point in Hasse's art was reached with his setting of *Didone abbandonata*, Metastasio's early masterpiece, first performed at Hubertusburg on 7 October 1742. For the title role, sung by Faustina, Hasse crafted several arias that spared the veteran singer's voice more than before. Her first aria, "Son regina e son amante," looks back to Vinci's setting (Example 2.5 on p. 90) in its choice of key and meter, also in melody (Example 4.9). Hasse, unlike Vinci, retains the three-measure module of the opening, then expands it to a four-measure one, followed by a five-measure unit. A moving bass in triple meter like the beginning invokes the minuet, which suits a text that is both noble and amorous (it is a couple dance). By leaping up a fourth for "regina" Hasse projects the queen's pride and energy at this point in the drama, before she learns for certain that Aeneas has resolved to leave her. Yet by the end of Act I she has become an uncomprehending and pitiful victim. Her aria, the penultimate one in the act, would become one of Hasse's most famous pieces.

Non ha ragione, ingrato!	No reason you say, ingrate!
un core abbandonato	has an abandoned heart
da chi giurogli fé?	by which you swore faith?
Anime innamorate,	Loving souls
se lo provaste mai,	if you have ever felt it,
ditelo voi per me.	say so for me.

Hasse chooses the key of g and a gentle duple meter, along with a quite simple declamation of the text (Example 4.10). The Lombard snaps increase the pathos, and the triplets add just enough vocal ornamentation. For the question posed twice, the voice rises and the music comes to a stop on the dominant chord, which is not resolved. Rather, the relative major arrives without preparation for the second tercet of the text. Perhaps Hasse originated the wistful mood associated so strongly with the key of g.

[35]Fürstenau, *Zur Geschichte der Musik und des Theaters*, p. 237.

EXAMPLE 4.9. *Hasse*, Didone abbandonata, *Aria*

EXAMPLE 4.10. *Hasse*, Didone abbandonata, *Aria*

Of all Hasse's operas *Didone* had the widest circulation after *Artaserse*. It even reached France. Under the auspices of the dauphine, Maria Josepha of Saxony, there was a performance of it at Versailles on 15 October 1753. It was surely Hasse's setting of "Non ha ragione" that Diderot referred to in his *Salon* of 1767 when criticizing a portrait of himself by Michel Van Lo.

By the Treaty of Breslau of July 1742 Austria ceded to Prussia upper and lower Silesia, retaining only a few small principalities on the border of Moravia. Frederick agreed to withdraw from the alliance against Austria, thus undercutting his French and Bavarian allies and allowing Austrian armies to chase them from Bohemia and Bavaria. Saxony gained nothing.

In the Second Silesian War of 1744–45 Saxony joined Austria in alliance against Prussia and France. Three days after the Prussians soundly defeated the Austrian and Saxon forces at Kesseldorf on 15 December 1745, Frederick entered Dresden as a conqueror. By his command *Arminio,* Hasse's latest opera, was given the next night. Hasse and Faustina were required to give chamber concerts for the king every night of his nine-day stay. By the Treaty of Dresden, signed on Christmas Day, Prussia retained its Silesian conquests and in return agreed to recognize Maria Theresa's husband, Francis of Lorraine, as Holy Roman emperor. Saxony was forced to pay Prussia an indemnity of one million rix-dollars.

Frederick Augustus, who had fled Dresden for Prague, returned on 4 January 1746. There was no opera in the court theater this carnival season, even though the Hasses were present. They did not leave for Venice until early summer.

The court soon showed that it could have an opera of sorts even without Hasse and Faustina. A Venetian impresario, Angelo Mingotti, requested and received permission to build a wooden theater near the Zwinger where he could stage operas in July and August. With a small company of his Italian singers, plus Joseph Schuster (father of the composer) borrowed from the royal cappella, he produced versions of Vinci's *Artaserse* and Hasse's *La clemenza di Tito.* Their majesties condescended to attend along with all their children. The general public could attend by paying for their seats, whereas in the court theater they received them gratis, but only upon invitation.[36] Dresden had its first commercial stage. The season must have been a success, because less than a year later Angelo's brother Pietro brought a similar troupe to the same theater for a more elaborate season.

In early 1747 the court hastened back to Dresden from Warsaw in order to witness the betrothal of Princess Maria Josepha to the dauphin, an occasion celebrated by a revised version of Hasse's *Semiramide riconosciuta* under the composer's direction, also by an opera in German, *Doris,* by Schürer. Then followed in June the double marriage of Frederick Christian with Maria Antonia Walpurgis of Bavaria, and of his sister Maria Anna with the Bavarian elector Maximilian Joseph III. The event could have come right out of a libretto by Metastasio, who was prone to mixing up sister-brother pairs, then sorting them out for a happy ending. The celebrations were capped by Hasse's *La Spartana generosa* on a libretto by

[36]Erich H. Müller, *Angelo und Pietro Mingotti: Ein Beitrag zur Geschichte der Oper im XVIII. Jahrhundert* (Dresden, 1917), pp. 52–55. Included are details about the theater's size and seat prices.

Giovanni Claudio Pasquini, who was appointed court poet in 1744 in succession to the deceased Pallavicino. *La Spartana,* given in the court theater, referred directly to Maria Antonia. She was about to play quite a role in cultural politics at the Saxon court.

That the Mingotti troupe in their temporary wooden theater were allowed to lead off the celebrations seems odd. They opened the season on May 25th in the presence of the entire ruling family with a performance of *Merope* set by Paolo Scalabrini, the troupe's music director. On 10 June they followed with a pasticcio *Didone,* then Scalabrini's *Demetrio* on 25 June. On 29 June the troupe gave Gluck's festival opera *Le nozze d'Ercole e d'Ebe* in a specially built open-air theater in the gardens of Pillnitz Palace upriver from Dresden. This is the earliest evidence that Gluck was connected with the Mingotti troupe, which he would subsequently follow to Hamburg and Copenhagen. For his labors in Dresden Gluck was rewarded with 412 thalers and 12 groschen. On the same list of 15 September Director Mingotti received 2,000 thalers; a young dancer from the Berlin court, Jean-Georges Noverre, received 140 thalers, while two dancers also destined for fame, Gaetano Vestris and his sister Teresia, received 100 thalers.[37] The star of the troupe beyond any doubt was the young wife of the director, soprano Regina Mingotti, who sang the role of Hercules in Gluck's opera. She was so successful the court hired her. By decree of 22 July 1747 Count Brühl ordered that she be put on the payroll at an annual salary of 2,000 thalers. The Mingottis brought to the stage as their final productions a pasticcio *Catone in Utica* with *Monsieur de Porsugnacco* as intermezzo.[38] Regina sang the role of Caesar in *Catone.*

One more composer who appeared on the scene in 1747 was Hasse's old rival Nicola Porpora. On 18 July Hasse directed a performance of *Filandro,* composed by Porpora for the court theater in celebration of Maria Antonia's twenty-third birthday. The prima donna was not Faustina but Regina Mingotti, who was a singing pupil of Porpora, as was Maria Antonia. Before this Hasse had directed only performances of his own operas (except for Pergolesi's *La serva padrona*) and the only prima donna who sang in them at Dresden was his wife. Hasse's pride must have been hurt. Not only did Maria Antonia hire Porpora and La Mingotti over his head, she also secured the title of maestro di capella for her singing teacher. In the new regime of Frederick Christian and Maria Antonia, it appeared that Hasse's supremacy would be in doubt.

For the carnival season of 1748 the court theater was enlarged and redecorated by Giuseppe Galli-Bibiena, who remained as the principal stage designer

[37]Ibid., pp. 68–72.

[38]Ibid., p. 72. Manuscript additions to the copy of the printed libretto in Dresden named the composers for most of the *Catone* pieces. The names ranged from Albinoni to Vinci and included Alberti (four arias and the final quartet), Fiorillo, Graun, Jommelli, Paradies, Scalabrini, Porpora, and Pergolesi. Surprisingly missing is Hasse, who set *Catone* for Turin in 1731. The manuscript additions are cited on pp. lxxv–lxxvi.

until 1753. *La Spartana* was revived to open the season and was followed by Hasse's setting of Metastasio's *Demofoonte,* in which both Bordoni and Mingotti sang. A quarrel erupted over who took precedence on the stage. Faustina sang the prima donna role of Dircea, a princess disguised as a handmaiden. Mingotti sang the seconda donna role of Creusa, a princess of lower rank but not in disguise. Such was the seriousness of the rivalry that Metastasio himself was consulted. He insisted in letters to Hasse, Pasquini, and Baron Diesskau, the court impresario, that Bordoni must indeed give precedence to Mingotti in the staging. Thus does the poet insist on the *vraisemblance* of his drama at the expense of the hierarchy among singers.

Meanwhile Maria Antonia was spreading her wings both as poetess and composer. She sent her verses to Metastasio, who had the temerity to rewrite them. As to her compositions, she apparently wrote the tunes to her verses and depended on Hasse to harmonize them. Metastasio had made a misstep, one of the few in his long life. Hasse was probably in jeopardy of making one too, no matter how he tried to stay in her good graces.[39]

The setbacks to Hasse turned out to be only temporary. If there was a crisis for him it was weathered. Porpora received his appointment on 13 April 1748 at an annual salary of 1,200 thalers, well below that of Hasse. Moreover, the court created, perhaps at Hasse's insistence, the title of Oberkapellmeister for him in 1750. Ristori became vice maestro. Porpora's salary stopped at the end of 1751, but he was given a pension of 400 thalers annually. He then moved on to Vienna. The pension ended in 1759 with the collapse of Saxony in the Seven Years War.

As Oberkapellmeister Hasse next bent his energies in a direction hitherto little explored. Chiaveri's Catholic court church on the banks of the Elbe was deemed ready for consecration in June 1751, although it was far from being completed. Hasse undertook the responsibility of writing the main music for the ceremony. The result is his impressive Mass in d and *Te Deum* in D. The Mass is really in D too, as might be expected on such a festive occasion. Only its Kyrie is in d, which makes the following Gloria seem all the more brilliant. It is heavily scored for an orchestra that included flutes, oboes, horns, trumpets, trombones, timpani, and probably bassoons as well. The four-part chorus is treated mostly in homophonic fashion, or as opposing duets between high and low, with many trumpet fanfares. Since the building, a long hall of stone, was extremely resonant there was no point in deploying contrapuntal skills or music of rapid harmonic change. Hasse's Gloria moves at a majestic gait with much surface activity but a slow harmonic rhythm. The orchestra unifies it by repeating an ostinato motif from the very beginning. A slight bow to tradition is made by setting the final words, "Cum sancto spiritu," fugally. It is a fugue that quickly dissolves after all four voices are

[39]Frederick Millner, *The Operas of Johann Adolf Hasse* (Ann Arbor, Mich., 1974), p. 23.

in, and the subject includes one chromatic rise that sounds more galant than traditional. The Credo also has a recurring motto in the orchestra that ties it together. For the Crucifixus Hasse follows tradition by invoking a chromatic descending bass line. The orchestra and chorus make the most of the fullness invoked by "Pleni sunt coeli" in the Sanctus. The Agnus Dei begins in a more intimate fashion. After a seven-measure ritornello a contralto solo begins the plea accompanied by strings, the first violins mostly doubling the voice an octave above (Example 4.11). Note that the habit of **a b b'** phrasing, acquired in operatic arias, pertains here as well. Typical of the composer is the way the half-cadence at the end of this excerpt arrives by way of a vii^7 of V chord that makes for a cross-relation between the G in the melody and the G♯ in the bass.

EXAMPLE 4.11. *Hasse, Mass (1751)*

Hasse's consecration mass for the new court church became a classic in Dresden that has been performed regularly to the present day. The same is true of the *Te Deum* written for the same occasion, which seems to take even more account of the building's echo, perhaps an indication that Hasse composed it after the mass and the experience of rehearsing in the hall. Hasse divides the long text of the *Te Deum* into three parts, two vigorous choruses in common time surrounding an elegiac aria for soprano in 3/4 at the words "Salvum fac." This meditative aria accompanied only by strings and continuo represents Hasse at his most mellifluous, with a smooth vocal line spanning two octaves. It eschews the da capo form of the opera aria for a large binary form concluded by a cadenza for the soloist. The two *Allegros* abound in brilliant fanfares, running scales, and unison passages for the orchestra, deployed so as to make the church's lengthy reverberation an advantage rather than a liability. Most impressive is the way Hasse unifies these long sections by an orchestral motto, stated over and over on various degrees. It is an upbeat figure taken from the very beginning (Example 4.12). In his mastery of this technique Hasse adumbrates its use by Viennese composers of following generations.

Hasse's *Te Deum* for the consecration of the court church provoked various critical reactions. Reichardt, after hearing a performance, wrote that he found Carl

EXAMPLE 4.12. *Hasse*, Te Deum

Heinrich Graun's setting of the text had more flowing harmonies and Handel's was more ingenious still (he means the work written to celebrate English victory at Dettingen, Bavaria, in 1743), but Hasse's made more effect than either.[40] One modern critic tried to explain why this might be so.

> To the whole work, which reaches the greatest effect by the simplest, yet genially handled means, clings something robustly folk-like. It is one thoroughly proper and worthy piece of church music, even if mixed with profane elements. From it speaks a free spirit and a joyful, eager faith, unfettered by dogma. It is the expression of conviction not only of its composer, but of the electoral court that has rendered it such continued favor.[41]

A more recent critic hints at the nature of the "profane" element by suggesting that the opening motto, the one that permeates the whole, is buffo in spirit, and comparing it with the octave leaps and repeated tones at the beginning of Pergolesi's *La serva padrona*.[42] Acoustics alone in the court church would prevent the motto from sounding comic.

Another debate has swirled around the building for which Hasse wrote his consecration mass and *Te Deum*. Reichardt already complained about the acoustics in the passage cited. Burney concurred. In the early nineteenth century Carl Maria von Weber advised a composer how to write for such a space.

> As far as your own composition is concerned, remember that our church is very large and excessively resonant; small figures are unclear, and longer appoggiaturas eat up a short main note. The music of Cherubini and Beethoven, for instance, of the kind that modulates quickly, with fast changes of harmony and where the voices are reduced in numbers, would sound in our circumstances like howling cats. Great broad figures, everything massed, but also the broad tones of wind instruments are very effective on the other hand.[43]

[40]Johann Friedrich Reichardt, *Briefe eines aufmerksamen Reisenden die Musik betreffend*, 2 vols. (vol. 1, Frankfurt and Leipzig, 1774; vol. 2, Frankfurt and Breslau, 1776), 2: 118.

[41]Müller, *Johann Adolf Hasse als Kirchenkomponist*, p. 109.

[42]Reinhard Wiesend, "Hasse und Mozart—ein ungleiches Paar?" *Hasse-Studien* 2 (1993): 5–27; 20.

[43]Letter of 26 December 1822 to Johann Gänsbacher, cited in Müller, *Johann Adolf Hasse als Kirchenkomponist*, pp. 42–43.

Abbé Vogler made a similar point when comparing the music of Hasse, which worked in large resonant halls, with that of Jommelli, which did not.[44] Gerber in his article on Hasse says that Gottfried August Homilius, a pupil of Bach's who became organist and later music director of the Frauenkirche in Dresden, often complained about the emptiness of Hasse's textures; but Gerber disagreed.

> Homilius should have remembered that Hasse, working with large spaces and a big orchestra, achieved with this empty texture a clarity in his composition that had far more effect on the listener, than the richest harmonies could have done. Moreover, it was not lack of knowledge in the science of harmony that accounted for this. He was sparing with his resources according to the place and the result he wanted to achieve. Then they also achieved wonders.[45]

Hasse's parsimonious textures found an even more convincing defender. When Burney visited Hamburg in October 1772 he conversed at length with Emanuel Bach, who at one point expressed his disdain for canons and maintained that many other things were necessary to make a good composer after counterpoint had been mastered.

> He said, he once wrote word to Hasse, that he was the greatest cheat in the world; for in a score of twenty *nominal* parts, he had seldom more than three *real* ones in action; but with these he produced such divine effects, as must never be expected from a crowded score; upon this occasion I observed, that as it is the part of a wise man in conversation, to wait for an opportunity of saying something to the purpose before he speaks; so a good composer should do in writing accompaniments. . . . to this he entirely assented.

Of course this may be Burney putting words in Emanuel Bach's mouth. Alas, no letters from Bach to Hasse survive.[46]

The early 1750s are reckoned as the high point of Hasse's reign over opera in Dresden and the apogee of the Saxon court. A visitor of 1753, Casanova, wrote, "I saw in Dresden the most brilliant court in Europe, and the arts which flourished at it."[47] Hasse grew from his early stage of being quite independent of Metastasio to relying more and more on an exact treatment of the Caesarean poet's every word. The case of *Attilio Regolo* well illustrates this. Metastasio wrote it for the

[44]Georg Joseph Vogler, *Betrachtungen der Mannheimer Tonschule,* 4 vols. (Mannheim, 1778–81; reprint 1974), 1: 164.

[45]Ernst Ludwig Gerber, *Historisch-biographisches Lexikon der Tonkünstler,* 2 vols. (Leipzig, 1790; reprint 1966).

[46]Those that have been preserved are gathered in *The Letters of C. P. E. Bach,* translated from the German and edited by Stephen L. Clark (Oxford, 1997).

[47]Giacomo Casanova, Chevalier de Seingalt, *History of My Life,* trans. Willard R. Trask, 12 vols. in 6 (New York, 1966–68; reprint 1997), 3:218.

name day celebration of Emperor Charles VI in 1740, who did not live to see Saint Charles Day on November 4th. In deference to the deceased monarch the libretto was set aside for a decade and not given to any composer until Hasse made the first setting for the carnival of 1750 in Dresden. Metastasio by this time was so close to Hasse that he wrote a long letter advising him how to treat the characters and the text, even specifying which words deserved treatment in obbligato recitative (they were very few).[48] Hasse meekly followed the poet's advice, almost down to the last detail. The opera had its premiere on 12 January 1750, sung by the brilliant cast of Faustina, Mingotti, Annibali, the tenor Angelo Amorevoli, Negri, Schuster, and Rochetti. To this company the soprano castrato Felice Salimbene was added for the following carnival. Dismissed at Berlin, where he earned 3,000 thalers a year, he was hired at an annual salary of 4,000 thalers. Salimbene made his debut on 7 January 1751 in the title role of Pasquini's *Leucippo,* a revival for which Hasse wrote all arias anew for him. Salimbene's triumph was short-lived for he died later the same year. Carestini, who was allowed to leave Dresden upon Salimbene's arrival, now replaced him in Berlin. Once again, and just as in the political arena, King Frederick outmaneuvered Elector Frederick Augustus.

The second opera of the 1751 carnival season was Metastasio's *Ciro riconosciuto* set by Hasse. Faustina and Salimbene appeared on stage for the last time in this production. After singing in Hasse's oratorio *I pellegrini al sepolcro* on Good Friday, Faustina retired, but kept her title of *virtuosa di camera* and her salary of 3,000 thalers annually in lieu of a pension. The following carnival of 1752 opened with Hasse's new setting of Metastasio's *Adriano in Siria,* with Mingotti singing the prima donna role of Emirena. She was released without a pension on 31 July 1752. Teresa Albuzzi, who was probably Count Brühl's mistress, was promoted to take her place. There were other changes as well. Angelo Maria Monticelli replaced Annibali. Giovanni Ambrogio Migliavacca replaced Pasquini as court poet. His *Solimano,* a work calling for elaborate stage spectacles, was set by Hasse and provided the second opera of the 1753 carnival, the first being a revival of Hasse's *Arminio* (poem by Pasquini). In March Hasse visited the court of Berlin, where he attended a performance of Graun's *Silla* and a revival of his own *Didone.* He received a snuffbox and ring as a gift from King Frederick. If there was also an attempt to lure him into Prussian service, it did not succeed. The carnival of 1754 opened with a revival of *Solimano,* followed by Hasse's setting of Migliavacca's *Artemisia.* In the summer the traveling company of Giovanni Battista Locatelli gave comic operas by Galuppi and a birthday piece for Maria Antonia on 18 July with music by Johann Georg Schürer. An imposing portrait of Hasse dates from about this time (Figure 4.9).

[48]Pietro Metastasio, *Tutte le Opere,* ed. Bruno Brunelli, 5 vols. (Milan, 1943–44), 3: 427–36. Letter dated Joslowitz [Moravia], 20 October 1749.

FIGURE 4.9. Pietro Rotari. Portrait of Hasse, engraved by Lorenzo Zucchi.

Precise information on the opera orchestra in 1754 reached Rousseau by way of his friend Melchior Grimm. Rousseau wrote in his *Dictionnaire de musique* (1767) "the greatest orchestra in Europe, as far as the number and intelligence of its performers is concerned, is that of Naples; but that which is best distributed and forms the most nearly perfect ensemble is the opera orchestra of the King of Poland at Dresden, directed by the famous Hasse" (Figure 4.10). An illustration shows two harpsichords, with Hasse's in the middle, continuo cello and bass behind both. In the two rows of violins facing each other there are eight firsts and seven seconds, between them four violas. To the left of Hasse were the winds: two flutes, two horns, five oboes, and five bassoons. Tribunes for trumpets and timpani flanked the orchestra on both sides.

The usual orchestral disposition in large Italian opera houses placed the two harpsichords at either end of the orchestral space, close to the stage, as illustrated

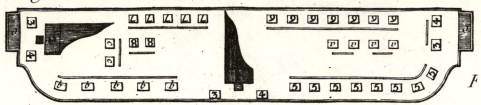

Distribution de l'Orchestre de l'Opera de Dresde,

Fig.1.   *Dirigé par le S.ͬ Hasse.*

Renvois des Chiffres.

1. *Clavecin du Maître de Chapelle*
2. *Clavecin d'accompagnement*
3. *Violoncelles.*
4. *Contre – basses.*
5. *Premiers Violons*
6. *Second Violons, ayans le dos tourné vers de Théatre.*

7. *Haubois, de même.*
8. *Flutes, de même.*
a. *Tailles, de même.*
b. *Bassons.*
c. *Cors de Chasse.*
d. *Une Tribune de Chaque côté pour les Tymballes et Trompettes.*

FIGURE 4.10. Seating plan of the Dresden orchestra from Rousseau's *Dictionnaire de musique.*

in the well-known painting of Pietro Olivero depicting the Teatro Regio at Turin upon its opening in 1740.[49] This allowed the harpsichords and their backup continuo players to provide an even harmonic support along the front of the stage, especially important to the singers during their long passages of simple recitative. But it placed the orchestra's director, seated at one of the harpsichords, at some distance from the center. By moving one harpsichord to the center and pointing it toward the stage, Hasse placed himself at a command post where all eyes could easily see him, whether in the orchestra or on stage (and throughout the house for that matter). He thus approximated the system used in French opera, in which the director, centrally placed, led the performance with a baton, as Rameau is depicted doing.[50] Hasse's orchestra is least modern in its proliferation of oboes and bassoons. Presumably all of them were used together only sparingly, in the

[49]Reproduced in Hellmuth Christian Wolff, *Oper Szene und Darstellung von 1600 bis 1900* (Musikgeschichte in Bildern, IV/1) (Leipzig, 1968), plate 83.

[50]At a performance of *La Princesse de Navarre* at Versailles in 1745. Drawing and engraving by C. N. Cochin fils, reproduced in François Lesure, *L'opéra classique français, XVIIᵉ et XVIIIᵉ Siècles* (Geneva, 1972), plates 3–4.

overture or other ripieno pieces, for instance, or in some ritornello passage in arias when the solo voices were not singing. Their reinforcement of the treble and the bass offers further comment on the subject of Hasse's "empty" textures.

Quantz, who played under Hasse's direction at Dresden before moving to Berlin in 1741, described an orchestral disposition for opera in his *Versuch* (1752) that is close to Rousseau's illustration.[51] He has the two harpsichords in the same position, and behind the first he places a cello and a bass, behind the second, two cellos. He also places the strings on the right and the winds on the left. He recommends that the leader of the first violins, the maestro di concerto, sit next to the maestro di cappella at the first harpsichord, and that his seat be slightly forward and elevated with respect to the other first violins to his right. There are differences in the orchestral forces between Quantz and Rousseau, but the overall picture is so similar that Quantz offers a confirmation for what Rousseau illustrates. Berlin followed the lead of Hasse and Dresden in this matter, as in nearly all musical matters.

In 1755 the court returned to Dresden in time for the carnival. *Artemisia* was revived on 7 January and the new opera on 20 January was Hasse's second setting of Metastasio's *Ezio*. Thus a pattern emerged in which the first opera, needing the least rehearsal, was a revival. A new opera came later. *Ezio* was staged with even greater spectacle than had been accorded the spectacular *Solimano*. It closed with a ballet choreographed by Antoine Pitrot to music of Schürer that lasted for forty-five minutes. Another pattern in the court's operatic activities was the celebration of the king's birthday on 7 October with a new opera staged in Hubertusburg, a country palace near Dresden where the main pastime was hunting. In 1755 the event was celebrated by Hasse's setting of Metastasio's *Il rè pastore*. This opera was repeated to open the following carnival season on 7 January, along with Hasse's *Ezio*. The new opera, on 16 February 1756, was Hasse's setting of Metastasio's *L'Olimpiade*. Summer again brought Locatelli's opera buffa troupe performing a Venetian comic repertory.

In 1755 Pietro Moretti constructed a small theater between the Elbe and the Zwinger that subsequently bore his name. He leased it to itinerant companies such as Locatelli's. It seated only 350 and was later acquired and rebuilt by the court as the Kleines Kurfürstliches Theater.

The memory of Hasse, his music and music making, lingered long in Dresden. Prince Beloselski, ambassador from Russia to the Saxon court when Burney visited Dresden in the fall of 1772, had his *De la musique en Italie* published at The Hague in 1778. In it he rated Hasse as the first among German composers and the equal of the best Italians. To him Hasse's greatest operas were three on Metas-

---

[51]Johann Joachim Quantz, *On Playing the Flute,* trans. Edward R. Reilly (New York, 1966), pp. 211–12. For further on Hasse's orchestra in Dresden at various times, see Mennicke, *Hasse und die Brüder Graun,* pp. 270–71.

tasian librettos: *Ipermestra* (1744), *Antigono* (1743), and *Il rè pastore* (1755). Apparently he was able to study scores of these at Dresden. The last-named well suited Hasse's strengths at the end of his Dresden years, for it and *L'Olimpiade* were cast by Metastasio in a more pastoral than heroic vein. Hasse was rarely the fiery dramatist he had been when setting *Artaserse* for Venice in 1730. Rather, he had become the docile follower of the Caesarean poet, a partner bent on capitalizing on his greatest musical strength, which was as a melodist and unsurpassed clothier of the human voice.

Dresden's Nadir

Court routine was about to be rudely interrupted in the fall of 1756. Hasse had already begun rehearsals in the late summer for the birthday opera on 7 October, which was to have been another setting of *Leucippo*. On 29 August a Prussian army led by King Frederick himself marched into Saxony in a surprise attack. Dresden was occupied on 10 September. The Saxon army, outmaneuvered and outnumbered, withdrew to the plateau above Pirna. Its Austrian allies were also surprised and unprepared. Frederick bypassed the Saxon army and marched into Bohemia. He defeated the Austrians in the battle of Lobositz, a victory that sealed the fate of Saxony. After a few attempts to escape their entrenchments near Pirna, the Saxon army surrendered on 14 October and was promptly impressed into Prussian service. Frederick August and Brühl fled to Poland, where they remained for the duration of the extremely destructive Seven Years War (1756–63). Its consequences for Dresden will emerge from Burney's accounts below.

King Frederick commandeered Brühl's palace on the Elbe as his temporary residence. He showed deference to Hasse and Faustina, who were invited to supervise sessions of music making there. He allowed them to return to Italy in December after Franz Benda and other chamber musicians called from Potsdam arrived to serve their master. Hasse's departure was not without stress, as we learn from a letter he sent from Venice on 3 September 1757 to Count Algarotti, who had requested Hasse's music to the *licenza* the poet had added to Metastasio's *Didone abbandonata* (1742). Hasse apologized for not being able to send it as he no longer had either the words or the music because he had abandoned his papers "during the high state of confusion in which he departed Dresden."[52] At this time Hasse anticipated being able to return to Dresden soon, but he did not do so as far as we know. About twenty of his operas in autograph somehow made

---

[52] *Johann Adolf Hasse e Giammaria Ortes: Lettere (1760–1783)*, ed. Livia Pancino (Speculum Musicum IV) (Turnhout, 1998), p. 354.

their way to safety before Hasse's house in Dresden was destroyed in the bombardment of 1760.

The electoral family of Saxony was dispersed because of the war. Prince Frederick Christian and Maria Antonia took refuge at Munich (Bavaria managed to stay neutral). Electress Maria Josepha remained with some of her younger children in Dresden. She died in 1757. Schürer, who also remained and was director of music in the court church, wrote the requiem mass that mourned this patroness of music.

Saxony continued to be a major theater of the war, along with Silesia and Bohemia. After a defeat by the Austrians and Russians at Kunersdorf in August 1759, Frederick retreated. Dresden fell to the Austrians on 4 September 1759. Returning the following summer Frederick besieged and bombarded Dresden, partly destroying it. Both sides were exhausted after the indecisive battle of Torgau in November 1760, the last great conflict of the land war. Russia withdrew from the anti-Prussian coalition, leaving only France among the great powers as Austria's ally, a France humbled and beaten by the British in the colonial and naval battles that raged around the globe. Both the Prussian army and the imperial army led by the Austrians were weakened to the point of impuissance. Peace negotiations dragged on until the final terms were adjusted on the *status quo ante* basis and signed at Hubertusburg on 15 February 1763. In other words, Prussia retained Silesia, which was lost to Austria forever.

The country that lost the most, aside from France, was Saxony, where the war had brought an appalling loss of lives in both civilian and military categories, as well as financial catastrophe. Its coinage debased, its trade ruined, Saxony was in a state of chaos that called for strong measures of order and reform.

The court of Frederick August in Warsaw forewent none of the pleasures of opera during the war and continued to mount Hasse's operas, some of them new, at enormous expense. Hasse himself, who had settled in Vienna with his family, probably went to Warsaw to direct the carnival operas of 1762 and 1763. The court returned to Dresden on 2 April 1763. Prince Frederick Christian and Maria Antonia had returned the previous spring, when it is possible that Hasse visited Dresden as well. He certainly returned in the spring of 1763. His destroyed residence had housed a collection of his manuscripts that had been prepared for publication by Breitkopf. Much of the court's collection of manuscripts had also not survived the bombing, including many Schütz autographs. In spite of the ruinous conditions the court decided to carry on as if the war had not happened. A decision was made to restore the great theater next to the Zwinger, which had been used as a storeroom by the Prussians. Here on 3 August 1763 Hasse's *Siroe* was mounted with the customary pomp. Few singers were left from the prewar troupe but new ones were brought in. Pisendel had died in 1755 and the orchestra had suffered subsequently, going without pay for the most part. Clearly, the elector was determined to make a show of it, to *far bella figura* on his terms, which meant mounting an old-style opera seria, in spite of all the obstacles and the ruin of his country. The folly of this act of pride and arrogance is matched by King Frederick's beginning the Neues Palais at Potsdam in spite of his empty treasury.

Hasse busied himself with readying a production of *Leucippo* for the birthday of Frederick August on 7 October. It was to be performed by members of the electoral family, including Maria Antonia. Just as in 1756 events intervened to cancel his plans. On the day of the dress rehearsal, 5 October, the elector died of a stroke. Brühl, dismissed and in disgrace, died 23 days later. The connection with Poland was at an end.

The great period of court opera in Dresden, led by Hasse and Pisendel, had in fact ended in the mid-1750s (Pisendel's death in 1755 was critical). The strange postlude of 1763 was no more than that, and was not to be repeated. Hasse composed no more operas for Dresden. In his obituary on Hasse in 1784, Carl Friedrich Cramer wrote, "he, with his wife Faustina, was the father and pride of the most glorious stage of Europe that was Dresden." That glorious stage in the following years was reduced to the Kleines Kurfürstliches Theater, supported in part by the court and in part by the public. The new elector, Frederick Christian, decided on the massive economies that were needed to begin reconstruction and brought in a group of ministers of his own determined to effect them. Hasse and Faustina were released without pensions. Out of respect for the dead king, whom he had served for over thirty years, Hasse composed the Requiem in C, one of his finest church works, and directed its performance in the court church on 22 November 1763. Within a month there was another loss to be mourned. Frederick Christian died on 17 December after an attack of smallpox. Hasse remained in Dresden longer than he planned, although he had been dismissed, in order to direct funeral services. He left Dresden having received 1,000 thalers for his expenses and the title of "honorary electoral Oberkapellmeister," which brought him no remuneration. On 20 February 1764 he and Faustina left for Vienna, where his services remained in demand.

Elector Frederick August III, the eldest son of Frederick Christian and Maria Antonia, was a boy of thirteen when he acceded to the throne. His uncle Prince Xavier was appointed guardian and set about healing the country's wounds with the help of the reform-minded ministers appointed by his father. The elector assumed the government in 1768 and during his long reign earned the respect of his subjects, who eventually bestowed upon him the title Augustus the Just. In 1791 he declined the proffered crown of Poland. The reduced musical life of his chastened court is described by Burney.

Burney Visits Dresden

Nine years after the decisive changes of regime in the fall of 1763 Burney visited war-ravaged Saxony. Coming from Bohemia, he traveled by carriage along the Elbe, stopping at Pirna briefly, then arriving at Dresden. On Friday 12 September 1772 he entered the city via the gardens of the Zwinger, which he called a "beautiful *Chateau*, or Villa, and pavilions, in a very good taste." That he was struck by the beauty of Pöppelmann's masterpiece half a century after it was built says something about the catholicity of his taste. In an era when severe neoclassical style was increasingly in vogue, some decried the ornate whimsies of the Zwinger, variously described by art historians as late baroque, rococo, or a mixture of both.

Not much could be rebuilt in the decade since the end of the war, Burney reported.

> The city itself has suffered so much in the last war, that it is difficult for a stranger to imagine himself near the celebrated capital of Saxony, even when he sees it from the most favourable eminence in the neighborhood, so few of its once many cloud-capt towers are left standing; only two or three remain intire, of all the stately edifices which formerly embellished this city: so that here, as well as at Prague, the inhabitants are still repairing the ravages of the Prussians; of whom it is remarkable, that though during the last war, they ruined many a noble city, they never took one by siege. They were in possession of Dresden three years: it was taken from them during the absence of the king of Prussia, by the prince of Deux-ponts, who commanded the army of the empire. In 1760, that monarch invested it again, and did incredible damage by his batteries, and bombardments, till it was relieved by general Lacy.

Among the hardest hit was the Kreuzkirche on the Altmarkt. Bernardo Bellotto painted a picture of the ruins in 1765.

Burney went at once to the English ambassador, Mr. Osborn, who welcomed him warmly and put him in touch with a musician whom Burney calls "Signor Bezozzi, the celebrated haubois player, in the service of this court." Antonio Besozzi and his son Carlo were both oboists in Saxon service at this time; Burney met the younger. On Saturday Osborn took Burney to a dinner with several other ambassadors and then to the prime minister, Count Sachen, who resided in the Brühl palace, where they waited until it was time to go to the opera. It was performed in the Kleines Kurfürstliches Theater in the presence of the electoral family. Burney was unusually critical of both the music and its performance. The work was not a local product but Antonio Salieri's second comedy for Vienna (1770) on a libretto by G. G. Boccherini.

> It was only a burletta, that was performed tonight in the little theatre, which is small, but neat; it has four rows of boxes, nineteen in each. *L'Amore innocente* was the name

of the piece, of which Signor Salieri was the composer. The music was as innocent of design, as the drama and performance: nothing in the least seducing or inflammatory was to be heard or seen; but all was tranquil, unmeaning, and as truly soporific as a nurse's lullaby. The best signer in this placid pastoral was Signora Calori. . . . Her performance passed as unnoticed as that of the rest, which was insipid to a very tiresome degree. I must mention, however, that in the second act of this opera, Signora Calori sung a long *bravura* song, accompanied on the violin, *obligato,* by M. Hunt, the principal violinist of this place, in which both these performers executed many great difficulties with little effect. He has indeed a very strong hand, and clear tone; but neither his taste nor expression are of the most delicate or touching kind.

How standards had fallen since the heyday of Hasse, Faustina, and Pisendel.

Burney's most intense musical experience in Dresden, surprising as it may seem, was the singing of chorales by the entire congregation in the Frauenkirche.

Sunday, 20th September. I went this morning to the *Frauen Kirche,* or great Lutheran church of our Lady, placed on the side of a spacious square; it is a very noble and elegant building, of white stone, with a high dome in the middle; this church is square without, but formed into an amphitheatre within. There is a projection for the communion table, over which is placed a most magnificent organ. This is the only instance I can recollect, of an organ placed at the *east* end of a church. I had hitherto only seen it at the west window, at the west end of the choir, or on one side. The singing here, with so fine an instrument, has a very striking effect. The whole congregation, consisting of near three thousand persons, sing in unison, melodies almost as slow as those used in our parish churches; but the people being better musicians here than with us, and accustomed from their infancy to sing the chief part of the service, were better in tune, and formed one of the grandest choruses I ever heard.

Gottfried Silbermann built the great organ in the Frauenkirche from 1732 to 1736. It was an instrument of three manuals and forty-three stops. Bach played it in the presence of the court on 1 December 1736. This magnificent church, built in 1726–43, withstood various dangers until the aerial raids on Dresden in February 1945. Two days after the bombing, the great stone building collapsed. Reconstruction using some of the original stones began only in the 1990s, supported with private money raised in a worldwide campaign. As a symbol of Dresden nothing excels it. King Frederick must have thought so too, as Burney implies.

The King of Prussia, in his last bombardment of Dresden, tried every means in his power to beat this church, as well as the other public buildings, about the ears of the inhabitants, but in vain, for the orbicular form of the dome threw off the balls and shells, and totally prevented their effect; however, he succeeded better in five or six other churches, which he totally demolished. This of our Lady constitutes the great feature of the city, like St. Peter's at Rome, and St. Paul's in London.

Burney was too late to hear the main service in the Catholic court church after his morning in the Frauenkirche. He did step into it on his way to the Residence and described it as "a new, large, and elegant building, adorned with several capital paintings, by Mengs, and Battoni."

Ambassador Osborn presented Burney to the elector at a reception attended by the various foreign ambassadors, one of whom, representing Russia, was young Prince Alexander Beloselsky. Then in another apartment of the Residence he was presented to the electress, who was a daughter of the prince of Deux-ponts who recaptured Dresden from the Prussians in 1759. The marriage of the nineteen-year-old elector in 1769 to the seventeen-year-old princess was the one occasion for which the court underwent the expense of reopening the great opera house attached to the Zwinger.

Having described the several members of the electoral family, then remarking that there was not much in the way of music to write about, Burney indulged his passion for visual art by writing a long guide to the picture gallery, which he called the largest and best in Europe. It was founded by Augustus, he says, and greatly enhanced by his son, who bought the duke of Modena's entire collection in 1745 and a large imperial collection housed at Prague in 1748. Burney's guide is still valuable, especially his remarks on the state of preservation of individual pictures. He noted in particular the rich collection of pastel portraits, still one of the great treasures of the Semper Gallery in Dresden, where they are accorded an entire room of their own.

> In the cabinet of crayon paintings, there are no less than a hundred and fifty-seven portraits by Rosalba, among which is that of Faustina, when young, and in the service of this court. She was very handsome when this was painted, or was very much flattered; there is likewise in this cabinet, a portrait, by Mengs, of Mingotti, when young, with a music paper in her hand; and if the resemblance was exact, she was then nearer a beauty, than it is now easy to imagine her ever to have been; she is here painted in youth, plumpness, and with a very expressive countenance.

Rosalba Carriera portrayed Faustina at Venice in 1724, well before her Dresden service, and did so with a sensuality that makes her look like a cross between a schoolgirl and the goddess Flora (Plate V).[53] Her disheveled hair, with flowers in it, conveys a certain nonchalance or *disprezzatura*. Female performers at the Pietà in Venice, where Faustina was once a student, were known for putting flowers in their hair to increase their attractiveness, but they certainly did not display the revealing décolletage when performing that Rosalba gives Faustina. Anton Mengs portrayed Regina Mingotti around 1750, during her Dresden stay (Plate VI). She

[53]Bernardina Sani, *Rosalba Carriera* (Turin, 1988), p. 298.

appears quite majestic, richly bejeweled as well as florally bedecked. Both portraits represent rococo art at its height. According to the latest evidence Faustina was born on 30 March 1697. The artist noted in her diary that she began the portrait of Faustina on 11 March 1724.

On Monday, at the English embassy, a special concert organized by Besozzi was put on for Burney's benefit. As Burney described it the program consisted of two parts, each begun by a symphony.

Part One.   A symphony [i.e., overture] of Hasse
           A solo on the violin by Tartini played by M. Hunt
           A German flute concerto played by M. Götsel
           An oboe concerto played by Signor Besozzi
Part Two.   A symphony by Vanhall
           A solo by Nardini played by Mr. Hunt
           Another concerto on the German flute played by M. Götsel
           A new oboe concerto performed by Signor Besozzi,
           who was prevailed upon to play, as an encore,
           "Fischer's well-known rondeau minuet."

Notable as a comment on the decline of Dresden is the use of old music (Hasse and Tartini), music from elsewhere (Nardini and Fischer), and music by Viennese composers (Vanhal here, and Salieri in the small opera house). Of the four concertos performed, only the second oboe concerto played by Besozzi qualified as "new."

The next day Burney went to the Frauenkirche to examine the Silbermann organ and hear it put through its paces by that church's organist, a man named M. Hunger.

From hence I went to the great theatre, where the serious opera used to be exhibited. It was built in 1706 [*recte:* 1717–19] by Augustus the second; but was afterwards decorated, and the stage much enlarged, by Augustus the third. I was extremely curious to see this celebrated scene of action, where *general Hasse,* and his well-disciplined troops, had made so many glorious campaigns, and acquired such laurels; all his best works having been expressly composed, as some of Metastasio's dramas were written, for its use. No money was ever taken for admission into this theatre, which is nearly as large as that at Milan. It has five rows of boxes, thirty in each, is in an oval form, like the theatres of Italy, and has an orchestra capable of containing a hundred performers. . . . At present, this theatre is shut up, for oeconomical reasons, no use having been made of it since the marriage of the present Elector, three years ago; at which time two operas were performed in it, one set by Hasse, and another by Naumann, the present chapel master of this court. The opera house being in the neighborhood of the picture gallery, I could not resist the desire of entering it again.

The opera by Hasse was a revival, not a new work. Johann Gottlieb Naumann, who held the title of chamber composer until he became maestro di cappella in 1776, composed Metastasio's *La clemenza di Tito* for the wedding festival. Burney errs on one point: Metastasio's only opera written expressly for the Saxon court was *Antigono.*

Other topics explored by Burney include the Silbermann organ in the court church, demonstrated for him by court organist Christlieb Binder, the church itself ("so great is the echo, and long the continuance of the sound in this building, particularly when empty, that no melody can be heard distinctly"), and the pantaleon, which Binder had studied with its inventor, Pantaleon Hebenstreit. Burney later went to Binder's house to see the original pantaleon, which was in an unplayable state because the cost of restringing it was more than the court would pay. This lamentable situation led Burney to draw some general conclusions on the poverty and ruin of the once-proud capital.

> Dresden is at present a melancholy residence; from being the seat of the Muses, and habitation of pleasure, it is now only a dwelling for beggary, theft, and wretchedness. No society among the natives can be supported; all must retrench; the court is obliged to abandon genius and talents, and is, in turn, abandoned by them! Except the wretched comic opera, there is not one spectacle, but that of misery, to be seen at Dresden; no *guinguette,* no public diversion in the city or suburbs for the people, and not a boat or vessel either of pleasure or business can be descried on the river Elbe, which is here nearly as wide as the Thames at London bridge.

By *guinguette* Burney means a public pleasure garden, such as Vauxhall or Ranelagh in London.

Burney concludes his section on Dresden with a disquisition on the singing boys in the streets, who hired out their services for various purposes such as weddings, funerals, and serenades. They originated before the Reformation he says, when all the churches had excellent boy choirs. The people of Dresden were gradually brought around to embrace Lutheranism, which they originally rejected, by the singing boys. Burney got his information on the boys by letter from Osborn, although he does not say so.[54]

On 24 September Burney left Dresden, traveling all night in an open wagon to Leipzig, Saxony's second city, which had also suffered occupation and depredations during the war. Here his main guide was Johann Adam Hiller, whose courtesies won Burney's praises. Hiller was another pupil of the Kreuzschule in Dresden, where the Grauns were trained before him and Naumann after him. His main teacher was Homilius, but his great idol was, and always remained, Hasse.

---

[54]Kerry S. Grant, *Dr. Burney as Critic and Historian of Music* (Ann Arbor, Mich., 1983), p. 321, n. 106.

The day of his arrival Hiller took Burney to the comic opera, which happened to be Monsigny's *Le déserteur* (mistakenly called Grétry's) performed in German by a visiting troupe from Berlin: "the performers did not charm me, either by their singing or acting; all were out of tune, out of time, and vulgar." Besides this, Burney did not like French music, even the Italianate kind of opéra-comique represented by Monsigny. The next day Hiller took Burney to a rehearsal of one of his own comic operas, an episode deferred until the consideration of Singspiel at the end of this chapter. Burney's other experience of note in Leipzig was a visit to the music presses of the industrious firm of Johann Breitkopf, whom Burney found uncommunicative.

Prince Frederick of Prussia

The first Prussian king, Frederick's grandfather, loved luxury and French culture, spending the small country's revenue in its pursuit. There was even a period of Italian opera at the Berlin court during his reign, although it was mostly due to the music-loving queen, Sophie Charlotte. This unlikely undertaking took place around 1700 under the musical direction of maestro di cappella Attilio Ariosto. Queen Sophie also invited Giovanni Bononcini to Berlin and he came for a short stay between 1703 and 1705. The Protestant clergy of Berlin were vociferous in denouncing opera as the work of the devil. Their view was shared by Frederick William I, who, when he succeeded his father in 1713, a year after the birth of Prince Frederick, dismissed the entire musical cappella and determined to do without a court music. Austere and puritanical, he detested French manners (while admitting that the French language was indispensable to diplomacy). He put his greatest efforts into building up his army and creating the sound financial infrastructure that would allow Prussia to become a military power. Called "the soldier king" or "the barracks king," he was famous for recruiting abnormally tall soldiers for his personal brigade at Potsdam. He was most famous of all for his treatment of his eldest son, whom he was determined to mold in his own image. But Frederick turned out, at least initially, to resemble his grandfather more than his father in his tastes and personality. The king laid down precise instructions as to the prince's education. It was to include instruction in German and French, but not in Latin, which the king deemed useless, along with the study of antiquity. The prince was to deny himself *belles-lettres*, operas, comedies, and other "follies" of the age. Piety (meaning Calvinism) was to be instilled into him daily, along with military discipline. Fortunately for the prince, Queen Sophie Dorothea was able to mitigate some of the severity of her husband's orders. Frederick learned Latin in secret and read widely in modern French literature.

Musical talent appeared at an early age not only in Frederick, but also in his elder sister Wilhelmina and younger sister Anna Amalia. The queen encouraged them to pursue musical studies. The king went along up to a point. As a present he gave Frederick a songbook containing the Psalms translated into French by Clément Marot and set to tunes that had become standard in the Calvinist liturgy. He also had him instructed at age seven by the cathedral organist, Gottlieb Heyne. The lessons included keyboard playing, thorough bass, and harmonization in four parts. At about the same time Frederick secretly began studying the flute, perhaps at the hands of his excellent French tutor, Jacques Duhan. The king, alternately cajoling and threatening in his attempts to make a soldier of his eldest son, came increasingly to believe that the prince was turning into an effeminate fop.

Frederick learned early the advantages of strict secrecy in the achievement of his goals. He also learned how to manipulate those around him to do his wishes in spite of all obstacles. Unlike his wavering father, who was now cruelly hostile and now permissive, Frederick never wavered in the pursuit of his ideals, only in his tactics. His high intelligence went along with a degree of ruthlessness that boded well for great accomplishment as well as great turmoil once he came to power.

In 1728, when Frederick was sixteen, the king took him on a visit to Dresden, the magnificent capital of Augustus. One of many persistent errors in the literature claims that he first encountered Hasse then: "On a visit to Dresden in 1728 the prince was overwhelmed at hearing his first opera, Hasse's *Cleofide.*"[55] Hasse did not arrive in Dresden until 1731, the date of *Cleofide*. There was an opera connected with the state visit to Dresden during the carnival of 1728 and it was Ristori's comedy *Calandro* of a year earlier, revived at the court opera on 2 February 1728. We know that Frederick saw it and enjoyed it because of a letter Ristori wrote to his superior, the directeur des plaisirs, saying that he was trying to have the score copied for a fee of 54 écus in order to honor the request for it made by the crown prince of Prussia.[56] In a letter signed "Frédérique le Philosophe" sent to his sister Wilhelmina and dated Dresden, 26 January 1728, the prince mentions Quantz, Buffardin, Pisendel, and Weiss, four stellar players in the Saxon cappella.[57] It is probably no coincidence that, when Augustus repaid the state visit by going to Berlin in May 1728, these four outstanding musicians accompanied him.

Frederick was an avid collector of both books and scores. In this he was assisted by his faithful Duhan, who secretly put together an enormous library of

[55]Eugene Helm, "Frederick II," in *New Grove.* The same error is enlarged upon in Eugene Helm, *Music at the Court of Frederick the Great* (Norman, Okla., 1960), pp. 9, 239.
[56]Curt Mengelberg, *Giovanni Alberto Ristori* (Leipzig, 1916), p. 6.
[57]Helm, *Music at the Court of Frederick the Great,* p. 9.

well over three thousand volumes, with the conspiratorial help of a Berlin banker and a town councillor, in whose house this library had been hidden. The king was given to bouts of alcoholic rages and stupors. Also he was very fat and slow moving. Deceiving him was not an insuperable problem, and his wife took pleasure in doing so. As for the conspirators, they could take certain chances buoyed by the thought that the old king would not rule much longer, given his excesses.

In the summer of 1730 the king was in the Rhineland inspecting his scattered possessions there. His reluctant crown prince was forced to accompany him. Frederick, aged eighteen, made the amazing decision to try to escape and seek exile in England. In this harebrained scheme he was aided by two young army friends, Lieutenant Keith and Lieutenant Katte, Frederick's lover. Keith escaped. Frederick and Katte were captured and brought before an army court martial. Katte was sentenced to life in prison, which the king changed to execution. He had Katte beheaded before Frederick's eyes. Any further insubordination by his son, the king made clear, would earn him the same fate. Perhaps it took this shocking experience to make Frederick fully realize that his father would prefer to be succeeded by one of his younger, duller, but less effeminate sons. Frederick was clapped into solitary confinement for his desertion in the fortress town of Küstrin on the Oder River, east of Berlin. He was still confined to the town of Küstrin in mid-1731 (when Hasse and Faustina were making their debut in Dresden with *Cleofide*). Gradually, he convinced his father that the sobering events of 1730 had made him an obedient son. The king pardoned him conditional on his good behavior and allowed him to attend Wilhelmina's wedding to the margrave of Brandenburg in November 1731. He was also readmitted to the army.

Five years later, Frederick began his famous correspondence with Voltaire, who strengthened in him a resistance to organized religion that led to his final repudiation of Christianity. He became a Freemason in 1738. These steps were not known to the king or the people at large. Brandenburg and Prussia were fervently Christian for the most part, and it would not do to have a sovereign who was openly an infidel. An atheist Frederick was not, since he believed in the existence of a supreme being. He later became the first monarch to publicly vaunt enlightened ideals, as propounded by the *philosophes*.

In 1736 Frederick produced a political tract, *Considérations sur l'état du corps politique de l'Europe*, in which he suggested that the military might of France and Austria should be checked by a third power, meaning Prussia. The king had already done his bit to defeat France, or at least to thwart French attempts to place its candidate on the throne in Warsaw, in the War of the Polish Succession. Frederick himself took part in the minor campaign against the French in the Rhineland in the winter of 1733–34 and had acquitted himself in a manner his father found satisfactory. The king was too timid in international politics, Frederick believed, and too ready to yield to the dictates of Vienna.[58] In fact, for all his military bluster, the king was wary of antagonizing a major power or committing his army to combat. His son suffered no such scruples.

Two issues threatened Frederick's future as a possible sovereign: his indifference to organized religion and his refusal to marry. His religious views shocked Protestant Prussia and Brandenburg. Frederick won his subjects over later too easily by becoming the conqueror of Silesia. As for marriage, the king simply forced his son to comply. Against his will Frederick married Princess Elisabeth Christine of Brunswick on 12 June 1733. Not even the king could force him to consummate the marriage. The spurned princess lived apart from him all her life, a wife in name only, but given full honors. She was niece to the princess of Brunswick of the same name who married Emperor Charles VI.

From the beginning of his residence at Ruppin in 1732 Frederick began to put together the musical forces that would later mark his reign. The violinist Johann Gottlieb Graun, who had visited Berlin during the festive summer of 1728, as had Pietro Locatelli, was with Frederick at Ruppin from the beginning. Franz Benda arrived in 1733, followed by his brother Johann a year later. These two Bohemian violinists came by way of the Dresden orchestra, and so did another Bohemian violinist, Georg Zarth, whose career closely followed that of Franz Benda. He joined the Ruppin band in 1734. By this time Frederick had been given Rheinsberg, some ten miles north of Ruppin. Georg Wenzelaus von Knobelsdorff, his favorite architect, was finishing an enchanting palace on the water at the site and it was ready for occupancy in 1736. At the time of the transfer to Rheinsberg in 1736 Frederick had an orchestra of seventeen that included, besides those just named, Christoph Schaffrath, cembalist; Michael Fredersdorff, flautist; Ernst Gottlieb Baron, theorbist; and, most import of all, Carl Heinrich Graun, who came in 1735 and was the maestro di capella.

Why did Frederick fail to go on a Grand Tour of Europe as did most other young princes? There are many reasons. His father was niggardly and despised other cultures; moreover, he disliked allowing his son and heir far out of his sight. Frederick himself was so proud and egotistical he could barely have tolerated a visit to Versailles. The newness of Prussian royalty rankled him. It availed little that his mother was a daughter of George I of England, because the Hohenzollerns looked down on the Hanover court, the ninth and last to achieve electoral status (in 1692). Frederick never wished to expose himself to quarrels about hierarchical rank. His hatred of the Habsburg and Bourbon monarchies was partly a response

---

[58]H. M. Scott, "Prussia's Royal Foreign Minister: Frederick the Great and the Administration of Prussian Diplomacy," in *Royal and Republican Sovereignty in Early Modern Europe,* ed. Robert Oresko, G. C. Gibbs, and H. M. Scott (Cambridge, 1997), pp. 500–26; 517. The author shows that Frederick served as his own foreign minister and ran the entire diplomatic service personally.

to his own perceived status as a parvenu among royal dynasties. He proclaimed the superiority of French intellectual life, as well as of French visual art, and the superiority of Italian singing, but he experienced neither France nor Italy. Apparently he did not wish to visit them even when as king, in peaceful times, he could have. A certain narrowness and rigidity in his tastes, an inability or unwillingness to change with the times, are perhaps related to his lack of direct experience with the cultures he admired the most.

In 1710 Frederick's grandfather called a talented French portrait painter, Antoine Pesne, to Berlin, where he remained throughout the philistine reign of Frederick's father. One of the only portraits of himself Frederick ever allowed was a fine one by Pesne of the young prince. Pesne was modest about his own abilities. He compared himself to Antoine Watteau by saying, "He has the genius I lack."[59] Queen Sophie Dorothea collected engravings after Watteau, which were greatly valued following the artist's early death in 1721. It may be through her that Frederick began to collect paintings by Watteau and his followers (mainly Nicolas Lancret and Jean-Baptiste Pater). At Rheinsberg he already possessed several. Moreover, there is some evidence that life imitated art in this semiprivate circle. One of the prince's intimates, Baron Bielfeld, compared the gaiety of life at Rheinsberg to a picture by Watteau, in contrast to the gloom surrounding the old king in Berlin, which he compared to a picture by Rembrandt.[60] This placing of the tenebrist and ponderous seventeenth-century past aside the light-filled and graceful rococo present is instructive as far as it goes. Yet the arts never stopped evolving and changing, except for Frederick. In constructing the Sans Souci palace at Potsdam, into which he moved in 1747, he chose French architectural modes of the 1720s as his model. The result was considerably inferior to the model, as was the case with almost all Frederick's endeavors in the visual and musical arts.

Conditions among the chamber musicians at Ruppin and Rheinsberg were not always as serene or harmonious as a *fête champêtre* by Watteau. In November 1735, after the move to Rheinsberg, Frederick wrote to Wilhelmina at Bayreuth in answer to her complaints about troubles with her musicians: "Je plains, ma chere soeur, que la révolte s'est mise dans votre musique; cette race de gens est très-difficile à conduire; cela demande quelquefois plus de prudence que la conduite des États. Je sais ce qu'en vaut l'aune et je m'attends à quelque nouvelle sédition parmi mes enfants d'Euterpe.[61] "Aune" has the double meaning of "ell," a unit of measure, and "alder tree," and it is probably the latter that is intended, in the sense of "taking the stick" to his musicians. Two years later on the same subject Freder-

[59]Helmut Börsch-Supan, "Frederick the Great and Watteau," in *Watteau 1684–1721*, ed. Margaret Morgan Grasselli and Pierre Rosenberg (Washington, 1984), pp. 546–55; 547.
[60]Ibid., p. 548.
[61]Letter of 26 November 1736, cited after Mennicke, *Hasse und die Brüder Graun*, p. 469.

ick wrote to his sister indicating that his particular favorite, Franz Benda, had given some trouble: "M. Benda, des enfans d'Apollon, est assez sage à présent; je dois louer leur bonne conduite, quoique je sois sûr qu'elle ne sera pas de durée."[62] What the trouble was with Benda may have had something to do with the promotion of Johann Gottlieb Graun to concertmaster when Frederick became king. Only after the elder Graun's death in 1771 did Franz Benda again become concertmaster.

Remaining aloof in Rheinsberg, surrounded by his chosen intimates, Frederick had the time and peace of mind to plan much of what he would do in his coming reign. On the musical side he imagined two separate spheres: a royal opera house in Berlin that would rival Dresden's as a center of Italian opera and over which Graun would preside; a chamber orchestra for his own private pleasure at Potsdam to be presided over by Franz Benda; and above all the presence of Quantz, as soon as he could pry his teacher loose from Dresden. Before the old king died Frederick had laid plans for building the opera house with his architect Knobelsdorff. After much deliberation Frederick decided the opera house would be a freestanding temple in Palladian style at some distance from the royal palace, on a broad avenue that led west from the center, Unter den Linden. It was a visionary move, one that foresaw the future Berlin on the scale of a great capital. Of actual temples Frederick had no personal need. He nevertheless donated a site behind the opera house for a great round and domed church, imitating the Pantheon at Rome (the temple of all the Gods).[63] His original intention was to make it a place of worship for all faiths, but eventually it became the Catholic cathedral of Saint Hedwig. This was certainly a convenience for the mainly Catholic Italian singers and French dancers of his opera house and was no doubt welcome as well for many of the embassies that sprang up nearby. The temple of the muses, which is all right angles, and the temple of the gods, which is almost all curves, still make a striking visual couple today. An engraving of ca. 1800 well conveys their interaction (Figure 4.11).

Berlin became an increasingly cosmopolitan city under Frederick. It had a large concentration of Huguenot exiles, as did Potsdam, and they were often skilled and well educated. Berlin also had the largest Jewish population of any German city. Surprisingly, its Catholic population was estimated as large as 10,000 in a city of ca. 100,000 around 1750. Frederick made religious toleration his state's policy. It brought him much political credit abroad and the admiration of Voltaire. It was also to his advantage when he sought alliances with Catholic states.

---

[62]Letter of 19 November 1738, ibid.

[63]Hans-Joachim Giersberg, *Friedrich als Bauherr: Studien zur Architektur des 18. Jahrhunderts in Berlin und Potsdam* (Berlin, 1986), p. 235. The author emphasizes that all building was done under Frederick's direct orders.

FIGURE 4.11. Opera house and Catholic cathedral in Berlin.

Carl Heinrich Graun

Graun was the youngest of three musical brothers. He was born either in 1703 or 1704 in Wahrenbrücke, Saxony, where Johann Gottlieb was born a year earlier, and August Friedrich four or five years earlier. Carl Heinrich and Johann Gottlieb were both pupils at the Kreuzkirche in Dresden. Carl Heinrich outshone his brother, receiving the distinction of "discant extraordinaire" for his beautiful soprano voice and artful singing. His report card as to conduct mentioned "industrius in literis et musicis." An early literary bent was an obvious advantage to the future operatic master. Graun's teachers included Schmidt, the Saxon court Kapellmeister, and Johann Zacharias Grundig, a singer and choir director whose duties included training the boys to function as a chorus in the court operas under Lotti and Heinichen in 1717–19. Thus both Grauns profited from the experience of singing Italian opera on the stage. Both enrolled in the University of Leipzig in 1717, but they remained nevertheless as choristers in the Kreuzkirche until 1721. Hiller in his biography of Graun claimed that as a sixteen-year-old he was so enchanted with Lotti's *Teofane* that he was able to write out the entire opera from memory after a few hearings. (This may well be a comment on Lotti's extreme simplicity as well as upon Graun's musicality.)

Graun's beautiful soprano matured into an equally beautiful tenor. He also played several stringed instruments. In 1723 he went with the Dresden contingent to Prague for Fux's coronation opera under the direction of Caldara, in whose orchestra he played cello. Johann Ulrich von König recommended Graun to the court of Brunswick in 1725. He was hired as a tenor and composer in the opera troupe under the direction of Georg Caspar Schürmann. History repeated itself. Another tenor four years earlier, Hasse, got his start as an opera composer at Brunswick, also recommended by König.

Brunswick and Hamburg were the two greatest centers of what is called "late baroque German opera." A commercial opera house opened in 1691 in Brunswick with a German-language *Cleopatra* by Johann Sigismund Kusser, who wrote several more German operas for the city, and for Hamburg and Stuttgart in the 1690s. Kusser's pupil Reinhard Keiser, a far greater composer, succeeded his teacher in Brunswick and went on to be the dominant figure in Hamburg. Opera in German (or German with large admixtures of Italian) such as developed in Hamburg was in the last phase of its long decline by the time Graun reached Brunswick in 1725. Among other things, its literary standards, never very high, condemned it to extinction. Its demise was inevitable even though it was led by such eminent musicians as Keiser and Telemann at Hamburg, and Georg Schürmann at Brunswick. Schürmann alone composed and directed some thirty operas for the Brunswick court between 1700 and 1730. With the arrival of Graun his output slowed, and Schürmann is said to have favored the young tenor by allowing him to alter and decorate his parts as he pleased. Graun wrote five operas on German texts for the court. It was the sixth, in Italian, that mattered the most for his future: *Lo specchio della fedeltà* for the marriage of Elisabeth Christine of Brunswick to crown prince Frederick in June 1733.

Frederick appreciated Graun's opera and his singing. Overtures about Prussian service were made to the young composer. On 23 October 1733 Frederick wrote his sister Wilhelmina that he believed Graun would join his service (and thereby join his older brother Johann Gottlieb). But Brunswick refused to release him as soon as this, although he was allowed to visit Frederick. Only with the death of Duke Ludwig Rudolph on 1 March 1735 did his successor decide to economize by greatly reducing the musical cappella. Graun was released. Frederick seized the opportunity to employ him at Ruppin, where Graun took charge of the band of musicians. On 15 August 1736 they moved into the new castle at Rheinsberg.

How pleased Frederick was with Graun can be gauged from a letter he wrote a year later vaunting the arias of "his composer" to his cousin William of Orange, whose wife had sent remarks praising Handel's operas. "Les beaux jours de Hendel sont passez, sa tête est épuisée et son gout hors de mode. . . . je vous enverai des airs de mon compositeur, que j'espère seront du gout de votre Epouse."[64] All too evident here is a spirit of competition and superiority that may have been based on little or no actual knowledge of Handel's works for London. This attitude almost guaranteed that Berlin would be closed to Handel, even though he was a Hohenzollern subject by birth.

Graun was useful to Frederick in several ways at Rheinsberg, although opera there was out of the question. He composed a number of Italian cantatas for himself as soloist to sing, and these works are regarded as among his best. He gave lessons in composition to Frederick, who formed a close bond with his new maestro di cappella. He also taught Franz Benda, another of Frederick's favorites and the original concertmaster of his orchestra. When the old king died on 31 May 1740 Frederick, in his typically autocratic and peremptory fashion, set aside his father's wishes to have nothing but Protestant chorales sung at his funeral and instead had Graun compose a funeral cantata in the Italian style. Since there were no Italian singers in Berlin to perform it, they were imported hurriedly from Dresden. This duty discharged, Frederick sent Graun to Italy to recruit a number of singers for his future opera. From July 1740 to March 1741 Graun visited Venice, Bologna, Florence, Rome, and Naples in search of talent. He rounded up five male and three female singers for Prussian service. None was ever to gain much success in Berlin. But the mere fact of seeking only Italian singers caused Mattheson in Hamburg to rumble in disapproving tones, saying that the royal prejudice forced good German performers to seek their fortunes elsewhere.

Frederick was away fighting battles in Silesia when his new Italian singers arrived. He did not hear them until he returned to Berlin in November 1741. An Italian librettist had also been hired in the person of Giovanni Bottarelli. But the royal opera house was nowhere near finished. The decision to place it on the site of an old fortress that was surrounded by a moat required Knobelsdorff to spend months just clearing the site for construction. Nevertheless Graun and Bottarelli brought their first opera to the stage in December 1741. *Rodelinda* was put on in a small theater in the city palace, a structure in the oldest part of Berlin, the small island surrounded by the waters of the river Spree. At least one witness claimed enchantment with the event, so novel in a Berlin long deprived of opera.

> For the beginning there was a symphony in which fiery and gentle sections were opposed. This was such a masterpiece of full, pure harmony, such a many-sided, artful mixture of tones, that it seemed as if the Muses and the Graces had united to draw our Frederick out of his own heroic sphere and to ourselves, where he could be held

---

[64]Letter dated 19 October 1737, cited after Mennicke, *Hasse und die Brüder Graun*, p. 469. William's wife, Princess Anne of England, was Handel's pupil.

back from the rude cares of war. The bewitching voices of the singers, the naturalness and beauty of action—everything was captivating to eye and ear. The whole spectacle, brought to such artistic perfection and executed with such skill, was received by the Monarch with high approval, and the public went forth from the theater lost in enchantment.[65]

The orchestra had swelled to thirty-eight players. Johann Gottlieb Graun presided as concertmaster in the theater. The singers recruited from Italy in 1741 by Carl Heinrich could not have given total satisfaction, because by the spring of 1742 Frederick was writing his contacts in Italy from the battlefields in Silesia in an attempt to get better singers.

By late 1742 the royal opera house, although unfinished, was at last ready to open. The new singers from Italy had arrived, as had the troupe of dancers from France. In his letters from that time Frederick shows the interest he took even in the most minute details of his opera company, from the rehearsal schedule to the costumes and machinery. Bottarelli and Graun wrote a *Cesare e Cleopatra* for the grand opening of the new house on 7 December 1742. The opera may have fallen short of being a masterpiece, but the theater was a complete success, even to having perfect acoustics, no small feat in such a large space. Its cost has been estimated at around 1,000,000 thalers.

For the next fourteen years the royal opera settled into a predictable routine as to the number and dates of its performances. The season, unlike elsewhere, usually began in late November. It ended on 27 March, the birthday of the Queen Mother. Another day often celebrated by a performance was Frederick's birthday on 24 January. Otherwise operas were normally given on Monday and Friday. A first opera (often a revival) ran until New Year's Day, when it became the custom to introduce the second opera. During his lifetime Graun was the only composer to have serious operas performed there, with the exception of Hasse (1743, 1747, 1753) and Johann Friedrich Agricola (1754). He received an annual salary of 2,000 thalers. In comparison, his concertmaster brother Johann Gottlieb received 800 thalers, with supplements added for his teaching activities.

Graun composed over twenty operas for the royal theater. These included six on librettos of Metastasio, concentrated in the years between 1743 and 1747. Then the court poet Leopoldo de Villati took over. Villati was called to Berlin in 1747 at an annual salary of 400 thalers to replace Bottarelli, who was dismissed the same year. Frederick chose the subjects for his librettists, just as he chose everything else in connection with his operas. He directed Villati to a series of adaptations from French plays or operas, all set by Graun (Table 4.1).

[65]Helm, *Music at the Court of Frederick the Great*, p. 94.

TABLE 4.1 French-Derived Librettos by Villati

Le feste galanti (1747)	after *Les fêtes galantes* by Joseph Duché de Vancy
Cinna (1748)	after *Cinna* by Pierre Corneille
Europe galante (1748)	after *L'Europe galante* by Antoine Houdar de La Motte
Ifigenia in Aulide (1748)	after *Iphigénie en Aulide* by Racine
Angelica e Medoro (1749)	after *Roland* by Philippe Quinault
Fetonte (1750)	after *Phaeton* by Quinault
Il Mitridate (1750)	after *Mithridate* by Racine
L'Armida (1751)	after *Armide* by Quinault
Britannico (1751)	after *Britannicus* by Racine
L'Orfeo (1752)	after *Orphée* by Michel Dubollay

Frederick had begun this trend earlier by directing Bottarelli to Pierre Corneille's *La mort de Pompée* for Graun's *Cesare e Cleopatra,* the work that opened the royal opera house in 1742. Besides his troupe of French dancers, Frederick had a troupe of French players, and it is likely that many classics of the French spoken theater turned into librettos were given as plays in Berlin. The literati there were not pleased with this infusion of seventeenth-century Gallic theater. Gotthold Ephraim Lessing, chief among them, found "little invention, order or verisimilitude" in Villati's librettos.[66] Lessing also wrote a satire on opera seria, *Tarantula* (1749), and used Villati's name. Villati died in Berlin in July 1752 and was replaced by Giampietro Tagliazucchi.

So marked a preference for direct adaptations of French literary models suggests an anti-Metastasian trend at work. A similar turn in court opera can be discerned somewhat later in the most advanced reformist centers of the time, namely Parma, Vienna, Stuttgart, and Mannheim. Frederick began to intervene more directly in musical matters during the second half of the 1740s. He forbade Graun to write any more French overtures; only Italian overtures appeared thenceforth. To Graun's 1746 setting of Metastasio's *Demofoonte* the king contributed three arias. He was not satisfied with Graun's setting of "Misero pargoletto," the crucial third-act aria for the primo uomo in *Demofoonte.* Graun composed it anew and the king was still not satisfied, whereupon he told his maestro di cappella to substitute a favorite setting by Hasse. The command must have mortified Graun.

Frederick turned away from the Metastasian war-horse librettos, if not their dramaturgical principles. Perhaps his political antipathies to Vienna extended to

[66]Gotthold Ephraim Lessing, *Nachricht von dem gegenwärtigen Zustand des Theaters in Berlin,* cited in Thomas Bauman, "Villati," in *The New Grove Dictionary of Opera.*

the works of the Caesarean poet and help explain Berlin's avoidance of Metastasio after 1747. During the years of peace between 1748 and 1756 he intervened ever more decisively in Graun's operas by becoming a co-librettist. With *Ifigenia in Aulide* (1748), *Coriolano* (1749), and *Merope* (1756) he wrote a sketch for the plot. With *Silla* (1753) and *Montezuma* (1755) he provided much more than a scenario. He wrote out a full prose libretto in French, which Tagliazucchi was obliged to translate into Italian and versify (as to the arias). *Montezuma* is regarded as the height of Frederican opera and will be considered its representative.

Berlin, the capital of music theory and music criticism, produced, not surprisingly, an elaborate treatise on Hasse-inspired, Graun-composed opera, *Von der musikalischen Poesie* by Christian Gottfried Krause. The author was a Silesian, born in 1719 to a family of musicians who gave him a good musical training. During the turmoil of the first Silesian war Krause studied law at the University of Frankfurt an der Oder, where Emanuel Bach preceded him as a student in the 1730s. Once established in Berlin, he rose rapidly in the legal profession, married, and bought a large house in Potsdam that became a meeting place for musicians, poets, and critics. Its large music room was decorated with mural paintings by Christian Bernhard Rode and earned a place among Potsdam's *Sehenswürdigkeiten*.[67] The house concerts Krause gave were among the most important of the time and enjoyed the participation of major court musicians such as Quantz and probably Emanuel Bach. Krause finished a version of his treatise in 1747 but held back from publication while it was being polished by several authors, including Graun himself, to whom it is dedicated. In the dedication, signed Berlin, 5 November 1751, Krause credits Graun as a quasi-author since he suggested it in the first place. Krause's main aim, he says in his preface, was to instruct both poets and composers about textual-musical matters. This he certainly does and at great length (484 pages), methodically attacking his subject from every angle and covering wide swaths of music history in the examples he cites. Krause praised the naturalness, elegance, and restraint of Graun's operas, as opposed to the bombast and exaggeration that he decried in the lately deceased Hamburg opera, which had been a truly baroque phenomenon, viewed in this light.[68]

Johann Adam Hiller wrote the main biography of Graun.[69] He believed that the composer was born in 1701. From Hiller comes the tale that, after hearing

---

[67]Friedrich Nicolai, *Beschreibung der königlichen Residenzstädte Berlin und Potsdam,* 3 vols. (Berlin, 1769–86), 2: 632.

[68]Chrisitan Gottfried Krause, *Von der musikalischen Poesie,* 2nd ed. (Berlin, 1752; reprint 1963), p. 184. On Krause's relationship to other theorists, see Gloria Flaherty, *Opera in the Development of German Critical Thought* (Princeton, N.J., 1978), pp. 167–75.

[69]Johann Adam Hiller, *Lebenbeschreibungen berühmter Musikgelehrten und Tonkünstler neuerer Zeit* (Leipzig, 1784), pp. 76–96.

three performances of Lotti's *Teofane*, Graun wrote out all the arias in a short score of treble and bass. Hiller also claimed that Graun composed a great number of instrumental trios as well as some dozen keyboard concertos, "which, if they fall short of exhausting the keyboard's potential, nevertheless do provide models of how to make an *Adagio* melodic and touching." When Graun died in Berlin on 8 August 1759 Frederick was quartered with his army in Dresden. Hiller reports that Franz Benda brought him the news, at which the king wept, saying, "Such a singer we shall never hear again." It is unclear whether Frederick meant his vocal talent or, in a more inclusive and figurative sense, his lyrical gifts as a composer. Hiller interpreted the remark in the former sense. "Thus Graun's singing was the first thing the king lamented, and yet he knew, and still knows, how to treasure Graun's compositions." In a parting remark, Hiller allowed himself a slight criticism of Graun. "It is too bad that his Adagio arias are almost all a little too long, especially since the first part must be repeated. A Graun or Salimbeni must perform them, if the auditor is not to become fatigued by them."

Being averse to religious music, the king probably never heard Graun's most successful work, a setting of Karl Ramler's Passion oratorio *Der Tod Jesu*, commissioned by Princess Anna Amalia and first performed at a concert in the cathedral on 26 March 1755. The style is operatic in the recitatives and arias, but learned and traditional in fine choral fugues, as well as popular in the simple chorales the audience was invited to sing.[70] Graun is at his most *empfindsam* in an obbligato recitative such as "Gethsemane!"[71]

MONTEZUMA

Frederick used a historical source relating the conquest of Mexico by a small band of Spaniards under Hernando Cortés as the basis for his story in *Montezuma*.[72] The choice was quite at odds with the usual subjects of serious opera at the time. It can be explained by the king's determination to flaunt his personal views on religion and morality. He blamed the destruction of Montezuma's ancient civilization squarely on Christian bigotry, as represented by a brutal and totally unsympathetic Cortés. Mass slaughter and destruction such as are unleashed in this libretto are nearly unheard of in operas of the mid-eighteenth century. They seem to portend the horrors of the Seven Years War, soon to follow. For shock value they rival Eugène Scribe's *Les Huguenots* for Giacomo Meyerbeer eighty years later.

---

[70] See Howard E. Smither, *A History of the Oratorio,* vol. 3: *The Oratorio in the Classical Era* (Chapel Hill, N.C., 1987), 401–34.

[71] Exemplified in Daniel Heartz, "Empfindsamkeit," in *New Grove,* an article that cites both praise and condemnation of *Tod Jesu* by contemporary critics.

[72] Antonio de Solis y Ribadeneyra, *Historia de le conquista de México* (Madrid, 1684) in a French translation of 1730.

In October 1753 Frederick wrote to his friend and collaborator Francesco Algarotti in response to the latter's missive from Italy (which does not survive). Algarotti must have complained about the low level of Italian operas he witnessed. Frederick began his reply with feigned modesty.

> If your operas are bad, you will find one here that perhaps will not surpass them. It is *Montezuma.* I chose the subject and I am working it out at present. You realize, I'm sure, that my sympathies are with Montezuma; Cortés will be the tyrant and consequently one can let fly, in music as well, some jibes against the barbarity of the Christian religion. But I forget that you are now in a land of the Inquisition, and I make my excuses, hoping to see you soon again in a heretic land where even the opera can serve to reform morals and destroy superstitions.[73]

Frederick's kingdom was of course not "heretic." Only he was. In the mentality of absolute monarchy the king was the country. Only in this light did his claim make sense.

Opera as a medium for reforming morals, or at least uplifting them, had been proclaimed from the genre's Italian beginnings, although rarely achieved or even seriously believed. Yet Frederick, for all his bantering tone (which is more evident in the French original) was dead earnest about destroying superstitions. His models in this respect can be found in Voltaire's plays, and especially in *Alzire.* Voltaire himself had been Frederick's guest in Berlin for a very stormy period of nearly two years beginning in mid-1751. As for Algarotti, another intimate of Voltaire, he would never return to Berlin; he died in Italy in 1763.

On 16 April 1754, as Frederick was working on the text of his opera, he wrote his sister Wilhelmina in Bayreuth, saying, "most of the arias are constructed so as to require no repetition; there are only four, two apiece for [the two principals] Montezuma and Eupaforice that are destined for [da capo] repetition." An explanation is in order. The full da capo aria is a textual construction in which the first stanza consists of a statement, a complete thought, modified or extended by the second stanza, so as to require the ensuing repetition of the first stanza. The cavatina often had two stanzas also. It differed in that the first stanza did not return, thus entailing a different function for each stanza. The second must conclude the thought, which the first was no longer required to do. In musical terms the two stanzas of the cavatina were applied to the first two parts of the full five-part da capo form, eliminating the **B** section of the music as well as da capo repetition. Frederick also used a single-stanza cavatina, repeated once in the music.

The cavatina had been winning many converts in the 1730s and 1740s, as the

---

[73]Carl Heinrich Graun, *Montezuma,* ed. Albert Mayer-Reinach (*Denkmäler deutscher Tonkunst* XV) (Leipzig, 1904), Preface. (Hereinafter in this volume, the abbreviation *DDT* will be used for this series.) The original letter is in French, as are those quoted subsequently, without further references.

style of aria composition made for longer and longer phrases, and consequently very long arias. It was Frederick's bold stroke to legislate that the cavatina should prevail almost entirely. Eupaforice sings da capo arias in the middle and at the end of Act I. Then she sings another (contrary to what Frederick indicated in his letter) to end Act II. This is a huge aria in which two horns are added to the usual strings. In such a crucial spot Frederick relied on the vocal heroics of his best singer, Giovanna Astrua, who was not paid the astronomical sum of 6,000 thalers a year in order to sing short arias. Montezuma sings only one da capo aria, an *Adagio* in D about his cruel destiny, placed after the confrontation with Cortés in Act II.

Frederick wrote again to his sister on 4 May 1754. By this time he had sent her his prose libretto in French. He tells her to try it out by having it performed (i.e., spoken) "by her admirable troupe of French comedians." He continues: "As to cavatinas, I have seen some by Hasse that are infinitely prettier than arias, and which pass quickly. Reprises are unnecessary except when the singers know how to vary the music, but it seems to me even so that repeating the same thing four times is an abuse." The thoughts of Gluck himself as recorded by Calzabigi in the famous preface to *Alceste* are not far distant from this reformist view about textual repetition. As for Hasse's model cavatinas, the modern editor of *Montezuma* faults the king and says he is mistaken because Graun had written in this short form earlier. Frederick must be taken at his word here. Graun may well have written any number of cavatinas, which is beside the point. What Frederick admired were some he had seen by Hasse.

After the opera went into rehearsal in the fall of 1754 Frederick mentioned it again to his sister in his letter of 21 November 1754. "I have heard the rehearsal of *Montezuma,* at which I directed the actors as to the sense of the drama. I believe this opera would give you pleasure. Graun has created a masterpiece. It is entirely in cavatinas." To remove the contradiction with what he wrote on 16 April about four da capo arias, he should have said "almost entirely in cavatinas."

Solely on the basis of its lengthy gestation and adequate rehearsal time this court opera stands far apart from the products of the commercial opera houses in Italy. The premiere took place on 6 January 1755. Frederick reported its success with an attempt at self-deprecating wit. "We have had *Montezuma* performed here. The decorator and the tailor saved the day for the poor author; above all two bad pistol shots were extremely applauded." And on a more serious note: "The Astrua played the last scene with admirable pathos, and Graun surpassed himself in the music." He says nothing about the title role. Graun composed it for a contralto, possibly Carestini, although he is said to have left Berlin for Russia in 1754.

Each of the three protagonists has an aide. Frederick to his credit keeps these subaltern characters out of romantic entanglements. Cortés (soprano) has the hot-headed and bloodthirsty Navrès (soprano), who makes his crafty chief look a little less evil by comparison. Princess Eupaforice, the intended bride of Montezuma, has a typical confidant in Erissena. Tezeuco is confidant to the naively confident emperor. In addition there is the clear-seeing Mexican general Pilpatoè (soprano), who warns Montezuma of the Spaniard's rapaciousness. In his long simple recitative that begins Act I, Montezuma describes the peace and prosperity that has blessed his reign, due to his wise leadership. The historical Montezuma, who reigned from 1502 until his death in 1520, was constantly at war with his neighbors and busy putting down uprisings against him of his own Aztec people, many of whom came to grief as human sacrifices. By making his fictional Montezuma a model ruler of an enlightened state, a philosopher-king such as Voltaire might have idealized, Frederick could only have been painting a picture of the king he imagined himself to be. In reality he should have seen himself as well in Cortés, who conquered Mexico through guile, boldness, superior organization, and ruthlessness, much as Frederick conquered Silesia.[74]

The arias, by which are meant both the cavatinas and the longer forms, number twenty-two. The primo uomo and prima donna have five apiece plus the love duet that they share. Cortés and Tezeuco receive three each, and the others have two apiece. They are distributed so that no character has to sing two in a row. Graun sets them in a variety of keys ranging from four flats to four sharps, taking care to avoid two consecutive pieces in the same key. Astrua is favored to the point of getting the big aria in C to end Act I and the even more brilliant aria in D to end Act II. The love duet in A is the second number in the third act, which ends tragically with two arias in the minor mode, hers in the key of b, and his in the key of f. Otherwise, there is only one minor-mode aria, in the middle of Act II, Pilpatoè's lament at Montezuma's being tricked, set in the key of g.

Besides the three-movement sinfonia in A, there is an orchestral piece to begin Act II, a *Vivace* in F and in common time. Its dotted rhythms, rapid scalar runs, and multiple trills summon back the arrogant strains of the old French overture in order to paint the ferocious Spaniards on their arrival. Navrès erupts in denunciations of the pagans and is restrained by Cortés, who tells him to dissimulate, after which a chorus of Mexicans welcomes the marauders with a bright *Vivace* in cut time, in the key of G. Lurking in the bass of this piece are the rapid runs of the previous *Vivace*, like whiplashes, conveying unmistakably the hatred and violence of the Spanish even as they are being welcomed.

Another instrumental piece is the short battle symphony in D for strings and

[74]The irony of Frederick's being in real life both a Cortés and an absurdly idealized Montezuma eludes Heinz Klüppelholz in "Die Eroberung Mexikos aus preussischer Sicht: Zum Libretto der Oper *Montezuma* von Friedrich dem Grossen," *Oper als Text: Romantische Beiträge zur Libretto-Forschung,* ed. Albert Gier (Studia Romanica 63) (Heidelberg, 1986), pp. 65–94. The author comments only on Frederick's identification with the "noble savage" Montezuma (p. 80).

two horns during which the Spaniards show their true colors by overwhelming Montezuma's palace guards, who flee at the first sound of pistol shots. Montezuma alone confronts Cortés, who claims Mexico for the king of Spain. "What right could your king have over Mexico?" Divine right of the true religion, which he intends to enforce, says Cortés. In an exchange that is far too long, Frederick puts in Montezuma's mouth such absurdities as "Our gods teach compassion and tolerance." He has made his point against Christianity and continues to hammer it home with a heavy hand. Eventually Montezuma is placed in chains. Cortés sings an aria asking him to do homage, to which Montezuma replies defiantly in his big da capo aria.

Eupaforice arrives and is stunned to see her betrothed in chains. Cortés lies to her and says that he was the one who was attacked: to Spanish treachery, add mendacity. She sees through him and to his claims of the one true god she hurls back, "Your only god is insatiable greed!" Montezuma is led out. The fiery princess sparks the flames of lust in Cortés, who maintains that Montezuma can be saved only if she gives herself to him. After three more arias that could easily be deleted, she gives vent to the explosion of wounded dignity and shame in her aria di bravura that ends Act II.

Act III opens in the dungeon where Montezuma is imprisoned. He bewails his fate in an obbligato recitative (peppered with diminished chords) in the strings. The *Largo e pizzicato* in common time in the key of E that he then sings is a short **A B A** form and open-ended, stopping on a dominant chord. Eupaforice enters, having bribed the guards with gold. Without ritornello he begins the love duet in A, which she answers by singing the same music to different words a fifth higher in E. For this piece flutes are added and the strings are muted. Graun shows a nice variety here but not enough to sustain such great length. Erissena enters with bad news that their plan to rouse the natives against the Spanish was betrayed. Tezeuco enters with more bad news: the Spaniards have slain every resistor. They urge Montezuma to flee but he vows to stay and die.

The scene changes to a great courtyard with a view of Mexico City in the distance. Spanish soldiers bring Montezuma and the others before Cortés, who sings a furious aria, *Allegro* 4/4 in G, which is quite unnerving in its chromatic rises for the strings in unison. The message has not changed. Only Eupaforice can save her betrothed by sacrificing herself to Cortés. At this she begins another piece without orchestral ritornello (Example 4.13). The cavatina in b is quoted up to the end of its first part, the cadence on the relative major. Note how the V - I cadence of the recitative is directly joined to the aria, which begins with the second chord. The first violins mostly double the voice, the violas the bass, while the second violins provide harmonic filler. At a few key points the first violins diverge from the vocal line and carry it higher, as in m. 5 and m. 11. A sense of urgency is maintained by plunging into the second key in m. 7, with the previous dominant chord

EXAMPLE 4.13. *Graun*, Montezuma, *Recitative cadence and Aria*

left unresolved. At the climactic melodic sighs in mm. 14–18 the strings provide full diminished-seventh chords. Graun wisely breaks the sequential pattern in m. 22 and sends the voice spiraling up to high A, exceeded then only by the precadential high B. The deceptive cadence in m. 27 helps him to increase tension. At the *fortissimo* in m. 29 the strings begin a clamorous ritornello, their first.

In the spirited directness of an aria like "Mostro!" and in its simple but effective rhythmic means, Graun seems as much or more a disciple of Vinci than he is of Hasse, who often opts for more subtle and complex rhythmic shapes. Graun's strong bass part, on the other hand, with its quasi-canonic dialogue as at the beginning of the piece, is more in character with his Saxon countryman. In any case Graun at his best is on a par with the two other masters in dramatic effectiveness.

The final aria is sung by Montezuma. It is curious as to text in having three stanzas, the first two in a defiant *Allegro* sung to Cortés, and the third, a tender farewell to his beloved sung to an *Adagio* in 3/8 time. The effect would seem like two separate pieces were the three sections not unified tonally by a progression from f to A♭ (first stanza), A♭ to c (second stanza), and C to f (third stanza). At his final repetition of "l'ultimo sospir" (the last breath) the orchestra breaks in with an agitated *Allegro* in common time, a diminished-seventh chord in reiterated dotted rhythms, to which the despairing Eupaforice sings conjugal endearments and further imprecations upon Cortés. An enharmonic change, a device of which Graun was very fond, moves the key from the flat to the sharp side of the tonal spectrum. Flames begin to leap from the city in the distance (as they do in another and more famous final scene, the end of Metastasio's *Didone*). The heroine taunts the villain, saying she ordered the arson, then she stabs herself to death, at which Cortés orders his troops "go slay them all." Reacting to this mass murder is the final chorus, a short *Presto* in 6/8 and in A (the key of the opening sinfonia), "Oh Cielo! ahi giorno orribile." The evening's entertainment was still not over. A ballet was added, as was the case with the first two acts as well. It depicted the rape and pillage committed by the Spanish and the flight of their few surviving victims.

The secondary characters inspired Graun less. Erisenna, for example, in her first aria was given an anodyne, overly optimistic text, "Godi l'amabile presente instante" (the eighteenth-century equivalent of "Have a nice day"). The composer could do little but invent a pleasantly pastoral but largely characterless musical raiment in G.[75] In this minuet-like *Allegretto* in 3/4 time two flutes double the treble in parallel thirds nearly throughout. The result is a sickly sweet sameness, not helped by the four-square rhythms. When Hasse set this kind of text he did resort to many of the same features, but managed to come up with an unusual twist or turn so as to lend more interest. Graun, on the other hand, is largely free of surprise or nuance. "Godi l'amabile" is a five-line single stanza, set like several texts in the opera of similar cast by repeating the entire text for the seconda parte.

Another disappointment in Graun's aria settings is his heavy reliance on the "wedge cadence." No fewer than six of the eight arias in Act I employ it. Hasse

---

[75]The aria is republished in its entirety in short score in *Historical Anthology of Music*, ed. Archibald T. Davison and Willi Apel, 2 vols. (Cambridge, Mass., 1947–50), 2: no. 282.

was much more sparing in its use. If Graun had had even one tenor voice at his disposal among the soloists, the monotony of soprano-alto sounds would have been broken. Even better would have been a tenor Cortés and bass Navrès.

For all its shortcomings *Montezuma* remains the high point of Frederican opera, and in Berlin the royal opera set the tone for every other kind of music. Graun was the center around which other composers revolved, even as early as his Italian cantatas of the 1730s. His premature death changed little. Frederick would not allow opera, or the court music in general, to advance beyond *Montezuma*.

Quantz and the Royal Chamber Music

Quantz was born in Scheden, a small village of the electorate of Hanover, in 1697. His father was a blacksmith and trained the boy to succeed him. This early practical training stood him in good stead to work with his hands later, as he did in making flutes and improving their mechanism. When his father died he was taken in by an uncle who was a town musician in Merseburg. It was during his apprenticeship there that he learned to play several instruments. His first trip from Dresden to Berlin was in 1728, during the state visit of Augustus. As he tells it in his autobiography, it was Frederick's mother, Sophie Dorothea, who then sought to employ him.

> After I had the honor of allowing myself to be heard several times before Her Majesty, the Queen, I was offered a position by Her Highness for 800 thalers a year. I was ready to accept, but the King, my master, would not agree. However, I did receive permission to go to Berlin as often as I was requested. In the same year, 1728, the Crown Prince of Prussia, now His Reigning Majesty, decided to study the transverse flute and I had the honor of teaching His Highness. For this reason I had to go to Berlin, Ruppin, or Rhinesberg twice every year. (p. 246)

When Frederick Augustus succeeded his father in 1733 Quantz's salary was raised to 800 thalers annually, and his permission to visit Berlin was confirmed. In addition he was allowed to visit Bayreuth to give flute lessons to the margrave (husband of Frederick's sister Wilhelmina). In a letter to Wilhelmina dated 12 January 1736, Frederick described the blacksmith's son as behaving like a *grand seigneur*: "You will find Quantz's high opinion of himself the more insupportable in that it is really without foundation. The only way to bring his haughtiness to an end is not to treat him too much like a grand gentleman."[76] He also looked the part of a

---

[76]Helm, *Music at the Court of Frederick the Great*, p. 158.

noble courtier according to an elegant portrait of him holding a flute, painted about this time by an unknown artist.[77]

Frederick's final offer to Quantz was so advantageous he had to accede. He would be required only in the king's small private band. This time he received permission to leave.

> In November 1741, I was called to Berlin by his Prussian Majesty for the last time, and offered a position by His Highness with such favorable conditions that I could no longer decline: two thousand thalers a year for life, plus a special payment for my compositions, a hundred ducats for each flute that I would construct, the privilege of not having to play in the [opera] orchestra, but only in the royal chamber music, and not having to take orders from anyone but the King. These justified my giving up a service from which I could never hope for such advantages. His Majesty, the King of Poland, was too merciful to refuse me for long the release which I sought in writing, especially since I was not obliged to His Highness as a subject, nor did the traveling money advanced me, in addition to my salary, oblige me to stay. Thus I left Dresden in December, 1741. (p. 246)

This suggests that had Quantz been born in the electorate of Saxony a release might not have been forthcoming so easily or quickly. It speaks well of Frederick Augustus that he allowed his great flautist to depart. Quantz became a very prolific composer in his Dresden years. He speaks in his autobiography of forming his personal style there and benefiting from "the constant intercourse with my dearest friend, Herr Concertmaster Pisendel, whose critical judgment, ever as correct as penetrating, did me uncommon good. The beautiful church music, the excellent operas, and exceptionally fine vocal virtuosos whom I could hear in Dresden constantly, brought me ever new pleasures and always rekindled my inspiration" (p. 245). Since Pisendel was a pupil of Vivaldi, and Quantz admitted earlier that he based his concertos on those of Vivaldi, he was in a sense doubly indebted to the Venetian master. His favorable remark about the church music is a tribute to Heinichen and Zelenka, just as his remark on the opera is a tribute to Hasse and Faustina.

In Berlin there was no royal church music as there was in Dresden, but the opera was as much like Dresden as Frederick could make it, although the commander was Graun, not Hasse. When writing his autobiography in 1754, Quantz was not loath to bestow high praise on Berlin's musical establishment, beginning with the opera.

> All of the royal music here—the reigning sensible-mixed and lovely style of theatrical composition; the various good Italian vocal virtuosos whom we have had, or still have;

---

[77]Reproduced in the article "Quantz," in *New Grove*. See also Charles Walthall, "Portraits of Johann Joachim Quantz," *Early Music* 14 (1986): 500–18.

the good orchestra, which already during the years 1731–1740 at Ruppin and Rheinsberg, was in such good condition that it charmed every composer and player and could give complete satisfaction; and which finally was enlarged into one of the finest orchestras in Europe after the beginning of the present reign: the various outstanding virtuosos who are in this orchestra—all this, I say, is already so well-known and famous that it would be superfluous to describe each in detail according to its merit. (p. 249)

Since Graun almost alone was allowed to compose for the opera, the remark on the mixed style (vernünftig-vermischte und reizende Geschmack) pertains to his music, which did indeed reign. There are elements of French as well as Italian style in Graun, who wrote his own ballet music and was partial to the French overture until Frederick told him to stop writing them. "Sensible" is what Quantz also used to qualify Lotti's operas for Dresden in 1717–19, and there it was a question of "the pure, but sensible, Italian style, from which the Italians have since strayed too far." In this light what Quantz praises in Graun comes close to meaning the early galant style. One can see here the beginnings of what became an official "party line." The remarks Quantz makes on the orchestra bear witness to the two fine violinists who were its concertmasters, Franz Benda up to 1740, and Johann Gottlieb Graun thereafter.

When Quantz began to specialize in the transverse flute during the 1720s the literature written for the instrument, or about it, was small and centered mainly in Paris. Visiting France in 1726–27 he had a second key added to the instrument. Among flute players he named as the best Michel Blavet, whom Frederick in vain tried to engage during the 1730s. Had Blavet, who made his debut at the Concert Spirituel in 1726, accepted the offers from Berlin, perhaps Quantz would have remained in Dresden.

Quantz mentions in his autobiography the paucity of music specifically composed for flute. He made it his mission in life to remedy that situation as well as deficiencies of the instrument. He published as his Op. 1 *Sei sonate a flauto traversiere solo* (Dresden, 1734), dedicating the sonatas to Frederick Augustus. This edition alone was authorized by the composer, although many of his sonatas achieved unauthorized publication, which shows that there was a demand for such works. In all he left some 300 solo flute concertos, 200 solo flute sonatas, and 45 trio sonatas for two flutes or one flute and another treble instrument. Much of his music was written for Frederick, either as prince or king. In one estimation over half of his voluminous production of concertos was written before he transferred to Berlin in 1741.[78] A more recent estimate places the break between Dresden and Berlin around Concerto No. 110.[79] In any case Quantz kept up his ties with Dresden, and particularly with Pisendel, his dear friend and mentor, who

[78] Edward R. Reilly, *Quantz and his Versuch: Three Studies* (New York, 1971), chapter 1.
[79] Meike ten Brink, *Die Flötenkonzerte von Johann Joachim Quantz: Untersuchungen zu ihrer Überlieferung und Form* (Hildesheim, 1995), p. 220.

received some of his Berlin works for his personal collection. Thanks to the intervention of the music-loving electress Maria Josepha, Pisendel's collection was purchased for the court and still survives in large part.

Quantz's concertos generally adhere to the prescription for such works by the composer himself in his invaluable treatise of 1752, *Versuch einer Anweisung die Flöte traversiere zu spielen*. They are in three movements, fast–slow–fast, all of which tend to be organized according to the ritornello principle. In the first movement he favored a five-ritornello, four-solo format. He preferred common time for the opening movement, but a lighter meter for the closing one. His slow movements usually provided either modal or tonal contrast. Concertos in the major mode most commonly resorted to the subdominant for the middle movement, or to the tonic minor. Very few concertos are available in modern editions, which reflects the situation in the composer's own lifetime, when this was a private repertory for his own personal circle and especially for Frederick. From the few that are available it appears that Quantz was at his most original and affecting in slow movements.

The Concerto in C that has become a favorite with modern flute soloists is not present in the Berlin manuscripts but is of undisputed authenticity.[80] It opens with an *Allegro* in common time that comes to an abrupt halt after three measures (Example 4.14abc). The closing *Presto* in 2/4 is much jauntier, with hints of the buffo in its unison writing. But it is the middle movement, *Amoroso* in 3/4, that is most memorable. It too is in the key of C, contrary to the composer's normal practice, and given to frequent and abrupt cadences, like the *Allegro*. The way the melody takes flight in m. 5 is arresting.

Quantz is not always so short-breathed or symmetrically chopped up in his melodic writing as in this example. In the Concerto No. 166 in G, dated ca. 1745 on the basis of paper studies and other evidence, the middle movement once again excels.[81] It is an *Arioso e mesto* in g, beginning with a melody that soars in long phrases up to the highest range of the flute. Quantz makes poignant use of the raised fourth coming after the flat sixth and fifth degrees, lending a rather Slavic character to the melody, perhaps a souvenir of his early years in Bohemia and Poland. Graun uses this same melodic trait in *Montezuma* (aria in the second act for Pilpatoè, also in g).

Music by Quantz completely dominated the evening chamber concerts that Frederick held at one or the other of his palaces. Quantz alone was allowed to comment on the king's flute playing, and this commentary was restricted to an occasional "bravo." The only other composer of instrumental music that we can be

[80]Johann Joachim Quantz, *Konzert in C-dur für Flöte, Streichorchester und Cembalo*, ed. Hanns-Dieter Sonntag (Corona No. 56) (Wolfenbüttel, 1959).
[81]Johann Joachim Quantz, *Concerto for Flute, Strings and Basso continuo in G major*, ed. Horst Augsbach (Wiesbaden, 1991).

EXAMPLE 4.14. *Quantz, Flute Concerto in C*

a.

certain had works played at these concerts was Frederick himself, who wrote a few flute concertos and many flute sonatas under the tutelage of Quantz and Graun in the Rheinsberg era (1736–40). Quantz did not normally play himself, unless two flutes were required. Yet he gave the tempo of each movement and started it going, acts normally reserved to the concertmaster. Not only this, he chose what was to be performed, in conjunction with Frederick. In every sense he was the director of the royal chamber music. Franz Benda, the elder Graun, and Emanuel Bach were all fine and prolific composers of concertos, but in the royal concerts apparently all they got to do was accompany. Quantz's official title was "chamber composer" according to the summary of the court's musical forces that Marpurg printed in 1754.[82] With respect to other composers of the royal chamber music, he appears to have been no less despotic than his master.

[82]Friedrich Wilhelm Marpurg, *Historisch-Kritische Beyträge zur Aufnahme der Musik*, 5 vols. (Berlin, 1754–78), 1: 75.

One of Frederick's generals, Count Egmont von Chasot, wrote a detailed description of the royal chamber concerts in his memoirs. He was an intimate of the king even before the coronation. After describing the music room at Potsdam he mentions the makeup of the chamber group that accompanied the king:

> The ensemble consisted of only one first and one second violin (seldom doubled), a viola, a cello, and as clavecin a fortepiano made by Silbermann, the flute, or two flutes when Quantz played with the king. Sometimes one or two castratos or one of the best female singers of the opera received orders and a royal coach for their journey to Potsdam. Only flute or voices were heard as soloists in the concerts; the other instruments were there only to accompany.[83]

Chasot also sang the praises of Quantz's "heavenly music" and says that Frederick paid him 30 louis for each new concerto, 20 louis for a trio sonata, and 10 louis for a solo sonata. Quantz had every inducement to be as prolific as he was.

Other Musicians in Prussian Service

Burney named Johann Gottlieb Graun as a favorite of Frederick's, but he was not favored in the same sense as his younger brother or Quantz. Like Quantz he studied with Pisendel, who taught him both violin playing and composition. His output of instrumental music was enormous: as many as sixty violin concertos, over a hundred symphonies and French overtures, and nearly two hundred trio sonatas. It stands to reason that some of this music must have been performed in the concerts of his royal master, but this cannot be proven. Outside of Frederick's concerts there were musical soirées given by the Queen Mother and other members of the numerous royal family, as well as by some members of the nobility. The compositions of Concertmaster Graun were known to have been cultivated by Frederick's younger sister Anna Amalia, who had many pieces by him copied for her collection.[84] Berlin also had a tradition of small public concerts. Perhaps the royal concerts in the first half of Frederick's reign were less rigidly structured than those in the second half.

Concertmaster Graun, although not achieving the cultlike devotion of his brother or Quantz, had a loyal following on the local level. When Burney dismissed his "overtures and concertos for violin" as being "still in high reputation at Berlin, though not of the first class for taste and invention" (p. 98), protests arose,

[83]Kurt von Schlözer, *General Graf Chasot: Zur Geschichte Friedrich des Grossen und seiner Zeit,* 2nd ed. (Berlin, 1878), pp. 226–27, cited after Meike ten Brink, *Die Flötenkonzerte von Johann Joachim Quantz,* p. 79.
[84]E. R. Bleckschmidt, *Die Amalien bibliothek* (Berlin, 1965).

first from his German translator, who felt obliged to contradict him, and then from Peter Schulz in his article "Symphonie" for Sulzer's encyclopedia; Schulz wrote that "in some of his chamber symphonies Johann Gottlieb has discovered the true spirit of the genre" (in einigen Kammersymphonien den wahren Geist der Symphonien getroffen).[85] Few of the composer's works were published during his lifetime and they have fared little better in modern editions. The Symphony in G that was advertized in Breitkopf's catalogue in 1762 is in three movements beginning with an ample *Allegro* in common time.[86] As head motif the composer chooses a unison passage ascending the triad with trills on the third degree and repeated eighth-notes as upbeat to the second measure on the fifth degree. His textures are full, and once the movement gets fully underway there are many sixteenth-note scales up and down in the violin. He displays the same *horror vacui* that plagued the "rushing violins à la Reutter" in Vienna.[87] When the trills take over the orchestra to the extent of answering back and forth between treble and bass in the same measure, the composer who comes to mind as a kindred soul is his colleague Emanuel Bach. One can understand how Burney might have reacted to such a movement as being too busy and having entirely too many notes, or as being deficient in cantilena. It is as obvious from the music that the composer is a violinist as it is that his brother's music was written by a singer.

There were two minds about the value of Johann Gottlieb's music even in Berlin, according to Burney. Those in favor found him to be "one of the greatest performers on the violin of his time, and most assuredly, a composer of the first rank; his overtures and symphonies are majestic, and his concertos are masterpieces, particularly those for two violins, in which he has united the most agreeable melody, with all the learning the art of counterpoint can boast." The opposite view, obviously Burney's as well, deprecates not just the music but the coarse way it was played.

> But less quarter is granted to this master, by the admirers of more modern music, than to his brother; they often find his overtures and symphonies too like those of Lully, and too full of notes to produce any other effect, when played at Berlin, than of stunning the hearers; and in his concertos and church music, when that is not the case, the length of each movement is more immoderate, than Christian patience can bear.

There is a Mass in E$^\flat$ that survives and perhaps Burney saw a score.

Of one violin concerto at least he heard a performance. The local musicians, as had happened at Dresden, assembled a concert in his honor. It took place on 3 October in the house of one of the royal violinists, a certain Kone, and was per-

[85]J. G. Sulzer, *Allgemeine Theorie der schönen Künste* (Leipzig, 1771–74).
[86]Mennicke, *Hasse und die Brüder Graun*, pp. 210–15, quotes the movement at length.
[87]*Haydn, Mozart*, p. 82.

formed by gentlemen as well as professional musicians. "I heard here a concerto of the late concert-master Graun's composition, performed by M. Kone, with more force than delicacy." The concert included symphonies by Hasse and Graun, a difficult flute concerto by Quantz played by Friedrich Lintner (showing that these works were not the exclusive property of Frederick), and another flute concerto composed and performed by Friedrich Wilhelm Riedt, "of which, both the style and the performance were rather coarse."

In Johann Gottlieb's favor it should be added that he had the confidence of Johann Sebastian Bach, who sent the fifteen-year-old Wilhelm Friedemann, his first and favorite son, to study violin with Graun at Merseburg in 1726. Moreover, Bach copied out two trio sonatas by Graun. This friendly relationship was presumably renewed when father Bach visited Potsdam in 1741 and 1747, the latter occasion giving rise to the meeting with Frederick that resulted in *The Musical Offering.* Emanuel Bach's relations with the Graun brothers were cordial. In late 1756 he wrote his godfather Telemann, who had requested some of their music, probably for the public concerts he supervised in Hamburg. With an ironic humor that is typical of him, Bach apologized for delays in forwarding the requested scores.

> The younger Herr Graun, in whom I noticed some concern about his Passion *[Der Tod Jesu]* will be heard from in writing in a few days. . . . The elder was supposed and prepared to send his concertos tightly wrapped to me early today, according to our understanding, on pain of having to mail them to you himself if he missed the present opportunity. Since I have not seen them yet, I suspect that he has willingly subjected himself to this punishment. I await Your Honour's further orders on this matter.[88]

Bach said, furthermore, that if he were more effective at collecting and sending the music requested, "this concert director [Telemann] would no longer doubt my good intentions."[89] In his better-known letter to Johann Forkel about his father's preferences among contemporary composers, the Grauns, along with Franz Benda, are named. Quantz is not.

> In his last years he esteemed highly: Fux, Caldara, Handel, Keiser, Hasse, both Grauns, Telemann, Zelenka, Benda, and in general everything that was particularly esteemed in Berlin and Dresden. Except for the first four, he knew the rest personally. In his younger years he was often together with Telemann, who was also my godfather. He valued him highly, especially his instrumental things. He was very severe in

[88]Letter dated Berlin, 29 December 1756, no. 2 in *The Letters of C. P. E. Bach,* ed. Clark, pp. 3–4.
[89]*Carl Philipp Emanuel Bach: Briefe und Dokumenten. Kritische Gesamtausgabe,* ed. Ernst Suchalla (Göttingen, 1994), p. 52. Suchalla's interpretation here differs from Clark's.

his judgment of works, *quoad Harmonium,* but otherwise he esteemed everything that was really good, and gave it his approval even if human weaknesses were to be found.[90]

What else could one expect of the great Bach than that he was a strict judge of musical works as to harmony? Yet he was able to appreciate what was really good in spite of weaknesses, a degree of tolerance that would have been needed in order to esteem much of what was fashionable in Berlin and Dresden.

Franz Benda, born in a small town northeast of Prague in 1709, was probably the least well trained composer on Bach's list, and the one about whose young life we know the most, thanks to his frank and entertaining autobiography, written at Marpurg's request in 1763 and amplified in another version three years later.[91] Between his duties as a choirboy in various Prague churches and his fiddling in taverns in order to earn his keep, Benda had little time or inclination for his studies. Around 1720 he ran away from the Jesuits in Prague in order to join the royal choirboys in Dresden, who were also under the tutelage of Jesuits. Still aged only eleven or twelve he became homesick in Dresden and ran away again in order to rejoin his parents. He was fourteen when the wide world of music descended on Prague in 1723 for the coronation of Charles VI. A prized vocal soloist, he took a contralto solo part in the secondary opera, Zelenka's *Melodramma de Sancto Wenceslas.* He undoubtedly heard Tartini as well as all the other virtuoso performers who came to Prague from Vienna, Dresden, and elsewhere. At age fifteen his voice broke and he began to practice the violin more seriously. He learned many concertos of Vivaldi by heart. In 1726 he was sent to Vienna in order to perfect his skills, and there he fell under the spell of the great cellist Francesco Alborea (alias Francischello), with whom he often played trios. After deserting three masters in Vienna in turn, he fled to Poland. He left the service of one Polish noble in order to join that of King Augustus, residing first in Warsaw, then in Dresden. By this time converted to Protestantism, he no longer wished to serve at a Catholic court. In 1733 he sought and found welcome at Ruppin as concertmaster of Frederick's quasi-secret chamber orchestra. He was valued for his excellent tenor voice and expected to sing a few arias almost every evening.

Not until Benda encountered the Graun brothers at Ruppin did he receive any systematic instruction in composition. Johann Gottlieb taught him how to set basses under melodies and also instructed him in some of the finer points of violin playing, especially in *Adagios.* He had already begun composing violin sonatas.

[90]Letter dated Hamburg, 13 January 1775, no. 76 in *The Letters of C. P. E. Bach,* pp. 72–75. The sentence about Telemann beginning "He valued him" was crossed out.
[91]On the two versions, see Heartz, "Coming of Age in Bohemia." The first is quoted in English translation in Paul Nettl, *Forgotten Musicians* (New York, 1951), pp. 204–45; the second is translated in part by Burney in his long chapter on Berlin.

Carl Heinrich instructed him in harmonizing chorales. Most of his music was composed between this time and 1750, he says, after which circumstances prevented him from composing much. In his autobiography he stated that he had composed eighty solo sonatas, fifteen concertos, a few symphonies, and many caprices for violin. These estimates were on the low side. Twelve concertos traveled as far as Vienna, if we may believe a tale told by Ditters about himself as a young violinist performing them. Still it was in the solo sonata with bass that he made his main contributions as a composer. As a performer he was unsurpassed, according to many witnesses.

Benda's violin sonatas are in three movements, usually all in the same key. The slow movement tends to come first in the manuscript copies but in the few printed versions it was often shifted to the middle, testifying to a gradually emerging preference for the fast–slow–fast design. No autographs survive. Our sampling is based on a critical edition of six sonatas for which one or more alternative versions of the solo part survive.[92] Benda's melodies tend to be quite flowery and ornamented to begin with, but no more so than those of Quantz. Benda is less predictable in his musical discourse than Quantz. He often favors a simple canonic dialogue between treble and bass in the final movements—his most advanced gesture in the direction of counterpoint. He is also prone to a certain mischievousness, such as inserting entire measures of silence where they are least expected. Not all his melodies in opening and middle movements are in the florid style.

The Sonata in e opens with an *Allegretto* that is relatively plain, its melody well-planned and cantabile (Example 4.15). Climbing from the first to the second to the third degree then turning back in m. 3 with a legato conjunct third downwards, Benda avoids a cadence in m. 4; he arrives at the tonic only on the third beat and supports it not by a chord in root position but by the third in the bass. He continues the melody, which has not really been interrupted, with the descending conjunct third, then suddenly soars up to high B, from which he descends into the half-cadence in m. 8, filling in the intervening melodic space. He has created a broadly spun eight-measure phrase, and to celebrate the feat, he repeats it, now *piano*, subtly varied, with expressive syncopations, the *piquanterie* of parallel sevenths in m. 12, and an expansive ascent in eighth notes up to the high B in m. 14. The gentle melancholy and extreme melodiousness of the theme suggests comparison with a rather similar theme by another Bohemian-born composer, Johann Baptist Vanhal, at the beginning of his Symphony in a.[93]

---

[92]Franz Benda, *Six Sonatas for Solo Violin and Continuo with Embellished Versions*, ed. Douglas A. Lee (Recent Researches in the Music of the Classic Era 13) (Madison, Wis., 1981). See also Douglas A. Lee, "Some Embellished Versions of Sonatas by Franz Benda," *Musical Quarterly* 62 (1976): 58–71.
[93]Exemplified in *Haydn, Mozart*, p. 459.

EXAMPLE 4.15. *Franz Benda, Violin Sonata in e, I*

Benda was very modest about his accomplishments as a composer. Subject to frequent depressions, he was often unable to compose anything at all. In the postscript to his memoir, dated 18 April 1763, he regrets that he never had the opportunity to learn the keyboard:

This instrument would have been of great service in my compositions; the fact that I did not master it made me shy away from "strong" things and fugues. Knowing my limited possibilities I endeavored all the more to write violin sonatas in a skillful and singable manner. Whether I succeeded in it may be left to the judgment of those violinists who tried to play my compositions for almost thirty years. The late Kapellmeister Graun used to keep me from brooding to which I was strongly inclined and always told me that I should follow the tracks of my innate singing voice whereby I would earn the gratitude of all music lovers. In short, I am not ashamed to confess publicly that I cannot be placed among the great contrapuntists. Everyone has his own gift and should try to do his best with it. I have admiration and due respect for those contrapuntists who also can express beautiful thoughts, for they are rare and therefore all the more to be admired. But those compositions which show an only apparent and inflated mastership remain rare too, for nobody asks for them and their composers are angry with the whole world. To make their creations rewarding, they increase their own enthusiasm and acclamation tenfold; and they never listen to the compositions of their colleagues to enjoy them, only to find something in them they can criticize.[94]

[94]Franz Benda, *Autobiography* (1763), translated by Paul Nettl in *Forgotten Musicians*, p. 244.

Not by coincidence was Benda encouraged especially by Graun, another singer turned composer.

The contrapuntists Benda believed capable of expressing "beautiful thoughts" surely included the Bachs and the Grauns. Who were those others? The answer may lie in his last word. By 1760 Berlin was spawning more music criticism than it was truly original compositions. The animus Benda displayed may have been directed against Johann Philipp Kirnberger, who had a brief time as violinist in the court orchestra before joining the chapel of Prince Henry in 1754, then that of Princess Anna Amalia in 1758. He was well known for his acrid criticism of other musicians and the pedantry of his own music.

Georg Zarth, born near Deutsch-Brod, Bohemia, in 1708, had a career closely parallel to that of Franz Benda. They fled Vienna together for Poland in 1729, eventually entering royal service there, then moving to Dresden. A flautist and violinist, Zarth followed Benda to Ruppin in 1734 and remained in Frederick's service until the Seven Years War, when he left Berlin for Mannheim. Around 1750 Boivin in Paris printed two sets of six solo sonatas with basso continuo by Zarth, one for flute, the other for violin. Marpurg lists him as a violinist of the royal orchestra in 1754.

An exact contemporary of Zarth's was Johann Gottlieb Janitsch, born in Silesia in 1708 and trained as a musician in Breslau. He studied law from 1728 to 1731 at the University of Frankfurt an der Oder, just preceding Emanuel Bach's years there. Janitsch must have been a talented composer even in his student days. He received several commissions for occasional pieces from the university and from the court, among them a cantata (lost) for the wedding of Princess Wilhelmina and the margrave of Bayreuth in 1731. In 1736 he was called to join Frederick in Ruppin. His primary instrument was the contrabass. He was commissioned in 1748 to compose a *Te Deum* (lost) for the laying of the cornerstone of Saint Hedwig's cathedral. His duties included composing and directing the music for the court balls in the opera house during carnival season. At his home in Berlin he maintained a series of weekly concerts, performed by professional and amateur musicians alike and known as the "Friday academies." These may very well have served as performance outlets for court musicians whose music found no place in Frederick's concerts. They were later imitated by three other concert series.

Johann Friedrich Agricola was born in Saxe-Altenburg in 1720 and was a student at the University of Leipzig from 1738 to 1741, at which time he was also a pupil of Johann Sebastian Bach. He moved to Berlin in 1741 and continued his studies with Quantz, also with Emanuel Bach. As a composer he was a follower of Hasse and Graun, in whose *Tod Jesu* he sang the solo tenor part at the work's premiere. His first success was an intermezzo, *Il filosofo convinto in amore*, performed at Potsdam in 1750, as a result of which Frederick appointed him a court composer with a salary of 500 thalers. He made the mistake of wedding one of the singers of the court opera, the soprano Benedetta Molteni, going against the royal command forbidding singers to marry. As punishment Frederick reduced their joint salary to 1,000 thalers (hers had been 1,500). Agricola remained more or less in royal disfavor for the rest of his career. When Graun died in 1759 Frederick named him director of the opera without benefit of the title of maestro di capella. Like many Berlin composers he was active writing musical criticism. His annotated German translation of Pier Francesco Tosi's *Opinioni de' cantori antichi e moderni* in 1757 claims a place in the history of singing.

Christoph Nichelmann was another composer who came to Berlin by way of Leipzig. Born in the province of Brandenburg in 1717, he attended the Thomasschule in 1730 and studied keyboard and composition with Friedemann Bach. He pursued his studies in Hamburg and moved to Berlin in 1739, where he subsequently had further lessons with Quantz and the elder Graun. Emanuel Bach also claimed him as a pupil. He published harpsichord sonatas in Nuremberg in 1745 and was most important for his sixteen concertos for harpsichord and strings. In 1744 he was appointed royal harpsichord player alongside Emanual Bach, a service he left in 1756, after which he apparently supported himself only by teaching.

The Seven Years War and its aftermath entailed a major decline in Prussian court music. With the demise of Graun in 1759, Frederick began to lose interest in opera. The opera had become senescent even before Graun died by the king's stubborn veneration of the Hasse ideal to the exclusion of any other. On the bright side of the picture, the numerous fine musicians hired for the royal chamber music and the opera began to exert a beneficial effect on musical life outside the court even before the Seven Years War. A case in point is the proliferation of concert societies, of which Marpurg described four already flourishing in 1754.

Burney in Berlin

A high point of Burney's tours is his description of his experiences at Berlin and Potsdam in late September and early October 1772. Burney swelled it to nearly 150 pages by including his translation and adaptation of biographies of three leading Prussian court musicians, Quantz, Franz Benda, and Emanuel Bach. Nowhere in his writing is Burney a keener observer of human nature or civic and courtly culture. His visit to the court at Potsdam particularly hits the mark and deserves to be widely read. Treated as a suspicious character by customs and other officials in his comings and goings, he was welcomed warmly by the musical elite. It would have been a mark of ingratitude to have been too severe a critic of Frederick's apparently tolerant but actually totalitarian state. For a more candid appraisal one can turn to the great Lessing, who minced no words in denouncing Berlin's sterility and repressive effects upon authors like himself. Here it will be possible to consider only a few of Burney's many telling observations, which are often couched in subtle irony.

Burney sets up his readers by admiring all the accomplishments of the Berliners in the realm of music theory and education, ticking off the major publications by Quantz, Emanuel Bach, Agricola, Marpurg, Kirnberger, and Sulzer, by title and date. He was eager to meet and learn from them all. He met Agricola on arrival along with the publisher Friedrich Nicolai, both of whom showed him every courtesy. A visit to the French theater his first night in Berlin gave him an opportunity to praise the theatrical company while decrying Monsigny's charming little opéra-comique *Le cadi dupé.* He inspected the royal opera house, was greatly impressed, and provided a heap of information about it without witnessing a production, for the season did not begin until later. What he could hear in person was the prima donna, the vaunted Gertrud Mara. Oddly enough she chose to introduce herself by singing a bravura aria by Traetta, followed by an *Andante* by the young Brunswick composer Johann Gottfried Schwanenberger, both praised by Burney as to music and performance. Only then did she favor him with an aria of Graun that she was studying for the impending revival of the composer's *Merope.*

At Potsdam Burney met the imposingly tall figure of Quantz, by this time a man in his midseventies. Seeking to put the best possible light on the master's three-hundred-odd flute concertos written for Frederick and played by him in regular rotation, he praised the king for his "constancy of disposition, but rarely to be found among princes." He followed this with a mock defense of old music, seemingly subscribing to the "golden age" theory by which all music was better in the times of yore.

> The compositions of the two Grauns and of Quantz have been in favour with his Prussian majesty more than forty years; and, if it be true, as many assert, that music has declined and degenerated since that time, in which the Scarlattis, Vincis, Leos, Pergolesis, and Porporas flourished, as well as the greatest singers that modern times have known, it is an indication of a sound judgment, and of great discernment, in his majesty, to adhere thus firmly to the productions of a period which may be called the Augustan age of music.

Note that this statement hangs upon a prepositional clause "if it be true." Burney did not believe for an instant that it was true. Detained for an extra day in Potsdam by an invitation to dine with the crown prince, Frederick's nephew and successor as Frederick William II, Burney found someone whose musical tastes were closer to his own. This devoted cellist and future patron of Haydn, Mozart, and Boccherini, Burney discovered, was "less strongly devoted to old music, and to old masters, than his majesty."

By the time Burney was ready to leave Berlin he allowed his descriptions to take on a more censorious tone. For true originality in music among the Berliners he was willing to name only two figures, Franz Benda and Emanuel Bach.

> The rest are imitators; even Quantz and Graun, who have been so much imitated, formed themselves upon the works of Vinci and Vivaldi. M. Quantz is an intelligent man, and talks well concerning music; but talking and composing are different things; when he wrote his book, more than twenty years ago, his opinions were enlarged and liberal, which is not the case at present; and Graun's compositions of thirty years ago, were elegant and simple, as he was among the first Germans to quit fugue and laboured contrivances, and to allow, that such a thing as melody existed, which, harmony should support, not suffocate; but though the world is ever rolling on, most of the Berlin musicians, defeating its motion, have long contrived to stand still.

Perhaps Burney realized that he too was far better at talking about music than composing it. Judging Quantz as a composer on hearing three of his concertos (a ratio of one in a hundred of the totality), and admittedly all early ones, incurred considerable risk, and Burney would later be taken to task on just this point.

It was not just the exclusive love for old music embraced by Frederick, and consequently by the country he ruled with an iron hand, that dismayed Burney. A consequence equally important was the reign of an older performance practice, one with little dynamic nuance or gradations of tone. Burney's ultimate deflation of his own concept of an Augustan age of music involves a comparison of the revered models with their less favored acolytes.

> It would be presumption in me to oppose my single judgment to that of so enlightened a prince; if, luckily, mine were not the opinion of the greatest part of Europe; for, should it be allowed, that his Prussian majesty has fixed upon the Augustan age of music, it does not appear that he has placed his favour upon the best composers of that age. Vinci, Pergolesi, Leo, Feo, Handel, and many others, who flourished in the best times of Graun and Quantz, I think superior to them in taste and genius. Of his majesty's two favourites, the one is languid, and the other frequently common and insipid,—and yet, their names are *religion* at Berlin, and more sworn by, than those of Luther and Calvin.

If Frederick ever saw this, or comprehended English well enough to understand the wry grin behind Burney's "luckily," he would be forced to admit, at least to himself, that the greater part of Europe managed to ignore the music of Quantz and Graun almost totally.

There is no missing Burney's unexpressed sigh of relief upon quitting Berlin. Perhaps he knew how it had gone with Voltaire and other intellectuals who provoked the king's ire. Safely in London when writing up his tour, he took literary leave of Frederick and his capital with some remarks that are even more scathing than those already quoted. He dared to draw an analogy between musical and military despotism. His subject was once again the Berlin opera.

> Though there are constantly Italian operas here, in carnival time, his Prussian majesty will suffer none to be performed but those of Graun, Agricola, or Hasse, and of this last, and best, but very few. And, in the opera house, as in the field, his majesty is such a rigid disciplinarian, that if a mistake is made in a single movement or evolution, he immediately marks, and rebukes the offender; and if any of his Italian troops dare diminishing a single passage in the parts they have to perform, an order is sent, *de par le Roi,* for them to adhere strictly to the notes written by the composer, at their peril. This, when compositions are good, and a singer is licentious, may be an excellent method; but certainly shuts out taste and refinement. So that music is truly stationary in the country, his majesty allowing no more liberty in that, than he does in civil matters of government: not contented with being sole monarch of the lives, fortunes, and business of his subjects, he even prescribes rules to their most innocent pleasures.

This passage he follows directly by a description of his agreeable surprise at arriving in Hamburg, where he perceived an air of liberty.

Burney's 1772 travel book as well as its German translation by Christian Daniel Ebeling and Johann Bode appeared in 1773. Various critics took Burney to task for what were regarded as views too dismissive of German music. Bode was one. He reproved Burney for denigrating Graun's early operas, saying they "have much more melody, expression and novelty, than one can find in many of the arias of his newer operas."[95] Yet Bode's view played into Burney's hand by seeming to confirm that Frederick had dampened Graun's talent.

Friedrich Reichardt was Burney's severest critic. At the age of twenty-one, he had completed a trip that took him through various music centers in North Germany and Bohemia (also Mannheim, he claimed, but this has not been proven). The result was his poorly organized but fascinating *Briefe* or *Letters concerning Music by an Observant Traveler,* the first volume of which was published in 1774. Born in Königsberg, East Prussia, in 1752, Reichardt had a desultory education at the university there and was taught music by, among others, a local organist, Carl Gottlieb Richter, who was an enthusiast for the keyboard works of Emanuel Bach. Reichardt's first letters give his impressions of Berlin and take up where Burney left off. In fact he is indebted to Burney for many of his ideas. At the same time he must have digested Burney's opinions hurriedly and incompletely, because he misquotes some of them. He accuses Burney, for instance, of punishing Schwanenberger, yet this composer was singled out for praise, not blame. After a long and rambling defense of Graun's operas Reichardt is forced to admit that they suffer in comparison with Hasse's. Patronage was responsible in the case of both mas-

---

[95]Grant, *Dr. Burney,* p. 85.

ters, he avers. In Dresden Hasse worked for a king, Frederick Augustus, who allowed him complete liberty to follow where his genius led. In Berlin Graun had no such liberty but was constrained by a king who dictated his every move."What did not please was cut, even if it was the best number in the opera. Being rather one-sided and stubborn [eigensinnig] in his tastes, the king allowed Graun no freedom and variety in his operas."[96] If Frederick read this he could not have been pleased. Burney could only have concurred.

Carl Philipp Emanuel Bach

The"Berlin Bach"stood out from other composers at the Prussian court both for his originality and for the high quality of almost everything he wrote. He often went against the grain of the galant style to the extent that, it could be argued, he does not belong under the rubric at all. But even he could not altogether escape the prevailing musical fashions, any more than could Gluck, his exact contemporary.

Emanuel was the second Bach son, born in Weimar on 8 March 1714. Friedemann, the eldest (born in Weimar on 22 November 1710), was sent away to study violin with the elder Graun at an early age, his father being determined to make him a well-rounded performer and composer. Emanuel, less favored by his father, did not make a special study of the violin. He was left-handed and probably took up the flute as a boy.[97] For the most part, he was trained by his father to be a keyboard player, and he became one without peer. He had no other teacher in this or in composition, as he emphasizes in the autobiography he supplied at the publisher's request for the German translation of Burney's tour in 1773.[98]

After studying law at the University of Leipzig, Emanuel pursued legal studies at the University of Frankfurt an der Oder from 1734 to 1738. He says that he also composed and directed music for all the public festivities at the university, as well as for a concert series. At this point he went to Berlin and received an attractive offer to accompany a young gentleman on the Grand Tour. The traveler was Heinrich Christian von Keyserlingk, son of the Russian ambassador to the Dresden court. Count Keyserlingk was the patron of Sebastian Bach for whom the"Goldberg Variations"were composed. He remained on good terms with Emanuel, as is

---

[96]Reichardt, *Briefe eines aufmerksamen Reisenden die Musik betreffend,* 1: 23.

[97]Günther Wagner, *Die Sinfonien Carl Philipp Emanuel Bachs: Werdende Gattung und Originalgenie* (Stuttgart and Weimar, 1994), pp. 244–45.

[98]A facsimile edition of the autobiography with copious annotations is published in Wili Kahl, *Selbstbiographen deutscher Musiker des 18. Jahrhunderts* (Cologne, 1948; reprint 1972), pp. 27–44. Another annotated facsimile is William S. Newman, *Carl Philip Emanuel Bach's Autobiography* (Hilversum, 1967). Quotations from the autobiography are given below without further attribution.

evident from his standing as godfather to Emanuel's son Johann Sebastian in 1748. The planned trip was to include Austria, Italy, France, and England.

An unexpected summons from Frederick called the young lawyer-composer to Ruppin. The tour had to be abandoned. By the time Emanuel wrote his memoir he clearly regretted not having taken the opportunity to travel abroad. The topic takes up more space in his story than any other. He rationalizes the loss by emphasizing the compensatory advantages of Leipzig, Dresden, and Berlin.

> My Prussian service never allowed me time enough to travel to foreign countries. . . .
> This lack of foreign travel would have been harmful to my profession had I not had the opportunity from youth on to hear first-rate masters perform and become acquainted with them, and sometimes their friend. I had this advantage already in my youth at Leipzig [from visitors to his father's house]. . . . About everything that was to be heard in Berlin and Dresden I need say little. Who does not know this era, in which music, as well as its most accurate and fine performance, began a new period during which the musical art climbed to such a height, whence I fear that, according to my view, it has already to a certain extent, greatly fallen?

The last sentence, starting out with a question, loses its thread in a heap of qualifiers. Unwilling to admit an absolute musical decline in Berlin and Dresden, he hedges his claim by saying "fear" that "according to my feeling" (nach meiner Empfindung) it has "to a certain extent" (gewissermassen) "already lost much" (schon viel verlohren habe).

In what follows he summons the judgment of other sage men, meaning the Berlin critics, to place the blame for the fall on the "comic."[99] This too is qualified. Then comes a digression that is surprising:

> I believe, along with many other insightful persons, that the now so-much-admired "comic" has the largest part in this [fall]. Without citing men of whom it could be objected that they have written little or nothing in the comic vein, I will name one of the greatest masters of the comic style still living, Signor Galuppi, who fully agreed with me when he visited my house in Berlin and cited some very ludicrous examples which he had experienced even in various churches in Italy. I must be satisfied, and am very happy to be satisfied that I have heard, besides the great masters of our country, the best of all kinds that foreign lands have sent to Germany; and I believe that there is no article of music existing of which I have not heard the greatest master.

He excuses himself from naming the composers, singers of both sexes, and instrumentalists of all kinds that he has come to know, saying it would take up

---

[99]The closely knit critical fraternity was unanimous in damning Italian instrumental music and calling it "comic" (as opposed to "serious" German equivalents). See Mary Sue Morrow, *German Music Criticism in the Late Eighteenth Century: Aesthetic Issues in Instrumental Music* (Cambridge, 1997), p. 53.

too much space and also tax his memory."So much I know for sure, that among them were geniuses that of this kind and greatness will not return."There is more than a whiff of Berlin's musical parochialism in such a statement. Yet it is softened in the next sentence by a lingering sense of remorse."In spite of all this, I do not deny that it would have been uncommonly dear and also advantageous to me, had I had the opportunity and means to visit foreign countries."

There follows the briefest mention of his personal life: marriage to the youngest daughter of a wine merchant in 1744, a union blessed with three children, two sons and a daughter. The elder son became a lawyer, the younger studied painting in Dresden and Leipzig. To these facts he appended a list of printed works that he acknowledged as authentic.

After listing his works that had been published, as far as he knew, and summarizing those that remained unpublished, Bach made a statement that seems part apology, part defense against criticism.

> I had to compose most of my works for certain persons and for the public and thus was always more circumscribed than I was in the few pieces I finished solely for myself. I even had to follow ludicrous prescriptions [Vorschriften] occasionally; nevertheless it could be that not altogether unpleasant circumstances of this kind moved my Genius to certain discoveries that I perhaps might not have made otherwise.

The apology pertains in part to the number of"easy"pieces he had written for the public and given to the press, with the main aim of supplementing his meager income. Who were the"certain persons"for whom he had to compose? Frederick comes to mind, yet he treated Bach not as a composer but as a mere accompanist. The two sets of keyboard works known as the *Prussian* and *Württemberg* Sonatas, published in Nuremberg, represent Bach at his best and certainly require no apology. In a letter to Forkel dated Hamburg, 10 February 1775, Bach mentions the latter set, saying he composed the sonatas at a clavichord with a short octave while taking a cure for his gout at Bad Töplitz in 1743. Then he appends,"subsequently, I have had to work mostly for the public, except for a few sonatas of the usual disposition that I play before amateurs now and then and are unknown."[100] Thus the "easy" works for the public followed the *Württemberg* Sonatas. A recent critic has expressed the unfashionable view that artistic quality and generic advancement would have been better served in Bach's case had he benefited from a generous aristocratic patron for whom to compose sonatas, instead of the bourgeois public.[101]

[100]*The Letters of C. P. E. Bach,* pp. 75–76.
[101]Günther Wagner,"Die Entwicklung der Klaviersonate bei C. Ph. E. Bach,"in *Carl Philipp Emanuel Bach und die europäische Musikkultur des mittleren 18. Jahrhunderts,* ed. Hans Joachim Marx (Göttingen, 1990), pp. 231–43; 243.

The piece written "according to ludicrous prescriptions" must be the well-known Trio Sonata in c, "Conversation between a Sanguinary and a Melancholiac" (Wotquenne 161/1; Helm 579), published in 1751 and described in the list of pieces in the autobiography as being "annotated" (mit Anmerkung). Bach was stung by the personal reaction to this piece as emerges in a letter to the poet Johann Daniel Gerstenberg in the fall of 1773, close in time to the autobiography. Gerstenberg related that incompetent attempts at program music in Copenhagen had raised derisive laughter. Sensitive on this point, Bach replied in a general way so as to put the poet off from inveigling him into the same. On one point he was specific.

> Of course one should not pour empty derision on the honest artist who wrote under his painted bird, "this is supposed to be a bird," especially when one says nothing about a sickness that might have occasioned certain experiments: indeed I remember when, many years ago, I had my *Sanguineus and Cholericus* printed, that I was not exactly insensitive when a good friend said certain things to me about it in jest, which he did not really mean maliciously but which did not please me. How weak we are![102]

Even if the experiment were undertaken in a delirium ("sickness"), it seems clear that it was undertaken willingly, that is to say that Bach himself was responsible for the "ludicrous prescriptions" he tries to disown. The identity of the friend who jollied him could not have been Burney, as has been suggested.[103] The affair goes back to the time of printing, over two decades earlier. (Besides this, Burney's German was scarcely adequate to making jokes about the verbal prescriptions.) The friend in question might have been Emanuel's half-brother, Johann Cristoph Friedrich of Bückeburg, whom Gerstenberg approached with a similar proposal in answer to which he was told about "a printed sonata *à 3*—two violins and basso—by my Hamburg brother, in which he has tried to convey a discourse between a melancholic and a cheerful man. In spite of the great deal of trouble he took with it, one would not tell the meaning of each movement if he had not carefully indicated his intentions with words."[104]

The rambling quality and disorganization of Bach's autobiography suggest it was written in haste. Just before the end, on the last page, he inserts a separate paragraph that should have appeared earlier. "Among all my works, especially for keyboard, there are only a few trios, solos, and concertos, which I made in all freedom for my own use." His remark throws a little light on his dedicated sets of key-

[102]Letter dated Hamburg, 21 October, 1773, in *The Letters of C. P. E. Bach*, pp. 41–42.
[103]Eugene Helm, "The 'Hamlet' Fantasy and the Literary Element in C. P. E. Bach's Music," *Musical Quarterly* 48 (1972): 277–96; 292.
[104]Letter dated 1 April 1733, quoted from Helm (ibid.), pp. 290–91, n. 19.

board sonatas (i.e., "solos"), suggesting that he did not regard them as personal in this sense, in which case their lack of complete freedom arose from taking account of the tastes or talents of the dedicatees.

Preceding this statement is one that takes music critics to task. Certainly it must be the Berlin circle that Bach had in mind, and the enforced unity of taste at Frederick's court.

> As I have never loved an overly large uniformity in composition and in taste, because I have heard so much that is both good and diverse, and because I have always been of the opinion that one should accept the good, wherever it is found, even if there are only small doses of it to be met in a piece, there arose, and with the help of my God-given natural ability, the variety in my works that will have been noticed. At this opportunity I must add that the Herr Critics, when they write without passion, which seldom happens, very often are unmerciful with the circumstances, the prescriptions [Vorschrifte] and the motivations of the piece. How very seldom does one meet in a critic sensitivity [Empfindung], knowledge, honor, and courage in appropriate degrees. These four qualities must absolutely be present in sufficient quantity. It is thus quite sad for the realm of music, that the otherwise very useful criticism is often a business of such heads as are not gifted with all these qualities.

The most combative of the Berlin critics were Marpurg, Kirnberger, and Agricola, but Bach was on friendly terms with all three. The objects of his remarks must be sought among less prominent figures. "Prescriptions" hints again at the Trio Sonata in c (W. 161; H. 579).

One critic known to have greatly irritated Bach was Christoph Nichelmann, who in 1755 published a treatise on harmony and composition under the misleading title *Die Melodie*. In it Nichelmann had the temerity to rewrite compositions by Bach and others purportedly showing how they could be improved. He was answered by a scathing anonymous reply, also printed, that has been shown to be by Emanuel Bach himself.[105]

Arrived at the end of his autobiography, Bach summed up with the credo that is often the only part quoted by his biographers.

> My chief study, particularly in recent years, has been directed toward playing and composing for the keyboard in as singing a manner as possible, notwithstanding the instrument's lack of sustaining power. It is no easy task, if one avoids leaving the ear too empty while still not spoiling the noble simplicity of song with too much noise. Music must above all touch the heart, in my opinion, and this goal will never be

---

[105]Thomas Christensen, "Nichelmann contra C. Ph. E. Bach: Harmonic Theory and Musical Politics at the Court of Frederick the Great," in *Carl Philipp Emanuel Bach und die europäische Musikkultur*, pp. 189–220.

reached by a keyboard player with mere rattling, drumming, and arpeggiating, at least not by me.

By 1773 the Alberti bass had become the bellwether of galant music for the keyboard. Bach's resounding rejection of it also figures in his negative reaction to the music of his half-brother Johann Christian.

The only works written to order for Frederick, it has been claimed, were some sonatas with a virtuoso solo flute part.[106] This may be true, but it is worth remembering that the composer himself was a flautist. Bach's personal relations with Frederick and his advancement, or lack of it, in Berlin require a look back to the beginning of his autobiography. "At Charlottenburg His Majesty accorded me the grace of accompanying all alone on the harpsichord the first flute solo he played as king." "All alone" is important, although usually omitted in translations. It was unusual not to have a bass instrument like the cello also accompany. "From this time [1740] on until November 1767 I was continually in Prussian service, although I had a few opportunities to accept advantageous offers from elsewhere. His Majesty was so gracious as to counter these offers through a considerable enhancement of my salary." Here Bach is guilty of enhancing the truth. He applied for three posts as far as is known: at Leipzig in 1750 and 1755, and at Zittau in 1753. For none was he selected or offered the job. Nor did Frederick counter any offers with preferment.[107] The truth is bitter. It obviously rankled the composer to the point of painting a false picture for posterity.

Bach was hired at an annual salary of 300 thalers, a scanty sum in 1740 (compare this with the salaries of Quantz and the Grauns). Ten years later he was paid the same. In 1755 he made a written complaint to the proper authority stating that even the second harpsichord players, his former pupils Agricola and Nichelmann, received twice as much as he did and that he could no longer live on his salary, and requesting an increase or release from his duties.[108] The question arises as to how he could have lived up to this time, with a wife and three children to support, on so paltry a sum. Royalties brought him some help, but fees for teaching wealthy pupils among the aristocracy probably counted a lot more. He never received royal gratification for compositions, unlike Quantz and Graun, as far as we know. The evidence can show only that he accompanied at the royal chamber concerts when it was his turn (he was spelled at regular intervals by the second

[106]Newman, *The Sonata in the Classic Era*, p. 422.
[107]William S. Newman, in "Emanuel Bach's Autobiography," *Musical Quarterly* 51 (1965), 363–72; 366, translated a crucial phrase too loosely as "although I had several opportunities to go after advantageous posts elsewhere," evidently in an attempt to bring the statement closer to the truth. On p. 372 he translates "Vorschriften" as "proscriptions" instead of "prescriptions."
[108]Hans-Günter Ottenberg, *C. P. E. Bach*, trans. Philip J. Whitmore (Oxford, 1987), p. 57.

harpsichord player). The only exception may have been a reward for the dedication of the *Prussian* Sonatas to Frederick in 1742, of which we have no record. Frederick was not loath to forbid dedications to himself. At the very least he permitted Bach this one, and it would have taken a very niggardly patron indeed to accept the obsequious flattery of Bach's Italian dedication without bestowing a commensurate reward.

Frederick's response to Bach's petition survives as comments in the margin: "Bach is lying; Agricola gets only 500 thalers. He [Bach] once played in a concert here, and now he's getting cocky. His pay will be increased, but he must wait for the next round of financial measures."[109] Bach was raised to 500 thalers in 1756 and there he remained. Frederick's remark about once playing in a concert means he played a solo, perhaps one of his harpsichord concertos. The uniqueness of this event speaks eloquently about Bach's place in the royal chamber concerts, as does Frederick's peremptory tone. Neither as a composer nor as a soloist was Bach honored or remunerated. In Frederick's eyes he remained an accompanist.

KEYBOARD SONATAS

When Emanuel Bach began composing sonatas for the keyboard alone around 1730 the genre was still without a strong profile. Mattheson in 1737 commented on its emergence from the traditional sonata for violin, saying it lacked a proper *Gestalt* and appeared to be more affected than affecting; it aimed, he said, at "moving the fingers more than the heart."[110] Dexterity per se was never chief among Bach's aims, but moving the heart was. Two sonatas by Bach that can be dated around 1731 show a fundamental distinction as to form. One for harpsichord and violin (W. 71; H. 502) follows the customary four-movement plan of the *sonata da chiesa*, beginning with an initial *Adagio*. Another, for keyboard alone, is the Sonata in B♭ (W. 62/1; H. 2), which begins with a *Presto* in 3/4 that is quasi-canonic, like a two-part invention in the style of Johann Sebastian, an *Andante* in 3/4 and in the relative minor, and a concluding *Presto* in 3/4. From the beginning Emanuel decided that the solo sonata for keyboard would emulate the fast–slow–fast pattern of the concerto. He wrote several such works before leaving the parental home in Leipzig and while a law student at Frankfurt an der Oder. That they were experimental in nature, and not yet ready for circulation, is evident from his using the same movements over again in different sonatas, as if searching for the best sequence.

Bach's international fame stemmed mainly from his keyboard sonatas, which were widely diffused in printed collections. The move to Berlin and secure

[109]Heinrich Miesner, "Aus der Umwelt Philipp Emanuel Bachs," *Bach-Jahrbuch* 34 (1937): 132–43; 139.
[110]William S. Newman, "A Checklist of the Earliest Keyboard 'Sonatas' (1641–1738)," *Notes* 11 (1954): 201–12; 203.

employment at Frederick's court gave him the stimulus to compose a set of six sonatas that began to establish his reputation. Printed at Nuremberg in 1742 by Balthasar Schmidt, they were dedicated to the king of Prussia and hence earned the sobriquet "Prussian." The title page is in a beautiful cursive script (Figure 4.12). The dedication belies the severely plain appearance of the title. It is anything but plain in its language, which is couched in the servile hyperbole expected of the genre (Figure 4.13). The following translation aims to be as literal as possible, with apologies offered in advance for the strain placed on plain English.

> The most singular genius with which Your Majesty alone regards musical compositions, united to my most humble and glorious servitude, oblige me to present, with respect, the present sonatas to Your Majesty with the sole aim that, having been composed with my most weak talent while in the fortunate service of Your Majesty, they carry a token most sincere of that vivid desire by which I shall again wish to render myself always in the vanguard among those capable of the honor of enjoying the pleasure of satisfying the fine taste of so renowned a monarch, with the advantages enumerated. Deign, by such august clemency as Your Majesty's, to receive them kindly

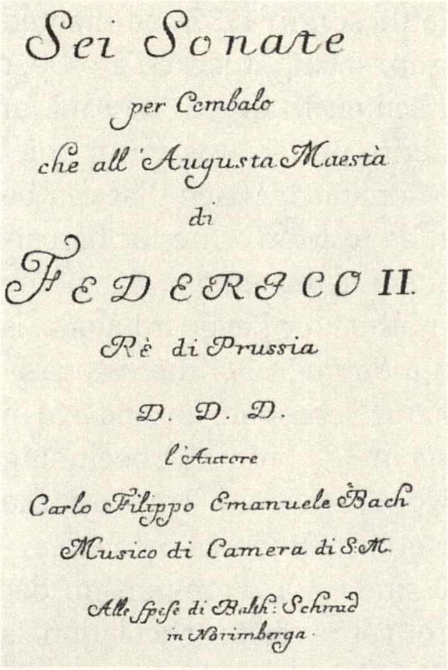

Sei Sonate
per Cembalo
che all'Augusta Maestà
di
FEDERICO II.
Rè di Prussia
D. D. D.
l'Autore
Carlo Filippo Emanuele Bach
Musico di Camera di S.M.
Alle spese di Balth: Schmid
in Norimberga.

FIGURE 4.12. Title page of Emanuel Bach's *Prussian* Sonatas, 1742.

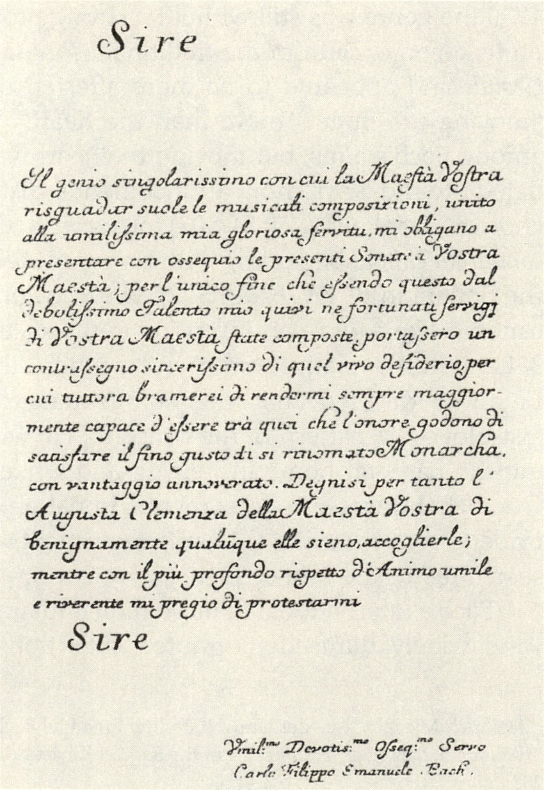

Sire

Il genio singolarissimo con cui la Maestà Vostra risguadar suole le musicali composizioni, unito alla umilissima mia gloriosa servitu, mi obligano a presentare con ossequio le presenti Sonate a Vostra Maestà; per l'unico fine chè essendo questo dal debolissimo Talento mio quivi ne fortunati servigj di Vostra Maestà state composte, portassero un contrassegno sincerissimo di quel vivo desiderio, per cui tuttora bramerei di rendermi sempre maggiormente capace d'essere trà quei che l'onore godono di satisfare il fino gusto di si rinomato Monarcha, con vantaggio annoverato. Degnisi per tanto l'Augusta Clemenza della Maestà Vostra di benignamente qualũque elle sieno, accoglierle; mentre con il più profondo rispetto d'Animo umile e riverente mi pregio di protestarmi

Sire

Umil.mo Devotis.mo Osseq.mo Servo
Carlo Filippo Emanuele Bach.

FIGURE 4.13. Dedication of the *Prussian* Sonatas.

whatever they may be; while with the most profound respect of the humble soul and reverently I have the honor of protesting myself, Sire, your most humble, most devoted, most respectful servant, Carlo Filippo Emanuele Bach.

Perhaps recourse for this verbiage was had to the court's Italian librettist, Giovanni Bottarelli.

All six sonatas are in three movements, with a middle slow movement marked *Andante* (twice) or *Adagio* (four times). The outer movements are all in binary form with repeats; the middle movements lack repeats. Five of the six sonatas are in the major mode. Their middle movements are in the relative minor except in the case of the first sonata, where the parallel minor is chosen.

Variety ranked high among Bach's aims in this path-breaking set of sonatas. No. 1 in F has the least idiomatic keyboard writing; its outer movements could easily be transcribed for trio sonata. No. 2 in B♭ illustrates an opposite pole, being free in texture and very idiomatic for the keyboard. It is also quite Italianate. Galuppi might have written the chains of descending parallel thirds that grace the finale, an *Allegro assai* in 2/4. One little passage in the finale, an arrival at a half-cadence, sounds like buffo repartee and has its equivalent in Pergolesi's *La Serva padrona* (Example 4.16ab).

EXAMPLE 4.16. *Emanuel Bach*, Prussian *Sonata No. 2, III*

Sonata No. 3 in E begins with a *Poco Allegro* in 3/4 that is broadly lyric, like an aria. By way of the parallel minor it quickly leads to an unexpected cadence in the key of G. Much of the movement is a duet between treble and bass. It could be thought of as a love duet, particularly as it deploys a favorite device of that genre: one voice holds a pedal, in this case trilled, against the other's roulades, and then the roles are reversed. Sonata No. 4 brings variety merely by being the only minor-mode work of the set. Its slow movement is an *Adagio* in 3/4 in the relative major.

Sonata No. 5 in C is the easiest to play and the most modern sounding. The opening *Poco Allegro* in 3/4 waxes quite galant, with its long static basses, quite rare with this composer. The bass pedal supports a theme in parallel sixths and thirds in the right hand that comes the closest in the entire set to approximating a"second theme."Bach repeats it in minor after the initial statement in major. The following *Andante* in 3/8 and in a is relatively light compared to the other middle movements. It also uses static basses and has no cadenza, unlike the other slow movements. They provide the opportunity for an improvised cadenza just before the close, with a fermata over the fifth degree in the bass, or over I_4^6 or I_3^6. The finale, *Allegro assai* in 2/4, exploits further the texture of sixths in the treble over a repeated note bass.

Sonata No. 6 in A has the longest movements and is in several other respects the most ambitious. The opening *Allegro* in 2/4 begins with a simple falling theme, *piano,* followed by a pause. A *forte* rejoinder ensues with a rapid run upward and thick broken chords. In the seconda parte on the way back to the tonic, the thick chords comprise as many as eight tones and demand that the right hand play four of them while encompassing the span of a tenth. The arrival of the tonic key along with the main theme might appear to be a double reprise but it is not. Rather, the moment is part of a long harmonic sequence in which V/V - V is followed by V/IV - IV. In the following *Adagio* in common time the theme has a drooping quality and covers a falling span of two octaves before it cadences in the sixth measure. This soft beginning is then framed by a loud, quasi-orchestral passage in octaves, serving as punctuation. The exchange goes on throughout the movement, hinting broadly at the tutti versus soli dialogues of the concerto and adumbrating a famous later example, the slow movement of Beethoven's Fourth Piano Concerto. The finale, an *Allegro* in 3/4, is also expansive, totaling over two hundred measures, and brings back some of the rapid arpeggiated figures of the first movement.

We return to the first sonata for more detailed consideration. Bach presumably took particular pride in it by giving it the place of honor as the first in his royal homage. The music engraving is a joy to behold (Figures 4.14–17). An opening *Allegro* in 3/4 begins in the character of a two-part invention, just like the earliest keyboard sonata mentioned above. The imitation between the two voices does not continue, but two-part linear texture does. Bach begins the modulation

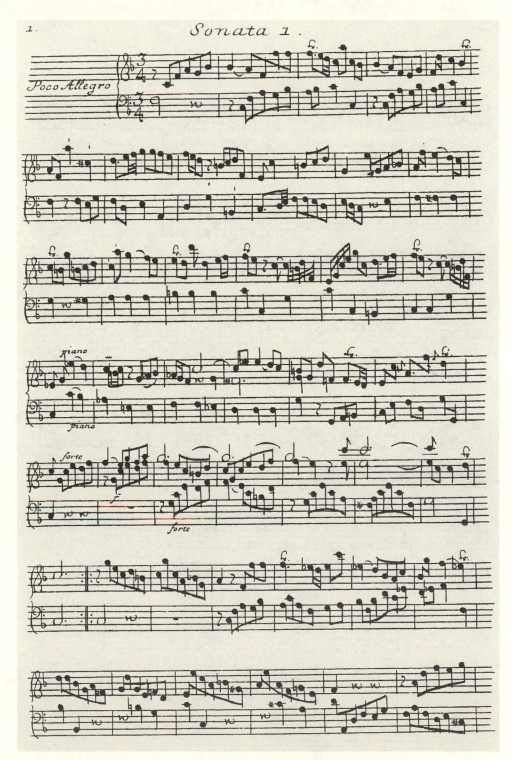

FIGURES 4.14–17. Emanuel Bach. Original edition of the first *Prussian* Sonata.

in m. 6 with a falling sixth in the treble, emphasized by wedges above, the harmonic progression being V/vi - vi, which is then transferred down a tone V/V - V by giving the bass the same figure beginning with the descending sixth with the wedges. This will not be heard as a canon but as contrapuntal exchange. In the rising sequence for the treble that follows, the left hand drops its pretense of being a contrapuntal equal and merely becomes a supporting bass. Note that the treble unhesitatingly lands on tones that make dissonances with the bass in m. 11 and m. 13 and that Bach singles out these tones by placing a slur over them. The new key is celebrated only briefly before turning into its minor equivalent, marked *piano. Forte* returns along with the main motive in a three-part imitation leading to an expressive vii^7/V in antepenultimate position, resolving to I$^6_4$ in the penultimate measure before the double bar. Contrapuntal and harmonic discourse take turns.

The seconda parte begins by inverting the main theme, just as happens in so many gigues. It is answered in the left hand by the theme right side up. Bach conducts the music to the relative minor and introduces his two- and then three-part canonic statement of the theme there, as happened at the end of the prima parte. This leads into a descending harmonic sequence, the two upper parts behaving like violins in a trio sonata sounding a chain of suspensions while the walking bass in eighth notes counterfeits the cello part. Here Bach comes close to a passage in his father's music, namely the descending sequence with chain of suspensions and walking bass in Prelude 24 of *The Well-Tempered Clavier,* Book I (Example 4.17). In a case like this it could be that Emanuel Bach has his father's music so much in his fingers at the keyboard that they resort to similar progres-

EXAMPLE 4.17. *Johann Sebastian Bach*, The Well-Tempered Clavier, *Book I, Prelude 24*

sions when he composes whether he knows it or not. The reprise follows the cadence on the relative minor with only the briefest of retransitions, a descending scale. Right after this Bach heads for the subdominant B♭, as would most composers of sonatas in the generations that came after him. He does this not only here but in many later sonatas just after the reprise. It is one of the more forward-looking features in his style, just as the chain of suspensions sequence is one of the most retrospective.

The second movement of the first *Prussian* Sonata has attracted particular attention. It is a landmark in the history of instrumental recitative, of which it represents one of the earliest printed examples.[111] No doubt remains as to what Bach is up to because he labels two passages *Recit*. They are both marked *forte* and alternate with the main movement, *Andante*, marked *piano*. The back and forth between these two suggests a dialogue, as if two quite different persons were speaking, and thus provides an example of what has been called the composer's *redende Prinzip* or "speaking principle." *Andante*, the first character, projects an elegiac, gently throbbing discourse, replete with many sighs, which create a plaintive mood. *Andante*'s first statement is not without one melodic boldness: the leap from G in the second measure (second tone of a melodic sigh from A♭ to G) up an awkward diminished octave to G♭, then down to the next sigh, B♭ – A♮. This pales beside the many boldnesses of *Recit.*, uttering but few tones at a time, broken by rests, as if groping for words. Its melodic compass is large, from the high G♭ (picking up on *Andante*'s most expressive moment) to low B♮.

The harmonic support, written as a figured bass in the true recitative style, progresses from surprise to surprise, adding as much to the impassioned quality as the declaiming treble itself. In Example 4.18 the first recitative passage is given with the chords realized, the appoggiaturas expected in this style written out, and an invented text added to convey more of the operatic flavor. The v_2^6 chord at the beginning, instead of resolving to B♭, moves up to a diminished chord, the E♮ of the bass making a particularly piquant dissonance with the E♭ appoggiatura required in the treble.[112] The diminished chord, chameleon-like as always, is resolved to a B_3^6 chord, taking the progression from B♭ far to the sharp side in short order. By the magic of another diminished chord, over D♮ in the bass, and an enharmonic change, the harmony is brought all the way back to f, four flats, where *Andante* began. At this cadence, *Andante* recommences, turning f into F♭, which, joined with the gentle throbbing, has a mitigating effect on recitative's outburst.

When *Andante* achieves a placid cadence on A♭, the relative major, at the beginning of the fourth system, it appears that its role is that of a pacifier. *Recit.* enters *forte* with the same destabilizing chord as the first time, the bass dropping a whole tone to anchor a $V_2^6/D^{♭6}_3$, but when the resolution arrives it is a surprising and unsettling $d^{♭6}_3$, leading to an augmented sixth chord (the raised sixth indi-

---

[111]Paul Mies, *Das Instrumentale Rezitativ: Von seiner Geschichte und seinen Formen* (Bonn, 1968), pp. 23–25.
[112]The move of the bass up a half step is often used for dramatic intensification in recitative. Richard Kramer, "The New Modulation of the 1770s: C. P. E. Bach in Theory, Criticism, and Practice," *JAMS* 38 (1985): 551–92; 570, posits a recitative origin for Bach's harmonic boldness in his "Heilig," in which he connects sections by rising a minor second. Bach's most stunning use of this device occurs in the first of six symphonies he wrote in 1773 on commission from Baron Gottfried van Swieten, when a *pianissimo* triad on A♭ gives way to a *fortissimo* triad on A (Symphony in G, W. 182/1; H. 657, first movement, mm. 80–81).

EXAMPLE 4.18. *Emanuel Bach, Prussian Sonata No. 1, II, recitative realized*

cated by a line through its curving top) over E♭ in the bass. The bass descends further to D, initiating a recitative cadence in g, far away from any place that could have been expected. *Andante* once again turns minor into major and slowly and calmly wends its way home to f via a series of secondary dominants and their resolutions, with one augmented sixth chord for good measure in the fourth measure from the end. The return of *forte* in the penultimate measure is the preparation for and arrival of an improvised cadenza signaled by the fermata over F in the treble. An astute performer could bring back a flickering of the seeming anger expressed by *Recit.* here, before extinguishing it in the final cadence.

Models for instrumental recitative as forceful and dramatic as Bach's second movement were few. The harmonic audacities remind us inevitably of his father. To find an inspiring example of keyboard recitative we need look no further than the famous Chromatic Fantasy and Fugue (BWV 903). It was one of father Bach's most sought-after works, with an unusually wide diffusion that took it even beyond Germany (no fewer than 38 copies exist—the autograph is lost). An important copy in the Berlin circle is that by Agricola of ca. 1740 marked "di J. S. Bach" in the hand of Emanuel.[113] An early version of the piece (BWV 903) is thought to date from Cöthen ca. 1720, the mature one from Leipzig ca. 1730. Note particularly the descent of the bass by chromatic steps that begins in m. 54 (Example 4.19). In m. 58 an enharmonic change from A♭ to G♯ occurs. In Emanuel's *Andante* G♯ becomes A♭.

Bach casts the theme of the Finale, *Presto* in 3/8, as an **a b b** shape to which he then adds two more measures as cadence. The octave leap in m. 4 has a buffo ring to it (cf. the first number of *La serva padrona*). Bach uses mm. 3–4 to modu-

[113]Johann Sebastian Bach, *Einzeln Überlieferte Klavierwerke* I, ed. Uwe Wolf (*Neue Ausgabe sämtlicher Werke,* Serie 5, Band 9.2) (Kassel, 1999), p. vi and facsimile on p. x.

EXAMPLE 4.19. *Johann Sebastian Bach, Chromatic Fantasy and Fugue*

late after the double bar in the middle, where the sequences are so numerous they become tedious. Most interesting about this finale is the rising progression over a chromatic bass, alternating chords in root position with ones in first inversion, then recast in a different form, *piano*. The passage sounds quite original and proved seminal for later composers such as Mozart, Haydn, and Brahms.[114]

Close to the *Prussian* Sonatas in time and in style is a second set of six known as the *Württemberg* Sonatas because they are dedicated to Count Carl Eugen of Württemberg, a guest in 1742–44 at the Prussian court taught by Bach, who mentions in the dedication that "he had the honor of giving him music lessons in Berlin." Formally, the set does not diverge from the first set. All are in three movements, the middle ones slow without repeats and with provisions for final caden-

[114]Mozart, Accompanied Keyboard Sonata in G, K. 9 (1764), first movement, mm. 10–14 (providing the transition to V); Haydn, Keyboard Sonata in F, Hoboken XVI:23 (1773), third movement, mm. 98–103; Brahms, Double Concerto for Violin and Cello (1887), third movement, mm. 313–20; and, most strikingly, Mozart, Piano Concerto No. 14 in E♭, K. 449 (1784), first movement, mm. 229–33.

zas, the outer ones fast or moderate with repeats. Three are in the minor mode, and Bach does not eschew keys with a great many accidentals, nor does he avoid rhythmic complexities. The invention is richer on the whole than in the previous set, and the demands greater. If the young duke could actually play these sonatas properly he was a fine musician indeed. In the *Prussian* Sonatas Bach calls for only two dynamic levels, *forte* and *piano*. In this set, first published by Johann Windter at Nuremberg in 1744, the second, third, and fifth sonatas call, in addition, for *pianissimo.*

Bach may have had a particular fondness for the last sonata of the *Württemberg* set. Marpurg tells an anecdote about Bach's playing it for a mutual acquaintance of theirs and the effect it made.

> Some time ago our Herr Bach played the sixth sonata from his second published set for a good friend of mine. This friend confessed to me that he normally suffered the misfortune of losing concentration before a piece of music was over; in this piece, however, he was able to perceive the formal design, and the performance was such as to retain his ardent and unshakeable attention throughout. This good friend is not a trained musician, and yet he understood the language of the music without the assistance of a text.[115]

The *Moderato* that opens the sonata in fact reaches a new level of intense rhetoric and "speaking" in tones. Its main theme alternates massive *forte* chords with a plaintive *piano* right-hand solo voice in dotted rhythms that acquires a left-hand counterpart before the half-cadence with a sigh in m. 7, followed by one of the composer's expressive moments of silence (Example 4.20). In the *Andante* of the first *Prussian* Sonata the declaiming solo voice remained singable, close to an actual recitative. Here the solo is more instrumental, particularly in the downward swoops and great leaps upward that begin the transition to the new key in m. 8, and in this sense is an example of a truly instrumental recitative (as opposed to a recitative merely transferred to an instrument). Whereas the former piece exemplified a *recitativo semplice* with continuo accompaniment, the latter one implies a stormy, orchestral *recitativo obbligato.* Perceiving "the formal design," as did Marpurg's "friend," was not difficult in the *Moderato* because Bach, as was normal practice, brought in the main theme at the beginning of the second part, and once again in the return to the key of b. This formal regularity conjoined with a wildly irregular and passionate musical discourse has struck one critic as an anomaly.[116]

---

[115]Friedrich Marpurg, *Der critische Musikus an der Spree* (Berlin, 1750; reprint 1970), p. 217, cited after Ottenberg, *C. P. E. Bach*, p. 41.

[116]David Schulenberg, *The Instrumental Music of Carl Philipp Emmanuel Bach* (Ann Arbor, Mich., 1984), p. 163, says of the movement, "Although its agitated harmony and halting phrasing render it the keyboard equivalent of a dramatic accompanied recitative the dramatic effect requires a sensitive performer to sustain it as it [the main theme] recurs, without relief, through all the sections of a ternary sonata form with retransition."

EXAMPLE 4.20. *Emanuel Bach*, Württemberg *Sonata No. 6, I*

The stormy discourse of the first movement is replaced by one of Bach's most simple and sublime ideas as the main theme for the *Adagio non molto* in B (Example 4.21). This movement too is often interrupted by skittish flights of passage work in dotted rhythm, which sound like refugees from the first movement, as well as by prolonged unstable chords and silences. But the serene first theme keeps returning to set things back on course, until a final fluttering of the dotted-rhythm passage leads to an incomplete I_4^6 chord with fermata, inviting the player to add a short improvised cadenza (Quantz, following Tosi, insisted that cadenzas should not exceed the length of a human breath). The frequent returns of the main theme in the tonic lend the movement a rondo character and presage the composer's later fascination with the possibilities of the rondo form.

For a finale, Bach writes the equivalent of a two-part invention in invertible counterpoint, an *Allegro* in 2/4 and in his normal sonata form with both parts repeated. Somewhat disappointing at first, after two stellar movements such as the *Moderato* and the *Adagio*, the *Allegro* grows on one with repeated playings and even reveals some points of kinship with the *Adagio*, such as the rapid descending passages in sixths or tenths.

Looking back on the life and works of Bach, Reichardt linked both early sets of printed sonatas together and assigned them an important place in music history: "There had never before then appeared any instrumental music in which such a rich, yet well-ordered harmony was combined with such noble lyricism, nor so much beauty, order and originality [bei solche originallen Laune] achieved,

EXAMPLE 4.21. *Emanuel Bach*, Württemberg *Sonata No. 6, II*

as in the first two sets of sonatas printed in Nuremberg, and the first concertos of this master."[117] Bach's early contributions to the concerto are briefly assessed in the next section.

Directly after the *Württemberg* Sonatas, and perhaps as a reaction to the level of complexity and difficulty that the general public must have found in them, Bach assayed some keyboard works along simpler lines. One such is the Sonata in G (W. 65/15; H. 43) that dates from 1745. It begins with an *Allegretto* initiated by a theme in **a b b'** form and moving in gentle syncopations à la Lotti or Hasse over a plain bass confined to only two tones, 5 and 1 (Example 4.22a). Bach's new direction prompted the work's modern editor to write, "The style of the sonata must be judged the result of a conscious effort to write in the simple, fashionable manner now usually termed *galant*."[118] Particularly effective is the raised fifth

[117]Johann Friedrich Reichardt, article on Bach in *Musikalischer Almanach* (Berlin, 1796), cited after Ottenberg, *C. P. E. Bach*, pp. 45–46.
[118]Carl Philipp Emanuel Bach, *Solo Keyboard Music,* ed. David Schulenberg (*Carl Philipp Emanuel Bach Edition,* ed. Rachel W. Wade and Eugene E. Helm, Series I) (Oxford, 1995), 18: 77.

EXAMPLE 4.22. *Emanuel Bach, Sonata in G (W. 65/15; H.43), I*
original and revised versions

degree in the melody in m. 7, leading in the transition to the second key. In the
following measure Bach reinterprets the high notes B - A of m. 5, putting them in
a different metrical position, sounding now a melodic sigh on the first beat. Bach
must have felt that he was giving in too much to fashion here, because he
changed mm. 7–8 in a revised version of the sonata by harmonizing the treble by
the eighth note, which has the effect of slowing down the motion. Moreover, he
reduces the expressiveness of the treble by making it just another tone in the harmony rather than a chromatically rising appoggiatura calling all attention to itself
(Example 4.22b). In m. 9 he added sixteenth notes, but otherwise he left the passage unchanged. Still, the changes in mm. 7–8 tell the whole story. His dalliance
with the galant sometimes went against his nature.

During the 1750s Bach continued to seek ways to make his keyboard style
more accessible to performers of modest talents. In August 1758 he fled Berlin
with his family at the approach of the Russian army and took refuge with his
friend Johann Friedrich Fasch, Kapellmeister of the court of Anhalt-Zerbst. The

Bachs returned to Berlin in early December (Fasch died on 5 December). While at Zerbst, Bach composed several sonatas that were subsequently published in *Sechs Sonaten fürs Clavier mit veränderten Reprisen* (Berlin, 1760) and dedicated to Princess Amalia. By writing out ornamented repetitions Bach not only helped novices, he also exerted more control over their performing. The sonatas were well received by the public, which led to the publication of two similar sets of six in 1761 and 1763 (without varied reprises).

The three sets of 1760–63 diverge from earlier ones by being in oblong format and using soprano clef for the right hand. Songbooks mainly used soprano clef for the melody, so it was familiar to many amateur musicians and was perhaps chosen for this reason. Other attempts to accommodate them may be read in Bach's simple textures and avoidance of sudden shifts in rhythm or texture. Yet Bach remains himself in the seriousness of his discourse. The Sonata in c (W. 51/3; H. 127) of the 1761 set begins smoothly as to rhythmic evenness between the hands and in its regular phraseology (Example 4.23). Its rapid melody is inaugurated by a falling diminished fourth and rising minor second, which Bach then

EXAMPLE 4.23. *Emanuel Bach, Keyboard Sonata in c (W. 51/3; H.127), I*

spins out into a convincing eight-measure phrase. This is one of the sonatas that Bach composed at Zerbst in 1758. He follows the opening movement, which is in his usual form, with a short *Molto Adagio* in C and in common time that does not forbear to include rhythmic and textural complexities, along with some traits that prompted one critic to hear it as a simulated recitative.[119] The finale, an *Allegro ma non tanto* in 3/4 time and in c, incorporates in its opening theme the same descending diminished fourth by step that opened the *Allegretto* by leap. Can it be a coincidence that Joseph Haydn, in his Symphony No. 52 in c of about ten years

[119]Darrell Berg, *The Keyboard Sonatas of C. P. E. Bach: An Expression of the Mannerist Principle* (Ann Arbor, Mich., 1975), p. 214.

later, used the identical diminished fourth as a leap to begin his first movement and as a conjunct descending interval to end his finale? Haydn was quite obsessed with this interval in several of his works around 1770, as a matter of fact.[120] If Bach's *Allegretto* theme is turned into the major mode, furthermore, it predicts one of Beethoven's, in his Overture to *Leonora* No. 1.

Bach had an admirer close to home in the person of Johann Gottfried Müthel, who was born in 1728 in Mölln, east of Hamburg. Müthel was the last student of Johann Sebastian Bach. After Bach's death in July 1750 he visited Hasse in Dresden, Emanuel Bach in Potsdam, and Telemann in Hamburg. In 1755 he became organist of the principal church of Riga, where he remained until his death in 1788. The first of his keyboard sonatas to be published came out at Nuremberg in 1756. Burney commented on the technical demands imposed by his sonatas and considered them among the most important of the time. Müthel's debt to Emanuel Bach is apparent in his jagged melodic lines and quirky rhythms. Diderot thanked Grimm for obtaining music for his daughter Angélique to play by Bach, Müthel, and Müller, meaning Gottlieb Friedrich Müller, organist in Dessau and composer of *Six sonates pour le clavecin* (Leipzig, 1762).

> My daughter has devoured the music you brought for her. . . . This Müller, this Emanuel, this Müthel, have a unique power which I rather admire. Moreover, since their music is difficult, you can imagine how much it has increased my daughter's skill in reading and in dexterous fingering—a good deal of technical proficiency is needed to play these composers in any event; there is plenty to occupy both hands and more besides. . . . I believe that she will be a good player, but I am practically certain that she will be a musician, and that she will learn the theory of this art well, unless some future husband should ruin everything, spoil her figure, and take away her appetite for study.[121]

Diderot made certain that she studied music theory by hiring Anton Bemetzrieder to teach it to her, then setting down in writing under Bemetzrieder's name a published treatise. Here again Diderot couples Bach with Müthel, this time in a comparison that contrasts the delicate taste of Domenico Alberti with the strong harmonies, thick textures, and modulatory variety of these German composers.[122] In 1774, on his return to Paris from Saint Petersburg, Diderot passed through Hamburg and asked Bach directly for some unpublished keyboard sonatas for his daughter, a request Bach fulfilled.[123]

---

[120]See *Haydn, Mozart*, pp. 292–93, 299–300, and 356–57.
[121]Letter of 2 November 1769, cited in Ottenberg, *C. P. E. Bach*, p. 223.
[122]Denis Diderot, *Leçons de Clavecin et Principes d'Harmonie par Mr Bemetzrieder* (Paris, 1751; facsimile reprint, New York, 1966), p. 152.
[123]Letter dated Hamburg, 30 March 1774, quoted in Ottenberg, *C. P. E. Bach*, p. 147.

CONCERTOS

Bach was the most prolific and important composer of keyboard concertos in northern Germany. In 1714, the year of his birth, his father was busy transcribing Vivaldi's violin concertos for organ. Later in Leipzig around 1730, Italian violin concertos inspired a stunning group of concertos for one or more harpsichords with accompaniments for strings from Johann Sebastian. These provided the foundation on which all the Bach sons built their keyboard concertos, as did some of father Bach's best pupils outside his family, notably Christoph Nichelmann. The techniques of linking ritornellos and solo episodes by using similar material were learned by Emanuel from his father's works.

Berlin knew another tradition of works for solo harpsichord and orchestra, and this even before Frederick ascended the throne in 1740. There is a harpsichord Concerto in C dated 1737 "del Signor Graun" that was the work, it has been argued, of Carl Heinrich.[124] Its proximity to Tartini's violin concertos in style and form would seem to indicate Johann Gottlieb, who had been a pupil of Tartini. The connection favors attribution to him, but the style does not. Johann Gottlieb preferred a denser and more contrapuntal style in his instrumental works, while Carl Heinrich favored a lighter and more modish style in all his works, and his mannerisms in melodic style do betray a strong resemblance to Tartini's. Frederick himself was in contact with the Paduan master, of whose music he possessed several autographs, and to whom he sent an aria he had composed.[125] Prince Frederick's little court at Rheinsberg may have been more receptive to keyboard concertos than it was later, when he was king. At the least he owned a fine collection of keyboard instruments, one of the prerequisites to the flourishing of keyboard concertos. Perhaps more pre-1740 keyboard concertos like Graun's would have survived had not the palace at Rheinsberg burned down on Maundy Thursday 1740.

The solo concerto in Berlin may have been especially linked with the several musical societies that sprang up, mainly in emulation of the king's music making, according to Forkel.

> After the reign of the present king of Prussia began such a general love of music arose in Berlin that, following the example of the king, everyone strove to contribute to the growth of this charming art. Not only did the king strengthen greatly the royal chapel, showing by this how much he wanted to further the cultivation of music in his states, but also private persons lent themselves to the project through the founding of special musical societies with the intention of supporting their great monarch. Among these societies a particularly distinguished one was founded in 1749 under the name

---

[124]Hans Uldall, *Das Klavierkonzert des Berliner Schule* (Leipzig, 1928), p. 73.
[125]Minos Dounias, *Die Violinkonzerte Giuseppe Tartinis* (Wolfenbüttel, 1935), p. 201.

Musikübende Gesellschaft, which had both honorary and ordinary members, governed by special rules and laws. . . . The society met weekly and also celebrated annually on the day of its founding.[126]

Forkel's brief article is a digest of Marpurg's long "Sketch for a Comprehensive Report on the Musikübenden Gesellschaft in Berlin," published in 1754.[127] Marpurg specified that Frederick's restoration of the court chapel's music to a flourishing state was responsible for the spread of private concerts and concert societies. The musicians he cites as directing the societies all held royal appointments.

The three professional musicians among the eight ordinary members of the 1749 society were the director, Friedrich Riedt, flautist, who became a royal chamber musician in 1741; Johann Gabriel Seyffarth, another royal chamber musician; and Johann Philipp Sack, organist of the cathedral. The society's twenty formal members met in Sack's house, which was on the corner of the Brüderstrasse across from the royal palace.

Besides the 1749 society Marpurg lists three others: the Akademie, which met every Friday under the direction of Johann Gottlieb Janitsch, royal chamber musician; the Assemblée, which met every Monday under the direction of Christian Friedrich Schale, also a royal chamber musician; and the Concert, which met every Saturday under the direction of Agricola, royal chamber musician and court composer. Of the last Marpurg specifies that not just instrumental music but also vocal music was performed, understandably so as Agricola composed more vocal than instrumental music. According to Burney (1772), he was "regarded as the best organ player in Berlin and the best singing master in Germany." By implication the other three societies did not cultivate vocal music. That they were devoted exclusively to instrumental music seems extraordinary for the time, but it is confirmed by Marpurg's detailed descriptions of the 1749 society, which reveal a typically Nordic passion for law and order.

Marpurg quotes twenty *Reglements* by which this society was governed. The twenty members were all instrument players. Even the noblemen among the twelve honorary members were enjoined to keep their instruments in good condition (rule 12). The next rule specifies that the clavecin and other instruments which were necessary for communal use be maintained by funds from the general treasury that paid for such necessities as heat and light. Every member could bring one or at most two good friends as guests. All pleasures other than music were strictly forbidden, that is, there was to be no gaming, smoking, or convers-

[126]Johann Nicolaus Forkel, *Musikalischer Almanach für Deutschland für das Jahr 1782* (Leipzig, 1782; reprint, 1974), pp. 179–81.
[127]Marpurg, "Entwurf einer ausführlichen Nachricht von der Musikübenden Gesellschaft zu Berlin," in *Historisch-Kritische Beyträge,* 1: 367–413.

ing; infractions incurred an automatic monetary punishment. Prussian seriousness begins to sound a little silly at this point, but perhaps the infractions were
more frequent than we imagine, else why these draconian rules?

The concerts of the society always began with an overture or symphony by
one of the best masters, followed by seven, or at most eight, other compositions,
consisting of concertos, trios, or solos. Musicians who were members of the royal
chapel but not members of the society often loaned their talents to the concerts.
Marpurg names several string players, including Georg Zarth, in this category,
along with two horn players and three bassoonists. Visiting composers were
known to bring their music to the concerts. Thus Bach's friend Fasch contributed
to a concert when visiting Berlin in 1751. The emphasis was on the very latest
compositions. Riedt brought a new flute piece every month. Seyffarth brought
various and excellent concertos for solo violin or solo oboe. Sack likewise brought
"some well-advised concertos for the harpsichord and earned the most perfect
applause in performing them."A certain Herr Wolff, registrar, did the same for the
violin. So much for Marpurg's account, which suggests a society for the performance of new instrumental music, with a special emphasis on new concertos.

The upshot of this is that Berlin was a prolific center of instrumental music,
and especially productive of concertos, ones for solo keyboard as much as or more
than those for solo violin. It can be no coincidence that three of the composers
mentioned as directors of concert series, Schale, Janitsch, and Seyffarth, are all
represented by surviving keyboard concertos.[128] Sack, according to Marpurg,
"composed various concertos and solos for the harpsichord, in which grace and
taste rule."[129] No evidence has yet been found to show that Bach's concertos or
Bach himself figured in any concert series. But at the least it is apparent that
organists of the caliber of Sack and Agricola were capable of performing Bach's
difficult harpsichord concertos in their respective concerts. An engraving of the
time shows a chamber orchestra accompanying a harpsichord player whose part
is identified with the word "Concerto" (Figure 4.18).

The effect of Bach's concertos on at least one witness may be told in the words
of Wilhelm Hertel, a native of Eisenach who visited Berlin in 1745 at the age of
eighteen and who wrote his autobiography late in life. Hertel, from an early age
a gifted keyboard player and violinist, sought out Franz Benda for lessons, was
accepted, and attended concerts in Benda's house."I heard Philipp Emanuel Bach,
recently appointed to royal service, play a concerto on the harpsichord, namely
the one in D major that has been printed."[130] This could be the Concerto in D of

[128]They survived, that is, at least into the 1920s. Uldall described and illustrated concertos by all three in *Das Klavierkonzert der Berliner Schule* (Leipzig, 1928), pp. 77–82.
[129]Marpurg, *Historische-Kritische Beiträge,* 1: 507.
[130]Johann Wilhelm Hertel, *Autobiographie,* ed. Erich Schenk (Graz, 1957), p. 24.

FIGURE 4.18. A harpsichord concerto with chamber orchestra.

1743 (W. 11; H. 414) that was printed at Nuremberg in 1745. Hertel himself was urged to play the violin and did so. He says further of the concert that he never before heard such beautiful music: "Particularly the Bach concerto made such an impression on me that I could scarcely think of anything else." He claims that he knew and had long practiced the manner of keyboard playing of the Bachs, but this concerto made him realize there was something more at stake than just being able to play a difficult piece purely, clearly, and perfectly. He bought a copy of the concerto before leaving Berlin with the intention "to practice it until it would sound close to what it should and what it still did in my memory." Two years later Hertel was again in Berlin, studying violin with Benda and keyboard with Bach, whom he heard play often and from whom he received pieces that he then played for the master.[131] He also heard the royal opera, in which he was allowed by concertmaster Graun to play the violin as a nonpaid visitor.

While the concerto for harpsichord surely would have flourished in Berlin without Bach, it would not have become the major genre that it did without the

[131]Ibid., p. 31.

three dozen or so concertos he wrote while in Prussian service. Nichelmann, from whom sixteen harpsichord concertos survive, is second only to Bach in this respect, and equal to him in the idiomatic quality of his keyboard writing. Between them, and together with a few others, they elevated the keyboard concerto to the point of being North Germany's most important contribution to instrumental music.

In opening movements of his keyboard concertos Bach often followed the four-ritornello and three-solo-section organization that was perhaps the most common throughout the century and was still recommended by Koch. Bach's solos are usually related to the opening ritornello in some way. In his *Versuch* Quantz allowed this possibility but also another:"If the opening ideal of the ritornello is not sufficiently singing or is not appropriate for the solo, a new idea quite unlike it must be introduced, and must be joined to the opening materials in such a way that it is not apparent whether it appears of necessity or with due deliberation."[132] Of course Quantz was talking about the solo flute, which was less rich in possibilities than a chordal instrument like the harpsichord. Bach delighted in turning his characteristically gruff and broad-ranged orchestral tutti themes into graceful lyric statements for the solo. A good example is the beginning of his Concerto in E of 1744 (W. 14; H. 417) in which he has the violins make great leaps against the conjunct descent of the bass, forming an alternation of chords in root position and in first inversion (Example 4.24a). The harmonic progression is nothing more than a cliché, but individual is the way Bach makes the melody careen from high to low in its large, unvocal range. The way the leaps grow in size is also typical: from a third, to a fifth, an octave, a tenth, and largest of all, two octaves. More impressive still is how Bach makes this material lyric for the solo, by a very skillful use of variation (Example 4.24b). Note how the conjunct falling fourth of m. 1 becomes a conjunct rising fourth with long, expressive rising appoggiatura in mm. 2–3, and how the ascent becomes even more expressive through chromatic tones in mm. 4–5, giving way to straightforward eighth notes and finally sixteenth notes before the half-cadence. As the movement progresses the solo sections become longer, so that the third and last is nearly twice the length of the first.[133]

When Bach uses the same type of wide-ranging and rhythmically vigorous tutti theme in the minor mode, the result can sound not just gruff and surly, but actually angry, especially when combined with the heightening effect of dotted rhythm and strategically placed trills. Such is the case with the opening of his Concerto in d of 1748 (W. 23; H. 427) (Example 4.25a). Underlying all the power expressed in this theme is the same orderly descending-bass cliché as in the previous examples. Moreover, the treble rising up a fifth in a sequence by the measure is also the same: 1–5; 6–3; 4–1. Yet the two beginnings make very different

---

[132]Quantz, *On Playing the Flute*, p. 312
[133]Ottenberg, *C. P. E. Bach*, p. 48, offers a diagram of the movement showing the relative proportions of each section.

EXAMPLE 4.24. *Emanuel Bach, Harpsichord Concerto in E (W. 14; H. 417), I*

impressions. The Concerto in d of 1748 is regarded as the greatest of all Bach's works in the genre, and it is certainly the best known. Bach's fondness for the long-held rising appoggiatura is demonstrated anew in the *pianissimo* codicil of mm. 8–10, where the basses drop out and allow the upper strings to make another half-cadence on their own. The composer perhaps savored the eerie harmony created by the D♯ as much for its discord as for its melodic expressiveness. It must have given his listeners a shudder at the time (and if they included Frederick, cause for a disapproving glare). Following the second half-cadence the music plunges directly into the relative major with strident triple stops in the violins announcing the chord tones of F. The movement is long, totaling 338 mm., but never loses power or interest. As in the example above Bach manages to make lyrical music for the solo harpsichord out of the tutti's theme. The main impression of the movement even so remains that of the stormy passions and seemingly irate discourse of the opening tutti. Quantz wrote that triple meter was not a good choice for the opening movement of a concerto, and he very rarely used it himself, favoring in almost all cases common time, the meter reserved for the most weighty arias in opera seria. Bach was not so loath to choose triple meter, as can be seen from this and the previous example. If works like Bach's Concerto in d had not existed, would Mozart eventually have written the stormy theme, with leaps from the first to second beat in 3/4 time, that begins his Piano Concerto No. 24 in c (K. 491)?

EXAMPLE 4.25. *Emanuel Bach, Harpsichord Concerto in d (W. 23; H. 427), I–III*

The second movement of the Concerto in d of 1748 is a *Poco Andante* in 2/4 and in the relative major, F. Bach begins it with a transition that also serves as the orchestral ritornello, as if gradually damping down the heated passions of the *Allegro.* The solo enters in m. 16, singing a melody that reaches higher and higher until sinking gracefully down to its cadence (Example 4.25b). The rhythm is relatively uncomplicated for this composer—an interlude obviously intended to serve as a moment of repose with respect to the first movement. It is rather modest in length at 114 mm. Not so the finale, an *Allegro assai* in 2/4, which is brusque and full of leaps and snarling trills like the first movement and which stretches out to a grand total of 462 mm. (Example 4.25c). A case could be made that the leap down an octave that begins the finale mimics the octave leaps that begin the first movement; also, that the important role of the flat sixth, B♭, in the theme of the *Allegro,* particularly the trill in m. 3 and the leap upward in m. 5 followed by a rest, has something to do with the leap up to B♭ followed by a rest in m. 3 of the *Allegro assai.* And then there is the trill on low B♭ in the finale's theme that sounds so threatening. In the gathering rhetoric of flat-sixth expressiveness over the generations it may be that Mozart's K. 491 is not the only heir of Emanuel Bach. Piano Concerto No. 1 in d by Johannes Brahms could lay claim to the same heritage.

Bach experimented with various modifications of the four-ritornello principle in search of a way to effect a double reprise such as he used in the first movements of his sonatas.[134] He never settled on a single solution that satisfied him, and in this sense he contributed less to the Viennese concerto than did his half-brother and pupil, Johann Christian. That he was aware of the more modern currents in musical style swirling in South Germany as well as in Austria and Bohemia is evident from revisions that he made in his concertos over time. It has been shown, for example, that the composer attempted to modernize his concertos by making the phrasing more regular, eliminating the odd measure here and there.[135] He made so many revisions in the slow movement of the Concerto in d of 1748 that eventually he recopied the whole movement and inserted the new manuscript into his score.[136]

The keyboard concertos were not necessarily composed by Bach for himself as soloist. A statement in his autobiography suggests that most of them were destined for others (some surely for his pupils): "There are only a few trios, solos and concertos that I have composed in complete freedom and for my own use." One

---

[134]Jane R. Stevens, "The Keyboard Concertos of Carl Philipp Emanuel Bach" (Ph.D. diss., Yale University, 1965), pp. 50–70, 97. See also Shelley G. Davis, "C. P. E. and the Early History of the Recapitulary Tutti in North Germany," in *C. P. E. Bach Studies,* ed. Stephen L. Clark (Oxford, 1988), pp. 65–82.
[135]Rachel W. Wade, *The Keyboard Concertos of Carl Philip Emanuel Bach* (Ann Arbor, Mich., 1981), pp. 205–10.
[136]Ibid., p. 294.

work identified as for his own use is the Concerto in c of 1752 that has a recita-tive for its middle movement (W. 31; H. 441). In a letter of 1784 Bach says it was formerly one of his showpieces.[137] Neither this work nor the imposing Concerto in d of 1748 saw print, but several of them did, including the attractive Concerto in E of 1744, printed by Georg Winter at Berlin in 1760. The print, as opposed to the autograph, supplies rests in the solo part throughout the ritornellos.[138] By this time Bach apparently had decided to confine the harpsichord to its solos, reliev-ing it of continuo duty in the tuttis. He regretted that the sound of the harpsichord was swallowed by the orchestra in loud tuttis and had this to say on the point in his *Versuch über die wahre Art das Klavier zu spielen.* "There are many things in music which, not fully heard, must be imagined. For example, in concertos with full accom-paniment, the soloist always loses those passages that are accompanied *fortissimo* and those on which the tutti enters. Intelligent listeners replace such losses men-tally, and it is primarily such listeners whom we should seek to please."[139] Pleas-ing intelligent listeners thus came before pleasing performers. The listeners Bach had in mind were perhaps multiplying thanks to Berlin's active concert life.

Bach gradually slowed his production of concertos but he never abandoned the genre. Toward the end of his years in Berlin he wrote twelve divertimento-like concertos for one or two keyboard soloists with an accompaniment mostly scored for strings, flutes, and horns, using a flexible number of short movements, most of which are arrangements of his character pieces for keyboard. He called these works sonatinas. They have been compared to the divertimentos of such Viennese composers as Wagenseil, who is said to have visited Berlin and displayed his prowess at the harpsichord in 1756.[140] After the move to Hamburg, Bach contin-ued to cultivate a scaled-down concerto with solo parts undemanding enough so that amateurs could play them. He published six concertos of this kind in 1771, advertised in the public press as follows.

> At the request of many amateurs of music six easy harpsichord concertos by Capellmeister C. Ph. E. Bach are to be published. Without losing any of their appro-priate brilliance these concertos will differ from the other concertos of this composer in so far as they are more adapted to the nature of the harpsichord, are easier both in the solo part and the accompaniment, are adequately ornamented in the slow move-ments and are provided with written-out cadenzas.[141]

[137]Uldall, *Das Klavierkonzert,* p. 39: "Das Konzert C Moll war vor diesen eines meiner Paradörs" (parade bears).
[138]Pippa Drummond, *The German Concerto: Five Eighteenth-Century Studies* (Oxford, 1980), p. 311.
[139]*Carl Philipp Emanuel Bach, Essay on the True Art of Playing Keyboard Instruments,* trans. and ed. William J. Mitchell (New York, 1959), p. 106.
[140]Drummond, *The German Concerto,* pp. 326–28. It is also claimed that Wagenseil had to cancel this tour.
[141]Leon Crickmore, "C. P. E. Bach's Harpsichord Concertos," *Music and Letters* 39–40 (1958): 227–41; 237.

Hope of financial gain is obviously behind these compositions, which may help explain the apologetic tone Bach struck two years later in his autobiography.

Bach's main keyboard rivals in Berlin were Nichelmann and Schaffrath. The sixteen surviving harpsichord concertos by Nichelmann exist in several copies but none was printed. These works are forward looking in several respects, such as their clear phrase structure and slow harmonic rhythm.[142] Their composer was more prone than Bach to have the solo part enter with music that was independent rather than restating the ritornello. Had Nichelmann lived another decade, perhaps he would have become an even greater rival to Bach (he died in 1761 or 1762). Concertos by both were still performed in Berlin as late as 1807–15 by, among others, one of Bach's pupils, Sara Levi, a great aunt of Felix Mendelssohn.

Christoph Schaffrath, born in the Saxon town of Hohenstein near Zwickau in 1709, applied in 1733 for the position of organist of the Sophienkirche in Dresden, but the post went to Friedemann Bach. He was in Frederick's service as a harpsichordist as early as 1734. In 1741 he switched to the service of Princess Amalia. Like Nichelmann he published harpsichord sonatas in the standard fast–slow–fast pattern of movements (Nuremberg, 1749) and wrote many concertos for harpsichord and strings, more than a dozen of which survive. Occasionally his style reflects aspects of Bach's, although he was more inclined to display his contrapuntal acumen, writing fugues even in his concertos, which Bach never did. He died in Berlin in 1763, a year or two after Nichelmann. With Bach's departure for Hamburg in 1767 Berlin was left with few keyboard artists of note. Permission for Bach to leave was granted with reluctance, and had he been a Prussian instead of a Saxon it might not have been granted at all.

Bach's Berlin symphonies were fewer than his concertos but no less audacious and original. He composed them in sporadic fashion. The earliest goes back to 1741 and the next was not written until 1755. Bach's lack of special training as a violinist has been blamed for his often awkward string parts, which do not lie easily for the hand.[143] The Symphony in e of 1756 (W. 177; H. 652) is a particularly powerful specimen of the genre and disposed in the three movements Bach always observed in symphonies as well as in regular concertos (as opposed to sonatinas). It was printed in Nuremberg in 1759. Gottfried van Swieten, appointed Austrian ambassador to Berlin in 1770, was captivated by Bach's music and commissioned the composer, by this time Hamburg's most famous, to write the superb set of six symphonies for strings of 1773 (W. 182; H. 657–62). A recent

[142]Douglas A. Lee, "Christoph Nichelmann and the Early Clavier Concerto in Berlin," *Musical Quarterly* 57 (1971): 636–55. Christoph Nichelmann, *Clavier Concertos in E Major and A Major,* ed. Douglas A. Lee (Madison, Wisc., 1977).

[143]Wagner, *Die Sinfonien Carl Philipp Emanuel Bachs*, pp. 244–45. The claim goes back to Reichardt's autobiography, as printed in Hans Michael Schletterer, *Joh. Friedrich Reichardt: Sein Leben und seiene musikalische Thätigkeit* (Augsburg, 1865), p. 163.

study of the symphony considers Bach's contributions as standing outside the main channels of music history.[144]

Disappointments with his post as a court musician in Berlin and Potsdam led Bach to hope that life would be better in a great capital of trade like Hamburg. These hopes, too, were disappointed. At least he was more of a free man than he was in Berlin, although burdened with the heavy responsibility of providing music for the city's five principal churches. What struck him deeply was the decline he observed relative to Hamburg's great past as a center of music.[145] After a long period of deterioration the Hamburg opera closed in 1738. "You are come fifty years too late" was the melancholy message Bach had for Burney. Even Telemann, Bach's revered godfather and predecessor, had been unable to stem the musical decline, which followed a downward curve as surely as the city's commercial fortunes followed an upward one. The sad facts Bach made clear to Burney, as recounted in Chapter 1. Bach wrote an earlier and less known account to Georg Kottowsky, a member of the Dessau court chapel that was threatened with dissolution, which led Kottowsky to sound out Bach about the possibilities for a professional musician to make a living in Hamburg.

> I pity you and your entire chapel of musicians from the heart. Perhaps God will give your Prince better ideas; I hope so from the heart. Hamburg is no place for a fine musician to stay. There are not many amateurs here, and very few connoisseurs. There is no taste here. Mostly queer stuff and no pleasure in noble simplicity. Everything is glutted. The musicians supported by the city must live mainly by playing dance music. Three, at most 4 thalers are given monthly for teaching, and everyone teaches here; the cheapest is the best. Prices are high. En fin, I cannot advise you to come here. Herr Abel [brother of the composer], the painter, whom you knew in England, has been here for a year and is earning almost nothing. The English colony understands its business and nothing more; may God grant that you do not have to leave![146]

"Noble simplicity" is a code expression for the kind of opera seria represented by Hasse, while "queer stuff" probably derided newer Italian styles. Elsewhere Bach used some hard words about the facile keyboard style of his younger half-brother, Johann Christian, together with that of Johann Schobert, saying that they filled the ear but left the heart empty.[147]

---

[144]Stefan Kunze, *Die Sinfonie im 18. Jahrhundert* (Laabe, 1993), pp. 243, 250: "The history of the symphony touches his eighteen works in the genre not at all, or only marginally."

[145]On the meager and poor musical forces he commanded, see Heinrich Miesner, *Philipp Emanuel Bach in Hamburg: Beiträge zu seiner Biograife und zur Musikgeschichte* (Leipzig, 1929), p. 15.

[146]Letter dated Hamburg, 6 December 1769. *The Letters of C. P. E. Bach*, p. 19.

[147]In a conversation with the poet Matthius Claudius, related by Claudius to Meinrich von Gerstenberg in a letter dated 5 July 1768, cited in Ernst Fritz Schmid, *Carl Philipp Emanuel Bach und seine Kammermusik* (Kassel, 1931), p. 37.

Bach wrote few concertos late in life, but one of his last works is the Double Concerto for Fortepiano and Harpsichord with strings, two horns, and two flutes (W. 48; H. 479), composed in 1788, the year he died. He was an innovator to the end, as this unusual choice of solo instruments shows. He will be remembered mainly for the concertos of the Berlin period, and particularly for the stormy ones such as the Concerto in d of 1748. Koch still considered Bach's concertos as models for the genre and in one surprising comparison likened their opposition of solo and tutti passages to the dramatic effect achieved by the ancient tragedians in alternating individuals with the chorus.[148] By analogy, Bach himself was the heroic individual of his solo concertos, ever at the mercy of the Philistines, whether in Berlin or Hamburg.

Schubart in his *Ideen* concludes his searching essay on Bach's music with a few remarks worthy to serve as a summary of the composer's position. "One notices in his newest pieces some accommodation with the present mode, but never a descent into the reigning taste for the petty. Trifling at the clavichord, sweetly enervating airs, and the tinkling baubles of today's composers are all abominations to his gigantic spirit. He remains, in spite of the fashion, what he is—Bach" (p. 179). Schubart makes clear his hostility to "the fashion," which is of course nothing other than the galant style.

Singspiel

Beginnings

German literature entered a golden age during the eighteenth century and northern Germany played a major part in its triumphs. Frederick paid no heed, except when excoriating the vernacular language and its practitioners. Yet his bellicose successes have been shown to be one of the causes of the wave of German pride that encouraged the literary efflorescence.[149] The Prussian capital was the home of several poets who contributed to what became known as the First Berlin School of Lieder.

Krause devoted some space to the Lied in his treatise *Von der musikalischer Poesie*, encountered earlier in connection with Graun. He recommended folk song as a model of simplicity to poets and composers alike, with an emphasis on the French chanson in particular. His ideal was to foster a song cycle so plain that the average person would be able to enjoy singing the verses, with or without accom-

---

[148]Heinrich Koch, *Versuch einer Anleitung zur Composition*, 3 vols. (Leipzig, 1788–93; reprint 1969), 3: 332; 337.

[149]T. C. W. Blanning, "Frederick the Great and German Culture," in *Royal and Republican Sovereignty*, pp. 527–50.

1. Antoine Watteau. *Fêtes vénetiennes*. (Edinburgh, National Gallery of Scotland)

II. Maurice Quentin de La Tour. *Portrait of Mme. de Pompadour.*
(Paris, Louvre)

III. Jacopo Amigoni. *Portrait of Farinelli.*
(Stuttgart, Staatsgalarie)

IV. Giovanni Paolo Pannini. *Teatro Argentina, 1747.*
(Paris, Louvre)

v. Rosalba Carriera. *Portrait of Faustina.*
(Dresden, Gemäldegalerie)

VI. Anton Raphael Mengs. *Portrait of Regina Mingotti.*
(Dresden, Gemäldegalerie)

VII. Giovanni Battista Tiepolo. *Armida and Rinaldo.*
(Chicago, Art Institute)

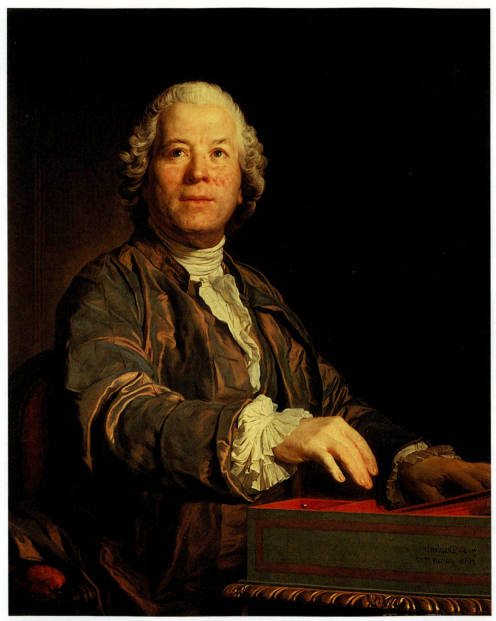

x. Joseph Silfrede Duplessis. *Portrait of Gluck.*
(Vienna, Kunsthistorisches Museum)

XII. Anonymous. *Portrait of Boccherini*
(Melbourne, National Gallery of Victoria)

XI. Thomas Gainsborough. *Portrait of Christian Bach.*
(London, National Portrait Gallery)

paniment. The plainer the melody, the better it would serve the multiple stanzas sung to it. Poetry was far more important than music in his scheme.

Krause's theories bore fruit. Together with the poet Karl Ramler, Krause coedited *Oden mit Melodien,* published in 1753 and succeeded by a second volume two years later. Ramler gathered the texts, Krause the music. Neither their names nor those of the many contributors were given, but Marpurg identified them by providing an index in the first volume of his *Historischer-kritische Beyträge* (1754). Among the poets were Otto von Gemmingen, Johann Gleim, Friedrich von Hagedorn, Ewald von Kleist, Lessing, and Ramler himself. The composers included Agricola, Emanuel Bach, Franz Benda, Graun, Krause, Nichelmann, and Quantz, an illustrious coterie.

Oden mit Melodien were followed by *Berlinische Oden und Lieder* edited by Marpurg in three volumes between 1756 and 1763 (exactly coinciding with the Seven Years War). This set, printed by Breitkopf in Leipzig, was the most extensive and highly respected of its kind, further enhancing the fame of the Berlin school. Musical settings were made by Agricola, Bach, both Grauns, Kirnberger, Krause, Marpurg, Nichelmann, Quantz, Sack, and others.

Bach had contributed five songs to *Oden mit Melodien* and he set no fewer than fifty-four poems in Christian Gellert's *Geistliche Oden und Lieder* (1758). The serious nature of these religious poems to be sung in the home prompted Bach to take more liberties than he did with secular songs. While remaining within the strophic format, he extended music's domain here and there by means of preludes, postludes, and interludes for the keyboard. A reviewer in 1766 remarked on Bach's greater musical demands.

> These *Odenmelodien* also bear the unmistakable imprint of Bach's fiery and imaginative spirit. Indeed they seem to have been conceived more in terms of the keyboard than the voice. None the less a well-trained and technically accomplished singer will find ample scope to improve his execution of small ornaments, to practice the accurate rendering of certain difficult melodic configurations and to develop his powers of expression.[150]

Gellert himself took notice of Bach's efforts. He wrote to his sister, "Bach, a court musician in Berlin, has composed settings of all my songs and has recently sent me a copy. . . . They are good, but too good for a singer who is not musical."[151]

Besides the ode, secular poets cultivated the fable and Anacreontic verse, in which shepherds and shepherdesses disported in idyllic landscapes bearing tra-

---

[150]*Allgemeine deutsche Bibliothek,* ed. Friedrich Nicolai, 118 vols. (Berlin and Stettin, 1766–96), 1: 302, cited after Ottenberg, *C. P. E. Bach,* p. 97, who gives impressive examples from the song "Bitten," pp. 98–99.
[151]Letter dated Leipzig, 25 March 1758, cited by Ottenberg, *C. P. E. Bach,* pp. 99–100.

ditional pastoral names such as Damon and Phyllis, Dafne and Chloe, etc. Poets also borrowed the French *romance,* a narrative tale of amatory content, told in the most naive style, frequently over many stanzas. Related to the *Romanze,* as the Germans called it, was the more dramatic and serious ballade, which often told of grisly events. First cultivated in the song literature, both these genres would become popular in German stage works as opera was gradually revived in the vernacular, generally in comic works called Singspiel or Operette.

The wide success of Lieder with the public encouraged poets and composers to create a new kind of popular theater using sung verses. This had happened early in the century in France with opéra-comique, a genre that helped give rise to ballad opera in England, beginning with John Gay's *The Beggar's Opera* (1728).[152] Several creative sparks were necessary before the successful ignition of Singspiel as a sustained, growing phenomenon.

Charles Coffey's ballad opera *The Devil to Pay* (1731) was transplanted at Berlin in 1742 as *Der Teufel ist los* and given by an itinerant troupe of players under the direction of Johann Friedrich Schönemann. The translator was an administrator in Frederick's service who masked his name under a pseudonym for fear of displeasing his superiors. The play traveled here and there without engendering any progeny until another theater director, Heinrich Gottfried Koch of Leipzig, commissioned a superior poet, the Saxon Christian Felix Weisse, to retranslate *The Devil to Pay* into German. He had his music director Johann Standfuss compose the songs. In this new guise *Der Teufel is los, oder Die verwandelten Weiber* (1752) became an ancestor of Singspiel.

Leipzig had two advantages that made it attractive to impresarios who wished to profit from opera: its great university, teeming with literary and musical talent, and its annual trade fairs, drawing travelers and money from far and wide. Opera had once flourished in the city. During the short reign of Elector Johann Georg IV his maestro di cappella Nicolaus Adam Strungk applied for and received permission to organize an opera company in Leipzig at his own expense. An opera house was built and inaugurated on 8 May 1693 with Strungk's *Alceste,* sung in German. Telemann directed this enterprise for a time beginning in 1702, when he was a student at the University of Leipzig. The company was dissolved in 1720. In 1730 Johann Christoph Gottsched, professor of poetry, logic, and metaphysics at the University of Leipzig, and no friend of opera, credited the increasing good taste of his countrymen for the declining fortunes of German opera.[153]

Gottsched advocated spoken tragedy according to the classical "rules." The

---

[152]Daniel Heartz, "*The Beggar's Opera* and Opéra-Comique en Vaudevilles," *Early Music* 27 (1999): 42–53.
[153]Reinhard Strohm, "The Crisis of Baroque Opera in Germany," in *Dramma per Musica: Italian Opera Seria in the Eighteenth Century* (New Haven and London, 1997), 81–96; 82.

first of his stage works was the tragedy *Der sterbende Cato* performed in Leipzig in 1731. A few years earlier he had become advisor to the Leipzig theatrical troupe of Johann and Caroline Neuber. Under their aegis Leipzig continued to have a lively theatrical scene, at least as to spoken plays. When young Lessing was a university student there in 1748 he was caught up in theatrical activities and wrote his first play at age nineteen. Traveling companies such as the Mingottis also visited Leipzig, offering serious and comic Italian operas.

During the Seven Years War, Koch took his troupe from Leipzig to Hamburg, out of harm's way. In 1759 he offered a sequel by Weisse and Standfuss, *Der lustige Schuster, oder Der zwete Theil von Teufel ist los.* Weisse also fled Saxony. In 1759–60 he visited Paris, where he became acquainted with Rousseau and witnessed the blooming of opéra-comique. After the peace of 1763 Koch returned to Leipzig as did Weisse, who revised his two Devil plays. Standfuss had died around 1760. Koch turned for help to Leipzig's leading musician, Johann Adam Hiller, who directed the city's foremost concert series (Grosses Concert) and was known as a composer mainly for his Lieder. In 1761 he published *Choralmelodien zu Gellerts geistlichen Oden und Liedern.* He had also attempted a setting of the songs in Gellert's *Das Orakel* (1747), a translation of Saint-Foix's two-act afterpiece *L'oracle.* As he says in his autobiography, "I shut myself up for three weeks from the noises of the fair and composed *Orakel,* which work I regard as no more than the raw material for a good composition that I would one day undertake, had not Fleischer in Brunswick made this effort superfluous."[154] Even though Hiller's work went for nought, Gellert's choice of model pointed the direction Singspiel would gradually take: away from the low comedy of the Devil operas and toward the more sentimental and pastoral plays popular in Paris.[155] But first Hiller would also make his contribution to the former by revising *Die verwandelten Weiber,* retaining twelve pieces by Standfuss, composing many more, and providing a new overture. This production of 1766, of which a keyboard score was issued in 1770, contained Hiller's first veritable "hit" song, the lusty "Ohne Lieb und ohne Wein, was wär unser Leben?" (What would our life be without love and wine?). The sequel was also revived, with seven new pieces by Hiller.

Impresario, poet, and composer differed on how best to bring the new German operetta fully to life. Koch wanted as popular a product as possible so as to fill his theater with paying customers. He wished for music so simple the audience could sing along with it. Weisse, an experienced playwright, dreamt of rais-

---

[154]Hiller, *Lebensbeschreibungen,* p. 299. Friedrich Fleischer set *Das Orakel* for Brunswick in 1771. On it, see Thomas Bauman, *North German Opera in the Age of Goethe* (Cambridge, 1985), pp. 85–88.
[155]By the 1760s opéra-comique was being widely performed throughout Europe. See Bruce Alan Brown, "La diffusion et l'influence de l'opéra-comique en Europe au XVIIIᵉ siècle," *L'opéra-comique en France au XVIIIᵉ siècle,* ed. Philippe Vendrix (Liège, 1992), pp. 283–342.

ing the literary level of the genre by emulating Charles-Simon Favart and Michel-Jean Sedaine, and in this he would succeed. Hiller mainly wanted to elevate taste by improving German singing along Italian lines, his idols being Hasse and Faustina in Dresden. He was a master teacher of singers himself and the author of an important treatise on singing. With the poet Daniel Schiebeler he collaborated on *Lisuart und Dariolette* (the text adapted after Favart's *La fée Urgèle*) which was produced in late 1766. It was not tuneful and light enough to please Koch, confessed Hiller in his autobiography, "and I gladly agree that Koch was not totally wrong, when the operetta consists mainly of scenes from the lower classes of people." In the preface of the next work, Hiller explained his turn toward simpler and shorter songs. Weisse adapted *Lottchen am Hofe* (1767) for Hiller from Favart's *Ninette à la cour*. Then a year later he adapted *Die Liebe auf dem Lande* from Louis Anseaume's *La clochette* and Madame Favart's *Annette et Lubin*. With these two works Singspiel assumed its classic form. Keyboard scores soon appeared in Leipzig that carried the works everywhere in the German-speaking world. In 1769 Hiller and Weisse capped their collaboration with *Die Jagd*, the work that is the quintessential representative of Singspiel.

HILLER'S *DIE JAGD*

Koch's Leipzig troupe gave the first performance of *Die Jagd* on 29 January 1770 in the Weimar court theater of Duchess Anna Amalia, to whom the work is dedicated. Weisse based his text mainly on Charles Collé's three-act spoken play *La partie de chasse de Henri IV* (1762). The successful opéra-comique on the same subject, *Le roi et le fermier* (1764) by Sedaine and Monsigny, also furnished Weisse some material. Collé's play accounts for the unusual cast of three pairs of rustic lovers, the king being the only other singing part. As in Collé the king remains Henri IV of France, but the milieu and society described are plainly those of rural Saxony. At the conclusion the six lovers each sing a stanza and then join to sing "Es lebe der König" (Long live the king), but the final stanza, sung directly to the audience, ends "Es lebe der Kurfürst" (Long live the elector). The Saxon elector at this time was young Frederick Augustus III.

Die Jagd was not only the most successful Saxon Singspiel but also the only one to benefit from a complete number-by-number description in print. The author was Hiller's pupil, Reichardt, who wrote *Über die Deutsche comische Oper* (On German Comic Opera) at the age of twenty-two. Breitkopf printed the pamphlet in Leipzig and it was published by Carl Bohn at Hamburg in 1774.[156] Reichardt held up *Die Jagd* as a model to young German composers who wished

---

[156]Johann Friedrich Reichardt, *Über die Deutsche comische Oper* (Hamburg, 1774), facsimile edition with commentary and an index by Walter Salmen (Munich, 1974). Reichardt's remarks on *Die Jagd* are quoted below without further attribution.

to write comic operas (they could scarcely have been much younger than the author himself). He praised Hiller's music as making good choices for the most part, while claiming in a few cases that better choices could have been made. "In my opinion Hiller outshines all comic opera composers of all other nations; he is to the genre what Hasse is to serious opera" (p. 11).

Reichardt felt compelled to give his German ancestors the honor of inventing comic opera, so he invoked the Quodlibets sung at reunions of the Bach family in the previous century as its point of origin. Then he invoked the comic operas of Telemann for Hamburg. This line of works for the theater had no future and was totally forgotten, he admits, for which he blamed bad German poems and the equally bad manner of German singing. Hiller, he maintained, had striven to improve German singing and was responsible for the present shape of German comic opera. "He knew the French and Italian comic operas and took from them what he pleased, discarded what was unsuitable, and made for himself a form that is tailored to nature and to our language, and necessarily even more so to our mediocre singers. He threw out long-winded arias because he knew they were not suited to comedy" (p. 7).

Hiller was indeed in a good position to learn from opera buffa. Whether in Dresden or in Leipzig, he profited from visiting Italian troupes. He knew opéra-comique perhaps even better because of its diffusion by means of printed scores. In two issues of his weekly newspaper on music in the fall of 1766 he included a penetrating review of Philidor's *Le sorcier* (1764).[157] Hiller called it a "happy mixture of French and Italian taste." He praised Philidor's harmony as "very pure, and chosen with care," and commended his accompaniments and instrumentation. Speaking of the sea storm in one of the arias, he wrote that "in this kind of description of nature the French are very often superior to the Italians."

The story of *Die Jagd* has two main plotlines. The king is lost in the forest in the gathering darkness after having been separated from his hunting party during a storm. Claiming to be one of the king's retainers, he is rescued by a commoner, the village judge Michel. It is this moment that is represented by the fine title vignette of the original keyboard score, which shows Michel, his lamp, and the more knightly figure of the king (Figure 4.19). Michel takes the king to his humble abode and gives him food and a place to sleep, all the while offering numerous examples of rustic virtue. The second plotline is domestic. Michel and his wife Marthe have two children. The elder, their son Christel, is engaged to marry Hannchen, the beautiful daughter of a tenant farmer. Röschen, their very high-spirited daughter, wants to marry the handsome but flighty Töfel. Permission is withheld pending the settlement of Christel's marriage to Hannschen,

---

[157]*Wöchentliche Nachrichten und Annmerkungen die Musik betreffend,* ed. Johann Adam Hiller, 5 vols. (Leipzig, 1766–70; reprint 1970), 1: 92 ff., an essay in two parts from the issues for 16 and 23 September 1766.

FIGURE 4.19. Title vignette of Hiller's *Die Jagd* (1770).

who has been abducted by the evil Count Schmetterling and held against her will for an entire month. Rumors circulate that Hannchen perhaps went off with the count willingly. The men believe these rumors. Röschen rejects them out of hand and argues firmly for the virtue of her brother's absent fiancée. If this turn of events sounds familiar, it may be because of the similar female solidarity against foolish male doubts in Mozart's *Die Entführung aus dem Serail,* which Gottlieb Stephanie derived from Bretzner's Singspiel *Belmont und Constanze* (Berlin, 1781).

The setting of Act I is a country scene with a rustic house in the background. Röschen is winding yarn and sings a strophic song vaunting Töfel. The key is A, as in the beautifully written overture: *Allegro con spirito* in common time; *Più tosto allegretto* in 3/8 and in D, a minuet; and *Allegro assai* in 2/4 with leaps of a fourth back and forth that suggest hunting music. After spoken dialogue with Marthe, Röschen sings a longer, nonstrophic piece in which she imitates Töfel's whistle. In later editions her two solos were labeled "Lied" and "Arie," respectively, but neither Weisse nor Hiller used these labels. All the characters sing both types of solo except Marthe, who has only one piece, a strophic song, near the beginning of Act III. She also sings in both ensembles of Act I, a quarreling trio (No. 7) and the penultimate quartet of farewells (No. 12). Act I ends with a chorus painting the royal exercise: "Der König jagt, der ganze Wald / Braust von Getümmel schon" (The king hunts and the whole forest reverberates already to the sound).

The high point of the first act is none of the above but the first appearance of Hannschen, who has escaped while the count was perforce occupied with the king's hunting party. She is not entirely alone because Töfel, in hiding, observes her and listens to her song addressed to the rustic setting.

Du süsser Wohnplatz stiller Freuden	Thou sweet dwelling of quiet joy
Du kleines Dörfchen, wohl, wohl mir!	Thou little village dear to me!
So find' ich nach so vielen Leiden	After so many trials will I find
Aufs neue der Liebe Glück in dir?	Love again and happiness in thee?

Weisse shows his mettle in lines like these, so full of the "m" and "n" and "l" sounds particularly favorable to music. Hiller seizes the opportunity to the full (No. 10). Hannchen is the only character who has no speaking before she sings. Rather, the orchestra of strings, two horns, and two flutes speaks for her in an expressive ritornello (Example 4.26). The key of E♭ appears here for the first time. The sweetness of so many sixths and thirds conveys one element in the very first line; the idea of stability inherent in "dwelling" perhaps generates the long tonic pedal at the beginning, "quiet joy" could be found in the slow-moving harmonies, and by itself "joy" could account for the opening triadic leaps of the melody. The ascending appoggiaturas with the raised fifth in m. 2 is not answered by its equivalent in m. 4 but by a sighing descent, a subtly effective touch. Hasse's operas for Dresden, of which Hiller says in his autobiography that he heard them all from *Semiramide* (1747) to *L'Olimpiade* (1756), were of greatest importance to Hiller's formation as a composer, and he shows how intimately he understood Hasse's lyric gift by writing so suave a piece as this. Hasse's traits are evident not only in the chromatic rise to the fifth over the subdominant harmony and the Lombard snaps of m. 5, but also in the accented and protracted weak third beat of m. 6, and the poignant cross-relation going into the half-cadence in m. 8. At the same time

EXAMPLE 4.26. *Hiller,* Die Jagd, *No. 10, Prelude*

there are traits that do not seem much like Hasse. The initial triadic figure of the treble is one, and even less Hasselike is the repeated descending triad in the bass, after full dominant seventh harmony in mm. 9–10, as if in response to the initial treble figure. These are the wonderful sounds of Hiller's own generation. It may have been a younger figure than Hasse, perhaps Philidor, who helped Hiller to discover them. If we were to imagine this piece with clarinets and bassoons as well as horns, its ethos comes close to the serenade in E♭ in triple meter offered by Ferrando and Guglielmo to their ladies in *Così fan tutte* (No. 21). The sighing parallel sixths of mm. 12–13 are particularly close.

The sensitive listener perceives from this ritornello alone, even before Hannchen begins to sing, the truth about her. She is a tower of virtue as well as sensibility. Töfel is not a sensitive listener and persists in his doubts. Her fiancé Christel also requires some persuading before they can sing their duet in Act II (No. 27). Without these doubts and their working out, the opera would be too short. Reichardt calls Hannchen's entrance piece "the favorite aria of all those who truly know this operetta" and says, "the aria's theme already expresses the sweetest satisfaction and one easily learns from the ritornello the content of the entire aria" (p. 49). The aria has a second strophe to be sung to the same music but Reichardt advises his readers, who presumably included many concerned with putting the Singspiel on the stage as well as young composers, to skip the second stanza and repeat the first, "because the composer has sung himself so completely into the feeling (Empfindung) of the initial words, no other words can fit"; in conclusion, he writes, "who knows Herr Hiller by this simple aria must of necessity love him; who cannot even feel how beautiful it is one must regretfully pity" (p. 50).

One of the characteristics of Singspiel is that a single character sometimes is given two or three solo pieces in a row to sing, interrupted only by the spoken dialogue. This is the case with Hannschen near the beginning of Act II, which is set in the forest. Töfel and Röschen have the first two numbers. They quarrel over Hannchen and then Töfel is called away. Hannchen appears. Röschen and Hannchen embrace and the latter almost immediately begins an aria expressing her concern that Christel no longer loves her (No. 16). Beginning with a broad eight-measure theme filled with musical sighs, the aria is one of the longest in the opera. Unlike others it has a contrasting middle section, a *Lento ma poco* in 3/4 and in f, during which she compares herself to the poor turtledove wrongly taken captive and returning home blameless. The first section comes back but ends, of course, in the tonic instead of the dominant. After a few lines of spoken dialogue, Hannchen sings a shorter piece, in 6/8 meter and in G, about how corrupt court and city people are (No. 17). Then, after more dialogue, she begins the *Romanze* "Als ich auf meiner Bleiche," the opera's most popular number. In it she relates how she was abducted and held captive, in six stanzas sung to the same music, half of them interrupted by spoken remarks. In opera with recitative the composer has the option of beginning without a ritornello. The Singspiel composer must have one, however short, to give the pitch to the singer. Hannchen's *Romanze* has one of the shortest. Two measures suffice to establish the key of A, in which the opera begins and ends, and the meter (No. 18) (Example 4.27). Absolute symmetry in phrase structure prevails: 4 + 4 + 4 + 4. The melody matches the **a a b a'** form of many German folksongs (also found in Beethoven's "Ode to Joy") except that **a'** begins while still returning to the tonic.

The *Romanze* in fact became a folk song, "because every person from the high-

EXAMPLE 4.27. *Hiller,* Die Jagd, Romanze

As I was in my laundry sprinkling a piece of wool,
There came out of the bushes a breathless maiden,
Said she: "Ah, Ah, have pity, help my father!
A fall has struck the poor man's leg in two."

est to the lowest sings, plays, and whistles it, even drums it, I should almost say, so much so that it is used in every conceivable way across all of Germany," wrote Reichardt in 1774 (p. 61). He also says that in hearing this tune sung many thousand times by the common people he never once heard them observe the two occurrences of D♯ in the last phrase. According to one of the current notions about what makes a folk song, it may originate with an individual composer but must be absorbed subsequently by the whole community and handed down in oral tradition that also transforms it.[158] The *Romanze* passes these tests. Even earlier than

---

[158]Klaus P. Wachsmann, "Folk music," in *New Grove.*

Reichardt, after *Die Jagd* had conquered Berlin within its first year, an anonymous reviewer there wrote, "Half the inhabitants know by heart the *Romanze* 'Als ich auf meiner Bleiche.' It is sung and played on every street, during every stroll, on every excursion on the water, during every promenade."[159] What can make a composer more happy, muses Reichardt, than the awareness of having contributed to the happiness of an entire people?

Hannchen and Christel, now fully reconciled, comment in their duet (No. 27) on the darkened skies and ominous thunder. Weisse and Hiller were not so bold in treating the approaching storm as were Sedaine and Monsigny, from whom Hiller nevertheless profited. Hiller chooses the key of d and an *Allegro moderato* in common time, with nearly continuous eighth-note movement, working up to a climactic phrase for orchestra alone after both lovers first sing. By the time the piece reaches the more calm area of the relative major, Weisse has kindly obliged Hiller with the sentiment that their love is now free of storms. The lovers leave the stage after the piece has returned to tonic d, and the orchestra then sounds its climactic phrase as a postlude. The storm proper (No. 28) is for orchestra alone, as in Monsigny. Hiller cleverly increases the tempo to *Allegro di molto* but otherwise keeps the same key and the incessant rhythmic motion, which builds up like a Mannheim crescendo to the climactic orchestral phrase of the previous duet. The storm is relatively brief (45 mm.), less than half the length of the duet, and would be quickly over at a very fast tempo. It winds down very skillfully to a *pianissimo* at the end, preparing the appearance of the solitary king.

Lost in the darkened forest the king blames himself and the folly of his passion for hunting for his plight. His spoken words are so few that the key of d is still ringing in our ears when the orchestra strikes up the ritornello of his aria (No. 29) in D, *Andante e con gravita* in 2/4. The words speak of human frailty, even in the most highborn, meaning himself. The music gives him a dignity that belies his words. Reichardt is especially good on it.

> Now the king appears. The music receives at once a totally different cast. One hears a song in which quiet greatness and true elevation reign. As gladly as I would otherwise allow the usual form of the large, extended aria as a mark of distinction to characters of high estate, what pleases me immensely in this aria of the king is its emphatic brevity and I believe this contributes the most to the majesty of its character. The poetry itself already precludes extensions and repetitions because it is of moral content. This is no king who always and solely thinks of his majesty but a friend of humanity, a man of fine feeling and tender heart, in sum it is Henri IV. (p. 79)

After a long spoken dialogue with Michel, the king sings again, this time a polonaise (No. 30), *Alla Polacca* in 3/4 and in A. Reichardt finds this also well chosen, as

---

[159]*Allgemeine deutsche Bibliothek* (1772) 17:2, 65, cited after Thomas Bauman, preface to Hiller, *Die Jagd* (German Opera 1770–1800, 1) (1985).

it lends a certain popular tone to the character, well suiting the words, as well as a proud, dignified one in keeping with this old national dance. But here Reichardt takes Hiller to task, as he did in the duet (No. 27), for repeating certain words. Michel and the king end Act II with a duet (No. 31), *Allegro moderato* in 2/4 and in G, in which the characters are not differentiated by the music, a treatment also censured by Reichardt. Weisse was more to blame than Hiller, if blame there be, because he had Michel strike up a drinking song in praise of their good king; failure of the incognito king to join in was not an option.

Act III takes place in Michel's rustic house. Songs are the natural means of celebration here to go along with supper. The king waxes philosophical again. Weisse's spoken dialogues become very long and tedious at some points, as when he has the king try to show a common touch by helping the women move the furniture. At length, in Scene 10, Hannchen arrives and inculpates Count Schmetterling, who himself arrives with threats two scenes later. Thus do the two plots finally come together. The king makes his identity known, banishes Schmetterling, settles a generous dowry on both young couples, and promises to be godfather to their children. A quartet of jubilation for the four lovers (No. 39), *Con spirito* in 2/4 and in F, precedes the divertissement (No. 40), *Allegretto* in 2/4 and in A, which is like a vaudeville with choral refrain.

Reichardt had high praise for the king's last aria (No. 38), *Andante ma non troppo* in 2/4 and in E♭, saying it was worthy of a Graun. The text, "Welche königliche Lust, seinen Thron auf Liebe gründen" (What a royal pleasure it is to base one's throne on love), nearly gives away the king's identity. Its sentiment smacks of platitude and repeats what has already been made clear. Not surprisingly, various practical editions indicate that the piece was usually omitted. Reichardt devotes to it one of his longest commentaries, calling it a "model for a serious aria in comic operas" (p. 93). This brings him back to his intended audience of young composers, whom he advises not to be satisfied with the keyboard score of the opera. All of Hiller should be studied in full score, he enjoins. But this could not have been easily done since the full scores were not printed, not even that of *Die Jagd,* of which manuscript scores also remain rare. From this point Reichardt launches into one of his frequent digressions on the unworthy German opera stage: "If we admire a countryman he must first go to Italy, forswear pure harmony and his religion . . ." (p. 94). It was Hasse, of course, who converted to Catholicism, but this diatribe is directed at Hiller, who did not. Reichardt implores him to "write Italian opera and earn the fame you deserve at least with foreigners; your country does not deserve your patriotism" (ibid.).

Hiller must have blanched at being lectured by his young student in this way and throughout the pamphlet. "I am convinced our friendship will not be affected by my criticisms," says the student at the end, rather disingenuously. Of Weisse's text he says (p. 25) that it is too bad that kings can never hear its wise teachings because they never listen to German operettas. The elector of Saxony was no longer king of Poland, so there was only one king in Germany—Frederick. Whatever his gaucheries, Reichardt was unstinting in his praise of Hiller, calling him "the first good composer of comic operas among the Germans, and also a very good model. He gave our comic opera the shape it now has" (p. 7).

The 1770s

The small duchies of Saxe-Weimar and Saxe-Gotha to the west of electoral Saxony became important centers of German opera in the 1770s. Both employed Abel Seyler's theater troupe. Under the patronage of the music-loving Duchess Anna Amalia, Weimar saw, besides the premiere of *Die Jagd,* the first performances of Anton Schweitzer's melodramma *Pygmalion* and serious opera *Alceste* (1773). Georg Benda composed his two melodrammas *Ariadne auf Naxos* and *Medea* for Gotha, as well as his two serious operas *Romeo und Julie* and *Walder,* both on texts by Friedrich Wilhelm Gotter, who also wrote *Medea.* Benda and Schweitzer will be encountered in the next chapter at Mannheim, where they reached the peak of their careers. Goethe, who as a student at Leipzig University had witnessed the triumph of Hiller and Weisse in the theater, arrived in Weimar in late 1775 to take up a court post. He served as librettist for several operas and even acted in the amateur shows. His *Erwin und Elmire* and *Das Jahrmarktsfest* were set to music by Duchess Anna Amalia herself.[160] Her main teacher was Friedrich Wilhelm Wolf, a disciple of Hiller who contributed several Singspiels to the Weimar stage.

Hiller composed four more comic operas in collaboration with Weisse after *Die Jagd.* Weisse derived the libretto of *Der Dorfbalbier* (Leipzig, 1771) from *Blaise le savetier* by Sedaine, set by Philidor with great success (1759). Hiller got his pupil, young Christian Gottlob Neefe, then a student at Leipzig University, to compose ten of the twenty-four numbers. Weisse's *Der Aerndtekranz* was an original libretto set in the environs of Dresden with a plot resembling that of his earlier *Lottchen am Hofe.* Hiller's setting (Leipzig, 1771) was so popular it remained a favorite on German stages for decades. Weisse and Ramler combined to write *Der Krieg,* after Goldoni's prose comedy *La guerra,* which Hiller set to music that was first performed in Berlin in 1772. Peasant couples populated Weisse's original *Die Jubelhochzeit,* which reached the stage with Hiller's music at Berlin in 1773. The venue for these comic operas in Berlin was the small theater in the Behrenstrasse, to which Koch gradually transferred his Leipzig troupe.

The opera Burney heard under Hiller's direction when he visited Leipzig in September 1772 was *Der Krieg.*[161] Its composer was not forceful enough with his wayward singers and players, thought Burney.

[160]For an illuminating discussion of all these works, see Bauman, *North German Opera,* chapters 4 and 5.
[161]Charles Burney, *Voyage musical dans L'Europe des lumières,* trans. and ed. Michel Noiray (Paris, 1992), p. 392, n. 5, citing a contemporary review of the production in Leipzig.

I found this music very natural and pleasing, and deserving of much better perform- ers than the present Leipsic company can boast; for to say the truth, the singing here is as vulgar and ordinary as our common singing in England, among those who have neither had the advantage of being taught, nor of hearing good singing. There is just the same pert snap in taking high notes, which they do with a kind of beat, and very loud, instead of a *messa di voce,* or swell. The instrumental parts went ill; but as this was the first rehearsal, they might have been disciplined into good order, if M. Hiller had chosen to bounce and play the tyrant a little; for it is a melancholy reflection to make, that few composers are well treated by an orchestra, till they have first used the performers roughly, and made themselves formidable.

Burney blamed the "bad manner of singing" on the lack of Italian opera in Leipzig. It is true that there was no resident Italian troupe as in Dresden and Berlin, but the fairs did attract itinerant Italian companies to Leipzig. Possibly some of the better singers Hiller trained had already moved or were moving to Berlin by this point. In his autobiography Hiller described the situation in 1766: "The theater had no proper singers of either sex; whoever was endowed by nature with a tol- erable voice and a little rhythmic feeling undertook to sing in the operettas."[162] He says he tried, step by step, to bring them closer to being real singers. Not much improvement was possible apparently. Reichardt in 1774 joined in calling the general level of singing miserable.

Schubart, looking back over the century in his *Ideen,* did not question that Hiller played the most important role in giving Singspiel its distinctive character.

Hiller. Director of music in Leipzig: the favorite composer of the Germans. However much Hiller studies Italian singing he studies German singing even more, which explains why his songs cut so deeply into our hearts that they have become common all over Germany. Which apprentice, which soldier, which maiden does not sing the lied "Als ich auf meiner Bleiche etc.?" "Ohne Lieb und ohne Wein etc.," and various others? No one has yet reached Hiller in the *Volkston.* He is the first after Standfuss to bring comic operas in the German language to the stage. His *Lustiger Schuster, Die Jagd, Dorfbalbier, Erntkranz* and several other operas have caused a general sensation in Germany. There is not a single theater among us where they have not been per- formed more than once. And this has to be attributed not so much to the texts, which are rather naive, but much more to the glorious songs with which Hiller knew how to animate his operas.[163]

Weisse would have disagreed and would have been dismayed to see what he regarded as the most important part of their operas thus treated, yet his texts were

---

[162]Hiller, *Lebensbegehreibungen.*
[163]Christian Friedrich Daniel Schubart, *Ideen zu einer Ästhetik der Tonkunst* (Vienna, 1806; Hildesheim, 1969), pp. 106–7.

but clever, well-crafted adaptations from the French. Hiller was more original and generally took care to avoid borrowing the music of opéra-comique.

Berlin had at least twice the population of Leipzig, and it was perhaps inevitable that the center of German opera should gradually shift from the university town to the teeming capital. Koch applied for permission to perform with his troupe in Prussia as early as 1767. He was granted this and the Berlin theater in the Behrenstrasse in 1771. A rival German company under Theophil Döbbelin was already established in Berlin. Döbbelin was more interested than Koch in serious German plays. He had given the premiere of Lessing's *Minna von Barnhelm* to an enthusiastic Berlin audience in 1767. An anonymous pamphlet comparing the two troupes was generally unfavorable to Koch, even in his own Leipzig repertory. The author conceded that Caroline Steinbrecher had the better voice in *Lottchen am Hofe* and *Die Jagd* but maintained that these parts were better acted by Döbbelin's wife Katharina.[164] Reichardt, on the other hand, specifically praised Steinbrecher for her acting as Röschen in *Die Jagd.* Koch died in 1775, leaving Döbbelin as the principal arbiter of Singspiel in Berlin.

Johann André, born in Offenbach in 1741, came to Döbbelin's attention with the songs he composed for Goethe's "Schauspiel mit Gesang," *Erwin und Elmire.* As performed in Berlin by Döbbelin's troupe in 1775, the work became an immediate and lasting success. It led Döbbelin to appoint André as the troupe's music director. André wrote more than a dozen operas for Berlin until 1784, when he returned to the Rhineland and took over his family's publishing firm. Abbé Vogler praised a comic song in André's *Der Töpfer* and bestowed upon its composer the title of "the German Galuppi."[165]

Throughout most of Frederick's reign Berlin also enjoyed a crown-sponsored French theater. In 1776 a new theater on the Gendarmenplatz, built for the French troupe, was opened. Two years later Frederick abruptly dismissed this troupe. Döbbelin took over the new theater and offered Parisian works, beginning with Grétry's widely acclaimed *Zémire et Azor.* Opéra-comique in German translation proved a formidable rival to Singspiel, not just in Berlin but all over Germany.

In Dresden the greatest resident composer since Hasse emerged in the person of Kapellmeister Johann Gottlieb Naumann, who refused Frederick's offer to succeed Agricola as the director of the Berlin court opera in 1774. Naumann did not contribute directly to Singspiel, but his two most eminent pupils, Joseph Schuster and Franz Seydelmann, did, when a new German company formed in Dresden in the late 1770s. Both had been with Naumann to Italy for immersion in Italian opera at the source during the 1760s. August Meissner was the poet of

---

[164]*Ueber die Kochische Schauspielergesellschaft* (Berlin and Leipzig, 1771), cited after Bauman, *North German Opera,* pp. 60–61.
[165]Vogler, *Betrachtungen der Mannheimer Tonschule,* 1: 397.

the short-lived triumph of German opera in Dresden. It began with his adaptation of a spoken comedy by Marc Antoine Legrand as *Der Alchymist,* set to music by Schuster (1778), that is ranked as one of the finest German operas of the decade.[166] By 1780 the Dresden court reinstated Italian opera and the German troupe was dissolved.

Singspiel of this era was confined to the cities and courts of German-speaking lands. Not even *Die Jagd* made it beyond them to the wider world. The German language had yet to achieve international currency, and even the best German plays did not travel abroad. Thus it cannot surprise anyone that Singspiel, conceived mainly as a vernacular play with added song, remained at home.

[166]Bauman, "The German Operatic Efflorescence at Dresden," in *North German Opera,* pp. 211–18.

5

Stuttgart and Mannheim

THE duchy of Württemberg was a hilly and largely wooded land that centered around the upper reaches of the Neckar River (Figure 5.1). On its banks stood the university town of Tübingen and the capital city, Stuttgart. Several pockets of independent territory interrupted the continuity of the duke's lands. These included the imperial free cities of Heilbronn, Esslingen, and Reutlingen, plus the small principality of Hohenzollern, ancestral seat of the Prussian dynasty. Some small enclaves across the Rhine River in Alsace and the county of Montbéliard near Belfort completed the ducal domain. These are not shown on our map.

The Palatine Electorate of the Rhine was even more amorphous in shape. Its territories stretched along the lower reaches of the Neckar River and included the cities of Heidelberg, seat of Germany's oldest university and for a long time the capital, and of Mannheim, at the confluence of the Rhine and the Neckar. The elector governed several possessions on both sides of the Rhine, split off from one another by the bishoprics of Speyer and Worms, and the archbishopric of Mainz. The duchy of Zweibrücken belonged half to the elector and half to a duke who held it as the elector's feudatory.

Much of South Germany and the Rhineland remained faithful to the Roman Catholic Church during and after the Protestant Reformation. Württemberg did not. Duke Ulrich I fought successfully against imperial incursions in the 1530s, and although he was forced to accept his duchy as an Austrian fief, he established Lutheran schools and churches throughout the state. He also accepted certain lib-

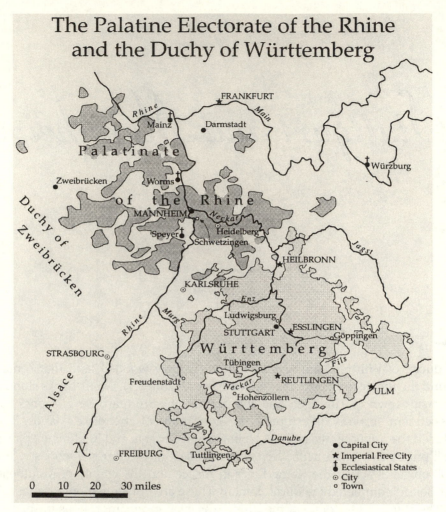

The Palatine Electorate of the Rhine and the Duchy of Württemberg

FIGURE 5.1. Map of southwest Germany in the eighteenth century.

erties granted the estates that laid the foundation for future constitutional rule. Protestants of the Calvinist sect predominated among the subjects of the Palatine elector.

The ruling family of Württemberg had split into two lines by the beginning of the eighteenth century. Duke Eberhard Ludwig of the senior branch ruled for the first third of the century and was responsible for building the magnificent palace of Ludwigsburg, a few miles north of Stuttgart. Carl Alexander, who headed the cadet branch, pursued a distinguished military career in the imperial army under Eugene of Savoy. Prinz Eugen, as he was known in German, the scourge of Louis

XIV and conqueror of Belgrade (1717), took a particular liking to Carl Alexander, who fought at his side in the Balkan wars and rose to become military governor of Serbia for thirteen years. Back in Stuttgart the duke had both a son and a grandson waiting to succeed him. Carl Alexander did not believe he would be called upon to rule the duchy. He became a Catholic, as was only natural for someone so long in imperial service, and in 1727 he wed a Catholic princess, Maria Augusta of the Thurn and Taxis family. This union was quickly blessed with three sons, Carl Eugen (born 1728), Ludwig Eugen, and Friedrich Eugen (striking testimony of Alexander's regard for his great protector). Then, to the surprise and dismay of the duchy, Eberhard's son and grandson both died. Carl Alexander became his heir. When the duke himself died in 1733 Protestant Württemberg was confronted with a Catholic ruler, the first since the Reformation.

Carl Alexander handled the difference of confession between himself and his subjects along the lines of the Dresden accords signed by Augustus the Strong. He guaranteed the Lutheran religion in churches and schools, while divesting himself as titular head of the state church. As a ruler who knew little about and had seen little of his duchy, he governed as might be expected of a military general: he gave orders. In so doing he violated the constitutional rights of the estates in tax matters. He brought in Joseph Süss Oppenheimer (known to history as the Jew Süss) to coerce direct payment of taxes and other levies. The populace, increasingly hostile to the duke and his chief advisor, was on the verge of revolt when the duke died suddenly in March 1737 after a reign of three years and a few days. The regency that took over had Oppenheimer publicly hanged. Carl Eugen, heir to the duchy, was nine years old.

Carl Eugen, Duke of Württemberg

The regency, formed to govern until Carl Eugen reached his majority, did not include his mother, contrary to his father's will. Even though he was and remained a practicing Catholic, the prince had grown up mostly in Württemberg, unlike his father. To accommodate him and his younger siblings the Catholic court chapel was continued. The duchy remained neutral in the war waged against Austria by France and Prussia in 1740–43 but was threatened by invasion. Frederick offered to take the three princes under his protection in Berlin, an offer accepted by their mother over papal objections.[1] The princes traveled to Berlin in December 1741 by way of Bayreuth, where Carl Eugen first saw the princess Elisabeth Frederica who would become his wife.

---

[1] Eugen Schneider, "Herzog Karls Erziehung, Jugend und Persönlichkeit," in *Herzog Karl Eugen von Württemberg und seine Zeit,* ed. Albert Pfister, 2 vols. (Esslingen, 1907), 1: 25–52, 30.

The duke's birthday on 11 February 1752 was celebrated by a performance in the opera house of Hasse's *Ciro riconosciuto,* composed for Dresden in 1751. Holzbauer may have provided the score. He had been associated with Hasse as ballet composer at Vienna and he added arias of his own to Hasse's. What the court needed in addition, in order to create original opera, was an Italian poet. A certain Luigi Lazarino was hired as such in 1752 at 500 florins. The duke took the sum from the funds of the state church over the protests of its custodians, who argued to no avail that their money had never been used for this purpose. Lazarino was let go in May 1755. Mattia Verazi was called to Stuttgart to take his place but was then appointed at Mannheim the following year.

Holzbauer and Lazarino were apparently responsible for the *Fetonte* performed on 11 February 1753 and described in the libretto as follows: "The poetry is drawn from the French (i.e., Quinault's *Phaëton* of 1683) and adapted to music. The arias are by Jommelli." Villati's *Fetonte* (Berlin, 1750) has also been cited as a model. Carl Eugen undoubtedly picked the subject. He had a certain partiality for the French kind of spectacle opera, reinforced by his visit in 1748 to Paris and Versailles, where he charmed Louis XV. The opera was a portent of the mixture of French and Italian traits often favored at Stuttgart under Jommelli, who had obviously become the duke's favorite composer. Sixteen arias, one duet, and four choruses, along with ballets, made up the 1753 *Fetonte.*

Holzbauer's departure from the ducal service in the summer of 1753 had partly to do with his wife, the soprano Rosalie Andreides, who sang minor roles in *Ciro* and *Fetonte.* He met her in Holešov, Moravia, where Count Rottal maintained a good-sized orchestra and gave Italian operas in the 1730s. According to printed librettos, she sang roles regularly with this company from 1733 to 1739. In 1737 she married Holzbauer, who tells in his autobiography at length about the courtship and the opposition to it by her powerful friends, who did not want her to sing on the stage (which she had already been doing). Librettos showed that she sang roles at Linz in 1742, Milan and Venice in 1744, and Verona in both 1745 and 1747. In his autobiography, written at the end of his life, Holzbauer boasted that his wife had sung in three of the most prominent theaters of Italy, which is true.

Holzbauer did not stint his praises for Carl Eugen. He had little choice, since the powerful duke was still alive and nearby when he wrote his brief memoir. About the duchess (who was dead by this time) he had fewer compunctions. After arriving in Stuttgart in 1751 (not 1750 as he remembers) they were graciously received and generously remunerated.

> I can say in truth that both rulers were the most adorable sovereigns and honored me with every grace, and we were also very well paid. Nevertheless one wicked married woman [böse Frau] who enjoyed the favor of the duchess, and always misused it, persecuted me because of my wife, who was younger and better looking than she

was. On this account we sought employment at this court [Mannheim], which then came about.[7]

The "böse Frau" could have been none other than the prima donna, La Pirker, known to enjoy the special protection of the duchess. This was obviously no dispute about beauty but an artistic quarrel of the kind Mozart portrayed in his *Der Schauspieldirektor* in the trio "Ich bin die prima donna hier!" The husband of La Pirker wrote his wife on 11 July 1753 eager to hear more about the Holzbauer affair, of which she had written him in an earlier letter. By this point the crisis had passed. Being the wife of the Kapellmeister did not entitle a soprano to challenge the prima donna.

Some kind friend at Mannheim (was it Stamitz?) got Holzbauer invited to compose the favola pastorale *Il figlio delle selve* staged at Schwetzingen on 15 June 1753. The libretto lists Holzbauer as "Cappel-Meister des Herrn Hertzog von Wuertemberg." It was the last time he used this title. His release from ducal service came in memoranda of 27 June 1753, 1 July, and a ducal decree of 11 July. His request for travel money to Mannheim was refused, and the departure from Stuttgart could be described as, if not exactly under a cloud, not in the best of graces either. Holzbauer landed on his feet with a contract as Kapellmeister for the opera at Mannheim, albeit with a reduction in salary from what he was paid in Stuttgart. Andriedes, on the other hand, went into rapid eclipse. Her last appearance on any stage was in the title role of her husband's setting of *L'Issipile* (Mannheim, 1754).

Carl Eugen came out of the affair getting what he most wanted, the services of Jommelli as Oberkapellmeister. During the early spring of 1753 Carl Eugen and his wife traveled to Italy, visiting Venice and, by Easter, Rome. Here the duke apparently met Jommelli in person. Not only Mannheim but Lisbon as well were then vying for the composer's services. Carl Eugen was a very handsome and commanding young prince, as can be seen from the full-length portrait of him painted by Pompeo Batoni at this time.[8] Jommelli broke off negotiations with Mannheim and Lisbon and agreed to come to Stuttgart in the duke's service.

---

[7] Ignaz Holzbauer, *Günther von Schwarzburg*, ed. Hermann Kretschmar in *DDT* 8–9 (1902), 8: vi–vii. The memoir is also reproduced in Friedrich Walter, *Geschichte des Theater und der Musik am kurpfälzischen Hofe* (Leipzig, 1898), pp. 356–61.

[8] The stunning portrait is reproduced in color as the frontispiece of the first volume of *Herzog Karl Eugen von Württemberg und seine Zeit*. For a discussion of the portrait, see 1: 769–70. Mattei in his *Elogio del Jommelli* wrote, "towards the end of 1753 the courts of Mannheim, Stuttgart and Portugal made the greatest efforts to secure Jommelli, who decided to prefer Stuttgart on account of the delicate taste of the Duke of Württemberg." Cited in Marita McClymonds, *Niccolò Jommelli: The Last Years, 1769–1774* (Ann Arbor, 1980) p. 790. Mattei errs slightly as to the date. The issue was settled by June 1753. Mattei also says that Jommelli wrote two masses in Stuttgart, "one a requiem for the death of the duke's mother in 1751" (p. 793). The date or place of composition must be wrong.

Jommelli arrived in Stuttgart in time to direct his setting of *La clemenza di Tito* for the birthday of the duchess on 30 August 1753. The details of his contract took a few months to negotiate. By its provisions he became Oberkapellmeister, and the sole person who would hold this title once Brescianello died. He was extremely well paid. Reports put his salary around 4,000 florins annually. His contract allowed him periodic visits to Italy, which he took advantage of by writing operas for Rome and Naples and directing them there in 1757. To celebrate the birthday of the duchess in 1754 he directed a setting of *Catone in Utica.* He was handicapped somewhat by the lack of an adequate Italian poet, until the arrival of Verazi. Together they produced *Pelope* for the duke's birthday in 1755, followed by *Enea nel Lazio* for the birthday of the duchess. These operas allowed the scenic splendor that Metastasio in his works on more historical subjects had sought to reduce. Verazi left Stuttgart for Mannheim within a year but remained available to Jommelli as a collaborator. The birthday opera on 30 August 1756 for the duchess was Jommelli's second setting of Metastasio's *Artaserse.*

At this juncture two drastic events interrupted the rounds of courtly life: the outbreak of the Seven Years War and the flight of the duchess back to her parents in Bayreuth, from which she did not return. Relations between the duke and his wife had long been strained, partly by his penchant for comely *danseuses* in the opera ballet. The son and heir to the duchy, so much hoped for, did not arrive. A daughter, born to the duchess in early 1750, died a year later.

When Frederick bid farewell to Carl Eugen in 1744, sending him back to Stuttgart to rule, he equipped him with a written guide, *Le miroir des princes,* in which Frederick warned his young ward to live within his means and to beware France and Austria. The duke heeded neither advice. He lived so far beyond his means he was obliged to pawn his state to the highest bidder. Unbeknownst to his advisors and against the constitution, which gave the estates consultative rights in foreign affairs, he signed a six-year agreement in 1752 to provide France with six thousand infantrymen, to be trained and quartered in Württemberg and used in case of war.[9] Louis XV paid 290,000 florins for this service directly into the duke's account, and an even larger amount for every year the treaty was in effect. Carl Eugen spent the money on his opera and other extravagances, with no intention of fulfilling his end of the bargain unless a war broke out. Amazingly, the French did not check to see how their money was being spent (if it had been Frederick instead of Louis XV, every soldier would have been accounted for). To make matters worse, the duke sought cash infusions secretly by securing them with crown properties. One of the investors he inveigled into this was Voltaire.

In the summer of 1756, after war broke out between France and England in

[9]James Allen Van, *The Making of a State: Württemberg, 1593–1793* (Ithaca, N.Y., and London, 1984), pp. 265–66.

the overseas colonies, Louis XV called the duke to account, sending an agent to Stuttgart to supervise the transport of the 6,000 troops. All that he found in the way of an army was a fancily dressed palace guard. To extricate himself from this scandal, the duke had the requisite number of citizens pressed into service, violating their civil liberties guaranteed in the constitution. With little or no training these men were hustled to the eastern front of the war, opened when Prussia invaded Saxony. Frederick was furious upon learning of the duke's actions in sending troops to the French and Austrian forces allied against him. The ill-trained troops from Württemberg were slaughtered en masse in the crushing defeat Frederick administered to the Austrians at Leuthen (5 December 1757). Less than one in three of the duke's six thousand mercenaries lived to return home.[10] Thus were the operatic triumphs in Stuttgart paid for in blood.

The story of Marianne Pirker illustrates another side of life under Carl Eugen. She was born in 1717, probably in ducal Württemberg (to her later chagrin), if not in Heilbronn, where she died in 1782. At age twenty she married the Salzburg violinist Franz Joseph Pirker, seventeen years her senior. Her career blossomed as a soprano in Italy from 1744 to 1747, after which she and her husband accepted the invitation to London from Lord Middlesex, impresario of the King's Theatre in the Haymarket. Next she became the prima donna of the Mingotti troupe and sang with great success in Copenhagen before becoming the pillar of Carl Eugen's first operatic company in 1750. She was responsible for getting her close ally and paramour Jozzi to Stuttgart from London as well as her husband. When the domestic strife between the duke and the duchess came to a head, La Pirker, a confidante and friend of the latter, openly sided with her. Without so much as granting a hearing, Carl Eugen clapped Pirker into the fortress of Hohenasperg near Ludwigsburg and left her to languish there for eight years. The same fate and fortress awaited Daniel Schubart when he incurred ducal displeasure in 1777. His confinement lasted ten years. Whereas her predecessor in Stuttgart, La Cuzzoni, ended up in a poorhouse of Bologna making buttons, Marianne was reduced to making straw flowers. Somehow she managed to send some of these artificial flowers to the empress Maria Theresa in Vienna, who took up her cause and sought her release, going so far as to have a medal struck in honor of the poor soprano. In terms of jurisdiction, Pirker descended from a Styrian family and was Austrian, and if she had been born in the free imperial city of Heilbronn, the offense of her incarceration was all the worse in the eyes of the empress. Pressure on behalf of Pirker increased when the other empress, Catherine II of Russia, joined the cause seeking her release. The duke finally relented in 1765. Nearing fifty years of age, the celebrated prima donna sang no more in public but retired

[10]Francis Carsten, *Princes and Parliaments in Germany from the Fifteenth to the Eighteenth Century* (Oxford, 1959), pp. 137–40.

with her husband to Heilbronn, where she taught singing. They were at the center of the city's musical life around 1770 when Schubart visited them.

In his early years as ruler the duke got his way mainly by playing the estates off against his privy council. By the time of the war he had gone so far in breaking his country's laws there was no turning back. His ruthlessness turned dictatorial and was enforced by the army he continued to impress into service. In 1759 he surrounded the office buildings of the estates in Stuttgart with soldiers and compelled the tax officials to hand over their money to him. A reckoning was coming. It took ten years to arrive. Revolution was not yet in the air as a possible answer, and in any case, the ruling class, the people necessary to any coup d'état, were suffering the least.

> Under such trying circumstances one might well wonder why the estates never considered getting rid of their ruler through some act of violence. That they did not do so testified to the deep-seated loyalty that eighteenth-century Germans still felt for their hereditary rulers. . . . More than pious sentiment restrained the territorial elite from a violent resolution of their difficulties. The brunt of Carl Eugen's arbitrary tax measures were falling upon the peasantry and the urban masses, not upon the magistrates.[11]

Rather than revolt against their sovereign's despotism, the estates waited out the war in the hopes that a changed balance of power in Europe might result in a better chance of redressing their grievances. They took recourse to the imperial law courts. Meanwhile, the duke continued to live on a scale of luxury that was unprecedented, and the opera became more magnificent than ever.

Along with his passion for operas the duke indulged in a frenzy of building palaces and theaters. Leopold Retti did the first remodeling of the beautiful Neue Lusthaus, built in 1580–83 (Figure 5.2). Retti gave way in 1751 to a great architect called from Paris, Major Louis Philippe de la Guêpière, who continued to renovate the Lusthaus and built the new ducal palace in Stuttgart, using as a model for the interior the Louis XV apartments at Versailles. Guêpière also extended and remodeled Ludwigsburg. His most famous buildings are the two ducal palaces built as summer retreats, Solitude (1763) and Mon Repos (1764). In 1758 he undertook a thorough rebuilding of the theater in the Lusthaus, tearing out the previous remodelings. He gave the auditorium a bell-shaped curve as in Italian opera houses, surrounded it with three balconies for loges, and provided a very elongated stage space that had no fewer than nine pair of wings and a large backstage behind those that could be opened for spectacular feats of perspective. In this case Guêpière's designs have been preserved (Figure 5.3). His massive columns with Corinthian capitals on the stage and Ionic capitals on the exterior

---

[11]Vann, *The Making of a State*, p. 280.

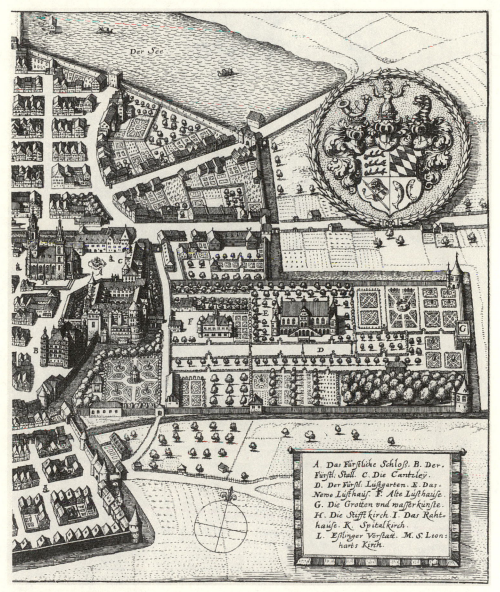

FIGURE 5.2. Stuttgart castle and pleasure gardens. Detail from map in *Topographia Sveviae* (1643).

show neoclassic grandeur. Yet the slender columns above the middle loge flaming out at the top could not be more rococo. Seven further ducal theaters have been credited to Guêpière. These are the small palace theaters at Ludwigsburg (1752), Grafeneck (1763), Solitude (1765), Tübingen (1767), and Teinach (1770), plus the extravagant great opera house at the rear of Ludwigsburg palace (1765). The last

Coupe du nouvel Opéra de Stuttgardt esquissé pour en voir l'effet sans aucunes regles de Perspective.

Plan où Projet de la restauration de l'Opéra de Stuttgardt.

de la Guêpièrre Del.   Benard Fecit.

FIGURE 5.3.
Louis Philippe
de la Guêpière.
Interior of the
theater in the
Lusthaus.

was a consequence of the duke's ongoing quarrels with the estates, which led him
to leave Stuttgart and make Ludwigsburg his capital.

The Treaty of Hubertsburg (15 February 1763) ended the war between Austria
and Prussia. Four days earlier Carl Eugen's thirty-fifth birthday was celebrated in
Stuttgart with two weeks of splendid entertainments centering around the latest
version of Jommelli's *Didone abbandonata*. Nearly all the princes from southern

Germany flocked to take part in the banquets, balls, hunts, and fêtes of every kind, bringing along hordes of courtiers and servants, all housed at the expense of the duchy.[12] Carl Eugen enraged the estates further by insisting that a large standing army be maintained even in peacetime. General opposition was mounting when he took the step of convening a general assembly or Landtag, the only one of his reign. It turned out to be a misstep from his point of view. Rather than divide and conquer as he planned, he emboldened the estates to file a formal complaint charging him with unconstitutional acts. This they sent to the Imperial Aulic Council (Reichshofsrat) at Vienna (30 July 1764). At the same time they sought support from the kings of Denmark, England, and Prussia, the powers that had guaranteed the religious settlement protecting the Württemberg church. Each king was also a power within the empire, as lord of Schleswig-Holstein, elector of Hanover, and elector of Brandenburg, respectively. In Frederick the estates found a formidable ally. Emperor Joseph II also came around to their side.

The Aulic Council of the empire was mostly ineffectual and noted for hearing cases over many years until they finally disappeared from public attention. In this case Frederick, still angry at Carl Eugen's defection, also for what he believed was mistreatment of his niece leading to the collapsed marriage, did not allow inaction. He pursued the matter like an avenging fury, or like a dog with a bone (not a bad analogy, since he was known for sleeping with his whippets). He even went so far as to get outside investigators authorized to enter the duchy, take depositions, and examine records. At this point the duke should have realized he was overmatched. The excessive expenditures went on as before, while the council was working out a settlement that would force the duke to capitulate and to restore all constitutional rights.[13] By the end of the 1760s the writing was clearly on the wall, and it signified the end of operatic extravagance. The duke had no choice but to sign the agreement in 1770.

Austerity became almost as much of a passion with the duke as had overindulgence before. He was encouraged in it by his liaison with a wise and charming mistress, Franziska von Leutrum, who was made a countess by Joseph II in 1774, at the duke's urgent request. When his wife died in 1780 he married Franziska, a Protestant, over the Pope's objections.

A school of music and dancing was founded by the duke in 1769 in Ludwigsburg, mainly for the children of those in court service, followed by a military academy, and an École de Demoiselles in 1773 near the Solitude palace. In 1775 the duke moved back to Stuttgart, and the military academy was transformed into the Karlsschule there. One of the purposes of these various schools was to train a

[12]Joseph Uriot, *Descriptions des fêtes données pendant quatorze jours à l'occasion du jour de naissance de son altesse Serenissime Monseigneur le Duc Regnant de Württemberg et Teck* (Stuttgart, 1763).
[13]Vann, *The Making of a State*, pp. 284–90.

generation of future musicians, singers, and actors who as state servants would be obliged to perform for little or no salary in the ducal theaters. Parents had to sign an agreement that their children could not leave this service without permission, a tyranny that drove the greatest product of the system, Friedrich Schiller, to rebel and eventually flee from Stuttgart to Mannheim in 1782.

Jommelli's Operas

When Jommelli returned to Stuttgart in 1758 from his leave in Italy he found a very changed situation. Marianne Pirker along with her husband were behind prison walls and would remain there. Jozzi, the primo uomo dependent on the Pirkers, had decamped, leaving Stuttgart for good (he later sang in Lisbon). The advantage of these losses, from Jommelli's point of view, was that he could begin to build an ensemble that was truly his own, not inherited.

The prima donna who replaced La Pirker in 1758 was Maria Masi Giura, a Roman soprano who made her operatic debut at Venice in 1746 singing a secondary role in Ferdinando Bertoni's *Orazio e Curiazio.* Her name then, according to the libretto, was Maria Masi and she was presumably around twenty years of age, which would mean she was around thirty-two when she arrived in Stuttgart. She sang in Berlin from 1747 to 1756 as seconda donna to Giovanna Astrua and visited other places as well.[14] In a performance of Tommaso Traetta's *Farnace* for the king's name day, 4 November 1751, at the San Carlo in Naples she took the part of Pompeo and is listed as Maria Masi Giura. Jommelli heard her either in Rome or Naples and remembered her voice. In Stuttgart she sang nothing but prima donna roles for him, a considerable testimony to her powers, because the company had two other very good female sopranos in Anna Cesari and Monica Buonani. All the singers and many of the orchestra under Jommelli were Italians.

Giuseppe Aprile, castrato, and one of the greatest male sopranos of the century, eventually replaced Jozzi as primo uomo. Born near Taranto in 1732, his principal teacher was Gregorio Sciroli in Naples, in whose comic opera *Lo barone deluso* he made his operatic debut at Rome in 1752. The following year he sang a secondary role in Jommelli's *Ifigenia in Aulide* at Rome. He was a member of the royal chapel in Naples from 1752 to 1756, after which he went on tour to various centers, one of them being Stuttgart for Jommelli's *L'Olimpiade* in 1761. From 1763 to 1769 he was in regular service at the Württemberg court, earning a salary that was close to Jommelli's own. He was a composer and thus better trained in music than most singers. Schubart praised his ability to improvise vocally and said that

---

[14]Johann Wilhelm Hertel, *Autobiographie,* ed. Erich Schenk (Graz and Cologne, 1957), p. 86, n. 75.

he was a valued artistic advisor to Jommelli. Schubart added that Jommelli was very generous in acknowledging the accomplishments of others, a point illustrated by the following tale."A flatterer was once denigrating German composers to Jommelli in my presence; 'be silent,' said the master, with a stormy glance, 'I have learned a great deal from Hasse and Graun.'"[15] Aprile was at the peak of his powers when he returned to Italy for good. In 1770 Burney heard him at the San Carlo in Naples in Jommelli's *Demofoonte.* In the same year Mozart heard him in Naples, Bologna, and Milan, from which he wrote his sister that "Aprile, primo uomo, sings well and has a beautiful even voice" (letter of 26 January 1770).

Jommelli's main tenor was Arcangelo Cortoni, who made his operatic debut in Bologna in 1756. He joined the Stuttgart company in 1760 and remained for eight years. Skilled in acting as well as in bravura singing, he inspired Jommelli to create for him the strikingly forceful part of Iarba in *Didone abbandonata* (1763). When Jommelli reached his home in Aversa near Naples in the spring of 1769 he received a letter from Pedro Bottelho, theater director in Lisbon, inquiring about the skills of various people who had left or were preparing to leave the duke's service, and specifically about Cortoni. Jommelli replied at once.

> He is one of the most skillful tenors presently making the rounds of the theaters in Italy, and under a diligent master, who knows how to hold him to duty, he will always make a good appearance. He sings much of the bravura and has the usual defect of modern tenors of wanting to sing in the upper register [contraltiggiare] too much. Still, he is otherwise docile (at least I have always found him so) and lets himself be easily directed.[16]

Cortoni sang in all three of Jommelli's late Neapolitan operas, another sign of the esteem in which he was held by the composer.

In the same letter to Bottelho, Jommelli gave favorable report on the castrato Giovanni Maria Rubinelli, who was in ducal service from 1766 to 1772."His contralto voice is very beautiful, and I could even say very rare: agile, strong, sonorous, well-in-tune. His figure is well-made although his short stature may be a detraction. His singing ability is optimum."For him Jommelli created the role of Epafo in *Fetonte* (1768).

The violinists under Jommelli's command included some of the period's most renowned. Pasquale Bini, born in Pesaro in 1716, was a pupil of Tartini who entered the duke's service in 1754 and remained for four years. No violinist of the

---

[15]Christian Friedrich Daniel Schubart, *Leben und Gesinnungen von ihm selbst im Kerker aufgesetzt,* 2 vols. (Stuttgart, 1791–93; reprint Leipzig, 1980), 1: 125–26. Note that after Jommelli's arrival no more operas by Hasse and Graun were performed.

[16]Letter of 13 June 1769, translated in McClymonds, *Niccolò Jommelli,* p. 63.

time was more famous than Antonio Lolli, born in Bergamo around 1725. He was appointed solo violinist of the ducal court in 1758 and remained in service until 1774, with frequent leaves to display his virtuosity and make money elsewhere. Jommelli's remarks on this dazzling technician convey his limitations as an ensemble player.

> Concerning the orchestra, the one subject of distinction is presently Sig. Lolli, aston-ishing solo violinist and therefore not too desirable for an orchestra. His playing is of an unsurpassable bravura and certainly unique, and if his Adagio corresponded to his Allegro, he would be a god. But a man of so much ability and so much reputation is full of bad habits and so eccentric that he not only demonstrates it very often in his own compositions, but also I must have much passion for music and for his ability in order to stomach him. The first violinist, Sig. [Pietro] Martinez, even though he is not a great player, is, however, such an excellent regulator of the orchestra that I would not know how to find a better one. There are many other good violinists but no one so extraordinary and of such rarity that their like could not be found elsewhere.[17]

Leopold Mozart concurred when he wrote about the violinist Anton Janitsch, "he plays in the style of Lolli, but his *adagio* playing is infinitely better."[18] At the oppo-site pole from Lolli and his fireworks on the violin was Pietro Nardini, favorite of his teacher Tartini. Born in Livorno in 1722, he served the ducal court from Octo-ber 1762 to March 1765. Of his playing Leopold Mozart wrote, "the beauty, purity and evenness of his tone and his cantabile cannot be surpassed; but he does not execute any great difficulties."[19] Both Lolli and Nardini make an appearance in the collected portraits of famous violinists depicted on Luigi Scotti's *Professori celebri di Suono* (see Figure 3.5 on p. 209). Lolli appears in the oval frame in the middle just above Nardini.[20]

Two wind players at Stuttgart who excelled were the oboists José and Juan Baptista Pla, brothers from Spain. In 1751–52 the Plas appeared frequently at the Concert Spirituel in Paris playing duets or concertos for oboes of their own com-position.[21] On some of these programs they shared the platform with the Mannheim musicians Johann Baptist Wendling, who played the flute, and his wife Dorothea, who sang Italian arias. To vary their offerings the Pla brothers played a concerto for psalterion and violin on the program of 28 March 1752. Then on 30 March they executed an oboe concerto "dont le fonds est un bruit de chasse" of their composition. On the same program Marie Fel sang an Italian aria accompa-

[17]Letter to Bottelho dated 13 June 1769, ibid., p. 63.
[18]Letter to his son dated Salzburg, 29 January 1778.
[19]Letter to Lorenz Hagenauer dated Ludwigsburg, 11 July 1763.
[20]On the violin concertos of these two rivals and associates see the discussion with musical examples by Chappell White, *From Vivaldi to Viotti: A History of the Early Classical Violin Concerto* (Philadelphia, 1992), pp. 111–14, 142–47.
[21]Constant Pierre, *Histoire du Concert Spirituel, 1725–1790* (Paris, 1975).

nied on the oboe by the composer, the elder Pla (Juan Baptista). It may be this piece that elicited the remark in the *Mercure de France* that Pla had an easy way of "wedding Italian audacity with French amenity." On 8 September 1753 the symphonies heard were by Hasse and Pla; at the next concert on 1 November the symphony is identified as being by José Pla, and it was heard again on 4 April 1755. In 1756 the Pla brothers entered the ducal service in Stuttgart. Ever since his trip to Paris in 1748 Carl Eugen had maintained an agent there to keep him informed of the latest fashions.

The Pla brothers moved Schubart to write one of his typically gushing portraits, not sparing us a classical allusion.

> If Castor and Pollux had played oboes, both divinely inspired, they could scarcely have blown better than these two. They were Spaniards transplanted to Germany, where they refined their tastes under Jommelli and reached an unusual degree of perfection on their instruments. This pair of brothers represented a quite uncommon musical phenomenon. As they loved each other deeply, so did this sympathy reign in their playing. Whoever heard them has listened to the last word in musical performance. One thought followed another, one breath raised another. This psychic oneness had never before been heard in Europe. Both composed in masterly fashion and it was impossible to say who was the better. No one has better expressed the intimate connection of the tones, the swelling of *portamento* and the cantabile, which intimated, if I may say so, both the friendly and the amorous.[22]

Schubart goes on to say that the younger died in Ludwigsburg, whereupon his brother threw away his oboe and went home. That makes a touching story but does not match the truth. Juan Baptista became an increasingly famous oboist in the 1760s, reappeared at the Concert Spirituel in Paris playing one of his oboe concertos, and at the end of the decade, as the Stuttgart orchestra was being decimated, found a well-playing position at the court of Lisbon, where he was greeted affectionately by Jommelli through letters Jommelli sent to Bottelho. Jommelli's writing for two oboes in his operas of the 1760s often calls for closely coordinated passage work, exposed and sometimes even unaccompanied—a tribute to the Pla brothers.

The orchestra also boasted very fine horn players in Jean Joseph Rodolphe (or Rudolph) and his pupil Johann Nissle. Rodolphe was born in Strasbourg in 1730. He studied with Jean-Marie Leclair in Paris and he may have been a violinist at the court of Parma in the 1750s. As a horn player he was trained by his father. He joined the ducal orchestra around 1760 but still retained many contacts with Paris. In the spring of 1764 he played horn concertos of his composition at the Concert Spirituel. At these same concerts was another master from Stuttgart, Lolli, play-

[22]Christian Friedrich Daniel Schubart, *Ideen zu eine Ästhetik der Tonkunst* (Vienna, 1806; Hildesheim, 1969), pp. 153–54. The brothers were too modest to publish their compositions, he says, and that is why they are hard to find.

ing violin concertos of his own composition. One could conclude in fact that Paris had gone quite concerto-mad at the time. Rodolphe, an innovator in the technique of horn playing, was also skilled in composition. Traetta is said to have been his teacher in Parma. He studied composition further with Jommelli. Schubart describes his horn playing in some detail. "His strong point was in the low range and he only used the high range as far as nature allowed it to this instrument. Tender passages he succeeded with in masterly fashion, and he was one of the first who expressed medium shading [Mezzotinto] with the horn." What Schubart says next about Rodolphe's ballets will occupy us below. Concerning Nissle, Schubart is deprecating about his compositions, but not about his horn playing. "As a second horn he scarcely has an equal. His double tonguing, his *crescendo*, the lightness with which he seized the pedal C, his easy tone production and especially his *portamento* raise him to the top of his profession."

Jommelli in his letter of 13 June 1769 to Bottelho in Lisbon, already quoted twice, specifically bewails the loss of Rodolphe, who left the ducal service in 1767, at the same time as Jean-Georges Noverre. Good leadership, good music, and good players were all necessary to success, he maintained.

> I have seen it a thousand times and am now experiencing it here [Naples] that a good concert master and good, well-regulated music make a good orchestra. The orchestra of his serene highness the duke of Württemberg has certainly been the best that ever was in Europe, but now it is no longer the same. After the departure of the two Pla brothers on oboe, of Rodolphe and his companion on French horn, and of so very many other good, young violinists, everything is changed. It is no longer what it was either in numbers or in quality. It is the same with the ballet as with the orchestra. The only dancer who would be a good acquisition is a certain Balletti, superb dancer of *mezzo carattere*.[23]

Jommelli implies that the Pla brothers left the ducal service together, so perhaps the younger did not die in Ludwigsburg as the less reliable Schubart claimed.[24] Had Jommelli ever heard the Mannheim orchestra, he might not have claimed priority for its Stuttgart equivalent. Also noteworthy is the attention he paid to ballet, even though he did not compose for it.

Karl Traugott Riedel, a Leipzig artist who specialized in engraved portraits of actors and musicians, sold by Breitkopf, included Jommelli, along with Hasse, Gluck, Grétry, and many others, in his gallery of famous composers (Figure 5.4). His oval portrait of Jommelli well captures the strong physiognomy, the renowned

[23]McClymonds, *Niccolò Jommelli*, pp. 63–64.
[24]Rudolf Krauss, "Das Theater," in *Herzog Karl Eugen von Württemberg und seine Zeit*, 1: 485–554; 507–8, says the younger Pla died at Stuttgart on 13 December 1762 at age 34 and was replaced by the well-paid oboe player Vittorino Columbazzo.

FIGURE 5.4. Karl Traugott Riedel. Portrait of Niccolò Jommelli.

fiery glance of the maestro, known for enforcing his will throughout the orchestra and on the stage.

L'OLIMPIADE

Jommelli made his first and only setting of Metastasio's famous *L'Olimpiade* for the duke's birthday in 1761. The printed libretto mentions that the music is newly composed and that Noverre created the ballets. By 1760–61 Jommelli had gathered several crucial members of his ensemble, vocal and orchestral. Most important, he had for the first time Giuseppe Aprile as primo uomo. Perhaps these circumstances explain why the opera was chosen to be the first in what was intended to be a series of commemorative scores, *Recueil des Opera composés par Nicola Iomelli à la cour du serenissime Duc de Wirtemberg,* printed in 1783 and available for purchase at the Academie Caroline (Karlschule).[25]

Lacking all the simple recitatives, the edition served no practical purpose. It was meant to keep the memory of the composer alive and enshrine his works as a monument to the duke's glory. Not surprisingly, there was no market for such scores, and the series was discontinued after the first volume. Even if the score had been complete, there would have been no market, because the music was too difficult and, by the 1780s, too dated for performance.

L'Olimpiade opens the richest period of the composer's long creative life. Its sinfonia is unusually elaborate even for him. An *Allegro spirituoso* in D and in common time deploys oboes, flutes, and horns in addition to the usual strings, divided so that the first violins sing the melody while the seconds provide the brilliance of nearly constant sixteenth-note motion in runs and other passage work. *Piano, forte,* and *pianissimo* alternate often, and the movement comes to a stop on the dominant, which leads to an *Andante* in 3/4 and in d that also ends

[25]Reproduced in the Garland edition, *Italian Opera, 1640–1770,* ed. Howard Mayer Brown (New York, 1978).

on V, resolved by the return of the first *Allegro* (the print is faulty and music is omitted between p. 12 and p. 13). A *Presto* 3/8 in D concludes the overture.

Megacle, the primo uomo (Aprile), sings the first aria, "Superbo di me stesso," preceded by a long ritornello in which the second violins are again in near constant sixteenth-note motion. The *Allegro* main part is in F and in common time. For the **B** section Jommelli switches to *Larghetto* 3/4 beginning in d, the relative minor and ending in B♭, the subdominant, a tonal procedure often chosen by the composer.[26] A full da capo repetition gave Aprile a chance to show his famed skills in improvisation.

The second aria, Licida's "Quel destrier, che all' albergo è vicino" (A steed that is close to the inn) is more brilliant still because of its key, D, and because of the *crescendo* in the first violins as they rise two octaves from the D above middle C. Jommelli is not the composer to neglect depicting the rhythm of a galloping horse. He conveys it by repeated anapests in the second violins. The **B** section begins in vi and ends in IV as in the previous aria. Francesco Guerrieri sang the demanding and very high part of Licida.

In a lovely scene for the seconda donna, the nymph Argene, Metastasio provides a "Coro di Ninfe e di Pastore," with solo entrances for her. They sing "O care selve! o cara felice libertà!" (O dear woods, and dear sweet liberty!—under Carl Eugen, Württemberg had more of the former than of the latter, but the irony probably went unremarked). Jommelli uses his winds to great advantage in creating a pastoral tone, calling on oboes (the Pla brothers), horns (Rodolphe and Nissle), and two piccolos. The higher instruments frolic in pairs, chasing each other in thirds up to high D and even high E. Monica Buonani sang the part of Argene.

Aristea, the prima donna (Masi Giura) enters after the pastoral scene (4) and in Scene 6 sings an aria to Argene. Jommelli accompanies her *Andantino* in B♭ and in 3/4 time with strings only but gives her abundant coloratura. The big moment everyone in the audience anticipated was the duet for Aristea and Megacle that ended Act I, "Ne' giorni tuoi felici ricordati di me," discussed earlier in Pergolesi's setting. Jommelli conveys the tension between the lovers in nervous little arpeggio figures in the violins, going rapidly up and down the triad, which would have needed to be very precisely executed to make their effect, and under his eagle eye doubtless were. The main section is a *Larghetto* in 3/4 and in the key of A, long favored for duets with two sopranos by the Neapolitans. The second time through the first stanza (**A2**) Jommelli achieves colorful harmonic effects by suddenly shifting to minor shadings and the Neapolitan sixth chord.

The tenor Cortoni took the role of Aristea's father, Clistene, king of Sicione.

---

[26]Reinhard Strohm, *Die italienische Oper im 18. Jahrhundert* (Wilhelmshaven, 1979), p. 297, suggests links with Pergolesi's setting of this aria.

Metastasio gave him an aria in each of the acts, the most famous text being his third-act aria, "Non so donde viene / quel tenero affetto," discussed earlier in a famous setting by Jommelli's mentor Leonardo Leo. Jommelli gave Cortoni something more by following this with a trio for Licida, Megacle, and Clistene. At this darkest moment of the drama the composer confected a text partly from Metastasio and set it as an *Allegro* in common time, *piano sempre,* and in the key of c. An intense ensemble throughout, it is not showy or overwritten. The strings accompany simply, with offbeats sounded by the violins.

The central event in any setting of the libretto is the treatment of Megacle's "Se cerca, se dice"in Act II, Scene 10. Aristea has fainted at the news that she must marry Licida. While she is unconscious Megacle tells Licida what to say when she revives (for text and translation, see p. 116). Caldara in 1733 established the pattern for setting the first stanza as a series of little interjections separated by rests, probably at Metastasio's suggestion.[27] Pergolesi followed him but chose the key of c instead of e in his setting of 1735 (see Example 2.12 on p. 118). Galuppi adopted the same hesitating diction in 1747 but chose the most expressive of major keys, E$^\flat$ (Example 5.1a). Hasse in 1756 followed him as to key and meter, managing to make the melody even simpler, while using the descending bass that is one of his trademarks (Example 5.1b). Four years later Jommelli also chose E$^\flat$, *Andante* in 2/4, and the same interrupted utterances. His setting acknowledges the great tradition while at the same time going far beyond it in subtlety and power.

EXAMPLE 5.1. *Settings of "Se cerca, se dice" from* L'Olimpiade

a. Galuppi (1747)

b. Hasse (1756)

[27]For the incipit see *Haydn, Mozart,* example 7.5, p. 506.

EXAMPLE 5.2. *Jommelli*, L'Olimpiade, *Aria*

All settings dispense with an orchestral ritornello. Yet Jommelli makes it clear from the first tones that the orchestra is his principal agent (Example 5.2). The violins in thirds sound a slurred rising second figure from offbeat to downbeat, imitated by the basses in the second measure and then by the voice as an eighth note and two quarter notes. These last do not inaugurate the motion in quarter notes, because the violas, sounding in the middle of the texture in mm. 2–3, anticipate the voice by calmly stating the tones 5 – 4 - 3, at which the process begins anew.

Every setting mentioned put the greatest weight of the first sentence on the word
"amico." So does Jommelli, by taking the voice up to the high tonic, as did
Galuppi and Hasse in the previous example. As the voice becomes more active,
the strings become less so, going from four to three parts as the violas join the

basses in m. 7 and their chords are cut off by eighth-note rests. The key word that
sets off Jommelli's imagination next is "infelice." He turns the dominant into a
minor v as the voice, now doubled by the first violins, weaves a stream of conjunct
eighth notes, first rising, then falling. The basses respond by imitating this snake-
like melodic line at the octave below and at the distance of one beat. The orchestra carries on the process even when the voice drops out in m. 15. A long wait for
the next word makes it seem as if Megacle is pondering what to say. To give him
more time, the strings resume their quarter-note motion. He utters "morì" as they
make their cadence, V - i. Independent violas reappeared in m. 14, and they lead

the way into the cadence descending 5 - 4 - 3 while the voice sounds ever so final and hopeless with its 5 - 1. This process, too, is repeated.

A vehement contradiction explodes in the orchestra before the voice utters "Ah nò! nò!" and it is characteristic of the composer to put the quick tonal movement and the gestures of obbligato recitative into the middle of set pieces. The strings rush up the scale of E♭ *forte* and are joined when they reach the top by reinforcing oboes and horns. After the V_5^6/V of mm. 28–29 it seems high time for the arrival of the dominant. Jommelli withholds it because he wants to paint "sì gran duolo" with a dissonant seventh that points the harmony in the direction of g via an augmented sixth yielding to V of g. Instead of g, the dominant, B♭, now arrives with éclat, the strings indulging in a point of imitation as the triadic figure is passed from high to middle to low, each time marked *forte piano.* The voice interjects "rispondi!" as the orchestra goes about its canonic business, reinforced the second time around by oboes and horns sounding pedal F. A tearful departure could hardly be painted better than here. Jommelli's excellent oboes sound all by themselves in the mournful key of b♭, where the violins respond to them in slurred rising seconds like those from the beginning, all this before the voice joins the melodic line for the cadence in mm. 47–49. After repeating this passage Jommelli adds a codalike extension with descending bass (mm. 55–58) that recalls the descending bass in mm. 16–19. He returns to earlier lines for the voice's "l'amico infelice," and the cadences become more frequent and more forceful, climaxing with *fortissimo,* the violins doing their rising seconds in diminution and the voice up to its highest tones so far, F and G♭.

How can Jommelli top this for the extraordinary third stanza of the poem? He begins with a B♭ pedal in the horns and basses, gradually building up tension. The voice achieves a new expressive level with its leaps of a sixth, a seventh, and finally an octave at "Che abbisso" in mm. 80–81, the very distance implied by an abyss probably inspiring them. The harmony goes through a rich circle-of-fifths sequence in supporting the voice until reaching the chord of g and its dominant in alternation and finally *fortissimo* in mm. 83–84. The way out of this climax is a shattering diminished-seventh chord for the final "pene" in mm. 85–86. It is resolved, sublimely, by a simple 6/3 chord in E♭ to support the vocal "Ah!" and then by the return to the beginning for the reprise.

Abbé Vogler in his comparison of various settings of "Se circa, se dice," mentioned three of those illustrated above. He admired Pasquale Anfossi's setting for being in the latest style of the new Neapolitan composers but he awarded the palm, as it were, to Galuppi. "The paramount aria of this great soul [Galuppi] is "Se cerca, se dice." It is bewitchingly beautiful, not so fiery and eruptive as Jommelli's nor so noble and sublime as Hasse's, but fuller of feeling."[28]

Jommelli posed great challenges to the performer who actually had to sing and act the part of Megacle; his "Se cerca, se dice" may begin softly, but the voice is on its own for much of the time, having its own line and many rhythmic subtleties. Schubart already noticed the composer's penchant for keeping the second violins in constant motion, a characteristic mentioned above in connection with Megacle's first aria. Schubart's observation was also more general. "One blamed Jommelli for making his instrumental accompaniments too deafening, keeping

[28]Georg Joseph Vogler, *Betrachtungen der Mannheimer Tonschule,* 4 vols. (Mannheim, 1778–81), 1: 130. The original passage is quoted in Daniel Heartz, "Hasse, Galuppi, and Metastasio," in *Venezia e il melodramma nel settecento,* ed. Maria Teresa Murano (Florence, 1978), p. 337, n. 19.

his violins, especially the seconds, in constant flowing motion, so that it took a very strong singer to penetrate through the storm of the instruments."[29] As difficult to negotiate as the orchestra's level of sound were the long silences in the vocal part, the many hesitations. These required a formidable acting ability on the part of the soloist. Jommelli would not have written them this way had not Aprile been as superior an actor as he was a musician. Aprile was still quite young in 1761, going on thirty years of age. A portrait of him in profile was engraved in his honor when he sang Megacle in Anfossi's *L'Olimpiade* at Perugia in 1778 (Figure 5.5). It shows an interesting countenance, if not as forceful a one as Jommelli's. Compare it with the profile of the singer in Figure 1.5 (p. 34), where he appears in an oval frame near the bottom.

FIGURE 5.5. Anonymous portrait of Giuseppe Aprile.

L'Olimpiade, the opera alone, must have lasted a good three hours when it was first performed in Jommelli's setting on 11 February 1761. It was only part of the entertainment. An initial prologue celebrated the duke's glory in fulsome measure. The stage opened to reveal a large image of his highness. Could this possibly be the lifesize standing portrait in full regalia painted by Pompeo Batoni in Rome? More likely it was an even larger reproduction of the same. The Muses laid their attributes before it, followed by Apollo, who sat his lyre in the same place, and Mars, who crowned it with laurel wreathes (a totally inappropriate reference to the duchy's miserable showing in the Seven Years War). As Terpsichore led in a ballet, the portrait ascended to the heights of Parnassus, where the gods arranged themselves in a decorous and admiring group.[30] This tasteless exercise in servility was presumably under the direction of Noverre. Jommelli left no music for it, nor did he for the three ballets by Noverre, one following each act of the opera.

[29]Schubart, *Ideen einer Asthetik der Tonkunst,* p. 57.
[30]Yorke-Long, *Music at Court,* pp. 56–57.

DIDONE ABBANDONATA

Metastasio made many revisions in successive versions of his earliest *dramma per musica,* probably to bring it more into conformity with his maturer works. Composers, too, were likely to make changes and cuts, especially in the overly long recitatives. Hiller noted in his biography of Jommelli that "he very often changed the texts of operas that he was to compose and here and there inserted his own poems."[31] Probably no composer before Jommelli departed so radically from *Didone* as he did in his third version of the work, first performed at Stuttgart on 11 February 1763. Not only did he greatly abbreviate the recitatives, he also shortened the aria texts by reducing almost all of them from two to one stanza, in effect turning them into cavatinas.

Jommelli's 1749 setting of *Didone* for Vienna, composed under the watchful eye of Metastasio, used all the blank verse intended for recitative, replaced one aria text, and added two aria texts in scenes that lacked them, which represents a very small amount of revision for the time.[32] Master of his own company in Stuttgart, the composer could make cuts at will. His drastic reduction of the text may well reflect the increasing importance and length of Noverre's ballets that went along with the opera. As in 1761 and 1762, independent ballets followed each of the opera's three acts, and they were reported in Joseph Uriot's festival book, *Description des fêtes données* (1763). The opera ended with *The Triumph of Neptune,* a ballet that stages a battle between the elements of Fire and Water. Instead of the Rhine River rising up to quench the flames that destroyed the Gibichung's palace, as at the end of the *The Ring,* the Mediterranean engulfs the fiery remains of Carthage.

One aria that Jommelli did not dismantle is the opera's biggest showpiece, "A trionfar mi chiama / Un bel desio d'onore," sung by Aprile as Enea near the beginning of Act III. Jommelli sets the long **A** section to a march rhythm with lots of wind color, and one wind in particular, the first horn (Rodolphe) engages in passage work and canonic imitations that vie with the voice in brilliance. The **B** section is very short, ending on the subdominant, but long enough to guarantee a da capo repetition of the concertante dialogue, presumably with still more elaborate figures.

Using only the **A** strophe of the other aria texts made for even more word repetition than usual for a composer already famished for words. The experiment was one he did not repeat. In his *Demofoonte* for the following birthday of the duke in 1764 the solo arias return to their two-stanza form, as Metastasio wrote them, and are set as da capo forms or in some modified version thereof. It is surprising that Jommelli experimented with shortening the texts in the first place,

---

[31]Johann Adam Hiller, *Lebensbeschreibungen* (Leipzig, 1784), p. 181.
[32]Audrey Lynn Tolkoff, "The Stuttgart Operas of Niccolò Jommelli" (Ph.D. diss., Yale University, 1974), p. 115.

because in other circumstances he complained that Metastasio's aria texts were too short and lacking in variety. "The poet economises by using the same words over again, as if he had to buy them at the market and pay a dear price."[33]

The opera begins with a sinfonia in D that outdoes even the overture to *L'Olimpiade* in verve and brilliance. The initial *Allegro,* as in that work, ends on the dominant, which is resolved by the middle movement, an *Andante* in 3/4 and in the key of d, with reduced orchestration, full of melodic sighs, appoggiaturas of various lengths, and falling melodic sevenths that are a characteristic expressive device with this composer. The *Andante* also ends on the dominant, which is resolved by the finale in 2/4, a surprisingly simple little dance that sounds as if it might well accompany a French nursery rhyme. The theme keeps returning after contrasting episodes, that is, it is a symphonic rondo, one of the early ones. Pairs of oboes and horns frolic in the episodes. Its refrain is an antecedent consequent melody in the tenor range, played by the strings (Example 5.3).

EXAMPLE 5.3. *Jommelli*, Didone abbandonata, *Overture, III*

Obbligato recitative is employed more extensively than ever, slowing down the performance, of course, and offering another possible reason for cuts in the aria texts. Jommelli creates what are small orchestral tone poems in several cases, painting words or sentiments before they are sung or commenting on them afterward. There are nine in all, compared to two in the 1749 *Didone* for Vienna. These elaborate poems provided the model for spoken melodrama with orchestral accompaniment, as cultivated by Benda and others during the 1770s. Jommelli inserts a fine example of the genre in the very first scene, which is in simple recitative up to the point where Enea relates to Selene and Osmida a dream in which his father, King Priam, upbraids him for tarrying in Carthage. Before his words the orchestra announces a striding, marchlike theme with dotted rhythm, very regal in effect. Only after it is well established do we hear from Priam: "Son, ungrateful son, is this the realm of Italy which you were commanded to conquer by Apollo, and by me? Unhappy Asia awaits the day when Troy will be reborn in another clime as the result of your valor." At the end of this noble harangue, interrupted

[33]Letter of 14 November to Gaetano Martinelli in Lisbon, preserved in the Music Library of the University of California, Berkeley. For the original see McClymonds, *Niccolò Jommelli* (1980), pp. 487–88 or Daniel Heartz, "Metastasio, 'Maestro dei maestri di cappella drammatici,' " in *Metastasio e il mondo musicale,* ed. Maria Teresa Muraro (Florence, 1986), pp. 315–38; 337.

repeatedly by the march, Priam commands his son to rise (Sorgi), at which the violins unleash rapid scales upward for two octaves, an example of postverbal painting.

Queen Didone makes her entrance in Scene 2 with a truly regal speech.

Enea, d'Asia spendore,	Aeneas, splendor of Asia,
di Citerea soave cura e mia,	sweet care of Venus, and of mine,
vedi come a momenti,	see how in a moment,
del tuo soggiorno altera,	proud from your sojourn,
la nascente Cartago alza la fronte.	nascent Carthage raises its brow.

These lines were so famous they gave rise to a comic parody by Goldoni.[34] After arias sung by Enea and Selene, Didone's sister, who is also in love with Enea, there is a march for the arrival of the Moorish king, Iarba, sung by the tenor Cortoni. Metastasio describes the arrival as being to the sounds of barbarian instruments (al suono di barbari stromenti) and specifies a large procession, including tigers and lions and other presents for the queen. Jommelli uses no outlandish instruments but lends his march in C a quite strident sound by means of loud multiple stops in the strings, and prominent horns and oboes, the latter in thirds unaccompanied some of the time. Iarba disguises himself as his own ambassador (as does Poro in *Alessandro nell'Indie*) but his speech and his manners are so arrogant there is no mistaking his high estate. He demands not only her hand in marriage (she is a widow), but also Enea's head. Lacking satisfaction of his two demands he will unleash his hordes upon Carthage and destroy it. Provocation has been built up to the point where the queen, summoning all her grandeur, replies "Son regina e sono amante, / e l'impero io sola voglio / del mio soglio e del mio cor." (For a translation, see p. 89.) We have seen how Vinci's simple and very effective setting in triple meter and in the key of C conveyed the majesty of the first two words by the expedient of a tonal rise, 1 - 2 - 3, and how Hasse followed Vinci in many particulars, while making the opening a little more majestic by substituting 1- 4 - 3. It is clear at several points that Jommelli knew Hasse's version of 1742, and this is one of them. He selects C major but opts for a broad singing *Allegro* in common time, initiated by the first violins stating 1-4-3 grandly in whole notes as the second violins provide rapid figuration. When the voice sings the same, the first violins double it softly. Note the three-measure phrases (Example 5.4). As a further demonstration of her *virtù*, Didone, embodied by Masi Giura, sings long coloratura passages in sixteenth notes. Even though the aria is shorn of its second stanza, it makes a splendid effect reduced to an amply pro-

[34]For Goldoni's parody see Daniel Heartz, "A Venetian Dancing Master Teaches the Forlana: Lambranzi's *Balli Teatrali,*" *Journal of Musicology* 17 (1999): 136–51; 151.

EXAMPLE 5.4. *Jommelli*, Didone abbandonata, *Aria*

portioned binary form. There is much text repetition even so. The word that seems most inspiring to Jommelli's vision here is "impero." The power and confidence of the imperium belongs to the queen for the last time in "Son regina." From this point on, hers is a long losing battle.

Jommelli does well by the two principals, also by the volcanic Iarba and the pitiful Selena, sung by Monica Buonani. The same cannot be said for the last two roles, Didone's treacherous minister Osmida and Araspe, Iarba's sidekick, who is a good man serving a tyrant. In Act I, Scene 6, Osmida, promised by Iarba the rule of Carthage for his treachery, sings a long aria on his bright prospects, "Tu mi scorgi al gran disegno" (You guide me in the grand plan), addressed to Iarba. The music is a rather neutral piece in common time and in G, with many Lombard snaps, overly long coloratura passages, and some rather crude-sounding tritones. It does little or nothing to give this unsavory character definition. Once Osmida is off the stage Iarba denounces him as a fool, upon which Araspe objects, "But you promised him." "He who betrays deserves betrayal," retorts Iarba. After singing an aria he exits, leaving Araspe alone for a solo scene concluded by a moralizing aria, "Se dalle stelle tu non sei guida" (If by the stars you are not the guide) addressed to "bella virtù." Jommelli gives him the full treatment of a big aria in D, with horns and oboes, plus long orchestral ritornello at the beginning and an orchestral postlude as well. All the attention to orchestral detail Jommelli lavished on this piece does not prevent it from sounding dry and boring, yet this one aria was selected for modern edition in full score.[35]

Metastasio made no provision for a duet in the opera. Jommelli remedied this lack by turning Didone's penultimate aria of Act I, "Non ha ragione, ingrato!" into a duet text. She upbraids Enea for abandoning her and reminds him of the faith he swore. It took little doing on the composer's part to turn this into a dialogue, giving Enea the usual excuses involving his destiny. In the second stanza of the aria Didone turns to the audience and asks its "loving souls" to take her part. The duet offers something close to this that both can sing together.

Oh affano!	Oh anguish!
Se questo è duol tiranno,	If this is overpowering grief,
Anime innamorate,	Loving souls,
Ditelo voi per me.	Say so for me.

The last two lines come from Metastasio. As for the music, Jommelli chose *Andantino* in duple meter and in the key of g, exactly as did Hasse in setting "Non ha ragione, ingrato!" as an aria (Example 4.10). The syllabic treatment of the text is quite similar at points, leaving no doubt that Jommelli had, as he told Schubart, "learned a great deal from Hasse."

Metastasio's Act II is not as strong as his first and third acts. It revolves around Didone's foolish strategy of trying to make Enea jealous by threatening to accept Iarba's suit for her hand. There is a secondary plot in which Araspe courts Selene. Jommelli borrowed the music for Iarba's aria in Scene 6, "Fosca nube il sol ricopra" (A dark cloud covered the sun) from his 1749 Viennese version of the opera,

---

[35]By Hermann Abert, "Die dramatische Musik," in *Herzog Karl Eugen von Württemberg und seine Zeit*, 1, Anhang 1 following p. 611.

apparently the only such borrowing in 1763. He decided to strengthen the end of the act by concentrating on the triangle at the center, putting together the text of a long trio for Iarba, Enea, and Didone, whereas Metastasio ends the act with arias for Iarba and Didone. The tone of these regal persons is lessened by undignified squabbling even in Metastasio's text, so it is not surprising that Jommelli resorts to an ensemble that is quite like a buffo finale. The terzetto is multisectional and through-composed. After some lovely vocal intertwining *à 3* over a pedal, Enea leaves the stage in despair, resigned to losing Didone to Iarba. Once he leaves, Didone no longer pretends to accept Iarba. He is insulted and also leaves. There is a stretch of obbligato recitative in the middle, and a slow section for Didone after she is left alone, then a moderate tempo in the original key to conclude the act.

Act III begins with a clash of arms between the Trojans and the Moors. Enea defeats Iarba in personal combat, decrees his death, then spares him, an act he regards as more consistent with his honor. *Honore* has triumphed over *Amore* in Enea's heart. He sings his great aria di bravura and leaves the stage for good. Osmida and Selene plead with Didone to save them by throwing herself upon Iarba's mercy. They leave her alone for the gruesome final scene. Vinci's famous setting of it in obbligato recitative was still praised as a model of its kind by Francesco Algarotti (1755). In this department no one excelled Jommelli. After his Didone hurls herself into the flames of her burning capital, there is a long symphonic section that winds down to a quiet conclusion, like a blessing.

The opera remained a favorite of Carl Eugen, who retained Jommelli's autograph, as he did all of the composer's autographs. Long after the last Italian singers had left the court it fell to the young wards of the state in the musical wing of the Karlschule to provide both orchestral and vocal forces in the performance of these great and exceedingly difficult operas. For the visit of Joseph II to Stuttgart on 8 April 1777 the students put on a performance of Jommelli's *Didone*. The emperor declared himself to be impressed (perhaps by the unusualness of an all-student German cast singing an opera in Italian). He requested a copy of the score, whereupon the duke gave him the original. When he later had the work performed in Vienna it failed to make the same impression.[36] Another witness of the tragic tale of Dido in operatic form must have been Friedrich Schiller, who was seventeen and a pupil of the Karlschule in 1777. The future master of the *Frauentragödie*, in *Maria Stuart* and *Die Jungfrau von Orleans*, for instance, made his plays so operatic in style that they were easily turned into librettos.

---

[36]Krauss, "Das Theater," 1: 519. No evidence has yet been found in Vienna to corroborate that this performance took place.

FETONTE

In June 1763 Carl Eugen had the famous Chevalier Giovanni Servandoni, principal scene designer of the Opéra in Paris, brought to Stuttgart, where he designed a number of scenes for the forthcoming season, including a famous prison scene for the last act of *Demofoonte,* the birthday opera of 1764. During the course of 1764 the duke resolved to leave Stuttgart, where his subjects were increasingly hostile, and withdraw to Ludwigsburg. Since the theater in this summer palace was of only modest size, work began on an enormous new opera house at the back of the palace. By dint of forced labor and the participation of even the ducal grenadiers, the new theater was ready for the birthday of 11 February 1765, celebrated with a revival of *Demofoonte.* For the birthday opera of 1766 Jommelli once again collaborated with Verazi, producing *Vologeso.* Schubart wrote that Jommelli "studied his poet and often improved on him, as was often necessarily the case with Verazi."[37] There was no birthday opera in 1767 because the duke was in Italy once again to enjoy the carnival season, having taken several of his musicians with him.

A comic opera was added to the court's entertainments in 1766, entailing different singers with much lower salaries than the regular ones. It also entailed the engaging of a fine Italian poet, Gaetano Martinelli. With him Jommelli wrote *Il matrimonio per concorso,* first performed at Ludwigsburg for the name day of the duke, 4 November 1766, followed by *La critica, Il cacciatore delusa* (4 November 1767 at Tübingen), and *La schiava liberata* (18 December 1768 at Ludwigsburg). The last, a *dramma serio-comico,* has been particularly acclaimed and was even successfully revived in the late twentieth century. Like Hasse, Jommelli had written comic music before with skill and verve, but only occasionally. Given a new poet as sympathetic to him as Martinelli was, Jommelli seemed to be opening up new horizons for himself.

Verazi received the visit of Casanova at Schwetzingen during the summer of 1767. The European traveler and bon vivant made some blunt remarks in his memoirs about Verazi's poetic ambitions and his relationship to Jommelli.

> As a poet, he is the greatest oddity I have ever known. To distinguish himself from the others, he cultivated eccentricity. He tried to bring into fashion a style completely opposite to that of the great master Metastasio, making harsh verses and claiming that, so fashioned they gave more scope to the science of the master who was to set them to music. Jommelli had persuaded him to accept this extravagant notion.[38]

According to Casanova it was Jommelli who induced Verazi to rebel against Metastasio, an action not inconsistent with the composer's complaints in letters

---

[37]Schubart, *Leben und Gesinnungen,* 1: 123.
[38]Giacomo Casanova, Chevalier de Seingalt, *History of My Life,* trans. Willard R. Trask, 12 vols. In 6 (New York, 1966–68; reprint 1997), 10:265.

to other librettists. Jommelli wanted longer and more irregular verses that would inspire him to new ideas and give him greater scope.

Fetonte, Jommelli's fifth opera with Verazi, became something of a *Götterdämmerung* with respect to Carl Eugen's serious opera. It was first given at Ludwigsburg to celebrate the duke's birthday on 11 February 1768. Aprile sang the title role. Masi Giura played his mother Climene, a tragic role like that of Didone. Buonani sang Libia, whose hand is sought by Fetonte, also by the Egyptian king Epafo, sung by Rubinelli. Orcane, the Moorish king of the Congo who presses his suit upon Climene, was sung by the tenor Cortoni. Anna Cesari sang Teti. Quinault's libretto of 1683 for Lully is the main ancestor of the libretto. Verazi took care to incorporate its spectacle and ballet into the opera in a way that was more French than Italian.

One of the many extraordinary features of the opera is its overture.[39] It is a sinfonia in three movements as usual, but stage action begins during its course. The *Allegro di molto* in common time and in D, with flutes, oboes, and horns in addition to the usual strings, comes to an end on V when the curtain opens to reveal "a dance of priests who circle an altar with lighted torches in hand." The music is a *Larghetto* in 3/4 and in d, to which Climene sings a solo with choral response by tenors and basses in thirds. For once Jommelli provides the dance music, an impressive chaconne with appropriately accented second beats. The final *Allegro di molto* in common time and in D accompanies an earthquake during which the sacred cavern is destroyed and replaced by the delightful underwater palace of Thetis, Climene's mother, where a dance of marine deities takes place. This is called Scene 2 in the libretto. Three years later at Milan, in *Ascanio in Alba,* Mozart and Parini followed suit by moving a ballet into the middle movement of the overture, then closing it with a choral chaconne and dance.

Schubart was an eyewitness to the first production of *Fetonte.* He relates the experience in his autobiography, which was dictated to a fellow inmate in 1778 and 1779 while he was imprisoned in the fortress of Hohenasperg, ostensibly for insulting the duke's mistress, Franziska von Leutrum. Schubart was twenty-nine years of age in February 1768 and had visited many of the towns and cities of southern Germany, yet he had never seen an opera before (or certainly not an opera like *Fetonte*).

> My wife and I were visiting her brother in Esslingen, whence I travelled in his company to Ludwigsburg in order to see the new opera *Fetonte* performed for the duke's birthday. Imagine such an incandescent person as was I, whose inclination was to the fine arts, especially music, and who had never heard such a magnificent orchestra, nor

---

[39]*Fetonte,* ed. Hermann Abert, *DDT,* 32–33 (Leipzig, 1907) is a complete edition of Jommelli's autograph, which lacks most of the ballet music.

seen an opera. Imagine, I say, how such a man was swimming in a thousand pleasures, witnessing the triumph of poetry,* painting, music, and acting. Jommelli still
presided over the best trained orchestra in the world. Aprili sang, and Buonani, and
Cesari. The spirit of the music was great and heavenstorming, and was expressed as if
every musician were one of Jommelli's nerves. Dance, decor, machinery—all was in
the boldest, newest, and best style.[40]

The asterisk after the word "poetry" leads to a footnote, apparently added by
Schubart before the work was printed: "triumph of poetry it was not, because
Fetonte is one of the most insipid and spiritless dramas among the works of
Metastasio." Schubart must have lacked a real appreciation of Metastasio's classi-
cal reserve if he believed the poet capable of something so irregular as Verazi's
Fetonte text. His critique is most valuable for pointing out how Württemberg opera
in its final phase under Jommelli had approached the ideal of a *Gesamtkunstwerk.*
Its like could scarcely be experienced elsewhere at the time.

The operas did not escape adverse criticism in Germany. Hiller, for one,
blamed Jommelli for allowing his orchestral accompaniments to swamp the vocal
solos.[41] Hiller was of course a strong partisan of Hasse. Schubart defended Jommelli, claiming that one had to have heard an opera under the composer's direction before criticizing his scores: "For the theater certainly there was scarcely
anyone greater than Jommelli. Hasse was as great, simpler, but more lyric and
longer lasting. And Gluck undeniably surpassed him entirely."[42] At this point
Schubart appended another footnote, a panegyric about Gluck added before publication: "Gluck's genius soared above Jommelli's. Deep and high, pure harmony,
bold transitions, novelty in tone, motion, and behavior, feeling for greatness, the
unusual, the Shakesperean characterize our Gluck." Phaeton's failed voyage driving the chariot of the sun evidently still lingered in Schubart's mind when he
compared Jommelli to an eagle flying into the sun, and then described Gluck as
flying even higher.

Act I of *Fetonte* ends with a *Ballo,* "a kind of military exercise for the Moors on
horseback." An elaborate scenario survives in the libretto but there is no music,
and consequently no proper act ending. We know from archival records that 341
soldiers and 86 horses were involved. The opera house at Ludwigsburg was
opened up at the back to enhance this vast spectacle. It is unfortunate that the
one opera by Jommelli available in modern edition is incomplete, lacking the vital
parts played by its ballets. Act III began with a ballet set in the realm of the sun,
as in Quinault's libretto.

[40]Schubart, *Leben und Gesinnungen,* 1: 109–110.
[41]Johann Adam Hiller, *Wöchentliche Nachrichten und Anmerkungen die Musik betreffend,* 5 vols. (Leipzig,
1766–70; reprint 1970), 3: 61.
[42]Schubart, *Leben und Gesinnungen,* 1: 123.

Jommelli himself preferred Verazi's *Vologeso* to the poet's *Fetonte*. He expressed this in a letter to Martinelli in Lisbon.

> Do not be surprised, my dear friend, but I also am more partial to the score of *Vologeso* than to that of *Fetonte*. The affections, and the passions in the former are better illuminated, of greater force, and more natural and true-seeming than in the latter. A historical tale is always superior to a mythical for tragedy. Be persuaded, therefore, that every effect that you experience, and that you can experience in listening, the composer, who writes with soul and mind, has experienced first. I do not know how to, nor can I create in myself the illusion that carries me to that grade of passion that I need to reach in order to write expressive music if my soul itself is not touched and does not feel it. A thousand times, I have found myself in similar, very difficult straits. It is my absolute duty not to betray and to express the words well, but it is neither my duty nor within my power to give them that acumen of sensibility and of passion that they, of themselves, by their nature are lacking. In comparison then, *Vologeso* will always triumph over *Fetonte*. The latter is a fable, and the former, historical. The former must touch and the latter can surprise. In the former, the heart of the listener is all passion, in the latter all admiration. Which of these two has the greater force in us? You, better than I, must know the answer.[43]

Rarely has an Italian composer of opera from the eighteenth century expressed his philosophy as to the act of creation so well. The heart must be moved initially by the text in order to convey passion in music to the listener. How close this is to the famous credo of Jommelli's great and close contemporary, Emanuel Bach: "A musician cannot move others unless he too is moved."[44]

The frequent tumult and excess of *Fetonte* should not obscure its many musical beauties and subtleties. Act I contains a tender love scene between Libia and Fetonte, who believe at this point that they must part forever because she is consigned to marry King Epafo. To her Fetonte sings an aria in B♭, "Le smanie celarti io dovrei" (I ought to conceal my desires from you). There is no opening orchestral ritornello. Rather, he begins by himself with a simple and winning melody (Example 5.5a). He is accompanied only by strings, with violins sounding on the offbeats. The piece is very long and includes abundant coloratura, a middle section more ample than usual, and a dal segno repetition of **A2** (where Aprile could display his famed skill for improvising). To terminate the aria the orchestra sounds a passage in which a sixteenth-note leaping figure climbs up to the high tonic and then tumbles down into the cadence (Example 5.5b). Nervous little figures like this and obsessive repetition are characteristic of Jommelli's string writing. His

---

[43]Letter dated Naples, 17 October 1769, as translated in McClymonds, *Niccolò Jommelli*, p. 484–85.
[44]*Essay on the True Art of Playing Keyboard Instruments,* trans. and ed. William J. Mitchell (New York, 1949), p. 152.

EXAMPLE 5.5. *Jommelli*, Fetonte, *Aria*

iron hand as a leader was vital to making them come out precisely together in performance. Not many other composers of the time made such demands. To this passage Fetonte makes his exit.

Libia ponders the meaning of his words. The music tells us so because Jommelli uses two motifs from his aria to introduce the following obbligato recitative for her (Example 5.6a). The initial melodic figure, *forte,* comes from his first cadence (Example 5.5a, mm. 5–6). The subsequent little nervous figure, *piano,* made more poignant by the Lombard rhythms, echoes his exit music (Example 5.5b). Her brooding is intensified by combining the two motifs, not in major where they had been heard, but in minor. At the section of the recitative marked *Andante* the orchestra transforms the Lombard rhythms into lacerating turns around the fifth degree of the key of g (Example 5.6b). These are followed by a *forte* outburst outlining a diminished-seventh chord, and then a quiet, conjunct melodic descent to the cadence. All three—the turns, outburst, and descent—figure in the main theme of her aria (Example 5.6c). She enters after a long ritornello, the orchestra having thoroughly explored her lamentable situation before she sings, "Spargerò d'amare lagrime" (I shall weep bitter tears). The aria has no da capo or dal segno repetition.

Musical linkage such as Jommelli uses to establish the closeness of the lovers is as advanced for the time as it is effective. Libia's recitative begins with motifs from Fetonte's aria, with one of them transformed into a main motif of her aria.

EXAMPLE 5.6. *Jommelli*, Fetonte, *Recitative and Aria*

a.

b.

c.

They sing in the keys of B♭ and g, the one being the relative of the other. As a complex, these two arias point ahead to the culmination of Mannheim opera in Mozart's *Idomeneo,* in which the lovers begin by singing arias in g and B♭ that are tied together by a repeated motif. Moreover, Mozart uses motifs from Ilia's aria in Act II, Scene 3, "Se il padre perdei," to begin the following obbligato recitative for Idomeneo, who ponders the meaning of her words. The first reminiscence he darkens by coloring in minor what had been in major.

The second number in Act II is a duet for Climene and Orcane. Choice of the key of A may be the most traditional thing about this duet, which also has no initial ritornello. It uses three different tempos and meters. The two sopranos warble together in long chains of thirds, although the text does not indicate they are in agreement. After its conclusion in A there is a direction, "Segue subito il Recitativo," at which the orchestra suddenly switches to the key of F, certainly not a common tonal move for the time. This is the beginning of a long obbligato recitative for Fetonte, leading to his biggest aria, "Sempre fido il primo affetto" (Always faithful the first love).

Act II, Scene 8, is a tomb scene, described as "a subterranean dark place of the royal sepulchers, sparsely lit by torches." Fetonte sings a somber invocation, "Ombra che tacite qui sede" (Spirits who reside here in silence). An *Adagio* in cut time, in the typical *ombra* key of E♭, its vocal solo commences in whole notes, descending the degrees 8 - 5 - 1. Climene also sings an aria, which turns into a trio when she is joined by Libia and Fetonte, who exits leaving the two women to finish the act as a duet.

Jommelli indulges in many metric and tempo changes within the arias and ensembles of the opera. These may be related to uneven line lengths and contrasts in Verazi's texts. In Act III, Scene 4, Orcane sings an aria, text and music, that is borrowed from Iarba's "Son quel fiume" in Jommelli's *Didone* of 1763. (The singer was the tenor Cortoni in both.) Metastasio's poem was perfectly regular and the musical setting is correspondingly straightforward, with no sudden *Adagio* sections or bursts of recitative. In the context of *Fetonte,* this aria sounds like an island of normalcy in a sea of eccentricity, and it serves to take the measure of the composer's stylistic change by the end of his years in ducal service.

Act III, Scene 6, brings the climactic moment of Fetonte's fatal driving of the sun chariot across the sky, prompted both by his mother's ambition and his desire to prove himself worthy of Libia. The skies redden in advance and seem to be catching fire, followed by the earth. This tour de force for the technical crew, machinists, and stage designer at Ludwigsburg astonished all. Their counterparts at Lisbon, attempting to stage *Fetonte,* sought instructions on how this scene could be done. Jommelli unleashes a long *"crescendo il forte"* for violins from their low D gradually up two octaves in active figuration to high D two octaves above.

Epafo and Climene describe the action in short lines that Verazi may have intended as a set piece. Jommelli composed it as an obbligato recitative over a slowly rising bass in chromatic steps. The lines themselves have an unpolished, slapdash character not much better than doggerel.

Epafo:	Numi! Che veggo!	Ye gods! What do I see!
	Qual ardor, quai lampi	What audacity, what flashes
	Super gli eterni campi!	Above the ethereal fields!
	Ahimè, La fiamma	Alas, The flame—
	Spettacolo tremendo!	Tremendous spectacle!—
	A momenti crescendo,	Growing moment by moment,
	E terra e il minaccia	And menacing both earth and sky—
	Tutto già quasi	All seems to nearly
	L'emisfero abbraccia!	Embrace the hemisphere.

Eventually a subterranean chorus is heard crying out to Jove for mercy. Jove responds with a lightning bolt that strikes Fetonte and hurls him, horses, carriage, and all, into the sea. The action is painted by the violins, descending from on high in little imitations, then in unison down to low G. There follows a trio for Climene, Epafo, and Orcane. The two kings quarrel as usual, while Orcane pleads with Climene to accept him as her champion. She refuses and finally tears herself away from them, runs to the shore, and throws herself into the sea, at which there is a short chorus sung by tutti bewailing "this wicked earth, inhuman place of hate, anger, and insane fury," followed by some reiterated orchestral chords on D ending the opera.

Thus the demise of Queen Climene is similar to that of Queen Didone. The point has been made that *Fetonte* is a *Frauentragödie* indebted to *Didone abbandonata* not just for its ending but in several details of its text.[45] The tragic outcome was not mitigated in any way. There was no tribute to Neptune for putting out the fire, as was the case at the end of *Didone abbandonata* at Stuttgart in 1763. The printed libretto claimed that the ballets were invented by the author (Verazi) and were derived from the subject of the opera. When *Fetonte* was revived for the duke's birthday in 1769, credit for the choreography was given to Antoine Dauvigny, Noverre's pupil and successor.

POSTLUDE

Jommelli had reason to be worried about his future at the duke's court when he saw the wave of economies that began to hit the theatrical establishment. Noverre left in 1767. Gaetano Vestris, the great solo dancer, no longer came annually for a visit. Rodolphe went back to Paris to stay. Masi Giura and Pla were

---

[45]By Hermann Abert in the Preface to his edition of *Fetonte*, p. xi.

released in April 1768. Innocenza Colomba, theater architect and stage designer, resigned in early 1768, complaining bitterly of nonpayment for his work. Aprile defected in March 1769, leaving many unpaid debts in his wake.

Carl Eugen suspected Jommelli of harboring plans to abscond, even though he was promised a pension and would jeopardize it by any rash action. Around 1767 Jommelli lost the easy access to the duke that he had always enjoyed. At the time of the *Fetonte* premiere Jommelli made a request to the duke for the autographs and copies of his scores that he could take on his forthcoming leave in Italy, where he intended to install his ailing wife. Rumors abounded that he did not intend to return, and it is not surprising that the duke believed them. Responding like the petty tyrant that he was, Carl Eugen forbade the composer access to both his autographs and the copies. Jommelli protested in a letter of 24 February 1769, saying that in his many years of service he had given his scores to the duke not as an act of duty but one of sincere attachment.

> Certainly no other composer or writer has allowed his autographs out of his hands or put them in the control of others. Neither Hasse and others at the court of Vienna, nor the celebrated [Domenico] Scarlatti and others at the Spanish court. . . . In sum, none of the thousands and thousands of others who create music. And if, when I had the fortune to be appointed to the service of Your Serene Highness, such a request had been made of me, frankly I would have said no at any cost. On the contrary, since at the time I was promised upon entering this service the same prerogatives and distinctions that the most worthy Master Hasse had at the Dresden court, I would never have believed myself duty bound to something that was not expected of the afore-mentioned Hasse or of any other Master and composer of music.[46]

Jommelli continued by explaining how necessary it was for an author to possess copies of his work and insisting that he would return after settling his wife in the family home of the Jommellis. The delicate matter of copies of Jommelli's scores being sold for profit also comes up in the same letter.

> I do not know how to justify myself because I have committed no wrongdoing. At least the copies of my works, even if I must give up my originals, are rightfully mine, but for the convenience, study, and benefit of myself, and not ever for shameful commercial enterprise that has been done with them by so many others. I do not know who they are, but they must exist because not only outside, but even in Stuttgart itself, as everyone knows, my compositions are being circulated and sold, compositions that now I myself am being denied that justly are my right to have.

Jommelli then pointed out that when the duke wanted the autographs of his predecessor Maestro Brescianello, he bought them from the widow. And he posed the question of why his enemies were circulating rumors about him.

[46]McClymonds, *Niccolò Jommelli*, pp. 694–95.

And on what are these suspicions founded? Perhaps on my refusal of the many requests that have newly been made to me in the last few days by a not-too-distant court? Perhaps on some other alleged commitment of mine elsewhere? Where then? Let them reveal it if it is true. I have never gone back on my word and particularly on the word given to the sacred person of the Reigning Sovereign who is yourself.

The not-too-distant court was surely that of the elector Carl Theodore at Mannheim, who was interested in Jommelli's operas before, during, and after his service to Carl Eugen. Jommelli was not being entirely candid about his other commitments. In 1768 he began negotiations to supply music for the court of José I at Lisbon. By the time he wrote this letter he had already made five shipments of his works to Portugal. On 29 March 1769 he left for Naples, never to return. It took two years of wrangling by letter, and negotiations in which Verazi played an important role, before the court and his private creditors in Württemberg were satisfied. He was accorded no pension.

Jommelli did for Stuttgart what Hasse had done for Dresden. He created a body of works and a level of performance that made it a capital of modern music. Lacking Dresden's superior resources of every kind, Stuttgart slipped back into musical mediocrity within a few years of Jommelli's departure. Carl Eugen gradually replaced all foreign musicians with his own subjects, a project mostly completed by 1774. In an effort to save face, Sacchini was brought in from Munich to compose the birthday opera for 11 February 1770, *Calliroe,* on a new text by Verazi. The composer actually came to Ludwigsburg and presided over the premiere. Perceiving the decline in the court's musical and theatrical forces at first hand, he reneged on providing another opera, even though he was paid in advance for one. *Calliroe* was revived many times at the ducal court. Sacchini's neo-Neapolitan style, with its relatively simple orchestral accompaniments and uncomplicated rhythmic and melodic style (compared to Jommelli's) made it much easier for average musicians to perform. Revivals were also made from the duke's treasured hoard of scores by Jommelli, as we saw in the case of *Didone,* although with what degree of completeness or competence must remain a question.

In April 1770 the little-known Antonio Boroni was hired as Oberkappellmeister in place of Jommelli. He would remain the exceptional foreigner in the ducal music. His duties were spelled out: compose and direct operas as well as church music, take part in concerts, and play the harpsichord in the theater. He in fact composed little for the opera, in which the duke rapidly lost interest. The most promising kind of spectacle at the ducal court in the early 1770s was comic opera, put on by the buffo troupe under the direction of Friderico Seemann, husband of Anna Cesari, and a skilled keyboard player long in ducal service.

Mannheim began to loom larger in Württemberg's musical life around 1770. It had frequently loaned the services of Verazi, of course, and would continue to do so. Other artists were now loaned as well. Claude Legrand, dancer and chore-ographer, came from Mannheim in 1770. The tenor Anton Raaff was hired for the revival of *Fetonte* in 1772. Parisian opéra-comique overwhelmed the ducal court in the 1770s as it did all of Germany. Boroni tried making his own setting of Sedaine's *Le déserteur* in 1774, but it was soon replaced by Monsigny's famous original setting. As in other German centers opéra-comique promoted the flour-ishing of Singspiel. Singers and actors became more confident performing in the vernacular. Theatrical troupes from elsewhere began to make regular stops at Stuttgart as well. Emanuel Schikaneder's came in 1778, playing, besides Shake-speare, Lessing, and Goethe, the beloved *Die Jagd* of Weisse and Hiller.

One aspiring young artist who emerged in Stuttgart was Schiller. Another was the cellist and composer Rudolf Zumsteeg, his friend of the same age and the most distinguished musical product of the Karlsschule. Grand opera at the court, limited mostly to the visits of foreign potentates, offered Zumsteeg an opportu-nity to shine as a composer in 1782, when Crown Prince Paul of Russia visited Stuttgart. The composer, born in 1760, was too young to have studied with Jom-melli, but he profited from Jommelli's musical legacy in Württemberg, especially the elaborate obbligato recitatives of the operas, as is evident in his songs and Singspiele. Schubart, finally released from prison in 1787, was appointed court and theater poet. He dreamed of emulating Mannheim's *Nationaltheater* but it was not to be. Death overtook Schubart in 1791 and Carl Eugen two years later.

Jommelli ended his life in a burst of compositional activity, writing works on demand for Rome, Naples, and Lisbon. His extensive correspondence with the Portuguese court represents one of the major discoveries in recent music history.[47] In his last works Jommelli was able to reuse much of his music written in Ger-many. The overture to *Armida abbandonata* (Naples, 1770), for instance, is none other than that for his *Didone abbandonata* (1763), not verbatim, but recollected, because he lacked the earlier score. Perhaps he reckoned that the two abandoned ladies had a lot in common.[48] To Armida and her enchanted garden Tiepolo devoted one of his greatest paintings (Plate VII).

In spite of personal loss Jommelli composed at a feverish pace. His wife, after a long decline, died in July 1770. The composer, mostly healthy up to this point, suffered increasingly from gout and was struck down by a paralytic stroke in 1771. Even this did not stop him entirely as he recovered enough use of his hands to keep writing. He succumbed at last in the summer of 1774. Gennaro Manna, primo maestro of the Neapolitan court, planned the public funeral, to which many poets and musicians contributed in an outpouring of respect for one of their greatest masters.

[47]The entire correspondence is reproduced in the original and translated into English in McClymonds (ibid.).

[48]On reuse of musical ideas from the composer's earlier works in his late ones, see McClymonds,"The Evo-lution of Jommelli's Operatic Style,"*JAMS* 33 (1980): 326–55.

Noverre's Ballets

For a brief period in the 1760s Stuttgart rivaled Paris and Vienna as a center for ballet, thanks to the presence of the century's greatest choreographer, Jean-Georges Noverre. Born in Paris in 1727 to a French mother and a Swiss military officer, he was trained early in dance, notably by Louis Dupré, first dancer of the Paris Opéra. By age sixteen he was dancing on the stage of the Opéra-Comique, then directed by impresario Jean Monnet. A year later, in 1744, he joined the ballet troupe directed by Jean-Barthélémy Lany at the court of Frederick in Berlin, whence he also visited Dresden for the marriage festivities in 1747, as noted above. After returning to France he worked at Marseilles and Strasbourg, where he choreographed his first ballets and probably met and married the actress and dancer Marie-Louise Sauveur. At Lyons in 1751 he staged his first serious pantomime ballet, *Le jugement de Paris.* At the Opéra-Comique in Paris during the 1754–55 season he created *Les fêtes chinoise,* with costumes by Louis René Boquet, a triumph that got him invited to London. During the seasons of 1755–56 and 1756–57 he directed a troupe of dancers at the Drury Lane Theatre run by David Garrick. He met little success because of the tense political situation that turned Londoners against anything French. On the other hand, he found in the acting of Garrick one of the inspirations to pursue serious pantomime further. During convalescence from an illness in London he drafted his famous *Lettres sur la danse et sur les ballets.* In the ninth letter is the following tribute.

> Mr. Garrick, the celebrated English actor, is the model I wish to put forward. Not only is he the most handsome, the most perfect and the most worthy of admiration of all actors, he may be regarded as the Proteus of our own time; because he understood all styles and presented them with a perfection and truth which aroused not only the applause and praise of his countrymen, but also excited the admiration and encomiums of all foreigners. He was so natural, his expression was so lifelike, his gestures, features and glances were so eloquent and so convincing, that he made the action clear even to those who did not understand a word of English. It was so easy to follow his meaning; his pathos was touching; in tragedy he terrified with the successive movements with which he represented the most violent passions. And, if I may so express myself, he lacerated the spectator's feelings, tore his heart, pierced his soul, and made him shed tears of blood.[49]

Noverre's prose, in which there is little of Gallic reserve, resembles a dramatic unfolding in its own right, as witness the way this paragraph makes an emotional

---

[49]Jean-Georges Noverre, *Letters on Dancing and Ballets,* trans. Cyril W. Beaumont from the revised and enlarged edition published in Saint Petersburg, 1803 (London, 1930; revised New York, 1966), p. 82. The original edition came out in Lyons in 1759 but is dated 1760 and is dedicated to Carl Eugen.

crescendo toward the end and concludes with dire images. Noverre also had high praise for the *drames bourgeois* and dramatic theories of Diderot.[50]

After London Noverre directed the ballet troupe in Lyons from 1757 to 1760, creating as many as thirteen new ballets, three of them in the serious genre. His musical collaborator was the composer François Granier, the first of several fine musicians Noverre had the good fortune to work with at length. Noverre took Granier's score for the ballet *Les jalousies, ou les fêtes du serail* with him to Stuttgart. He submitted it in 1766 along with many other documents to King Stanislaus of Poland, with whom he was negotiating for a position. Some of Granier's music, along with Joseph Starzer's, turned up in the ballet *Le gelosie del seraglio* by Noverre's pupil, Charles Le Picq.[51] The ballet accompanied Mozart's *Lucio Silla* (Milan, 1772) and Mozart notated its dances for himself.

Stuttgart provided the conditions that allowed Noverre to put his theories into practice on a larger scale than at Lyons. Carl Eugen had founded an independent corps de ballet in 1758. Under the direction of François Sauveterre, it consisted of six male and five female dancers, and sixteen figurants evenly divided. The dancers were mostly French or Italian, and divided into *serieux, demi-caractères,* and *comiques.* On 11 February 1760 the ballets between the acts of Jommelli's *Alessandro nell'Indie* had for subjects "The Indians from the realm of the grand Mogul" and "Orpheus and Euridice." Sauveterre left after these productions and was replaced by Noverre in March 1760.

Noverre and his wife joined the ducal service for an engagement of six years. Their joint salary was initially 5,000 gulden plus travel money and it was raised in subsequent years. The size of the ballet troupe grew larger under Noverre, reaching a high in 1764 of seven *danseurs,* seven *danseuses,* twenty-three *figurants,* and twenty-one *figurantes.*[52] Boquet of Paris designed many of the costumes. Another expense was required by the visit of the highly regarded and well-remunerated Gaetano Vestris of the Paris Opéra as a guest artist every carnival season. The duke lavished support of every kind on his ballet, allowing Noverre to indulge his superb taste in costumes, scenery, and all the technical aspects of staging, of which he was a master. He was particularly famous for the graceful grouping of his large forces. Most of all he was famous for his dramatic pantomimes, which were not dances so much as poems of gesture and movement, aided by music. For his actions he often chose French classical tragedies (which were also being

---

[50]On Noverre's indebtedness to both Garrick and Diderot, see Daniel Heartz, "From Garrick to Gluck: The Reform of Theatre and Opera in the mid-Eighteenth Century," *Proceedings of the Royal Musical Association* 94 (1967–68): 111–27.

[51]Kathleen Kuzmick Hansell, "Opera and Ballet at the Regio Ducal Teatro of Milan, 1771–1776: A Musical and Social History" (Ph.D. diss., University of California, Berkeley, 1979), pp. 748–53.

[52]Kraus, "Das Theater," 1: 512–14.

played at court) or subjects from Greco-Roman antiquity. Some of his ballets were independent but most of them were attached to operas.

Music was of supreme importance to pantomime ballet. It was to the genre what words were to opera, said Noverre in his *Lettres.* He claimed that he did not create his choreographies to existing music. Rather, he composed a sustained action or plot, then instructed the composer as to how the music should support it and explain it. If this were indeed his normal method, it can be readily understood why Jommelli, fourteen years his senior, longer in ducal service and of higher rank, did not compose music for ballets. Exceptions may have been two works of 1763 by the poet Giampietro Tagliazucchi called "pastorale," *Il trionfo d'Amore* and *La pastorella illustre.* Possibly these entertainments approached the genre of opéra-ballet, with which the poet would have been acquainted from his years of service at the Berlin court. Noverre's regular musical collaborators in the ducal service were two outstanding younger composers, both protégés of Jommelli, the hornist Rodolphe and Florian Deller.

Deller came from Lower Austria, having been baptized on 2 May 1729 in the little hill town of Drosendorf on the Moravian border, just north of Horn. Of his early education in music nothing is known. He became a violinist and presumably studied in Vienna, where he could have come in contact with Holzbauer or Starzer, both eminent ballet composers, or with Jommelli himself during his 1749 visit. He arrived in Stuttgart together with the Austrian tenor Christoph von Hager. By decree of 12 February 1751 his annual salary was set at 300 gulden. He played as a ripieno violinist in the court chapel and also in the opera. His salary was increased by 50 gulden while he still remained at the lowest step among the violinists. In 1756 he requested permission of the duke to study counterpoint and composition with Jommelli. Granted this, he began his lessons when the master returned from his leave in Italy during 1757. He was involved with the ballet troupe before Noverre's arrival, accompanying rehearsals alone as a solo violinist.[53]

Deller was responsible for the music to Noverre's *Admète et Alceste, ou Le triomphe de l'amour conjugal,* which was given with Jommelli's *L'Olimpiade* in 1761. A happy outcome of the opera with the union of the lovers evidently decided the choice of subject for the ballet. A year later Deller wrote the music for *Amore e Psiche* and *La morte d'Ercole* while Rodolphe wrote that for *La fête persiane,* three ballets by Noverre that accompanied Jommelli's *Semiramide riconsciuta.* For the ducal birthday in 1763 Jommelli made his new setting of *Didone abbandonata.* Noverre added *Médée et Jason* (music by Rodolphe) after Act I, *Orfeo ed Euridice* (Deller) after Act II, and in conclusion *Le bassin de Neptune* (Deller).

In London for a successful season in 1781–82 at the King's Theatre Noverre

[53]The source of this paragraph is the introduction to *Ausgewählte ballette Stuttgarter Meister aus der 2. hälfte des 18. jahrhunderts (Florian Deller und Johann Joseph Rudolph),* ed. Hermann Abert, *DDT,* 43–44 (1913).

revived several of his Stuttgart ballets, including *Médée et Jason,* of which John Boydell published an engraving in 1782 (Figure 5.6). It shows the main figures in exaggerated poses and rather old-fashioned costumes (the lady on the right certainly wears a hoop skirt, although Noverre had inveighed against panniers in his *Lettres*). Three droll orchestral musicians labor in the pit. The notated music illustrates the overture to Gluck's *Iphigénie en Aulide.*

DELLER'S *ORFEO ED EURIDICE*

At Lyons Noverre had already created an Orpheus ballet, *La descente d'Orphée aux Enfers,* for which no music or scenario survives. In 1763 a program in French described the nine scenes of *Orfeo* in considerable detail. There follows a condensed version of these.

In Scene 1 Orfeo laments the loss of Euridice. He touches his lyre and pleads for passage over the river Acheron. Charon, enchanted, ferries him across. The gates of Hades creak open. Scene 2 is set in the Elysian Fields. The blessed spirits are surprised to see a mortal. They surround Orfeo and express their pleasure with dancing. He looks for Euridice and eventually finds her. They embrace. He leaves to seek the favor of Pluto. Scene 3 shows Pluto's palace. Pluto and Proserpine are on their thrones. Orfeo enters trembling and casts himself down before the thrones. Specters and furies surround him menacingly. By singing to his lyre he softens the heart of Pluto, who grants him Euridice, with the single caveat that he must not look upon her until they have left death's realm. In Scene 4 Euridice is brought in. She is frightened and flies to her spouse, who offers her a trembling hand, without looking at her. She pleads for a glance. At his refusal she despairs and lets go of his hand. He calls to her and tries to find her without looking up. Failing in this he looks at her. Vigilant demons appear to enforce Pluto's stricture. They try to take her away from Orfeo, who touches his lyre, at the sound of which they weaken. Tisiphone rallies the demons and they separate the lovers. In Scene 5, Cupid, distressed at the lovers' cries, flies through the air and pursues the furies who are taking Euridice away. The scene changes to Mount Rhodope and the meandering Hebrus River. Orfeo, disconsolate, plays his lyre. Nymphs, charmed by the sounds, surround him and invite him to join them. In the next scene (7) trees come to flower and wild animals gather around him to listen. In Scene 8 the nymphs, spurned, become bacchantes and beat Orfeo to the ground. The last scene is the most splendid. Bacchus descends. The earth opens to reveal Cupid and Euridice. Bacchus revives Orfeo and the lovers are reunited. Fawns and many other creatures join in a general celebration.

Noverre's elaborate creation seems more like a full ballet than an entr'acte. It requires three different sets: before the gates of Hades, Pluto's palace, and Mount Rhodope. Magical transformations such as trees that bloom, plus the menagerie in Scene 7, testify to Noverre's famed ability to control all aspects of theatrical

FIGURE 5.6. Noverre's ballet *Médée et Jason* (London, 1782).

spectacle. Deller's main task was to provide music in the traditional French dance forms for the long sequences that are divertissements, namely, the dances of the blessed spirits in Scene 2 and the final celebration. He acquitted this task very well. He excelled in the more original moments required by pantomime. In all there are thirty individual numbers in the score.[54]

A short overture in F, a kind of intrada, takes little time. It leads to No. 1 in B♭, a *Larghetto* in cut time for strings that conveys Orfeo's sadness. No. 2, an *Adagio*, corresponds to his first touching of the lyre. Pizzicato violins provide a simple yet effective suggestion of the plucked lyre, in support of a lovely melody for solo oboe that stands in for the voice of the divine singer of Thrace (Example 5.7). A

[54]Modern edition by Abert in *Ausgewählte ballette Stuttgarter Meister*, 1–63.

EXAMPLE 5.7. *Deller*, Orfeo ed Euridice, *Pantomime*

third piece in B♭, an *Allegro* in common time for strings and flutes, accompanies Charon's ferry ride and the opening of Hell's gates. Deller cleverly changes key for the change of scene. He selects E♭ for the Elysian Fields and dances of the blessed spirits, straying from it only briefly in the sequence of conventional dances in Nos. 4–10, which include a Rondo, a Gavotte, and a Chaconne.

The change of scene to Pluto's palace evoked from Deller a *Maestoso* in common time and in B♭ that is like a pompous French overture, with lots of dotted rhythms and runs in the strings, which are supported by two horns. This return to B♭ was strategic because it was followed by its relative minor, g, No. 12, to paint Orfeo's trembling approach with little hesitations and a melody that seems to stutter. No. 13 is an *Adagio* in G and in 3/4 time for strings and flutes that conveys Orfeo's pleading. The crucial Scene 4, Orfeo's attempt to lead his beloved away without looking at her, is pure pantomime. Deller wrote an *Allegro furioso* in g and in 3/4 time (No. 14) that seems to paint the menacing furies and that is interrupted by *Adagio* passages of a sighing nature that convey Euridice's plight. The last part of this impressive number brings back the pizzicato strings representing Orfeo's lyre, here supporting a melody for two oboes that is left open (Example 5.8). The following section, with the strings col arco, is suitably furious for the demons, with rushing runs down to a throbbing diminished chord that is not resolved. Then the sighing *Adagio* that suggests a verbal plea alternates with the *Allegro* of the furies and demons, who win out. The free combinations and boldness of Deller's pantomime music stand out in this example. For his models he had the obbligato recitatives of his teacher Jommelli, which are replete with similar pauses and short contrasts of rhythms, textures, and tempos. Another source was Noverre himself, who was often explicit in requesting accompaniments for his pantomimes.

Cupid's flight through the air in Scene 5 was brief, judging by the short *Allegro* for strings in 3/8 time and in D, No. 15. Lamenting Orfeo on the Hebrus River in Scene 6 brings back the key of g, which has become characteristic of his grief and was evidently as much a favorite of Deller as it was of Jommelli. When Orfeo again plays his lyre the texture reverts to solo oboe and pizzicato strings. Reminiscences like this are so clear they cannot be missed. Deller was aiming at nothing less than an overall unity. He achieved this in spite of the looseness of the

EXAMPLE 5.8. *Deller*, Orfeo ed Euridice, *Pantomime*

genre and Noverre's demands that the ballet end with a huge divertissement. Keys on the flat side that have dominated the entire work give way after No. 22, an *Adagio* in B♭ and in 3/4 time for flutes and strings. The following *Marcia,* scored for strings, flutes, and horns, proclaims the key of G, and D soon follows in the attractive *Louré,* No. 25. Two numbers later D is celebrated by an *Allegro* in 6/8 in which the violins climb up two octaves from their low D in a long passage gradually growing louder, what is usually called a Mannheim *crescendo* but should be called, after its inventor, a Jommelli *crescendo.* Deller even uses the master's precise terminology: "crescendo il forte." The ballet is rounded out by three pieces in 2/4 time, a *Rondo Allegretto* for strings in the key of A, a *Finale Allegro* in many sections for strings, flutes, and horns in D, and a jolly *Contre-Danse* in D in which bassoons are added to the aforementioned.

Lavish praise for *Orfeo,* its principal dancers, and its music appeared in Uriot's festival book. The role of Orfeo was taken by one Lepy, a dancer recruited from Paris. Mademoiselle Toscani played Euridice, and Pluto was none other than

Vestris. On Deller's music Uriot wrote in his festival book:"He imitates the rolling of thunder. He lets us hear the lapping of the waves. He paints the delights of Olympus and the horrors of Hades. He even knows how to express the souls, feelings, and passions of every character who appeared on the stage." Ballet reached a very high level in Württemberg under Noverre and his composers, of whom the favorite was Deller. Indeed, a modern authority on the genre has gone so far as to say of Noverre that"during his tenure Stuttgart could claim the world's outstanding ballet company."[55]

Schubart was a friend of Deller's who praised him in quite specific terms. It was Deller's music, he said, that gave life and color to Noverre's great and unique ballets."Deller's style was light, natural, plain, and flattered the ears of connoisseurs and amateurs alike. . . . Even the most common people could retain his melodies, so happily had he heard them in nature."[56] The assessment seems to suit Example 5.7 quite well. In his lighter pieces Deller attains the kind of grace that made Grétry such a good ballet composer. Schubart's other remarks on Deller pay more heed to the serious and sublime style he could deploy.

> Deller is an excellent man who came under the mild influence of Jommelli but did not slavishly imitate him because he soon discovered a source within himself from which to create. Deller admired the genius of Jommelli. Yet he was proud and original enough to resist being disturbed by it in his own circle. . . . Noverre, first ballet master of the world, contributed greatly to the emergence of Deller's spirit. Deller provided music for his magical ballets and did this so magnificently that these ballets are still considered masterpieces all over Europe. Noverre himself claimed that he had never found a better translator for his mimed creations than Deller. The great tragic ballet *Orfeo* is rich in grand, shattering, heavenly, and ravishing passages. Novelty in thought, grace and delicacy in sentiment, melting loveliness in the transitions, rich rhythmic variety—in a word, beauty shone forth everywhere in the musical character of this man.[57]

Schubart goes on to say that Deller played the violin with uncommon sweetness and wrote for it in masterly fashion. He praised also the comic operas Deller wrote for the court after Noverre left, of which the best known is *Il maestro di cappella*, and regretted that the composer did not write for the German theater. Deller was never paid well by the ducal court, from which he repeatedly requested his leave. It was granted in June 1771. He returned to Vienna and died in Munich two years later.

Noverre's program for *Médée et Jason* is in nine scenes, like that for *Orfeo*, and

---

[55]Marian Hannah Winter, *The Pre-Romantic Ballet* (London, 1974), p. 115.
[56]Schubart, *Leben und Gesinnungen*, 1: 129–30.
[57]Schubart, *Ideen zu einer Asthetik der Tonkunst*, pp. 151–52.

nearly as long; Rodolphe's music for *Médée,* on the other hand, is considerably shorter than Deller's for *Orfeo,* consisting of only fifteen numbers after a brief sinfonia in one movement.[58] The longest piece is a huge chaconne, No. 4. Other formal types are a Marcia and a Gavotte. Rodolphe also favors the *crescendo* and dramatic pauses in the form of empty measures surmounted by fermatas. At the most gruesome part of the action, at No. 14, as Medea kills her children, Rodolphe deploys a multisectional, quickly shifting sequence that is like an obbligato recitative. He was perhaps directed to this choice by Noverre.

By all accounts Noverre was a hard taskmaster, as vain as he was irascible. He quarreled with the ducal court about the amount of money owed to him for giving dancers private lessons, and this led to his leaving Stuttgart. He negotiated with London and Warsaw but ended up going to Vienna. Even so, he looked back fondly on his Stuttgart years and later explored the possibilities of returning. It was impossible at the level of expense he required. Only a Paris or a London could afford him. Michael Kelly tells a story in his memoirs about Noverre from the time Kelly was managing the King's Theatre in the Haymarket in 1793. It bears both upon the master's irritability and his genius.

> Paisiello's charming comic opera, *I Zingari in Fiera,* was produced that season; its popularity lasted many years. The ballets were of the first class; the great Noverre was the ballet-master, and there was a numerous and well-chosen corps de ballet. . . . Noverre produced his magnificent ballet of *L'Iphigénie en Aulide;* the splendour of the spectacle, the scenery, the richness of the decorations and dresses, could not have been surpassed: the dancing was of the first order, and the acting of D'Egville, as Agamemnon, inimitable; the triumphal cars, with horses; the grand marches, processions, and above all the fine grouping of the corps de ballet, all was *vrai* classicality, and proved Noverre to be the greatest of his art. But he was a passionate little fellow; he swore and tore behind the scenes, so that, at times, he might really have been taken for a lunatic escaped from his keeper. . . . I was standing behind the scenes, talking to one of the men, in my supernumerary dress, and perhaps rather loudly; Noverre, who was all fire and fury, came behind me and gave me a tremendous kick."Taisez-vous, bête!" exclaimed he; but when I took off my vizor, and Noverre found he had been kicking his manager, he made every possible apology.[59]

A portrait of Noverre was drawn and engraved in London showing his visage ringed with flames, suggesting the incandescence of his genius (Figure 5.7). The accompanying quatrain explains: "With the fire of his genius he animates the dance / Calling it back to life from its great days in Greece. / Recovering through him their antique eloquence, / The gestures and steps learn how to speak."

---

[58]*Ausgewählte ballette Stuttgarter Meister,* pp. 245–96.
[59]Michael Kelly, *Reminiscences,* 2 vols. (London, 1826; reprint New York, 1968), 2: 34–36.

FIGURE 5.7. Anonymous portrait of Jean-Georges Noverre.

Ballets by Noverre continued on the stage in many cities into the nineteenth century. Following an 1803 performance of *Médée* in Saint Petersburg directed by his pupil Le Picq, Emperor Alexander I commanded the printing of the *Lettres* in a new edition. Noverre sent a preface in which he reviews his career and states, "I have achieved a revolution in dancing, as striking and as lasting as that achieved by Gluck in the realm of music."

The Building of Mannheim

Heidelberg, long the residence of the Electors Palatine of the Rhine, was badly damaged by French armies in the late-seventeenth-century wars. Elector Johann

Wilhelm moved his residence to the castle at Düsseldorf on the lower Rhine, capital of the duchies of Berg and Jüllich, which were also family possessions. At his
death in 1716, his brother and heir, Elector Carl Philipp, moved the government
back to Heidelberg. Religious quarrels among his subjects there decided him to
build a new city and palace at Mannheim, a small fortified market town strategically located at the confluence of the Neckar and Rhine rivers. When Carl Eugen
opted to leave Stuttgart for Ludwigsburg, he had a completed castle and surrounding town ready to receive him. Carl Philipp created a capital afresh. Under
his successor, Carl Theodore, it became a leading music center.

The new palace at Mannheim was mostly the work of French architects. Initial plans for it have been attributed to Louis Rémy de La Fosse. The first phase of
execution between 1720 and 1731 required the services of several other architects:
Johann Herwartel of Mainz, Jean-Louis de Froimont of Speyer, and Guillaume
Hauberat of Cologne, who had been a pupil of Robert de Cotte, French royal
architect. The opera house was the work of Alessandro Galli-Bibiena from 1737 to
1741. Nicolas de Pigage was responsible for most of the palace interiors, including the famous library, the pride and joy of Elector Carl Theodore.

An anonymous engraving of 1726 shows the shape the palace would eventually take (Figure 5.8). It bears the inscription "Edifice Jean Clemen de froimon." In
its size the palace rivaled Versailles, though its decorative style was plainer, more
Italian, and owed something to Johann Fischer von Erlach's designs for Schön-
brunn palace.[60] The creation of a *cour d'honneur* in front of the palace certainly
evokes Versailles. The 1726 engraving also shows the beginning of the city facing
the palace. It was designed on a gridiron pattern in the new way. William Penn
laid out Philadelphia similarly in 1681, as a gridiron about two miles long and one
mile wide. Saint Petersburg, founded in 1703, was planned along similar lines. The
ramparts behind the Mannheim palace apparently were to be planted with rows
of trees. Several open squares with verdure graced the town. Vauban-style fortifications ringed the entire city.

At the center of the new palace was a grand octagonal hall with a staircase
over two hundred feet in height leading to the Knight's Hall or Rittersaal that
overlooked the fortifications and the Rhine. A place for formal receptions and
masked balls during carnival season, the Rittersaal was also the site of the orchestral "academies" for which Mannheim's court music was to become most famous.
The palace suffered heavy damages in World War II. A point was made of quickly
restoring it to former glories. The great stairwell and Rittersaal now gleam once
again and are used for festive events at Mannheim University, to which the palace
has been assigned.

---

[60]Alastair Lang, "Central and Eastern Europe," in *Baroque and Rococo Architecture and Decoration,* ed.
Anthony Blunt (New York, 1978), pp. 276–77.

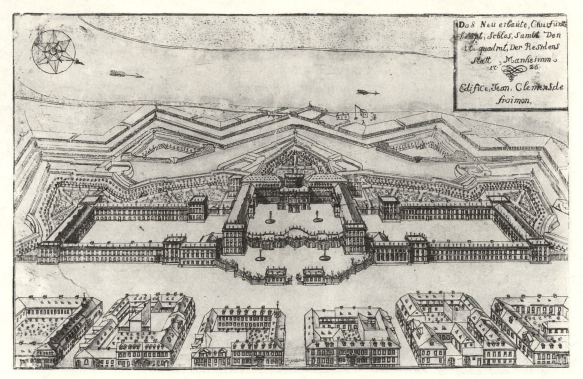

FIGURE 5.8. Jean Clemen de Froimon. Plan for the palace at Mannheim, 1726.

The opera house was installed in the wing of the palace the furthest to the right as depicted in the 1726 engraving. Adjoining it on the river side was the ball house. Following the fences from the two outer gate houses the eyes alight on the right upon the chapel, with its seven windows across, and on the left upon the similar building that housed the library, which also has seven windows across. Living quarters for the electoral family were mainly in the two central buildings on either side of the Rittersaal.

A palace the size of Mannheim's proclaimed Wittelsbach pride. Construction was hastened along by the elderly elector Carl Philipp, so that by 1741–42 he was able to receive as guests the two most potent princes of the Wittelsbach clan, his distant cousins Carl Albert, elector of Bavaria and emperor, and Carl Albert's younger brother Clemens August, archbishop and elector of Cologne. On 17 January 1742 Clemens August officiated in the court chapel at the wedding mass uniting Elizabeth Auguste, grandchild of Carl Philipp, to her cousin Carl Theodore. She was twenty-one, he was seventeen. It was actually a double wedding, for her younger sister Maria Anna at the same time married Duke Clemens of Bavaria. In political terms the various branches of the Wittelsbach house were being tied together, a move that had far-reaching consequences. The close alliance between Bavaria and the Rhenish Palatinate would eventually result in bringing both under the rule of Carl Theodore.

Besides sumptuous guest quarters and a finished chapel, Carl Philipp needed a finished opera house in early 1742. No dynastic event of the magnitude of these marriages could go uncelebrated by the performance of a new grand opera. On the day following the weddings the court and all its guests gathered in the opera house of Alessandro Galli-Bibiena to witness the first performance of *Meride,* with music by Kapellmeister Carlo Luigi Pietro Grua to a libretto by Giovanni Claudio Pasquini. Grua contributed another festive opera to the court with his setting of Metastasio's *La clemenza di Tito,* first performed on 17 January 1748, which was Elizabeth Auguste's birthday as well as her wedding day. She exercised great weight in artistic and even political matters in Mannheim. On this occasion it was her husband, Carl Theodore, who decided what to present as an anniversary offering. Librettos but no music survive for these two operas, thus the first chapter of Mannheim's operatic history is incomplete.

Burney, during his visit to Mannheim in July 1772, was impressed as much by the city as by the palace, although he was incorrect in saying that the government impinged so greatly on the town.

> The expense and magnificence of the court of this little city are prodigious; the palace and offices extend over almost half the town; and one half of the inhabitants, who are in office, prey on the other, who seem to be in the utmost indigence. . . .The town itself is more neat, beautiful, and regular, than any I had yet seen; its form is oval; the streets, like those of Lille, are *tirées au cordeau,* running in strait lines from one end to the other. It has a great number of squares; contains about 1548 houses; and, in the year 1766, its inhabitants amounted to 24190.

It is true that many servants of the court, including musicians, dancers, and actors, lived in the quarter nearest the palace, as was only practical since they were always on call to rehearse or perform. Burney may have assumed wrongly that they occupied government-owned quarters or "offices." He seems also to have exaggerated the indigence of the noncourt inhabitants.

Friedrich Jacobi called Mannheim a musician's paradise. The Mozarts certainly concurred, and their judgment had to do not just with the quality of the elector's musical establishment. It reflected the dignity and opportunities to rise in social standing that were accorded to musicians, many of whom were able to own their own houses, a quite rare phenomenon elsewhere. An expert on the subject recently concluded, "Obviously it was not only Mannheim's above-average remuneration of artists that attracted them, but also the conditions of civic

integration under which musicians gladly lived and worked, supported by a network of social relationships."[61]

Elector Carl Theodore

The Wittelsbach dynasty had several branches besides the main Bavarian and
Palatine ones. Moreover, there was more than one Palatinate. This term was used
to designate any state that was ruled by a count or duke palatine and derives from
palatini, attendants of the emperor in late Roman times. Besides the Rhenish
Palatinate there were parts of Bavaria and other lands north of the Danube River
known as the Upper Palatinate (Oberpfalz). *Pfalz* is the German term for palatinate, and *Kur* for electoral. Kurpfalz was the state ruled from Mannheim, Kurbay-
ern was that part of Bavaria ruled from Munich. Neuburg on the Danube was the
seat of the duchy of Pfalz-Neuburg. Pfalz-Sulzbach was a duchy east of Nuremberg that included the towns of Sulzbach and Weiden, near which Gluck was
born. Closely tied to the rulers in Mannheim were the Palatine dukes of
Zweibrücken, another branch of the Wittelsbachs.

Carl Theodore was the last surviving male from the house of Pfalz-Sulzbach.
His heritage was small compared to that of Carl Philipp, ruler of Pfalz-Neuberg,
of the duchies of Berg and Jüllich along the lower Rhine river, and of Kurpfalz.
When Carl Theodore was born in 1724 Carl Philipp was already sixty-three, and
despite three marriages, without male heir. Even when Carl Theodore was a small
child he was designated to succeed Carl Philipp. The marriage of state with Elizabeth Auguste, the elector's eldest granddaughter, was planned as early as 1733.

Carl Theodore himself was the issue of a political marriage, one arranged by
Carl Philipp. His father, Johann Christian, was born in 1700. His mother came
from the high French and Flemish nobility. She was born Duchess Marie Henriette of Arenberg and Aerschott (near Louvain), and she inherited the marquisate
of Bergen op Zoom. Her father was a count from the ancient French family of La
Tour d'Auvergne. She married Johann Christian in 1722 and gave birth to Carl
Theodore on 11 December 1724 in a chateau near Brussels. The child's mother
died when he was four, bequeathing him his first title, marquis of Bergen op
Zoom.

The future elector was raised as a French prince. Taught mainly by Jesuits, he
learned Latin. He began to learn German at age seven when he was taken by his

---

[61]Gabrielle Busch-Salmen, " . . . 'Auch unter dem Tache die feinsten Wohnungen': Neue Dokumente zu
Socialstatus und Wohnsituation der Mannheimer Hofmusiker," in *Die Mannheimer Hofkappele im Zeitalter
Carl Theodors,* ed. Ludwig Finscher (Mannheim, 1992), pp. 21–35; 35. The quotation in her title stems from
a letter of Leopold Mozart dated Mannheim, 3 August 1763.

father to Sulzbach. In 1732 Johann Christian succeeded his father as ruler of the duchy, but he lived only one year more. Thus Carl Theodore, at age eight, became duke of Pfalz-Sulzbach. Carl Philipp became the boy's guardian. There was a contingency plan put in place to assure that, should the elector die before his ward's maturity, the guardianship would devolve upon one of the princes of the Bavarian house. Carl Theodore showed an aptitude for study that prompted the elector to send him back to the Low Countries in 1738–40 for study at two famous universities, the Protestant University of Leiden and the Catholic University of Louvain.[62] As the young duke would eventually rule people of both confessions, it was thought appropriate that he study law, finance, and letters at both, a quite enlightened viewpoint for the time. There were plans to finish his education by sending him on the Grand Tour. But Carl Philipp, who turned eighty in 1741, pressed ahead with the more important plan, scheduling the marriage to occur during the coronation festivities at Frankfurt for the Wittelsbach emperor and the visit of the elector of Cologne. On 16 June 1742 Carl Theodore was declared to have reached his majority by Emperor Charles VII. The newly wed pair traveled to Sulzbach during this summer to receive the homage of their subjects there. Back in Mannheim, Carl Theodore turned eighteen on 11 December 1742. Three weeks later, on 31 December or 1 January, Carl Philipp died.

With the extinction of the senior family line, the junior line of Sulzbach assumed leadership, headed by Carl Theodore. Although females could not inherit in most of Germany, the young elector's claims to several thrones were greatly strengthened by his marriage to the eldest grandchild of his predecessor. Strengthening his legitimacy was vital because of the greed of the great powers. Frederick of Prussia coveted the duchies of Jüllich and Berg. Eventually the Habsburgs set their sights on Pfalz-Neuburg and Pfalz-Sulzbach. Another great power, France, loomed ominously on the very borders of Kurpfalz. As head of six separate states (including Bergen op Zoom), all with different administrations, the young ruler could have had little time to pursue music, art, letters, and science, to all of which he was attracted. One of his first acts was to begin the castle and park at Schwetzingen near Mannheim in 1743. In 1744 on 29 April he received the homage of the citizens of Mannheim, not in the palace, but in the large market square (Figure 5.9). It has been suggested that he did not do so earlier because of the volatile and perilous political climate created by the War of the Austrian Succession.[63]

---

[62]On the youth's education see Hans Rall, *Kurfürst Karl Theodor: Regierender Herr in sieben Ländern* (Mannheim, 1993), pp. 12–13.

[63]Hermann Weber, *Die Politik des Kurfürsten Karl Theodor von der Pfalz während des österreichischen Erfolgekrieges (1742–1748)* (Bonn, 1956), p. 30. Maria Theresa scornfully refused to accredit an embassy from Carl Theodore in 1743 and demanded that he withdraw from alliance with Bavaria.

FIGURE 5.9. Klauber. Market square in Mannheim.

Wittelsbach power peaked with the coronation of Charles Albert as Emperor Charles VII in February 1742. At this time Frederick withdrew from the alliance against Maria Theresa, whose armies drove the French and Bavarians out of Bohemia, where Charles Albert had been crowned king, and then began driving their opponents out of Bavaria itself. Charles VII in Frankfurt became an emperor in exile as opposing armies ebbed back and forth across the plains of the Danube valley, laying waste his own country. His fortunes improved in 1744 when he was able to reenter Munich, but then the unfortunate emperor died unexpectedly in January 1745. His son and successor, Maximilian III Joseph, declined to pursue any imperial claims and agreed to support the candidacy of Francis Stephen of Lorraine, Maria Theresa's husband, in exchange for a guarantee securing his hereditary states.

Elector Clemens August of Cologne did not attend the imperial election in Frankfurt in 1745. His vote, along with that of the elector of Bavaria, went, as promised, to Francis Stephen. Two other electors neither attended nor voted:

Frederick and Carl Theodore. The latter managed to steer a course of neutrality in dangerous waters until the Peace of Aix-la-Chapelle ended the wars in 1748. In 1751 Carl Theodore began accepting subsidies from France. He was little interested in military matters and maintained a minimal army. An English diplomat wrote of him flatteringly: "Few living princes, with the exception of the king of Prussia, have educated themselves with more industry or with greater success. His knowledge from reading is extraordinary, and what he has learned from books is supplemented by travel and a keen insight into human behavior."[64]

Elizabeth Auguste was also well educated and well endowed with the qualities of a ruler. An experienced keyboard player, she lived in her own apartments separate from those of her husband, which was nothing unusual for princely marriages of the time. The longed-for heir failed to appear. An illegitimate son was fathered by Carl Theodore in 1750. There were additional natural children, born of various mistresses. History has blamed him for being solicitous of their welfare and granting them titles and benefices. After nearly two decades of marriage a son was born to Elizabeth Auguste on 28 June 1761. He died the following day.

The couple's happiest moments were spent in the summer residence at Schwetzingen, in parklike surroundings, to which a theater had been added so that no pleasures of the city, such as opera, had to be forgone. During the summer of 1753 the outside world came to visit this terrestrial paradise in the person of Voltaire, who had fled Berlin after a stormy two years at Frederick's court. Frederick was incensed that the philosopher had taken with him a copy of the private edition of the king's poems, which Voltaire had labored to improve, and claimed as a gift from the king.

Voltaire arrived at Frankfurt, a free imperial city, on 31 May 1753. Frederick ordered his resident minister there to seize the contested book and some royal honors that had been bestowed on Voltaire. The Prussian underlings went further by incarcerating Voltaire and seizing all his money and jewels. Then they compounded the outrage by doing the same to Voltaire's niece, Madame Denis, who came to his rescue. Frederick refused to disavow the brutal actions of his underlings, which revealed him to all the world for what he was. Emperor Francis was no help in the affair. The city council of Frankfurt, terrified of Frederick, finally set Voltaire free on 7 July. He crossed the Rhine and stopped at Mainz to recuperate from his many ailments. His pen never flagged in defense of himself and his niece. After Mainz he traveled to Mannheim. In his letter to Madame Denis in Paris dated Schwetzingen 3 August, Voltaire says that he wanted to thank the elector in person for the part that Carl Theodore and his ministers played in setting them free.

[64]Rall, *Kürfurst Karl Theodor*, p. 59.

C'étoit un devoir indispensable pour moi de faire ma cour à leurs altesses électorales, et les remercier des bontés extrêmes dont elles m'ont honorés. Je suis actuellement dans la maison de plaisance de monseigneur l'électeur palatin. Il ne manque que de la santé pour y jouir de tous les plaisirs qu'on y goûte. Comédie française, comédie italienne, grand opéra italien, opera buffa, ballets, grande chère, conversation, politesse, grandeur, simplicité, voilà que c'est la cour de Manheim. Je sens que je serais enchanté si je me portais bien, et si les agréments de cette cour ne perdaient dans mon coeur beaucoup de leur prix par l'impatience et le besoin que j'ai de me rejoindre à vous.[65]

Holzbauer's *favola pastorale* on an old text by Carlo Sigismondo Capace, *Il figlio delle selve,* was given its first performance at Schwetzingen on 15 June 1753. It is probably the "grand opera" that Voltaire heard there. Holzbauer wrote at least three more operas for Schwetzingen up to 1756. Unlike the case of *Il figlio delle selve* the music is lost or survives in only a few arias.

Voltaire remained for two weeks in Schwetzingen where the French troupe gave his plays *Zaïre, Alzire,* and *Nanine* to honor him. His relations with the ruling pair were cordial and he was urged to return, which he did for another visit in July 1758. Meanwhile, he and the elector had struck up a correspondence. Carl Theodore patronized many endeavors besides music. In 1756 he invited Paul Hannong of Strasbourg to start a porcelain factory in Frankenthal, across the Rhine from Mannheim. Hannong had been trained at the royal French factory, which moved from Vincennes to Sèvres in 1756. Carl Theodore bought the Frankenthal factory outright in 1762. Its products ranked among the best of their kind in Germany and were marked with the elector's monogram "C T." This china came along at a time when the most famous German factory, that at Meissen established by Augustus the Strong in 1710, no longer functioned because Frederick, in an act of spite during the war, had completely sacked it. As in music, Saxony's desolation was followed by Mannheim's good fortune.

Elizabeth Auguste took special interest in the ballet. She went so far as to lure two French dancers away from the closely allied court of Clemens August, offering them higher salaries.[66] This did not sit at all well with the venerable elector of Cologne, who remonstrated with Carl Theodore when they met in Munich in January 1755 that he expected greater consideration, and that wives should be kept in line. Clemens August was still complaining a year later when he received the visit of the electoral pair to his residence in Bonn. Elizabeth Auguste held her ground and the incident eventually passed. It was a matter of some importance

---

[65]Voltaire (François Marie Arouet), *Voltaire's Correspondence,* ed. Theodore Besterman, 150 vols. (Geneva, 1953–1965), 23: 119–20.
[66]Rall, *Kürfurst Karl Theodor,* p. 52.

for artistic matters at Mannheim because one of the dancers, André Bouqueton, became the court's ballet master.

The Wittelsbachs made frequent visits to each other's courts. From January to April 1752 Carl Theodore and Clemens August were in Munich visiting Maximilian III Joseph. On this occasion Clemens August played first viola da gamba in a trio, Carl Theodore played second viola da gamba, and Maximilian played "Basselet" (an instrument somewhere between a cello and a contrebass).[67] Carl Theodore was mainly a flute player and is so depicted in some of his portraits. Burney calls him "a very good performer on the German flute, and [one] who can, occasionally, play his part upon the violoncello."

In appearance Carl Theodore was no match for the well-proportioned and strikingly handsome Carl Eugen. He was short instead of tall, his visage was rather round with pronounced eyebrows, long nose, small mouth, and weak chin. Portrait artists were hard pressed to give him a noble look in spite of all his finery. His wife looked more noble in her portraits. Carl Theodore was also swarthy of complexion according to James Boswell, whose account of his unhappy visit to Mannheim in 1764 is offered in the Appendix.

Other visitors to Mannheim were more generous to Carl Theodore than Boswell and took pains to visit his library and his excellent natural history collection. He opened the library to the public in 1763, the same year that he founded an academy of drawing and of sculpture. Goethe was one visitor who declared himself impressed by how much the elector had done for the arts and sciences. In 1766 Carl Theodore issued an edict of religious toleration, anticipating Joseph II's edict in Vienna by fifteen years.

A turning point in the court's theatrical life was Carl Theodore's dismissal of the French players in 1770, over the objections of his wife, who henceforth refused to take part in running the theaters and who in any case lived much of the year in her country retreat at Oggersheim across the Rhine. Count Andreas von Riaucour, ambassador from Dresden, reported to his court in a dispatch dated Mannheim 27 October 1770 that the elector was about to give notice to the French players. "One does not believe that the Electress, who only recently resigned from the direction of spectacles, concurs in this decision."[68]

Elizabeth Auguste as director of the theaters opens a new perspective on this unhappy princess. It lends more meaning to the mentions of "given by order of the Electress" on many printed librettos. She also took particular singers under her

[67]Thomas Anton Henseler, "Musik und Theater unter Clemens August," in *Kurfürst Clemens August, Landeherr und Mäzen des 18. Jahrhunderts,* Austellung in Schloss Augustusburg zu Brühl 1961 (Cologne, 1961), pp. 92–98.

[68]Quoted in the original French in Paul Corneilson, "Opera at Mannheim, 1770–1778" (Ph.D. diss., University of North Carolina, 1992), pp. 373–74.

protection. Similarly to the unfortunate duchess of Württemberg in the case of that court's prima donna, her favorite was prima donna Dorothea Wendling, a favor that extended to Dorothea's beautiful young daughter named—what else?—Elizabeth Auguste. This Elizabeth was eighteen when she caught the eye of the elector, whose previous mistress was the defunct Josepha Seyffert, a dancer in the court ballet for whom he had arranged a marriage with Count Heydeck. Riaucour reported to Dresden on the situation in his letter dated Schwetzingen, 14 July 1772.

> One noted that Madame Electress was not too gay during the spectacle [Sacchini's *Isola d'amore*], and alleged the reason to be that the Elector has chosen young Wendling in place of his deceased mistress named Seyffert. The Electress has always been particularly good to this young person, and above all to her mother, the prima donna, who played a specific role in this sordid drama. As the latter is an intriguer, it is greatly feared that she will gain ascendance over the Elector. . . . He continues to support the extraordinary expenditures his wife makes at Oggersheim and still pays her the respect she is due, at least outwardly. But inwardly she is chagrined and does not hide this from her confidantes."[69]

The liaison did not last many months before the elector moved on to his next mistress. Life at court evidently offered intrigues quite like those in operas and plays.

Schubart visited Mannheim in the summer of 1773 and formed a favorable impression of the elector. He was summoned to Schwetzingen, a command he was delighted to receive, inasmuch as it was difficult, he says, to get a hearing from Carl Theodore. He found the prince attended by a few nobles and some court musicians in his Badhaus, which he described as a small but uncommonly tasteful building in the Schwetzingen garden.

> He had deposed almost all splendor—the suspicious glance of majesty, as Klopstock puts it. He seemed only a good man and a likable member of society. His friendly glance, which he beamed on stranger and subject alike, softens his fearsome power and presence. One almost forgot, in seeing his smiling countenance, the glittering star on his chest that proclaimed his princely greatness. He received me so cordially that my usual bashfulness changed into candour.[70]

It was as an eminent musician that Schubart was thus honored, and he leaves the impression that the elector received all accomplished visitors with comparable warmth.

---

[69]Corneilson, "Opera at Mannheim, 1770–1778," p. 378.
[70]Schubart, *Leben und Gesinnungen*, 1: 208–9.

Stamitz: Life of a Virtuoso Violinist

Johann Stamitz was baptized on 19 June 1717 in Německý Brod (Deutschbrod), a town some forty miles east of Prague. His mother Rozyna was the daughter of a lawyer and town councillor. His father Antonín was organist of the dean's church and later rose to prominence as a merchant, landowner, and town councillor. Johann was one of eleven children, four of whom died in infancy. He was the third born and first to survive. Antonín was probably his first music teacher. Burney stresses the musical training of the schools of Bohemia and credits the local one for the boy's success.

> In these common country schools now and then a great genius appears as was the case at Teuchenbrod, the birth-place of the famous Stamitz. His father was *cantor* of the church in that town; and Stamitz, who was afterwards so eminent, both as a composer and performer, was brought up in the common school, among children of common talents, who lived and died unnoticed; but he, like another Shakespeare, broke through all difficulties and discouragements; and, as the eye of one pervaded all nature, the other, without quitting nature, pushed art further than any one had done before him; his genius was truly original, bold, and nervous; invention, fire, and contrast, in the quick movements; a tender, graceful, and insinuating melody, in the slow; together with the ingenuity and richness of the accompaniments, characterise his productions; all replete with great effects, produced by an enthusiasm of genius; refined, but not repressed by cultivation.

Clearly Burney was reacting to the great leap forward represented by the symphonies of Stamitz, although he does not neglect to mention his eminence as a performer (on violin and other stringed instruments). The passage quoted occurs in the second volume of his *German Tour*, where he describes his visit to Bohemia. In volume one, describing his visit to Mannheim, he wrote of "the late celebrated Stamitz, from whose fire and genius the present style of *Sinfonia,* so full of great effects, of light and shade, was in considerable degree derived."

In 1728 Stamitz entered the Jesuit gymnasium in Jihlava (Mahler's later home as a boy) where he remained for six years. The Jesuits put strong emphasis on developing musical skills wherever they taught. In 1734 the young musician, aged seventeen, enrolled in the Faculty of Philosophy at Prague University, just as Gluck, three years older, had done at seventeen. Neither Gluck nor Stamitz remained long at the university. Around the age of twenty in 1734 or 1735 Gluck sought his fortune in Vienna, as another Bohemian musician destined for fame, Franz Benda, had done before him. Did Stamitz also seek his fortune in Vienna at some time in the second half of the 1730s? The temptation is strong to believe that he did, although no evidence has yet emerged. For a Bohemian youth, Vienna was the logical place to finish perfecting one's performing skills, to hear the greatest music and performers, and to find wealthy patrons.

Stamitz's mother died in early 1735. When his father died thirty years later a memorandum of the mayor and town council of Německý Brod stated that "Johann Stamitz had sought, but could not find, an appropriate salaried position as a virtuoso musician in Bohemia, and for this reason emigrated to the Palatinate."[71] This may well be true and even seems to be confirmed by Burney's reference to "difficulties and discouragements." But it also sounds oversimplified as well as a trifle provincial, as if the local officials believed the world revolved around their little town and a reason had to be found for losing a famous son. Mannheim was a great distance from Německý Brod in all senses at that time, and it is difficult to believe that a musician could have made the transfer in one jump.

The political situation in 1740–41 may help explain what really took place. Frederick began the War of the Austrian Succession in 1740 by seizing Silesia. Elector Charles Albert of Bavaria joined with France in attacking Austria and Bohemia. They succeeded in capturing Prague, where Charles Albert was crowned king of Bohemia in 1741. This affront to Maria Theresa was just a prelude to the main goal of Charles Albert, his coronation as Holy Roman Emperor Charles VII in succession to her father, Charles VI. The imperial election began in Frankfurt on 20 November 1741, with electors gathering in the large house called the Römer, near the cathedral. Charles Albert attended the wedding of Carl Theodore in Mannheim in mid-January 1742, then on 31 January made his entry into Frankfurt. He was crowned emperor on 12 February. The ceremonies continued with the coronation of his wife as empress. Stamitz was apparently one of many musicians attracted to Frankfurt for the festivities, and he may well have come from Bohemia in the suite of Charles Albert. A notice dated 26 June 1742 alerted music lovers that the "famous virtuoso Stamitz would give a concert on the 29th in the Scherffschen Saal that would include a concerto with two orchestras newly composed by him and at which he would perform solos on various instruments such as the violin, the viola d'amore, the cello, and the contrebass."[72] Carl Philipp was in Frankfurt the same summer to celebrate the emperor's birthday. Stamitz, "famous virtuoso," was perhaps already in his service.

Stamitz does not appear in the court lists at Mannheim until 1743, when he was given an increase of salary of 200 gulden by decree of 17 June and styled as "Erster Hoff Violinist."[73] In 1744–45 his salary rose to 900 gulden, higher than that of any other instrument player at the court. Only the Kapellmeister, Carlo Grua,

[71]Eugene K. Wolf, *The Symphonies of Johann Stamitz: A Study in the Formation of the Classic Style* (Utrecht, 1981), pp. 13–14.

[72]Carl Israël, *Frankfurter Concert-Chronik von 1713–1780* (Frankfurt, 1876), p. 32, cited after Wolf, *The Symphonies of Johann Stamitz*, p. 19, n. 27.

[73]Wolf, *The Symphonies of Johann Stamitz*, p. 14. All subsequent biographical information comes from Wolf.

at an annual salary of 1,000 gulden, was paid more. By 1745 or 1746 Stamitz was given the title of *Concertmeister.* Then in February 1748 he received the offer from Stuttgart for a salary of 1,500 gulden, to which he replied with further demands and conditions, saying that "a beneficent court like Mannheim would not be easy to leave."[74] In support of negotiating his position he claimed that he had been "leading the direction of the entire electoral music to the complete satisfaction of his Highness going into his eighth year." If this statement is exact, it would mean that he was hired in 1741. He may well have exaggerated here, as he did in the matter of directing "the entire electoral music," for Grua as Kapellmeister was responsible for church music and opera. What Stamitz wanted was a post that gave him independence and absolute authority over instrumental music. He got this at Mannheim, perhaps with some help along the way from Stuttgart's competing offer. In the court calendar of 1755 the composer is called Instrumental-Music-Director and is listed alone below the two Kapellmeisters, Grua for church music and Holzbauer for opera, and above the two concertmasters. Here is more evidence that concerts were on a par in importance with other kinds of performance at Mannheim.

On 1 July 1744, a year or two after entering the service of the Palatine elector, Stamitz married Maria Antonia Lüneborn, who may have descended from one of the Tyrolean families that came west with Elector Carl Philipp in 1716. From their union were born Carl Philipp in 1745, Maria Franziska in 1746, and Anton Thadäus in 1750, as well as two children who died in infancy. Husband and wife traveled to Německý Brod in 1749 in order to witness the installation of Johann's younger brother Antonín Tadeás as dean of the main church, at which their father was organist. Another brother, Václav Jan, visited Mannheim the same year. Johann returned to Mannheim in March 1750 accompanied by his brother Antonín while his wife remained behind, giving birth to Antonín's namesake in November. Possibly Johann recruited further Bohemian musicians for the Mannheim orchestra on this trip.

Stamitz's spreading fame is manifest from the performance of a symphony by him with horns, trumpets, and timpani to open the Concert Spirituel in Paris on 12 April 1751.[75] On the same concert the audience heard a flute concerto composed and performed by Mannheim's premier flautist, Johann Baptist Wendling, who surely was the agent by which Stamitz's symphonic score or parts reached Paris. The following spring both Wendling and his then new wife, the soprano Dorothea Spurni from Stuttgart, appeared at the Concert Spirituel of 27 March. Not long after, Stamitz himself followed the trail that led to the French metropolis and handsome monetary rewards.

[74]Wolf, "Driving a Hard Bargain: Johann Stamitz's Correspondence with Stuttgart (1748)," 1553–69; 1565.
[75]Pierre, *Histoire du Concert Spirituel,* no. 436. The chief candidates for this symphony are D-8 and D-11 in Wolf's *Thematic Catalogue.*

In the summer of 1754 Stamitz arrived in Paris. He came perhaps at the invitation of Alexandre Jean Joseph Le Riche de La Pouplinière, who installed the composer in his chateau in Passy, then a suburb, and made him the leader of his private orchestra, of which François-Joseph Gossec was a member and Jean-Philippe Rameau the previous director. According to a memoir written much later by a nephew of La Pouplinière, Stamitz's duties included composing dance music; specific mention is made of horns and clarinets, and of "Menuets, Contredanses, and Allemandes or what we now call Waltzes."[76]

The Concert Spirituel of 8 September 1754 opened with a symphony by Stamitz, described as "nouvelle," that included horns and oboes. On the same program the composer played the solo in one of his violin concertos and executed a sonata for viola d'amore of his composition. As in 1742 he called attention to himself as a virtuoso performer. At the Concert Italien where he also appeared he won praise for both his compositions and his violin playing.[77] On 26 March 1755 the Concert Spirituel offered a symphony of his composition with horns and clarinets that was repeated the next day. On 4 August a mass of his was performed in the Jacobin's church, an event for which tickets could be purchased. The work is believed to be the Mass in D written for Mannheim.

Parisian music publishing, then in a flourishing state, beckoned as another avenue to fame and perhaps to fortune. Stamitz applied for a royal privilege to protect his rights and on 29 August 1755 received a decree that allowed him to publish "de la musique instrumentale de sa composition" for ten years. The first fruit of his labors to appear under this privilege were six orchestral trios, Op. 1, published under the title *Six sonates à trois parties concertantes qui sont faites pour Exécuter ou à trois, ou avec toutes l'orchestre* (Figure 5.10). Stamitz dedicated the set to his pupil Thomas Erskine, Lord Pittenweem (later earl of Kelly), who became a published composer in his own right. Mademoiselle Vendôme was responsible for the engraving, also for selling copies in her shop. The somewhat mysterious initial address, "A Paris chez l'auteur, rue St. Jacques chez Mlle. Vendôme," means that he was the publisher and she the agent for selling the copies belonging to him. Two other merchants' addresses appear below hers. Stamitz's title is printed as "Directeur de la Musique de S. A, S^me Monseigneur l'Electeur Palatin," which is misleading since it omits "Instrumentale." The trios have many traits in common with the late symphonies of Stamitz and may well have been written in Paris specifically for publication.[78] Such trios were quite at home there.[79]

Stamitz returned to Mannheim in the late summer or autumn of 1755. His

[76]Georges Cucuel, *La Pouplinière et la musique de chambre au xviiie siècle* (Paris, 1913), pp. 192–96. The memoir was written in 1808. It mistakes the year of Stamitz's visit as 1753.

[77]Wolf, *The Symphonies of Johann Stamitz*, p. 21, n. 59.

[78]Eugene K. Wolf, "The Orchestral Trios, Op. 1, of Johann Stamitz," in *Music in the Classic Period: Essays in Honor of Barry S. Brook*, ed. Allan W. Atlas (New York, 1985), pp. 297–322.

[79]Hubert Unverricht, *Geschichte des Streichtrio* (Tutzing, 1969), pp. 108–15.

symphonies remained in great demand in Paris, where the active music publishing industry was about to release a flood of them. The *Mercure de France* for March 1757 announced that six new symphonies of his composition had just been published as his Op. 2. He reaped little or no reward from these and many other subsequent publications because he died in Mannheim at the end of March 1757, just short of completing his fortieth year. His widow and three children may or may not have benefited from the flurry of publications that made his works famous throughout Europe. Christian Cannabich, his former pupil, replaced him at the head of the Mannheim orchestra in 1758.

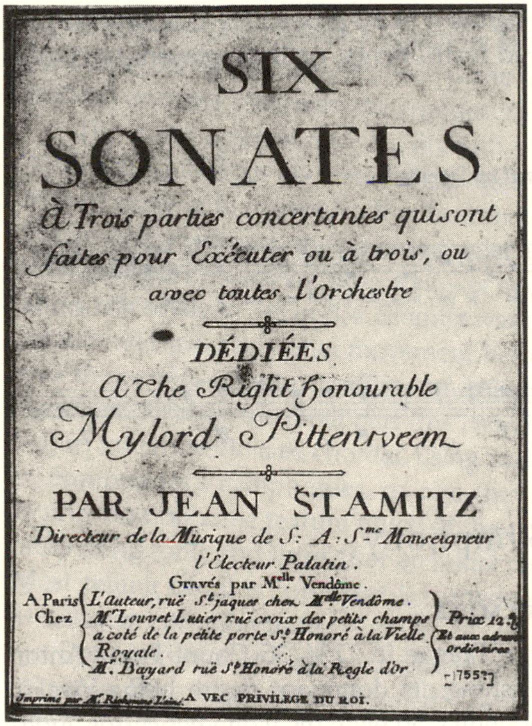

FIGURE 5.10. Title page of Stamitz's trio symphonies.

Bohemia was not forgotten in the bloom of Stamitz's European fame. There were many Bohemian musicians in his orchestra at Mannheim: whole families of hornists (Mastuska, Swoboda, and Ziwiny), of trumpeters (Stulick and Tuzeck), and of woodwind players (Ritter).[80] He may well have been responsible for hiring some of these. His *Sinfonia pastorale* in D (D-4) testifies to another kind of link with the Bohemian past.[81] It is a very late work that is saturated with the closing strain of a Bohemian Christmas carol. The pastorella tradition, particularly cultivated in Bohemia, encouraged some musical or dramatic expression of the Nativity scene to demonstrate the Christmas Eve Gospel. Stamitz's symphony may have sounded in the court chapel at Mannheim on Christmas Eve 1755 or 1756. The *Presto* first movement is unusual in that it opens softly with a passage that is like a long, slow curtain sweeping open, with the bass twice descending an octave from D to D against a constant pedal D in the first violins. Then the theme appears in m. 9 using a motif from the climactic

[80]Roland Würtz, "Die Organisation der Mannheimer Hofkapelle," in *Die Mannheimer Hofkapelle im Zeitalter Carl Theodors*, pp. 37–48; 38.

[81]Johann Stamitz, *Sinfonie Pastorale D-Dur*, ed. Walter Upmeyr (Berlin, 1931). One manuscript source described in Wolf, *The Symphonies of Johann Stamitz*, p. 400, listed both clarinets and oboes on the title page.

tremolos, often over long pedal harmonies. Chords change normally by the measure instead of the half-measure. Phrases are more melodic and regularly double in size with respect to the early works, a process also found in Wagenseil around 1750.[85]

Stamitz's fame rests principally on the handful of symphonies, only nine in number, that are attributed to his last four years; that is to say, the time just before his trip to Paris in 1754–55, the Paris stay, and the last months in Mannheim. To these symphonic masterpieces should be added the stylistically similar orchestral trios of Op. 1. These works confirm the tendencies noted in his middle period and bring them to culmination. They constitute his best-known works, both at the time, and since their modern revival in editions and recordings. In printing a selection of them in 1758 in a collection subtitled "La Melodia Germanica," the publisher Venier claimed, with some justification, "les Simphonies de Stamitz de Cet OEuvre sont les dernieres, et les meilleures que ce Célébre Auteur a Composé." Clarinets appear in them as a possible replacement for oboes. *Crescendo* passages are not used with consistency until these late works, and they appear both in first and last movements (of which three are in 6/8 meter). In first movements the norm is three *crescendo* passages, distributed as follows: near the beginning of the prima parte, near the beginning of the seconda parte (in V), and near its ending (in I). These passages have taken on a life of their own, like themes that one wants to hear again. Because of the expansion of the movement, due in part to the *crescendo* passages, repeat signs are eliminated. Expansion of another kind is represented by the clearly lyrical second themes, which lengthen to eight measures, or even sixteen (referred to as "a double period"). Cantabile traits become more prominent throughout the movement and not just in the second theme area. Texture becomes more variable, with less reliance on the drum bass in eighth notes, more reliance on orchestral unison passages, and a spirit of repartée between the strings and the winds.

The late symphonies by Stamitz are without equals in the 1750s. They may help explain why concerts came to play such a prominent role at the Mannheim court, sometimes taking place once or twice a week in the Rittersaal of the city palace, or at Schwetzingen during the summer. Even the famous Burgtheater concerts in Vienna were more restricted than this, being limited to certain holy days or seasons, and limited also by sharing a hall mostly used for stage works. Stuttgart had no parallel tradition of concerts and no locale particularly assigned to them. That Mannheim and Vienna did must have had something to do with the flourishing of the symphony in both. An orchestral-vocal concert, as elsewhere, began with a symphony and often ended with one. The more concerts there were, the more symphonies came to the fore.

[85]On Wagenseil's symphonies and keyboard sonatas, see *Haydn, Mozart,* pp. 97–108.

Burney very astutely divined the importance of concerts at Mannheim. He even ventured to credit Jommelli as the grandfather whose opera overtures sired the modern symphony as fashioned by Stamitz.

> But it has not been merely at the Elector's great opera that instrumental music has been so much cultivated and refined, but at his *concerts* [Burney's italics], where this extraordinary band has "ample room and verge enough," to display all its powers, and to produce great effects without the impropriety of destroying the greater and more delicate beauties, peculiar to vocal music; it was here that Stamitz, stimulated by the productions of Jommelli, first surpassed the bounds of common opera overtures, which had hitherto only served in the theatre as a kind of court cryer, with an "O Yes!" [oyez!] in order to awaken attention, and bespeak silence, at the entrance of the singers. Since the discovery which the genius of Stamitz first made, every effect has been tried which such an aggregate of sound can produce; it was here that the *Crescendo* and *Diminuendo* had birth; and the *Piano*, which was before chiefly used as an echo, with which it is generally synonimous, as well as the *Forte*, were found to be musical *colours* which had their *shades*, as much as red or blue in painting.[86]

Burney went on to express his disappointment that the oboes and bassoons started out too sharp the night he heard them in Schwetzingen, and proceeded to get sharper to the end of the opera.

Other commentators of the time have similar things to say about the *crescendo*, the origins of which they attribute to Jommelli. Reichardt in 1774 says he experienced the wonder of it at Mannheim. "They tell us that when Jommelli first introduced this in Rome, the auditors gradually rose from their seats during the *crescendo*, and only at the *diminuendo* noted that it had taken their breaths away. I myself have experienced this process at Mannheim."[87] Abbé Vogler, writing at Mannheim four years later credited Jommelli as inventor: "to him belong the thanks . . . for the waxing and waning of the parts and especially for the raging, fiery *crescendo*."[88] Schubart, an authority on all matters musical pertaining to Mannheim and Stuttgart, confirmed the point. "Jommelli also raised himself to the level of a musical inventor. . . . The more precise specifications of musical color and especially the overpowering *crescendo* and *decrescendo* are his!"[89] Certainly Jommelli was responsible for the spread of the *crescendo* north of the Alps, both by his widely diffused opera overtures and by his direct presence.

---

[86]Wolf, *The Symphonies of Johann Stamitz*, p. 288, n. 8, identifies the quotation "ample room and verge enough" as coming from Thomas Gray's *The Bard*. Burney's mention of Jommelli occurs only in the second (1775) edition of his *German Tour*.

[87]Johann Friedrich Reichardt, *Briefe eines aufmerksamen Reisenden die Musik betreffend*, 2 vols. (Frankfurt, 1774–76), 1: p. 11, n.

[88]Georg Joseph Vogler, *Betrachtungen der Mannheim Tonschule*, 4 vols., (Mannheim, 1778–81), 1: 162.

[89]Schubart, *Ideen zu einer Ästhetik der Tonkunst*, p. 47.

Jommelli himself was pursued by the Mannheim court. Short of obtaining him in person, Carl Theodore sought out his operatic scores for performance. In 1751 he wrote to Giovanni Coltrolini, his resident minister in Rome, instructing him to pay Jommelli 100 ducats for his score of *Artaserse.*[90] Coltrolini replied that he could have had the score cheaper the ordinary way, by relying on copyists who worked for the theater, to which the elector replied that he treasured Jommelli too highly to use this route. Jommelli's *Artaserse* was performed as the carnival opera at Mannheim in 1751. It was followed the same year on the elector's name day by Jommelli's setting of Verazi's *Ifigenia in Aulide,* which had had its premiere at Rome only seven months earlier.

The late Symphony in D by Stamitz (D-2) shows that he too treasured Jommelli. It is one of those that begins with the call to order and to silence by stern unisons, *forte,* immediately followed by a contrasting passage of softer and more playful character. Jommelli does this in his overture to *Ipermestra* (Spoleto, 1751), then repeats the opening verbatim (Example 5.10a). Stamitz follows a similar procedure (Example 5.10b). Where the Italian is happy with his three-measure phrases (1 + 2), a module very common in arias written on certain verse types, the Bohemian opts for the 2 + 2 phraseology that is characteristic of most dances. In both movements the opening is followed by a *crescendo* passage spanning several measures and climbing from the violin's low D to high D two octaves above, of which Stamitz's is given in illustration (Example 5.11). After fanfare figures rock-

EXAMPLE 5.10. *Symphonic incipits*

a. Jommelli, Overture to *Ipermestra* (1751)

b. Stamitz, Symphony in D (D-2), I

---

[90]Adolf Sandberger, "Aus der Korrespondenz des pfalzbayerischen Kurfürsten Karl Theodor mit seinem römischen Ministerresidenten," in *Ausgewahlte Aufsätze zur Musikwissenschaft,* 2 vols. (Munich, 1921), 1: 218–23.

EXAMPLE 5.11. *Stamitz, Symphony in D (D-2), I*

ing back and forth between D and A, Stamitz settles on A, which gives way to a *piano* theme for strings alone. Here the inspiration was the subsidiary theme of an overture to Jommelli's *Eumene* dating from 1742 but known to have been applauded in Paris in 1753–54 (Example 5.12ab).[91] The expressive leap downward of a melodic seventh was a favorite of Jommelli, and it is not difficult to understand why Stamitz was attracted to the passage, another winning feature of which was the smooth progression by the half-measure of the second violins and violas to a deceptive cadence on vi in support of the violin melody. Stamitz avoids the repetitiveness of the model by making the second half of the melody contrast

EXAMPLE 5.12. *Secondary themes*

a. Jommelli, Overture to *Eumene* (1742), I

b. Stamitz, Symphony in D (D-2), I

[91]Helmut Hell, *Die neapolitanische Opernsinfonie in der ersten Hälfte des 18. Jahrhunderts: N. Porpora, L. Vinci, G. B. Pergolesi, L. Leo, N. Jommelli* (Tutzing, 1971), p. 575.

with the first, its even eighth notes slurred in twos following nicely upon the big half-note syncopation of the first half. The singing character of this subsidiary theme is not affected by the change. The 4 + 4 plan of Jommelli's secondary theme was still quite novel in the early 1740s, although his mentor Leonardo Leo had used it before him.

Stamitz wanted still more lyric content in his movement, and so he opted for another subsidiary theme, this one expanded to 6 + 6 measures and sung by the woodwinds over minimal string accompaniment, a pedal A in which the horns softly join (Example 5.13). Only in the precadential measures do the strings and horns exert themselves to full harmonization. The *crescendo* passage comes back in V to begin the seconda parte. When the tonic returns to the opening unisoni statements of D, Stamitz resorts immediately to the first of his subsidiary themes (Example 5.12b) in I. Everything returns in due course, the *crescendo* passage in the tonic last of all. When the subsidiary lyric theme returns, now sung in tonic D, the horns support it as before for the first six measures, then on the repetition they reveal that they can also sing the melody when it is in the key to which they are tuned. This simple but marvelous fact of nature must have come as a revela-

EXAMPLE 5.13. *Stamitz, Symphony in D (D-2), I*

tion at the time. Stamitz was the symphonist who established the practice, which prevailed for as long as there were natural horns.

Symphony D-2 continues with an *Andante non Adagio* in 2/4 and in the key of A, for strings alone. The theme features an expressive appoggiatura of a rising major second in its very second measure, over subdominant harmony, answered by a more conventional rising minor second appoggiatura in the corresponding part of m. 4 (Example 5.14). The rising major second appoggiatura was regarded as less Italian than French, and was even proscribed in Italian recitative by some writers on the subject. The full orchestra returns for the earthy third movement, a minuet that is strangely labeled "Menuè." Sources for Stamitz's symphonies usually settle for "menuet," or their diminutives "menuetto" and "minuetto." The woodwinds come to the fore as soloists in the Trio.

EXAMPLE 5.14. *Stamitz, Symphony in D (D-2), II*

Each of the first three movements began with the rise of an octave. The finale *Prestissimo* in 2/4 follows suit. Further kinship with the first movement's beginning emerged with the finale's alternation of *forte* and *piano* at short range, and with the recurrence of the tones 3 - 2 - 1 (Example 5.15). There is more evidence still that Stamitz was linking the finale and first movement in an effort to unify the cycle in the last movement's subsidiary theme, for strings alone (Example 5.16). The basses drop out, leaving the accompaniment in smoothly moving long notes to the second violins and violas supporting a lively treble in the first violins with expressive melodic sighs. In this 8 + 8 period clinching reference back to the "Jommelli theme" of the first movement is the calm rise of the lowest part by step to the sixth degree, a deceptive cadence that makes us welcome hearing the theme again, ending with a regular cadence. It might be objected that this winning theme, because of its very fast tempo in 2/4 time, sounds more like 4 + 4 than 8 + 8. In another late symphony Stamitz created a subsidiary lyric theme that truly sounds like 8 + 8 in its phrasing.

EXAMPLE 5.15. *Stamitz, Symphony in D (D-2), IV*

The Symphony in E♭ (E♭-1) begins with an *Allegro assai* in common time, initiated by three hammerstroke chords, played in double stops by the violins in quarter notes, followed by a descent down the triad in eighth-note octave leaps (which only a well-disciplined orchestra could have negotiated without embarrassments). A long *crescendo* over a tonic pedal up to high E♭ follows eventually, succeeded by another, totally different kind of intensification that in five measures

EXAMPLE 5.16. *Stamitz, Symphony in D (D-2), IV*

takes the strings in unison from a *piano* low A♭ by chromatic degrees to a *fortissimo* F (V/V) nearly two octaves higher.[92] More than one kind of *crescendo* passage belonged to the composer's armory. The agitation created by the chromatic surge perhaps decided him to opt for an unusually broad subsidiary theme for winds, supported by all the strings in unisons and octaves (Example 5.17). The horns play a few sustained tones when the oboes (or clarinets) play the theme in B♭. When it is time for the theme to sound in the seconda parte, it is in tonic E♭. For the first eight measures the horns remain subservient, then upon its repetition the horns play most of it themselves. The innovation here seems even more striking than the theme's equivalent in Symphony D-2 (Example 5.13), partly because of the added breadth and partly because of the reduction of the strings to strict time beating in quarter notes, like the ticking of a clock.

The musical quality and orchestral ingenuity of Stamitz's late symphonies outstripped those of all other works in the genre composed in the mid-1750s, including those of Wagenseil for Vienna. These stunning works opened a path for others to follow. The consequences can be heard most directly in the younger generation of composers working in Mannheim and in Paris, particularly Gossec.

[92]Gossec, in the most Stamitz-like of his *Sei sinfonie a Più Stromenti* (Paris, 1756), Op. 3 No. 6 in D, deploys in the opening *Allegro* both a diatonic and a chromatic *crescendo,* in succession.

EXAMPLE 5.17. *Stamitz, Symphony in E♭ (E♭-1), I*

RICHTER AND HOLZBAUER

Not long after Stamitz became its concertmaster, the Palatine court appointed two established composers in the persons of Richter and Holzbauer. They were older than Stamitz but destined to long outlive him. All three, elder statesmen of what would come to be called the Mannheim school, hailed from Habsburg-ruled central Europe.

Franz Xaver Richter was born in 1709, in Holešov, Moravia, according to Gerber. He is said to have trained in Vienna, and perhaps he studied with Johann Joseph Fux, a connection that would help explain his lifelong commitment to counterpoint. In 1740 he became vice maestro di cappella of the prince-abbot of Kempton in southern Germany and also served in the Benedictine abbey of Ettal. He married at Kempton in 1743. In 1744 he enjoyed the distinction of having a set of symphonies for four-part strings published in Paris as *Six grandes symphonies.* One of these, available in modern edition, is a three-movement work in F consisting of an opening *Allegro* in cut time with a plethora of dotted rhythms and triplet figures that make a rather fussy effect, dissolving into a protracted circle-of-fifths sequence; an *Andante* in 3/4 and in the relative minor; and a *Presto* in 3/8 beginning with a six-measure opening theme sung by the violins in unison against the basses and violas in octaves.[93] The work, whatever its deficiencies, leaves no doubt that Richter was a mature composer who had formed his own style before he arrived in Mannheim.

Richter's name appears on the court list of 1747 as a bass singer (virtuoso da camera). According to printed librettos he sang the roles of Publio in Grua's *La clemenza di Tito* in 1748 and of Aminta in Galuppi's *L'Olimpiade* in 1749. His name appears in no further librettos, which suggests that his singing duties were confined thereafter to church music. In 1748 he composed the Lenten oratorio *La deposizione dalla croce* at Carl Theodore's request. Marpurg included him as a second violinist on his 1756 orchestra list for the court, but this function is not confirmed elsewhere. His writing for stringed instruments shows that he knew them well in any case. He received a further appointment, chamber composer, at some point in the 1760s, at which time he wrote *Harmonische Belehrungen,* a treatise on counterpoint after Fux and Meinrad Spiess that he dedicated to Carl Theodore.

Burney neglected to mention Richter in the Mannheim section of his *German Tour*, but he made up for the lack by devoting an entertaining page to him at the end of the second volume.

> M. Fr. Xav. Richter should have been distinguished among the musicians of Mannheim; his works, of various kinds, have great merit; the subjects are often new and noble; but his detail and manner of treating them is frequently dry and sterile, and he spins and repeats passages in different keys without end. The French and Italians have a term for this tediousness, which is wanting in our language, they call it *Rosalie,* or *Rosalia:* an Italian cries out, upon hearing a string of repetitions, either a

[93]Franz Xaver Richter, *Five Symphonies,* ed. Bertil H. van Boer (The Symphony, Series C, vol. XIV) (New York, 1985), Symphony No. 2 in F major. Symphony No. 1 in B♭ major, dated by the editor "before 1750," is a much less mature work. Its opening *Allegro* is rhythmically stiff, divided into brief two-measure segments, and lacks any sense of a continuous line. A crassly mechanical circle-of-fifths sequence takes over after the first modulation.

note higher, or a note lower, of the same passage or modulation, *ah, santa Rosalia!* Indeed this species of iteration indicates a want of invention in a composer, as much as stammering and hesitation imply want of wit or memory in a story-teller.

Burney explains in a footnote that the saint in question was remarkable for repeating her Paternoster or saying her rosary more frequently than even the most pious of worthies. Burney was rarely as negative as this about individual composers, and he may have tried to soften his criticism by adding "great" before "merit" with regard to Richter's works. What he heard as novel and "noble" is perhaps illustrated by the beginning of the Symphony in g, a work of the later 1760s that was offered for sale by Breitkopf in his Supplement of 1769 (Example 5.18).[94] Richter was fonder of the minor mode than other composers at Mannheim. The theme is stark and powerful. It is cogent as well, deriving its logic from the recurrence of the interval of the third, at first by step in eighth notes, then falling by

EXAMPLE 5.18. *Richter, Symphony in g, I*

skip in quarter notes in m. 2, by half notes in m. 3, and exploding up to the high tonic in quarter notes, which leads to a repetition of the whole. This is a sinfonia *à 8* in which two oboes and two horns join the strings. The oboes enter after the strings pause in the opening movement, not so much as to announce a secondary theme of their own, for the composer is unwilling to follow Stamitz so far in this direction, but to continue the discourse begun by the strings and provide it with a cadence. The movement is very broad, encompassing 253 measures, and has a clear double reprise in the second part. It is followed by an *Andantino grazioso* in 2/4 and in B♭. Then in conclusion comes the characteristic signature of this composer that makes him so unlike his younger colleagues at Mannheim, a finale entitled *Fugato,* in cut time and in g. Rarely did Richter follow Stamitz to the extent of including a minuet as a third movement in a four-movement symphony. When he did, he was likely to include some reminder of his contrapuntal acumen elsewhere in the same work, as if to say, "this far, but no further."

Another side of Richter's art emerged during his last years in Mannheim, evident in the set of six string quartets published in London in 1768.[95] The Quartet

---

[94]Modern edition in Richter, *Five Symphonies,* No. 3.
[95]Ed. Hugo Riemann in *Denkmäler der Tonkunst in Bayern,* Jg. XV (vol. 27) (1914). (Hereinafter in this volume, the abbreviation *DTB* will be used for this series.)

in C consists of three movements, an *Allegro con brio* in 3/4, an *Andante poco* in 3/4 in the key of F, and a finale, entitled *Rincontro (Presto)*, in cut time, a movement that alternates fugal and homophonic textures. Most impressive is the middle movement, showing how Richter was able to integrate imitative writing with a rich harmonic palette (Example 5.19). Particularly suave is the way the ii$^6_5$ chord in m. 2 becomes V$^6_5$/V with the chromatic rise of the bass. These sonorities sound quite Mozartian. So does the main idea, a slurred descending motive in dotted rhythm with multiple afterbeats that prefigure the "Idamante motif" in *Idomeneo*.

EXAMPLE 5.19. *Richter, String Quartet in C, II*

Richter's *Harmonische Belehrungen* was not printed, perhaps because he quit the electoral service in 1769, thereby forgoing what may have been a necessary source of subsidy with which to achieve publication. He assumed the position of Kapellmeister of Strasbourg cathedral in succession to Joseph Garnier, a post he occupied for twenty years until his death in 1789, in his eightieth year, and during which time he is thought to have composed a large part of his imposing body of works for the church. The treatise has a few passages on such modern genres as the trio sonata, concerto, sinfonia *à 4* (for strings) and *à 8* (for strings, two oboes, and two horns). Speaking of the opening *Allegro* movement he advises composers that, in the case of the last genre, they should not deploy several different themes because excessive length would result if they did.[96] He allows that the oboes can have pretty and short solos in both the first and second parts, in which case the violins and violas should accompany them softly and the bass should drop out of the texture. His own symphonies bear this out in that he favors

---

[96]Jochen Reutter, "Franz Xaver Richters Bemerkungen über das Komponieren einer Sinfonie in Kompositionstheorie und Kompositionspraxis," in *Mozart und Mannheim: Kongressbericht Mannheim 1991*, ed. Ludwig Finscher, Bärtel Pelker, and Jochen Reutter (Frankfurt, 1994), pp. 221–31.

giving the oboes short or partial secondary themes (at most of four bars) but nothing of the scope lavished upon them by Stamitz in his longer secondary themes for winds. Richter warns composers against reducing the sinfonia *à 4* main theme to a mere two-part texture, with the violins doubled in unison and viola col basso "as the present-day Italians make a habit of doing, as I can testify from the wretched and naked four-part writing in a dozen symphonies that have passed through my hands, pieces that should be condemned to perpetual incarceration." Perhaps he forgot that he used this very same reduced texture to open the finale *Presto* of his Symphony in F printed in 1744. Or perhaps he regarded the latter as a youthful indiscretion by his last decade in Mannheim. No other composers at Mannheim, with the exception of Vogler, put their ideas in prose. Richter deserves to be regarded as a Rhenish musical Nestor.

A portrait of the aged master leading his musicians in the cathedral was engraved at Strasbourg in 1785 (Figure 5.11). With dignified and care-worn features he faces ahead, his musicians behind him, as Rameau is depicted doing at Versailles in 1745. He beats the tactus with an upraised right arm holding a furled scroll of music. His large score contrasts with the small sheets used by the singing boys on the right and the mature performers on the left, one a violinist and one singing through his nose in the way then accepted for filling large spaces.

FIGURE 5.11. Christophe Guerin. Portrait of Franz Xaver Richter, 1785.

Mozart encountered Richter when he stopped at Strasbourg on his way back from Paris to Salzburg in the fall of 1778. In his letter dated Strasbourg 26 October 1778, he poked fun at Richter's consumption of wine in an attempt to amuse his father. He added in a postscript, "last Sunday in the cathedral I heard a mass newly composed by Richter that was charmingly written." Rarely did Mozart pay so high a compliment to anyone.

Ignaz Holzbauer was born in Vienna in 1711. As a youth he studied the *Gradus ad Parnassum* of Fux, whom he persuaded to look over his exercises. As Holzbauer tells it in his autobiography, Fux was satisfied with the work and urged the young composer to seek further study in Italy, which he did.[97] After a brief period in Venice in the mid-1730s he took a post in Moravia, where he met and married the soprano Rosalie Andreides (30 April 1737). They were based at Vienna in the 1740s and made several trips to Italy, where she sang on several stages. Holzbauer found a niche for himself in Vienna as a composer of ballet music, without being appointed to a high-level position in the imperial court music.[98] He provided the ballet music accompanying Hasse's *Ipermestra* (1749) and *Arminio* (1747). His appointment to Stuttgart in 1751, discussed earlier, was as Oberkapellmeister, overseeing both opera and the Catholic services. He was an experienced composer in many genres before his appointment to Mannheim two years later.

Holzbauer was a well-traveled, cosmopolitan figure. In 1756 he visited Rome and returned to Mannheim by way of Vienna, where he retained contacts. His symphonies were often performed in Burgtheater concerts and in 1761 his oratorio *La Betulia liberata* was heard there. After a visit to Turin in 1758 he returned by way of Paris so that he could attend the Opéra and the Concert Spirituel.

He may have composed as many as a hundred symphonies, only a small fraction of which are available for study. Comparisons with the symphonies of Stamitz or others are scarcely possible under such conditions. According to his autobiography Holzbauer composed many concertos, symphonies, and the like even before he joined the service of Count Rottal in Moravia during the 1730s. Those composed before 1750 have survived only sparsely, but they may have included some works of the Austrian-Bohemian Parthia type that contained a minuet as the third of four movements.[99] In other words, Holzbauer could have been a possible model for Stamitz in this regard, especially had they met in Moravia or in Vienna (if Stamitz went to Vienna). An early Symphony in d purportedly by Holzbauer bears on the manuscript parts some performance dates, the earliest of which is 1749.[100] It begins with an *Allegro* in 4/4 that is so stiff it suggests a beginner, with suspended basses, abundant sequences, and a clumsy facture that could hardly have inspired any other composer, least of all a Stamitz. The attribution to Holzbauer is probably a mistake. The symphony continues with an *Adagio,* amounting to a transition passage of a few chords, a dull *Fuga* (alla breve)

[97]The autobiographical sketch was written in 1782 and published in 1783. It is reprinted in the foreword of Holzbauer, *Günther von Schwarzburg*, 8: vi–vii.

[98]Gustav Zechmeister, *Die Wiener Theater nächst der Burg und nächst dem Kärntnerthor von 1747 bis 1776* (Vienna, 1971), pp. 205–6. He was paid 1,000 gulden for the 1748–49 season, during which Wagenseil received 1,650 gulden.

[99]Wolf, *The Symphonies of Johann Stamitz*, p. 88.

[100]Ignaz Holzbauer, *Three Symphonies*, ed. Richard J. Agee (The Symphony, Series C, vol. 5), (New York, 1983), No. 1. The preface gives an inaccurate précis of Holzbauer's autobiography.

in d, and a final *Allegro* in 3/8 in binary form, also in d. If the work is in fact by Holzbauer, it must be very early indeed.

Holzbauer's long association with Italian opera in Moravia, Vienna, and Italy itself prepared him well to adapt its type of overture to the purposes of the concert symphony. In addition he had the advantage over Stamitz of having worked directly with Hasse (in Vienna) and with operas by Hasse and Jommelli (in Vienna and Stuttgart). It stands to reason that he went through some of the same stages of assimilation and adaptation as did Stamitz with regard to the birth of concert symphonies.

However he arrived at his symphonic path, Holzbauer emerges as a modernist on a par with Stamitz in the collection *Six simphonies à quatre parties obligés avec cor de chasse ad libitum,* Op. 2, published by Huberti in Paris, with a privilege dated 1757. His outer movements use a wide range of dynamics in an essentially homophonic and thematic style. He favors sharply profiled secondary ideas as much as does Stamitz. The minuet as third movement of four has become his norm. The works underwent many reprintings, an indication that they were well received. Huberti's use of the designation "Opus 2" suggests that there may have been a previous publication of Holzbauer's symphonies.

An undated Op. 3 followed in Paris, *Six simphonies à huit parties obligés* published by Madame Berault, followed by Op. 4, *Trois simphonies à grand orchestre . . . dans lequel il y a La Tempête . . .* listed by Sieber. Breitkopf, in Supplement IV of 1769, included incipits of several symphonies from both publications. The Symphony in C (Op. 3 No. 1), a work with oboes and horns, begins with an *Allegro* in common time, both parts repeated, continues with an *Andante Spirituoso* 2/4 in c, also with repeats, a *Menuetto gratioso ma non troppo lento* in 3/4 that has no trio but seems to run on into a chaconne-like movement, concluded by a *Presto* in 3/8.[101] The first movement features long *crescendi* of the kind favored by Stamitz in his late symphonies and by his followers.

Holzbauer's best-known work in the genre is the Sinfonia *à 10* in $E^\flat$ scored for strings and pairs of oboes, horns, and bassoons, which became known as *La Tempesta.*[102] It opens with a broad theme sung by the violins in unison, against a rocking bass in eighth notes reinforced by the bassoons, while the rest of the orchestra sustains the harmonies (Example 5.20a). The rise of a conjunct fourth up to the high $A^\flat$ (x) makes this a fine example of a "singing *Allegro.*" The melodic cadence in m. 6 is undercut by the arrival of the bass at C for a restatement (x^1) of the rise and fall of the treble in mm. 3–4. A condensed repetition consisting of only the fall (m. 8) then leads not to a cadence on the tonic but to a half-cadence, *forte,* punctuated by dotted rhythm on the second beat, like a march. The new key

---

[101]Ibid., No. 2.
[102]Ed. Hugo Riemann in *DTB,* Jg. VII/2 (vol. 13) (1906).

EXAMPLE 5.20. *Holzbauer, Symphony in E♭* (La Tempesta), *I*

is reinforced in martial manner with this rhythm and with scales, *forte.* A new harmonic plane having been established, forcefully, as Stamitz did often in his late works, the way has been prepared for a contrasting secondary idea. With Stamitz, it would have introduced the most lyrical moment yet heard, and usually with timbral contrast. Holzbauer, having endowed his opening material with so much lyric content, has to depend heavily on the timbral contrast supporting the secondary idea (Example 5.20b). He does so by giving a saucy little repeated figure to the two bassoons, accompanying the singing violins. A tertiary idea soon follows in which the bassoons in thirds cavort at short range with the oboes in thirds. Concertante exchanges like this could well have prepared the way for Holzbauer's role as an early and perhaps seminal creator of the symphonie concertante. There follows a series of *forte* and *piano* contrasts reinforcing the key of B♭, with a *tutti fortissimo* and a repeat sign ending the prima parte. To scale down the seconda parte, which is longer (54–48 mm.), the composer touches briefly on the secondary idea, now in modulatory guise but unmistakable because of its texture and timbre, which leads quickly back to tonic E♭, ushered in by the tertiary idea, followed by a greatly abbreviated appearance of the opening material. He concludes with a rousing *crescendo* to *fortissimo.*

An *Adagio—Maestoso e Gratioso,* in common time and in the key of c, follows.

Frequent dotted rhythms, trills, and suspended dissonances, as well as the absence of much lyric content, lend this short movement the character of an introduction, as if leading up to a majestic speech by some exalted character (Neptune, perhaps?). In keeping with this the movement ends, after twenty measures, on its own dominant, like a preparation. Without ado the *Menuetto* in 3/4 restores the original keynote of E$^\flat$. Its trio is begun and largely dominated by the bassoons, along with the oboes. The finale, labeled "La Tempesta del mare," is in common time like the opening movement, with which it shares several features. Dynamic contrasts at short range, tremolos, and scales running rapidly up and down do their best to portray the storm and obviously were effective in making the work such a favorite that it was advertised on the title page of *Trois symphonies à grand orchestre*. The arresting feature that may be lost in all the churning is that Holzbauer has taken care to unite the first and last movements thematically, by making prominent use of the same rising conjunct fourth in the violins.

Stamitz, Richter, and Holzbauer form the first generation of Mannheim symphonists. Burney gave pride of place to Stamitz, although he took care to include Holzbauer as well, even naming him first, before mentioning the composers of the second generation, who were mainly pupils and followers of Stamitz. Richter is omitted from his summary, perhaps because he was too idiosyncratic to be classed in this way. Burney witnessed at first hand the emergence of Mannheim's symphonic eminence that he described in his *History*.

> At the court of Mannheim, about the year 1759, the band of the Elector Palatine was regarded as the most complete and best disciplined in Europe; and the symphonies that were produced by the maestro di capella, Holtzbaur, the elder Stamitz, Filtz, Cannabich, Toeski, and Fräntzel, became the favourite full-pieces of every concert, and supplanted concertos and opera overtures, being more spirited than the one, and more solid than the other. Though these symphonies seemed at first to be little more than an improvement of the opera overtures of Jomelli, yet, by the fire and genius of Stamitz, they were exalted into a new species of composition, at which there was an outcry, as usual, against innovation, by those who wished to keep Music stationary. . . . It has long seemed to me as if the variety, taste, spirit and new effects produced by contrast and the use of the *crescendo* and *diminuendo* in these symphonies, had been of more service to instrumental Music in a few years, than all the dull and servile imitations of Corelli, Geminiani, and Handel, had been in half a century.

Burney minced no words when it came to what was truly important. The dull imitations were of course those made by his countrymen (it was left to foreigners like Christian Bach and Carl Friedrich Abel to establish the modern symphony in England). To Stamitz belonged the credit of exalting what he took from others into "a new species of composition."

ANTON FILS

A second generation of composers and performers came to the fore in Mannheim under the aegis of Stamitz in his last years. They were members of the orchestra who had been appointed by him and also taught by him. The most prominent were Christian Cannabich, born in Mannheim in 1731; Carl Joseph Toeschi, born in Ludwigsburg the same year; Johann Anton Fils, born in Eichstätt, Bavaria, in 1733; and Ignaz Fränzl, born in Mannheim in 1736. Fils, often called Filtz, is connected by his name to Württemberg where Fils is a small tributary of the Neckar River (see Figure 5.1 on p. 442).

Fils was appointed second cellist in Mannheim on 15 May 1754, at a salary of 300 gulden. At the same time Innocenz Danzi (born in Italy around 1730) was appointed first cellist. Fils received an increase in salary when he got married in February 1757. By 1759 his salary was 450 gulden. The future looked secure, and he took on a debt of 800 gulden in order to buy his own house in May 1759. Within a year Fils died, in March 1760, six months short of his twenty-seventh birthday. Besides his widow he left behind an infant daughter.[103] They were provided for by Carl Theodore in characteristically generous fashion.

Sets of six symphonies by Fils were quickly taken up by Parisian publishers, Op. 1 and Op. 2 (La Chevardière), both appearing in 1760. His chamber music was also sought after. A set of trio sonatas appeared as his Op. 3, on the title page of which Fils is described as a court chamber musician to the elector and as a pupil of Stamitz. He probably did some accompanying at the elector's private concerts. Many of his chamber works with flute may have been played by Carl Theodore himself.

The early death of Fils was partly responsible for the cult that made publications of his music profitable well into the 1770s and that led to Schubart's extravagant praise for the composer as "the best symphonist who ever lived." The works have moments of charm and some that, on closer inspection, might have profited from revision, greater polish, or better technique. On the whole Fils does not approach late Cannabich in fertility of invention or professional skill. Oddly enough, Fils was not performed at the Concert Spirituel, unlike Fränzl, Toeschi, and Cannabich.

Stamitz was not the only model taken by Fils. The overture to Galuppi's *Il filosofo di campagna* (1754), a comic opera performed at Mannheim in 1756, provides a closer prototype for the first movement of the familiar Symphony in A by Fils than does any symphony by Stamitz, it has been argued.[104] The opening *Alle-*

---

[103]Hubert Unverricht, "Johann Anton Fils (1733–1760): Zur Herkunft und Bedeuting des Komponisten," in *Johann Anton Fils (1733–1760): Ein Eichstätter Komponist der Mannheimer Klassik,* ed. Hermann Holzbauer (Tützing, 1983), pp. 11–32.

[104]Wolf, *The Symphonies of Johann Stamitz,* pp. 359–60. The Symphony in A by Fils was published by La Chevardière as *Symphonie périodique,* No. 2. A modern edition by Hugo Riemann is in *DTB,* Jg. III/1, p. 227. There is a keyboard score of Galuppi's *Il filosofo di campagna,* ed. Virgilio Mortari (Milan, 1965).

gro in 3/4 time of each work commences with a theme that rises up the triad through one octave, then repeats the same an octave above, a *crescendo* that is both written out in the sense of the rising tessitura and specified by various dynamic markings. The most telling resemblance between the two beginnings is their reliance on a six-measure module, one for the lower octave (mm. 1–6), and one for the higher (mm. 7–12). Fils repeats this beginning, Galuppi does not. Their second themes also are akin. Galuppi's is a sudden *piano* as the violins in thirds fall gently down the octave over a pedal, a repeated two-measure phrase. Fils writes the same fall for his two flutes in thirds and sixths over the violins' soft pedal E, with the difference that there is expansion to four-measure phrases (a process already encountered in Stamitz). The biggest difference between the two movements occurs at the beginning of the second part. Galuppi, forgoing a double bar with repeat signs, modulates quickly back to his tonic, D, for the reprise, using only eleven measures. Fils is more expansive here, using twenty-seven measures to reach his reprise. He indicates repeats for both first and second parts.

The aforementioned Symphony in A is a work in four movements with minuet. An *Andante* in D and in 2/4 time for strings and two flutes has an attractive singing quality in spite of all the clichés (Lombard rhythms, melodic sighs, and three-note snaps). The minuet is short and not especially memorable. Its trio is entirely taken up with a florid solo for flute in the subdominant key of D (a moment for the excellent Wendling to shine?). The finale *Presto* in 6/8 opens with one of those rapid ascents in the two violins that have been called "Mannheim rockets." Its second idea harks back to the first movement's, offering a similar descending idea in thirds and sixths against a soft pedal in the strings. If the idea had greater distinction, its composer could be congratulated for thinking in terms of unifying the cycle by bringing it back. Since it is so pale, the temptation is to fault him for lack of invention.

The six symphonies brought together and printed as Op. 2 by La Chevardière in Paris offer a range of works in three and four movements, in the keys of A, g, B♭, F, D, and E♭.[105] Symphonies 2, 3, and 4 dispense with a minuet. A symphony in minor is a rarity for Mannheim. Fils opens No. 2 in g with the rapid motion up and down a third. The following *Andante* in 2/4 and in B♭ he begins the same way. Moreover, he begins the first symphony of the set with the same figure. He relies more on such stereotyped figures than does Stamitz.

Op. 2 No. 5 opens with an *Allegro* in D that matches Stamitz in his blustery mode—the work was attributed to Stamitz in several sources, in fact, but the correct composer is Fils.[106] The second theme is soft and involves only the two vio-

[105] Antonín Fils, *Sei Sinfonie per Orchestra Op. 2*, ed. Jan Racek (Prague, 1960) (Musica Antiqua Bohemica, 44). Symphonies Nos. 5 and 6 are edited by Hugo Riemann in *DTB*.
[106] According to Wolf, *The Symphonies of Stamitz*, p. 451.

lins, for which there is precedent in Stamitz. With only two voices the composer needed to pay attention to questions of euphony as well as melodic interest (Example 5.21). In m. 24 Fils puts a little motion into the second violin part at the expense of forming intervals of a fourth then a fifth with the first violin part. The lower part then rests, leaving the first violin by itself, a very thin-sounding moment that becomes even thinner. The rise up to the third, with melodic turn, then in thirds together, with the treble rising to the fifth, is often used by this composer when he cannot think of anything more interesting to do.

Fils was mostly known as Filtz before his baptismal record was discovered in Eichstätt. He was considered to be of Bohemian ancestry by Dlabač.[107] His father was also a cellist and had taken up a position in the small episcopal court at Eichstätt before the birth of his son. Critics have looked for signs of a possible Bohemian heritage in the music of Fils, and one has pointed to the rather exotic-sounding "Lydian fourths" near the end of the Symphony in D published in Paris as *Symphonie périodique* No. 10 (Example 5.22).[108] Folk elements have been claimed especially in minuets by Fils and cited in explanation of why these movements were so popular in collections.[109]

EXAMPLE 5.21. *Fils, Symphony Op. 2 No. 5, I*

EXAMPLE 5.22. *Fils*, Sinfonie périodique *No. 10, IV*

CANNABICH

Christian Cannabich, foremost of the post-Stamitz symphonists in Mannheim, was a second-generation member of the famous orchestra. His father Martin was a flautist in electoral service who followed Carl Philipp from Düsseldorf to the

[107] Jan Bohumír Dlabač, "Filtz, Anton," in *Allgemeine historische Künstler-Lexikon für Böhmen* (Prague, 1815).
[108] Edited by Riemann in *DTB*. Karl Michael Komma, "Filtz, Anton," in *Die Musik in Geschicte und Gegenwart* (Cassel, 1949–), cites the passage but mistakenly calls it m. 115.
[109] By Roland Würtz, "Filtz," in *New Grove*.

Palatinate and retired with a pension in 1756. Christian joined the orchestra as a violinist in 1744 at age twelve. By 1746 he was receiving an annual salary of 135 gulden. His teacher Stamitz must have thought him very gifted and capable even of becoming a maestro di cappella. At Stamitz's recommendation he was sent off with an electoral stipend to study with Jommelli in Rome. Musicians did not go to Jommelli to study violin playing. They went to study the higher forms of composition, namely, counterpoint, sacred music, and serious opera. In summer 1753 Cannabich accompanied Jommelli to Stuttgart and apparently remained with the master until early 1754, when he returned to Italy to study in Milan, perhaps with Sammartini. It had become clear at some point that he was destined to become concertmaster, not a Kapellmeister.

Cannabich returned to Mannheim and resumed his orchestral duties. Secure in his position at court, he was able to marry. At Mannheim on 8 January 1759, he was joined with Marie Elisabeth de la Motte, who had been a lady of the bed-chamber to the duchess of Zweibrücken, wife of Duke Christian IV. The close ties between the two courts played a role not only in his marriage but also in his career. Symphonies by Cannabich appeared in print in Paris as early as 1760. Then in 1764 the composer journeyed to Paris and stayed as a guest of Christian IV in the Hôtel des Deux Ponts, a visit repeated two years later.

Privilege was accorded to Cannabich by the royal authorities to publish for his own profit two sets of his compositions. He dedicated *Six simphonies* (La Chevardière's Op. 4) to Christian IV and six trio sonatas (La Chevardière's Op. 3) to the duke's morganatic second wife, comtesse de Forbach. Just as Stamitz had conquered the capital with trio sonatas and symphonies, so did his emulator a decade later. Cannabich's symphonies were less conquering, or at least they were heard more rarely at the Concert Spirituel. Not until the 1770s did Cannabich have a success as great as that of Stamitz in Parisian concert life. On 29 April 1772, in Paris again for a prize contest and a benefit concert for the École Gratuite de Dessin, he won the first prize, a gold medal worth 300 livres, for a Symphonie Concertante in E♭ for two solo violins, two solo oboes, and orchestra.[110] The second prize went for a symphony by Ernst Eichner, violinist and bassoonist at the court of Zweibrücken.

Cannabich emerged slowly as a symphonist in his own right. The shadows cast by his two great masters, Stamitz and Jommelli, were not easily dispelled. Of his early symphonies it has been stated, "these works reveal an exceptionally strong influence of the Italian opera overture, especially the overtures of . . . Jommelli."[111] Up to 1764 he invariably followed the four-movement pattern with min-

[110]Jean K. Wolf, *The Symphony at Mannheim* (Thematic Catalogue No. 42) (New York, 1984). She quotes the *Mercure de France* for June 1772 as identifying the solo violinists as the elder Leduc, head of the first violins, and Guénin, head of the seconds (p. 50, n. 22).
[111]Wolf, *The Symphony at Mannheim*, p. liii.

uet pioneered by Stamitz. Then he switched to the three-movement form favored in Paris after 1760, with two exceptions. His prize-winning Symphonie Concertante of 1772 follows the French fashion by having only two movements. The other exception is a surprising Symphonie Concertante in F for solo winds and orchestra that has four movements, including as the third a *Tempo di Minuetto* with trio. Perhaps it was written before he had knowledge of the French genre. The work probably dates from the late 1760s and thus constitutes one of the earliest of its kind. Holzbauer was another early contributor to the genre, for which Vienna and Mannheim as well as Paris may lay maternal claims.[112]

Few of Cannabich's more than six dozen symphonies are available in modern editions.[113] Symphony No. 22 in C, dating from ca. 1764, is in three movements and requires two oboes, two horns, and strings. The opening *Allegro molto* in 4/4 begins with hammerstroke repeated chords against fast-rising and descending scales in the bass. A *crescendo* passage leads to V/V, followed by a calm secondary theme for the two oboes. Another *crescendo* passage, over G, signals the end of the first part. There is no double bar. After a transition tonic C is restored, without recourse to the hammerstrokes. The movement ends with a *crescendo* over pedal C. Stamitz is obviously the model, with his three-*crescendo* pattern, one near the beginning, the second in the middle, and the third at the end. An *Andante con brio* in 2/4 and in G follows, unmemorable and relying less on melody than on violinistic figurations with repeats. In the finale, *Un poco Presto* in 6/8 time, also in binary form with repeats, there are again *crescendo* passages. The reprise begins with the secondary thematic material. A touch of imitative dialogue involving the two violin sections and the bass enlivens the beginning of the second part, but on the whole the symphony lacks the flair and originality of Stamitz.

Symphony No. 32 in D, dating from ca. 1765–66, is one of those from the collection dedicated to Christian IV. It requires both flutes and oboes, as well as horns and strings. The first movement, *Allegro molto spirituoso* in 4/4, also begins with hammerstrokes, here combined with a rocking figure in eighth notes that reappears, simplified, at the beginning of the finale. *Crescendos* occur in the same places as in Symphony No. 22. Were they beginning to be so common as to become routine and tiresome? Interplay between flutes, oboes, and violins makes up the secondary material of the *Allegro,* a three-way conversation that goes beyond anything in Stamitz. Here, in the timbral realm, Cannabich exploits new combinations, which make his greatest contributions to the symphony.[114] Flute and oboes remain prominent in the second movement, an *Andante* in 2/4 and in

[112]See *Haydn, Mozart,* p. 52, n. 58.

[113]Wolf, *The Symphony at Mannheim,* offers Nos. 22, 32, 57, and 73.

[114]A similar conclusion is reached by Sabine Henze-Döhring, "Orchester und Orchestersatz in Christian Cannabichs Mannheimer Sinfonien," in *Mozart und Mannheim* (1994), pp. 257–71.

G that has more melodic content than its counterpart in Symphony 22. The finale, *Presto* in 2/4, is the most attractive movement, one of considerable span that shows the composer's contrapuntal strengths and increasing interest in the possibilities of thematic development.

Two contemporary observers took care to assess Cannabich's abilities as both composer and concertmaster. One was Schubart, whose frequent hyperbole and enthusiasms placed him firmly in the *Sturm und Drang* camp. The other was Mozart, a sober and hard critic rarely given to praise or superlatives.

Schubart was appointed organist and teacher at Ludwigsburg in 1769. In 1773 he was dismissed and banned from the duchy of Württemberg because of a satirical poem he wrote. He began a year of wandering with a visit to the Pirkers in Heilbronn, then on to Mannheim. His most vivid impression of this visit was hearing Cannabich's music played by a large ensemble.

Schubart's memoirs antedated by several years his *Ideen* (ca. 1784–86), also dictated while in prison. The memoirs often served as a springboard for the *Ideen*, and this is true of his famous description of the Mannheim orchestra in the latter, first sketched in a more inchoate but no less interesting version in the memoirs.

> To hear the symphonies of Cannabich performed by the entire Palatine orchestra then seemed to me to be the non plus ultra of the symphony. The experience is not merely one of voices clanging against each other, like the screeching of an enraged mob, but of a musical totality, the parts of which make a complete impression on the soul. The listener is not only inundated by the sound, but utterly shaken and penetrated by the overwhelming and indelible effects. The justly famous Palatine orchestra had this man [Cannabich] to thank more than any other for its perfection. Nowhere are light and shade better marked, the tonal surge and support more cutting; nowhere is better captured the cataract of the harmonic stream at its highest peak. Most young members of this superb ensemble have been trained by Cannabich himself. (1:210)

What Schubart might have heard in 1773, besides symphonies by Cannabich, is the ballet *La Foire de village hessoise,* revived from the previous summer, when it gave Burney such delight, with music (lost) by Cannabich. Then at the great opera in Mannheim in November 1773 there was a revival of the previous year's *Temistocle* by Christian Bach, with entr'acte ballets by Toeschi and Cannabich.

In the *Ideen* Schubart goes into welcome detail about how Cannabich played and directed, raising questions about the source of his skills.

> Nature herself formed him as a concertmaster! No one better knows the duties of a Ripieno player. His bowstroke is entirely original. He has found a completely new means of bow control and has the gift of holding even the largest orchestra in order, with a mere nod of the head or movement of the elbow. It is he who created the even execution that reigns in the Palatine orchestra. He discovered all those magical effects

that hold Europe in their thrall. Perhaps no one has studied violin coloring so thoroughly as he has done. Determining the model of his bow stroke is most difficult. It is far from Tartini's stiffness, and still further from the looseness of [Domenico] Ferrari. (p. 137)

Stamitz is an obvious answer to the source of such skills, for he surely was as influential here as he was in composition. Schubart never heard the orchestra under Stamitz. Consequently he cannot claim so much for Cannabich and nature. He continues his remarks as follows.

He controls the bow with a freedom that can scarcely be imagined, bringing to full power both the high and low registers, the louds and the softs, and with the finest shadings in between. As great as he is as a concertmaster, he is equally great as a teacher. Solo violin players as well as the finest Ripieno players emerge from his tutelage. His original way of painting sounds with the bow has brought forth a new cult of the violin. In orchestra leading and in teaching lie his greatest distinctions.

One of Cannabich's most famous violin students was Wilhelm Cramer, born in Mannheim in 1746. After several years in the Mannheim orchestra Cramer went to Stuttgart, was celebrated at the Concert Spirituel in Paris (1769), and finally settled in London in 1772.

Having built up Cannabich so high, Schubart was about to deflate him.

As a composer he amounts in my eyes to not much. Unusual bow strokes, a deep study of musical timbres, and some modish busy work account for the character of his compositions. His ballets are not bad but in fifty years no one will look at them. Cannabich is a thinker, an industrious, tasteful man, but no genius. Industry compiles, and its compilations gather dust. Genius invents and its inventions do battle with eternity. It could be that Cannabich's fire is weakened because his life long he has never drunk wine. (p. 138)

Schubart had no direct contact with Cannabich after 1773. He probably had no idea that Cannabich was changing. Mozart knew better.

The Mozarts first encountered Cannabich in the summer of 1763, as they were beginning their Grand Tour. In his letter to Lorenz Hagenauer dated Schwetzingen, 19 July 1763, Leopold described his relief at leaving the military atmosphere of Ludwigsburg. He bore letters of recommendation to Carl Theodore from Prince Clemens of Bavaria and the prince of Zweibrücken and hence was warmly welcomed.

Yesterday an academy was ordered especially for us, the first held here since May. It lasted from five until nine in the evening. I had the pleasure of hearing, besides good male and female singers, a flautist, M. Wendling, who is worthy of admiration. The orchestra is the best in Germany and is staffed by young people of good morals who are neither drinkers and gamblers, nor country bumpkins, so that their conduct is as praiseworthy as their orchestral playing. My children have set all of Schwetzingen in motion and given inexpressible pleasure to their electoral Highnesses. Everyone was amazed.

In his travel diary Leopold notated the names of several musicians he met or heard. They included the violinists Franz Wendling, Johann Georg Danner, Fränzl, and the Toeschi brothers, the soprano Dorothea Wendling, bassoonist Georg Ritter, and clarinetist Johann Michael Qualenberg. He concluded his list with "Cannabich und seine Frau."

Near the end of their long trip the Mozarts encountered Cannabich again in Paris, in May 1766. They were not impressed with his symphonies from around this time, of which Symphonies No. 22 and No. 32 may give a fair sample. A change in Mozart's attitude began to take place in Mannheim when he arrived there in the fall of 1777. In a postscript to his mother's letter dated Mannheim 31 October 1777, Mozart wrote to his father: "This day I went with Danner to call on M. Cannabich, who was unusually courteous. I played something for him on his fortepiano, which is a very good one, and we went together to the rehearsal" [directed by vice maestro di cappella Abbé Vogler]. Mozart began his letter of 20 November 1777 with a scathing denunciation of Vogler's compositional abilities, followed directly by: "Cannabich composes much better now than when we knew him in Paris, but what Mama and I both noticed about the symphonies here is that the one like the other always begins in long notes [langsam] and in unison." Several symphonies by Cannabich from around 1776–77 do exhibit such beginnings.

Cannabich treated Mozart as if he were another son and did all he could to secure for him a court appointment. Mozart was a frequent recipient of hospitality at the home of the Cannabichs and gave piano lessons to their young daughter Rosa. Then in early 1778 he made the acquaintances of Fridolin Weber and his family, who quickly gained his confidence and allegiance. In his letter of 24 March 1778 he was all enthusiasm for them. Their worthiness and gratitude he contrasted with the ingratitude of the Cannabichs. Leopold failed to see through the comparison, which was nothing more than an attempt to build up the one by denigrating the other. He replied by return letter of 6 April 1778.

Now do you believe that such a wretched scribbler of symphonies as Cannabich would want seriously to see you appointed to the same service? Especially as you are young and he is old? I do not believe it! The Mannheim compositions have, if truth be told, never pleased me. The orchestra is good—strong—but their taste is not the fine, true one that moves the listener [aber ihr gusto ist nicht der feine wahre rührende Geschmack].

From "the best orchestra in Germany," as Leopold called them in 1763, the Mannheimers had declined (without his having heard them again) to a lesser status. What ensemble of the time, if any, did please Leopold?

The Mannheimers came to the fore again in Mozart's letters as he was contemplating with dread his impending return to Salzburg in mid-1778. On 9 July he wrote his father saying, "one of my chief reasons for detesting Salzburg is those coarse, slovenly, and dissolute court musicians." Whether he realized it or not, the idea merely reiterates Leopold's Mannheim-Salzburg comparison of 1763.

> Ah, if only the court music were regulated as it is in Mannheim! The discipline that reigns in that orchestra! The authority wielded by Cannabich—everything is executed to perfection there. Cannabich, who is the best director I have ever seen, is both loved and feared by his subordinates. Moreover he is respected by the whole town and so are his soldiers. They behave differently from ours, have good manners, are well dressed, and do not go to the taverns to swill.

Perhaps Mozart wished to undo the claims that led to Leopold's railing against Cannabich a year earlier.

Cannabich and Mozart's other highly placed Mannheim friends, Raaff and Wendling among them, prevailed on Carl Theodore in the end. The much-sought-after commission for an opera resulted in *Idomeneo,* brought to the stage in Munich two years after most of the Mannheim court music moved there. In his first letter from Munich after arriving there in the fall of 1780, Mozart's strongest impressions were of the orchestra and of Cannabich, this time as composer.

> Yesterday the play *Essex* was performed in the electoral theater. There was a magnificent ballet and the theater was completely illuminated. A symphony [Ouverture] by Cannabich opened the evening, a work I did not know since it was one of his latest. I assure you, if you had heard it yourself it would have pleased and moved [gerührt] you as much as it did me, and if you had not known ahead of time, you would not have believed that it was by Cannabich. Come soon then and hear the orchestra and admire it! (8 November 1780)

By using the very word *rühren* that Leopold had denied the Mannheimers, Mozart reproved his father's earlier remarks. More importantly, he told of another advance in Cannabich's symphonic composition, one so astounding as to be difficult to believe.

Symphony No. 57 in E♭ dates from Cannabich's first years in Munich, 1778–79, and is scored for two oboes, two clarinets, two bassoons, two horns, and strings. It begins in long notes (as Mozart claimed they all did) and with a rhythmic diminution similar to that favored by Mozart himself to open several works in the same key: | ○ | ♩ ♩ ♩ | ♪♪♪♪♪♪♪♪ |. Cannabich draws great variety from the rich orchestration. The clarinets are prominent, as may be perceived from the secondary material from the first movement in Example 5.23. Cannabich's harmonic palette sounds more sumptuous than before, with a greater use of secondary dominants. The source of this new-found richness may well have been the inspiration provided by the many pieces Mozart wrote or played while in Mannheim, including the piano sonata for Mademoiselle Cannabich, K. 309. The routine *crescendo* of earlier years plays no part in Symphony No. 57, which is rounded out by an *Andante con moto* in 2/4 and in B♭ for clarinets and strings, and an *Allegro non tanto* in 6/8 with a catchy and folk-song-like main theme.

EXAMPLE 5.23. *Cannabich, Symphony No. 57, I*

Ballet music was one of Cannabich's special assignments. His contributions to the genre once rivaled his symphonies and chamber music in scope, but few scores have survived. As early as 1758, not long after his return from Italy, he wrote some ballet music to a burlesca, *Arlichino fortunato nell'amore,* in which Fränzl, the younger Toeschi, and Lorenzo Quaglio played roles. During the same season he composed the music for the heroic ballet by Bouqueton *Ulisse, roi d'Ithaque,* an entr'acte in Holzbauer's *Nitteti.*

Cannabich's ballet music runs the gamut from the light and pastoral to the serious and tragic. His music for Bouqueton's hunting ballet *Le rendes-vous* (1769) illustrates the former.[115] The score has sixteen short dances preceded by a very short one-movement *Ouvertura*. Cannabich unifies it tonally and reinforces its unity by frequent returns to one of the traditional hunting calls, "La Queste" (used also by Haydn in the "Hunting Chorus," No. 23, in *The Seasons*). The instrumentation for small orchestra is varied throughout and imaginative. No. 9, a rondo with episodes in vi and i, would sound quite at home at the Opéra or Opéra-Comique, for which the composer's frequent sojourns in Paris are obviously responsible. The rondo theme, with its many repeated tones, has a folklike character and could possibly have been associated with a text. A hunting ballet was a perfect complement to the fall season at Schwetzingen, where Carl Theodore enjoyed his favorite sport.

Tragic ballets engaged another side of the composer's artistic personality. *Medea*, by Euripides, the most grizzly and shocking of ancient tragedies, was one source for Etienne Lauchery's *Ballet tragique Médée et Jason,* the second ballet in Christian Bach's opera *Temistocle* (1772).[116] Lauchery, who was a dancer at Mannheim as early as 1747, returned to the city as successor to Bouqueton in 1769, after eight years at the court of Kassel. Cannabich's score consists of twenty-seven numbers scored for large orchestra of flutes, oboes, bassoons, horns, trumpets, timpani, and strings. Some are simple dances in binary form, like almost all those in *Le rendes-vous.* Others are through-composed, sometimes going through different tempos. The *Ouverture*, in 4/4 and in D, begins like the first movement of a symphony and has a *crescendo* to *fortissimo* but ends on V, being only a prima parte. It gives way to a fanfare in D for eight trumpets, four on stage and four in the orchestra. The most impressive piece is the Chaconne, No. 9, in 3/4 and in D. It totals nearly three hundred measures, rivaling the great chaconnes of Rameau, with which it shares several features, and looking forward to the specimen of the genre for these same musicians that Mozart would write to end his *Idomeneo* in 1781. There is a concentration of numbers in the minor mode two-thirds of the way through the ballet, evidently coinciding with gruesome parts of the action. Tragedy seems to be well within the composer's compass. The ballet ends softly, in E♭, as the flames engulfing Jason's palace die down. Lauchery's treatment of the story was perhaps influenced by Noverre's famous *Médée* for Stuttgart.

Cannabich responded to the vogue for melodrama with a setting of *Electra* by

---

[115]*Ballet Music from the Mannheim Court,* Part. I. Christian Cannabich: *Le rendes-vous, ballet de chasse;* Georg Joseph Vogler: *Le rendez-vous de chasse, ou Les vendanges interrompues par les chasseurs,* ed. Floyd K. Grave (Recent Researches in the Music of the Classical Era, 45) (Madison, Wis., 1996).

[116]*Ballet Music from the Mannheim Court,* Part II. Carl Joseph Toeschi: *Mars et Vénus;* Christian Cannabich: *Médée et Jason,* ed. Nicole Baker (Recent Researches in the Music of the Classical Era, 47) (Madison, Wis., 1997).

Heribert von Dalberg, who had been director of the national theater since it was formally instituted by Carl Theodore in 1778. *Electra* was first performed in the new theater (Nationaltheater) on 4 September 1781 as an afterpiece to Hiller's *Die Jagd.* The composer was presumably present, at least his duties as director of the orchestra in Munich were slight at this particular time of year. The score survives by a thread.[117] Yet it may be the greatest of all compositions in the genre, and certainly the most symphonic. Benda, the most celebrated composer of melodrama, was somewhat limited as a symphonist by the narrowness of his background at the Berlin court. His strengths were the same ones he brought to Singspiel. Cannabich brought to the task a fiery orchestral imagination and long stage experience writing ballet music. He aimed to write an orchestral drama that could almost stand on its own even without the spoken drama. He took care to unify the tragedy by bringing back the music of Electra's opening monologue at the moment of matricide. One critic took him to task for being too generous with music in his interludes.[118] In fact he rescued the genre from sounding like a quodlibet of snippets, a patchwork quilt. His use of an offstage female chorus is admirable, as is concentration on the tonic minor as the epitome of tragedy. The *Allegro moderato* part of the *Introduzione* returns to conclude the work.

FIGURE 5.12. Egide Verhelst. Portrait of Cannabich.

Electra came only a few months after Mozart's *Idomeneo* in Munich, which was vigorously rehearsed and led in performance by Cannabich, to the great satisfaction of the composer. Possibly Cannabich was inspired when writing his melodrama by the dark and funereal strains (in c minor) of the chorus "O voto tremendo" in the last act of *Idomeneo.* In any case, the subjects were related.

Cannabich was a polished courtier, of striking mien (Figure 5.12). In Munich he continued to advance in status. After the death of Carlo Grua in 1773, his salary was increased by 150 gulden to 850 gulden per annum, which implies that he inherited some of Grua's duties. In 1774 he was given the title director of instrumen-

[117]Christian Cannabich, *Electra,* ed. Thomas Bauman (German Opera, 1770–1800, 10) (New York, 1986).
[118]Edgar Istel, *Die Enstehung des deutschen Melodramas* (Berlin and Leipzig, 1906), p. 85. The author complained that Cannabich's long musical interludes "betray the absolute musician." Bauman (ibid.) demurs. See also Emilio Sala, "Melodrame. Définitions et métamorphoses d'un genre quasi-opératique," *Revue de Musicologie* 84 (1998): 235–46.

tal music, bestowed before only on Stamitz. As of October 1778, when most of the orchestra moved to Munich, his salary rose to 1,500 gulden. Kapellmeister Holzbauer remained in Mannheim. Normally it would be his responsibility to rehearse and direct a court opera. Mozart's experiences with *Idomeneo* make it clear that these tasks fell entirely on the shoulders of Cannabich, who had become Kapellmeister for the Munich opera in all but name. In a final raise in salary, Cannabich advanced in 1790 to 1,800 gulden, following the death of Toeschi.

After 1780 the popularity of Cannabich's symphonies waned and he composed fewer and fewer. It was inevitable this would happen once Haydn's symphonies eclipsed those of all other composers in public favor. Cannabich himself directed Haydn's symphonies and evidently knew them well. He paid a kind of homage to Haydn, his close contemporary, in his very last symphony, numbered 73 and dated December 1794 in his own hand, a fine work that lacks a third-movement finale to complement the opening *Allegro* in C (4/4) and *Andante* in G (2/4). The latter treats a typically Haydnesque theme to variation, with a *minore* middle section.

Cannabich's best-known symphony is No. 72 in B♭.[119] There is reason to believe that it is also very late—the composer's numbering of his symphonies is indeed a chronological one. Symphony No. 72 begins softly, with the second violins executing a melodic turn around the tonic preceded by two staccato upbeats, answered by the first violins tripping down the triad. Paired clarinets complete the phrase in their most dulcet tones. After a resounding V^7 of V, with pause, the clarinets enter again, singing a second theme over rocking bassoons that begins not in F but in f minor (Example 5.24). The melody is close to the second theme of the *Allegro di molto* of Mozart's four-hand piano sonata in F (K. 497, dated 1 August 1786). In this late symphony Cannabich becomes so lyrical throughout as to approach Mozart more than anyone else. Particularly Mozartian is the deceptive cadence to the lowered sixth degree that followed the second theme in m. 48 and the close part writing allowing all voices to move in conjunct motion, with the help of secondary dominant harmonies, pushing to a cadential I$^6_4$ chord. Then follows the Mannheim signature device, a *crescendo* gradually mounting over an F pedal, using the motif that opened the movement. A first movement as lyrical as this poses challenges for the succeeding movements. The *Andante* in 3/4 and in E♭ uses the same orchestral forces and they manage to sigh even more plaintively. The concluding *Allegro* in cut time recycles some ideas from the first movement, including the Mozartian second theme, in both major and minor, followed by an excursion to the distant reaches of the flat side.

[119]Ed. Hugo Riemann in *DTB,* Jg. XV/2 (1907).

EXAMPLE 5.24. *Cannabich, Symphony No. 72, I*

The last years of Carl Theodore's reign in Munich (he died in 1799) were difficult and marred by wars. Financial and political problems plagued the court. Cutbacks were made in salaries paid to musicians, forcing Cannabich and others to go on concert tours in order to supplement their incomes. Reichardt claims that Cannabich was in Vienna in 1796. Cannabich died at Frankfurt in early 1798 while visiting his son Carl. He had outlived his own fame.

TOESCHI AND FRÄNZL

There were three Toeschis in the Mannheim orchestra at one time. Alessandro, born in Italy before 1700, may have been a student of Vivaldi. He was engaged as a violinist by the Darmstadt court in 1719, moved in 1725 to Stuttgart, which he left in 1737, and was in Mannheim before 1743, when he composed the ballet music to go with Grua's *Meride.* On the 1748 court calendar both he and Stamitz are listed with the title *Concertmeister.* Of his two sons, the younger, Johann Baptist, born in Stuttgart in 1735, was a pupil of Stamitz and Cannabich who became an orchestral violinist by 1755. His duties included leading the orchestra in the ballets that accompanied the gala operas for the elector's name day and other celebrations. One of the dancers in the ballet troupe was his sister Barbara, born in Ludwigsburg in 1733. She married the cellist Innocenz Danzi, from which union sprang the composer Franz Danzi and the singer-composer Franziska, who married the court oboist Ludwig August Lebrun. Networks of such familial relationships were common in the Mannheim orchestra and theater personnel.

Carl Joseph Toeschi, baptized on 11 November 1731 and henceforth called simply Toeschi, pursued a career closely parallel to that of Cannabich, who was almost identical in age (baptized 28 December 1731). He is said to have been a pupil of Fils as well as of Stamitz.[120] With the death of Stamitz in 1757 and of Alessandro Toeschi in 1758, the concertmaster positions became open in the orchestra, of which Toeschi had been a member since 1752. He and Cannabich were appointed joint leaders in 1759. As first violin Cannabich was paid 700 gulden annually, 200 more than Toeschi, who led the second violins. A generation later the two remained joint concertmasters at Munich, and Cannabich still took precedence, as Mozart amusingly described, recounting a clash between them that involved the cellist Johann Baptist Mara (letter of 24 November 1780).

Toeschi was elevated to the post of *Direktor der Kabinettsmusik* in 1774 at the same time his brother was promoted to the status of concertmaster. *Musique de cabinet* referred to the private chamber music in which Carl Theodore himself played. The elector was somewhat timid as a flautist. When Schubart visited Mannheim in 1773 he was called to Schwetzingen where, after being drawn into conversation about himself by the elector, his highness "performed, almost rather fearfully, a flute concerto accompanied by the two Toeschis and the cellist Danzi."[121] Toeschi wrote many flute concertos. Schubart's *Flötenkonzert* was perhaps not a concerto but a flute quartet. Toeschi wrote several such quartets for solo flute, two violins, and cello. A set of six was issued by La Chevardière as Op. 2 in Paris in 1765.[122] Junker considered Toeschi's flute quartets of epochal importance for the modern style. He extolled, in particular, their harmonic richness and independence of parts.[123]

Six symphonies by Toeschi were published by La Chevardière in Paris as Op. 1 in 1762, and six more issued by the same publisher as Op. 3 in 1765. It is difficult to get much impression of these early works because they have not attracted modern editions, with few exceptions. Op. 3 No. 3 in B^b may not be representative.[124] The opening *Allegro* in 3/4 has no repeat signs, and the entire movement is dominated by an upbeat rhythmic figure from the very opening. There is no clear secondary idea, only the same rhythmic motif in a different guise. The *Allegro*

---

[120]By Robert Münster, *New Grove.*

[121]Schubart, *Leben und Gesinnungen,* 1: 209.

[122]One quartet from this collection is edited by Hugo Riemann in *DTB* XXVII, Jg. XV (1914). It makes modest demands on the flute.

[123]Carl Ludwig Junker, *Zwanzig Komponisten: Eine Skizze* (Bern, 1776), pp. 95–99. Neither the flute quartet nor the flute quintet by Toeschi edited by Riemann merits these tributes, both being thin in texture (often no more than two parts sounding at a time) and tepid in harmonic inspiration.

[124]Ed. Hugo Riemann in *DTB,* Jg. VIII/2 (1907).

sounds like an experiment. Could an entire opening movement be built upon a single rhythmic cell? If such was the wager, it failed in the sense of retaining interest for the listener. Yet it may be this very quality of monotony, of preserving a single affect, that led Hiller to praise the symphony, along with the one in A that followed it in the same set, as "pleasing the most, because the composer did better at holding himself within the confines of the serious."[125] Otherwise, he faulted the composer for being uneven and repetitious, and for his pseudocontrapuntal treatment of material that is too thin.

Toeschi follows his curiously straight-laced *Allegro* with an *Andante* in 2/4 time and in F. Here he does offer a clear secondary idea, but it is of little interest, being a rather rudimentary three-part canon. The *Menuetto* that follows repeats the *cadence galante* that had already become tedious in the *Andante.* Lacking any melodic inspiration worthy of the name, the composer resorts in the trio to an imitative beginning between treble and bass. The finale, *Allegro* in 2/4, consists largely of triplet figuration, lending the movement a giguelike character. The triplets cease for the advent of the secondary idea, played by the two violins alone, a device used effectively by Stamitz and somewhat less so by Fils. Toeschi's duet merely sounds thin and wan (Example 5.25). The result could be called watered-down Fils. What the composer intended, clearly, was a contrapuntal dialogue.

A Symphony in D by Toeschi, of uncertain provenance and date, belongs much more to the norm for Mannheim symphonies.[126] It is in three movements,

EXAMPLE 5.25. *Toeschi, Symphony Op. 3 No. 3, IV*

[125]Hiller, *Wöchentliche Nachrichten,* 1: 210–12. In another passage (2: 92) Hiller allowed that Toeschi joined fire, cantabile, and invention with good thematic working out.
[126]Carlo Giuseppe Toëschi, *Symphony in D,* ed. Adam Carse (London, 1936). The principal study is Robert Münster, "Die Sinfonien Toeschis: Ein Beitrag zur Geschichte der Mannheimer Sinfonie" (Ph.D. diss., University of Munich, 1956).

probably indicating a post-1765 dating. In the opening *Allegro* in common time there is a vigorous unison beginning in the strings, supported by chords in the oboes and horns. After a stop on the tone A, the oboes launch a soft secondary theme, a descent in thirds down through the octave over a pedal in the violas, rather like the descent in the first movement of the Symphony in A by Fils. But here the violins retort perkily with their own descent in thirds. The ensuing *Andante* is in A and in 2/4 time. It begins with a little imitative dialogue between the violins. The finale, *Presto* in 3/8, returns to the exuberant slides and leaping triads in unison of the opening *Allegro*.

Schubart could be describing a symphony like this in his *Leben und Gesinnungen*, the earlier of his pronouncements on the subject.

> Toeschi's manner is not so original as Cannabich's, but more readily understood, and more in the honeyed taste of fashion. Serious majesty at the beginning, then connection of the stream from the babbling *pianissimo* to the cloudstorming *fortissimo*, a flattering Andante and comic Presto—these are the characters of all his symphonies. If one hears two or three one has heard them all. (1:211)

Inasmuch as Toeschi composed more than sixty-six symphonies, it would be rash to judge them by a mere few.

In his *Ideen* Schubart has a lot more to say about Toeschi, and he extends the comparison with Cannabich.

> Toeschi is the second concertmaster of the Palatine-Bavarian orchestra. In bow control he is far from being a Cannabich. The latter commands armies, the former scarcely a battalion. Nevertheless he possesses something quite original. He has made himself at home in a certain style of symphony with exceptional power and effect. They begin with majesty and swirl on into the *crescendo;* they deploy the *Andante* with grace and end with the jolly *Presto.* Yet he lacks variety, because if one has heard a single symphony by him one has heard them all. Cannabich brought matters further by drinking water than did Toeschi by drinking wine. Toeschi won a laurel, languidly wrapped it around his brow, and then proceeded to fall gently asleep. (p. 138)

Junker went through a more drastic change of mind about Toeschi's music between his *Zwanzig Komponisten* of 1776 and his *Almanach* of 1782. In the former he praised the symphonies for their natural melodic flow and for a mixture of the sublime and sensuously beautiful. In the latter he complained that they sounded monotonous, with too much reliance on sequence [rosaliert], and were poorly structured.[127] Schubart claimed Junker as one of his sources in the *Ideen,* and he may well have changed his view of Toeschi because of Junker.

---

[127]Karl Ludwig Junker, *Musikalischer Almanach auf das Jahr 1782* (Leipzig, 1782), pp. 63–64, cited after Roye E. Wates, "Karl Ludwig Junker, 1748–1797: Sentimental Music Critic" (Ph.D. diss., Yale University, 1965), p. 172.

Schubart had high praise, on the other hand, for Toeschi's ballet music. He claimed he could envisage the dancer in action just by looking at the composer's scores. This would seem to confess that he never witnessed one of the ballets danced. Here would have been the place to mention Toeschi's *Roger dans l'isle d'Alcine*, the first ballet in Bach's *Temistocle* (1772–73), had he actually seen it when in Mannheim.

Toeschi began writing ballets as early as 1758, when he wrote the music for *Thamangul, chef des Tartares*, the first of Bouqueton's entr'acte ballets in Holzbauer's *Nitteti*; Cannabich contributed the music for the second, *Ulisse, roi d'Ithaque*.[128] In 1766 Toeschi composed music for Bouqueton's ballet *Mars et Vénus*, performed between the second and third acts of Francesco de Majo's *Alessandro nell'Indie*. His score survives and seems amazingly long and complex for an entr'acte.[129] There were seven main roles, with Bouqueton himself as *premier danseur*. Toeschi provides an overture and thirty-two numbers, quite varied in mood and colorfully orchestrated, the total effect unified by tonality. The impression created by the score is of a full-length ballet. More modest in dimension is Toeschi's score for Bouqueton's *Céphale et Procris*, the first entr'acte in Holzbauer's *Adriano in Siria* (1768).[130] It consists of thirteen numbers preceded by a very short overture of eighteen measures. The initial key of D is well suited to the opening scene of the hunt, as is the 6/8 meter. Moving by the interval of a third or a fourth from number to number, the music travels as far afield as four flats when Procris enters the underworld and implores the goddess of revenge to smite Aurora for having abducted Cephalus. Toeschi chooses an *Adagio* in 3/4 dominated by two bassoons, instruments quite at home in the rare key of A♭. Schubart in the *Ideen* characterized this major key as "the tonality of the grave. Death, the tomb, decomposition, and eternity lie within its compass." Toeschi works his way back to D by a similar maneuvering, using only the intervals of a third or a fourth between numbers. He ends with a grand chaconne.

Ignaz Fränzl was born in Mannheim in 1736, the son of a trumpet player in the court orchestra. He was so precociously gifted as a violinist that Stamitz placed him as a boy at the last desk of the first violins in 1747.[131] Three years later he became a paid member. By age twenty he was earning an annual salary of 500 florins. In 1758 he composed one act of a pantomime burlesca, *Arlichino fortunato nell'amore*, in which he played the role of Pantalone. Most of his compositions, aside from ballet music, were chamber music for strings, symphonies, or violin

---

[128]Both ballet scores are lost. See Paul Corneilson and Eugene K. Wolf, "Mannheim Ballet Sources, 1758–1778," in *Ballet Music from the Mannheim Court*, Part I, xxvii–xxxii.

[129]Modern edition in *Ballet Music from the Mannheim Court*, Part II.

[130]Modern edition in *Ballet Music from the Mannheim Court*, Part III, ed. Paul Cauthen (Recent Researches into the Music of the Classical Era, 52) (Madison, Wis., 1998).

[131]Roland Würtz, "Die Organization der Mannheimer Hofkapelle," in *Die Mannheimer Hofkapelle*, pp. 37–48; 39.

concertos, but very little survives. Only five symphonies are now known.[132] Seven violin concertos have survived, not many for a performer who was the most sought-after violin virtuoso among the Mannheimers. He was a frequent soloist in his own violin concertos at the Concert Spirituel in Paris from 1768 on. In these concerts he soon moved to the most prestigious spot on the program, the penultimate work, just before the closing motet or piece with sacred text.

Schubart in his memoirs praises Fränzl as "the violinist of love—one can hear nothing sweeter or more insinuating than his way of playing and his compositions." In the *Ideen* Schubart expands this and becomes a little more technical.

> Fränzl is one of the loveliest violinists of our time, equally strong in accompanying and in solo playing. His bow stroke has so much delicacy and enchantment that no one can hear him without being deeply moved. He is no slave to his own manner, but gladly performs the works of others with warmth. The violin pieces he composed belong among the best of the genre. They are not stormy or fiery, yet all the more deeply felt, more inward, and full of new melodic ideas. . . . His *Allegro* rolls along so lightly and without constraints that he seems to do nothing when he actually does everything. (pp. 144–45)

Fränzl's manner of making difficult things seem easy was also noted by Junker.

Fränzl was promoted to the status of concertmaster in 1774, at the time the Toeschis and Cannabich were also elevated and given new titles. This does not mean that Toeschi and Cannabich ceased serving as concertmasters but that Fränzl and the younger Toeschi served as such on some occasions. Mozart heard him at the height of his powers playing a violin concerto in an academy held in the Rittersaal on 21 November 1777 (the third gala celebrating the name day of Electress Elizabeth Auguste). He wrote his father about it that night, speaking as one violinist to another.

> Today, the 21st, before noon, we received your letter of the 17th. I was not at home but at Cannabich's where Wendling was rehearsing a concerto for which I had written the orchestral parts. At six o'clock today the gala academy took place and I had the pleasure of hearing Herr Fränzl (who is married to a sister of Mme. Cannabich) play a concerto on the violin. He pleases me very much. You know that I am no great lover of difficulties. He plays difficult passages but one is not aware they are difficult and believes one could readily play the same oneself. That is the true way. He also has a very beautiful, round tone and never misses a note. One hears everything and all is distinct. He has a beautiful staccato done with a single bow stroke, up as well as down. Such double trills I have never heard before. In a word, he is, in my opinion, no charlatan, but a very solid violinist.

[132]Ignaz Fränzl, *Three Symphonies*, ed. Roland Würtz (New York, 1982). As a symphonist, Fränzl does not come up to the level of the other post-Stamitz Mannheimers.

Was the concerto Fränzl's composition? Mozart does not specify. Perhaps it was, but this superb violinist was generous when it came to playing the works of others, as Schubart noted.

When Mozart returned to Mannheim in the fall of 1778 on his way home to Salzburg he found that the great migration was well underway. Most of the orchestra had chosen to move to Munich with Carl Theodore, including three of the four concertmasters (Cannabich and both Toeschis). Those in service to the court were free to remain in Mannheim if they so desired, without reduction in pay. Fränzl chose to stay, and so he automatically became the leader of what remained of the orchestra, which henceforth saw duty mainly in the Nationaltheater, where he was music director until his death in 1811. Fränzl also laid plans for a concert-giving orchestra to be made up of nonprofessional musicians, which would take the place of the court academies in the Rittersaal. He deserves much credit for rebuilding Mannheim's musical life as a civic enterprise. Mozart reported to his father in a letter dated Mannheim, 12 November 1778, "An Académie des Amateurs modelled on the one in Paris is about to begin here, directed by Herr Fränzl, first violin, hence I am now composing a concerto for keyboard and violin." Had he been allowed by Leopold to stay in Mannheim for six weeks to two months as he wanted (the excuse being a commission from Dalberg to write a melodrama), he would have finished this double concerto, intended as a tribute to Fränzl's violin playing and for himself to play at the keyboard. He completed fifteen pages of a noble, marchlike *Allegro* in D (K. 315f), but no more. Yielding to his father's commands to return as soon as possible, he left Mannheim in short order. The concerto remained a torso, the melodrama an unfulfilled dream.

Fränzl flourished in his new role as music director, although it meant that he was able to compose little more. He became a highly respected citizen, with a house and a garden that ran down to the Neckar. An inventory of his property after his death revealed richly appointed furnishings and many other appurtenances of wealth.[133]

Palatine Court Opera

Holzbauer dominated opera in Mannheim in the years directly following his appointment. The main fare was provided by Metastasian librettos, of which Holzbauer set three, *L'Issipile* (1754), *La clemenza di Tito* (1757), and *Nitteti* (1758). The last is the only one for which the music survives. No name-day opera took

[133]Gabriele Busch-Salmen, " . . . Auch unter dem Tache die feinsten Wohnungen," in *Die Mannheimer Hofkapelle*, 21–35; 25.

place in 1755 because Carl Theodore and Elizabeth Auguste were visiting their states ruled from Düsseldorf and did not return until May 1756. The name-day opera that fall was Galuppi's setting of *L'Olimpiade,* revived from its first Mannheim production in 1749. Rosalie Holzbauer made her one and only stage appearance in Mannheim singing the title role of *L'Issipile.*

Nitteti was a relatively new libretto. Metastasio wrote it for Farinelli in Madrid, where Nicola Conforto made the first setting in 1756. It was repeated at the San Carlo with Teresa Castellini in the title role, Filippo Elisi as primo uomo, and Anton Raaff as tenor. The following year there were settings by Piccinni, Traetta, and Hasse for other Italian stages, followed by Holzbauer's setting for Milan as the carnival opera of 1758. For Mannheim the following fall Holzbauer shortened the opera by four arias but enriched his orchestration.[134] Mannheim's practice of substantial entr'acte ballets (in this case by Toeschi and Cannabich) may help explain why Holzbauer made several cuts in his score.

Holzbauer was commissioned by Milan to set *Alessandro nell'Indie* for the carnival of 1759. He remained in Italy throughout the spring and could have witnessed the production at Parma in May of Traetta's *Ippolito ed Aricia* on a libretto derived by Carlo Innocenzo Frugoni from *Hippolite et Aricie* by Simon-Joseph Pellegrin and Rameau, the most discussed operatic event of the year. Oddly enough, Holzbauer's *Alessandro* was not selected for repetition at Mannheim. Instead, the name-day opera of 1759 was *Ippolito.*

Mystery surrounds the production of *Ippolito ed Aricia* at Mannheim in the fall of 1759. The printed libretto makes no mention of Frugoni, although his text was altered only slightly.[135] Verazi was responsible for these small changes. He may well have been behind the whole enterprise, since he was a leading figure in moving the Italian libretto away from Metastasio and toward French models, particularly with regard to increasing spectacle and incorporating ballet within the acts. *Ippolito,* in imitation of *Hippolite,* incorporated both in each of its five acts, eliminating the need for entr'acte ballets. At Parma the production relied on Rameau for dances and for such spectacular orchestral effects as the storm music. According to the printed libretto for Mannheim the opera was newly composed by Holzbauer, its ballet music by Cannabich. No score for either has ever been found, nor has their existence been so much as mentioned in old records. The temptation is strong to believe that what Mannheim heard in the fall of 1759 was largely Traetta and Rameau, not Holzbauer and Cannabich. Although no score of an

[134]Nicole Baker, "Italian Opera at the Court of Mannheim, 1758–1770" (Ph.D. diss., University of California, Los Angeles, 1994), pp. 111–56.
[135]Klaus Hortschansky, "Ignaz Holzbauers *Ippolito et Aricia* (1759): Zur Einführung der Tragédie-lyrique in Mannheim," in *Studien zur deutsch-französischen Musikgeschichte im 18. Jahrhundert,* ed. Wolfgang Birtel and Christoph-Hellmut Mahling (Heidelberg, 1986), pp. 105–16.

Ippolito by Holzbauer exists, there is one extant by Traetta that is connected with Mannheim.[136] Connoisseurs who collected librettos must have been amazed that Mannheim gave no credit to Frugoni. If the borrowing involved the Parma score as well as the libretto, and on a large scale, Holzbauer could well have been compromised. It was one thing to revise and rewrite under the banner of "newly composed." Massive borrowing under false ascription, on the other hand, contained the seeds of scandal.

The principal singers at Mannheim had long careers. Rosa Gabrieli, soprano, who appeared in a minor role in Grua's *Meride* (1742), advanced to the prima donna role of Vitellia in the composer's *La clemenza di Tito* (1748), by which time she was known as Rosa Bleckmann, having married the orchestra's first oboist. The tenor Pietro Sarselli sang Tito and his wife Carolina took the primo uomo role of Sesto. The Sarselli clan's most famous singer was to be their daughter, Elisabeth Sarselli Wendling. Rosa Bleckmann continued to sing prima donna roles under Holzbauer, the exception being in *L'Issipile,* when she yielded to Madame Holzbauer. If there were a battle about the latter's status in Mannheim, as there had been in Stuttgart, and there probably was, it was won by La Bleckmann. Her challenger and eventual replacement was Dorothea Spurni, who married the orchestra's first flautist and became Dorothea Wendling. (Elisabeth was her sister-in-law.)

A major shift in direction took place in 1760. Verazi took charge and Holzbauer composed no more operas for several years. The reasons for this could have been manifold. They may have had something to do with the demands of Madame Holzbauer, with the authorship of the *Ippolito* score, or perhaps only with the whims of the ruling pair. Instead of Holzbauer the choice fell upon such distinguished outsiders as Jommelli, Traetta, Majo, Piccinni, and Christian Bach.

Carl Theodore was more easygoing with the artists who served him than were such hard taskmasters as the king of Prussia or the duke of Württemberg. Unlike them he incarcerated no one for insubordination, as far as is known. Let us suppose that his intendant relayed the resolve of his Kapellmeister to compose no more operas until his wife was again chosen and paid for singing the principal part. Faced with such a contretemps the elector could well have avoided crisis by telling the intendant to employ another composer for the name-day opera. These operas were not to be taken lightly because of the astronomical sums they required of so small a state as the Palatinate. Economy of a kind was exerted by staging a new one only every other year and making do with revivals to fill the odd years. Thus every even-numbered year from 1760 to 1772 saw a new production, in most cases repeated the following year.

---

[136]Paul Corneilson and Eugene K. Wolf, "Newly Identified Manuscripts of Operas and Related Works from Mannheim," *JAMS* 47 (1994): 244–74; 261.

Holzbauer's retreat from composing operas may also have been related to his increased duties in other areas. He was needed to sustain the composition and direction of sacred music after 1760 because the aged Grua became increasingly infirm (he died in 1773). Throughout his long career Holzbauer was a prolific composer of oratorios, masses, and other sacred music. His earliest datable composition is a mass of 1739 and his last completed score was a German mass (1780). In one case he revised and modernized an early mass around 1770, bringing it up to date by adding chromatic appoggiaturas and slowing down the harmonic rhythm.[137] Holzbauer's masses were well received and widely diffused in copies. A Prussian visitor to Mannheim in 1772 wrote that on Saint Charles Day he attended a gala service in the court chapel "where a mass well worth hearing by Kapellmeister Holzbauer was performed."[138] Further proof of Holzbauer's reputation as a composer of masses came after the court moved to Bavaria in 1778. Apparently unsatisfied with what he was hearing in Munich's court chapel, Carl Theodore requested that a parcel of masses by Holzbauer be sent from Mannheim (in this way they were rescued from later conflagrations). Finally, there is the testimony of Mozart in a letter dated Mannheim, 4 November 1777: "Today, Sunday, I heard a mass by Holzbauer that he wrote twenty-six years ago, but which is really well done. He is a very good composer, has a good church style, knows how to write well for voices and instruments, and invents good fugues."

TRAETTA'S *SOFONISBA*

The rise to eminence of Mannheim's orchestra in the 1750s was paralleled during the following decade by its opera, abetted of course by the famous orchestra. What Holzbauer was not quite able to achieve in the 1750s was brought to pass by a distinguished series of visitors who were invited to write operas celebrating the elector's name day. The first opera to earn the reputation of an undisputed masterpiece was *Sofonisba,* created by court poet Verazi and the peripatetic Neapolitan master Tommaso Traetta, who had just come from operatic triumphs in Turin, Parma, and Vienna. Verazi modeled the libretto after one that Jommelli set for Venice in 1745, attributed to Antonio Maria Zanetti. It became one of the most dire of *Frauentragödien,* a drama centered upon the suffering and death of a noble heroine.

The subject may well have been chosen because of the woman who became Mannheim's greatest singer, Dorothea Wendling. She replaced Rosa Bleckmann, whose last appearance was in the revival of Holzbauer's *Nitteti* in 1760. La

---

[137]The original and revised versions are exemplified by Klaus Altmann, "Ignaz Holzbauer als Messenkomponist," in *Mannheim und Italien: Zur Vorgeschichte der Mannheimer,* ed. Roland Würtz (Mainz, 1984), pp. 223–43; 237–43.
[138]Paul Corneilson, "Opera at Mannheim, 1770–1778," p. 33.

Wendling was a great actress as well as a superb singer. She would require both talents in abundance to negotiate the title role of *Sofonisba,* brought to the stage of the court opera on 5 November 1762. There is no proof to show that Traetta traveled to Mannheim for the event. Such proof does exist regarding his successors, Gian Francesco de Majo and Johann Christian Bach, which makes it at least likely that Traetta did preside over his opera during the rehearsals and first performances.

A possible visual stimulus for the choice of subject was the image of Sofonisba that once hung in the electoral picture gallery at Mannheim (Figure 5.13).[139] Francesco Solimena, the great Neapolitan artist who lived from 1659 to 1749 and was active to the end of his long life, painted it. Solimena depicts the proud daughter of the Carthaginian general Hasdrubal as she raises the cup of poison to her lips and her eyes to heaven, determined to die rather than become a Roman captive.

FIGURE 5.13. Francesco Solimena. *Sofonisba,* engraved by Heinrich Sintzenich.

In the opera Sofonisba is the wife of Siface, king of Numidia, sung by Pietro Sarselli, tenor. She had been promised originally to Massinissa, who tries to regain her, a role sung by the soprano castrato Lorenzo Tonarelli. They are all oppressed by the conquering Romans, led by Scipione and Lelio. The other female part, Cirene, was the first major role sung by Elisabeth Sarselli, not yet married to Franz Wendling.

The martial character of the opera strikes the audience from the outset, when the third movement of the overture is treated as a battle

[139]Karl J. Svoboda, *Galerien und Gala im kurfälzischen Hof zu Mannheim* (Heidelberg, 1979), p. 54.

symphony, with fanfares depicting the defeat of the Numidians by the Romans, enacted on stage with curtain up.[140] Massinissa sings the first aria and Sofonisba the second, followed by a march for the arrival of the victorious Scipione and his troops on horseback. The march, in F, gives way to a magnificent obbligato recitative for Scipione that begins in the distant key of b. Here Traetta portrays majesty with dotted rhythms and a bass descending by suspensions that show how greatly he profited from the encounter with Rameau's operas at the court of Parma. This is followed by a chorus sung by the Roman warriors *à 3* (TTB), leading to music for the gladitorial games (a ballet insert within the act as in *Ippolito*) composed by Traetta and framed by another chorus sung by the warriors. The first chorus begins darkly in c and ends on the chord of D (functioning as V). Without ado the ballet established B$\flat$ while the second chorus, without transition, launches forth in D, the key of jubilation.

Act I ends with an imposing solo scene for Siface, going from simple to obbligato recitative, then an ample aria in F, with passages for a lonely solo bassoon eerily conveying Siface's anguish at the thought of losing his wife (he believes, wrongly, that she wishes to return to her first suitor). Verazi deserves credit for integrating spectacle so thoroughly with music throughout the act. He does this even in solo arias by means of stage directions minutely specifying pantomime by the singers. It was an original stroke to make the first chorus, "Morrendo rinasce" (In dying we are reborn), a somber moment, seized perfectly by Traetta in a dirge-like canonic lament that sounds for all the world like Gustav Mahler. The following gladiatorial contest was so important it earned choreographer Bouqueton an extra mention in the libretto, besides citation for the entr'acte ballets (composed by Toeschi and Cannabich). Traetta shows how well he knew the strengths of the orchestra by beginning the second, triumphal chorus with a rapid ascent in the violins up two octaves to high D, what has been called a Mannheim rocket. Touches like this add to the likelihood that the composer was indeed present in Mannheim. Moreover, he puts a long, sixteen-measure *crescendo* with ascent of the violins up to high D in the first movement of the overture, once near the beginning and again at the end.

Act II begins with arias for the secondary characters (scenes 1–3, omitted in the modern edition). The setting then changes to the temple of the sun. A chorus *à 4* (SATB) sings praises to the god.

Nume adorabile	Adorable god
Che in ciel risplendi	who lights the sky
Coi raggi fervide	with fervid rays
A Noi discendi!	descend upon us!

[140]Tommaso Traetta, *Sofonisba*, ed. Hugo Goldschmidt, *DTB*, 25 (1914) and 29 (1916). The edition is far from complete.

These are five-syllable lines the first and third of which end with two weak sylla-bles (*quinari sdruccioli*). Traetta responds with the time-honored choice of triple meter with dotted rhythm for the second measure: | ♪ ♪ ♪ | ♪. ♪ ♪ |. The most famous example of *quinari sdruccioli* was Calzabigi's chorus of the furies in the second act of *Orfeo ed Euridice,* set the same way by Gluck. The first production of *Orfeo* in Vienna preceded that of *Sofonisba* by one month. Traetta, who was well acquainted and friendly with Gluck, probably traveled to Vienna in early 1761 for the production of his own *Armida,* after which he was back in Parma for his *Enea e Lavinia.* His whereabouts in 1762 are unknown, and the only clue is an *Alessandro nell'Indie* composed for the spring season at Reggio-Emilia. In his chorus sung to the sun god, Traetta shows excellent part writing. He conveys the main idea of the words by making descent the principal musical idea.

At the center of the opera is Sofonisba's aria in Scene 4 of Act II. Siface, believed dead, intervenes at the altar in the nuptials between his wife and Massi-nissa. Condemning herself, she asks for punishment and death. Verazi conveys her anguish in a short-breathed series of lines, full of hesitations and exclamations.

Crudeli, aimè! Che fate?[1]	Cruel men, alas! What are you doing?
Se il sangue voi bramate,	If it is blood you are seeking,
Prendete, eccovi il mio. . . .	Take it, here is mine. . . .
Ma dove? . . . Oh Dio!—Sentite:	But where? . . . Oh God!—Listen:
A me ferite . . . il sen.	Strike me . . . in the heart.
Ferite: io vi perdono. . . .	Pierce it: I forgive you. . . .
Misera! a chi ragiono?[2]	Miserable me! To whom do I speak?
Barbari affanni miei	My cruel misfortunes
Oh Dei, che piu volete?	Ye Gods, what more do you want?
Ah m'uccidete . . . almen.	Ah kill me . . . at least.

The numerals attached to the Italian lines are cued to the poet's stage directions. The first says, "turning now to Siface, now to Massinissa, who look askance at her menacingly, and who try to leave the temple but are stopped either by her pleas or by Scipione and Lelio, who accost them, and from whom they break away twice while clashing and threatening blows." That is a lot of stage business in competition with the music for the audience's attention. The second footnote says, "seeing that no one any longer listens to her, and terrified to the point of des-peration, she abandons them." By not listening to her, the men set another bad example for the audience. Verazi presented no small challenge to the composer and singer.

Traetta emerged triumphant, as did Dorothea Wendling. His setting of "Crudeli" to an agitated *Allegro* in the key of g established a model for a whole series of arias that would become like signature pieces for this singer. First violins provide a constant ostinato, beginning with a wavering figure in sixteenth notes back and forth between the fifth and flat sixth degree (Example 5.26). The vocal line comes in short bursts, following the shape of the text. Note that the violins drop their *sforzati* on the first sixteenth note when the voice comes in. The harmonic progression is rich: $| i | ii_2^6 | V_5^6 | i | {}^{\flat}II^6_3 - V| i$. A quick modulation to the relative major follows the opening phrase. Traetta mixes up the short exclamations at will, just as Diderot had recommended for lyric tragedy. At two places in the aria he calls for "un urlo francese," (a French scream). The French singers employed at Parma had apparently indulged in nonnotated cries of anguish at high points of tension, a step in the direction of realistic theater one would not expect an Italian composer to condone (and which Mozart condoned only in *Don Giovanni*). Twice the movement breaks off for short passages of recitative. It is through-composed,

EXAMPLE 5.26. *Traetta*, Sofonisba, *Aria*

the second stanza set as a kind of coda, marked *Allegro agitato,* in which the voice climbs to the melodic peak note, high B♭, just before the end.

At the apex of La Wendling's pathos-laden pieces in g stands Ilia's first aria in Mozart's *Idomeneo,* "Padre, germani, addio," which is adumbrated by "Crudeli." Another link between Mozart and Traetta's "Crudeli" will not have escaped some. The aria's lingering on E♭ - D, then on D - C (first violins) adumbrates the beginning of Symphony No. 40 in the same key (K. 550), a movement in common time marked *Molto Allegro.* Moreover, Mozart's harmonic progression duplicates the first five measures of the aria. Could Mozart possibly have studied a score as old as *Sofonisba?* Yes, he could have. A copy was in the collection of operatic scores possessed by Count von Sickingen, Mannheim's envoy to Paris, which Mozart specifically cited (letter dated Paris, 29 May 1778).[141]

Verazi ended Act II of *Sofonisba* with a trio for the three principal parts, "Muore!" Traetta begins with an *Allegro agitato* in common time and in the key of E♭. This gives way to an *Andantino grazioso* in 3/8 meter in canon, a plea to heaven for help, a return to *primo tempo,* another *Andante grazioso* in 3/8 but with different music, and one last return to *primo tempo,* with Sofonisba climbing up to high B♭. The ensemble amounts to a sizable 340 measures altogether. One curious feature of it is that Sofonisba and Siface exit before the very end, leaving Massinissa alone to vent his rage. The ensemble of diminishing forces is a resource that Verazi also deployed in his *Fetonte* for Jommelli.[142]

Act III takes place in a palatial room with a large curtained window giving on the port. Verazi turns up the pathos, as it were, by bringing Sofonisba's and Siface's young son on stage, which necessitates tearful farewells and a great deal of minor-mode lamenting in an opera already replete with the same. The role of young boy was a nonsinging one in the original production, but for the revival a year later it was made into a singing part for Dorothea's little daughter, whose name was added to the newly printed libretto as "Elisabetta Augusta Wendeling [sic]."

Sofonisba confides her son to the care of Cirene, as she and Siface are about to be shipped as prisoners to Rome. Sofonisba is alone momentarily (Scene 10). In her monologue, an obbligato recitative after a few measures of simple recitative, she asks why her hands tremble so. The violins shudder away in triplet unisons, painting her trembling in the key of a, *Largo ma non troppo.* At her words "Ah! I did not believe how terrible it would be to face death!" the violins let out a rapid scale up two octaves from middle C to high C (the violas doubling an octave below).

[141]Corneilson and Wolf, "Newly Identified Manuscripts of Operas and Related Works from Mannheim," p. 253.

[142]Jörg Riedlbauer, *Die Opern von Tommaso Trajetta* (Hildesheim, 1994), pp. 283–86, argues that *Sofonisba* influenced *Fetonte* in both text and music.

The curtains at the rear are suddenly opened to reveal prisoners in chains being marched onto the waiting ships. Traetta reinforces this *coup de théâtre* by a simultaneous march for a band of winds on stage, in an incongruously gay and bright C major. Sofonisba has already raised the cup of poison to her lips. As soldiers enter with torches and chains to take her away, she drinks the poison. The last scene begins in simple recitative, Scipione announcing the news that the Roman senate has relented and granted Siface and Sofonisba their freedom. In a final quintet of farewells, Traetta boldly modulates from the initial key of d, through f, b♭, B♭, g, a, and finally to d. But more boldly still, he takes the middle movement of his overture, an *Andante* in 2/4 that seems to waver in key between d and g, from this quintet. Thus does the overture forecast the final tragedy. Sofonisba does not die on stage, but staggers off, supported by her handmaidens. A final chorus, *Allegro strepitoso* in cut time and in the key of F, ends the opera.

Majo's *Ifigenia in Tauride*

Gian Francesco de Majo was the next composer to be called to Mannheim. Born in Naples of a musical family on 24 March 1732 (one week before Haydn), Majo had by 1758 been appointed second organist of the royal chapel there. Only at this rather late date did he begin to compose operas. Traetta became maestro di cappella at Parma the same year. For the following carnival season in Parma, Traetta wrote the first opera, *Solimano,* on a libretto of Migliavacca, and Majo wrote the second, *Ricimero, re dei Goti,* by Zeno and Pariati, given its first performance on 7 February 1759. These were followed a few months later by Traetta's *Ippolito ed Aricia,* first performed on 9 May 1759. Traetta must have been instrumental in getting Majo invited to Parma. Majo wrote no further operas there. He did compose several for other centers. During the period from April 1761 to February 1763, while he was mainly in northern Italy, Majo studied with Padre Martini in Bologna, but an apologetic letter to Martini from the young composer suggests that he was an erratic student because of various amorous distractions. Majo's health may have also been a factor. He suffered a first attack of tuberculosis in 1760 and the disease would kill him ten years later.

In the spring of 1764 Majo was invited to Vienna, for which Traetta may also have been responsible. The court was celebrating the coronation of Archduke Joseph as king of the Romans (meaning he would automatically succeed his father, Francis of Lorraine, as Holy Roman emperor when Francis died a year later). In honor of the event it commissioned Majo to set Marco Coltellini's *Alcide negli orti esperide,* given at Laxenburg on 9 June 1764. The composer spent the summer at leisure in Vienna and was mentioned by Metastasio in his letters to Farinelli. In the letter of 25 August 1764, the poet wrote, "Our ardent and languid Majo, stimulated by his friends and by his duty, is at length set off for Mannheim, where he is engaged to compose an opera for the Elector Palatine" (2: 296).

Verazi wrote the libretto and probably chose the subject. Not to be excluded is the possibility that Carl Theodore chose it, or indeed that his wife did, since the opera was given "by command of the Electress," as the title page of the libretto states, in order to celebrate the elector's name day. Standing on the success of his *Sofonisba,* Verazi chose to overburden the famous Greek tragedy with even more spectacle and dramatic pantomime. The time was not yet ripe in the 1760s for a return to the simplicity of Euripides, who confined himself to four characters: Ifigenia, Orestes, Pylades, and Thoas. At Vienna in 1763 Coltellini came fairly close to Euripides in his *Ifigenia in Tauride,* set by Traetta, but he added a female companion of the title role, Dori, who was needed so that the two women could enhance the opera with duets. Mannheim could also boast an excellent pair of female sopranos in Dorothea Wendling and Elisabeth Sarselli. It would have been a pity not to use both. Verazi decided to infuse the healthy rivalry between them into the story itself by creating the role of Tomiri, daughter and sole heir of the rightful ruler of Tauris, whose throne has been usurped by Toante. To further embroil things, and following traditional patterns consecrated by Metastasio, Verazi has Tomiri in love with Toante and jealous of Ifigenia, upon whom Toante has amorous designs. He needed one more character to bring the number up to the usual six. He made the mistake of inventing Merodate, a comic-opera kind of sovereign from a neighboring kingdom. Toante tries to marry Tomiri to Merodate, both to get rid of her and to strengthen his hold on the throne that is rightfully hers. The resulting mishmash wavers fitfully between the sublime and the ridiculous, and would have daunted a composer far more experienced than Majo. To his credit Majo drew many moments of beauty from an excessively long, wordy, and confusing libretto.

The Greek myth suffered one further touch of comic opera at Verazi's hands. Orestes, we are told, had killed his mother Clytemnestra by accident, when she darted in front of the blow that was intended for her paramour Aegistes, an action suggesting a Punch and Judy show. Verazi baldly asserted in the preface of the libretto, "Without altering the most essential circumstances, we have allowed ourselves the discretion to diverge in part from the common opinion of the myth," and furthermore, "we have tried to make its subject more interesting and its success less uncertain and perilous."[143] What Verazi has done is layer intrigue upon intrigue onto a straightforward tale. One visitor to Mannheim took a dim view of Verazi's changes and "improvements." Wilhelm Heinse in his novel *Hildegard von Hohenthal* (1795–96) looked back on the experience with praise for Majo's music but scorn for Verazi.

> It is incomprehensible how someone could make something so mediocre out of Euripides's masterpiece. The poor-village King Merodate and Tomyris must unravel

---

[143]Gian Francesco de Majo, *Ifigenia in Tauride,* ed. Paul Corneilson (Madison, Wis., 1996), p. xii.

the plot and rescue the Greeks in a pitiful manner. Except for several beautiful arias and situations, there is none of the feeling in this opera that Euripides summons from innermost Nature with delightful results. Unfortunately, two of the greatest composers [Majo and Jommelli] have wasted their genius on it. [144]

Heinse went on to explain why intentional matricide was important.

The truth of the myth consists in the following: Orestes must, according to the judgement of the gods, after many afflictions, still endure fear of death because of his mother's murder; his youngest sister and his bosom friend rescue him in the end and make him happy again. The whole is charmingly veiled and decorated through religion. The librettist Verazi had no inkling of all this. Childishly, he changed the story and allowed Orestes to murder his mother Clytemnestra against his will, because she unexpectedly stepped between them as he was about to stab Aegisthus.

Some reaction against Verazi must have declared itself in court circles at Mannheim as well at the time. Henceforth he was reduced to the function of revising works of Metastasio and other poets for local setting. Majo, on the other hand, was invited to compose another opera for Mannheim two years later. He obliged with a setting of *Alessandro nell'Indie,* an odd choice in a way. Kapellmeister Holzbauer had made his own setting of this favorite libretto by Metastasio (Milan, 1759). Commissioning another setting by the young Neapolitan can only have seemed like a reproach to Holzbauer. It could be that both Verazi and Holzbauer were in some electoral disfavor for a while.

Having opened the stage curtains on the last movement of the overture to *Sofonisba,* Verazi called for all three movements to correspond to pantomime in *Ifigenia.* The first movement accompanied a storm and shipwreck of the Greek forces. The second represents a calm after the storm. During the third there is enacted the capture of the surviving Greeks by the Scythians. Majo would have reached Mannheim by about the first of September 1764; thus he had a good two months to sound out the local forces and learn from them. His overture is a disappointment and does little honor to Mannheim's symphonic tradition. Its key, E♭, is unusual in Italian overtures. But otherwise Majo conjures the storm rather weakly, with octaves in runs up and down, or twelfths, and, at one point in the opening *Allegro con brio* in common time, a prolonged diminished seventh chord outlined by unisons. In order to reach the reprise Majo modulates in a crude, almost schoolboyish manner, by rising thirds in the violins until they finally reach the third and fifth degrees of the dominant. This very tame storm gives way to a transition at the end leading in the calm, which is a frilly flute solo in G marked

[144]Wilhelm Heinse, *Sämmtliche Werke,* 10 vols. (Leipzig, 1903), 5: 290, quoted from Majo, *Ifigenia in Tauride,* xi–xii.

cantabile (at least G was a much better key than E♭ for the transverse flute, and flautist Wendling was one of the orchestra's great strengths). Another transition leads to the innocuous finale. Majo was no symphonist.

Majo's biggest asset was an ability to display the individual voice to maximum advantage. Many Mannheim composers traveled to Italy in search of this precious gift, but it was attained by very few. Majo's sparing use of the Mannheim orchestra, looked at from the singer's point of view, was an advantage. A lot can be learned from the very first aria, assigned to Dorothea Wendling in the title role, "De' tuoi mali esulterei" (I would exult in your misfortunes). She sings this to Pylades, explaining that her own misfortunes make her pity him. She tells just enough of her story to serve the purpose of dramatic exposition. Majo sets the text to *Allegro moderato* in common time and in the key of B♭. Wendling was partial to flat keys and almost always got them in her arias, either because composers studied her previous roles or because she demonstrated her voice directly to them, perhaps accompanying herself at the keyboard. Majo restricts the orchestra to strings alone in this piece. They begin with a texture *à 3*, the violins singing the melody in thirds and sixths, or in unison, with a liberal sprinkling of chromatic appoggiature. One appoggiatura, at the first unison in the violins (at which the violas stop doubling the basses) is so insistent it lasts for two measures before being resolved, having entered as the top tone of an augmented triad—an audacious, surprising tonal maneuver. Soon after this the violins sing what will become the smooth and sensuous second theme. Ifigenia enters in m. 24 singing a simplified version of the main theme, without the sixteenth-note decorations introduced by the violins in the opening ritornello. Her line is almost totally conjunct and moves about easily in a modest range, except for the two touches of coloratura that end the **A** section and its repetition. Majo's orchestration may be sparing but it is also deft. Particularly effective is the way he lets the orchestra take the lead in the second theme, giving the voice a rest, and bringing it in to double the first violins only at the end of the two-measure phrase (Example 5.27). A little flurry of coloratura and the "wedge cadence" end the section. Of the five parts of the old da capo aria (**A1 A2 B A1 A2**) less than three remain. Majo ends **A1** on V, as usual, eliminates **A2**, introduces a contrasting *Larghetto* in 3/8 time and in c minor for the **B** stanza, then returns to tonic B♭ at the equivalent of the second theme for an abbreviated version of the initial **A** ending on I. He uses this modified and shortened kind of ternary form often throughout the opera. The result, in the case of Dorothea's first aria, is an ample and satisfying musical experience, although relatively short at 122 mm., or at least a lot briefer than the full da capo forms of the previous generation.

Majo makes an exception to the through-composed norm in the case of Ifigenia's jealous rival, Tomiri, who can hardly be considered a seconda donna because her part is nearly equal to Dorothea's and indeed superior to it as to vocal

EXAMPLE 5.27. *Majo*, Ifigenia in Tauride, *Aria*

display. Elisabeth Sarselli was obviously developing into a fiery coloratura soprano. She is given the opera's third aria, "È specie di follia la gelosia" (Jealousy is a kind of madness). She sings this to Ifigenia, plunging into an *Allegro brillante* in common time and in the key of A with only one measure of orchestral introduction. Brilliant runs up into the stratosphere, some with staccato articulation, sound like madness itself. Just as flat keys suit the more sedate roles of Dorothea, sharp keys often displayed the vocal fireworks of the volatile Elisabeth. Majo uses the full five-part form here, abbreviating only **A1** on its return after **B** by a dal segno indication. The total number of measures rose to 191 and, in time elapsed, considerably more than in the first aria for Dorothea. The opera's creators made it up to Dorothea by giving her a great solo scene to end the second act. Having learned of the death of Clytemnestra, her mother, Ifigenia gets to sing an *ombra* aria in which pairs of oboes and horns are prominent. It is an *Allegro* in common

time and in E$^\flat$, with themes admirably adumbrated in the preceding obbligato recitative. "Ombra cara che intorno t'aggiri" (Dear shade that hovers around me) is a cliché of Italian opera in both text and music but well executed, and perhaps modeled after the *ombra* aria for Telaira in Traetta's *I Tintaridi* (Parma, 1760). Dorothea also receives a tearful recitative and aria in Act III (Nos. 26–27), beginning in g.

All the spectacle accompanying the arrival of King Merodate in Act I, with the staging of gladiatorial games in his honor, forms a strange counterpoint to his niggling, ill-bred behavior. Majo, unlike Traetta and Jommelli, had no experience writing comic opera, but he gives an appropriately buffo tone to Merodate's aria, No. 9, an *Allegro* in G and in 3/8 time that proceeds in symmetrical little units separated by rests. The part was sung by the tenor Pietro Pablo Carnoli.

Tonarelli, the court's leading soprano castrato, played the role of Orestes, and his faithful sidekick Pylades was taken by the alto castrato Giovanni Battista

Coraucci. Verazi has guards separating them with violence at the end of Act I. A duet of sweet warblings in chains of thirds and sixths, however musically effective, seems dramatically inept here, because the music contradicts the stage action. Tonarelli must have had a soprano to match Elisabeth Sarselli's voice, because he is given a huge aria di bravura (No. 28) just before the dénoument. It is the only other dal segno aria besides hers.

Giovanni Battista Zonca was an Italian bass who had been hired by the court the previous year. His first major role was Toante, and it was a big one. Basses were confined to comic opera in Italy for the most part. It was a breakthrough to have a powerful bass voice and a good actor along with it in serious opera. Zonca was the only singer besides Dorothea Wendling given an aria in each of the three acts, and he also had the task of ending the opera with his third aria, as he throws himself into the flaming ruins, like Metastasio's Didone. Verazi wrote a long last scene for him shamelessly pillaging the senior poet for verbal expressions. Majo had the good sense to make a large cut in the text. He set this last aria of rage in the key of E♭, where the overture had begun the opera. Mozart had a favorable opinion of Zonca's singing and acting abilities. He first thought the role of Idomeneo would go to him. After it was assigned to Anton Raaff he said he would have preferred Zonca, for whom he would have written music more expressive of the text (letter dated Munich, 27 December 1780).

Verazi systematically sought to reduce the number of arias in his text. In the second and third acts there are only three apiece. Their place was taken by short cavatinas or by ensembles, in which the opera is rich (two duets, two trios, and one quartet). As in *Sofonisba* he was partial to the action ensemble of diminishing forces. Thus the trio at the beginning of Act III becomes a duet for the two ladies in praise of constancy after the boorish Merodate leaves. One of the few redeeming features of Verazi's libretto is the way the ladies, after previous disagreements, make common cause toward the end against both Merodate and the tyrannical Toante.

Lorenzo Quaglio, the scene designer and theatrical engineer at Mannheim, was kept very busy by Verazi's demands. There were no fewer than eleven changes of scene in the opera, plus five more in the two entr'acte ballets (which do not survive). Verazi's scenic extravagance reached its Mannheim peak in *Ifigenia.*[145]

JOHANN CHRISTIAN BACH

After the excesses of *Ifigenia* Mannheim turned toward more conventional operatic fare, evident in the return to librettos by Metastasio, which required fewer

---

[145]In 1771 Jommelli had to write an opera on short notice for the San Carlo in Naples. He asked his friend Verazi to revise *Ifigenia in Tauride* for him. Verazi did, by eliminating all the ensembles and the choruses. This suggests that they were not essential in the first place. What Naples saw was an unadulterated aria opera. Even though the singers were good, inadequate rehearsal time, Jommelli's orchestral demands, and the lack of understanding on the part of the public doomed the opera to failure.

stage sets. The turn is seen as well in the choice of Piccinni and Christian Bach as outside composers. After Majo wrote *Alessandro* in 1766, no more luminaries from the Parma-Vienna orbit were called upon. Some interest was shown in Gluck's *Alceste,* the first act of which was rehearsed before the court in July 1769, with an intention of public performance during the following opera season. It did not happen. Gluck was an honored guest of the elector when he passed through Schwetzingen in August 1774 but he wrote nothing for Mannheim. Nor were Jommelli, Traetta, and Majo tapped for further complete operas. A special dynastic occasion had to be celebrated in early 1769 when the Wittelsbach princess Amalia Augusta of Zweibrücken wed Elector Frederick August of Saxony. For this family affair it was certainly appropriate that the court's Kapellmeister resume the reins as opera composer and he did. Holzbauer made a setting of Metastasio's *Adriano in Siria* to celebrate the wedding. His score has been lost. Like those of most other operas he composed, it fell victim to the Austrian bombardment and destruction of the opera house in 1795.

Niccolò Piccinni of Naples was commissioned to make a setting of Metastasio's *Catone in Utica* to celebrate the elector's name day in 1770. The second version of the ending was chosen, in which Cato kills himself offstage. Piccinni set sixteen of the poem's original twenty-six arias, plus four additional ones (perhaps by Verazi). The only ensemble was a trio to end Act II. That Piccinni worked from afar and did not come to Mannheim is clear, because Burney was visiting him in Naples as the rehearsals were taking place in October 1770. That he worked with the knowledge of Mannheim's singers is also clear, else he would not have written arias for Dorothea Wendling as Marzia in the keys of g and $E^\flat$.

Anton Raaff was apparently the conduit by which the new opera traveled from Naples to Mannheim, where the famous tenor arrived to take up residence in August 1770. Born near Bonn in 1714, Raaff had sung at Carl Theodore's wedding in 1741 when he was in the service of the elector of Cologne. In 1761 he sang the title role in Christian Bach's very successful *Catone* for Naples and would do the same in Piccinni's new setting for Mannheim. There were borrowings from the earlier libretto that show Raaff's hand, notably a big scene in the coveted spot before the *scena ultima.* Here in 1761 he received one of his most famous arias, "Per darvi alcun pegno" (To give you some token), sung as he prepares to die. Bach set the piece as a long slow aria, a *Larghetto* in the key of $B^\flat$. Raaff retained this advantage in Mannheim, and it cannot be a coincidence that Piccinni set "Per darvi alcun pegno" similarly, in the same key.[146] Mozart followed suit in *Idomeneo* by giving Raaff a big, slow, penultimate showcase, "Torna la pace al core" in $B^\flat$.

[146]Wolfram Enslin, *Niccolò Piccinni: Catone in Utica: Quellenüberlieferung, Aufführungsgeschichte und Analyse* (Quellen und Studien der Mannheimer Hofkapelle, 4) (Frankfurt, 1996), pp. 232–33. Enslin, on pp. 172–73, gives other examples that show Piccinni knew Bach's setting.

Piccinni's autograph of *Catone* survives and shows several changes in the hands of Mannheim copyists, plus one major addition. An alternative aria by Sacchini, "Ovunque m'aggiri sol veggio perigli," (Wherever I wander I see only perils) was substituted for No. 14. According to a note in the manuscript, this was done at the request of the electress.

Raaff was a musician well along in years when he returned to Mannheim in 1770. His ideas about opera were those of the midcentury. He did not like to sing in ensembles and only wanted lyric opportunities to "spin out his voice," as he complained to Mozart, who complained accordingly to his father (letter of 27 December 1780). It cannot surprise that the composer invited to write the name-day opera for 1772 was Christian Bach himself, another of Raaff's favorites. He was commissioned to set Metastasio's *Temistocle,* which provided another title role for Raaff. Unlike Piccinni, Bach came to Mannheim. His presence is attested by Riaucour as early as 12 September 1772—plenty of time to assess the local strengths. Aside from the great singers he would have heard for the first time the finest of orchestras, an ensemble under Cannabich superior to anything he could have experienced in Berlin, Italy, or London.

Bach had another strong connection with Mannheim. During the spring of 1772, the Wendling family—father, mother, and daughter—visited London. They stayed in Bach's house and participated in his concerts. Returning the favor, they became Bach's hosts in Mannheim. Bach proposed marriage to the daughter, who was compromised by an affair with the elector. The marriage came to naught, but by residing at the Wendlings Bach could often try out the music he was composing with them.

Verazi asserted himself once again by making major alterations in the *Temistocle* libretto. He retained only ten of the original arias and revised two of these, while adding six arias of his own, plus a duet. Most striking of all, he ended Act II and Act III with free-flowing ensembles of several sections. Act II closes with a quartet of diminishing forces, one of his favorite devices. Aspasia, the prima donna part sung by Dorothea Wendling, begins and ends the piece, in which Raaff did not participate. She is abandoned by the others soon after the beginning. What emerged was a great solo scene for Mannheim's finest singer, who inspired the composer to the highest degree. By this time she had taken on a quite matronly mien, as a silhouette of her shows (Figure 5.14).

Major opportunities for Raaff had already occurred in Act I, with a long dal segno aria in E♭.[147] For Dorothea Wendling Bach wrote an agitated aria in g that

---

[147]Johann Christian Bach, *Temistocle,* ed. Edward O. D. Downes and H. C. Robbins Landon (Vienna, 1965), pp. 30–41. This edition is nearly useless for scholarly purposes, being a potpourri of several Bach works. In the aria in question the B section is eliminated without any indication. For a scholarly edition, see that of Ernest Warburton in *The Collected Works,* vol. 7 (London, 1988). On p. ix Warburton refers to the edition of Downes and Landon as a version "best described as a pasticcio."

FIGURE 5.14. Silhouette of Dorothea Wendling.

paid homage to a special tradition stretching from Traetta's "Crudeli" to Mozart's "Padre, germani." Wendling again revealed her penchant for touching the degrees 1 - 5 - 8 in this key (Example 5.28). To end the last act Raaff as Temistocle received an obbligato recitative and slow aria that blossomed into an ensemble of several sections. In the recitative the orchestra sounds independently a motif that recalls Aspasia's initiation of the quartet ending Act II. Furthermore, the orchestra sounds chains of descending conjunct fourths that occur in that earlier piece. These are orchestral "plants" that prefigure the first postrecitative item, the *Largo* in D sung by Temistocle. Thematic integration of this kind has been observed in Jommelli's Stuttgart operas and link up with future Mannheim operas such as Holzbauer's *Günther von Schwarzburg* (and Mozart's *Idomeneo*). In moving freely from recitative sections to those in various tempos, keys, and meters, Bach never loses the high tone of serious opera or approaches anything that sounds like opera buffa, a genre he never cultivated. The opera as a whole can be viewed as a happy expansion of the seria genre by poet and composer alike.

EXAMPLE 5.28. *Christian Bach*, Temistocle, *Aria*

Bach's relations with Mannheim were mutually satisfactory and warm. Two of his serenatas written for concert performances in London, *Endimione* and *Amore vincitore,* were revived at the Palatine court, the former with revisions by Verazi and additions by Jommelli. Not surprisingly, Bach was invited to compose another name-day opera for 1774. The choice fell upon Giovanni de Gamerra's *Lucio Silla,* which Mozart had set for Milan in 1772–73.

Lucio Silla was somewhat ill-starred from the beginning. Bach made the setting in London. There was no need for him to return to Mannheim since the singers who would perform it were nearly all known to him. His score was shipped from London by a diplomat in Palatine service. Unfortunately, a part of it was lost in transit, which postponed performance from the name-day celebration of 1774 to that of 1775.[148] One dire consequence was that no serious opera graced the carnival season of 1775, which was given over entirely to comic operas composed for other centers. The musical invention in *Lucio Silla* has been described as not being on as high a level as that of *Temistocle*.[149] Mozart reported to his father by letter of 13 November 1777 that Bach's second opera pleased less than the first, which can only be the opinion of his musician friends. Mozart was eager to see the score of *Lucio Silla*, having set the same opera himself. Holzbauer told him to borrow it from Vogler, which he did. According to the same letter Vogler, to Mozart's great annoyance, denigrated Bach, particularly his setting of Cecilio's "Pupille amate" (Beautiful eyes).

Mozart's sublimely beautiful but simple setting of "Pupille amate" defies comparison, except with Gluck.[150] Bach's setting shares with it 3/8 time and the key of A (Example 5.29). His melody seems stunted, especially in mm. 3–4, where repeated tones were dictated by the decision to paint "lagrimate" by chromatic descent in the bass. Rhythmically rather stiff, the musical idea does not soar or impress itself on the memory as does Mozart's. But it had less need of doing so, being no longer the high point of the act, as in Mozart. This function went to Raaff in the title role, who sang a long, slow additional piece in his accustomed penultimate spot, a concertante aria, with solo oboe, horn, and bassoon, in which he could shine along with the famous Mannheim wind players. Verazi had increased Silla's arias from two to four. Raaff was known for demanding and getting his way in such matters.

EXAMPLE 5.29. *Christian Bach*, Lucio Silla, *Aria*

Lucio Silla was well received at its first performance on 5 November 1775 according to Riaucour's dispatch written two days later. A cloud hung over the event even so. The court was expecting news from one moment to the next announcing the death of the duke of Zweibrücken. Carl Theodore and Elizabeth

---

[148]Paul Corneilson, "The Case of J. C. Bach's *Lucio Silla*," *Journal of Musicology* 12 (1994): 206–18.
[149]By Ernest Warburton, "Bach, Johann Christian" in *The New Grove Dictionary of Opera*, ed. Stanley Sadie (London, 1992).
[150]*Haydn, Mozart*, p. 554.

Auguste were visibly distraught, says Riaucour. The news came at the end of the performance, entailing a six-week period of mourning.

In public Vogler had nothing but praise for Bach, which casts doubts upon Mozart's assertions. He summed up the composer's strengths and individuality in an interesting way, with stress upon the multinational facets of his style.

> Bach is one of the greatest composers, a musician of whom Germany can well be proud. . . . In general his musical compositions incorporate a mixture of Italian taste, in which the main sonorities are very simple; of German, which surprises with unexpected harmonic turns; of French, in which the minor mode rules; and of English, that occasionally brings forth quite cool and bracing melodies: a mixture that was never attempted before.[151]

For more on Vogler's comments about Bach, see pp. 918–19.

Opera buffa made few inroads at Mannheim before 1770 but then it began to take over. For the missing name-day opera by Bach in 1774, Salieri's *La secchia rapita* (Vienna, 1772) was substituted. Both Salieri and his teacher Florian Gassmann had been represented by Italian comic operas in Mannheim during 1772. Other comic operas were composed by Galuppi, Piccinni, Guglielmo, Giuseppe Gazzaniga, Anfossi, and Paisiello, in other words, the phalanx of opera buffa composers beginning to prevail everywhere. None of these works was written for Mannheim. The singers of the Italian comic operas were mainly those who sang in the serious ones, including Zonca and the Wendlings. Raaff did not deign to sing in comic opera. Perhaps he felt that appearing in comedies was beneath his dignity. His roles in the serious operas were usually those of sage or virtuous rulers, elder statesmen, or patriotic heroes.

Mannheim's years as a center for the creation of new operas were apparently drawing to a close, just as at Stuttgart. Yet during the same time, the first half of the 1770s, a new current began stirring with the cultivation of operas sung in German. Within a few years Mannheim forged to the head of this movement.

Theater in German: Melodrama

Carl Theodore began to take interest in German theater toward the end of the 1760s. In 1768 he attended plays performed by Joseph Sebastiani's Mainz-based troupe in a temporary theater on Mannheim's market square. In consequence he allowed the actors to style themselves his "Palatine court players." A year later he directed his French troupe to perform the *drame Eugénie* by Caron de Beaumarchais. Squabbles within the troupe about casting delayed the production, which

---

[151]Vogler, *Betrachtungen der Mannheimer Tonschule*, 1: 63–66, quoted in the original German by Corneilson, "The Case of J. C. Bach's *Lucio Silla*," p. 216, n. 31.

enabled the poet and publisher Christian Friedrich Schwan to make a German translation of the play in haste and have it performed first by the visitors.[152] From this point on, the French troupe gradually lost the elector's favor. In his dispatch dated Mannheim, 27 October 1770, Riaucour reported that Carl Theodore was, on the one hand, dissatisfied by the negligence with which the French comedians attended to their duties, and, on the other hand, he wished to avoid their very great expense during an unfortunate time when his subjects were scarcely in a position to pay their ordinary taxes. The troupe was to continue only through Easter and then was to be released and replaced by a less expensive one.[153]

Theobold Marchand, born in Strasbourg in 1741, was largely responsible for the flourishing of German theater in Mannheim in the 1770s. He had gone to Paris to study medicine at the age of seventeen but instead began studying French theater and especially the newly blooming genre of opéra-comique. He joined Sebastiani's troupe in 1764 and by 1770 became its director. Marchand's success in Mannheim led the elector to invite the troupe to make the city their main residence.

Opéra-comique, as elsewhere in Germany, provided the catalyst that stimulated Singspiel. Parisian works by Duni, Philidor, Monsigny, Grétry, and others, sung in German translation, dominated Marchand's lyric offerings, to which were added a few works by Gluck (*Die Pilgrimme von Mekka*), Gassmann, Galuppi, Piccinni, and Sacchini.[154] The only locally composed work was Vogler's one-act *Der Kaufmann von Smyrna* on a libretto that Schwan translated from Nicolas-Sébastien de Chamfort's *Le marchand de Smyrne*. When Burney arrived in Mannheim in August 1772 he saw a performance of Grétry's *Zémire et Azor* sung in German. He was highly complimentary:"I was astonished to find, that the German language, in spite of all its clashing consonants, and gutterals, is better calculated for music than the French."

The principal singers who emerged from Marchand's troupe were Barbara Strasser and Franziska Danzi, sopranos; Franz Hartig, tenor; and Ludwig Fischer, bass, the future Osmin in Mozart's *Die Entführung.* Fischer tells in his autobiography how the court's intendant, Count Louis Savioli, surprised Carl Theodore by presenting a Marchand Singspiel in the Schwetzingen theater. It was Duni's *Les deux chasseurs et la laitière* translated by Schwan as *Das Milkmädchen.* The elector was very pleased with it and wanted to hear more. From this point on German comic opera eclipsed opera buffa at Mannheim, says Fischer. The German singers were taken into direct electoral service. One of their great triumphs was the pro-

---

[152]Günther Ebersold, *Rokoko, Reform und Revolution: Ein politisches Lebensbild des Kurfürsten Karl Theodor* (Frankfurt, 1985), p. 40.
[153]Corneilson,"Opera at Mannheim, 1770–1778," pp. 373–74.
[154]The Marchand troupe's repertory in Mannheim from 1770 to 1776 is catalogued from printed librettos by Corneilson (ibid., pp. 124–25).

duction of a serious German opera, Anton Schweitzer's setting of Christoph Martin Wieland's *Alceste,* written for the small court of Saxe-Weimar in 1773. In 1774 Marchand produced this *Alceste* in Frankfurt, probably using the printed score (Leipzig, 1774).

Anton Klein, a former Jesuit from Alsace, was, with Schwan, one of the founders of Mannheim's German Society in 1775. A poet, dramatist, and professor of philosophy, Klein took it upon himself to write Wieland in Weimar telling him of Marchand's plans to perform *Alceste* at the Palatine court. Wieland was flattered and flustered to the point that he was afraid Klein meant Gluck's *Alceste,* not Schweitzer's.[155] Marchand had put his main singers into the four roles required (Weimar could muster only four good solo singers in 1773). Strasser sang the title role, Hartig her husband Admetus, Franziska Danzi was Parthenia, and Fischer was Hercules. The first performances took place at Schwetzingen on 13 and 20 August 1775 and were generally accounted to be a triumph. Riaucour wrote Dresden that the work "has certainly brought honor to German literature and to the national genius for music." The success of *Alceste* led Carl Theodore to commission two serious operas in German, *Günther von Schwarzburg* from Klein and Holzbauer, and *Rosamunde* from Wieland and Schweitzer.

Not everyone at court was pleased with the turn toward theater in German. Electress Elizabeth Auguste, still smarting from having been removed from the direction, showed hostility to Schweitzer's *Alceste* in 1775, attributed by Riaucour to her general distaste for German plays.[156] She may have sided with the established singers against the newcomers.

Schweitzer's *Alceste* was a success with the public wherever it was performed, while professionals damned both Wieland and Schweitzer for it. Goethe, in *Götter, Helden und Wieland* (1773), took the poet to task for making a sentimental hodgepodge out of Euripides. Actually Goethe put his finger on the very element that made the opera so successful—the public saw instead of a Greek tragedy a *drame bourgeois* full of characteristically mid-eighteenth-century *Empfindsamkeit.* A young German composer, Joseph Martin Kraus, excoriated both the libretto and the music in *Etwas von und über Musik fürs Jahr 1777* (Frankfurt, 1778). Gerber summed up: "many and diverse things have the critics found to fault in it, and indeed not without cause. In spite of this, it has now held up on our German stage for sixteen years, always with the same enthusiastic praise and applause."[157]

A close look at one of Schweitzer's pieces is in order at this point. The trio from Act II will serve (Example 5.30). This moment was chosen to illustrate the

[155]Ibid., pp. 126–27.
[156]Letter dated Schwetzingen 15 August 1775, ibid., p. 384.
[157]Ernest Ludwig Gerber, "Anton Schweitzer," in *Historisch-biographisches Lexikon der Tonkünstler*, 2 vols. (Leipzig, 1790–92), cited after Thomas Bauman, *North German Opera in the Age of Goethe* (Cambridge, 1985), p. 105.

EXAMPLE 5.30. *Schweitzer,* Alceste, *Terzetto*

title page of the printed score.[158] Alceste begins by saying that if she had a thousand lives to give in rescuing her husband's life, she would given them all with joy. "What a love, great gods!" exclaims Admetus, "What a model of pure desire!"

[158]Klaus Hortschansky, "Musiktheater in Mannheim als gestelltes Bild," in *Mozart und Mannheim*, pp. 65–80; 75–78.

chimes in Parthenia. Schweitzer has a good melodic inspiration at the start, the paired notes with slurs in conjunct descent being in the best Italian operatic style and used often by Hasse. The bass, on the other hand, calls attention away from the voice, which Hasse never would have done, by descending to A♭, suggesting a modulation to IV even before the tonic has been established. A simple V, with F in the bass, would have kept the focus on the melody. As it is written, the melody's

B♭ (middle tone of a melodic turn) clashes with the bass. The A♮, although only a decorating tone (low one of the turn), clashes even more by coming on the first half of the fourth beat. In m. 2 it would have been easier for the voice to return to F instead of leaping down to C after quick notes. A chromatic rise as in m. 3 adds a nice melodic touch and is very modish—its like can be found in Hasse's *Alcide al bivio,* printed in Leipzig in 1763. Once again the clash between bass and treble takes away from the latter. Having the violins break into sixteenth notes conveys the idea of multitude expressed by "tausend," as do the obstinate repetitions in the vocal line in mm. 7–8. For the comments of the other characters Schweitzer switches to *Allegretto* in 3/8, adding further rhythmic nervosity to a musical fabric that is already very fussy. Giving the man bassoons as accompaniment and the ladies flutes shows care and discernment in choice of tone color. The vocal lines in 3/8 time invoke a whole series of melodic sighs. This, too, is Hasselike and surely raised many a tear. If gentle tears are the highest aim of *Empfindsamkeit,* this piece rises toward the goal.

Wieland cast *Alceste* in five short acts, like a spoken tragedy. He emulated in German Metastasio's beauty, precision, and economy of language with remarkable success. Also Metastasian is the way he eschews spectacle, ballet, and chorus (of which there is little). The concentration is on the poetry and, secondarily, its musical setting. *Alceste* fit well with the move toward greater austerity in opera at Mannheim but did not prevent grand opera in all its excess from soon returning.

Mozart met Schweitzer in Mannheim and wrote a number of impressions of him, his *Alceste,* and his subsequent *Rosamunde.* He accorded *Alceste* its rightful place as a path-breaker and respected the composer as a person.

> Herr Kapellmeister Schweitzer is a good, worthy, honest man, dry, and plain like our [Michael] Haydn, but better-spoken. There are some very beautiful things in his new opera and I believe that it will succeed. His *Alceste,* which is not half so beautiful as *Rosamunde,* pleased greatly. That it was the first German Singspiel contributed to its success of course. Now it no longer makes such an impression on spirits carried away by novelty alone. Herr Wieland, who wrote the poetry, is also coming here this winter. I would gladly make his acquaintance. [Letter dated Mannheim, 3 December 1777]

Thus *Alceste* was the first serious opera in German of the new era. But what of all those operas in German at Hamburg and elsewhere two generations earlier? They were forgotten and might as well never have existed. As for Hiller's *Die Jagd,* no matter how serious it was in parts, its spoken dialogue placed it in a different league from *Alceste,* which was sung throughout, much of it in recitative, like an opera by Metastasio.

Rosamunde irritated Mozart when he got to know it better. He even directed one of the rehearsals of it at Wendling's in place of the indisposed Schweitzer (letter of 18 December 1777). His mother reported in the same letter what he was saying in private. "The new opera by Schweitzer is being rehearsed daily. It does not please Wolfgang at all. He says there is nothing natural about it, and all is exaggerated, and that it is not composed to suit the singers. How the production will come out we must wait and see." The production, scheduled for a first performance on 11 January 1778, was scrapped. On New Year's Day Carl Theodore received the news of the Bavarian elector's death. A period of mourning canceled the opera and all other carnival festivities. The opera was rescheduled for the carnival of 1779 in Munich, with Aloysia Weber singing the role of Emma. Mozart made his most scathing remarks about Schweitzer in this connection.

> It saddens me to think that when the Salzburgers flock to Munich next carnival when *Rosamunde* is performed the poor little Weber will probably not please, or at least people will not be able to judge her according to her merits, for she has a miserable part, almost a mute one, and sings only a few verses between the choruses. One aria she does have, where the ritornello might lead you to expect something good, but the vocal part is *alla* Schweitzer, as if the hounds were yelping. In the second act she has a kind of Rondeau where she can sustain her voice a bit and show her ability. Pity the poor singer, male or female, who falls into Schweitzer's hands, for his life long he will never learn how to write well for voice. [Letter dated Paris, 11 September 1778][159]

This performance too was canceled and in its stead *Alceste* was revived. Mozart noted the event in one of his last letters before returning home.

> Now in Munich they are performing Schweitzer's dismal *Alceste*! The best of it, along with the beginnings, middle passages and conclusions of some arias, is the beginning of the Recitative "O Jugendzeit!" Raaff made it so by showing Hartig, who sings Admetus, how to phrase, and through this achieved true expression. The worst part of all (although most of the opera is bad) is certainly the *ouverture*. [Letter dated Kaysersheim, 18 December 1778]

Schweitzer had reverted to an old-fashioned French-style overture in the minor mode to introduce *Alceste,* which then began with two arias in minor.

Another theatrical genre that flourished in Mannheim was melodrama. Jean-Jacques Rousseau was a forerunner with his spoken *scène lyrique Pygmalion* written ca. 1762 and performed at Lyons in 1770 with music by Horace Coignet. Rousseau's text was translated into German and used as the basis for new music by Schweitzer (Gotha, 1772) and Franz Asplmayr (Vienna, 1772). Both scores are lost. The two most famous melodramas were *Ariadne auf Naxos* and *Medea* with music by Georg Benda (Gotha, 1775).

[159]The rondeau-like aria in Act II is "Wie ein Kind, in Mutterarmen." Anton Schweitzer, *Rosamunde,* ed. Jutta Stüber, 2 vols. (Orpheus, vol. 87) (Bonn, 1997), 1: 238–47.

Abel Seyler's theatrical troupe at Gotha provided the incubator for German melodrama. The famous actors who declaimed these works were Johann Böck as Pygmalion, Charlotte Brandes as Ariadne, and Sophie Seyler as Medea. Johann Brandes wrote *Ariadne* for his wife. Gotter wrote *Medea* as a vehicle for Seyler's wife so that she could compete with Charlotte Brandes. As to the music, Benda had at his disposal the expressive and fiery kind of obbligato recitative pioneered by Hasse in *Artaserse* (Venice, 1730) and brought to its peak by Jommelli. In trying to explain the genre to his father Mozart wrote that it was nothing other than obbligato recitative, but spoken rather than sung. In his letter of 12 November 1778 he says that he first saw Benda's *Medea* during his previous stay in Mannheim (fall-winter, 1777–78).[160] Thus melodrama, and Benda's *Medea* in particular, was being performed in Mannheim well before the Seyler troupe took up residence there in the fall of 1778, at which time Mozart could have seen the original Medea, Sophie Seyler, play her most famous role. Both *Medea* and *Ariadne* were printed in keyboard scores (Leipzig, 1778). These are presumably what Mozart carried around with him ("because I love them so much").

Benda was twenty-eight in 1750 when he managed to get discharged from his duties as a violinist at the Berlin court and accepted the post of Kapellmeister at the small court of Saxe-Gotha. He became a prolific composer of cantatas and instrumental music during his early years in Gotha. Many of his symphonies date from this time. They are sprightly and pleasing but somewhat stunted in melody by the desiccated musical atmosphere of Berlin, and they sound like miniatures compared with Mannheim's symphonic best. In 1766 Benda went to Italy as the beneficiary of a six-month leave with pay. He met Hasse in Venice and became acquainted with the latest operatic currents on the peninsula. His true career opened up as a creator of German stage music after the Seyler troupe settled in Gotha during 1774. His setting of *Ariadne* in early 1775 was soon followed by that of Gotter's Singspiel *Der Jahrmarkt* and then by *Medea*. In 1776 he set Gotter's librettos *Walder* (after Marmontel's *Silvain*) and *Romeo und Julie*, adapted from Shakespeare, two works that approach serious opera.[161] He resigned his post at Gotha in 1778 and traveled to Hamburg, Mannheim, and Vienna in search of fame and fortune. Not finding a suitable post, he returned to Gotha in 1779.

Medea opens with a short orchestral prelude, with sweeping scales and dotted rhythms that set the tragic tone effectively and economically. Medea utters her first despairing words as the orchestra plays a wrenching descent with Lombard snaps in the key of d, an idea that will become a kind of *Leitmotif* for Medea's grief. There is a certain amount of dramatic exposition. She calls herself a mother without children—custody of them has gone to Jason, who drove her away and

---

[160]The letter is quoted at length in *Haydn, Mozart,* pp. 676–77.
[161]Bauman, *North German Opera*, pp. 116–29.

married Creusa. She watches this pair arrive to a jaunty march in the key of G, first played offstage. Fragments of the march recur after it has finished, surrounding her words, almost as if we were hearing them through the medium of her distracted mind (Example 5.31). She muses on Jason's being "more handsome than on the first day of our love." Another fragment sounds, "Majestic and certain, like a god." The music ascends in dotted rhythm with D triads. "Shall I follow?" "Shall I transform this joyful noise into dread sounds of mourning?" The instruction here says that she continues on without break. "Verwandeln" (transform) is placed so that its last two syllables arrive with the tonal transformation from high D to a low placement of the totally unrelated triad of A♭ at *Grave.* This uncanny sound holds as she thinks of entering the temple and confronting the shameful pair at the foot of the angry statues and strangling them. At the verb "strangle" (würgen), according to the careful text placement in the 1778 keyboard score, the violins fly up a scale, *Allegro,* over a B♭ chord. "Or should I wait until they are carousing and drinking to the defeat of their enemies, to Medea's defeat?" The boldness of Benda's tone painting found a resonance in Mozart, who wrote something similar to introduce Scene 6, Act III in *Idomeneo* (No. 23 in the *Neue Mozart Ausgabe*). In the

EXAMPLE 5.31 *Georg Benda*, Medea, *Scene*

opera it is a case of pantomime music for the three estates who enter here in order: the royal party to a pompous *Maestoso* in the key of C, with dotted rhythm and a rise of the violins to high C; the priests to an eerily quiet and low-placed chord, A♭, marked *Largo*; and the populace, agitated, to a bustling *Allegro* over the chord of B♭. Mozart meant what he said about loving Benda's *Medea*.

The tragic music in the key of d that marked Medea's first words returns at the very end when Jason sees the bodies of his dead children, murdered by their mother, whereupon he throws himself on his sword. *Medea* fulfilled the ambitions of *Sturm und Drang* theater to be shocking, as did the Seyler troupe's production of *Hamlet,* to which Vogler wrote an impressive overture.[162]

When the elector moved his court to Munich in 1778 he took the Marchand troupe of actors with him. Their legacy in Mannheim included a new playhouse, the Stadttheater or Nationaltheater, across the street from the Jesuit church (Figure 5.15). It was designed and built in 1775–77 by Lorenzo Quaglio, theater architect and stage designer long in electoral service. In Marchand's place the elector appointed Freiherr von Dalberg director of Mannheim's Nationaltheater ("national"in this sense refers to the use of the German language).

Carl Theodore continued to rule in Mannheim as well as in Munich. He took a lively interest in all cultural matters having to do with his former capital, which he also visited regularly. Under Dalberg the German theater became preeminent and in a sense restored Mannheim to capital status. One of its greatest triumphs was the first performance of Schiller's play *Die Räuber* in January 1782. Schiller himself received a one-year appointment as Mannheim's theater poet in July 1783.

Holzbauer's *Günther von Schwarzburg*

Klein and Holzbauer must have worked on *Günther von Schwarzburg* throughout much of the year 1776. Although it has only five characters, it is a full-scale opera with a very detailed libretto, complicated staging, and an intricate and powerful score. Perhaps it was originally intended for performance on the elector's name day in November but was not ready on time. In any event, Schweitzer's *Alceste* was revived again on 5 November 1776 and given in the great opera house, where it must have looked rather puny, having no spectacle or ballet and only four characters. The economical nature Wieland imposed on *Alceste* was quite the opposite of *Günther,* which brought back spectacle, pantomime, ballet, and imposing choruses. *Alceste* was not the last opera performed in the court theater. That honor

---

[162]See Floyd K. Grave and Margaret G. Grave, *In Praise of Harmony: The Teachings of Abbé Georg Joseph Vogler* (Lincoln, Neb., 1987), pp. 185–87. Vogler had sensible ideas about orchestration, as advanced in Daniel Heartz, "Abbé Vogler on the horn parts in Peter Winter's Symphony in D minor (1778): A View from within the Mannheim Orchestra," *Historic Brass Society Journal* 12 (2000): 89–101.

Das teutſche Comödienhaus.   *La Comédie allemande.*

FIGURE 5.15. Klauber. The National Theater.

went to Paisiello's *Il finto spettro* on 26 November 1776. *Günther* opened Quaglio's new national theater outside the palace on 5 January 1777. There has been some doubt on this point, but Riaucour specifies that the performance took place in "la nouvelle salle de spectacle."

Anton Klein was not a man of few words. He prefaced his libretto with a lengthy explanation in which he justified celebrating German heroes and subjects from German history.[163] He found Günther in a history of the Holy Roman Empire during the first half of the fourteenth century, from which he quoted: "Count Günther von Schwarzburg was a brave and experienced soldier . . . who stepped forward to aid the Palatinate, Bavaria, Emperor Louis the Bavarian, and the archbishop of Mainz" during a time of war and turmoil. Local patriotism and a desire to magnify the Wittelsbach dynasty clearly played a role in the choice,

[163]Corneilson ("Opera at Mannheim, 1770–1778") includes the document in his Appendix C-6.

which may have been made by Carl Theodore. Klein confuses the reader of his preface after citing history by not making clear what is fiction in his story. He crowns Günther emperor (fiction). He paints a confusing picture of Emperor Charles IV, the actual successor of Louis the Bavarian. There is an unstated analogy with the imperial succession in the 1740s: a Wittelsbach emperor (Charles VII) dies and is succeeded by an outsider (Francis of Lorraine).

It may help to set the historical record straight before proceeding further into Klein's farrago. Louis the Bavarian was crowned emperor in 1314. In the 1340s he was challenged by Charles, eldest son of King John of Bohemia and of Elisabeth, sister of Wenceslas, the last Premyslide king of Bohemia. King John was one of the most Romantic figures of that time. A member of the Luxembourg dynasty, he is known to music history as the patron of Guillaume de Machaut. He went blind about 1340. In 1346, acting in union with Pope Clement VI, he had Emperor Louis deposed and his son Charles elected. War was gathering between them in Germany when Louis suddenly died in 1347. King John's last act was in aid of the French king Philip VI. He fell at the battle of Crécy on 26 August 1346 attacking the English invaders and died a heroic death. Charles, at his side, survived. As king of Bohemia Charles founded the University of Prague in 1348. As Emperor Charles IV he was instrumental in promulgating the Golden Bull of 1356 by which the rights and duties of the imperial electors were spelled out for the first time. He corresponded with Petrarch. Much of his youth was spent in the city of Lucca. He married Blanche, sister of King Philip VI.

Klein sets his libretto in the year 1349. His Karl is seen as an unworthy candidate for emperor because of his non-German upbringing. Günther, on the other hand, is truly German and is supported for the crown by Count Palatine Rudolf, whose daughter Anna loves Karl and is loved by him in return. The other female character is Karl's mother Asberta, a villainess who intrigues on behalf of her son and against Günther, whom she finally poisons before killing herself. Günther dies happily, blessing the union of Karl and Anna, which brings peace between the warring factions. The fashion for medieval settings and clashing knights in armor, known in German as *Ritterdrama,* lies behind *Günther.* Goethe wrote the outstanding example in his spoken play *Götz von Berlichingen* (1773).

Here is an alternate explanation that does not begin with Klein. Capitalizing on the success of Schweitzer's *Alceste* at Mannheim, *Günther* was built around the same four singers who triumphed in that, plus one other who was won over to the cause of opera in German—Anton Raaff. The most famous and highly paid of Palatine singers, Raaff had never sung German in an opera before. Once his participation was assured, so was the subject, or at least its main outline. It would be a title role for him culminating in one of his signature death scenes. Klein rummaged around in German history until coming up with an appropriate vehicle, which was shaped accordingly. Raaff regarded Günther as his greatest role. He chose to be depicted holding a score of the opera in his late portrait, painted after he sang the title role in Mozart's *Idomeneo* (Munich, 1781).

A mixture of both explanations is possible. A search for a medieval subject with local overtones led to the story of the German hero Günther. Once Raaff was persuaded to join the enterprise, Klein made him emperor and shaped the story so that he died at the climax of the opera. Of the singers who created the five roles, all except Raaff had come to prominence in the Marchand company.

TABLE 5.1. The Original Cast of Holzbauer's *Günther von Schwarzburg*

Anna, countess palatine . . . . Franziska Danzi, soprano

Karl, Bohemian king . . . . Franz Hartig, tenor

Rudolf, count palatine . . . . Ludwig Fischer, bass

Asberta, Karl's mother, ... Barbara Strasser, soprano
    dowager queen of Bohemia

Günther von Schwarzburg . . . . Anton Raaff, tenor

The reception of the new opera was mixed. An anonymous critic in the *Mannheimer Zeitung* praised it to the skies.

> Germany may be proud of the general and enthusiastic applause that today greeted *Günther von Schwarzburg*, the first opera on the electoral stage that is German not only in language but also in subject. It elicited approval from connoisseurs and non-connoisseurs (whose hearts are otherwise moved to only a moderate degree of human sympathy). A crowd of visiting and local spectators was all ears, all sentiment [alle Empfindung]; in every eye one read a glowing, patriotic refutation of the former taste for foreign operas.[164]

The reviewer went on to thank Professor Klein, "who expressed the most tender and most noble sentiments in our manly German language, who knew how to paint them and make them felt." He thanked "our Holzbauer, who showed here how the magic strength of the tonal art stood at his command; the task rejuvenated him so that he could feel with the young lovers and commune in manly fashion with heroes." Note the emphasis again on masculinity. Next it was the turn of the singers. "Never have the great Raaff and our singers Danzi, Strasser, Fischer and Hartig felt so strongly and vividly what they were divinely singing, not ever, as they did today." Lastly the critic thanked Carl Theodore not by name, but as "the greatest connoisseur and most generous benefactor of the sciences, under whose mighty protection the end result soared aloft. . . . " In conclusion

---

[164]Helga Lühning, "Das Theater Carl Theodors und die Idee der Nationaloper," in *Die Mannheimer Hofkapelle*, pp. 89–99; 96.

came this odd coda: "One looks down on all the ill-tempered faultfinders and laughs at their powerless rage! One sees German honor rescued. What delight does not the rescuer feel in the thought: this is my work." The rescuer was presumably Carl Theodore. Who had impugned German honor over the opera?

The dispatches sent from Mannheim to Dresden by Riaucour help illuminate the controversy surrounding the opera's premiere. Riaucour's duty as a diplomat was to report not so much his impressions as those of the Palatine court. In his letter of 31 December 1775 he wrote that the opera would be first performed in public on January 5 in the new theater, "having been censured without mercy in the Frankfurt papers."[165] Presumably it was the printed libretto that was circulating before the premiere. "One replied in few words but with force in the local gazette," he continued, "while making it clear how inconsiderate and indecent such criticism was, and calling on the judgment that an impartial public will make." Then a few doubts crept into Riaucour's report. "It is true that the drama's style is quite far-fetched [fort recherché] and that several passages are even unintelligible." He too may have been reacting to the printed libretto, or he may have been at a rehearsal. We know from his other reports that he often attended rehearsals. He wrote more on *Günther* on 7 January 1777, two days after the Sunday premiere. "It was strongly applauded as to the music, which is of great beauty, to which the words are far from responding. The more one pays attention to them the more one finds faults." From this it would appear that he did not know the opera first through the libretto. "An affected style [style recherché], false and obscure ideas, plus forced situations make up the character of this drama." Wieland was equally negative and resolved to remain silent in *Der teusche Merkur,* which he founded in 1773. "In Mannheim, I hear, there is a great noise about the Ex-Jesuit Klein's so-called opera Günther von Schwarzburg. The thing is so monstrous that I fear the Mannheimers will accuse me of envy or ill will if it is reviewed in the *Merkur,* as planned."[166]

Klein's "false ideas" from a political point of view, which would have been Riaucour's worry, included harping on the theme of a German nation, a free and democratic nation at that, concepts that had no equivalent in reality, either in the fourteenth or the eighteenth century. It was one thing to express local patriotism by a devotion to Pfalz-Bayern, quite another to advocate pan-Germanism and to boast of Teutonic superiority in morals and manly courage, ideas acceptable only in the most outspoken *Sturm und Drang* literary circles. How different were the sentiments of Lessing, who was invited to Mannheim at precisely this time, early 1776, with a view to making him director of the national theater. He had had his fill of the failed Hamburg national theater of the previous decade, which he ridiculed, exclaiming, "We Germans are still not a nation! I speak not of political

[165]Corneilson, "Opera at Mannheim, 1770–1778," pp. 389–90.
[166]Ibid., p. 215.

unity but of cultural character."[167] Lessing left Mannheim not long after he arrived, his only impact having been to recommend hiring the Seyler troupe and founding a theater school.

The *teutsch* movement in southern Germany had its strongest proponent in Schubart, who had praised the German Society in Mannheim as epochal in his *Deutsche Chronik* of 1775.

> Dawn has already broken in the Palatinate; posterity will be thankful to both Klein and Schwan, these intense zealots for the glory of the fatherland, for what they accomplished in the spreading of good taste in the Palatinate. As long as the Italian taste and as long as French *esprit* still tyrannize over strength and manliness . . . long I fear the delay of the full day.[168]

Schwan might have been a better choice than Klein as librettist. He had translated many comic librettos into German, while Klein's previous operatic experience consisted of translating Metastasio's *Didone.* At least Schubart was clear as to what he saw as the enemies of German "manliness." He does not mention effeminacy outright, but its French and Italian source is clearly implied. According to Burney, Schubart could speak neither French nor Italian.

Klein was content denouncing foreign customs without further specification. In Scene 8 of Act I he gives Günther these lines, referring to Karl.

Gab fremde Sitte nicht ihm niedern Trieb	Did not foreign customs give him the base trait
Zur Herrschucht—zur Herrschsucht über Brüder?	of seeking to rule—seeking to rule over brothers?

Holzbauer paid his librettist the compliment of not setting this pair to music, but he had to set many others that were of the same order, such as these.

Nein! Karl kann unser Haupt nicht sein!	No! Karl cannot be our chief!
in fremder Länder erzogen, kennnt er nicht	raised in foreign lands he does not know
deutscher Männer Pflicht, mit Königstoltz	the duties of a German man, with royal pride
blickt er auf freie Helden. . . .	he looks upon free heroes. . . .

[167]*Hamburgische Dramaturgie,* 19 April 1768, cited after Lühning, "Das Theater Carl Theodors und die Idee der Nationaloper," p. 89.

[168]Roland Würtz, "Ignaz Holzbauer and *Das Teutsche,*" *Studies in Music from the University of Western Ontario* 7 (1982): 89–98; 94. Vogler took a dimmer view, writing in 1790, "a German Society was founded, in which we were all infected with a bigotry toward German, in which we feared it a sin to use a naturalized foreign word, wanting to substitute *Nasenkrautstaubschachtel* for *tabatière.*" Grave and Grave, *In Praise of Harmony,* p. 136.

Holzbauer, raised mainly upon Italian opera, dutifully set these in simple recitative and Raaff, also trained in Italy, dutifully sang them in the title role. He sang even worse in celebrating Günther's victory in battle over Karl's forces at the end of Act I, praising his warriors.

Vater Teut! Die hier—sie sind von deinem Stamme!	Father Teut! These here—they are of your line!
Wie wider die Entarteten ihr Auge Unmuth winkt!	How their eyes flash in anger against the degenerate!

Equating otherness with degeneracy smacks of xenophobia and has a repugnantly twentieth-century ring.

The libretto poses problems of many other kinds as well. Characterization is one of them. Anna is the most consistent of the characters. She is intent on marrying Karl from the first to the last. Her father Rudolf is less firm. Asberta asks Rudolf (Act I, Scene 3) an apt question: if Karl is unworthy of being emperor, how can he be worthy of marrying your daughter? Rudolf makes no direct answer, only saying he has given his word to Günther for emperor. His aria that follows is about the sanctity of keeping promises. A German man never goes back on his word, he sings. This is hardly the stuff out of which a composer can make a great operatic scene. Wieland knew as much and warned poets not to give singers moral axioms. He also warned them not to put politicians on the stage, so it is no wonder that he was negative about *Günther.* Klein sinned against Wieland's dicta particularly in the character of Günther, who does next to nothing but spout morals. Rudolf tells us repeatedly what a bold, decisive, heroic patriot is Günther, but we never see him do anything that would convince us of as much. This weakness in the title role makes the repulsive Asberta seem all the stronger as a character. At first she tries to talk Rudolf and Günther into accepting her son Karl as emperor (I, 10), and when this fails she poisons the pious old windbag. As the dupe of his mother and at the same time the idol of Anna, Karl has a serious dichotomy to his character, and nothing Klein writes explains it away.

Günther's death oration is not only his nadir but Klein's. The Greek way, followed by Calzabigi and Gluck in *Alceste,* is to have a short oration followed by a long choral threnody to convey the event's true magnitude. Klein and Holzbauer do exactly the opposite, giving Günther a very verbose departure followed by a paltry choral dirge. Holzbauer cannot be blamed for this. He was probably exasperated with Klein for being so wordy and hence shut down the mourning as quickly as possible.

Günther gets the last aria, a slow piece in E♭, "O süsse End meiner Plage" (Oh sweet ending of my troubles). Then he goes on in recitative. His final words are as follows:

O Deutschland! Wie klein—bist du—	Oh Germany, how small you are
Zerteilt durch Zwietracht!	when divided by discord!
Wie gross durch Brüdereinheit!	How large through brotherly
	unity!
Karl! Rudolf!—Meine Brüder!	Karl! Rudolf! My brothers!
Entnervender als Zwietracht ist Hang zu	More unnerving than discord is
fremder Sitte—	the inclination to foreign customs.
Stolz—deutsch zu sein—ist eure Grösse!	Pride in being German is your
(er stirbt)	greatness! (he dies)

Thus Klein uses Günther's dying breath to reiterate his main moral. Then follows the one-line chorus, "Der Held des Vaterlandes stirbt" (The hero of the fatherland dies), set by Holzbauer to six measures of *Adagio*, in c minor. The opera was a success in spite of its text. It was revived in November for the name-day celebrations with one change in the cast. Danzi was on leave and her role of Anna was taken over by Elisabeth Wendling.

The Mozarts, mother and son, arrived in Mannheim on 30 October 1777. They observed the gala celebrations, on which she reported first, in a letter dated 8 November 1777. "The second day they performed a grand opera in German titled *Günther von Schwarzburg* which is very beautiful and has incomparable music, accompanied by a wonderfully beautiful ballet." (The ballet was Lauchery's *Cortes und Telaire* with music by Cannabich.) "The third day there was a great Academy at which Wolfgang played a concerto and at the end, before the final symphony, he improvised and played a sonata out of his head. He received uncommon applause from the elector and electress as well as from all who heard him." On the fourth day there was a play, *The Earl of Essex* by John Banks, given in German along with a heroic ballet.

Mozart reported his reactions to the opera in his letter dated Mannheim, 14 November 1777. "The music by Holzbauer is very beautiful. The poetry is not worth such music. I am astounded that a man so old as Holzbauer still has so much spirit, for it it is unbelievable how much fire there is in the music." Next he described some of the singers. Elisabeth Wendling was sickly and ill at ease in a role not written for her, one that was too high for her voice (and yet not much higher than what Mozart wrote for her as Electra, taking her voice up to high B and high C). Mozart was disappointed in Raaff's singing, acting, and stage presence.

In the opera he has to die, and do so while singing a very long aria in slow time. Well, he died with a smile on his face. Toward the end of the aria his voice failed so badly one could hardly stand it. I was sitting next to the flautist Wendling in the orchestra. He objected earlier that it was unnatural for a man to go on singing until he died, an event for which one could hardly wait. I told him have patience, he will soon be there, for I hear it. I too, he said, and laughed. The seconda donna is a certain Mlle Strasserin (not a streetwalker despite her name), who sings very well and is outstanding as an actress.

Thus Strasser as Asberta captivated him, and indeed it is the opera's most potent role, one that left traces upon Electra in *Idomeneo* and the Queen of the Night in *Die Zauberflöte.* Mozart had no comment on Hartig as Karl or Fischer as Rudolf.

EXAMPLE 5.32. *Holzbauer*, Günther von Schwarzburg, *Act I, Scene 1*

Holzbauer chose E♭ as the key of his overture and of Raaff's last aria. It recalls the choice made by Majo for *Ifigenia* twelve years earlier, and the two operas also have their spectacular battle and conflagration scenes in common. Whereas Majo was no symphonist, Holzbauer had the advantage of being a superior one. His overture used the full resources of the orchestra to fine advantage and alternated between a *Maestoso* in dotted rhythm and a bustling *Allegro,* adumbrating

Mozart's overture to *Die Zauberflöte*.[169] The *Allegro* section that begins the seconda parte in B♭ returns in E♭ as the curtain opens to reveal Anna in a solo scene that becomes more and more animated (Example 5.32). At the first tutti in m. 5, *forte* and *piano* exchanges punctuate a rising conjunct fourth in sixths similar to the same figure exemplified above in one of his symphonies (Example 5.20a on p. 528). Violins in octaves in mm. 7–9 betray Viennese practice. At mm. 11 and 13 the tutti stamp their feet in contredanse fashion with an almost Beethovenian brusqueness. Then the *crescendo* begins, rising to *fortissimo* by m. 20 along with a rise in pitch and an increasingly thick texture. Anna must perform a pantomime to this music that is minutely keyed to the score. She sits, inscribes a portrait she is holding, gazes intently at it, and rises as the orchestra rises to the peak of its *crescendo*, the descent from which and chordal punctuation in m. 22 prepare for her vocal entrance. Mime this elaborate can be considered a legacy of Verazi, on the one hand, but also, from the point of view of the composer, of pantomime ballet and Benda's melodramas, on the other. Already in this opening scene we can hear what Mozart meant by the fiery qualities manifest in the aged Holzbauer's music.

Anna believes that her love for Karl is doomed and that her life is near an end. What she wrote on his portrait, as we find out at the beginning of Act II, is "For you only have I lived." Her obbligato recitative passes through several phases then moves seamlessly into a short aria, "Ihr Rosenstunden!" then back directly into obbligato recitative, leaving no possibility of applause (Example 5.33). Holzbauer delays the arrival of the tonic, D, until the fourth measure of the *Andantino*. Mozart makes a similar tonal maneuver before the first aria in *Idomeneo,* sung by the conflicted and lovelorn Ilia after a long solo scene in obbligato recitative. Mozart also uses a figure very like Holzbauer's fourth-beat dotted rhythm with *sforzato* over a pedal in mm. 63–64 to introduce the love duet in *Idomeneo* (Nos. 20a and 20b). Holzbauer often uses another figure, a falling conjunct fourth or fifth in dotted rhythm, to which Mozart would assign a particular significance in *Idomeneo* (the "Idamante motif"). But he is not the only Mannheim composer to do so. The same figure was observed in Richter (Example 5.18 on p. 523) and can be heard in the symphonies and ballets of Toeschi and Cannabich (e.g., Example 5.19 on p. 524).

Asberta enters. The recitative suddenly reverts to *semplice,* a simple way of showing that she is from a different and colder world. Asberta attempts to present herself as a caring mother in her first aria (as does the Queen of the Night). The demonic and near-maniacal side of her will emerge later. Following Asberta's aria Anna sings a full-fledged aria with coloratura display, which leaves no doubt that she is the prima donna here. Günther's first aria comes next, and it is followed by his patriotic hymn to victory with responding chorus. Mozart in his let-

---

[169]Michael Schwarte, "Musikalisierung von Zeit- und Bewegungsabläufen in Ignaz Holzbauers Oper *Günther von Schwarzburg,*" in *Mozart und Mannheim*, pp. 101–17; 116–17.

EXAMPLE 5.33. *Holzbauer*, Günther von Schwarzburg, *Act I, Scene 1*

ter of 16 November 1777 mentions that Raaff as Günther had four arias. He must have included the battle hymn as one of them. It is an effective act ending and makes one forget the words because of the music.

Act II begins with Karl finding his portrait with Anna's inscription in a grotto on the banks of the Main River near Frankfurt. The grotto is illustrated with the story of Tusnelda, the faithful German wife of Arminio, who saved him from death at the hands of the Romans. The allegorical reference to Anna and Karl is not made clear enough but furnishes Karl with the impetus to sing an aria filled with noble sentiments. A trio ensues in which Asberta breaks the lovers apart and orders Karl back to battle, leaving Anna alone to sing a pathetic aria asking who will protect her. The rest of the act is taken up mostly with Günther's coronation celebrations in Frankfurt. Its most memorable music is Rudolf's aria describing the silver-haired Günther, in tones that have long been recognized as precursors to Sarastro's "In diesen heil'gen Hallen."

The dramaturgy of *Günther* was described in the older literature as being closely indebted to that of Metastasio. Recent study has pointed out that the massive scenic directions and spectacle are quite unlike both Metastasio and Wieland, who is a closer follower of the Roman poet. They are in fact close to Verazi and Mannheim's well-developed tradition of pantomime ballets. Another departure from Metastasian dramaturgy is the placing of arias and other closed numbers not at the end of scenes but midway through them, which is true in half of the twenty numbers and represents a considerable advance beyond Wieland.[170]

Schubart, who praised Klein in 1775 for being such a zealous patriot, changed his tune in the *Ideen,* where the emphasis is on Holzbauer's triumph in *Günther.*

> The poetry is by Professor Klein, who is otherwise known for his accomplishments in our literature. Only for this task he did not show the best judgment and his composer soared far beyond him. The overture of this German opera is written with much art and insight. In it lies embedded the character of the whole opera so that the following scenes only spin out what is already in the overture. Most of the arias have new and beautiful themes and are very well carried out. The duets are masterful in their working out and the choruses rise aloft through their solemnity and grandeur. Holzbauer knows especially how to use the instruments with great effect, although at the same time it appears that here and there he overuses them. (p. 132)

Schubart goes on to praise the word setting in the various kinds of recitative and the transitions into *arioso* as uncommonly attractive. Critics who were more aligned with Hasse, such as Hiller, blamed Holzbauer for using the orchestra too much and for overwhelming the singers with it, the identical faults they found in Jommelli, Holzbauer's great model not only here but also in his generally nervous and rhythmically intricate style.

---

[170]Helga Lühning, "Aufkündigung einer Gattungstradition: Das Metastasianische Drama, Wielands Singspielkonzept und die deutsche Oper *Günther von Schwarzburg,*" in *Mannheim und Italien,* pp. 162–99; 177–79. The author writes persuasively on Anna's "Ihr Rosenstunden," pp. 184–89. For a summary of recent work on *Günther* see Karl Böhmer, *W. A. Mozart's Idomeneo und die Tradition der Karnevalsopern in München* (Mainzer Studien zur Musikwissenschaft, 39) (Tutzing, 1999), pp. 143–47.

One aria that did not begin with a "new" theme was Rudolf's moving lament in the key of c at the beginning of Act III, in which he mourns the double loss of Anna, whom he believes dead, and of Günther, whose death is impending. Probably without realizing it, Holzbauer began the aria with the descending theme with sobbing Lombard snaps that is the main idea of Benda's *Medea*, where it occurs on the first page and at the end. Oddly enough, the composer does not return to this initial theme in the course of the aria, which goes through three tempos, with no returns to previous material. Many of the arias are in individual schemes such as this, so far from any formulaic habits that they must have been especially challenging for the singers to learn.

Holzbauer took the unusual step of having the full score of *Günther* engraved at Mannheim by Götz, all at his own expense. He dedicated the publication to Carl Theodore with an homage that is simple and dignified, uncommonly so in contrast with the fustian of most dedicatory epistles of the time (Figure 5.16). In translation: "To Carl Theodore, the most illustrious patron of music, under whose sublime protection the Palatine stages first celebrated a German hero. This work, crowned with highest praise, is dedicated to you as a monument from your faithful, grateful, and loving first Kapellmeister, Holzbauer."

Publication made it possible for the rest of Germany to assess what had happened in its leading operatic center. A critic writing for a Hamburg paper sniffed

FIGURE 5.16. Title page and dedication of Holzbauer's *Günther von Schwarzburg*.

disdainfully at both text and music and recommended that composers who set German to music get better acquainted with the noble simplicity of a Handel and the correct knowledge of the language of Telemann. An anonymous amateur in Mannheim answered the critic with an insertion in Vogler's *Betrachtungen* (1778).[171] He descends to invective. How could the critic form the right conception of music in Hamburg, where it will always be impossible? London has never had a musical theater worthy of being compared with ours in Mannheim, and so on. Getting down to cases the defender writes that "on the first of November last year, we had a chance to judge the simplicity of a Handel when our best singers and players performed the so highly acclaimed *Messiah*. They did everything possible to earn the applause of the court." The defender continued, "Everyone there yawned. What else but unbearable dryness, not the noble simplicity of the music, sunk us in this deathly apathy! How great was the contrast, when at the same event a Psalm-Magnificat by our second Kapellmeister [Vogler] was performed and brought us back to life." The author of this effusion may of course be Vogler himself, who has adopted the guise of an amateur. Mozart went to the rehearsal for this concert on 31 October 1777 and reported on it to his father in a letter dated the same day. He heard Vogler's piece, which lasted nearly an hour, then left before the Handel was rehearsed.

Günther had consequences for the next German opera written for the court. Wieland was determined to make *Rosamunde* a true Mannheim opera. He disregarded his own principles enunciated in defense of *Alceste* and opted for a full-blown spectacle opera that would rival and, he hoped, surpass *Günther*. He chose a subject from medieval history, not German but English, and worked it out for six characters, with multiple ensembles, choruses, scenic transformations, and even a ballet within the first act. He based it on a play by Joseph Addison that he found in *The Spectator* concerning Eleanor of Aquitaine, queen of England, her consort King Henry II, and his paramour Rosamunde, a drama which ended with Rosamunde replacing Eleanor on the throne. Wieland must have been obtuse in not foreseeing what objections this would bring from the electress, plagued as she was by a straying husband. The libretto had to be drastically rewritten so as to end with the death of Rosamunde.[172]

Our discussion will be limited to how Wieland's correspondence throws light on the singers who were to play the title role. Danzi was the original choice, but she was given leave to perform in London, Paris, and Milan in 1777–78. In his letter of 16 April 1777 the poet lamented, "they now have no Rosamunde. . . . My lit-

---

[171]Corneilson ("Opera at Mannheim, 1770–1778") gives the document in full as his Appendix C–8.
[172]See Corneilson (ibid.), pp. 216–29, for a discussion of the changes, based on Wieland's extensive correspondence.

tle piece, which with the lovely nymph Danzi should, could and would have made the most supreme effect, now from lack of an actress, who looks like Rosamunde and sings like a Rosamunde, is going to the dogs."[173] Schwan answered Wieland in May, reassuring him that her substitute, Dorothea Wendling, would do even better.

> Your opera loses nothing by that, but rather it gains more thereby. Without a doubt Madame Wendling sings much better than Danzi; her voice is no longer as youthful and she does not have the high notes of Danzi; but in comparison she is more certain, more complete and lovelier, and she is the same as an actress, and indeed she is a good actress, a talent that the other entirely lacks.[174]

Wieland had the grace to admit he had been mistaken. He came to Mannheim in December 1777 to hear the rehearsals of Schweitzer's music and on 24 December he wrote to his friend the author Sophie La Roche about Wendling.

> Her style of singing surpasses everything I have ever heard, even the famous Mara. This alone is true song—language of the soul and heart, every note living expression of the purest, tenderest feeling; the entire song a rippling line of beauty. In short I could chatter for hours about this delightful woman and not grow tired. You must hear her, dear Sophie! For sensitivity [Empfindsamkeit] like yours there is going to be a real feast.[175]

Wendling's career did not end with the collapse of the *Rosamunde* production. She went on to sing a few other major roles before capping her career by creating Ilia in Mozart's *Idomeneo* (1781).

Holzbauer was increasingly infirm during his last years in Mannheim, but he did not give up composing. Nor did he shrink from trying again to bring *Rosamunde* to the stage, although he had mixed feelings about the quality of its music. On 20 January 1780 he led a performance of the opera in the Nationaltheater, two years after its aborted first production. Younger local singers took the place of the original ones, who had mostly departed. According to Wilhelm Heinse, Holzbauer worked feverishly to whip the production into shape; Holzbauer opined to Heinse about Schweitzer, "when he hits the mark it is divine; many times otherwise it sounds as if he had been swilling brandy."[176] Equally adverse were the criticisms made by Holzbauer that reached the ears of Wieland:

---

[173]Ibid., p. 217, Corneilson's translation, as with the next two quotations.
[174]Ibid., p. 218.
[175]Ibid., p. 61.
[176]Letter to Jacobi dated 14 July 1780, in Heinse, *Sämtliche Werke* 9: 11, cited after Anton Schweitzer, *Rosamunde*, ed. Jutta Stüber (Bonn, 1997), 2: 599.

"through overly German thinking Schweitzer allowed himself to be led to unsingable, exaggerated, and unharmonic passages, and thus sometimes became baroque and unintelligible; in tender passages he became so boring that one wished impatiently for the end to come."[177] Vogler took Schweitzer to task for writing such a large work without a preconceived tonal plan.[178] There were no more public performances of *Rosamunde* after the first. Holzbauer died in Mannheim on 7 April 1783.

The current of national celebration initiated in German opera by *Günther* was continued in works by Vogler and Johann Gottlieb Naumann, among others. Vogler composed Karl Theodor von Traitteur's *Albert der Dritte von Bayern* for Stuttgart in 1781, and Johan Henrik Kellgren's *Gustav Adolf och Ebbe Brahe* for Stockholm (first performed in 1788). Naumann's very successful setting of Kellgren's *Gustaf Wasa* is considered the capstone of opera under Gustavus III and was long regarded simply as the national opera of Sweden. A third German composer who worked for Gustavus III was Joseph Martin Kraus. Trained by Richter in Mannheim, Kraus had a few interesting words to say about the city, Holzbauer, and Vogler in 1777.

> We still have in one place, where what is unquestionably the best orchestra resides, and where the best stage could be, two great men, Holzbauer and Vogler. The first set *Adriano* and now *Günther von Schwarzburg* to music, both in the good old Italian way [auf gutalte Italienische mode]. In Vogler, we awaited on his return from Italy the most fiery and original composer. We received—a skilled theorist.[179]

Kraus was not wrong in assessing Holzbauer as a product of the best Italian tradition, by which he probably understood the operas of Jommelli. *Günther* was colored nevertheless by the solidity and brilliance of the Mannheim orchestra, an achievement of truly European scope.

[177]Julius Maurer, *Anton Schweitzer als dramatischer Komponist* (Leipzig, 1912), pp. 29–30.
[178]Grave, *In Praise of Harmony*, pp. 181–83.
[179]Joseph Martin Kraus, *Etwas von und über Musik fürs Jahr 1777* (Frankfurt, 1778; reprint 1977), p. 93.

6

Paris

Institutions

THE French refer to the reign of Louis XIV from 1648 to 1715 as their *grand siècle*. They call the period that began with the accession of Louis XV and ended with the revolution of 1789 *le siècle des lumières*. Rococo decorative style had its roots in the last years of Louis XIV but bloomed especially during the following reign until the 1760s. Cutting across both centuries was a perceived *age classique*, represented in the theater by the dramatists Corneille, Molière, Racine, and Voltaire. French literary classicism reached its zenith simultaneously with the perfection and grandeur represented by Versailles in all the arts. Scarcely a principality, no matter how small, did not attempt to duplicate some of the trappings with which Louis XIV surrounded his august rule. In literature the waves of classicism emanating from Paris had several consequences outside France, including the founding of the Arcadian Academy at Rome and the reform of the Italian libretto by Zeno and Metastasio. The resulting genre, opera seria, and its musical accoutrements eventually came to triumph, like Italian music in general, all over Europe.

Italian opera held sway everywhere except in France, where the followers of Lully defended an older kind of opera, likewise Italian in origins. French music had more idiosyncracies than any other; hence, it had the most to lose (or gain, depending on one's point of view) in submitting again to Italian hegemony. A battle ranged partisans of the national style of music against those who, like Diderot and Rousseau, championed *la musique ultramontane*.

By the eighteenth century France was already becoming a country so centralized that its cultural life was played out largely upon a single stage—Paris. Under Louis XIV, the court at nearby Versailles set the tone; now it was Paris that dictated fashions under the regent and Louis XV. Much that emerged in the way of great artistic talent in the provinces was quickly drawn to the capital, where the financial reward was greatest. Particularly instructive on this point are the memoirs of the playwright Charles-Simon Favart, who scoured the provincial towns for actors, dancers, and musicians good enough to be brought to Paris and who also supplied personnel to the court theater at Vienna. The main musical institutions at Paris were the larger churches and the four theaters or theatrical companies inherited from the seventeenth century: the Académie Royale de Musique, or Opéra for short; the Comédie Française; the Comédie Italienne; and the Opéra-Comique, initially associated with the twice-yearly trade fairs. New was the Concert Spirituel, established in a specially designed hall in the Tuileries palace.

CHURCHES

Hundreds of churches, large and small, dotted Paris during the ancien régime. Even the small terrain of the Ile de la Cité, the large island in the Seine, housed several besides the cathedral of Notre Dame and the Sainte Chapelle within the royal palace, that exquisite Gothic reliquary built by Louis IX to house the Crown of Thorns (Figure 6.1). Even the smallest parish churches had music, and most had an organ as well. The cathedral did not necessarily have the best sacred music, but it, along with the Sainte Chapelle, has had the benefit of more archival study to date than most other churches.

Guillaume-Antoine Calvière succeeded Médéric Corneille as the cathedral's organist in 1730, and the quarter-century during which he held the post is celebrated as a high point of French organ building and organ playing. Calvière persuaded the chapter (the body of canons governing the cathedral) to have the great organ at the rear of the nave under the west window fully restored and a new case for it made by the royal organ builder, François Thierry. As a virtuoso improvisor, Calvière was reputed to be a genius to whom all things came easily, even fugue. Like other successful organists he accumulated post after post, being named to the chapel royal (Versailles) in succession to Louis Marchand (1739), the abbey of Saint Germain des Prés, Sainte Marguerite in the Faubourg Pincourt, and finally the Sainte Chapelle. At Calvière's death the chapter decided to adopt a practice long followed by the chapel royal: employ four organists serving each a quarter-year (for a salary of 200 livres). The four were Armand-Louis Couperin, Calvière's

FIGURE 6.1.
Central Paris;
detail from the
Plan Turgot,
1739.

pupil René Drouard du Bousset, Louis Claude Daquin, and Charles-Alexandre Jolage.[1]

The choirmasters at the cathedral during this period were less distinguished. The succession included Louis Homet (1734); Antoine Goulet (1748), who had been music master at Saint Germain l'Auxerrois; Antoine de Mongeot (1761); and

[1]Félix Raugel, *Les grandes orgues des églises de Paris et du département de la Seine* (Paris, 1927), p. 85.

Guilleminot Dugué (1780), who also came from Saint Germain l'Auxerrois, a church that had long functioned as a kind of parish church for the Louvre and thus was not without its advantages when it came to royal preferments. Royalty often attended the cathedral too, which was as much a national symbol then as it is now, although sovereigns were crowned at Rheims and buried at Saint Denis. Dugué was a frequent contributor of compositions to the Concert Spirituel and was mentioned as one of the only three Parisian choirmasters whose compositions were deemed worthy of praise by the royal organist Nicolas-Jean le Froid de Méreaux in 1774.

It was the duty of the cathedral's choirmaster to preside over the *maîtrise* or choir school and regulate all the service music, to which he was expected to contribute new compositions. The musical forces were not large, relative to the size of the building. Twelve choirboys had been the rule since 1550 and the number remained the same until the Revolution. At least as many *chantres* among the clerics sang the lower parts, and these were regularly doubled by instruments such as the serpent, bassoon, and contrabass. Violins were introduced by André Campra, choirmaster from 1694 to 1700, but their use was not frequent. Under these circumstances it is not surprising that Dugué sought to rectify the choir's vocal imbalance. In 1783 he complained that "the voices of the children, placed in the center, are covered by the musicians who surround them."[2] The chapter conceded the provisional use of two benches upon which to place the children. The choir did not always perform from the floor of the chancel. A journal entry for Sunday, 28 May 1719, specifies: "Le Roi alla à Notre Dame, ou il entendit chanter le *Te Deum*. La musique était dans les voûtes de l'église."[3]

In 1785 an attempt was made to suppress the practice of executing a motet *à grand choeur et symphonie* before the altar of Our Lady on Holy Saturday, but Dugué prevailed and the practice continued. The following year he retired and was replaced by Jean-François Le Sueur, the teacher of Berlioz, who had been choirmaster at Saints Innocents, another church with a reputation for concerted sacred music and with strong ties to the monarchy. Le Sueur initially succeeded in persuading the chapter to pay for elaborate, oratorio-like works with orchestra and soloists to be performed on Easter, Pentecost, Assumption, and Christmas. This challenge to the traditional domain of the Concert Spirituel did not last long,

[2]F. L. Chartier, *L'ancien chapitre de Notre-Dame de Paris et sa maîtrise d'après les documents capitulaires (1326–1790)* (Paris, 1897), pp. 120–21. Chartier, pp. 109–10, shows that in the seventeenth century at Notre Dame on great feast days a single psalm and the Magnificat were sung in polyphony, but all the rest remained in plainchant. For further information on the administration of the cathedral see Craig Wright, *Music and Ceremony at Notre Dame of Paris 500–1550* (Cambridge, 1989), pp. 165–95.
[3]Chantal Masson, "Journal du Marquis de Dangeau 1684–1720," *Recherches sur la musique française classique* 2 (1961–62): 193–223.

the new operatic personnel proving scandalous to the canons. Le Sueur was dismissed and Dugué recalled. He served until the dissolution of the chapter in 1791, thus becoming the last choirmaster in a continuous tradition stretching back to the early thirteenth century.[4]

The *maîtrise* attached to cathedrals and other sizeable churches deserves some attention because it was one of the few means to a musical education under the ancien régime. A small boarding school that offered instruction in singing, playing (and talent permitting, composition), as well as Latin grammar and theology, it took in boys around the age of seven or eight and kept them for about ten years, after which a professional career either as a cleric or a musician (or both) often followed. It has been estimated that there were some 800 choir schools in France during the eighteenth century: 130 attached to cathedrals, and a like number attached to colleges, while the rest "were even more educationally dubious: they were small abbey and monastery schools."[5]

A wealthy church like Notre Dame at Paris made life fairly comfortable for its young charges. Its *maîtrise* moved into new quarters in 1740 and produced a very talented composer in François Giroust. Extraordinary vocal talent in a boy brought its own perils, as there were princes of the church and even kings who attempted to raid Notre Dame for good sopranos. Castration was not practiced in France, and in fact was much criticized as an Italian vice contrary to nature (which did not prevent an adulatory public from listening with rapture to the greatest castrati at the Concert Spirituel). Most boys, at the mutation of their voices, did not become a Philidor or a Giroust, but went on to drab and ill-paid jobs on the fringes of the musical or clerical establishments.

Burney is our best witness to the peculiarities of Gallic church music in his day since most French critics took them for granted, hence unworthy of note. He was surprised to find that, throughout France, plainchant was sung mostly without accompaniment, although organs were to be found in all the larger churches—they were used only on Sundays and at the great festivals, independent of the voices, or in alternation with them. At Lille in 1770, at the outset of his first musical tour, he found that the choirboys were taught exclusively from Gregorian notation. On each side of the choir a serpent gave the tone in chanting and played the bass when parts were added above the plainchant.

A latter-day kind of improvised discant, called *chant sur le livre* or *fleuretis*, was practiced in many French churches, although frowned upon at Notre Dame in Paris and the chapel royal. Henri Madin, writing about the practice in 1742, men-

[4]Martin M. Herman, "The Turbulent Career of Jean-François Le Sueur, Maître de Chapelle," *Recherches sur la musique française classique* 9 (1969): 187–215.

[5]Ibid., p. 192.

tioned its use in a choir as large as thirty.[6] The practice had detrimental effects on the chants, which were altered so as to facilitate cadences, according to Abbé Jean Lebeuf, in his *Traité historique et pratique sur le chant ecclesiastique* (Paris, 1741). From the *Nouvelle méthode ou principe raisonnées du plein-chant* (Paris, 1780) by Imbert de Sends, serpent player at the small parish church of Saint Benoît on the Left Bank, it emerges that entire cadenzas were added between the lines of plainsong hymns, further altering their original character.[7]

Burney was present in Notre Dame for the feast of Corpus Christi in June 1770. He was somewhat surprised by the circulation of people around the choir and in the great aisle, but the niggardly character of the music surprised him even more:

> Though this was so great a festival, the organ accompanied the choir but little. The chief use made of it, was to play over the chant before it was sung, all through the Psalms. Upon enquiring of a young abbé, whom I took with me as a *nomenclator,* what this was called? *C'est proser,* 'Tis prosing, he said. And it should seem as if our word *prosing* comes from this dull and heavy manner of recital. The organ is a good one, but when played full, the echo and the reverberation were so strong, that it was all confusion; however, on the choir-organ [which he elsewhere calls by its French name, *positive*] and echo stops I could hear every passage distinctly. The organist has a neat and judicious way of touching the instrument; but his passages were very old fashioned. Indeed what he played during the *offertorio,* which lasted six or eight minutes, seemed too stiff and regular for a voluntary. Several motets, or services, were performed by the choir, but accompanied oftner by the *serpent* than organ. . . . These compositions are much in the way of our old church services, full of fugues and imitation; with more contrivance and labour than melody.

Relegated to the end of this chapter are Burney's impressions of the two leading organists at Paris in 1770, Claude-Bénigne Balbastre and Armand-Louis Couperin. They throw further light upon the "modern" taste, or lack of it, in French sacred music.

Parisian churches, then as now, were more celebrated musically for their organists than for their choirs. The organists constituted a kind of professional guild, as demonstrated by their concerted action when challenged by the

---

[6]Henri Madin, *Traité du contrepoint simple ou chant sur le livre* (Paris, 1742). See Abbé Jean Prim, "Chant sur le Livre in French Churches in the 18th Century," *JAMS* 14 (1961): 37–49; 42. Prim writes (p. 38): "Madin was at that time Music Master of the Royal Chapel but, having directed many cathedral choirs (among others those of Bourges, Angers, and Rouen) he knew the practice of chant sur le livre from personal experience." See also Jean-Paul Montagnier "Le *Chant sur le Livre* au xviiie siècle: Les *Traités* de Louis-Joseph Marchand et Henry Madin," *Revue de musicologie* 81 (1995): 37–63.

[7]Walter Hillsman, "Instrumental Accompaniment of Plain-chant in France from the late 18th Century," *Galpin Society Journal* 33 (1980): 8–16.

Ménétriers in 1750. In his listing of famous French organists in 1754, Marpurg names no fewer than thirty-three professional players.[8] Some of these who can be identified by their principal church are: Calvière (Notre Dame), Daquin (Saint Germain de l'Auxerrois and Saint Paul), Louis-Nicolas Clérambault (Saint Sulpice), Jean-François Dandrieu (Saint Merry), Balbastre (Saint Roch), A.-L. Couperin (Saint Gervais), Michel Forqueray (Saint Séverin), Pierre-Claude Foucquet (Saint Eustache), Michel Corrette (Jesuits), François Dagincour (chapel royal), Nicolas Séjan (Saint André des Arts), and Jean-Philippe Rameau (Sainte Croix de la Bretonnerie). Even this small selection gives an inkling of the richness of organ playing in Parisian musical life at midcentury.

The career of Guillaume Lasceux conveys some idea of what organists underwent at the collapse of the ancien régime. He was a student of Charles Noblet, whom he succeeded as organist at the church of the Mathurins. Then he succeeded J. N. Ingrain at the Cloister of Sainte Aure (before 1769) and at Saint Étienne du Mont. Besides serving these churches, he was organist at the Church of the Minimes in the Place Royale (1779), at the Collège de Navarre, and at the Seminaire Saint Magloire. Most of these institutions disappeared during the Revolutionary period, during which Lasceux, in order to save his organ and earn a living, played for the sect of the Théophilanthropes, which met in Saint Étienne du Mont (renamed Temple de la Piété Filiale). When Catholicism was restored in 1807 he returned to his old post in the same church and served until his retirement in 1819.

It has been claimed that the rococo style contributed nothing to ecclesiastical architecture in France and that efforts to adopt the new principles of salon decoration to church interiors, as in Saint Louis du Louvre, were unsuccessful.[9] This may be true, but the situation changed with the neoclassic revolution, felt so powerfully in Paris shortly after midcentury. Witness Jacques Soufflot's Sainte Geneviève replacing the Gothic church dedicated to the patron saint of Paris, and known to later generations as the Panthéon. The anonymous *Lettre sur le mechanisme de l'opéra italien* (1756), after speaking about grand theaters in the Greek and Roman style, praised this church as follows: "un Temple superbe, consacré à la Patronne d'une cité immense, sera dans la posterité la plus reculée, un monument mémorable de la piété du Monarque qui le fit ériger, et de l'édification du peuple qui en ait jetté les fondements. . . . un édifice majestueux, digne de la plus belle antiquité. . . ."[10] For grandeur of scope and a vision in line with the *noble simplicité* of the new ideals, an obvious Parisian landmark to range beside the Pan-

---

[8]Friedrich Wilhelm Marpurg, *Historisch-Kritische Beyträge zur Aufnahme der Music,* 5 vols. (Berlin, 1754–78; facsimile reprint, Hildesheim and New York, 1970), 1: 448–65, contains "Nachricht von verschiedenen berühmten französischen Organisten und Clavieristen itziger Zeit." The list of professional players is followed by the names of several women harpsichord players, headed by Madame Mondonville.

[9]Arno Schönberger and Halldor Soehner, *The Rococo Age* (London, 1960), p. 106.

[10]See *Haydn, Mozart,* pp. 158–64, for a discussion of this pamphlet and its likely author.

théon is Gossec's monumental *Messe des morts* of 1760, first given by some two hundred performers at the Jacobin church in the rue Saint Jacques. It was greatly admired and performed often to the end of the century and even beyond.

L'Académie Royale de Musique

The first theater of the Académie, or Opéra, was in a wing of the Palais Royal, located on the right side as one faces the structure from the rue Saint Honoré. Built originally in 1637 and the home of Molière's troupe before it was assigned to Lully in 1674, this theater was small by Italian standards. The most careful estimates place its capacity at thirteen to fourteen hundred spectators.[11] In its eighteenth-century guise it was decorated with garlands of flowers, fluttering cupids, and other rococo ornaments in stucco, as can be seen from a charming gouache drawing by Gabriel de Saint-Aubin, showing a revival of Lully's *Armide* in 1761.[12] Under Lully and his successors, the Académie was not, contrary to what its title might suggest, a training ground for young talent (unlike the Académie des Arts, also founded by Louis XIV), but a company entirely devoted to putting on operas. These were choral-balletic spectacles deploying elaborate stage machinery in service of the grand heroic style that Lully inaugurated at the court of Louis XIV, that is, the essentially aristocratic tragédie-lyrique. A true conservatory of music, the need for which was keenly felt and often expressed, had to wait until 1784 and the founding of the École Royale de Chant et de Déclamation, which replaced an earlier but ineffectual branch of the Opéra. The theater in the Palais Royal was totally destroyed by fire in April of 1763.[13]

For its next home the Opéra was given a part of the Salle des Machines in the Tuileries palace, a wing of the huge complex of the Louvre that was incinerated at the time of the Paris Commune in 1871 and subsequently razed. This theater, one of the largest in Europe and often compared with the Teatro Farnese at Parma for vastness, was begun in 1660 under the auspices of Cardinal Jules Mazarin, who planned to install an Italian operatic troupe there with which to divert the young Louis XIV and his court. Its amphitheater, which was more rectangular than oval, could hold as many as eight thousand spectators, according to several estimates of the time.[14] But this part of the theater was only half the length of the stage,

---

[11]Henri Lagrave, *Le théâtre et le publique à Paris de 1715 à 1750* (Paris, 1972), p. 86. Lagrave reproduces six manuscript sketches of the theater's interior, plates 7–12.

[12]It is reproduced in François Lesure, *L'opéra classique français* (Iconographie Musicale 1) (Geneva, 1972), p. 18. Lesure's estimate of 2,200 possible spectators (p. 23) is not supported by the documents elucidated by Lagrave.

[13]For a colored print of the time depicting the event, see Lesure, *L'opéra classique français*, p. 22. (The plate is reversed.) The conflagration happened in the morning, when the theater was empty, except for workmen who were drying some painted canvas scenery, which caught fire. No lives were lost, but all was destroyed except the ancient harpsichord, said to be invaluable, which was rescued.

[14]Lagrave, *Le théâtre et le publique*, p. 92.

which was well equipped to deploy all the marvels of perspective and stage machinery for which seventeenth-century opera was celebrated. Typical of so many colossal enterprises under Louis XIV, the Salle des Machines was literally superhuman; singers could not make themselves heard in it. Thus it was used infrequently for opera, but was employed from 1734 to 1758 for a spectacular series of pantomime shows directed and designed by Jean-Nicolas Servandoni, machinist-designer at the Opéra who was responsible for the façade of Saint Sulpice (1732–54). No subject was too grandiose or exotic for Servandoni's talents; the labors of Hercules, the conquests of Kublai Khan, the fall of the rebel angels (after Milton's *Paradise Lost*) were all staged as pantomime ballets with machinery and orchestral music. At least one orchestral score from these extravaganzas has survived. Francesco Geminiani, who visited Paris often around 1750, contributed the music to *La forêt enchantée* (after Torquato Tasso's *Gerusaleme liberata*) in 1754; he returned to London the next year and published the work under the title *The Inchanted Forest*. It is a curious mixture of old-fashioned Italian music, Handelian gestures, and attempts to be modern and at the same time to please the French penchant for descriptive orchestral effects. Its colorful and full orchestral textures were at any rate well calculated to fill the vast spaces of the seventeenth-century hall.

When Soufflot and Ange-Jacques Gabriel, two of France's greatest architects, were called upon to install a new theater in the same place, after the fire at the Palais Royal, they used only the stage portion of the old Salle des Machines and adopted the plans and small scale of the destroyed hall, but they eliminated the rococo ornament. A revival of Rameau's *Castor et Pollux,* the last within the composer's lifetime, opened the sparsely decorated new theater on 24 January 1764. During the rest of the decade this substitute theater served the Opéra, a time which saw the beginnings of a departure from older tragédie-lyrique, especially with Philidor's epochal *Ernelinde* of 1767.

By 1770 a splendid new theater, built by the architect Jean-Michel Moreau in neoclassical style, allowed the Opéra to return to its old location in the Palais Royal.[15] Its auditorium was more circular in shape than that of its predecessor and had an additional fourth tier of loges, which allowed the accommodation of three hundred more spectators (see the floor plan, Figure 8.1 on p. 809). Faithful as ever to the past, the directors of the Opéra offered a revival of Rameau's *Zoroastre* to inaugurate the new hall on 20 January 1770. But the days of Lullian and Ramellian revivals were quickly drawing to a close. The challenge of Philidor's *Ernelinde* had been a portent, preparing the way for the triumph of Gluck at Paris in the 1770s, as well as for the success of several of his Italian rivals. Moreau's theater lasted little more than a decade before it too burned, in 1781. The Opéra was then

---

[15]Lesure, *L'opéra classique français*, pp. 23–24 and 34–37. See also Jean Gourret, *Histoire des salles de l'Opéra de Paris* (Paris, 1985).

obliged to move into a theater hastily erected at the Porte Saint Martin, whence it was shunted to several other locations during the Revolutionary period.

The Opéra, like the other theaters to be discussed shortly, was public, although endowed by the king and run by his appointees.[16] One could gain entrance by showing up at the theater with the proper attire and the price of a ticket. There were several performances a week: Tuesday, Friday, and Sunday (also Thursday during the winter). Receipts were highest on Friday because there was no competition from the other royal theaters on this day.[17] The evening performance began at five o'clock and was announced by the tolling of a bell that could be heard by strollers in the adjacent garden of the Palais Royal. Diderot, at the end of his *Neveu de Rameau,* irreverently compares the clang of the bell and its effect upon opera lovers with a summons to vespers. Performances lasted about three hours. In 1758 it cost 40 sols (two livres) to purchase a ticket to stand in the parterre and more than three times that amount to gain admission to the first rank of loges or the *amphithéatre* (on the same level at the rear of the hall). Many of the best box seats were rented by the season or belonged by privilege to the aristocracy. A servant in livery was not allowed entrance. Given the relatively high price of admission (a laborer earned 40 sols for two days of work), the audiences were limited mainly to the nobility and wealthier artisan and bourgeois classes. The same is true for the carnival balls held at the Opéra throughout the era (Figure 6.2).

FIGURE 6.2. Poster for a carnival ball at the Opéra.

There were days of free admission also, in order to celebrate events such as royal births, marriages, or state visits. Thus on 14 September 1750, the public could have seen a free performance of Rameau's opéra-ballet *Les Indes galantes* (originally produced in 1735), for the duke of Burgundy was being honored that day. In addition the Opéra gave an annual concert in the garden of the Tuileries,

---

[16]In 1749, after years of mounting deficits, the king transferred control of the Opéra from private enterprise to the city of Paris, but directors' appointments remained subject to his approval. Control shifted between these two poles several times subsequently.

[17]Elizabeth Giuliani, "Le public de l'Opéra de Paris de 1750 à 1760; mesure et definition," *International Review of the Aesthetics and Sociology of Music* 8 (1977): 159–81.

free to the public, on the eve of the king's name day, the feast of Saint Louis (25 August).

A considerable number of functionaries of the realm or luminaries of the stage had right of entry to the theater without fee. These were divided into two classes, the inferior one having passes to the parterre (the painter Maurice Quentin de La Tour, Jean le Rond d'Alembert, and the Abbé Guillaume Raynal belonged in this group) and the superior one given entry to the *amphithéatre,* a distinction accorded, for example, to the two Crébillons, playwrights, and to the royal painter François Boucher. Ladies were excluded from the ground floor and took their places only in the loges. The first loges were for the social elite, the second for the bourgeois, and the third, or "Paradis," being the least favored places, went to less favored elements of society. The artisan class was well represented in the parterre, as has been deduced from a close reading of several criminal cases directed against individuals for creating a disturbance there.[18] Especially revealing is a novel of 1744 about a pretty young duchess who disguised herself as a commoner in order to experience what life was like in places such as the Paradis at the Opéra, where she met quite a variety of lower-class Parisians and was propositioned.[19]

The opera public at Paris in the mid-eighteenth century was not unlike the public for opera today. While some attended more for social than for artistic reasons, the majority (including many who had to devote a substantial part of their hard-earned income to this purpose) did so because they belonged to that intrepid species of opera lover that never tired of the sights and sounds of musical theater. Among the latter were the *philosophes* who were transforming intellectual life everywhere by planning and executing the great *Encyclopédie,* even though some of them were among the harshest critics of the Opéra's traditionalism. Tragédie-lyrique remained an expression of aristocratic values and ideals, reflecting its origins at the court of Louis XIV. But no matter how contrary it was to the middle-class spirit of the Enlightenment, led by the *philosophes,* French opera remained so stunning a musical-visual experience that not even a Diderot could resist its magic spell. Rousseau relates in the *Confessions* that during his early days at Paris, when he was an aspiring but impoverished composer of operas, he somehow found the means to go twice weekly "au spectacle."

OTHER THEATERS

The Opéra had to yield pride of place to another and older institution founded by Louis XIV, the Comédie Française. Spoken tragedies and comedies in French were

---

[18]Lagrave, *Le théâtre et le publique,* pp. 238–44.
[19]Gaillard de la Bataille, *Jeannette seconde, ou La nouvelle paysanne parvenue,* cited by Lagrave (ibid.), pp. 234–44.

the prerogative of this theater, which continued the traditions of its classics—Corneille, Racine, and Molière—while not neglecting new dramas, whether serious (Voltaire and the Crébillons) or comic (Lesage, Marivaux, and Beaumarchais). More than its present-day successor, the Comédie assigned an important place to music. Theoretically, the Opéra's royal charter prohibited singing in French outside its domain. But the Comédie had its own orchestra, singers, and dancers, as well as composers, who provided overtures, entr'actes, dances, and songs, the last two coming to the fore especially in the divertissements concluding comedies and in comedy-ballets. To avoid attracting lawsuits from the Opéra, recitative was avoided, and the vocal music was kept as simple as possible. Many fine composers worked for this theater, including Jean-Claude Gillier and Jean-Joseph Mouret in the early eighteenth century.

Since 1689 the Comédie Française had been located on the Left Bank, at No. 14, rue de l'Ancienne Comédie, not far from the Carrefour de Buci—the café setting for *La bohème.* In size it was about the same as the Opéra in the Palais Royal. Spectators had to pay roughly half the cost of entry to the Opéra. The lack of spectacular scenic effects must have accounted for some of this discrepancy. As the century advanced, the theater of the Comédie became increasingly dilapidated. After the Opéra left the Soufflot-Gabriel theater in the Tuileries in early 1770, the Comédie moved in. It was here that the aged Voltaire was crowned with a laurel wreath in 1778, at a performance of his last tragedy *Irène,* an event recorded in prints preserving one of few visual records of this hall.[20]

For twelve years the Comédie remained at the Tuileries, while a beautiful and sternly neoclassical hall was being built for it on the Left Bank near the Luxembourg palace: the Théâtre de l'Odéon, which still stands. *Le mariage de Figaro* by Beaumarchais, with songs by Antoine Laurent Baudron, leader of the orchestra, had its premiere in this theater on 27 April 1784.

The Comédie Italienne was inferior to both the Opéra and Comédie Française in prestige and position. In a sense it was the oldest of all, being heir to the various troupes of Italian players that began visiting Paris in the sixteenth century. Dismissed by Louis XIV in 1697, allegedly for satirizing the grand monarch's prudish mistress, Madame de Maintenon, the Italians, under Luigi Riccoboni, were invited back in 1716 by the regent, Philip of Orleans. They were reinstated in the same old sixteenth-century playhouse, the Hôtel de Bourgogne, located in the populous quarter of Les Halles, near Saint Eustache. Refurbished many times in its long history, this theater too had once housed Molière's troupe. Although

---

[20]It is reproduced in Nicole Decugis and Suzanne Reymond, *Le décor de théâtre en France du moyen age à 1925* (Paris, 1953), p. 126, and in John Lough, *An Introduction to 18th-Century France* (New York, 1960), p. 288, plate 43. For a floor plan of this theater see the article "Paris" in *The New Grove Dictionary of Opera,* ed. Stanley Sadie (London, 1992).

small, it was able to accommodate about as many spectators as the Opéra in the Palais Royal. Daily playbills, attendance figures, and financial receipts have survived for the entire eighteenth-century existence of the theater, and they show that the record attendance was reached on 2 February 1742 for a spectacle comprising *Petit-maître amoureux, Oracles,* and *Divertissement:* 1,367 spectators, bringing in a revenue of 3,911 livres.[21]

Italian plays and pantomimes were the original province of this troupe, and as in Italy they were often drawn from the ever-popular *canevas* of the commedia dell'arte and largely improvised. It was not long before the public, tiring of a language that was not its own, clamored for plays in French, which the troupe gave them, bringing down the wrath of the Comédie Française. (Marivaux began his career as a playwright at the Théâtre Italien in 1720 and wrote his masterpiece *Le jeu de l'amour et du hasard* for it in 1730.) Music and dancing were included in the entertainments to the extent that the troupe dared, without infringing on the Opéra's privilege, and the *Divertissement* mentioned above was surely a spectacle involving both. An instruction sheet engraved by Gabriel de Saint-Aubin, entitled "La Bionni Contredanse, tirée du Waxhall Hollandois," shows the final contredanse of *Le Wauxhall hollandais* (1761), a divertissement by the choreographer of the Théâtre Italien, a certain Bionni (Figure 6.3).[22] It is just possible to make out a few of the commedia dell'arte characters among the dancers: Harlequin and Harlequine with their motley, Pierrot in white with his floppy hat, and Pulcinella with his tall hat.

When the Comédie Italienne merged with the Opéra-Comique in 1762 it became, for several years, the most interesting lyric theater in France, the Opéra having become quite unenterprising by comparison. A representation of the theater in the Hôtel de Bourgogne during the heyday of Philidor and Monsigny exists in the form of a 1767 drawing by Wille that has been identified as depicting Monsigny's *Le roi et le fermier.*[23] It shows in welcome detail some features characteristic of most Parisian theaters of the time (see Figure 7.8 on p. 771). Behind the orchestra of some twenty-odd players, there were several rows of benches filled with men. This was the parquet. Behind this was the pit of the parterre, also men only, and all standing. Burney, in a letter to his daughter Fanny of 13 June 1764, complained: "I am just come from the Comick Opera which is called here

[21]Clarence D. Brenner, *The Théâtre Italien: Its Repertory 1716–1793* (University of California Publications in Modern Philology, 63) (Berkeley and Los Angeles, 1961), p. 130. Total capacity was around fifteen hundred. The figure cited did not include boxes rented by subscription or free passes (p. 16).

[22]The entire plate is reproduced in Jean-Michel Guilcher, *La contredanse et les renouvellements de la danse française* (Paris, 1969), following p. 96, and in Daniel Heartz, *Mozart's Operas* (Berkeley, 1990), pp. 188–89.

[23]Daniel Heartz, "Opéra-Comique and the Théâtre Italien from Watteau to Fragonard," in *Music in the Classic Period: Essays in Honor of Barry S. Brook,* ed. Allan W. Atlas (New York, 1985), pp. 69–84.

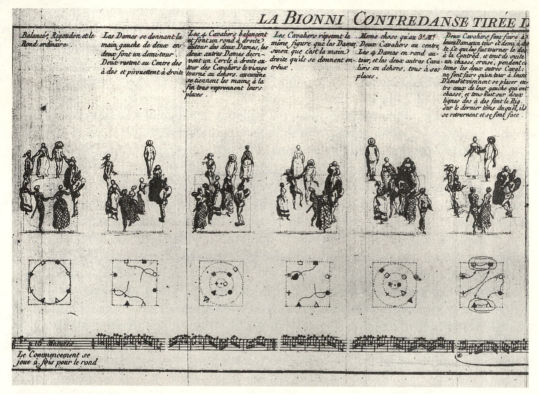

FIGURE 6.3. Gabriel de Saint-Aubin. *La Bionni, Contredanse.*

Comédie Italienne, where I have been extreamly well entertained [by *Le roi et le fermier*], but am so tired with standing the whole time, which everybody in the pit does." Ladies are to be seen only in the boxes, of which there are three tiers. One reason they were not welcome in the parquet has to do with the high hairdos then in fashion, on top of which large hats were also frequently worn.

French plays formed a part of the repertory of the Comédie Italienne only at certain times during its existence, but the Italian plays were a continual feature of the company, along with the Italian players to perform them. These plays did not draw a large public, in fact, they often played to pitifully small houses. The fortunes of the company at midcentury had sunk quite low, partly because of financial mismanagement. Like the Comédie Française, the Italian troupe was a cooperative in which the profits, if any, were shared by the permanent members of the company. The responsibility of overseeing the financial management passed from member to member—an arrangement that often proved disastrous. What rescued the Italians from a final decline and dissolution was their ability to put on musical comedies. This came to the fore especially in the 1750s, when

Favart worked regularly for them. As a result they were able to challenge the brilliant Opéra-Comique under Jean Monnet with their own productions. The merging of the two companies in 1762 was in reality a victory for the Italian company, because they absorbed a potent rival and integrated its best singers and most acclaimed productions. Orchestral forces grew larger and more diverse after the merger, and the chorus gained in importance.[24]

There was another event in 1762 which gave a needed boost to the company. Carlo Goldoni, fresh from a decade at Venice during which he became Italy's leading dramatist, accepted an invitation to Paris. He immediately helped rejuvenate the Italian part of the repertory with his own works and enabled the Italian players to continue. Plays in Italian were not finally abandoned until the spring of 1780. Thenceforth the offerings were totally devoted to lyric shows with spoken dialogue in French, in other words, to opéra-comique in its classic formulation. In 1769 the Comédie Italienne petitioned to move from the Hôtel de Bourgogne to the 1763 hall in the Tuileries about to be vacated by the Opéra, giving as the chief reason their unfortunate location and citing the difficulty of access through the narrow streets around Les Halles. The authorities refused and favored the Comédie Française instead, as we have seen. Not until 1783 did the Comédie Italienne (which was no longer Italian except in name, save for the Italianate character of much of the music) have the opportunity to move to a new theater. It was especially built for them near the location of the present Salle Favart off the boulevard des Italiens, so named after the troupe, and held upwards of two thousand spectators (see Figure 7.11 on p. 793). Finally, in 1793, the company changed the name of its hall from Théâtre Italien to the more appropriate Théâtre de l'Opéra-Comique National.

The expression *opéra-comique* emerged early in the eighteenth century as an appellation for the musical entertainments given at the Parisian trade fairs. There were two main fairs, one in the Faubourg Saint Germain during February-March, the other occupying the terrain now covered by the Gare de l'Est in the Faubourg Saint Laurent during August-September. These musical shows and the companies that put them on led a precarious existence at best, hounded by the Opéra, the Comédie Française, and the Comédie Italienne in turn. One advantage enjoyed by the three royal troupes, aside from their subsidies and privileges, was the lucrative invitations to play before the court at Versailles or Fontainebleau, which they did annually. The court thus got to see what had been tested and found successful at Paris. Special gratuities often resulted. The lowly Théâtres de la Foire, or "Forains" for short, enjoyed no such avenue to extra earnings. They

---

[24]David Charlton, "Orchestra and Chorus at the Comédie-Italienne (Opéra-Comique), 1755–99," in *Slavonic and Western Music: Essays for Gerald Abraham,* ed. Malcolm Hamrick Brown and Roland John Wiley (Ann Arbor, Mich., and Oxford, 1985), pp. 87–108.

made do with inadequate facilities and an unruly public, and had to overcome the strictures of the privileged theaters by ruse and guile.

At one point (around 1712) in their checkered existence, the Foraíns sought to go beyond mere pantomime and introduced sung verses accompanied by banners (*écriteaux*) with large lettering that were somewhat similar in effect to the cloud-shaped speeches of the comic strips. The *Pièce à écriteaux* became in fact the earliest type of true opéra-comique.[25] When the small orchestra struck up a familiar tune (vaudeville) the audience sang the new text off the banner—nothing in the privilege of the Opéra prevented this. Little by little the Foraíns also introduced spoken comments, thereby challenging the prerogative of the Comédie Française.

As this repertory developed, poets and musicians were able to manipulate hundreds of vaudevilles, each having some prior significance for the audience, and combine them into new comedies with a wealth of allusions. An art of double entendre emerged that was often scabrous by intention, especially in the early days under the Régence. But after Favart became the main poet of these comedies in the 1730s, he raised the level of the whole genre, while not giving up its popular foundations in the tunes of the vaudeville repertory. Favart played a role in refining French lyric comedies rather similar to that of Goldoni in Italy.

In order to survive at all, the companies putting on opéra-comique had to pay fees to the Opéra. The more successful they were, the more likely it became that one or more of the privileged theaters would put an end to their existence. Thus in 1745, for example, the Comédie Française and the Comédie Italienne combined to have the Foraíns suppressed. Their genial impresario Jean Monnet was forced to leave the capital and lead an itinerant life in Dijon, Lyons, and London for several years. After returning to Paris in 1752 he had a greatly admired theater constructed at the Foire Saint Laurent (see Figure 7.2 on p. 707). When the Opéra-Comique was assimilated by the Théâtre Italien in 1762, the theater was bought by the crown, dismantled, and reassembled in the rue Berger as "La Salle des Menus Plaisirs du Roy."[26] As such it was used for the entertainment of the court upon its rare visits to Paris and also served to house the Opéra for a few months in 1781. Even more important, it became the seat of the Conservatoire, in its earliest existence as the École Royale de Chant (1784–95), to which it afforded an excellent concert hall. The theater was remodelled in Empire style under

[25]Donald Jay Grout, "The Opéra Comique and the Théâtre Italien from 1715 to 1762," in *Miscelánea en homenaje a Monseñor Higinio Anglés*, 2 vols. (Barcelona, 1958–61), 1: 369–77; Donald Jay Grout "The Origins of the Opéra Comique" (Ph.D. diss., Harvard University, 1939); Daniel Heartz, "Terpsichore at the Fair; Old and New Dance Airs in Two Vaudeville Comedies by Lesage," in *Music and Context: Essays for John M. Ward*, ed. Anne Dhu Shapiro (Cambridge, Mass., 1985), pp. 278–304.

[26]J. G. Prod'homme and E. de Crauzet, *Les menus plaisirs du roi: L'École Royale et le Conservatoire de Musique* (Paris, 1929), p. 43.

Napoleon and continued as the Salle de l'Ancien Conservatoire until the building was demolished in 1910.

Besides the theaters already mentioned there were several others that sprang up along the spacious boulevards that were replacing the old ramparts of Paris in the eighteenth century. The boulevards served as parks for the multitudes of the capital, and the entertainments offered there were gaudy and popular in nature, like the Vauxhall at London, and probably best approximated today by the Tivoli Gardens at Copenhagen. Burney, when in Paris in 1770, observed: "The Boulevard is a place of public diversions, without the gates of Paris. It is laid out in walks and planted. In the middle is a wide road for carriages, and at the sides are coffee-houses, conjurors, and shows of all kinds." He was most impressed with how well dressed the people were, and with a pavilion for dancing called the New Vauxhall, "which is square . . . with two rows of corinthian pillars ornamented with festoons and illuminations. This is a very elegant room, in which are *minuets, allemandes, cotillons,* and *contre danses.*" Lastly, mention should be made of the many private salons and theaters of the nobility, at which concerts and operas were frequently given, offering another source of employment for musicians.

THE CONCERT SPIRITUEL

With the Concert Spirituel, founded in 1725 and lasting until 1790, Paris acquired an institution that was of European scope. It became the premier concert series of the Continent, and the only one for which the repertory is known, year by year, concert by concert.[27] In 1725 one of the royal musicians, Anne Danican Philidor, sought and received permission to organize concerts on the thirty-odd religious holidays when the theaters were closed and to transform one of the rooms in the Tuileries palace for this purpose. In return for paying 1,000 livres to the Opéra annually, he obtained permission to give public concerts of "musiques spir- ituelles" for three years. In return he promised not to include any operatic music or music written to French texts. Posters were used, as at the public theaters, to advertise the concerts, which began at 5 or 6 P.M. and lasted for two hours or more. Tickets could be bought in advance or at the door; in the early days the price of a seat was from 2 to 4 livres.

The concert hall was located on the upper floor of the central pavilion of the Tuileries palace, in a room known as the Salle des Cent Suisses. It was nearly square and it rose to a height of three stories. Surmounting the room was a vaulted wooden ceiling, which certainly contributed to the resonant qualities of this hall.[28] The original installation comprised an elevated tribune for the musi-

---

[27]Recorded in a landmark publication, Constant Pierre's *Histoire du Concert Spirituel 1725–1790* (Publica- tions de la Société française de Musicologie, 3e Serie, Tome III) (Paris, 1975).

[28]See Daniel Heartz, "The Concert Spirituel in the Tuileries palace," *Early Music* 21 (1993): 241–48.

cians erected against the south wall, measuring thirty-six feet wide, nine feet deep, and ten feet high. It accommodated a chorus and orchestra of sixty in total. When Philidor sought renewed permission for the series in 1727, it was modified to allow for more performers, and modifications were made continually during the long history of the concert series. An organ was installed at the back of the musicians' tribune. Wooden bleachers in an amphitheater arrangement were built for the audience, with loges around the sides and back for the ladies. A balcony ran around the top of the hall. Figure 6.4 shows an undated drawing of a floor plan, inscribed "Salle de Concert aux Thuilleries. Plan du parquet."

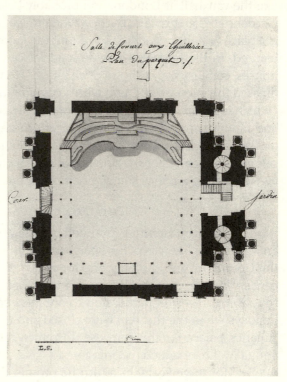

As to acoustics, the concert hall in the Tuileries was judged a success by most critics. The dissenting voices came from those who felt it was too vast for the softer instruments. Although in absolute terms it was not very large by later standards, the only measurement that matters was that of the musical ears of the time, which perceived the space to be enormous. One critic in 1740 complained that the Tuileries provided "une salle énorme en grandeur, une salle d'espace immense"—one of the earliest charges that a concert hall was too large.[29] He claimed also that

FIGURE 6.4. Plan for the Concert Spirituel in the Tuileries palace.

the "violin sought out this great space where, in being distant from the auditors, it can flatter them, and where its sharp tone [ton aigu] can be absorbed by the multitude of the clothes." There were evidently several hundred auditors at a typical concert. The advantages of the violin family over the viol family in such a situation are undeniable. Emergence of a brilliant school of violinists and cellists at Paris after 1725 can be tied directly to the auspices of the Concert Spirituel and the physical fact of its large and quasi-permanent concert hall.

[29]Hubert Le Blanc, *Défense de la basse viole contre les entreprises du violon et les prétensions du violoncel* (Amsterdam, 1740), cited after Michel Brenet, *Les concerts en France* (Paris, 1900), pp. 154–55.

Composers were often well rewarded for their effort if they supplied music to the Concert Spirituel, which helps explain why the series gradually became an international forum for new music. In a letter of 3 December 1777 from Mannheim, Mozart related that the flautist Johann Baptist Wendling told him that a symphony was rewarded with 5 louis d'or from the Concert Spirituel or the rival Académie des Amateurs at the Hôtel de Soubise. Wendling had played often in Paris and was in a position to know. His appearances there spanned three decades. He first played one of his flute concertos at the Concert Spirituel on 12 April 1751. At concerts of 19 and 27 March 1780 Wendling is described as having been soloist in a new flute concerto of his own composition. The composer-flautist who dominated the 1780s was François Devienne.

When the Concert Spirituel began in 1725, Philidor used his connections as a royal musician to obtain copies of several of the forty-two grand motets for soloists, chorus, and instruments by Michel-Richard de Lalande, the favorite church composer of Louis XIV. These motets served for several decades as one of the mainstays of the series. *Dominus regnavit* was in fact performed as late as the concert Burney attended in June of 1770. It was the last of Lalande to be heard in the series, unbeknownst to Burney, who seized the occasion to rail against French traditionalism in music. Along with Lalande on the opening program of 1725 was "La Nuit de Noël" by Corelli, that is to say, the so-called *Christmas* Concerto, Op. 6 No. 8. Italian violin music thus had a prominent place from the earliest days of the concerts. A revue of the first concert in *Mercure de France* for March 1725 specified that the concert was made up of "motets à grand choeur et de symphonies françaises et italiennes des meilleurs auteurs" and furthermore that there were sixty musicians, selected from the Opéra, the king's music, and the larger Parisian churches.[30]

Many of the greatest Italian violinists throughout the century came in person to play their sonatas and concertos at the Tuileries, beginning with Jean-Pierre Guignon of Turin in 1725. Cello solos were frequent as well, the greatest name on the long list of cellists heard at the concerts being Boccherini. Oboe and bassoon virtuosi, as well as flautists, were prominent on the concert's programs, as were, towards the middle of the century, horn players (Bohemians and Germans mainly). The clarinet was first heard in 1750 but did not become a frequent solo instrument until the 1770s. Around 1760 the harp became a modish salon instrument with the Parisian ladies, in large part because of its antique associations at a time that was rife with neoclassical fads of all kinds. Audiences at the Tuileries concerts were not deprived of enjoying this newly fashionable instrument.

At the concert of 12 May 1765 Mademoiselle Schencker, the precocious daughter of a hornist in the service of the prince de Conti, "played charming

---

[30]Pierre, *Histoire du Concert Spirituel,* p. 16.

pieces on the harp" according to the *Mercure de France*.[31] A young Danish artist then studying in Paris, Cornelius Høyer, sketched the occasion, providing a rare glimpse of actual music making in this concert series (Figure 6.5). Although barely twelve years old at the time, the young lady is dressed and coiffed like a grown-up, as was the fashion with children then. Seated in the middle of a specially raised platform, she plays her elaborately scrolled harp while reading from music on a stand placed in front of her. Surrounding her are the much larger figures of grown musicians, violinists on either side, also playing from separate music stands, and behind them the outlines of an orchestra with winds, horns, and double basses (on either side at the back). The heads of the audience in the foreground reach up to the bottom of the soloist's platform, which is about waist level of the nearby violinists. Two rows of musicians behind them occupy a middle level and a higher level. The orchestra's disposition for accompanying a soloist seems eminently practical.

The prohibition against French texts or operatic music was enforced only intermittently. From 1728 to 1733 French secular cantatas by Colin de Blamont, Clérambault, and others were frequently heard, but these were performed at

FIGURE 6.5. Cornelius Høyer. Mademoiselle Schencker, soloist at the Concert Spirituel.

[31]Florence Gétreau, "Une harpiste au Concert Spirituel. Mlle Schencker en mai 1765," *Musique. Images. Instruments. Revue française d'organologie et d'iconographie musicale* 1 (1995): 178–81. The author discusses the new chromatic harp with pedals, perfected by the Bavarian maker Hochbrucker, which arrived in France only in 1749, by way of Georges-Adam Geopffert, harpist in the orchestra of La Pouplinière.

"extra" concerts in addition to the thirty-odd regular ones.[32] During this period one of the directors of the series, succeeding Philidor, was Mouret, who added eleven French cantatas and four Latin motets to the Concert's repertory. Under the next management, that of François Rebel and François Francoeur (1734–48), who also ran the Opéra, the original strictures prohibiting works in French were enforced and the "extra" concerts abolished. (The two directors had made their debut together at the Concert Spirituel in 1726, playing violin duets.) A favorite composer of new motets who emerged in the 1730s was Jean-Joseph Cassanéa de Mondonville.

Strictures against operatic music evidently applied only to French opera, because Italian arias were frequently heard, as were a succession of the most prominent Italian opera singers. Oratorios and sacred cantatas in French became common again after 1760. Mondonville had started this trend in 1758 with his short oratorio, *Les Israëlites à la montagne d'Horeb.* The Concert Spirituel became more and more secular over its long history, but it never lost all connection with its original purpose, contrary to what has been claimed.[33] The last concerts of 1790 still offered Latin motets, along with symphonies, concertos, and French-texted works on sacred subjects.

Italian music and musicians took ever greater part in the programs of the Concert Spirituel over the decades. A glimpse of the content of this concert series amply illustrates the Italianization of French music. When Philidor founded the concerts there was another, quasi-public rival known as the Concert Italien, at which nothing but Italian music was played. It was supported by sixty subscribers who payed 400 livres each.[34] The Concert Spirituel never became exclusively Italian, but it was the center for Italian musicians visiting Paris. Singers from the Royal Academy of Musick at London were frequent soloists, and they served as the vehicles by which a few operatic arias of Handel were heard at Paris. Handel's London rival, Giovanni Bononcini, appeared in person as the leader of some of his Latin church music at the Concert Spirituel in 1733. Telemann, who was in Paris during 1737–38, directed a grand motet of his composition at the Tuileries. It was not repeated. No new compositions of this period were deemed sufficiently attractive to oust the motets of Lalande from their central position in the repertory, and the only ones to challenge them were provided by the young Languedocien composer, Mondonville.

---

[32]See David Tunley, *The Eighteenth-Century French Cantata* (London, 1974), pp. 6–12; the extra concerts were called "Concerts français."

[33]William Weber, *Music and the Middle Class: The Social Structure of Concert Life in London, Paris and Vienna* (New York, 1975), p. 4; the author also errs in stating that the Opéra and Concert Spirituel were run by aristocrats and state officials; they were run by professional musicians (who might also, as in the case of the elder Philidor and Mouret, enjoy positions in royal service).

[34]Brenet, *Les concerts en France,* p. 162.

Instrumentalists appearing at Paris in the 1730s included several luminaries attached to the court of Savoy at Turin. Among these were the violinist Lorenzo Somis, who played a concerto and a sonata in 1733 (and published a collection of sonatas in Paris the following year) and the Besozzi brothers, who offered duets for oboe and bassoon in 1735. A special connection between Savoy and the Tuileries concerts prevailed in later years as well. Felice Giardini and Gaetano Pugnani both came from Turin and made their debuts at the Concert Spirituel in 1750 and 1754, respectively. Parisian publications of their music followed both events.

Debuts of two notable young French violinists took place in 1741: Pierre Gaviniès, aged thirteen, and Joseph-Barnabé Saint-Sévin L'abbé le fils, one year older. They played a sonata for two violins by Jean-Marie Leclair (who had published collections of such sonatas, both unaccompanied and with bass, during the 1730s). The occasion represents a watershed. Leclair was rarely performed at the Concert Spirituel after this point. Henceforth violinists turned increasingly to more recent Italian styles for a model. In vocal music the case was similar. The French cantata during its heyday in the 1730s was stylistically linked to the earlier Italian cantata of the type that Alessandro Scarlatti had brought to a peak of perfection. Another pair of young Frenchmen made their debut at the Concert Spirituel in 1743 as the composers of Latin motets, both lost, Jean-Baptiste Cardonne and François-André Danican Philidor (stepbrother of the founder of the series). From their surviving vocal music we are able to range them alongside the most galant of the midcentury Italians.

When Philidor first appeared at the Concert Spirituel his irreverent modernism could not prevail against the public's devotion to Lalande, whose motets have been described as representing the dusk of the *grand siècle* and the dawn of the rococo.[35] Protracted as was this long twilight, it seems more appropriate to consign Lalande's lingering shadow to the aftermath of Louis XIV's reign, while recognizing the rococo ideals of the reign of Louis XV (or at least the first part of it, up to ca. 1760) in such masters as Mondonville and young Philidor.

The newer Italian styles of vocal music represented by Leo, Hasse, and Galuppi scarcely made any inroads in France until midcentury. By then the change in French musical tastes began to accelerate to a remarkable degree. All three of the composers just mentioned were represented in performance at the Tuileries concerts, but only after 1750, at a date when they had long since arrived at their mature styles (and in the case of Leo, years after his death in 1744). In France it was the newer Italian violin music which anticipated and stimulated the changes that gradually overcame every other kind of music. "We have attained

---

[35]Ibid., p. 122. James R. Anthony, *French Baroque Music from Beaujoyeux to Rameau,* rev. ed. (New York, 1978), p. 194, wrote that the composer mingled "the official Versailles style and galant airs borrowed from opera."

their excellence in instrumental music," claimed the author of the mysterious *Lettre sur le mechanisme* (1756), "and we can do so in vocal music."

The Concert Spirituel held competitions for newly composed motets. They attracted submissions from far and wide. Antonio Soler in Spain wrote his chief patron in 1767 saying that he had completed a motet for the Paris series: "Although I do not expect to win the prize, for lack of *Hombre,* nevertheless I hope in God that I shall not fail to bring some lustre to our Spain."[36] There is no record in Paris of his motet's being performed.

The end of the series was ignominious. After the fall of the Bastille and the disturbances at Versailles in 1789 the king and his family were forced to move back to Paris, where they took up residence in the Tuileries palace. Shunted from place to place, the concerts ended on 13 May 1790. In 1791 Ginguené commented that "the general disorder, suppression of privileges, and above all the lack of a locale since the arrival of the king at the Tuileries banished all spectacles there, have united as causes to strike a blow at the Concert Spirituel from which it will not likely recover."[37] He saw clear.

Music Publishing

The Ballard family retained sole privileges of printing music in France for several generations from the time of the founding of their firm in 1551 by Adrian Le Roy and Robert Ballard. They perfected the method of printing music by a single impression from movable type introduced by Pierre Attaingnant. Like him they set up shop on the Left Bank near the Sorbonne, always remaining at the same address on the rue Saint Jean de Beauvais. Several challenges to the Ballards' monopoly arose but were mostly overcome. What eventually ruined the Ballards was the newer technique of engraving music on copper plates, which was better suited to almost all kinds of music, by the end of the seventeenth century.

Henri Foucault, a *marchand papetier,* challenged Christophe Ballard's monopoly by setting up a music-selling business at the beginning of the rue Saint Honoré (near the rue du Roule) at the sign of "La Règle d'Or" between 1690 and 1692. This Right Bank location was not far from the Académie Royale de Musique in the Palais Royal, which had long since become the center of French musical life. By 1697 Foucault was selling many kinds of music, including André Campra's score to *L'Europe galante* printed by Ballard, who had sued Foucault in 1690 but later came to an accommodation with him. During the eighteenth century the Ballard

---

[36]George Treutt Hollis, "'El diablo vestito de fraile': Some Unpublished Correspondence of Padre Soler," in *Music in Spain during the Eighteenth Century,* ed. Malcolm Boyd and Juan José Carreras (Cambridge, 1998), pp. 192–206; 202. The expression *Hombre* was apparently a polite circumlocution for testicles.
[37]Article "Concert Spirituel" in *Encyclopédie Methodique: Musique,* ed. Nicolas Étienne Framery and Pierre Louis Ginguené, vol. 1 (Paris, 1791).

firm became increasingly marginal with regard to the mainstream of music publishing. Their printed music, still reproduced by the old method, came to consist mainly of popular airs and theoretical treatises.

Music engraving did not come under the monopoly of the Ballards and was thus free to expand as an industry. The process of printing from engraved plates made it possible to make very few copies, on demand, or up to as many as three hundred.[38] Such flexibility suited marketing. Henri de Baussen, who styled himself "graveur ordinaire de l'Académie royale de musique," engraved Lully's operas around 1710 (after they were first printed by the Ballards). In 1711 Louis Hüe, aged about twelve, apprenticed himself for a three-year period to Baussen and went on to become one of the finest music engravers in a career that spanned over fifty years, from 1714 to at least 1765.

François Boivin succeeded to the music shop at the Règle d'Or on the rue Saint Honoré in 1721, and at his death in 1733 his widow carried on the business for another twenty years. By 1753 when she sold the shop to Marc Bayard, her stock in music was worth no less than 36,400 livres. Meanwhile the Le Clerc brothers, both practical musicians, set up two more music stores in the same neighborhood. Jean-Pantaléon Le Clerc, born before 1697, entered the "Vingt-Quatre Violons du Roi" in 1720. His residence in the rue du Roule, at the sign of "La Croix d'Or," offered a large stock of music for sale from 1728 to 1758, the last years of which were in partnership with his daughter, from whom Louis Balthazard de La Chevardière took over the business. La Chevardière was the first to publish quartets by Haydn (in 1764). In 1780 he turned the business over to his daughter, who sold it to Pierre Leduc in 1784.

Charles-Nicolas Le Clerc (1697–1774) was even more enterprising as a music publisher than his older brother. He became a violinist at the Opéra in 1729 and one of the "Vingt-Quatre Violons du Roi" in 1732. His talents as a violinist merited him frequent mention in the *Mercure de France.* When he began publishing in 1736 he resided on the rue Saint Honoré at the sign "à la Ville de Constantinople" near the Oratoire, which was next to the oldest part of the Louvre. The younger Le Clerc had the foresight to commission music from many of the foreign musicians who were attracted by good pay to the nearby Concert Spirituel in the Tuileries. The famous Telemann, for instance, who arrived in the autumn of 1737 for an eight-month stay in Paris and who contributed a motet to the Concert Spirituel on 25 March 1738, had instrumental works of his advertized in Le Clerc's catalogues of 1738–39. Le Clerc published music by a long list of other visitors to the Concert Spirituel, including Alessandro Besozzi, Bononcini, Geminiani, Giar-

[38]Anick Devriès, *Édition et commerce de la musique gravée à Paris dans la première moitié du XVIIIe siècle: Les Boivin, Les Leclerc* (Geneva, 1976), p. 6. This groundbreaking work, based on original research, served as my main source for the whole section.

dini, Pugnani, Somis, and Carlo Zuccari.[39] According to the music historian John Hawkins, Geminiani was attracted to Paris partly by the excellence of its music engraving and publishing. Le Clerc also published music by French composers such as Leclair, Louis-Gabriel Guillemain, and Jean-Baptiste Cupis. Until the 1750s he published instrumental music. Then he became an important publisher of opéra-comique.

Women were prominent in Parisian music publishing, and several became expert music engravers. Rameau's *Premier livre de pièces de clavecin* (1706) was engraved by Claude Roussel. His daughter, Louise Roussel, engraved Rameau's *Nouvelles suites de pièces de clavecin* in 1729. The following year she became Madame Leclair (wife of the great violinist-composer), and many a title page bore this form of her name until 1764, when she became "La veuve Leclair." Marie Charlotte Vendôme was active over an equally long period as an engraver. Her name appears in this form on the *Pièces de clavecin* by Jacques Duphly in 1744. Twenty years later she engraved Mozart's first harpsichord sonatas, described on the title page as "Gravées par Mme Vendôme ci-devant rue St Jacques à présent rue St Honoré vis à vis le Palais Royal."[40] She too gravitated to the center of Parisian music making and music publishing. Leopold Mozart referred to her as old in a letter of 23 December 1764, but she apparently went on engraving music for another twenty years.

In some cases publication of a new work happened nearly simultaneously with its first presentation at the Concert Spirituel. One curious instance is Charles Henri de Blainville's *Essay sur un troisième mode, presenté et approuvé par Mrs. de l'academie des Sciences, joint la Symphonie Executée au Concert du Chateau des Thuilleries 30. May 1751.* This print was "gravé par Mme Leclair" and sold at the addresses of the author, the widow Boivin, and the elder Le Clerc, and by "Mlle Castagnery, rue des Prouvaires à la Musique Royale." Some notices of concerts mention use of specific music prints. Thus in the same summer of 1751 the concert of 15 August (Assumption of the Virgin Mary) began with the "6e symphonie du 14e oeuvre" by Guillemain, a reference to *Deuxième livre de symphonies en trio dans le goût Italien* published in 1748. The next concert on 8 September (Annunciation to the Virgin Mary) began with François Martin's "1re ouverture du 4e oeuvre," a reference to *Six symphonies et ouvertures pour deux violons, altoviola et basso* advertised in the *Annonces* of 28 October 1751. If we possessed similar repertories for other concert series there would no doubt be many more cases showing close ties between the publishing business and what was being performed.

New publishers and engravers arrived on the scene around 1760, swelling the ranks of an industry that did not cease growing. Antoine Bailleux first attracted

---

[39]Ibid., pp. 83–84.
[40]The title page is reproduced in *Haydn, Mozart,* p. 500.

attention as a composer of *Sei sinfonie a quatro, due violini, alto viola e basso . . . composte da Antonio Bailleux,* announced on 13 December 1756 and sold by Bayard, the elder Le Clerc, and Marie-Anne Castagneri. His penchant for Italian titles figured as well in the many publications he brought out and sold at his shop, as successor to Bayard at the Régle d'Or. He was the first to publish Boccherini's string trios of 1760 (in July 1767). A music teacher as well as a composer and publisher, he advertised his stock by several one-sheet lists, the first in 1767: "Catalogue de Musique Françoise et Italienne, Vocale et Instrumentale, que Mr. Bailleux, Maitre de Musique a fait graver depuis peu, qu'il continue et vend à Paris rue St. Honoré près celle de la Feronnerie à la Régle d'Or."[41] At the bottom of some subsequent catalogues Bailleux stated his willingness to send music to any dealer or private person in or outside the realm of France.

Three other major figures joined the field. Anton Huberty was employed by the Opéra in 1756. His Parisian catalogues date from 1760 and he began advertising in Vienna a decade later; in 1777 he betook himself and his family to the imperial capital, where he worked mainly as a music engraver. Jean Baptiste Vénier, who flourished from the mid-1750s to 1784, was the first to publish a symphony by Haydn (in 1764). Jean-Georges Sieber, a Bavarian, arrived in Paris in 1758 at age twenty and became a noted hornist at the Opéra and the Concert Spirituel, as well as one of the greatest and most scrupulous of Parisian music publishers. He continued publishing into the following century, sometimes in partnership with his son. All three firms remained in the same *quartier* on or around the rue Saint Honoré near the Palais Royal, favored for the music-selling business ever since Foucault and the Le Clercs.

The combination of the Concert Spirituel and other Parisian concert series, and a flourishing industry of music publishing lent the French metropolis an unparalleled centrality in European musical life. Music publishing and the abundant concert and operatic life in Paris were in fact closely tied together: the one fed the other in a dizzying spiral of production and consumption.

Rameau

One keen observer of eighteenth-century musical trends opined that French instrumental music was improving (by which he meant coming closer to Italian ideals) but he doubted that French vocal music was capable of doing the same (Leopold Mozart, letter of 6–11 May 1778). It is true that French instrumental

[41]Cari Johansson, *French Music Publishers' Catalogue of the Second Half of the Eighteenth Century,* 2 vols. (Stockholm, 1955), 2: facsimile 1.

music led the way toward a more modern style. Not far behind, nevertheless, and gradually opening up to newer fashions, French vocal music followed suit.

The Sphinx who dominated both vocal and instrumental music in France was Jean-Philippe Rameau. Born at Dijon in 1683, two years before the great triumvirate of Bach, Handel, and Domenico Scarlatti, Rameau was more influential with regard to the music of his own time than any of the other three. Bach responded to some musical currents of the middle third of the century that he encountered at Dresden, but he did not influence them. While Scarlatti's sonatas gave rise to a cult of devotees, they found almost no imitators even among keyboard composers. Handel's influence was confined mainly to England, where it was enormous, but served to inhibit rather than to stimulate younger composers.

Rameau was as central to musical life in France as Handel was to that in England. The difference between their positions was great even so. Handel remained for the most part an Italianized German, vintage 1710. Rameau capped several generations of indigenous musical tradition while transforming it so as to incorporate some of the strengths of recent Italian music. Instead of declining, as English music did after Handel, French music after Rameau, especially opéra comique, became a European phenomenon.

Besides spending many years in his native Burgundy, Rameau worked as an organist, violinist, and composer in several other provincial cities, including Lyons, Clermont (Auvergne), Montpellier (Languedoc), and Avignon (Provence). He was thus well acquainted with the colorful folklore of southern France. An early trip to Paris coincided with the printing of his first collection of *Pièces de clavecin* in 1706. Apparently he did not settle in Paris until 1722, at which time his *Traité de l'harmonie* first appeared.[42]

His second collection of harpsichord pieces followed in 1724. Rameau began working for the stage at this time, and some of his keyboard pieces reflect the songs and dances he contributed to the fair theaters, in collaboration with his fellow townsman, the poet Alexis Piron. In 1727 he tried to gain access as a composer at the Opéra by writing a letter to Antoine Houdar de La Motte, author of *L'Europe galante* (music by Campra) and several other librettos. In this long and important letter Rameau sought to dispel the notion that he was mainly a learned theoretician, and hence unfit to work for the Opéra.[43] He cited his cantatas, which had "recitative and well-defined airs" (in the Italian style) as proof of his dramatic skills, along with his harpsichord pieces: "You have only to come and hear how I

---

[42]On the complex early biography of the theorist-composer, see Neal Zaslaw, "Rameau's Operatic Apprenticeship: The First Fifty Years," in *Jean-Philippe Rameau Colloque Internationale*, ed. Jérôme de La Gorce (Paris and Geneva, 1987), pp. 23–50.

[43]Cuthbert Girdlestone, *Jean-Philippe Rameau: His Life and Work* (New York, 1969), translates the entire letter, pp. 9–10.

have characterized the song and dance of the savages who appeared at the Théâtre Italien two years ago. . . ."He refers to"Les sauvages"in his *Nouvelles suites de pièces de clavecin* (ca. 1729) (Example 6.1).

EXAMPLE 6.1. *Rameau, "Les sauvages"*

On 10 September 1725 a pair of nearly naked dancers entertained the audience at the Théâtre Italien. A critic in the *Mercure de France* for the same month wrote:

> Two savages recently arrived from Louisiana, tall and well-built, about twenty-five years of age, danced three kinds of dances, together and separately, and in a style which left no doubt that they learned the steps and leaps very far from Paris. . . . The first dancer represented a Chief of his Nation, dressed a bit more modestly than in Louisiana, but still with sufficient nudity. . . . He presented the *peace pipe* that one offered to one's enemy. Then together they danced the dance of *peace*. The second dance called *war*, expresses a gathering of savages. . . . Then they dance together the dance of victory.[44]

Perhaps Rameau translated the leaps on stage into the vigorous leaps of both right and left hands of his magnificent character piece (such leaps were nevertheless present in many of his other pieces). More likely, he captured some rhythmic feature that caught his attention. He reused this music as the "Dance of Peace" in the entrée "Les sauvages" added to his opéra-ballet *Les Indes galantes* in 1736, layering a vocal duet, and then a chorus, over the original melody.

[44]Howard Brofsky,"Rameau and the Indians: The Popularity of *Les Sauvages*,"in *Music in the Classic Period*, pp. 43–60. The translation is his. Brofsky speculates on the possible American Indian content of Rameau's piece, pp. 48–49. He exemplifies several parodies and variation sets engendered by"Les sauvages,"the popularity of which endured throughout the century. See also Thomas Betzwieser, *Exotismus und "Türkenoper" in der französischen Musik des Ancien Régime* (Laaber, 1993), pp. 174–77.

Rameau was probably introduced by Piron into the circle of Alexandre Le Riche de La Pouplinière, a royal tax collector *(fermier général)* and his main patron. Here he met Abbé Simon-Joseph Pellegrin, a successful librettist at the Opéra. Pellegrin agreed to write *Hippolyte et Aricie* for Rameau. Its music was given privately at the house of La Pouplinière in the spring of 1733, rehearsed throughout the summer at the Opéra, and given its first public performance on 1 October, a few days after Rameau's fiftieth birthday. The greatness of Rameau's music for *Hippolyte* impressed Voltaire so much that he hurriedly wrote *Samson* and got Rameau to set it, but the work never passed the censors and its music was distributed subsequently into other operas.

It was not unusual for a composer to wait so long before being entrusted with composing a full-fledged tragédie-lyrique for the Opéra. Philidor did not do so until his *Ernelinde* of 1767. Gossec had to wait until his *Sabinus* of 1773. Like Rameau they began in the theater by writing for the comic stage.

Tragédie-lyrique, as formed by Quinault and Lully, remained throughout the eighteenth century a huge enterprise, involving solo singers and chorus, a substantial and variegated orchestra, solo dancers and corps de ballet, brilliant spectacle and elaborate machinery—in other words, the total art work, and one in which the literary quality of the libretto mattered as much or more than anything else. Voltaire defined it deftly in a quatrain quoted by Jean-François Marmontel in his *Poétique françoise* (1763):

> Voila l'idée qu'on peut se former d'un spectacle qui réunit le prestige de tous
> les Arts:
>> Où les beaux vers, la danse, la musique,
>> L'art de tromper les yeux par couleurs,
>> L'art plus heureux de séduire les coeurs,
>> De cent plaisirs font un plaisir unique.
> Dans ce composé tout est mensonge, mais tout est d'accord; et cet accord en fit
> la verité.

The quality of the visual spectacle in French opera remained at the same high level first achieved by Jean Berain in Lully's time. Designers of genius were never lacking in Paris. François Boucher designed sets and costumes for the Opéra. Jean-Baptiste Martin succeeded him in 1748. Louis René Boquet did the costumes for Rameau's ballet *Pygmalion* of the same year. Boquet's delicate and ethereal designs, in perhaps the purest rococo style of all, persisted throughout the 1760s and even into the 1770s. Martin's costume designs were so popular that a series was gathered in colored engravings, sold to the public as *Collection de figures théâtrales* (1762), and revised and expanded as *Gallerie des modes* (1779). The illustrations here come from the first set and show a Neptune with his trident and an *Indienne* (Figure 6.6). In addition to the allusive richness of their dress, the fig-

Neptune.   *Indienne.*

FIGURE 6.6. Jean-Baptiste Martin. Costume designs for the Opéra.

ures exhibit typical gestures, which were as highly stylized as everything else at the Opéra. An expert on this subject has demonstrated that the famed chorus of the Opéra moved scarcely at all—the dancers did the moving for them—but they did gesture.[45] Bringing a new work to life on the stage of the Opéra required months of rehearsal and great expense, which helps to explain why, throughout the period from Rameau to Gossec, the Opéra often played it safe by reviving the tested works of the past, especially those of Lully.[46]

Rameau shook the Opéra out of some of its lethargy and earned the hostility of Lully's devotees for his efforts. He far excelled Lully with respect to harmonic richness, melodic intensity of expression, and sensitivity to instrumental color. Yet he was not above profiting from some of the more effective moments in the Florentine's operas. It has been pointed out that the choral statement on the heroine's death in Lully's *Alceste* was in Rameau's mind when he wrote the chorus announcing the death of Hippolyte.[47] What should be pointed out as well is how Rameau improved upon his model (Example 6.2ab).

[45]Mary Cyr, "The Dramatic Role of the Chorus in French Opera: Evidence for the Use of Gesture, 1670–1770," in *Opera and the Enlightenment,* ed. Thomas Bauman and Marita Petzoldt McClymonds (Cambridge, 1995), pp. 105–18. See also Dene Barnett, *The Art of Gesture: The Practices and Principles of 18th-Century Acting* (Heidelberg, 1987).

[46]Paul Marie Masson, *L'opéra de Rameau* (Paris, 1930), pp. 18–21.

[47]James R. Anthony, *French Baroque Music from Beaujoyeulx to Rameau* (New York, 1978), p. 75, places the two passages side by side. Anthony also quotes a parody of the same passage in Lully sung at an opéra-comique, *Les funerailles de la Foire* (p. 152).

EXAMPLE 6.2. *Cadences in Lully and Rameau*

a. Lully, *Alceste* (1676) b. Rameau, *Hippolyte et Aricie* (1733)

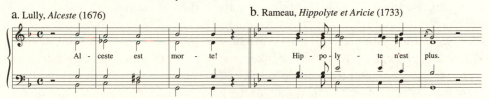

Lully's part writing is bland and does little to enhance the tragic moment. Using the same harmonic progression, Rameau resorts to unusual spacing and doubling, so that the tenors are in their most expressive high range. He provides dissonances that intensify the drive toward the cadence. The seventeenth-century master was content with a penultimate dominant chord that is a simple triad. His eighteenth-century epigone adds the dominant seventh and, to make the moment all the more intense, substitutes the minor sixth for the fifth degree. The resulting augmented chord appears frequently in Rameau's music, so much so that it is one of his trademarks. Burney, who made many visits to Paris, remarked on its presence in *Castor et Pollux* in his *History* and complained, "the superfluous fifth . . . makes all nature shudder except our Gallic neighbors."

In *Hippolyte* Rameau already showed an ability to differentiate characters by their music, and the roles of Theseus and Phèdre are particularly powerful examples of this. The work is his most unstintingly tragic and grandiose construction. Its great fugal chorus, "Que ce rivage retentisse," may be compared with Handel at his best and deserves the appellation "baroque" in several senses of that much belabored and originally pejorative term: colossal, pompous, overtly learned and intricate, densely built, and sublime. Rameau never repeated the experiment of using a vast fugal piece in subsequent operas, and in this sense he may be said to have put his own "baroque" behind him.

Castor et Pollux, written four years after *Hippolyte,* is quite different in character. It is more galant in subject, with many shades of amorous emotion serving as a principal thread in the drama. The composer shows great delicacy in differentiating the two pairs of crossed lovers. *Castor* goes further than any other opera of the time in one important aspect. It deploys keys and contrasting moods so as to unify long stretches of musical time, even to the extent of pitting one act (the Underworld) against another (the Elysian Fields).

Ballet is skillfully integrated into every act of *Castor* and into the Prologue as well. There is more of it than in *Hippolyte,* which suggests that the opéra-ballet, in which dance was uppermost to drama, was impinging more and more on tragédie-lyrique. Rameau was so superb a composer of dances that his ballet music, by its very force and variety, was bound to bring such an evolution to pass. He had not spent many years in the provinces without profit. The rich variety of regional dances observed, their gestures, rhythms, and melodic traits assimilated, permeate Rameau's music. Working for the Opéra-Comique brought him in touch with the vaudeville repertory, itself a repository of old and new dance songs that was national in scope. It also brought him into direct contact with dancers. The sharp perception that characterized the song and dance of "Les sauvages" went on to ever greater feats of capturing bodily movement in music at the Opéra. Here Rameau could write constantly for the great solo dancers and a corps de ballet that was unsurpassed. Not surprising, then, is the gestic element that is so strong in all his music.

Rameau's importance for dance music was not confined to France, or to his own lifetime. One critic claims to have seen Rameau's dances on all the stages of Italy and Germany; what is more, he says, "the famous Jommelli confessed that without Rameau Terpsichore would have had to forsake Italy."[48] There was indeed a wide diffusion of French dancers and, with them, French dance music in Italy, where the operas were regularly given with ballets (but without integration of the two), and in Germany, where Jean-Georges Noverre and Joseph Gardel both worked for a time. In his *Lettres sur la danse* (1760) Noverre paid tribute to the aged Rameau in no uncertain terms: "Dancing owes all its progress to M. Rameau's varied and harmonious writing, to the *traits* and witty conversations that prevailed in his tunes." Gardel, one of the century's greatest ballet masters, along with Noverre, wrote of Rameau in a treatise of 1775: "He divined what the dancers themselves did not know; we look upon him rightly as our first master."[49] Elsewhere Gardel maintained that the perfection of the dance was due to "l'expression pittoresque" of Rameau's music and the prodigious variety of his *airs de ballet*.[50]

An advanced stage of rococo art called "le genre pittoresque" was represented especially by Jacques de La Joue, whose stage sets for the Opéra almost took on qualities of dance and bodily movement themselves (Figure 6.7). The curvilinear cannot go much further than this—scarcely a straight line can be seen. Critics complained of excessive femininity.

In 1739 the Opéra brought forth two new works of Rameau, the tragédie-lyrique *Dardanus* and the opéra-ballet *Les fêtes d'Hébé.* Both came under heavy attack from the critics for the quality of their texts. *Dardanus* was subsequently revised and revived a number of times, but it never attained the success of *Castor* or *Hippolyte. Les fêtes d'Hébé,* also called *Les talents lyriques,* was praised for its abundance of beautiful dance music, but damned even so because of its meager literary quality.[51]

[48]In the *Journal des théâtres,* December 1777, quoted in Girdlestone, *Jean-Philippe Rameau,* p. 467.
[49]Girdlestone, ibid., p. 563.
[50]Albert de Croix, *L'ami des arts ou justification de plusieurs grands hommes* (Amsterdam, 1776), p. 101.
[51]Mary Cyr, "Rameau's *Les fêtes d'Hébé*" (Ph.D. diss., University of California, Berkeley, 1975), pp. 22–24.

FIGURE 6.7. Jacques de La Joue. Stage set for the Opéra.

Rameau, like many practical musicians of all times and places, was not as sensitive to literary values as he might have been, a deficiency not easily tolerated in Paris. True enough, there was no poet working for the Opéra who had the stature of Quinault, Lully's partner in a dozen tragédies-lyriques, written in as many years. Indeed, it was Quinault more than Lully to whom the "old wigs" were devoted. The music of the Lullian operas underwent considerable rewriting upon successive revivals, but not so the text. Rameau changed poets often but still did not find the perfect match for his talents. *Dardanus* proved that the public had a limited tolerance for new tragedies, no matter how grand the music. Its fourth act takes place in a prison, and this provided French stage designers with the opportunity to deploy some memorably gloomy and Piranesi-like dungeons.[52]

During the decade of the 1740s Rameau was occupied in the main with revising, and writing, occasional works for the court. The greatest of these is *Platée*

[52]See especially the design by Michel-Ange Slodtz for the 1763 revival in Nicole Decugis and Suzanne Reymond, *Le décor de théâtre en France,* No. 59; so stark and pre-Romantic a conception would not be out of place in *Fidelio.* Slodtz did the sets for Rameau's *Naissance d'Osiris* (1754) and they are already neoclassical in style (while the costumes remained rococo). See François Souchal, *Les Slodtz, sculpteurs et decorateurs du roi* (1685–1764) (Paris, 1967), P1.65B; the sets for the revival of Lully's *Alceste* in 1754 (P1.67A–B) are also remarkably severe and neoclassical.

(1745), a hilarious comédie-lyrique (originally called a *ballet bouffon*) that mocks the conventions of tragédie-lyrique and ridicules its mythological gods and god-desses.[53] Rameau is truly a man of his century in being able to laugh at what was most solemn and serious in his art, to laugh, in other words, at himself. *Platée* was first staged at Versailles for the marriage of the dauphin. There was no precedent for such a work at the Opéra, but the critics, while being nonplussed for this reason, were generally favorable upon its revival there in 1749, especially the *philosophes*, who praised the naturalness and vivacity of the vocal music. D'Alembert saw it as a presage of the success that Italian comic opera was about to have in Paris: "Who knows whether *La serva padrona* would have pleased so greatly if *Platée* had not accustomed us to that kind of music?"[54]

Zoroastre of 1749 was a pivotal work in several respects. It was Rameau's last tragédie-lyrique on this grand a scale created at the Opéra (*Les Boréades* of 1764 did not reach public performance). The librettist, Louis de Cahusac, was an expert on ballet who wrote most of the articles on dance in the *Encyclopédie*. He worked earlier with Rameau on some shorter works that called forth extraordinary music from the master. In *Zaïs* (1748) the overture represents the "disentangling of Chaos and the conflict of the elements when they are separated," which Rameau expresses by the clash of distant tonalities in rapid succession: D - f - e - D. In *Naïs* (1749), an occasional work to celebrate the Treaty of Aix-la-Chapelle, the prologue deploys a huge choral battle in which the Titans storm the gods. Cahusac went further than his predecessors in putting action on the operatic stage. He worked dance and pantomime into the fabric of the opera, rather than as divertissement, and he even took an interest in coordinating the machinery and scenic aspects of the whole. *Zoroastre* represents the culmination of these tendencies.

There was much in *Zoroastre* for the modernists to admire, and the opera did win their acclaim. It was a tragedy without prologue, like an opera seria. The overture in fact took the place of the prologue. Rameau was among the first to integrate the overture into the opera. He did this in various ways. The overture to *Hippolyte* leads directly into the opening chorus. *Castor* ends with an apotheosis, the music of which is already foreshadowed in its overture. In all his later works the overtures contain material from the body of the opera. In the *acte de ballet* *Pygmalion* (1748), the overture depicts the chipping of a sculptor's chisel.[55]

Zoroastre has a program overture that is spelled out in so many words in the

---

[53]Jacques Van den Heuvel, "Platée, opéra-bouffe de Rameau au milieu du XVIIIᵉ siècle," in *Jean-Philippe Rameau Colloque Internationale,* pp. 101–7.

[54]Quoted after Girdlestone, *Rameau,* p. 440.

[55]According to Jean le Rond d'Alembert, *De la liberté de la musique* (Paris, 1759), p. 460 (reprinted in *La Querelle des Bouffons,* ed. Denise Launay [Geneva, 1973], 3: 2198), who describes the programmatic content of several other overtures by Rameau as well.

libretto. The first part is a strong and pathetic picture of Abramane's barbarous power (unison attacks and triadic figures, plus rushing figures, in the key of c) and of the groaning people whom he oppresses (melodic sighs in sixths for unaccompanied flutes, as if they were saying, "Hélas!"). A sweet calm ensues and hope is reborn (expressed by a gracious menuet in C). The last part is a lively and smiling image of the salutory power of Zoroastre and the happiness of the people he has delivered from oppression (expressed by a jaunty contredanse in c). Hardly a vestige of the old French overture is left in this tone poem, except for the repeat of the first part, which is no longer slow and pompous but *"vive."* The sustained dominant-seventh chord at the end of the first part is built up throughout the strings and with the two flutes sounding their high D and high F. Such a striking sonority, and many other features of Rameau's imaginative scoring, foreshadow the music of the generation to come.

A catalogue of novel orchestral devices in *Zoroastre* would be out of place here, but we should not fail to note the modern and coloristic use of two horns in Zoroastre's ariette "Accourez" in Act III. The solo air in this opera is sometimes used as the peroration of a scene, in the manner of opera seria, a practice new to tragédie-lyrique and an example of what has been called "creeping Italianism."[56] Clarinets were first introduced at the Opéra in *Zoroastre.* Rameau did not rest on his laurels as the greatest French composer of the age. He continued to absorb the new in music, even to the point of approximating in some pieces the trio style of Sammartini.[57] Parisian orchestras owed all their progress to Rameau, according to Ancelet's small but discerning *Observations sur la musique, les musiciens, et les instrumens* (Amsterdam, 1757).

Rameau's last decade (he died in 1764) was embittered by increasingly acrimonious disputes with the most prominent Encyclopedists, among them Diderot, D'Alembert, Rousseau, and Grimm. These turned mostly on matters of music theory, in which Rameau had made the most important advance of the century with his elaboration of *la basse fondamentale.* D'Alembert, celebrated as a mathematician, initially won Rameau's praises for explaining the new theory in *Elémens de musique théorique et pratique suivant les principes de M. Rameau* (1752). His attempt to simplify and rationalize complex issues so as to reach the widest possible public defined what is meant by Enlightenment as well as any simple statement could. Unfortunately, D'Alembert, although expert as a scientist and writer, was not enough of a musician for the subtleties of the task, and when Rameau eventually perceived certain falsifications of his ideas, the two of them came to verbal blows.[58]

Diderot described the aged Rameau as a great composer in *Le neveu de*

[56]Girdlestone, *Rameau,* p. 293.
[57]See ibid., p. 297 and example 159.
[58]Thomas Christensen, *Rameau and Musical Thought in the Enlightenment* (Cambridge, 1993), chapter 9.

Rameau (written mainly in the 1760s) but also as an apocalyptic misanthrope whose theories neither Rameau nor anyone else could understand. The painter Jean-Baptiste Greuze, one of Diderot's favorites, may have intended to show the wild stare of a mystic in his portrait of Rameau nearing life's end. Bizarrely crowned with laurel, the great man seems to be in a rapture, perhaps contemplating *Le corps sonore* (overtone series) that he came late in life to regard as the key to the universe, and not just to music. The last words Diderot wrote on Rameau deserve attention. In the *Leçons de clavecin et principes d'harmonie* (1771), ghost-written for his protégé Anton Bemetzrieder, he chided Rameau for twisting facts to fit his theories. "I have long been aware of the defects in Rameau's system—I and many others. But how can one dispute a great authority who penned such magnificent works [of music]?"[59]

Violinist-Composers

Leclair

Jean-Marie Leclair was born in Lyons on 10 May 1697. He was destined to become, if not the founder of the French violin school, the musician who brought it to international prominence by his flair for idiomatic invention combined with contrapuntal solidity. He published five sets of sonatas for solo violin. Like other great masters of the violin concerto he entranced listeners with his *élan vital* and control of driving rhythms, qualities suggesting the world of dance. Unlike those other masters Leclair was actually a professional dancer as a youth, having been listed among the ballet personnel of the Lyons opera before his nineteenth year. In 1722 he served as a ballet master at Turin, where he also profited from violin instruction under Somis, himself a pupil of Corelli. Later he came into contact with Locatelli.

In 1723 Leclair was in Paris living with a wealthy patron, Joseph Bonnier, "Trésorier General des États de Languedoc," to whom the composer dedicated his first collection of twelve sonatas, *Premier livre de sonates à violin seul avec la basse continue.*[60] These were of the *sonata da camera* type and included three works in the minor mode. Louis Hüe engraved the sonatas and they were sold by Boivin at his shop in the rue Saint Honoré. The newly flowering industry of publishing music from engraved plates may well have been the attraction that first drew Leclair to Paris. For the publication of his second book of twelve sonatas he was again in Paris in 1728, when he made several appearances as a soloist at the Concert Spirituel, playing both sonatas and concertos.

---

[59]Ibid., pp. 302–3. The translation is his.
[60]Jean-Marie Leclair, *Sonatas for Violin and Basso Continuo Opus 1,* ed. Robert E. Preston (Recent Research in the Music of the Baroque Era, 76) (Madison, Wis., 1995). The editor disproves the claim of an earlier manuscript version of the sonatas dated 1721.

Leclair cut a dashing figure as a person, handsome of mien, elegantly dressed, and bewigged, as shown in the well-known engraved portrait by Jean Charles François after a painting by Alexis Loir. His abilities as a courtier can be read from the stylish dedications he wrote to his several aristocratic patrons, some of whom were also his violin students. He reached one peak of his career in late 1733 when he was appointed *ordinaire de la musique du roi*. In consequence he dedicated his third set of twelve sonatas to Louis XV, cleverly working into the expected disquisition a reference to Louis XIV's patronage of Lully. Sonatas in the minor mode had increased from three to four in the second book, and from four to five in the third. Thus Leclair seemed to be tracing a path opposite the one that made the major mode ever more triumphant with early galant composers. His best-known work is Sonata No. 6 in c from the third book, which came to be known as "Le tombeau" during his lifetime. The opening *Grave* in common time is chromatic and very expressive in both melody and bass line (Example 6.3). It begins with a bass tone that becomes a suspended dissonance resolving downward on the fourth beat, one of the composer's favorite harmonic moves.

By 1737 Leclair resigned his royal position because of disagreements with the violinist Guignon, to whom he refused to become subordinate in the king's band.

EXAMPLE 6.3. *Leclair, Sonata Op. 5 No. 6 ("Le tombeau"), I*

This same year saw the publication of a superb collection of concertos for solo violin and string orchestra, his Op. 7, which would be followed by another six concertos for the same forces published as Op. 11 in 1745. Leclair patterned his violin concertos on Vivaldi's. Their overreliance on harmonic sequences reflects the Venetian master, but the effect is less crass because of greater refinement in part writing.[61]

[61]Penny Schwartze, "Styles of Composition and Performance in Leclair's Concertos" (Ph.D. diss., University of North Carolina, 1983), shows how Leclair retained French traits even while imitating Vivaldi.

Leclair kept up a steady stream of publications at Paris, but he gradually began to lose the favor of the Parisian public (perhaps as fickle as any), or so it appears from the programs of the Concert Spirituel. The last sonata by him heard there was in 1745 and his last piece of any kind executed at this series was a violin concerto played by a certain Vogin in 1750. On the other hand, his lyric tragedy *Scylla et Glaucus* had a decided success at the Opéra in 1746.

After nearly thirty years of married life with the former Louise Roussel, who engraved all his works beginning with Op. 2, the couple decided to separate in the late 1750s. Madame Leclair remained in the city, but the composer purchased a suburban house north of Paris in the Faubourg du Temple. Here he led a solitary existence, without servants, well enough off so that his life was at least comfortable, but by no means luxurious. This rather strange self-isolation in a sparsely populated neighborhood of gardens and sheds (the Plan Turgot of 1739 shows that the rue de Carême prenant where he lived had very few houses) came to a violent end on an October evening in 1764. Leclair was stabbed to death and his body found by a gardener in his house, to which the door was open. The police investigated three suspects: the gardener, a disgruntled nephew of the composer named François Vial, and Madame Leclair. Their depositions make as fascinating reading as any whodunit. Even more interesting is the extremely detailed inventory of possessions drawn up for both households, that of Leclair and his widow.[62] His surroundings were considerably more modest than hers. Charges were never brought for the murder.

A memorial service for the composer took place on 2 December 1764 in the church of the Feuillants on the rue Saint Honoré near the Place Vendôme. His widow did not attend. The chorus and orchestra, made up largely of forces from the Concert Spirituel, performed Mondonville's motet *De profundis* and Leclair's "Le tombeau," arranged as a *grande symphonie* for the occasion. Eulogies were printed in several publications.

The violinist-composer Blainville offered a comparison involving Leclair and the leading Italian masters of the violin in 1754. Tartini came first because his was the art "de faire chanter le violon" and because his music suggested words, passionate ideas, and painterly images. Locatelli was less original and less rich in imagination and expression, but more gay. Geminiani, without being so original as either, held the middle ground between them. Leclair, while conserving his national character, betrayed a talent equal to theirs in both composing and playing—he deserves to be called the Corelli of France.[63]

---

[62]For details of these inventories, the police depositions, and everything else to do with Leclair's life and works, the best source remains Lionel de La Laurencie, *L'école française de violon de Lully à Viotti*, 3 vols. (Paris, 1922), 1: 298–310.

[63]Charles-Henri Blainville, *L'esprit de l'art musical ou réflexions sur la musique et ses différentes parties* (Geneva, 1754; reprint 1974), pp. 87–88.

MONDONVILLE

It was Leclair's lot, as it was Vivaldi's, to be overshadowed before the end of his career by several younger performers on the violin. Among the new violinists who triumphed at the Concert Spirituel, the most prominent were Guignon, Guillemain (born, perhaps at Paris, in 1705), and Mondonville (born at Narbonne in 1711). The last and youngest was the first to have his music printed. His Op. 1, six sonatas for solo violin with basso continuo, appeared at Paris in 1733. In the Rondeau refrain of the fifth sonata the composer uses a written-out Alberti bass accompaniment (Leclair had anticipated him in the Sarabande of his Op. 1 No. 9).

A set of *Sonates en trio* constituted Mondonville's Op. 2 of 1734. These pieces are filled with brilliant violinistic writing. Although the title page says "pour violons ou flûtes," mention of the latter may be a publisher's addition. The fifth

sonata, in D, gives a good sampling of the set: it begins with an *Allegro* for the two violins alone, without bass, a piece in which the melody, played in double stops, is exchanged between the two trebles, the phrasing being irregular (sometimes of two measures, sometimes three). Mondonville charms with his exuberance and originality.

Mondonville titled his Op. 3 *Pièces de clavecin en sonates, avec accompagnement de violon* (Figure 6.8). This set not only finished the process of naturalizing the Italian sonata in France, but also promoted a new texture. Nothing of the kind had been published before, although there are reports of performances in which a violin softly accompa-

FIGURE 6.8. Title page of Mondonville's Op. 3. nied idiomatic keyboard playing. Mondonville made it clear in his preface that he was attempting something novel. His dedication to the duc de Boufflers, governor of the city of Lille, has made it possible to fix the date of publication around 1738.[64]

The set begins, appropriately, with an overture in the French style, a first movement succeeded by a lyrical middle movement called simply Aria, in gavotte

[64]Bruce Gustafson and David Fuller, *A Catalogue of French Harpsichord Music 1699–1780* (London, 1990), p. 179. The authors comment that the first three of these sonatas were frequently performed at the Concert Spirituel between 1749 and 1757 as "mises en grand concert." See also Roberte Machard, *Jean-Joseph Cassanéa de Mondonville: virtuose, compositeur et chef-orchestre* (Béziers, 1980).

rhythm, and a final Giga. The other sonatas are in the same three-movement form, and thus point not so much to the Italian solo sonata (which was just beginning to adopt this pattern) as to the concerto and Italian sinfonia. The last sonata begins with an *Allegro* called Concerto and it deploys the ritornello form appropriate to the genre. A wide range of possibilities is explored regarding how the two instruments relate to each other. The harpsichord can provide a written-out chordal accompaniment to the violin, but so can the violin for the harpsichord (e.g., in the *Aria gracioso* of the second sonata). In the opening movement, *Allegro,* of the fourth sonata the violin at first provides the bass, then sings the treble of the **a b b** theme in thirds with the harpsichord (Example 6.4). In the middle movement of the third sonata there is real trio writing, with three parts sharing equally. Here the "accompaniment" of the violin is obviously essential, but this is equally true of the homophonic example just discussed. The impression Mondonville leaves is one of delight in showing how many possibilities there were in his new idea.

Looking back at the accomplishments of Mondonville, Marpurg pointed to his keyboard sonatas with violin accompaniment, saying that that they differed from Sebastian Bach's in that the texture was not limited to a certain number of voices.[65] Today we are more apt to regard his feat in generic terms as the forced and ever so fruitful marriage between an old French tradition, the *Pièces de clavecin,* and a recently imported Italian one, the chamber sonata for solo violin. It is the triumph of this marriage that neither partner prevails unremittingly and that the compromises between them can have as many nuances as a Proustian novel.

Mondonville first appeared at the Concert Spirituel during Lent of 1734 and was praised by the *Mercure de France* for playing several violin concertos "d'une manière très brillante." If the concertos were his own, they have not survived. It is typical of the whole school that few concertos were printed (Leclair is an exception), the reason being not only their difficulty for amateurs, but also the necessity for the virtuoso to keep this kind of material from falling into the hands of his rivals. In 1738, when Mondonville next appeared at the Concert Spirituel, he directed the performance of several of his own motets. One of those to have survived is his *Jubilate.*[66]

The grand motet was a piece in several movements, involving soloists, chorus, and orchestra, with a duration of from twenty to thirty minutes. *Jubilate* is unified by its key, B♭, and by its general tone of exuberance. The first section, "Jubilate," is set for a soprano solo, who sings a jaunty Bourrée-like tune marked

---

[65]Friedrich Wilhelm Marpurg, *Klavierstücke,* I (Berlin, 1762), p. 6; cited after David Fuller, "Accompanied Keyboard Music," *Musical Quarterly* 60 (1974): 230.

[66]It is edited with an introduction and notes by Edith Borroff, *Mondonville: Two Grand Motets.* (Jubilate and Cantate Domino) (Pittsburgh, 1961).

EXAMPLE 6.4. *Mondonville, Sonata Op. 3 No. 4, I*

"Gai," which is first put forward by the orchestra. (The Bourrée characteristics lie in the alla breve duple meter, the single quarter-note upbeat, and the falling by melodic leap onto an accented quarter note.) After an episode in the relative minor, using the same melodic material, there is a reprise of the original, followed by a traversal of the same by a five-part chorus. Whereas the dance aspects of this movement and its melodic-harmonic framing are typically French, the brilliant commentary provided by the violins is modern and Italianate, quite beyond anything in Lully or Lalande. The second piece, a Duo for soprano and bass on "Introite," is an almost perfect gavotte from beginning to end, its four-square phraseology being broken only so that the soloists can sing roulades in triplets and dotted rhythms at the intervals of the tenth and the sixth. The whole piece is framed according to the rule of the controlling parallel tenths between the outer voices, an old French practice that was still lively enough to engender quantities of music in the eighteenth century, and not just by French composers.

If we place ourselves in the persons of the auditors of the Concert Spirituel listening to such a movement, it becomes obvious that much of the appeal is physical, through the feet. The listeners were accustomed to dancing gavottes that sounded just like this. Moreover, they had witnessed similar pieces danced and sung simultaneously with infinite grace at the Opéra. The theatrical overtones must have been all the more vivid because, although it was sung to sacred words in a place that called itself the sacred concert, the soloists were none other than the adored stars of the Opéra. Many eighteenth-century writers pointed out that the Concert Spirituel was only a substitute for hearing what one was accustomed to hearing at the theater. Mondonville's *Jubilate* does not refute this charge. A very theatrical accompanied recitative in dotted rhythm, "Sciote" for the soprano, leads to an air with unison chorus, "Populus Ejus," scored in trio with violins and flutes only. This is the most Gallic number of all, in that it is a menuet of a peculiarly old and ingrained national type that relies on three-measure phrases—a derivative of the sixteenth-century branle de Poitou, which is also well represented in the popular tunes of the vaudeville and noël collections. Mondonville follows this with an air, related to the first, that is even more pronouncedly Bourrée-like, sung by the soprano to "Laudate nomen Ejus."

The chorus then begins the doxology, invoking a menuet of the more usual 4 + 4 phrase structure. "Sicut Erat in principio" is set fugally in long notes at first, but later joined to the Bourrée elements that refer back to the beginning. The whole is brilliant and facile. Mondonville's light touch with motets such as this kept these pieces in the repertory for decades. For all their public success, his motets did not escape the charge of being trivial and banal—qualities that indeed may help explain their long-lived favor with the public. Marmontel made this accusation, but he was looking at the matter from the point of view of a partisan of Piccinni in the 1770s.[67] As such he was immune to the charms of the old French dances, even adorned in an Italian raiment.

Mondonville was, among other things, a good businessman with regards to his talents as a composer and performer. He managed to keep his motets under

---

[67]La Laurencie, *L'école française de violon,* 1: 421–22.

his own control and did not allow copies made or performances other than those under his direction. He was paid handsomely by the Concert Spirituel for their use. At one point (1762) when he decided to withdraw them, they were sorely missed. He considered having them engraved but decided against it, with the result that many are now lost.

Emboldened by his successes at the Concert Spirituel, Mondonville decided to challenge Rameau for supremacy at the Opéra. In this he failed, although at least one of his operatic efforts, *Titon et l'Aurore* (1753), was a decided, if temporary, success. It is as an innovator that Mondonville is best remembered. His combining of two distinct genres in his Op. 3 is only one example of this, albeit the most rewarding one, historically speaking. He published his second set of six violin sonatas (Op. 4) under the title of *Les sons harmoniques.* They utilized natural harmonics—the first extensive use of this resource anywhere. Some of the singularity that critics pointed out in Mondonville's playing probably had to do with his use of the same resource. A decade later, at the Concert Spirituel, he was experimenting with concertos that combined violin solo with the voice of Marie Fel, the most renowned soprano in France at the time, who was acclaimed as much for her mastery of the Italian style of singing as for the French. His innovations did not stop there. As an accompaniment to Mademoiselle Fel, he conceived the idea of having the ritornellos sung by the chorus, varying their tones from soft to loud, an effect highly praised in the *Mercure de France.*[68]

No such concertos survive, but a hint of the inspiration that went into them may well be present in the composer's Op. 5 of 1748, *Pièces de clavecin avec voix ou violon.* These are elaborate harpsichord solos "with a part to be sung by soprano, or played by the violin." Latin psalms provide the texts. Since the vocal lines are far too demanding for the ordinary soprano to sing while playing her clavecin— it would have taken a Mademoiselle Fel to do justice to them—a violin accompaniment was the more likely solution adopted in practice. If the composer had primed his muse by meditating upon the words for inspiration, he would have been following Tartini's manner of using texts. But advertisements for the set say that he chose the psalms after composing the music.

Mondonville had an extraordinary knack for taking advantage of the artistic resources at hand and combining them in new ways. No better example of this exists than his masterpiece, the opera *Daphnis et Alcimadure* (1754). He himself wrote the text, in his native tongue, Languedoc, so as to take advantage of the presence at the Opéra of three singers who came from southern France: Fel, Jean-Baptiste de Latour, and Pierre de Jélyotte. The music is the composer's most inspired and lyrical. Each of the three acts is structured around a central tonality,

---

[68]Pierre, *Histoire du Concert Spirituel,* pp. 100–101. The review makes it clear that these pieces were indeed like the instrumental concertos of the time in form.

in succession: E, G, and A (the fine three-movement overture and the prologue are also in G).

Charming pastoral effects abound in *Daphnis et Acimadure*. The old traditional dances come in for their due. In no other work do they evoke more nostalgia for the French countryside. They are enhanced and made more theatrical by the brilliant violin writing.[69] To gain an idea of Fel's flexible throat, there is no better specimen than her air "Gazöuillats auzelets" in Scene 2 of Act I. Mondonville had written *Titon et l'Aurore* in haste, in response to a request from Madame de Pompadour. It has some strong features, such as the painting of the sunrise in Act I. *Daphnis* is more even in quality throughout and has that special poignancy attaching to a labor of love. The overtures to *Daphnis* and *Titon* were favorite concert pieces at the Concert Spirituel as played on the organ by Balbastre. In his portrait of the composer, Maurice Quentin de La Tour captured him with violin in hand and with a strikingly lively countenance (Plate VIII).

Guignon and Guillemain

Jean-Pierre Guignon was judged to be the finest violinist in France by his contemporaries, and especially in the highest echelons at court, where he was showered with privileges and benefices by Louis XV. When he died in 1774, the same year as his sovereign, he was the richest musician in the kingdom. Born at Turin in 1702, Guignon was a pupil of Somis. By 1725 he was already at Paris, where he made his debut during the first year of the Concert Spirituel, playing in alternation with the French violinist Jean-Jacques-Baptiste Anet. Each played in his respective style—a kind of duel between the French and Italian manners, as the *Mercure* commented. In a letter of 1730, André Cardinal Destouches, at the time director of the Opéra, complained that, whereas many French violinists could play in the Italian style, the reverse was not true, and that even Guignon was but an indifferent violinist when he assayed the French style. His explanation for this invoked a painterly metaphor in which bow strokes became brush strokes: "Bold strokes are easier to imitate than strokes of a certain finesse. A Capuchin friar is easier to paint than a pretty woman. Likewise more people are capable of being trained in Italian music than in French."[70]

At the Concert Spirituel in 1728 Guignon won praises for playing the solo part in concertos by Vivaldi ("Spring" and "Summer" from *The Four Seasons*). His increasing fame won him invitations to court, where his first appearance in 1730,

---

[69]See J. G. Prod'homme, "La musique à Paris, de 1753 à 1757, d'après un manuscrit de la Bibliothèque de Munich," *Sammelbände der Internationalen Musik-Gesellschaft* 6 (1904–1905): 568–87; 582 on *Daphnis*. This anonymous report on Parisian music was sent to Elector Carl Theodore in Mannheim.

[70]Cited after the translation by Lowell Lindgren, "Parisian Patronage of Performers from the Royal Academy of Musick (1719–28)," *Music and Letters* 38 (1977): 4–28; 27.

as described by the *Mercure,* sheds some light on the relationship of amateur and professional music making in the royal circle. Summoned to Marly by the queen, who was the Polish princess Marie Lesczyńska, he performed solo sonatas accompanied by a harpsichord (played by Colin de Blamont, superintendant of the Musique de Chambre from 1726 to 1760) and by a bass viol (played by a distinguished amateur, Monsieur de Dampierre). The king subsequently requested him to play Vivaldi's "Spring" Concerto, and as the royal band was not present, an orchestra of courtiers formed "who were glad to accompany Guignon in order not to deprive his Majesty of hearing this beautiful concerted piece [cette belle pièce de symphonie] which was perfectly executed."[71] The Concert Spirituel had anticipated what happened at court.

Royal preferment was not long in coming. In 1733 Guignon was put at the head of the royal band of violins, along with Leclair; their rivalry did not last long because the latter saw fit to leave the royal service. Enchanted with his first violin, the king was persuaded to revive the ancient title and office of Roi des Ménétriers for Guignon, who took it seriously enough to start promulgating regulations for all other professional musicians. At this, some thirty organists and *clavecinistes* in Paris and the provinces bridled and in 1750 got the courts to set aside Guignon's claims to hegemony over them. By this time Guignon had installed himself as violin instructor to Princess Henriette and her brother the dauphin, which entailed further stipends. The latter appointment, upon which Mondonville had set his hopes, led to a cooling of relations between the two violinists, heretofore closely connected in duet performances both in Paris and on tour in the provinces. Guignon selected as a new partner the young Pierre Gaviniès. He remained, as he had been for a long time, a frequent partner in concert with the flautist Michel Blavet.

In 1737 Guignon took out a nine-year privilege to protect the works he wished to publish. His Op. 1, as had become customary, consisted of solo sonatas for violin with basso continuo, pieces that he had presumably had in his portfolio for some time. His Op. 2, on the other hand, was quite unusual: *Six sonates a deux violoncelles, basses de viole ou bassons.* Within a decade he had brought out eight more publications, covering the usual genres of trio sonata, sonatas for two violins without bass, and variations on well-known airs. His concertos, for which he was the most famous of all as an executant, were not printed, and only two survive in manuscript; they show him to be an adept follower of Vivaldi. The printed collections of chamber music do not come up to the level of Leclair and Mondonville. Ancelet summed up Guignon's talents by saying that he was a better orchestral leader than Leclair, by the force of his bow, and that perhaps he

---

[71]*Mercure de France,* 1 December 1730, cited after La Laurencie, *L'école française de violon,* 2: 45.

would have been the best all around, if his compositional talent had equaled Leclair's.

Louis-Gabriel Guillemain remained throughout his life somewhat under the shadows of Mondonville as a composer, and of Guignon as a violinist. Like the latter he studied as a youth with the renowned Somis at Turin. His first position was as a violinist with the opera at Lyons in 1729 and member of a concert society (founded in 1725) at Dijon, where his Op. 1, sonatas for solo violin and basso continuo, was printed in 1734. By 1737 his fame had spread sufficiently for him to be taken into royal service, where he remained until his death, but always as the proverbial "second fiddle" to Guignon. Many documents survive recording their performance of duets together. Guillemain's shabby personal life came to a sad ending in 1770. Debt-ridden for many years, a poor manager of his affairs, yet devoted to living well and consuming inordinate quantities of eau-de-vie, he committed suicide.

Guillemain had eighteen collections published between 1734 and 1762, some of a very popular nature. Besides writing the usual solo and trio sonatas, and many duets without bass, he was an early practitioner of the concertino for two violins, viola, and bass (Op. 7, ca. 1740). Following Mondonville's lead, he produced a collection of *Pièces de clavecin en sonates, avec accompagnement de violon* (Op. 13, 1745). He claimed these could also be played without the violin, but this is scarcely true and no more than an attempt to increase their salability. As in Mondonville, the violin contributes vital chord tones and contrapuntal parts. Some of his titles testify to the same aim of increasing sales. *VI Symphonies dans le goût italien en trio* (Op. 6, 1740; second book, Op. 14, 1748) offered precise information, by title, of what to expect—namely, orchestral trios, the genre pioneered by Sammartini.[72] Op. 8 is called *Premier amusement à la mode pour deux violons ou flûtes et basse.* These are easy pieces, mostly dances, written for the inexperienced amateur. French catalogues offer many such "easy" duets and solos, and almost all the composers mentioned here contributed their share. Guillemain contributed more than his share. His *Pièces pour deux vielles, deux musettes, flûtes ou violons* (Op. 10, ca. 1741) capitalize on the rage for rustic instruments such as the hurdy-gurdy and the bagpipe, which was particularly intense at the court of France, to the point where depiction of these instruments became a genre unto itself.[73]

A more solid accomplishment of Guillemain, although adorned with one of his characteristically glib titles, is the *Six sonates en quatuors, ou conversations*

---

[72]The *Presto* Finale of Op. 6 No. 1 in D, cited by La Laurencie (ibid.), 2: 25, bears a resemblance to the "Posthorn octaves" of the Finale of Sammartini's Symphony in D, discussed in chapter 3.

[73]Richard D. Leppert, *Arcadia at Versailles: Noble Amateur Musicians and Their Musettes and Hurdy-gurdies at the French Court (c. 1660–1789): A Visual Study* (Amsterdam and Lisse, 1978). Guillemain's *Pièces* are not mentioned.

galantes et amusantes entre une flûte traversière, un violon, une basse de viole et la basse continue (Op. 12, 1743). The composer announced in the *Mercure de France* that each part was within the grasp of anyone [chacque partie etait à la portée de tout le monde], but this is an exaggeration. His model was Telemann's *Quatuors* for the same combination, brought out at Paris by subscription in 1736 and 1738, and to which several of Guillemain's colleagues, including Mondonville, Guignon, and Blavet, had subscribed. Guillemain is at least as modern and Italianate as is Telemann in these pieces.

The exposition of the first quatuor shows how far Guillemain advanced towards a truly bithematic structure (Example 6.5ab). While the two treble parts chat away in this *Conversation galante* as equals, the bass viol has a little more trouble getting a word in and often must wait for one of the trebles to pause before having a chance to accompany; the basso continuo is functional rather than thematic and often rather sparsely used, as, for example, during the "second theme." After the double bar the main theme is sounded on V, followed by a lengthy discourse between the two trebles slightly related to it, which takes place over the usual sequences via the circle of fifths to a cadence on vi; the tonic then returns as the bass viol comes into its own by proposing a florid new idea with trills, accompanied at first by the others, and then taken up successively by the two trebles, which leads to the "second theme" in the tonic. In other words, the movement in form is a completely rounded sonata *allegro*, except that Guillemain avoids, and wisely too, a tonic reprise of his main theme. Since the main theme's interest is more textural than anything else, we welcome a new melody along with a new texture at the point of tonal return, more than we would a third statement of the rather fussy initial idea. The ambling gait of this movement and certain other features such as the 4 - 3 suspensions may be old-fashioned, but its overall thrust is not. Philidor and other younger composers learned much from such amiable "conversations" as these.

Guillemain had favored bithematic construction before, particularly in his sonatas for two violins without bass (Opp. 4 and 5, 1739). Moreover, he was not averse to using a tonic reprise of the main theme, as in his trio symphonies, but he did not care to use both features together:[74] that would have stretched the limits of the form and style beyond an appropriate length. It is already stretched very far in a movement such as the opening one of Guillemain's first quatuor, just discussed, which totals 108 measures. The movement that follows is called an Aria

---

[74]For a monothematic example with tonic reprise see the opening *Allegro* of the Trio-Symphony in d, Op. 14 No. 5, printed in Barry S. Brook, *La symphonie française dans la second moitié du XVIIIe siècle,* 3 vols. (Paris, 1962), 1: 72–75. The second "Quatour" (in b) also has an initial *Allegro* with tonic reprise of the main theme, but no distinct second theme. On bithematic movements, see further Lionel de La Laurencie and Georges de Saint-Foix, "Contribution à la histoire de la symphonie française vers 1750," *L'année musicale* 1 (1911), pp. 1–123, especially pp. 31–32.

EXAMPLE 6.5. *Guillemain, Quartet* (Conversation galante), *Op. 12 No. 1, I*

and marked *Allegretto grazioso*. Also in G, and in 3/8, it is like an Italian minuet and keeps recurring after episodes that establish V, vi, and i. Large rondo structures of the kind are frequently encountered in this repertory, and the name "Rondeau" is not uncommon to designate them.

The last movement seems hardly necessary in a tonal sense, the ascendancy of G having been sufficiently challenged and sustained in the long Aria (of 168 measures). But the need for a fast movement to conclude the cycle was ingrained. Guillemain provided a giguelike *Allegro ma non presto* in 6/8 in binary form with repeats. The gigue remained a favorite choice for a finale for a long while. As the *giga* it appeared in Mondonville's Op. 3. It appears also in the finales of Parisian symphonies from the 1750s by François Martin, L'abbé le fils, and Gossec. Even as an idealized type later in the century, in countless finales of symphonic and other persuasion, the gigue still carried the association of being a French dance, a legacy of the old suite.

Others

Jean-Baptiste Cupis de Camargo, brother of a famous ballerina, "La Camargo," and of François Cupis, cellist and composer of cello sonatas, published his Op. 1, six sonatas for solo violin with basso continuo, in 1738. He followed them with another six (Op. 2) that include an interesting Sonata in g with many syncopations and the renowned "Menuet de Cupis" (the finale of the last sonata), which became a favorite tune for variations. Op. 3 of Cupis contained *VI Simphonia à quatre parties* (Paris, before 1751), one of which is also in g. All three sets begin *con brio,* with showy works in D. The choice is characteristic to open a publication. The Symphony in A, Op. 3 No. 3, is particularly attractive and has a finale opening with the folklike figure of 5 - 3, 4 - 2, 3 - 1, 2. A critic writing in the *Mercure de France* in June 1738 opined about the playing of Cupis at the Concert Spirituel that he combined the surprising fire of Guignon with the tender sentiment of Leclair.

Joseph-Barnabé Saint-Sévin, known as L'abbé le fils, was a child prodigy who matured into one of the best violinists of the time. Born in 1727, he became a pupil of Leclair and made his debut in print in 1748 with a set of solo sonatas for violin and basso continuo. The first sonata is a brilliant piece in D, with considerable technical demands. It begins with an *Andante*, followed by a long and elaborate *Allegro presto*, an Aria, a *Chasse* (very popular items in this repertory, and always in D and in 6/8), a *Minuetto*, and a *Giga,* all in the same key. In other words, what begins as an Italian sonata ends as a French suite. The solidity of the part writing and the prominence of the bass, which is often suspended, hark back to the older strict style. Quite a different matter is provided by a four-movement Symphony in D; in its opening *Allegro* the bass rattles on with many repeated notes, mainly on V and I. Also quite modern are the *Six symphonies à trois violons et une basse par M. L'Abbé le fils* that appeared in 1753. After this point he returned to writing virtuoso works for solo violin, especially variations on popular tunes from the operatic repertory. He is also remembered as the author of the foremost French violin tutor of the time, *Principes du violon* (1761), which ranks in importance with the treatises of Geminiani and Leopold Mozart in the literature of the instrument. A modern authority on the subject chose 1761 as his terminal date because of this tutor and wrote: "It is a date which also serves to mark the gradual decline of the Italian school of violin playing and the gradual assumption of leadership on the part of the French."[75]

André-Noël Pagin was another violinist who, like L'abbé le fils, first appeared in print with a collection of solo sonatas in 1748. He made his debut at the Concert Spirituel on 8 December 1747, playing a solo sonata of his own, very likely the brilliant Sonata in D that opens his Op. 1. At the next concert, Christmas Eve, he was heard as the soloist in a concerto of his teacher, Tartini. Violin concertos continued to be central at the Tuileries concerts to the end. Pagin is the only French player who figures in the portrait gallery of famous violinists, where he is depicted faintly just behind Tartini (see Figure 3.5 on p. 209).

A frequent soloist in concerts up to 1750, Pagin stopped playing in public because, it was said, he displeased auditors by always playing Tartini. According to the annals of the Concert Spirituel, he played a concerto of Locatelli in 1749, and following this two concertos by Vivaldi, "La tempesta di mare" and the ever-popular "La Primavera." The more likely reason for his early retirement is that he did not sustain comparison with the brilliant Gaviniès, who also played Tartini, or with some of the visiting Italians. Felice Giardini made his Parisian debut at the Concert Spirituel in March 1750, the same month Pagin quit.

From Pagin's published sonatas it is not difficult to recognize the disciple of Tartini. The first sonata, for instance, opens with an *Andante* in 12/8 that recalls the lovely pastoral effects so characteristic of the Paduan master, who is also recalled in the deft use of double stops, sometimes as pedal harmonies, to achieve a maximum of euphony from the instrument. The *Allegro* in 4/4 is also in D. Besides the expected brio, there are hints of the cantabile model as well—we are not far removed from an aria such as one of the heroines in an opera seria by Galuppi might sing. The main theme is graced with a galant extension, and there is a discreet closing theme, a kind of summary paragraph that shows how well the composer could differentiate the various parts of the form. A Minuetto with *minore* trio concludes the Sonata. It is often in the last movements that popular and dance elements are most prominent, that the masters of the French violin school show themselves to be most inventive. Pagin's fourth sonata has such a concluding movement (Example 6.6). A new type of finale is in the making here, one that is dancelike and catchy, but not beholden to any particular dance.

[75]David D. Boyden, *The History of Violin Playing from its Origins to 1761 and Its Relationship to the Violin and Violin Music* (Oxford, 1965), p. vi.

EXAMPLE 6.6. *Pagin, Sonata Op. 1 No. 4, III*

Two other Italian violinists who appeared in Paris around 1750 and challenged the local players with the virtuosity of their performances at the Concert Spirituel were Ferrari and Chabran. Diderot noted their passage in his *Neveu de Rameau* and linked them with Locatelli's music. Domenico Ferrari, a Tartini pupil, appeared at the Tuileries in 1749 and had his *Sei sonate a violino solo e basso*, Op. 1, beautifully engraved by Mademoiselle Vendôme, published two years later. They cost 9 livres, three more than Pagin's sonatas of 1748. Once again, the first Sonata is in D, and especially brilliant, and the set ends with variations. The initial sonata adopts the sequence *Allegro–Largo* (in A)–*Allegro*, an arrangement of movements that alternates in this set with the older practice of placing the slow movement first.

Ferrari is idiomatic in the extreme, but not very inventive. He does not avoid resorting to routine harmonic sequences. There are no sonatas in the minor mode, which appears, as in Pagin, only in *minore* trios. Harmonics (Sons harmonique) are required in the fifth sonata, and the last sonata of the set, in its initial *Adagio e Cantabile*, calls for an improvised cadenza after the piece has come to a stop on a I_4^6 chord with fermata. (L'abbé le fils included written-out cadenzas in his sonatas of 1748.)

Carlo Francesco Chiabrano, better known as Chabran, was a pupil of Somis. He made his debut at the Concert Spirituel in 1751. His set of *Six sonates a violon seul et basse continue*, Op. 1, engraved by Vendôme the same year, was dedicated to no less a person than the dauphin. The title page mentions that they were to be purchased at the composer's residence "chez Mr. Vanloo" in the Louvre. This would be the history painter Carle Vanloo, who, like Boucher and other official painters, was given working and living quarters in the Louvre. Vanloo was married to Christine Somis, a skilled singer and keyboard player who was the niece of the famous violinist. The first sonata by Chabran is in D, as we have come to

expect. It is showy but also rather empty despite some colorful harmonic progressions; the second theme consists almost entirely of double stops repeating
the dominant chord (the tonic in the reprise, of course). All but one of the sonatas
adopt the sequence *Allegro–Largo–Allegro* (to which the last sonata adds a final
Minuetto a Variazioni). The fifth sonata, in G, enjoyed a particular renown and
longevity, being reprinted as late as Jean Baptiste Cartier's *L'art de violon* of 1798.
The *Allegro Rondau* [*sic*] with which it concludes gives a sampling of what
Chabran had to offer. Chabran's adaptation to certain French practices is apparent from this rondeau, which lives up to its name in the formal sense in that the
refrain comes back after an episode on V and again after a *minore* episode. In addition to the six sonatas of the set, there is a hunting piece at the end, "La Caccia,"
a kind of character piece that has particularly old and close French associations. It
is an *Allegro* in D in the mandatory 6/8 meter, which returns after a contrasting
Andante.

In 1754 Marpurg published a critique of the leading Parisian instrumentalists,
based on what he knew of their reputations and their works.[76] At the head of his
ranked list he placed Leclair, Mondonville, Guignon, Cupis, and Guillemain. Of
the last he wrote, perhaps with the *Quatuors* in mind, "His compositions are rather
bizarre and he studies daily how to make them even more bizarre." Ancelet says,
as if in reply, that Guillemain's *first* works were too prodigious of difficulties,
which implied that he outgrew this stage. Marpurg concluded his list with thirteen other violinists working in Paris, almost all of whom left publications of their
own: Pagin, Petit (both pupils of Tartini), Gaviniès, Joseph Canavas, Louis Aubert,
Étienne Mangean, Greff, Louis-Antoine Travenol, Guillaume-Pierre Dupont,
Francoeur, Joseph-Antoine Piffet, Jean-Baptiste Quentin, and L'abbé le fils. Of
this group, Gaviniès was the most important as a teacher and as a composer,
especially for his violin concertos.

Following his list of French violinists, Marpurg enumerates the leading
flautists active at Paris: Blavet, Evrard Taillard, Jacques-Christophe Naudot,
Toulon, Le Clerc, Benoît Guillemant, and Joseph Bodin de Boismortier. Of the first
he says, "a virtuoso of the first rank"; the voluminous output of the last as to solos,
duets, trios, quartets, quintets, and concertos drew less favorable comment. The
extensive publications of the whole school had no counterpart elsewhere, and
even Quantz conceded that Blavet was unsurpassed (1: 238).[77] As might be
expected of an instrument long associated with French music, the flute did not
engender a repertory as modern as did the upstart Italian violin. But it could not

[76]"Nachricht von verschiedenen berühmten Violinisten und Flötenisten itziger Zeit zu Paris," in Marpurg,
Historisch-Kritische Beyträge zur Aufnahme der Musik, 1: 466–72.
[77]For summary treatment of the instrument and its music, see Jane M. Bowers, "The French Flute School
from 1700 to 1760" (Ph.D. diss., University of California, Berkeley, 1971).

remain untouched by newer fashions, if only because so much of the best chamber music being written involved both flute and violin. Duets between the two were commonplace at the Concert Spirituel, and Blavet was at one time or another the partner of Cupis, Guignon, Guillemain, Mondonville, and L'abbé le fils. Paris remained the center of flute playing and flute making throughout the century, towards the end of which François Devienne wrote the classic manual for the instrument, *Nouvelle méthode théorique et pratique pour la flûte* (Paris, 1794).

Quite in keeping with the ideals of the midcentury, when the treble-dominated galant style was sweeping all older music before it, Marpurg enumerated the famous flautists and violinists but neglected the cellists. Yet there was a flourishing school in France for this Italian challenger to the supremacy of the bass viol. Before 1750, Martin Berteau (the teacher of Jean-Pierre Duport, one of the century's most celebrated cellists), Jean Barrière, and François Martin had all published music for cello solo (mostly sonatas with basso continuo) and played sonatas or concertos for cello at the Concert Spirituel. Martin will occupy us next as an early French symphonist. François Cupis should also be added to the list for his prolific output for cello, including his *Méthode nouvelle et raisonnée pour apprendre à jouer du violoncelle* (Paris, 1772).

Gossec and the Symphony

A precursor of Gossec among French symphonic composers was François Martin. Born in 1727, he became a cellist at the Opéra by 1746, when he received a privilege to publish his music. Three collections soon appeared, two of which were cello sonatas with bass, Op. 1 and Op. 2. Overly modest and shy, according to reports in the *Mercure de France,* he triumphed nevertheless at the Concert Spirituel of 3 April 1747 with a cello concerto of his composition and the following year with a motet: "Martin, the skilled cellist of the Académie Royale de Musique, known for the finesse of his playing and for some estimable symphonies, had his 'In Exitu,' *motet à grand choeur,* performed on 10 April [1748], with great success."[78] This motet does not survive, but at least four of Martin's sacred compositions do, along with some secular cantatas of his ("Cantatilles") that were printed. They show him to be so adept that he could be, and was, mistaken for Rameau himself.[79]

The latest Italian style was not a matter of easy mastery for the young composer. In his Op. 3, *Six trios ou conversations à trois pour deux violons ou flûtes et un*

[78]Pierre, *Histoire du Concert Spirituel,* p. 103, and Brook, *La symphonie française,* 1: 107.
[79]Mary Cyr, " 'Inclina Domine': A Martin Motet Wrongly Attributed to Rameau," *Music and Letters* 58 (1977): 318–25. The author justly calls attention to the "rich expressive harmonies" of an orchestrally accompanied recitative, p. 324, a passage that prefigures Berlioz in its modal inflections.

violoncelle (1746), Martin retains the chamber sonata pattern of slow - fast - slow - fast, with all movements sharing the same tonality and often related cyclically by similar motivic beginnings. In style these pieces are not as advanced as the earlier quatuors of Guillemain. They cling to thematic *Fortspinnung,* for one thing, and do not approach Guillemain's bithematic experiments or otherwise attempt to differentiate the function of various parts of the movement. Their cello part is not figured, but rarely differs in function from basses that are.

It is quite a different matter with the symphonies that appeared as Op. 4 in 1751. These are divided into *Ouvertures* and *Symphonies*, three apiece. The former are distinguished by slow introductions to the first movements—an updating of the old Lullian overture that was to have wide consequences. The *Allegro* section of their first movements preserves at least an initial showing of fugal texture, betraying the model of the French overture. The first piece in the set is in D, typically, and an *Ouverture.* It begins with a majestic chordal progression in dotted rhythms: I - vi - I - I^6 - ii - V - I (Example 6.7abc). A running figure in sixteenth notes, the fugal subject takes the first violins quickly up to high D in the *Allegro*, followed by the second violins, violas, and basses in turn. After the modulation to V, there occurs a truly singing "second theme," *piano,* which is immediately echoed an octave lower, *pianissimo.* Martin's earlier lack of differentiation with respect to the function of passages is no longer evident. Here he could not be more clear as

EXAMPLE 6.7. *Martin*, Ouverture *in D, Op. 4 No. 1, I*

to what is primary and what is secondary. As eloquent as this first movement is, the second, an *Andante* in d, is even more so and shows the composer to have an excellent command of chromatic harmony. The third movement is a "Giga. *Allegro*" that goes from 6/8 to 2/4 for its closing theme. What seems equally extraordinary in this finale are the hints of the harmonic progression with which the symphony opened. These may be no more than a subconscious holdover from cyclical habits acquired in writing chamber sonatas. But they are a prediction, as well, of how later masters will relate their slow symphonic introductions, which are one of the major legacies of the French school, to their rapid finales.

Martin's *Ouverture* in D inaugurated the Concert Spirituel of 8 September 1751, and a splendid opening it must have made. Other slow introductions to initial symphonic movements appeared at the same time as Martin's in printed works by the cellist Pierre Davesne and the violinist Charles-Joseph Sohier. This Parisian practice was adopted a few years later by Gossec and, following him, by Simon Leduc.

The second of the three *Symphonies* by Martin is in g, which was rapidly becoming one of the favorite keys in Paris as well as in Vienna. Its opening movement, a furious *Allegro*, has an impressive development section.[80] An *Andantino* in B♭ and an *Allegro* in g with curious accents on the third beat of triple meter round out the work. Martin's frequent dynamic markings extend from *pianissimo* to *fortissimo*.

Discovery of an excellent group of symphonists in the most modern style, operating at Paris around 1750, should raise questions about the traditional belief that it took Stamitz and others from across the Rhine to plant the symphony in France. Departing from the same Italian models, the Mannheimers—and the Viennese too, for that matter—could not help but come to some of the same results as the French symphonists. Children with ancestors in common are likely to resemble each other.

Little else is known of Martin except that he acquired another privilege in 1752, for his own compositions, and one in 1753 "pour un recueil de musique instrumentale étrangère." He died in 1757, at only 30 years of age. The significance of his symphonies of 1751 has been summed up as follows: "They are remarkable for their form—bi-thematic, with substantial development passages, well-designed recapitulations—and for their sense of orchestral sonority . . . with a large dynamic range calling for both *crescendi* and *diminuendi* without using these words."[81]

Around 1750 an important change took place at the Concert Spirituel, under the new direction of Joseph-Nicolas-Pancrace Royer and Gabriel Capperan (1748–54). Until then it had been customary to begin concerts with a grand motet, followed, typically, by a concerto or sonata. But in 1749 most of the concerts began with a symphony—this year's offerings included examples by Domenico Alberti

[80]See Brook, *La symphonie française,* 3: 3–11, for a complete transcription.
[81]Ibid., 1: 113.

and Geminiani ("Symphonie terminé par un menuet"), and Mondonville's newly orchestrated Op. 3. In 1750 all the concerts but three began with a symphony or, more often, a "grande symphonie." Some of these items may have been orchestral suites in the old style, masquerading under the title of symphony, but this type was rapidly dying out. The banner year for symphonies was 1751. Besides Sammartini, Geminiani, Fortunato Chelleri, Telemann, and Stamitz (represented for the first time in Paris, by "Symphonie à timballes, tromps et cors de chasse" on 12 April), there were many symphonies by French composers, including Guillemain, Martin, Duplessis le cadet, Guillemant, J.-J. Rousseau, Blainville, and Davesne. On All Soul's Day one symphony followed another to open the concert, the first by the prolific Davesne, the second by Sammartini. It is rarely made clear which specific symphony was heard—the case of Martin's Op. 4 No. 1 mentioned above is exceptional but proof enough that the orchestra players used parts that were then hot off the Parisian presses.

By giving the Italian-style symphony pride of place at the Concert Spirituel, the new directors were bringing the concerts more in line with the typical "academy" elsewhere. The first flowering of the French symphony took place under these auspices. With it the stage was set for the career of Gossec. Among the many other accomplishments of his long life, he carried the French symphony to its highest peak of excellence between 1756 and 1770. Only after this peak did the wave of Austrian symphonies, led by those of Haydn, gradually begin to inundate the French symphony.

François-Joseph Gossec was born on 17 January 1734 at Vergnies, a village in the province of Hainault between Maubeuge and Philippeville. His ancestors may have come from Gozée, a village north of Vergnies. The son of a farmer, he was trained as a choirboy at Walcourt (near Gozée) and at Maubeuge. His promise was such that he was sent to finish his musical apprenticeship at the cathedral of Antwerp, under the tutelage of the choirmaster André Blavier of Liège. (Hence the qualification "di Anversa" after the composer's name on many title pages.)

Armed with a recommendation to Rameau, Gossec arrived in Paris in 1751. Through Rameau he came to know an immensely rich and munificent patron, La Pouplinière. According to Choron and Fayolle's *Dictionnaire historique des musiciens* (1810), Gossec was already a violinist in the private orchestra of La Pouplinière in 1752, when Rameau was still its leader. This orchestra numbered about fourteen professional musicians and was probably enlarged by a few domestic servants as well. La Pouplinière had in his service two clarinetists and two hornists: Gaspard Procksch, Flieger, Schencker, and Pierre Louis.[82] After the rupture

---

[82]Georges Cucuel, *Études sur un orchestre au xviiie siècle: l'instrumentation chez les symphonistes de La Pouplinière* (Paris, 1913), p. 17. This study completes the more biographical and general work by the same author, *La Pouplinière et la musique de chambre au xviiie siècle* (Paris, 1913).

between Rameau and La Pouplinière that took place in 1753, Mondonville is believed to have become orchestra leader.

Gossec's Op. 1 was a set of six trios for strings, *Six sonates à deux violons et basse,* that appeared in 1753. They are all in three movements, two being slow–fast–dance, and four being fast–slow–dance. The "duetting" of the two violin parts, which swap idiomatic figurations freely, suggests Sammartini as a likely model; La Pouplinière is known to have possessed manuscript music by Sammartini in his rich collection of scores. Gossec's first sonata contains the explicit direction *crescendo* and is richly provided with other dynamic markings. The second sonata shows Gossec to be a melodically fluent composer in the latest galant style, and somewhat more vigorous and direct than most French imitators of Italian music.[83] A case in point is the Minuetto of the second sonata, which begins with a measure of unisoni D, marked *forte,* then arpeggiated figures leaping up the octave, marked *piano* (Example 6.8). The initial three-measure phrases are followed by four-measure phrases. Gossec's part writing is not without contretemps (at least Rameau would have regarded them so) such as the parallel octaves in

EXAMPLE 6.8. *Gossec, Sonata Op. 1 No. 2, III,* Minuetto primo

Minuetto II which is a *minore* that varies the thematic content of Minuetto I. Gossec was only nineteen when these sonatas appeared and he had much to learn, but he was already on the way to becoming a symphonic composer. The step from trios to symphonies was small, and indeed these sonatas already seem orchestrally conceived.

Gossec's Op. 2 of ca. 1754 consisted of six duets for flute or violin, pieces that survive only in the incipits in the Breitkopf Supplement of 1779–80.[84] One of the sonatas is in the minor mode. By the flexible choice of instruments it is apparent that the works were of the "easy" sonatina type, intended to earn for the composer more reward than glory. The publication cost 4 livres, 4 sols. (Op. 1 sold for 6 livres.)

Gossec's next publication, Op. 3 of 1756, shows the composer making strides

---

[83]Cucuel, *Études sur un orchestre,* Appendix, pp. 3–11, gives a transcription of the entire trio.
[84]Brook, *La symphonie française,* 2: 266–67, quotes the incipits, as he does for all the instrumental works of Gossec that have survived.

towards maturity. This set of six symphonies sold for 9 livres and survives by the thread of a single copy once owned by André Mayer. All the works are in three movements, fast–slow–fast, for four-part strings, except for the last, which has two obbligato wind parts. The Italians remained Gossec's model here, as is evident from several features besides the three-movement format. The slow movements, all but one, are in the minor mode. The violino primo dominates most of the time, to the extent that it is possible to get a fair impression of the whole from its part (Figure 6.9).

The opening *Allegro* of Op. 3 No. 1, aside from showing the composer's customary vigor and directness, has the rhythmic snaps and the melodic extensions in the minor mode that are particularly characteristic of the operatic overtures of Leo and Jommelli. The long *crescendo* of the violins from their low A up to high E (beginning at the end of the seventh brace) would seem intended to make audiences rise to their feet involuntarily, just as did the famous *crescendi* of Jommelli, and those by Stamitz in imitation of him. In the *Adagio* that follows, there is a range of dynamics from *pianissimo* to *fortissimo*. The beginning of the third symphony resembles a particular Italian overture that was used by Pergolesi for his *L'Olimpiade* and other works. Reliance on Italian models is less evident in the last symphony of the set, which has oboes and is

FIGURE 6.9. Gossec. Violino primo part of Symphony Op. 3 No. 1.

the most mature of the lot, and probably the last to be composed.[85] The rhythmic

---

[85]A modern edition is in Brook (ibid., 3: 23–33).

clichés, *crescendi,* and lack of a development section in the large-scale outer move-ments still point to the Italian overture, although in the final *Presto* Gossec makes telling use of the two oboes, which have the second theme to themselves, as is often the case in the late symphonies of Stamitz.[86]

The introduction of horns and other obbligato winds into symphonies at Paris came about gradually. A lost "Symphonie à 2 cors de chasse" by L'abbé le fils was heard at the Concert Spirituel on 1 November 1750. The overtures and symphonies of François Martin (1751) are believed to have had added horn parts.[87] But horn parts were not sold in Paris with parts for the strings until the publication in 1754 of *VI Sinfonie* by the flautist Antoine Mahaut and the *Six ouvertures* (with slow introductions) by Pierre Davesne, who was a cellist at the Opéra. The last work in Davesne's set has, in addition to two horns, two oboes and two bassoons. A "Sym-phonie à cors de chasse" by Jommelli, presumably one of the composer's operatic overtures, was played to open the Concert Spirituel of 19 April 1754.

Attributed to Gossec are some dubious "Notes concernant l'introduction des cors dans les orchestres."[88] A historical farrago at best, these "Notes" are interest-ing even if forged. They claim that Alessandro Scarlatti and Antonio Lotti intro-duced horns into theatrical music in Italy and were followed in the practice by their pupils Hasse and Domenico Alberti (with mention of a superb "Caro Sposo" employing horns and oboes by the latter). Under the rubric "Introduction des cors et clarinettes en France," Stamitz is said to have counselled La Pouplinière about adding these instruments to his orchestra, which he did, but Gossec is said to have been the first to introduce them at the Opéra, in 1757, in two airs written to be sung by Sophie Arnould at her debut. If this information does indeed come from Gossec, his memory was faulty. Rameau's use of La Pouplinière's clarinet-tists and hornists at the Opéra in 1753 is known. Furthermore the "Notes" claim that La Pouplinière called three trombonists from Germany, along with the two clarinettists and two hornists. With regard to the trombones, this claim seems planted only to prepare for a later statement, which is true, that Gossec used three trombones in his *Messe des Morts* of 1760, a work of such massive proportions as to prefigure the bands of the Revolutionary period.

Gossec succeeded Stamitz at the head of La Pouplinière's orchestra according to some biographers, but again there is no documentary evidence. At the least, the wealthy patron held the young composer in considerable esteem, because he

---

[86]Brook (ibid., 1: 154) describes a "close contact with Stamitz" in this symphony, which he hears especially in the first movement, with its long *crescendo* passages, sudden *fortes,* and tremolos above long pedals, used to create tension.

[87]La Laurencie and Saint-Foix, "Contribution à l'histoire de la symphonie française," 79.

[88]Printed in *La revue musicale* 5 (1829): 217–23. François-Joseph Fétis says the "Notes" come from a manu-script in the hand of Gossec. Cucuel, *La Pouplinière,* p. 432, was suspicious, having found no such autograph among the papers of the composer at the Paris Conservatoire.

stood as godparent to one of his children in 1760. Gossec was certainly the most prolific composer among La Pouplinière's musicians in the years just preceding and following 1760. There is reason to believe that Gossec enjoyed the same latitude in experimenting with orchestral effects that was such a blessing to Haydn a few years later. Mastery of the symphonic medium was not slow in coming under such ideal conditions.

Gossec's Op. 4 opened the most prolific and in many ways the most important epoch of his long creative life. It consisted of *Six symphonies à plusieurs instruments,* dating from 1758. The symphonies required four string parts and two horns (except for the first, which also had two oboes, and the last, which required no winds). Each symphony is in four movements, with a Minuetto and Trio preceding a final fast movement. In this departure (anticipated already by L'abbé le fils in 1751–52) critics discern the unmistakable model of Stamitz.[89] Gossec's Op. 5 also contained six symphonies in four-movement form. After this point the composer gradually reverted to the three-movement format with which he began, and which is typical of the French (and Italian) symphony in general. Composers at Mannheim did likewise beginning in the mid-1760s.

La Pouplinière died at the end of 1762 and his possessions were impounded. On 26 May 1763 Gossec appeared before a magistrate to reclaim several scores of his own and of other musicians who had been in La Pouplinière's employ. He laid claim specifically to "seven symphonies with clarinets, of which four were in E♭, two in D and one in F, plus one symphony with muted strings and oboes in A, plus a book of harpsichord sonatas by Domenico Alberti, all of which books and musical scores belonging to him had been loaned to Monsieur de la Pouplinière and his wife."[90] The symphonies mentioned can be identified among those published in the composer's Op. 5 and Op. 6, which must therefore date before the demise of La Pouplinière in 1762. The sonatas of Alberti were presumably the *VIII Sonate di cembalo del sigr Domenico Alberti* printed at Paris in 1760, and they were no doubt destined for Madame de La Pouplinière, for she was a keyboard player, unlike her husband. Besides his own music and his copy of Alberti's sonatas, Gossec reclaimed for his colleagues' benefit the printed cello sonatas of Carlo Graziani, a cellist from Asti who made his debut at the Concert Spirituel in 1747, and five symphonies with horns and clarinets by Schencker, who played the horn and the harp in La Pouplinière's orchestra.[91] Schencker was the father of the

---

[89]La Laurencie and Saint-Foix, "Contribution à l'histoire de la symphonie française," p. 104, consider the insertion of minuets in Gossec's Op. 4 the most concrete evidence of the influence of Stamitz on the French symphony, "but only on its exterior order; in detail, the composer remained rather close to his first, entirely Italian manner."

[90]Cucuel, *La Pouplinière,* pp. 360–61, followed by a detailed commentary on the works in question.

[91]One of Schencker's symphonies, which were printed in 1766, is edited by Cucuel in *Études sur un orchestra,* Appendix, pp. 37–46.

young lady who played a harp solo at the Concert Spirituel in 1765 (see Figure 6.5 on p. 614).

Other composers who emerged from the same circle included the Roman flautist and composer Filippo Ruge, active in Paris from 1753 to 1775. He is the author of *Sei sinfonie a quattro parti obligate con corni da caccia ad libitum,* which appeared in 1756, and a celebrated storm symphony, *La nuova tempesta,* heard many times at the Concert Spirituel from 1757 on and printed in 1761.[92] After the death of La Pouplinière, Gossec entered into the service of the prince de Conti, whose palace in the rue du Temple contained a large music room that is familiar from the painting of 1766 showing Mozart accompanying the singer Jélyotte. He encountered the outstanding harpsichordist Johann Schobert in Conti's service.

The full brilliance of Gossec's symphonic achievement becomes apparent with the twelve symphonies of Op. 5 (1761–62) and Op. 6 (1762), some of which have attracted modern editions and recordings. Op. 5 opens with a distinguished Symphony in F for four-part strings and pairs of flutes, horns, and bassoons. The opening *Allegro* in common time begins with a boldly assertive theme that rises through the triad, then explodes in eighth notes up to high D, whence the melodic inversion of the beginning brings it down (Example 6.9). The structure of the melody in three plus three measures is at odds with changes of harmony, creating a tension that the composer exploits to full advantage throughout the

EXAMPLE 6.9. *Gossec, Symphony Op. 5 No. 1, I*

movement. He also exploits the wavering back and forth between fifth and sixth degrees, introduced as if it were of no consequence by the second violins as a commentary on the end of the theme in m. 6. After a long *crescendo* passage both violins introduce the wavering figure on the high C and D, rhythmically augmented and in tremolo. The penetrating sonority of this passage cannot help but fix it in the listener's ear, and that is what Gossec must have intended: the wavering figure will return as a kind of punctuation special to this symphony in the second movement and again in the last movement.

There are other signs of the economic and telling use of thematic material in Gossec's Op. 5 No. 1. The second theme of the first movement, given to the

---

[92]It is edited by Brook, *La symphonie française,* 3: 37–53.

winds, is derived from the rising triad of the first, and so is most of the development, which traverses several minor chords before reaching its main goal, vi. Gossec saves the return of his opening material in the first movement for the coda. He does not begin his tonic reprise with it, which is not surprising, given the amount of attention it has received throughout the movement.

The heart of the symphony is the noble *Adagio*, the broad main melody of which has melodic affinities with the concluding portions of the lyric second theme of the initial movement. Again there is a sense of continuity and of dialogue from movement to movement. The key of the *Adagio* is the subdominant (B♭), which becomes Gossec's most frequent choice from this point on; this movement, too, is bithematic with a substantial development section. The wind doublings of flutes and bassoons at two octaves' distance, coupled with the long-breathed, elegaic melody, resemble some of the sonorities that are best known from Gluck's Parisian works.

Both the Minuetto and Trio use the rising triad and both are forthright country-type dances with little trace of anything resembling the mannerisms of the old court dance. They could easily be mistaken for Haydn's dances of a later date, but then so could much of Gossec's music from Op. 5 on. Perhaps there is more than mere coincidence in the circumstance that both composers came from sturdy peasant stock, and both were too poor to make the tour of Italy once thought essential to polish young musicians.

The final *Presto* in 2/4 completes the cycle, invoking the rising triad for its main material, using the wavering figure 5 - 6 - 5 for punctuation and adding a delightfully jaunty second theme for the winds that resembles "Malbrough s'en va-t-en guerre," the melody of which even the horns can play when it comes back in the tonic (but not when it first appears in the dominant). The submediant is again the main goal of the development. In a symphony with this much feeling, wit, and polish, Gossec emerges as a composer of more than local consequence, one who has assimilated Italian models and struck out on his own path.

A good representative of Gossec's symphonies is his Op. 5 No. 2 in E♭ requiring pairs of flutes, clarinets, and horns, in addition to four-part strings.[93] The first movement, an *Allegro moderato* in 3/4, begins with a theme resembling the *Adagio* of the previous symphony, a carryover that does not indicate a lack of inspiration in the composer so much as the wish to exploit a choice idea in several different settings. Inasmuch as the symphony begins with a lyric idea, and *pianis-*

---

[93]It is edited by Cucuel, *Études sur un orchestre*, Appendix, pp. 12–36. For Cucuel's evaluation of the symphony see pp. 51–54. Brook, *La symphonie française*, 2: 278, does not mention clarinets. On the aesthetics of French orchestration in Gossec's day, see Robert James Macdonald, "François-Joseph Gossec and French Instrumental Music in the Second Half of the Eighteenth Century" (Ph.D. diss., University of Michigan, 1968).

simo, with the flutes and clarinets doubling the melody in the violins, the horns and violas providing the bass, Gossec can set off the unusual beginning by following it with one of his characteristically gruff and triadic themes, *forte,* a unisono passage in all the strings that will recur several times in the movement, notably in the development and at the end to close the movement. As soon as the strings make their unisono pronouncement, the flutes and clarinets take up the end of it, *piano,* and harmonize it, as if in commentary on the proposed material. There are several other thematic ideas in the first theme group, which stretches out to considerable length before the modulation and second theme, played by flutes and clarinets. The exposition of eighty measures is followed by eighty-four of development, leading via a prominent deployment of the relative minor to a complete recapitulation of eighty-two measures.

After this expansive and well-proportioned movement comes a *Romanza,* an *Andante* in cut time that is also in E♭. Its theme is related to the opening theme of the first movement and is even sweeter, with its insistence upon thirds and sixths. Clarinets and flutes doubled at pitch, and doubled by the first violins an octave lower, play the tune. It is of the gavotte type, like many operatic *romances.* As a type the *romance* was intensely sentimental, verging on pathos, often with a flowing accompaniment figure (lending a serenade-like touch), while retaining its nursery-rhyme simplicity and folk-tone earnestness.[94] Gossec's symphonic *Romanza* lacks none of these qualities. The movement as a whole has a five-part rondo structure, the first episode being in V and the second beginning on vi and ending on V. Thus it is a *romance en rondeau,* an early example of a type and a form that was to become quite characteristic in French instrumental music for decades thereafter and destined for much use in non-French music as well—Haydn's Paris symphonies of 1785–86 provide some examples.

Gossec's is not the first symphonic *romance,* to be sure. L'abbé le fils included one in a symphony of his nearly a decade earlier. But Gossec's masterly symphonies from Op. 5 on quickly overshadowed the works of earlier French symphonists, and he became the model for others to follow. His Symphony in E♭ of Op. 5 ends with a Minuetto and Trio (both thematically related to the beginning of the first movement) and a long *Presto* in 2/4 (336 measures). There is a danger of tonal monotony when all the movements of such a long work are in the same key. Why, then, did the composer not put his *Romanza* in the subdominant, A♭? For one thing, A♭ posed too many problems of intonation. Gossec never used it for slow movements in his several works in E♭, preferring instead B♭, c, or E♭, as here. Moreover, the expressive qualities of the *romance* naturally allied themselves with a key that was coming to be regarded as the most expressive of all. Possibly

[94]Daniel Heartz, "The Beginnings of the Operatic Romance: Rousseau, Sedaine and Monsigny," *Eighteenth-Century Studies* 15 (1981–82): 149–78.

Gossec conceived this whole symphony starting with the beautiful wind color of the *romance,* which is the work's most extraordinary feature. In any case, his touch is that of a master of orchestration. With him the winds become not just a prominent feature of a symphony, but often the decisive feature that gives each work its individual personality.

Two of the symphonies of Gossec's Op. 5, Nos. 3 and 5, have slow introductions, possible links in the chain that led Haydn to adopt this feature as standard. There is a slow introduction to the second symphony of Op. 6 as well. The latter collection, which followed Op. 5 by about a year, has an informative title page and a dedication to a prominent musical patron at Paris: *Six simphonies, dont les Trois premières avec des hautbois obligés et des cors adlibitum et les Trois autres en quatuor, pour la commodité des Grands et Petits Concerts, dediées à Monsieur le Baron de Bagge.* Implicit in this distinction between large and small concerts is the suggestion that a work employing winds needed a larger complement of strings for a balanced sonority.

Some figures as to what constituted a large concert are available from the annals of the Concert Spirituel. In 1751, the year when the French symphony began its ascendant path, the orchestra at the Tuileries concerts consisted of twenty-six strings and ten winds; by 1762 the strings had increased to thirty and the winds to twelve; by 1773–74, when the new regime of Gaviniès, Gossec, and Leduc roused the Concert Spirituel from its lethargy under Antoine Dauvergne's direction, the orchestra numbered sixty: twelve first and twelve second violins, four violas, twelve cellos, four basses, two flutes, three oboes, two clarinets, four bassoons, two horns, two trumpets, and timpani.[95] This disposition was not enlarged subsequently but prevailed with few changes until the end of the series. By "small concerts" Gossec means to remind his public that the symphony can also be played as chamber music in the home. Indeed, it must have taken many households to absorb the three editions of his Op. 5 and the two of his Op. 6. Some symphonies made excellent string quartets (the extreme of a small concert). Mastery of one led to mastery of the other. Gossec was one of the first French composers of string quartets, which he published as his Op. 14 in 1770.

One of the most precocious aspects of the modern French school around 1760 was a growing attachment to symphonies, sonatas, and other works in the minor mode. The sonata for solo violin was the first medium to show a particular indulgence in this regard, especially to the key of g. Opéra-comique was not far behind, and in a work like *Le Prétendu* by Gaviniès (1760), there are weighty pieces in g neighboring equally expressive ones in E♭. Two of the six symphonies of Gossec's Op. 6 are in minor. No. 3, the third of the grand symphonies, is in c,

---

[95]Pierre, *Histoire du Concert Spirituel,* pp. 77–78, and Brook, *La symphonie française,* 1: 238. For the makeup of the orchestra of the Concert Spirituel in 1778, see Brook, 1: 320.

and this departure entailed a corresponding one in form, the three movements being *Allegro*, *Minuetto gratioso* (in C and c), and *Fugato* (beginning and ending in c). Apparent from the last movement is a link in the composer's mind between the minor mode and the old strict style.

The fifth symphony of the set, a chamber work for strings without winds, is in g. Its three movements are *Allegro*, *Allegretto* (in E♭), and *Non troppo Presto*, beginning and ending in g. The work reaffirms Gossec's allegiance to the Italian symphony, as is evident from its three movements without minuet, and certain other details. But this work is more terse and dramatic than any Italian symphony or, for that matter, any Mannheim work. Its powerful beginning, with unisoni thrusts against double-stopped chords, jagged diminished sevenths, and convoluted minor-second passages, evokes the whole world of what has been called *Sturm und Drang* and associated with Viennese music of a later date. At the same time this symphony is chamber music, exquisitely wrought down to the last detail. It does not depend upon mass for its effect. Rather, it relies upon clarity of texture (especially evident in the lyric second theme of the first movement) and a control of rhythmic momentum within sonata allegro form, attained only by the greatest masters.

If Gossec had stopped composing symphonies in 1762 he would still deserve a place in the history of music as a pioneer of the genre. In fact he went on to write many more. The works in his Op. 8 of 1765, *Trois grandes symphonies* employing clarinets, oboes, and horns, have been praised as the equal of symphonies written anywhere in Europe at the time.[96] The first and third are in E♭, a favorite choice of the composer when clarinets are involved.[97] The second has a slow introduction with muted strings in f to the first movement, which is in F. The most widely disseminated of his collections was his Op. 12, *Six symphonies à grande orchestre* (1769), which went through five editions, including one at London by Bremner, the last edition being as late as 1784.

One intriguing feature of these fine works is that they contain tempo and performance directions in French, followed by the Italian equivalent, as if the composer were aware and proud of being the leading French symphonist. After his Op. 12, Gossec wrote symphonies only sporadically, perhaps because he had amply supplied the need for such works by himself and others. As founder and

[96]Brook, *La symphonie française*, 1: 157: "Parmi les plus belles symphonies de cette période il faut compter les trois de l'Opus VIII (1765), qui soutiennent la comparaison avec n'importe quelle oeuvre symphonique de l'Europe de la même époque."

[97]Op. 8 No. 3 was edited (from a manuscipt in the Library of Congress) by Sidney Beck and published by the New York Public Library in 1942. In the slow movement, *Larghetto, Tempo di Romanza*, which is in E♭, the clarinets carry the theme by themselves. In his preface, Beck questions the usual judgments about Stamitz and Gossec, passed ad infinitum from one secondary work to another: "compared with many composers of the day, Gossec has a healthy naturalness and sincerity which is often lacking in the Mannheim school."

orchestra leader of the Concert des Amateurs (1769) in the Hôtel de Soubise (now the Archives de France), he had an excellent forum through which to perform his own symphonies and those of other composers. He used this series, which was supported financially by a group of highly placed nobles, to introduce the Parisian public to the symphonies of Haydn, starting in 1773, the same year that he also took over the Concert Spirituel with Gaviniès and Leduc. These and other duties at the Opéra reduced his time for composing and slowed his output. The leadership in Parisian orchestral composition had passed to Leduc in the 1770s, which may offer another reason why Gossec eventually went on to other fields of musical endeavor. In all, about sixty of his symphonies have survived.

Before Haydn's triumphs in Paris the major competition for French symphonists came from the second generation of Mannheim composers, namely Fils, Toeschi, and Cannabich, plus the older Holzbauer. Grimm had a correspondent, the marquis de Croismare, who lived in rural Normandy and who depended upon him for sending music as well as information.

> I admire the fecundity of Mannheim and the continuity of your good deeds for us. . . . I confess the desire to know more about these exciting [terrible] composers of Mannheim. For example, Cannabich. Is he aged, tall, short, married, lively, amiable, etc.? Toeschi, Holzbauer, this young adept who opens himself to the world. *Quoy? Quis? Quid, ubi, Cur, quando?* Forgive, dear friend, a provincial curiosity that has neither head nor tail. Did Filtz die young, without children? He was a stout-hearted composer![98]

Curiosity about the creative artist as an individual being, physical as well as spiritual, sounds a sympathetic note that is quite in tune with the ideals of the Enlightenment. The epitome of such an attitude was reached in Boccherini's declaration, written to his publisher Pleyel in Paris, that he was "a man of probity, honest, sensitive, sweet-natured and affectionate, as my works show me to be."[99]

Gossec dedicated his *Messe des morts* in its 1790 publication to the directors of the Concert des Amateurs, shortly before this celebrated concert series ended. In so doing he made some telling remarks about the dignity that he believed belonged to creative artists. He mentioned that, of the many encouragements given by the aristocratic directors of the series to musicians, "the most powerful is the noble distinction with which you treated them: to elevate artists' souls is to work towards the elevation of the arts." Musicians were less well treated in many

---

[98]Letter to Grimm dated 30 August 1763 from Marc-Antoine-Nicolas, Marquis de Croismare, resident of Lasson in Normandy, in François Lesure, "Mozartiana Gallica," *Revue de musicologie* 38 (1956): 115–24. Note that Franz Beck does not figure among the Mannheimers.

[99]Elisabeth Covel Le Guin, "'As My Works Show Me to Be': Physicality as Compositional Technique in the Instrumental Music of Luigi Boccherini" (Ph.D. diss., University of California, Berkeley, 1997), p. xiii.

other places. Humiliations the Mozarts say they suffered at the hands of Archbishop Hieronymous Colloredo are well known. When urging his son on to Paris, Leopold Mozart argued that "there the nobility treat men of genius with the greatest deference, esteem, and courtesy" (letter of 11–12 February 1778). Gossec's remarks bear out what Leopold claimed.

Other than Gossec, French symphonists did not fare very well with the critics. Gasparo Angiolini, in his *Lettre à Monsieur Noverre* of 1773, lumped together French and German symphonies, implying that they were easy to read from sight in spite of their quantity of notes. Laurent Garcins in his *Traité du mélo-drame* (1772) says that in instrumental music "one seems to agree in giving the preference to the German symphonists, and especially the Bohemians." In his 1770 essay "Quelques réflections sur la musique moderne," Nicolas Étienne Framery reproved French composers because Gossec was the only one of them who could march beside the great men—he mentions Stamitz, Toeschi, and Pierre van Maldere in the genre of the symphony. Having named composers of Bohemian, Italian, and Flemish descent, he asks, rather inappropriately, "Was not Gossec himself a pupil of the Germans?"[100] La Borde a decade later in his *Essai sur la musique ancienne et moderne* pronounced an emphatic negative answer to this question, saying Nature was Gossec's only master: "his works prove this because his music is not imitative of any Italian or German master, and if some critics, jealous of his talent, say that it is, they do more harm to themselves than to him."

An anonymous critic writing in the *Mercure de France* for April 1772 ranged the symphonies of Stamitz, Holzbauer, Toeschi, and [Christian] Bach heard at Paris in the previous twelve to fifteen years alongside those by Gossec, "devenu le musicien de notre nation pour cette partie." J. J. O. de Meude-Monpas was more specific than usual in his *Dictionnaire de musique* of 1787 (article "Symphonie"): "of all the French composers who have cultivated the symphonic genre, Gossec is without doubt the most skillful; no one commands better than he does the harmonic effects, the proper manner of writing, in sum everything that derives from the rules of the art, as for example, how to dialogue, to vary the movement, to make the wind instruments speak appropriately, etc." By the time Choron and Fayolle brought out their *Dictionnaire historique des musiciens* in 1810–11, they were eager to place the pioneers of the symphony in relation to Haydn: "The symphony, cultivated since the middle of the century by Gossec, Toeschi, Vanhal, and Emanuel Bach, was perfected by Haydn." On strictly chronological grounds, Toeschi and Vanhal cannot be considered to belong with those who cultivated the genre from the 1750s on, but Gossec can. Haydn did not begin composing symphonies until the late 1750s.

---

[100]Nicolas Étienne Framery, *Journal de musique historique, théorique, et pratique,* 5 vols. (Paris, 1770–71), 1: 357.

Gossec had a worthy follower in the person of Marie-Alexandre Guénin, who also came from the north. Born at Maubeuge in 1744, he was sent to Paris at an early age in order to perfect his precocious talent as a violinist. Nicolas Capron and Gaviniès were his violin teachers. He dedicated his Op. 1, a set of six trios published before 1769, to Gossec, his composition teacher. Like the similar collection by Simon Leduc (1768), the works were equally divided between solo and orchestral trios, as the title page makes clear. The first trio is an impressively somber work that remains in the key of g for all three of its movements.

Gaviniès and Leduc

One of the most sympathetic musicians of the time was the virtuoso violinist Pierre Gaviniès. The son of a violin maker, he was born in Bordeaux on 11 May 1728. The family moved to Paris by 1734, and before the end of the decade young Pierre was delighting listeners with his violin playing in private concerts. On 8 September 1741 he made his debut at the Concert Spirituel, playing with L'abbé le fils one of the sonatas for two violins by Leclair, a performance that roused the enthusiasm of a large audience, according to the *Mercure de France*. Two months later, on All Saints' Day, he played the solo in Vivaldi's "La Primavera." Records of his subsequent activities or studies (did he go to Italy?) are missing until 1748, when he reappeared at the Concert Spirituel playing solos often and in duet with Blavet, Guignon, and Marie Fel during the next five years. Another hiatus from the concert life of Paris from June 1753 until April 1759 has never been explained. One story handed down by his biographer Constance Pipelet has him entangled in a romantic liaison with a lady of the court that resulted in his imprisonment for a year, during which he wrote his famous *romance*.[101] In his *Observations sur la musique, les musiciens, et les instrumens* (1757), Ancelet wrote that "Gaviniez was born with all the dispositions that one could wish for the violin: he has taste, mastery of the bow and of fingering. . . . His playing embraces all styles [caractères]. He is touching because of the beauty of his tone and astonishing in his dexterity."

Gaviniès held back from publishing compositions until 1760, when Madame Oger engraved his Op. 1, *Six sonates à violon seul et basse.* The *Mercure de France* welcomed them with words suggesting that they were not new: "The superior talents of the author, in composition as well as in performance, made us wait for a long time before he consented to having his works engraved; and we do not

---

[101]Constance D. T. Pipelet [Princess de Salm], *Éloge historique de Pierre Gaviniès* (Paris, 1802), p. 7, cited after Arthur Pougin, *Viotti et l'école moderne de violon* (Paris, 1888), p. 38, in Pierre Gaviniès, *Sonatas for Violin and Basso Continuo Opus 1*, ed. Anthony F. Ginter (Recent Researches in the Music of the Classic Era, 43) (Madison, Wis., 1995), p. xv. Ginter's preface is the source of all the information in this paragraph.

doubt that this sample will suit the taste of the public so agreeably that it would soon wish to see the other works of this versatile and gracious artist."[102] The composer obliged by publishing a second set of six sonatas of the same kind in 1764 as his Op. 3. Meanwhile, as if in demonstration of his versatility, his fine opéra-comique, *Le Prétendu,* was published in score (Op. 2).

The first set of sonatas for violin and bass by Gaviniès represent a high point in the achievements of the French violin school and in galant chamber music. They should, with the help of a scrupulous new edition, prove attractive to concert violinists possessing enough technique to meet their demands. The six sonatas are in D, g, b, G, B♭, and A. In the third, fifth, and sixth sonatas, all three movements share the same key. The tempo pattern of the movements is fast–slow–fast or fast–slow–dance, the exception being Sonata No. 3 in b, which begins with an *Adagio,* continues with an *Allegro* in sonata form, and concludes with a *Grazioso* theme decorated with nine variations. Sonata No. 2 in g begins with an *Allegro moderato e dolce* that illustrates both the poignant, cantabile style favored by the composer (main theme) and his rather mechanical use of floridly decorated harmonic sequence (transition to the relative major). The phrases are regular and foursquare, a closed cadence in m. 4 being followed by an open cadence in m. 8, in other words, an inverted period. Double and triple stops are common. In the *Adagio* of Sonata No. 6 in A the violin marches up and down the scale in parallel thirds, projecting music very like that sung by two sopranos in some buffo finale by Galuppi.

Gaviniès was prized as a teacher and orchestra leader, as can be seen among other ways from the many music prints dedicated to him by his pupils and colleagues, in an age when dedications were usually made to wealthy patrons in hope of financial reward. As concertmaster of the Concert Spirituel in 1762 he was the first to introduce the Italian manner of leading the orchestra with his bow arm.[103] Of his many pupils, Simon Leduc (sometimes called "l'ainé", [the elder], to distinguish him from his brother Pierre) was by far the greatest composer. The filial line between Gaviniès and Leduc is most apparent in slow movements, in the playing of which Gaviniès was especially praised. There is a lyrical quality in some of the slow movements of Op. 1 by Gaviniès, but still more so in those of his Op. 3 of 1764. In the latter set, half the sonatas are in the minor mode: No. 3 in g; No. 4 in d; No. 6 in f♯. The fifth sonata of the set is in G and begins with an *Allegro* in 2/4 that has a second theme in which the violin plays moving voices against pedal tones in double stops—an effect very like the drones that Leduc

[102]The original French is cited by Ginter in his edition of Op. 1 by Gaviniès, p. xv, n. 38.
[103]La Laurencie, *L'école française du violon,* 2: 285, an innovation applauded in the *Mercure de France.* La Laurencie devotes a long chapter entirely to Gaviniès and quotes liberally from his sonatas and concertos in musical examples.

uses as a second theme in the first movement of his first published sonata (Op. 1 No. 1, 1767).

The ensuing movement is an *Andante* in C of very lyrical character (Example 6.10). Typically galant traits abound, most notably the chromatic appoggiaturas, the sanglots, and the generally flowery nature of the discourse. But there is a quality of poetry and originality too, apparent in the detour to vi in m. 3 (a favorite first destination of Leduc's as well), and in the way the melodic turn here is reinterpreted harmonically in the next measure, which leads to an arrival back at the tonic using the same turn in the following measure. Melodic extensions have stretched the process out to five measures and given it a certain wayward fancy, like a reverie. In what follows, the harmonic rhythm slows down to the point where there is not much for the bass to do other than repeat notes. Realization of the chords by a keyboard is still quite necessary. Leduc would arrive at a point at which it was less essential, and he would also abandon some of the galant clichés, but not the poetic quality and the delicacy of shading with ornamental tones. Gaviniès concludes his sonata with a *Tempo di minuetto* in 3/8 that has a *minore* trio.

Following his Op. 3, Gaviniès published his epochal *Six concertos à violon principal, premier et second dessus, deux hautbois, deux cors, alto et basse*, Op. 4, 1764 and *Six sonates à deux violons*, Op. 5 (n.d.). He twice played one of his concertos at the Concert Spirituel (2 February and 26 March) when the Mozarts were in Paris in 1764. Subsequently they collaborated, Gaviniès having been hired to lead the small orchestra at the Mozarts' second concert in a private theater at the porte

EXAMPLE 6.10. *Gaviniès, Sonata Op. 3 No. 5, II*

Saint Honoré (9 April 1764). In the end, the famous violinist refused to take his fee, a typical gesture in a lifetime filled with generous acts. From 1769 to 1772 he organized charity concerts to support the École Gratuite de Dessin. From 1773 to 1777, when he ran the Concert Spirituel with Gossec and Leduc, his role was as concertmaster and leader of the first violins, while Leduc led the seconds. At the École Royale de Chant (1784) and the Conservatoire that succeeded it, he was professor of violin until his death in 1800. His pupils, besides Guénin and Leduc, included Capron, Jacques Lemière, Jean-Baptiste Moria, Isidore Bertheaume, Louis-Henri Paisible, Alexandre-August Robineau, Antoine-Laurent Baudron, Jean-Jérôme Imbault, and enough others to staff an entire orchestra with violinists. There is evidence, in fact, that the orchestras he led were largely filled with his pupils.

The compositional importance of Gaviniès lay especially in his violin concertos of 1764, the first to be published in Paris since those by Leclair in 1745. His dramatic flair as a soloist combined in these works with the powerful symphonic language of Stamitz and Gossec, leading to a synthesis that was influential both for Mozart's violin concertos and for the so-called *concerto héroïque* identified with Giovanni Battista Viotti, who made his debut in Paris at the Concert Spirituel in 1782. According to an authoritative critic, "they became the first of an increasing flow of brilliant, attractive works that made Paris the most significant center of the violin concerto."[104] At least one of the many French writers on music of the time made some pertinent remarks on the violin concerto. In his *Réflexions sur la musique* of 1763, C. R. Brijon used the concept *solo,* by which he meant sonata, as well as symphony, to define the genre.

> The concerto is the combination of the symphony and the *solo.* The *tutti,* with which it commences, exposes the propositions that are to be discussed in the course of the piece; the contradictions that result from this then form a musical combat between the *solo* and the *tutti,* a combat that terminates with a reunion of sentiments and ideas. Ordinarily, the end of the piece ought to ally force with charm, and energy with gaiety.[105]

It is unusual to find a definition of this date that emphasizes struggle and contradiction. Most eighteenth-century writers on the subject were more bland.

The year 1760 that saw the first prints by Gaviniès was also the year of publication of the solo violin sonatas, Op. 1, by Pierre Vachon. Born in 1731, Vachon emerged in the 1750s as a rival to Gaviniès at the Concert Spirituel. His first pub-

[104]Chappell White, *From Vivaldi to Viotti: A History of the Early Classical Violin Concerto* (Philadelphia, 1992), pp. 217–24; 218. The musical examples White offers bear out his claims for the composer.
[105]C. R. Brijon, *Réflexions sur la musique et sur la vraie manière de l'exécuter sur le violon* (Paris, 1763), p. 3.

lic appearance was on Christmas Eve, 1756, when he played a violin concerto of his own composition that, like so many other solo concertos, has not survived. More than a year went by before he was heard there again, playing his own concertos (again lost) and the eternally verdant "La Primavera" by Vivaldi. Vachon's sonatas show a ready command of the violin, but a rather vapid inspiration, overly reliant on melodies in parallel sixths. Several of the pieces are in the showy vein of Chabran, Vachon's teacher. One of the six sonatas is in minor, or rather begins in the minor mode. The "Sonata Quinta," after a first movement in g, *Cantabile* in 2/4, turns to G for an *Adagio* and a concluding *Allegro*.

Simon Leduc was born at Paris on 15 January 1742 and baptized the same day in the parish of Saint Roch.[106] He was thus not a child prodigy when he began appearing in public, contrary to what had been suggested by a false birthdate of 1748.[107] In 1759 he is listed as a member of the second violins at the Concert Spirituel. From the following year comes the dated manuscript in the Paris Conservatoire inscribed "Sonata a violino solo del Signore Le Duc, 1760."[108] It is in three movements, *Allegro*–*Grave*–[Rondeau], and in the key of A. The rigid two- and four-measure phrases of the opening movement and their failure to generate much forward momentum betray the neophyte. Stylistically, the movement is indebted to Gaviniès and shows all the usual galant traits. The slow movement, by contrast, is a sparsely ornamented song in the parallel minor that displays a surprising command of chromatic harmony. Best of all is the final Rondeau, which begins with a fall from the fifth to the third degree, and subsequently to the tonic, a melodic kernel that generated some of Leduc's finest movements (Example 6.11). Note that the bass is unfigured, as it is throughout the sonata. This may be no oversight, inasmuch as the parallel tenth structure and the tendency of the violin to supply more than one chord tone per bass note make for self-sufficiency— as if the composer were thinking in terms of a violin–cello duet.

In 1763 Leduc was promoted from the seconds to the first violins at the Concert Spirituel and he also began making solo appearances: on 22 March he played "airs en trio" with Gaviniès and Lemière (most likely arrangements of opéra-comique tunes); on 25 March he played "airs en quatuor" with the same and the

---

[106]A happy archival discovery made by Anik Devriès, "Deux dynasties d'éditeurs et de musiciens: Les Leduc," *Revue belge de musicologie* 28–30 (1974–76): 195–211; 199. She shows that Simon Leduc published only his own compositions (as Brook deduced earlier), unlike his younger brother Pierre, who was born in 1755 and became one of the main Parisian music publishers.

[107]Provided by A. Choron and F. Fayolle, *Dictionnaire historique des musiciens* (Paris, 1810–11) and followed by Fétis. Brook argued astutely that this date was several years too late. See his *La symphonie française,* 1: 263–67, and the related discussion in his article "Simon Le Duc l'aîné, A French Symphonist at the time of Mozart," *Musical Quarterly* 48 (1962): 498–513.

[108]For a facsimile of the first page of the sonata (taking the opening *Allegro* up to the double bar in the middle), see Brook, *La symphonie française,* 1: 276; Brook doubts that the manuscript is an autograph.

EXAMPLE 6.11. *Leduc, Sonata in A (1760), III, Rondeau*

cellist Nochez; on 8 September he played a violin concerto by Gaviniès; and finally on Christmas Eve he played a sonata of his own, a concert that the Mozarts surely would have heard had they not that very day left Paris for Versailles.

Leduc did not rush into print with this and five other sonatas after his debut, as had so many others. Like his teacher he waited a few years before producing his Op. 1. Yet it is tempting to believe that the Sonata in D with which this collection begins, after a touchingly earnest and unflowery dedication to Gaviniès, is indeed his debut sonata played at the Tuileries.[109] This is by no means the last Op. 1 No. 1 in D of the French violin school, but it surely is the best. In it Leduc manages to make even the mandatory passage work interesting and melodious, in which regard he is akin to Mozart of a later date (but not Mozart at the time of his first visits to Paris). His harmonic and rhythmic control could also be compared with that of the mature Mozart. The resemblance of the second theme of the first movement with similar pedal effects in Gaviniès has been noted. Progress made beyond Leduc's early sonata of 1760 is everywhere evident, and nowhere more decisively than in his ability to keep the momentum going, achieved by avoiding strong cadences and tonic arrivals.

Similar qualities are evident in the lovely slow movement, *Amoroso Cantabile* in G, the long spun-out cantilena of which, taken together with the most delicate *broderies,* evoke and surpass the similar reveries of Leduc's teacher. The initial harmonic movement to vi resembles the example from Gaviniès above. Pauses in the middle of the movement and at the end over 6/4 chords provided for the improvisation of cadenzas. The resolution of the latter led without a break into the final *Rondo alla francese,* a relatively lightweight movement compared to the first two, but not inferior in quality. There are episodes on V and on vi, both using vari-

[109]Modern edition in Simon Le Duc, *Vier Sonaten für Violine und Basso continuo,* ed. Elma Doflein (Mainz, n.d.) (Edition Schott 4708-09, 2 vols; vol. 1 has Op. 4 Nos. 1 and 6, vol. 2 has Op. 1 No. 1 and Op. 4 No. 4).

ants of the main theme, surrounding the three statements of the main theme in the tonic; everything is written out, and the subtle transitions belie the rigidity of the old formal scheme. The designation *alla francese* refers not only to the form, but to certain melodic features (e.g., the falling conjunct fourth in even eighth notes encountered in so many gavottes).

The most appealing sonata of Leduc's altogether winning Op. 1 set is the third one in A. Its first movement, *Commodo e espressivo,* begins with the falling from the fifth degree already noted in his early sonata in A. The chromatic appoggiatura is still in evidence, as are the penultimate triplets, as may be seen from Example 6.12a, showing the beginning and ending of the movement, but the discourse is far more straightforward than in the first movement of the 1760 sonata. Swell marks such as occur in the violin part, m. 2, are frequently used by Leduc. After an expansive development section, led off by the first theme in the dominant, the reprise cuts in with material following the main theme. The big leaps and the dynamic level up to *fortissimo* at the end of the movement seem to predict an ensuing cadenza, but none is forthcoming. Instead, the cadence is undercut by a diminishing of the dynamic level ("smorzato"), and the prolonged A in the violin leads without a break via a chromatic rise into the slow movement in 3/4 *Amabile con grazia,* marked "piano sempre" (Example 6.12b).

The melodic line of the middle movement is relatively bare of ornament at first, a simple cantilena falling from the fifth degree. This eight-measure phrase (with its two preliminary measures) must be all in one long breath, which the violin is more capable of than the voice, its obvious model here. Upon repetition there is more melodic elaboration, and it is exquisitely wrought (especially the ever-changing position of ornamental and linear functions of the sixteenth notes in mm. 14–16).

The chromatic appoggiaturas that one has come to expect are here more than just an added seasoning to render the dish piquant. A chromatically raised B in the melody in m. 5 (which one hears in relation to the chromatic rise inaugurating the movement) becomes the bass line of a subtle reharmonization in m. 11 and recurs again in the melody, in accented position, over a subdominant harmony, in m. 14. Each occurrence is more expressive than the previous one. Leduc is so pleased with his lovely falling melody that he makes it the second subject as well, and it sounds even more beautiful occurring in the dominant, in the rare key of B major. There is a substantial development section, leading to the repeat of the entire main theme, *fortissimo,* in double-stopped thirds. At the end of the movement the theme comes back once again in the coda, which is extended by putting another half-step rise in the bass, producing a deceptive cadence to the flat sixth, which gives way to a minor tonic in 6/4 position (via a diminished-seventh chord, with bass motion A♯ to B, as in the melody at the beginning of the movement). The fermata over the major tonic 6/4 chord in the next measure signals a cadenza.

EXAMPLE 6.12. *Leduc, Sonata in A, Op. 1 No. 3*

c. II (ending) -- III

Again there is no break between movements. The violin carries its E over ("di seguito") as the first tone of the third movement, a rondeau marked *Brillantino* (Example 6.12c). This finale can be compared with that of the early sonata in A. Whereas in 1760 Leduc was content with the usual proliferation of triplets, here he makes every note of the melody count. The two-part counterpoint in the violin, *fortissimo,* upon restatement of the idea is almost Haydnesque. In addition to being a pithy tune in its own right, the Rondeau theme, with its 5 - 4 - 3, 4 - 3 - 2, 3 - 2 - 1 melodic motion, sums up and ties together the previous two movements (cf. their initial themes). It is truly the *summa* of this tightly knit and carefully planned multimovement cycle. With works like this—and all the sonatas are on a very high level—Leduc has moved, like Gossec, beyond the limits of the earlier galant style, to what is best called its second phase. Mozart would do so only later, and Leduc was perhaps one of the sympathetic spirits who was inspired enough to help show him the way.

Leduc represents the culmination of a long Parisian tradition of excellence in the Italianate sonata. Tartini's lyricism, planted in local soil by Pagin and others, joined Leclair's solid virtues and those of his disciples to produce a first peak of artistry in Gaviniès, who made it possible for his pupil to attain an even higher level. Not to be dismissed either is the refulgence from those parallel peaks, just as lofty, reached by Gossec in the symphony, and simultaneously, around 1760, by Philidor and Monsigny in opéra-comique. A great composer need not be generically limited as to his inspiration.

In the music of Leduc there is an occasional hint that he, along with Philidor and a few other initiates, was not immune to the formidable charms of Gluck. Count Giacomo Durazzo sent a score of *Orfeo ed Euridice* (1762) from Vienna to Paris, where it was first published two years later. The last sonata in Leduc's Op. 1 ends with a Tempo di Minuetto that has a simple closing idea of two successive falling conjunct fourths, matching the phrase "Non lagnarti" in the chorus ending Act II of *Orfeo*. It is typical of Leduc that, when he repeats this idea, he enhances it with a chromatic progression, emphasized by a *rinforzando*. Also typical is the way he repeats it once again, quite simply, as a coda to the whole movement, thus drawing the maximum effect out of a truly lyric idea, one that we are glad to hear again as a final farewell.

Leduc's output as a composer was modest in size, about a collection a year in the decade between his Op. 1 of 1767 and his early death. For this reason alone he will never be accorded major status, nor perhaps even the status of many prolific but mediocre composers who came before and after him. His Op. 2 of 1768 consisted of *Six trios pour deux violons et basse, dont trois à pleine orchestra et trois à trois concertants* (note the use of the last word in the sense of solo performers). These are the greatest of all orchestral trios, and their restoration became possible only in recent times with the finding of the missing violino primo.[110] The first trio, in D, is headed with the further explanation: "I Primi tre Trio sono per grande Orchestra. Li altri sono per sonarsi a trè." It is in three movements, fast–slow–fast, as are the other two orchestral trios. The second trio is in g, with a slow movement in E♭.

Some excerpts from the recovered first violin part will convey the salient virtues of this symphony (Example 6.13abc). The *Allegro* begins *fortissimo*, the three parts in unison, with a rocket that also launches the development, after the double bar, in a sequence descending by thirds. The movement ends on the dominant, which leads as in a deceptive cadence, V - ♭VI, to the Cantabile, *pianissimo*, another of the composer's dreamy movements in 3/4, with broad-arched melody and in this case a minuet-like gait. There is another transition at the end of this movement, taking the music without a break into the *Presto* Finale. The last movement is derived from the first not just in the rising triad of their openings, but also in that the *Presto* theme echoes the falling-third sequence of the first movement's development. Besides this cyclic linking of movements, there is the meshing of one movement with another so that the whole becomes one flowing stream of sound from the initial tone to the cadence of the finale.

---

[110]Brook made a conjectural restoration of this part in *La symphonie française*, 1: 282–83. For the complete orchestral trio in g, Op. 2 No. 2, with original violino primo restored see Simon Le Duc, *Five Symphonic Works*, ed. Barry S. Brook and David Bain (The Symphony 1720–1840, Series D, Vol. 4) (New York, 1983), pp. 1–23.

EXAMPLE 6.13. *Leduc, Symphony in g, Op. 2 No. 2*

a. I

b. I into II

c. III

Leduc carried over the search for continuity from his solo sonatas. For him a symphony is an enlarged sonata, and the "full orchestra" need not be treated very differently, except in that he chooses more blunt and forceful language for the themes of the fast movements. The chamber trios, Nos. 4–6, confirm this as well. Two of them, Nos. 4 and 5, are in only two movements, ending with a minuet, but the sixth is almost as grand as the orchestral trios and includes a *misterioso* passage in chromatic harmony and a slow movement in the unusual key of B♭ minor, marked *Lento assai expressione mesta,* indication enough that the composer regarded his extraordinary creations in the minor mode as sad and even tragic, which is our reaction to them too. In none of these works is the bass figured.

Six duo pour deux violons constitutes Leduc's Op. 3, followed by his *Second livre de sonates pour le violon,* Op. 4, of 1770. The duos are without bass, a genre frequently cultivated in France after Leclair, notably by Gaviniès. They allow full scope to the composer's penchant for the long, elegaic *Adagio,* followed by the jolliest of popular-type Rondeaux. Some of the latter come close to Haydn in the delight they take in melodic inversion (e.g., the rising chromatic line that disturbs the sunny finale of Op. 3 No. 3 in C and turns at one point into a falling chromatic line).

The second set of sonatas shows the composer at the height of his powers. The sonata was a serious matter for him, more weighty, for instance, than the duet or the chamber trio. Two of the sonatas are in minor, No. 4 in c and No. 6 in f. In general Leduc continued to simplify and refine his style, so that Op. 4 represents as much of an advance over Op. 1 as the latter represented over the 1760 sonata. Gone are the wordy tempo and movement directions, as well as the frequent and rather fussy dynamic indications. It is as if the composer had resolved to let the notes speak for themselves. There are no figures in the bass, but keyboard realization is still helpful to explain the often rich and subtle harmonic implications. At the same time, performance as a violin-cello duet should not be ruled out as a possibility.

In the first Sonata in A, the opening Cantabile begins with a V^4_2 of IV, the bass having a G♮, while the violin rises through the tonic triad. The second theme, related to the first, is also triadic, so that in both cases the melody instrument explains the harmony. This movement is ample in proportion. It has an exposition of forty-six measures, a development, mostly in the minor, of thirty-two measures, and a full recapitulation, beginning with the main theme, of thirty-nine measures. Both the second theme and closing theme begin with the progression from tonic to submediant, which is also used to initiate the intensely moving *Adagio* in E. The *Rondo Allegretto* that concludes the sonata has the same rising triad motif as the opening movement, but here the mood is less serious and indeed rather like an opéra-comique song. Technical display is abundantly present in the outer movements, but it is subordinate to a genuine melodic interest that marks Leduc's work more strongly than ever. His mastery of harmony is such as to place him in a class with few other composers of the time.

In Leduc's *Second livre de trio pour deux violons et basse* (Op. 5, 1772), two of the works are in minor. What is even more surprising, the next opus, although devoted to "easy" duets *(Six petits duo pour deux violons de la plus grande facilité),* comprises no fewer than three works in the minor mode. Leduc's penchant for the minor emerges logically from a longstanding trend within the French violin school. His command of chromatic harmony, developed by writing so many fine works in the minor, was put to telling use in his major-mode works as well. What sets him apart from many others is his use of chromaticism in a structural way, so as to make it vital to the harmonic progressions of a given movement. In this regard he is distinctly different from a figure like Franz Beck, the symphonic composer born in Mannheim who was resident in France from about 1760 until his death in 1809 and who has been proposed as a formative influence on Leduc because of the minor-mode symphonies in his Op. 1 (Paris, Venier, 1758), Op. 2 (Paris, Chevardière, 1760), and Op. 3 (Paris, Venier, 1762).[111] Beck, who left Mannheim early, uses chromaticism in a more old-fashioned way, mainly in descending lines that generate harmonic sequences (for instance, in the outer movements of Op. 3 No. 3).[112] Leduc's subtle, organically conceived use of chromaticism, on the other hand, is astonishingly forward looking. His music is treated here at more than usual length in the conviction that it adumbrates the mature Mozart.

In his last three years when, alongside his cohorts Gaviniès and Gossec, Leduc helped restore the Concert Spirituel to its former excellence (1773–76), he again took up writing for orchestra, which he had neglected since his Op. 2 of 1768. The three symphonies for full orchestra from this period are worthy to stand beside those of Gossec. The one in E♭[113] has a slow introduction that adumbrates the rising line of the *Allegro Vivace* that follows, and a sombre and very chromatic *Adagio sostenuto* in c, followed by a cheerful *Rondo Moderato*. Both outer movements emphasize the relative minor. The other two symphonies are in D. One has a slow introduction that passes from *Largo* (a two-measure fanfare in dotted rhythm) to an *Andante poco lento* of several measures, consisting of a chromatic melody and bass line that will shape the second theme of the ensuing *Allegro molto assai* (or, to look at it the other way around, the second theme was planted in the introduction as a unifying feature). The *Andante poco lento* that follows is in A and displays again Leduc's favorite melodic motif of falling from the fifth degree to the tonic; when this fall becomes chromatic, we realize that it, too, is related to the slow introduction, a relationship that is made more explicit in the reprise. Falling thirds from the fifth degree generate the final *Presto non troppo*, which is a sonata allegro form with a single theme, used for both tonic and dominant areas and with a lengthy development section. The other symphony in D, without slow introduction, has a unifying thematic principle as well in that all three movements make a point of emphasizing the supertonic as a melodic and harmonic goal.[114]

Leduc also composed several violin concertos, three of which were printed.

---

[111]Brook, *La symphonie française*, 2: 70, says "it is without doubt to this influence that Simon Le Duc owes the unusual employment he makes of chromaticism and the minor mode." Beck's Op. 1 No. 1 is in g, with a slow movement in B♭, as is Op. 2 No. 2 and Op. 3 No. 3. Op. 3 No. 5 is in d.

[112]Burton Stimson Carrow, "The Relation between the Mannheim School and the Music of Franz Beck, Henri Blanchard, and Pierre Gaveaux" (Ph.D. diss., New York University, 1956), p. 131. The insistence of Parisian publishers on title pages that Beck was a disciple of Stamitz and chamber musician of the Palatine elector, in the absence of any direct evidence, raises suspicions that he was neither one nor the other.

[113]Edited in Brook, *La symphonie française*, 3: 57–81.

[114]Edited in Le Duc, *Five Symphonic Works*, pp. 59–119.

His first concerto, in D, is a paraphrase of his violin sonata in A, Op. 1 No. 3, quoted in Example 6.12 on p. 669 (another reason to believe that this sonata was a favorite of his); only the Rondeaux are different. The opening movement is freely adapted, necessarily, since it involves a double exposition, but the glorious slow movement remains very close to its original form. From this it may be seen that Leduc regarded the concerto as an outgrowth of the solo sonata, and in his case it is true that the sonata is at the heart of his creative life.

As a virtuoso performer, Leduc yielded to his younger brother Pierre, which betokened a modesty that is in accord with what little we know of his personal life. Indeed, he was reproached by a critic in the *Mercure* in 1773 "for reducing himself to an ordinary orchestral player; his talent could show itself with far greater éclat if he undertook more."[115] Pierre Leduc played a violin concerto by his brother as early as 1770 at the Concert Spirituel. The "Nouvelle symphonie concertante" for two violins by the elder Leduc that was heard at the Concert Spirituel on Christmas, 1774 and 1775, had as soloists Pierre Leduc and Gossec's pupil Guénin. This is presumably the Symphonie Concertante in G that originally had sixteen parts, but was reduced to ten parts by the publisher, Henry, "in order to facilitate its execution and render it more useful for *petits Concerts.*"[116]

Leduc brought to his orchestral compositions the same refinements that are so much in evidence in his sonatas and chamber music. Yet he is most at home in the intimate chamber works, where he himself, as violinist, was the boldly passionate singer-protagonist. The *Adagio* of his most mature symphony, the one in E$^\flat$, is nevertheless on a level with the highest poetry of his Op. 4 sonatas. Fittingly, it served as a kind of *tombeau* when Leduc died, just having passed his thirty-fifth birthday, in early 1777. As reported in the *Journal de Paris,* an event shortly thereafter provoked a most touching response to the man and his music:

> The Concert [des Amateurs] began Wednesday last, 26 February 1777, with a symphony by the late M. Le Duc; which had produced an effect at the rehearsal well worth being reported. In addition to his superior talents in both composition and performance, M. Le Duc possessed moral qualities that endeared him to all who knew him. In the middle of the Adagio of this symphony, the celebrated Monsieur [le chevalier] de Saint Georges, moved by the expressiveness of the piece and recalling that his friend existed no longer, dropped his bow and began to weep; this emotion communicated itself to all the artists and the rehearsal had to be suspended.[117]

[115]Brook, "Simon Le Duc," p. 503.
[116]Brook, *La symphonie française,* 2: 415–17. Subsequent to Brook's work, parts for the original version *à 16* have been acquired by the British Library, London.
[117]Brook, "Simon Le Duc," p. 503.

Concerto and Concertante

Around 1770 a new kind of concert piece involving a few solo performers and orchestra became popular. It acquired the designation of symphonie concertante. Music publishers in Paris were quick to capitalize on the fad, which led to a new and rapidly expanding rubric in their catalogues. The term concertante in the sense of composed for solo performers was commonly used around this time and it is this sense that Rousseau understands in his *Dictionnaire de musique* of 1767. The same year Venier published *Sei sinfonie concertante, o sia quintetti . . . dell Sig. Misliwecek il Boemo* and followed them a year later by a similarly titled set by Cannabich. These works for five solo performers have only their title in common with the new orchestral genre, which is more indebted to the concerto than to the symphony.

The earliest examples of the orchestral symphonie concertante published in Paris were scored for two violins as soloists. Duets between two violinists had long been one of the most ingrained of Parisian tastes—recall the duel of Guignon and Baptiste Anet back at the beginnings of the Concert Spirituel, the debut of both Gaviniès and L'abbé le fils, paired together, in the 1740s, and the many other similar performances, plus the large number of published sonatas for two violins, with or without bass. Giving such duets an orchestral background, so that the symphonic band would not sit idly by, seems like such a logical employment of the forces at hand, it is a wonder that someone did not think of it sooner. Gaviniès, for instance, wrote symphonies (which are lost), violin concertos, and duet sonatas for two violins, all the ingredients, as it were, of the early symphonies concertantes. Leduc is reputed to have written a concerto for two violins that was performed in 1770 at the Concert Spirituel, but this is an error that comes from conflating two distinct events.[118]

What, indeed, is the difference between a double concerto for two violins and orchestra and the new genre? There is none in externals. Like the concerto, the symphonie concertante begins with a fast movement having a double exposition. But the new genre is blithely melodious, thin textured, and lightweight compared to the ponderous double concertos of the past; at its most typical it has only two movements, *Allegro* and Rondeau.[119] The comparison is irrelevant in a sense because the double concerto for two violins was little practiced in France and

[118]Brenet, *Les concerts en France*, p. 294: "Leduc jeune et Rougeon, qui jouérent un concerto à deux violons de Leduc l'ainé." According to Constant Pierre, Rougeon played a violin concerto on 9 April 1770, while Pierre Leduc played his brother's violin concerto a few days later on 14 April. La Laurencie, *L'école française du violon*, 2: 381, quotes the review in the *Mercure* that mentions the debut of both violinists but makes it clear that they played in different works.

[119]Barry S. Brook, "The Symphonie Concertante: An Interim Report," *Musical Quarterly* 47 (1961): 493–516.

rarely encountered at the Concert Spirituel. Violin duets were so common, on the other hand, as to be a fixture there and in publishers' catalogues. They tended to be less demanding musically, but not technically, than the solo violin sonata (of the prestigious Op. 1 variety, that is to say, not the "easy" sonatina).

Facile melodies in thirds and sixths, arching pyrotechnics vaulting one violin over the other, and a preponderance of effect over affect marked the duet repertory. These are the very characteristics that shaped the symphonie concertante at its inception. Increasing popularization of concert life at Paris, where audiences gradually became less aristocratic, seemed destined to lead to the symphonie concertante.[120] The composers who best typified the popular aspects of the symphonie concertante were two professionals, Carl Stamitz and Giuseppe Cambini, and two amateurs, Jean-Baptiste Davaux and Joseph Boulogne, Chevalier de Saint-Georges (Figure 6.10).[121]

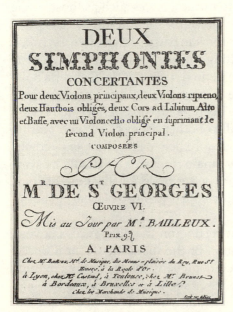

FIGURE 6.10. Title page of Symphonies Concertantes by Saint-Georges, 1775.

The introduction of the new genre at the Concert Spirituel did not happen until Gossec, Gaviniès, and Leduc took over the direction in early 1773. Lacking the annals of the Concerts des Amateurs under Gossec, we can only surmise that symphonies concertantes figured earlier than this in their repertory. (Meude-Monpas says in the article on Gossec in his *Dictionnaire de musique* of 1787 that the orchestra for these concerts was the best staffed and disposed of all.) Framery throws some light on the subject in two essays in the *Journal de musique.* In the issue for August 1770, while reviewing the *Essai sur l'union de la poësie et de la musique* (1765) by François-Jean Chastellux, he takes issue with the following passage about German symphonists: "Leurs symphonies sont des espèce de *Concertos,* où les instruments brillent tous à leur tour, où ils s'agacent et se repondent, se disputent et se raccomodent" (p. 23). "It is clear from this description," says Framery,

[120]Barry S. Brook, "The Symphonie Concertante: Its Musical and Sociological Bases," *International Review of the Aesthetics and Sociology of Music* 6 (1975): 9–27.

[121]The Symphonie Concertante No. 13 in G of 1782 by Saint-Georges is edited in Brook, *La symphonie française*, 3: 147–69; it is in the "easy" violin key of G and consists of two movements, *Allegro* (with double exposition) and Rondeau. For samples of similar works by Davaux and Cambini, see Brook, 2: 308–12 and 417–25.

"that the author is not talking at all about ordinary German symphonies, which are masterpieces of unity and motivic simplicity, but about symphonies concertantes, a genre infinitely superior to concertos, extremely agreeable, and little known in France except at Paris, in some private houses, because of the difficulty of uniting enough skilled artists on all instruments in order to execute such pieces to the point of perfection."

The reference to private concerts points to musical forces such as those of the prince de Conti (under Gossec's musical leadership), the duc de Noailles (led from 1770 on by Carl Stamitz), and the baron de Bagge, who often recruited orchestral musicians in order to show off visiting soloists. In the March 1771 issue of the *Journal de musique,* while reviewing the Lenten season of the Concerts Spirituel, Framery painted a vivid picture of the institution's decline under Antoine Dauvergne's leadership. The old motets have been heard too often to pique one's curiosity, he says, and few composers cared to bother themselves with writing new ones, since they were not paid enough for their pains. That left tedious sonatas and long-winded concertos as the two main resources. "It should be symphonies concertantes that replace them. What better place for this kind of composition than that which should unite the most skilled virtuoso players of Paris of all kinds?"

Framery then caught himself up short, reflecting on the differences between what should be and what was. The disposition of the orchestra at the Concert Spirituel was abominable, he says, and would prevent the execution of such pieces. The first and second violins could neither see nor hear each other, and consequently lacked any kind of ensemble. The flutes and oboes were buried in the basses and lost all their effect, while the horns were badly placed as well, and the miserable organ, in the middle of everything, divided and destroyed the entire harmony. The chorus was far too numerous, but this would be easy to remedy.

To this unlovely picture Framery added another factor bearing on the financial condition of the concerts: "What opposes the innovation represented by the symphonies concertantes in addition to this: if one would have them, not only must they be well executed, but it will also be necessary to pay the price for them. Glory, as one knows, must be the principal motive of every artist, but glory is a distant goal, while profit is an immediate one, and it takes precedence." The implications of these remarks are several. Soloists would have to be paid better if the best players were to be lured back to the Tuileries to perform the latest kind of symphony with concertante parts. The orchestra, which needed a thorough shaking up, would have to rehearse more in order to succeed with them, because the symphonic part of the new genre demanded more coordination than the perfunctory accompaniments given the solo concertos Framery found so boring. And the parts for such works had to be paid for, too. Anything so much in demand by the public as the symphonies concertantes was bound to send their cost soaring, and there is some evidence that this actually happened.

Framery's hoped-for reform triumphed two years later in 1773. Immediately after the takeover of the Concert Spirituel by Gossec, Gaviniès, and Leduc, a symphonie concertante figured on nearly every program. It was placed in the middle of the concert and received more attention from the press than did the mostly anonymous symphonies that opened the programs. At their first concert on 25 March 1773, the new directors offered a symphonie concertante by Carl Stamitz with solo violin played by Pierre Leduc and solo oboe played by Gaetano Besozzi. This may be the same as the one that appeared under the composer's name in Sieber's catalogue of 1773. Three days later Capron and Guénin, violinists, appeared as soloists in a symphonie concertante by Davaux, presumably one of the two for this combination published by Bailleux in 1772, or else one of the two published in 1773; all four are in two movements without *Adagios.* On 4 April, the two Leduc brothers played the concertante parts in a work by Christian Bach. Sieber's catalogue of 1773 announced a symphonie concertante by this composer; it required cello and violin soloists.[122] Capron and Guénin reappeared on the concerts of 7 and 8 April 1773, a symphonie concertante by Davaux being specified as their vehicle on the second occasion.

On 9 April 1773, Pierre Leduc and the renowned cellist Jean-Pierre Duport appeared as soloists in a symphonie concertante (composer unknown, as is quite often the case). There was no symphonie concertante on the program of 10 April, but instrumental soloists were heard in a "Quatuor executé par quatre instruments." On 11–12 April there were symphonies concertantes of unspecified composers and executants. On 18 April, a symphonie concertante by Christian Bach was heard, and likely it was the same one that was heard two weeks earlier (most new works got at least two hearings). Two new violinists, Cambini and Imbault (the pupil of Gaviniès and later publisher), made their debut as soloists in a symphonie concertante by the former on 20 May. For some reason, the annals fail to describe concerts on the usual holy days until 8 December, when Paisible, Guénin, and Guérin appeared as soloists in a symphonie concertante by Davaux. The memorable year of 1773 ended with the traditional noëls at the two Christmas concerts, but these were not played at the organ by Balbastre, as in previous years. The mania of the public for the concertante brought forth from Simon Leduc a "Suite de noëls à plein orchestre mêlés de solos et d'echos concertants." The work has not survived, but its mere title is enough to show that the concertante idea was spilling over into other genres. Introduction of concertante wind parts into operatic arias furnishes another instance.

---

[122]Cari Johansson, *French Music Publisher's Catalogues,* facsimile 104; the cost of Bach's work, like the one by Carl Stamitz just mentioned, was 3 livres 12 sols, while single symphonies on the same list sold for 2 livres 8 sols; what is more, Sieber raised the prices of the former to 4 livres 4 sols in 1775, while symphonies stayed the same—an indication that the public could be made to pay more for what it preferred.

SAINT-GEORGES

The most colorful figure in Parisian music at the time was known simply as "the American." Born ca. 1739 on Guadeloupe, one of France's several colonies in the Caribbean, he was the son of a black woman and a French official, Monsieur de Boulogne. There cannot be many if any earlier instances of a musician born in the New World achieving fame in Europe. Joseph Boulogne de Saint-Georges first distinguished himself as an athlete and swordsman in Paris, where his father took him at an early age. He became a royal gendarme in his twenties, by which time he was also renowned as a dancer and as a violinist, the toast of Paris and, according to legend, a great favorite of the ladies. The whole improbable story seems like a fiction and did in fact give rise to a long novel. Could a mulatto have risen so high in the rival colonial empires ruled from London, Madrid, and Lisbon?

The standing of young Saint-Georges as a performer was such that, even before he was thirty, several works were dedicated to him. Gossec provided a biographical clue in the dedication of his trios Op. 9 of 1766, "À M. de Saint-George, Ecuyer, Gendarme de la Garde du Roi." He wrote: "Sir, the celebrated reputation you have acquired by your talent, and the favorable reception you have given artists, made me take the liberty of dedicating this work as an homage to the merit of so enlightened an amateur."[123] Gossec's delicately put "favorable reception" surely means that he had received money from the young man for music lessons, presumably in composition. The same year Antonio Lolli, one of the greatest virtuosos of the violin, dedicated *Deux concertos à violon* to Saint-Georges, an unlikely act of homage to so young a violinist unless Saint-Georges could play them, which he could, as his own concertos show. A certain Avoglio, violinist of the Concert Spirituel, dedicated *Six sonatas à violon seul* (Paris, 1768) to him. A poet sang his praises with this verse, published in the *Mercure* in 1768. Note that, as a child of the Muses, his acumen in dancing takes precedence even over his musical talents.

> Offspring of taste and genius, he
> > Was one the sacred valley bore,
> > Of Terpsichore nursling and competitor;
> And rival to the god of harmony,
> > Had he to music added poesy
> > Apollo's self he'd be mistaken for.[124]

In 1769 he joined Gossec's recently formed Concert des Amateurs. A master newly arrived in Paris, Carl Stamitz, dedicated his flute quartets as Op. 1 (1770) to

---

[123]La Laurencie, *L'école française de Violon,* 2: 454.
[124]Ibid., 2: 457. The English translation is from Lionel de La Laurencie, "The Chevalier de Saint-Georges: Violinist," *Musical Quarterly* 5 (1919): 74–85; 75.

Boulogne père with praises for having produced such a prodigy as a son. The violinistic exploits of young Saint-Georges suggest that he was a counterpart to
Schobert, the capital's most celebrated young harpsichord player during the 1760s.

The violin concerto and string quartet were two of Saint-Georges's main genres as a composer. Two concertos he had played with success at the Concert des
Amateurs were printed by Bailleux as Op. 2 in 1773, and nine more followed up
to Op. 8. His Op. 1, brought out by Sieber in 1773, was *Six quatuors à deux violons,
alto et basse.* There had been a flurry of flute quartets published in Paris, led by the
Mannheim composers Toeschi, Cannabich, and Carl Stamitz. Not until the
appearance of Boccherini in Paris during 1767–68 and the printing of his string
quartets (1767–69) did the new genre catch on definitively. Gossec led the way
with his Op. 15 in 1772. Carl Stamitz also contributed. Saint-Georges was another
pioneer with his 1773 set. When he returned to the genre in 1778 the set bore the
title *Six quartetto concertans.* Another set of six quartets came later. Besides string
quartets and violin concertos, his other specialty, as might be expected, was the
symphonie concertante with violin solos.

The violin concertos retain the three-movement sequence standard for the
genre. Their first movements adopt a sonata-form pattern, with clear second
themes and complete recapitulations.[125] High demands are made of the soloist,
with exploitation of the upper register exceeding that in any concertos before
Viotti's with the exception only of Lolli's.[126] Saint-Georges loved plunging from
high to low (Example 6.14). Lolli himself appeared at the Concert Spirituel playing sonatas and concertos of his own in 1764 and again in 1766, during which vis-

EXAMPLE 6.14. *Saint-Georges, Violin Concerto Op. 2 No.1, I*

its he met Saint-Georges, who may have taken the Italian's pyrotechnics as a
model for his own. For his slow movements Saint-Georges preferred the key of
tonic minor, enhancing the jocular and often folklike themes of his final Rondeaux. Formally, these finales are quite predictable, having one episode in the
dominant and one in tonic minor, surrounding returns of the refrain.

Some dozen symphonies concertantes were once known, of which eight are
extant. Bailleux printed the earliest, *Deux symphonies concertantes pour deux violons
principaux,* in 1775 (see Figure 6.10). The first is a work in the key of C with an ini-

[125]White, *From Vivaldi to Viotti,* p. 244.
[126]Ibid. The author quotes a stunning example from the third concerto as his example 4-10, p. 64.

tial *Allegro moderato* that stretches to three hundred measures, with a written-out cadenza.[127] The concluding movement is a Rondeau in cut time that observes the same predictable form as in the quartets. One unusual feature of the print was the presence of a complete part for cello as a possible substitute for the second violin.

Much of the composer's prolific output is lost. He wrote several opéras-comiques for the Théâtre Italien, of which little survives. His instrumental oeuvre has also suffered some regrettable losses. At the Concert Spirituel, for instance, he was represented by an often-performed clarinet concerto (lost) and a bassoon concerto (also lost). Grétry mentions a symphony "by the skilled artist Saint-George" that incorporated and reiterated the cadence formula of the forlana.[128] It does not survive. There are other symphonic works as well that are known only by catalogue entries, references, or incipits.

The composer was a man of wealth but hardly of leisure. In 1776 he succeeded Gossec as director of the Concert des Amateurs. He was tapped for the post of codirector of the Opéra around the same time. His appointment was withdrawn after Mademoiselles Arnould, Duplant, and Guimard complained in a petition to Queen Marie Antoinette that they could not possibly take orders from a mulatto. In early 1781 the Concert des Amateurs disbanded. Saint-Georges directed its replacement, the Concert de la Loge Olympique, a series satellite to one of the most famous Masonic lodges of the capital. He was an intermediary for the count d'Ogny in commissioning Haydn's six Paris symphonies for this orchestra.[129] His other responsibilities included a post in the service of the duke of Orléans as one of his huntsmen, for which he received a substantial annual salary. At the same time, he served the duke's morganatic wife Madame de Montessori as director of her private theater and concerts.

Saint-Georges's fortunes began to take a downturn with the death of the duke of Orléans in 1785. To recoup his losses the composer, among other enterprises, gave exhibition matches at Angelo's Fencing Academy in London. It was on this occasion that a young artist from Boston, Massachusetts, who was studying in London, Mather Brown, painted his portrait with sword in hand and violin in the background (Figure 6.11). Once again the New World recompensed the old one.

The vicissitudes of the composer-violinist's life during and after the Revolution have only occasionally to do with music. They bear mainly upon his prowess

---

[127]Le Chevalier de Saint-Georges, *Three Symphonic Works*, ed. Barry S. Brook and David Bain (The Symphony 1720–1840, Series D, Vol. 4) (New York, 1983).

[128]André-E.-M. Grétry, *Mémoires, ou essais sur la musique*, 3 vols. (Paris, 1789–94; reprint 1971), 2: 75. On the Forlana cadence, see Daniel Heartz, "A Venetian Dancing Master Teaches the Forlana: Lambranzi's *Balli teatrali*," *Journal of Musicology* 17 (1999): 136–51; 146–47.

[129]Bernard Harrison, *Haydn: The "Paris" Symphonies* (Cambridge, 1998), p. 1.

FIGURE 6.11. Mather Brown. Portrait of the Chevalier de Saint-Georges.

as an army captain and have been recounted at length elsewhere.[130] The exploits of a swashbuckling mulatto in the military are the stuff of novels. Of interest here are the heights that an amateur musician could reach in those days. Saint-Georges died in Paris at about the age of 60 in 1799.

A parallel figure among musical amateurs in Paris was the less colorful but equally talented Jean-Baptiste Davaux, born in 1742 at La Côte-St André in Dauphiné (the town where Berlioz was born in 1803). He went to Paris about 1767 and became one of the leading composer-violinists of the capital. Besides string quartets, his favorite genre was the symphonie concertante with two solo violins. His first were published around 1772 and were performed at the Concert Spirituel after 1773. Some thirteen of his symphonies concertantes survive, and they compare favorably with those of the professional composers in the same genre, the prolific Carl Stamitz (at least thirty-eight exemplars) and the incredibly fertile but shallow Giuseppe Cambini (over eighty).

Mozart heard one of Cambini's quartets at Mannheim and praised it when he subsequently met the composer at Paris. On 12 April 1778, a symphonie concertante with four winds by Cambini was performed at the Concert Spirituel. Wind soloists became more usual in the symphonie concertante toward 1780, but four winds was still a novelty at the Concert Spirituel in 1778. Mozart may have attempted to duplicate the work with his own symphonie concertante for the same four wind soloists. It did not come to performance at the Concert Spirituel, a failure for which Mozart blamed the machinations of Cambini.

The quatuor concertant produced a literature at Paris more abundant even than the symphonie concertante. It falls mainly in the last quarter of the century and will be considered here but briefly, as representing an appendage in the domain of chamber music to its symphonic cousin. As elsewhere, in France the string quartet evolved only gradually into a major genre. There were many isolated examples of the combination of two violins, viola, and cello, and it has been

---

[130]La Laurencie, *L'école française de violon*, 2: 449–500.

mentioned that the chamber symphonies of Gossec and others could also be played with only one on a part.

The string quartet was evidently deemed appropriate only to the more intimate dimensions of the salon, not to public concerts. Those of Boccherini are concertante in a sense peculiar to him, in that he made the cello part not only more obbligato than usual but also more prominent in display passages (Mozart's last string quartets likewise favor the cello, the instrument of the Prussian king for whom the pieces were written). After Boccherini's visit to Paris, publishers' catalogues began to fill up with "quatuors" and "quatuors concertants." Antoine Laurent Baudron's quartets published in 1768 are lost. Gossec's first string quartets (Op. 15, 1772) were preceded and prepared by his string trios (Op. 9, 1766) and his flute quartets (Op. 14, 1769). Other composers at Paris writing quartets, besides Saint-Georges, included the baron de Bagge himself, Carl Stamitz, Cambini, Gossec, Davaux, Guillaume Navoigille (a violinist who was also patronized by the baron de Bagge), Vachon, and Leduc (whose published quartets have been lost, unless they have survived in a manuscript of "Divertimenti à 4" attributed to him).[131]

Some of these works are called quatuors concertants when they are not particularly marked by concertante elements—either because the publisher is using the term in the older sense of one instrument to a part or, more likely, because the publisher wants to take advantage of a term that had become modish because of the symphonie concertante. Whether the label "concertant" was applied or not, concertante treatment of the instruments, especially the two violins, became increasingly frequent in French literature during the course of the 1770s. With the works of Étienne-Bernard-Joseph Barrière and Cambini published in 1776, the quatuor concertant achieved its classic formulation and became synonymous for the rest of the century with "Parisian quartet."[132]

The predominant scheme of the quatuor concertant is *Allegro*–Rondeau, without slow movement, a disposition that shows the close relationship to the symphonie concertante. *Allegro* movements do not deploy a double exposition, unlike their symphonic counterparts. Rather, they tend to have lyric ideas, one after another, for the majority of concertante exchanges. The minor mode becomes rare to the point of extinction in both quartets and symphonies of this type. A waning of interest in the minor mode, except as a means of contrast in the episodes of Rondeaux, goes along with a general lightening of content.

The seriousness with which Gossec and Leduc endowed French instrumen-

---

[131]On the remarkably fine and diverse production of string quartets in France see Philippe Oboussier, "The French String Quartet, 1770–1800," in *Music and the French Revolution,* ed. Malcolm Boyd (Cambridge, 1992), pp. 74–92. The author maintains that Paris was second only to Vienna in this genre.

[132]Janet M. Levy, "The Quatuor Concertant in Paris in the Latter Half of the Eighteenth Century" (Ph.D. dissertation, Stanford University, 1971). Includes a first movement from Barrière's Op. 1 of 1776, pp. 72–78.

tal music is rarely met in the tuneful but trivial works of Cambini, who led all others in productivity with his 174 quatuors concertants.[133] Publishing so many similar works points to a clientele of non-professional string players, insatiably eager to buy new music of easy accessibility and play it at home. If the quatuors concertants were not very challenging in content, they were at least moderately so in technique, and notably in the violin parts. The exchange of idiomatic figurations between the two violins, a heritage that stems especially from Sammartini and from Italian string music in general, led as naturally to the quatuor concertant as it did to the hundreds of symphonies concertantes with two solo violins.

The Keyboard

French keyboard music after 1730 rarely attained the high level of the French violin school. When François Couperin brought out the fourth and last book of his *Pièces de clavecin* in 1730, the art of music for solo harpsichord in France reached a pinnacle never again to be equaled in quality. Couperin le grand was inimitable, which may help explain why his successors looked elsewhere for inspiration—to Tartini (Barrière), Handel (Pierre Février), D. Scarlatti (Duphly and Armand-Louis Couperin), and more modern Italians like Alberti and Galuppi (Duphly and Balbastre).[134] Rameau alone seemed able to take Italian music in his stride, absorbing what he fancied while never abandoning his own musical personality, which was forged upon the richness and breadth of his early professional activities. Figures such as Balbastre, Daquin, and Duphly, however interesting and idiomatic they may have been, and although they were the best among a host of lesser lights, come nowhere near the stature of Couperin and Rameau. Armand-Louis Couperin, born in 1727, had a difficult time living up to the great name he bore, yet he was one of the most solidly grounded keyboard artists of his time. Compared with the best French violinists who were his contemporaries, he cuts a disappointing figure.

There was no falling off in the quality of keyboard instruments made in

---

[133]See Dieter Lutz Trimpert, *Die Quatuors Concertants von Giuseppe Cambini* (Mainzer Studien zur Musikwissenschaft 1) (Tutzing, 1967). Trimpert brings evidence that Parisian critics considered Cambini "un génie heureux et facile" (p. 26) but that a later German critic considered him far inferior to Boccherini and Pugnani (p. 25). Concerning his Op. 1 quartets, another critic wrote, "On y reconnoit la manière brillante qui caractérise toutes ses symphonies" (p. 28).

[134]David Fuller believes that the French grounding in the forms inherited from the seventeenth century—the various traditional dances, rondeaux, and chaconnes—did not prepare composers to grapple with the free expansion of material and dramatic use of modulation that characterizes the sonata (personal communication). Yet the French violinist-composers did succeed here, where the keyboard composers so often failed, which suggests how potent the violin was per se as a liberating (and Italianizing) force.

France. Superb harpsichords were constructed by François Étienne Blanchet and Pascal Taskin, and superb organs by the Cliquot family. Technical improvements were many, and they tended in the direction of giving both instruments more tone colors and greater dynamic range, with the possibilities of flexible dynamics as well. Little music survives worthy of those grand French organs of the later eighteenth century. Much of it was improvised, of course, as it had been for centuries and still is today. If such improvisations were of value, more of them ought to have been written down, if only for the commercial purpose of selling them to amateurs and organists in the provinces. Alas, there is only the pale reflection left in manuscripts and in the *Journeaux d'orgue* of Lasceux and Beauvarlet-Charpentier (father and son), and in the published works by these organists and by Corrette, Daquin, and Balbastre.

Claude-Bénigne Balbastre was the best-known Parisian organist of his day. Burney describes him at the height of his success in 1770 upon a visit to his fashionable church on the rue Saint Honoré.

> I went to St. Rocque, to hear the celebrated M. Balbastre, organist of that church, as well as of Notre Dame and the Concert spirituel. . . . The organ is an immense instrument, made not above twenty years ago [by Cliquot]; it has four sets of keys, with pedals; the great and choir organ communicate by a spring: the third row of keys is for the reed stops, and the upper for the echoes. This instrument has a very good effect below; but above the keys are intolerably noisy. M. Balbastre took a great deal of pains to entertain me; he performed in all styles in accompanying the choir. When the *Magnificat* was sung, he played likewise between each verse several minuets, fugues, imitations, and every species of music even to hunting pieces and jigs, without surprising or offending the congregation, as far as I was able to discover.

The eclectic and perhaps dubious tastes of Balbastre emerge as well from his organ solos at the Concert Spirituel, which were greatly applauded. He was partial to arrangements of opera overtures and variations on popular airs. His Concerto in D for organ solo is the first of its kind in France and profits from his familiarity with both Rameau and Vivaldi.[135]

Burney also heard Armand-Louis Couperin play at his church, Saint Gervais, where his ancestors had been organists. He praised him more highly than Balbastre but with some reservations: "his taste is not quite so modern, perhaps, as it might be; but allowance made for his time of life, for the taste of his nation, and for the changes music has undergone elsewhere, since his youth, he is an excellent organist; brilliant in execution, varied in his melodies, and masterly in mod-

---

[135]Claude-Bénigne Balbastre, *Organ Works,* ed. Nicolas Gorenstein, 3 vols. (Fleurian, 1994), 1: 20–39.

ulation."What Burney heard on this occasion were improvisations upon the alternate versets of the *Te Deum;* no written record survives of such music.[136]

There is no dearth, on the other hand, of surviving music for solo harpsichord. In this enormous literature, the old style in all its whimsy often sits cheek by jowl with insipid attempts to profit from the Alberti bass. Jacques Duphly, born in 1715, was a pupil of François Dagincour and brought out four books of *Pièces de clavecin* (1744, 1748, 1756, and 1768) that take the instrument to the last possible degree of idiomatic sophistication. It is symptomatic that Duphly, unlike most other keyboard artists and teachers, renounced the organ "pour ne pas se gâter la main." The third book by Duphly has two sonatas accompanied by violin disguised among its pieces. It reaches a new level for subtle nuances of articulation and ornamentation, and is the highest in quality, after which the fourth book is largely a letdown, a capitulation to the banalities reigning in other keyboard collections. Duphly died the day after the storming of the Bastille, and Armand-Louis Couperin died a few months earlier. Balbastre had the dubious luck to live on longer and write variations for fortepiano on the "Marseillaise." Meanwhile, the proud old clavecin and its music gradually went the way of the ancien régime.

ACCOMPANIED AND SOLO WORKS

It is a comment of some severity on the *clavecinistes* that the most original departures affecting the literature of their instrument were made by musicians who were not primarily keyboard players. Mondonville, the virtuoso violinist, enriched the last decades of the harpsichord by marrying it with the Italian sonata for solo violin. This combination of violin and harpsichord on an equal basis represented such an original idea that many imitations followed, among them, collections by Boismortier and Corrette (1742), by Charles-François Clément (1743), and by Guillemain (1745). Even the great Rameau paid hommage to Mondonville and cites him as a model for his own *Pièces de clavecin en concerts* (1741), although they are quite different, having three independent parts—harpsichord, treble instrument, and viol—and their texture owes more to the extremely skillful orchestral writing in Rameau's operas.

Accompanied keyboard sonatas preceded the sonata for keyboard alone in France and paved the way for it. The cellist Jean Barrière published the first French solo sonatas for harpsichord. He was in a good position to make this innovation, having studied cello in Italy with Francischello (Francesco Alborea) from 1736 to 1738. On his return to Paris, Barrière appeared at the Concert Spirituel as a soloist playing cello sonatas of his own composition and published a third volume of sonatas for his instrument. A fourth volume followed in 1740, after which came a

---

[136]*Armand-Louis Couperin: Selected Works for Keyboard,* ed. David Fuller, 2 vols. (Recent Researches in the Music of the Pre-Classical, Classical and Early Romantic Eras, 1–2) (Madison, Wis., 1975), Preface, p. vii.

volume for treble viol *(Livre V),* then the *Sonates et pièces pour le clavecin (livre VI).* The six keyboard sonatas of the last collection (ca. 1741) are free arrangements of the preceding viol sonatas. In the course of his published works (1733–ca. 1741), Barrière made the transition from the four-movement Italian chamber sonata to the newer three-movement patterns and to a very galant idiom. The Aria that serves as the finale of his Op. 6 No. 2 provides a typical specimen.

A parallel case to Barrière is that of the Chevalier d'Herbain, born in 1739, a French military officer who was in Italy in the early 1750s and wrote some Italian intermezzi. Their success led to subsequent stageworks written for Paris. He also put his Italian experiences to good use by enriching the French harpsichord literature with its most progressive works to that date, *VI Sonates de clavecin avec un violon ou flûte d'accompagnement* (1756). With these works the galant keyboard sonata, adumbrated by Mondonville and by Barrière's arrangements, made a decisive appearance in France. A year earlier Philidor's *Art de la modulation,* a set of instrumental quartets, achieved a similar breakthrough.

Perhaps the most blithely melodious sonatas in this repertory are those by an Italian, Felice Giardini. Born at Turin in 1716, he appeared as a violin soloist playing a concerto and duets (with Venier) of his own composition at the Concert Spirituel in 1750. Two years later he married the French singer and dancer Violante Vestris. His *Sei sonate di cembalo con violino o flauto traverso* (ca. 1755) were printed at London and at Paris, where he evidently picked up this Franco-Italian genre. He was a keyboard player himself, although he is said to have given up appearing as a harpsichord soloist after he heard the outstanding playing of a Rameau pupil, Madame de Saint Maur. In any case, his sonatas are perfectly idiomatic for both instruments, although not very demanding, and his melodic invention is more vocal than that of Mondonville or any of the other French composers of his generation. Most of his career was spent in England, where he ranked as one of the greatest violinists and orchestra leaders.

During the 1760s keyboard composers continued to deliver accompanied sonatas to the voracious music publishing houses at Paris. Armand-Louis Couperin made obeisance to the fashion in 1765 with his Op. 2, *Sonates en pièces de clavecin avec accompagnement de violon,* but these are not among his best pieces. A more interesting set that came out the same year was by Philibert Cardonne, royal chamber musician, *Premier livre de sonates pour le clavecin, avec accompagnement de violon obligé* (Op. 3). Three fine keyboard composers who came to Paris from elsewhere are the Alsatian Leontzi Honauer; Johann Gottfried Eckard of Augsburg, who appeared in print with *Six sonates pour le clavecin, dédiées à Monsieur Gaviniès* (1763); and Johann Schobert, a Silesian according to Grimm, among these the most prolific. They bring us into the immediate artistic vicinity of Mozart himself, who capped the whole evolution with his solo and accompanied sonatas.

Keyboard pieces with parts for more than one accompanying instrument, pioneered by Rameau, were published in 1766 by Philippe Valois. They followed three years behind the Op. 4 of Anton Fils, *Six sonates en trio pour le clavecin, violon et basse,* published by La Chevardière. Armand-Louis Couperin contributed to this medium in 1770 with his *Sonates en trio pour le clavecin, violon et violoncelle* (Op. 3). According to their modern editor, his model was not the Germans working in France, as one might have expected, but the chamber music of Italians such as Giardini, Sammartini, Pugnani, and Ferrari.[137] In this field too, then, as we have seen above with the violinists, the massive wave of Italian inspiration passing over French instrumental music did not give way until sometime after 1770. Galant chamber music with obbligato harpsichord is represented in a few more collections by French composers such as Simon Simon and Jean-François Tapray in the years around 1770.

By 1781, when Marie-Alexandre Guénin published three fine accompanied sonatas as his Op. 5, this genre reached its high point in France.[138] His collection was called *Trois sonates pour le clavecin ou le piano forte avec accompagnement de violon* and bore a dedication to the daughter of the prince de Condé. Guénin sounds amazingly close to Mozart, which provides a further argument for those critics who have maintained that Mozart was indebted to French instrumental music. Carl Friedrich Cramer in the first volume of his *Magazin der Musik* (1783) wrote that Guénin's sonatas deserved preference over the mass of keyboard sonatas published in France: "they are very euphonious and brilliantly written, and the violin is no mere accompanist, but also has its full share of work." Guénin's sonatas often betray symphonic ambitions, with *crescendi* and *decrescendi, coups d'archet,* and other orchestral effects.

SCHOBERT

The most successful keyboard artist in Paris from ca. 1760 until his untimely death in 1767 was Johann Schobert. Estimates of his birthdate range from 1730 to 1740; thus, he was roughly contemporary with his main rival Eckard, born in 1735, like Christian Bach. Grimm is our best source of information on Schobert, and there is no reason to distrust his claim, made twice in the *Correspondance littéraire,* that the composer came from Silesia. Up until its conquest by Prussia in the 1740s,

---

[137]Ibid., p. xiii.

[138]La Laurencie, *L'école française de violon,* 2: 413–15, lists the prolific production of keyboard and violin sonatas at Paris from 1760 to 1780 and gives his highest praise to those of Guénin, who represents "une sorte de Mozartisme avant la lettre, avant Mozart." Eduard Reeser, *De Klaviersonate met Vioolbegleiding in het Parisjsche Musiekleven ten Tijde van Mozart* (Rotterdam, 1939) concludes his detailed study of this repertory with twelve sonatas in score, including some of Guénin's. Reeser quotes examples from the Op. 1 sonatas (1772) by Nicolas Séjan that offer particularly attractive examples of the "singing *Allegro*" (pp. 98–99).

Silesia belonged to the Habsburg empire. It was populated by more Slavs (Czechs and Poles) than Germans. A young Silesian musician would naturally gravitate to Vienna, just as did young Czech musicians in the persons of Gluck, Franz Benda, Joseph Anton Steffan, and possibly Stamitz. If Schobert did go to Vienna in the 1750s, a likely teacher for him would have been Wagenseil, whose galant keyboard sonatas were models for many students and whose musical importance for Schobert has been demonstrated.[139] The virtuoso keyboard demands made by Wagenseil's pupil Steffan are even more in line with Schobert's.

Gerber in his *Lexikon* (1792) claimed that, before arriving in Paris around 1760, Schobert was a teacher in Strasbourg, his native city. Gerber was correct about Schobert's teaching in Strasbourg—it is corroborated by other evidence. Burney elaborated on Gerber by claiming that Schobert also published an early collection in the Alsatian capital, but it has never been found. Strasbourg was close to Mannheim and there were many musical connections between the two centers, as instanced by Richter's relocation from one to the other. One of Schobert's dedicatees was an official of the Palatine duke of Zweibrücken, a close ally and relative of Carl Theodore. Of course the connection could have been made in Paris. What seems certain in any case is that Schobert knew music by Stamitz and other Mannheimers. He may even have heard the famous orchestra under Cannabich.

Schobert's talents earned him the patronage of one of the peers of the realm, Louis François de Bourbon-Condé, prince de Conti, the king's cousin, who lived in great splendor at the Hôtel du Temple.[140] Conti had taken many of La Pouplinière's musicians into his service, loved music, and provided a locale for concerts second to none. Thus Schobert fell heir to a tradition of fine chamber and orchestral music. He resided on the rue du Temple near his master and sold publications of his music there. Unlike many other musicians newly arrived in Paris, he did not perform or compose for the Concert Spirituel (although one of his concertos for keyboard was played there as late as 1783).

Schobert reaped monetary rewards not only from selling his many publications: almost all of them bore dedications. Several women figure among his dedicatees and some were surely wealthy personal pupils. One nonpupil is the city's most celebrated harpsichord player, Madame Brillon de Joüy, whose musical salon rivaled those of the prince de Conti and baron de Bagge. Financial success allowed the composer to marry a Frenchwoman, to whom their son Antoine was born on 9 March 1765.

Table 6.1 presents the works as they are described on title pages. All are for

[139]Hans David, *Schobert als Sonatenkomponist* (Leipzig, 1928), p. 62.
[140]Herbert C. Turrentine, "The Prince de Conti: A Royal Patron of Music," *Musical Quarterly* 54 (1968): 309–15.

solo harpsichord, accompanied or not. None bears a date, but Op. 7 was advertised in 1764. The titles say precisely what forces are required or suggested. Thus Op. 4 has no violin part ad libitum. In the concertos of Opp. 11, 12, 13, and 15, the horns alone are ad libitum, the rest of the orchestral parts being essential to play the tuttis. All three parts are essential in Op. 16. The titles of Opp. 9 and 10 suggest that "ad libitum" and "qui peuvent se jouer" mean the same thing. Much effort went into the subordinate parts. It is a pity to omit them. The horn parts of Opp. 9 and 10 in particular invent a new kind of chamber music, inspired no doubt by Conti's fine horn players.

TABLE 6.1. Publications of Schobert's Music in Paris during the 1760s

---

Opus 1. *Sonates pour le clavecin qui peuvent se jouer avec l'accompagnement du violon*

2. *Sonates pour le clavecin qui peuvent se jouer avec l'accompagnement du violon*

3. *Sonates pour le clavecin qui peuvent se jouer avec l'accompagnement du violon*

4. *Sonates pour le clavecin*

5. *Sonates pour le clavecin avec accompagnement de violon ad libitum*

6. *Sonates en trio pour le clavecin avec accompagnement de violon et basse ad libitum*

7. *Sonates en quatuor pour le clavecin avec accompagnement de deux violons et basse ad libitum*

8. *II Sonates pour le clavecin avec accompagnement de violon*

9. *Sinfonies pour le clavecin avec accompagnement de violon, cors ad libitum*

10. *Sinfonies pour le clavecin seul qui peuvent se jouer avec accompagnement de violon et cors de chasse*

11. *Concerto pour le clavecin avec accompagnement de deux violons, deux cors de chasse ad libitum, alto et basse*

12. *Concerto II pour le clavecin, avec accompagnement de deux violon, deux oboe, deux cors de chasse ad libitum, alto et la basse*

13. *Concerto pastorale pour le clavecin, avec accompagnement de deux violon, deux cors de chasse ad libitum, alto et basse*

14. *Six sonates pour le clavecin . . . les parties d'accompagnement sont ad libitum*

15. *Concerto IV pour le clavecin avec accompagnement de deux violons, deux cors de chasse ad libitum, alto et basse*

16. *Quatre trio pour le clavecin, violon et basse*

17. *IV Sonates pour le clavecin avec accompagnement de violon*

18. *Concerto V pour le Clavecin avec accompagnement de deux Violons et une basse*

Schobert sought to expand his professional activities in 1765 by writing an opèra-comique for the Théâtre Italien, a failure that elicited Grimm's first description of the master. Grimm refers to him as the young harpsichordist of the prince de Conti's music. His highest praises went to Eckard, whom he considered the stronger composer and whose playing was full of sensibility, done with a surprisingly light touch, he said.

> Schobert is Silesian. He has been in France for five or six years. . . . He is the more brilliant player and the more agreeable, which are also the characteristics of his compo-

sition. Thus he generally pleases more than his rival, but he does not come close to him as to the value and choice of ideas. The opera *Le Garde-Chasse* is his trial piece in vocal music. This musician knows musical effects; his harmony is pure and does not lack magic, but his ideas, although agreeable, are common. . . . He earns lots of money from his engraved harpsichord pieces. I believe he will do well to stick to them and give up this project of writing for the voice.[141]

What Grimm found common in Schobert's musical ideas might possibly be illustrated by a piece like the Sonata in D of Op. 5 (Example 6.15). Here the composer is at his most symphonic. The three hammerstrokes spread over four octaves suggest a hundred Italian opera overtures in the key of D or, more specifically, Stamitz's several symphonies in this key that begin the same way. The following unison and octave passages also seem symphonic. Chromatic rises in octaves as *crescendo* passages are not unknown in Stamitz's symphonies (for instance, in the late E♭-1). Of course, the harpsichord could not reproduce such an orchestral *crescendo* literally, but the rising pitch may have created the illusion of one in the ears of listeners. There is also a chromatic rise in unison from the third to the fifth degree in the very first number of Pergolesi's *La serva padrona*. Grimm's "common" could mean low class or buffo. Might his slight antipathy to Schobert be that of a German toward a Slav?

Burney returned from Paris to London in 1766 with numerous works by Schobert, whom he claimed to have introduced to the English, works that subsequently enjoyed an enormous vogue in England. Publishers in both London and Amsterdam took them up. In the *History* Burney explained that "Schobert is well entitled to a niche in an English history of Music, his pieces for the harpsichord having been for many years the delight of all those who could play or hear them." He explained this partly in terms of the harpsichord's continued supremacy.

> His style never pleased in Germany so much as in England and France. Those of Emanuel Bach's party allowed him to be a man of genius, but spoiled by his affectation of a new and extraordinary style, accusing him of too frequently repeating himself. The truth is, the spirit and fire of his pieces require not only a strong hand but a *harpsichord,* to give them all their force and effect. They are too rapid, and have too many notes for clavichords or piano fortes, which supply the place of harpsichords in Germany.

Daniel Schubart heaped praises in his *Ideen* on the "fiery harpsichord player" and said he completely understood the nature of this instrument. "The *Adagio* was his

[141]*Correspondance littéraire, philosphique et critique par Grimm, Diderot, Raynal, Meister, etc.,* ed. Maurice Tourneux, 16 vols. (Paris, 1877–82), December 1765, translated after Georges de Saint-Foix, "Les premiers pianistes parisiens, Jean Schobert, vers 1740–1767," *La revue musicale* 3, no. 10 (1922): 121–36. Saint-Foix disagreed with Riemann on nearly everything touching Schobert, except that both of them struggled against the evidence to make him a pianist.

EXAMPLE 6.15. *Schobert, Sonata Op. 5 No. 1, I*

only weakness, and this was because he failed to study the clavichord enough, and strangled expression with runs and overdone ornaments." Schubart's claims that Schobert was his relative with a misspelled name are generally dismissed.

To Burney's great credit he guessed the source of Schobert's thunderous fulminations.

> The novelty and merit of Schobert's compositions seem to consist in the introduction of the symphonic, or modern overture style, upon the harpsichord, and by light and shade, alternate agitation and tranquility, imitating the effects of an orchestra. The general use of piano fortes, for which the present compositions for keyed-instruments

EXAMPLE 6.16. *Schobert, Trio Op. 16 No. 4*

are chiefly written, has more contributed to lessen the favour of Schobert's pieces, than their want of merit.

By the time this was published in 1789 the harpsichord was in full retreat.

French harpsichords were celebrated for their delicacy and sweetness of tone. Those by the Blanchet dynasty and its successor, Taskin, were highly prized. Typically they were two-manual instruments, with strings of 8', 8', and 4', a sliding

b. III

coupler, and a compas of F' to f'''. Schobert seemed determined to show off their power. He often took advantage of the lowest bass tones with his left-hand octave doublings. His partiality to flat keys, particularly F and B♭, may have been connected to his desire to sound the instrument's lowest tone. In fact he ranged quickly in his pieces over the entire compass, and this does not seem at all characteristic of his French contemporaries among *clavecinistes*. His rattling octaves up and down the keyboard often bear resemblance to latter-day transcriptions of Stamitz; for example, the "Klavierauszug" included with the editions by Hugo Riemann in the *Denkmäler der Tonkunst*.

Gerber praised Schobert for the orginality of his brio and passion [Schwärmende], saying he knew how to mix them here and there with a judicious cantabile. He also saw in him a progression toward greater sophistication:"his last works have, besides a greater variety in modulation, a nobler gait and more simplicity." Mozart must have agreed because he made his most direct borrowing from the late and possibly posthumous Op. 17.[142] The Trio in F Op. 16 No. 4 offers another test case for Gerber's claims (Example 6.16ab). The violin shares the the-

---

[142]The *Andante* of K. 39 is from Schobert's Op. 17 No. 1 and saw further use in Mozart's A minor piano sonata, K. 310, composed in Paris in 1778. See *Haydn, Mozart*, p. 593.

matic material with the harpsichord. The bass, well suited to a cello, sustains tones that the left hand of the keyboard player only touches briefly and has some dialogue with the other two players. The main theme of the *Andante* is a catchy tune, easily remembered, although constructed over the cliché of a bass that descends an octave. In the seconda parte this complex returns in tonic minor, which is nothing unusual in either Steffan or Wagenseil but is more protracted here, and emphasized by a change of key signature from one to four flats before *Majeur* returns. Note that a welcome three-measure phrase intervenes before the return of the initial four-measure one in the violin. Although much of Schobert's music falls into strictly regular periods, an exception such as this does lend occasional relief. By answering with the main theme in the dominant the violin revives a characteristic of the old trio sonata.

The two middle movements of the Trio in F are less interesting than the outer movements—all movements are in tonic F, which works against the variety needed to maintain interest. The first is a Polonaise in 3/4 marked *Andante*. A Menuetto in 3/4 follows, sounding too much like the Polonaise, even though the violin and bass combine to sing the main melody together, and a *minore* trio is added. Schobert was fond of *minore* trios, and some of them sound quite as mournful as those of Steffan. Relief from the sameness of motion of the middle movements comes with the sparkling *Presto* finale in 2/4 (Example 6.14b). Here the harpsichord unleashes a torrent of sixteenth notes well suited to the right hand and to the violin, which then takes up the theme. The effect is similar to that in some of Haydn's "Gypsy" rondos in perpetual motion. Formally, the *Presto*, like the opening *Andante,* is a sonata form with both parts repeated. The similarity of this theme and its descending bass to the opening of the first movement belies the claim that "the interrelation of movements by similar incipits appears not to have interested Schobert."[143] This is a mature and attractive feature of the Trio, which, all in all, justifies Gerber's claims to a greater sophistication in the last works. Much of Schobert's keyboard writing is blustery and symphonic, but here there is no denying him finesse in a truly chamber music style.

Schobert's brief life ended horribly on 28 August 1767 after he, with family and friends, mistook poisonous mushrooms for safe ones. Grimm related the incident at length and in gruesome detail, with obvious intent to create a shudder in his elite readership. From this he went on to reiterate his preference for Eckard, which can only sound like self-justification after Schobert had published so much and Eckard so little.

---

[143]William S. Newman, *The Sonata in the Classic Era,* 3rd ed. (New York, 1983), p. 632.

The compositions of Schobert were charming. He did not have the precious ideas of his rival but he had a superior knowledge of the effects and magic of harmony, and he wrote with great facility, while Eckard achieved things of genius only with difficulty. The latter pardoned himself in nothing, and Schobert was in all of a more easy character. He perished in the flower of his age. Schobert was Silesian.[144]

Schobert was inventive in many respects and his harpsichord works with accompaniment helped mold one of the predominant genres of the time. Boccherini, who arrived in Paris just after Schobert's death, learned from him how to write his Op. 5 harpsichord sonatas with violin, which he dedicated to Madame Brillon de Joüy in 1768. Many others imitated Schobert's manner, said Gerber, "but they were mostly unfortunate, being able to match his dexterity, but not his spirit." A French critic of more recent times judged that Schobert stood far above the other foreigners in Paris: "Honauer, Eckard, Raupach and the harpists Meyer and [Christian] Hochbrucker were scarcely more than competent performers . . . sometimes a pretty and expressive *andante,* derived very often from memories of our opéra-comique and notably from the romances of a Philidor or Monsigny, but how many examples of *allegros* as empty as they are brilliant!"[145]

FORTEPIANO VERSUS HARPSICHORD

The fortepiano did not gain a firm foothold in France until the 1760s. First mention of it on a title page appeared in Eckard's *Deux sonates pour le clavecin ou le pianoforte* (Paris, 1764); he had mentioned the instrument in the preface to his 1763 collection. Eckard requested a dynamic range from *pianissimo* to *forte,* with several gradations in between. La Borde erroneously says that Eckard was one of the first to use the Alberti bass in France, but fails to note that he was a pioneer of the fortepiano, at least with respect to Paris. Part of the reason for the longevity of the clavecin lay in the ingenuity of builders like Taskin, whose knee levers and other devices gave the older instrument some of the dynamic flexibility so admired in the violin. But the days of the quilled instrument were numbered when the fortepiano was gradually altered and its volume increased to the point that it became a viable concert instrument. Its inventors had never intended it as more than a chamber instrument. The newcomer appeared in public at Paris in 1768, perhaps for the first time, at the Concert Spirituel, where some solo pieces by Romain de Brasseur were executed by his fifteen-year-old pupil, Mademoiselle

---

[144]*Correspondance littéraire,* 15 September 1767. The second sentence began, "Il n'avait pas les idées précieuses de son émule," mistranslated in the article "Schobert," *New Grove,* as "He had no valuable ideas to be emulated." This nonsense is contradicted by his many emulators, including Mozart both in his early accompanied sonatas and later. The error remains uncorrected in *New Grove,* 2nd ed.
[145]Saint-Foix, "Les premiers pianistes parisiens," pp. 125–26.

Lechantre (in May of 1771 the *Mercure* advertised under his name *Trois sonates pour le clavecin ou pour le pianoforte, Op. 1*). In 1769 two still younger soloists capitalized on the same novelty at the Concert Spirituel, but pianists began to assume a large place in the offerings of this series only in the 1780s.

When Burney was in Paris in the spring of 1770 he heard Madame Brillon de Joüy play her own sonatas, "both on the harpsichord and *piano forte,* accompanied on the violin by M. Pagin." The prolific Henri-Joseph Rigel dedicated one of his several sets of accompanied sonatas (Op. 7, ca. 1771) to the same lady, described as "célèbre pianiste mondaine" (thus coining the word *pianist*?). In 1771 Christian Bach and Burney were commissioned by Diderot to select a small square piano made by Johannes Zumpe for the philosospher's only surviving child, Angélique, who was described by both Philidor and Burney as one of the best keyboard players in Paris and for whom Grimm had procured a supply of Italian and German keyboard sonatas. Another lady amateur, Madame Victor Louis Bayon, brought out *Six sonates pour le clavecin ou le piano forte dont trois avec accompagnement de violon obligé* in 1768. These are charming Italianate pieces in two or three movements, good enough to attract the attention of Christian Bach, who once owned the copy now in the British Library. The association of women musicians with the keyboard was as strong in France as elsewhere. In Michel Corrette's *Maître de clavecin pour l'accompagnement* (1753), there is an engraved frontispiece showing a lady at a double-manual harpsichord, reading from music, while a gentleman violinist stands behind and accompanies her (Figure 6.12). Other visual illustrations that make the same point are very numerous throughout the century, and not only in France. The keyboard instrument most often pictured from the 1780s on is the fortepiano.

A ton gré, divine harmonie,
Je sens, avec ravissement,

Le feu rapide du génie,
Ou la douceur du sentiment.

FIGURE 6.12. Michel Corrette. *Le maître de clavecin* (1753), frontispiece.

Even the last masters of the clavecin—the professional musicians, that is to say—began to take up the fortepiano in the 1770s. Balbastre told Taskin when he first heard an English piano, "This newcomer will never dethrone the majestic harpsichord."[146] He must have changed his mind as he encountered more and better instruments. At the Concert Spirituel of 18 April 1770, there is mention of "Plusieurs morceaux composés et executés par Balbastre sur son forte piano auquel il a ajouté un jeu de flûte executé par Cliquot." Shortly thereafter Balbastre published a *Recueil de noëls formant quatre suittes avec variations pour le clavecin et le forte-piano* (Paris, without date, but announced in a catalogue of December 1770). There is also evidence to show that Balbastre took his fortepiano with him to play in Parisian homes. One of the century's most illustrious salons was that of Madame du Deffand, who wrote to Voltaire on 24 November 1774, that she had already secured Balbastre to play noëls at her Christmas Eve supper, "Je me suis déjà assuré de Balbastre qui jouera sur son forte-piano une longue suite de Noëls." Voltaire replied testily, calling the piano "un instrument de chaudronnier [ironmonger] en comparison du clavecin."[147] He, and many others who had been raised to the sounds of the noble harpsichord, remained loyal to it.

The first of Balbastre's published noël variations is of the variety that progresses with ever smaller diminution, variation by variation, but in general he avoids so mechanical a procedure. His use of hand-crossings in the variations on the fourth noël ("Ah ma Voisine es-tu fachée?") is similar to that in the fourth variation of Mozart's keyboard Sonata in A (K. 331 with the "Rondo alla Turca" finale). Armand-Louis Couperin wrote his *Aria con Variazione*, a manuscript work of 1781, so as to take advantage of the dynamic possibilities of the fortepiano.[148]

There is evidence that the fortepiano and harpsichord fought for supremacy in France right up to the end of the century. Taskin was still making new harpsichords and repairing old ones in considerable quantity in 1792. Some composers pitted the fortepiano against the harpsichord in the same work, as did Rigel in three sonatas (ca. 1775) and Tapray in four symphonies concertantes written between 1778 and 1782. If the older instrument prevailed at Versailles, as seems to have been the case,[149] it was not so at Paris. When the École Royale de Chant opened in 1784, there were seven pianos on hand for lessons but only one harpsichord, which was for continuo playing (the continuo practice remained an indispensable technique of compositional training to the end of the century and beyond). Taskin made his first fortepiano in 1776, and in 1784 he imported four

[146]*C. B. Balbastre: Pièces de clavecin, d'orgue, et de forte piano*, ed. Alan Curtis (Paris, 1974), p. iv (Le pupitre 52). See *Haydn, Mozart*, plate IV, for a reproduction of the painting of a harpsichord once in the possession of Balbastre, depicting scenes from Rameau's *Castor et Pollux*. Unfortunately, the plate is reversed and its colors fail to convey the original's contrast of red (Hades) with the cool shades in green and blue (Elysium).
[147]Béatrice Didier, *La musique des lumières* (Paris, 1985), p. 264.
[148]According to David Fuller, who includes the piece in his edition *Armand-Louis Couperin: Selected Works*, 2: 26–30.
[149]Sibyl Marcuse, "The Instruments in the King's Library at Versailles," *Galpin Society Journal* 14 (1961): 34–36.

Broadwood pianos from London.[150] By this time a whole new school of pianoforte makers was springing to life in France, led by the brothers Erard, who established their long-lived firm at Paris by 1777.

The experts on this subject selected 1780 as the cutoff date for their inventory of harpsichord music, citing the prominent organist Nicolas Séjan as a pivotal figure and "one of the very best French keyboard composers of the period."[151] Séjan's first book of ca. 1772, *Six sonates pour le clavecin,* with an optional violin part, carries an annotation on the title page saying that "some of these pieces can be played on the piano forte." The composer's next publication, *Recueil de pièces pour le clavecin ou le piano forte dans le genre gracieux et gay* (1783) is liberally sprinkled with dynamic markings, clearly showing preference for the fortepiano. The triumph of the newer instrument was sealed by the time Meude-Monpas brought out his *Dictionnaire de musique* in 1787. He defined "Forte-Piano" as "un instrument à touches, semblable à peu près au clavecin, mais qui lui est supérieur, en ce qu'il marque les *forte* et les *piano* que le clavecin ne peut pas rendre." That the instrument's main attraction was epitomized by its very name did nothing to hinder its conquering advance.

Burney, in his article on Johann Schroeter in the Rees *Cyclopaedia,* claimed that Schroeter was the first in England to demonstrate the true art of playing the fortepiano.

> We were unwilling to give up the harpsichord, and thought the tone of the piano-forte spiritless and insipid, till experience and better instruments vanquished our prejudices and the expression and the *chiar'oscuro* in performing music expressly composed for that instrument, made us amends for the want of brilliancy in the tone so much, that we soon found the scratching of the quill in the harpsichord intolerable, compared with the tone produced by the hammer.

Schroeter flourished in London mainly between the death of Christian Bach in 1782 and his own early death in 1788. Burney's evaluation confirms the triumph of the fortepiano over the harpsichord by the 1780s.

[150]Raymond Russell, *The Harpsichord and Clavichord* (London, 1959), p. 60.
[151]Bruce Gustafson and David Fuller, *A Catalogue of French Harpsichord Music 1699–1780* (London, 1990), p. 13.

7

Opéra-Comique

Vaudeville Comedy

SPRUNG from lowly origins, opéra-comique was destined to become one of the century's most highly prized genres of musical theater. Its principal Parisian homes were the Théâtre Italien and the Théâtre de la Foire. The real reasons Louis XIV abolished the former in 1697 were personal disinterest and financial considerations.[1] The Italians left behind a large repertory of plays. Those in French benefitted from two collective editions put together by Evaristo Gherardi, the Harlequin of the dismissed company.[2] The Théâtres de la Foire, or Forains as they were called, appropriated much from the repertory of the Italians. No copyright existed to prevent them from doing so. They entered the new century in a relatively flourishing state, although they continued to be harassed by the Opéra and the Comédie Française. Their shows teemed with popular songs (vaudevilles), dancing, gymnastics, and bawdry.

Little of lasting value might have come from these coarse entertainments at the fairs had not a prominent author, Alain Lesage, joined ranks with the Forains.

---

[1]Virginia Scott, *The Commedia dell'Arte in Paris, 1644–1697* (Charlottesville, Va., 1990), pp. 330–31.

[2]Evaristo Gherardi, *Le théâtre italien, ou le recueil de toutes les scènes françoises qui ont esté jouées sur le théâtre italien de l'Hostel de Bourgogne* (Paris, 1694); and *Le théâtre italien, ou le recueil général de toutes les comédies et scènes françoises jouées par les comédiens du roy, pendant tout le temps qu'ils ont été au service*, 6 vols. (Paris, 1700).

He had already triumphed with two literary comedies for the Comédie Française, *Crispin rival de son maître* (1707) and *Turcaret* (1709). In 1712 Lesage wrote *Arlequin, roi de Sérendib,* which was successfully staged at the Foire Saint Germain of early 1713, even though the characters could not sing (a ban enforced at the time by the Opéra) but had to rely upon the audience to sing the verses, which were unfurled on banners above the stage. In this three-act play Lesage parodied over sixty existing tunes, ranging all the way from street songs to favorite airs by Lully.[3]

Lesage was a master at picking just the right song for the dramatic situation, and often its original label (*timbre*), text, or music—possibly all three—served as commentary on his new verse. He also used parody in the wider sense with great flair by satirizing what was being played in the official theaters. Thus *Arlequin roi de Sérendib* ends with a hilarious takeoff on the sacrifice scene in *Iphigénie en Tauride* by Henry Desmarets and André Campra then being performed at the Opéra. In *Télémaque* (1715) Lesage parodied the entire tragédie-lyrique of the same name by Pellegrin and Destouches (1714). This work managed to introduce some spoken dialogue between songs (in spite of the monopoly on speaking in French held by the Comédie Française). It is therefore held to mark the arrival of opéra-comique at its first stage of generic perfection. The term by which the genre became known is as old as the genre itself.[4]

The Régence (1715–23) was a heady time for the Forains, as Lesage and several scarcely less talented poets among his collaborators soared from one triumph to another. Suffice it to mention Lesage's *Le monde renversé* (1718), which was revived many times in Paris, to which it held up a mirror reflecting corruption and fatuity. Other cities saw it, too, for it provided the basis for Telemann's Singspiel *Die verkehrte Welt* of 1728 for Hamburg and for Gluck's opéra-comique for Vienna in 1758. In 1716 the regent called to Paris a troupe of Italian players under the leadership of Luigi Riccoboni. Such was the popular success of the Forains that the new Italians were often forced to imitate them. But the Italians once again became a royal troupe, which eventually gave them the upper hand. Opéra-comique, like the Théâtre Italien, was accorded the tribute of a multivolume edition, edited by Lesage and D'Orneval, *Le théâtre de la Foire ou l'opéra comique,* ten volumes brought out in several editions at Paris between 1721 and 1737 and copied in pirated form in other centers. Bernard Picart added a pretty engraved frontispiece dated 1730 to the first volume of the collection (Figure 7.1). It shows, as the caption explains, how "the Muse of Comedy assembled Poetry, Music [with a hurdy-gurdy], and Dance to produce the little entertainments under the name

---

[3]Several tunes and texts are illustrated and discussed in Daniel Heartz, "Terpsichore at the Fair: Old and New Dance Airs in Two Vaudeville Comedies by Lesage," in *Music and Context: Essays for John Ward,* ed. Anne Dhu Shapiro, (Cambridge, Mass., 1985), pp. 278–304.

[4]The beginnings and evolution of the genre, along with the term, are explored by Maurice Barthélemy, "L'opéra-comique des origines à la Querelle des Bouffons," *L'opéra-comique en France au xviiie siècle,* ed. Philippe Vendrix (Liège, 1992), pp. 8–78.

of opéra-comique." On a balcony above, various actors disport. Harlequin strikes a characteristic pose as Pierrot doffs his hat.

FAVART

Lesage, born in 1668, was an old man by the time Rameau made his debut at the Opéra in 1733 with *Hippolyte.* It fell to Lesage's brilliant successor, Charles-Simon Favart, born in 1710, to parody Rameau's operas for the Forains. Favart was, if anything, even more skillful than Lesage in revealing ludicrous aspects of the tragedies at the Opéra, and he did it with an even lighter touch.[5] His greatest contributions, nevertheless, lay elsewhere.

Favart's true poetic bent emerged in a more delicate and sentimental vein, apparent already in *Les jumelles* (1734). The following year in a prologue, *Le génie de l'opéra comique,* he counselled an author writing for the Forains to make "couplets galants," because love is inspired more by the heart than the mind—"L'esprit moins que le coeur inspire la tendresse."

The intellectual climate at Paris in the 1730s was particularly favorable for a man of Favart's talents. *Sensibilité* was in the air, and Marivaux turned it to advantage in his novel *Marianne,* the first two installments of which came out in 1731. Nivelle de la Chausée gave his first "comédie larmoyante" at the Comédie Française in 1733. Even the proud Voltaire, who had begun his dramatic career at the Comédie Française in 1718 with *Oedipe,* a stark and powerful tragedy, yielded to the taste of his audiences to the point of creating a sentimental and tearful heroine in *Zaïre* (1732). In 1737 Favart tried to turn Marivaux's *Marianne* into an opéra-comique; its lack of success served as a lesson without discouraging him in the least from

La Muse de la Comédie rassemble la Poësie, la Musique, et la Danse pour composer ses petits divertissemens, sous le nom d'Opéra Comique.

FIGURE 7.1. Bernard Picart. Frontispiece to *Théâtre de la Foire,* 1730.

---

[5] On the parodies of Rameau's operas by Favart and others, see the masterful essay of Michel Noiray, "*Hippolyte* et *Castor* travestis: Rameau à l'Opéra-Comique," *Jean-Philippe Rameau* (1987), pp. 109–25.

portraying other young ladies just awakening to love. Resounding and lasting success came to him in 1741 with *La chercheuse d'esprit,* which had a run of two hundred successive performances at the Foire Saint Germain.

A tale by Jean de La Fontaine, *Comment l'esprit vient aux filles,* provided the source for *La chercheuse d'esprit.* Librettists often fell back upon La Fontaine and other French classics with good results during the eighteenth century. The literary standards by which their works were judged remained higher at Paris than anywhere else, even when it was a question of a popular entertainment for the fair theaters. The texts were printed and subjected to critical appraisal in the press just as if they were plays. *La chercheuse* is in a single act of twenty-one scenes and mixes spoken prose with seventy sung vaudevilles in verse. It requires only one set: a village with the farmhouse of the widow Madré in the background. She is the mother of Nicette, aged fourteen, who will eventually get her way and discover *esprit* by seducing young Alain, son of the notary Subtil.

Although Favart uses only short tunes, he chooses them so cleverly that there is a sense of unity and development even on a musical level. The first three pieces are in G or g and of the gavotte rhythmic type that dominated the vaudeville repertory, just as it did French folk song in general. The first three also have similar beginnings, and they expand in range and melodic activity as they go along. No. 4 brings a marked contrast (Example 7.1). It is in triple meter, with phrases of three measures, that is, the old branle de Poitou type that survived as one kind of menuet into the eighteenth century. This type must have had amorous associations, because it was frequently used when sentiments of love and passion came to the fore, and it was the direct forerunner of the earliest operatic *romances* in the 1750s (e.g., "Dans ma cabane obscure" in *Le devin du village*).

Favart uses six-syllable lines to cloak the short three-measure phrases, and his easy way with verse should not obscure the skill with which he interprets the rising ardor of Subtil, especially with the hesitations in speech towards the end and the final epigrammatic twist.

Sa taille est ravissante,	Her figure is ravishing,
E l'on peut déja voir	And one can already see
Une gorge naissante	An incipient bosom
Repousser le mouchoir:	Pushing back the kerchief:
Elle a, par excellence,	She has, in surpassing fashion
Un teint . . . des yeux . . . elle a . . .	A complexion . . . eyes . . . she has . . .
Elle a son innocence	She has her innocence
Qui surpasse cela.	Which surpasses all that.

We can see this young lass, before she appears; she is the idealized rustic ingénue that François Boucher loved to paint.

EXAMPLE 7.1. *Favart,* La chercheuse d'esprit, *No. 4.*
(Timbre: Tes beaux yeux, Nicolle)

Subtil: Sa taille est rav - vis - san - te, Et l'on peut dé - ja voir U -

ne gorge nais - san - te Re - pous - ser le mou - choir. Elle a

par ex - cel - len - ce Un teint... des yeux... elle a... Elle a

son in - no - cen - ce, Qui sur - pas - se ce - la.

   La chercheuse d'esprit became so well known and loved that Favart could cite
its verses as *timbres* in his next works, most notably in *Le prix de Cythère* (1742), *Le
coq de village* (1743), another phenomenally successful work, and *Acajou* (1744).
There is a falling-in-love scene between two innocent and naïve young people at
the center of *Le coq de village,* and the message of this proto-*romance* epitomizes
the galant:"Le talent le plus beau est le talent de plaire."The last word alone would
be our choice to sum up the age, if faced with so drastic a choice. It is the key word
by which Voltaire defines the term *galant* in the *Encyclopédie,* as we saw earlier.
   Even after opéra-comique *melée d'ariettes* came to the fore in the 1750s, the
most beloved vaudeville comedies continued to be savored. *La chercheuse* was
revived at the Comédie Italienne in 1762. This version, which had only a short
run, was apparently the one in which Duni, La Borde, and Baron Gottfried van
Swieten of Vienna collaborated on setting the text to new music (which is lost).
Framery, in reviewing a 1770 revival in his *Journal de musique,* says that their music
was charming but the play less good than the original one. He explains why a
vaudeville comedy, in which every word counts, could not be made into a satisfactory operatic libretto without losing all the salt of the former: operatic arias
required much word repetition and few verses; vaudeville comedy operated with
no word repetition and scores of verses. The revival of 1770 was of the original,
which won Framery's unqualified praise, although he admitted the decline of the
musical part of the old genre:"If the Vaudevilles ever lose enough of their credit
so that one can no longer tolerate listening to them, the only change necessary
would be to put everything in verse and play them without music. But it must be
the author himself who accomplishes the task. Who, other than M. Favart, would
dare lay a hand on *La chercheuse d'esprit?*" A tribute of this kind to a theater poet
was made to few others, the most notable being Metastasio, whose lyric gift and
versifying skill Favart matches.

Nicette found love and Favart found both fame and love at the same time. Like Pygmalion he had created a female image of the ideal beauty, and lo she soon came to life. Marie Duronceray, the future Madame Favart, was aged fourteen in 1741. The role of Nicette was not written for her, but it soon became hers. Of delicate proportions and small stature, she too was an innocent and wide-eyed ingénue from the country (a Provençale). They were married in 1745, at the peak of Favart's first successes. With her help he would later go on to create such roles as Bastienne, Ninette, Roxelanne, and Annette, but not before a dangerous interlude that interrupted both their careers.

Jean Monnet, who became the impressario of the Opéra-Comique in 1743, published a memoir of his life much later that provides some glimpses of theatrical life in his early days.[6] When he took over he found nothing but disorder in the behavior of players and audiences alike, or so he says, but he is obviously exaggerating for effect and in order to enhance his own reforming role. The orchestra was composed of a scruffy lot "who played at weddings and taverns," according to him.[7] They were led by none other than the disreputable fiddler and scion of the Rameau family satirized by Diderot in *Le neveu de Rameau*. Monnet hired Favart as his director at a salary of 2,000 livres annually. The latter's *Le coq de village* opened the season. Boucher was responsible for the sets and costumes. Favart's records as régisseur for the Saint Laurent fair of 1743 have survived and they show that the troupe was quite large.[8] There were twelve actors and twelve actresses, seven male dancers, of whom the first was Noverre, and seven female dancers, the first being Mademoiselle Lany. The orchestra expanded to eighteen musicians, of whom the chief was Adolfe-Benoît Blaise and the second in command, the flautist Joseph Bodin de Boismortier. Besides these two there were six violins, four basses, two horns, two bassoons, one flute, and one oboe. Total seasonal expenses for the actors amounted in francs to 10,600; for the dancers, 4,150; and for the orchestra, 4,500. From the same source it emerges that the daily expense could be as high as 572 francs and that an author was paid 50 francs an act per performance.

The size of the orchestra indicated that it was capable of doing more than just accompanying the vaudevilles. Indeed, there is evidence in Favart's works that, increasingly, the music was not just compiled but composed afresh. This is particularly true of *Le prix de Cythère*, which included some fairly elaborate airs. Blaise,

[6]Jean Monnet, *Supplément au Roman comique, ou Mémoires pour servir à la vie de Jean Monnet,* 2 vols. (London, 1773).

[7]Ibid., 1: 79: "l'Orchestre était composé par des gens qui jouait aux noces et aux guinguettes." See also Clifford R. Barnes, "Instruments and Instrumental Music at the 'Théâtres de la Foire,' (1697–1762)," *Recherches sur la musique française classique* 5 (1965): 142–68.

[8]Auguste Font, *Favart, l'Opéra comique et la comédie vaudeville au xviie et xviiie siècles* (Paris, 1894), p. 124.

in addition to being a violinist and a bassoonist (at the Comédie Italienne), was a talented composer and the most likely candidate to have supplied some of the freshly composed items. The number of dancers employed also hints at increasing elaboration. Opéra-comique was becoming more and more like what could be seen and heard in the privileged theaters, and this was bound to cause trouble. The very success of opéra-comique under Monnet and Favart led to its suppression in 1745. Both men left Paris to seek their fortunes elsewhere. Favart was hired to direct a theatrical troupe by Maurice, count of Saxony, commander of the French army warring in the Low Countries and marshal of France. When the marshal's attentions to Madame Favart went beyond the bounds of decency, the couple fled back to France. Favart went into hiding and his wife was clamped into a convent by the all-powerful marshal. His sudden death in 1750 ended the threat to the couple, and they were reunited.

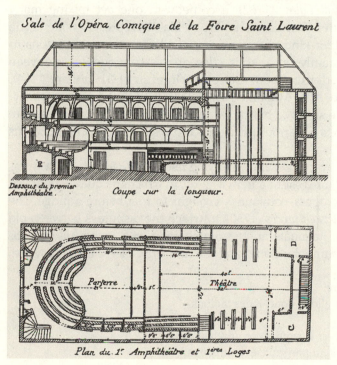

Monnet returned from London to Paris in 1752, struck a new bargain with the Opéra, and ushered opéra-comique into an age of even greater accomplishment. He commissioned from Boucher the designs for a new theater at the Foire Saint Laurent, which was rapidly built and put into operation. It had only two rows of boxes, framed by simple arches in an elegant neoclassical style, as may be seen from the diagrams in Gabriel Dumont's *Parallèle de plans des plus belles salles de spectacles d'Italie et de France* (Paris, 1763) (Figure 7.2). Ancelet claimed in 1757 that the superiority of opéra-comique under Monnet was due to the excellent acoustics of this hall.[9]

FIGURE 7.2. Section and floor plan of Monnet's theater at the Foire Saint Laurent.

[9]Ancelet, *Observations sur la musique, les musiciens, les instruments* (Amsterdam, 1757; reprint, Geneva 1984), p. 11.

In 1751 Favart began working for the Comédie Italienne, where his wife had become an actress-singer and his coauthor. She was taught music by Charles Sodi, composer-violinist of the troupe, and is portrayed by François-Hubert Drouais playing a double-manual harpsichord (Plate IX). The Favarts parodied several of the greatest successes at the other theaters: Mondonville's *Titon et l'Aurore* became *Raton et Rosette;* Rousseau's *Le devin du village* became *Les amours de Bastien et Bastienne* (later set by Mozart in Friedrich Wilhem Weiskern's translation); Goldoni's *Bertoldo* became *Le caprice amoureux ou Ninette a la cour.* The last was translated into several languages and played all over Europe.[10] It was also revived at Paris with new music by Louis-Joseph Saint-Amant as late as 1791. Madame Favart's *Annette et Lubin* (1762), a comedy in one act mixing many vaudevilles and a few ariettes (composed in part by Blaise), represents one of the last high points for the older kind of opéra-comique.[11] Favart's contributions to the newer kind, relying mainly on ariettes ("les opéras-comiques du nouveau genre," as he wrote in a letter to Count Giacomo Durazzo of 31 January 1764), belong to a later discussion. After Madame Favart died in 1772, the poet wrote little more for the theater. He survived her by two decades. His declining days were spent in relative ease, thanks to various pensions, and often in the company of his good friend Goldoni.

As a final example of Favart's wit and versifying talent, here is a scene from his skit *Le procès* put on at the Foire Saint Laurent in 1760, in which the quarrel between the old and newer kind of opéra-comique is brought to trial before a judge. The model is Lesage's *Les couplets en procès* (1730), in which the dispute is between old and new vaudevilles.[12] The Italianate ariettes are charged with being full of leaps and curves, filled with instrumental clatter and the nonsense of vocalizing vowels:

Timbre:
> Et allons donc, jouez violons
>
> C'est la troupe des ariettes
> Allant par sauts et courbettes,

---

[10]Alfred Iacuzzi, *The European Vogue of Favart: The Diffusion of the Opéra-Comique* (New York, 1932), pp. 354–56. In Weisse's translation of *Ninette* as *Lottchen am Hofe* it was set by Hiller (1767); Sacchini set an anonymous translation as *La contandina in corte* (1765); in Bertati's translation as *La villanella rapita* it was set by Bianchi (1783). The story of an attempted rape of a young country girl by a powerful courtier had a quite personal significance for the Favarts. The legacy of this theme also includes *Le mariage de Figaro* by Beaumarchais.

[11]It receives extensive discussion in David Charlton, "The *Romance* and Its Cognates: Narrative, Irony and *Vraisemblance* in Early Opéra Comique," in *Die Opéra comique und ihr Einfluss auf das europäische Musiktheater im 19. Jahrhundert,* ed. Herbert Scheider and Nicole Wild (Hildesheim, 1997), pp. 43–92; 74–79. This and several of the author's other essays have been reprinted in facsimile in David Charlton, *French Opera 1730–1830. Meaning and Media* (Aldershot, 2000), with an Addenda et Corrigenda at the end.

[12]Lesage's comedy is described in Heartz, "Terpsichore at the Fair." See note 3 above.

Chantant sans cesse A, a, O, o;
    C'est l'eternelle
    Ritournelle
Qui vient toujours sans qu'on l'appelle:
    C'est le Duo
    C'est le Trio
Le Quatuor ou le Quinto
Avec les Piano, les Presto
Echappés de cent concerto,
En un mot toute la séquelle
De cette musique nouvelle
Qu'en France la mode introduit
Pour ne produire que du bruit.

The satire specifically concerns Philidor's *Blaise le savetier* of the previous year, which is filled with ensembles, up to and including a quintet. Favart next introduces several ariettes. The first evokes a sea storm and shipwreck (cf. Vinci's widely parodied "Vo solcando un mar crudele"). The second paints the bliss of lovers, and so on. After introducing the *Ritournelle,* "which walks about with a long tail, hands in pockets because it knows not what to do with them," and a few other choice personifications of operatic clichés, Favart brings on the "Duo contradictoire Et oui, et non, et si, et mais, non, non, non, non, si, si, si, si." The judge condemns the vaudevilles and ariettes to live together in harmony, a practice to which Favart heartily subscribed but which became infrequent with the gradual disappearance of the former after 1760.

La Querelle des Bouffons

The practice of reviving works from the previous reign was not without its political overtones at a royal institution like the Opéra. Louis XV, hemmed in by the various *parlements*, no longer possessed the absolute power of his predecessor, and there were some around him, if not the king himself, who would willingly turn the clock back to the days of Louis XIV. One of these revivals was at issue when Melchior Grimm wrote his *Lettre sur Omphale*[13] and published it in January of 1752. *Omphale* by Destouches went back to 1701. Grimm, born at Regensburg in 1723, came to Paris in 1749 as a secretary to the Saxon embassy and fell under the spell of Diderot. He had an easy task of demonstrating how much French music had advanced since *Omphale.* His pamphlet represents a minor skirmish

---

[13]The *Lettre sur Omphale* and all the pamphlets of the succeeding quarrel are published in facsimile in *La Querelle des Bouffons,* ed. Denise Launay, 3 vols. (Geneva, 1973).

preceding the battle. The broadside attack on the Opéra did not begin here, as has often been mistakenly assumed,[14] but with Grimm's spirited satire of a year later, *Le petit prophète de Boehmischbroda.*

In his first pamphlet Grimm took the lofty position that it was up to men of letters like himself to enlighten the multitude ("d'éclairer la multitude par leur lumières"). The court gives the nation its fashions, he went on, and the *philosophes* give it its laws (a bold proposition!). He pursued the parallel by referring to d'Alembert's inspired "Discours préliminaire" to the *Encyclopédie.* France had surpassed antiquity by emulating it, Grimm agreed. But in music the Enlightenment was yet to come, and it would only come when the public could be taught to listen and judge with the same finesse and delicacy brought to bear in other fields of endeavor. Rameau is spared any criticism for this state of affairs. In fact, his music is praised. What is decried is the singing and acting at the Opéra and the return to such superannuated works as *Omphale.* Critical response to the *Lettre sur Omphale* amounted to no more than a flurry, compared to what was to come a year later.

Meanwhile, during the summer of 1752, a few comic players of intermezzi, who had been touring the French provinces, arrived in Paris. Revenues at the Opéra were declining at the time, and the Italian players, featuring Pietro Manelli, were hired to put on their shows alongside the regular offerings in the hope of stimulating public interest. They began by staging Pergolesi's *La serva padrona* in early August. The work was not new to Paris, having been given at the Comédie Italienne in 1746, when it caused little stir. Comic intermezzi in Italian had been played at the Opéra as early as 1729. Before the end of 1752 Manelli and his singers had put on, in addition to *La serva padrona, Il giocatore* (a pasticcio involving Vinci, Pergolesi, and others),[15] *Il maestro di musica* (another pasticcio), *La finta cameriera* by Gaetano Latilla, and *La donna superba* by Rinaldo da Capua.

Attendance at the Opéra increased for a time, but it is doubtful if the itinerant Italian players could have continued to hold the public's attention had not Grimm and Rousseau made them a cause célèbre. Dauvergne's *Les amours de Tempé* (November 1752) rallied the partisans of French opera, as, to an even greater degree, did Mondonville's *Titon et l'Aurore* (January 1753). The program music in the latter depicting a sunrise was particularly singled out for praise.

The hero, or rather antihero, of Grimm's *Le petit prophète* is Waldstorch, a wretched fiddler from the outskirts of Prague. As a student at Leipzig and courtier at Dresden, Grimm was well acquainted with the phenomenon of Bohemian *Musikanten.* The parallel intended is with the wandering Manelli, not with Johann

---

[14]In spite of the conclusive article of Paul Marie Masson, "La Lettre sur *Omphale* (1752)," *Revue de musicologie* 27 (1945): 1–19.

[15]O. G. Sonneck, "*Il giocatore,*" *Musical antiquary* 4 (1912–13): 160–74.

Stamitz, who was a highly paid and respected master violinist. Perceived through the eyes and ears of Waldstorch, who is transported through the air to Paris, the Opéra had nothing but defects (exception made only for the singing of Pierre de Jélyotte and Marie Fel). The spectacle is dismissed in sum as consisting of two and a half hours of dances—menuets, gavottes, rigaudons, tambourins, and contredanses—interlaced with scenes in plainchant (i.e., French recitative) and some vulgar chansons. The prophetic Voice then begins to speak through Waldstorch in reproof of the haughty French. I raised you, says the Voice, from the superstition and squalor of the Middle Ages to become the first among European peoples, by enlightening you with the torch of the sciences, letters, and arts. The genius given to you has been abused.

Lully, Grimm continues, was given to you in order to adopt the peculiarities of the French language to music (as if this had never happened before!). Rameau "the precursor" was given in order to make you forget Lully and Mouret. (One can imagine how the still vigorous Rameau reacted to being relegated to the status of a precursor—the same as Berlioz did, no doubt, when cast as John the Baptist by the Wagnerites.) My last gift to you was Manelli, unworthy though he was to represent his Italian brothers, in order to humiliate the vain and proud people I no longer esteem, with the divine music of Pergolesi. If you will renounce the "Merveilleux," I shall still show you the way to an opera of passions and grand tableaux such as I have given the Italians, an opera that can express the gamut of character from the tragic to the comic. By way of an example I have already had one *Intermède* performed by Fel and Jélyotte (the reference is to Rousseau's *Le devin du village,* first given at Fontainebleau in October 1752). If you persist in your ways I shall harden your ears until you hiss at Tartini and his envoy, Pagin, and the scales will not fall from your eyes until after you have banished my servant Servandoni.

Finally the Voice chastised the French for their critical mistakes in preferring mediocre works to *Phèdre, Le misanthrope,* and *Zoroastre* and of preferring the Opéra-Comique to the Comédie Française. Grimm the would-be aristocrat (he got a wealthy friend to buy him his title of baron) could be expected to side with the more aristocratic Comédie Française against the lowly Opéra-Comique. That he should link in one breath masterworks by Racine, Molière, and Rameau shows how paradoxical his position still remained with respect to the last. Perhaps the linkage is intended to put Rameau into the past with the others, thus reinforcing his "precursory" role. In any case the party line and even much of the critical vocabulary of the *philosophes* concerning music is established for the first time in *Le petit prophète.* It seems odd that it should have taken a Bavarian to do this, yet no stranger than the case of Rousseau, another outsider, who set himself up as supreme arbiter in matters of musical taste.

In three months' time a couple dozen responses to Grimm saw print, mostly by outraged traditionalists. Rousseau had already written his virulent *Lettre sur la musique française,* but held back from publishing it until the end of 1753, when it caused another couple dozen pamphlets to be written and published in protest.[16] Ancelet in 1757 put the pamphlet war in a proper musical perspective:

> I shall not enter into those eternal and tiresome disputes between the different parti- sans of French and Italian music; I recognize but one music: that which makes a tableau, which best paints the passions and the different characters, that, in a word, which employs with discrimination both melody and harmony, according to nature and to truth, following the subject and the words.[17]

The battle subsided but left some issues smouldering that burst into the flames of another pamphlet war in the late 1770s between Gluckists and Piccinnists.

Diderot stood somewhere in the middle of the quarrel, siding with his friends Grimm and Rousseau (with whom he had not yet broken relations) in vaunting Pergolesi, while being by no means deaf to the beauties of Rameau. He gave a very favorable review to *Le devin du village* when it had its premiere at the Opéra on 1 March 1753.

ROUSSEAU'S *LE DEVIN DU VILLAGE*

After a year in Venice during 1743–44 as secretary to the French ambassador, Rousseau was fired for insubordination. His stay afforded him opportunities to become acquainted with the comic intermezzo and perhaps with one or two full-length comedies in music (not yet called by their later designation of opera buffa). After returning to Paris he remained a firm partisan of French music in his writings.[18] He resumed work on an opéra-ballet begun earlier, *Les muses galantes,* and submitted it to the Opéra, then under the direction of François Rebel and François Francoeur. The work went as far as a general rehearsal before Rousseau withdrew it. He came to the attention of the court, which commissioned him to adapt a *comédie-ballet* by Voltaire and Rameau, *La princesse de Navarre* as *Les fêtes de Ramire.* Basking in his new role he wrote to Voltaire and received a flattering reply. He corresponded as well with Madame de Pompadour, mistress of Louis XV and virtual ruler of France. Through his friend Grimm he became acquainted with Marie Fel, reigning diva of the Opéra, and with the tenor Jélyotte, who would cre- ate the principal roles in *Le devin.* All these connections helped open doors. He

---

[16]The quarrel's complexities—political, social, and literary-historical—are deftly examined by Philippe Ven- drix,"La reine, le roi et sa maîtresse: Essai sur la représentation de la différence durant la Querelle des Bouf- fons," *Il saggiatore musicale* 5 (1998): 219–44.

[17]Ancelet, *Observations sur la musique,* p. 5.

[18]Georgia Cowart, *Controversies over French and Italian Music, 1600–1750: The Origins of Modern Musical Crit- icism* (Ann Arbor, Mich., 1980), pp. 228–30. The study places the Querelle des Bouffons in the context of earlier disputes about the French and Italian styles.

was determined to impress his new friends in Paris among the *philosophes,* and especially Diderot, by writing an opera, text and music alike.

In his *Confessions* Rousseau described the genesis of *Le devin* as occurring in the spring of 1752, when he was taking the waters at Passy as the guest of his friend Mussard, a cellist. They reminisced together about the opere buffe they had seen in Italy. These were nothing like what was being given at the Opéra, mused

Rousseau, who dreamt of supplying the lack himself. (The lack hardly pertained after the buffo troupe arrived at the Opéra in the summer of 1752 and began their offerings with *La serva padrona,* which perhaps sped his resolve.) In short order he sketched the verse and music for Colette's opening monologue, "J'ai perdu mon serviteur"; the aria for the Soothsayer, "L'amour croit"; and the final duet of Colin and Colette. Then he filled in the rest, except for the final celebrations, which were added later. He wrote this solely for his own pleasure, he claimed, and he would have preferred to hear it performed all by himself (cf. Wagner's wishes to hear *Tristan* alone). The score was copied and rehearsed, and a performance at the Opéra was imminent in the fall of 1752 when, after disputes, it was secured by the court. The first performances took place at Fontainebleau in October 1752, with Fel and

FIGURE 7.3. Title page of Rousseau's *Le devin du village,* 1753.

Jélyotte as the lovers and the baritone Cuvillier le fils in the title role. Francoeur and Jélyotte, not content with Rousseau's recitatives, supplied replacements. In the prefatory note to the printed score the composer says he insisted on restoring his own, and so it was performed for the public at the Opéra for the first time on 1 March 1753. By this stage the overture and final celebrations in dance and song had been added. As such it was printed, the title page citing the dates and places of its first performance (Figure 7.3).

By calling the work an "Interméde," a term going out of use in France, its creator sought to reinforce the link with his model, the Italian comic intermezzo. In its brevity and restriction to a few characters there was an affinity, but in little else.

The simple tale, a sentimental pastoral in the vein of Favart, had almost no equivalent in Italian opera. Colette loses her lover Colin to the lady of the manor, visits the local soothsayer for advice, and is told to make him jealous, a strategy that works in getting him back. There are no subplots or distractions, only tropes upon the same theme of rustic virtue corrupted then redeemed (as retold in pantomime in the concluding ballet). Nothing could be further from the world of *La serva padrona*, it appears.

The work begins with an overture in the Italian style, in three movements, in the keys of D, d, and D. Far better imitations were soon to come from the hand of Gossec. Without any transition, the orchestra launches into the key of F for the ritornello of the first air, Colette's monologue "J'ai perdu mon serviteur." Aside from playing the tune, which is so simple as to be folklike, the violins, doubled by flutes and oboes, indulge in a few ornamental triplets, notably a triadic sally before the cadence, not enough to qualify as Italian in style but certainly more frisky than found in most post-Lullian works at the Opéra, including those of Francoeur. The melody is in the rhythm of a slow gavotte or *gavotte tendre*, earthbound, as it were, to the five tones above the tonic initially, then making it up to the high tonic in its concluding phrase. Everyone could sing this melody, or try to, even the tone-deaf Louis XV. It was memorable. It was also quintessentially French. So was the overall form of the air, a five-part rondeau. The first episode modulates to C to the words "Hélas! il a pu changer!" translated by Burney as "Ah! since he has learn'd to rove."[19] The virtues of creating both text and music are evident here. Modulation to the dominant provides a neat tonal equivalent of roving away from home. After repeating the refrain Rousseau changes to longer lines of text, which he sets in a simple recitative that approaches *recitativo semplice*, giving it only continuo accompaniment over a figured bass. The first auditors must have thought this a passage coming after the air was over, but the return of the refrain shows that it was only the second episode. Spoken text, normal for such a passage at the Théâtre Italien or the fair theaters, would have been an affront to the dignity of the Opéra, where everything was sung. It was daring of Rousseau to make recitative function as an episode of his rondeau. The idea is so novel and striking it may have inspired Gluck to set Orfeo's "Chiamo il mio ben così" (1762) as a five-part rondeau with episodes in recitative.

Colette approaches the house of the village soothsayer, who arrives on stage to begin the second scene. Rousseau provides a little entrance music in the form of a prelude, *Grave et marqué*, for violins and bass. Colette is instructed as to the

---

[19]Jean-Jacques Rousseau, *Le devin du village*, ed. Charlotte Kaufman (Recent Researches in the Music of the Classical Era, 50) (Madison, Wis., 1998). This scholarly edition published by A-R Editions, Inc., has the virtue of offering Burney's entire translation in parallel with the original text and of printing as a supplement Burney's adaptation, *The cunning man* (1766).

pantomime she must perform by directions placed in the score: she counts the money of the fee she must pay him, shifts it from hand to hand, and hesitatingly approaches him. She describes her plight in a dialogue recitative, which leads to her outburst in song, "Si des galants de la ville," a *gavotte gai* in d, another five-part rondeau, but short and direct, and explains that she could have had many beaux had she listened to the propositions of the village's young gallants. The devin (soothsayer) is older and worldly wise. Appropriately, his air strikes a much more Italian tone, as does his advice: a little coquetry will make her shepherd more constant.

FIGURE 7.4. Jean-Michel Moreau. Scene from *Le devin du village,* 1753.

Stage pictures for this work have scarcely survived, an odd lacuna given its extreme popularity over such a long period. Two artists working in Paris, Jean-Michel Moreau le Jeune and Pietro Antonio Martini, make up for the lack with their faithful illustration of Scene 2 for the complete works of Rousseau edited in 1779, a year after the author's death (Figure 7.4). The original libretto specifies a corner of the devin's house with trees and fountains, in the distance a village. Colette is weeping and drying her tears with her apron. The artists show a nattily attired devin and a village, its rustic houses covered with thatch, over which looms the manor house with a round tower. Diderot praised the original scenery for its asymmetry and likened it to a painting by Teniers.[20]

Rousseau set the devin's air *moderato* in 3/4 time beginning on the second beat, like a chaconne. Here the violins are quite in the Italian manner with their three-note snaps, octave leaps, and repeated cadential gestures (Example 7.2). The vocal line well expresses the text by rising for Love's increasing and descending for his falling asleep. If the basic idea once again derives from a French dance pattern, there is no question as to the lineage of the violin writing. A passage from

[20]Denis Diderot, *Les trois chapitres ou La vision de la nuit de mardi-gras au mercredi des cendres* (Paris, 1763), reprinted in *La Querelle des Bouffons,* 1: 491–511; 505. A rural stage set graces an early plan for the Fontainebleau theater and may have been connected with *Le devin.* It is reproduced in the article "Paris," in *New Grove.*

EXAMPLE 7.2. *Rousseau*, Le devin du village, *Scene 2*

EXAMPLE 7.3. *Pergolesi,* La serva padrona, *Scene 2*

Pergolesi's *La serva padrona* shows the wide leaps and repeated cadences that enliven the buffo style as the treble and bass rush onward from upbeats to downbeats (Example 7.3). Rousseau knew his Pergolesi well. He sold copies of *La serva padrona* from his house, where he worked as a music copyist.

Even in the devin's air, the most Italianate piece that can be mustered in the little work, Pergolesian brio is something external, layered onto the surface of a conception that is traditional and French. Rousseau knew this full well. When listing a number of self-contradictions about himself in the article "Copiste" in his

Dictionnaire de musique (1767) he confessed, "I loved only Italian music but composed only French music."[21] One of his severest critics dismissed *Le devin* as "a little opéra-comique on known vaudevilles, with accompaniments that made every effort to pass for being Italian, but which are not so well disguised."[22] At the end of his life Rousseau rewrote several of the airs in an attempt to make them more Italian, but these destroyed the unity of the work, which does have a distinct tincture. Burney realized this when he wrote in his *History* describing the work as "being composed in a familiar ballad style, neither entirely French nor Italian." It was more French than he believed, and in spite of his disdain for Gallic music, he mostly succeeded in preserving Rousseau's melodic *estro* in his adaptation. Rousseau had a lyric gift that was channelled, to his chagrin, almost entirely into the traditional French dance types, particularly menuets and gavottes.

Rousseau was proud of the success of *Le devin* nevertheless. Its quality, which flags notably in the second half, was not a matter of concern to him. He even denigrated the work in a conversation with Christian Felix Weisse, the leading poet of German Singspiel, who visited him at Montmorency in 1759. Weisse had just come from a performance of *Le devin* in Paris, eliciting from its creator, "C'est une bagatelle, je ne l'ai faite que pour voir, quelles bêtes sont ces François-la, pour pouvoir goûter une telle misère."[23] A remark in the *Confessions* that rings more true is that he created it to set himself apart from the *philosophes,* to accomplish something that they had not.

The premiere of *Le devin* at the Opéra on 1 March 1753 was also the occasion for the performance of another new work, *Le jaloux corrigé,* "opéra-bouffon." Michel Blavet was responsible for this agreeable pastiche, which had been performed for his patron, Count Clermont, the previous autumn. The term *opera buffa,* rare and perhaps nonexistent in Italian practice at this time, was just being coined in Paris to describe comic operas put on by the buffo troupe. Blavet was first flute at the Opéra and hence in a good position to observe the Buffoni and parody their music. His librettist in this case was Charles Collé, a companion of Rameau in the celebrated drinking and singing club called Le Caveau. There are only three characters, M. Orgon, "bourgeois de Paris," Madame Orgon, and her servant, Suzon. The scene is the interior of Orgon's house, and the plot consists of teaching the unnecessarily jealous husband a lesson, which the ladies do by having Suzon dress up in male attire and pay court to Madame (an idea perhaps derived from the incident in *La serva padrona* when Vespone mascarades as a suitor to Serpina).

---

[21]I have pursued this point in an article describing the entire work. See Daniel Heartz, "Italian by Intention, French of Necessity: Rousseau's *Le devin du village,*" in *Échos de France et d'Italie: Liber amicorum Yves Gérard,* ed. Marie-Claire Mussat, Jean Mongrédien, and Jean-Michel Nectoux (Paris, 1997), pp. 31–46.

[22]Jourdain, *Seconde lettre du correcteur des Bouffons à l'écolier de Prague* (Paris, 1753); *La Querelle des Bouffons,* 1: 582–84.

[23]Christian Felix Weisse, *Selbstbiographie* (Leipzig, 1806), p. 73.

The musical novelty lay in the adaption of twelve of the best Italian pieces from four intermezzi played at the Opéra: *La serva padrona* (three); *Il giocatore* (five); *Il maestro di musica* (three); and *I viaggiatori ridicoli* (one). The sprightly air in g, "Non, non, Madame Orgon," adapted to an aria from *Il giocatore,* furnishes a good example of the process.[24] Favart would use the same piece to good effect a few years later in *Ninette à la cour,* and Sedaine used it again in his first opera, *Le diable à quatre* (1756), whence it passed to Gluck's arrangement of the same. Blavet, with a few changes in the vocal line, easily adapted Collé's parody texts to the Italian arias. The French language did not suffer greatly thereby, although perhaps it did in the mouths of the Buffoni, who were singing their first work in French. (*Le devin,* the other half of the double bill, was sung by the Opéra's regulars.) To the basic stock of borrowed Italian numbers, Blavet added a simple connecting recitative, one that was more Italianate than Rousseau's in *Le devin.* He also added a lively one-movement overture, marked *Presto,* which is quite concerto-like.

At the end Blavet placed a divertissement, a ballet suite mostly of his own composition. An excuse had to be found to introduce dancing, even in an "opéra-bouffon." In this case, Suzon goes outdoors to recruit some guests who will help celebrate the reconciliation of Monsieur and Madame Orgon. Since it was carnival time she had no difficulty finding in the streets of Paris some *zani,* that is, people dressed as commedia dell'arte characters. The dances include a chaconne, passepied, musette, two tambourins, and a very vigorous final contredanse, which was often the last dance in stage ballets.[25]

Prior to the contredanse the three singing characters launch into a vaudeville finale of the usual type. The impinging of opéra-comique practices in the hallowed hall of the Opéra is to be noted no less than the inroads of the intermezzo. Mingling the French and Italian comic traditions here, as Blavet has done, albeit in a fashion that is less a marriage than a cohabitation, pointed the way to further and more original works along the same lines.

Contant d'Orville expressed satisfaction with *Le jaloux corrigé* but with some reservations.[26] The work is gay, he says, the situations are pleasing, and the ariettes well chosen. While he approved of "naturalizing" the best Italian pieces on the French stage, he still found that musical parody would always leave something to

---

[24] The melody and accompaniment are illustrated in *New Oxford History of Music,* vol. 8: *The Age of Beethoven, 1790–1830,* ed. Gerald Abraham (London, 1994), 205–6, example 103. Rousseau in his *Devin* never achieved anything like the rhythmic momentum of this piece. The statement that the tune is "probably by Gluck himself" should be disregarded. Its author must have ignored the several parodies in question.

[25] The musette, tambourin, and contredanse figured among the "Airs nouveaux" in *Les couplets en procès,* given at the Foire Saint Laurent in 1730; René-Alain Lesage with D'Orneval et al., *Le théâtre de la Foire ou l'opéra comique,* 10 vols. (Paris, 1721–37), 7: 234.

[26] André Contant d'Orville, *Histoire de l'opéra bouffon,* 2 vols. (Amsterdam and Paris, 1768), 1: 11–12.

be desired. The public success of the work was modest and short-lived but started a vogue. Meanwhile, an original comic opera of far more consequence was in the making by one of Blavet's colleagues in the orchestra of the Opéra, the violinist Dauvergne.

DAUVERGNE'S *LES TROQUEURS*

Antoine Dauvergne was one of six violinists of the Opéra receiving 600 livres a year in 1753 (Blavet received 700). Besides this employment he was a royal chamber musician, and had been since 1744. Like Rameau, he had to wait some time before being invited to compose for the Opéra. His *Amours de Tempé* was given its premiere in November 1752; critics found its violin airs livelier than those in Mondonville's more successful *Titon* of a few months later. Jean Monnet, impressario of the Opéra-Comique at the fairs in 1753, was impressed with Dauvergne to the point of putting him to work on a very novel project.

In his *Mémoires pour servir à la vie de Jean Monnet* (1773), Monnet gives a detailed account of the situation in mid-1753, just as the pamphlet war was reaching its peak.

> After the departure of the Bouffons [Monnet errs; they did not leave until early 1754, but their departure had long been rumored], I conceived the project, founded on the impartial judgment which people of sure taste made upon their opera performances, of having one of our own musicians write an opera somewhat in the same style. M. Dauvergne appeared to me to be the composer most capable of opening this path with success. I brought him together with M. [Jean-Joseph] Vadé and gave a simple indication of a subject from La Fontaine. The plan of the work was done in fifteen days. We had to take account of the cabale of the Bouffonistes, those fanatics for Italian music ever persuaded that the French had no music [a direct reference, it would seem, to the end of Rousseau's *Lettre sur la musique française*], and who would not have failed to bring my project to ruin. In collusion with the two authors, we kept the strictest secrecy. Then in order to throw off the scent those enemies I was about to create for myself, I let it be known outside and had the news spread that I had sent the text to Vienna, where an Italian musician who knew French was eager to try his talents at setting it.

Les troqueurs was a success and played to packed houses from the end of July into September, when the Opéra, still master of the Opéra-Comique by way of the patent leased to Monnet, forced him to change shows. Among other audacities Dauvergne employed recitative, a prerogative of the Opéra. Bouffonistes complimented Monnet on finding a good composer in the style they approved. Monnet says further in his memoirs: "I was as charmed by their good faith as by the happy deception I had worked upon them; I then revealed M. Dauvergne as the veritable Orpheus of Vienna." Consternation was great on all sides. The Bouffonistes were at some pains to denigrate Dauvergne (because he was French) while hailing the success of *Les troqueurs* as a confirmation of Italian superiority. The anonymous critic reporting to the court at Mannheim wrote:

> The poem is entirely after the cut and conduct of the Italian intermezzi given here; the composer has sought no less to imitate those ultramontain Orpheuses by the way he adapted the music, which, weak as it is in comparison with that of the masters he wanted to imitate, has nevertheless had the greatest success, surely because this kind of music, in which the accompaniments mix with the voice [se marient avec la voix], is the only true kind and which has the right to please all ears.[27]

Rousseau had to come to terms with the success of *Les troqueurs* too, which he did in his paradoxical fashion.

The engraved score is entitled *Les troqueurs. Intermède par M^r. Dauvergne.* On the first music page is another name: "Opera Bouffon." Its "Ouverture," like that of *Le devin,* is a three-movement sinfonia of an entirely Italianate cast. It begins with a *Presto,* 2/4, in F, the familiar hammerstroke chords giving way to a unison and octave descending figure from the sixth degree down to the tonic.[28] Two horns join the strings. As a second theme Dauvergne introduces a canonic dialogue in the minor, quite in the manner of Leo or Jommelli. The four-measure module reigns supreme throughout and is often reinforced by dynamic changes. A fairly extensive development ends on vi, after which there is a complete recapitulation. Idiomatic use of the string tremolo makes for a brilliance of effect.

Dauvergne had a distinct advantage over Rousseau in that he was, like Stamitz, a brilliant violinist himself, a favorite pupil of Leclair, and had begun by publishing collections of instrumental chamber music. In the *Andante* second movement of the overture he introduces the parallel minor, f, and an abundance of galant triplets and melodic sighs. The last movement, *Presto* 3/8, restores the major. Lacking any rhythmic subtlety at all, it is a good example of a *minuetto galante* (as opposed to a *menuet*).[29]

Scene I begins with Lubin alone, singing an air in B♭, *Allegro* 3/4, about wishing to set up a household in a hurry, hence marriage is his lot, in Vadé's pithy verse:

[27]J. G. Prod'homme, "La musique à Paris, de 1753 à 1757," *Sammelbande der Internationalen Musik-Gesellschaft* 6 (1904–5): 570. See also Lionel de La Laurencie, "Deux imitateurs des bouffons: Blavet et Dauvergne," *L'année musicale* 2 (1913): 65–125; 98–99.

[28]For musical illustrations from the overture and other parts of the opera, see La Laurencie, "Deux imitateurs des bouffons," pp. 116–24.

[29]The printed score of *Les troqueurs,* along with a vast array of other French music in all genres, belonged among the holdings of the Esterházy library in 1759. Janos Harich, "Inventare der Esterházy-Hofmusikkapelle in Eisenstadt," *Haydn Yearbook* 4 (1975): 76.

> On ne peut troptôt
> Se mettre en menage,
> J'ai beaucoup d'ouvrage,
> Et le mariage
> Est mon vray balot.

The connection of the air with the overture is tonal, as in a tonic resolution that follows a dominant preparation, and melodic, as the prominent eighth notes descending to the tonic of the overture's *Presto* inaugurate the piece. Lubin's musical speech is as blunt and straightforward as his verbal message. It remains totally syllabic except in painting the "flighty humour" (humeur volage) of his intended spouse, Margot, which he says "is almost the guarantee of an unhappy fate." French opera audiences expected vocalises on "volage" and many other clichés in their airs, but they must have laughed at the musical parody of this little chromatic spell, with its augmented-sixth chord harmonies, usually reserved for the most serious matters. The absurdly funny melismas of Uberto in *La serva padrona* (e.g., on "morire" in the first air) had not been lost on Dauvergne.

Lubin, like Uberto, is that rarity in early French opera, a comic bass. His air, a da capo piece that is urged along constantly by its upbeat figures, has good modulatory progressions. Of French "langeur" there is nary a trace. Yet the French musical mind at work here cannot be denied. Belying all the Italianism is a reliance on a predominantly parallel-third structure between the voice and the bass line.[30]

Dauvergne's recitative mimics the melodic fourths and many repeated notes of Italian *semplice* but does not give up the French practice of frequently changing meter. The recitative following Lubin's air lays out the plot with the minimum of explanation: Lucas is engaged to marry the indolent Fanchon, Lubin the volatile Margot. The second air, sung again by Lubin, is a portrait of Margot, and its key (A following upon the flat keys heard earlier) and its 6/8 *Allegro* pace, like a gallop, are well chosen to render the message: "Margot parbleu est par trop joyeuse." Little melodic hiccups in the violins betray their models in *La serva padrona*.

In the following recitative, the men decide upon a swap ("un troq") of their intended spouses, upon which they launch into an energetic swapping duet, "Trocquons, trocquons." It is in E, *Allegro* 8/4, with imitative counterpoint between the two voices and a good modulatory scheme, this time without da capo structure. Duets for men are rare in any kind of opera at this time, which insured that this excellent piece was received as a novelty. The men's changed intentions are relayed to the girls with utmost economy; a few words, amounting to seven meas-

---

[30]La Laurencie, "Deux imitateurs des bouffons," p. 116, says that the first air is modeled on a preexisting vaudeville tune, "Tout cela m'est indifférent."

ures of recitative, suffice. The quartet that follows is the first minor piece since the overture. It is in a, and begins with alternating *piano* and *forte* passages and the driving upbeat rhythms that the composer has made his own, even if the model is Pergolesi. A typically Italian ensemble of perplexity ("Oh no it's he; Oh no it's me," etc.) results, one that could not but have had the audience in gales of laughter, as the women try in vain to adjust to their new suitors.[31] Contant d'Orville found that nothing in the score was more lively and brilliant than this ensemble. The brilliance, again, is due partly to the excellent string writing, as, for example, when the strings end the quartet with a clatter of sixteenth notes and suspended dissonances, the first violins going up to the highest pitch in the piece.

After this resounding cadence on a, the orchestra begins an *Allegro* in F, 3/4, its melody filled with sighs, sanglots, and trills. Is this the middle section of the quartet just heard? Ambiguity can be dramatic in and of itself, and this moment must have been heard as such by the astute auditor. The new music turns out to be a piece, not a section, an aria da capo for Margot, who is at this point rather subdued and is given music suitable to her text, which muses upon love and inconstancy. Dauvergne is up to his task here as well, although he is more than routinely Italianate with his irregular phrases, unpredictable extensions, and unprepared melodic leaps. On the other hand, one harmonic progression he uses has become too predictable by this time: V^7/IV - IV; V^7/V - V. Margot is the ancestor of Fiordiligi, while Fanchon anticipates Dorabella—she sings her one solo piece of the opera here, "On dit que l'hymen est bien doux," *lentement*, to an old vaudeville. Dauvergne, by resorting to a vaudeville, may be satirizing not only the lazy Fanchon but also the creators and partisans of the older opéra-comique.

Another quartet consecrates the change in partners, "Changeons ma chère" (Example 7.4). It is brief, very Pergolesi-like and serves as a prelude to the big aria for Margot in the same key of G, which begins *Allegro* 2/2, as she warns Lucas not to be jealous, and concludes in a furious *Presto* 6/8 in g, in which she shows herself to be a veritable shrew. "I should sooner marry the Devil," says Lucas after this display, in an orchestrally accompanied recitative following her exit. It leads to a *Larghetto* in E♭, 4/4, "Pauvre Lucas," that becomes an *Allegro* 12/8 in order to paint Margot's fracas—another piece composed to the requirements of the text, rather than to some preconceived form. Dauvergne manages to avoid direct quotations of his models for the most part, but here he falls into Uberto's "Finir si può" (second air, *La serva padrona*).

Next it is Lubin's turn to express his disappointment in the exchange, which he does in an *Allegro* in D, 2/4, quite clearly inspired by the beginning of "Si, si

[31] According to La Laurencie (ibid., p. 121), there are parallels between this quartet and the duet in *Il cinese rimpatriato*, "Sei compito e sei bellino." *Il cinese* was given by the Buffoni at the Opéra in June of 1753. On ensembles in general see the excellent study by Elisabeth Cook, *Duet and Ensemble in the Early Opéra-Comique* (New York and London, 1995).

EXAMPLE 7.4. *Dauvergne*, Les troqueurs, *Quartet*

maladetta" from *Il giocatore* (which had been parodied by Blavet as "Non, non, Madame Orgon"). Brilliant orchestral writing alternates with hilarious mimicking of Fanchon's slow speech and soporific gait—a more subtle kind of musical humor than in the Italian models. Margot and Lubin then sing an *Allegro gratioso* in G, 3/8, as he tries to ingratiate himself with his original intended. The poet cleverly has Margot answer in one syllable, corresponding to the last sound of Lubin:

Lubin:	Margot:
Sans Rire, Comment va le désir Conjugal?	Mal.
Oh dés ce Soir tu porteras mon nom,	Non.
Vas, vas, tu ne pens pas ainsi,	Si.
Méprise-tu mon tendre effort?	Fort.

The final quartet, following a short and quasi-obbligato recitative, calls for an orchestra with horns for the first time since the overture, to which are added two oboes as well. The piece is in B♭ and 2/4 time, with a variety of textures, as the pairs of crossed lovers combine and recombine, or the ladies respond as a duet to the pleading of the men, who get down on their knees, provoking hilarity.

The dramatic ensemble has gone beyond the Pergolesian model here, and indeed into territory that Galuppi had only begun exploring with his first ensemble finales of 1749. This is not to suggest that a French composer would necessarily have known these in 1753. More likely Dauvergne, starting from common models, was hitting upon similar solutions independently. It is to his great credit that he applied the whole range of possibilities opened up by the developing buffo style and created a short opera that is well constructed as to variety and sequence of keys and meters, and makes a satisfactory whole.

No small credit goes to Monnet for the choice of subject and to Vadé for the verse, which is just as interesting and perhaps a little more polished than anything Italy had to offer. Contemporary critics did not fail to see in *Les troqueurs* the seeds of many comic operas to come. A Suite de Ballet in G, using very imaginative orchestration, follows the final quartet. There is no clue in the score as to the dramatic content of the ballet, but the key suggests a rustic or pastoral divertissement, such as at the end of *Le devin du village*. The dances included those that the Forain audiences had come to know well and probably expected: tambourin, menuet, and contredanse. Ancelet paid tribute to *Les troqueurs* in his *Observations* (1757), saying that he preferred "Dauvergne's ingenious comedy to several grand opéras, which are boring and maintained only by cabal and protection, those twin scourges of the public." It held the stage for many years.

Rousseau must have cast a wary eye upon the success of *Les troqueurs* in the summer of 1753, a time when he had written his *Lettre sur la musique française* but not yet published it (which he did the following November). His famous parting shot, to the effect that the French have no music and cannot have any, and if they do, it will be so much the worse for them, called for some sort of extenuation to deal with Dauvergne. Like a shifty graduate student dealing with negative evidence, Rousseau tucked his remark in an inconspicuous footnote printed at the end in small type:

> I don't call having a music mere borrowing that of another language and trying to apply it to one's own, and I should rather that we kept our own dull and ridiculous singing [chant] than to associate, even more ridiculously, Italian melody to the French language. This disgusting combination, which will perhaps become the aim of our composers, is too monstrous to be admitted, and the character of our language will never allow it. At the most, a few comic pieces can pass, on the strength of their orchestral writing [à faveur de leur symphonie]; but I make so bold as to predict that the tragic genre will never even be attempted [Gluck's successes at Paris in the 1770s made him retract this]. Last summer at the Opéra-Comique one applauded the work of a man of talent who seems to have listened to good music with good ears, [how patronizing in view of the mediocre ears of the writer!] and who translated the genre into French as closely as was possible; his accompaniments are well imitated after their models, without being copied, and if he did not make true lyric melody [s'il n'a point fait de chant], that is because it is impossible to do so on this basis.

Dauvergne could not have ignored the cutting edge of these verbal daggers, which perhaps helps explain, along with his expanded managerial duties at the Opéra in subsequent years, why he did not attempt to repeat the experiment of *Les troqueurs*. The way was prepared for others to do so, notably Duni and Philidor. But not before a mighty pen sprang to Dauvergne's defense. Rameau answered a number of Rousseau's sophistries in his *Observation sur notre instinct pour la musique* of 1754. The creator of *Platée* was no stranger to the problems and possibilities of comic opera, nor to the resources offered by the Italian style. He believed that sentiment was the dominant force in tragédie-lyrique and opéra-ballet, and that it was best served in vocal music by the rhythmic vagaries of the old French style. On the other hand, "the comic genre, which almost never has sentiment for its object is in consequence the only one that is constantly susceptible to the strict rhythms [mouvement cadencés] for which one pays honor to Italian music. These are quite happily employed by our musicians in the small number of essays that the delicacy of French taste has permitted them to risk, essays where one has proven, in performance, how easy it is to excel in this genre."[32] He then cites by name *Les troqueurs*.

Rameau puts his case delicately, but truly. Taste had to be led step by step in

---

[32]In *La Querelle des Bouffons*, 3: 1739. Rameau also cites *La coquette trompée*, a one-act comedy by Favart set to music by Dauvergne and given at Fontainebleau in November 1753.

the rejuvenation of French music, as no one knew better than he did. Dauvergne had met the buffo style on its own terms and mastered it. Although he gave the field over to others in succeeding years, he still deserves credit as the main pioneer who brought the French and Italian comic traditions into something that was more than a mere cohabitation. He deserves the credit, in other words, for accomplishing what Rousseau set out to accomplish in *Le devin du village*.

INTERLUDE

There followed a number of operatic adaptations and translations of the Italian intermezzi brought by the Buffoni, who left Paris in March 1754, giving as their last spectacle, appropriately, *I viaggiatori*. Pergolesi's *La serva padrona* became *La servante maîtresse* at the hands of Pierre Baurans at the Théâtre Italien the same year. *Il cinesi rimpatriato* by Giuseppe Sellitto, a prolific Neapolitan composer, was parodied by Favart as *Le chinois* (1756). *La zingara*, when given along with *Il cinesi* by the Buffoni at the Opéra in June of 1753, had already diverged greatly from the original intermezzo by Rinaldo da Capua.[33] Parodied as *La bohémienne* (1755) by Favart, the work was further modified by the addition of other music.

The scores of these French parodies were published, so it is easier to study them than the Italian originals, which exist, if at all, in manuscript and often in only one corrupt version. Such is the case with the most famous and successful of the pastiches, Favart's *Ninette à la Cour* (1755). It was based on *Bertoldo in corte*, an intermezzo put on by the Buffoni at the Opéra in late 1753. This version had already strayed far from what Goldoni and Ciampi had staged at Venice in 1748 as a full-fledged *dramma giocoso* in three acts, *Bertoldo, Bertoldino e Cacasenno*.[34] To make the matter more complicated, there was another parody of the intermezzo, *Bertholde à la ville*, translated by Louis Anseaume and others, performed at the Opéra-Comique in 1754. Favart went back to Goldoni's original in devising his three-act *Ninette* in 1755. But the following year he reduced *Ninette* to two acts, and it is this version of which the score was printed.

Goldoni's *Bertoldo* of 1748 was an early example of his special kind of *dramma giocoso*, a full-length comedy for several characters, mixing opera seria types (such as noble lovers) with rustics, servants, and other buffo types. Being one of the first of its kind, it is quite crude, especially when judged by the standards Goldoni achieved shortly thereafter in collaboration with Galuppi. For the seria characters' arias he was not loathe to make several outright borrowings from Metastasio. The rustics play jokes on each other that stem from the age-old vulgarities of com-

[33]Claudio Gallico, "Rinaldo da Capua: *Zingara o Bohémienne*," in *Venezia e il melodramma nel settecento*, ed. Teresa Muraro, 2 vols. (Florence, 1978–81), 1: 425–36. One aria, "Ombra che pallida," was taken from *Vologeso*, an opera seria by Rinaldo da Capua.

[34]O. G. Sonneck, "Ciampi's *Bertoldo, Bertoldino e Cacasenno* and Favart's *Ninette à la Cour*," *Sammelbande der Internationalen Musik-Gesellschaft* 12 (1911): 524–64.

media dell'arte, and one such scene had furnished Ciampi with the makings of a small act-ending ensemble, an incipient buffo finale.[35]

Quite unusually, in a work for the lyric stage, the rustics also indulge in some surprisingly frank and egalitarian talk, which may be the element that attracted Favart to Goldoni's original libretto. In any case, he preserved this feature, while changing it so as to incorporate one of his pet themes. In the original, Bertoldo teaches the king a lesson in speaking honestly, set to a vigorous and amusing aria by Ciampi ("Quando s'incontrano"). Favart turns the same music into a duet between the rustic lovers, Colas and Ninette ("Tu nous perdras Colas") in which a grand seigneur tries to abduct Ninette—a good example of an action ensemble.[36] François Parfaicte compared the original poem with the parody in his *Dictionnaire des theatres de Paris* for 1756 and concluded, "If the author of the coarse *Bertoldo* had more delicacy, he could have achieved something approaching *Ninette à la cour,*" and stated furthermore that, in the latter, "Molière himself would have recognized the model of a good comedy."[37]

The music for *Ninette* came in only small part from Ciampi. There were liberal borrowings as well from Vinci, Pergolesi, Sellitto, Jommelli, Latilla, and Rinaldo da Capua—a veritable Neapolitan anthology. Parfaicte, in the critique just mentioned, found fault with this: "If Pergolesi still lived, he would have made music expressly suited to the French words, which are more worthy of his talents than the Italian words of *La serva padrona,* and he would not have suffered that they be dishonored by a music much inferior to his, and which would often be boring were it not in the mouths of Mme. Favart and M. Rochard." Pergolesi was venerated with special fervor in Paris, where performances of his *Stabat mater* as well as *La serva padrona* continued throughout the century.

What if Pergolesi had lived to collaborate with Favart, who was his exact contemporary? The history of opéra-comique would have doubtless taken fewer twists and turns in the incipient stages, and its telling would have required less space. Parsing the contents of a pastiche remains one of the more complicated scholarly labors. In *Ninette* the pieces range far and wide, going back as far as Vinci's *Artaserse* of 1730, from which the heroic shipwreck aria so much admired by Grétry and Burney is taken (but without middle section or da capo reprise, and transposed down a tone). It is sung by the prince, a soprano, as "Le nocher loin

---

[35]A short excerpt is given in Daniel Heartz, "The Creation of the Buffo Finale in Italian Opera," *Proceedings of the Royal Musical Association,* 104 (1977–78): 69.

[36]The beginning is exemplified in Daniel Heartz, "Les Lumières: Voltaire and Metastasio; Goldoni, Favart and Diderot," in *Report of the Twelfth Congress of the International Musicological Society, Berkeley, 1977,* ed. Daniel Heartz and Bonnie Wade, (Kassel, 1981), p. 236.

[37]Sonneck, "Ciampi's *Bertoldo, Bertoldino e Cacasenno,*" quotes the whole passage in the original French, p. 550.

du rivage." Also from Vinci's *Artaserse* is an aria of lighter weight, "Per pietà, bell'i-dol mio" (which becomes "Un doux penchant m'entrain," again without middle section and da capo reprise).

Among the unidentified pieces are some that belong to the traditional French dance types, that is, there are airs as well as ariettes involved. Most of the action is conveyed in the spoken dialogue; but there are action ensembles as well. One such, a duet derived from an aria by Ciampi, has been mentioned. Another action duet, equally up to date, is the charming bell song from Latilla's *La finta cameriera*, rendered by Favart as "Comme la cloche de village." Ninette sings here of her heart's pounding like a little bell "din, din," while Colas has a heart that pounds, predictably, like a big bell, in the bass range, "don, don." The inevitable combination that happens in duets produces "din, din—don, don," an alternation providing one ancestor of the second Duettino between Mozart's Figaro and Susanna, probably by way of many intermediaries, because Latilla's duet was widely admired and copied. The score requires pairs of flutes, oboes, and horns (which last are documented in the orchestra of the Théâtre Italien from 1751). With *Ninette* the ingredients of the new opéra-comique were at hand: spoken dialogues, airs, ariettes, ensembles, and dances. Lacking only was the single composer to stamp the whole with his musical personality. Egidio Duni led the way in the next few years and brought the formative period of adaptations to an end.

A poster from the Foire Saint Germain survives from January 1759, advertising *Les troqueurs*, Favart's parody *Raton et Rosette*, and *Ninette à la cour* (Figure 7.5). The troupe called itself a variety of names, including "Italian" (note the Harlequin on the left), but could not call itself "royal" (in spite of the *fleurs de lys*) until amalgamation with the Théâtre Italien in 1761.

Duni

Many poets and composers were working to bring about the so-called *comédie mêlée d'ariettes* during the final pentad of the fair theaters, 1757–61. The three composers recognized as forming a kind of triumvirate by contemporary critics were Duni, Philidor, and Monsigny.[38] Other musicians who contributed important works were Blaise, the singer Jean-Louis Laruette, and the Rameau pupil and lexicographer La Borde. Duni was the earliest among these. Judged by his music alone, Duni would not seem to deserve such a distinction. Had he remained at home, he would merit no more attention here than several of his Neapolitan con-

---

[38]Nicolas Étienne Framery, "Quelques réflexions sur la musique moderne," *Journal de musique,* May 1770: 11–12 (an essay of extraordinary vitality, mainly in praise of Philidor); Pierre Louis Ginguené, "Chanson," in *Encyclopédie méthodique,* vol. 1 (Paris, 1791).

FIGURE 7.5. Poster for the Opéra-Comique.

temporaries of less than first rank, composers such as Nicola Logroscino, Sellitto, and Gennaro Manna. Duni's rise to fame began when he was called to the court of Parma as an instructor to the prince's daughter, Isabella. As a consequence of the Treaty of Aix-la-Chapelle in 1748, Parma had acquired a Bourbon ruler, Don Philippe, infante of Spain, a great-grandson of Louis XIV who married Louise Elizabeth, eldest daughter of Louis XV. Under the powerful ministry of Guillaume du Tillot, Parma became a center of French culture second to none in Italy.[39] It was at Parma that Goldoni first experienced Molière played by French actors. His stunned reaction is set down in detail in his memoirs.

The French theatrical forces at Parma in the 1750s were considerable—sizable enough to put on not just comedy, tragedy, and opéra-comique, but also opéra-ballet and even Ramellian tragédie-lyrique.[40] Duni and Goldoni collaborated to produce the first *Buona figliuola* at Parma in 1756 (Piccinni's famous setting of the same libretto came four years later for Rome). The original setting was disap-

[39]The indispensable study of the Parmesan court under the Bourbons remains Henri Bédarida, *Parme et la France de 1748 à 1789* (Paris, 1928). See also *Parma in Festa,* ed. Luigi Allegri and Renato di Benedetto (Parma, 1987).

[40]Daniel Heartz, "Operatic Reform at Parma: *Ippolito ed Aricia,*" in *Atti del Convegno sul settecento Parmense nel 2o centenario della morte di C. I. Frugoni* (Parma, 1969), pp. 271–300.

pointing, partly because the singers were inadequate, says Goldoni in his memoirs. Although the opera was attractive enough to warrant several productions in northern Italy in the next few years, a score has yet to be located. In 1756 Monnet received a request from Parma for a new French libretto to be set by Duni for Paris. Whereas Monnet had invoked a fictitious Italian composer working at Vienna in the case of *Les troqueurs,* this time he repeated the experiment with a live composer working at Parma. The courts of Vienna and Parma (linked by princely marriages) were at this time the most important centers of French opera outside Paris.

Duni was no stranger to the metropolises of the north. He is said to have sought his fortune as a keyboard player on more than one occasion in Paris. His *Sei sonate a tre* (Rotterdam, ca. 1736) coincided with a soujourn in Holland, where he was under the treatment of a famous doctor for nervous disorders. These trio sonatas are advanced stylistically but not well written; they lack melodic inspiration and continuity from one idea to another. A rather feeble set of dances for harpsichord bearing Duni's name appeared in London in 1738 with a dedication to a lady patron. A year earlier there appeared *Arie composte per il regio teatro, cantate dal Signor Carlo Broschi Farinello; e dedicate all'Illustrissima Signora Madamigella Caterina Edwin dal suo umillissimo servo Egidio Duni. Londra nel MDCCXXXVII.* These arias are so lacking in melodic invention and rhythmic interest it is difficult to believe that Farinelli sang them at the royal or any other theater, but perhaps Lady Edwin (a pupil?) did at home. What few sparks of life they show often correspond with passages in the arias of the recently defunct Pergolesi, a fellow student and friend of Duni's. The third aria, for instance, a setting of "Prudente mi chiedi?" from Metastasio's *Demofoonte,* uses the beautiful diminished-seventh progressions and melody of the final section of Pergolesi's "Se cerca, se dice" from *L'Olimpiade,* an aria that also inspired Galuppi and others when setting the same text.

Duni's *Nerone* is supposed to have outshone Pergolesi's *L'Olimpiade* at Rome in 1735, whereupon Duni counselled his moribund friend to adopt more broad and vulgar strokes for the theater. This legend, like so many connected with Pergolesi, cannot be verified. It goes back to sources claiming to have it firsthand from Duni, which does not make it any more credible.[41] Duni's early publications suggest a composer who was none too scrupulous, and more opportunistic than genial.

[41]Charles Boyer, "Notices sur la vie et ouvrages de Pergolèse," *Mercure de France,* July 1772. La Borde picks up the tale and amplifies it. From La Borde it passes, with further embroideries, to subsequent lexicographers and is apparently the source of the similar anecdote in Grétry's memoirs. La Borde places Duni in Parmesan service from 1748, whereas the only documented years for Duni's stay at Parma are 1754–56.

LE PEINTRE AMOUREUX DE SON MODÈLE

Duni's success in comic opera was assured when he set *Le peintre amoureux de son modèle* in 1757. The text, based on an older intermezzo, possibly *Il pittore* by Latilla,[42] was by Louis Anseaume, a poet who also worked as prompter at the Opéra-Comique under Monnet. Duni took a leave of absence from Parma in order to supervise the rehearsals at the Foire Saint Laurent in the summer of 1757. The success of the opera decided him to stay in Paris. La Borde paid Duni the compliment of parodying *Le peintre* at the following winter fair.[43]

Desboulmiers, the first historian of opéra-comique, was careful to place *Le peintre* in the context of *La serva padrona.*

> This piece is absolutely in the style of the Italian Intermezzi, is well made, and won much success. It had the honor, in some respects, of fixing this genre on our stage, upon which *La servante maîtresse* [the translation by Baurans for the Théâtre Italien] had made it known to advantage. But as the earlier work was only a translation, one has a greater debt to its indigenous successor. M. Anseaume wrote the words and M. Duni the music, which will always pass for a masterpiece with those who prefer graces of singing and true expression to the useless sounds of a noisy harmony that is often out of place dramatically. It was sent to Italy expressly for being set to music, and was not parodied on arias already written, as claimed by the *Histoire de l'Opéra* [Contant d'Orville].[44]

"Harmony" and "noise" are two clichés directed against the Opéra by its enemies, and most likely Desboulmiers is ranging Duni against Rameau here, as did Diderot in *Le neveu de Rameau.*

A printed score soon followed the performance of *Le peintre,* according to the Parisian custom. In it the composer placed an *Avertissement* in which he tried to explain his relationship to Rousseau: "While at Paris an author tried to prove that the language spoken there was not made for being set to music, I, an Italian living at Parma, was setting nothing but French words." [An untruth: in order to make his point Duni conveniently forgets *La buona figliuola* and other Italian works of the time.] The address continues rather in the vein of a political speech: "I have come here to render homage to the language that has furnished me with melody, sentiment, and images." This is an impressive statement, but it loses some

---

[42]Given at Leghorn in 1739 and Vienna in 1745 according to Irène Mamczarz, *Les intermèdes comiques italiens au XVIIIᵉ siècle* (Paris, 1972), p. 455. A later edition of Duni's *Peintre* (Paris, 1768) is described as a "Pièce en deux Actes, parodiées dal Pittore Inamorato, Intermède Italien . . . par M. Anseaume."

[43]*Gilles garçon peintre.* Cucuel quotes three attractive musical excerpts in *Les créateurs de l'opéra-comique français* (Paris, 1914), pp. 99–100, from which it appears that the overture (with clarinets!) and first air were related motivically.

[44]Jean-Auguste Desboulmiers, *Histoire du théâtre de l'opéra comique,* 2 vols. (Paris, 1770), 1: 69.

force in the light of Duni's reportedly poor command of spoken French. "The anti-French author [Rousseau] should have gone to Italy and set only Italian words; instead he created *Le devin du village:* never was there a more amiable inconsequence. It is a pity he has not continued in this path. Doubtless he feared that his operas would give the lie to his theories." The last *boutade* has the lightness of touch and revelling in paradox that is so characteristic of Gallic wit. Perhaps Monnet really wrote it, although one would have expected him to promote *Les troqueurs* over *Le devin.*

Le peintre has a charming subject. Alberti is a portrait painter, an Italian to judge from his name.[45] The scene opens, after a one-movement overture in D that is quite unmemorable, as he is working in his Parisian atelier at a large easel. Next to him his apprentice, Zerbin, is at work at a smaller easel. In his first air Alberti berates his young assistant and tells him he would be better off wielding a rake than a paintbrush. His vocal line contains some embarrassingly literal echoes of *La serva padrona,* for instance, the "giù e su" motif of Uberto's "Sono in contrasti" upon the repetition of Zerbin's name. The resemblance may be intentional. It could not but have contributed to the mirth of a Parisian audience well acquainted with Uberto and his music.

Alberti is very like Uberto, in fact. A crochety old miser, he leers fatuously at the young girl he tries to lure into his studio as a model. It is as if Uberto, somehow rid of Serpina, had turned up in Paris posing as a painter (for we cannot believe that this old fool and his blowzy Venuses would be allowed into the biennial salon at the Louvre). Jacinte, a housekeeper who has seen many years herself, enters and remonstrates with Zerbin about "frivolous idle youth" in an ariette that begins something like "Lo conosco" in *La serva padrona.* Zerbin then sings, and Duni is revealed as clearly incapable of portraying a sentimental young man by musical means, although he invokes the serious key of E♭ and marks his piece "gravement et doux." More within his powers is the farcical Jacinte, who, in her ensuing ariette, "Quand j'étois jeunette Fillette," mimics the pleas of her various suitors. Alberti then sings an air to "Reveillés-vous, belle endormie," one of the oldest tunes in the vaudeville repertory. The music is not printed in the score; since everyone knew the tune, there was no need to include it. In terms of the drama, the tune prepares us for the entrance of the young lady, Laurette, who is veiled and led by her duenna, upon which Alberti sings "Ah! que vous êtes belle" to the vaudeville air "Je vous adore."

Vaudevilles were still an important resource at the Opéra-Comique, as may be seen from the uses just cited and others to come. Since they are associated par-

---

[45]There was a licentious Italian painter in Paris of a similar name, Giuseppe Amadeo Aliberti, whose portrait was drawn by Bouchardon. The drawing is reproduced in the catalogue *France in the Eighteenth Century* (London, 1968), fig. 203, p. 72.

ticularly with Alberti in this work, they help set him apart and enhance his character as a "dirty old man." When Alberti next addresses Laurette, it is with a written-out air that is *like* a vaudeville, a piece in d that resembles "Si des galans de la ville" in *Le devin du village;* Anseaume's text includes some amusing lines parodying the high-flown language used at the Opéra, such as "je vole au devant de mes fers." This is followed by yet another vaudeville, "L'honneur dans un jeune tendron" (young girl), one traditionally used to cast aspersions on a maiden's virtue, which Alberti sings while toying with the audience by asking the equivalent of "Do you take my meaning?"

Laurette sings in quite a different style. Her languishing menuet-like air in g, very French with its many little ornaments, tells us that her thoughts are all of Zerbin. Alberti responds with a pompous and marchlike ariette in D. It proclaims his *italianità* and at the same time makes him more ridiculous than ever. By absurd repetitions ("Tu roulera-ra-ra-ra-ra . . . en carosse") he advises Laurette to seize this moment that will make her rich. Just as Alberti is about to pounce upon his prey, the others arrive to rescue Laurette in an act-ending quartet. The piece is not particularly noteworthy, except that its first word, "Courage," is sung to a falling triad, which anticipates the beginning of the "Letter Duet" in Mozart's *Figaro* ("Sull'aria").

The second act of *Le peintre* begins with Laurette alone on the stage—always an effective dramatic situation. She sings a Neapolitan-style ariette in A about her ardor, replete with inverted dotted rhythms, roulades, and the favorite cadential motion of thirds descending against a rising bass (i.e., the "wedge cadence"). Jacinte follows with a vaudeville that must have sounded as prosaic in context as the thought she utters: nothing to be gained by her if either Alberti or Zerbin marries Laurette. As if to prove her versatility, Laurette sings two more solos, interspersed with vaudevilles for Jacinte and Zerbin, the first a very French-sounding ariette in C, with flute obbligato, the second an air in G, "Amoroso," which could not be more Gallic, employing as it does a mainly conjunct melody and the three-measure phrases in triple meter of the branle de Poitou, associated since Favart and Rousseau with the stage *romance* (Example 7.5). Also French is the double suspension in mm. 3–4. Duni's strong point, it has been claimed, is his preference for free forms as opposed to patterns such as **A B A**.[46]

Duni exhibits a kind of naive charm when copying the French style. He also succeeds with the farcical, as when Jacinte paints a picture of the continual fracas of married life in a lively 6/8 ariette in A (the obverse of the frequent lovesick significance of this key in Italian opera, deployed at the beginning of the act). Then she quarrels with Alberti in a little duet, as if in demonstration. Her words give

---

[46]Cook, *Duet and Ensemble in the Early Opéra-Comique,* p. 156.

EXAMPLE 7.5. *Duni*, Le peintre amoureux de son modèle, *Ariette*

him pause. He goes to his easel and unveils a large painting of Venus receiving Mars in her embrace (of Rubenesque proportions and tint, we imagine, rather than those of Watteau). Laurette enters, and the most theatrically effective scene in the opera begins. As Alberti sings an ariette in d (with accompaniment figures in the violins like those from the end of Pergolesi's *Stabat mater*), he perceives that Laurette's cheeks become inflamed. The cause of this he does not perceive: Zerbin has entered behind him, unnoticed, and an elaborate pantomime is played out by all three *during* the aria. As Alberti moves to embrace Laurette, he discovers the truth.

Resolution comes swiftly. Jacinte admires Alberti for consenting to the marriage of the young lovers and proposes marriage to him. He accepts at once. There is nothing left to do but celebrate felicity, which is done by a pastoral piece with oboes in the typically rustic combination of G and 6/8 meter; drone effects increase the similarity with some of the dances in *Le devin du village.* In sum, the composer has taken advantage of both French and Italian traditions to fashion a highly effective if uneven comic opera in two acts. It was revived several times over the following three decades.

Duni made some additions to *Le peintre* for its presentation at the midsummer fair the following year, 1758, and these too were printed. Having won his audience, he moved to make the opera a little less local in flavor by cutting down on the number of vaudevilles and the amount of spoken dialogue, and substituting for them a trio, a duet, and another ariette for Jacinte. In place of one air of Laurette (see Example 7.5) he substituted another trio. The work thereby gained more musical brilliance and a more Italianate tinge, but in the process it lost some of the dramatic characterization of the original version. The mixture of French airs and dance types with Italian buffo arias and ensembles found in *Le peintre* set the standard for several years to come. In this sense the opera was quite as epochal as Diderot claimed, when he had Rameau's nephew cry out: "The prophecy of Duni will be fulfilled, and I wish to die if, in four or five years' time from *Le peintre amoureux de son modèle,* there is so much as an alley cat to be skinned in the celebrated Impasse [of the Opéra]."[47]

SUBSEQUENT WORKS

Duni's revisions in *Le peintre* might lead one to think that in subsequent works he would revert more and more to his Italian stock in trade. Such was not the case. He varied the mixture of French and Italian components depending on the drama and the theater. During the same summer fair of 1758 that saw his revised *Peintre,* he provided the Opéra-Comique with *Nina et Lindor,* a pastoral work very much in the vein of *Le devin du village.* It has a *romance* sung by Lindor, "Quel Amour fut aussi tendre," which is preceded by "le son d'une guiterre ou d'un instrument qui l'imite," which lends it a serenade character. The tune is nothing out of the ordinary, but it is remarkable how many written-out appoggiaturas have been added to grace it, a practice consistent with French tastes, not Italian ones. Little sung dances abound in the score—gavottes, branles gays, menuets. In one of Nina's airs,[48] the composer even seems to be attempting to copy Rameau, for the piece is an old-style *récit-air* with suspended bass tones slowly resolving, augmented melodic intervals, and several other trappings of French music that were anathema to Italophile critics. The Pergolesian elements are present, too, and they rub uneasily against the preciosity of the French style, as purveyed by Duni.

In March of 1758 the Théâtre Italien had given the premiere of *La fille mal gardée ou le pédant amoureux,* a parody of "La Provençale" (an act of Mouret's *La fête de Thalie*). This was Duni's first direct collaboration with Favart, and the pieces he supplied were decidedly in the Italian buffo style. A duet won special praise, as performed by Madame Favart; Antoine d'Origny wrote of it in his *Annales du théâtre italien* (1788): "one hears the poorly articulated sounds of a young pupil who spells while sobbing, mixed with the brusque outbursts of the Magister, making this a very agreeable painting." In 1759, Duni contributed to the Opéra-Comique *La veuve indécise* (text by Vadé and Anseaume). Its success was mediocre compared to that of two other works of the same year, Philidor's *Blaise le savetier* and Monsigny's *Les aveux indiscrets.* These resulted in such an abundance of spectators at the fair that the Comédie Italienne began to suffer as a result. By 1760 the latter company had started a campaign to suppress the Opéra-Comique and take over its repertory.

Duni allied himself with the Comédie Italienne in 1760, giving up the fair the-

---

[47]Daniel Heartz, "Diderot et le théâtre-lyrique: le 'nouveau stile' proposé par *Le neveu de Rameau,*" *Revue de musicologie* 64 (1978): 229–52; 239.
[48]Air in e, pp. 62–63 of the original edition.

aters to Monsigny and Philidor. The Comédie's hall needed repairs (again) in 1759–60, which necessitated a temporary stay in one of the boulevard theaters. When the troupe moved back into its renovated premises in the Hôtel de Bourgogne, Favart celebrated the opening on 8 October 1760 with a Prologue, *Le boutique du poète,* for which Duni wrote the music. Attendance dropped markedly in the next month, until *Le prétendu* by Gaviniès briefly revived public support by the brilliance of its music, following which Duni brought forth his *L'isle des foux* in December 1760. There were twenty performances to modest-sized houses before it was withdrawn the following February. D'Origny blames the weak and episodic libretto for the work's only moderate success. Anseaume fashioned the text after Goldoni's *L'Arcifanfano,* a libretto of 1750 for Galuppi, and in truth one of his weaker ones. Favart's play *Soliman second, ou les trois sultanes* (with Madame Favart as Roxelane) rallied interest in the offerings of the Théâtre Italien in the spring of 1761, but Duni's *La buona figliuola* apparently did not please: it had only five performances and was then replaced by *L'isle des foux.* By summer attendance fell to a couple hundred an evening or less.[49] The score of *L'isle des foux* was printed with a title vignette by the celebrated artist Charles-Nicolas Cochin depicting the miser Sordide singing one of his ariettes, "Je suis un pauvre misérable." The choice seemed an ironic commentary on the fortunes of the Comédie Italienne and of Duni.[50]

The competition offered by the Opéra-Comique at the Foire Saint Laurent in 1761 consisted of two stunning new works: *Le maréchal ferrant* by Philidor, and *On ne s'avise jamais de tout* by Monsigny. Duni countered with *Mazet* on a text of Anseaume after La Fontaine, but it did not succeed in bringing large houses to the Comédie Italienne. Negotiations compelling the union of the two groups were finally completed in late 1761. Five singers from the Opéra-Comique were taken into the Comédie Italienne. But the fairs' most important legacy was the works of Philidor and Monsigny. The unified spectacle opened to a large house on 3 February 1762. On the program was *Blaise le savetier, On ne s'avise jamais de tout,* and the ballet *Le Wauxhall hollandais.*

Duni had no new work to offer, so his *Peintre* was revived (for the first time at the Comédie Italienne, since it had belonged to the repertory of the Opéra-Comique). It had only three performances, while his rivals' works enjoyed scores of performances. Duni had reached a low point. He complained bitterly in a letter that Favart had put aside working on *La plaideuse* for him in order to write

[49] All these attendance figures come from Clarence D. Brenner, *The Théâtre Italien: Its Repertory, 1716–1793* (Berkeley and Los Angeles, 1961).

[50] Heartz, "Diderot et le théâtre-lyrique," reproduces the title page of *L'isle des Foux;* it also includes excerpts from the three pieces in it praised by Diderot, one of which is "Je suis un pauvre misérable." See also Bruce Alan Brown, *Gluck and the French Theatre in Vienna* (Oxford, 1991), pp. 377–78.

Annette et Lubin (premiered on 15 February 1762).[51] He signed this letter, "Je suis un pauvre misérable." *Le procès ou la plaideuse* had its premiere on May 19, but it was not a success and was quickly withdrawn. Two new works by Philidor (*Sancho Pança dans son île*) and Monsigny (*Le roi et le fermier*) rounded out the year with far greater acclaim.

Duni's *Le milicien* of early 1763, on a text by Anseaume, did please the public. One suspects that the Neapolitan composer was catching on to certain virtues of his chief rivals and profiting from them. He had several successes after this point, notably *Les deux chasseurs et la laitière* (1763), *La clochette* (1766), both on texts by Anseaume, and *La fée Urgele* (1765) and *Les moissoneurs* (1768), both on texts by Favart. Even so, it was becoming clear to even the most partisan Italophiles that Duni was not all they had made him out to be. Diderot, in a letter to Burney of 1771, dismissed Duni as being capable only of putting French to Italian music, while Philidor he considered to be the true founder of a new Franco-Italian musical style.[52]

Grimm, the staunchest of the Parisian *Italianissimi,* also began to cool with respect to Duni. In 1763 he still found much to admire in *Les deux chasseurs,* while admitting that Duni's style was beginning to age; *La clochette* of three years later elicited a harsher judgment: "The music is pretty although in a taste that is rather old and a style that is a little weak; our good papa Duni is no longer young—ideas are beginning to fail him and he no longer works except from habit."[53] From this patronizing disdain it was but a step to outright condemnation of the final works as lacking in color, except for an overall greyness, leading Grimm to counsel a retirement in favor of Philidor and Grétry. Duni did retire from writing for the stage in 1770, five years before he died.

Philidor

APPRENTICESHIP

François-André Danican Philidor was born in Dreux on 7 September 1726. He came from a family of musicians with a long history of service to the crown. As a

---

[51]The letter, addressed to L'Abbé Voisenon, a friend of Favart, is printed in Julien Tiersot, *Lettres de musiciens écrites en français du xvᵉ au xxᵉ siècle,* 2 vols. (Turin, 1924), 1: 82–84. *Annette et Lubin* is now ascribed to Madame Favart.

[52]Letter of 15 May 1771. The relevant passage is quoted in the original in Heartz, "Diderot et le théâtre-lyrique," p. 247.

[53]*Correspondance littéraire, philosphique et critique par Grimm, Diderot, Raynal, Meister, etc.,* ed. Maurice Tourneux, 16 vols. (Paris, 1877–82), 7: 105, cited after Kent Maynard Smith "Egidio Duni and the Development of the *Opéra-Comique* from 1753 to 1770" (Ph.D. diss., Cornell University, 1980), pp. 281–82. The author kindly sent me a copy of his thesis, for which I thank him again.

page in the royal chapel at Versailles from the age of six, he enjoyed the best musical education possible in France. He was probably tutored by chapelmaster André Campra himself. From his fellows in the chapel Philidor learned to play chess, a pastime indulged in every morning as the musicians waited for the arrival of the king to hear mass. As early as 1738 a motet by Philidor was rewarded by Louis XV with 5 louis d'or. Two years later the composer left Versailles for Paris, where he sought to make his living by giving music lessons and copying music. A *motet à grand choeur* of his composition inaugurated the Concert Spirituel on the Feast of the Assumption, 1743. The program also included motets by Lalande and Mondonville, and a concerto by Blavet. Since it was the custom for composers to direct their new works in person at the Tuileries concert hall, we may assume that Philidor, although only seventeen years of age, led the choral and orchestral forces by beating time with a scroll in the traditional way as F. X. Richter is depicted doing at Strasbourg cathedral (see Figure 5.11 on p. 525). Philidor's motet was not repeated, and it was a long time before he was heard again at the Concert Spirituel. The mastery of chess continued to occupy him, and according to his own account, "he applied himself so closely to the game that he neglected his scholars and they consequently took another master."[54]

In 1745 Philidor helped Rousseau complete his opéra-ballet *Les muses galantes,* a fact that is not confessed in *Les confessions* but admitted by Rousseau in a letter to a friend. Later the same year Philidor left for Holland on a concert tour planned with Geminiani and some other Italians. When the tour fell through, leaving the young composer stranded in Rotterdam without funds, he supported himself by his expert chess playing. From Holland he went to London and astounded the chess experts there. An itinerant life between the Continent and England during the next few years did not prevent him from writing the classic exposé on the game, *L'analyse des échecs* (London, 1749). Philidor must have had one of the most analytical brains of any musician who ever lived. To what extent, as a composer, he was helped or hindered by this mental brilliance is open to question. His keen memory, an asset in chess, sometimes retained music by others that he may have thought was his own.

Philidor's fame as a chess player led to invitations from various courts. In 1751 he traveled to Berlin at the request of Frederick II of Prussia. During his *Wanderjahren* he could not help but hear the latest in Italian music, whether Galuppi's works in London or the Italian operas of Hasse and Jommelli in Germany. La Borde says specifically that wherever he traveled, he took pains to become acquainted with the works of the best composers of Italy. Returned to Paris in 1754, he tried to win a post in the royal chapel with a motet *Lauda Jerusalem,* but

---

[54]Richard Twiss, "Anecdotes of Mr. Philidor, communicated by himself," in *Chess* 1 (1787): 149–71; 2 (1789): 215–18. Reprinted in *Pour Philidor,* ed. Jean François Dupont-Danican (Coblenz, 1994), pp. 51–58.

failed because the piece was judged to be too Italianate. It was perhaps a blessing in disguise that he did not, unlike his ancestors, get taken into royal service. His musical bent was strong and original when he finally found his métier as a the-ater composer. It might have been stifled had he tried to please Versailles more than Paris. Mozart claims that he was offered one of the organist posts at Versailles in 1778; he regarded the possibility as tantamount to being buried alive and wrote his father, "Whoever enters the King's service is forgotten in Paris" (letter of 3 July 1778).

Philidor's early sacred music is not likely to be recovered. As we have seen in the case of Mondonville, French motets remained in manuscript, for the most part, and many have been lost. Even the most national and voluminous repertory, the motets for the Concert Spirituel, survive in pitifully small number. Some man-uscripts were probably destroyed as a consequence of Revolutionary fervor, oth-ers because they were regarded as artifacts having lost any utilitarian value. The most prominent and prolific French masters of sacred music in Philidor's day were Mondonville, Gauzargues, and Giroust. They supervised music at the royal chapel in succession from 1745 to the end of the monarchy. Charles Gauzargues, a pupil of Rameau, replaced Mondonville in 1758. He is the author of treatises on harmony and composition and, exceptionally, he had his motets printed in 1775 (by the ancient firm of the Ballards and using their sixteenth-century printing technique). In the same year he retired and was replaced by François Giroust, born in 1737.

It was presumably music under the direction of Gauzargues, if not indeed by him, that Leopold Mozart both praised and scorned when attending services at the royal chapel at Versailles in 1764: he excoriated the vocal solos as "empty, cold, miserable, and consequently French," but pronounced the choruses good, even very good, and made sure his son missed no opportunity to hear them (letter of 1–3 February 1764). Imitative choral textures were a part of the technique of French motet composers, and Philidor's contrapuntal skill can be ascribed to this part of his heritage. The airs were as likely as not to be dance movements clothed in sacred texts, as we have seen in the case of Mondonville; this, along with both Mozarts' disdain for French solo singing, helps explain the negative part of Leopold's reaction.

Philidor's failure in competing with Gauzargues and Giroust can be explained by his whole-hearted embracing of the latest Italian aria styles. Even after the period of his greatest musical successes, in 1767, Philidor lost a motet competi-tion for a setting of "Super flumina" at the Concert Spirituel. Giroust, many of whose motets for the royal chapel do survive, won the competition with two motets in different styles. Burney, while detesting most of the Concert Spirituel he heard on Corpus Christi, 1770, had a moderately kind word for a solo motet by Philidor, sung by his wife, the soprano Elisabeth Richer (they were married in

1760): "Madame Philidor sang a motet next, of her husband's composition, who drinks hard at the Italian fountain; but though this was more like good singing and good music than any vocal piece that had preceded it, yet it was not applauded with that fury, which leaves not the least doubt of its having been felt."

L'ART DE LA MODULATION

A set of six instrumental quartets printed in 1755 and sold by the composer at his house in Paris represents the earliest music by Philidor to survive. Each quartet is headed by the title "Sinfonia" in the separate parts but they have little in common with the Italian concert symphony, as represented, for example, by Sammartini. The full title of the set is *L'art de la modulation, quatuors pour un haut-boy, deux violons et basse, composé par Mr Philidor, dédiés à Monseigneur le Duc d'Ayen.* Specific indication of the wind instrument intended appears on the individual quartets. Thus the first four are marked "Flauto Traversiero,"[55] the fifth "Flauto" (i.e., recorder), and only the last "Oboe." The first quartet is in the key of g, which was such a favorite with the French violin school, the second in F.

The third quartet begins with a *Moderato* that gives a good sample of the collection and of Philidor's "modulatory art" (Example 7.6). Typically galant is the long, chromatically inflected, double appoggiatura in m. 2 as well as the triplet figures, emphasis on the subdominant, melodic sighs, and dynamic contrasts at close range. A little more unusual is the slowing of the harmonic rhythm for an entire measure of tonic (m. 3) followed by an entire measure of dominant. Upon repetition of the opening, *forte,* the flute gains a few decorative tones. The ensuing path of modulation toward the dominant is strewn with sequences, the sigh motif being tossed back and forth between the flute and the answering violins until, at the *forte,* the same sequential progression is accelerated and the figuration in the first violin and answering flute becomes more elaborate. The chromatic rise of the bass to the cadence on V of V sounds an appropriate response to the long chromatic descent of the treble.

Philidor's harmonic skill is evident, and so is his care to balance instrumental sonorities. These factors and the elaborate care with which the bass is figured argue in favor of viewing *L'art de la modulation* as a kind of treatise on the galant style. The man who explained the intricacies of chess in his previous publication is now setting forth an *Analyse de l'harmonie.* Its ideals are not quite as simple as Galuppi's definition of good music—"Vaghezza, Chiarezza, e Buona modulazione"—exemplified in practice by his *Salve regina* of 1746 (see Example 3.14 on p. 262), with which the example by Philidor may be compared. Whereas, for

---

[55]The attempt to be Italian at all costs emerges even in this nomenclature. The proper term is *flauto traverso.* What Philidor comes up with is a transliteration of the French *traversière.* It is difficult to imagine a more characteristically Parisian instrument than the transverse flute.

EXAMPLE 7.6. *Philidor, Quartet Op. 1 No. 3, I*

Galuppi, "modulation" must have meant good melodic continuation, for Philidor it obviously had more harmonic implications. Rameau's example, in precept and in practice, was not lost on Philidor just because he chose to adopt a more galant attire.

The subtlety of Philidor's discourse and also his didactic purpose come more clearly to the fore in the passage that follows our example. He introduces a long passage marked *Minore* in all the parts, and what is more, he changes the key signature to two flats for some eight bars before reverting to the original key signature at *Majore.* There are several diminished-seventh chords in this *Minore* passage, and a continuation of the kind of dialogue between all four instruments with which the movement began, but with more prominence for the second violin and a more motivically integrated role for the cello. The movement as a whole is binary, with tonal but not thematic, reprise. It is followed by an Aria marked *Gratioso* in G with a Seconda Aria in g as Trio, and a concluding *Giga* in G.

Each of the last three quartets (B♭, C, and D) begins with a slow introduction such as has been observed in the works of François Martin and other Parisian symphonists. Each work remains in the same key throughout. The fourth quartet continues with a common-time *Allegro* in complete sonata form and concludes with an Aria marked *Gratioso,* which is in fact a minuet. The fifth has a Fuga Moderato as its second movement, an *Andante* in 3/4 as its third, and an Aria in 2/4 with four *Variatione* [sic] as its finale. In the last Philidor follows his slow introduction with an *Allegro* that is imitative in texture and a concluding Tempo di Minuetto. The models Philidor could have taken for his *Art de la modulation* quartets are quite diverse. Guillemain's *Conversations galantes* quartets of 1743 offer parallels not only in instrumentation but in texture, style, and form (notably, the use of a discrete second theme in sonata form movements) as well. Telemann's Parisian quartets are another possible source of inspiration. The slow introductions seem to reflect more recent trends at Paris. It is not such an anomaly as it might seem for Philidor to appear as an instrumental composer before writing the operas that we mainly associate with him. Rameau, Mondonville, and Dauvergne did the same thing, and so did Grétry. Italian instrumental music, which *L'art de la modulation* tries to be without completely succeeding, led the way at Paris to a slightly later and more gradual conquest of French opera by the new Franco-Italian style.

SEDAINE

Aside from Philidor's contributions to the stageworks of Rousseau, his first efforts for the lyric theater were blessed by the collaboration of a poet who was to become the finest librettist of his time in succession to Favart, Michel-Jean Sedaine.[56] Before he wrote *Le diable à quatre* for the Foire Saint Laurent in 1756, Sedaine was known only for a few collections of poetry. Born in 1719, he was a friend and imitator of Favart, who was only nine years his senior, although a generation more experienced as a theater poet. Sedaine was a humble man, without airs, and to some he appeared without grace. Whereas Favart, a baker's son, rose

---

[56]The importance of Sedaine to the genre is emphasized by Karin Pendle, "L'opéra-comique à Paris de 1762 à 1789," in *L'opéra-comique en France au XVIIIe siècle,* ed. Philippe Vendrix (Liège, 1992), pp. 79–177; 94–104.

to mingle with the highest level of society at court, Sedaine, a stonemason, remained just that even after his successes in the theater. He was the son of a failed architect, grew up an orphan, and adopted as his son a young man destined to become a great painter, Jacques-Louis David. His skill with homely, familial subjects reflects his own life. As a disciple of Favart, Sedaine profited from the strides made in drama by the older poet, and he had an equal flair for the truly theatrical, although he never achieved Favart's easy grace as a versifier. His sometimes rough and blunt lines represented a new departure in the libretto, less polished perhaps than the pastoral prettiness of Favart and Rousseau, but more direct. The parallel with the visual arts is not to be missed. Just as some artists in Paris were rejecting the florid rococo style, Sedaine did away with frilly conceits in his lyrics. Moreover, he showed the way to Philidor and others to do the same in music. An astute biographer compared Sedaine to the painter Chardin, while Favart she equated with that equally great artist, Boucher.[57]

Monnet was responsible for getting Sedaine to adapt Charles Coffey's ballad opera *The Devil to Pay,* which he had seen in London. The result, *Le diable à quatre,* is typical in that Sedaine worked not with the original play in English, which he probably did not understand, but with a translation, Claude-Pierre Patu's *Choix de petites pièces du théâtre anglais* (Paris, 1756). The music involved all three of the major possibilities then being cultivated: vaudevilles, parodies of Italian arias (à la *Ninette*), and newly composed airs—"airs nouveaux." Besides Philidor, Pierre Baurens and the singer-composer Jean-Louis Laruette had a hand in the musical arrangement.[58] Although thrown together in a great hurry, as usual, the work had an immediate success upon its first performances. The intrigue of the play resembles that of *The Taming of the Shrew,* but with added elements of magical transformations so beloved in French opera of all kinds. There are nearly seventy vaudeville tunes used, and each of the three acts contains two bravura arias, either Italian or newly composed.

In 1757, according to La Borde, Philidor offered a one-act work to the Opéra, but it was refused. The director, Rebel, was scandalized by the traces of Italian style and told the composer not to introduce ariettes within the scenes. (They were thought to be appropriate only in the act-ending divertissements, as Rameau had used them.) The following year Philidor composed new airs for an old vaudeville comedy, *Les pèlerins de la Mecque.* The success of this revival prompted Julien Corby, one of the directors of the Opéra-Comique in succession

---

[57]Louise Parkinson Arnoldson, *Sedaine et les musiciens de son temps* (Paris, 1934), p. 68. This study has been superseded by *Michel-Jean Sedaine (1719–1797): Theatre, Opera and Art,* ed. David Charlton and Mark Ledbury (Aldershot, 2000).

[58]Paulette Letailleur, "Jean-Louis Laruette chanteur et compositeur: Sa vie et son oeuvre," *Recherches sur la musique française classique* 8 (1968): 161–89; 9 (1969): 145–61; 10 (1970): 57–86. The question of who wrote what for *Le diable à quatre* is discussed in 9: 156–61.

to Monnet, to have Sedaine and Philidor do a comedy mainly in ariettes and ensembles, following in the wake of Duni's *Le peintre.* The result was *Blaise le savetier* (cobbler). Its phenomenal success determined Philidor's course in the theater: eleven comic operas by him followed between 1759 and 1765.

BLAISE LE SAVETIER

Not long after *Blaise* was seen at the Foire Saint Germain in early 1759, the score was printed, entitled "Opéra bouffon" and dedicated to the marquis de Marigny. Philidor aimed high with his dedication. Marigny was none other than the brother of Madame de Pompadour. In charge of royal building projects, Marigny also directed the French party at the excavations in Herculaneum, which included the architect Jacques Soufflot. He was responsible for getting Soufflot the commission (1756) to begin what became the Panthéon, the most imposing new building at the time anywhere in Europe.

Philidor took account of Marigny's labors in his dedicatory address, which is not overly flowery or servile, as such things go, and which ends on a prophetic note: "In the celebration of the Arts, this century, under your auspices, will leave to the one that preceded it only the honor of having prepared for it." This was a bold statement in a France still crushed by the weight of *le grand siècle* of Louis XIV. (An entire volume, *Les deux ages du goût,* was published in 1766 by Bricaire de la Dixmérie dedicated to comparing the accomplishments of the two reigns of Louis XIV and Louis XV.) The implication of Philidor's statement is that Soufflot's Panthéon both derives from and surpasses the great buildings of Louis XIV, a claim with which many would agree. Soufflot's Italian experience of antiquity at its most monumental made the difference. There is a further implication that arises from the mere presence of such a statement prefacing a musical score: opéra-comique, lowly as the genre was thought to be, was overtaking prior forms of operatic entertainment. In retrospect, few could reasonably disagree with this proposition either. A great decade of opéra-comique was just opening with *Blaise,* and it would reach a stunning conclusion with Monsigny's *Le déserteur* of 1769.

By calling his work an "Opéra bouffon," Philidor was laying claim to the heritage left by the visiting Italian troupe of Buffoni and of Dauvergne's *Les troqueurs,* which was similarly titled. Duni's *Le peintre* was called an "Opéra comique" when printed. Philidor uses only Italian tempo markings and directions, whereas Duni was not reluctant to use French ones. The one determined to prove himself more Italian than the Italians, while the other was content to try and assimilate the language and fashions of his adopted home. In certain ways this same dichotomy applies to the music of the two composers. Duni could be ostentatiously French on the surface, in a way that Philidor almost never was. Philidor, for all his attempts to be purely Italian, achieved something that, at its best, superseded both French and Italian norms.

Blaise is a young cobbler who prefers drinking and parties to his work, much to the distress of his wife Blaisine. As the first scene begins (there is no overture), Blaisine complains that they cannot pay the rent, while Blaise expresses his care-free nature by singing the praises of wine to a vaudeville tune, which is subsequently made to serve for a quarreling dialogue. The concerted duet in G that follows, "Hélas, que je suis malheureuse," makes clever use of the orchestra, invokes frequent chromatic appoggiaturas, and contrasts staccato triplets with legato sighs. Such contrasts prefigure the "mi perdoni" section of the first finale to Piccinni's *La buona figliuola* of the following year, but there is surely no relationship between the two operas, except that both masters succeeded in raising common buffo elements to new heights of expression. Also in common with Piccinni (and later Mozart), Philidor uses many sonorities consisting only of thirds, without the fifth of the chord. There can be no doubt that he was in touch with the very latest in Italian opera and that, paradoxically, he was in this respect more *au courant* than Duni, whose musical language seems to have stopped assimilating the latest Italian currents sometime before Piccinni burst upon the scene in the second half of the 1750s.

Philidor also shows, in the first duet, an uncommon descriptive talent in reinforcing the text. Blaisine says they are reduced to extremities. "What extremities?" replies Blaise, climbing an octave by step, in which he is joined in unison by all the strings, so that the point cannot be missed. Her distress is painted by a turn to the minor, prepared by an augmented sixth chord. The first part of the duet, an *Andante,* ends on V, followed by an *Allegro* in 6/8 to which she rattles off the names of all their creditors in eighth notes. Blaise responds in longer note values that his credit is good at the cabaret. This middle section ends in the key of e as they sing their statements simultaneously. The *Andante* returns, without Ritornello and with the reprise rewritten so as to make it end on the tonic. Sedaine has deftly set up the whole piece, using a contrasting poetic meter for the middle.

This substantial duet is followed by a little syllabic air in the key of e, an *Andante* in 3/8 of only thirty-one measures for Blaise, "Tien ma femme je t'en prie." It is in the nature of opéra-comique to range tiny airs (the vaudeville inheritance) alongside lengthy concerted pieces (the Italian buffo inheritance). Later in the century, the same disparity of very long and very short pieces begins to appear in Italian opera, both serious and comic (Mozart's *La clemenza di Tito* furnishes an example). A carryover from opéra-comique could offer one explanation for this phenomenon (in Mozart's case by way of Singspiel, as well as directly from Parisian models, which he knew well).

In the second scene of *Blaise* two bailiffs arrive and start taking inventory of the household goods. This is done in a quartet with Blaise and Blaisine—actually a trio, because the bailiffs do not sing together; the one dictates in a droning fashion while the second echoes his words: first, "une armoire"/second, "une armoire," etc. The armoire or wardrobe closet becomes an essential stage property in the last scene of the opera. After a complex duet, and then the inventory ensemble, Philidor astounds us with an elaborate quintet. The piece, which he proudly labels "Quintuor," is an *Allegro assai* in C with full orchestra (strings, plus oboes and horns). It begins after only a few words of spoken dialogue, taking us quite by surprise, just as Madame Pince, the landlady, bursts in and takes Blaise and Blaisine by surprise. Her initial words, "Ah vous ne voulez pas payer votre loyer," are set to a long rising line that conveys her mounting anger (Example 7.7). The young couple try to calm her down, using longer note values, a kind of musical pun on their words ("Madame Pince donnez-nous du temps"), but she keeps babbling away, and as if this were not enough, the two bailiffs enter the texture

EXAMPLE 7.7. *Philidor*, Blaise le savetier, *Quintet*

after the dominant is reached and resume their droning inventory—a domestic scene such as Hogarth himself might have drawn! Philidor has created here the first great ensemble in opéra-comique and a worthy successor to the comic ensembles in Rameau's *Platée*.

The quintet in *Blaise* has a good modulatory scheme, including several secondary dominants. Philidor's most genial stroke is to plant a long stretch of the minor tonic at the moment of reprise, after which the major tonic seems all the more brilliant, the stage drama all the more frenetic. What is rare in comic opera of any kind at this time is an extended ensemble using the resources of modulation and reprise to dramatic effect. Galuppi had done so in coining the buffo finale, and he, not Duni, is the closest parallel to which one can point for what Philidor achieved here.

The drama resumes, again with only minimal spoken dialogue, as Blaisine sings a little air consisting of an *Andante* in gavotte rhythm as she reminds Blaise of his conjugal vows, then an *Allegro* in 6/8 for contrast as she reproaches him with the verity of his running about ("Tu cours, tu cours," etc.), a point that the violins get across also by running up and down in sixteenth notes. Two measures of recitative, a rare but not unheard of occurrence in Italian arias, lead to the reprise of the *Andante.* One of the qualities that contemporaries especially prized in Philidor was his ability to paint effects orchestrally while keeping the voice part simple, of which this is a good example.

Blaisine follows the quintet with a vaudeville, the first since the opening scene, then continues her remonstrances in a written-out air in G, another gavotte type, this one with a prominent part for solo oboe. In spite of the vivid instrumental color, the piece is relatively uninteresting, its melody rather stiff and awkward. This could be an indication that Philidor is less inspired when writing for solo voice or that he could not warm up to the nagging-wife side of Blaisine. French tradition is manifest not only in the gavotte rhythm, but also in the long melisma on "un Epoux vo-*la*-ger" (an errant husband). The solution to their difficulties lies close at hand, for they discover in the following dialogue that not only does Monsieur Pince (Mr. Pinch) have amorous intentions toward Blaisine, but Madame Pince has an eye for Blaise. The amorous entanglement of an older and younger couple is typically Gallic and very frequent in opéra-comique. A plot is quickly hatched—everything happens quickly in Sedaine. Blaise will hide as Blaisine plays the beaten and abandoned housewife to Pince, an *Allegro* in F in which Philidor makes good use of minor inflections and orchestral *crescendi.*

In the following dialogue Pince woos Blaisine, who gets carried away with her acting to the point of sobbing. Pince, a tenor, like Blaise, begins a "tell me where it hurts" duet in the key of c, with descending chromatic tetrachords to depict the feigned injuries, just as Figaro will complain of having injured his leg in the second-act finale of *Le nozze.* Other premonitions of the later opera appear as Blaisine repeats the word "sensible" several times to the same three-note ostinato sung by Susanna ("discaccia i sospetti") toward the end of the second duettino. Duets in the minor mode are a rare item in Italian opera of the time, and it is evident that Philidor is blazing his own path here. Unable to win Blaisine on his own merits, Pince offers to buy her ("L'Argent seul fixe les caprices"), sung to a pompous "Majestuoso" [*sic*] in E$\flat$, a full da capo aria of the old stripe; horns are used prominently here, and it is possible that they have the cuckolding significance that they had already assumed in Galuppi.

Blaise bursts in, pretending to be the jealous husband, at which Pince is hustled into the armoire. The action and music take on some of the characteristics of a buffo finale at this point, with Blaise playing both himself and his wife (in falsetto). Since she refuses to give him the key to the armoire, he goes, like the count in *Figaro,* to find a hammer, forbidding Blaisine to leave. Then he pretends to come back with the hammer, forcing Blaisine to confess the "truth," which leads to a very funny trio in d, during which Pince trembles in repeated eighth notes. Madame Pince enters and, with a little encouragement, sings endearments to

Blaise. Upon hearing this, Pince tries to kick his way out of the armoire. A brilliant quartet follows, *Allegro* in D, an ensemble of perplexity in which the two sopranos in thirds are pitted against the two tenors in thirds.

Pince emerges from the armoire sheepishly, while Madame Pince is furious because she believes her husband has misbehaved with Blaisine. This is the situation superbly captured by Fragonard in an etching entitled *L'armoire* (Figure 7.6). An electric charge of energy flows from right to left in his picture.

The denouement comes as a boy from the cabaret invites Blaise and Blaisine to the wedding of their friend Mathurin, which they accept; this leads to a final duet, a kind of homily. Between even the most peaceful spouses there arise trouble and fracas (painted musically), but by lowering their tone (which they do) a couple can achieve unity (unisons in the orchestra, later in the voices). A vaudeville finale then ends the work in the accustomed way.

The strengths of Philidor's art are already fully apparent in *Blaise*. His ability to characterize different personalities or actions simultaneously represents a breakthrough in opera, and not just in France. Grétry claimed that Philidor was the inventor of pieces with several contrasting rhythms, and that he heard nothing of the kind in the theaters of Italy (where he studied in the 1760s). He went

FIGURE 7.6. Jean Fragonard. *L'armoire.*

on to draw a parallel between Philidor's mastery of difficult combinations in music and in chess. Grétry also put Philidor on a par with Gluck "par la force de l'expression harmonique."

LE MARÉCHAL FERRANT

After the success of *Blaise le savetier,* Philidor collaborated again with Sedaine on *L'huître et les plaideurs* later the same year (1759) and then with Anseaume on *Le soldat magicien* for the Foire Saint Laurent, 1760. Sedaine furnished him next with an excellent libretto, *Le jardinier et son seigneur,* put on at the Foire Saint Germain in early 1761. Social satire, often present in the genre, emerges here in strong terms: a lord, using his hunting privileges, ravages the garden of a peasant, who retaliates by killing a guard—a situation rescued at the end by the lord's contrition. (Diderot particularly relished the part attacking wigs.) Philidor responded with an impressive array of solos and ensembles, including one very pictorial aria painting the ravage created by the hunt. Still more successful was *Le maréchal ferrant* (The Blacksmith) of a few months later. It was not on a libretto by Sedaine, but somewhat after his manner, written by several hands.

Country life at the raw, barnyard level is the subject of *Le maréchal ferrant.* A robust peasant, the blacksmith Marcel, has a chattering sister Claudine and a daughter Jeannette, who is courted by the coachman LaBride but is in love with his nephew Colin. Besides these characters there are two peasants, Eustache and Bastien, who come to consult Marcel. Jeannette and Colin meet and exchange professions of love with minimum sentimentality. Marcel has left some drugged wine for Colin to drink in order to get him temporarily out of the way and bestow his daughter on LaBride. Having drunk the potion, Colin sings the dying sobs of "Mon coeur s'en va" in the key of e, a piece that Diderot thought an excellent painting of a moribund.[59] Jeannette, terrified by his collapse, has his body carried off by the two rustics. When Colin wakes up in Act II he is in an unfamiliar dark place, Marcel's wine cellar. He is barely able to push open the trapdoor to the room above, a struggle conveyed by Philidor in an extremely moving and detailed obbligato recitative, the first in opéra-comique (except for a slight adumbration in *Les troqueurs*).

The overture to the opera is a typical three-movement work (G - g - G) with oboes and horns. In the opening scene Marcel sings of his *joie de vivre* to music of extraordinary pith and freshness. It is used, moreover, in subsequent scenes as a recurring motif. Marcel works at his forge, first fanning the flames ("en soufflant") then striking his anvil ("battelant à l'enchaine"), as indicated by the crosses on a separate staff (Example 7.8a). The melodic and rhythmic drive of the passage is

---

[59]Heartz, "Diderot et le Théâtre-lyrique," quotes the beginning of the piece.

.

element in *Le maréchal,* and appropriately so, for this old Gallic strain well complemented the earthy humor of the libretto. Burney took sharp exception to their intermingling, as he noted in his *Journal:* "went to the Mareschal Ferrant. . . . I detest that mixture of old French vaudevilles with Philidor's Italian plunder."[60] Favart, on the other hand, heartily approved of Philidor's forays abroad, as he wrote on 21 March 1763 to Durazzo about *Le bûcheron:* "Our musical savants claim that Philidor has stolen from Italians. What does it matter, if he enriches our nation with the beautiful things of foreign lands which we should perhaps never have known without him?"[61]

Framery insisted upon Philidor's originality in "Réflexions sur la musique moderne" for the May 1770 issue of his journal.

> Because the composer did not try to give all the ariettes [in *Blaise*] the square and monotonous cut of a Romance or a Brunette, people denied that he had melody [du chant]. . . . He was not given credit for his vigourous tableaux, his use of wind instruments, and the boldness with which he dared paint the different and contrasting passions of five or six persons in the same piece of music, without confusion, without embarrassment, without allowing them to lose the character he had given to each. We had choruses before, and fugues as well, but a quintet "dialogué" with so much spirit and harmonic force—that is what no one had conceived before, either in Italy or in France. The *Maréchal* rallied all the wits, one sang all the ariettes (while continuing to deny that the composer had melody, because first impressions are powerful). Other authors adopted this new genre, which was not at all that of Italy; its turns of phrase, the one part consequent of the other, and which derived nothing from the first mixture [Duni's?], became the model upon which the genius of other musicians was formed. This change came about without being perceived, without even any thought being given to it; one was far from believing that one owed something to Philidor, and scarcely did one reflect that his manner was new, that it was not what was in use up to that moment.[62]

Framery's remarks are all the more valuable because he was a practical musician and man of the theater. He goes on to suggest that Philidor profited from the scores of such Italianized Germans as Hasse, Holzbauer, and, improbably, Christian Bach, also from Gluck. The last certainly made a major impression on Philidor. Holzbauer, along with Stamitz and the whole Mannheim symphonic school, were of course idolized in Paris.

---

[60]*Music, men and manners in France and Italy, 1770: Being the journal written by Charles Burney during a tour through those countries,* ed. H. Edmond Poole (London, 1969), pp. 221–22. Burney deleted this observation from his official, printed version of the tour.

[61]Charles-Simon Favart, *Mémoires et correspondance littéraires,* 2 vols. (Paris, 1808), 1: 79.

[62]Nicolas Étienne Framery, *Journal de musique,* 1: 352–53.

LE SORCIER AND TOM JONES

Philidor and Sedaine drew apart in the years after *Le jardinier et le seigneur,* with consequences that eventually boded ill for the composer. *Sancho Pança dans son isle,* Philidor's first work for the united troupes at the Comédie Italienne in 1762, was done in collaboration with the poet Antoine Poinsinet, whose reputation did not stand high. D'Origny, reporting on the first performance, complained that the poet should have been able to draw better advantage from the ingenious *roman* of *Don Quichotte.* Favart ascribed the success of the opera to Philidor's music and had nothing to say on the poet (whom he called "Poinsinet le mystifié," a pun on "point-si-net," meaning "not so clear"). There are many ensembles, but none so striking as in *Blaise;* the ariettes also seem less interesting than before, and there are too many in 6/8. Grimm complained that Philidor in places imitated Monsigny's *On ne s'avise jamais de tout* and even *Annette et Lubin,* that is, the French folk-song types that Grimm so detested. The work's *romance,* sung by a shepherdess, bears out his point.

Sancho Pança was followed in early 1763 by *Le bûcheron,* on a libretto by Jean-François Guichard and Nicolas Castet. D'Origny praised it as the best new opéra-comique since the two companies joined forces. He liked it better than *Le roi et le fermier* by Sedaine and Monsigny of three months earlier (but the public liked them equally well). Favart pronounced it Philidor's masterpiece in a letter to Durazzo of 21 March 1763:

> The melody, of a clear and tranquil cantilena, always rises above the harmony of the accompaniments, which do not suffocate it at all, although they are well worked out; there is a great variety in the ariettes and each has a distinctive character—one finds the second better than the first, the third wins out over the second, the fourth is preferable to the third, and so on to the end of the work.

Philidor's range of melodic types was indeed quite extensive. "Clear and tranquil" is not a bad description of some, especially if the latter adjective is read in the sense of undisturbed by superfluous melisma and ornamentation. But it does not go far enough in describing the boisterous quality of a piece such as the Axe Song sung by Blaise, who is the *bûcheron* (woodcutter). The brash exuberance of this C major descriptive piece, with its great leaps and triadic melody, its highly effective use of rhythmic blows, represents Philidor at his best. In the overture to *Le bûcheron* Philidor combined Italian style with Rameau's practice of citing music from the opera.[63]

Le sorcier marks a crucial point in Philidor's operatic career. Put on in early

---

[63]David Charlton, "The Overture to Philidor's *Le Bûcheron* (1763)," *D'un opéra l'autre: Hommage à Jean Mongrédien,* ed. Jean Gribenski, Claire Mussat, and Herbert Schneider (Paris, 1996), pp. 231–42.

January 1764, it had an immediate success. D'Origny recounts that the public clamored for "l'auteur," which had happened before at the Comédie Française (in the case of Voltaire's *Mérope*) but never at the Comédie Italienne. When Monsieur Poinsinet stepped out, there were cries of "l'autre, l'autre," obliging the poet to retire in favor of the composer, who was greeted with a "ravishment of admiration" on account of his "musique intéressante, sublime et savante, sans cesser d'être gracieuse."

Philidor, like Rameau, was courting risk in being considered *savant,* and he even explained in the preface of the printed score of the opera, inscribed "Au Public," how he dared to write as he did: "If ever I allowed myself some deeper vistas, and perhaps some boldnesses, in a new genre which a part of the nation would still resist (but which it loves), that is because true connoisseurs in music, those ears that are in love with harmony, have seemed to order me along this course when applauding my first essays." What are these boldnesses?

The overture begins with an *Allegro* in common time and in G, a symphonic movement in sonata form of more than usual breadth and interest. Next comes an *Andante* in g, 6/8. The auditors thought they were hearing the middle movement, as was the case with many other overtures, including Philidor's to *Le maréchal.* Sixteen measures into the piece the curtain goes up, as the score specifies, and we witness the rustic heroine singing her thoughts while ironing the wash under a great tree. Her tune is the same as that of the peasant chorus in the first act of *Le nozze di Figaro.* The piece goes into the major (without the same tune), returns to the minor, and becomes a duet when Agate is joined by Blaise. Such fluidity of dramatic movement, and also the playing with conventions and breaking down of same, are found before in French opera (cf. Rameau's uses of the overture), but rarely joined. In Act II of *Le sorcier,* where sorcery and hallucination come into play, the grandest moment is an enormous obbligato recitative, foreshadowing the celebrated ones to come in *Tom Jones* and *Ernelinde.* The truth of Burney's remark that Philidor drinks deep of the Italian spring is nowhere more apparent than in such a scene. Only the Opéra enjoyed the privilege of using recitative. Philidor flaunted his defiance. Dramatic fluidity is the touchstone of obbligato recitative. The audience, being new to such procedures, must have found them very demanding.

A deepening and refining of Philidor's harmonic skills are evident in *Le sorcier.* They appear even in one of the work's shortest pieces, Agate's "Rien ne peut bannir de mon âme mon amour" in Act I. It is a simple ternary form in which **A** consists of a rather ordinary triadic melody, deployed in two eight-measure phrases, the second modulating to V, after a four-measure orchestral introduction. The middle section, **B**, makes the return journey to tonic B♭ via a descending harmonic sequence employing secondary dominants and their resolutions (Example 7.9). The chromatic rises in the bass in mm. 21–22 and 25–26 lend the harmony a richness and subtlety that is anything but ordinary. There follows a reprise of sorts in B♭, but it encapsulates **A** rather than repeating it, reducing it to only 12 mm. Hiller, discussing *Le sorcier* in the first volume of his periodical, selected Agate's song as his musical illustration, saying he chose it not only because it was the shortest, but also because it was very good ("sehr artig").[64] In general he praised *Le sorcier* as a happy mixture of French and Italian tastes, and described the harmony as very pure and chosen with intelligence. It could well have inspired him when he came to write *Die Jagd*. Richer harmonies help define the galant style's second phase.

There is boldness of another sort in *Le sorcier*, which suggests that something was amiss with Philidor as a creative artist. In 1763 Favart, after being refused by Mondonville and Duni, asked Philidor to prepare the score of Gluck's *Orfeo* for printing. Philidor kept the score for four months and did nothing; for results Favart had to turn to Charles Sodi.[65] The work was printed in Paris in the spring of 1764. There is little doubt that Philidor's particular tap into the Italianate spring

EXAMPLE 7.9. *Philidor*, Le sorcier, *Act I, Scene 3, Ariette*

[64]Johann Adam Hiller, ed., *Wöchentliche Nachrichten und Anmerkungen die Musik betreffend*, 5 vols. (Leipzig, 1766–70; reprint 1970), 1: 92–96; 101–102.
[65]Brown, *Gluck and the French Theatre in Vienna*, p. 377.

of obbligato recitative in *Le sorcier* was furnished by *Orfeo,* and here he acquitted himself honorably, matching and perhaps even surpassing the inspiration of his model. It was another matter with the *romance* in A, "Nous étions dans cet âge," in the first act of *Le sorcier.* The piece is nothing other than Orfeo's "Chiamo mio ben così," with a slightly different beginning tacked onto it and different ornamentation. In *Tom Jones* and in *Ernelinde* Philidor compounded the felony with further larcenies from the same score, and there was one more in his late comic opera *La belle esclave* (1787).

Philidor's plagiarisms were recognized as such at the time. The originals were but thinly disguised, and his action was deemed unworthy of so great a composer. In his article "France" in the *Encyclopédie methodique* (the continuation of Diderot's *Encyclopédie* in various special fields, of which *Musique* came out in two volumes, dated 1791 and 1818), Ginguené summed up the case rather sadly: "A little laziness probably accounts for this deficiency. Nourished as he was from early on by the study of great masters, Philidor could doubtless have imitated their style, as he often did, without confusing legitimate imitation with unpardonable plagiaries." Eighteenth-century views about what was permissible in the way of borrowing were generous. There were limits even so, and plagiarism was beyond the bounds. In this matter Philidor's legendary acuity and subtlety of mind betrayed him.

Tom Jones took time to win over the public. Henry Fielding had satirized Samuel Richardson's ever-virtuous and long-suffering Pamela in several works, most memorably *Tom Jones* (1749), whose (almost always) virtuous and long-suffering hero travels from adventure to adventure, in the tradition of Cervantes. Philidor and Poinsinet adapted the first half of this savory portrait of English country life and brought it to the stage on 27 February 1765. Their "Comédie lyrique" (as it is called in the later printed score) failed utterly at its first performance, which must have been a particular embarrassment to the composer because he had as guests in his box David Garrick and other London friends. Philidor, on account of his lengthy sojourns in England, most likely chose the subject himself; to his misfortune, he apparently had no choice of librettist other than Poinsinet. Ineptitudes in the drama and poor dialogue were the reasons for the opera's failure, although the music was praised from the first. The show was withdrawn after only seven performances and replaced by Gossec's *Le tonnelier* (The Cooper). A year later, after Sedaine had made many revisions in the text, *Tom Jones* reappeared in three acts, and it is this version of the score that was printed.

Although *Tom Jones* in its revised form held the stage until 1790, it was not as popular a success as some of his earlier works, such as *Le maréchal.* Musically, it represents an advance beyond its predecessors, and particularly with regard to tonal planning and the dramatic use of keys. The one-movement overture in B$^\flat$ calls for horns in F; in the exposition they have the second theme to themselves, accompanied by the strings. Act I opens with several pieces in either F or B$^\flat$, the horns remaining in F. The point of remaining on the flat side of the tonal spectrum becomes clear in Squire Western's sensational descriptive aria about his hunting exploits, "D'un Cerf dix cors." It begins in f and passes through several keys and meters. In the middle the horns change crooks to D, the traditional key of hunting calls, some of which are now heard. "Fanfare" is accompanied by the orchestral strings playing harmonics, which represents another innovation. At the end, as the call of victory over the stag, "Hallali" is sounded. A coda broadens to include other solo voices, forming an impromptu chorus. The effect is exceedingly brilliant, partly because the composer so successfully plays off the brightness of D against the foil of the flat keys. Philidor is nowhere more in his element than in this great al fresco painting of the hunt, with all its sounds and sights. The piece inspired many imitations, leading to Haydn's great Hunting Chorus concluding "Autumn" in *The Seasons* (which also passes through several keys, requiring the horns to change crooks in the middle, and ends likewise with "Hallali").[66]

Philidor plays the flat keys against the sharp ones again in Act II, which ends with a stunning septet in D for all the characters, following after four pieces in F, B♭, c (a duet), and F. The final ensemble of perplexity is concluded by an elaborate pantomime, carefully spelled out in the score, a kind of tableau without words such as Diderot propounded in his various treatises on theater. Act III, set in a tavern at Upton, begins with a catch for four drinkers, without orchestral accompaniment. Sophie and her maid Honora, fled hither, are greeted by the drunken moans of the men, which convey a sense of the danger they are in. Philidor rises to his greatest heights in the obbligato recitative for Sophie (Example 7.10). It is followed by a magnificently broad and sustained invocation to her lover, the ariette in E♭. The recitative is an agitated painting of her distress that begins in g and ends in G (the ariette's under-third relationship to the recitative is then pointed up in its development section by moving from V into the reprise by falling-third tonalities without connecting transition: B♭ - G - E♭). The minor ninth appoggiatura in the solo bassoon at m. 6 predicts Mozart.

Jones arrives in time to rescue the ladies from the drunkards; he then sings a rather bland love duet in G with Sophie, following which the plot is resolved by the revelation of his true identity; this leads to the conventional vaudeville finale, which is in B♭. The score has great variety and power, and the drama, in its final form, is conducted with logic and considerable suspense.

[66]Daniel Heartz, "The Hunting Chorus in Haydn's *Jahreszeiten* and the 'Airs de Chasse' in the *Encyclopédie*," *Eighteenth-Century Studies* 9 (1976): 523–39. The article reproduces the five plates of hunting calls from the *Encyclopédie*. Haydn's lyrical interlude in A♭ before he introduces "Hallali" has a parallel in Philidor's softening at "L'animal forcé succombe"; in both cases a note of pity is introduced for the stag. Baron van Swieten, the librettist and to a certain extent the musical architect of *The Seasons* (he specified which horn calls were to be used) was in Paris in the 1760s and was the composer of an opéra-comique, *Colas, toujours Colas* (a rejoinder to Monsigny's *Rose et Colas* of 1764) that uses horn calls.

EXAMPLE 7.10. *Philidor*, Tom Jones, *Sophie's obbligato recitative*

Modern critics who dismiss the work because it incorporates so little of Fielding's novel fail to understand how opera works in general, or what were the outer limits permitted by the conventions of opéra-comique.[67] One critic of the time did better. Laurent Garcin in his *Traité du meló-drame* (1772) wrote the following about Sophie's aria:

[67]A case in point is Eric Blom, "*Tom Jones* on the French Stage," in *Stepchildren of Music* (London, n.d.), pp. 45–54. For a detailed and sympathetic criticism of the opera, see Charles Michael Carroll, "François-André Danican-Philidor: His Life and Dramatic Art," 2 vols. (Ph.D. diss., Florida State University, 1960), 1: 348–82; vol. 2 consists of a complete transcription of *Tom Jones*.

Here, without doubt, is the most pathetic aria in *Tom Jones,* and one of the most beautiful and effective pieces that our theater possesses. The composer prepares us by a slow and soft melody for all the fire of the *Allegro,* and all the agitation of the *forte-piano* contrast. Sometimes the soul of Sophie appears to calm itself, sometimes a new movement transports it, and carries it out of herself. The entire aria is really a sublime commentary on the words "je m'égare" [I lose my way]. . . . What cannot be accomplished when imagination, genius and taste soar upon the chords they have struck. There is nary a musician alive to whom this piece could not serve as a model. It is the triumph of modern opéra comique. (pp. 225–26)

As great as is Sophie's aria, its reprise condenses rather drastically and sounds a little short-breathed. This trait was observed on a smaller scale in the aria from *Le sorcier* discussed above.

Philidor wrote several more works for the Comédie Italienne in the decade following *Tom Jones,* but his earlier success eluded him in nearly every case. Working mainly with lesser poets, he experienced one failure after another. Only when he again collaborated with Sedaine, on *Les femmes vengées* (1775), was the result deemed worthy of several revivals; his other later operas were quickly forgotten after a few performances of the first production. A large part in Philidor's declining fortune as an opera composer can be ascribed to the triumph of Grétry. A lingering doubt about Philidor remains even so. If he, and not Grétry, had received the fine new librettos of Sedaine and Jean François Marmontel to set, would he have succeeded with them? The initial rupture with Sedaine assumes all the more importance in light of these speculations.

ERNELINDE

While the sun of opéra-comique shone ever more brightly, the Opéra was eclipsed for want of new or bold works.[68] An exception was Philidor's most ambitious stagework, *Ernelinde, princesse de Norvège,* on a libretto by Poinsinet, first staged at the Opéra in 1767 and revived two years later. The history of *Tom Jones* repeated itself. Not until Sedaine undertook a thorough revision of the libretto did the opera gain a measure of success, at the revivals in 1773 and 1777. Ginguené wrote of the work that it "marked an epoch" as the first tragedy at the Opéra to use "simply declaimed recitative, with arias, duets, trios, and other pieces of measured music in the Italian style, instead of the ancient and soporific French psalmody."[69] Framery devoted a long and penetrating article to *Ernelinde* in the *Journal de musique* for July 1770. He points out that Philidor wanted to demolish the remains of the old French style with a single blow. Choice of an old Italian libretto by Francesco Silvani as a model was especially guaranteed to insult the partisans of Lully and Rameau. There was no "Merveilleux" for them, and not enough dancing. Instead there were all the ingredients of opera seria: pseudo-history instead of fable, arias within the drama and used as scene-ending perorations, ensembles (rare but present in Italian works), and most important of all a completely Italianate recitative, both of the simple and complex varieties. Framery was unrestrained in his admiration of Philidor's bravado here. The partisans of the older opera claimed that the one thing that could never triumph at the Opéra (even if the ariette was allowed in here and there) was Italian recitative. French-style recitative was the last bastion of the old style to fall, and it was *Ernelinde* that

[68]Lois Rosow, "French Opera in Transition: *Sylvie* (1765) by Trial and Berton," *Critica Musica: Essays in Honor of Paul Brainard,* ed. John Knowles (Amsterdam, 1996), pp. 333–63.

[69]Julian Rushton, "Philidor and the Tragédie Lyrique," *Musical Times* 117 (September 1976): 734–37, citing Ginguené's article "France" in the *Encyclopédie méthodique.* Rushton offers valuable insights on *Ernelinde* and also on the composer's later *Persée* (1780) and *Thémistocle* (1786). He has also edited *Ernelinde* (1769 version) in the series French Opera in the 17th and 18th Centuries, vol. 56 (1992).

started the walls tumbling down. Philidor prepared himself by working in opéra-comique, of course, with several superb examples of obbligato recitative, as we have seen. But the celebrated example of *Ernelinde's* monologue, an *ombra* scene in which the heroine reacts to having sent her lover to death (forced as she was to choose between him and her father), surpassed his previous efforts and brought to the Opéra an intensity hardly known since the great works of Rameau.[70]

Monsigny was the first of the opéra-comique composers to write for the Opéra, with his *Aline, reine de Golconde* (1766), a heroic ballet on a libretto by Sedaine. Framery relates the work to the "revolution" represented by *Ernelinde* as follows: "Monsigny commenced the attempt with the *Reine de Golconde,* but this work was only a ballet; the style of Monsigny, agreeable though it is, does not depart enough from the French genre in order to combat it: this was only a light attack. Philidor's work allowed no middle ground between victory and defeat. It was a tragedy, a huge machine, which did not allow for only partial success." The stirrings of reform at the Opéra, during the period of its sojourn in the Soufflot-Gabriel theater in the Tuileries, is also reflected in the addition of Jean-Claude Trial to the institution's directorate from 1767 to 1769. Trial was an opéra-comique composer himself, and his younger brother Antoine made his debut in the role of Bastien in *Le sorcier* on 4 July 1764. So great a departure as the Opéra ventured with *Ernelinde* can be explained in part by Philidor's links with the Trial brothers.

Philidor had every resource at his command when he came to write *Ernelinde* (except the all-important one of a worthy librettist). His experience as a motet composer put him at an advantage over Monsigny when it came to writing the choruses expected at the Opéra. The magnificent choruses of *Ernelinde* are one of the work's chief glories. One chorus with tenor solo in particular, "Jurez sur ces glaives sanglants," in which the hero Sandomir swears his soldiers to allegiance, was extravagantly praised—Framery pronounced it the "most beautiful chorus known in France, and perhaps in the world." The interaction of soloist and chorus is an original feature of *Ernelinde* for which Traetta's reform operas of the 1760s offer the closest parallel.

Philidor's ballet music is also distinguished.[71] The harmonic richness with which the composer sometimes overwhelmed his audiences at the Comédie Italienne would seem to be at least properly deployed in the temple devoted to the operas of Rameau. For all its wealth of beauty and power, *Ernelinde* remained a

[70]The beginning of the monologue is reproduced in plates VIII–IX in Heartz, "Diderot et le Théâtre-lyrique," which article also contains a detailed description of the piece.

[71]The ballet music is found in the 1769 orchestral score but not included in the vocal score edited by César Franck (1883). Framery included a vigorous "Polonaise. Air des Cosaques" in 12/8 as a "Pièce de Clavecin ou de Forte piano de l'Opéra d'Ernelinde de M^r. Philidor" in the June 1770 issue of the *Journal de musique*, pp. 514–17; the *cresc. poco a poco* from p to ff makes the piece more appropriate to the latter instrument; in the middle of both strains of the dance the composer falls back upon the "anvil motif" of his *Maréchal ferrant*.

flawed masterpiece, a work so doomed by the dramatic ineptitude of its libretto that not even Sedaine could fully rescue it. Yet it helped prepare the way for Gluck to triumph at Paris with his *Iphigénie en Aulide* in 1774.

Having prepared the way for Gluck at the Opéra, Philidor later found himself on the outside looking in, just as was the case in opéra-comique, where he had opened the gates to Grétry. That Philidor was still capable, in his later years, of writing a superb orchestral-choral piece on the grand scale is proven by his setting of Horace's hymn for the Roman games, the *Carmen seculare*.[72] This secular oratorio was first heard in London in 1779 under Masonic auspices; successful performances followed at the Concert Spirituel in 1780. It was the composer's last great success. In a letter of 1782, his old friend Diderot reproached him for his unnerving feats of showmanship at chess (such as playing three games simultaneously while blindfolded) and admonished him to "write excellent music for us, and do it for many years to come; don't expose yourself any more to becoming what so many people we despise are by birth."[73]

FIGURE 7.7. Charles Cochin. Portrait of Philidor.

Philidor did not fully heed Diderot's advice, in that he continued to devote

[72]The work is discussed and exemplified in Donald H. Foster, "The Oratorio in Paris in the 18th Century," *Acta musicologica* 47 (1975): 67–133; 94–101. Its origins and history are further explored by Charles Michael Carroll, "A Classical Setting for a Classical Poem: Philidor's *Carmen Saeculare*," *Studies in Eighteenth-Century Culture* 6 (1977): 97–111.

[73]This letter, dated Paris 10 April 1782, is one of the last that Diderot wrote. His exact words are: "Croyez moy, faites nous d'excellente musique, faites nous en pendant longtemps et ne vous exposez pas davantage à devenir ce que tant de gens que nous méprisons sont nés." Denis Diderot, *Correspondance*, ed. Georges Roth and Jean Varloot, 15 vols. (Paris, 1955–70), 15: 293–95. The letter is reprinted in *Pour Philidor*, p. 50.

most of his energies to chess. Yet his last musical works, such as the *Te Deum* (1786) and the *Ode anglaise* (1789, for the recovery of George III), show that his muse had not forsaken him. He died in exile at London in 1795.

Charles Cochin portrayed Philidor in profile, in a drawing engraved in 1772 by Augustin de Saint-Aubin and accompanied by a quatrain praising the composer's "masculine harmony" (Figure 7.7).

Aux Français etonnés, de sa mâle harmonie,	To the astonished French, by his strong harmony
Il montra dans son art des prodiges nouveaux;	He shows new prodigies in his art;
Dans ses délassemens admirant son génie,	As to his recreations, admiring his genius,
On voit qu'en ses jeux même il n'a point de rivaux.	One sees that he has no rivals even in his games.

Philidor's virile harmony most impressed his contemporaries, along with his ingenious orchestral portraits and text paintings. The engraving gives the composer a rather weak countenance that is at odds with his muscular music. A more forceful image of him is the 1783 bust sculpted by Augustin Pajou that has remained to this day with the composer's descendents.[74] It captures both the strength and the affability of Philidor, and includes symbols of his two passions, music and chess, surrounding his name.

Monsigny

The musical advantages with which ancestry and upbringing endowed Philidor were altogether lacking in Monsigny. Yet he was to become a dramatic composer of equal importance to his slightly older colleague, and one who had an even greater knack for pleasing the public. Born to an impoverished noble family in a tiny village near Saint-Omer (Artois) in 1729, he went to one of the local Jesuit schools, where he received violin instruction as an incidental part of his training. By 1749 he was already working in Paris as an accountant, in order to support his widowed mother. According to early biographies, he studied composition for five months under the direction of Pietro Gianotti, a contrabass player in the orchestra at the Opéra and author of *Le guide du compositeur* (1759). Nothing else about Monsigny's early musical efforts is known until three works of his were staged at

---

[74]Illustrated in *Philidor musicien et jouer d'échecs* (Recherches sur la musique française classique 28) (Paris, 1995), figure 1.

the Opéra-Comique: *Les aveux indiscrèts* (1759), *Le maître en droit* (1760), and *Le cadi dupé* (1761).

The last won praise in the *Mercure de France* for a quality that was essential to the successful theatrical composer: "The music was applauded; it must be of a more general taste than certain other works in that it is easy to retain by memory almost all the principal airs."[75] Contant d'Orville singled out the same quality. It is true that Monsigny's melodies often have a lilt or some arresting and unexpected feature that makes them more easy to retain than those of Duni or Philidor. The most significant result from *Le cadi dupé* was that Sedaine, after four successes in collaboration with Philidor, wished to combine his talents with Monsigny's. The first result, based on a fable of La Fontaine, was the eminently successful *On ne s'avise jamais de tout* (1761), followed by several other happy collaborations: *Le roi et le fermier* (1762), *Rose et Colas* (1764), *Aline* (1766), *Le déserteur* (1769), and *Félix* (1777).

ON NE S'AVISE JAMAIS DE TOUT

The first opera with Sedaine is one of those that popularized the "motto-title," along with Leo's *Amor vuol sofferenza,* Paisiello's *La precauzione inutile* (alias *Il barbiere di Siviglia,* which derives its story from the work in question), and Mozart's *Così fan tutte.* That is to say that the title of the work is sung at the end of the opera as a kind of homily: "One cannot be prepared for everything," in this case. It occurs as the refrain of the vaudeville finale (Example 7.11). From the motto alone it is possible to gather how astutely Monsigny used the old French tradition of conjunct melodies in dance rhythms. There are no vaudevilles per se in the work, but this has more to do with the poet than the composer; Sedaine was in the process

EXAMPLE 7.11. *Monsigny,* On ne s'avise jamais de tout, *Scene 19, vaudeville*

of banishing the traditional *timbres* altogether. To say this risks distorting a true picture of the sources of Monsigny's musical airs, which are inherently more French and popular than Philidor's. At the same time Monsigny does not fail to profit from the Italian idioms current in Paris, and from Philidor himself. The opera has only four characters, plus the commisaire who arrives to put things in

---

[75]Arthur Pougin, *Monsigny et son temps* (Paris, 1908), p. 44.

order at the end: the soubrette Lise (Rosina), her aged guardian Dr. Tue (Bartolo), her suitor Dorval (Lindoro/Almaviva), and her duenna Margarita.

The published score of the work is entitled "Opéra bouffon" in one printing and "Opéra-comique" in another. It begins with an overture that shows Monsigny quite abreast of the Italian sinfonia and its Parisian imitations. Opening with a fast movement in D, cut time, with double stops in the violins for brilliance, and *crescendi* up to the high D (à la Pergolesi and Jommelli), the fast scalar rushing passages already suggest the opening movement of Mozart's *Paris* Symphony. A lyric second theme is given to the oboes and horns alone, and the effective repeat in the reprise takes the oboes, up to their high D (the upper limit for orchestral oboes according to Mozart's instructions to Thomas Attwood). There follows an *Andante* in G without winds that has more individual and Gallic melodic traits; in particular, the drooping melodic sevenths recall a favorite air in Rameau's *Indes galantes*, "Obéissons sans balancer," and are used again prominently in the same composer's *Pygmalion*. The concluding *Minuetto Presto* in D, 3/8, could not be more Italianate, because it has no hint of rhythmic complication and because of its fast tempo.

Dorval is the first to appear and sing, outside the house where Lise is kept under close surveillance. The piece is an *Amoroso* in G in cut time, a langorous melody that is related to the *Andante* of the overture (thus prefiguring Mozart's procedure in the work that bears so many traces of its opéra-comique inheritance, *Die Entführung aus dem Serail*). Monsigny follows his initial six-measure phrase (2 + 2 + 2) with three three-measure extensions, throwing the listener off balance (Example 7.12). Yet the melody is haunting and likely to be retained. There is a naturalness about it that belies the art with which the third measure contracts the melodic motion of the first two, or the manner in which the melodic later peaks is also made the high point harmonically by the viola's dissonance. Note also the frequent parallel tenths in the outer voices, a feature that could not be more tra-

EXAMPLE 7.12. *Monsigny*, On ne s'avise jamais de tout, *Scene 1, Ariette*

ditional or French. As for the harmonic progression, Monsigny writes what pleases him rather than what the rules sanction.

Instructive is a comparison with Rameau's just-mentioned "Obéissons," on a similarly lovesick text. For all the similarities, and the overriding quality of "tendresse" common to both, they differ in that the older master's irregular meters have given way to the straitjacket of regular barring, if not regular phraseology. Monsigny is of course far more interested in the treble melody. Grétry says that Monsigny composed not at the keyboard, but by playing his violin, and one can almost hear him arriving at the melody of "Dieu des Amours" in this manner.

After a short spoken dialogue between Dr. Tue (literally, "kills") and Margarita, the former sings an *Allegro* in E♭, cut time, which has more melodic leaps and a more regular rhythm than the opening number, although the tenths are still prominent in the outer voices. The strings, which are joined by two horns here, are given lots of busywork, long *crescendi* and *decrescendi,* and they also comment on the text, as, for example, when Tue says that a doctor is always running, trotting from one place to another, at which there is a kind of gallop in the orchestra: ♫ ♫ ♫ ♫ . Monsigny is quite as pictorial in orchestral characterization as Philidor, from whom he has obviously learned much. In another short dialogue, Dorval appears in the first of his disguises (*en servant*) and listens as Tue instructs Margarita how to guard Lise. He has bought an amatory thesaurus in Florence, *Compendium Cythereum,* that makes him all-wise in the ways of young ladies. Margarita responds indignantly in an aria that there is no ruse a girl could invent that would elude her, at which a prominent blast on the horns makes mockery of her. She is from considerably further south than Florence, as confirmed by Sedaine's amusing line, "Je suis de Raguse, Et j'arrive de Syracuse." Pergolesian touches abound in her music—"I am arriving from Syracuse" begins like "Sempre in contrasti" from *La serva padrona.* But they are appropriate to her and constitute a kind of musical joke in their own right, as with Duni's Alberti in *Le peintre.*

Dorval, *en captif,* begs Tue and Margarita for alms in a brilliant trio. Monsigny's control of rhythm is quite as admirable as Philidor's here; moreover, the climactic drives already begin to suggest a later, post-1770 phase of comic opera. Even Grimm, who was forever disparaging Monsigny's music for being too French, admitted that this ensemble was a masterpiece. In a final quintet, Lise asks her guardian for permission to be united with Dorval, which is reluctantly granted. There follows the vaudeville finale with its motto refrain, quoted above.

Monsigny, according to the *Dictionnaire historique des musiciens* by Alexandre Choron and François Fayolle, was called the French Sacchini, which is suggestive in its way of how lyric a master his countrymen perceived him to be. The same source says that *On ne s'avise jamais de tout* "completed the musical revolution at the Opéra-comique." Because the French and Italian styles are beautifully integrated, without recourse to any of the traditional vaudevilles, the claim seems viable.

LE ROI ET LE FERMIER

Sedaine created in *Le roi et le fermier* a prototype of *drame lyrique*. Its emphasis upon some darker sides of contemporary life, including class conflict, is one that he had already shown in his *Le jardinier et son seigneur* for Philidor. The committee of the Comédie Italienne that passed on new librettos was reluctant to accept the work, which helps explain why Philidor delayed composing it. The court was involved too, as the opera was to be played there. Favart was a key figure in the altercation, which tested the friendship between him and Sedaine, as the latter implies in a letter of 25 November 1762, sent with a copy of the printed libretto to Favart. Philidor had begun to set the libretto but discontinued, says Favart (letter of 7 July 1762 to Durazzo), because he did not find that the poem presented him with enough *"tableaux et d'harmonie imitative;* Monsigny has not been so difficult and has taken on the task."

Sedaine took as his main source for the libretto Robert Dodsley's "dramatic tale" *The King and the Miller of Mansfield* (1737), which he knew from a French translation of 1756. The story is a simple one. The monarch (Henri IV in Charles Collé's play) loses his way in the forest at night returning from a hunting party. He stumbles upon a peasant, who rescues him and takes him to his cottage; "and there he sees, perhaps for the first time, what a man is vis-à-vis another who is stripped by his ignorance of the profound respect that he ought to have for his king," as Sedaine wrote in the preface to his libretto (an indication in itself of the seriousness of the endeavor).

There was hardly a precedent in French theater for putting a monarch of the reigning dynasty on the stage, and certainly none for lecturing him there. To gain some distance and a more exotic setting, Sedaine returned the story to England, which allowed him to have a stage set for the first two acts described as, "Une Forêt; des arbres plantés ça et là sur le Théâtre, et sans ordre" (i.e., the opposite of a typical, well-groomed French forest). Paradoxically, French composers with their long experience at orchestral tone paintings were the best equipped at this time to do justice to so romantic a setting.

Act I ends with a duet for the "noble peasant" Richard and his fiancée, the orphan Jenny, into which the sounds of the retreating hunt intrude (painted in the orchestra), as well as the threatening noises of a gathering storm (likewise painted). The singers comment on both aural phenomena. Much of this act and the opera as a whole is disposed in ensembles, Philidor's special strength (*On ne s'avise jamais de tout,* on the other hand, written especially for Monsigny, consisted mainly of solos). Monsigny shows that he can paint hunts and storms in his orchestra just as well as Rameau or Philidor. His gathering storm takes the form of slippery chromatic progressions and shudders in the strings, marked with a long *crescendo* and *decrescendo* by explicit wedge signs (Example 7.13). The storm proper breaks into full fury as an entr'acte in g. Cloud machines, lightning, rain, and thunder effects were frequent enough at the Opéra, but here it was a case of

EXAMPLE 7.13. *Monsigny*, Le roi et le fermier, *Duet*

the Comédie Italienne's stealing some of the thunder, literally, of its elder sister. The spectators at the Hôtel de Bourgogne particularly enjoyed the fright caused by this "orage en musique" according to one eyewitness.[76]

Laurent Garcin, commenting on the duet of Richard and Jenny, points out the many irregularities of this somber piece of tone painting. In a symmetrical, Italian-style duet, the singers are obliged to remain rooted to their positions, as stiff as statues. But in an action duet such as Sedaine has imposed, he says, they must follow the situation as it develops. The duet between Jenny and Richard, concludes the confident but overemphatic author, is a model that no Italian lyric melody will ever approach. Action ensembles may have been rare in opera seria, but they existed. They were common in opera buffa, especially in finales. Summing up the virtues of Sedaine as a librettist Garcin wrote this strong paragraph, ending with a panegyric of the poet's path.

> Whoever appreciates the works of Monsieur Sedaine without prejudice will agree that it is not an easy matter to attempt setting his *Drames* in music. The loftiness of his intentions, the force of his characters, the energy of his dialogue, and the picturesque qualities of his stage pictures [tableaux], together with the masculine concision of his style—all these qualities impose on the composer a task that is all the more arduous because they subjugate him, whatever he does, and do not permit him to seize on any ideas except the ones given him to paint. . . . Under the appearance of simplicity in subject and in tableaux, Sedaine, in *Le roi et le fermier, On ne s'avise jamais de tout,* and *Rose et Colas,* has sown the seeds of that interest that, in *Le déserteur,* would one day cause the shedding of so many tears.[77]

All these works were set by Monsigny, and the last named even bears the title "Drame" on the title page of the score.

Act II of *Le roi et le fermier* begins with a duet, a scene of low comedy between two peasants groping their way through the now-dark forest. The dignified figure of the king follows directly upon this farce. Monsigny establishes his character in an orchestral ritornello in E♭ (the key of the overture), which sounds solemn and imposing after the duet in g of the rustics, and it begins a huge obbligato recitative followed by an ariette for the king. Contrary to the dictates of the French classical tradition, Diderot, in his treatises on theater of the late 1750s, took the Shakespearian view that the serious—the tragic, even—should rub shoulders with the grotesque, just as happens in nature and in real life. We are witnessing here some of the first consequences of his ideas on the operatic stage. Sedaine looked up to Diderot as a spiritual father, and so did Duni, Monsigny, Philidor, and Grétry.

[76]Jean Desboulmiers, *Histoire anecdotique et raisonné du théâtre italien, depuis son rétablissement en France jusqu'à l'année 1769,* 7 vols. (Paris, 1769), 6: 487.
[77]Laurent Garcin, *Traité du mélo-drame, ou Réflexions sur la musique dramatique* (Paris, 1772), pp. 230–31.

The heart of the drama comes in Act III, set in the humble cottage of Richard, who has rescued the king. First we see his mother, his little sister Betsy, and Jenny engaged in various domestic pursuits such as spinning (the libretto specifies a spinning wheel as a stage property). To the consternation of the women, Richard brings in the strange nobleman. His mother is agitated because she has little to feed him. (When she finds out too late who he is, she regrets she did not feed him better, which she could have done: "Ah! si j'avais su que c'étoit le roi! moi, qui avois des poulets tout prêts!"—a typical example of Sedaine's insight into character). In Scene 10 the king sits down and has a remarkable spoken dialogue with Richard, while Jenny looks on. Richard's wisdom surprises his guest. It is one of your aristocratic presumptions, says Richard, that only courtiers can think. You do not intend to flatter me, responds the king, to which Richard replies that he only flatters those whom he despises. The exchange becomes more frank and turns upon a king's possible wisdom, surrounded by flatterers as he is. Richard concludes that he has seen more than a king is often allowed to see. Of what, asks his guest? "Des hommes."

The enlightened message of this capital scene cannot be mistaken. No wonder it was chosen by Wille for the stage picture completing his detailed drawing of the theater in 1767 (Figure 7.8). The moment shared by the three central characters is a long one. Jenny entertains the men by singing a *romance* about rustic life; the poem is directly inspired by Rousseau's "Dans ma cabane obscure" while the music is not, being in common time and accompanied by the slow triplets that from this time on often mark the genre.[78] Richard responds with a more lively piece, the ariette "Ce n'est qu'icy, oui, ce n'est qu'au Village que le bonheur a fixé son sejour." The king seizes the idea of happiness and sings a gavotte-like air that could not be more national or more simple. Happiness is in its spreading, in pouring it on humankind, and making blossom from your hands everything they have a right to expect:

> Le bonheur est de se répandre
> De le verser sur les humains
> De faire éclorer de vos mains
> Tout ce qu'ils ont droit d'attendre.

The king has given his identity away, almost, by the end of this air, which proclaims that the sovereign who is beloved of his people must be the happiest of men. Sedaine's ideal ruler is not without precedent in opera. Metastasio's *Tito* and Goldoni's *Bertoldo* had their lessons for rulers, too, and they were similar; Favart was also capable of some remarkably egalitarian speeches, such as "On nait égaux

---

[78]It is reproduced and discussed in detail in Daniel Heartz, "The Beginnings of the Operatic Romance: Rousseau, Sedaine, and Monsigny," *Eighteenth-Century Studies* 15 (1981–82), 149–78; 176–77.

FIGURE 7.8. Georg Wille. Scene from *Le roi et le fermier.*

dans nos Bois" in *Le prix de Cythère* (1742).[79] For the real monarchs of the time, whether Bourbon, Habsburg, Hannoverian, or Hohenzollern, the enlightened lesson librettos would teach them were not so easily put into practice.

The denouement arrives when Lord Lurewell (a wicked seducer who intends

[79]Heartz, "*Les Lumières*, p. 238.

to deflower Jenny) and a courtier enter the cottage seeking the sovereign, whom they recognize at once. In the septet that follows, the four peasants express their astonishment, repeating over and over to each other, "C'est le Roi?" while the two courtiers unctuously praise their master, who is aloof and questioning. It is a masterpiece of drama and music converging to form something higher, and an example of how much Monsigny has learned from Philidor's complicated ensembles with various rhythms for different characters. In spoken dialogue the king banishes Lurewell, tries to ennoble Richard, who refuses, then settles a dowry on Jenny and promises to come to their wedding. A choral ensemble for all praising royal generosity accompanies the king's exit. Then comes the vaudeville finale in the same key of C as the previous chorus. It is a typical gavotte, and the refrain after each verse draws the moral of the evening's entertainment: "Il ne faut s'étonner de rien, Il n'est qu'un pas du mal au bien."

Goldoni arrived in Paris in time to witness the premiere of *Le roi et le fermier* on 22 November 1762. He makes a point of this in *Mémoirs de M. Goldoni pour servir à l'histoire de sa vie et à celle de son théâtre* (Paris, 1787):

> I saw *Le Roi et le Fermier* at its first performance and was extremely pleased . . . ; it had an infinite number of performances and one still sees it with pleasure. Monsieur Sedaine has been ably seconded by the composer. . . . I find the music of Monsigny expressive, harmonious, agreeable: his motifs, his accompaniments and his modulations enchant me, and if I had dispositions to write comic operas in French, this musician would be one of those to whom I should turn.

This is considerable tribute, coming from so genial a playwright and librettist.

Grimm had high praise for Sedaine but not for Monsigny; he expressed a hope that the libretto would be translated by an Italian poet so it could be set by a good musician. It was adapted (along with other models using the same plot) as the subject of an Italian libretto by Goldoni, *Il re alla caccia*, which he then sent to Galuppi, who brought the opera to the stage at Venice in 1764. A comparison of the Parisian and Venetian scores does not redound to the credit of the latter; Galuppi was quite at a loss when it came to painting the hunting party or the oncoming tempest with his orchestra. The buffo finales that had become obligatory in Italian comic opera, along with the mandatory number of solos for each singer, allowed Goldoni little latitude to capture the essence of the original, and the enlightened elements that remained seem to have escaped Galuppi altogether.

Le roi et le fermier also traveled to Vienna. Favart, acting as Count Durazzo's agent at Paris, sent him Monsigny's score, and the work was performed at the Burgtheater in the fall of 1763. Durazzo wrote Favart on 19 November 1763:

> We have just given *Le roi et le fermier,* which is at its tenth performance; never has an opéra-comique had more success in this country. I can easily conceive the reason for

this. . . . Here one wants neither the *trop tendre,* nor the *trop amoureux,* and still less the *trop bas. Le roi et le fermier* falls precisely in the middle, being neither *bas* nor *trop tendre.* One seized with avidity the moral maxims which are spread throughout the work; its simple and sometimes elevated style made much effect.

Durazzo has hit upon an excellent definition of what could be called Enlightenment opera: moral maxims projected by a simple but elevated style. It would do as well for *Die Zauberflöte.* Vienna was aware of a huge store of Parisian music in the 1750s and 1760s, by way of its resident French companies. Paris knew but an insignificant amount of Viennese music until it came to know Gluck and Haydn in the 1770s.

By the time d'Origny published his *Annales du théâtre italien* in 1788, *Le roi et le fermier* had had over two hundred performances and earned its authors 20,000 livres, paid them out of receipts, with costs previously deducted. From this it can be seen that a popularly acclaimed opéra-comique brought its creators considerable wealth.

None was more popular than *Rose et Colas,* Sedaine's Favart-like tale of two young peasant lovers who prevail over adversity only at the very end. It offered a perfect vehicle for Monsigny's lyric gifts. From its first performances at the Comédie Italienne in 1764, *Rose et Colas* won the acclaim of the multitude and was rarely absent from the boards for more than a few months during the following three decades. D'Origny attributes this not only to the excellence of the libretto but also to "une musique dont l'effet incontestable est de toujours plaire."

LE DÉSERTEUR

In March 1769 *Le déserteur* continued the path opened by *Le roi et le fermier* and *Tom Jones.* It is no longer a comedy at all, but a serious work of great dramatic tension, with a few comic scenes. Conforming to the theory of Diderot as to what a *drame* should be, it describes a situation in the life of ordinary people of the contemporary period. The action takes place in an army camp in Flanders, on the French side of the border.

Alexis, a soldier, is duped into believing that his fiancée Louise has married someone else, and out of despair he mentions deserting the army, upon the mere threat of which he is arrested and incarcerated. Act II and most of Act III take place in prison. Sedaine cleverly strings out the coming to awareness of Alexis that he was duped, and of Louise that he is condemned to die. A fellow prisoner, Montauciel, who is a drunkard, provides some Gallic humor to what is otherwise an increasingly tense and black situation, and Louise's doltish brother is also comic. These two end Act II with songs of their own, which they then combine as a duet, an original idea that was greatly admired by Berlioz:

sense of theater was so strong that he unerringly tied the whole experience of this gripping drama together by musical means. The subsequent composers of "rescue operas" down to and including Beethoven could and did learn much from *Le déserteur.*

A vast body of critical reaction grew up in response to this masterpiece of Sedaine and Monsigny. Chosen among many writers here is Heinrich Heine, who was one of the foremost art and music critics of nineteenth-century Paris, because he brings together something quite rare, a synthesis of musical and visual perceptions. Heine witnessed *Le déserteur* in 1844, as adapted by Adolphe Adam.

> Voici de la vraie musique française! The most serene grace, an ingenuous sweetness, a freshness similar to the perfume of wild flowers, a true *naturel,* verity and even poetry, yes poetry, but without the shudder of the infinite, without mysterious charms, without bitterness, irony and *morbidezza*—I should say a poetry enjoying good health; and this health is at once elegant and rustic. Monsigny's opera reminded me at once of the works of his contemporary, the painter Greuze. . . . in listening to this opera I understood clearly how visual and musical arts from the same epoch always breathe a single and same spirit, and that contemporary masterpieces carry the characteristic marks of the most intimate brotherhood.[81]

Monsigny fulfilled Heine's intuitive leap, claiming that he was inspired by Jean-Baptiste Greuze's painting *La bénédiction du père de famille* when setting to music the culminating trio in *Félix.*[82]

Much can be learned from adaptations of *Le déserteur.* In 1770 Francesco Badini made an Italian libretto out of it that Pietro Guglielmi composed and brought to the stage in London. The action is rendered incongruous in several places from the need to include solos for secondary characters and furnish the interminable finales with enough bickering to sustain them. Of the Act II finale a modern critic has written that "it trivialises the drama by introducing a set of irrelevant scenes during which unimportant characters express their hopes of love and marriage and squabble about who was responsible for Alessio's arrest."[83] He notes further in comparison of the two operas:

> Another very common fault of Italian comic opera, exemplified by *Il Disertore,* is the weakness of its ending. In the French *Déserteur* the denouement, when Alexis and Louise meet in freedom, comes as the climax of the final ensemble which also happens to be the largest musical item in the work [and the first music heard in the opera,

[81]Pougin, *Monsigny,* p. 139; Druilhe, *Monsigny,* pp. 94–95. Heine's criticism has been edited by Michael Mann, *Heinrich Heine: Zeitungsberichte über Musik und Malerei* (Frankfort, 1964).

[82]Michel Noiray, "Monsigny," in *The New Grove Dictionary of Opera,* ed. Stanley Sadie (London, 1992).

[83]Michael F. Robinson, "Two London Versions of The Deserter," in *Report of the Twelfth Congress of the International Musicological Society, Berkeley, 1977,* pp. 239–45.

at the outset of the Overture]. In *Il Disertore* Alessio and his girlfriend meet not in an ensemble but during a passage of recitative. They then have a love duet. The other characters subsequently assemble on stage during further recitative. Only after that does the last finale commence, a short piece with conventional congratulations to the happy couple. In other words the denouement is sensibly associated in the one case with a finale that is substantial enough to be considered the musical climax of the opera. In the other case it occurs before the end, leaving the finale devoid of any action whatsoever.

The rigidity of Italian opera when compared with opéra-comique emerges clearly enough here, and also apparent is how much Italian poets had to learn from advances in Paris with respect to theatrical effectiveness.

It comes as no surprise, then, that Italian opera in the last third of the eighteenth century turned increasingly to French models, even for musical features such as the *romance,* rondo, recurrent motif or theme, and the program overture (of which *Le déserteur* offers an example with its alternating calms, storms, and shepherd's pipes). Guglielmi's version included none of these features yet, but it was at least musically competent, which cannot be said for Charles Dibdin's *The Deserter,* put on at Drury Lane in 1773 as a pastiche of Monsigny, Philidor, and Dibdin himself. London had a long history of mangling the best French stageworks, so this was nothing new. The critic of these three operas on the same subject concludes that the cultural climate in Hannoverian England was all wrong for Monsigny's "intensely felt blend of social comment and musical expression." Little could be done because Italian opera in London was badly managed, and not even Christian Bach or Antonio Sacchini could arrest its declining standards.

Monsigny wrote little after *Le déserteur.* His failing eyesight contributed to his decision to give up the theater altogether after *Félix ou l'enfant trouvé* (1777), again with Sedaine, who tried to lure him out of retirement with the libretto for *Richard Coeur-de-lion.* The composer returned it and counselled Sedaine to call upon Grétry. During his long life (he died greatly honored in early 1817), Monsigny was a generous friend to other artists, young and old alike. In a letter of 31 August 1795, written when he was indigent himself through loss of his pensions from the house of Orléans that he had long served, he addressed the associated artists of the Opéra-Comique National:

Citizens, when in 1775, I asked you to grant to the celebrated Philidor the pension that you had the kindness to offer me, I told you that Philidor merited it more than I for his talents. I told you that it would be unjust for me to take from a great artist the only recompense for which (at that time) he had the right to hope. Today, my dear fellow citizens, I am going to make you another request. Philidor is dead and leaves a widow without means. Do me the extreme pleasure of permitting me to see the enjoyment of this pension go to her. For thirty-five years, I have received from you the marks of esteem and friendship; put the seal on these marks of esteem and friendship in granting me what I ask for the widow of the famous Philidor. The happiness of obliging the widow of a great artist is so sweet to my heart that you will not refuse this moment of delight. *Salut et fraternité*.[84]

This moving testimony says much about the noble spirit of the artist who wrote it.

Grétry

LIÈGE, ROME, AND GENEVA

The memoirs of Grétry rank with those of Ditters von Dittersdorf as a portrait of eighteenth-century musical life and will consequently be mined at some length for their richness of detail.[85] Baptized on 11 February 1741, André-Ernest-Modeste Grétry was one of six children born to a poor and loving family in Liège. The city was an independent principality ruled by an archbishop, like Salzburg, and a part of the Holy Roman Empire, with strong ties to the courts of Vienna and Brussels. Like his father and brother Grétry became a violinist at the collegiate church of Saint Denis. His teachers included several competent local musicians, one of a brutality he never forgot. What inspired him to become a musician, he says, was not their teaching but a troupe of Italian singers under the direction of (G. F.) Crosa and (Natale?) Resta who visited Liège during 1753–55 and performed buffo operas by Pergolesi, Galuppi, and others: "That is where I formed a passionate taste for music" (1: 15).

Grétry was also trained as a singer. His triumph as a church soprano came when he sang a solo motet with words praising the Blessed Virgin, a contrafactum of an Italian aria, he says. There was nothing unusual about this. Extraordinary was the way he sang it "in the Italian taste as purely the best opera singers" (1: 17–18).

After his voice broke he applied himself more and more to composition. Church music he wrote in abundance, he says, but also six symphonies, which do not survive. They were performed with success, according to him. His early compositions helped win him the patronage that sent him to Rome for further study, probably in March 1760.[86]

Liège was not isolated in a musical sense during the 1750s, as the visit of an

---

[84]The original is printed in Pougin, *Monsigny*, p. 201, and Druilhe, *Monsigny*, pp. 38–39.

[85]André-E.-M. Grétry, *Mémoires, ou essais sur la musique*, 3 vols. (Paris, 1789–94; reprint, New York, 1971). Volume 1 appeared in 1789; the second and third volumes were written by 1794. Subsequent references in this chapter will cite only the volume and page number in the text.

[86]David Charlton, *Grétry and the Growth of Opéra-Comique* (Cambridge, 1986), p. 21.

Italian buffo troupe indicates. Also, the city had its own musical periodical, *L'écho, ou Journal de musique françoise et italienne,* published by Benoît Andrez. The May 1758 issue included two numbers from *La fausse esclave,* Gluck's first opéra-comique for Vienna, which had its premiere only four months earlier. The September 1759 issue included two airs from Gluck's setting of *Le diable à quatre* for Vienna, one of them the famous tobacco song.[87] Political connections between Liège and Austria obviously entailed cultural ones.

Grétry recounts more about people than places in his memoirs, in which respect they are like those of Dittersdorf, who may possibly have read Grétry's. An eye for human characterization is, of course, one aspect of what made them both such masterly composers for the stage. Yet how we would have enjoyed more about the scenery encountered on the long trip from Liège to Rome. Grétry quotes his hero and model, Jean-Jacques Rousseau, as saying the only way to really see the countryside is to walk. That is what the fledgling composer did, although he had a frail constitution and a lung disease that caused him to spit blood. Not for nothing was his first name André (from the Greek meaning "manly" or "courageous"). He deserved it quite as much as the other two, "earnest" and "modest."

In 1760 the Seven Years War was at its height, but the Continental battles were confined mostly to Saxony, Silesia, and Bohemia. Grétry, accompanied by a few others, traversed the Ardennes forest and the Rhineland, going by way of Trier, an electoral court of the empire. Presumably he passed by way of neutral Bavaria in order to reach Austrian territory. He crossed the Brenner Pass and the South Tyrol into Italy, by way of Trent. It was spring and the realization of leaving icy mountainous terrain for warm fertile plains did stir his pen to a brief rhapsody. Like many a sensitive northerner, he had long been dreaming of Italy and Italian music. The only city he mentions specifically before Rome is Habsburg-ruled Florence.

Once in Rome he settled into one of the fellowship posts at the Collège de Liège, which was good for five years. Students sought teachers in their special fields outside the college. Grétry became a pupil of Giovanni Battista Casali, maestro di cappella at Saint John Lateran, with whom he studied counterpoint for two years. (Casali is not to be confused with Giovanni Battista Costanzi, director of the Capella Giulia of Saint Peter's, to whom Boccherini came for study in 1756.) Grétry also mentions studying composition and harpsichord with a Roman organist he does not name; in order to please this master he wrote many keyboard fugues patterned on those of Francesco Durante, whose *Sonate per cembalo divise in studii e divertimenti,* widely diffused through prints and copies, did

---

[87]Brown, *Gluck and the French Theatre in Vienna,* pp. 211, 219. For the tune of the tobacco song, see Brown's example 6.9b, p. 230. It is also quoted in *Haydn, Mozart,* p. 272.

include fugues. Perhaps these harpsichord pieces by Grétry resembled the two "fugues" he appended to the third volume of his memoirs (3: 396–410); both are contrapuntal exercises in two voices based on well-known themes. He wrote church music as well, but little survives. Six string quartets published in Paris in 1773 do survive, on the other hand, and the title page claims that they were "composed in Rome." Their suavity and assurance in handling the quartet texture make it difficult to believe that he wrote them so early.

Grétry confesses that he was "dying with desire" to meet Piccinni, whose setting of Goldoni's *La buona figliuola* was written for Rome in 1760 and held the stage for two years running, an unusual feat for any Italian opera he says (1: 88), and indeed it was. An abbé of his acquaintance introduced him into the study of Piccinni, who took little notice of his young admirer, also dressed as an abbé, as college rules required. The famous composer ignored the visitors and went back to work on the oratorio he was composing. After an hour in silence they left. "I deserved no better then," says Grétry, "but how much the slightest encouragement from him would have pleased me." He resolved to behave differently to budding talents should he become famous. The *Mémoires* as a whole are meant to instruct young musicians.

A Magnificat for eight voices (lost) culminated Gretry's lessons with his teacher Casali, who urged him to work by himself henceforth. Grétry insisted that, even when in Rome, he never intended to become a church composer, although, with the help of Padre Martini, he passed the counterpoint examination for admission to the Accademia Filarmonica of Bologna. Never does Grétry deny the importance of contrapuntal skill for a theater composer. In fact he insists "one cannot be simple, expressive and above all, correct, without having exhausted the difficulties of counterpoint" (1: 92). "I loved the music of Galuppi, Piccinni, Sacchini, Majo, and Terradellas, but I loved even more that of Pergolesi—nature called me toward his genre and I was persuaded that I would never arrive at creating good music, for the theater above all, unless I took his declamation for a guide" (1: 96).

Pergolesi's music by itself was not quite all that Grétry needed for inspiration. His own efforts failed to satisfy him, he says, and he became so despondent that he took to his bed with a fever and remained there for six months. Once he was strong enough to walk again he went into the country outside Rome where he met a hermit and accepted his offer of a simple, rustic existence for three months. "The sweetest satisfaction of my life occured in these conditions. . . . one day when I decided to compose an aria on the words of Metastasio. Imagine my ravishment when my ideas flowed purely and clearly and I could arrange them as I wished! Now I could add or subtract without harming the principal idea, which I saw embellished at every turn" (1: 100). Once again the great Roman poet was the cause of a musical epiphany. Ginguené claims that Grétry took some months of lessons with Sacchini at this time, a circumstance about which Grétry says nothing.[88]

Soon after his idyll in the country, Grétry wrote for the Roman carnival of 1765, two intermezzi for the Alibert theater entitled *La vendemmiatrice* (The Lady Grape Picker). The libretto survives but not the music. As was standard practice, he, as composer, directed the first three performances from the first harpsichord. The work succeeded, he says, and the public clamored for one aria to be repeated. Piccinni now took notice of Grétry and made his approbation of the work known. People in the streets sang tunes from his new opera to him. A wealthy English flautist, thought to be the fourth earl of Abingdon, who was his own age, commissioned some flute concertos (lost) and was so pleased with the results he gave Grétry a pension for further compositions.

A friend in the French embassy at Rome showed Grétry a printed score of *Rose et Colas.* This genial *paysannerie* by Sedaine and Monsigny, first performed in March 1764, revealed to Grétry his true calling. He now realized he wanted to work in Paris (whereas a Liègois would more normally gravitate to Vienna because of political and cultural ties). It appears that Grétry instinctively recognized his deep kinship with the music of Monsigny, whom he called the most lyric of all composers ("le plus chantant des musiciens" [3: 386]). Perhaps he gained at the same time his first knowledge of Sedaine, with whom he would eventually achieve his greatest success of all, *Richard Coeur-de-lion* (1784).

In early 1766 Grétry made his way to Geneva, where Lord Abingdon had a residence. He no longer traveled by foot but by carriage, a fact he cleverly uses to make an epigram about Rousseau's dictum. His route took him by way of Turin and over the Mont Cenis Pass. Geneva was where he hoped to earn enough money to make his way as a composer in Paris. He says he gave singing lessons to some twenty ladies there, an occupation he did not enjoy. The Genevans had just acquired their first theater, after fierce disputes as to the propriety of such an institution in the city of Calvin. A French troupe arrived and played several recent opéras-comiques, among which Grétry named his favorites as *Rose et Colas, Le maréchal,* and *Tom Jones,* the last two by Philidor. "They gave me great pleasure once I got used to hearing French sung, which at first appeared disagreeable to me. It required still more time to get used to hearing speaking and singing in the same work" (1: 130). He began to search for a libretto with which to create such a work, his first in French.

Voltaire lived close to Geneva just across the French border at Ferney (from which he could flee France once again if forced). Grétry made so bold as to send a letter to Voltaire asking his help. The great man bade him come for a visit and

[88]Pierre Louis Ginguené, "France," in *Encyclopédie méthodique: musique,* ed. N. E. Framery and P. L. Ginguené, vol. 1 (Paris, 1791).

received him warmly. He declined at first to write a libretto, saying "I am old and scarcely know the opéra-comique fashionable in Paris today, on account of which people abandon *Zaïre* and *Mahomet*" (1: 33) (two of his most successful plays for the Comédie Française). Grétry turned elsewhere and while still in Geneva made a setting of Favart's *Isabelle et Gertrude,* which was based on a poem by Voltaire. The opera, performed in Geneva's new theater in December 1766, survives only in fragments.[89] It undoubtedly helped the young composer's career that he had an imposing mien and was, in spite of his lung disease, relatively robust. Madame Elisabeth Vigée-Lebrun, famous French court painter, portrayed the mature Grétry as an elegant figure, with broad forehead and neatly curled hair (Figure 7.9).

FIGURE 7.9. Elisabeth Vigée-Lebrun. Portrait of Grétry.

FIRST YEARS IN PARIS

In the course of 1767 Grétry, fortified with his earnings in Geneva, took the decisive step of his life. He went to Paris and attempted to break into the circle of composers working for the Théâtre Italien. It was no easy task, as poets were loathe to take their chances with a novice, and poets were in control in the sense that the libretto had to be voted up or down by the company, usually before the music was composed. Duni, Philidor, and Monsigny had all had a string of successes, so librettists were naturally content to rely upon them. It is a tribute to all three that they welcomed Grétry and tried to smooth his path. Philidor induced Roger Pleinchesne to offer his libretto *Le jardinier de Sidon* to the newcomer, but after a few days the poet changed his mind and would agree only if Philidor shared in the composition, which Grétry refused. Philidor's setting proved unsuccessful.

An anecdote Grétry tells puts his situation in clearer light. He was visiting an actor from the troupe of the Théâtre Italien one day. "He did not disguise how difficult it would be to succeed alongside of the three composers who worked for their company. Then he sang me Monsigny's Romance 'Jusque dans la moindre chose' in its entirety" (1: 149) (Example 7.15). "There is melody for you, sir; that is

---

[89]For details, see Charlton, *Grétry and the Growth of Opéra-Comique,* pp. 24–26; in what survives, Charlton detects influences of Pergolesi, Philidor, and Monsigny.

EXAMPLE 7.15. *Monsigny*, On ne s'avise jamais de tout, *Romance*

what you must do, but it is very difficult." Grétry left his challenger, he says, and began composing melodies that he compared with those of Monsigny.

The example is the first part of the *romance* sung by Lise in *On ne s'avise jamais de tout* (1761), the first collaboration between Sedaine and Monsigny. It is followed by a middle section in the minor mode, then a return to the main section with different words, the form given to many *romances.* Lise's lovesong makes a good case for its composer. There is a subtle motivic unity and balance achieved by various rising or falling conjunct thirds or fourths. The climactic line "Pour moi tout est son image" becomes also the melodic climax, heightened by a change of tempo to *Adagio* for the last two syllables. Melodic ornamentation is carefully indicated. Well might Grétry wonder if he would ever achieve Monsigny's lightness and grace.

Grétry's first work for Paris was *Les mariages samnites* on a libretto by Pierre Légier that was turned down by the Italians as too noble for their theater. A trial performance followed in early 1768 with some forces of the Opéra in the salon of the prince de Conti (the same room depicted by Michel Barthélemy Ollivier two years earlier with the boy Mozart at the harpsichord and Pierre Jélyotte tuning his guitar). The performance was a failure because of the desultory way it was sung by all except Jélyotte, who had only a minor role. Even so, Gretry's music was strong enough to win him important supporters such as Count Gustav Philip Creutz, the Swedish ambassador, and the influential writers Jean Baptiste Suard and Abbé François Arnaud. These supporters persuaded Marmontel to write a true opéra-comique for Grétry.

Jean-François Marmontel was a disciple of Voltaire who was a distinguished literary figure, author of a celebrated collection of *Contes moraux,* and member of the Académie Française. He had collaborated with Rameau in the 1750s and had written at least one opéra-comique, *La bergère des Alpes,* a pastoral set by Josef Kohaut without much success in 1766. Less a man of the theater than Sedaine, he was an equally good poet and had the great advantage, from a composer's point of view, of being pliable to the demands of music in opera. He based the libretto of *Le Huron* on a recent short story of Voltaire, in which a savage raised in North America showed, after being transplanted to France, more natural goodness and bravery than the locals. He allowed Grétry considerable say in shaping the story for musical setting. It was evidently the composer who gave Marmontel indications about the verse forms he required.[90] Grétry modestly remained silent about this in his memoirs.

LE HURON AND LUCILE

Grétry's music for *Le Huron* still met some resistance among the actors who had to sing it, but they were won over by the excellent singer-actor Joseph Caillot, who played the title role. It was Caillot who took the young composer to the house of Madame Laruette, where he played the whole opera at the harpsichord for the singers. She was to create the leading female role in this opera and several subsequent ones by Grétry. After surprisingly little rehearsal time in the theater, the opera was offered to the public for the first time on 20 August 1768. The libretto had profited from Voltaire's satirical humor, some of which Marmontel managed to preserve, but it was the music that carried the day, thanks to the singers. Grétry showed that he could project the text with appropriate melodic accents, free from clichés. This is well illustrated in the opera's best-known number, "Ou est l'Huronie?" (Example 7.16). Caillot sang it with such verve he brought the house down.

Grétry used the same musical example in his memoirs as a lesson about how to set the mute *e* in words like *Huroni–e, Turqui–e,* and *Arabi–e.* The first two he

EXAMPLE 7.16. *Grétry,* Le Huron, *Act I, Scene 8, air*

[90]Edouard A. Fétis, preface to his edition of *Le Huron,* A.-E.-M. Grétry, *Collection complète des oeuvres* (Leipzig, n.d.), 14: v.

sets to weak melodic notes; the third gets no note at all. As he explains, "all notes that carry the mute *e* are without consequence, and can even be suppressed without damage to the melody" (1: 135). In a comic piece of this type Grétry was obviously more interested in catching the declamatory rhythms of the text than he was in metric regularity.

About this first big success in Paris, Grétry recounts in humble and winning manner his nervous anxiety before the premiere (much as did Salieri before his first opera two years later in Vienna) and his elation immediately thereafter. Now the poets who had turned him down earlier came swarming around to present their librettos. It is characteristic of the man that he wanted to thank Marmontel by turning them down and writing another opera in collaboration with him. Within a short time their *Lucile* reached the stage (premiere on 5 January 1769).

At the fourth performance of *Le Huron,* Grétry was seated next to Monsigny, who intuited that cuts had been made in the little duet "Ne vous rebutez pas." The older composer exclaimed, "Your complaisance made you spoil this piece, for it is impossible that you created it as I have just heard it sung" (2: 308). Grétry, like the other composers of the Théâtre Italien, was constantly adjusting his music. In this case he admitted that Monsigny was right. The cuts Grétry made in the last rehearsals disturbed the proportions of the piece. He restored the music to its original form. Grimm praised *Le Huron* precisely for Grétry's skill in knowing how to end a piece and give it the right length.

Philidor's *Ernelinde* was one source of inspiration for the type of energetic melody in march time with wide leaps that Grétry used, but he was more sensitive to declamation than Philidor.[91] Without making comparisons with his Parisian predecessors Grétry wrote to Padre Martini as early as 1 December 1767, saying that he believed he was on the path of finding a way to match Italianate music with correct French prosody.[92] What did he consider good declamation in French? The answer may seem surprising. He took as his model the stylized speech of the actors and actresses at the Comédie Française, he says, and even sought guidance from them in person. One day Marmontel took him to visit the famous Mademoiselle Clairon, for whom he played the duet "Dans le sein d'un père" in *Sylvain* (1770), his third collaboration with the poet. She was content with the music except for a few lines that were insufficiently emphatic. She declaimed them, and Grétry copied her declamation while singing and revised his setting accordingly (1: 201).

The single most celebrated piece in Grétry's first operas for Paris is the quartet in *Lucile* "Où peut-on être mieux qu'au sein de sa famille?" It occurs at about

---

[91]Charlton, *Grétry and the Growth of Opéra-Comique,* p. 32, compares "Né dans un camp" in *Ernelinde* with No. 6 in *Le Huron.*

[92]*La correspondance générale de Grétry,* ed. Georges de Froidcourt (Brussels, 1962), pp. 29–32.

the middle of this one-act comedy and is set for an unusual combination of one soprano, two tenors, and one bass. Lucile and Dorval are about to be married, hence this blissful outpouring seated around a table with their respective fathers. The lovers begin by singing in tenths, which neatly ties them together (Example 7.17). Lucile's lovely melody is almost entirely conjunct and hints that its composer has indeed profited from studying Monsigny. The harmony is more regular

EXAMPLE 7.17. *Grétry*, Lucile, *Quartet*

than is often the case with that master. In m. 5 harmonic interest is quickened by the IV^7 chord coming after $IV - V^4_3 / IV - IV^6$. A sense of relaxation emanates from abundant use of the subdominant. Here it is the full measure of subdominant in m. 3 that lends a particular sweetness to the notion of well-being from reposing in the bosom of one's family. The entire quartet is organized as a large five-part rondo, with episodes made mostly out of contrasting duets suggested by the text.

Marmontel and Grétry placed their quartet of family bliss just before a peripeteia. In a powerful monologue composed in very free form following the outbursts of the text, the peasant Blaise reveals that he, not the rich bourgeois Timante, is the father of Lucile. She is mortified and afraid that Dorval will no longer want her. Will he desert her? Of course not, for the message of this opera, quite in line with what Voltaire and the *philosophe* party were preaching, is that low birth does not matter where the heart is concerned. The opera ends with choral celebration and choreographic spectacle. Grétry's instrumental piece, called simply "Danse," is such an inspired piece of gavotte-like music (in a, with a middle section in A) that he appears here to be the heir of Rameau.

The quartet in *Lucile* became so well known that its celebration of domestic virtue took on a political significance, the home in question coming to mean the French royal family. By the time of the Bourbon restoration in 1815, the piece had virtually been transformed into a royalist hymn. This is ironic in a sense, because Grétry's sympathies were more republican than royalist, in spite of all the patronage he enjoyed from the crown, and in spite of excesses committed in the name of the republic that he deplored in print. The first volume of his memoirs was written before the bloody events of July 1789. In it he makes many references to the famous quartet, including this one so earnest it shows he truly deserved the first of his two middle names.

> This comedy [*Lucile*], where I found the means of deploying domestic sensibilities, so natural to a man born in the land of good people [Liège], awoke, if I dare say so, this same precious sentiment here. The quartet "Où peut-on être mieux qu'au sein de sa famille" made tears flow from the spectators, surprised to be moved by new means in the land of *galanterie* [Paris]. (1: 173)

Tear-jerking comedies were nothing new in Paris, especially in the spoken theater. Voltaire made fun of them repeatedly, while not missing any opportunity to profit from the vogue himself. Pathetic or philosophical elements were certainly nothing new to opéra-comique after Sedaine's *Le roi et le fermier* of 1762. Marmontel, who died in 1799, claimed in his memoirs, written late in life, to have created a new genre by raising the character of opéra-comique with *Lucile*. But this seems little more than a gratuitous insult to Sedaine, who died in 1797.

ZÉMIRE ET AZOR AND AFTER

The long alliance between Paris and Vienna culminated in 1770 with the arrival in France of Marie Antoinette, youngest daughter of Empress Maria Theresa, as the bride of the dauphin, grandson of Louis XV. She was fourteen, he a year older. Trained in music since she was a small child, Marie Antoinette sang, played the keyboard, and may even have composed, quite in line with the tradition of her Habsburg ancestors.[93] Perhaps she became fond of opéra-comique before leaving Vienna, where it was well known both as a local product and as a Parisian import. In France she would become its greatest patron. Her older sister Maria Carolina carried a love of opéra-comique from Vienna to Naples, of which she became queen in 1768.

To celebrate the royal marriage many operas of various kinds were performed, some new, some old. Tragédies by Lully and Rameau were revived. Most of the entertainments at Fontainebleau in the fall of 1770 were of the lighter operatic variety. No fewer than eight opéras-comiques were given, plus Rousseau's *Le devin du village.* The court requested Grétry to set two new librettos. A year later,

[93]Daniel Heartz, "A Keyboard Concertino by Marie Antionette?" in *Essays in Musicology: A Tribute to Alvin Johnson,* ed. Lewis Lockwood and Edward Roesner (Philadelphia, 1990), pp. 201–12.

in celebration of the marriage of the comte de Provence (the future Louis XVIII), he was asked to set two more. All were performed at Fontainebleau by the forces of the Comédie Italienne before being given in Paris (Table 7.1).

TABLE 7.1. Operas Set by Grétry in 1770–71 That Were First Performed at Court

Title	Libretto	Fontainebleau	Paris	Dedicatee
1. *Les deux avares*	Charles Fenouillot de Falbaire	27 October 1770	6 December 1770	Duc d'Aumont
2. *L'amitié à l'épreuve*	Charles-Simon Favart and Claude Fusée de Voisenon	13 November 1770	24 January, 1771	Marie Antoinette
3. *L'ami de la maison*	Jean François Marmontel	26 October 1771	14 May 1772	Duc de Duras
4. *Zémire et Azor*	Marmontel	9 November 1771	16 December 1772	Madame du Barry

The four new operas were quite different in character, as can be gathered even by their geographical settings. Charles Fenouillot de Falbaire, a wealthy courtier, set *Les deux avares* in Smyrna. *L'amitié à l'épreuve* is set in London. Marmontel gave *L'ami de la maison* a setting outside Paris. His masterpiece, *Zémire et Azor,* is a fairy tale on the legend of Beauty and the Beast, set in exotic Persia.

Grétry's star was not merely on the rise. He had arrived to the extent of becoming the favorite composer of both the court and Paris, especially with *Zémire et Azor.* The dedications tell their own story, all the more so in an age when the dedicatee's permission was required. D'Aumont was first gentleman of the king's bedchamber, who was in charge of the festive operas at Fontainebleau, an office to which the Duras succeeded the following year. The dauphine, Marie Antoinette, was pleased to accept a dedication, and so was Madame du Barry, *maîtresse en titre* of Louis XV. Royal recognition was not long in coming. As Grétry wrote with pride to Padre Martini on 24 January 1772, the king had awarded him a pension of 1,200 francs and a gratuity of 200 louis d'or. In addition to this, the Comédie Italienne decided to award him a salary of 100 livres a month for his exclusive service to their troupe as composer and music director.

After settling in Paris, Grétry fell in love with a Frenchwoman from Lyons, Jeanne-Marie Grandon. A daughter, Jenny, was born to this couple on 1 December 1770. Their marriage did not take place until July 1771, by which time it appeared that their financial prospects were bright enough to raise a family. Two more daughters were born to them, Lucile, in 1772, and two years later Antoinette, named after Marie Antoinette, who was her doting godmother and who became queen of France on the death of Louis XV and accession of Louis XVI in May 1774.

Zémire comprises some twenty-five numbers plus the three-movement overture. The overture's finale depicts a storm leading without a break into the first number, a reaction to the storm and its waning by Ali, the timorous servant of the merchant Sandor; both have been set down in an abandoned palace after escaping a shipwreck. A table laden with food and drink appears by magic. Ali gorges himself and then cannot help from falling asleep (all his characteristics are traditionally associated with Harlequin). Grétry deploys the Italian buffo style to good advantage in characterizing Ali. The tone changes abruptly when Sandor plucks a rose from the palace arbor as a gift to take back to his youngest daughter Zémire. Azor, disguised as a beast, erupts on the scene and says that this insult to his hospitality must cost Sandor his life, but he yields to Sandor's pleas to go back to his three daughters before he dies.

Zémire learns what has happened from Ali and resolves to die in her father's place. She goes to Azor. In his palace she finds a room with her name over the door. At this point some genies perform three graceful dances in her honor. Azor appears wearing a hideous mask for a face. Frightened at first by his appearance, she is impressed by his gentleness of manner and speech. At his request she sings an elaborate coloratura aria with flute solo about a bird. He asks what he can do in return to please her. She misses her family and asks to see them. Azor conjures a magic picture of them on the wall, behind a scrim, and they sing a stunningly beautiful trio lamenting her absence. The scene inspired an engraving that brims with details of staging, costume, and Azor's disguise (Figure 7.10).

After more travel back and forth, Zémire returns to Azor of her own free will. When she declares her love for him, the spell of enchantment is broken. Instead of being a beastlike figure he becomes a proper young prince on a throne, welcoming her to his side. Grétry attributes some of the opera's success to the public's knowledge that its favorite tenor, Jean Baptiste Clairval, a handsome man, was under the mask.

Grétry's score abounds in novel sonorities, inventive touches, and inspired lyricism. Two instances must suffice here as examples. The ballet welcoming Zémire to Azor's palace consists of three dances, all in the rarified key of E, heretofore unused in the opera. The first is rather slow and dignified, the second an *Andante* in 2/4 labeled "Pantomime," the third a lively Passepied. The Pantomime shows Grétry at his superb best as a ballet composer (Example 7.18). Melody is everything to the composer, as he insisted repeatedly in his memoirs. The charm of this melody is the slurred B - A sigh in m. 2 over incomplete subdominant harmony, answering the detaché eighth notes in m. 1. It would have been easy for Grétry to maintain the implied three-part texture of the beginning, the oscillating bass supplying two chord tones not present in the melody. But this he could have done only by writing a more active bass, which would have called attention away from the melody. He purposefully kept the bass as simple as possible, even if it duplicated tones in the melody.

FIGURE 7.10. Jacques Louis Touzé. The magic picture scene in Grétry's *Zémire et Azor*.

 The magic picture trio had an unusual genesis both as to dramatic idea and musical realization. Grétry confesses that the idea of this theatrically effective ensemble, an early telepicture, was his and not Marmontel's. "I had composed the piece twice, when Diderot came to visit me; he was unhappy with both undoubtedly because, without approving or blaming, he began to declaim the beginning, "Ah! lais-sez moi, lais-sez moi la pleu-rer!" as follows: ♪♪♪|♪♪♪|♪♪♪|♩. I substituted tones for the declaimed sounds of his beginning and the rest of the piece fell into place" (1: 225) (Example 7.19). The final version, with simple

EXAMPLE 7.18. *Grétry*, Zémire et Azor, *Pantomime Entrée*

melodic repetition of the opening descent, casts an almost hypnotic spell. Grétry chose a timbral spectrum that few could have heard before: six wind instruments behind the stage, pairs of clarinets in B♭, horns in E♭, and bassoons. The dulcet effect of the key was enhanced by its coming after the bright sonorities in the key of G sounded at such length in Zémire's preceding birdsong extravaganza, the longest aria in the opera. In *Così fan tutte* Mozart introduces the same six instruments sounding alone on stage in No. 21 as the lovers arrive on a barque, an *Andante* in triple meter and in E♭, coming after a recitative cadence in G. One of the printed scores in Mozart's library was *Zémire et Azor*. Moreover, the opera was in repertory when Mozart visited Paris in 1778, having been given seven times from April through September.

As early as December 1771 Marmontel wrote Voltaire that he was going to say farewell to Grétry and opéra-comique in order to move on to more serious projects. The process was gradual and apparently hastened by worsening relations

EXAMPLE 7.19. *Grétry*, Zémire et Azor, *Act 3, Scene 6, Trio*

*(Winds on stage behind the screen)

between Marmontel and the Théâtre Italien, which rejected several of his librettos. It did not help that his poem was blamed for the cool reception given to Grétry's opéra-ballet *Céphale et Procris, ou L'amour conjugal* (1773) at court and at the Opéra. The composer worked only once again with Marmontel on a completed opera, *La fausse magie,* an opéra-comique of 1775 that enjoyed considerable success.[94] Thereafter Marmontel turned in a different direction, writing several tragedies for the Opéra, mainly in collaboration with Piccinni, whose works he championed while denouncing those of Gluck. Thus Grétry was in danger of being left without a prominent poet upon whom he could depend.

Sedaine was still linked with Monsigny, but the first signs of a change came when he offered Grétry *Le magnifique* (1773), claiming that Monsigny had two unset librettos by him already. According to Grétry, the intermediary who gave him the poem was Madame d'Epinay, the friend and close collaborator of Grimm and Diderot, who both supported Grétry. *Le magnifique,* based on an amorous tale of La Fontaine, who got the story from Boccaccio's *Decameron,* is set in Florence. It opens with a procession of former slaves freed by Il Magnifico, mingled with the chanting priests in the square outside a window. Sedaine probably thought this up as a way of capitalizing on Monsigny's skills of deploying two musical ideas then combining them, as demonstrated in *Le déserteur.* Grétry succeeded in the task just as well as his musical mentor. His overture depicting the procession is a tour-de-force of orchestral color, truly a landmark in the annals of the program symphony. He brings back memorable strains from the overture at various crucial points in the drama. The score requires trumpets (a first in opéra-comique), horns, side drum, and timpani, all offstage. Sedaine favored ensembles over arias in order to move the action forward, which may explain why audiences came around to the work rather slowly. The libretto took advantage of the Italian setting by moving toward opera buffa. It offered comic patter that Grétry skillfully set in the buffo style, and the continuous action of the buffo finale. The composer even uses this Italian spelling in his score.

Further collaborations with Sedaine did not ensue immediately, and Grétry was somewhat cast in the shade by the disputes about Gluck and Piccinni that broke out in 1777, when he still lacked a steady source of librettos. At this point an English or possibly Irish librettist, Thomas Hales, called D'Hèle in France, came to the rescue. His story is so improbable it deserves to become a libretto in its own right. Born around 1741, he served as a young man in Britain's Royal Navy, where he ruined his health drinking punch and other strong liquors (as was frequently the case). In 1763 he settled in Havana, made and lost a fortune, then around 1770 moved to Paris. Suard recommended him to Grétry as a man full of original ideas. His French was sufficient for prose, but Anseaume was enlisted to help with the

[94]Karin Pendle, "The opéras comiques of Grétry and Marmontel," *Musical Quarterly* 62 (1976): 409–34, ranks the work as a high point, as did the composer himself.

verses of *Le jugement de Midas,* which was set by Grétry and given its premiere at
the Théâtre Italien on 27 June 1778. Mozart, who lived nearby, was probably not
in the audience because of his mother's final illness (she died on 3 July). The public found the new opera intriguing and many performances followed. Poet and
composer collaborated successfully again on *L'amant jaloux,* first performed on 20
November 1778, and on *Les événements imprévus* (11 November 1779). The buffo
finale made further inroads in French opera with these works, but Meude-Monpas specifically blamed Grétry for the muddle he perceived in the first finale of *Les
événements.* In the article "Finale" in his *Dictionnaire de Musique* (1787) he said that
Grétry did not attain the clarity and precision of Italian models. The collaboration
ended with the death of Hales in 1780.

Opéra-Comique had long outgrown its physical premises, the old Hôtel de
Bourgogne in the Marais, which was difficult of carriage access. In spite of
repeated strictures imposed by the Opéra, the orchestral and choral forces of the
troupe had kept growing even in this limited space. By 1780 the prestige of the
troupe's offerings was such that a new theater was planned, a handsome, freestanding structure near the boulevard des Italiens, known as the first Salle Favart,
on the location of the present Opéra-Comique. It opened in early 1783 (Figure
7.11). This temple in neoclassical style shows by itself how far opéra-comique had
come from its humble beginnings in the fair theaters.

FIGURE 7.11. The first Salle Favart, 1783.

RICHARD COEUR-DE-LION

During the 1770s Sedaine became increasingly interested in medieval subject matter, which had begun to fascinate French scholars and playwrights even earlier. After two ordinary librettos, *Les femmes vengées* set by Philidor (1775) and *Félix* set by Monsigny (1777), he offered Grétry *Aucassin et Nicolette ou les moeurs du bon vieux temps* (1779). It was based on a thirteenth-century fable that had been published in modern French (1756, and again in 1760) by a distinguished scholar, Jean-Baptiste de la Curne de Sainte-Palaye. Grétry's music shows some attempts to capture archaism matching the subject matter, although these had to be mostly imagined in the absence of much knowledge about thirteenth-century music. The work was only a partial success with the public. Auditors were perhaps puzzled as much as entertained or edified by this new fashion. The opera nevertheless prepared the public and its creators for an even more daring departure along the same lines. Meanwhile Grétry enjoyed one of his greatest successes at the Théâtre Italien with *L'épreuve villageoise,* a *paysannerie* by Pierre-Jean Desforges playing on jealousy, reconciliation, and rustic virtue versus urban evils, quite in the tradition of *Le devin du village.*

Sedaine submitted the libretto of *Richard Coeur-de-lion* to the Théâtre Italien by April 1782. He intended it for Monsigny and made every effort to induce him to set it. Monsigny was not persuaded to reenter the operatic lists, partly because of his poor eyesight (cataracts), but also because he realized his limitations better than did the poet. He recommended Grétry. After a longer than usual period of gestation, the opera had its premiere at the Théâtre Italien on 21 October 1784. One enthusiastic member of the audience was a diplomat newly arrived in Paris, Thomas Jefferson.

Richard was based on the misfortunes of a real person, King Richard I of England, the Lion-Hearted. Returning from the Third Crusade in 1192 or 1193, he was imprisoned and held hostage by Leopold of Austria in the fortress of Dürrenstein high above the Danube River west of Vienna. Sedaine changed the setting to the castle of Linz on the Danube, specifying a gothic fortress with battlements and towers, against the background of a dark forest and barren mountains. (He obviously never saw the valley of the Danube, but Grétry must have on his way to Rome, and it may be apposite that the printed score gives even more complex scenic directions than the printed libretto.) On the side of this gloomy stage picture is a gentleman's house, owned by Sir Williams, a Welshman who had served in battle under King Richard in the Holy Land. The overture is played with the curtain up. It begins in g (dungeon music), which becomes G as peasants cross the stage returning home at dusk from the fields with rakes on their shoulders. They soon start singing a pastoral-sounding chorus in praise of a fiftieth wedding anniversary in their midst to be celebrated on the morrow. Williams has a daughter, Laurette, who is in love with Florestan, master of Linz castle. This subplot, along with others, will eventually be shown to bear upon the main plot, Richard's liberation by his faithful troubadour Blondel.

All classes of society are represented in the opera and their interaction is a testimony to Sedaine's admiration for Shakespeare. Grétry enhances this variety with a very mingled chime of musical types, from the downright popular, including strophic songs, one being the exotica of a crusader's chanson sung by Blondel, to the two grand and very serious arias, alloted only to Richard and Blondel. The famous *romance,* sung ultimately by everyone, is in a class by itself and will be discussed presently.

Blondel enters in disguise as a bearded blind man. He is led by young Antonio, who sings couplets about his love for Colette. This simple music in G is followed by Blondel's soliloquy "O Richard! ô mon roi! L'universe t'abandonne," an aria the elevated quality of which can be sensed from its long orchestral ritornello. The orchestra opens *Allegro* in common time, and in the key of C, with a simple melody with reiterated cadences repeated up a tone (Example 7.20a). Blondel removes his beard and enters to a slower tempo, with a melody that is new (Example 7.20b). Gretry's sense of declamatory melody is equal to the sublimity of the words. He places the word "roi" in lowest position, as if to indicate how this particular king has been cast down. A leap of a tenth upward then helps capture the immensity of "L'univers." The initial harmonic progression is I - V^6 - vi, with bass descending by step from C to A. After a modulation to the dominant, the first section is repeated with a higher and more emphatic melodic cadence, followed by a feint to the relative minor but a quick return to C and an *allegro* tempo. Here

EXAMPLE 7.20. *Grétry*, Richard Coeur-de-lion, *Act 1, Scene 2, air*

Blondel sings of his fidelity and exhorts other monarchs to prize this quality. The aria seems ready to end when Grétry brings back the opening lines without their opening melody (Example 7.20c). What was cast down is now elevated, and the pertinence of the orchestral ritornello (Example 7.20a) is made clear. Also clear is an uncanny adumbration of Claude Joseph Rouget de Lisle's rousing "La Marseillaise" of 1792.

Blondel has so much to do throughout the opera, singing while acting, speaking, and playing a violin (or miming this), he is the linchpin upon which everything turns. The role was created by Clairval, the first Azor. It could even be claimed that poet and composer wrought what they did because of Clairval. Born in 1735, he was still attractive and at the peak of his powers as singer and actor. Grétry was unstinting in his praise.

> Clairval filled the role of Blondel in an inimitable manner. The nobility of a knight, the finesse of a clear-seeing blind person who directed a great intrigue: he knew how to use turn by turn those delicate nuances, with an exquisite taste. A role never suffers with this actor; he knows how to hold back at passages that are doubtful or too new for the public; but as one gradually gets accustomed to them he deploys all the energy of which the role is susceptible. A mechanical actor is the same every day—he fears only hoarseness; but Clairval does not have the misfortune of being the same at every performance; the perfection of his acting depends on the state of his soul, and he knows how to please us, even when he is displeased with himself. (1: 370–71)

A fellow actor-singer, Michael Kelly, visited Paris after Vienna in 1787 and had this say: "My favorite theatre of all was the Théâtre Italien, in the Rue Favart, where French comic operas were performed; the orchestra was very good, and the actors and singers equally so." He enlarged on one work in particular:

> I saw there "Richard Coeur de Lion," and enjoyed its charming music, I thought it always Grétry's masterpiece. Clairval, the original Blondel, gave the air of "O Richard! O mon Roi!" with great expression. His acting in the scene when he heard the voice of Richard from the prison, was electrifying: his joy, his surprise, at having found his king, the trembling of his voice, his scrambling up the tree to let Richard hear his voice, and the expression altogether, made an impression on me that never can be effaced; and while I remained at Paris, I never missed going to see him. Monsieur Philippe played Richard remarkably well, and gave the bravura air, "L'univers que j'ai perdu," ["Si l'univers entier m'oublie"] with great skill and animation.[95]

Richard's bravura aria at the beginning of Act II is preceded by a somber orchestral entr'acte, a *Larghetto* in 2/4 and in E♭. "During this march soldiers

---

[95]*Reminiscences of Michael Kelly of the King's Theatre and Theatre Royal Drury Lane*, 2 vols. (London, 1826; reprint 1968), 1: 286–87.

appear on the terrace and others exit the castle to take a turn around the ramparts," say Sedaine's stage directions. Richard is not seen at first in the predawn darkness, but his presence is felt from the very first notes of the orchestra, playing the progression I - V⁶ - vi. The gradual lighting of the scene reveals the king behind a grill, stage left. Blondel will appear playing his violin outside the prison, stage right (Michael Kelly's is the only mention of a tree for him to climb).

We are at the center of the drama, the moment of recognition. A violin in the wings behind Blondel sounds the famous *romance*, which is familiar from its appearance in Act I. The original printed score shows how its strains are interrupted by spoken words (Figure 7.12). Blondel pauses to listen after singing the first stanza, say the directions at the bottom of the page. When Richard sings the second stanza to the same music, Blondel knows he has found his man.

The *romance* was so crucial to the success of the work that Monsigny turned down the task for fear he could not do this piece well enough, according to what Sedaine told Grétry, who goes on to say, "I confess that the *romance* disturbed me

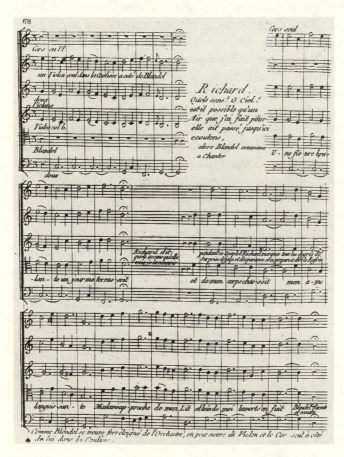

FIGURE 7.12. Romance from *Richard Coeur-de-lion* by Sedaine and Grétry, 1784.

as much as my colleague; I composed it in various manners without finding what I sought, that is the old style capable of pleasing a modern audience" (1: 368–69). Part of the music's old style resides in its extreme simplicity and alternation of trochaic and iambic rhythms, as in many dances of the old branle family, including the menuet (probably the oldest music known to Grétry). In this it resembles another famous *romance,* Rousseau's "Dans ma cabane obscure." Another antique trait is the quirky declamation of the text, with unimportant syllables or words falling on the strong beat of the measure. Given Grétry's care in such matters in his normal settings, these irregularities take on the color of archaisms and reinforce the fiction that it was Richard himself who composed this *romance* in honor of his lady, Marguerite, countess of Flanders and Artois.

Sedaine was taken to task for relying too much on coincidence. It does strain credibility that Williams should have taken a house outside Linz castle, and that Marguerite with her soldiers and Blondel should arrive there unbeknownst to each other at the same time. The story's resolution did not come easily. Various versions were tried. Originally Florestan, master of the castle, handed Richard over without resistance. The public decried this as dereliction of duty and a lame ending. Poet and composer disagreed on what to do. Sedaine opposed the rescue of Richard by force, claiming that rescues had become too common in the theater. (And perhaps he wanted to avoid a similarity with the ending of his *Déserteur.*) Grétry, on the other hand, wanted just this and wrote Sedaine suggesting, "The back curtain will rise as in your *Déserteur,* and Blondel will be seen, sword in hand, leading Richard out, with the garrison arrested by the knights escorting the countess."[96] This solution prevailed. After the assault on the fortress and rescue to lively battle music, there is general celebration (foreshadowing *Fidelio*). The chorus and all the many characters join in a composite finale in several sections, the most memorable of which, after a moment of silence, is the *romance,* now in D and sung to new words celebrating faithful friendship.

Grétry composed many more operas after *Richard* but none of them was so successful. His followers among younger composers, including Jean-Paul Martini, Stanislas Champein, Nicolas Dezède, and Nicolas-Marie Dalayrac, began replacing him in public favor even before *Richard.* He adapted somewhat to newer styles but never ceased to exalt melody above all other elements. The personal tragedy of losing his three daughters to tuberculosis at a young age slowed but did not stop him. Lucile, born in 1772, was musically gifted and wrote an opera at the age of fourteen, a sequel to *Richard, Le mariage d'Antonio,* performed several times with success at the Théâtre Italien (her father supplied harmonizations and instrumentation). She died in March 1790. By this time the first volume of Gretry's memoirs had received critical acclaim and he was at work on the next two. When

---

[96]Charlton, *Grétry and the Growth of Opéra-Comique,* p. 249. The letter dates from 23 October 1786.

the public decidedly turned its back on him as a composer, it was not because of any of the several melodists among his followers, but because of the more potent and harmonically dense operas by Étienne-Nicolas Méhul, Jean-François Le Sueur, and Luigi Cherubini. He named these three as the hope of lyric theaters (3: 372), but considered them followers of Gluck, not of himself (3: 432). He retired to L'Ermitage at Montmorency, the former home of his idol Rousseau, and wrote further memoirs (*Réflexions d'un solitaire*) and treatises; he died there in 1813. No other eighteenth-century musician left such an extensive literary oeuvre. None better summed up the world of eighteenth-century opéra-comique as a writer and as a composer.

Meude-Monpas in his *Dictionnaire* of 1787 included an article on opéra-comique (unlike Rousseau in 1767). It described the evolution of the genre since the 1750s succinctly and with general accuracy.

> It was at the Foire Saint Laurent that several poets . . . had performed various *comédies mêlées d'ariettes,* composed by different musicians, such as Duni, Philidor and Mon-signy, etc. This kind of spectacle pleased the public so much that soon [1762] it was united to Harlequin's Theater. . . . Since that time poets, or rather versifiers, have not disdained working for the genre of opéra-comique. Among their number are brethren Sedaine and Marmontel, Laujon, etc. It is true that the dramas they have given us are not entirely comic, but it matters not since they interested, and that is the point. After the naive Duni, the too learned Philidor, the incorrect and natural Monsigny, came the *spirituel* and celebrated Grétry, an intelligent man but perhaps too prodigious of that spirit that everyone recognizes in him. Nevertheless it would be unjust to reproach Grétry for some excesses of coquettishness, when one ought to be grateful to him for twenty-five charming opéras comiques that he has given us.[97]

The truth of this last remark cannot be gainsaid. The number of Grétry's operas that held the stage far outnumbered those of the next-ranking rival in this respect, who was Monsigny.

Several years before Meude-Monpas, opéra-comique received official recognition from the crown as France's most influential musical export. Louis XVI, by letters patent of 31 March 1780, changed the decree governing the Comédie Italienne. The plays in Italian were suppressed entirely, and the last remaining Italian players pensioned, while the other parts of the repertory were confirmed.

> French music, which used to be the object of foreigner's scorn or indifference has today spread all over Europe because the French comic operas are performed in all the northern courts and even in Italy, where the greatest Roman and Neapolitan com-

---

[97]Meude-Monpas includes a footnote here sending the reader to his article "Finale," in which he criticizes Gretry's *Les évenements* as we have seen.

posers applaud the talents of our French composers. It is works of this genre that have formed taste in France, accustomed ears to a more learned and expressive music, and prepared the revolution that occured even on the stage of our Académie de Musique, where one now sees applauded masterpieces of which the merit would have failed to be recognized or appreciated had they been performed twenty years earlier. Thus it cannot be doubted that this revolution is anything but the fruit of the *opéras bouffons* composed for the Comédie Italienne and the continued efforts of the artists who performed them.[98]

The document goes on to say that this miracle occurred because creators consulted public taste and sought ways to satisfy and perfect it.

Opera since its beginnings has always been a form of cultural politics. Rarely has a head of state admitted as much so candidly. Equally rare is the candor of acknowledging that it was opéra-comique which allowed Philidor, Gluck, and others to shake lyric tragedy out of its torpor. Gluck did this first on Viennese ground. Without the stimulation of opéra-comique he could not have begun his reform movement even there, a process he subsequently crowned with his works for Paris.[99]

---

[98]Richard Langellier-Bellevue and Roberte Machard, "La musique à Paris et à Versailles d'après les actes du Secrétariat de la Maison du Roi de 1765 à la Révolution," *Recherches sur la musique française classique* 19 (1979): 211–302; 269–70.

[99]*Haydn, Mozart,* chap. 3. David Charlton, "'L'art dramatico-musical': An Essay," in *Music and Theatre: Essays in Honour of Winton Dean,* ed. Nigel Fortune (Cambridge, 1987), pp. 229–62, makes this point with regard to Paris and supports it from the voluminous prose writings of Grétry.

8

Gluck at the Opéra

Preparations

CHRISTOPH GLUCK first visited France in 1745 while accompanying Prince Ferdinand Lobkowitz from Milan to London.[1] Later his direct relations with the country were the result of Count Giacomo Durazzo's plans for promoting *Orfeo ed Euridice*, first performed in Vienna in 1762. Durazzo sent a score of the work to Paris to be printed and instructed Gluck to go there in the spring of 1763, following the production of *Il trionfo di Clelia* in Bologna (14 May 1763), ostensibly to oversee publication. In his letter to Favart of 6 May 1763 Durazzo foretold Gluck's arrival and admonished the poet that he would have to force the composer to correct the proofs because "he is naturally indolent and very indifferent to his own works."[2] This characterization of Gluck hardly corresponds to the energetic figure who drove his performers without mercy throughout an unheard of number of rehearsals. But perhaps it does correspond to his more relaxed behavior outside the theater, to moments at home with his wife. Both were fond of fine wine and the pleasures of the table.[3] Favart responded with a warm letter of invitation sent

---

[1]Georg Kinsky, "Glucks Reisen nach Paris," *Zeitschrift für Musikwissenschaft* 8 (1925–26): 557–66.

[2]Charles-Simon Favart, *Mémoires et correspondances littéraires, dramatiques et anecdotiques*, ed. A.-P.-C. Favart, 3 vols. (Paris, 1808), 2: 111.

[3]They are so depicted in a joint portrait, reproduced in Bruce Alan Brown, *Gluck and the French Theatre in Vienna*, (Oxford, 1991), plate 1.

directly to Gluck, offering him a guest apartment in his house in the Marais: "You will find furnished rooms, a good harpsichord and other instruments, a little garden, and complete liberty."[4] Favart gave his address as "rue Mauconseil, près la Comédie Italienne, vis-à-vis la grande porte du cloître Saint-Jacques-de-l'Hôpital."

The composer did not go to Paris at this time. Durazzo summoned him back to Vienna from Bologna. As Louis Dancourt explained in a letter to Favart of 5 July 1763, "Since the Opéra has burned, Gluck's trip to Paris would, according to the Count, be useless."[5] Evidently Durazzo had in mind more than just correcting the proofs of *Orfeo.* He was pushing for performance of the work at the Opéra. The "indolent" composer was being prodded into an endeavor with which he may initially have had little or nothing to do. Favart's enthusiasm for renovation went so far that when writing Durazzo he "wished it had pleased God that the conflagration at the Opéra had also consumed the entire traditional repertory of French music."[6]

The following winter, in late February or early March, Gluck did finally reach Paris, along with Durazzo, shortly before they were both due in Frankfurt for the coronation of Joseph II as king of the Romans. The German engraver Johann Georg Wille, long established in Paris, noted in his diary for 9 March 1764: "Chevalier Gluck, the famous composer known all over Europe where good music is esteemed, came to see me; he is a very fine man moreover and he stayed with me several hours. He is in the service of the empress and was accompanied by the poet Coltellini, also in the service of the house of Austria."[7] Wille executed the drawing reproduced earlier of *Le roi et le fermier* by Sedaine and Monsigny on the stage of the Théâtre Italien (Figure 7.8 on p. 771).

The Opéra had reopened in January 1764 in a temporary theater built in part of the Salle des Machines in the Tuileries palace. Gluck could have seen the revival of Rameau's *Castor et Pollux* on this stage and heard Sophie Arnould as Telaire. The Théâtre Italien, for which both Favart and Goldoni worked, offered the premiere of a new masterpiece by Sedaine and Monsigny, *Rose et Colas,* in March 1764. The Mozarts were also in Paris.

The 1760s represented a low point for new music at the Opéra, being a time devoted mainly to revivals. Perhaps as a consequence the public was more inter-

[4]Favart, *Mémoires,* 2: 114. The letter is undated. In *The Collected Correspondence and Papers of Christoph Willibald Gluck,* ed. Hedwig and E. H. Mueller von Asow, trans. Stewart Thomson (London, 1962), p. 22, the mistake is made of translating "clavecin" as "clavichord."

[5]Favart, *Mémoires,* 2: 279. For further on the corresponence see Brown, *Gluck and the French Theatre in Vienna,* pp. 374–81.

[6]Favart, *Mémoires,* 2: 88 (letter of 8 April 1763): "Plût à Dieu que l'incendie parvenu jusqu'à l'entrepôt de l'Opéra, eût encore consumé toute la bibliothèque de notre musique française!"

[7]*Mémoires et Journal de J. G. Wille, graveur du roi,* 2 vols. (Paris, 1857), 1: 259; 2: 182, 186, 392. Wille lived and worked on the quai des Augustins.

ested than ever in dancing, less in music. The same could be said, surprisingly enough, for Italian serious opera, which had to be propped up by dancing, most especially in London. A diplomatic exchange between London and Paris shows how important it was for each of them to enjoy the exclusive services of a rising young dancing star, Jean Dauberval, in 1764, just after the Seven Years War. The question was treated like a matter of state. In order to prevail, London offered Paris the following political concessions in a letter sent by minister Horace Walpole to the British ambassador in Paris: discharge in full of Canadian war debts and of the ransoming of French prisoners, plus permission for Monsieur D'Estain to retain command in the West Indies. The reply was negative and telling: "As the taste for music declines, the great expense of this *spectacle* makes it necessary to support it with dancing which . . . is essential to a French opera."[8]

Dancing had always been central to French lyric theater. It flourished before full-fledged opera in such older forms as the *ballet de cour*. The theater merely reflected the centrality of dancing in French society as a means of promoting grace of movement and savoir faire. No more enchanting visual representations of this exist than those by Watteau.

A visitor to Vienna in 1767, Monsieur de Sevelinge, reported to Count d'Escherny a conversation with Gluck that indicates the composer's increasing preoccupation with working for Paris. It was at a dinner given by Sevelinge at which Gluck was a guest.

> Gluck began to praise Lully to the skies, encomiums well deserved no doubt, but unexpected from a composer of Italian operas. He praised in Lully a noble simplicity, vocal writing close to nature and intentions that were truly dramatic. He had studied, he said, the scores of Lully, and this study was for him an eye-opener; he perceived there the true genius of opera, which only needed to be developed and perfected, and that if he were called to work for the Opéra in Paris he hoped that, in preserving the genre of Lully as well as French *cantilène,* he would obtain from it true lyric tragedy.[9]

If this account is accurate it helps confirm that Gluck had studied the score of Lully's *Alceste,* as is suggested by the parallel between the repeated refrain of "Alceste est morte" and its Italian equivalent in his own *Alceste* (1767). "Noble simpicity," "natural vocal writing," and "true drama" are refrains themselves, destined to figure prominently in Gluck's subsequent declarations.

Around 1770 Gluck befriended an attaché to the French embassy in Vienna

[8]Horace Walpole, *Correspondence,* 48 vols. (New Haven, Conn., 1937–83), 38: 460–61, 483, cited after Curtis Price, Judith Milhous, and Robert D. Hume, *The Impresario's Ten Commandments: Continental Recruitment for the Italian Opera in London, 1763–64* (Royal Musical Association Monographs 6) (London, 1992), p. 28.

[9]Le comte d'Escherny, *Mélanges de littérature, d'histoire, de morale et de philosophie,* 2 vols. (Paris, 1811), 2: 356–58, cited after Gustave Desnoireterres, *Gluck et Piccinni 1774–1800,* 2nd ed. (Paris, 1875), p. 77.

with the imposing name of François-Louis-Gaud Lebland, bailli du Roullet, whom he may have met earlier in Rome. The bailiff was a military nobleman, born in Normandy in 1716, thus two years younger than the composer. Whether it was Du Roullet or Gluck who suggested turning Racine's tragedy *Iphigénie en Aulide* into a libretto remains a question. There was no want of encouragement to do just this. Diderot had proposed the play as a fine resource from which to make an opera in *Entretiens sur le fils naturel* of 1757, singling out the monologue of Clytemnestra as she imagines her daughter Iphigenia immolated on the sacrificial altar. Two years earlier Francesco Algarotti published the first edition of his reform treatise *Saggio sopra l'opera in musica,* which ended with a short libretto intended to be exemplary, a prose sketch in French for an *Iphigénie en Aulide* after Racine and Euripides. Racine's tragedy was also performed by the French troupe in the Burgtheater on 29 July 1770. Thus it was still current, although nearly a century old.

When Burney arrived in Vienna on 31 August 1772 he wasted no time seeking the most prominent musicians. Countess Thun arranged a meeting with Gluck on Wednesday 2 September: "She had been so kind as to write a note to Gluck on my account, and he had returned, for *him,* a very civil answer; for he is as formidable a character as Handel used to be: a very dragon, of whom all are in fear" (Burney's italics). That afternoon Lord Stormont, the British ambassador, conducted Burney to the dragon's lair.[10]

> At five o'clock Lord Stormont's coach carried Madame Thun, his lordship, and myself, to the house of the chevalier Gluck, in the fauxbourg St. Mark. He is very well housed there; has a pretty garden, and a great number of neat, and elegantly furnished rooms. He has no children; Madame Gluck, and his niece, who lives with him, came to receive us at the door, as well as the veteran composer himself. He is very much pitted with the small-pox, and very coarse in figure and look, but was soon got into a good humor; and he talked, sung, and played, Madame Thun observed, more than ever she knew him at any one time. He began, upon a very bad harpsichord, by accompanying his niece, who is but thirteen years old, in two of the capital scenes of his own famous opera *Alceste.*

This recital by Mademoiselle Gluck, who was a singing pupil of the soprano castrato Giuseppe Millico, did not end before she had sung solos by various other composers, and in different styles, "particularly by Traetta."

Gluck himself was then prevailed upon to sing: "With as little voice as possible, he contrived to entertain, and even delight the company, in a very high degree; for, with the richness of accompaniment, the energy and vehemence of

---

[10]Gluck's summer residence at the time was in the Saint Marx suburb (today Wien 3, Rennweg 93). See Walther Brauneis, "Gluck in Wien—seine Gedenkstätte, Wohnungen und Auffuhrungsorte," *Gluck-Studien* 1 (1989): 42–61; 54.

his manner in the *Allegros,* and his judicious expression in the slow movements, he so well compensated for the want of voice that it was a defect which was soon entirely forgotten."Burney then specified what was sung:

> He was so good-humored as to perform almost his whole opera of *Alceste;* many admirable things in a still later opera of his, called *Paride ed Elena;* and in a French opera, from Racine's *Iphigénie,* which he has just composed. This last, though he had not as yet committed a note of it to paper, was so well digested in his head, and his retention is so wonderful, that he sung it nearly from the beginning to the end, with as much readiness as if he had had a fair score before him. His invention is, I believe, unequalled by any other composer who now lives, or has ever existed, particularly in dramatic painting, and theatrical effects. He studies a poem a long time before he thinks of setting it. He considers well the relation which each part bears to the whole; the general cast of each character, and aspires more at satisfying the mind, than flattering the ear. This is not only being a friend to poetry, but a poet himself.

Burney goes on to quote from the preface to *Alceste* and to describe Gluck's relationship to the old French operas of Lully and Rameau. The evening must have beeen well advanced by the time Gluck had sung for his guests as much as Burney claims, but it was not over. Stormont at length carried Burney across the city to the residence of the Danish ambassador, General Valmoden. "There was an assembly of foreign ministers, and his lordship did me the honour to present me to the whole *Corps diplomatique.*" Perhaps he met there the other creator of *Iphigénie en Aulide,* le bailli du Roullet.

Burney may have been mistaken about the existence of a score for the new opera or misled because Gluck chose to perform the music without reference to one. On 1 August 1772, a month before Burney's visit, Du Roullet sent a long anonymous letter from Vienna to Antoine Dauvergne, one of the directors of the Opéra in Paris. He went into detail about how the libretto was adapted from Racine's play and spoke of having heard several performances of the opera's music.

> It has seemed to me that this great man had exhausted all the resources of art in this composition. Simple, natural songs, always imbued with the most true and sensitive expression and with the most flattering melody; an infinite variety of ideas and of nuances; a most impressive use of harmony to express terror, pathos and tenderness alike; a fast-moving recitative which is also noble and expressive; finally, perfect examples of French recitative at its most declamatory, a great variety of dance-airs of a new kind and most agreeably fresh choruses, duets, trios and quartets all equally expressive and moving, with scrupulous attention to the prosody; in short, everything in this work seems very suited to our taste and nothing seemed to me strange to French ears.[11]

---

[11]Gluck, *The Collected Correspondence,* pp. 32–35.

The letter, which has the character of a public manifesto, was in fact published in Paris, in the second October installment of the *Mercure de France.* It ends by informing the directors that Gluck was prepared to travel to France if assured that the opera would be produced. A postscript adds that the writer was prepared to send the text on ahead so the directors could make their own judgment. Paris being Paris (and quite unlike Vienna), Du Roullet's letter caused quite a stir. Michel-Paul-Guy de Chabanon published a very long "Lettre sur les propriétés musicales de la langue française" in the *Mercure de France* for January 1773, elaborating on several points in response and dismissing Rousseau's objections to opera in French.[12]

Next it was the turn of Gluck himself. His letter appeared in the *Mercure de France* of February 1773, modestly disavowing the praises of *Iphigénie* in the October *Mercure* and giving credit to Calzabigi for having made possible "the new form of Italian opera." The letter is cleverly put and very polished; its ease of expression probably owes much to the courtly Du Roullet. It disowns any advantage that Italian had over French as an operatic language, contradicting Rousseau, and yet ends by singing the praises of Rousseau's *Lettre sur la musique française:*

> [T]he language which will always appeal to me the most is that in which the poet provides me with the most varied opportunities to express the emotions; this is the advantage I believe I have found in the text of the opera *Iphigénie,* in which the poetry seemed to me to have all the vigour required to inspire good music. Although I have never been in the position of offering my works to any theatre, I cannot hold it against the writer of the letter to one of the Directors that he proposed my *Iphigénie* to your Academy of Music. I confess that I would have been pleased to produce it in Paris, because by its effect and with the help of the famous M. Rousseau of Geneva whom I intended to consult, we might together, in seeking a noble, moving and natural melody with a declamation in keeping with the prosody of each language and the character of each people, have succeeded in finding the medium I have in mind for producing a type of music suited to all nations and in eliminating the absurd distinctions between national forms of music. The study I have made of this great man's works on music, amongst others the letter in which he analyses the monologue of Lully's *Armide,* prove the depth of his knowledge and his sureness of taste and have filled me with admiration.[13]

Had Rousseau devoted himself fully to opera, concludes Gluck, he would have achieved the prodigious effects attributed to music by the ancients.

Without saying it in so many words, Gluck painted himself as the saviour who did devote his entire life to opera and would now achieve those prodigious ancient effects in Paris, while creating a supranational opera and healing the rifts

---

[12]Ibid., pp. 35–44.
[13]Ibid., pp. 30–32.

still left from the Querelle des Bouffons of two decades earlier. A tall order to fill, surely, yet Gluck with his supreme self-confidence went about it almost like a military campaign. With such a barrage of propaganda in the press, the directors of the Opéra were under pressure to accept Gluck's offer. After receiving the first act of *Iphigénie* Dauvergne responded evasively: "If the chevalier Gluck promises to deliver six opera scores to the Académie de musique nothing could be better; otherwise *Iphigénie* will not be produced because such a work is made so as to kill all our old French operas."[14]

Gluck held a trump card in his hands with which to coerce the royal academy of music. Marie Antoinette, the Austrian dauphine, had been his pupil in Vienna, although in what kind of instruction is unclear. According to the *Mémoires secrets*, the directors of the Opéra did not accept Gluck's proposal because they had little interest in foreign music and feared it would discredit their own. "Happily the Sr. Gluck thought fit to arrive, and as he has the honour to be known to Madame la Dauphine, it is to be hoped that he will enjoy enough protection to have his opera produced. This princess has given him permission to call on her at any time."[15]

In April 1773 Grimm took notice of the turmoil surrounding Gluck's offer and reported on it in the *Correspondance littéraire*. At the end of a favorable review of a new translation into French by François-Jean Chastellux of Algarotti's *Saggio sopra l'opera*, Grimm adds: "his essay ends with two operas in prose, *Enée à Troie* and *Iphigénie en Aulide;* the latter has been put into French verse, set to music by Chevalier Gluck and performed in Vienna, where it had the greatest success. Subsequently it has been offered to our directors, who, as usual, refused. These gentlemen have vowed to bore us forever with the same old operas."[16] Grimm errs on two counts. Du Roullet's libretto in verse was not a translation of Algarotti's prose sketch, although indebted to it for several scenes.[17] Misled by the anonymous letter sent by Du Roullet to Dauvergne of August 1772, Grimm assumed there had been public performances of *Iphigénie* in Vienna. There were none, and for good reason. Du Roullet and Gluck conceived the opera for Paris. The *Mémoires secrets* stressed the importance of the poet in creating the work: "It was he who led Gluck from Vienna to France and who recast Racine's tragedy in a form appropriate for musical setting."[18]

[14]Anton Schmid, *Christoph Willibald Gluck: Dessen Leben und tonkünstlerishes Werken* (Leipzig, 1854), p. 180.
[15]Gluck, *The Collected Correspondence*, pp. 31–32, note.
[16]Cited after Yves Giraud, "Iphigénie entre Racine et Du Roullet," in *L'opéra au xviiie siècle*, ed. André Bourde (Aix and Marseilles, 1982), pp. 163–84; 171.
[17]Julian Rushton, " 'Royal Agamemnon'; the two versions of Gluck's *Iphigénie en Aulide*," in *Music and the French Revolution*, ed. Malcolm Boyd (Cambridge, 1992), pp. 15–36; p. 22, n. 17, denies the connection and says that Calchas does not appear in Algarotti's version. He does so to the extent of dominating the final scene. (It is Racine who only mentions Calchas, without having him appear.)
[18]*Mémoires secrets*, 24 March 1774, cited after Giraud, "Iphigénie entre Racine et Du Roullet," p. 174.

The Visit of 1774–75

The Opéra of the 1770s offered composers the advantages or burdens of a nearly century-long unbroken tradition, which proved for Gluck to be both inspiration and impediment. It also possessed the most modern and most beautiful theater in Europe, completed in 1770 after six years in the planning and building. Jean-Michel Moreau, the architect, was born in Paris in 1727 and profited as a young man from being sent as a royal pensioner to Italy, where he studied among other things the great opera houses. His theater in the Palais Royal occupied a wider space than its burnt-out predecessor, obtained by suppressing the famous Cul-de-sac de l'Opéra and some adjoining private properties. While still modest in size by comparison with Italy's largest, the new house provided its patrons with optimum comfort, sight lines, and acoustics.[19] The graceful curve of its auditorium was repeated in smaller curves elsewhere in the design, as may be seen from the plan of the ground floor (Figure 8.1). Moreau himself made some drawings of the theater's interior that were etched by Malbeste. One shows the fashionable audience leaving and about to enter the vestibule on the rue Saint Honoré (Figure 8.2). The curved wall (to the left of letter E in the floor plan) offers a perfect foil to the sternly plain and neoclassical pilasters. Curves were the essence of rococo art, and they remained essential to the work of a neoclassical architect like Moreau. One floor above the vestibule was a large foyer for promenades by the spectators, an amenity altogether lacking in its predecessor. It was in this public foyer, with its tall windows looking out on the street, each with a balcony, that splendid marble busts by Jean-Jacques Caffieri of Lully, Quinault, and Rameau stood guard.

In the autumn of 1773 Gluck returned to Paris accompanied by his wife and niece. Aged fifty-nine and, as Burney called him, a "veteran composer" with dozens of successful operas to his credit, he could scarcely have imagined what trials awaited him at the Opéra. Although the new theater was one of the finest in Europe, conditions had changed little since Grimm painted them with devastating wit in *Le petit prophète de Boemischbroda* twenty years earlier. Louis-Sébastien Mercier in his *Tableau de Paris* (1770) compared the orchestra to "an old coach drawn by skinny horses and led by someone born deaf."[20] Grimm had called the leader of the orchestra the "woodchopper" because of the blows he landed on his desk with a large wooden baton in order to be heard by all the performers. Rousseau returned to the same charge in his *Dictionnaire de musique* (1767) article "Battre la mesure," citing Grimm and adding the sarcasm that Italian and German musicians got along without this barbarity because they were able to sense the meter, unlike their French counter-

---

[19]Jean Gourret, *Histoire des salles de l'Opéra de Paris* (Paris, 1985), pp. 61–80.
[20]Cited after Gustave Desnoireterres, *Gluck et Piccinni,* p. 91.

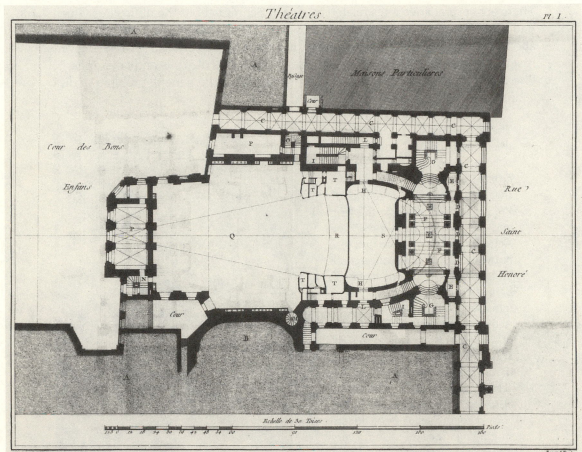

Théatres

Pl. 1.

Salles de Spectacles, *Plan au Rez de Chaussée du Parterre de la Nouvelle Salle de l'Opera, Executée au Palais Royal sur les Desseins de M.* Moreau *Architecte du Roy et de la Ville.*

BB

FIGURE 8.1. Jean-Michel Moreau. Floor plan of the Opéra, 1772.

parts. The chorus was apparently worthy of the orchestra and inured to the custom of standing in rows, immobile, on either side and at the back of the stage.

Once he arrived, Gluck presumably had a voice in casting his opera. The cast chosen was as shown in Table 8.1.

TABLE 8.1. Gluck's Cast for *Iphigénie en Aulide*

Iphigénie	Mlle. Sophie Arnould, soprano
Clytemnestre	Mlle. Rosalie Duplant, mezzo-soprano
Agamemnon	M. Henry Larrivée, baritone
Achille	M. Joseph Legros, tenor (haute-contre)
Calchas	M. Nicolas Gélin, bass
Patroclus	M. Durand, bass
Arcas	M. Beauvalet, bass

There are several anecdotes related by Anton Schmid about the difficulties Gluck had with his principal singers, but they cannot be verified.[21] Grétry tells a tale about the female lead at a rehearsal of his opéra-ballet *Céphale et Procris,* given first at Versailles in 1773 for the marriage of the comte d'Artois and later at Paris. She was Rosalie Duplant, and her case may illustrate the general problem of discipline with the performers at the Opéra.

The Actress on stage: "What does this mean, sir, a rebellion, I believe, in your orchestra?" *Batteur de mesure* in the orchestra: "How is that, mademoiselle, a rebellion? We are all here to serve the king and we do so with zeal." The Actress: "I wish to serve him too, but your orchestra disconcerts me and prevents me from singing." *Batteur de mesure:* "And yet, mademoiselle, we are keeping time." Actress: "Keeping time! What sort of a beast is that? Follow me, sir, and know that your orchestra is the very humble servant of the actress who recites." *Batteur de mesure:* "When you recite, I follow you, mademoiselle; but you are singing a measured air, very measured." Actress: "Come now, no more of this foolishness. Follow me."[22]

FIGURE 8.2. Vestibule of Moreau's opera house after a performance.

Grétry writes of another singer, Pierre Garat, that he dared add no ornaments when singing Gluck's dramatic scenes, not even in concert, where this luxury was more readily tolerated (3: 369). The case conveys something of the rigor that Gluck introduced on the stage of the Opéra.

The premiere was announced for 13 April 1774, to be attended in Paris by the dauphin, the dauphine, and many other members of the royal family. Suddenly Larrivée came down with a cold that badly affected his voice. Gluck would hear nothing of using an understudy for the role of Agamemnon, so crucial to the fate

[21]Schmid, *Christoph Willibald Gluck,* pp. 199–200.
[22]André-E.-M. Grétry, *Mémoires, ou essais su la musique,* 3 vols. (Paris, 1789–94; reprint New York, 1971), 1: 280–81. Subsequent references in this chapter will cite only the volume and page number in the text.

of the opera. He exclaimed he would rather throw his opera into the fire than expose it in public to an inadequate interpretation. So the court had to rearrange its plans and wait for six days, until the premiere was given on Tuesday 19 April.

Sophie Arnould was reputed for her beauty and the number of her admirers. She was thin and did not have a powerful voice but one that was well trained (by Marie Fel). Born in 1740, she had been a leading soprano at the Opéra since the age of seventeen, singing over thirty roles in works by Lully, Mouret, Rameau, and Rousseau (*Le devin*). She was prepared somewhat for a more modern and Italianate style by singing the title role in the ballet-héroique *Aline, reine de Golconde* (1766) by Sedaine and Monsigny. Creating the title role in *Iphigénie* was the climax of her career, and all the critics agreed in praising her, even those who did not like Gluck's music. She managed to project the virginal innocence of the adolescent heroine despite being in her midthirties and very *mondaine.* Of the five principal singers, all of whom were lauded for both their singing and their acting in the *Mercure de France* of May 1774, she received the most notice:"Mlle Arnould charms as much as she astonishes in *Iphigénie* by her noble and interesting acting, by the soul and assuredness of her singing, by an expression that is always true and *sensible,* by her voice even, which seems in this opera to take on more body, force, and range."

Rosalie Duplant was about the same age as Arnould. More ample in figure, she had a powerful voice and she used it to maximum advantage in the role of Clytemnestra. Perhaps she was in awe of the terrifying Gluck to the point of behaving better for him than she had for Grétry. For whatever reasons, Gluck did not call on her for roles in any of his subsequent operas for Paris, although he considered her for La Haine in *Armide.* Dismissed by the Opéra, she was reinstated at Gluck's demand in 1779.[23] After having mentioned the principal singers, the reviewer in the *Mercure de France* for May 1774 singled out a certain Mlle. Rosalie who "sang several airs very agreeably in the divertissements."The reference is to a younger soprano, Rosalie Levasseur, who was to become Gluck's favorite female interpreter in Paris.

Gluck must have been satisfied with Larrivée, his Agamemnon, because he chose him for several subsequent leading parts. Larrivée had a flexible baritone voice with extensions up into the tenor range. He lacked the noble bearing to play a king, said some critics, let alone the "king of kings," yet he continued to sing the role of Agamemnon as late as 1797 (he died, like Arnould, in 1802).

Joseph Legros was Pierre de Jélyotte's successor at the Opéra in the difficult *haute-contre* roles of Rameau. He also sang roles in the more Italianate style, such as Sandomir in Philidor's *Ernelinde* (1767); thus he was not without preparation for the demands made on him in creating Achilles. Gluck paid him the tribute of adapt-

[23]Desnoirreterres, *Gluck et Piccinni,* p. 277.

ing the part of Orfeo to his voice in 1774 and choosing him subsequently for Admète, Renaud, and Pylades. During his visit to Paris in 1764 Gluck could have heard this fine tenor making his debut at the Opéra in the revival of *Castor et Pollux.*

IPHIGÉNIE EN AULIDE

Open rehearsals helped prepare the public somewhat for the shock administered to the audience of the Opéra on that memorable opening night of 19 April 1774. From the first tones of the overture there sounded a language of power, pathos, and terror undreamed of before. The pathos unfolds in the *Andante* in the many minor second dissonances, rising and falling, that express the suffering in Agamemnon's soul (Example 8.1). Gluck took this from a passage in his *Telemaco* (1765) and the situation is not dissimilar, there a boy crying out for his lost father, here a father agonizing over the daughter he is obliged to sacrifice.[24] Terror is unleashed by the ensuing unison *Grave* in all the strings, pausing on the unstable tone of the second degree, then on the even more unstable tone of the fourth degree, heard as a dominant seventh (Example 8.2). The power of the entire orchestra, with woodwinds, horns, trumpets, and drums, explodes in m. 29 after the direction *Animé.*

The livelier part calls forth mighty chords in the brass and winds, animated by marchlike anapestic rhythms and by the incessant sixteenth-note agitation of the violins. Up the octave to high C the music strides in quarter notes, like a giant, and then down again in 6/3 chords. There is a softer passage with more melodic content, but it is only a brief contrast before a *crescendo* to *fortissimo* for the arrival of the dominant. These elements, put through modulations to a number of keys and supplemented by soft minor second cries, sufficed Gluck to construct his mightiest overture. At the end the *Grave* returns, but this time it leads straight into the first vocal number, Agamemnon's "Diane impitoyable," sung to the *Andante* that opened the overture, now in g. The recurrence is touchingly effective. Another way to view it is that Gluck moved Agamemnon's plea back to the beginning of the overture (probably composed later). Mozart used a similar strategy to integrate the first vocal number of *Die Entführung aus dem Serail* with its overture.

Abbé François Arnaud wrote an elaborate critique of the opera shortly after its premiere and published it in the *Gazette de littérature* for April 1774. It is couched in the form of a letter to a lady who had written to him about the opera and was the forerunner of many other essays on the work.

> Listen to the overture, see how, after having linked the beginning to the subject, not by vague connections but by the forms themselves, the composer suddenly hurls all the instruments on the same note, how, after ascending together at the unison, up to

[24]For the passage from *Telemaco* see *Haydn, Mozart,* example 3.9, p. 216. On p. 699 I say that the rising second motif Mozart took from Gluck as the "duol" motif of *Idomeneo* comes from the end of the overture. This should be corrected to read from the end of the overture's *Andante.*

EXAMPLE 8.1. *Gluck*, Iphigénie en Aulide, *Overture*

EXAMPLE 8.2. *Gluck*, Iphigénie en Aulide, *Overture*

the octave above this note, these instruments divide and combat each other in preparing the soul for a great event, how in order to conserve the sentiment of the rhythm, weakened by the speed with which the upper parts move, he makes the other instruments strike anapests, of all feet the one best suited to songs of war; how, in order to rest the ear and at the same time indicate the soft and *sensible* parts of the drama, he causes to emerge from the center of these warlike and passionate forms a melody which, without slowing down, takes a more amiable and gracious turn; with what exquisite sentiment and with what skill he conducts the melody to noble and touching plaints, establishing the pathetic and tragic of the action.[25]

---

[25]*La Querelle des Gluckistes et Piccinnistes,* ed. François Lesure, 2 vols. (Geneva, 1984), 1: 29–30.

Arnaud's eloquence loses something in my translation. Still, it is remarkable how he succeeds with mere words in conveying a series of musical events with no text to help him—a difficult feat then and no less so today.

Agamemnon's plea to the goddess moves easily between recitative and its main section, which is more like an arioso than an aria, judged by Italian norms. Next comes what is called an air, addressed to Apollo, "Brilliant auteur de la lumière," a *Moderato* in common time and in e. It is a small **A B A** form that is comparable with only the simplest and shortest kind of *aria parlante*, such as might be given a minor character in Italy. The minimum of dramatic exposition needed to understand the situation is accomplished in its *Andante* middle section: "the faithful Arcas is deceiving the queen and my daughter by saying that Achilles has found another love, so that they will return home." After the return of the **A** section the piece disintegrates into an agitated recitative: "If my daughter arrives in Aulis nothing can save her from the homicidal transports of Calchas, the Greeks, and the gods." These hordes are no sooner mentioned than seen and heard. A chorus of Greeks erupts, *Allegro* in common time, *forte*, in a strident G coming after Agamemnon's e and with no break. The chorus sings partly in unison and in vehement rhythms that recall the fast music of the overture. Calchas, the seer-priest, engages the Greeks in dialogue then goes into a trance, *Andante* in g; he claims the goddess orders him to spill the purest blood. This is followed by a duo, *Moderato* in common time and in E♭, which has a very somber effect after so many sharp keys.

Calchas now implores Diana. He begins the duo declaiming syllabically and in a near monotone, "Tu veux que par ma main tremblante le sang le plus pur soit versé." The orchestra provides the musical content, and particularly the rising bass, with chromatic inflections appropriate to the horror of the situation. Agamemnon joins in as Calchas begins to repeat the initial music, as if this were a strophic hymn. He imitates at the distance of one measure the falling fifth of Calchas, like a trio sonata in texture, and especially because of the old-fashioned "walking bass" in even quarter notes. They end by singing together in sixths and thirds, a novel sonority in this opera. Duets for two deep male voices were rare in any kind of opera of the time, although not unknown. The chorus of Greeks renews its cries, now demanding the victim's name, now imploring Diana to lead them to the shores of Troy. At this juncture Calchas promises that a victim will be on the altar fulfilling their demands that very day. The chorus exits at this point. Choruses in action throughout, as Gluck required, were new to the Opéra. One wonders how he imposed this without insurrections, and perhaps there were such.

Scene 3, between Calchas and Agamemnon, continues on without a break, alternating the keys of c and E♭ as in the previous scene. Calchas has a portentous unison string figure introducing his recitative (Example 8.3). Agamemnon replies that he hates the gods, prompting the priest to upbraid the king in very strong

EXAMPLE 8.3. *Gluck*, Iphigénie en Aulide, *Act I, Scene 3*

terms (foreshadowing a similar confrontation a century later in another opera for Paris, Verdi's *Don Carlos*). Agamemnon then begins his air in c, *Andante* in cut time, "Peuvent-ils ordonner qu'un père," a more elaborate piece than his previous air but still completely syllabic, as is the entire opera, Gluck having renounced even the slightest hint of melisma. He grows defiant, "Je n'obéirai point à cet ordre inhumain." Then the orchestra takes over.

Oboes (doubled by flutes according to the printed score) emit an appoggiatura of a falling second against the strings throbbing in eighth-note chords, *pianissimo,* and answered by another whole note in the bass. The appoggiaturas and their resolutions keep climbing step by step (Example 8.4). Agamemnon responds to them with an independent melodic line of his own. He hears sounding in his breast, he says, the plaintive cry of nature that speaks to his heart, and its voice is more sure than the oracles of fate. These cries of the oboes, representing nature's voice, are recognizably similar to the minor ninth and other two-note cries in the softer parts of the overture. We have been prepared for them, but hardly for their full significance in this human context, powerfully conveyed by the long ascent of the oboe line, joined on some pitches by the voice part two octaves below. The piece ends as the king reiterates his refusal to obey, sung to agitated dotted rhythms and short melodic thrusts quickly rising and falling.

Several early commentators singled out this passage and they always refer to oboes, not oboes and flutes; maybe the combination fooled their ears, perhaps because Gluck had the flutes play softly. Of Agamemnon's air in c Arnaud wrote as follows.

EXAMPLE 8.4. *Gluck*, Iphigénie en Aulide, *Act I, Scene 3*

What is sublime, and can only belong to a profound sensibility awakened to and moved by genius, is the way in which the composer announces and expresses the cries that nature raises at the bottom of Agamemnon's heart. This groaning voice of the oboes, the somber response of the basses, the chromatic progression of the vocal melody and the instruments which accompany it, that harmonious and intermediary murmuring, which fills out the space between the plaintive and monosyllabic accents of the oboes and the basses, tunes and informs all the parts of the orchestra without damaging the effect of the dialogue. Those are beauties of which one alone would suffice to make up for a thousand faults. Oh! And how you felt them when you wrote me that you started forward involuntarily in your chair with a motion of pity for the unfortunate father.[26]

Calchas, for one, is not impressed and not to be deflected from his morbid plan. After more dialogue between them, the chorus of Greeks crosses the stage, announcing the arrival of a chariot bearing Clytemnestra and her daughter (as in Algarotti, not Racine). Calchas sings a very short air. The actual arrival follows and is hailed by a chorus behind the stage to melodious strains in C, "Que de graces," *Andante grazioso* in 3/4, the first use of triple meter in the opera, a fresh resource that Gluck has saved for just this moment. His means may be simple, but the tenderness and relief attained by them are out of all proportion to their weight because they are placed exactly right. An aura of grace and femininity, the first in the opera, sweeps over the stage. The music grows louder by slow degrees as the procession accompanying mother and daughter marvels at their beauty. Many repetitions draw out this tableau to great length.

Clytemnestra descends from the chariot and sings of her pleasure at their reception in an *Air gracieux* in cut time and in G, which leads to a chorus in D, *Gracieux sans lenteur* in 3/8. For Iphigenia's first utterance Gluck invents an air in D, *Andante* in 2/4, that is like a little dance, with both strains repeated. The piece is so simple it could have figured in one of Gluck's opéras-comiques. It perfectly expresses her youth, innocence, and candor. Following it is an actual dance air in D, *Lentement (mouvement de passepied)* in 3/8. Enhancing the emotions of the moment by dance and instrumental music is what Rameau himself would have done at this point, and Gluck's inventiveness is not inferior to that of his great predecessor at the Opéra.

A peripeteia is at hand. Clytemnestra returns, distraught with the news from Calchas that did not reach them in time to prevent their arrival. They must leave at once, she declares, or suffer in person the shame of Achilles' betrayal because he is falsely said to no longer wish to marry Iphigenia. The affronted matron now takes on the bellicose tone of the Greek army, even imitating their anapest rhythms, in her air "Armez vous d'un noble courage." This is the closest Gluck has

---

[26]Ibid., 1: 31.

yet come in this opera to an Italian-style aria in its length and in its opening orchestral ritornello of four measures stating the entire theme. Moreover, Clytemnestra exits at its conclusion, as she would in an opera seria (probably to applause for the role's creator, Mademoiselle Duplant). Her departure in high dudgeon breaks the flow so carefully maintained up to this point, but for dramaturgical reasons it was necessary to give Iphigenia a soliloquy here in which to ponder her changed fate.

Conflicting emotions of love and hate for Achilles give wing to her impassioned multipartite air in g, another piece comparable to an aria in length. It conveys her suffering very effectively and lends her the emotional maturity necessary to confront Achilles, who immediately appears, struck with surprise by seeing her in Aulis. They straighten out the misunderstanding at length in recitatives and an air apiece. He concludes with an orchestral climax almost certain to induce applause, as if Gluck wanted to reassure Legros that he was still the public's favorite tenor, even though the new opera differed radically from most of his previous triumphs. The way was now prepared for the duet of reconciliation ending the act.

Nothing could be closer to Italian operatic practices than placing the love duet at the end of the first act. As Arnaud wrote to his lady correspondent, "The shape [coupe] and forms of the duo are Italian, I admit, but you will agree that the composer knew how to bend them and adapt them without doing the least violence to our language." Lacking altogether are the typically dulcet billing and cooing in vocalises so characteristic of Italian love duets. Gluck chooses a martial key, D, and writes an *Andante* in common time for the beginning that seems too marchlike to suit the declarations of love being sung, in spite of what Arnaud claimed. The tempo becomes faster as the lovers start singing together in thirds, sixths, and tenths, but changes to slower-moving intonations of the magic word "Hymen!", effectively accompanied by the winds. At the duet's climax the lovers take turns reaching their high A, also very effective, and Gluck adds a considerable orchestral postlude, *fortissimo,* almost guaranteeing the sought-after thunder of hand clapping. No one should belittle the composer for springing the applause trap here. Even Mozart did the same, changing the whole ending of Act II in *Die Entführung* so as to assure applause.

Du Roullet placed the full-scale divertissement for chorus and ballet expected at the Opéra in the middle of Act II and made of it a tribute to the military exploits of Achilles. Some deride Gluck for bowing to the French tradition of having related ballets within the acts (as opposed to the Italian practice of unrelated entr'acte ballets composed by another). Did Rossini and Verdi demean themselves by composing extensive ballet sequences to be integrated into *Guillaume Tell* and *Aida?* No. Nineteenth-century grand opera, generally agreed to have coalesced with Gaspare Spontini's *La vestale* (Paris, 1807), would have taken shape more slowly had not Gluck conquered the Opéra in the 1770s. He was a direct model for Spontini.

Act II begins in the key of C with a chorus of women reassuring Iphigenia that she is loved by Achilles. This may seems superfluous at first, but not so when we realize that she is upset by more rumors of his betrayal emanating from her father. In effect this puts us in mind again of Agamemnon's terrible dilemma, the central issue of the opera. After Iphigenia sings an air of foreboding in F, Clytemnestra arrives with her suite of followers; Achilles and Patroclus also enter. Achilles begins a martial air, *Maestoso* in cut time and in the key of C, in which Legros must have been especially effective in high tessitura. He urges the people to celebrate their queen, "Chantez, célébrez votre Reine," in the most brilliant music heard so far. A dialogue of soloist versus full chorus like this makes one wonder if Gluck had not profited from some of Handel's splendid examples.[27] This particular chorus could be more elaborate musically than those in Act I, says Arnaud, because it was sung standing still.

The praises next begin to rain upon Achilles himself, first as the object of an *air gracieux,* then of an even more vigourous chorus in the same key of C, "Ami sensible, enemi redoutable." The prominent dactyl rhythms in both tie these two choruses together, as does their common tonality. Had Paris ever heard such electrifying martial strains sung by the chorus at the Opéra before this? Probably not. Gluck deserves credit for being one of the first to unleash that *élan terrible* later associated with the music of the Revolutionary period and further adumbrated by Grétry in his *Richard.*

The pieces that follow the choruses in C lead up gradually to one of the great glories of the 1774 score, a large *Passacaille* in D enclosing gavottes in A and in a, constituting the central ballet. Since the overall tonal movement of Act I was from C to D, we cannot but hear the rightness of this plateau of D projected for several minutes coming after the impressive choruses in C. Arnaud singled out the *Passacaille* as one of the most beautiful pieces of instrumental music ever heard at the Opéra, adding that "it was something well thought out for the composer to have tempered its noble and elevated style with two gavottes that Rameau would have been glad to claim as his own." Mozart was impressed to the point of taking several of its features into the Chaconne of his concluding ballet for *Idomeneo,* and notably Gluck's transitional passage back to the tonic after the first big cadence on the dominant. Unfortunately for the cohesion of the whole, Gluck dismantled the sequence of pieces leading up to the *Passacaille,* which piece he then moved to the Act III ballet for the revival of the opera in January 1775.[28] He replaced them with a set of dances, three borrowed from his earlier works, that maintained the key of C or its relative, a. The replacements do not come up to the quality of what was replaced; performers would be wise to reinstate the original sequence.[29]

[27]The culminating chorus in C of *Israel in Egypt,* "Sing ye to the Lord, for he hath triumphed gloriously," offers several parallels.

[28]Rushton, " 'Royal Agamemnon'; the two versions of Gluck's *Iphigénie en Aulide,*" pp. 15–36. See especially table 2, Act 2 divertissements, p. 28.

[29]As did John Eliot Gardiner in his superb 1987 recording of the opera for Erato, 2292-45003-2.

A superior set of pieces in the 1775 ballet that may go back to the original production is represented by the entry, chorus, and dance of the slaves (who are freed by Iphigenia), which move tonally from a to F. In his *Lettre* of April 1774 Arnaud discusses the dance of the slaves directly after his words on the *Passacaille,* which suggests that this is the sequence he observed on the stage in the first production. In the printed score the slaves' dance appears in the final ballet of Act III. Arnaud's correspondent had called the *air d'esclaves* by the name *Tirolois,* and indeed the rapid triadic figure in the opening melody might have resembled a yodel to Parisian ears, the foot-stamping vigor of the whole, a clog dance such as mountain people might well have been imagined to perform.

> The air that you call Tyrolean is a dance for the slaves who have just been freed. I admit that this piece is not noble, but why should it be? You will agree at least that it is piquant and truly original, and you were undoubtedly struck by the variety of modulations that the composer negotiated in such a short space. It is a kind of harmonious labryinth in which one is happy to reorient oneself after experiencing more than once the distress of being lost beyond hope of recovery.[30]

Gluck does modulate quickly and often in the course of the dance, venturing far to the flat side of the tonal spectrum. Constant sixteenth-note figures suggest the Viennese *alla Turca* idiom.[31]

The main action resumes with an impressive quartet for Iphigenia, Clytemnestra, Achilles, and Patroclus, with choral interjections, "Jamais à tes autels le plus saint des serments." This hymn in praise of marriage shares its key of F with the preceding dance, which provides an element of continuity. Disjunction follows the news revealed by Arcas that Iphigenia is going to the altar not as a bride but as a sacrificial victim. An angry chorus of men, the followers of Achilles, express general outrage in a *Presto* in cut time and in the key of c, "Nous ne souffrirons point ce sacrifice impie." They will all die, they say, in order to save her.

Clytemnestra kneels to embrace the knees of Achilles in the following recitative, which cadences in D, followed by a plaintive oboe solo in b, a sorrowful melody that serves as the ritornello of her air, "Par un père cruel à la mort condamnée." That the oboe signifies the victim condemned to die has been made clear in Agamemnon's air in c in Act I (see Example 8.4 on p. 816). "Only you can save her," sings Clytemnestra to Achilles in this moving appeal, which ends with the same haunting ritornello for solo oboe. "You are to her in this place father, husband, refuge, and her gods," argues the distraught mother. Achilles reassures the queen, but Iphigenia is unwilling to defy her real father, whom, she says, she

---

[30]Lesure, *La Querelle des Gluckistes et Piccinnistes,* 1: 33.
[31]As argued persuasively by Thomas Betzwieser, *Exotismus und "Türkenoper" in der französischen Musik des Ancien Régime* (Laaber, 1993), pp. 193–94. Brown, *Gluck and the French Theatre in Vienna,* p. 307, shows that the theme of this dance goes back to one of Gluck's ballets of 1761.

still loves. These emotions in conflict are played out in the following trio, the most substantial vocal ensemble so far, which stretches out to over a hundred measures. Mother and daughter exit, leaving Achilles and Patroclus, the latter of whom is sent after them with renewed assurances of protection, a clumsy way of clearing the stage for the confrontation between Achilles and Agamemnon.

Agamemnon enters with Arcas and his soldiers, announced by a unison dominant seventh in descent, with menacing effect. Yet the king's first words reveal weakness: "There is Achilles. Can he have learned?" Achilles leaves no doubt about what he knows, beginning a verbal attack that spares nothing. Agamemnon is quick to take offense, greatly wounded by such audacity from a young subordinate. The dialogue escalates in fury until it finally bursts out in a duo, *Presto, animé* in cut time. Much of the time they sing the same words, being equally offended, in parallel thirds and sixths. The tessitura is once again very high for Achilles, who reaches B♭ at the climax. Exit Achilles in great agitation, singing in recitative to words of extreme emotion: the king will have to kill him first before immolating his daughter.

The rest of Act II belongs to Agamemnon, who rages against himself in a long obbligato recitative, during which he hears the cries of the Eumenides and blames the gods for his plight. At length he wavers and sends Arcas to accompany his wife and daughter at once back to Mycenae, out of harm's way. Then he begins a tender lament in the key of a and in 3/4 time, addressed to his absent daughter, "O toi, l'objet le plus aimable," begging pardon. At the concluding *Allegro* the plea turns from a to A and from *Moderato* to *Allegro* in common time as he denounces Diana and cries to her, "If you want blood, take mine!" The defiant part is a little too short musically for an act ending, but Gluck extends its fury with an orchestral postlude of eight measures.

The chorus is called upon to play several roles in the opera. It begins Act III as the Greek army once again angrily clamors for the human sacrifice they believe will propitiate Diana and unleash winds that will propel their becalmed fleet to Troy. For the music Gluck chooses a fast-moving march in cut time and in G, reminiscent of the first appearance of the chorus in Act I. Iphigenia emerges in the middle of their frenzy, asking Arcas why he opposes the army's demand. The plan to escort her far away has foundered because of her resistance. Achilles appears and urges her to flee under his protection. She will hear none of it. She refuses. Her air in B♭, "Il faut de mon destin subir la loi suprême," recaptures the calm and simple movement of her first air in Act I, and like it is in a short binary form with both halves repeated. The effect is uncanny. She has reverted to being the innocent young princess we first encountered, before the trials and tribulations of love gave her musical language more complexity to match her rapidly emerging emotional maturity. She is resolved to die. Achilles rages to no avail.

She sings the first of her farewells to him, a serenely beautiful air in E♭, in triple meter marked *Lent.* The vocal line of this binary form is almost completely conjunct in motion. Both strains are repeated so that, although the piece is short, it lingers long at this slow tempo. At the beginning of the second strain Gluck allows the orchestra to continue the melody as she falls silent, as if too moved to continue (Example 8.5). Continue she does, asking him not to forget that she cherished life only because of him and will love him until her death. At this thought her melody soars up to high G, and on the next sally moves to A$^\flat$, before descending to the cadence with little two-note sobs (sanglots) in inverse dotted rhythm. Her last word is "Adieu." Few eyes could remain dry after this.

Achilles throws her unearthly serenity into further relief by erupting in a bellicose showpiece of an air, *Allegro* in cut time and in C with trumpets and drums. As if lit by a match the chorus repeats the same angry demands it sang before. Clytemnestra enters. Mother and daughter attempt to console each other, which leads Iphigenia to sing the second of her farewells, an air that is even shorter than her entrance air in Act I and lacking repeats, "Adieu, vivez pour Oreste, mon frère." Bidding her mother to live for her younger brother is an idea that does Du Roullet credit. It hints at the grisly tragedies to come for this family. It also plants the seed of a sequel in which Iphigenia will encounter Orestes many years later in Tauris, a libretto on which Du Roullet was in fact already working.

Once again the army repeats its threats, and since these outbursts come closer and closer together in time, the effect is ominous, unsettling. Iphigenia leaves to prepare for her immolation (victims sacrificed to Diana required a special garb). Clytemnestra's big moment is not exactly a monologue because she is attended by her ladies. She wants to die in place of the victim. She imagines the scene of horror as Calchas plunges the knife into her daughter's breast and removes her bloody heart to fulfill his duty as a seer. This imagining is the very scene in Racine's play, with some of the same words, that led Diderot to propose the work in 1757 as a basis for renewing lyric tragedy. Once again B$^\flat$ (her agitated air) leads to E$^\flat$, as a chorus behind the scene intones a solemn hymn to the goddess, while Clytemnestra interjects her pitiful lamenting.

The scene opens up to reveal the seashore, on which stands an altar. Iphigenia in sacrificial garb is kneeling on the steps by the altar, behind which Calchas extends both arms to heaven, the sacred knife in one hand. The Greeks now flood the stage, repeating the choral dirge. Achilles rushes in to seize Iphigenia, threatening the unarmed Greeks as he advances. The ensuing altercation ends suddenly as Calchas feels or feigns a rapture, signaled by the same mysterious rising figures that heralded his warnings to Agamemnon in Act I, Scene 3 (see Example 8.3 on p. 815). He proclaims the goddess has relented after all. This, the original version, was denounced by nearly all the critics, who said it made Calchas look more fearful of Achilles' sword than of the goddess. In the revival of early 1775 the creators brought Diana herself down from the skies to the same music, to pronounce her change of heart *viva voce.*

EXAMPLE 8.5. *Gluck*, Iphigénie en Aulide, *Act III, Scene 3*

Calchas bids the crowd to sing praises of the goddess, which they do. Breezes begin to stir the waves (painted by the orchestra), which shows that Diana was in earnest. The family that has been spared can manage at first to utter only a few words or each others' names, a device as simple as it is moving and copied by Mozart after the divine reprieve in *Idomeneo*. There follows for father, mother, daughter, and fiancé one of the greatest treasures in all Gluck's music, the quartet "Mon coeur ne saurait contenir l'excès de mon bonheur." It expresses wonderment and joy in equal measure in a series of soaring progressions that take the voices to their highest peaks on the words "excès" (Achilles) and "délire" (Iphigenia and Agamemnon). The quartet (in F) serves as a kind of plagal cadence to the chorus in C hailing the impending marriage of the young couple. So ended the 1775 revision of the opera, according to its edition in the complete Gluck works. In 1775 as in 1774 there was surely much added celebration in dance by the ballet, as would have been expected at the Opéra.

It would be a pity to lose such admirable music as Gluck composed for the final divertissement. This is especially true of the great Chaconne in D, the direct model for Mozart's Chaconne in the ballet ending *Idomeneo.* Gluck reused his Chaconne in D in the Paris version of *Orfeo, Orphée et Euridice,* which had its first performances in the summer of 1774. This may help explain why he moved the *Passacaille* in D from the second act to the end of the third for the revival of *Iphigénie* in January 1775. In compensation he transferred the lambent strains of the *Air pour les esclaves* from the end of the opera to the middle of Act II, extended with a rollicking *Allegro,* and prepared it with a *Gavotte gracieuse* in a, a chorus of female slaves from Lesbos (also in a), and a recitative in which Iphigenia consoles them. The celebration of Achilles' capture of Lesbos parallels Algarotti's *Iphigénie* (Act II, Scene 5) and is present neither in Euripides nor in Racine.

At the end of the Chaconne in D, Calchas breaks in singing a recitative, "Partez, volez à la victoire." The Chaconne then concludes and the chorus, representing the whole of Greece, takes up his words in an extraordinarily powerful unison chorus in d, darkly chromatic and punctuated with strokes on the bass drum on the first beat of every measure. This primitive-sounding battle cry makes a magnificent end to the opera and forecasts the terrible war about to be fought with Troy. Left in doubt is the issue of the marriage between Achilles and Iphigenia. According to Euripides the young hero went off to combat with the rest, postponing the greatly desired and celebrated marital union until the end of the war, from which he did not return.

One Parisian critic who remained curiously silent about Gluck was Diderot. The composer was probably unaware of the enmity that had developed between Rousseau and the other *philosophes* in the 1760s. By cultivating Rousseau so assiduously, Gluck all but insured the silence of Diderot, who once had prophesied the arrival of a genial poet-musician in France who would create true lyric tragedy. Diderot abstained from any mention of *Iphigénie.* Rousseau, on the other hand, basked in the attentions Gluck paid him and was willing to see his canard about the impossibility of opera in French revealed for the hoax that it was. As early as Du Roullet's letter of 1 August 1772, Gluck was heralded as a revolutionary in opera. In 1775 *Iphigénie* was called "an opera that can produce a revolution in French music, and which forced M. Rousseau of Geneva to agree that we can indeed have an opera; its success has been extraordinary."[32] Even Marmontel, embittered as he was by his own experiences at the Opéra, had to admit that *Iphigénie,* although deprived of Racine's eloquence, "still retained enough indestructible beauties to make the most magnificent opera."[33]

Gluck had various effects on French composers. Some envy was to be expected of a foreigner's triumph at the Opéra. A young Provençal composer, Étienne Joseph Floquet, had a major success at the Opéra in 1773 with his *ballet-héroique, L'union de l'Amour et des arts* (sixty performances up to January 1774). Another work of his in the same genre, *Azolan,* had the misfortune of falling between *Orphée* and the revival of *Iphigénie;* it fared much less well. Grétry stated in his memoirs that he felt crushed ("écrasé") by Gluck's harmonic power (3: 431). Some regarded Gluck as the new champion of Italian music in Paris, but since Grétry claimed this role for himself, he decided that Gluck's music emerged instead from the German symphony (by which he meant Haydn, whose symphonies he frequently praised): "All the geniuses of Italy could not produce an overture such as that to *Iphigénie en Aulide*" (1: 284). Grétry got the relationship between Haydn and Gluck backwards. Gluck, a generation older than Haydn, was the source of some of Haydn's symphonic ideas. Another composer who felt crushed by the greatness of Gluck was Gossec. He had been successful with a setting of Chabanon's *Sabinus* for the Opéra, first staged on 22 February 1774, as *Iphigénie* was in rehearsal. After Gluck's premiere *Sabinus* was relegated to secondary status. In a letter of 1778 Gossec lamented that as long as Gluck held the stage there would be no place for Gossec: "I am too small to reach so high."[34]

If Gluck was aware of Philidor's purloinings from the printed score of *Orfeo* (Paris, 1764) he did not take offense over them. Writing from Vienna to Du Roullet in the summer of 1776 in reaction to Piccinni's being summoned to the Opéra from Italy, Gluck opined: "You are right in saying that the French composers are too greatly neglected; for I am very much in error, if Gossec and Philidor, who understand the style of the French opera so well, could not serve the public better than the best of Italian composers, if people were not too enthusiastic over whatever is new."[35]

Judging by the impact of *Iphigénie* on Parisian fashions, we can say that Sophie Arnould made the greatest impression as she knelt at the altar awaiting her death as a sacrificial victim. She wore her hair piled up and surmounted by

---

[32]*Almanach des Muses* (Paris, 1775), p. 322, cited after Giraud, "Iphigénie entre Racine et Du Roullet," pp. 163–84; 169.

[33]Jean François Marmontel, *Oeuvres complètes,* 6 vols. (Lièges, 1777), 5: 444, cited after Giraud, "Iphigénie entre Racine et Du Roullet," p. 170.

[34]Julian Tiersot, ed., *Lettres de musiciens écrites en français du xve au xxe siècle* (Turin, 1924), pp. 200–201.

[35]Gluck, *The Collected Correspondence,* p. 85.

black roses, from which a kind of veil trailed behind. Parisian ladies copied this fashion in a headdress called *à l'Iphigénie.*[36] A search through millinery fashions of the time might uncover some visual documentation of the fad. Even in the absence of such evidence there is the telling testimony of the sculpture executed by Jean-Antoine Houdon in 1775 known as *Mademoiselle Arnould* (Figure 8.3). She lifts her eyes to heaven in prayer. Over her right breast is a sash with stars and the crescent moon of the goddess Diana.

FIGURE 8.3. Jean-Antoine Houdon. Bust of Mademoiselle Sophie Arnould.

That her left breast is exposed to view derives from artistic tradition (and perhaps from the wishes of the sitter). An extraordinary sidelight on Houdon's genial creation is the contract made between sculptor and singer for its manufacture. Dated 5 April 1775, it specifies that Houdon was to deliver the marble bust the following August, along with the terra cotta that served as its model; moreover, he promised also to deliver the unusually large number of thirty plaster of Paris copies (enough, quipped one wag, to satisfy all her lovers).[37] The eminent specialist on Houdon describes the bust as "one of his most rococo concepts, theatrical in pose and expression, at once delicately feminine and chastely erotic, elegant and abandoned."[38] He goes on to say:

> It is obvious that the sculptor, though his theme is classical, is here in no sense concerned with the imitation of antiquity. What he gives us is antiquity as interpreted in the classical French drama (or in this case opera), in which there was no concern for anachronisms in costume; and the more violently an emotion was torn asunder the better pleased were both audiences and actors. Iphigenia appears to us here as she undoubtedly did on the stage, her hair and dress in careful disarray, one charming breast exposed, face turned up to the heavens and exaggerated eyes rolling even higher as she prays for the mercy of the goddess. Although Houdon's bust is deliberately theatrical in the stage sense, it does remind us of several works by Bernini in

[36]*Correspondance secrète* (London, 1787), 1: 64 (4 September 1774), cited after Desnoiresterres, *Gluck et Piccinni,* p. 100.
[37]H. H. Arnason, *The Sculptures of Houdon* (New York, 1975), p. 36.
[38]Ibid., p. 35.

which the emotion expressed is both more violent and more authentic. The ecstasy of Saint Theresa is apparent not only in the gasping mouth, but in the eyes.

May it soothe whatever passions are aroused by Houdon's bust of Sophie Arnould to learn that, contrary to this expert's opinion, decorum did not allow the exposure of bare breasts on the stage of the Opéra.

ORPHÉE AND *ALCESTE*

The death of Louis XV on 10 May 1774 cut short the first production of *Iphigénie.* Throughout the early summer of 1774 in Paris Gluck worked at the transformation of *Orfeo* into *Orphée* with the young poet Pierre-Louis Moline. The premiere took place on 2 August. He needed do little more in many cases than transpose the contralto part written for Gaetano Guadagni down a fourth for the tenor Legros.[39] In order to make the work a full-length opera he added several pieces. Thus Act I received new solos for Orpheus (the disputed bravura aria "L'amour renaît") and for Amour, sung by Rosalie Levasseur. He recast the infernal scene, Act II, Scene 1, from its taut key structure of E♭ and c giving way to f and F into a less satisfactory sequence of several keys, which undermined the magical arrival of Elysium with the key of F. A happy addition, on the other hand, was the new air for Eurydice, "Cet asile." Sung by Sophie Arnould, the role of Eurydice, even as enhanced for Paris, was much smaller than that of her partner and did not win her the public adulation that she enjoyed as Iphigenia. To Act III Gluck added a trio for the principal singers and several dances to the final ballet. The opera was a resounding success, perhaps in part because its original creators in Vienna were already dreaming of Paris. Gluck took control of the staging to a degree unprecedented for a composer. Not only did he make the chorus move, he made the ballet dancers sing in the infernal scene, where they had to utter "Non!" as Furies, along with the chorus. They protested, to no avail, that singing even a single note went against the stipulations of their contract.

A revised form of Gluck's opéra-comique *L'arbre enchanté* (1759) was staged at court in February 1775 to welcome Archduke Maximilian, the queen's younger brother. It was performed by the forces of the Théâtre Italien and raised little enthusiasm. Gluck returned to Vienna shortly afterwards, having signed a *pro memoria* contract with the Opéra to provide it with three more operas: *Alceste, Electre,* and *Iphigénie en Tauride.* He left behind the score of another of his earlier opéras-comiques, *La Cythère assiégée,* which was performed as an opéra-ballet (with many additional dances composed by Pierre-Montan Berton) in the sum-

---

[39]For a number by number comparison of the 1762 and 1774 versions, with keys indicated, see Jeremy Hayes, "Orfeo ed Euridice," in *New Grove Dictionary of Opera,* ed. Stanley Sadie (London, 1992). See also Alessandra Martina, *Orfeo-Orphée di Gluck* (Florence, 1995).

mer of 1775. In a letter to Du Roullet of 1 July 1776 Gluck predicted that *Cythère* would succeed only under his personal direction, and he was right. The public did not take to lightweight works by Gluck after experiencing *Iphigénie* and *Orphée*.

Du Roullet was the poet of Gluck's choice for transforming *Alceste* into a French opera. Much more labor was involved here than was the case with *Orphée*. *Alceste* was longer and more complex. Also, Gluck and Du Roullet decided to make many changes in the story and order of its events, which necessitated extensive recomposition. The resulting opera is not so much a revision as a reconception of the original version.[40] It stands in its own right as one of Gluck's greatest works. So intense were Gluck's emotions when re-creating this tragedy that the process nearly caused him a nervous breakdown, evident from his detailed reports to Du Roullet. Not surprisingly, he became seriously ill and for four months was unable to compose.

Work on *Alceste* resumed in the fall of 1775, and by the end of the year Gluck managed to send the first two acts of the score ahead to Paris. In March 1776 he made the arduous three-week trip to Paris by himself, his wife remaining behind to care for his seriously ill niece, Marianne. At the premiere on 23 April the first two acts went well but the last was not well received, which meant that the whole was judged a failure. Gluck was devastated by this, and even more so by the news from Vienna that Marianne had died. He cut short his stay in Paris and returned to Vienna in May. Had he remained, he would have been gratified to see the audience at the Opéra gradually come around to *Alceste* and recognize it for the masterpiece that it is.

Rosalie Levasseur was chosen for the title role, to the mortification of Sophie Arnould. Gossips of the time blamed Arnould for trying to spoil the premiere by rallying various anti-Gluck factions. Some of the credit for turning the tide in the opera's favor must surely go to Levasseur. She was no beauty, although her favors were appreciated by the Austrian ambassador to France, who housed both her and Gluck in his mansion near Saint Sulpice. She commissioned no sculptures of herself as far as is known. She may have won the role by being the ambassador's mistress, but she won over the public by the warmth of her acting and singing.

One great person was in a position to compare Levasseur's Alceste with Antonia Bernasconi's original Alceste in Vienna. He was Joseph II, who visited his sister and the French court in 1777, while *Alceste* was still playing at the Opéra. Joseph praised Levasseur as "the best I have yet heard, with respect to both acting and singing."[41] This is a choice compliment coming from the emperor, whose vanity rarely permitted him to admit that anything Parisian could surpass its Viennese equivalent. Gluck paid a similar compliment to the singer in his undated let-

---

[40]See Jeremy Hayes, "Alceste," in *New Grove Dictionary of Opera*.
[41]Hans Wagner, "Die Reise Josephs II nach Frankreich 1777 und die Reformen in Oesterreich," in *Salzburg und Oesterreich* (Salzburg, 1982), pp. 335–60; 356.

ter from the summer of 1776 to Du Roullet, who had committed the impertinence of comparing *Orphée* and *Alceste,* to the detriment of the former (of which he was not the poet). Works so dissimilar cannot be compared, thundered Gluck in answer, and"if *Alceste* were performed by inferior actors, or by anyone other than Mlle. Levasseur," it would lose such a contest to *Orphée.*[42]

Houdon sculpted a bust of Gluck in plaster in 1775 (Figure 8.4). His image of the master is as rough and commanding as Arnould's is smooth and softly yielding. The artist's concern was to make a unity of the portrait bust between the individual portrayed and the "design of the torso and accessories of dress."

His face was deeply pockmarked, and the sculptor used this fact to establish his theme. He clothed him in a heavy coat, whose texture is an overall pattern of slashed grooves, free and direct in their expressive impact. Here there was no attempt to simulate the appearance of the actual material, but rather, in a manner almost Rodinesque, to bring out the quality of the clay. The open shirt, the unbuttoned vest, the short dishevelled hair, and the alert, tilted pose of the head all emphasize the impact of genius.[43]

A year later the cellist Jean-Baptiste Janson initiated a subscription to commission a marble copy of the bust from Houdon. Joining him were several of Gluck's most important supporters: Gossec, Du Roullet, Larrivée, Simon Leduc, Berton, and Joseph

FIGURE 8.4. Jean-Antoine Houdon. Bust of Christoph Gluck.

Legros (in order of signing).[44] It was exhibited at the salon of 1777 and then placed by order of the king in the grand foyer of the Opéra, next to three busts honoring Lully, Quinault, and Rameau.[45] There could be no more telling sign that Gluck had taken his place among the titans of French opera.

Another French artist who portrayed Gluck in 1775 was the painter Joseph

[42]Caroline Bouju, "Rosalie Levasseur, la créatrice d'Alceste à Paris," in *L'avant scène opéra* 73 (1985): 92–93, with a portrait of the singer. The passage in question is omitted from Gluck, *The Collected Correspondence,* p. 83.

[43]Arnason, *The Sculptures of Houdon,* p. 34.

[44]Patricia Howard, *Gluck: An Eighteenth-Century Portrait in Letters and Documents* (Oxford, 1995), p. 164.

[45]Gourret, *Histoire des salles de l'opéra de Paris,* p. 66. When Moreau's opera house burned in June 1781 only the busts of Lully and Quinault could be saved, and they were destroyed in their turn during the conflagration of the theater in the rue Le Peletier in 1873.

Silfrede Duplessis (Plate X). He shows the composer at the keyboard, beautifully dressed and looking both beatific and inspired. Gluck liked the flattering portrait and hung it in his home in Vienna. Reichardt saw it there on a visit to Gluck during his last years and admired it, whereupon Gluck ordered a copy made to give him. Outliving the insolence of his youth, Reichardt was child enough of the Enlightenment to resist pointing up the contrast between the craggy exterior of the real-life Gluck and the flowing graces of the idealized portrait. He described it, in the context of relating his visit to Gluck, as "the beautiful, life-size oil painting by Duplessis of Paris, which shows the artist brimful of vitality, heaven in his eyes and love and goodness on his lips."[46]

An Homage to Lully and Quinault: *Armide*

On 6 March 1764 during the visit of Gluck and Durazzo to Paris, the Opéra revived for a final time *Armide* by Quinault and Lully, which held the stage until the following December. The tenor Legros made his debut at the Opéra singing Renaud in this production, and Gluck could well have heard him. Quinault's masterpiece was no stranger to Gluck even before this. It provided the basis for the Italian *Armida* (Vienna, 1763) arranged by Durazzo and versified by Giovanni Migliavacca for Traetta, the Italian composer most admired by Gluck. A more recent reminder was the Viennese *Armida* of 1771 by Coltellini and Gluck's young protegé Salieri.[47] It was Gluck's good fortune in Paris to inherit as his Renaud, in the person of Legros, the last actor schooled in the tradition of Lully's hero.

After returning from Paris to Vienna in 1775 Gluck wrote to his collaborator Du Roullet a long letter dated 1 July, mostly concerning the work on *Alceste*. At the end he revealed that he intended to bring another opera with him back to Paris, along with *Alceste:*

> In doing *Iphigénie en Tauride,* be guided by my observations. Do not press anyone else to write operas for me, for I have already decided on my third, which I will bring with me to Paris. I will not tell you the subject yet, because you might dissuade me. I feel that you have too much power over my mind, and I will only tell you the subject when I am too far advanced to be able to turn back.[48]

The "third opera" after *Aulide* and *Alceste*—a formulation meaning that he did not consider even *Orphée* to be in their category, not to mention his lesser operas—was to be *Armide.* Gluck confessed this to Du Roullet in a letter of 31 January

---

[46]*Allgemeine Musikalische Zeitung,* October 1813, cited in Gluck, *The Collected Correspondence,* pp. 201–2.
[47]On this fine work see John Rice, *Antonio Salieri and Viennese Opera* (Chicago, 1998), pp. 162–75.
[48]Gluck, *The Collected Correspondence,* p 67. Subsequent translations from Gluck's letters are from this edition.

1776: "I had conceived several scenes of the opera *Armide* before my illness [July to October 1775] and after." He was reluctant to tell the truth in July for the reason given above, but Du Roullet must have guessed it or discovered it in any case. In his letter of 14 October 1775 Gluck wrote as if in answer to a reproof from Du Roullet (whose half of the exchange we do not have): "As for *Armide* I visualize a new method, for I am not going to remove one verse of Quinault's opera." Perhaps as a result of even stronger objections he softened his position in his letter of 22 November 1775: "As to *Armide,* I shall not consign the music to paper [fixera la Musique] until I am in Paris, because I want to consult you to see whether we should leave the poem as it is or make cuts." Setting Quinault's poem as it stood meant dispensing altogether with a live librettist, so it is no wonder that Du Roullet published a pamphlet pointedly signaling what he regarded as superfluities and faults in the old poem, a line of argument probably similar to what he had written in several lost letters to Gluck.

Du Roullet published his *Lettre sur les drames-opéra* (Amsterdam, 1776) anonymously, but by singing the praises of the libretto of *Aulide* at several turns in this essay of fifty-odd printed pages he fatuously gave way his identity. He divided operatic poems into three types, "Le tragique, le pastoral ou galant, et le bouffon." This pamphlet, considering only the first, was to be followed by treatments of the others, but they apparently never materialized. The poet must put his dramatic exposition *en action,* he counsels, as in the case of *Aulide.* At the end he takes on Quinault's *Armide* and gives it short shrift.

> *Armide* is Quinault's masterpiece but its first act is without movement or action, and used only in part for dramatic exposition, for which one scene of 30 lines would have sufficed. You will find there a totally useless person named Hidraot. The first two scenes of the second act are certainly unsatisfactory, the first being deadly cold, and easily supplanted by four or six lines in the first act, and the second apparently there so that Armide and Hidraot can announce that the action is about to begin. What could be more ridiculous than Quinault's nymphs and shepherds dancing around the sleeping Renaud since he can neither hear nor see them?[49]

Du Roullet descends to such a petty and literal reading here as to make one wonder how he could have made the *Aulide* and *Alceste* poems as good as they are, and the more one wonders, the more likely will emerge an answer that involves a firm guiding hand from the composer. A lack of theatrical sense goes hand and hand with Du Roullet's surprising lack of empathy. (It follows from his line of reasoning that the audience should be deprived of seeing and hearing the fairies dance around Verdi's sleeping Falstaff, since he can neither see nor hear them.) Du Roullet continues:

[49]Lesure, *La Querelle des Gluckistes et Piccinnistes*, 2: 156–61.

It is true that the arrival of Armide makes up for the fastidious *remplissage* that preceded it. Nothing is better constructed, more sublime or truly tragic than this scene of Renaud sleeping and Armide dagger in hand. Never has a dramatic action *begun* with such warmth [author's italics]. . . . The third act is totally episodic and useless, filled with an allegory, ingenious, in truth, but misplaced, both for Armide, who, vanquished by Love, should not have left Renaud, and for the spectator, impatient to see these two lovers together again. Even the enthusiasts for Quinault have not dared to try justifying the fourth act. The poet resumes his action finally with the fifth act, the composition of which is admirable in its entirety.

In sum, Du Roullet proposed (initially by letter to Gluck, presumably) heavy cuts in the first and second acts of Quinault, and elimination of his third and fourth acts, which would have made for a very short opera. Follow the Greeks, not Quinault, urged Du Roullet. "*Iphigénie en Aulide* provided us with the least defective opera that has yet appeared in our theater."

Gluck could not have been happy with Du Roullet for publishing a manifesto of this kind, from which enemies of the new *Armide* could and did draw ready ammunition. To understand what the composer found in Quinault's poem that was so attractive, one should take the trouble to read it from beginning to end. There are moments of less than capital interest, for sure, and Gluck did not deny this. After writing to Du Roullet on 14 October 1775, "I am not going to remove one verse from Quinault's opera," he added, "but in many scenes one must be able to trot, or, to put it still better, gallop with the music in order to conceal the coldness and *ennui* contained in the pieties expressed." Still, as a total construction Quinault's poem is sound, its language seductive, and its psychological penetration admirable. Gluck concluded his remarks on it just cited by saying, "When I study the fifth act I have to weep despite myself, so realistic and tender is the situation."

Du Roullet errs concerning the expository functions of Quinault's first act. In the first two lines, Armide's confidante Phénice conveys the air of celebration following Armide's victory over the Christians and poses the question to her mistress around which the whole opera turns:

> Dans un jour de triomphe, au milieu des plaisirs,
> Qui peut vous inspirer une sombre tristesse?

In what turns out to be a dialogue with another confidante, Sidonie, the two women declaim in simple song, one note per syllable, with no repetitions, explaining the situation with admirable clarity and concision. At first they sing to menuet-like strains of an *Andante* in 3/4, but at the mention of war and its ravages Gluck switches to cut time and introduces in the accompaniment a rhythmic and melodic figure that corresponds to the main theme of his overture, marked *Allegro*. The overture is in C and begins with a slow introduction comprising several bars of fanfares followed by minor mode inflections and melodic sighs, *piano*, that can only be interpreted as Armida's "dark sadness," especially since this passage recurrs at the end of the overture as a transition into the first air sung by Phénice.

The title page of one edition of the score, an elegant example of neoclassical restraint, magnified the name Gluck (Figure 8.5). But hostile critics belittled *Armide* even before the premiere on 23 September 1777. Later Jean-François de La Harpe, the most stringent of them, wrote at length of the opera in the *Journal de politique et de littérature* for October 1777 castigating Gluck for abandoning his own "truly lyrical plan of a drama interspersed with airs" and saying "there is no melody or cantabile in the new work; everything is carried on in recitative," concluding "above all I want to hear airs."[50]

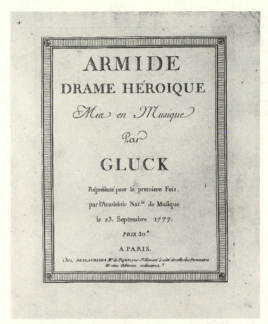

FIGURE 8.5. Gluck. Title page of *Armide*.

What La Harpe called recitative and would not dignify by the name air is well exemplified by the first vocal number (Example 8.6). The piece continues in this 4 + 4 phraseology, as does all the subsequent music sung by the two confidantes. Thus Gluck did not sin here against the concept of La Harpe's revered metric regularity ("la période"). His fault, in the eyes of this and likeminded critics, was to have resorted to the simplicity of age-old French dance airs. Instructive is a comparison of an air sung by "Le Menuet" in René Lesage's vaudeville comedy *Les couplets en procès* of 1730 (Example 8.7). Moving up the scale an octave in conjunct motion and then down to the fifth for the first cadence lends these two pieces a similarity that is obvious and no doubt coincidental. Countless French dance airs deploy this same smooth stepwise motion. With his experience setting vaudeville comedies in French for the Viennese court, Gluck was long steeped in an old Gallic tradition of melody. Most of his public in Paris must have felt quite at home with such music, and even willing to regard tunes like this as "airs." *Armide* has earned the title of being Gluck's "most French opera."[51] Partisans of Italian music wanted from Gluck and every other composer not just the

[50]Desnoireterres, *Gluck et Piccinni*, p. 209.

[51]Jeremy Hayes, "*Armide*, Gluck's Most French Opera," *Musical Times* 123 (1982): 408–10.

EXAMPLE 8.6. *Gluck*, Armide, *Act I, Scene 1*

EXAMPLE 8.7. *Lesage*, Les couplets en procès (1729), *air*

sainted *période* but the singing *Allegro* type of melody over largely static harmonies, at which Neapolitan composers were so successful and to which Gluck himself had contributed.

Quinault brings in Armide after her chattering companions reach the point of saying how many valiant warriors she has subdued. At this Armide says, in direct terms, with no prevarication:

> Je ne triomphe pas du plus vaillant de tous
> Renaud, pour qui ma haine a tant de violence.

Only he has resisted her potent physical charms, hence the violence of what she calls her hatred. Hades had predicted a hundred times that our arms will be useless against this warrior, she says. Moreover, she has dreamed of his delivering her a mortal blow himself. It does not take training in psychology to interpret Quinault's subtle and often double-edged language metaphorically.

Gluck characterizes Armide at her first vocal entrance with a marchlike swagger. He switches to common time from the cut time of the confidantes while the tempo stays the same. Her vocal line is broad and imperious, quite set apart from theirs, and the phraseology becomes irregular (3 + 2 + 2 measures constitute the first period). The confidantes revert to cut time and a dainty, even mincing, musical speech, regularly phrased, which contrasts strongly with the impassioned dignity of Armide. Gluck claimed in a letter to Du Roullet (undated, summer 1776) that one could tell from the music whether it was Armide or her servants speaking—no idle boast. Armide resumes singing to her broad march rhythms. Her vocal line soars to a climax at the words "His image troubles my sleep in spite of myself." The climax comes on a long high A♭ as she repeats her last two words, "malgré moi." Up to this point Gluck avoided repeating a single word of text. The sustained high A♭ acts as a musical exclamation point before sinking to the cadence on F over churning sixteenth-note accompaniment figures in the orchestra, which lead straight into the music over which she will recount her dream in recitative (real recitative, that is).

Continuity is one of Gluck's main concerns throughout the opera. Armide's relation of her dream encounter with Renaud is a good example of it. (Uncannily close in effect is another narration in obbligato recitative, Donna Anna's tale of how she was attacked by Don Giovanni). Emerging without a break out of Armide's martial strains, her recitative comes to a resounding cadence in c that is transformed immediately into soothing soft music in E♭ and in 3/4 time as Sidonie tries to exorcise "cette vaine chimère."

Enter Hidraot and his followers to a ludicrous march in C, so simple it sounds like a parody (or an anticipation of how Gilbert and Sullivan might introduce an eastern potentate). This elderly ruler is Armide's uncle, who lends his voice to her praises and then gets down to business. He is failing and has but one dying wish: to see her married and future mother to the royal succession. To convey this homely message is not a "useless" function (*pace* Du Roullet). It could have been put in the mouth of a mother or an aunt, but then Act I would have no male soloist. It also throws a different light on Armide. Enchantress with hellish powers, yes, but even so she is a woman susceptible to the wishes of her family, a human being with more at stake than merely her obsessive love that she calls hate.

Hidraot's air, "Je vois de près la mort qui me menace," is sung to a jaunty air in 2/4 time and in the key of a. It lends him neither fatherly nor kingly weight and sounds less like grand opera than opéra-comique, as Gluck's detractors did not fail to point out. Gluck's intention was perhaps to throw Armide into relief as much more regal in comparison, which he does in her intricate and lyrically attractive response in A, "La chaîne de l'Hymen m'étonne." The sinuous melodic line is begun by the orchestra, with ties over the bar line providing the audiovisual equivalent of "chains." She wishes to preserve her liberty, she says, and yet when she repeats the first line, Gluck departs from his rapid, totally syllabic word setting for a long-held tied note of three measures on "l'Hymen." This music may tell us more than her words about what is really on her mind. An orchestral postlude *à 2* continues and concludes the idea of "chains" in a series of dissonant ninths in the violins (with ties over the bar lines) pushing the bass to resolve downward by step, ending with a thin cadence in only two parts, presumably because Gluck rejected the usual cadential texture of at least three parts as calling too much attention to itself.

Hidraot comes back with more patter, *Tempo giusto,* 2/4, again in a, this time picking up the scherzando motif from Sidonie's earlier chatter. The orchestra mocks him with little slides upward in the violins. For the first time there is a substantial textual repetition, which may also serve to characterize the elderly uncle's inclination to garrulity. After a short dialogue in recitative between Armide and Hidraot, she launches into a *Maestoso* in cut time and in G that restores the regal temper. Only valor, not riches, will conquer her. This short and emphatic music should be over with the resounding cadence on G with fermata. But there are two unequal lines in addition, treated as if an afterthought.

> Le vainquer de Renaud, si quelqu'un le peut être,
> Sera digne de moi.

For these Gluck pushes to a cadence on e, enhancing the uncertainty of the proposition. The tonal ambiguity may also hint at some deeper, hidden meaning—the vanquisher of Renaud will be Armide.

A double chorus bursts upon the scene as the people of Damascas sing the praises of Armide, a radiant *Andantino* in 3/4 that profits from the celebratory choral music in the key of C so prominent in *Aulide.* Trumpets and drums enhance its splendor. The hemiola cadences hint at dance music, and this appears to be the first of a series of dances. To set "Que la douceur d'un triomphe est extrême," Gluck resorts to a chorus in B♭ and in gavotte rhythm; this idyll is interrupted only after an ominous move to g, when Aronte, a wounded soldier, bursts in with the news that the prisoners have escaped, liberated by a solitary, invincible warrior. "Un seul geurrier!" sing the astonished people in staggered entrances. Armide does not need to be told who he is. She blurts out his name: "O ciel! c'est Renaud." The following chorus of revenge, "Poursuivons jusqu'au trépas," restores B♭ and ends the act with so much power that it still served as an inspiration to Giacomo Meyerbeer when he wrote *Les Huguenots* for the Opéra many years later.[52]

---

[52] Act II, Scene 7, "Par l'honneur." The nearly constant triplets in fast common time of Gluck's chorus may also have inspired Mozart's "Corriamo, fuggiamo" chorus ending Act II of *Idomeneo.*

In Act II we first meet Renaud, although it seems as if we know him already. He is introduced in dialogue with Artémidore (another high tenor), whom he has just rescued and who wishes to accompany the great warrior on his quest. Renaud has exiled himself from Godefroi's army over a perceived slight (cf. Achilles and Agamemnon encamped before Troy). Asked by Artémidore where he will choose to settle, Renaud answers with talk of glory and justice, but Gluck answers the question in a tonal sense by choosing the key of A, last heard in Act I in association with Armide's exalted ideas about "l'Hymen." As if picking up this cue, Artémidore warns against the dangerous charms of the enchantress (in the key of a). As Renaud is replying, the music moves to the key of F and stays there, making multiple use of high A in the solo voice. They exit.

Armide and Hidraot enter. After a short recitative they sing an invocation to the spirit of hatred, *Andante* in cut time and in E, a piece Gluck had used earlier in *Telemaco* and elsewhere. They spy Renaud approaching. Hidraot suggests an ambush but Armide demurs, saying she wants to kill him herself. They withdraw as Renaud enters and gazes at the verdant riverbank while removing his armor. Gluck's orchestra, led by a full complement of winds, paints the magical glade in softly murmuring strains, seamlessly multiplying in long melodic extensions. As this liquid continuum goes on, he sings the sublime "Plus j'observe ces lieux, et plus je les admire" to the initial melody. To paint nature's spell Gluck reverts to the vein of gurgling brook cum birdsongs of Orfeo's "Che puro ciel" but is more continuous than he chose to be in that quasi-arioso interrupted by recitative cadences. The piece is in D and reaches one climax when the voice enters on high A and descends into the cadence on the dominant, another when it sustains high A after the tonic returns. As Renaud falls asleep, D as tonic becomes D as dominant in a little postlude leading to a pastoral dance and song in G, with echoes, and this in turn leads to a more lively antiphonal chorus and dance in C. The enchantment goes on with instrumental dances, a *Moderato* in C and in 3/4 with all the earmarks of a menuet,[53] then an *Andante* gavotte, a beautiful song by a shepherdess, and a reprise of the antiphonal chorus.

Armide enters with a dagger in her hand, and with a spring in her step to judge by the orchestra's *Spiritoso* in constant dotted rhythms and in the key of a: "Enfin il est en ma puissance / Ce fatal enemi, ce superb vainqueur." She declaims these famous lines unaccompanied, the only orchestral punctuation coming between them. Before she can act, the orchestra evokes the softer tones of pity (clarinets in sixths), forecasting the love motif that will emerge later. Furious music alternates with a pathetic chain of rising chromatic seconds in descent. She wavers. (This is the scene Rousseau attacked in Lully's setting because the music

[53]Is this the "Menuet d'Armide" that Grétry in his *Essais sur la musique* (3: 300–301) calls "le plus beau menuet de Gluck"?

did not foreshadow the words, an argument countered by Rameau.)[54] Eventually the parallel sixth motif, inverted to parallel thirds, leads into the air, "Ah! quelle cruauté de lui ravir le jour! . . . Il semble fait pour l'amour." In the following aria in e, Armide gives in. She calls for demons to come and carry them together to the ends of the universe. Demons transformed into zephyrs do her bidding during the lengthy orchestral postlude that ends the act.

Armide opens Act III with a solo scene in which she laments her lost liberty in a big **A B A** aria. Her *suivantes* reappear with their typical scherzando chatter. In a long dialogue with them, Armide comes to realize that Renaud's love for her, procured through enchantment, is not the equal of hers for him. She resolves to call in Hatred to cure her of her love. If Quinault were not such a great poet, the appearance of such an allegorical figure could seem incongruous and outmoded, even in a magic opera such as this. Gluck thrives on the challenge. Hatred ("La Haine") arrives after blustery music with rocking martellato thirds in the bass for emphasis (and in the key of A, perhaps with ironic intent). She is reinforced in a series of solos and choruses by her followers, an admirably developed sequence mostly borrowed from earlier Gluck operas. Ballet music ensues (some borrowed from the duel scene in *Don Juan*). This demonstration of horror is so convincing that Armide asks Hatred to leave, which she does, with curses hurled at Love. The whole spectacle is great theater, and no other composer could have done it as much justice as Gluck (perhaps a clue to his choice of both libretto and the extraordinary option of setting it uncut?). Quinault ended the act with Hatred to the fore, but Gluck wanted to refocus attention on Armide, so he added four lines to the old poem:

Armide: Oh ciel! quelle horrible menace!
Je frémis, tout mon sang se glace
Amour, puissant Amour! vien calme mon effroi
Et prends pitié d'un coeur qui s'abandonne à toi.

The music seems to calm down in comparison with what came before, but in its midst on the second beat of the 3/4 time is a pedal A (the dominant) that bursts out with a flurry of quick notes marked *sforzato,* an orchestral translation of Armide's shuddering, as it were, and also a premonition of trouble ahead.

In his long letter to Du Roullet of 1 July 1775, Gluck complained that the intensity of reliving the music of *Alceste* was driving him mad: "It seems to me that I have a hive of bees constantly buzzing in my head. Believe me, these types of opera are very vicious; I am now beginning to understand the shrewdness of

---

[54]Their quarrel over it is discussed at length in Cynthia Verba, *Music and the French Enlightenment: Reconstruction of a Dialogue, 1750–1764* (New York, 1993).

Quinault and Calzabigi in filling their works with secondary characters, thus enabling the spectator to relax." His remark surely pertains to the *Armide* poem, and specifically to its much maligned Act IV, which introduces the secondary characters Ubalde and the Danish Knight. Quinault knew full well what he was doing. Renaud's friends and rescuers need equal time with Armide's confidantes to maintain balance between the two principals. Moreover, Renaud's crisis in the last act takes on greater weight by having each of these two companions experience a trance and throw it off in turn, with the aid of magic weapons that will eventually be used to free Renaud.

Ubalde (tenor) and the Danish Knight (baritone) enter the scene with a golden scepter and a sword destined for Renaud, which allow them to fight off the monsters let loose from the underworld that block their way. Gluck excelled at painting battles with demons, and this scene is no exception. After overcoming the first onslaught the knights sing a duet about redoubling their defenses against more sweet enchantments awaiting them. A pastoral ballet in 6/8 and in the key of F introduces Lucinde, a demon who has taken the form of the Danish Knight's beloved. The main enchantment follows in her air in B♭, "Jamais dans ces beaux lieux," with reinforcing chorus and ballet. Unceasing undulation in eighth notes, *Grazioso* in cut time, provides a movement that anticipates nothing less than the "Scene by the Brook" movement of Beethoven's *Pastoral* Symphony. Eventually the lovers sing a charming duet, "Jouisons du bonheur extrême," after which she disappears when touched by the magic scepter. Quinault used many fewer lines for the parallel temptation and bewitching of Ubalde by a demon impersonating his beloved Melissa.

Gluck's music for Act IV is no less genial than that in the other acts. Indeed, one of his most sensitive and fervent admirers, Berlioz, declared this act to be his favorite after he witnessed a performance of *Armide* under the direction of Meyerbeer in Berlin in 1843. Only a composer sensitive himself to the high poetic art of painting scenes in music could have written the following:

> But for sheer beauty and subtlety of expression nothing equalled the scenes in the Garden of Delights. A gliding, voluptuous languor, a kind of hypnotic ease, seemed to waft me inside the enchanted palace of love (dream picture of two poets, Gluck and Tasso) and to offer it to me for my own. I closed my eyes and let that divine gavotte lap over me with its caressing melody and the hum of its soft, unchanging harmonies, and heard the chorus murmuring of endless felicity: "Jamais dans ces beaux lieux"; and as I listened saw around me arms coiled in seductive arms, delicious feet entwined, the ripple of perfumed hair, and everywhere bewitching smiles and the gleam of sparkling eyes. Pleasure seemed to open like a flower at the soft insistence of the music, loosing a stream of harmonious sounds and scents and colours from its luxuriant corolla. And Gluck wrote this: Gluck—the composer who sang the griefs of mankind and made Tartarus roar and evoked the harsh shores of Tauris and the sav-

agery of its inhabitants—found music to catch this vision of an ideal sensuality, a love without care![55]

Gluck kept the love duets between the two temptresses and the Christian knights in Act IV to a relatively modest length so as to allow himself more scope when arriving at the main event in the last act. A much grander duet was obviously in order for the archtemptress and the knight of all knights. Renaud, in Armide's palace, garlanded with flowers, opens Act V singing, "Armide, vous m'allez quitter!" She answers, also using the formal "vous" to him, saying that her art required solitude and a consultation with the infernal powers. She promises that a royal entertainment will divert him until she returns, which thus sets up another grand divertissement. The duet proper begins at "Aimons nous, tous nous y convie," after a long dialogue. It is an *Andante* in common time and in the seemingly neutral key of C. The music is so sensual its composer claimed it would be the cause of his perdition should he be consigned in afterlife to burn in Hell. Renaud is at the top of his voice much of the time, singing in thirds with his beloved. Not even melismas are spared, and when Gluck arrives at the words "ma flamme" he gives the voices long chains of sixths and thirds to sing, an extraordinary liberty that he allows nowhere else in the opera.

The Pleasures plus the Fortunate Swains and Happy Damsels come on to console the hero in the work's largest ballet. Dance songs and choral responses follow an imposing Chaconne in B♭. One of the Pleasures (soprano) then starts a song about birds in F, with choral refrain, built partly over a repeated descending fourth bass. The flute eventually adds a chromatic rise to the complex, answered by the clarinet (Example 8.8). The ballet goes on until another Pleasure sings Quinault's entry into the *carpe diem* poetic sweepstakes: "Jeunes coeurs tout est favorable, / Profitz d'un bonheur peu durable." Gluck sets it to a lilting melody in G, in 3/4 time. This, too, is decorated with a choral response in kind, leading to the second Chaconne (in G/g). Renaud dismisses his entertainers, who gradually dance off.

The two knights make their appearance. This is the moment captured in one of Tiepolo's sublime visual translations of Torquato Tasso's poem (see Plate VII). His knights look grizzled as they spy on the enamoured couple from behind a garden wall. In Quinault the knights first encounter Renaud alone and show him the diamond-studded shield, which blinds him. Ubalde then takes the lead with a martial song (in C) recalling him to duty. Renaud removes the garlands of flowers and receives the shield and sword during Ubalde's air—without the preparations in trance breaking offered by Act IV, this quick renunciation by Renaud

---

[55] *The Memoirs of Hector Berlioz, Member of the French Institute. Including His Travels in Italy, Germany, Russia, and England, 1803–1865,* trans. and ed. by David Cairns (London, 1969), pp. 330–31.

EXAMPLE 8.8. *Gluck*, Armide, *Act V, Scene 2, chorus*

would seem too sudden. The three men hasten to leave when they encounter Armide (C becomes c). Her pleas to Renaud, alternately eloquent, touching, and finally piteous, fall on deaf ears, but they make her one of the most fascinating female characters in all opera. He must leave, he says, but she will always reign in his heart—a lame remark to be sure. A rumble of sixteenth notes in the bass of the orchestra (similar to the breezes starting up at the end of *Aulide*) signals the igniting of Armide's anger, which grows steadily. The knights drag Renaud away. Armide alone begins singing softly, "Le perfide Renaud me fuit," which allows her to work up step by step to the full measure of her fury. She flies off in a chariot led by dragons while her demons raze and burn the enchanted palace. The 1710 reduced score of Lully's *Armide* printed by Baussen illustrates the scene with a picture that may suggest how it was actually staged—the palace is built to be dismantled (Figure 8.6). Gluck was of course in his element, creating an orchestral firestorm such as only he could write, and had earlier created for the end of *Don Juan*. As in that epochal pantomime ballet of 1761, the conclusion seems to settle

FIGURE 8.6. Lully. *Armide.* Final scene, engraved by Henri de Baussen.

on the key of d, only to be replaced at the last moment by D (and thus the D at the end of Act IV was prophetic). Gluck knew that he had created a masterpiece for the ages. He said so. His *Armide* was so genial it outraged the partisans of the old French opera and of Italian opera to an equal degree. The latter clamored for a new champion.

A Neapolitan Rival: Piccinni

The attempt to import Piccinni to combat Gluck went back to early 1774 and is thought to have originated with the desire of the king's mistress, Madame du Barry, to rival Marie Antoinette as a cultural patron. An important intermediary between the composer and the French court was the Neapolitan ambassador in Paris, Domenico Caracciolo. With the death of Louis XV, Madame du Barry passed immediately out of the picture, but Marie Antoinette, now queen of France, was brought around to the idea that she could sponsor both Gluck and Piccinni, who left Naples in mid-November 1776 and arrived in Paris on the last day of the year. Gluck, who may have known Piccinni from his visits to Rome and Naples, and who certainly knew the composer's music from performances in Vienna among other places, was not happy when he learned that the Neapolitan master was to write a *Roland* adapted by Marmontel from Quinault for the Opéra.

The rumor spread in Paris that Gluck was also working on a *Roland,* which led one wag to say, "now we shall have both an *Orlando* and an *Orlandino,*" the latter referring to the burlesque *Orlando* written by the macaronic poet Teofilo Folengo. In other words, Gluck's work was being placed on a par with Ludovico Ariosto's *Orlando* and Piccinni's with Folengo's comic travesty. Gluck apparently went along with the joke by claiming that he had already started composing his *Roland* to the same poem. His claim is not believable. His discernment with regard to librettos never would have allowed him to consider setting such a botch as Marmontel made of Quinault in this case. There is also something odd about the timing of Gluck's claim, written in a letter from Vienna to Du Roullet assigned to the summer of 1776, although he mysteriously maintained that he was answering a January letter from Du Roullet. The letter is more likely from early 1777.

> I have just received your letter of 15 January, my friend, in which you urge me to continue work on the words of the opera *Roland;* that is not possible, because when I learned that the administration of the Opéra, who were not unaware that I was setting *Roland,* gave this same work to Piccinni, I burned all that I had already composed, which perhaps did not amount to much, and in this case the public ought to be obliged to M. Marmontel for having prevented it from hearing bad music. Besides, I am not a man made for entering competitions. M. Piccinni would have too much of an advantage over me, because, in addition to his personal merit, which is assuredly very great, he would have that of novelty, while I have given four works in Paris, good or bad makes no difference; this uses up one's invention; also, I prepared the way for him, which he only has to follow.[56]

Whatever the truth about Gluck and *Roland,* there is no disputing the Parisian lust for novelty, as Piccinni would sadly learn in the 1780s when he was shunted aside at the Opéra by Salieri and Sacchini. Gluck's revolution in Paris had indeed prepared the way for all who followed at the Opéra. Not the least of Gluck's benefactions to his successors was taming the orchestral and choral forces of the establishment and training its greatest soloists—Larrivée, Legros, and Levasseur—as singing actors who could execute demanding new music bereft of the fripperies of the older French style. These three singers in fact carried the day for Piccinni when they were transferred from *Armide* to *Roland.* Piccinni, after a year's work and coaching in the French language by Marmontel, saw his *Roland* given with success in January 1778.

Gluck continued his letter to Du Roullet in a way that allowed his resentment to show, and even expressed a kind of controlled anger through bantering.

> I shall not speak of his [Piccinni's] protectors. I am certain that a certain political figure of my acquaintance [Caracciolo] will give dinner and supper to three quarters of

---

[56]Gluck, *The Collected Correspondence,* pp. 83–84. I have retranslated the letter from the French, quoted in the preface to Niccolò Piccinni, *Roland,* ed. A. Pougin (Paris, 1880).

Paris in order to make proselytes, and that Marmontel, who knows so well how to tell tales, will tell the entire kingdom of the exclusive merit of M. Piccinni. I pity, in truth, M. Hébert for having fallen into the claws of such people, the one an exclusive lover of Italian music, the other a dramatic author of operas that pretend to be comic. They will make him see the moon at midday. I am truly annoyed, because M. Hébert is a galant man and this is the reason I do not retract my *Armide,* but under conditions that I laid down in my previous letter, of which the essentials are, I repeat, that I be given at least two months when I am at Paris in order to form my actors and actresses; that I shall be the master able to call as many rehearsals as I believe necessary; that no role be doubled; and that another opera be held in readiness in case one of the actors or actresses is indisposed. These are my conditions, failing satisfaction of which I shall keep *Armide* for my own pleasure. I have composed the music in a manner that it will not soon grow old.

Gluck probably intended this letter to be published all along. In any case it was printed in *L'année littéraire* with the disclaimer that neither the writer nor the recipient were responsible (how could Du Roullet not be responsible in some sense for its publication?). The letter became the opening salvo of the war proper between Gluckistes and Piccinnistes. Piccinni himself stayed out of the fray and has been seen as the only figure who came out of it with his honor intact.

ROLAND

Roland opens with a three-movement overture. Its middle movement, *Andantino amoureux* in 3/4, deploys a subtly constructed melody, mostly in thirds and tenths, that resembles a beloved minuet by Christian Bach (see Example 9.11a on p. 928). Marmontel discarded Quinault's prologue and began with a series of scenes for the heroine, Angélique. She cannot reconcile her love for Médor, the follower of an African king whom she had rescued after he was wounded in battle, with her more exalted status as queen of Cathay. Perhaps to reinforce the regal tone, Piccinni calls for a trombone to join the winds that accompany her first obbligato recitative, sung to her patiently listening confidante Thémire.[57] She then conveys her troubled state in an air in the key of c, with a roulade on "gloire" and sustained high A♭ followed by the Neapolitan sixth chord for "mon coeur." La Borde in his *Essai sur la musique ancienne et moderne* numbered this among his favorite pieces in *Roland* and called it a "cavatine." It was just a prelude to the aria proper, a common time *Allegro* in B♭ with some surprisingly buffa traits, such as the flurry of four sixteenth notes on the second beat of the accompaniment. Indecision does not make for much drama, if carried out at this length (Lully's rapid setting of the

---

[57]Berlioz, in *A travers chants* (Paris: 1927), pp. 222–23, complained that modern hands added trombones to *Armide* in both Paris and Berlin. Trombones had been used by Gluck in both *Orphée* and *Alceste* at the Opéra, but not in *Armide.*

text in recitative or arioso was more proportionate to its interest). Adding to the problem at the premiere, the rather homely Levasseur was more at ease in a maternal role (Alceste) or as the terrible-tempered Armide than she was as an equivocating Chinese enchantress. Thémire reminds her of her regal status and plumps for the knight Roland over Médor. As the ladies withdraw, Médor (Legros) himself appears. His *Andante amoroso* brings coloratura for "ma flame." When Piccinni repeats the melisma in I instead of V, it is transferred to the word "offenser" (Example 8.9). Another "a" sound would have been preferable here. Gluck in his reform mode did not allow lengthy roulades.

EXAMPLE 8.9. *Piccinni*, Roland, *Act I*, *Scene 2, Aria*

Angélique returns and decides to banish Médor from her presence. They sing a long duet (157 measures) expresssing regrets about parting. It is in the traditional key of love duets in Neapolitan opera, A, and has much to recommend it. After this outpouring Angélique has to sing the line, "Terminons les regrets que pourraient trop s'étendre," which must have raised a few smiles. After sending him away she laments having done so in a dramatic recitative which leads to an aria in E♭ that is beautiful but spoiled by Marmontel's ineptitudes (heavy musical accents needed words of more consequence and better sonority than he gave his composer). She sends Thémire to bring Médor back, then recalls her and utters words to the effect "go and console the unhappy one at least," which has to be one of the lamest remarks possible. The act ends with the appearance of a troupe of "oriental island people" come to praise Angélique and Roland. This ballet, by no less than Jean-Georges Noverre, did not manage to please, so Piccinni's stirring Marche in D was wasted. His following chorus, "Triomphez charmante Reine," coming after the strong choruses of *Armide,* was considered too slight. In his letter of 28 February 1778 from Mannheim, Mozart reported that the choruses in *Roland* were found "too bare and weak [zu nachend und schwach] because in Paris people were used to Gluck's choruses."

Act II begins with a long divertissement next to the fountain of love in a forest. Piccinni responded with some lovely dance music, including a gavotte-like *Andantino* in A. When Angélique and Thémire start conversing in recitative again, the situation is exactly the same as we left it in Act I. Roland appears but Angélique makes herself invisible to him by means of a magic ring. He sings his complaints to Thémire in a big aria in D, calling the name "Angélique," anticipated by drooping sixths and thirds in the flutes that sound as if they may have been inspired by a similar motif in Armide's monologue, "Enfin il est en ma puissance." Thémire makes the case for Roland to her mistress, who will hear none of it. They hear Médor's voice saying he will kill himself over the loss of Angélique. This turns the tide finally and she yields, telling him to live on, but to be patient until she has dealt with Roland, with whom she sings a duet in C that was another of La Borde's favorite pieces in the opera. The music is somewhat trite but perhaps suits the falsity with which she leads him on in order to be rid of him.

The scene changes to a seaport. Médor and Thémire are joined by a band of sailors who sing a chorus and dance. Médor launches into an aria about being rescued from a shipwreck, a vehicle for vocal display that gets the full bravura treatment it would in an Italian opera. Legros entertained his many admirers with coloratura up to high B♭ and an improvised cadenza following a fermata. This old-fashioned kind of piece ended with the stereotyped "wedge cadence." In the final scene Angélique reappears and bids him to a rustic temple to receive her faith. A chorus sings "Régnez en dépit de l'envie." Act II ends with the customary dancing. Although Italian and French elements still sit uneasily beside each other, the composer seems somewhat more comfortable in carrying out his tasks than in the first act.

It was Act III that rescued the opera as a whole, particularly the music for Roland and its projection by Larrivée. The stage represented a grotto in the middle of a grove. Roland is introduced by an *Allegro animato* in E, the prelude to his first recitative. He sings a very galant *Andantino amoureux et vif* in the same key, "De l'aimable objet qui m'enchante." He has no inkling of what has happened to Angélique, but the audience did know, which makes for an interesting situation, the first one in the opera, it might be claimed. Astolphe attempts to persuade his friend Roland to return to duty, singing of "gloire" to march rhythms in a duo in D. Roland answers without the dotted rhythms, singing of love. Astolphe leaves and Roland's famous monologue begins. After his invocation of night, "O nuit favorisez mes désirs amoureux," which seems to be in f, the composer places a little wavering figure and a pause—a small but telling detail that Mozart may have picked up in Paris during his visit in 1778 (Example 8.10).[58] Piccinni repeats the figure after "tranquilité profonde," in which case the slight agitation of the music

EXAMPLE 8.10. *Piccinni*, Roland, *Act III, Scene 2*

seems to contradict the words. Then Roland begins a gavotte-like tune in F for "Le charmant objet de mes voeux," which could not sound more French, because of both the rhythm and the restricted melodic ambitus and conjunct motion. Surprisingly, the piece works its way into the key of g. Roland discovers the grotto, and then some words written above, as the music progresses to B♭. A first shock is signaled in the music by unprepared hammerstroke chords (three times) in C after B♭, then D after C, resolving to g as Roland recognizes the handwriting of Angélique. Next he sees the name "Médor" and suspects the worst, although he tries to fight off suspicion. Learning through the writing that Angélique had yielded to the happy Médor, to more orchestral outbursts, he rises to an explosion of wrath in the aria, "Que l'insolent qui m'outrage tremble et redoute ma fureur."

[58]Cf. the similar wavering figure in dotted rhythm in Ilia's opening recitative in *Idomeneo,* after "oh sorte."

Piccinni prepares it with an orchestral ritornello of fifteen bars in B♭, effective here because he has been sparing throughout the opera with orchestral introductions. The aria is an *Allegro assai* in common time, with a distinct middle section for "Elle aurait trahi sa gloire," an *Andante soutenu* in 2/4 that begins in f and ends in F as preparation for the return of the first part in B♭. The aria is one of the biggest in the opera, but not a coloratura showpiece such as given to Médor; it has no cadenza. As a continuous *scena* using various kinds of recitative and arioso all coursing toward a grand outpouring in the form of a tripartite aria, Piccinni's Act III, Scene 2, can stand beside the greatest scene complexes of its time, either in the operas of his Italian contemporaries or in those of Gluck.

Rustic music breaks in upon Roland's solitude as a chorus of shepherds arrives singing an *Andantino gracieux* in 6/8 and in the key of D. Of course they sing of love and the charms of this wooded spot that invites to dalliance. Next comes a dance, a blithe *Allegro* in 2/4 and in A that is put through many melodic extensions and keeps returning to its refrain, variously orchestrated (Example 8.11). This must be the "longue et charmante gavotte" that the master added to his score in response to a request for a solo by Mademoiselle Marie Madeleine

EXAMPLE 8.11. *Piccinni*, Roland, *Act III*, *Scene 3*, *dance*

Guimard.[59] It certainly ranks with the best of all dance music at the Opéra. Following the dance, two of the young lovers sing a duet in the same key. One of them next sings "Angélique est Reine et belle" to an *Andantino* in 6/8 and in the key of d. Médor is mentioned as well, and in the next scene Roland learns that they have sailed away to seek a safe haven.

His vengeance thwarted by their flight, Roland goes on a rampage and scatters the rustics. In another solo scene (Scene 6), he rages against Angélique to an

---

[59]The episode, along with many others concerning the composition and performance of *Roland,* is narrated by Pierre Louis Ginguené, *Notice sur la vie et les ouvrages de Nicolas Piccinni* (Paris, 1800–1801), pp. 38–39.

Allegro vif in common time and in the key of f, during the long orchestral postlude of which he destroys the inscriptions on the grotto, overturns the rocks, and pulls up the trees. A powerful recitative follows in which Roland laments his fate: "O supplice horrible! Je dois montrer un exemple terrible des tourments d'un funeste amour." The orchestra follows these words by performing a wordless *Andantino amoureux* in E♭ and in 3/4 time, a perfect example of a menuet galant. A good fairy, Logistile (soprano), appears and calms Roland's spirits, after which it is left for a chorus of French knights and their ladies to welcome Roland back to the paths of glory, in an *Allegro sans presser* in common time and in D. Roland sings in the middle, welcoming the chance to arm himself again, and the opera ends with a *Marche guerrière* in cut time.

One of the immediate consequences of the premiere of *Roland* was a verse by Framery praising the title role, published in the *Journal de Paris* of 4 February 1778. Framery was an anti-Gluckist who had compromised himself by falsely charging Gluck with plagiarizing Sacchini (*Mercure de France,* September 1776). He couched his praises as a rebuke of Larrivée for having said, "there is only one truth in the world and Gluck has found it."[60] What was so extraordinary in this affair is that the singer answered with a reply one day later, 5 February, in the same paper, when he must have had time or energy for little else other than concentrating on a very demanding role during the opera's first run.

> I did not say that there was only one truth in the world, only that there was one truth in music, and M. Gluck had discovered it. . . . I have a superb role in *Roland* and if self-esteem sometimes leads to perfection, often it gives only the emulation to attain it. It is in this last class that I place myself with justice, too happy to have been able to satisfy the two authors of this work. With respect to my particular opinion in music, I do not pretend to be a judge of either composer, but I could not have failed to be seized by enthusiasm. My heart has been transported by the accents of M. Gluck, moved, *attendri,* enraptured; I agreed to this and I still do. What this composer has done to my sense for music, I had experienced only partially before, even through what was esteemed the best possible [Lully? Rameau?]. In the present moment my senses are affected but not at all enraptured.[61]

What this fine artist seems to be attempting to say, from his priviledged position as an insider, is that Gluck inspired not only him but Piccinni as well.

One of the two "authors" of *Roland,* Marmontel, was not happy with his share of the credit or his treatment financially by the Opéra. On 4 May 1778 he wrote the director of the Opéra claiming that his work on *Roland,* and on Quinault's

---

[60] "Epitre de M. Framery à M. Larrivée jouant le rôle de Roland; sur ce qu'il avoit dit: qu'il n'y a qu'une vérité dans le monde, et que c'est M. Gluck qui l'a trouvé."

[61] "Réponse de M. Larrivée," in Lesure, *La Querelle des Gluckistes et Piccinistes,* 1: 407–11.

Atys as well, was so extensive that he deserved to be paid as an author, not as just an adaptor. He described his labor as accommodating the old poems to the tastes of Italian music.

> It would have been as impossible for the great Italian masters—Pergolesi, Jommelli, Sacchini and Piccinni himself—to write melodies [faire du chant] on the verses of Quinault as on the prose of Fénelon. These verses were made for recitative; regularly measured song demands verbal forms that are analogous. It is up to the poet to design what the composer must paint. Difficulties beyond imagining must be overcome by repeated trials in this operation so as to make the verse supple and docile to musical requirements.[62]

Director Anne-Pierre-Jacques Devismes du Valgay answered his request four days later with a refusal, saying he could not get around the strict language of the law governing fees for authors and adaptors. He might have added that Marmontel needed further study of Metastasio in order to serve Italian composers with what they needed, most particularly soft vowel sounds at the ends of stanzas capable of taking melismas. The poet mentioned in his letter having read aloud his version of *Atys* to the approval of Devismes. Perhaps this working method helped him, because his *Atys* is a much better poem for music than *Roland.* Both poet and composer were able to improve over the uneven quality of their first collaboration. Although Marmontel threatened to withdraw *Atys* unless he was better paid, he did not do so. The work reached the stage of the Opéra on 22 February 1780 and was well received; it had an even more successful revival in 1783, which engendered a fine critique from Ginguené.[63]

When Duplant, in retirement, had her portrait painted by François Vincent, she alluded to one of her favorite roles by a piece of music placed open on the desk of the piano. It was not by any role from Gluck or Grétry that she wanted to be remembered but by that of Cybèle in Piccinni's *Atys.* The "Air d'Atys" displayed in a vocal score that included obbligato flute, "Je resens un plaisir extrême à revoir ces aimables lieux," opens Act II.

In spite of his success Piccinni's lot at the Opéra was not easy. He had a large family, a wife and seven children, of whom five survived infancy, and was lured to Paris with promises that he would be able to earn a better living with which to support them. Once he arrived he had to struggle to learn French and the conventions of French opera. Obstacles were placed in his way and the financial rewards were never as great as he hoped, but through it all he behaved with dignity.

La Borde was finishing the writing of his *Essai* in 1778, while *Roland* was in its first run. Of all the contradictory and often partisan reports about Piccinni from

---

[62]Desnoireterres, *Gluck et Piccinni*, pp. 239–40.
[63]Lesure, *La Querelle des Gluckistes et Piccinnistes,* 2: 595–621.

that time and long after, his assessment remains the best. He wrote several pages on the Neapolitan master in his third volume, ending his précis with Paris and *Roland.*

> At Paris where, in spite of ridiculous criticisms and bitter enemies, he won the applause of all sensitive people and all the connoisseurs, he made an opera on a poem lacking in interest, in a language that he scarcely understood, and of which he knew not the accent and prosody, for a nation whose taste, genius and theatrical system were absolutely unknown to him. He made an opera full of delicious pieces [he names eleven] and above all the terrible aria "Que me veux-tu, monstre effroyable." These are in every mouth, on the desk of every keyboard, and will always be heard with transport in the theater as long as one sings French words in France.

Oddly enough, the "terrible aria," which was Roland's last, was cut from the third act, which was obviously too long, and does not appear in the original printed score. Another critic writing on *Roland* praised the opera "in spite of the meager resources offered by the poem," signaling several of the same favorites, ending with the "sublime ariette" sung by Roland, "Que me veux-tu spectre effroyable!"— "nothing in Gluck is so theatrical, so true, so tragic," says this enthusiast.[64]

In his dedication of *Roland* to Marie Antoinette, Piccinni mentioned some of the difficulties he had encountered: "Transplanted, isolated, in a country that was entirely new to me, intimidated in my work by a thousand difficulties, I needed all my courage, and my courage abandoned me." If Marmontel told the truth about his tutoring the composer daily, it cannot be true that he was isolated. And perhaps he was intimidated as much by the poet as by Gluckist partisans. There are many tales of how the personnel at the Opéra behaved as rudely to him as they had initially to Gluck. What turned the situation around for Piccinni? A kind glance from the queen, he claimed, restored his courage. There is at least good operatic precedent for the marvels a single glance could work, as when Vitellia emboldens Sextus to become an assassin by granting him a look in Metastasio's *La clemenza di Tito.*

The Opéra followed up the success of *Roland* by engaging Piccinni to direct a season of opera buffa performed by Italian singers. Opera buffa had made sporadic inroads at the Théâtre Italien in Paris but hardly at the Opéra. The repertory chosen included comic operas of Anfossi, Paisiello, Sacchini, and Traetta as well as several by Piccinni himself. Grimm, one of the strongest partisans of Italian opera and of Piccinni, attempted to push Mozart toward this enterprise in the summer of 1778, after his mother died in Paris. Despondent over her death and dispirited with his failure to earn money in the French capital, Mozart was adamant to the

---

[64]Claude-Philibert Coquéau, *Entretiens sur l'état actuel de l'Opéra de Paris* (Amsterdam, 1779) in Lesure, *La querelle des Gluckistes et Picinnistes,* 2: 458–72.

point of not even going to see Piccinni. In his letter of 11 September 1778, Mozart wrote of Grimm, "He kept trying to get me to run after Piccinni and also to see Caribaldi [primo tenore]—for they have here now a miserable opera buffa—but I always replied that I would not take a single step in that direction. In a word, he is of the Italian faction." At this point Mozart was of the Gluck faction, if only to annoy Grimm.

It has been argued, on the other hand, that if Mozart had managed to get a commission for a tragedy from the Opéra, his work would have owed more to Piccinni than to Gluck.[65] *Idomeneo,* in many ways the artistic result of Mozart's 1778 stay in Paris, owes much to both composers. For all its French origins and scenic construction, *Idomeneo* is still closer to an Italian-French compromise like *Roland* and *Atys,* in which there are distinct arias and other large numbers. Boundaries may be blurred at the beginning and ending of pieces sometimes, but not to the extent of the continuum typical of older French operas and raised to a new level by Gluck in *Aulide* and *Armide.* Gluck was well aware of Piccinni's merits as a composer and did not begrudge him his success. Perhaps it was the triumph of *Roland* over all obstacles that helped decide Gluck to have his long-planned *Iphigénie en Tauride* structured with large discrete numbers and big solos for his three favorite principals, who had also carried the day for *Roland.* Whatever the cause, Gluck reverted to his own "truly lyrical plan of drama interspersed with airs" that La Harpe had blamed him for forsaking in *Armide.*

Final Triumph: *Iphigénie en Tauride*

The contract Gluck signed with the Opéra in early 1775 specified that, after *Alceste,* he would provide two more works, an *Electre* and an *Iphigénie en Tauride.* He was thus thinking to follow *Aulide* with the next installment on the horrors besetting the House of Atreus: Clytemnestra and her paramour Aegisthus murder Agamemnon on his return from Troy, to avenge which Orestes murders his mother and Aegisthus in complicity with his sister Electra. (Some sources soften Clytemnestra's guilt by having her act in revenge for what she believed was Iphigenia's death at the hands of Agamemnon.) Both Sophocles and Euripides left an *Electra.* In the eighteenth century, Voltaire and Friedrich Wilhelm Gotter, among others, wrote plays on the same myth. It would have made a superb vehicle for Gluck's dramatic strengths and perhaps given us a great trilogy by him. Nothing more is heard about *Electre* in the surviving correspondence. In his letter to Du Roullet of 1 July 1775, Gluck urged compliance with his wishes in preparing

---

[65]Julian Rushton, "The Theory and Practice of Piccinnisme," *Proceedings of the Royal Musical Association* 98 (1971–72): 31–46.

Iphigénie en Tauride. At some time that cannot be specified, Du Roullet stepped to the background and turned the versification over to the young poet Nicolas-François Guillard. Besides Euripides the librettists took as their model the tragedy in five acts by Guymond de la Touche introduced with success at the Comédie Française in 1757, which attracted the favorable criticism of Grimm and a flattering parody by Favart.[66] It was an advantage of this drama over earlier eighteenth-century treatments to have pared the characters down to four: Iphigenia, Orestes, Pylades, and the barbarian king Thoas. Especially odd for a French play was the absence of any love interest. Love of sibling, of friend, and of country made up for the lack.

The Opéra had attempted to put Gluck in direct competition with Piccinni by having him set *Roland,* or so Gluck claimed. When Gluck left Paris in March 1778 another scheme of the same sort was hatched. Director Devismes offered Piccinni in secret an *Iphigénie en Tauride* libretto by Alphonse Dubreuil. Piccinni was reluctant to rise to the bait, knowing that Gluck's version was forthcoming. Only when the director promised that Piccinni's opera would be performed first did the composer agree. Gluck returned to Paris in November 1778 with his score nearly complete. Devismes broke his promise to Piccinni, whose work was postponed until after Gluck's and not performed until 1781.

Gluck's new opera had its premiere on 18 May 1779 after months of rehearsals, with Levasseur in the title role, Larrivée as Orestes, Legros as Pylades, and the bass Moreau as Thoas. Unlike most of his previous works for Paris, the opera pleased from the beginning. A report three days after the premiere expressed this with some astonishment.

> The opera was strongly applauded. It is in a new genre, being a veritable tragedy, declaimed more knowledgeably than at the Comedie Française, a *tragedie à la grecque.* There is no overture, only one very characteristic dance and no ariettes. Yet the diverse accents of passion expressed with such energy imbue it with an interest hitherto unknown to lyric theater. One can only applaud the Chevalier Gluck for having found the secret of the ancients, which he will no doubt perfect. Some spectators were seen weeping from one end of the show to the other.[67]

In place of an overture the orchestra commences with a gentle menuet-like piece in 3/8 and in D, sounded first by strings then joined by flutes, representing *Le calme.* After 28 bars of this idyllic strain there is a rude interruption: the tempo and

---

[66]Julie E. Cumming, "Gluck's Iphigenia Operas: Sources and Strategies," in *Opera and the Enlightenment,* ed. Thomas Bauman and Marita Petzoldt McClymonds (Cambridge, 1995), pp. 217–40; 222–23.

[67]*Mémoires secrets,* XIV, 58 (21 May 1779). The original is quoted in Gluck, *Iphigénie en Tauride,* in *Sämtliche Werke,* ed. Gerhard Croll, Abteilung 1, Bd. 9 (Kassel: 1973), p. viii. Croll's edition incorporates the elaborate stage directions in the printed libretto.

meter switch to *Allegro* 4/4 as the strings, joined by timpani, announce a storm in the distance. By degrees it becomes louder and more furious, marked with explicit directions in the score: Gluck indicates "storm a little nearer" (m. 37), and at the *fortissimo* (m. 45) after a *crescendo* he brings in the whole orchestra ("Tempête très fort"). The curtain is up from the start, revealing the following stage picture, according to the printed libretto.

> The stage represents, in the background, the entrance to the temple of Diana; in the foreground the sacred grove that surrounds it. One hears from the beginning a few strokes of thunder which then becomes more frequent as the piece continues, until it becomes a furious storm. Day has dawned, but it is obscured by clouds, and the scene is lit only by flashes of lightning.

Rain and hail fall according to the score in m. 69, signaled by the upper winds, including two *flauti piccoli*, swirling up to the heights, with marvelously shrill effect, above a pedal $F\sharp$ pushing the key toward b. In m. 76 Iphigenia enters, confirming the key of b. She implores the gods for help and for an end to the revengeful ire unleashed on innocent heads. The priestesses echo her words in a chorus divided into Soprano I and Soprano II. The storm ebbs but persists. Iphigenia sings two more strophes, to which the priestesses respond with their same initial refrain. There is a gradual return to calmness and the key of D after several intermediate tonal destinations; *pianissimo* is reached in m. 227 as Iphigenia sings, "Le calme reparaît." But there is no tonal closure finally, because Gluck leaves this stunning tone poem hanging on the dominant, A, unfinished business, as it were, and quite appropriate to her next words, sung in recitative: "Calm returns, yet in my heart, alas! the storm still dwells." Outer storm thus represents inner turmoil.

French opera offered many precedents for Gluck's storm scene. The original *Iphigénie en Tauride* on a poem by Joseph-François Duché de Vancy (1696) set to music by Henri Desmarets and André Campra (1704, revived at the Opéra until 1762), contained a tempest in the third of its five acts.[68] Gluck's own opéra-comique *L'isle de Merlin* of 1758 began with the models of his 1779 storm music and calm, in this order. Meanwhile *Ifigenia in Tauride* by Verazi and Majo for the Mannheim court in 1764 had begun with a three-movement overture depicting in turn the shipwreck of Orestes and Pylades in a storm, a calm, and their capture after a battle with the Scythians. Gluck visited Mannheim on his return from Paris to Vienna in the fall of 1775 and could have seen the libretto, the score, or both there.[69]

---

[68]The context is a celebration of the Scythians together with various sea creatures, interrupted by a furious *Tempeste* sent by Neptune. Duché's libretto is typical of its time in that he has Electra trailing behind her brother to Tauris, being enamored of Pylades, and inducing Thaos to fall in love with her.

[69]The opera is discussed in Chapter 5.

Beginning the work with a storm comes from operatic tradition, not from Euripides or Guymond de la Touche, who begin with a short exposition of Iphigenia's past and continue with her dream in which she saw all her family destroyed, including Orestes by her own hand. Guillard and Gluck have individual priestesses ask her to explain why she is so troubled. Gluck prepares her anguished answer with a unison F$^\sharp$ in the strings, *pianissimo,* sustained for two measures. She begins her narration singing F$^\sharp$ - G over a diminished triad, which recalls her first entrance in the storm. This is one of many small touches that show Gluck's tonal and motivic economy; they work as unifying factors in the listener's ear, whether conscious or unconscious.[70] Iphigenia has dreamt of her ancestral home and of her father's embrace, these warm memories effacing his later actions at Aulis and fifteen years of misery since then. Gluck picks out for emphasis (*fortissimo* in the strings) "et quinze ans de misère. . . ." Next she relates seeing her home devoured by flames, depicted in the orchestra with a brief *Presto* interlude, leaping up a triad then falling down to emphasize the tones of a diminished-seventh chord (vii^7 of b). At the mention of her murdered father ("mon père sanglant") the key of b is reached again. The other high points are underlined with strong dynamic accents followed by pauses after "ma mère!" and "Oreste!" As in Euripides, she sees herself as her brother's executioner. An abrupt V - i cadence in e ends her narration and she falls senseless. The two-part chorus of priestesses next comment on the horrors of her dream, very much as would a chorus in a Greek tragedy, to a slow and sad dirge that moves from e to the key of a: "Hear our cries, oh Heaven! and have mercy."

Iphigenia revives and continues musing on the fate of her family in recitative, but now the emphasis is all upon her brother, who will never come to dry her tears, she says. She sounds more composed even so. Supposing that she was about twelve at the time of Aulis, she would now be a mature twenty-seven. Her little brother, mentioned only once in Gluck's *Aulide* but in one of her most compelling airs, the second farewell, would have been about ten years younger (Euripides calls him a baby). This recitative is of the conventional sort leading up to an aria but accompanied throughout by slowly moving chords in the strings (there are no simple recitatives in the opera). It ends with the sharp punctuating chords V^7 - I, the traditional signal for an aria in Italian opera, the last chord being the triad of E. The aria that follows is in A and is announced by four measures of orchestral ritornello stating the main theme, which Iphigenia then sings (Example 8.12). The melody of this plea to the goddess Diana begins very smoothly, the

[70]For a sensitive and telling analysis of the dream narration see Julian Rushton, "*Iphigénie en Tauride:* The Operas of Gluck and Piccinni," *Music and Letters* 53 (1972): 411–30; 419–21. Rushton points out that the woodwinds are used at the words "voix plaintive" in a way that recalls Agamemnon's second monologue in *Iphigénie en Aulide* (Act II, Scene 7).

EXAMPLE 8.12. *Gluck*, Iphigénie en Tauride, *Act I, Scene 1, Aria*

first leap being a characteristic rising third reached from a quick note in m. 6, then a large leap up to F♯ for the name of the goddess. The orchestra first provides the continuation and it takes the melody up to the high tonic, with *sforzato* on the leap from quick note up a third, at which point Gluck brings in the oboes to double the violins (mm. 12–13), an act of kindness to the soprano, who had only to follow the orchestra's example. It was not a question of the highly skilled Levasseur's needing any prompting from the orchestra, but rather of Gluck's desire to emphasize a melodic motif and harmonization (IV - I⁶) that he is going to bring back later in the opera. The aria is in a simple **A B A** form, with middle section ending on iii.

The chorus of priestesses enter at once, picking up the last chord on A as the beginning of their *Largo* expression of sympathy for Iphigenia, which ends in the key of a. These short choruses are not numbers in the Italian sense, but rather framing appurtenances for the title role. They replace the confidantes of earlier operas, still prominent in Gluck's *Alceste* and *Armide*. As with any chorus, by the very nature of grouped voices, they seem to represent the communal response; what they express is readily transferred to that other community of people watching the spectacle. Reacting to their cries of despair in this case is the tyrant Thoas, for whose entrance Gluck merely lowers the bass one tone to G, support for a secondary dominant leading off his concise and energetic recitative in which he tells Iphigenia to propitiate the gods not with tears but with blood sacrifices. His aria "De noirs pressentiments" begins without orchestral ritornello except for a burst of throbbing accompaniment in the strings. It is in the key of b already so prominent in the storm music. Subject himself to terrifying visions, he imagined the earth opening under his feet and swallowing him up, described in words sung to a striding figure rising up an octave in the basses, an idea that goes back to Gluck's *Semiramide riconosciuta* of 1748 but which could not be more appropriate here. Thoas has a vocal line that is much less melodious than that given Iphigenia. Mostly he declaims on single tones against the raging torrent of the orchestra, but at the end he sings some of the descending passages along with the orchestral basses. After this powerful outburst, at which the original Parisian audiences must have cringed, came another and happier surprise, a vigorous and exotic dance, with piccolos, side drum, and cymbals for special effects.[71] The gleeful Scythians (three-part male chorus) sing this *Allegro* in D and in 2/4 announcing that the gods have sent them victims to be sacrificed—a gruesome message sung to jolly music that must have sounded to French ears like a traditional *tambourin.*

Two young Greeks have been captured on the shore after a fierce struggle, announces a Scythian in recitative, one of them raving of his crimes and remorse, wishing himself dead. At this the chorus repeats its *tambourin.* Iphigenia, in an aside sung in the following recitative, asks the gods to stifle in her "le cri de la nature."Thoas orders her and the priestesses to the temple for the impending sacrifice and they leave; then he orders his warriors to intensify their celebrations. At this, the chorus of Scythians bursts into another vigorous *Allegro* in D, this one in common time, "Il nous fallait du sang," sung to the same compliment of exotic-sounding percussion, with a triangle added to amplify it. Both this and the preceding chorus suggest athletic dancing or mimed representation of their *joie barbare.* The second chorus, having begun in D, ends in b and is followed by an orchestral air in the same key and others in D, which amount to a substantial ballet in several sections. When the dancing stops after a cadence of the final piece in D, Gluck eerily raises the bass a half-tone to D♯ to begin the final recitative of the act as Thoas interrogates the two chained Greek youths, who answer defiantly. He condemns them to death as they are led away. Orestes has the last word, sung to Pylades:"O mon ami! c'est moi qui cause ton trépas."The act ends with

---

[71]This dance also goes back to an early ballet by Gluck according to Brown, *Gluck and the French Theatre,* p. 297.

a reprise of the second chorus. It has been confined almost entirely to two main keys, D and its relative, b. Iphigenia's aria in A offers the only relief from the grip of their domination.

The second act belongs to Orestes, just as clearly as the first act belonged to Thoas and Iphigenia. Gluck's sense for continuity is so strong he begins Act II with the same sixth chord erected on D$\sharp$ in the bass with which he commenced the final recitative of Act I. In a little prelude the orchestra paints the silence and desolation of the two friends in chains, who are held in an interior room of the temple designated for sacrificial victims. An altar stands to one side. Pylades sings first, commenting on the fearful silence of the place and questioning Orestes, who continues to blame himself for their predicament. The recitative is worked up to a climax of self-accusations, punctuated by orchestral interjections, the first violins carrying their line upward by step to high D, which arrives with the recitative cadence, V^7 - I. The aria of Orestes, "Dieux! qui me poursuivez," is heroic and agitated in the extreme, an *Allegro* in common time and in D, borrowed from *Telemaco* (1765), with trumpets and drums as well as oboes, clarinets, and horns. It is economical, a mere sixty-six measures encompassing a modulation to the dominant, retransition, and reprise. The constant sixteenth notes in the strings and the heavily accented first beats abetted by three-note slides upward in the winds convey more than the words about the character of Orestes. His nobility, haughty pride, and valor shine through in spite of his misfortunes. Mozart achieved a similar result using many of the same means in Donna Anna's "Or sai chi l'onore."

Pylades tries to soothe his friend. Death has no terror for him as long as they die together. The recitative cadence ends on E, which is then resolved by the aria, a *Grazioso* in the key of A, "Unis dès la plus tendre enfance." Eight measures of orchestral ritornello set the mood with a first theme filled with tender melodic sighs. A solo bassoon is the only wind that joins the strings. Mostly it doubles the cellos and basses, but after the cadence on the dominant midway through the piece, it sustains long notes in its highest range, like a protracted sigh. Gluck repeats the second half of the aria, the return to the tonic. Close to the end he takes the tenor up to the high tonic by stepwise motion. Since he had favored Legros with many opportunities to shine with his high A before, the choice of key may have been decided by this factor, as well as by the tonal nearness of A to D as an emotional expression of the two men's close personal relationship.

The most cruel blow Pylades can imagine, separation from Orestes, now happens. A minister of the temple forces him to leave, over the objections sung jointly in recitative by the two men, a third apart. Gluck's first of several uses of this device to express their union was an afterthought on his part. They are also in close physical embrace as the stage direction of the printed libretto makes clear: "Pylades tears himself from the arms of Orestes with pain." He must leave for dramaturgical reasons as well as those cited by the minister, in order to isolate Orestes on stage for his upcoming dream scene with the Furies.

Scene 3 opens with a strident unison figure in dotted rhythm for nearly full orchestra. This elaborate recitative paints the hero's despair. He asks the gods to thunder upon him, which the orchestra does with quick notes and rapid scales up and down in the strings, and to destroy him. He falls and becomes delirious, ending the recitative with a sudden calm. His question at the end of it, "What is this sudden tranquility?" is set in traditional fashion to a Phrygian cadence, the bass moving a half-tone down from B♭ to A. The piece that follows, an *Andante* in 2/4 with two sharps in the key signature, is no aria in the ordinary sense. The tone A from the recitative ending becomes a pedal rarely absent in the course of the piece as he falls into an exhausted sleep. The violas sound it in a menacing way, with *sforzato* on the first beat followed by syncopated eighth notes: . Not once in the course of the *Andante* is this figure absent. It tells the true state of his heart as opposed to his words, "Le calme rentre dans mon coeur." Gluck often works marvels with the slightest means, but here he deploys some of his fabled harmonic richness in what is in fact a long transition. To the strings he adds only a solo oboe holding a very long C♯ then vacillating between C♯ and D. The violins keep up the same two-measure accompanying figure throughout, often touching the same tones as the declamatory voice part. The *Andante* ends as it began, without tonal closure.

The harmonic tension of so long a pedal is broken by the arrival of D at the beginning of the next scene, along with the strident orchestral unison heard before. Here Gluck reinforces the orchestra with three trombones, harbingers of the other world beyond mortal life. From the back of the stage the Eumenides issue forth and surround the unconscious Orestes. Some dance a "Ballet-Pantomine de terreur" around him while others speak to him. The Eumenides become a four-part chorus, the first one heard in the opera. "Let us avenge both nature and the angry gods," they sing to an *Animé* in cut time and in the key of d, using many repeated tones in a rise up the octave (sopranos) then a chromatic descent to the fifth, while the large orchestra reinforces them by sustained tones outlining the same progression. To an eighteenth-century audience the combination of church instruments like trombones with prominent chromatic fourth descents spoke the very language of death. A sudden hush falls as the chorus intones in longer notes, "Il a tué sa mère," with the longest-held tones reserved for the first syllable of the last word to drive the point home; the winds add a *sforzato* here for good measure. Then, to reduced orchestration (solo flute, solo clarinet, and strings), Orestes cries out in his sleep, "Ah! ah! ah!" and this inarticulate cry becomes, after more taunting and a change of key to F, "Ah! quels tourments." The chorus repeats its accusation, and this time, after "mère," the specter of Clytemnestra appears in the middle of the Furies, then disappears. Gluck extends the piece with further exchanges between Orestes and the chorus until a final cadence on d seems inevitable, but there is no proper cadence. On a protracted diminished-seventh chord (which should lead to i - V - i) the doors open to reveal Iphigenia and her priestesses, at which sight the Furies vanish. Orestes, now awake, mistakes her for their mother and pronounces simply to the same diminished chord, "Ma mère! Ciel!" Iphigenia speaks calmly to him and tells the priestesses to remove his chains.

It was Gluck's idea to introduce the stunningly theatrical mistaking of Iphigenia for Clytemnestra, as is clear from his long letter of instructions to Guillard dated 17 June 1778. He had seen how effective this was in Traetta's *Ifigenia in Tauride* for Vienna in 1763. But Traetta had not made the most of this dramatic idea, relegating it to simple recitative.[72] One of Gluck's own works provided the main musical ideas for the tormented dreams of Orestes, or perhaps they should be called nightmares. In his pantomime ballet of 1765 with Gasparo Angiolini, *Sémiramis*, it is the queen who has nightmarish visions in her sleep, including the appearance of the ghost of her husband Ninus, whom she murdered. Gluck derived from the sinfonia to *Sémiramis* the strident unison figure in dotted rhythms that introduces the chorus of Furies. For the opening choral rise up an octave and chromatic fall down a fourth, he used the first number of the ballet, a pantomime in which the ghost of Ninus appears.[73]

The questioning of Orestes by Iphigenia is one of the key scenes of the tragedy. Euripides drew it out at length in a rapid-fire exchange of one-line questions and evasive answers from Orestes about himself—he was more forthcoming on the end of the Trojan wars and the deaths of Achilles and Agamemnon. Orestes almost comes to awareness when he sees how moved Iphigenia is at the mention of their father. Yet the play cannot allow recognition to happen as soon as this. Thus Euripides deflects the exchange to other subjects, to the still living Electra. Iphigenia has a plan to send a letter to Electra if she can manage to save the unknown Greek who stands before her and get him to carry it back to Argos.

Iphigenia's last question is the most important. What has happened to Orestes? Euripides has him answer, "Not dead but not in Argos." Guillard and Gluck had to change this to "He met the death he long sought" in order to set up the last two numbers of the act, the heroine's great lament, "O malheureuse Iphigénie" and the funeral rites she orders the priestesses to perform in honor of the dead hero, "Contemplez ces tristes apprêts." A major misreading of the text led one critic to mistakenly identify Agamemnon as the beneficiary of these rites.[74]

---

[72]Cumming, "Gluck's Iphigenia Operas," p. 229 and table 11.4.

[73]Its beginning is given as example 3.8, p. 214, in *Haydn, Mozart*.

[74]Hermann Abert's introduction to his Eulenberg edition of *Iphigénie en Aulide* (Leipzig, n.d.), pp. v–vi.

For the opera to reach the maximum degreee of pathos and efficiency, it is important to bear in mind that Orestes remains the object of both the lament and the funeral chorus. His plight dominates the entire act.

Gluck introduces the last complex of pieces in the act with a short chorus for the priestesses, "Patrie infortunée," *Lentement* in common time and in the key of g. It is followed directly by the glorious oboe melody in G that begins the lament, borrowed from a famous aria in Gluck's *La clemenza di Tito* (1752), "Se mai senti spirarti."[75] Once Gluck decided to adapt this aria into French, he sent the most precise instructions to Guillard (letter of 17 June 1778).

> I wish to have an air in which the words explain both the situation and the music. The meaning should always be complete at the end of the line, not at the beginning, nor in the middle of the following line. This is as essential for airs as it is bad for recitatives—the difference distinguishes between them—and makes airs more susceptible to a flowing melody. As to the meter of the air I require, here is the Italian poem, where I have put signs indicating which syllables ought to be long and sonorous; the lines are of ten syllables. . . . I wish the third line to begin with a monosyllabic word as in the Italian, for example, "Vois nos peines, entends nos cris perçents." The last line ought to be somber, if possible, in order to match the music.[76]

Gluck went on to ask the poet to excuse him if he explained things unclearly because his head was overheated with the music. "And if you do not understand me we shall leave the matter until my arrival and then it will be done first thing." Perhaps they did leave the final solution until their meeting, since Guillard's verse does not fulfill Gluck's verbal directions, consisting as it does of two eight-syllable lines followed by two Alexandrines. (Gluck's elisions are indicated with ‿).

> Ô malheureuse‿Iphigénie
> Ta famille‿est anéantie!
> Vous n'avez plus de rois, je n'ai plus de parents;
> Mêlez vos cris plaintifs à mes gémissements!

The Italian aria was sung by Sesto as a last farewell to his beloved Vitellia as he is led off to his death. Iphigenia begins as if in a soliloquy, but then turns to her priestesses to sing the third and fourth lines. She asks them to mix their plaintive cries to her groans. As an afterthought, Gluck added to his score the priestesses response: "Mêlons nos cris plaintifs à ses gémissements." He brought them into the aria at just the point that had made it so controversial in the first place, the sustained high pedal on G holding firm against shifting harmonies, which

[75]*Haydn, Mozart*, p. 150, with musical example.
[76]My translation from Gluck's original French quoted in the preface of Croll's edition.

resulted in poignant dissonant clashes (Example 8.13). Thus he answered his critics by reinforcing what annoyed them. After this pinnacle of pathos, the aria gradually subsides. The priestesses have the last words over a long pedal G in the bass. "Nous n'avions d'espérance, hélas! que dans Oreste: / Nous avons tout perdu, nul espoir ne nous reste!" The final six measures are marked by several long signs for a *diminuendo.*

Iphigenia, in her greatly perturbed state at hearing of the death of Orestes, momentarily forgets her other sibling, Electra. First in the recitative just before she tells the mysterious Greek (Orestes) to leave her presence, she says to herself, "It is over! All your family have died." Then in her aria she sings, "Je n'ai plus de parents," which means not "parents" in the English sense but "relatives." This oversight will be corrected soon, as carrying the letter to Electra becomes a main focus of Act III.

After the aria of Iphigenia "will come the chorus, 'Contemplez ces tristes apprêts,' which is very appropriate for the situation," wrote Gluck in the same letter of 17 June 1778 to Guillard, whose French text for this piece must have been acceptable to the composer. Gluck also mentioned the possibility of having the aria return, or at least the first part of it, after the chorus, da capo. This is not surprising, since he derived the music of the chorus from the middle part or **B** section of "Se mai senti spirarti sul volto." It is a slow and gentle strain in 3/8 and in C, vacillating with a minor-mode version of the same. Its affect translates to perfection the second strophe of Metastasio's masterly original poem, which it is now time to examine.

Se mai senti spirarti sul volto	If ever you feel blowing on your face
lieve fiato che lento s'aggiri	A light breeze that slowly surrounds you
dì: "Son questi gli estremi sospiri	Say: "These are the last sighs
del mio fido, che muore per me."	Of my true love, who dies for me."
Al mio spirto, dal seno disciolto	To my spirit, freed from my breast,
la memoria di tanti martiri	The memory of such sufferings
sarà dolce con questa mercé	Will become sweet with this blessing.

The bittersweet quality of remembrance after death haunts Gluck's lovely middle section of the original aria and seems "very appropriate" indeed to honor the memory of Orestes, whose supposed death is further mourned by the presence of three trombones.

The many repetitions and extensions for Paris of the original aria's short middle section (already used for "Que de graces" in *Aulide*) had something to do with the stage action. Not only did the priestesses and Iphigenia take part in the funeral rites but also the corps de ballet, as is made clear from a remark in the main Paris score copied from Gluck's autograph. At the point where the chorus finally stops singing, the scribe notated, "faire partie Les choeurs et la Danse." The

EXAMPLE 8.13. *Gluck*, Iphigénie en Tauride, *Act II, Scene 6*

orchestra alone sounds the rest to an emptying stage, very softly, one of the minor sections, repeated, and then to end, the original eight-measure phrase in C from the beginning. As an act ending, this quiet dignity could not be more effective, especially in the light of all the brilliance ending Act I and the heroic splendor to come that will end Act III. In the Vienna of Joseph II, where ballet played a minimal role in opera, Gluck replaced this superb choral ending with a simple march in the key of c. Its loss to the German version of the opera in 1781 (and apparently to subsequent productions in Paris as well) can only be regretted. Lament and funeral chorus share a natural symbiosis that comes from having been originally conceived as complementary parts of the same aria.

Even before the opera's premiere there were rumors circulating that its greatest beauties were to be found in the third act, an opinion widely held after public performances began. Act III does what was essential for the work's total success: it raises Pylades to a degree of distinction that makes him in every sense worthy of Orestes and his sister. Equal in valor to his companion, he exceeds him in mental stability and a toughness that will bring the drama to its dénouement.

The hitherto unused key of B♭ opens Act III with a short prelude after which Iphigenia announces to the priestesses that she will send a letter to Electra announcing the death of their brother by one of the two captives, for she can save only one from death at the sacrificial altar. Which one? She has chosen the young Greek so miserable in his sufferings. "My heart reaches out to him by secret bonds. . . . Orestes would have been of his same age and this unhappy captive reminds me of his image, retracing for me a portrait of his noble pride."Thus ends the recitative, on D, leading to her air"D'une image, helas! trop rechérie,"marked *Gracieux et lentement.* It is in the key of g and in 3/4 time, with little leaps from a quick note up a third that are in common with her air in Act I, which it resembles in general for its modest length and mostly conjunct melodic style.

The captives, who have remained separated, are ushered in. Orestes rushes to embrace Pylades. Iphigenia explains that she cannot save them both, at which point the trio begins, *Un peu lentement* in common time and in B♭. She can save at least one of them, she sings, at which the two burst in singing together at a faster tempo,"My friend, you shall live."The contrast between her slow music and their excited responses continues for two more exchanges. Since they sing exactly the same words to the identical rhythms and at close melodic intervals, further repetitions might skirt the comical, turning them into Tweedle Dee and Tweedle Dum. Gluck halts the process at three exchanges, then gives the orchestra a poignant passage in the gloomy key of c as Iphigenia prepares to make her decision:"Il faut donc entre vous choisir une victime."To intensify the moment, also to enhance musical unity, Gluck has her sing these words to a version of the famous dissonant passage with high pedal that expressed her agony in Act II. The piece breaks down into recitative, and then into slow orchestral sobs before she finally gives the nod to Orestes: "C'est vous qui partirez." He responds with disbelief. She orders him to prepare his departure at once, then exits to a little animated orchestral music, which turns B♭ as tonic into the dominant seventh of E♭ and leads to an agitated recitative.

Pylades, in a state of exaltation, expressed by the tremolo in the strings, commences in recitative, "O moment trop heureux! Ma mort à mon ami va donc sauver la vie."Orestes demurs, and the argument quickly escalates into the duet, *Fièrement et animé* in cut time and in the key of c. Orestes begins imperiously,"And you still pretend that you love me?" Pylades answers calmly, saying that his sacrifice is the will of the gods. Soon they respond to each other at close range, then their voices overlap. A moment of silence is followed by the orchestra, which proposes a new theme, less lively in tempo, and marked by the skip from rapid note up a third and recovery by conjunct descent, a melodic trait heard most recently in the air sung by Iphigenia at the act's beginning. "Gods, soften his heart," they sing to each other in their simultaneous vein, followed by canonic overlappings. Then Gluck takes them to an accented melodic peak, tenor up to A♭, baritone up to F. The whole section is so beautifully wrought for Legros and Larrivée that it alone could explain the early partiality for Act III—this was their finest hour. Gluck repeats the section with the canonic entrances, this time beginning *pianissimo.* He repeats the climactic passage up to the high A♭ followed by descent several times, then closes with an orchestral postlude, the violins murmuring in minor seconds back and forth in eighth notes, over an oscillating two-note bass in quarter notes.

Unable to overcome the steadfast purpose of his friend, Orestes lapses into one of his fits. We know this is serious business when the trombones join the threefold hammerstroke chords of punctuation in the strings, as the violins sound lacerating arpeggios. He sees the Eumenides again, armed with serpents. At the height of his delirium (*crescendo* to *fortissimo* of the whole orchestra), he believes that Pylades has abandoned him. Then he sinks into the arms of his friend, who brings him to his senses.

In a purely musical sense, one can hear the turning point of the drama right here, as the key returns to the mollifying B♭ of the act's beginning, while Pylades implores his friend for pity to a motif transforming from minor to major the slower theme of the previous duet of altercation (Example 8.14). There is some-

EXAMPLE 8.14. *Gluck*, Iphigénie en Tauride, *Act III, Scene 4*

thing about the even-toned confidence of Pylades, as expressed more by the music than by his words, that signals an eventual end of misfortunes. The melodic turn around the fifth degree, at *Andante,* and the subsequent descent of the melody accompanied by sixth chords has an illustrious follower at the beginning of Beethoven's Violin Concerto. The piece is short and filled with original traits. At the injunction "obey the choice of the priestess," the oboes emit a falling second sigh that seems to revive the imagined cries of the victim the oboes sounded in *Aulide.* Just before the reprise, and joining its first tones, Orestes enters to sing a single word, "Pylade!" and again when the section is repeated. The orchestra finishes the piece by completing its initial figure (1 - 3   1 - 3) with an answer that pushes from the fifth up to the tonic (5 - 1   5 - 1).

Pylades sang his plea at the feet of Orestes. In the following recitative Orestes abruptly raises him up and says he will save him no matter what. Iphigenia expresses pity for the victim. Orestes insists he is the one who must die, a proposition which she says she cannot accept, being hindered by some unknown and powerful instinct. She finally yields to the insistence of Orestes, who bids Pylades carry the letter to Electra. He will obey, he says. Meanwhile, he has formed his own plan to rescue Orestes from the sacrificial knife. Gluck worked the recitatives so as to end on G, preparing the arrival of C in the aria. Since the entire act has taken place on the flat side of the tonal spectrum, the arrival of C comes as a particularly bright revelation. It is also the first time that Pylades has had the stage to himself.

Gluck borrows the music from the aria "Contro il mio destin" in his *Antigono* (1756). After only five beats of orchestral preparation, a kind of galloping motion with dotted rhythm in the violins over steady quarters in the basses, Pylades launches his soliloquy, climbing the tonic triad then descending. The resemblance to Beethoven's kind of heroic triumph (especially the finale of his Fifth Symphony) cannot be missed. The words, on the other hand, "Divinité des grandes âmes, Amitié! viens armer mon bras," show some inspiration in the incipit of another invocation to the gods, "Divinités du Styx" (which ended the first act of the Paris version of *Alceste*). After his first invocation and a silence, the orchestra starts throbbing in even sixteenth notes over the two-note figure in eighth notes in the bass. A solo oboe emerges over this orchestral shimmering with what sounds like a message of hope in answer to the singer's call; it too affirms the rise through the triad after a strong emphasis on the seventh above the dominant: $\|: \frac{3}{1} | \frac{4}{V} - 3\,2 \,| \frac{1}{I}\, 3\, 5 :\|$. Such an accentual weight given to the dominant seventh seems by itself another anticipation of Beethoven's sonorous world. The line with which Pylades responds to the orchestra implores the divinity to fill his soul with celestial flames, and perhaps the orchestra's continual sixteenth-note agitation is meant to represent them. His final line is: "I shall rescue Orestes or go to my death." A first high A comes just before Gluck switches to what sounds like a stretto, at the entrance of the trumpets and drums. The tempo does not actually change here but sounds faster because of the orchestral triplets. A more sustained high A leads to the last vocal cadence. Final word goes to the sublime oboe solo, sounding one last time, *piano.* Then the galloping motions from the very beginning bring this show-stopper to a rousing close.

Act IV takes place inside the temple of Diana, with the statue of the goddess elevated in the middle and the sacrificial altar off to one side. The act opens with an energetic orchestral noise in the key of A, a tonality not heard heard since Pylades' air in Act II. Iphigenia, alone, says she cannot perform her horrid duty in a very brief recitative, which leads directly into her aria imploring the goddess for help, in the same key of A. This aria, too, comes from Gluck's *Antigono,* and he used the music subsequently in *Telemaco.* It is a vigorous dialogue between orchestral treble and bass in common time, marked *Fièrement, un peu animé.* At its basis is the freely adapted Gigue of the first keyboard Partita by Johann Sebastian Bach, who engraved the set of six partitas as the first part of his *Clavier-Übung* (Leipzig, 1731). How Gluck came across Bach's music has never been explained, but it is worth noting that, while the great German master was still alive, Gluck came to the Saxon court in 1747 for a royal wedding, an occasion for which he wrote his opera *Le nozze d'Ercole e d'Ebe.* Gluck could even have met Bach. (He probably met Rameau and certainly met Handel.) Bach's contrapuntal dialogue between high and low (via hand crossings) in the Gigue surround a middle-range accompaniment in triplets. Gluck changed the accompaniment to sixteenth notes, and they are rarely absent, which lends this plea, sung at the foot of the altar, an urgency that, joined with its bright key and winds that include oboes and horns, approaches the ferocious. It stands out in one's memory as all the brighter because of what follows: a solemn entrance of the priestesses singing, "Ô Diane, sois-nous propice," a dirge in the key of a minor consisting mostly of even half-notes in common time. The ritual sacrifice has begun.

Orestes arrives in the middle of the solemn procession, surrounded by the priestesses. Now he faces Iphigenia, who is bowed in grief. He urges her to do her duty, thereby satisfying the thirst of the gods for vengeance. The touching recitative between them breaks into an arioso of eleven measures for him, as he sings of being comforted in his last moments by her tearful regrets—the kind of lyrical but brief outburst so characteristic of *Aulide.* Next the priestesses begin their *Hymne,* "Chaste fille de Latone," which is less dirgelike than the last chorus because it is in cut time, in the key of G, and more lyrical, although still moving in ponderous half-notes (Example 8.15). It comes from Gluck's pantomime ballet *Sémiramis* (1765) along with much other music for this opera, and had been used subsequently by the composer in *Le feste d'Apollo* (1769). Note how Gluck gives the melodic line to the orchestra in m. 5—he is saving the high G in the sopranos until later in this multisectional hymn. Of all Gluck's pieces of this type, at which

EXAMPLE 8.15. *Gluck*, Iphigénie en Tauride, *Act IV*, *Scene 2*, hymne

he was particularly excellent, none has a more direct resonance in Mozart, whose last two operas exploit the same melodic incipit.[77] During the several strains of the hymn, Orestes is bedecked with garlands and conducted to the altar, where perfumes are burned around him and libations poured on his head.

Iphigenia can barely drag herself to the altar, assisted by four of her priestesses. What resources of expressive recitative could Gluck have possibly left unexploited by this point? None, perhaps, but his orchestra by itself was a resource that the composer now used in a manner so modern as to stun. Shuddering, Iphigenia fixes her eyes upon Orestes. A priestess hands her the sacrificial knife, which she accepts. To this pantomime, the strings play a distortion of the priestly

[77]In *Die Zauberflöte* for the "March of the Priests," and in *La clemenza di Tito* for the duet in A of the two women (No. 7), the latter having the same final reharmonization of the theme with a flat seventh leading to IV that Gluck uses at the words "En tous temps on te consulte."

processional music, its foursquare phrase in plodding half-notes becoming an uncanny chromatic caricature of the original (Example 8.16). There cannot be many parallels with this in the music of the eighteenth century. From a later period there is the wrenching distortion of the main theme with which Beethoven closes the *Marcia Funebre* of his *Eroica* Symphony. In both cases the composers have brought their themes to the verge of annihilation. Another composer who springs to mind is Gluck's greatest admirer, Berlioz, who was able to profit

EXAMPLE 8.16. *Gluck*, Iphigénie en Tauride, *Act IV, Scene 2*

from Beethoven's rhythmic disfiguring as well as from Gluck's chromatic one (in *Roméo et Juliette*). For all its chromatic pathos, Gluck's *Lento* obeys the rules of good part writing, the violas maintaining an independent voice until joining the basses at the octave for their last two tones. Especially effective is the use of the Neapolitan chord in the third measure, arrived at by taking the bass up to D and quitted by having the violas descend to their lowest tone, B♮.

The issue of how to bring about the recognition of brother and sister caused Guillard and Gluck to create three distinct versions. At first Guillard was too verbose. He also put the crucial words of Orestes too early in his sentence. Only with the third version did they come last, where Gluck wanted them: "Ainsi tu péris en Aulide, Iphigénie, ô ma soeur!"

Iphigenia sings, "Ô mon frère!" in recognition at the same time Orestes pronounces what he thinks are his last words, "Ô ma soeur!" The priestesses immediately throw themselves down prostrate before him, acclaiming their king. Gluck presses the action forward at the speed of spoken drama.

Iphigenia explains how she escaped immolation at their father's hands by the intercession of Diana. The music moves from recitative into arioso as she tries to put the horrors of the past behind them: "Laissons là ce souvenir funeste, laissez moi resentir l'excès de mon bonheur!" expressing her joy in the key of C. It is short-lived as a Greek woman enters and to an agitated *Allegro* in d announces that the tyrant has been informed and is hurrying to punish them. Iphigenia places her brother in the sanctuary, but that is all she can do before Thoas himself arrives, breathing fire. His music is fast and filled with urgent dactyls as in Act I, *Très animé* in cut time. But Gluck does not resort at first to the key of b associated with him in the first act. Thoas begins in F and moves to d as he orders his guards to seize Orestes and drag him to the altar. Iphigenia tries to intervene, explaining that he is her brother and her king, the son of Agamemnon (whose name is set here but nowhere else with the second syllable long and accented). The anger of Thoas reaches its peak, and the music does move to the key of b as he tries to kill both of them. Before he can strike a blow, Pylades enters quickly and kills Thoas with a single blow, singing, "C'est à toi de mourir!" (strong cadence on b). Following him is a band of Greeks, who clash with the soldiers of Thoas. The mêlée continues as an antiphonal struggle between imploring priestesses and the two contigents of male combatants until a voice from above cries out sternly, "Arrêtez." It is the goddess herself, who descends on a cloud.

FIGURE 8.7. Gabriel de Saint-Aubin. Sacrifice scene of *Iphigénie en Tauride.*

Gabriel de Saint-Aubin sketched an impression left upon him by the climactic scene (Figure 8.7). Diana descends into the middle of a circular temple surrounded by pillars with Doric capitals. Pylades is on the left with sword still in hand, flanking Iphigenia and Orestes, all three in loose, flowing costumes *à la Grècque,* and Pylades sports a warrior's plumed helmet. King Thoas lies on the floor head down, his scepter beside him. In the absence of scenic and costume designs from the golden age of the Moreau theater, this impression by a first-rate artist is especially precious. The semicircular temple on stage nicely complements the neoclassical design of Moreau's opera house (see Figures 8.1–2 on pp. 809 and 810).

Moreau himself designed

sets and Gluck was one connoisseur who greatly admired them. In his letter dated 3 January 1781 from Vienna to Franz Kruthoffer, Gluck's close friend and agent at the Austrian embassy in Paris, the composer mentioned that he was looking forward to receiving Moreau's designs for the Viennese *Iphigenie auf Tauris.* In the next letter to Kruthoffer, dated Vienna, 28 March 1781, he wrote, "Embrace M. Moreau some dozens of times on my behalf. He has completely delighted me with his designs."[78] Then on 2 November 1781, after the premiere, he wrote this same correspondent in more detail.

> I must inform you that *Iphigenie* was produced here on the twenty-third, to great acclaim. The designs by Herr Moreau contributed substantially to the good reception. I am sending you back the sketches, which I wanted to keep; this is a hard sacrifice for me, and only for you have I been able to resolve to deprive myself of them. Congratulate him warmly on them, on behalf of the public here. When I am again in a condition to get out into the world, I shall not fail to try to get something for him from the emperor.[79]

This touching evidence of Gluck's attachment to the visual side of opera, and to great visual art per se, should come as no surprise in the master who remarked that he had striven (in *Armide*) to be more painter and poet than musician.

The total work of art achieved on Gluck's terms at the Opéra by *Iphigénie en Tauride* won him supporters even among those who had previously resisted his music. One such was Saint-Aubin, who, upon viewing Houdon's famous bust of Gluck at the 1777 salon (see Figure 8.4 on p. 829), dismissed the composer as "dur à l'oreille comme aux yeux."[80] The artist, like so many others, was converted and swept off his feet by the beauties of the 1779 work.

Guillard fails to explain how or where Pylades found weapons and Greeks to wield them. Euripides offers a possible solution. He does not wreck the ship on which the two captured youths arrived but has it lie in waiting with "fifty stout oars," ready to bear them and the statue of Diana back to Greece.

Diana tells the Scythians to return her statue to the Greeks, to the sound of throbbing chords in the key of b. As the music moves into the tonal realm of a, she says she will take charge of the fate of Orestes, who is no longer subject to divine retribution, having removed his guilt by suffering. "Go, Mycenae awaits its king, go to reign in peace there, and restore Iphigenia to an astonished Greece." Only with this speech, after which the goddess ascends to the heavens, does Pylades learn to his astonishment the identity of the high priestess. In a very simple arioso,

[78]Patricia Howard, *Gluck: An Eighteenth-Century Portrait in Letters and Documents* (Oxford, 1995), p. 222.
[79]Ibid., p. 227.
[80]Thomas Bauman, "The Eighteenth Century: Serious Opera," in *The Oxford Illustrated History of Opera,* ed. Roger Parker (Oxford, 1994), pp. 47–83; 74.

Andante modulating from a to C, Orestes sings the last solo music of the opera, "In this touching object who has saved my life . . . behold my sister Iphigenia."

The final chorus in C is sung by all present—Greek men, the priestesses, and the Scythians. Gluck adapted it from the final chorus of *Paride ed Elena* (1770) where it bore the text "Vieni al mar." This too is a marine chorus, and its central message is "a peace profound and sweet reigns on the bosom of the seas." Audiences probably expected shouts of triumph here such as they heard from Pylades at the end of the previous act. The chorus projects a different mood altogether. Its nearly constant eighth-note motion, often in undulating major seconds, back and forth, paints the calmness of nature and, by extension, the peace that has descended on Greek and Scythian alike. Gluck uses trumpets and drums, but mostly they sustain and reinforce. He avoids almost totally taking the sopranos up to the high dominant, keeping them close to tonic C. If triumph there is here, it is that of humanity.

However superb the work's ending, audiences at the Opéra had been long accustomed to something more at this point, namely, a formal ballet. Before the first production had finished its run, the directors gave the public what it wanted in the form of "Les Scythes enchaînés par les vainqueurs," with music by Gossec. Expanding superfluously on the words and spirit of the final chorus, the new divertissement had the Scythians hold out their hands for manacles while bowing before Orestes and his sister, who give them their liberty, cause enough for protracted dances of joy. The critics approved and Gluck, in this case, objected in vain.

Gluck was seriously ill during the summer of 1779 in Paris, suffering his first stroke in late July. He had brought two operas with him from Vienna on this trip, the second being the pastoral *Écho et Narcisse*, on words by Baron Ludwig Theodor von Tschudi, a Swiss poet and essayist, and member of the diplomatic corps in Paris as representative of the prince-bishop of Liège. Rehearsals of *Écho* were delayed because of Gluck's illness so that it did not become the "summer opera" (i.e., lighter entertainment) that was intended. The premiere took place on 24 September 1779 and it met the same indifference that earlier greeted *La Cythère assiégée*.[81]

Gluck's obstinacy and determination to be hailed in Paris as a master of the lighter genre had brought him to grief once again. The libretto of a poet inexperienced in the genre did not help, and one can only imagine that Gluck put his friendship for the author above his usual hard-headed judgment in such matters. When Gluck went to Queen Marie Antoinette to take his leave, she insisted that he must return and remain in Paris after settling his affairs in Vienna, to which

---

[81]Michael Fend, "Der Fehlschlag von Glucks *Écho et Narcisse* und die Probleme einer 'musikalischen Ekloge,'" in *D'un opéra l'autre: Hommage à Jean Mongrédien,* ed. Jean Gribenski, Marie-Claire Mussat, and Herbert Schneider (Paris, 1996), pp. 31–43.

purpose she offered him the lucrative sinecure of music master to the royal children. The failure of *Écho* rankled so greatly that he vowed never to return. Nevertheless he was tempted again to do so in 1782 but sent Salieri in his stead.

Successors

Iphigénie en Tauride set a standard by which all subsequent serious operas for Paris were measured. It was no easy task to match its lofty tone or economy of means, but Piccinni came close in his best work, which did not include his own *Iphigénie en Tauride,* flawed as it was by a poor libretto.[82] His finest contributions were *Atys* (1780), *Didon* (1783), and *Pénélope* (1785), all three in collaboration with Marmontel. They were successes with the public and remained so. Several new singers came to the fore during these "Piccinni years." The most outstanding was

Antoinette Cécile de Saint-Huberty, who created the title role of *Didon,* in which she was portrayed. The picture deserves study for both costume and gesture (Figure 8.8). Of Piccinni's nine serious French operas, *Didon* was the most successful, enjoying continued performances at the Opéra until 1836 and favorable reception in French, German, and Italian versions throughout Europe.

The Opéra suffered a blow when the beautiful and practical theater of Moreau burned down on 8 June 1781 in spite of all the precautions taken to prevent such a catastrophe. After inhabiting temporary quarters the company took up residence in a hastily built theater at the Porte Saint Martin in the fall of the same year and remained there until 1794. The impetus unleashed by the renewal of tragédie-lyrique under Gluck and Piccinni was too great to be brooked by a mere physical disaster.

FIGURE 8.8. Portrait of Madame de Saint-Huberty in the title role of Piccinni's *Didon.*

What Gluck and Piccinni wrought in Paris was so powerful and inspiring it opened up the Opéra to other non-French com-

---

[82]Rushton, "*Iphigénie en Tauride:* The Operas of Gluck and Piccinni," p. 423, shows that Marmontel got things exactly wrong when heaping invective on Gluck for his orchestral noise and lack of consideration for the voice: "It is Gluck who is restrained, Piccinni who is extravagant; Gluck who concentrates interest in the voice, Piccinni who takes every opportunity for orchestral elaboration."

posers eager to follow in their path. Christian Bach and Antonio Sacchini, the main representatives of Italian music in London, both came to Paris at the behest of the Opéra. Salieri, Gluck's successor in Vienna, also answered the call. Between the three of them, they composed several dozen Italian operas before coming to Paris. Yet in each case the individual experts on their music claim that what they wrote for the Opéra brought them to the pinnacle of their creative achievements.

Christian Bach was the first to come. His contribution was a setting of *Amadis de Gaulle* (1779) on a libretto derived from Quinault. Legros sang the title role. The number of performances was not great for various reasons, but the response was positive enough that the Opéra offered him a contract for another work, a setting of *Omphale*. It was not completed before the composer's death on 1 January 1782, which cut short what might have been a series of works as rich as those by Piccinni.

Sacchini was born in Florence in 1730 and trained in Naples from an early age. After a string of successes in both comic and serious opera in the major Italian centers he went to London in 1772 and dominated Italian opera there for a decade, then moved to Paris. His contemporaries considered him the greatest melodist of the age. Grétry was one of those who accorded him this distinction. For the Opéra he wrote several works, including *Renaud* (1783), *Chimène* (1783), *Dardanus* (1785), and finally the work always acclaimed as his masterpiece, *Oedipe à Colone* (1786). Lully was the first Florentine musician to conquer Paris, Sacchini was the second, and the third was Luigi Cherubini, who made his debut at the Opéra at the age of twenty-eight with *Démophon* (1788). Grétry considered Cherubini to be a follower of Gluck.

Salieri was predisposed to follow Gluck's Viennese reform operas of the 1760s as early as his skillful setting of Coltellini's *Armida* (Vienna, 1771) when the composer was only twenty. Another opera of this kind was his setting of Verazi's *Europa riconosciuta,* written on commission from La Scala for its opening in 1778. Salieri's first work for Paris came about indirectly, because he was Gluck's protégé and assistant.

Calzabigi sent *Ipermestra, o Le Danaïde* to Gluck in Paris in 1778, along with a *Semiramide.* Both these subjects had been successfully worked by Metastasio in librettos set by Gluck for Venice (1744) and Vienna (1748). After returning from Vienna to Italy in 1773, Calzabigi remained spiteful toward Metastasio and proprietary toward Gluck. With his eye on the Parisian successes of *Orfeo* as *Orphée* and of the French *Alceste,* he resolved to try another libretto based on Greek tragedy. Metastasio had made his *Ipermestra,* originally a wedding piece for Maria Theresa's sister set by Hasse, an aria opera for seven characters of his usual stamp and with a happy ending. Calzabigi insisted on all the gruesome details of the Greek legend: the fifty daughters of Danaüs revenge him by slaying the fifty sons of Egyptus on their wedding night. As unlikely as such a black story seemed at the height of the Enlightenment, Gluck saw its possibilities in terms of a great spectacle opera dominated by chorus and orchestra. He went so far as to arrange for two of his recent librettists, Du Roullet and Tschudi, to collaborate on a translation and adaptation into French. The Opéra continued to encourage Gluck and invite his return. Gluck resumed work on the project in 1782, by which time he had suffered several crippling strokes. Salieri got involved at first as an amenuensis, taking down Gluck's ideas as musical dictation. In early 1783 Gluck informed Paris that he was too ill to come in person but would send Salieri to complete the work as a joint effort. Salieri, with the skills of a diplomat, gradually owned up to being the composer, while insisting that he worked under Gluck's inspiration. Joseph II went along with the duplicity and promoted the opera by carefully worded letters.[83]

Gluck, who did not speak languages with ease according to Salieri, sent his pupil off to Paris with a blessing that must have approximated the mish-mash of French, German, and Italian with which he generally communicated.

> Gluck, whose native tongue was Czech, expressed himself in German only with effort, and still more so in French and Italian, a difficulty only increased by the paralytic condition he suffered during his last years. Usually he mixed several languages together during a conversation, and so the farewell speech to his favorite protégé went as follows: "Ainsi . . . mon cher ami . . . lei parte domani per Parigi. . . . Je Vous souhaite . . . di cuore un bon voyage. . . . Sie gehen in eine Stadt, wo man schätzet . . . die fremden Kunstler . . . e lei si farà onore . . . ich zweifle nicht," and as I embraced him he said in addition: "ci scriva, mais bien souvent."[84]

Gluck's prediction came true. Salieri did himself honor with *Les Danaïdes.* Paris did itself honor, too, by embracing the work of yet another foreign artist.

Salieri arrived in Paris with the score during the last days of 1783. On 5 January 1784 he and Du Roullet signed a contract with the Opéra. Rehearsals began at once, with an aim of producing the work when the theater reopened after Easter. Excitement about the opera was great. The premiere took place on 19 April 1784 and stunned the audience with its spectacular effects. Madame Saint-Huberty sang Hypermnestre, while the two principal male roles of Lyncée and Danaüs were taken by Étienne Lainez and Larrivée.

Gluck's name appeared with Salieri's as co-composer in the public announcements. It was withdrawn by Gluck himself soon after the premiere by

[83]The full details of these ambiguous dealings awaited the magisterial work of Rice, *Antonio Salieri and Viennese Opera,* chapter 10, "*Les Danaïdes*," pp. 307–29.

[84]Salieri's memoirs were translated into German and published by Ignaz von Mosel, *Über das Leben und Werke des Antonio Salieri* (Vienna, 1827). Citation from Daniel Heartz, "Coming of Age in Bohemia," *Journal of Musicology* 6 (1988): 510–27; 524.

means of a letter to the press. Salieri acquiesced but still insisted that all his inspiration came from Gluck. Grimm, a sworn enemy of Gluck from as far back as the Parisian *Orfeo* score of 1764, was furious at Salieri's presumption and at the trick played by the Opéra. He condemned the music and compared it unfavorably with Piccinni. The drama did not fare any better at his hands.

> This opera is even more boring than atrocious. It is less a lyric drama than a tragic pantomime with one or two scenes in each act that explain it but slow down the action. . . . The recitative, so important in our lyric dramas, is in general vague, without accent, and cut up too often by orchestral sallies that render it cold and insignificant. Some choruses and dance airs are the work's most estimable parts, but what leaves the most to be desired is that truth of expression, that pure and sensitive melody of which the operas of Piccinni, and above all *Didon,* offered us such sublime models, lacking which no work can have a durable success on our lyric stage.[85]

Contrary to Grimm's words *Les Danaïdes* did have a lengthy run, especially after its revival in 1817. When Berlioz first came to Paris in 1821 he credited the opera, along with Gluck's *Tauride,* for having changed his life.

> I was about to become a student like so many others, destined to increase by one the disastrous number of bad doctors when one evening, I went to the Opéra. They were performing Salieri's *Les Danaïdes.* The splendor and brilliance of the spectacle; the sheer weight and richness of sound of the orchestra and choruses; the pathos . . . disturbed me and thrilled me to an extent which I will not attempt to describe. I was like a young man born to be a sailor who, having seen only the little boats of his native mountains, found himself suddenly transported to a three-deck ship on the high seas.[86]

Within a few days of the first performances of *Les Danaïdes* Paris witnessed *Le mariage de Figaro* at the Comédie Française, a production Pierre-Augustin Beaumarchais brought to pass against all obstacles posed by the censors and the crown. A jocular quatrain circulated on these two novelties, maintaining that the one scandalized by its violence, the other by its sexual license.

> Que pense-tu, dis-le moi sans mystère
> Des nouveautés qu'au jourd'hui chez Molière
> Et chez Quinault, on court avec fureur?
> —L'un fait honte et l'autre fair horreur.[87]

---

[85]*Correspondance littéraire philosophique et critique par Grimm, Diderot, Raynal, Meister, etc.,* ed. Maurice Tourneux, 16 vols. (Paris, 1877–82), quoted in Adolphe Jullien, *La cour et l'opéra sous Louis XVI,* (Paris, 1878; reprint 1976), pp. 179–80.
[86]Translation by Rice, *Antonio Salieri* (1998), p. 329.
[87]Jullien, *La cour et l'opéra sous Louis XVI,* p. 188.

An odd conjunction here is that Beaumarchais soon began courting Salieri to set a libretto he had been working on, *Tarare,* originally intended for Gluck. The Opéra was more officially involved in another project for Salieri. Guillard, the poet of Gluck's *Tauride* and a member of the institution's Comité de Lecture, offered the composer *Les Horaces,* adapted from Corneille's famous tragedy. Salieri, after two years in Vienna, returned to Paris in mid-1786 to complete these works and see them onto the stage. *Les Horaces* was an abject failure and was withdrawn after three performances in December 1786.[88] The critics and the public villified the libretto as a debasement of Corneille, which shows how risky it was, even for a poet of Guillard's talent and experience, to attempt an opera on a great French classic. *Tarare,* on the other hand, a mongrel derived from an obscure English tale blending comedy, tragedy, and an exotic setting, succeeded. Thanks to the poet's carefully managed publicity campaign, the public stormed its initial performances in June 1787. The music in *Tarare* was far too dominated by the overly long, complicated, and wordy text. The opera's interest was consequently more political than musical. It has been described as a lesson in "what an enlightened ruler should be."[89] Nevertheless, its text was skewed this way and that to suit various regimes from the Revolution to the Restoration.[90] When Salieri returned to Vienna for good in the fall of 1787, he had Lorenzo Da Ponte recast *Tarare* in Italian as *Axur, re d'Ormus* and recomposed much of his music. The revised opera became a favorite of Joseph II and the public as well.[91] Gluck did not live to see the premiere on 8 January 1788, having died on 15 November 1787.

Guillard had his greatest success at the Opéra with the libretto of *Oedipe à Colone,* based loosely on the play of Sophocles, which demonstrated that an opera made from a classic could please sooner if it was not a French classic. The collaboration with Sacchini was a happy one and led to the creation of a masterpiece that was performed at the Opéra nearly six hundred times up to 1830, more than any opera of the time, even those by Gluck. Guillard reduced the story to three acts and began it with a meeting between Theseus, ruler of Athens, and Polyneices, who had exiled his father Oedipus from Thebes. He added a love interest (other than the love of family in Sophocles' play) by creating the character of Eriphile, daughter of Theseus given in marriage to Polyneices. Perhaps he would have done the same in *Tauride* had not Gluck stopped him. Great opera composers like Gluck and Mozart tyrannized their librettists. The addition allowed

[88]Julian Rushton, "Salieri's *Les Horaces:* A Study of an Operatic Failure," *Music Review* 37 (1976): 266–82. The author blames Salieri as much as Guillard. The painter Jacques Louis David had his first great success, a famous *Oath of the Horatii,* in 1785, a year earlier.

[89]By Ludwig Finscher, "Opera and Enlightenment," in *Report of the Twelfth Congress of the International Musicological Society, Berkeley, 1977,* ed. Daniel Heartz and Bonnie Wade (Kassel, 1981), p. 254.

[90]Jullien, *La cour et l'opéra sous Louis XVI,* pp. 269–76.

[91]Rice, *Antonio Salieri and Viennese Opera,* pp. 418–20.

him to end Act I with an impressive choral scene in which the people implore the gods for a blessing on the couple. Their pleas produce silence, painted eerily in the music by a hesitating unison figure in the strings, *pianissimo* (Figure 8.9). Both Rousseau and Diderot extolled the powers of music in depicting silence and this is a good example. Then thunder and a raging storm in the orchestra signal divine disapproval. All flee to end the act.

Oedipus appears in Act II, enfeebled and blind, led by his daughter Antigone, as in the first part of the play by Sophocles. The people try to drive him away in another impressive choral scene. Theseus restrains them and proves to be an enlightened king himself. Sacchini was genial at every part of operatic discourse

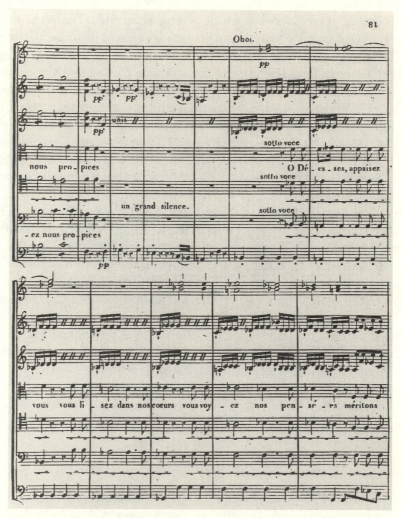

FIGURE 8.9. Sacchini. *Oedipe à Colonne.* Final scene of Act I.

but never more than when the drama naturally allowed, as here, for an expansive solo aria, of which there are few. Ensembles predominate and cadences are regularly undercut so that the music is nearly continuous from beginning to end of the acts. The most famous ensemble came in Act III as peripeteia. Oedipus, at the pleading of Antigone, forgives Polyneices, which leads to a heart-wrenching trio of reconciliation. While it is not Sophocles, and consequently lamented by purists, it is nevertheless operatic drama of the highest degree. Philidor was in London when the work had its premiere at the Opéra. His son André relates that his first questions upon returning concerned its reception.

> "Did it succeed?""Yes father.""What was said about it; was a particular piece picked out?""Oh yes father! above all there was a trio in Act III that everyone found superb." "Go seek it out for me at once." The young man ran for the score and brought "Où suis-je, où suis-je, mes enfans," to his father's attention. A profound silence followed. Philidor took the piece and read it without saying a word, and his son, to his astonishment, saw copious tears fall from his father's eyes, so moved was he: a beautiful and worthy homage that did honor to all, sincerely paid to a sublime work![92]

Perhaps Philidor wept as well for the composer, who did not live to see the premiere at the Opéra in 1787, having died in Paris on 6 October 1786. Berlioz relates in his memoirs that he wept silently at a performance of *Oedipe* in 1826, and at the same spot, which he identifies by the words sung when the three voices combine, "O doux moment." He knew the entire opera by heart.

Grétry, summoning up various approaches to opera in the first volume of his memoirs (1789), placed his method somewhere between that of Gluck and that of Sacchini. Of the former he wrote: "It is legitimate to express something with much harmony and an active orchestra, to which song is often accessory, or declaimed with minimal lyricism: that, in general, is what Gluck did" (1: 243). His approach to words and music was different. "It is legitimate as well to express something by making declamation produce a pure and easy melody to which the orchestra provides only an accessory accompaniment: that, in general, is what I tried to do." He went on to describe a third way. "One can make a melody even sweeter and more pure, which, in painting nothing, nevertheless has nothing intentionally contrary to the expression of the words: that is what Sacchini did." He concluded, "as long as music is composed, these three methods will prevail." His generalization about Sacchini has some truth to it. Even in *Oedipe*, declamation of the French text is not as finely nuanced as Grétry's, and sometimes there are musical accents on inappropriate words or syllables. This did nothing to stop the opera's circulation around the Continent. It was given in French at Liège, Hamburg, Cologne, Copenhagen, and Saint Petersburg; and in German at

---

[92]*Pour Philidor*, ed. Jean François Dupont-Danican (Coblenz, 1994), p. 75.

Hanover, Berlin, Munich, and Vienna. It was also translated for performance into Italian, Swedish, and Russian. Burney errs on this matter in his article on Sacchini for the Rees *Cyclopaedia* and also shows his hostility to the whole Gluck-Piccinni legacy: "It is manifest in the operas that he composed for Paris, that he worked for singers of mean abilities; which, besides the airs being set to French words, prevented their circulation in the rest of Europe, which his other vocal productions in his own language had constantly done." *Oedipe* had a greater success than any of his Italian operas, but conditions were not such in London that it could be produced there.

The circumstances that made Paris a great capital of serious as well as comic opera during the 1780s were largely owing to Gluck. In his article "France" in the first volume of the *Encyclopédie méthodique* (1791), Ginguené spelled out exactly what Gluck had accomplished.

> When one recalls the state this spectacle [the Opéra] was in before Gluck, the coldness of the actors and actresses, the immobility of the choruses, the inability of the orchestra, and when one thinks about the warmth that animates all these parts today, and of what moral authority and physical force were necessary to produce such a metamorphosis, one will admit that Monsieur Gluck was precisely the man needed to bring about this happy revolution.

Gluck's reform of serious opera in Paris, as earlier in Vienna, was predicated on a dictatorial control of soloists, chorus, orchestra, and every facet of stage production.

With Gluck gone in person from the Opéra, local composers came more to the fore. Grétry emerged from Gluck's shadow and wrote several *tragédies-lyriques* in the 1780s. None was as successful as his opéra-comique *Richard* (1784) for the Théâtre Italien or his opéra-ballet *La caravane du Caire* (1783) for the Opéra. The public accorded him its favor especially for his lighter works, the domain they refused to concede to Gluck. Philidor had no particular success with his last tragic operas, *Persée* (1780) and *Thémistocle* (1785). Monsigny's *Pagamin de Monègue* on a libretto by Sedaine was refused by the Opéra in 1785. Gossec returned to the Opéra with *Thésée* in 1782, his last *tragédie-lyrique,* arranged after a libretto by Quinault. The French composer who created the greatest stir at the Opéra was Jean-Baptiste Lemoyne, who dedicated his *Electre* of 1782, on a libretto by Guillard, to Queen Marie Antoinette, with flattering references to Gluck, whom he claimed to imitate. It was followed by two other tragedies, *Phèdre* (1786) and *Nephté* (1789).

Gluck's triumph at the Opéra prompted one French critic to claim even more than the "happy revolution" described by Ginguené. Jean Baptiste Leclerc, a politician who represented Challans in the Convention Nationale, held Gluck responsible for nothing less than the great Revolution itself.

Although the constitutive laws of modern society take no account of music's influence, music is no less powerful than it was in ancient times; we believe that it plays a much greater part in modern politics than is generally supposed. . . . Marie Antoinette, a victim of national pride, attracted to France some years ago the celebrated German to whom we are indebted for the creation here of dramatic music. This was an unwise thing to do. It is not too much to say that Gluck's musical revolution must have made the government tremble. His vigorous harmonies stirred the warm hearts of the French, which were moved to lament past errors. There were signs then of a power which was to burst forth, shortly afterwards. The throne was shaken. The friends of liberty in their turn enlisted music's help—music which employed those manly accents that the German composer had taught it.[93]

Marie Antoinette did not lure Gluck to France, contrary to what Leclerc wrote. The composer's campaign to conquer the Opéra was long in the planning and independent of any connivance with the French monarchy. Gluck first got his foot inside the door of a very reluctant Opéra by cunning and subterfuge, as described above. This said, it is also possible to believe that the elevation of his former pupil to a position of prestige as dauphine further emboldened Gluck to act as he did.

---

[93]Jean Baptiste Leclerc, *Essai sur la propagation de la musique en France, sa conservation, et ses rapports avec le gouvernement* (Paris, 1796), as translated in Peter le Huray and James Day, eds. *Music and Aesthetics in the Eighteenth and Early-Nineteenth Centuries* (Cambridge, 1981), pp. 240–45.

9

Three Apostles of
the Galant Style

Christian Bach in London

APPRENTICESHIP: GERMANY AND ITALY

FEW composers have had better musical training than Johann Christian Bach, whose teachers included, in succession, his father Johann Sebastian, his half-brother Emanuel in Berlin, and Padre Martini in Bologna. He was born in Leipzig on 5 September 1735 and is thought to have been introduced to the keyboard by his father at an early age. This youngest son of Bach's second wife, Anna Magdalena, became a helpmeet by taking on certain secretarial tasks when declining health and poor vision beset his father. Bach designated Christian as the recipient on his demise of three "claviers," a bequest that was contested by his half-brothers Friedemann and Emanuel. It was Friedemann who escorted Christian to Emanuel in Berlin within a few months of their father's death (28 July 1750). Christian was never close to Friedemann. He held Emanuel in great respect. His favorite brother was Johann Christoph Friedrich Bach, only three years his senior. Friedrich gave up his study of law at Leipzig University in early 1750, by which time their father was seriously ill, in order to take a position as chamber musician to Count Wilhelm of Schaumburg-Lippe at Bückeburg. His annual salary was only 200 thalers but it helped him to support the soon-to-be destitute Anna Magdalena. The count was a generous and knowledgeable patron of music. In 1751 he accepted the dedication of two famous trio sonatas by Emanuel, who may have been instrumental in securing the appointment.

Christian blossomed quickly in the hothouse climate of musical Berlin during the early 1750s. He contributed songs to the newly fashionable genre of odes with melodies fostered by Marpurg and Krause, alongside those of Emanuel. Most impressively, he composed and performed concertos for harpsichord and four-part strings, emulating Emanuel's pathbreaking works in the genre. These come down to us in Christian's hand, with annotations by Emanuel.[1] Preserved in the latter's *Nachlass,* they are in three movements, make frequent use of the minor mode, and conform to the intense seriousness of the North German school.[2] While they do not attain the drama and profundity of Emanuel's own concertos, they are sturdy representatives of their kind, able to stand beside similar works by Christoph Nichelmann and other Berlin masters in Emanuel's orbit.

Christian had the good fortune to experience Berlin opera at the peak of Carl Heinrich Graun's achievement. He was also a witness to the success of Graun's *Tod Jesu* at its first performance on 26 March 1755, with Emanuel presiding as leader from the harpsichord. A few months later Christian left for Italy. Johann Nicolaus Forkel commented in his *Musikalischer Almanach für Deutschland* of 1783 on the young musician's friendships with many Italian singers in Berlin, "one of whom persuaded him to travel with her to Italy"; in his *Lexicon* of 1790 Gerber embroidered on Forkel by stating that Christian's desire to see Italy was inflamed by several of the female singers of the Berlin opera.[3]

Emanuel, when compiling his chronicle of the Bach family in the 1780s, entered an annotation to the effect that Christian departed on his Italian trip in the year 1754. He erred by one year. Marpurg specified in mid-1755 that Christian had just left for Italy.[4] War was imminent and the young musician, approaching his twentieth birthday, was fortunate to depart when he did. Saxony lay directly on the route to the south. Did he visit his home in Leipzig and see his mother for a last time? (She was to die in poverty in 1760.) Perhaps he was supported for this very costly journey by the court in Dresden. Hasse's role in his subsequent advancement suggests as much. It is possible that his main goal all along was Naples, where opera reigned supreme, and over which the music-loving

[1]Johann Christian Bach, *The Collected Works,* ed. Ernest Warburton, 48 vols. (New York, 1984–99), vol. 32, *Six Early Concertos,* ed. Richard Maunder (New York, 1985).

[2]For an illuminating discussion of Christian's indebtedness to Emanuel's works in these concertos, see Stephen Roe, *The Keyboard Music of J. C. Bach: Source Problems and Stylistic Developments in the Solo and Ensemble Works* (Outstanding Dissertations in Music from British Universities, ed. John Caldwell) (New York and London, 1989), pp. 117–25. The dissertation was presented at Oxford in 1981.

[3]Charles Sanford Terry, *John Christian Bach,* 2nd ed. (London, 1967), p. 11. Terry quotes both in the original German.

[4]Hans-Joachim Schulze, "Wann begann die 'italienische Reise' der jüngsten Bach-Sohnes," *Bach Jahrbuch* 69 (1983): 119–22, and 74 (1988): 235–36.

Saxon princess Maria Amalia ruled as queen. Whatever his goal, he did reach Italy in the second half of 1755. Emanuel could only have sighed with envy that his young ward was embarked on the Grand Tour he himself had so longed to make.

Milan, a city of intellectual ferment that challenged Naples as foremost center of the Italian Enlightenment, became Christian's main domicile. He found a patron there in the young scion of one of the oldest and noblest families, Count Agostino Litta. Lessons with Padre Martini had apparently begun as early as 1755. In a letter dated Milan, 10 January 1756, the mathematician Giovanale Sacchi reported to Martini that he had encountered "suo valoroso scolare Monsieur Bach" in the house of Litta.[5] Christian may have come to the attention of Litta through a connection with Prince Ferdinand Philipp Lobkowitz, Gluck's patron at Milan in the 1740s, who was an intimate of Frederick the Great in Berlin and a confidant of Emanuel.[6]

Padre Martini maintained a voluminous correspondence with the learned figures of Italy and elsewhere, a network that often made it possible to track the movements and behavior of his students. Bach's letters to him before 1757 do not survive. One correspondent reported meeting Bach in late 1756. Girolomo Chiti, the venerable music master of Saint John Lateran, wrote to Martini in a letter dated Rome, 20 November 1756, "On the 16th your most worthy pupil Signor Bach the Saxon paid me a gracious visit and I gave him the welcome and courtesies he was due."[7] According to the modern editor's summary of the rest of the letter, Chiti says that Bach "plays the cembalo in the manner of the Great Saxon." Born in 1679, Chiti was old enough to have heard and appreciated Handel's visits to Rome between 1708 and 1710. But it is more likely he was referring to Hasse. The summary continues, "Chiti found him truly charming, but with Northern ideas, and more Prussian than Saxon," a curious comment that may bear upon the gravity of his Berlin concertos. Finally, "he stayed only a brief time, having to leave for Naples."

Why was Bach hurrying to Naples in mid-November? He had already missed the name-day celebrations when King Charles III was feted in the San Carlo with Michelangelo Valentini's *Solimano,* an opera that won little success.[8] Did he seek an audience with Queen Maria Amalia? He would not have missed Piccinni's first serious opera for the San Carlo, a setting of Metastasio's *Zenobia,* given its pre-

[5]Ann Schnoebelen, *Padre Martini's Collection of Letters in the Museo Bibliografico Musicale in Bologna* (New York, 1979), no. 4802.

[6]Heinz Gärtner, *John Christian Bach: Mozart's Friend and Mentor,* trans. Reinhard G. Pauly (Portland, Ore., 1994), pp. 104–7.

[7]Schnoebelen, *Padre Martini's Collection of Letters,* no. 1641: "Li 16. Stante fu de la visita gratiosa del Signor Giovanni Bach Sassone suo degnissimo Scolaro, a cui feci quel poco d'accoglienza, e Cortesie, che dovevo."

[8]Valentini knew Bach and mentioned him by name in his letters to Martini dated 22 May and 15 September 1756; ibid., nos. 5442–43. Other musicians Bach met through Martini included Naumann, Farinelli, and Francesco de Majo.

miere with success on 18 December 1756, after which he protracted his stay into the carnival season. At this juncture came the first of his many surviving letters to Martini, dated Naples, 18 January 1757, in which he apologizes: "I intended to visit Bologna last month . . . but Cavaliere Litta's particular favor granted me another month's stay here, due to the inclement weather. . . . I hope to find myself in Bologna by the middle of February."[9] How convenient of the weather! It allowed him to witness Pasquale Cafaro's opera *L'incendio di Troia*, first given at the San Carlo on 20 January 1757.

Christian was an assiduous student of Martini, despite what his feeble excuses might suggest. He probably began with a protracted study of strict counterpoint, as did other students. He then went on to settings of liturgical texts in the old style (with Palestrina as a model), as well as in a freer, more modern but still sedate style. The training was carried on partly by correspondence, sometimes including musical examples, and makes fascinating reading.[10] The pupil kept sending pieces to Bologna for corrections and approval, dutifully provided by Martini. Many of the pieces were then performed in various churches in Milan, on which performances Bach also reports at length. He was serious about attaining an ecclesiastical position in Italy with which to support himself, urged on by both Litta and Martini, who believed he had the makings of a maestro di cappella. That this quest also entailed his conversion to Roman Catholicism does not mean that he was lacking in religious conviction. In the changed circumstances of his later life in London, he could easily have reverted to Protestantism. He remained loyal to his adopted faith.

Some of Bach's autograph sacred works composed when in Milan and Bologna have recently come to light again. Such is the case with his setting dated 1758 of the Psalm *Laudate Pueri*.[11] The text, rather long and in several sections, provided Bach an opportunity to organize a work in many movements and to design a coherent tonal progression between them. He solves the task by beginning in the key of E, progressing by the circle of fifths toward C, then to e, and finally to E for the ending, "Sicut erat in principio:" E - A - D - G - C - e (ending on B) - E. His orchestra requires, besides the usual strings, flutes, oboes, horns, and trumpets, all in pairs, but never all at once. The music is bright, almost exclusively in major, and in sprightly tempos. At the beginning of the first number Bach relies on the fashionable but somewhat tired cliché of the "wedge cadence." Bach's fondness for his early sacred works can readily be understood. In them is evident

[9]Ibid., no. 303, quoted in the translation by Terry, *John Christian Bach*, p. 15.

[10]Terry, *John Christian Bach*, pp. 14–58, translates most of the letters, includes their musical quotations, and illustrates several pieces of church music composed by Christian.

[11]Johann Christian Bach, *Laudate pueri* for soprano solo and orchestra, ed. Richard Charteris (Classical Music Series, PRB Productions 4) (Albany, Cal., 1998). The work is also in *Music Supplement*, ed. Ernest Warburton (*The Collected Works* 48: 3) (New York, 1999), 249–328.

an artist determined to increase his powers, to stretch his creative muscles.[12] He took these autograph scores with him to England, whence they landed eventually in Hamburg, along with many manuscripts by Hasse, and to which they have been recently returned after a long postwar exile in the former Soviet Union.

Secular music also occupied Bach, who became a prolific composer in Milan. He wrote many keyboard works with accompanying violin(s). Count Litta required such chamber music in his city palace as well as in his country resort, where the young composer worked on occasion. The active concert life of the city made further claims upon him. His fame began to spread even beyond Italy. In his letter to Martini dated Milan, 14 February 1761, he wrote, "for some time past I have almost had to put my studies aside, being every day called to write something for concerts—a Symphony, Concerto, Cantata, and so forth—for Germany or Paris."[13]

Opera was of increasing concern to Bach as he was preparing for a career as a church composer and attracting attention for both sacred and secular works. In Milan opera seria was flourishing, especially works by Galuppi and by local son Giovanni Battista Lampugnani. Christian was in direct contact with Lampugnani, the harpsichordist of the opera, and mentions him in his letters to Martini. In 1759 Litta asked him to write a substitute aria for Filippo Elisi in Giovanni Ferrandini's *Temistocle*—nothing less than a setting of "Misero pargoletto." His setting succeeded to the extent that Elisi had to repeat it at every performance. Although Bach generally played down any connections with opera in his letters to Martini, he did mention this.[14] In his letter dated Milan, 17 June 1760, he apologized once again for failing to call at Bologna, although he passed nearby. He told the truth as to the reason why.

> I hoped from week to week to visit Bologna, but was disappointed. True, I was a week at Reggio, but so pressed that I only heard the last performance of the opera. Thence I went to Parma, where I stayed but two nights, and from there returned to Milan after only six days' journeying. My purpose was to hear two singers who are to appear at Turin next Carnival: for, being engaged to compose for that theater, I was anxious to learn something of their qualities.[15]

The opera Bach heard in Reggio was Giuseppe Ponzo's *Demetrio*, the two singers being prima donna Maddalena Parigi and seconda donna Teresa Mazzoli (his fondness for female singers and dancers was marked and may help explain the

---

[12]Whatever Chiti meant by saying that Bach struck him as "more Prussian than Saxon" might find further explanation in Bach's meticulously neat autograph scores from the Milanese years.

[13]Terry, *John Christian Bach*, p. 50, mistakenly identifies "Parigi" as the singer of this name.

[14]Letter dated Milan, January 1759, in Schnoebelen, *Padre Martini's Collection of Letters*, no. 319.

[15]Terry, *John Christian Bach*, p. 48, "della virtù di questi due personaggi."

eagerness to meet them). Visiting Parma he presumably encountered the court's maestro di capella, Traetta, and may even have heard one of the performances of Traetta's *I Tintaridi.*

The hoped-for appointment in Milan arrived around the same time as the opera commission. In his letter to Martini dated Milan, 28 June 1760, Bach announced, "I have been appointed organist of the Duomo here, a post which will give me 800 lire and not much to do."[16] His new position of second cathedral organist did not require Bach to compose, for that duty fell to the cathedral's maestro di cappella, Giovanni Fioroni. Neither did it require very much in the way of organ playing. Bach hired a substitute and was away from Milan for most of 1761, as Litta complained to Martini in his letter of 7 April 1762.[17] Bach returned to his duties in Milan soon after this complaint, but he did not long remain.

The year 1760 was decisive. Not only did he compose his first opera and see it staged in one of Italy's finest theaters; he was also obliged to spread his wings as an instrumental composer. In September of this year Princess Isabella of Parma made a royal progress through northern Italy en route to Vienna for her marriage with Archduke Joseph. Bach was involved with the celebrations and could write to Martini with bona fide excuses for neglecting his lessons, which he did in his letter dated Milan, 30 August 1760.

> I have been ordered to travel soon to Casal Maggiore and to Mantua. There I am to direct two major concerts of instrumental music given by the city of Milan in honor of the princess of Parma, who is passing through both places. You will understand, Reverend Father, that writing so many symphonies and concertos has kept me more than busy, especially since I have a serious competitor, San Martino [Sammartini]. You probably know him by name; he is an expert at this kind of composing. God only knows what kind of an impression I shall make. I find comfort in the thought that I do not have to establish my reputation with these compositions.[18]

Martini did know Sammartini by reputation. A correspondent informed him in 1756 of a concert directed by Sammartini in Milan and of Sammartini's intentions to send music to Vienna.[19] Bach evidently thought he would make his reputation as a church composer. Yet it was his operas that made him famous.

Hasse, the arbiter of Italian opera as much as Martini was of Italian sacred music, was behind the invitation to Bach from Turin. The "great Saxon" had been in honor at this court ever since writing an *Arminio* for it in 1730. The council of

[16]Ibid., p. 49.
[17]Ibid., p. 57.
[18]Gärtner, *John Christian Bach,* p. 141.
[19]Schnoebelen, *Padre Martini's Collection of Letters,* no. 1956. For Sammartini's influence on Bach, see William S. Newman, *The Sonata in the Classic Era,* 3rd ed. (New York, 1983), pp. 708–9.

noblemen who ran the opera invited Hasse to compose two operas for the coming carnival season of 1760–61. Hasse, in exile from Dresden because of the war, responded that he might be able to compose the second (and more prestigious) carnival opera but in case of peace he was obliged to return to Saxony.[20] He named a monetary figure should he be present for the opera, and a lower one in case he had to send the work. For the first opera he recommended that the council write to maestro di cappella Bach, whose agreement was secured by 30 May. Hasse was in negotiations elsewhere as well. While Bach's *Artaserse* was playing in Turin in early 1761, Hasse's third version of the same libretto went on the stage of the San Carlo in Naples. The second opera for Turin, *Tigrane,* was not by Hasse but by Piccinni, whom Bach met already during his visit to Naples in 1756–57.

Bach's score for *Artaserse* reveals all the exhilaration one might expect to find from a twenty-five-year-old composer entering into a promised land. For primo uomo he had the great singer-actor Gaetano Guadagni, about whom much is known—especially in connection with Handel and Gluck, whose Orfeo he became two years later. Less is known about Maddalena Parigi. The other principal, for the role of Artabano, was Pietro DeMezzo, a fine singer whose baritone had a tenor extension. The importance of singers to the enterprise can be gauged by their payments. Bach received 130 gigliati; Mazzoli, 150; DeMezzo, 160; Parigi, 550; and Guadagni, 800. The first dancer, Vincent Saunier, together with his wife, received 580. Filippo and Colomba Beccari, second dancers, received 500. The opera was a success, as confirmed by the many invitations that followed, including one from Turin to compose another opera in 1763. Bach was by then becoming established in London and did not accept.

Artaserse opens with an overture in D, cast in the usual three movements. Remarkably, none of the arias has a full da capo return. Bach places the first aria, sung by Parigi as Mandane, in the key of G. Then follows a more elaborate aria for Guadagni as Arbace, in the key of F, in which Bach writes quite athletic sung triads up and down. The keys of the succeeding arias keep descending by step. Artabano's first aria is appropriately in E$\flat$ because the text is of the *ombra* type. Artaserse sings his aria No. 4 in D, then Semira breaks the chain with a simple aria in B$\flat$ and in 2/4, with syncopations that Bach often associated with this key. Artabano follows, singing, "Non ti son padre!" to a through-composed aria in the key of g that makes a stunning effect. It was a brilliant stroke to set the next aria, Semira's "Torna innocente," in the distant key of A, as a simple melody in 3/4 that features three-measure phrases and eschews all the usual decorations. It also is through-composed. Mandane follows with her vigorous self-justifications in B$\flat$, and the act ends with Arbace all alone, singing Metastasio's grand shipwreck aria,

---

[20]Johann Christian Bach, *Artaserse,* introduction by Ernest Warburton (*The Collected Works* 1) (New York, 1984), p. ix .

"Vo solcando un mar crudele," in heroic C major, reinforced by march rhythms and trumpets as well as horns and oboes.

Bach must have planned the tonal symmetry between the two halves of Act I, each of which has four numbers in a row related by step (Table 9.1).

TABLE 9.1. *Artaserse,* Act I										
Overture	No. 1	2	3	4	5	6	7	8	9
D - G - D	G	F	E♭	D	B♭	g	A	B♭	C

The simple recitatives permit him to maneuver gradually from one key to the next, of course. Mostly these are very long, although shortened from Metastasio's original. On the other hand, some are very short, as is the case between Nos. 6 and 7, which allows Semira's soothing key of A to follow hard upon Artabano's seething g minor. A scene change occurred between Nos. 5 and 6. The opera was blessed with outstanding sets by Fabrizio Galliari, Turin's great scenographer.[21] Bach carried the autograph of *Artaserse* with him to England, where it reposes today in the British Library. Several arias, including Artabano's two arias in Act I, have been torn out, presumably for use in other circumstances, or as gifts.[22]

Acts II and III give the impression here and there that its young composer at this stage of his development still lacked enough variety to sustain an entire opera. When Mandane sings her furious aria in Act II, "Và tra le selve ircane," Bach gives her the rapid triads up and down that suit her irate state but take something away from Arbace's use of this device in his first aria. For the ultrapathetic leave-taking aria of Arbace from his father, "Per quel paterno amplesso," on the other hand, Bach excelled himself. He improved on the smooth triple meter of Semira's No. 6 by greater subtlety in phrase construction (Example 9.1). After a "curtain" of two measures he gives Guadagni a charming melody in three-measure phrases, with vocal climax last.

The Turin *Artaserse* eliminated nearly a quarter of the dialogue in Metastasio's original libretto. This saved time in the simple recitatives, but Bach lengthened the opera by including three obbligato recitatives. His boldest economy was in avoiding full da capo returns in the arias.

Artaserse was the most frequently set of all Metastasio's librettos. Who chose it in this case? Almost certainly not Bach. Choosing the libretto was an honor that composers could aspire to only after many years of success in the theater, not a decision entrusted to neophytes. The libretto was so highly respected it may have served as a kind of proving ground for young talent. Gluck made his operatic

[21]Galliari's sketches for the sets are reproduced at the appropriate places of the score in *The Collected Works* edition, with admirable effect.

[22]Terry had only the autographs to go on, and so his thematic catalogue is missing several items.

EXAMPLE 9.1 *Christian Bach*, Artaserse, *Act II, Scene 12, Aria*

debut in 1741 with a setting of it for Milan. It was chosen for Hasse when he wrote his first opera for Venice in 1730.[23] Later it served for the Venetian debuts of Domenico Terradellas (1744) and Francesco de Majo (1762). The libretto's prestige helps explain why it was selected to open new opera houses. Graun's setting for Berlin inaugurated the Stuttgart Opera in 1750. Galuppi's setting for Vienna was revised as the opener of the Teatro Nuovo in Padua a year later. Jommelli's first opera for Mannheim in 1751 was a revision of his version for Rome in 1749. Thomas Arne attempted to found a new genre of serious opera sung throughout in English with his *Artaxerxes* of 1762.

Bach probably remembered little of opera in Berlin after five years in Italy. His experiences at the San Carlo in Naples would have been more potent. Those in Milan itself contributed to forming him as a composer of opera seria. The main (i.e., second) carnival operas there were all on librettos by Metastasio: *Ezio* (1757) and *Ipermestra* (1758) by Galuppi; *Alessandro nell'Indie* by Holzbauer; and *Demetrio* (1760) by Wagenseil, who is known to have come to Milan for the event. The presence of the last-mentioned in Milan was possibly important for Bach's instrumental music as well. Unlike the Italian masters (except Galuppi), Wagenseil was a prolific composer of symphonies, keyboard sonatas, and keyboard concertos, and an acclaimed keyboard player.

The reputation Bach gained with the success of his *Artaserse* quickly spread.

---

[23]Daniel Heartz, "Hasse at the Crossroads: *Artaserse* (Venice, 1730), Dresden, and Vienna," *Opera Quarterly* 16 (2000): 24–33.

In Naples he was already known for his keyboard playing and for single arias he had written at the request of Piccinni and of the castrato Giovanni Amadori.[24] Bach was being considered to set *Andromaca* for King Ferdinand's name day on 30 May 1761, but the choice fell instead on Sacchini, whose first opera seria resulted. The impresario Gaetano Grossatesta then commissioned Bach to set *Catone in Utica* celebrating the name day on 4 November of Charles III, king of Spain since 1759. The change of regime in Spain meant a return to Italy of two famous singers, Farinelli, who settled in Bologna, and the tenor Anton Raaff, who took up an engagement at the San Carlo. Raaff may be the main reason why Metastasio's *Catone in Utica* was chosen. It offered him not just a title role as Catone, but the kind of part he loved to play: a hero who goes to his death. The libretto explains in a note to the reader that the text of the opera would be the shortened version used at the San Carlo since 1746 (in a setting by Egidio Duni). As much as a third of the dialogue was cut from Metastasio's original libretto. Besides Raaff, there was one other singer involved who would play a role in Bach's later career, the castrato Tommaso Guarducci, who sang the part of Caesar.

Catone in Utica in Bach's setting outstripped most Italian operas of its day, as can be seen from the unusual number of revivals in other centers. There were nine productions following the first. The success was so great that Bach was soon pressed to write a second opera for Naples.

Catone for Naples was less adventurous than *Artaserse* for Turin, where Bach had taken unusual liberties in abbreviating arias. In Naples he reverted mostly to the da capo ideal, as was clearly expected there. *Catone* thus projects a more conventional appeal, and this may help explain why it was favored by producers elsewhere. The most forward-looking aspects of *Catone* were built-in by Metastasio: the quartet in Act III, and the ending of this act with a simple recitative. Bach's greatest moment in the opera is not the quartet, but his inspired music for the work's sole obbligato recitative, for Raaff/Catone, preceding his final aria. The piece comes in two sections, separated by simple recitative. In the second, as Catone bids farewell to his daughter Marzia, Bach goes as far afield as A$^\flat$, the funereal key, in which he proposes a syncopated figure that also occurs in the following aria. Moreover, he anticipates in an uncanny way the entrance of Idamante robed for his immolation in the last act of Mozart's *Idomeneo,* twenty years later (Example 9.2ab). Here the correspondence is so specific, the placement and meaning of the passage so similar, that it seems idle to claim both as reflective of some more widespread practice. Raaff sang in both operas.

Hasse was involved again with respect to Bach's second opera for Naples. At first Grossatesta intended to revive Hasse's successful *Artaserse* of a year earlier

---

[24]Ulisse Prota-Giurleo, "Notizie biografiche intorno ad alcuni musicisti d'oltralpe a Napoli nel settecento," *Analecta musicologica* 2 (1965): 112–43; 114.

EXAMPLE 9.2.
a. Christian Bach, *Catone in Utica,* Act III, Scene 12

b. Mozart, *Idomeneo,* Act III, Scene 9

for Naples. Objection was raised on the grounds that its music graced the music stands of all the harpsichords in the capital and that there was nary a dilettante who did not possess its arias; that is, it was too well known and loved. Thus a new setting of *Alessandro nell'Indie* was proposed to Hasse. He declined to accept because of obligations in Vienna. Hence Bach was asked to make the setting, which was to be sung by the same forces as in *Catone.* The offer was another moment of triumph for the young composer. To fulfill it he needed permission to extend his leave from Milan.

Opera in those days was an affair of state as serious as any, short of war and dynastic survival. This was necessarily so because of its huge drain on the state's treasury and because it put the prestige of the state squarely on the line. When Bach arrived in Naples in September 1761, he bore with him a letter of recommendation to the first minister, Marquis Bernardo Tanucci, from Count Karl von Firmian, the governor of Austrian Lombardy. Soon after the premiere of *Catone,* the authorities realized that they both desired and needed Bach to compose *Alessandro.* Tanucci wrote to Firmian requesting leave for him to stay through carnival season. Firmian acquiesced, saying he was delighted that Bach had drawn the applause of a city so preeminent in music. Firmian probably did not learn from Tanucci or anyone else that Bach was also warned by the Neapolitan authorities to desist in his indiscreet attentions to the married ballerina Colomba Beccari. His attentions may have begun earlier, when she danced in the *Artaserse* at Turin. Propriety had to be observed, at least in public, for it too reflected on the state's prestige.

Alessandro nell'Indie was first performed on 20 January 1762, the birthday of Charles III, preceded by Bach's cantata celebrating him. The public once again applauded Raaff in the title role. Bach was lavish to the point of including four obbligato recitatives, and notably one for Raaff before he sang his aria in Act III, "Non sò d'onde viene." Borrowed from *L'Olimpiade,* Metastasio's beautiful verse did not suit its new situation very well. Bach's setting, on the other hand, became the most successful of all his arias, not only Raaff's favorite of favorites, but also Mozart's.[25]

Two successes in the Teatro San Carlo were enough to alert any enterprising company that put on opera seria as to Bach's merits. They were so appreciated in Naples itself that an invitation was being worked out for him to compose another name-day opera for Charles III the following November. Negotiations were in the works as well to invite him to Venice for an opera. London got ahead of both these options with a firm and generous offer to compose two serious operas, tendered by Colomba Mattei, soprano, who with her husband Joseph Trombetta managed the King's Theatre in the Haymarket. The offer arrived soon after Bach returned to Milan in April. He requested a one-year leave from his superiors in order to accept, "having been offered the opportunity to go to London to compose two operas for an excellent stipend and at great personal advantage."[26] His request, dated 27 May 1762, was granted. In a final letter to Martini before leaving Italy, dated Milan, 9 June 1762, Bach announced his imminent departure for England, but says nothing about returning after a year.[27]

THE KING'S THEATRE

An older tradition of scholarship had Bach going to London as a successor to Handel in royal service after that great master died in 1759. A more recent error

---

[25]Terry, *John Christian Bach,* quotes the main theme, p. 33. See also Stefan Kunze, "Die Vertonungen der Arie 'Non so d'onde viene' von J. Chr. Bach und W. A. Mozart," *Analecta musicologica* 2 (1965): 85–111.

[26]The document is published in facsimile by Claudio Sartori, "A Milano J. C. Bach in disaccordo con il tesoriere," *La Scala: Revista dell opera* (Milan, 15 November 1955): 29–31.

[27]This letter is lacking in Schnoebelen, *Padre Martini's Collection of Letters.* A facsimile and translation are found in Howard Brofsky, "J. C. Bach, G. B. Sammartini, and Padre Martini: A *Concorso* in Milan in 1762," in *A Musical Offering: Essays in Honor of Martin Bernstein,* ed. E. H. Clinkscale and C. Brook (New York, 1977), pp. 63–68; 65.

had him going to London by way of Strelitz in northern Germany, from which he purportedly received 100 thalers travel money on 8 July 1762.[28] This attractive hypothesis had the advantage of linking Bach with the court whence came Princess Charlotte Sophia of Mecklenburg-Strelitz, the queen of England who married George III in September 1761. The travel grant is authentic and its receipt is signed by hand "Bach," the handwriting being that of Carl Philipp Emanuel, who went regularly to Strelitz and was the keyboard teacher of Charlotte and other members of the princely family.[29] It is possible that Emanuel might have taken young Christian along to Strelitz on one of his visits from Berlin. This would help explain how Christian came to compose John Lockman's *Ode on the auspicious Arrival and Nuptials of her present most gracious Majesty Queen Charlotte,* "set to Music by Mr. Bach," a manuscript that belonged to the queen. Of course, Christian could have set the ode well after the events related by its text. Not impossible is the hypothesis that Emanuel, then the most famous Bach, had something to do with Christian's invitation to London through his connection with Queen Charlotte. The English court, on the other hand, did not support financially or meddle with the management of the London opera, even though it was called "Royal." A more likely person to have recommended Christian to Mattei is the soprano Filippo Elisi, who was primo uomo of the 1761–62 London opera season under Mattei's management and whom Bach had pleased in Milan by his setting of "Misero pargoletto." Unfortunately for Bach, Elisi left London after one season, and his replacement, along with the rest of the company, left a lot to be desired.

Bach's immediate predecessor as house composer at the King's Theatre was Gioacchino Cocchi, an experienced opera composer with successes in Naples, Rome, and Venice, before he went to London in 1757. Cocchi wrote or arranged both comic and serious operas in London for five years until, as Burney claimed, his inspiration ran dry. His last season was 1761–62, when Bach was engaged as his replacement. Cocchi remained for about ten years in London, where he was a fashionable teacher of singing, but he wrote no more operas. Bach was at first reluctant to write for the company he supervised, which had neither prima donna nor primo uomo worthy of the name. Burney in his *History* said that Bach "for some time totally declined composing for our stage, being unwilling, as a stranger, to trust his reputation to such performers."

By a stroke of fortune Mattei had hired the De Amicis family to perform comic operas, and Bach perceived in Anna greater possibilities. "Having heard the De Amicis sing two or three serious songs in private," recounted Burney, "it suggested to him the idea of giving her the first woman's part in his serious opera; and having communicated his design to Mattei the impresaria, matters were soon arranged." Most of the texts Cocchi set in London were the warhorse librettos of

[28]Terry, *John Christian Bach,* pp. 59–60.
[29]Gärtner, *John Christian Bach,* p. 167.

Metastasio, locally revised of course. Bach received or sought out an original libretto by Giovanni Bottarelli, the house poet, who may be the same person of this name who worked with Graun in Berlin during the early 1740s. Casanova tells of meeting Bottarelli as an impoverished hack poet at London in 1763.[30] *Orione, o sia Diana vendicata* went on the stage and Anna De Amicis triumphed in the prima donna role of Candiope. Up to this time Bach had limited his contributions to writing overtures or individual numbers in pasticcio operas. His first major contribution to the London stage proved to be a resounding success. Its several choruses were especially remarked. Writing choruses was well within the powers of a composer so well trained in sacred music.

Orione, unlike Bach's operas in Italy, was based not on historical figures from antiquity, as seen through Metastasio's rose-colored lenses, but upon myth, like most French opera of the serious kind. Possibly Bach had already passed by way of Paris, where he had many contacts with music publishers, and had experienced tragédie-lyrique at the Opéra, where an *Orion* had in fact been staged. This would help explain the choice of subject and the strong role given to choruses in the work. Another explanation, offered by a contemporary commentator, is that Bach intended to flatter the ears of the English public with choral music because of its fondness for Handel. In either case it appears that the composer, not the poet, took the lead in shaping *Orione*.

Burney was unstinting in his praises of *Orione* in his *History*, although not of the singers, with the exception of De Amicis.

> Mr. Bach's first opera in England . . . was honoured with the presence of their Majesties on the first night, February the 19th, 1763, and extremely applauded by a very numerous audience. Every judge of Music perceived the emenations of genius throughout the whole performance; but were chiefly struck with the richness of the harmony, the ingenious texture of the parts, and above all, with the new and happy use he had made of wind-instruments: this being the first time that *clarinets* had admission in our opera orchestra. Their Majesties honoured the second representation likewise with their presence, and no other serious opera was wanting for near three months.

Bach's contractual agreement to furnish two operas was fulfilled by his setting of Bottarelli's *Zanaida*, first staged late in the season, on 7 May, with less success. "The principal songs of these two operas, though excellent," wrote Burney, "being calculated to display the compass of voice and delicate and difficult expression and execution of De Amicis, were not likely to become common or of much use out of the Opera house. The rest of the airs were so indifferently sung, that they

---

[30]Giacomo Casanova, Chevalier de Seingalt, *History of My Life,* trans. Willard R. Trask, 12 vols. in 6 (New York, 1966–68; reprint 1997), 9: 339.

were more admired as instrumental pieces, than compositions for the voice."Neither *Orione* nor *Zanaide* has survived in complete form. Only ten of nineteen arias from *Orione* remain. They show a variety of forms that link them more with Bach's *Artaserse* than with his two Neapolitan operas, which suggests that he was once again free to do as he wished. Burney credits him with being the first to banish the da capo aria. This is misleading on two accounts. He was not the first composer working to reduce the aria in scale—recall the cavatinas of Hasse and Graun. Moreover, he continued to employ a few full da capo forms in his operas. Both of his 1763 operas were accorded the honor of publications in the form of *The Favourite Songs.*

Bach's leave of absence from his post of organist at Milan cathedral expired in the summer of 1763. Surprisingly, his contract at the King's Theatre was not renewed by the new management team of Felice Giardini and Regina Mingotti. What decided him to stay in England was the favorable attention of the monarchs, not only to his operas but also to his playing and to his person. In his letter to Martini dated London, 1 July 1763, he wrote, "It was my intention to go to Italy this year, but the infinite kindness of their Majesties the King and Queen obliges me to obey their request that I should remain here."[31] An official appointment as music master to the queen was not long in coming.

Giardini had run the opera once before as impresario, in 1756–57, with mediocre results. Before this and again later he led the opera orchestra, with better results, commensurate with his standing as one of London's best violinists. He also aspired to compose operas. Burney opined that "he had not sufficient force or variety to sustain a whole opera." The public agreed.

Giardini realized he needed at least one composer of stature. He attempted without success to hire Piccinni. In his place he settled for a little-known and inexpensive Neapolitan working at Venice, Mattia Vento. There is apparent in Giardini's attitude toward Bach a scarcely disguised hostility to non-Italian-born composers that was shared by most of the expatriot Italian musicians in London. That Bach stood in high favor with the queen did not alleviate their disdain. In a letter of 15 July 1763 Giardini wrote sarcastically, "Trombetta, Mattei, and Bach are set out this day for Paris—bountiful tears were shed but they can be dried with a large handkerchief."[32]

Bach returned from Paris to London by the fall of 1763. Previously he had resided with Mattei and her husband; his Op. 1 keyboard concertos on 17 March 1763 were advertised as "to be had of him at Signora Mattei's, in Germyn-Street, St. James." Next he moved north into the newly built and fashionable suburb of

[31]Terry, *John Christian Bach*, p. 74.

[32]The story of Giardini's peremptory and disastrous direction is told in documents transcribed and translated by Curtis Price, Judith Milhous, and Robert D. Hume, *The Impresario's Ten Commandments: Continental Recruitment for Italian Opera in London, 1763–64* (Royal Musical Association Monographs 6) (London, 1992).

Soho, taking lodgings together with Carl Friedrich Abel, who would be his business partner in concert giving for nearly two decades. The first of their series was advertised in February 1764 and invited the public to buy tickets at half a guinea apiece "at Mr. Bach and Mr. Abel's Lodgings, in Meard's street, St. Ann's Soho." The concert took place on 19 February in the Great Room in Spring Gardens, near Saint James Park, and consisted of several new instrumental works by Abel and a lost serenata by Bach, thought to have been a setting of Metastasio's *Galatea*. During the same month Bach published his Op. 2 keyboard sonatas with accompaniment. George III had granted him protection against piracy of his printed works by decree of 15 December 1763.[33]

By 1765 Bach and Abel had moved to a longer-lasting address near Soho Square, given on the title page of Bach's Op. 3 symphonies, "Printed for the Author and Sold at his House in King's Square Court, Dean St. Soho." The address can easily be found on Jean Rocque's 1763 map of the area (Figure 9.1).

The opera season of 1763–64 placed Giardini into debt for years. He was obliged to give up the managerial reigns to his former partners John Fermier and

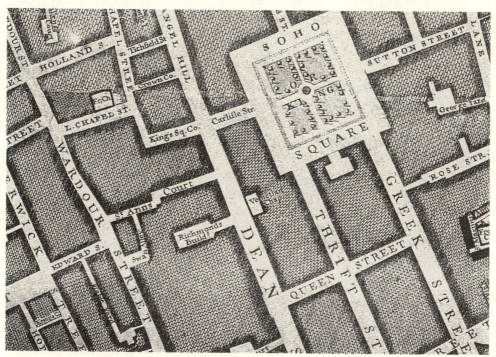

FIGURE 9.1. Jean Rocque. Map of London, 1763, detail.

[33]Ten years later Bach took the publishers Charles Lukey and James Longman to court for copyright violations and eventually won a decision against them in 1777. John Small, "J. C. Bach goes to Law," *Musical Times* 126 (1985): 526–29.

Peter Crawford for the following season, which promised a new beginning with the arrival of the famous castrato Giovanni Manzuoli. Others hired were Bach's close friend Ferdinando Tenducci, the tenor Ercole Ciprandi, and as prima donna Teresa Scotti. Vento remained the house composer. The season opened with a pasticcio *Ezio* on 24 November 1764. Horace Walpole judged Manzuoli to be past his prime and less touching than Elisi, but the public, including Burney, praised the new star to the skies. Ciprandi was successful singing the aria "Non sò d'onde viene" Bach had composed for Raaff in Naples. (Individual arias by Bach frequently graced the London seasons whether or not he contributed a new work.) Tenducci may have helped Bach to get a foot in the door with the new managers, who were more impressed by Bach's high standing at court and growing fame than were the generality of Italian singers. Manzuoli sided with the latter to the point of declaring he had made a vow (which he soon broke) not to sing a note of Bach's music.[34]

Bach's third London opera was Metastasio's *Adriano in Siria*. One advantage of an old warhorse like this from the point of view of the singers was that they would have already sung the long dialogue texts between the arias and were not required to memorize entirely new words. London opera was singer dominated as much or more than ever, which made a departure from the norm such as *Orione* all the more of an achievement. *Adriano* was first performed on 26 January 1765. The seventh and last performance took place on 16 February, honored, like the first, by the presence of the sovereigns.

There are some signs of innovation in *Adriano in Siria*. To the principals Bach allowed long arias with middle sections and dal segno repetitions. The secondary singers, on the other hand, had to be content with much shorter arias, in three cases (Nos. 5, 17, and 18) on texts shorn of their second stanzas. Substitute texts from other Metastasian operas were introduced for the prima donna and primo uomo in Act I. Several new texts replaced those of Metastasio in Act II, presumably written by house poet Bottarelli. They involve two for Emirena, the prima donna, and one for Farnaspe, sung by Manzuoli, plus an act-ending trio for these two with Ciprandi. The substitute aria for Farnaspe is "Cara la dolce fiamma," a piece that has attracted attention because of a decorated version of the vocal line written out by one of the Mozarts (probably Leopold). They were in London throughout the opera season and were befriended by Manzuoli. Speculation arises as to whether the embellishments reflect what Manzuoli actually sang.

Individual arias of *Adriano* were successful but the opera as a whole failed, according to Burney, who surmised that expectations were too high, the theater too crowded, and the Italian cabal too strong. The opera that followed it was

---

[34] Letter of Mrs. Gertrude Harris to her son at Oxford, dated London, 19 October 1764, cited by Terry, *John Christian Bach*, pp. 81–82.

Vento's setting of *Demofoonte.* It had more success, "which seemed matter of great triumph to the Italians," as Burney wrote. He found Vento's opera "natural, graceful, and pleasing, always free from vulgarity, but never very new or learned." Still another opera followed for Manzuoli and company, a setting of *L'Olimpiade* by Arne, intended as homage to this worthy master whose *Artaxerxes* had won converts to serious opera in English two years earlier at Covent Garden. Burney had to admit, reluctantly, that Arne was out of his element at the King's Theatre after writing so long for playhouse singers and audiences. He confessed also that Arne mangled the Italian language as much as a newly arrived Italian in London might have mangled English.

Two years passed before Bach was again requested to compose an opera for the King's Theatre. For the 1766–67 season managers Crawford, Thomas Vincent, and John Gordon, brought several singers from Italy, forming companies for both comic and serious opera. Three of the comic singers, Giovanni Lovatini, Andrea Morigi, and Gaspero Savoi, had performed in the first production of Piccinni's *La buona figliuola* at Rome in 1760, and they now introduced the fall season with this very work, which was new to London. It triumphed. Morigi and Savoi also sang in the serious troupe, which was led by Guarducci, primo uomo, who had sung in both of Bach's operas for Naples. The serious operas did not even begin until 20 December 1766, with a revival of the pasticcio *Ezio.* Meanwhile Bach and Bottarelli were planning the creation of an opera that would hark back to *Orione* and capture, they hoped, some of the luster that an original subject, unusual settings, and choral splendor could lend the stage. The result was *Carattaco,* first performed on 14 February 1767.

Tacitus had long proved a fruitful source for librettists. His vivid descriptions of the Roman war against the Germans provided Antonio Salvi with material for his *Arminio,* set most memorably by Handel for London during the 1736–37 season. Thirty years later there were but few London operagoers who would have remembered that. Bottarelli chose an English subject from Tacitus, the Roman capture of Britain (also chosen by a contemporary playwright, William Mason). Foregoing the so-called unity of place, the subject offered great historical sweep, moving from Druidic ceremonies in Celtic England, through the Roman conquest, marine transport of captives, and a final act in Rome itself, in an amphitheater where they were about to be killed. At the end Caesar pardons everyone, a nice eighteenth-century touch, of which Metastasio would have approved.

The chorus begins and ends Act I, and the choral singing received much praise. Comparisons with Handel were not lacking. One spectator wrote the local press, "His Chorusses elevate the Soul and put us in mind of those of the immortal Handel, and of his own favourite *Orione.*"[35] The arias received comparable

---

[35]Ibid., p. 107.

praise. Bach was even more economical as to their length than before. Only four out of twenty-one were of the dal segno type, and these went to the principals, of whom Guarducci in the title role received the most. The prima donna role was intended for Cecilia Grassi, Bach's future wife, but because of illness she was replaced in the first performances. There are more secondary characters than usual, so it was vital for Bach to limit the lengths of their arias, which he did to an average of about a hundred measures. The conventions were not slighted even so. There is a love duet in the key of A for Guarducci and the prima donna in Act III as they face death (or so they imagine). Caesar forgives all in a *Tempo di Minuetto* aria that is a five-part rondo, one of the most fashionable aria types of the 1760s. Caesar was sung by the same tenor, Morigi, who sang Tagliaferro in *La buona figliuola*. Insofar as it was still possible for any opera seria to stand up to Piccinni's comic masterpiece, Bach had succeeded once again. The sovereigns, like everyone else, were thrilled with the English subject and attended all but two of the six performances.

Carattaco was not only lauded in the public press. It evoked there requests for more employment of Bach:

> The masterly Stile of the Music, and particularly the Grandeur of the Chorusses, makes it to be wished that Signor Bach may meet with further Encouragement, as his Genius and Judgment seem admirably calculated to reform the present corrupted Taste of our modern Music, and, like a second Handel, once again restore that Elegance and Perfection we have for some Time been Strangers to.[36]

The Italians in power at the opera were not about to allow any reformist changes in the status quo. At most, Guadagni got to sing his special role as Gluck's Orfeo by his own request during the 1770 season. To make *Orfeo ed Euridice* of a sufficient length and palatable to London audiences, Bach and Guglielmi padded it with new recitatives and arias to texts by Bottarelli. Burney lamented the damage done to a masterpiece. The composer who succeeded in nearly ousting Bach from the King's Theatre was not Guglielmi but Sacchini, who arrived in London in 1772 and dominated its opera for a decade.

Bach wrote no new operas for the King's Theatre between 1767 and 1778. He made occasional forays into the area of operas and cantatas in English, of which the largest was *The Fairy Favour* for Covent Garden in 1767, a masque for which only the text survives. In 1770, besides contributing to *Orfeo,* he took refuge at Covent Garden theater by producing an oratorio on the text of Metastasio's *Gioas, re di Giuda*. The work was not particularly well received, and Bach's attempts to play an organ concerto between the two parts, as was the custom since Handel, were ridiculed. On 6 April 1772 his Serenata for four singers on the text of Metas-

---

[36]Ibid., pp. 106–7.

tasio's *Endimione* was produced at the King's Theatre. *Orione* was revived there with success in May 1767, bringing his operatic strengths to the attention of the London public again, after his successes abroad at Mannheim. It prepared the way for the last and greatest of his London operas.

La clemenza di Scipione was the work of an anonymous librettist, believed to be a foreign ambassador in London, "a Person of Taste and Learning, who softens the Cares of Negotiation by sacrificing in secret to the Muses," as a public newspaper announced just after the premiere on 4 April 1778.[37] The work was advertised as a "new Serious Opera, with Grand Choruses"; the choral emphasis makes it almost certain that the libretto was prepared specifically for Bach. There were only five characters. The three principals were Valentin Adamberger from Munich, tenor; Francesco Roncaglia, primo uomo, for whom Bach had composed in Mannheim; and Franziska Danzi, daughter of Franz, first cellist at Mannheim, prima donna. Two other musicians of Mannheim were prominent in the London opera, Wilhelm Cramer, first violin, and Ludwig August Lebrun, first oboe (in the course of the eight performances Mademoiselle Danzi became Madame Lebrun). The whole musical enterprise was suffused with a glow from Mannheim, not least of all in Bach's orchestral writing. Possibly the librettist too hailed from the Palatine court. Carl Theodore's ambassador in London was Count Joseph von Haslang.

Scipione begins with an overture that lacks the usual three movements observed by Bach. Instead there is an *Allegro assai* based on a strong triadic motif in unisons and octaves, punctuated by a knocking rhythm in staccato eighth notes (Example 9.3). While still in the tonic the basses reiterate this motif, making it

EXAMPLE 9.3. *Christian Bach*, La clemenza di Scipione, *Overture*

more of a theme by adding an answer, a tone higher, against which the upper strings sound tremolo accompaniments. A long crescendo taking the violins up to high D, as in many a Mannheim symphony, follows the modulation to V. The musical periods are broad yet deployed with an economy and cogency that sound quite new in Bach's discourse. Woodwinds are often independent, as when they state the second theme. A double reprise leads in the return of tonic D. The *Allegro assai* can be regarded as a one-movement overture, in which case it is in keeping with Holzbauer's for *Günther* a year earlier. There is another way to perceive

[37]Ibid., p. 157.

it. The short *marcia* in G (played on stage?) that comes next, joined with the following obbligato recitative, also short and peppered with the *Allegro assai*'s opening motif, could be heard as a middle movement, then rounded out with a return to D by the rousing chorus "S'oda il suon de la Tromba guerriera." As the chorus approaches the cadence on V, the violins climb above it with a striking melody that sounds very much like Mannheim (Example 9.4). The melodic turn in eighth notes leading up to A, rapid descent down a tritone, with afterbeat, then expansion to a major sixth leap could be by Cannabich, or indeed by Mozart.[38]

EXAMPLE 9.4. *Christian Bach*, La clemenza di Scipione, *Act I, Scene 1,* chorus, "S'oda il suon"

John Welcker printed a full score of *Scipione* but it lacked the simple recitatives, and no copy of them has yet been found. The score reader is therefore shocked by an aria in C major following without the tonal transition a recitative would have provided after the trumpet chorus in D. Words for the recitatives survive in the printed libretto. They should be reset, failing discovery of the originals, at least to the extent of providing the essential connective tissue. Everything is terse in this opera, including the recitative dialogue and the orchestral introductions to the arias, none of which has dal segno returns. Act I ends with a modest-sized love duet in the key of A, consisting of a ternary-form *Larghetto* in 3/4 and a concluding *Allegro* in 4/4, with prominent gavotte rhythms—an approximation of the new two-tempo rondo that is to arrive full-blown in Act III.

Act II, after the obligatory *aria di sorbetto* for a secondary character, continues with a chorus (and another chorus in the libretto not given in the score) and works its way up to three of the opera's most effective numbers: an obbligato recitative for Luceio/Roncaglia followed by his pathetic aria "Frena le belle lagrime" set to a *Larghetto* in 3/4; an obbligato recitative and concertante aria with flute, oboe, violin, and cello for Lucinda/Danzi, an *Allegro maestoso* in 4/4; and an

[38]See *Idomeneo*, duet, No. 20A, mm. 17–18.

act-ending terzetto for these two plus Scipione/Adamberger, set as an *Allegro* in 4/4. Each was praised in letters to the public press.

It was a challenge for Bach to surpass himself in Act III, yet he managed to do no less. The high point of the opera is Luceio's rondo "Nel partir, bell'idol mio," preceded by an obbligato recitative that anticipates the *Andantino* with which the rondo begins. Here Bach wrote a full-fledged, two-tempo rondo of the most modern cast, with both slower and faster parts informed by gavotte rhythms, and both with returns after contrast. Moreover, the middle section of the *Allegro assai* returns to the main theme of the *Andantino.* In another return that is very effective, Bach brings back the main motif of the overture during the final number in praise of love and honor, sung in dialogue between soloists and chorus.

Scipione prompted a correspondent to one of the newspapers to admonish the opera's managers "never to let a Winter pass without employing this great Master in composing at least one Opera."[39] The advice went unheeded. At best, because *Scipione* was so superior to the rest of their operatic fare, the managers decided to retain Bach's name among the list of the theater's official composers, but he supplied no more original works. Posthumous life was granted *Scipione* many years later when Mrs. Billington, the daughter of Bach's pupil Mrs. Weichsell, had the work revived as a vehicle for her benefit in 1805. The version was condensed to two acts and may have born little resemblance to the original, although based presumably on Welcker's printed score. It was among the last full scores of an Italian opera to be printed locally during the period. According to one assessment, *Scipione* "represents the high-water mark of Italian opera in London during the second half of the eighteenth century."[40] The praise loses some force because the same authors assess the general level of London opera as dismal.

INSTRUMENTAL MUSIC

Italian opera brought Bach to London. A royal appointment, teaching, and successes in concert giving and publishing kept him there. Visiting composers from Italy were frequent in the two decades before Bach's arrival. They included Gluck, Ciampi, Galuppi, and Lampugnani, among others. None stayed long enough, or made enough impact, to change English musical life in any decisive way. Those who did stay longer, like Cocchi, Giardini, and Vento, lacked sufficient depth as composers to make much of a difference. The weight of Handel's genius fell heavily on native composers such as William Boyce, master of the royal music from the 1760s until his death in 1779. Boyce wrote "symphonies" that continued the Handelian or even the Corellian concerto grosso. According to one critic, it took a Bach to break the spell.

---

[39]Terry, *John Christian Bach,* pp. 157–58.
[40]Curtis Price, Judith Milhous, and Robert D. Hume, *Italian Opera in Late Eighteenth-Century London,* vol. 1: *The King's Theatre, Haymarket, 1778–1791* (Oxford, 1995), p. 195.

Within a few years, perhaps even at the very time Boyce was writing these works, J. C. Bach arrived in London and a new era in English musical life began. This meant that unlike Germany and Italy the process of transformation from the high baroque to the classical manner, which can be called "rococo," never really took place in England. England has no equivalent of Hasse, Vinci or Telemann, either native or visitor; nor does it seem to have acquired the taste for a truly decorative style. Its favourite composers were soon Haydn and Beethoven. It may be that some national characteristic, abhorring the purely decorative, may be traced in this, since much the same may be said of English architecture. Without any doubt, in music it was due in no small measure to the vogue for Corelli and its extension in the music of Georg Friedrich Handel.[41]

Music by Hasse, Vinci, and Telemann was well known in England, of course, that of Vinci being championed by none other than Handel himself. Yet it is true that Handelian *gravitas* prevailed right up to the 1760s, and in some circles beyond. Contrary to what the author says, it was Christian Bach, a follower of Hasse and his true heir in many respects, who imposed the "decorative style" in London, called the galant style in this book. As for comparisons with the visual arts, the author omits French influences, without which there could have been no Thomas Gainsborough.

John Hawkins, in his preface to Boyce's *Cathedral Music*, put the blame for Boyce's fall from favor squarely upon the shoulders of Bach and Abel, particularly their "new-fangled Trios, Quartettos, Quintettos and overtures" (i.e., symphonies).

We no more hear the solemn and pathetic *Adagio*, the artful and well-studied Fugue, or the sweet modulation of the keys with the minor third: all is *Allegro* and *Prestissimo*, and if not discord, such harmony as the ear sickens at hearing. Such music Mr. Handel was used to listen to and laugh at, and comparing it to a game of cards would exclaim, "Now D is trumps, now A," in allusion to those vulgar transitions from the key-note to its fifth, with which such sort of music, especially when accompanied with French Horns, abounds.[42]

If Handel ever made such a remark, it was astute of him to observe how tonic-dominant polarity had taken over music in the major mode, and what a light-hearted sport it had become, like a game, in comparison with the heavier *Allegros* it had replaced. Nor was Hawkins mistaken in connecting this state of affairs with the limited tones of the natural horn.

Bach's eminence as teacher, performer, and composer was reinforced by a series of publications, usually headed by dedications to wealthy patrons and

[41]Denis Arnold, "The Corellian Cult in England," in *Nuovi studi corelliani*, ed. Giulia Giachin (Florence, 1978), pp. 81–88. In agreement is Roger Fiske, "The Galant Style Comes to Britain," in *Music in Britain: The Eighteenth Century*, ed. H. Diack Johnstone and Roger Fiske (Oxford, 1990), pp. 206–20.
[42]Percy Young, *A History of British Music* (London, 1967), p. 343.

members of the royal family (Table 9.2). Note how many women figure among the dedicatees, especially of keyboard music. The series began, appropriately, with six harpsichord concertos dedicated to the queen, Bach's principal patron. In his dedication Bach mentions his relationship to her under two guises, as his singing pupil and as an indulgent listener. This suggests that Bach himself played the harpsichord in these small chamber concertos. The queen was also able to serve as soloist, for the part was not very demanding and she played well. It remains a question whether Bach wrote these works in Italy or after his arrival in London. We know that he composed concertos as well as symphonies for festivities celebrating Isabella of Parma in 1760, performances that he also supervised and very likely appeared in as a keyboard soloist. The first concerto of the set, Op. 1 No. 1 in B♭, has an opening movement *Allegretto* with the main theme resembling the parallel movement in Bach's first Berlin concerto, another *Allegretto* in B♭ (Example 9.5). The syncopations and melodic movement up to the high tonic are similar. Alberti basses do not see use in his Berlin concertos.

Bach's Op. 1 Concertos are Italianate in texture. They abandon the four-part string writing of the Berlin concertos by using only three string parts, without violas. They often substitute the two-movement sequence of *Allegro* and minuet in the same key for the three-movement fast–slow–fast sequence of the older concertos. In other words, they are very like the small chamber concertos by Wagenseil that Bach could have encountered in Milan or for that matter in London, where John Walsh published Wagenseil's *Six Concerts for the Harpsichord or Organ with Accompaniments for Two Violins and a Bass* (London, 1761).

EXAMPLE 9.5. *Christian Bach, Harpsichord Concerto, Op. 1 No. 1, I*

TABLE 9.2 Bach's Works with Opus Numbers Published in London during His Lifetime

Opus	Date	Title	Dedicatee
1	1763	*Six concerts pour le clavecin, deux violons, et un violoncelle*	Queen Charlotte
2	1763	*Six sonates pour le clavecin accompagnées d'un violon ou flûte transverière et d'un violoncelle*	Princess Augusta of Brunswick-Lüneburg, sister of George III
3	1765	*Six simphonies a deux violons, deux hautbois, deux cors de chasse, alto viola, et basse*	Duke of York, brother of George III
4	1765	*Sei canzonette a due*	Lady Glenorchy, viscountess
5	1766	*Six sonates pour le clavecin ou le piano forte*	Duke Ernest of Mecklenburg, brother of Queen Charlotte
6	1766	*Sei canzonette a due*	Duke Joseph Frederick of Sachsen-Hildburghausen
7	1770	*Sei concerti per il cembalo o piano e forte con due violini e violoncello*	Queen Charlotte
8	1772	*Six quartettos for a German flute, violin, tenor, and violoncello*	Sir William Young
9		*Trois simphonies* (The Hague: B. Hummel, after a London edition?)	
10	1773	*Six Sonatas, for the Harpsichord or Piano Forte; with an Accompagnment for a Violin*	Lady Melbourne, viscountess
11	1774	*Six Quintettos for a Flute, Hauboy, Violin, Tenor, and Bass*	Elector Carl Theodore
13	1777	*A Third Sett of Six Concertos for the Harpsichord or Piano Forte*	Mrs. Pelham
14	1778	*La Clemenza di Scipione*	
15	1779	*Four Sonatas and Two Duetts for the Piano Forte or Harpsichord, with Accompaniments*	Countess of Abingdon
16	1779	*Six Sonatas for the Harpsichord or Piano-forte, with an Accompaniment for a German-Flute or Violin*	Misses Greenland*

*One of Bach's lawyers was Augustine Greenland and the dedicatees were presumably his daughters.

Another difference with the early concertos written at Berlin is that Bach rarely calls on the right hand to play more than a single melodic line, that is, the typical "singing allegro." Burney observed the phenomenon and explained it in his *History:*

> In general his compositions for the piano forte are such as ladies can execute with little trouble; and the allegros rather resemble bravura songs, than instrumental pieces

for the display of great execution. On which account, they lose much of their effect when played without the accompaniments, which are admirable, and so masterly and interesting to an audience, that want of hand, or complication in the harpsichord part, is never discovered.

Burney could have added that Bach requires the left hand to provide chordal accompaniments such as the Alberti bass when the strings are silent. Less convincing is Burney's previous account, said to derive from the composer himself, of how facility at the keyboard was lost in Italy from years of disuse.

> [Christian Bach] was for some time a scholar of his elder brother, the celebrated Charles Phil. Emanuel Bach, under whom he became a fine performer on keyed-instruments; but on quitting him and going to Italy, where his chief study was the composition of Vocal music, he assured me, that during many years he made little use of a harpsichord or piano forte but to compose for or accompany a voice. When he arrived in England, his style of playing was so much admired, that he recovered many of the losses his hand had sustained by disuse, and by being constantly cramped and crippled with a pen; but he never was able to reinstate it with force and readiness sufficient for great difficulties.

The explanation, even if Bach did tell Burney something along these lines, sounds too pat and is self-contradictory. If his style of playing was so admired when he arrived in England, it must be because he had already perfected his "singing Allegro." If he had lost so much prowess at the keyboard from composing while in Italy, how could he have made such an impression with his playing in Naples and in Rome? In an earlier version from Burney's papers dating from ca. 1779, there is no mention of Bach's having told Burney he neglected the keyboard in Italy.[43]

The fourth and sixth concertos of Op. 1 depart from the others in that they are in three movements and are titled "Concerto o Sinfonia." A "sinfonia" to Bach evidently entailed three movements. Moreover he experimented, making the two initial movements more like symphonies than concertos by putting them in binary form with repeats. This experiment was also tried by Tartini in some violin concertos. Bach eliminated the double exposition found in the other concertos by bringing the soloist in with the second theme in the dominant. In effect he eliminated the first exposition. With both parts repeated, the running time amounted to roughly the same in both forms. There is a nice local touch in the sixth concerto, which Bach ends with six simple variations on "God Save the King" followed by a coda. The tune is first stated unadorned except for a few trills and a *cadence galante* in place of the penultimate measure.

---

[43]Roe, *The Keyboard Music of J. C. Bach*, pp. 199–200.

The accompanied sonatas of Op. 2 are not very different in texture from the concertos, except that the accompanying parts for violin and cellos have much less to do, and the first movements are all in binary form with repeats. Some opening ideas in them assume quite expansive proportions, such as the **a b b**[1] theme that begins Op. 2 No. 1 in F.[44] In a later set of accompanied sonatas, Op. 10, Bach allots a more important role to the violin. The theme that begins Sonata No. 1 will be familiar as the Preludium to the First Partita for keyboard (BWV 825) by his father (Figure 9.2). The first four measures remain the same except for ornaments, added dotted rhythm, and the altered cadence. Upon repetition Christian gives the violin a vital accompanying part without which the harmony

FIGURE 9.2. Christian Bach. Accompanied keyboard sonata, Op. 10 No. 1.

would be incomplete. Father Bach continued the melody with a good example of *Fortspinnung*. His son continues with little balanced phrases of two measures, a lyric melody played by the right hand on the keyboard, leading to a half-cadence introduced by typically galant triplets and followed by a second theme imitated by the violin. The rewriting furnishes a fine lesson in how the galant style differs from what came before. The title page of Op. 10 is as light and airy as the music (Figure 9.3).

[44]Example given by Newman, *The Sonata,* p. 710, and Roe, *The Keyboard Music of J. C. Bach,* p. 211, ex. 2.

FIGURE 9.3. Title page of Christian Bach's Op. 10.

Symphonies required large musical forces. In origin, at least, they were for professional players. Both chamber concertos and sonatas belonged to the public of dilettante players, although they may well have been heard in the professional concerts for which Bach and Abel became famous. Bach's symphonies certainly were heard there. They were often promoted on the basis of having been heard in the latest professional concerts. Thus, an advertisement for the Op. 3 set by Bach announced on 3 April 1765 "Six new Overtures, in 8 parts; as they were performed at the Wednesday Subscription Concert, in Soho-square."[45] Two months earlier a series of six subscription concerts at 5 guineas a seat had been announced in Carlisle House by Mrs. Cornelys, the impresaria.[46] They were directed alternately by Bach and Abel, beginning with Bach. It is possible that the six new overtures or symphonies were the works that in turn began the six concerts. The series was so successful it was expanded the following year to fifteen concerts.

Bach's Op. 3 symphonies went through several reprints from the original plates, which indicates that they were avidly taken up by amateur orchestras, of

---

[45]Johann Christian Bach, *Twelve Early Symphonic Works from Eighteenth-Century Printed Sources,* ed. Ernest Warburton (*The Collected Works* 26) (New York, 1984), p. vii.
[46]Terry, *John Christian Bach,* pp. 94–95.

which there were many. Huberty in Paris and Hummel in Amsterdam quickly had their own plates engraved after the original publication, which further diffused its contents. Works dedicated to important personages usually required both title and dedication in French. Bach followed the custom, at least as far as the citation of his address. The set offers only works in the major mode and confined to the most common keys, in turn D, C, E♭, B♭, F, G. Each has three movements. Nos. 3 and 6 have *Andante* middle movements in tonic minor; otherwise, Bach chooses as contrasting tonality either the subdominant (Nos. 1 and 4) or the dominant (Nos. 3 and 5).

The Symphony in D, Op. 3 No. 1, opens with an *Allegro con spirito* in common time, the main theme of which is begun with a scalar rise through the octave. The answering rise of an octave upward on V is confined to the bass, while the violins deploy their tremolo on a pedal A and the winds sustain chords. Coming to a complete stop on the tonic before modulation, as here, seems to be an Italian practice.[47] A clear second theme as well as a closing theme in the dominant appear before the double bar in the middle with a repeat sign at m. 65. The second part stretches to m. 145 and lacks a repeat sign as well as a double reprise.

The *Andante* in 2/4 scored for strings only is pure cantilena for the first violin from beginning to end. Both parts are repeated and both end with a *cadence galante.* The melody moves within its two-octave range mostly by step, as if written for voice. It is typical of Bach to reach higher and higher for melodic climaxes as the movement unfolds.

Mozart's Symphony No. 7 in D (K. 45), composed in Vienna during January 1768, owes a particular debt to Bach's Op. 3 No. 1. Its opening *Molto Allegro* in common time comes to a full stop on eighth notes, just as in Bach, and there is further similarity in what follows, when the theme takes to the bass under a torrent of sixteenth-note pedals in the upper strings, while tracing a route around the circle of fifths. But it is in the finales of the two symphonies that the debt is most specific. Bach opens with a unisono theme clambering up and down the tonic triad in 6/8 at great speed (Example 9.6). The continuation is a soft murmur of even eighth notes up and down a conjunct third gradually rising in pitch and volume until it reaches a *fortissimo* statement of the opening motif in the bass, once on the tonic, and once on the dominant, with another torrent of pedal tones in the violins. The horns join the basses for the statement on the tonic. Mozart's finale is also very fast, beginning with a unison rise through the tonic triad and stepwise descent (Example 9.7). This is followed by a soft flurry of even tones, up

---

[47]This could bear on the question of which works were written before London. Manuscript copies of all the Op. 3 symphonies exist in Milan but they are thought to be later than the print rather than earlier. There were other manuscript symphonies of Bach in Milan not duplicated in London prints, as Burney attested when hearing them there in 1770. These were presumably some that Bach had written when in Milan.

EXAMPLE 9.6. *Christian Bach, Symphony in D, Op. 3 No. 1, Finale*

and down a conjunct third, in the violins. Mozart eventually puts the main idea in the bass with the violins sustaining a high pedal against it, but he waits until the movement has reached the secondary key of A to do so (which, of course, becomes tonic D in the reprise). Mozart's dotted rhythms in 2/4 must be integrated with his triplets when they occur together, and thus should be played as triplets from the beginning. Possibly Mozart knew Bach's symphony from hearing it in London in early 1765. He may have imagined that his notation conformed to Bach's. In any case the boy composer profited from his model, learning how to get brilliant chiaroscuro effects from the orchestra.

Bach took the symphony as a genre more seriously than he did the keyboard sonata, or even the keyboard concerto. Often displeased with his compositions, he was wary about publishing a good number of his symphonies that date from

EXAMPLE 9.7. *Mozart, Symphony No. 7 in D (K. 45), Finale*

around 1760, his last few years in Italy, and they remain in manuscript.[48] Under his personal supervision the set of six symphonies published in London as his Op. 3 achieved a nicely balanced variety in key, form, and content, either because he chose judiciously among his existing works or composed anew in order to reach this goal. The lengths to which he went in attempting to protect his works from being pirated can be read in the royal warrant of 1763.[49] It forbade the king's subjects from copying, reprinting, or publishing his works for a period of fourteen years. Furthermore, it interdicted importing or selling music of his published abroad, which gave him about as much protection as could be hoped for, there being none possible against foreign pirates. He had several links with the music publishers of Paris, who presumably remunerated him for new works.

Breitkopf in Leipzig offered many of Bach's symphonies for sale, beginning with those in his *Thematic Catalogue* of 1766, in which the incipits shown in Figure 9.4 appeared. They give an idea of what was circulating under the composer's name on the Continent and of the bibliographical complexities surrounding his symphonies. No. 1 in B♭ first survives in print in the set of six symphonies by Bach printed as Op. 6 by Hummel in Amsterdam in 1770. One critic has called it the weakest work in the set and one of his weakest symphonies overall.[50] As if to con-

---

[48]Several are gathered in Symphonies IV, *Eight Symphonic Works from Eighteenth-Century Manuscript Sources*, ed. Ernest Warburton (*The Collected Works* 29) (New York, 1989). The editor includes an important preface addressing the questions raised here about dating.

[49]Terry, *John Christian Bach*, p. 78.

[50]Fritz Tutenberg, *Die Sinfonik Johann Christian Bachs* (Wolfenbüttel, 1928), p. 275.

tradict him, another selected it for inclusion in an anthology.[51] Breitkopf offered it for sale again in his catalogue of 1770, and the publisher Markordt of Amsterdam reprinted it in his *Six simphonie* [sic] . . . *composées par Jean Chretien Bach: Opera 8.* Breitkopf's second incipit of 1766 refers to a work not published in any surviving print until *An Overture in Eight Parts* brought out by Welcker in London ca. 1770.

No. 3 in D is the overture to *Artaserse* (1761), first published by Vénier in Paris. No. 4 in F turns up in Markordt's Op. 8 No. 5 in E♭ and in Hummel's Op. 6 of 1770. No. 6 in D is a lost work that may not be by Bach at all—its incipit resembles none of his other symphonies.

FIGURE 9.4. Detail from Breitkopf's *Thematic Catalogue*, 1766.

Bach may have had no control over so fundamental a source as the set of six symphonies published by Hummel in 1770 as Op. 6. Unlike the well-planned Op. 3, Op. 6 has two symphonies that are in the same key, both No. 3 and No. 5 being in E♭, and rather alike, especially in that both have dull middle movements in the relative minor. The first movements of the set show Bach undecided about how to compress primary and secondary thematic material in the reprise so as to keep the seconda parte a reasonable length. In No. 5, a favorite with the public, to judge from the number of reprintings, he eliminated the second theme altogether from the reprise, although it was quite striking and its loss is thus regretted.[52] In other first movements (Nos. 2 and 3) there is only a partial return of the secondary material, and in No. 4 there is no clear secondary theme at all. Op. 6 has one extraordinary work, on the other hand. The last symphony of the set is the Symphony in g first offered to the public in Breitkopf's catalogue of 1769. With this impressive work, which has a fiery middle movement in the key of c minor, Bach in his only surviving minor-mode symphony joins a vogue for dark and passionate symphonic outbursts pioneered by Joseph Haydn in the late 1760s.[53]

Bach's very best symphonies almost put him alongside Haydn and Mozart at the highest level of symphonic practitioners the age could boast. His mediocre

---

[51]Johann Christian Bach, *Six Symphonic Works*, ed. Ernest Warburton (New York, 1983), pp. 117–45.
[52]Available in modern edition in *Six Symphonic Works*, pp. 147–77.
[53]*Haydn, Mozart*, pp. 285–94.

works, which he may never have cleared for publication, fall short of Boccherini's consistently high degree of inspiration. At the head of the list of Bach's best, along with the Symphony in g, are the symphonies for double orchestra in *Six Grand Overtures, Three for a Single, and Three for a Double Orchestre . . . Opera XVIII* published by William Foster in London ca. 1780. In one sense the latter revive the contrasting sonorous bodies of the old concerto grosso, which never lacked partisans in England. Viewed from this perspective, the works were an ingenious bow to a local tradition. Three other works derive from Bach's overtures to *Endimione, Temistocle,* and *Lucio Silla* for Mannheim. The *Endimione* overture goes back to 1772 and appears to be Bach's first essay in the double-orchestra genre, which enjoyed great popularity in London, there being no fewer than twenty-three mentions of performances of such works by Bach between 1772 and 1781.[54]

The Symphony in E♭ for double orchestra begins with both bands stating a unisono theme in dotted rhythm, so jagged and forceful it could have been invented by Emanuel Bach (Example 9.8). The running passage in sixteenth notes that follows in Orchestra I could also be Emanuel's, especially in the way it overlaps with a return of the main motif in Orchestra II. There is a third distinct idea,

EXAMPLE 9.8. *Christian Bach, Symphony in E♭, Op. 18 No. 1, I*

rising softly by step before the modulation, after which a distinct contrasting theme in gavotte rhythm is heard, framed before and after by the main motif, in the latter case by overlapping.

The movement works so well partly because of the sharp contrast between the downbeat-oriented main motif and the dancelike gavotte motion of the main secondary theme. Its broad outlines permit a full development section, during

[54]Johann Christian Bach, *Seven Symphonic Works,* ed. David Wyn Jones (*The Collected Works* 28) (New York, 1989), p. viii.

which the gavotte theme appears in minor, and a full reprise, attaining an ample 170 measures in all. Ending softly with a mere *pianissimo* whisper invites attention to what follows directly (*attacca*), a lovely *Andante* in 2/4, delicately outlined by continual triplet sixteenth notes in the first violins of Orchestra I. Bach chooses the key of B$^\flat$ and gives oboes to his first band, flutes to his second. The interplay between the two groups reaches a state of quick repartée in the jocular finale, *Allegro* in 6/8 time.

Fifteen orchestral works are extant that belong to the type loosely defined as symphonies concertantes. Only three were printed, all in Paris, where they were given this title. Italian or Italian-trained composers more often used plain concertante, concertone, or just concerto in designating such works, and Bach uses the last in labeling several pieces that remained in manuscript. Returning from Mannheim in the late fall of 1772 or early 1773, he may have stopped in Paris. Two excellent violinists there, the brothers Simon and Pierre Leduc, played the solos in a symphonie concertante by Bach at the Concert Spirituel on 4 April 1773. This is surely the excellent work in E$^\flat$ with two solo violins printed by Sieber in Paris the same year. The *Mercure de France* reported that they opened the second half of the concert with it: "MM le Duc frères ouvrirent la second partie par un concertante de Bach chantant et bien coupé."[55] The last two words regard the long and regular melodic periods of this exquisite work in three movements. In the opening *Allegro* the first solo violin sings by itself a theme still in the tonic, while the second enters with another theme, after the modulation to the dominant. Another delight is the Symphonie Concertante in A for violin and cello solo, a work that is possibly Bach's most French in style. It has only two movements, sharing the same key, the preferred form in Paris. The second is an ingratiating Rondeau that has an episode in the minor mode resembling Rameau's "La Timide" in the *Pièces de clavecin en concerts* (Paris, 1741).

Bach's most imposing symphonie concertante is one in B$^\flat$ that was not published, thought to be his latest.[56] The solo instruments are violin, oboe, cello, and pianoforte. To accommodate the four soloists Bach enlarges the movements considerably. The opening *Allegro* in common time stretches to 317 measures, a record for him. An *Adagio sostenuto* in E$^\flat$ and in common time yields to a *Rondo Allegretto* in 2/4 in which there is a lot of Alberti bass for the pianoforte. The grander scale on which the whole work was planned and executed gives an indication where Bach was headed in the last years of his life.

---

[55]Johann Christian Bach, *Eight Symphonies Concertantes,* ed. Richard Maunder (*The Collected Works* 30) (New York: 1985), viii. The work in question is Maunder's No. 6.
[56]Johann Christian Bach, *Seven Symphonies Concertantes,* ed. Richard Maunder (*The Collected Works* 31) (New York: 1985), No. 9. No. 3 is a unique example among the fifteen works in the genre of a score in Bach's hand. Maunder uses physical evidence relating it to other autographs of Bach's sacred music written in Italy to show that it dates from around 1760. If this is true, the genre was being widely cultivated before it became such a vogue in Paris.

The Piano Concerto in B♭, Op. 13 No. 4, is a particularly attractive example of Bach's most mature style. Haydn admired it to the point of making an arrangement of it for keyboard solo.[57] The opening *Allegro* begins with a potent unison theme that is far removed from the composer's usual frills. Consider in this respect the opening sixteen measures, which fall into four melodic segments (Example 9.9). The first, *forte*, announces a terse motif, a descending triad that fastens on repeating the return up to the fifth. The second, *piano* and accompanied, is begun by an upbeat in sixteenth notes, declaims in four even quarter-note beats, then reverts to the fixation of mm. 2–4, enhanced by dotted rhythm. The

EXAMPLE 9.9. *Christian Bach, Piano Concerto in B♭, Op. 13 No. 4, I*

[57]Hans-Bernd Schmitz, *Die Klavierkonzerte Johann Christian Bachs* (Würzburg, 1981), p. 215. (Not in Hoboken's catalogue.)

third, *forte,* takes up the sixteenth-note upbeats of m. 4 and extends it backward and forward as a rocketing scale up to the high tonic, after a nod to the rhythm of two eighth notes and a quarter note from m. 2; the dotted-rhythm version of the same (as in m. 6) tops the ascent and leads to a welter of sixteenth-note figures descending over precadential harmony. Failure of the melody to reach the lower tonic in m. 12 allows a fourth segment, divided between *piano* and *forte,* covering new melodic ground (a very galant raised tonic degree included) while reverting to the four even beats of m. 5 and repeating the move up to high B♭, leading this time to a half-cadence. The material is rich and tightly integrated. It suffices the composer for much of the *Allegro,* but he is generous with new melodic ideas as well. Bach was clearly moving in the same direction as Mozart, and moreover the Mozart of the first great Piano Concerto, K. 271 in E♭ of 1777. After the soloist has played the orchestral material quoted, the piano launches a new theme in the dominant, F, beginning with high C and a rapid fall down a fifth. Mozart does something similar when beginning the second theme on high C in the first movement of his last Piano Concerto in B♭, K. 595 of 1791, with the difference that he changes to the minor mode. Bach does this too, but he reserves the minor-mode treatment of the figure for its recurrence in the reprise. Both composers prefer modulatory excursions with passage work for the soloists rather than motivic development for the area that begins the seconda parte. Bach prepares his double reprise with a long pedal on the dominant, with return to one of the lyric themes from the exposition. There is a *fermata* just before the reprise, which gives the soloist an opportunity to improvise an *Eingang,* but none at its end, where the Mozartian concerto required a cadenza.

The second movement of Bach's concerto does provide opportunity for the pianist to improvise a cadenza at the end. It is an *Andante* in common time and in E♭ that foreshadows the wistful, elegiac mood of Paisiello's Rosina in her revery and Mozart's "Porgi, amor" for the same Rosina as Countess Almaviva. The return to B♭ for the finale is begun by the piano solo, an *Andante con moto* in 3/4 time that is nothing other than the lovely Scottish song "The yellow-haired Laddie." One of the many delights of folk songs from the British Isles is the way the melody, after soaring to what sounds like the highest tone or peak, then soars still higher, as happens in "Laddie," which is treated as a theme and variations. Before the tune is finished, there are some endearing "Scotch snaps" over subdominant harmony. Bach's own melodic invention profited from tunes such as this, both as to the snaps and the shaping according to melodic peaks (a good example is the soaring melody Mozart borrowed in one of his early concertos adapted from Bach's keyboard sonatas).[58] It may be such qualities that account for what Georg Joseph

---

[58]*Haydn, Mozart,* p. 687.

Vogler perceived as a "cool" and "bracing" legacy of English melody in Bach, alongside his German, Italian, and French legacies.

The English piano was being developed into a powerful instrument during the 1770s. It took no less to execute the long *crescendo* passages Bach requires of the soloist in the concerto just discussed. The master builders were John Merlin, John Broadwood, and Americus Backus, also the Saxon emigré Johannes Zumpe, whose specialty was the spinnet. Burney gives Bach the main credit for this revolution in taste.

> After the arrival of John Chr. Bach in this country, and the establishment of his concert, in conjunction with Abel, all the harpsichord makers tried their mechanical powers at piano-fortes; but the first attempts were always on the large size, till Zumpé, a German, who had long worked under Shudi, constructed a small piano-forte of the shape and size of a virginal, of which the tone was very sweet, and the touch, with a little use, equal to any degree of rapidity. These from their low price, and the convenience of their form, as well as power of expression, suddenly grew into such a favour, that there was scarcely a house in the kingdom where a keyed-instrument had ever had admission, but was supplied with one of Zumpé's piano-fortes, for which there was nearly as great a call in France as in England. In short, he could not make them fast enough to gratify the craving of the public.[59]

Bach purchased a square piano by Zumpe for 50 pounds in June 1768. On 2 June 1768 he played the first public solo performance on a piano in England. His concertos of Op. 13 from the later 1770s presume a grand piano.

Another Saxon composer who promoted the instrument in English public concerts was Johann Samuel Schroeter, a protégé of Bach's. His family, consisting of father, sister, and younger brother, after concertizing widely on the Continent, arrived in London, where they all participated in a Bach-Abel concert on 2 May 1772. Only Johann remained in London. His published collections of sonatas and concertos advanced the cause of the pianoforte, and he replaced Bach not only as the public's favorite pianist but also as music master of Queen Charlotte. He died young, in 1788, his widow Rebecca later becoming a student and intimate of Haydn in London. Mozart wrote cadenzas for three of Schroeter's piano concertos. Nevertheless it remains clear that, in genres involving the keyboard, no composer was more important to Mozart than Christian Bach.[60]

Leopold Mozart actually urged the model of Bach upon his son when the latter was struggling to make a living in Paris during the summer of 1778. In his letter dated Salzburg, 13 August 1778, he advised composing some short, easy, and popular pieces expressly for publication.

[59] "Harpsichord," in *The Cyclopaedia*, ed. Abraham Rees, vol. 17.
[60] John Irving, *Mozart's Piano Sonatas: Contexts, Sources, Style* (Cambridge, 1997), pp. 24–29.

> Did Bach in London ever publish anything but small-scale works? The *small* is *great* if written in a natural, flowing and easy style, and soundly composed. Creating in this manner is more difficult than all those complicated harmonic progressions, unintelligible to most, and those melodies that are difficult to perform. Did Bach lower himself by such work? Not at all! Good writing [der gute Saz], order, *il filo* [the thread]—these distinguish the master from the bungler even in small works.

Leopold's evaluation of Bach, with its emphasis on natural and easy discourse, one idea leading to the next as expressed by *il filo,* was quite similar to what Schubart had to say about Bach in his *Ideen,* although there could have been no connection between them. Praising Bach as a master of all musical styles, he singled out the serious operas for their "natural flow of thought and lovely melodies" (p. 202).

SACCHINI AND OTHER RIVALS

Bach was five years younger than Sacchini and must have known the Italian master as early as 1756 when they were both in Naples. Recall that Sacchini was chosen over Bach to set *Andromaca* for the San Carlo in May 1761. At the same time, Gennaro Manna retired as maestro of the Loreto conservatory. He was succeeded by Pietro Antonio Gallo, while Sacchini was appointed vice maestro. The following year Sacchini was granted leave to go to Venice to write operas. He was so successful in Venice and other operatic centers that he gave up his conservatory post and lived for several years as an itinerant composer and teacher of singing. In 1768 he settled in Venice and was deputized as music director of the Derelitti conservatory (Ospedaletto) for Traetta, who was on leave in Russia. He continued to supply operas to a number of Italian cities and in early 1770 had successes in Germany as well, at Munich and Stuttgart.

In the fall of 1772 Sacchini took up the post of house composer at the King's Theatre. For the next nine years he was the dominant figure in London's operatic life, eclipsing all other composers, including Bach. He brought on average two operas of his own before the public every year, not always new works but new to London, and largely rewritten for the singers on hand if they were older works. One of his older works that had a great success was *Il Cidde* on a libretto by Giovacchino Pizzi for Rome in 1769. Bottarelli revised the libretto for London and it led off the procession of Sacchini's operas in January 1773.

Burney first encountered Sacchini in Venice during the summer of 1770. He rated very highly both his sacred music and the singing of it at the Derelitti under the composer's direction. In Venice, he claimed, only Galuppi surpassed Sacchini. And he made so bold as to assay a ranking.

> Were I to name the living composers of Italy for the stage, according to my idea of their merit, it would be in the following order: Jomelli, Galuppi, Piccini, and Sacchini. It is, however, difficult to decide which of the two composers first-mentioned, has

merited most from the public; Jomelli's works are full of great and noble ideas, treated with taste and learning; Galuppi's abound in fancy, fire, and feeling; Piccini has far surpassed all his contemporaries in the comic stile; and Sacchini is the most promising in the serious.

Sacchini's arias were heard in London pasticcios as early as 1765. Burney's praise of Sacchini's *Salve regina* heard in Venice sets the tone for his later appraisals: "it was new, spirited, and full of ingenious contrivances for the instruments, which always *said* something interesting without disturbing the voice."

In his *History,* Burney looked back upon Sacchini's reign in London during the 1770s as something of a golden age.

> Antonio Sacchini, of Naples, arrived in England in 1772, after having composed for all the great theatres in Italy and Germany, with increasing success. And here he not only supported the high reputation he had acquired on the Continent, but vanquished the natural enemies of his talents in England. His operas of the *Cid* and *Tamerlano* were equal, if not superior, to any musical dramas I had heard in any part of Europe.

Tamerlano was the composer's second opera for London, brought forth in May 1773. Both works were quickly followed by the publication of *Favourite Songs* anthologies, as were most of Sacchini's London operas. Among composers there was only one "natural enemy" on Sacchini's level in England at the time, namely, Bach. Burney may also mean that Sacchini was able to tame the notoriously arrogant behavior of the Italian singers at the King's Theatre. Burney goes on to vaunt Sacchini's treatment of individual voices, bringing the best out of all, even secondary singers. He concludes with more general observations on the two operas of 1773.

> Each of these dramas was so *entire,* so masterly, yet so new and natural, that there was nothing left for criticism to censure, though innumerable beauties to point out and admire. It is evident that this composer had a taste so exquisite, and so totally free from pedantry, that he was frequently new without effort; never thinking of himself or his fame for any particular excellence, but totally occupied with the ideas of the poet, and the propriety, consistency, and effect of the whole drama. His accompaniments, though always rich and ingenious, never call off attention from the voice, but, by a constant *transparency,* the principal melody is rendered distinguishable through all the contrivance of imitative and picturesque design in the instruments.

If he was as occupied with the poem as Burney claims, it is a pity that he had such hacks to deal with as the house poets of the King's Theatre. Of the more adventurous new librettists on the Continent, they took advantage only of Giovanni de Gamerra, whose *Erifile* was set by Sacchini in 1778. Sacchini had set Gamerra's *Armida* for Milan just before going to London, where it was revised as *Rinaldo* in

1780. At the end of his London years Sacchini was possibly choosing the poet or libretto himself, a prerogative normally belonging to the theater manager.

Burney was not blind to Sacchini's human failings. In his article on the composer for Rees's *Cyclopaedia* he begins with a lurid tale of how, fulfilling his first operatic commission, purportedly at Milan, Sacchini fell in love with the prima donna and neglected his compositional duties. There might be some truth in this tale, but Sacchini did not, as far as we know, compose for Milan until *Armida* during the carnival of 1772. That he was addicted to wine and women as well as song cannot be denied. His dissipations led to gout, which left him incapable at times of directing operas from the harpsichord and also slowed his creative work. Nevertheless, his powers of invention in London remained supreme and were certainly not "beginning to diminish," as has been claimed.[61]

Sacchini's operas before London are relatively well preserved in scores. The London scores have disappeared, apparently consumed in the fires that destroyed the King's Theatre on 17 June 1789. An exception is the comic opera *L'amore soldato* of 1778, a score of which was printed. From the serious operas we have only the *Favourite Songs,* and these are incomplete in several senses. As a rule they omit almost everything but arias. In the *Favourite Songs in the Opera "Il Cid,"* there are a few obbligato recitatives and one SATB chorus, the last number, which is an impressive *ombra* lament in E♭ with flutes, clarinets, horns, and bassoons. Altogether there are thirteen numbers included, plus the overture (in keyboard score), which cannot represent more than about half of the set numbers. Other publications of this type can have as few as eight numbers, as is the case with *Tamerlano.* Burney praised Sacchini in the *History* for his choruses and explained at the same time one of many deficiencies at the King's Theatre.

> The late exquisite composer Sacchini, finding how fond the English were of Handel's oratorio choruses, introduced solemn and elaborate choruses into some of his operas; but though excellent in their kind, they never had a good effect; the mixture of English singers with the Italian, as well as the awkward figure they cut, as actors, joined to the difficulty of getting their parts by heart, rendered these compositions ridiculous, which in still life would have been admirable.

Given these circumstances it is no wonder that both Bach and Sacchini wrote their greatest operas for Paris, where choral acting and singing were both taken seriously.

---

[61]Price, Milhous, and Hume, *Italian Opera in Late Eighteenth-Century London,* 1: 52. The insularity of the authors reaches the extreme (p. 276) of mistaking Monaco (which had no opera at the time) for Munich, where Sacchini composed two operas in early 1770. Their view of the composer is so limited they probably are unaware of what he went on to accomplish in Paris.

Possibly the choral situation improved at the King's Theatre. In any case Sacchini kept including choruses in his operas. Another survives in the *Favourite Songs in the Opera "Montezuma"* (1775) and is also a piece in E♭ of an *ombra* nature. A more complicated opera still was *Rinaldo* (1780), which house poets Antonio Andrei and Francesco Badini adapted from an *Armida* by Jacopo Durandi. It required not only choruses but three ballets integrated with the singing. The title role was sung by Gasparo Pacchiarotti, whom the dancing Furies handled so roughly on stage that he complained of his bruises.[62] William Napier, who usually brought out the *Favourite Songs* after an opera as successful as this one, failed to do so. Robert Bremner a year later published *The Favourite Songs in the Opera Rinaldo Composed by Sigr. Sacchini,* which includes several pieces that Sacchini wrote for the revival. In the absence of Pacchiarotti, the title role was taken by the Mannheim castrato Roncaglia, who had sung for Sacchini a decade earlier in Munich. Rinaldo's big rondo in Act II, "Dolce speme" was a two-tempo piece, *Andantino* in 2/4 leading to *Allegro* in 4/4. For Roncaglia Sacchini made a totally new setting in the same key of G and the same form. The vocal demands of the two pieces differ little. It was perhaps a matter of pride for the second singer to have his own rondo, a type of piece in which Sacchini excelled, as Piccinni stated in his obituary.

Sacchini wrote one of the loveliest of his many rondos in his last London opera, *Mitridate* (1781). It was for the primo uomo role of Farnace sung by Roncaglia, of whom Burney wrote in his *History* that he "had an elegant face and figure; a sweet toned voice, a chaste and well disciplined style of singing; hazarded nothing and was always in tune." Of the three requisites of a complete stage singer—pathos, grace, and execution—Burney continued, "he was in perfect possession of only the second." Sacchini capitalizes on his forte in his setting of the rondo "Resta in pace amato bene" (Example 9.10). The key of A, a favorite with the composer to express sentiments of love, enters softly on the second half of the measure, like a *gavotte tendre* (gavotte rhythm was very frequent in the vocal rondo). The first violins double the melody, while the seconds weave a web of murmuring sixteenth notes or sustain when the treble takes over the quicker notes. The bass is unobtrusive but nevertheless makes a statement by becoming legato in m. 12 and introducing a chromatic rise that creates a false relation with the treble. Possibly Roncaglia lacked enough breath control for the execution of long roulades. After the half cadence in m. 13 the theme recommences as expected, but without the voice, conveying the effect that the lover is too choked with emotion to continue. In reshaping the treble so as to reach a full cadence,

---

[62]Ibid., 1: 239.

EXAMPLE 9.10. *Sacchini*, Mitridate, *Rondo*

Sacchini takes the voice up to F# for another descending third in mm. 15–16, accompanied by the first violins in unison, then takes the voice up to the high tonic by itself, from which perch the descent by disjunct thirds into the cadence begins. Next the violins seize upon the high A with a dynamic accent followed by a new rhythmic figure. Here the orchestra proposes with its harmonies I⁶ - V⁷, which the voice calmly answers, supported by a sustained chord, "Resta in pace,"

the rhythm the same as the rondo theme. Resolution, V^7 - I, nicely conveys the idea of "resting in peace." The process is repeated to the following words of the text, after which the voice, doubled in thirds by the strings, rises and falls in little waves melodically related to m. 12, each slurred pair being separated by tiny rests, a sobbing effect that breaks up the word into "con - ser - va – mi." The strings stop on the tonic triad but the voice goes higher, reaching F# over subdominant harmony by the sounding of a chromatically raised fifth, a move so consummate it approaches Mozart. When the two young men come back in their original personae in the second finale of *Così fan tutte,* Mozart deploys the same rise, fermata and all.

The rest of Sacchini's "Resta in pace" is equally fine and worthy of study. In the second episode the composer shows his modulatory skills, taking the music to the tonic minor, then to C major, nicely attuned to the text and its outbursts of suffering at the thought of leaving the loved one. The following harmonic preparation for the return of the lovely rondo theme is equally fine. This piece alone should convince a sensitive listener what a treasure London was losing to Paris in the person of Sacchini.

Several other Italian composers tried their fortunes in London during Bach's time. Although Piccinni refused Giardini's invitation to replace Bach, his *La buona figliuola,* first performed in London in 1766 and almost continuosly thereafter, was the greatest operatic success of all. Pietro Guglielmi, Sacchini's predecessor for five years at the King's Theatre, had his biggest success there with another opera buffa, *I viaggiatori ridicoli* (1768), on a libretto Bottarelli adapted after Goldoni. It was the most frequently performed opera after *Buona figliuola.* Traetta returned from Russia to his post in Venice in 1775, then took another leave in order to accept an offer from London, for which he composed the opera seria *Germondo* on a text by Goldoni, first performed at the King's Theatre in January 1777. This was followed by another seria, *Telemaco,* on a text by Zaccaria de Seriman. The first was given the distinction of being excerpted in a *Favourite Songs,* but not the second. Burney in his *History* explains why the composer did not remain in London: "Though an able master of great reputation, he arrived here too late: for Sacchini had already taken possession of our hearts, and so firmly established himself in the public favour, that he was not to be supplanted by a composer in the same style, neither so young, so graceful, or so fanciful as himself." By the "same style" Burney may mean only that they were both trained in Naples, indeed at the same conservatory, Santa Maria di Loreto, and by the same principal teacher, Durante. Traetta was only three years older than Sacchini but he may have looked much older because of the ill health that had begun to plague him in Russia. He died in Venice on 6 April 1779.

The new composers at the King's Theatre after 1777 were of lesser stature than Guglielmi, Sacchini, and Traetta and cannot be considered Bach's rivals with respect to musical quality. They included Ferdinando Bertoni, Francesco Bianchi, Pasquale Anfossi, and the soprano castrato Venanzio Rauzzini, who created a scandal by accusing Sacchini of plagiarism, a charge that Burney dismissed. Whatever semblance of order in the theater Sacchini had been able to impose was weakened by increasingly feeble and incompetent management. The result was an artistic and financial decline that could not be arrested, even by the successes of Jean-Georges Noverre and his ballets.

Carl Friedrich Abel, Bach's friend and partner, was his rival as a symphonist, but not his equal. He was born in Cöthen in 1723 and may have studied with members of the Bach family in Leipzig. By the age of twenty he was employed as a viola da gamba player in the court orchestra at Dresden under Hasse. Like several other Saxon musicians, he fled Dresden in 1757–58 to escape the siege of the city by the Prussians. Within a year he was in London, where he would remain. A set of six symphonies by him, presumably composed earlier, was published as his Op. 1 in London in 1760.[63] These are in the most commonly used symphonic keys, all major, and methodically arrayed: B♭, C, D, E♭, F, G. All are in three movements, which are generally briefer and less Italianate than those in Bach's Op. 3 (Bach chose the same six keys, but not in ascending sequence). Comparisons must have been made by the auditors at their joint concerts. Bach was much the superior as a melodist and in his rhythmic élan.[64] While Bach soared, Abel tended to plod along. Schubart in his *Ideen* dismissed Abel as less genial than industrious ("mehr Kunstfleiss als Genie").

Another refugee from Dresden was Johann Christian Fischer, famous for his oboe playing and oboe concertos. He was introduced by Bach and Abel in the same concert in 1768 in which Bach first played a piano in public. The three Germans became intimates of Thomas Gainsborough, who also played the gamba. He painted marvelous portraits of all three. Abel was portrayed seated by his gamba, pen in hand; Fischer, standing in front of his oboe, pen in hand, leaning on a large keyboard instrument that bears the inscription "Merlin Londini fecit." Bach sat for a portrait at the request of Padre Martini (see Plate XI.)

Gainsborough executed two closely related portraits of Bach, one for the sitter, one for shipment to Bologna. The former remained in England and is the source of our reproduction. In his letter dated London, 22 May 1776, Bach wrote Martini, "You do me too much honour in desiring to place my portrait among persons so celebrated, of whose company I do not think my own worthy. Still, my

---

[63]Carl Friedrich Abel, *Six Symphonies, opus 1,* ed. Franklin B. Zimmerman (The Symphony, 1720–1840, Series E, 2) (New York, 1983).
[64]Stefan Kunze, *Die Sinfonie im 18. Jahrhundert: Von der Opernsinfonie zur Konzertsinfonie* (Laaber, 1993), pp. 213–31, offers an overview of the symphonies by Bach and Abel. The author's untimely death rendered this work uneven and its coverage spotty—Boccherini, for instance, is missing.

respect for your commands compels me to obey without question. The portrait is already finished, and only awaits an opportunity to come to you, along with some music."[65] The right opportunity did not arise until two years later, when primo uomo Roncaglia was traveling to Italy after the final performances of Bach's *La clemenza di Scipione*. Meanwhile, Martini had sent a letter to Burney asking him to remind Bach of the portrait. In his letter dated London, 28 July 1778, Bach wrote Martini, "I have placed in Signore Roncaglia's charge an excellent portrait of myself by one of our best painters. He is passing through Bologna and, no doubt, will deliver it into your hands. I beg you graciously to accept it as a small token of my heavy debt to you."[66]

The year before Bach sat for Gainsborough, Sacchini was portrayed by Sir Joshua Reynolds.[67] The similarities between the portraits of the two musicians suggests a little friendly rivalry between the two great artists. Reynolds chose to depict his subject in half-length, with a dark background that makes a striking contrast with the illuminated face and neck ruff. Sacchini, a handsome man with rather thin, angular features, is shown looking off to the right into the distance, as if inspired. Gainsborough also chose a half-length pose and dark background against which Bach's broad and kindly face is luminous, as is the white neck ruff, the main difference being that Bach shows both hands and holds music pages in his right hand. He gazes off into the distance to the left. The delicacy of the modeling and the airy lightness with which Gainsborough depicts the fabrics make a wonderful match with Bach's supreme command of everything that is light and graceful in the modern music of his time.

Bach and Sacchini alike were fond of a melodic type that moved in moderate triple meter, like a minuet, with treble descending a conjunct third, in parallel thirds, from the fifth degree, against a bass rising a conjunct third from the tonic. This very smooth progression occurs in the earliest works both composers wrote in London, the implication being that they brought it with them from Italy. Sacchini used it in both of his first operas for London. Bach wrote one of his gems of this kind as the central movement of his overture to Galuppi's setting of Goldoni's opera buffa *La calamita de' cuori* (The magnet of hearts) (Example 9.11a). With great economy Bach makes the treble's descending third the bass in m. 2, then brings it back in m. 4 in the treble, reharmonized as a weak cadence. Other conjunct thirds (rising) slip into the treble in m. 3 and into the bass (across the bar line from m. 3 to m. 4). Characteristic of Bach, besides the smoothness and utter economy, are the tinge of chromatic color in m. 2 and a vii[7] chord in m. 3. Bach's overture was widely diffused by prints in London and Paris.

[65]Terry, *John Christian Bach*, p. 151.
[66]Ibid., p. 160.
[67]Reproduced in Price, Milhous, and Hume, *Italian Opera*, vol. 1, plate 9.

EXAMPLE 9.11.
a. Christian Bach, *La calamita de' cuori*, Overture (1762)

b. Mozart, *Acht Menuette*, No. 4 (K. 315a) (1773)

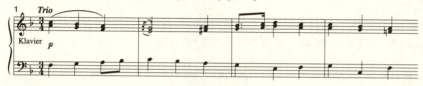

c. Mozart, *La finta giardiniera* (1775), Aria, "Dolce d'amor"

d. Mozart, Piano Concerto in A (K. 414) (1782), II

Mozart was also partial to this *Andantino grazioso*. He used it in the trio of a minuet for keyboard in the *Acht Menuette* (K. 315a) that probably dates from 1773 (Example 9.11b). He did not follow Bach beyond the first four bars, but in these he changed almost nothing. In 1775 he made the same incipit flower into a beautiful declaration of love in an aria sung by the castrato Tommaso Consoli, who took the seria part of Ramiro in *La finta giardiniera* (Example 9.11c). The text is "Dolce d'amor compagna speranza lusinghieri" (Agreeable hope, sweet love's companion). It helps interpret the amorous affect clinging to all versions of this graceful minuet. The dance's particular rhythm was reinforced by the three "knocking" eighth note upbeats in m. 3. Mozart came back to Bach's theme one more time, in 1782, at the very beginning of which year Bach died in London. The *Andante* of the Piano Concerto in A (K. 414) reverts even to Bach's original key of D (Example 9.11d). At the same time it picks up the three "knocking" eighth notes from the aria. Mozart makes Bach's theme a little richer by deploying a full, four-member vii^7 chord in m. 3, and a full V^7 with double appoggiatura preparation at the beginning of m. 4.

In the summer of 1778, Bach and Mozart met for the last time in Paris, where Bach had come to listen to the singers who would perform his *Amadis de Gaule.* Mozart wrote movingly about him in the letter to his father dated Saint Germain, 27 August 1778: "I love him (as you know) with all my heart and respect him highly; and as for him, there is no doubt that he has praised me, not only to my face, but to others also, not in an exaggerated way like some, but seriously, truly." Bach's praises probably helped persuade Elector Carl Theodore to commission *Idomeneo* from Mozart two years later. In a letter dated Vienna, 10 April 1782, Mozart wrote his father, "You will surely know already that the English Bach is dead? A pity for the world of music!" The *Andante* of K. 414 can be read as a final tribute to the composer Mozart considered his mentor. It is an irony of history that Mozart has so thoroughly eclipsed two composers of such eminence as Christian Bach and Sacchini, who in their lifetimes eclipsed him.

Paisiello in Saint Petersburg

RUSSIA UNDER THE TSARINAS

Peter I (the Great), who ruled Russia for thirty-six years beginning in 1689, was determined to open up his country, hitherto closed to most outside influences. He sought commercial, diplomatic, and even artistic links with Western Europe. He was the first Russian ruler to travel there, visiting, among other places, Dresden, Amsterdam, London, and Vienna as an incognito observer in 1697–98. He founded Saint Petersburg with the idea not just of opening a window on the Baltic toward Western Europe but also of rivaling its capitals. Since Russian architects were hardly able to build a great modern city, skilled though they were at constructing churches of wood, he called to his service numerous architects and builders from the West. Jean-Baptiste Le Blond was responsible for laying out Saint Petersburg on a grid system, with canals. Bartolomeo Rastrelli, born in Paris and the son of an Italian sculptor, became the city's leading architect.

Peter's interests in the shipbuilding and military weaponry he had observed abroad were colored by martial ambitions for his country. Determined to form a modern army and navy with which to challenge two hostile neighbors, Sweden and Turkey, he eventually made war on both, with ultimate success. Little interested in music per se, he decided nevertheless that his Western-style armies needed Western musicians. These he imported, mostly from Germany. Not until the reigns of his successors did Western music begin to make serious inroads at the Russian court.

One of Peter's legacies was a law that gave the ruler the right to name his successor. His only surviving son, Alexis, married a German princess, Charlotte of Brunswick. A magnet for intriguers who wanted to overthrow or murder his father, Alexis died in prison, a fate not uncommon for males of the Romanov dynasty. Peter himself died in 1725 without naming his successor. The palace guard elevated his second wife to the throne as Catherine I, but she lived only two years, naming as her successor a grandson of Peter I, a boy of twelve, as Peter II. He lasted only three years and was replaced by a niece of Peter I, Anna, who reigned from 1730 to 1740.

Empress Anna was not a strong ruler in comparison with her uncle, but she did much to lay the foundations for Russia's future greatness in music.[68] She married Duke Frederick of Courland and surrounded herself with German statesmen who ran the government. Anna requested from Augustus the Strong the loan of a troupe of actors and musicians who would celebrate her coronation in Moscow. Augustus accorded a year's leave of absence to a company of twenty-two actors and musicians under the direction of Tommaso Ristori, a commedia dell'arte troupe that had split its time between Warsaw and Dresden. In addition to plays, the troupe was able to offer comic intermezzos in music, and before they departed they put on the *commedia per musica Calandro* by Tommaso's son Giovanni, in December 1731. *Calandro* is generally considered the first Italian opera performed in Russia—a harbinger of many to follow. The Ristori company visited Saint Petersburg on their way back to Poland. Anna understood some French but no Italian. She ordered that Russian translations of the plays and libretti be made and printed, establishing a precedent. Often there were translations into both Russian and French.

Even before the Ristoris left, Anna sent Johann Hübner to recruit replacements at Hamburg, where six singers and nine instrumentalists were hired. Then Hübner went to Italy to hire more musicians in 1732. His efforts yielded results. In 1733 he secured the services of an excellent violinist from Venice, Luigi Madonis, who remained at the Russian court for many years. In 1738 he published a set of suites for violin, cello, and continuo in Saint Petersburg and dedicated them to Anna.

In 1734 Anna sent the violinist Pietro Mira to Venice to recruit an opera troupe and an Italian maestro di cappella. This foray resulted in the hiring of an experienced Neapolitan composer, Francesco Araia, as maestro. He reached Saint

---

[68]This and the following paragraphs are indebted to R. Aloys Mooser, *Annales de la musique et des musiciens en Russie au XVIIIe siècle*, 3 vols. (Geneva, 1948–51).

Petersburg in 1735 and was assigned an annual salary of 1,220 rubles, plus lodging and other perquisites. By the following year he had sufficient forces under his control to offer an opera seria, *La forza dell'amore e dell'odio,* which he had composed for Milan in 1734. He followed this with new serious operas, setting Francesco Silvani's *Il fino Nino, overo Semiramide* (1737) and Metastasio's *Artaserse* (1738). Comic opera also flourished, at least that of the intermezzo type. Girolamo Bon came to Saint Petersburg in 1735 as scenic designer, along with his wife Rosa Ruvinetti Bon, a famous actress and singer in comic intermezzos. Her longtime partner Domenico Chricchi also came to Russia, but they did not remain long before moving on to Dresden and Berlin. Among the instrumentalists hired in the mid-1730s was Domenico Dall'Oglio, violinist, a prolific composer of instrumental music; his cello-playing brother Giuseppe came with him. Domenico remained many years and married a daughter of Madonis.

The acculturation of Italian music in Russia was a multidirectional affair. From the 1730s on Russians were sent to Italy to study. These were young serfs who later returned to swell the number of trained singers and instrumentalists in the imperial capital. The first music school in Russia was founded under Anna in January 1740. The same year Araia was sent to Italy with the task of recruiting additional forces for the opera troupe. Anna died in 1740, but Araia remained in favor. When he returned to Saint Petersburg in 1742 he brought performers and a production team, including poet and librettist Giuseppe Bonecchi. He went on writing operas and directing them until 1755. That year he produced *Cephalus and Procris,* a serious opera sung totally in Russian, to a libretto by Alexander Sumarokov, another first for the court.

Anna was succeeded by Elizabeth Petrovna (daughter and youngest child of Peter I), who had many of the strengths and passions of her father. Raised by a Parisian governess, she spoke fluent French. During her reign of twenty years she particularly favored her French theatrical troupes. Like her father, she was a great builder. Chief architect Bartolomeo Rastrelli worked on several vast buildings at her behest: the Smolny convent (begun in 1748), the rebuilding and enlarging of Peterhof (1746–58), the palace of Tsarskoye Selo (1749–56), and the Winter Palace in Saint Petersburg (1754–68), also called the Hermitage, his masterpiece (Figure 9.5).

The contingent of Italian musicians at court continued in favor under Elizabeth. In fact one of them, Madonis, was of sufficient stature to participate in the plot that placed her on the throne, deposing the legitimate heir designated by Anna, Ivan VI, an infant who was imprisoned and later murdered, not under Elizabeth but under her successor Catherine in 1764.

Elizabeth was crowned in Moscow on 25 April 1742, an event celebrated by a performance of Hasse's *Clemenza di Tito,* on the Metastasian libretto favored for coronations. Moscow was still the legal and ecclesiastical capital. Tradition dictated that coronations take place there. Madonis contributed arias to Hasse's

letter from Naples to Madame D'Epinay dated 27 July 1776 describing Paisiello's departure: "he will be a great resource this winter for Grimm, who is mad for his music, and rightly so."[81]

Paisiello, thirteen years younger than Traetta, was thirty-six years of age when he left for Russia. He was offered a three-year contract at 3,000 rubles per annum plus travel expenses. In order to accept, he had to cancel an agreement to compose the festival opera for the San Carlo (4 November 1776), which was granted him by the first minister, Bernardo Tanucci. He and his wife, the singer Cecilia Pallini, traveled by way of Vienna, where they paid their respects to Metastasio and witnessed a triumphant performance of the composer's *La Frascatana* in the Burgtheater.[82]

The Paisiellos arrived in Saint Petersburg during September, in time to hear the two performances of Salieri's *Armida* put on by the Italian opera company in the theater of the Winter Palace on 2 and 5 October. Few outstanding singers remained except the tenor Antonio Prati, who had created the parts of Galuppi's Thoas and Traetta's Creon, and in this production sang Ubaldo. Nevertheless Paisiello, quite unlike his two predecessors, soon set to work composing a new opera for them. Thanks to the correspondence that survives between Grimm and Galiani, we have a description of Paisiello's first appearance before Catherine. Grimm's letter dates from 3 December 1776.

> His success was the most brilliant and general possible. On the day of the presentation there was an academy at court which he directed and in which only his music was heard. The empress, who is not passionately fond of music, was struck singularly by the vigor [nerf] of his style and the novelty of his ideas. The grand duke and grand duchess, the entire court, were enchanted and people clapped hands in the throne-room as if at a public spectacle. After the first piece and the *baciamano* by Paisiello the empress began to play cards but she deputized the grand equerry and other messengers of the kind to make the most agreeable compliments to him, and as she forbad me to approach her table for fear of distracting me from the music, she later deputized me in addition as an ambassador to compliment him on this success, so general and so complete. The great Paisiello is now occupied setting the opera *Nitteti* of Metastasio, and as he wishes to bring it onto the stage in fifteen or twenty days, we do not play much together at the moment. The grand duchess at once took him as her teacher.[83]

The lady in question had just married Grand Duke Paul, his first wife having died. She was the niece of Carl Eugen of Württemberg, rechristened Maria Feodorovna, and she would bear her husband a son, Alexander.

[81]Ibid., 2: 194. "Il sera d'une grande ressource à Grimm, cet hiver, car il raffole de sa musique, et avec raison."

[82]*Haydn, Mozart*, p. 75.

[83]Mooser, *Annales de la musique*, 2: 194–95.

Nitteti was a resounding success. Catherine herself attended the dress rehearsal on 17 January 1777. Concerning the premiere the next day, we again have Grimm's description, written in a letter to Galiani dated Saint Petersburg, 28 January 1777.

> Paisiello has had the most brilliant success. It is now ten or twelve days since the premiere of his *Nitteti.* I possess it to the extent that it keeps me from sleeping. It won not only the applause of the empress and the court; when the clapping stopped and Her Majesty departed from her loge, the general public gave three or four more rounds of applause specifically to the composer. The next day the empress entertained Paisiello and all the actors, as well as the theater director; during dinner she sent presents to the principal actors. Paisiello received a superb box of diamonds that was, as is proper, the most beautiful of the gifts. . . . I was in her cabinet when she chose these presents, among which she had placed, as if by chance, a superb box, enriched with diamonds and decorated with her portrait, that she obliged me to keep. I asked her what I had done for the opera. She replied, "you listened to it well. . . . make your compliments to Paisiello, and agree that we do not treat badly those friends that you have ceded to us."[84]

The opera departed from Metastasio by adding choral scenes and dances between the acts.[85] Unlike most operas given in the theater of the Winter Palace, *Nitteti* did not disappear after the first performances. There were two revivals the same year, another the following year, then in 1780 another for the meeting of Catherine with Joseph II, and yet another in 1788.

Paisiello was also rewarded by an invitation from the sovereign to him and his wife to spend the summer of 1777 at her country palace of Tsarskoye Selo, where he took delight in the gardens according to a letter from Catherine to Grimm dated 24 August. He was working on another opera. This time the libretto was a new one by Coltellini, an *azione teatrale* for four characters, *Lucinda ed Armidoro*. It was the last work of the poet, who died in November 1777 at Saint Petersburg. Catherine wrote to Grimm in a letter dated 22 December 1777 showing a warmer reception than usual: "Savez vous bien que l'opéra de Paisiello était une chose charmante? J'ai oublié de vous en parler; j'ai été toute oreille pour cet opéra, malgré l'insensibilité naturelle de mon tympan pour la musique. Je mets Paisiello à côté de Galuppi."[86] Note that she ranks the composer as high as Galuppi (making no mention of Traetta) and perhaps even higher because he has awakened in her a response to music that made her "all ears."

The birth of Catherine's grandson Alexander in December 1777 was cele-

[84]Ibid., 2: 203.

[85]Jacques Joli, "Il Fragore delle Armi nella *Nitteti,*" in *Metastasio e il mondo musicale,* ed. Maria Teresa Muraro (Florence, 1986), pp. 99–132.

[86]Mooser, *Annales de la musique,* 2: 208.

brated the following month with Paisiello's setting of Metastasio's *Achille in Sciro,* reduced from three acts to two at the express wish of the empress. She began to acknowledge taking more interest in music, but she continued to dislike long operas.

A strong element of caprice in Paisiello's music was not without an equivalent in his personal behavior. Strengthened by the obvious favor he had attained with the empress, he began to make demands of the theater director, Ivan Yélaguine, who complained that his orders were being ignored by Angiolini, the ballet master, by the violinist Antonio Lolli, and most of all by Paisiello. The last impinged on the director's prerogatives by demanding to choose what he was to compose in the way of operas. His contract specified that he should compose music in all genres, but since it did not specify comic operas in so many words, the composer balked at writing them. He did this with a view to obtaining a higher salary when it was time to renew his contract in 1779. What he wanted was the same compensation as Galuppi, 4,000 rubles a year. Grimm wrote to Catherine supporting his cause. She was reluctant to contravene Yélaguine and pointed out that Paisiello had an advantage over his predecessors in the country apartment granted him for four months every summer at Tsarskoye Selo, plus an additional salary of 900 rubles from the grand duchess. She did not mention the special presents lavished upon him. In the end she relented, and Paisiello's new contract called for parity with Galuppi's former salary.

Decorum or ingrained habit kept opera buffa off the stage of the imperial theater in Saint Petersburg until relatively late, but not out of the city altogether. Visiting troupes offered not only opera buffa but also opéra-comique and Singspiel in some abundance, and opéra-comique was to prove particularly influential in the emergence of an equivalent genre in the Russian language. Paisiello's refusal to compose opera buffa may have been partly for practical and artistic reasons. The Italian troupe in imperial service were seria singers, mostly lacking in experience in the buffa genre, which required different kinds of acting as well as singing. The first tentative steps toward change came in 1777 when Yélaguine advertised for a tenor "who could sing in both genres of spectacle, opera seria and opera buffa."[87] The singer engaged, Matteo Babbini, was indeed skilled in both. A year later, the well-traveled poet Giovanni Battista Casti arrived in Saint Petersburg, for which he wrote his first libretto, an inferior comedy entitled *Lo sposo burlato.* Paisiello treated it as a pasticcio, applying some of his own music to the words as well as that of other composers. The first performances were in July 1778 at Petershof. Babbini participated, as did prima donna Caterina Bonafini and other seria singers.

A decisive step toward indigenous opera buffa came when Paisiello in early

[87]Ibid., 2: 197.

1779 took an old libretto by Giovanni Bertati, *I visionari,* and set it under the title of *I filosofi immaginari.* Catherine wrote to Grimm in a letter dated 5 February 1779 informing him that Paisiello, his conditions having been met as to salary, composed a comedy in very short order. "He entertained us the day before yesterday on the stage of my theater in the Hermitage with a comic opera composed in three weeks, after his fashion. It has us dying of laughter. There is an aria with coughing set to music . . . that no living being could resist. The work earned Mme. Paisiello a flower of diamonds and her husband a box."

Shortly before this Catherine had written Grimm, in a letter dated 17 December 1778, about an opera buffa company directed by Mariano Mattei and Angiola Orecia that came to the capital and gave one of Paisiello's most successful earlier comedies: "A troupe of bad Italian buffo players performed *La Frascatana* and people ran to it just as at Naples and Paris." Her social condescension to other capitals, and these two capitals in particular, must have amused Grimm. Her scorn notwithstanding, the best of these lowly buffo singers were later taken into her service.

I filosofi generated such enthusiasm that Catherine wanted to witness several more performances. After one of them at Petershof in mid-July she wrote Grimm:

> The more I see it the more astonished I am at his singular control of tone and sounds. Even a cough becomes harmonious and full of sublime follies. You cannot guess how this magician makes even the less sensitive organs, like mine, pay attention to the music. I leave the performance with my head full of music; I can recognize and almost sing his composition. Oh what an extraordinary head is Paisiello's! I have ordered the score transcribed for you, who will find it full of sublime things. It passes understanding.[88]

Two weeks later, after another performance, she wrote Grimm that, upon encountering the composer, she sang one of the arias to him, which he did not fail to boast about to his acquaintances. Paisiello provided two other operas in 1779, one a revival of his earlier comedy *L'idolo cinese,* and the other Metastasio's *Demetrio,* another older work, reduced now from three acts to two. They evoked less enthusiasm. After a further performance of *I filosofi* Catherine wrote Grimm on 23 August:

> You should know, by the way, that there is not an aria in it that I do not know by heart. Consequently I believe that Paisiello can make one laugh, weep, and impress upon the soul, mind, and heart whatever sentiment he pleases, like a conjuror. I'm having the work copied for you and I believe firmly that it is his masterpiece, inasmuch as neither *L'idolo cinese* nor *Demetrio* can come near its music.

It was performed again in May 1780 at her meeting with Joseph II. He too wanted a copy and had it translated into German, then staged at the Burgtheater in

---

[88]Ibid., 2: 230. Letter dated 14 July 1779. The last sentence is one of the rare cases when she switches from French into German: "das ist unverständlich."

Vienna a year later. It was translated as well into singing versions in French and in Russian.

In sum, Catherine modified her stance about music and her relationship to it thanks to Paisiello, and to *I filosofi* in particular. In her letter to Grimm dated 15 September 1779, she wrote, "Paisiello continues to work miracles. He made me see operas without being bored and listen to music with attention and with interest."[89] It should be added that the opera is noteworthy for several cavatinas of great beauty.

In the fall of 1779, Grand Duke Paul commissioned an opera from Paisiello for the opening of the new theater in his palace of Kammenïy Ostrov, at the gates of the city on the right bank of the Neva. The choice fell not upon an opera seria, as was customary for a theater opening, but on a comic libretto, Pietro Chiari's *Il marchese villano,* previously set by Galuppi (Venice, 1762) and by Paisiello himself, now recomposed and rechristened *Il matrimonio inaspettato.*

The meeting between Catherine and Emperor Joseph II refered to earlier took place at Mogilev on the Dneiper in White Russia. She brought the entire operatic troupe with her to this provincial center. Besides *I filosfi,* Paisiello revived several other works for the occasion: *La Frascatana, L'idolo cinese, Il matrimonio inaspettato,* and *Nitteti.* He wrote afresh a comic opera, *La finte amante,* on an anonymous libretto. The celebrations at Mogilev in May moved to the capital in June. Paisiello was richly rewarded by Joseph II, as well as by Henry, prince of Prussia, who was also visiting.

Serious opera began disappearing from the offerings of the Italian troupe around 1780. At the same time, seria singers began leaving Russia. Without an Italian poet on hand, Paisiello resorted to Metastasio's *festa teatrale Alcide al bivio* to celebrate Catherine's name day in November 1780. Hasse's original setting was made for Joseph II's first wedding in 1760 and was a great favorite with the emperor. When in Russia, Joseph may have had a role in interesting Catherine or the composer in the work. Paisiello was relieved that his setting of *Alcide* pleased, perhaps because he feared that a noncomic opera no longer would, perhaps because he was wary of comparison with Hasse, whom he greatly admired. Hasse's score was readily available in print from Breitkopf in Leipzig.

Paisiello wrote often to Galiani in Naples, to which he hoped to return. Most of the correspondence is lost, but beginning in 1781, remarkably, a few letters survive. In January 1781 the composer reported to his friend about *Alcide:* "By the grace of God, it had a good success. . . . I worked very hard on it because I wanted to free myself from the inconveniences to which one is accustomed in the theaters of Italy, and have completely suppressed vocal *passagi,* cadenzas, and ritornellos, and have set nearly all the recitatives with orchestra."[90] He may have wanted to

---

[89] Ibid., 2: 238, n. 2.
[90] Andrea della Corte, *Paisiello* (Turin, 1922), p. 60.

make all the recitatives orchestral because he began the opera this way, but time apparently became short and he reverted to simple recitatives by the middle of the work, although introducing more orchestral ones at the end.[91] By renouncing the showy parts of Italian opera in the seria mode and promoting recitative closer to parity with arias, Paisiello was edging closer to the operas of Paris, whether by Gluck, Piccinni, or Grétry, whose opéras-comiques were creating a furor in Saint Petersburg just as they were everywhere else.

The three-year contract Paisiello had with the court was due to expire in 1782 and he began agitating for a renewal well in advance. Catherine was willing to give him a four-year contract or one without limit of time. Unbeknownst to her, he was actively seeking a royal post at Naples, to which he sent copies of all his works written in Russia, via the diplomatic service. Galiani was enjoined to plead his cause with King Ferdinand.

Prospects for Italian opera in Saint Petersburg would remain less than ideal as long as there was no resident librettist. Requests for new works from afar did not avail the composer. He wrote to his earlier collaborator Giovanni Battista Lorenzi in the hopes of getting a new libretto but received no answer, as he complained to Galiani in a letter dated 5 May 1781.

> I wrote some time ago to Lorenzi asking him to send me his librettos written since I left Naples. I requested that he write a new one expressly for this court, explaining to him in detail how to conceive the characters of the players, and insisting on brevity, because Her Majesty is unwilling to remain more than an hour and a half in the theater. I pray you urge him to do this, which would permit me to obtain for him the recompense that he merits.[92]

Galiani's efforts did nothing to change the situation. Lorenzi was too busy writing librettos for Naples.

Further depredations among the seria singers took place in early 1782. Caterina Bonafini requested and received permission to leave the imperial service as of 1 March 1782. The same month soprano castrato Giuseppe Compagnucci died. Paisiello's main singers were now those taken over from the Mattei-Orecia buffo troupe, soprano Anna Davia de Bernucci and basses Baldassare Marchetti and Luigi Paganelli. They were joined by the strong tenor Guglielmo Jermoli and his wife Maria Anna, soprano, who had been members of Haydn's troupe at Esterháza from 1777 to 1781.

Catherine ordered an operatic celebration for the name day of her little grandson Alexander in August 1781 at her country palace of Tsarskoye Selo. The most famous of all intermezzo texts was selected, Gennaro Federico's *La serva*

[91]Michael F. Robinson, *Naples and Neapolitan Opera* (Oxford, 1972), p . 86.
[92]Mooser, *Annales, de la musique,* 2: 311.

padrona, perhaps because it would be the most readily comprehended by a five-year old. Marchetti sang Uberto and Anna Davia sang Serpina. Paisiello was not happy about putting himself into competition with Pergolesi, as can well be imagined. He expressed his thoughts on the subject in a preface to the printed French translation of the libretto, dedicated to Catherine.

> Madame, the intermezzo of *Serva Padrona* that I have the honor of presenting to Your Imperial Majesty, was put to music 36 or 40 [*recte:* 48] years ago by the famous Pergolesi. The reputation this master's music enjoys throughout all Europe explains why no one has made a new setting of these words, either out of respect for his memory, or to avoid the danger of comparison, or for fear of being reproached by the public for temerity. The same reasons kept me from touching it, and I never would have done so of my own volition, had I not received orders, which for me are those of Your Majesty herself. Thus putting aside any other consideration I composed this new music on the same words in view of creating something agreeable to Your Imperial Majesty.[93]

The performance, attended by Alexander's parents as well as Catherine, was a success and enjoyed by all, including, presumably, the little boy. Posterity has been less kind, and more inclined to share Paisiello's doubts on being compared with Pergolesi. The episode points up even more clearly the dilemma of an opera company without a librettist.

IL BARBIERE DI SIVIGLIA

Great plays have often been and continue to be transformed into operas. The risk for the opera is that it will be found wanting in comparison. Paisiello, after setting himself in competition with Hasse, then Pergolesi, courted another kind of risk by fashioning a libretto and opera after one of the greatest plays of the century, Beaumarchais's scintillating *Le barbier de Séville.* Its creator intended the original version (1772) as an opéra-comique for the Comédie Italienne in Paris. His final version, accepted as a play by the Comédie Française in 1775, still bore many marks of an opéra-comique—the principal characters all have to sing—to the point that purists condemned the play. Audiences in general loved it and wanted to see it over and over. The mordant witticisms that made Beaumarchais the true heir of Molière were soon on everyone's lips and inscribed on ladies' fans (according to Mrs. Thrale). No theater of standing could do without the play. Catherine had it performed by her French players at Tsarskoye Selo with success in the summer of 1776, after which it soon conquered Saint Petersburg. A visiting Parisian troupe brought it to the attention of the capital again in 1781, so it was freshly in mind when Paisiello decided to risk transforming it into an Italian opera, first performed at the Hermitage on 26 September 1782.

[93]For the original French, see Michael F. Robinson, *Giovanni Paisiello: A Thematic Catalogue of His Works,* 2 vols. (Stuyvesant, N.Y., 1991), 1: 305.

Beaumarchais chose one of the oldest plots possible as a framework for his play: young love triumphs over all obstacles, even over a greedy and powerful old tutor who tries to marry his ward himself, and nearly succeeds. Molière's *Le malade imaginaire,* in which the young lover manages to visit the young lady in the disguise of a music master, provided one model. Another was *On ne s'avise jamais de tout,* the proverbial title that headed one of the *Contes* by Jean de La Fontaine, inspiration for the opéra-comique of the same name by Sedaine and Monsigny (1761). In a preface to *Le barbier* Beaumarchais answered an objection that there was too much resemblance to the latter with an insouciance worthy of Figaro: "It does not resemble that work; it is *On ne s'avise jamais de tout.*" Novel is the Spanish setting, also the jack-of-all-trades character Figaro, whose adventures and misadventures in Spain carry echoes from the author's own experience, especially his multiple legal battles. To the four main characters of Rosina, Almaviva, Figaro, and Bartolo he added the venal cleric and music teacher Basilio. Marcellina is mentioned as being present in Bartolo's house but does not appear. Two servants and a few officers of the law make up the rest. The paucity of characters became an advantage to Paisiello, constrained as he was by a time limit as well as meager personnel.

Paisiello described his singers without naming them in another plea for help to Galiani in a letter of uncertain date. He spelled out his needs for a new libretto tailored to the forces at hand.

> The libretto should be in a single act, or two at the most, and call for only four or five persons, whose characters I shall explain in terms of the artists currently in imperial service. 1) A buffo caricato who sings excellently the roles of an old man, father, jealous tutor, philosopher; 2) a second buffo caricato who could be compared with Gennaro Luzio; 3) a tenor comparable to Grimaldi, who also plays roles in high comedy and sings well; 4) a female comic who plays excellently any caricato part; 5) another woman who plays mezzo carattere roles, equal to the preceding one. There should be very few recitatives because Italian is not understood here. As to the musical numbers, arias, cavatinas, duets, trios and finales can be used, within the boundaries of the plot, as is the practice at Naples. The libretto must be entirely in Italian [i.e., no dialect]; it should not require low comic, but rather half comic, which will suffice if it is a comedy of character.[94]

Most of the three men and two women described can be identified. No. 1 is surely Baldassare Marchetti, who had played Uberto and for whom the part of Bartolo

[94]Della Corte, *Paisiello,* pp. 71–72. Della Corte dated the letter September 1781, changed to September 1782 by Daniela Goldin, "Il Barbiere di Siviglia da Beaumarchais all'opera buffa," chap. 5 in her *La vera Fenice: Librettisti e libretti fra Sette e Ottocento* (Turin, 1985), pp. 164–89; 186, n. 9. The two singers mentioned by Paisiello for comparison's sake were stalwarts of the Neapolitan comic stages and had sung under him. The tenor Niccolò Grimaldi began his singing career in 1753 and created the part of Gafforio in Paisiello's *Socrate imaginario* (Naples, 1775). The bass Gennaro Luzio began in 1751 and was still singing comic roles in 1800. He created Buonafede in Paisiello's *Il credulo deluso* (Naples, 1774).

was created. No. 2 could be Luigi Paganelli, also from the Mattei-Orecia company, who created Basilio, or possibly the Figaro, a newly arrived buffo, Giovanni Battista Brocchi. No. 3 is the tenor Guglielmo Jermoli. No. 4 must be Anna Davia de Bernucci, who sang both Serpina and Rosina. No. 5 could be Madame Jermoli.

This important letter only confirms what we have known from studying Mozart's *modus operandi* in the theater. A great opera was typically built upon the acting and singing abilities of the individuals who were at the disposal of the poet and composer. Paisiello was a model for Mozart in this respect, as in so many others.

Brocchi obviously played a key role in *Barbiere*. He must have been quite young when he came to Saint Petersburg, because he had a long career thereafter and was still singing on stage as late as 1807 at Milan (as Don Alfonso in *Così fan tutte*). He began his career in Venice (1776–77) then sang in Warsaw (1780–81). No less demanding of acting ability was the part of Almaviva, who had to impersonate in turn an indigent student improvising a serenade, a drunken cavalryman, and a singing teacher claiming to be Basilio's assistant, before assuming his true identity as a splendidly dressed grandee in the final scene. Marchetti was well prepared to cope with the role of Bartolo, a large one. Anna Davia de Bernucci had a fine line to tread in creating Rosina, who is wily in some ways, innocent of guile in others. Beaumarchais has Almaviva describe Rosina to Figaro (Act I, Scene 4) as a young lady "of noble blood, orphaned, and married to an old medical doctor named Bartolo." Figaro quickly disabused him as to her marital status. It contributes to our understanding of Almaviva's character development to learn that he thought he was pursuing an affair with a married lady, only to come to terms with a more serious purpose—marrying her himself.

The libretto's authorship has been the source of speculation and controversy. Paisiello sent the score to Naples in the fall of 1782, following his practice with all the operas written in Russia. In a letter to Galiani of 15 February 1783 he was apologetic about its literary merits. "I had it translated into verses in Italian. I hope you will like the distribution of musical pieces, which I made myself. You will not like the poetry, for which I had to comply with necessity, given the lack of poets here."[95] The author of the poetry remained anonymous in all the early librettos. There can be no doubt that it was concocted under the supervision of the composer, maybe with his participation. Deciding where the musical numbers should go in the text was, after all, the first crucial step in its creation. Possibly one of Paisiello's new buffo singers had a hand in the task. At Esterháza the tenor Carl Friberth helped Haydn by revising and even creating texts for musical setting— Haydn suffered from the same dearth of poets. Could the tenor Jermoli have per-

---

[95]Robinson, *Paisiello: A Thematic Catalogue*, 1: 324. "Io l'ho fatta tradurre in versi in lingua italiana. Spero che gli piacerà la distribuzione delli pezzi di musica da me fatta, ma non sarà contento della Poesia, avendo dovuto uniformarmi alla necessità della mancanza che qui abbiamo riguardo a Poeti."

formed a similar service with *Barbiere?* Another possibility was one of the Italian diplomats in the Russian capital.

Within a year the opera was conquering many stages, beginning with Vienna, where it achieved more than sixty performances. The poet remained anonymous wherever the libretto was printed during the 1780s for over twenty different productions until, in 1789, at the King's Theatre in London, there appeared the statement, "Poesia di Giuseppi Petrosellini." The principal expert on Paisiello doubts claims for the Roman poet Petrosellini, not only on grounds of lack of evidence but also because the text falls below the standards of a professional librettist.[96]

A professional opera buffa libretto of the time was divided into two long acts, each ending with a monster finale in which all the characters congregate on stage. Managing plots so as to create these finales gave poets fits, as so vividly described in his memoirs by Lorenzo da Ponte. By the 1780s these conventions became so overblown that complaints began to be heard about the tedium of overlong finales.[97] *Barbiere* followed no such conventions. It remained very close to the four-act play, in which the acts were short and the last act very short. This meant ending Act I with a duet for Figaro and Almaviva and Act II with a soliloquy for Rosina. A relatively brief finale to Act III begins with the quintet in which the unexpected Basilio is persuaded that he is sick and must go to bed. Act IV is made to end with another finale, although not a very long one. By slavishly following the play, the creators of *Barbiere*, harboring their resources of necessity, managed to break through the mold of long finales. In another respect also, by fielding as many ensembles as arias, they pointed to the future of Italian opera.

Much of the play's rapier wit had to be sacrificed in the libretto. Beaumarchais larded his text with puns, proverbs, and anagrams, also with subtle references to other stage works and rich literary allusions, all of which find no place in a libretto. Preserved at least are many of the occurrences of the word *precaution*, which alludes to the work's subtitle, "The Useless Precaution," taken over from the play. The finale that ends the opera concludes, "What has happened here can truly and with good cause be called useless precaution." Brevity exacted a particularly heavy toll on the scene preceding this finale, forcing deletion of some of the play's vital information about Rosina's character. When Almaviva threatens to punish Bartolo, she says, "Non, non, grâce pour lui, cher Lindor! Mon coeur est si plein, que la vengeance ne peut y trouver place." Their diverse reactions help define the differences between Count and Countess Almaviva to come in the sequel.

The play is an economical vehicle in spite of its verbal virtuosity. It follows the so-called unities of place, time, and action, valued highly in French classical the-

---

[96]Ibid.

[97]Daniel Heartz, "The Creation of the Buffo Finale in Italian Opera," *Proceedings of the Royal Musical Association* 104 (1977–78): 67–78; 73.

ater. As to place, there are only two sets, the street outside Bartolo's house, with windows grilled, and the same but inside the house, with the grilled windows in the background. The time is constricted to one day, from dawn to midnight. Almaviva's conquest, pursued from his first words throughout the play until his final triumph, furnished the central action around which everything revolves. In his dedication of the opera to Catherine, Paisiello was as breathtakingly brief as the matter he describes.

> Madame! *Le barbier de Séville* having been to the taste of Your Imperial Majesty I thought that this same play as an Italian opera could not displease you; in consequence I have made an extract of the play, which I have tried to make as brief as possible while conserving (insofar as the genius of Italian poetry allows) the expression of the original, without adding anything.[98]

To this the anonymous versifier added in the printed libretto, "If in translating I abbreviated it was done solely to adapt the play to the genius of this imperial court, in the hopes that music would enhance the beauty of the scenes that I had of necessity to cut in order to make the spectacle as short as possible."[99] The librettist has been taken to task for sacrificing too much and for chasing rhymes at the expense of precise meanings.[100]

Antoine Laurent Baudron, first violinist of the Comédie Française, composed the stage music for the play, which is unusually elaborate. Ruault, publisher of the play's first edition in 1775, also offered for sale an engraved score of the music that had a wide diffusion.[101] Aside from the songs sung on stage, the play required an orchestral thunderstorm as entr'acte music, setting the emotional tone for Act IV. Here Beaumarchais owed inspiration to his friends Sedaine and Monsigny, who deployed an entr'acte storm to wonderful effect in *Le roi et le fermier*.[102]

From the outset, Paisiello achieves an unusual degree of fluidity between recitative, short songs, arias, and ensembles. In what is called in some sources an *Introduzione*, Count Almaviva begins the dramatic exposition singing an *Andante*

---

[98]See Robinson, *Paisiello: Thematic Catalogue*, 1: 324, for the original French.

[99]Della Corte, *Paisiello*, pp. 74–75.

[100]By Goldin, "*Il Barbiere di Siviglia* da Beaumarchais all'opera buffa," p. 170. See also on the relationship of the operas by Paisiello and Rossini to Beaumarchais and to each other Marvin Tartak, "The Two 'Barbieri,'" *Music and Letters* 50 (1969): 453–69.

[101]It is reproduced in E. J. Arnould, *La genèse du "Barbier de Séville"* (Dublin and Paris, 1965), plates XII–XIV. According to the author, p. 87, *Barbier* was played 118 times up to the theater's closing in 1792. By July 1962 it had been played 1,098 times, 19 more than *Le mariage de Figaro*.

[102]Walter E. Rex, "The 'storm' music of Beaumarchais' *Barbier de Séville*," in *Opera and Enlightenment*, ed. Thomas Bauman and Marita Petzoldt McClymonds (Cambridge, 1995), pp. 243–59. The plates from the original edition are reproduced on pp. 252–55. The author includes a penetrating discussion of the events in Act III leading to the storm and of the character of Bartolo, who was truly his own worst enemy.

in 2/4 and in D that is more song than aria, lasting only thirty-eight measures. Its gavotte rhythms lend the count courtly graces. He withdraws at the approach of Figaro, who is making up a song in praise of wine and struggling with the words. The latter's tune is much more plebian. It is a singsong 6/8 meter in the key of G, without the gracious upbeat afforded Almaviva. His efforts break down after only twenty-five measures, lapsing momentarily into recitative. Baudron, whose stage music Paisiello evidently knew, provided the model with his jingling ditty in 6/8 meter. Deficient in musical inspiration as Paisiello makes Figaro sound in improvising his melody, it was just this humdrum quality that Mozart wanted for the eruption of the peasants in Act I of *Le nozze di Figaro,* who also sing in 6/8 meter and in the key of G, confining the rustic melody mostly to the five tones above the tonic.[103]

Figaro's drinking song gives way as he and Almaviva spot each other. The orchestra strikes up a lilting *Moderato* in common time and back in the key of D. A one-measure rhythmic and melodic motif in the violins, using dotted rhythm and a melodic turn, keeps repeating as the music gathers momentum, modulates, and moves higher in pitch. Orchestral continuity music of this kind originated in the buffo finale. It allows the two men to drop in and out of the texture as they gradually recognize each other, interjecting their comments, and sometimes intertwining. Their duet accelerates to a final *Allegro* back in the tonic, with the patter, emphatic cadences, and repetitions characteristic of the buffo style. No wonder Catherine was enchanted by the sheer verve of such music.

Almaviva begins the following recitative with an ironic compliment, saying that Figaro had become so corpulent as to be hardly recognizable. In fact Figaro had become just the opposite due to all the miseries he had recently suffered; this sets up Figaro's big catalogue aria recounting his misfortunes. In the middle of this recitative as he explains how he lost one good post, Figaro bursts into arioso lament on the subject of envy. It is short and pseudotragic, invoking the minor mode, g, accompanied only by strings, a sonority almost unique in the opera (Example 9.13). Note how the third phrase begins like the first but ends like the second. Mozart exploited this passage for Alfonso's pseudolament "Vorrei dir, e cor non ho" in *Così fan tutte* (Act I, Scene 3), using the minor mode and the same accompanimental figure to the same agitated *Allegro,* also set for strings alone.[104]

---

[103]For further comparison of these two pieces, see Daniel Heartz, "Constructing *Le Nozze di Figaro,"* *Journal of the Royal Musical Association* 112 (1987): 77–98, reprinted in Daniel Heartz, *Mozart's Operas,* edited, with contributing essays, by Thomas Bauman (Berkeley, 1990), pp. 133–55, examples 5 and 6. (Subsequent citations refer to the later printing.)

[104]Bruce Alan Brown, "Beaumarchais, Paisiello and the Genesis of *Così fan tutte,"* *Wolfgang Amadé Mozart: Essays on His Life and His Music,* ed. Stanley Sadie (Oxford, 1996), pp. 312–38; 315–19. The author traces Figaro's outburst into song to Beaumarchais's use of a rhymed couplet at this point, a single Alexandrine supposedly quoted from one of Figaro's own poems.

EXAMPLE 9.13. *Paisiello*, Il barbiere di Siviglia, *Act I, Scene 2, Arioso*

When Figaro's aria proper arrives, it is introduced by the orchestra's rise of one scale degree per measure from the tonic in a motif that offers another combination of the melodic turn and dotted rhythm. This rise, first in unison then in thirds, gave Paisiello the idea that begins his pert and winsome one-movement overture, also in the key of C. Figaro commences his aria by intoning the first of the *ottonarii* lines in half notes, beginning on the first beat, "Scorsì già molti paesi" (I have traveled many lands already) but snapping off the last two syllables as quarter notes. He repeats the descending seventh melodic idea in dialogue with the initial orchestral statement, after which the orchestra launches into chattering sixteenth notes, to which Figaro responds in eighth-note patter cataloguing his travels. There is a little pause with fermata just before the arrival of the dominant, at which Paisiello switches to gavotte rhythm for the line, "Ma però di buon umore" (And nevertheless of good humor). Mozart's Figaro also switches to gavotte rhythm at the onset of the dominant in "Non più andrai" ending Act I of *Le nozze di Figaro*. The poet of *Il barbiere* changes meter at this point of his catalogue, probably at the behest of Paisiello, who decided to end not with a still faster section, but a slower one, *Andantino* in 3/8, rather like a menuet, in order to reflect the words, which concern Figaro's present state of living simply in Seville as a barber because he has no money. In the most famous catalogue aria of all, "Madamina! il catalogo è questo" in *Don Giovanni,* Mozart gave Leporello an *Allegro* in common time filled with patter, followed, at the point where the poetic meter shifts, by an *Andante con moto* in 3/4 time. Its ancestry in Paisiello could not be clearer. Mozart profited the most from Paisiello in his continuation of the Figaro saga, but all three of the comic operas created with Da Ponte are beholden to *Barbiere.*

The Venetian blinds of the house open and reveal Rosina's presence to her unknown admirer. She sings what seems to be an aria, praising the fresh air she is enjoying out of the sight of her watchful tutor. Paisiello moves to the flat side of the tonal spectrum, choosing the key of F, which exudes relaxation and sonorous beauty, especially when colored as here by solo flute (which suggests a state as free as a bird) and expressed in a smoothly flowing *Andantino* in 3/8 time. She is at once gracious, sentimental, and clever, with little melismatic bursts and a final vocal flurry up to high A showing that, however weak her position, she is a personality to be reckoned with. After full closure, her aria becomes a duet at the change of meter and tempo. Bartolo has been watching her and is upset by a paper he sees in her hand, and which she lets flutter down to the street, much to his distress. Still within the same duet he goes out to retrieve it, but of course it is gone. He returns and locks the shutters.

Rosina's paper was a note to her admirer. She asks him to sing to the tune of a certain air from "The Useless Precaution" declaring his name and intentions, as soon as Bartolo has left. Bartolo departs, giving orders that no one be allowed to enter the house. Count Almaviva is nonplussed: "But how shall I sing?" Figaro answers, "However you can. Everything you say will be excellent," a play on the count's manner of address as "eccelenza." Figaro gives his guitar to the count, who proceeds to pluck out a tune (played by a mandolin in the orchestra). As in the play, the text is slow in getting to the point, as if the count were truly bumbling at this game. The first stanza goes no further than urging that she listen and he will reveal his name. He does this at the beginning of the second stanza, sung to the identical music. Baudron relied on pizzicato violins to convey the plucking accompaniment in an orchestra reinforced by flutes and horns. He chose the key of $E^\flat$ and wrote a melody for the count that is simple but has a pleasing contour as it arches up to the high tonic for the second line. Here it is transposed to $B^\flat$ and given the words at the beginning of the second stanza (Example 9.14ab). Mozart liked Baudron's melody enough to write variations for keyboard on it when in Paris in 1778 (the "Lindor" Variations, K. 354/299a). The word setting is atrocious, yet this too lends the serenade further verisimilitude, like the plucked strings. That

EXAMPLE 9.14. *The count's serenade*

a. Baudron, *Le barbier*, Act I, Scene 6

b. Paisiello, *Il barbiere*, Act I, Scene 6

Paisiello knew Baudron's setting and wanted to capitalize on the likelihood that his audience also knew it seems all but certain. He began his melody with the most expressive part of Baudron's tune, the turn around high tonic and skip down to the fifth, and eventually reached a half-cadence with the same melodic fall. By the third time around, for the third stanza, this strictly strophic and very slow song may begin to sound tedious. The special tone color of the mandolin solo helps rescue it, as do the two clarinets in B♭, used here for the first time; they have a lot to do with rendering the *amoroso* quality required.

Rosina begins to answer the count to the same music. She gets no further than two lines when the window is slammed shut, cutting her off in midstream (the effect is so theatrical Alban Berg could still use it in *Wozzeck*). The count, enamored further by her voice, declares that Rosina will become his wife. He rewards Figaro for his services and promises more of the same, eliciting from Figaro a long melisma of joy on "*vo*-la alla fortuna." Figaro invites the count to his house and tells him to bring a soldier's outfit, an order for billeting, and lots of gold. The act's concluding duet begins in the key of G, associated with Figaro's improvised drinking song, as the count promises to bring gold, reinforcing the rustic association by singing a lusty melody, *Allegro presto* in common time, that has no orchestral introduction at all but plenty of precedents in folksong: 5 - 3 - 4 - 2, 4 - 2 - 3 - 1. It became the model for Mozart's "Non più andrai," Figaro's jolly ending to Act I of *Le nozze di Figaro*. An argument has been made that the peculiar *tinta* of putting the earthy key of G up against the prolonged *amoroso* outpouring of B♭ in *Barbiere* had multiple consequences for using these two keys in sequence in *Nozze*.[105]

[105]Heartz, "Constructing *Le Nozze di Figaro*," pp. 148–50.

Having Rosina begin to sing the same song as the count is an improvement on the play, in which she begins to answer with a different tune. The words Beaumarchais gives her, on the other hand, are far more effective than those by the anonymous librettist. Slavish to the point of a mechanical reaction in the duet is the libretto's retention of the description of Figaro's shop sign, including the Latin motto "Consilium manuque" (Counsel and dexterity). Beaumarchais used this motto knowing his audience in Paris would associate it with the Royal College of Surgeons (barbers and surgeons had long been linked).[106] Who would have known this in Saint Petersburg?

Act II begins with Rosina finishing a letter to her Lindoro. Figaro enters and asks her to write one, upon which, to his surprise, she gives it to him. Figaro exits. Bartolo enters vituperating against Figaro, who has administered a narcotic to one servant, Svegliato ("Alert"), and a sneeze powder to another, Giovanetto ("Youth"). Moreover, he has confined Marcellina to her bed after bleeding her foot. Bartolo calls the two servants to him as the terzetto begins, a *Moderato* in common time and in the key of A. An orchestra of two horns, two oboes, and strings plays a short introduction establishing the main motif as an unusual accent pattern, with *forte* emphases on the second and third beats, as against the *piano* of the fourth and first beats, which are connected by a dotted rhythm upbeat. It is as simple as it is original. Bartolo interrogates the two in turn: "Did someone besides Figaro enter the house and visit Rosina?" Alert can only respond with yawns in long notes that reinforce the orchestra's rhythmic pattern. Bartolo sings in eighth-note patter. The process is repeated with Youth, who hobbles in on a cane. He can only respond by sneezing, "Ec-cì . . . ec-cì . . . ec-cì. . . ." Renewed questioning produces combined yawning and sneezing, accompanied by Bartolo's exasperated patter. The two servants eventually sing their own patter in eighth notes, saying that if it were not for Rosina they would no longer serve such a master. At this the piece ought to be over, having undergone a full cycle of modulation to the dominant and back to the tonic. One is only too delighted to hear them go once more through their sneezing and yawning routine. After a vigorous full cadence on the tonic, Paisiello puts a measure of silence with fermatas. Surely it is over? No, it is not. The orchestra recommences and Youth builds up to the mother of all sneezes: "Ec . . . ec . . . ec . . . ec . . . ec . . . ec . . . ec . . . ec . . . ec . . . ec . . . ec . . . cì."

Paisiello was nowhere more in his element than when controlling rhythm for the purposes of comic effect (it was the same with the hilarity caused by his setting coughs to music in *I filosofi*). He was inimitable in such pieces. When Rossini and his librettist Cesare Sterbini took up the subject of the opera again in 1816, they did not even try to compete with this terzetto.

---

[106]Arnould, *La genèse du Barbier de Séville*, p. 430, reproduces the surgeons' coat of arms with this motto.

EXAMPLE 9.15. *Paisiello*, Il barbiere, *Act II, Scene 8, Trio*

Connoisseurs, especially among the aristocratic ladies who had boxes at the Burgtheater, probably preferred the next number, Rosina's act-ending cavatina, "Giusto ciel," a musical poem in E♭ projecting the most tender longing, colored by murmuring bassoons in thirds answered by the even more amorous-sounding clarinets in B♭—their first return since the count's serenade in Act I. This piece prepares the way for the similar affect voiced by a sadder and wiser Rosina after marriage to the count, "Porgi, amor," the cavatina that opens Act II of *Le nozze*.

Act III begins with a duet between Bartolo and the count, newly arrived as Alonso, pretended pupil of and substitute for the indisposed Basilio. Alonso proceeds to bore Bartolo to distraction with his repeated invocations of joy and peace, sung (often nasally) to a monotone G (the piece is in C and in 3/4 time). In the following recitative Bartolo is quickly duped as the newcomer produces the letter Rosina wrote to Lindoro/Almaviva. Rosina appears. Still smarting from Bartolo's ill-

tempered behavior, she refuses to take her music lesson with a substitute, then instantly changes course when she recognizes him. They move to the harpsichord. She announces an aria from "The Useless Precaution." He seats himself to accompany her. In the play Baudron provided an Ariette on Beaumarchais's long poem describing the return of spring and a lonely shepherdess who awaits her lover, Lindor. Italian poetry provided Paisiello with a beautiful equivalent verse by Metastasio, "Già riede primavera" (see p. 25).[111] Given the excuse for composing a veritable aria in the grand style, Paisiello does not stint. An orchestra of two oboes, one clarinet (in B♭), one bassoon, two horns, and strings sounds a leisurely ritornello in which the two solo instruments frolic together, an *Andante con moto* in 3/4 and in B♭. The proceedings resemble the first movement of a concerto, the orchestral ritornello

---

[111]Not "Deh riede la primavera," as in Mary Hunter, *The Culture of Opera Buffa in Mozart's Vienna: A Poetics of Entertainment* (Princeton, N.J., 1998), p. 46, a demonstration of how one false consonant-vowel sound can destroy Metastasio's delicate balance of sonorities.

opera. Key jokes in opera did not begin with Almaviva's "Quà la chiave!" in the second-act finale of *Le nozze*. The ample concluding section, *Allegro presto* in common time and in E$^\flat$, is given over to Bartolo's rage and accusations, Rosina's angry reaction, and general pandemonium in a series of varied textures, mainly three against one.

Beaumarchais's Act IV is the briefest of all. The libretto dutifully follows suit. Night has descended along with the rainstorm. Bartolo sends Basilio to fetch the notary who will marry him to his ward. Rosina appears. He produces her letter to Lindoro, surprises her by naming its real recipient as Almaviva, and dupes her into believing that the count has betrayed her. In revenge she agrees to marry Bartolo at once. She confesses to the stolen key. At this Bartolo, newly enraged, goes out to get the police. Enter Figaro and count, dripping wet. She plays along with them at first, then denounces Lindoro: "You have sold me to Count Almaviva!" Another *coup de théâtre* occurs as he throws off his great cloak to reveal a magnificent outfit: "I am Count Almaviva!"

Paisiello sets the proceedings in simple recitative up to the point of Rosina's accusation, when the first and only obbligato recitative of the opera takes over (Metastasio would approve such parsimony). Being so rare, it admittedly makes a superb effect. The opera could risk such a long swath of recitative only because the play was so well known. A short finale ensues. Although the dénouement has just taken place in recitative, various strands remain to be resolved. Rosina and the count begin, singing the equivalent of a love duet, in B$^\flat$, *Larghetto* in 3/4 time, with clarinets in B$^\flat$. The music approaches that of Sacchini in its delicate lyricism. We know how much Paisiello admired his Neapolitan colleague—in 1785 he told a pupil that Hasse's mantle as the god of song had passed to Sacchini.

Figaro interrupts the warbling lovers with the news that the ladder they brought has been removed. The music changes to *Allegro moderato* in 2/4. Basilio enters with the notary, who marries the young pair by mistake while Basilio, won over by another purse, signs as witness along with Figaro. The music slows to *Andante* for a section in E$^\flat$ as they muse together on the power of money. Bartolo enters with the forces of the law and demands that everyone be arrested (*Allegro* in cut time). A confused magistrate has to have the situation explained to him slowly, step by step (*Andante* in common time and in F). The return to B$^\flat$, *Allegro* in common time, brings the end near, with the deflation of Bartolo. At last comes the moral, *Un poco più mosso:* "When the god of love is in accord with two young hearts, all the precautions in the world are useless."

Barbiere begins in C but ends in B$^\flat$, a descent that brings relaxation rather than the intensification that might be expected in so scintillating a comedy. Serenity has been used as a concept to characterize Paisiello's overall musical personality.[113] Oddly enough, Haydn adopted the same tonal scheme, C giving way to B$^\flat$,

---

[113]Lippmann, "Paisiello und Mozart in der Opera Buffa," p. 140.

as the grand plan for *The Creation.* Perhaps it was not so odd. Haydn made extensive changes of all kinds in most of the operas he adapted for presentation at Esterháza. In *Barbiere* he made only a few small cuts and changed almost nothing.[114]

Of all Catherine's *maestri,* including Giuseppe Sarti, Domenico Cimarosa, and Vicente Martín y Soler, who came later, Paisiello was the most productive. In his last year (1783) he composed a setting of Metastasio's full-length oratorio *La Passione di Gesù Cristo* for performance during Lent in the Catholic cathedral of Saint Petersburg. To celebrate the anniversary of Catherine's coronation in October he composed another opera, *Il mondo della luna,* a reduced version of Goldoni's libretto with added dance scenes. He had set the libretto before in Naples as *Il credulo deluso,* but this new work was almost entirely rewritten. The success of all three last works did not make the composer's departure any easier. His duties were increased by the committee that ran the theaters without any increase in salary. At this Paisiello balked. He was held in contempt and threatened with prison. Catherine stood by her favorite once again. She granted him a year's leave of absence with full salary in order to return home, the only stipulation being that he send any new scores he wrote. He departed in early 1784, never to return.

FIGURE 9.7. Elisabeth Vigée-Lebrun. Portrait of Giovanni Paisiello, 1791.

Paisiello was painted by the famous portrait artist Madame Elizabeth Vigée-Lebrun, who fled Paris for Italy in 1790. She depicted the composer at the keyboard in a canvas that still survives.[115] As engraved (Figure 9.7), his pose recalls the

[114]Dénes Bartha and László Somfai, *Haydn als Opernkapellmeister: Die Haydn-Dokumente der Esterházy-Opernsammlung* (Budapest and Mainz, 1960), pp. 356–57. Dénes Bartha, "Haydn's Italian Opera Repertory at Esterháza Palace," in *New Looks at Italian Opera: Essays in Honor of Donald J. Grout,* ed. William W. Austin (Ithaca, N.Y., 1968), pp. 172–219; 204–5.
[115]In the Musée de Versailles. It is reproduced in Michael F. Robinson, "Paisiello," *New Grove.*

famous portrait of Gluck by Duplessis (see Plate X). The heads are similarly turned, and the eyes raised as if receiving inspiration from above.

Paisiello persevered against the odds to achieve what even Galuppi and Traetta could not: he created works of such charm and verve for the Russian capital that they were eagerly sought by other countries. It was a cultural coup on a par with Catherine's appointment of Diderot as her librarian (she bought his library) and her commission of Étienne Maurice Falconet's greatly admired equestrian statue of Peter the Great. Saint Petersburg did indeed become a great European capital, and that was what Peter set out to accomplish in the first place. If London could boast in Christian Bach a sterling representative of the newest and most fashionable kind of Italianate music, Russia could claim no less for Paisiello. Our third expatriate composer, Boccherini, brought similar honor to Spain.

Boccherini in Madrid

VIRTUOSO CELLIST

The facts about Boccherini's early years are few. He was born to a musical family in Lucca on 19 February 1743 and christened Ridolfo Luigi. His father Leopoldo was employed from 1747 on as a supernumerary performer on the contrebass and cello by the Signoria of Lucca. He was Luigi's first teacher. Together with his brother Giovanni (born in 1742), Luigi sang as a chorister in the cathedral from age eight. Leopoldo requested and received permission in 1754 to accompany his son to Rome for further study, but which son is not specified. Giovanni was an aspiring poet and ballet dancer as well as a singer. Luigi was certainly in Rome for study in 1756–57, when he was taught by the cellist-composer Giovanni Battista Costanzi, who became director of the Cappella Giulia of Saint Peter's in 1755.[116]

The peak of Lucca's musical life came annually in September, at the festivals of the Holy Countenance and the Holy Cross, with performances in the cathedral and in the theater. Maestro di cappella and organist positions at the cathedral were filled by the same master, Giacomo Puccini (direct ancestor of his famous namesake, also from Lucca). He contributed grand motets for chorus and orchestra to the annual festivals, in which Luigi took part from age ten. Puccini insured that his positions, the only well-paid musical ones in the small city, stayed in the family. There were thus no hopes in the long term for the Boccherinis to earn a good living from music by remaining in Lucca.

As early as August 1756, young Luigi, aged thirteen, appeared as soloist in a cello concerto in his native city. He may also have been its composer. An entry in

---

[116]The composer's biography has long been encrusted by myths and clichés. For a careful marshaling of what facts there are, with documentation, see Remigio Coli, *Luigi Boccherini* (Lucca, 1988; 2nd. ed., revised and amplified, Milan, 1992). Subsequent references are to the second edition.

Puccini's diary for 4 August 1756 records a payment to "Luigi Boccherini . . . per fare un Concerto di Violoncello che Lo fece il giorno dopo il primo Salmo e suonò ancore per favorire me, a Messa e Vespro."[117] This could be interpreted to mean "for composing a cello concerto which he played the day after the first Psalm, and then, in order to oblige me, at Mass and Vespers."

The young cellist at such a tender age presumably played some scaled-down size of cello. On the other hand, Benjamin Hallet, a child virtuoso on the flute and cello, was depicted by Thomas Jenkins managing to play an instrument that was at least a head taller than himself (Figure 9.8). The caption reads, "A Child not five Years Old who under the Tuition of Mr Oswald Performed on the Flute at Drury Lane Theatre An.° 1748 for 50 Nights with extraordinary Skill and Applause, and in the following Year was able to Play his part in any Concert on the Violoncello." Hallet's flute is shown resting on the music stand. His entire right hand is needed to grip the cello bow. Compare the delicate grasp of the bow with the fingers in the portrait of Boccherini as a young man (Plate XII). Hallet's left hand is in a relatively low position on the strings. Boccherini's is much higher, in keeping with the often stratospheric heights reached in his cello sonatas and concertos.[118]

FIGURE 9.8. Thomas Jenkins. A child prodigy playing the cello, 1749.

Leopoldo Boccherini took another leave of absence in March 1757 in order to go to Venice, where Giovanni made his debut as a dancer in the San Salvator theater and his sister Maria Esther also danced.[119] Then

[117]Gabriella Biagi Ravenni, "Calzabigi e d'intorni: Boccherini, Angiolini, La Toscana e Vienna," in *La figura e l'opera di Ranieri de' Calzabigi,* ed. Federico Marri (Florence, 1989), pp. 29–71; 40.

[118]Elisabeth Covel Le Guin, " 'As My Works Show Me to Be': Physicality as Compositional Technique in the Instrumental Music of Luigi Boccherini" (Ph.D. diss., University of California, Berkeley, 1997), devotes her second chapter to the techniques demanded by the cello sonatas. She posits (p. 5) that in the early portrait reproduced as plate XII Boccherini is getting ready for an F above middle C with the index finger of his left hand.

[119]Elisa Grossato, "Luigi Boccherini e Venezia," *Chigiana* 20 (*Luigi Boccherini e la musica strumentale dei maestri Italiani in Europa tra sette e ottocento*) (1993): 135–50.

Leopoldo to see Luigi holding his own with maestro di cappella Puccini. Leopoldo did not survive another year, dying on 30 August 1766.

Filippo Manfredi, born at Lucca in 1731, was a pupil of Pietro Nardini. In a sense he replaced the departed Leopoldo. He was a frequent partner with Luigi in duets and his main companion on subsequent concert tours. Filippo was also a composer of sonatas and other music for strings but little has survived.[125] He was also something of a free spirit, as is evident from the following incident. In 1764 he shocked the city fathers by playing at one of their banquets dressed in "a colored coat with a vest brocaded with gold," whereas regulations prescribed "black habit with cloak and wig." The elders who enforced such rules evidently still harked back to seventeenth-century Spanish etiquette. They complained to maestro Puccini and the affair then went all the way up to the General Council.[126] In a city as small as Lucca the slightest affront to dignity became a major scandal. It could be that Luigi took a cue from his friend as to dress. In the early portrait (see Plate XII) he sports a colored coat of a gorgeous light brown hue and a waist-coat that is gaily embroidered, partly with gold, the whole topped by an outra-geously large bowtie that contrasts markedly with his small white wig. Luigi's sensitive and thin face, his widely spaced dark eyes, elegant nose, and pursed lips offer the very picture of galant sensibility. This splendid portrait was once attrib-uted to Pompeo Batoni of Rome (a native of Lucca). Art historians today go no further than ascribing it to the Italian school.[127] Note that he holds the cello between his knees.

Nardini left Stuttgart in 1765, visited the court of Brunswick, and returned to his native Livorno in May 1766. Around this time a string quartet was said to have been formed with him as first violin, his former pupil Manfredi as second, Luigi as cello, and the young Giuseppe Cambini of Livorno as a willing violist, accord-ing to an anecdote told by Cambini many years later.[128] There is no corroborating evidence. Cambini says the ensemble performed quartets by Boccherini, Haydn, and other celebrated masters. With Boccherini there is no difficulty in believing that they would have played his first set of six quartets, composed in 1761 accord-ing to their creator. Both Nardini and Boccherini had been in Vienna, and it is pos-sible that the one or the other might have collected some of Haydn's early *Divertimenti a 4*. Impossible, on the other hand, is the claim made by Cambini, or

[125]Carol Bellora, "L'opera strumentale di Filippo Manfredi," *Chigiana* 20 (*Luigi Boccherini e la musica strumen-tale dei maestri Italiani in Europa tra sette e ottocento*) (1993): 231–45.

[126]Coli, *Luigi Boccherini*, p. 36.

[127]*Catalogue of Paintings, National Gallery of Victoria*, ed. Ursula Hoff (Melbourne, 1996), pp. 141–42.

[128]Giuseppe Cambini, *Nouvelle méthode théorique et pratique pour le violon* (Paris, ca. 1795, facsimile reprint, Geneva, 1972), pp. 19–22. The passage gives detailed advice on performing two passages, one the begin-ning of Boccherini's String Quartet No. 1 in c, the other the beginning of the *Andante* in Haydn's Symphony No. 53.

under his name, that they played quartets from Haydn's Opp. 9, 17, and 21 (*recte:* 20) in the mid-1760s, before these works had been written and published.[129] The "Tuscan" Quartet, as it has been called, did not last long, if it ever existed.

Manfredi and Boccherini left Lucca and headed north in 1767. They resided for a time in Genoa, whence they set their sights on two great capitals, Paris and London, gathering letters of recommendation to both, partly through a web of supporters who, like them, were Freemasons.[130] A surviving letter dated Genoa, 7 September 1767, was addressed by Ivan Schousallow to Prince Galitzin, Russian ambassador to the court of France.[131] It recommended to his protection "Les Sieurs Filippo Manfredi excellent violon, et Luigi Boccherini, virtuoso di Violoncelle" and added finally, "Ils se proposent de passer en Angleterre après un Séjour de quelque mois à Paris." Their next stop was Nice, from which a letter of recommendation to Felice Giardini in London was written on 5 October 1767.[132] They reached Paris by late October.

Boccherini was known by his compositions in Paris before he was known in person. The *Mercure de France* dated 1 April 1767 announced the publication by Vénier of the first set of his string quartets as Op. 1. In July Bailleux published as Op. 2 the set of six string trios. In his catalogue the composer reversed these two opus numbers, giving the trios Op. 1 and the date of 1760, the quartets Op. 2, dating from 1761 (opus numbers cited hereafter are the composer's own). Their publication at Paris before he arrived there reinforces his claim that they were indeed composed as early as he says. When he appeared as a soloist playing one of his cello sonatas at the Concert Spirituel of 20 March 1778, the *Mercure* noted that he was "déja connu par ses trios et ses quatuors qui sont d'un grand effect" and that he executed his sonata "en maître."[133] Manfredi was less successful at the Concert Spirituel. Both were given further opportunities to display their performing talents at the salons given by the baron de Bagge (a prominent Freemason).

Customers who purchased Boccherini's first set of string quartets might have learned something about the identity of the composer even before he appeared in Paris. The slow movement of the first quartet begins with a solo for the cello that is more generous than ordinarily found in early string quartets (Example 9.17). The main key of the quartet is c, which gives Boccherini opportunity to introduce as contrast the key that was a great favorite of his, E♭. The first violin, used to having the lion's share of the musical interest in this literature, remains

[129]Giuseppe Cambini, "Ausführung der Instrumentalquartetten," *Allgemeine musikalische Zeitung* 47 (22 August 1804): 781–83. Friedrich Rochlitz, the editor, may have fabricated this article on the basis of Cambini's *Méthode*.

[130]Coli, *Luigi Boccherini*, pp. 47–48.

[131]Ibid., facsimile reprint as plate 7.

[132]Ibid., p. 49.

[133]Constant Pierre, *Histoire du Concert Spirituel, 1725–1790* (Paris, 1975), p. 148.

EXAMPLE 9.17. *Boccherini, Quartet in C, Op. 2 No. 1 (G. 159), 1*

silent for the length of the cello's opening oration, which is characteristic of the composer in its many downward turns of phrase and lends the melody a melancholic aura. Cello solos as prominent as this are relatively few in the first set of quartets, but the cello is treated in general with more independence than in quartets by other composers, in which the instrument is most often relegated to providing only a jogging bass line.

The beginning of the second quartet offers several typical traits (Example 9.18). Boccherini thinks in four-measure phrases and in melodies very often deployed as chains of thirds or sixths. He extends his thoughts by repeating them with roles exchanged. Here all four parts begin the second phrase in mm. 5–8 by taking on a part played by another instrument in mm. 1–4. This inverts the melody from sixths to thirds, lowers it by an octave, and lets the cello play what the first violin did, until they reverse roles in mm. 7–8, with the first violin resuming its treble part. The rapid-arpeggio descending triads first added by the viola in mm. 1–2 go to the second violin in mm. 5–6. Over the static harmony of mm. 8–10 there is a typically Boccherinian canonic interplay, followed by a delightful new theme in the dominant, F. The seconda parte begins with the initial theme on V, leading to a double reprise, which is not typical, the composer generally eliding into the second theme area. Both parts are marked for repetition. After a *Largo* middle movement in E♭, with initial cello solo, the quartet ends with an excellent and rousing fugue.

Boccherini made an important musical conquest in Madame Brillon de Joüy, the keyboard player so highly praised by Burney. He composed for her *Sei sonate*

EXAMPLE 9.18. *Boccherini, Quartet in B♭, Op. 2 No. 2 (G. 160), I*

The end of the reign became increasingly morose. In the wake of the great earthquake that destroyed Lisbon on 1 November 1755, the king closed the theaters for a year. Scarlatti died in 1757, Maria Barbara died in 1758, and her husband succumbed the following year after an agonizing dementia. They had no issue. Farinelli was pensioned and returned to Italy.

Charles III, henceforth called Carlos III, was the greatest of the Spanish Bourbon kings. He acceded the throne in 1759 at the age of 43 after ruling in Naples for 25 years, where he supported opera mainly to oblige his wife, Queen Maria Amalia. Unfortunately, she died within a year of reaching Spain. To his credit the king pursued the realm's economic recovery, begun earlier, and surrounded himself with able advisors such as Count Fuentes and Count Aranda, who became prime minister in 1766. Aranda determined to revive opera as a necessary enhancement of the king's glory. Thus came into being the Compañía de los Reales Sitios, a troupe that followed the court as it moved from place to place according to a rigidly determined schedule. Upon their arrival in Spain, Manfredi and Boccherini joined the orchestra of this troupe, whose director was the Venetian composer, and later publisher, Luigi Marescalchi.

We do not know what sort of promises, if any, brought Manfredi and Boccherini to Madrid. No contracts nor letters of recommendation have been found. Except for a very few printed librettos that survive, the repertory of the opera company remains obscure. Boccherini contributed several arias with obbligato cello solo for himself to play. His inspiration, like that of Tartini a generation earlier, came mainly from the verses of Metastasio. An example that may come from this time is his setting of "Se d'un amor tirano" (G. 557), an aria sung by Mandane in Act II of *Artaserse* (Example 9.19ab). He gave the poet's typical *settenarii* a simple, syllabic setting, which resulted in short, symmetrical phrases that prevail throughout. For his earlier solo he ornamented the melody and indulged in broken triads in high range. He must have particularly like this melody because he used it again, in even more ornamented guise, in a solo cello sonata with bass (G. 4/1) and as a solo for flute in the Sextet in C (G. 466/1) of 1773. He revived his 1765 Symphony in D (G. 490) to go with Piccinni's *La buona figliuola* at Aranjuez in summer 1769, the same year he provided a symphonie concertante for two solo violins and orchestra for a Lenten academy at the Caños del Peral theater in Madrid (G. 491). The Reales Sitios company performed in the Coliseo del Buen Retiro. One indication that Boccherini was gaining a public in the capital is his dedication of the six quartets of Op. 9 (1770) "alli Signori Diletanti di Madrid."

Two princes of the blood, unlike the king, took a lively interest in music. One was Crown Prince Carlos, who came with his father from Naples and bore the title prince of Asturias. To him Boccherini dedicated six string trios, Op. 6 (1769). The other was the king's younger brother, Don Luis, infante (the title given a royal son not heir to the throne). He stood high in the king's favor for having resisted

EXAMPLE 9.19. *Boccherini*, Artaserse, *Aria with cello solo (G. 557)*

all plots to set him on the throne during the year-long final anguish of Fernando VI.[139] Boccherini dedicated to him his Op. 8 string quartets (1769).

Boccherini's earliest trios and quartets were as much orchestral in derivation and intention as they were products of chamber music, it has been claimed.[140] (Some printed copies of Op. 2 were entitled *Sei sinfonie o sia quartetti*). With the trios and quartets of the later 1760s there is no doubt that they are very much chamber music. An early trio by Boccherini was one possible stimulus for Mozart's earliest quartet.[141]

[139]Charles C. Noel, "The Crisis of 1758–1759 in Spain: Sovereignty and Power during a 'Species of Interregnum,' " in *Royal and Republican Sovereignty in Early Modern Europe,* ed. Robert Oresko, G. C. Gibbs, and H. M. Scott (Cambridge, 1997), pp. 580–608.

[140]By Christian Speck, *Boccherinis Streichquartette: Studien zur Kompositionweise und zur gattungsgeschichtlichen Stellung* (Studien zur Musik 7) (Munich, 1987), pp. 82–92, 152.

[141]Ludwig Finscher, "Mozarts erstes Streichquartett: Lodi, 15. März 1770," *Analecta musicologica* 18 (1978): 246–70; 251–53. See also for a comparison, *Haydn, Mozart,* example 7.16ab, p. 560.

During the 1760s Boccherini compiled an impressive list of instrumental works. Those he intended for publication he assigned opus numbers and dates of composition in his catalogue. Excluded were his numerous cellos sonatas and concertos, also vocal works. Table 9.3 reproduces the data from his catalogue and in addition cites place, publisher, and date of first edition. To avoid discrepancies in early titles (between manuscripts and prints, for instance) titles are given in English.

TABLE 9.3. Boccherini's Works with Opus Numbers Composed 1760–70

Opus	Title and Date	Publication
1	6 String Trios, 1760	Paris, Bailleux, 1767
2	6 String Quartets, 1761	Paris, Vénier, 1767
3	6 Duets for two violins, 1761	Paris, La Chevardière, 1769
4	6 String Trios, 1766	Paris, Vénier, 1768
5	6 Keyboard Sonatas with obbligato violin, 1768	Paris, Vénier, 1768
6	6 String Trios, 1768	Paris, Vénier, 1771
7	Symphonie Concertante for two solo violins and orchestra, 1769	Paris, Vénier, 1769
8	6 String Quartets, 1769	Paris, Vénier, 1769
9	6 String Quartets, 1770	Paris, Vénier, 1772

Not since Vivaldi had a composer put so much music for strings on the market within a few years. There are other parallels between the two composers. Both led hectic lives as virtuoso performers in addition to composing and teaching. Each extended the technique of his chosen solo instrument. Descriptive music appealed to both. Perhaps more than any other composers, they not only sought but obtained ready acceptance of their music by the public. Of importance in their formation, neither was trained to become a maestro di cappella. The absence of this superior professional status, equivalent to that of a history painter in art, freed both to become great painters in instrumental music.

IN THE SERVICE OF INFANTE LUIS

The year 1770 was the turning point of Boccherini's life. Destiny guided him, as he probably saw it, to his greatest patron, the homonymous Infante Luis. Boccherini had made a special veneration of his patron saint, King Louis IX of France, as he declared in his last will and testament.[142] The youngest son of Elizabeth Farnese and Philip V was anything but saintly. His mother, untroubled by scruples and hoping there would be another Farnese pope, had him created cardinal arch-

---

[142]Germaine de Rothschild, *Luigi Boccherini: His Life and Works* (London, 1965), pp. 82–85. The will, dated Madrid, 6 September 1799, contains the expected citations of the Holy Trinity, the church, and the Blessed Virgin Mary, then invokes "my Guardian Angel, the Saint of my name and of my special devotion," a point of which Coli, *Luigi Boccherini,* p. 166, makes nothing, calling the whole a formula.

bishop of Toledo and Seville as a boy. Within a decade the young man, loving life and women in particular, was separated from his ecclesiastical benefices. Eccentricities of his kind in a prelate of the highest birth might be tolerated in Italy but were not condoned by the Spanish church, not even in Don Luis de Borbón y Farnesio.

Don Luis deferred to his brother the king in all matters. With the permission of Carlos III he appointed Luigi chamber violoncellist and composer in a decree dated Aranjuez, 8 November 1770. The annual salary was a relatively high 14,000 reales, and it kept rising in subsequent years. Francisco de Goya was appointed royal painter in 1786 at 15,000 reales a year.

Life changed for Boccherini under Don Luis. He was twenty-seven, about the same age as Christian Bach when royal favor persuaded him to remain in his adopted land. Luigi may not have intended to stay in Spain any more than Bach intended to stay in England. A generous appointment made many things possible, notably marriage. In the spring of 1771 Luigi married Clementina Pelliccia, one of the sopranos in the Sitios Reales company. He sent to Lucca for his widowed mother, who moved to Madrid, perhaps in time for the marriage. Both Luigi and his wife left the opera company.

The year 1771 was an extremely productive one for Luigi. He composed his first two sets of six string quintets, Opp. 10 and 11, and his first set of six symphonies, Op. 12. His string quintets with two cellos became the greatest favorite of Don Luis, for whom no fewer than seventy were composed. The second set, Op. 11, contained the Quintet in E (G. 275) with the celebrated "minuet of Boccherini." It kept the composer's memory alive when almost all his music was forgotten by the late nineteenth century. To the age of Massenet it evoked powdered wigs and rococo prettiness. Such images obscured Boccherini's exquisite craftsmanship, his unerring sense for getting the best sounds out of his instruments, and above all his felicity of melodic invention. A trill and melodic turn begin the famous minuet tune, followed by a syncopated line and melodic sighs. The lightest of accompaniments supports this ethereal melody, a continual pizzicato in the lower strings, perhaps suggesting the guitars of Mediterranean climes.

Another work of 1771, the Symphony in d, Op. 12 No. 4 (G. 506), represents the composer's dark and turbulent side, often remarked by his contemporaries. Its finale takes for its subject nothing less than the culminating "Dance of the Furies" in Gluck's ballet *Don Juan* (Vienna, 1761), an epochal work on a theme that was not just Spanish, but Sevillian, about a don whose womanizing brought him down. Boccherini portrays the descent to hell, borrowing freely from the Viennese master he obviously adored, composing what in earlier times would have been called a parody. Some early manuscripts refer to the devilish symphony as "Della casa del diavolo." Boccherini may well have performed Gluck's *Don Juan* during his third stay in Vienna. In any case it was an admirable connection of his Viennese past with his Madrileño present.

Manfredi was less fortunate in Madrid. He too composed arias with obbligato solos for himself, there being one in the *Montezuma* given at Aranjuez in 1768 as well as in *L'Almeria,* in which Luigi inserted an aria with cello obbligato to end Act II.[143] Manfredi apparently found no patron and no wife (he never married). In 1771 or 1772 he returned to Lucca and died there in 1777.

Gaetano Brunetti, violinist and composer, was the most prominent musical figure then in Madrid. He was probably a pupil of Nardini in Livorno. A year younger than Luigi, he moved to Spain with his parents in 1762. He entered the service of Carlos III as twelfth violinist in the royal chapel in 1767 and was also appointed music and violin teacher to the prince of Asturias. He gradually moved to the front desks of the orchestra. His various duties included composing for the court, and in 1779 he was made director of festivities at Aranjuez, the post held by Farinelli until his departure. Like Boccherini he was mainly a composer of instrumental music, although there were a few works written for the church or for stage performance. He composed chamber music and symphonies in abundance. Vénier in Paris printed sets of trios and sextets by him. His symphonies, along with Viennese ones, dominated music at court.[144]

Madrid's enthusiasts for playing and listening to chamber music could choose in the 1770s among the works of Brunetti and Boccherini, and the quartets of Haydn, prints of which were taken up avidly. Tomás de Iriarte sang the praises of Haydn in his poem "La música" (1779), which shows how much his works were appreciated there; specifically praised were Haydn's string quartets. Iriarte also praised the operas of Gluck. Spain, though isolated in many ways from the rest of the Continent, was obviously not immune to its musical mainstreams, at least not in court circles. Brunetti and Boccherini became professional rivals in supplying their patrons with the latest and most modish kinds of music. Don Luis patronized both composers.

Prominent solos for cello such as we have seen in Boccherini's first set of string quartets endeared him to good performers on the instrument but not to everyone. The composer cut down on the number of cello solos in his string quartets of Opp. 8, 9, and 15 (1768–72). The reasons may have been less artistic than commercial. The change could even have emanated from his publisher Vénier in Paris, who perhaps saw a sales advantage in keeping the master's string quartet textures close to the norm for the genre. This is not to suggest that Boccherini reverted to the jogging, hum-drum basses all too common then. Rather, he integrated the cello's voice in a consort of four equals and treated it less often as the star of the show. What is true of his quartets is also true of his trios. The quintets

[143]Coli, *Luigi Boccherini,* pp. 66–67.
[144]David Wyn Jones, "Austrian Symphonies in the Royal Palace, Madrid," in *Music in Spain during the Eighteenth Century,* ed. Malcolm Boyd and Juan José Carreras (Cambridge, 1998), pp. 125–43.

presented a whole new world of possibilities with their two cellos. If one tended mainly to bass-line duties, the other could be freer to soar on its own.[145]

Another way in which Vénier may have had some say in the quartets relates to their length and the number of minor-mode works in a set. In the case of both Op. 8 and Op. 9 Boccherini included two quartets in the minor, in c and d in Op. 9. These sets he qualified in his catalogue as "opera grande," that is, substantial works in three or four movements. He used the same description for his first set. When Vénier brought out the next set, Op. 15 composed in 1772, there was only one quartet in the minor, No. 6 in c, and it concluded with a minuet-like movement in C. All six have only two movements, both in the same key, and the composer lists them as "opera piccola." In other words, they approach the most typical movement sequence of the lightweight symphonie concertante, so popular in Paris at the time.

The quintets in particular made Boccherini's fame. They are cited often by his contemporaries, always with praise. A group of teachers at the Paris Conservatoire recommended them in a method for cello published ca. 1804. They had no doubts as to who created the genre.

> If there is a genre that seems to have been made for the violoncello, it is the quintet as the celebrated Boccherini conceived of it; in making the instruments heard as both accompanying part and a reciting part he gives the medium a double charm, and becomes a creator of this genre as Haydn has done for the symphony and Viotti for the concerto: his original style, full of grace, freshness and purity, and of an expression so special, compels us to cite him as a model for those who study the violoncello, and who search to make it speak its true language in the three principal kinds of movement.[146]

The authors quote liberally from Boccherini in exemplifying slow, moderate, and fast movements. Their remark about Boccherini's making the cello speak its "true language" is akin to Burney's praise of the composer for writing "in the true genius of the instruments."

Once Boccherini settled into a comfortable life in the service of Infante Don Luis, his career resembled that of Haydn, not Vivaldi. He became even more prolific, as can be seen from Table 9.4 showing works he dated 1771–76. The Italian titles are retained here so that a distinction can be observed between full-scale

---

[145]A good example can be seen in the autograph score Boccherini wrote for his own use of the Quintet Op. 18 No. 5 in d of 1774, the first page of which is reproduced in Gérard, *Catalogue of the Works of Luigi Boccherini,* plate 2. The cello at the bottom of the score uses bass clef and plays a real bass. The one above uses tenor clef and plays florid melodic turns.

[146]Pierre Baillot, Nicolas Baudiot, Charles-Simon Catel, and Jean Henri Levasseur, *Méthode de Violoncelle et de Basse d'Accompagnement . . . adoptée par le conservatoire impérial de musique* (Paris, 1804; reprint 1974), p. 2.

works ("grande") and those in fewer and shorter movements (designated by a diminutive title).

Table 9.4. Boccherini's Works with Opus Numbers Composed 1771–76

Opus	Title and Date	Publication
10	6 Quintetti, 1771	Paris, Vénier, 1774
11	6 Quintetti, 1771	Paris, Vénier, 1775
12	6 Sinfonie, 1771	Paris, La Chevardière, 1776
13	6 Quintetti, 1772	Paris, Vénier, 1776
14	6 Trio, 1772	Paris, La Chevardière, 1773
15	6 Quartettini, 1772	Paris, Vénier, 1773
16	6 Sestetti (flute), 1773	Paris, La Chevardière, 1775
17	6 Quintettini (flute), 1773	Paris, La Chevardière, ca. 1775
18	6 Quintetti, 1774	Paris, La Chevardière, 1775
19	6 Quintettini, (flute), 1774	Paris, Vénier, 1777
20	6 Quintetti, 1775	Paris, Vénier, 1777
21	6 Sinfonie, 1775	Paris, La Chevardière, 1776?
22	6 Quartettini, 1775	Paris, La Chevardière, 1776?
23	6 Sestetti, 1776	Paris, Sieber, ca. 1780

In a new flurry of activity the composer was delivering as many as three sets a year to the voracious music publishers of Paris. These first editions were taken up for the most part by other publishers also. Many manuscript copies circulated as well all over Europe. Note that the weighty chamber works ("opera grande") shifted from quartets to quintets. Flute quintets and sextets (with one flute and strings) joined the list. Two superb sets of symphonies for strings and winds gave notice that Boccherini was a serious rival to Christian Bach or any other symphonist of the time.

The Op. 21 symphonies of 1775 are even more inventive and diverse than the Op. 12 symphonies of 1771. Throughout Op. 12 Boccherini calls for two cello parts, and in No. 4 in d ("Della casa del diavolo") plus No. 5 in B♭ he calls for two viola parts as well. Op. 21 is less elaborate in orchestration. No. 4 in D (G. 496) is an Italian overture in three movements in which the third repeats the opening *Allegro* in abbreviated form (like Mozart's Symphony No. 32 in G of 1779). Boccherini's opening movement begins with a canon, the first violins being imitated at the unison by the seconds at a distance of two measures. This device is similar in melodic shape to the opening of the composer's earliest surviving symphony, G. 490 of 1765, which is also an overture. The pair invite comparison.

G. 490 begins with a canon at the distance of one measure, the two violin parts tumbling over each other, then giving way to a tutti doing the same (Example 9.20). After arriving at the dominant they repeat the same process, which gives the impression of one of those children's rounds like "Row, row, row your boat"

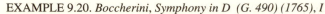

EXAMPLE 9.20. *Boccherini, Symphony in D (G. 490) (1765), I*

that become more tedious with every repetition. For contrast Boccherini resorts to a lame sequence, a circle-of-fifths progression with suspended dissonances layered on top, surprising for a composer who was going to become so inventive. The general impression here is that he has not advanced beyond Sammartini. His *Allegro* ends on the dominant, as is characteristic of many Italian overtures, which leads directly into the slow middle movement in the same key of D (Example 9.21). Violins in octaves play the smooth and beguiling theme in octaves, supported by violas and a bass that moves in quarter notes, like a minuet. Christian Bach could gladly have written the chromatically raised tone in the second measure, the seventh chord in the middle of the following measure, or the rise to a melodic peak in the fifth measure, as well as the many conjunct thirds, both in the melody and the bass. In fact he did write something very like this (see Example 9.11 on p. 928) and Mozart copied him. G. 490 ends with a brief and perfunctory *Allegro assai* in 3/8 time that also begins with a canon.

Assigning the melody to two violins in octaves is a Viennese practice. It was roundly attacked by North German music critics, who blamed Haydn, and defended by a critic in Vienna, who credited Haydn with its invention.[147] There is evidence to show that Joseph Starzer used the device in his ballets as early as 1752, when Haydn had scarcely started to compose.[148] Surely it was a practice from popular dance music in Vienna, in which Haydn did play violin as one means of eking out a living. Starzer transformed it into a texture worthy of higher things. He was the composer and orchestra leader whose ballets dominated the musical repertory of the Kärntnerthor theater in the 1750s and 1760s. Boccherini, as a cellist in the same orchestra during his three sojourns at Vienna, had ample opportunity to become acquainted with Starzer's music. The texture of violins in

[147]*Haydn, Mozart*, p. 257.
[148]In a minuet from the ballet *Psiché et l'amour* (Vienna, 1752), exemplified in *Haydn, Mozart*, p. 131.

which provokes a different response by the tutti, then on the tonic. Everything comes back in order. A little coda ensues when the violins again begin their canon. But it is cut off by the tutti after only two measures with rousing cadential gestures. The sense of dialogue so evident here has actually been a constant throughout the movement, an ongoing exploitation of the question and answer so marked in mm. 1–8. Those commentators of the time who heard the master's music in terms of dramatic action were far from wrong.

The middle movement is an *Andantino con moto* in 3/4 time and in d, tonic minor being a frequent choice for slow movements with this composer. As in G. 490 the violins begin singing the melody in octaves. They soon switch to parallel thirds. The movement as a whole is wistful and poignant, providing enough justification for the return of the boisterous *Allegro* to close the symphony.

The circumstances that led Boccherini to compose quintets with two cellos may have been purely musical, postulated above as a splitting of duties between bass function and more elaborate, often high, florid writing. Practical concerns involving the musicians available to him may also have played a role. Don Luis had in his employ from 1771 Francisco Font, a viola player on an annual salary of 9,000 reali and father of three string players gradually added to the payroll, Antonio, Pablo, and Juan.[150] Together the Font family made up a string quartet and probably got to play many of Luigi's works in the genre for Don Luis. If Luigi added himself as performer (presumably of the more florid cello parts) we have the ensemble for the quintets, of which he wrote even more than quartets. The string quintet with two violas was perhaps more prevalent throughout Europe, and Mozart's personal favorite, but the quintet with two cellos, inspired by Boccherini, had partisans in Brunetti and Cambini.[151] The general richness of sound of Boccherini's quintets has been claimed as an influence on Christian Bach, in some of his late works.[152] Boccherini favored duet against duet even in his Op. 2 quartets of 1761, which may have influenced Haydn.[153] The quintets gave him still more possible combinations for duetting, and he exploited them to the full. His first quintet provides examples (Example 9.23).

Until 1776 Boccherini followed the court on its fixed rounds as did his master, although there may also have been months of repose at one or the other of the palaces allotted the infante. Don Luis was a collector—of clockworks, ancient

---

[150]Coli, *Luigi Boccherini*, pp. 71–72.

[151]Ellen Iris Amsterdam, "The String Quintets of Luigi Boccherini" (Ph.D. diss., University of California, Berkeley, 1968), pp. 109–27.

[152]Stephen Roe, "J. C. Bach and 'New Music, at a More Reasonable Expense,'" *Musical Times* 126 (1985): 529–31; 531.

[153]Haydn is at his most Boccherini-like in the opening movement of the Quartet in C of Op. 20 (1772), which not only opens with the cello playing the theme, but also dissolves into lacy open-work duetting. See *Haydn, Mozart*, pp. 342–43.

coins, and specimens of natural history, among other things. According to family history Boccherini's mother died in 1776, when he was at Aranjuez, which the court visited annually during spring.

Don Luis wished to marry. Carlos III, who never remarried, was naturally opposed to the idea, for fear that a male heir of Luis might eventually challenge the succession of his son, the prince of Asturias, who was an unpopular figure and foreign born (in Naples). Henry Swinburne was visiting the court at Aranjuez in early May 1776 and wrote a discerning portrait of its austere monarch, his passion for hunting, his children, and lastly the infante.

> Don Lewis, the king's brother, after having been a cardinal and an archbishop, is now on the eve of matrimony with a pretty Arragonese girl, whom he took a fancy to last year, as she was running across the fields after a butterfly. As he has made a collection of natural history, this similarity of taste made a great impression upon him. This wedding, which the king has consented to with reluctance, has produced a total revolution in the marriage-laws of Spain. A new pragmatica or edict is published, to prevent all matches betwixt persons of unequal rank and quality. . . . Don Lewis's bride is not to be allowed the title or rank of a princess of the blood, nor are her children to be deemed qualified to succeed to the crown; he is to reside near Talavera, where I make no doubt but he will lead a happy life, as he has a great taste for music and natural history; his cabinet already contains a very valuable collection of rarities, especially such as are found in the Spanish dominions. This prince is cheerful, humane, affable, and full of pleasantry; good qualities that render him the darling of the nation.[154]

He was also, from the moment of his marriage, virtually banished from court, which he was allowed to visit only once a year, without his wife. She was the seventeen-year-old Maria Teresa de Vallabriga y Rosas and she bore her fifty-one-year-old husband three beautiful children, lovingly painted for posterity by Goya in his 1783 portrait of their household at the palace of Arenas, some ninety miles southwest of Madrid, in the mountains. One grave and handsome man standing in the right forefront of the painting has been identified as Boccherini.[155]

Boccherini's family also grew at Arenas, as did his list of compositions. Don Luis, being an affable and generous prince, may have allowed his eminent cellist-

[154]Henry Swinburne, *Travels through Spain in the Years 1775 and 1776* (London, 1779), letter dated Aranjuez, 6 May 1776, reproduced as "At the court of Charles III," *FMR* (English edition) 5 (1986), 66–68. The author was the fourth son of Sir John Swinburne and a Catholic who had been educated in France.

[155]Francisco de Goya, *The Family of the Infante Don Luis de Borbón*, oil on canvas, Fondazione Magnani-Rocca, Corte di Mamiano. Reproduced as a whole and in details to illustrate Vittorio Sgarbi, "Goya and Don Luis," *FMR* 5 (1986): 50–71. Also reproduced in Coli, *Luigi Boccherini* (plates V–VI), which identifies the composer, p. 102, and in *Goya and the Spirit of Enlightenment*, ed. Alfonso E. Perez Sanchez and Eleanor A. Sayre (Boston, 1989), no. 5, with summaries of the scholarly literature on the picture and on Don Luis.

EXAMPLE 9.23. *Boccherini, Quintet in A, Op. 10 No. 1 (G. 265), I*

composer liberty to attend musical affairs in the capital from time to time. Still, the exile at Arenas was not unlike what Haydn complained about at Esterháza, only worse, because it was twice the distance from the metropolis. Oddly enough, Boccherini tried to make contact with Haydn at just this period, sending his compliments to the master via their common publisher, the Viennese firm of Artaria. In a letter dated February 1781 Boccherini wrote describing Haydn as "a composer admired in the highest degree by me and by the whole world. . . . I am one of the most ardent appreciators and admirers both of his genius and of his musical compositions, which are received here with all the esteem that in strict justice they merit."[156] Haydn wished to reply in kind and tried to locate Arenas so he could

[156]Rothschild, *Luigi Boccherini: His Life and Works*, pp. 45–46.

write to Boccherini, but Artaria did not or could not supply a more exact address. Of the works Boccherini sent, Artaria published Opp. 25, 26, and 32. In them he lessened his usual reliance on manipulating blocks of differing textures and opted for more motivic development, a process begun in his Op. 24 quartets of 1776–78.[157] In other words, he wrote quartets and quintets that were more Viennese, more like his greatly admired idol Haydn, without ever losing his own voice, so distinctive that it can be recognized almost instantly. Few composers of the time were so Protean as to manage a feat like this. One who boasted that he could counterfeit any musical style was, of course, Mozart.

Whereas Boccherini remained as productive as before at Arenas, at least up to 1782, the works went increasingly unpublished, as may be seen from Table 9.5.

[157]Christian Speck, *Boccherinis Streichquartette* (Munich, 1987), pp. 125–26.

Table 9.5. Boccherini's Works with Opus Numbers composed 1776-84

Opus	Title and Date	Publication
24	6 Quartetti, 1776–78	Paris, Sieber, 1778?
25	6 Quintetti, 1778	Vienna, Artaria, ca. 1785
26	6 Quartettini, 1778	Vienna, Artaria, 1781
27	6 Quintettini, 1778	Venice, Zatta, 1782?
28	6 Quintettini, 1779	
29	6 Quintettini, 1779	
30	6 Quintetti, 1780	
31	6 Quintetti, 1780	
32	6 Quartetti, 1780	Vienna, Artaria, ca. 1782
33	6 Quartettini, 1781	
34	6 Trios, 1781	Paris, Naderman, ca. 1782
35	6 Sinfonie, 1782	
36	6 Quintettini, 1784	(Redated 1786 for presentation to the prince of Prussia)*

*Marco Mangani and Remigio Coli,"Osservazioni sul Catalogo autografo di Luigi Boccherini: I Quintetti a due violoncelli," *Rivista italiana di musicolgia* 32 (1997): 315–26.

Failure to achieve publication could be attributed to a number of factors. Lack of popularity with the public was not one of them—music publishers in Paris and London continued to reprint his earlier works throughout the 1780s. Vénier went out of business by 1784. The remoteness of Arenas made communication more difficult. Artaria, as far as we know, published only a portion of the music Boccherini sent him. Economic conditions were in decline, both in Vienna and in Paris, where his connections had been the strongest. After the upheavals of the Revolution in France the composer reestablished communications with Paris. Unfortunately for him, he sent the quintets of Opp. 28, 29, and 31 to Ignace Pleyel there, a publisher he respected as a composer. He lived to rue this decision because Pleyel arbitrarily disrupted the carefully planned sets of six and printed some quintets but not others, beginning only in 1798 and stretching beyond the composer's death in 1805. We have Pleyel to thank, on the other hand, for the amazing series of protesting letters from Boccherini, in which he said some remarkably personal things about himself.

"THE TRUE GENIUS OF THE INSTRUMENTS"

Signs of slackening in the composer's steady output began to appear by 1783. Perhaps they were due to an illness. Disruptions soon followed. His wife died in the first part of 1785, leaving six children. The death of Infante Luis followed on 7 August 1785. Boccherini requested a pension from the king in recompense for his long service. He was granted 12,000 reali per annum for a sinecure in the royal chapel. The move back to Madrid was accomplished by late 1785. He took a small house in the capital's populous northern sector.

The following year opened new chapters in his life. He had earlier sent to Berlin copies of some of his quintets for Frederick William, the cello-playing prince of Prussia. On 27 January 1786 he received an appointment at 1,000 ducats a year as chamber composer in absentia to the prince, who succeeded his uncle Frederick II as Frederick William II the same year. To this remote patron Boccherini added a nearby patroness, the countess-duchess of Benevente-Osuna, who named him as composer to and leader of her small orchestra. She commissioned him to write an opera, or rather a zarzuela, for performance in her palace by members of her family. He fulfilled her wishes with *La Clementina,* a Spanish play in two acts by Ramón de la Cruz to which he added some eighteen arias and ensembles, plus an overture. Opera returned in a bigger way to Madrid during 1786 with the engagement of a professional Italian company at the Caños del Peral theater. After years of exile at Arenas, Boccherini could enjoy attending the latest comic operas of Paisiello, including *Il barbiere di Siviglia.*

Difficult though it must have been with several children in a small house and a once-again hectic professional life, Boccherini gradually resumed his former diligence as a composer. He remarried in 1787. Between 1788 and 1799 he inscribed Opp. 40 to 56 in his catalogue. He wrote many new quartets and quintets, including four quintets for pianoforte and strings in Op. 56 of 1797. After this point many of his sets are quintet arrangements in which two violas are substituted for two cellos, or a guitar is substituted. The guitar quintets originated to satisfy a request from the marquis de Benevent, an able guitarist. Two more sets of original quintets with two violas were composed as late as 1801 (Op. 60) and 1802 (Op. 62), both being dedicated to another patron, Lucien Bonaparte, French ambassador to Madrid. Illnesses rendered the year 1803 infertile, but in 1804 Boccherini set out to compose another set of six string quartets. He completed only the first, leaving the second unfinished.

Boccherini's artistic lineage invites comment. Eximeno, the Spanish music theorist, probably did not know the composer personally because he was banished from Spain as a Jesuit in 1767 and settled in Rome, where he wrote his masterwork. He placed Boccherini among numerous other string players and composers inspired by Tartini, who in his turn had been inspired by Corelli.

The works of Corelli will always be admired for their variety of beautiful and well-sustained subjects, for the exact observation of the rules of harmony, for the solidity of the basses, and for the attitude toward exercising the hand of the performer. Tartini added to these more charm and more rapidity in managing the bow. And in this school founded by Corelli and perfected by Tartini, were formed Constanzi, Boccherini, Bottesi, Pugnani, Nardini, Giardini, Manfredi, Lolli, Ferrari, Freddi, and so many other valorous performers with the bow, who are today the delight of Europe.[158]

Thus performing excellence was not to be separated from composition in this select company, of whom the last and greatest was Boccherini.

The Italian tradition of string playing and composing, as refined by Tartini, suffices to explain the inspiration behind the cello sonatas and concertos of Boccherini. He may well owe something to Sammartini's string trios as well, but as the liberator of the cello, he stands as the inventor of the modern string trio with his Op. 1 of 1760. As for the modern string quartet, he is, with Joseph Haydn, its co-creator.[159] One critic wrote of Boccherini: "the instrumental music of Italy, Spain, and even France profited especially by him, in that he was the first there to write quartets in which all the instruments play obbligato parts; at least, he was the first to find general acceptance there with such works."[160] He and Haydn each profited from the musical ferment in Vienna initiated by Mathias Georg Monn, Wagenseil, Starzer, and others that led both masters to excel at quartets and symphonies.

Paris cannot be omitted any more than Vienna in the formation of the mature Boccherini. His visit there in 1767–68 marked his music for life, both by showing him how to arrange his sets and market them, and by leading him to adopt certain fashions such as those connected with the rondeau and the symphonie concertante. Fully mature by the time he went to Madrid in 1768, might he have become the same great master wherever he settled? No. The invention of the string quintet with two cellos and cultivation of it extensively as his most original and important genre have a lot to do with his principal patron, Don Luis. This raises the question of what isolation for years in the mountains at the heart of Spain did for his musical inspiration.

Descriptive music appealed to Boccherini and he left some stunning examples of it in his quintets. In his Op. 11 there is a good example. He probably considered the set's high point not the Quintet in E, No. 5 (with the celebrated minuet) but No. 6 in A, to which he attached the label "L'ucceliera" (The Aviary). Don Luis was a bird lover and maintained aviaries at his various residences. An equivalent in chamber music hardly surprises. The work begins with a short slow introduction, *Adagio*, followed by an *Allegro giusto* in A in which the upper strings emit various chirpings and bird calls, against the more sustained harmonies of the

---

[158]Antonio Eximeno y Pujades, *Dell'origine e delle regole della musica* (Rome, 1774), p. 437. All names mentioned have been encountered before with the exception of Bottesi and Freddi, who must have been string players Eximeno heard in Italy. The Roman Constanzi, cited first, just before Boccherini, was, of course, his teacher.

[159]Finscher, *Studien zur Geschichte des Streichquartett I* (Kassel, 1974), p. 23.

[160]Anonymous obituary of the composer in the *Allgemeine musikalischer Zeitung* of 21 August 1805, quoted from Le Guin, "As My Works Show Me to Be," pp. 246–47.

lower strings. There follows an *Allegro* in 6/8 time that he labels "I pastori et le cac-ciatori" (The shepherds and the hunters). The first are represented by a repeated eight-measure section in the key of a minor over drone harmonies. It is followed by a section twice as long in the key of C major and given over to hornlike fan-fares and hunting calls, as if in interruption of the shepherd's pastoral life by the passage of horses, hounds, and huntsmen (Example 9.24). The shepherd's drone in a minor eventually returns to finish the movement, after a contrasting section in 2/4 time, with canon between the viola and cello 1, who is instructed to play "harmonics on the third and fourth strings near the bridge." Such special effects were dear to the composer.

"The Aviary" is Boccherini's equivalent in subject matter to Beethoven's *Pastoral* Symphony. Although lacking a thunderstorm, it does not want for dramatic tension. The conflict between aristocratic hunters and country people was a wide-

EXAMPLE 9.24. *Boccherini, Quintet Op. 11 No. 6 ("The Aviary") (G. 276), II*

spread topos of the time and even went on the stage as the subject of an opéra-comique, *Le jardinier et son seigneur* (Paris, 1761) by Sedaine and Philidor. Boccherini might have known it, but he hardly needed a stagework to prompt him. Noblemen trampled fields and forests in every country pursuing the stag and other game, nowhere more passionately than in Spain, whose monarch was hunting mad and often drew Don Luis into his favorite pastime. Swinburne's description of Carlos III, written from Aranjuez in May 1776, gives a hilarious account of the king's obsession with the hunt. Boccherini follows his shepherds and hunters with a serene *Tempo di Minuetto* in A, perhaps implying reconciliation, then with a return to a portion of the bird music from the *Allegro giusto*. He was very fond of cyclic returns to end a work.

Much of Boccherini's music sounds dramatic and descriptive even though he rarely labeled exactly what he was describing. It struck his contemporaries the same way. The Neapolitan savant Saverio Mattei, when celebrating the poetic power of Metastasio and Jommelli, digressed with an apostrophe on instrumental music.

Music and Poetry are sisters. In the happy times of Greece poetry without music was not known, and the poet was the same as the singer, even as to his name. Perhaps music without poetry was also unknown, because absolute instrumental music did not exist, or was what pantomime is with respect to drama, which imitates and represents actions in dance that ought to be expressed by words and singing. In fact the finest composers of instrumental music among us do not write at random, but propose a poetic theme, a picture, and their sonatas also have titles like storm, springtime, and so on, as anyone can see in Corelli [does he mean Vivaldi?]. The admirable trios, quartets, quintets, and sextets of Boccherini will always be the most perfect models of instrumental music because, besides the inspiration, learning, invention and precision, they always have joined with these qualities that of cantabile, which renders these notes not just a capricious melody of warblings, but a measured and harmonious, poetic cantilena.[161]

Boccherini himself wrote that music meant nothing if it was without sentiment or failed to speak to the human heart.[162] Emanuel Bach agreed.

Another descriptive quintet, even better known than "The Aviary," is the composer's "Night Music of the Streets of Madrid," the sixth and last work in Op. 30 of 1780 (G. 324). Did this bit of nostalgia serve to console the exiled prince at Arenas? It has five movements, depicting in order a sounding of the bells for the Ave Maria, the minuet of the beggars ("the violoncellists will hold their instruments across their knees and, using all the nails of their hand, will imitate the sound of a guitar"), the chanting of the Rosary, a passacaglia of the street singers, and finally the military retreat. The last is a theme with eleven variations: "One will imagine that the retreat begins to be heard in the distance, so that it must first be played *piano,* so softly that it is scarcely audible; the indications *crescendo* and marcando must then be strictly observed." The retreat fades away to nothing, giving the illusion of spatial distance. This trick was familiar from the theater, as well as from real life on the streets of Madrid.

Famous, too, in this category is the "Fandango" Quintet, Op. 40 No. 2 (G. 341), dated April 1788. The conception must have begun earlier because the composer described it as "Quintettino that imitates the fandango that Padre Basilio played on his guitar for his royal highness Don Luis." Thus the prince, who died in 1785, had listened willingly to Spanish popular music such as this dance. Boccherini cultivates its hypnotic repetition of two harmonies, i and V, almost to the exclusion of anything else for over two hundred measures of moderate 3/4 time. A section in the middle is marked "castanets," calling either for use or imitation of these instruments to accentuate the rhythm. Ravel's *Bolero* is no more intoxicating or seductive. Other uses Boccherini made of popular Spanish dances include a "Follia" trio of the minuet in Quintet No. 76 (Op. 40 No. 1) and "La tiranna," a *Presto* in 3/8 time in Quartet No. 65 (Op. 44 No. 4). The "Fandango" Quintet tops all his uses of Iberian folk music. He later arranged it for guitar quintet (G. 448), making it sound even more Spanish. Visual artists also captured national folk dances. In the anonymous picture shown in Figure 9.10, a couple in native costume uses castanets while dancing to the music of a single guitar player. Even the landscape says Spain: vast arid plains extend to distant mountains.

Several of Boccherini's contemporaries were struck by a dark and melancholy strain they perceived in his music. Junker could not listen to his music for long, he

---

[161]Saverio Mattei, *Memorie per servire alla vita del Metastasio ed elogio di N. Jommelli* (Colle, 1785; reprint Bologna, 1987), p. 61.
[162]Letter to Lucien Bonaparte dated Madrid, 8 July 1799, cited by Rothschild, *Luigi Boccherini: His Life and Works,* pp. 76–77.

said in *Zwanzig Componisten* (1776), finding it "too shadowed, too dark, too morose"; Junker also complained of improvisatory capriciousness.

> Boccherini seems to me discontinuous, chasing after his every momentary, particular feeling,—he seems to allow too decisive a role to accident,—to momentary products of his imagination,—to momentary feelings of his breast, too particular to relinquish, and so, inevitably, in the putting together of sections, here and there a part is missing; here and there a section too few or too many sticks out. The most appropriate sentiment in response to Boccherini is, on the whole, a shudder. . . . Since I have come to know his Quintets for two violoncellos, the man begins (at least for me) to seem warmer, and to have a more decisive influence on my feelings; there he seems to have worked following a plan, an outline. They are beautiful,—pathetic. It seems meanwhile that in the Allegros he has made himself more acquainted with the Germans; they have a German cut and flow: but the Adagios in them, over which the Italians will be beside themselves, are and remain for Germans—intolerable.[163]

FIGURE 9.10. Anonymous engraving of a couple dancing with castanets.

The critic himself, a spokesman for south German *Empfindsamkeit,* was prone to throwing his thoughts down in a helter-skelter way. At least he shows that the quintets, within five years of their first publication, were making their way through Europe and causing a sensation. If anything, they were less Germanic than the quartets and trios that preceded them. The richer medium encouraged the composer to think even more in terms of timbre and sonority than of motivic development. His legacy to posterity was the creative freedom to glory in sound for its own sake.

Another critic, in 1779, compared Boccherini's somber qualities in the quartets to Edward Young's *Night Thoughts,* poems on death first published in London in 1741 and subsequently in innumerable editions and translations; contrasted

---

[163]Carl Ludwig Junker, *Zwanzig Componisten: Eine Skizze* (Bern, 1776), pp. 17–21, cited after Le Guin, "As My Works Show Me to Be," pp. 211–13, with some retranslation.

with them, as an example of good cheer, were sonatas by Giardini.[164] In 1783 Burney and his friend Thomas Twining exchanged opinions on the question of who was the more serious and pathetic in his music, Boccherini or Haydn. Twining argued that Boccherini was more given to pathos, and Burney yielded to the extent of writing, "I'll allow that Boccherini is more constantly serious than Haydn—nay that he is always serious & Charming."[165] Pairing of Haydn and Boccherini became frequent. In his 1784 *Treatise on the art of music*, William Jones called the two "moderns" and credited them for invention but faulted them for the way in which they worked out their ideas.

> As for Haydn and Boccherini, who merit a first place among the moderns for invention, they are sometimes so desultory and unaccountable in their way of treating a subject, that they must be reckoned among the wild warblers of the wood: and they seem to differ from some pieces of Handel as the talk and laughter of the Tea-table (where, perhaps, neither Wit nor Invention are wanting) differ from the Oratory of the Bar and the Pulpit.[166]

Jones hit the nail on the head: Handel's harangues in comparison sounded like a pompous lawyer or a sermon, with which Jones, being a clergyman, was well familiar.

Grétry, one of Boccherini's few peers among composers of the time, cited Haydn's symphonies in his memoirs as an example of drama that could be achieved in music even without words. An anonymous reviewer took care to add another.

> We can say as much of Boccherini, the sentimentalist par excellence, whose melody is so pure and harmony so complete, who is turn by turn somber, tender, heart-rending, graceful, and yet very gay, all by fits and starts. A young man had just played the following phrase for the first time, from one of the less known and quoted of his quintets:

[164]Pascal Boyer, *L'expression musicale, mise au rang des chimères* (Amsterdam, 1779), pp. 14–15. "One knows that the Sonatas of the celebrated Giardini are sprightly and gracious, and that the Quartets of Boccherini have something, I know not what, of sombreness which makes them comparable to the Nights of Young." Cited after Le Guin, "As My Work Shows Me to Be," p. 214. The ascription to Boyer (Boyé in the Dutch print) is uncertain.

[165]*The Letters of Charles Burney*, vol. 1: 1751–1784, ed. Alvaro Ribeiro. (Oxford, 1991), pp. 376–400. The exchange is summarized in *Haydn, Mozart*, p. 402.

[166]William Jones, *A Treatise on the art of music, in which elements of harmony and air are practically considered* (Colchester, 1784), p. 49, cited after Leonard Ratner, *Classic Music: Expression, Form, and Style* (New York, 1980), p. 27.

The bow fell from his hands, and he cried out: Behold the first accent of Ariadne's grief at the moment when she was abandoned upon the island of Naxos! Fontenelle would have said: Sonata, what do you want of me? Haydn and Boccherini respond: We want sensibility, and you have nothing but wit: go make your epigrams and your calculations.[167]

This reproof of an older generation's lack of sensibility was nothing new. The venerable poet Bernard Le Bovier de Fontenelle, who allegedly posed the famous question, was taken to task for it by Rousseau among others.[168]

The pairing with Haydn received very prominent support by Gerber in his article on Boccherini in the first edition of his *Lexicon* (1790). "No Italian knows how to use the treasures of harmony, none wanders the field of modulations with such freedom and abandon, as does he. And then how often melting, how heartfelt is his melody! and notwithstanding the great quantity of his compositions, how ever new and almost inexhaustible!"[169] Gerber next mentions the correspondence with Haydn as a further proof of Boccherini's renown, not realizing that it remained a failed attempt. "It seems that it is only Haydn whom we Germans can set against this Italian," continued Gerber.

Boccherini's harmony is indeed prone to caprices little known by music theorists. His recourse to modal passages and modal degrees provides an example.[170] His frequent chromatic passages, especially melodic descents in any part of the texture, help explain the melancholy he projected to many of his listeners. A fine Spanish composer, the Catalan Carlos Baguer, left a dozen or more symphonies that delight by their proximity to Haydn's style. The Symphony No. 12 in E♭ is one of his most sturdy and beautiful. Its mournful strains, with frequent drooping chromatic lines, suggest a further model in Boccherini.

We have seen already how Cambini, in order to demonstrate bowing, selected passages from Boccherini and Haydn in his *Nouvelle méthode* (ca. 1795): "I shall choose only two phrases for the moment, one taken from the elegant and tender Boccherini, the other, from the celebrated Haydn." He also cited Fontanelle's

---

[167]Anonymous review (signed "P") of Grétry, *Mémoirs, ou essais sur la musique,* in *Journal des Savans,* 30 ventôse an VI (1797): 171, cited after Le Guin, "As My Works Show Me to Be," pp. 223–24. The quintet in question is Op. 20 No. 6 (G. 294) composed in 1775 and published by Vénier two years later.

[168]Walter E. Rex, "A Propos of the Figure of Music in the Frontispiece of the *Encyclopédie*: Theories of Musical Imitation in d'Alembert, Rousseau and Diderot," in *Report of the Twelfth Congress of the International Musicological Society, Berkeley, 1977,* ed. Daniel Heartz and Bonnie Wade (Kassel, 1981), pp. 214–25. A revised version of the essay figures as Chapter 7 in Walter E. Rex, *The Attraction of the Contrary: Essays on the Literature of the French Enlightenment* (Cambridge, 1987), pp. 108–24.

[169]Ernst Ludwig Gerber, "Boccherini," in *Historische-Bibliographisches Lexikon der Tonkünstler,* 2 vols. (Leipzig, 1790–92).

[170]In the first movement of the Symphony No. 16 in A, Op. 37 No. 4 (G. 518), dated 1787, there is a perverse insistence upon vi, *followed* by V⁷, that is, the chords of a deceptive cadence, only backward.

famous question, answering it by saying it could only be asked of music indifferently performed, never of sonatas played by Tartini or Nardini, both of whom he had heard.

The last word should go to Burney. In the fourth volume of his *History*, published in 1789, he summarized Boccherini's place in the world of music with his usual acumen and sensitivity. Not knowing the conditions of the composer's life in the 1780s, he assumed that the hiatus in new works being published meant a decrease in productivity. From his own experience as a performer he realized how special a treat the quintets were to the discerning, with the caveat, "when well executed."

> Boccherini, who is still living at Madrid, and whose instrument is the violoncello, though he writes but little at present, has perhaps supplied the performers on bowed-instruments and lovers of Music with more excellent compositions than any master of the present age, except Haydn. His style is at once bold, masterly, and elegant. There are movements in his works, of every style, and in the true genius of the instruments for which he writes, that place him high in rank among the greatest masters who have ever written for the violin or violoncello. There is perhaps no instrumental Music more ingenious, elegant, and pleasing, than his quintets: in which invention, grace, modulation, and good taste, conspire to render them, when well executed, a treat for the most refined hearers and critical judges of musical composition.

In his old age Burney contributed the article on Boccherini to the *Cyclopaedia* of Abraham Rees. He saw fit to change nothing in the above, and to add only that the composer's works had lost little of their worth, nor would they ever wholly lose their bloom.

Epilogue

A new musical style emerged in Italy during the early eighteenth century. At Naples Leonardo Vinci led the way in his comic and serious operas beginning around 1720, followed by the visiting Hasse, Pergolesi, and other composers born or trained in Naples. They fashioned a simpler, more direct musical language in their vocal music by rejecting contrapuntal complexity and other intricacies of the past. The greatest rival to Naples at the time was Venice, which also cultivated the newer operatic fashions and was supreme in instrumental music. By 1720 Vivaldi and other Venetian composers had already completed a new framework for the concerto and given it an ideal form that long shaped the genre. The symphony also emerged in northern Italy, following the concerto, as did the modern sonata.

All these achievements spread quickly across the Alps. They found especially fertile ground in Dresden, where the musical establishment was closely tied to Venice, later to Naples. The Dresden court orchestra under maestro di cappella Heinichen and concertmaster Pisendel became the most famous of its day, and both masters were eminent practitioners of the Vivaldian concerto. Heinichen, in addition, was a leading music theorist, one whose vivid attacks on counterpoint still make lively reading.[1] Then came Hasse, who made Dresden the leading center of Italian opera in Germany.

Music historians have often identified the dominating type of eighteenth-century music as Italian court opera (*Hofoper*), by which is meant the international type of opera in Italian that graced the wealthier courts throughout Europe. This cosmopolitan phenomenon was contrasted with its nineteenth-century successor, described as being national and bourgeois. One drawback to such a crude and simplistic formulation is that it minimizes the extent of bourgeois sentiment and subject matter, sympathetically treated, in eighteenth-century opera. No one today, surely, will deny that the international vogue of Italian opera constituted the leading current in eighteenth-century music. To what extent it was court ordained, court connected, or even courtly by nature, can be argued.

All capital cities that have been studied here were ruled by courts. There were many princely courts during the eighteenth century that, regardless of size and power, vied with larger royal and imperial courts with regard to the prestige of their operas. To lump these together as "court opera" is to erect a monolith, as if there were no difference among them. It will prove more informative to make distinctions and pose questions as to who ran the opera at the various courts. Many rulers placed these responsibilities in the hands of a skilled impresario or a committee of directors. A recent archival study of the impresarial system then prevailing reveals how often the opera directors were in league with each other throughout Italy and beyond.[2]

Naples and Venice differed somewhat in the degree to which impresarios were empowered to run musical affairs. Noblemen owned the theaters of Venice, which often remained in the same family for several generations. They and the impresarios whom they employed were quite free of interference from the doge and his court, which consisted of several layers of government. The senate, made up only of aristocrats of centuries' standing, was the deliberative body and had jurisdiction over foreign affairs, finance, and commerce, although it could be overruled by the Council of Ten that stood even closer to the doge. Galuppi, maestro di cappella of the doge's church, the basilica of San Marco, and hence the state's highest-ranking musician, had to obtain approval from the senate to accept an invitation for a three-year stay at Saint Petersburg. This was treated as a matter of state. The Venetian Republic was of course honored to oblige the empress of all the Russias, Catherine II. Otherwise, it is difficult to see how the doge's court had much to do with Galuppi's operas, comic or serious.

---

[1]George J. Buelow, *Thorough-Bass Accompaniment according to Johann David Heinichen* (Berkeley, 1966), pp. 268–70.

[2]William C. Holmes, *Opera Observed: Views of a Florentine Impresario in the Early Eighteenth Century* (Chicago, 1993).

The impresarial system prevailed also at Naples, with the difference that the court made these appointments. Also, the main opera house was a royal institution, located in or near the king's palace (the Teatro San Carlo after 1737). The high level of music in the many churches of Naples, directly related to the flourishing of its four conservatories, and moreover the widely admired excellence of Neapolitan opera, declined very little, or not at all, when the government in 1734 passed from the vice regency of the Austrian Habsburgs to the personal rule of King Charles, a Spanish Bourbon. By the 1750s, on the other hand, the king, under the influence of his reforming minister Tanucci, began withdrawing support from the conservatories, and this led to a gradual decline in every phase of Neapolitan music.

Dresden and Berlin presented quite a different picture from each other. In the former, generous electors gave Hasse the power to decide nearly all matters touching music and abundant financial support with which to pursue his aims. The Saxon court was consequently regarded as a paradise for musicians. This happy state of affairs barely survived the scourging of Saxony by Prussia in the midcentury wars. Frederick II of Prussia took all matters musical into his own hands—in fact, all matters whatsoever. He served as his own prime minister, impresario, occasional librettist, and sometimes even composer. The rigidity of his taste led ultimately to a desiccated formalism and to the defection of so great a composer/performer as Emanuel Bach. But the brighter side of Frederick's legacy to music is that he poured such large sums into the court orchestra and opera that several of his servants were able to inaugurate a lively urban concert life in Berlin as a sideline. The moral may be that all expenditure in support of music does good in the end.

Stuttgart and Mannheim, comparatively modest courts, were not small in musical importance. Carl Eugen, a ruthless tyrant along the lines of Frederick II, ruined his duchy of Württemberg by maintaining an impossibly lavish opera and ballet under the direction of Jommelli and Noverre. Jommelli became the greatest representative of Italian opera in Germany after Hasse. Mannheim's Carl Theodore, no less passionate about music than Carl Eugen, was a wiser head. With meager resources he managed over many years to sustain a court that was distinguished in opera, ballet, sacred music, and, above all, symphonic concert music, which became the pride of Germany. His small court rivaled for a time the great court of Vienna, where musical monarchs were the norm and where high musical standards were demanded as a matter of course.

Courts played the central role in running the musical establishments at Vienna and the German capitals just mentioned. A tourist visiting one of them, such as Boswell at Mannheim in 1763, could sample gratis the rich musical offerings of church, theater, and concert hall, all of which were directly responsible to the court, and often to the ruler. Orders from on high decided what was performed, and the requisite financial underpinning with which to carry out the orders came from the same source. The Russian court was no different from the German ones in this respect. In Spain the court was more peripatetic than most, Madrid being only one of its many residences. The connection between the sovereigns' personal whims and the court music, which was close in Saint Petersburg, was less strong in Spanish musical life.

London and Paris, the two largest capital cities, present a picture very different from that of the German capitals. Both were very old and surprisingly independent of royal or court governance. A recent essayist on the history of London, upon being asked if he discovered that he had left out anything when he finished the book, answered that he had omitted nothing he intended to put in: "There's nothing in there about royalty, but I don't think they're a part of the essential London. The real London has always been democratic and egalitarian in spirit and hasn't had much use for the royals."[3] Paris shared the same spirit, perhaps to an even greater degree than London. Magistrates of the Parisian Parlement, although appointed by the king, fought doggedly to resist his influence, often managing to evade his direct commands.[4] The French monarchy under Louis XV was not so absolute as it looked. As in England the king was forced to share many of his powers.

The French court, even before the building of Versailles, was more often to be found moving around the chateaux of the Loire valley than resident in Paris. The regency of 1715–23 was an exception, during which time Paris became the seat of government, and after which Versailles regained the court and most of the governing functions. Royal appointees were in overall charge of the Opéra and the Opéra-Comique (after 1762) while the practical management from day to day was done by committees of professionals. The public paid entrance fees for seats or subscribed in advance for boxes. Music at court was in comparison relatively obscure and, in the case of opera, mostly brought from Paris for command performance. Accepting one of the four posts of court organist at Versailles, claimed Mozart, was tantamount to being buried alive. The Concert Spirituel in Paris, on the other hand, was an international showcase for new music and performing talent. Mozart did compose for it, and was well remunerated. It was a royal institution, like almost everything of any prominence in France. Yet there seems to be no case during its long history when it was actually attended by royals. Neither Gluck nor Grétry came to Paris at the invitation of the court, although after their arrival they were encouraged and supported by the music-loving Marie Antoinette, both as dauphine and as queen.

---

[3]Peter Ackroyd, *London: The Biography* (New York, 2001). The author was interviewed by Kenneth Baker in the *San Francisco Chronicle* dated 23 December 2001.
[4]John Rogister, *Louis XV and the Parlement of Paris, 1737–1755* (Cambridge, 1995).

London, one of several residences of the English court, remained a seat of government to a greater extent than did Paris at the time, but its musical life depended little on the crown. Christian Bach went to London in 1762 because he was hired for a year's service by the impresarios of the King's Theatre in the Haymarket. His subsequent appointment to the largely ceremonial post of music master to Queen Charlotte may well have helped persuade him to remain. Also important were other incentives: his success as an entrepreneur running a popular concert series with Abel; a supply of wealthy pupils; a lively commerce with the music publishers; and in general all those amenities afforded by the vast metropolis, not least of all its unwavering support for the greatest and most expensive Italian singers.

Opera seria is often regarded as the supreme example of court music. This connection makes more sense in the German-speaking lands than it does in Italy or in England. The two greatest centers of opera seria, Naples and Venice, adopted the impresarial system, as did London, the center where the most money was spent on this genre. That the plots of most operas were courtly in subject matter made them no different from those of the preceding century, gave them no specifically eighteenth-century tint. The creative artist responsible for doing this was Metastasio, and he was distinctive for being "the most galant poet of all"— "galantissimo" as Baretti put it. His suave and polished diction was received as the antithesis of seventeenth-century pomposity. The most salient feature of opera seria, which is virtually synonymous with Metastasian opera, was not that it epitomized courts, but that it was galant.

Extending the galant or modern rubric from Metastasio to his favorite composers requires no great leap of faith. The galant style in music meant freedom of dissonance treatment and, just as important, freedom to vary the number of voices in the texture. Vinci and his followers often switched from three structural parts in the texture to only two, melody and bass. This economy of means can be compared readily with Metastasio's setting strict limits on his vocabulary. Never did the aphorism "Less is more" seem more apt than when describing the ideals of the Arcadian poets and their composers.

Around the middle of the century some voices were raised suggesting that, while composers should be free to use what was felicitous about the new galant style, the old virtues of solidity and contrapuntal skill should not be sacrificed altogether. Marpurg dedicated his *Abhandlung von der Fuge* (Berlin, 1753) to Telemann. He praised the venerable composer, saying, "the masterworks of your pen have long contradicted the false opinion that the so-called galant way of writing [Schreibart] could not be united with some traits borrowed from counterpoint." Quantz argued the same proposition at length in his *Versuch einer Anweisung* (Berlin, 1752). Some Italian composers demonstrated a similar integration of old and new. Jommelli had from his beginnings favored considerable rhythmic and harmonic intricacy, as did his teacher Leo. Partisans of Hasse complained that Jommelli allowed his orchestral accompaniments to be too interesting at the expense of the solo voice. When Jommelli returned to Naples after his years in Germany, audiences complained of the same thing. The ideal balance was achieved, according to Burney, by Sacchini, who wrote interesting and novel accompaniments but never smothered the vocal soloists. Piccinni and Traetta took even more interest than Sacchini in enriching the harmonic language of Italian opera. These enhancements after 1750 can be regarded as a second phase of the galant style.

In France the violinist-composers who took up the Italian instrumental genres were at the same time not immune to the harmonic richness of Rameau. Mondonville excelled in sonatas and Pierre Gaviniès in concertos. Simon Leduc refined and polished the style of these predecessors and showed an attraction to expressive and often chromatic harmonies in sonatas, concertos, and symphonies. Gossec was almost equally skilled and much more prolific (Leduc died young). Italian vocal music also had an impact on French composers, especially after Pergolesi, Galuppi, and others began to be heard frequently at the Concert Spirituel around 1750. Great strides were made particularly in opéra-comique as it was reconstituted in the 1750s, at first by the Neapolitan Duni, then more skillfully by Philidor and more lyrically by Monsigny. Grétry praised Philidor specifically for his forceful harmonic expression, and it was Grétry who capped this whole line of Italianate melody merged with French harmonic sensitivity, another manifestation of the galant style's second phase.

German Singspiel profited greatly from opéra-comique, which largely provided not only its textual basis but also many of its musical traits. Hiller's *Die Jagd* (1770) was a key work in the evolution of Singspiel. In it Hiller went beyond his idol Hasse to deploy a full and euphonious harmonic language, very smoothly handled. Hasse himself, in one of his last works, the *intermezzo tragico Piramo e Tisbe*, composed primarily for his own pleasure, indulged in harmonic richness without sacrificing his supremely lyrical melodic gift, and in so doing joined the second phase of the galant style; he was the only master still living who had been among the creators of its first phase.

No composer of the 1760s and 1770s was more successful in adapting galant melody to an enriched harmonic palette than Christian Bach, who inherited a typically solid grounding in his craft before imbibing Italian vocal lyricism at the source. One of the most astute critics who commented on the subject wrote:

> This German worshiped Italian ideals of beauty and form with singular tenderness and became the consummate master of the style galant, but of a style galant born from the union of a German father and an Italian mother. His melodies, polished with

emery, were captivating and seductive, and his construction fused with infinite skill and artistry the contradictory elements in opera and instrumental music.[5]

Another master who was consummate in the style, who carried it further and lived longer, was Boccherini. He was, if anything, even more lyrical, although paradoxically an instrumentalist who wrote little music for voices. On his special medium of the string quintet with two cellos he lavished not only the most exquisite melodies, but also harmonic boldness, rhythmic élan, and a range of textural variety that defies easy description.

Around 1780 there was a massive changing of the guard at the top echelons of European music. Most of the giants who had dominated the mid-eighteenth century died a few years before or during the 1780s. Leaving the stage forever were Farinelli and Metastasio, Hasse and Gluck, Emanuel Bach, Jommelli and Holzbauer, Galuppi, Traetta, Sacchini, and Christian Bach. An era had clearly ended, one that was perceived at the time as a great musical moment, and one that could not justly be relegated to the status of a mere prelude to what followed.

In 1778, when Abbé Vogler began publishing his commentaries on music, he sought to establish his credentials for the task with this boast:"One must possess an intimate, wide, and exact knowledge of an artform before being able to erect a tribunal of galant aesthetics."[6] He did not return to the concept in his subsequent writings, which were extensive, but perhaps he regarded his total oeuvre as the tribunal in question. The excellent Mannheim orchestra alone, especially famed for its wide and fluid dynamic range, certainly represented a peak of"galant aesthetics." It is also possible that Vogler let the subject drop because, by the 1780s, the term *galant* and what it signified in music no longer represented the acme of modernity. As recently as 1768 Hiller had praised Haydn for his"most fiery and galant symphonies."[7] He probably would not have used the latter term to describe them after 1780.

The leading German theorists of the late eighteenth century, Koch and Türk, continued to justify what they defined as the free or galant style as an attractive alternative to the strict or learned style. They offered, in fact, the best definitions of the galant style. Not for the first or last time in the history of music were theorists rather tardy in keeping abreast with practice. By the end of the century the term *galant* was beginning to acquire pejorative nuances. It took on a meaning akin to"old-fashioned."In this respect the concept and the term suffered the same fate as others such as *rococo, Pompadour,* and *Louis XV.*[8]

[5]Paul Henry Lang, *Music in Western Civilization* (New York, 1941), p. 639.
[6]Johann Georg Vogler, *Betrachtungen der Mannheimer Tonschule,* 4 vols. (Mannheim, 1778–81), 1: 49.
[7]*Haydn, Mozart,* p. 313.
[8]Jean Weisgerber,"Qu'est-ce que le Rococo? Essai de definition comparatiste,"in *Études sur le XVIIIᵉ Siècle,* vol. 18: *Rocaille. Rococo* (Brussels, 1991), pp. 11–23.

Not all music theorists of the late eighteenth century were slow to apprise the situation. In his 1796 treatise Galeazzi proclaimed that "galant motives and pleasing passages" no longer sufficed to make a good composition, the measure of which was to be taken in "the rigorous motivic conduct of an entire piece of music."[9] If this sounds like a call to restore some of the standards of pregalant music, that is evidently what Galeazzi intended. Haydn, paramount in integrating galant melody with a more obbligato style of writing, was one of Galeazzi's heroes and models, while Mozart's music was apparently unknown to him. No so with E. T. A. Hoffmann, who revered the music of both masters and called each "romantic" (his highest accolade).

Hoffmann and other writers of the early nineteenth century were selective as to what they admired in Mozart's multifaceted works, not all of which met their approval. Hoffmann took exception to Mozart's two Masses in C of 1779–80 (K. 317 and K. 337) and in general deprecated church music like this for lacking solemnity: "Mozart, however *galant* his style in the two better known masses in C major, has splendidly overcome this problem in his Requiem; this is truly romantic-sacred music, proceeding from his innermost soul."[10] The Requiem of 1791 (K. 626) came a decade later than the two Masses, but this surely mattered less to Hoffmann than the differences in character—smiling C major versus gloomy d minor. He greatly admired *Don Giovanni* as well, particularly the overture and the second finale. Mozart's two Masses of 1779–80 had by way of contrast relegated the minor mode to a relatively unimportant role during some interior movements. Romantic melancholia had to be slaked by ever larger doses of the minor mode and its host of related musical traits.

Carl Maria von Weber shared Hoffmann's fascination with *Don Giovanni*. He reported in a letter to his brother the effect the opera had on him at a performance in Munich in early 1811: "a large orchestra raised ocean waves to heaven in the overture, finale and chorus of the Furies. What terror! What power! I am so moved just thinking about it that I could throw away my pen."[11] Fortunately Weber did not throw away his pen; he went on to compose *Der Freischütz*. In another letter, written to a colleague who was commissioned to compose a new mass for Dresden, Weber warned that the court there preferred the galant style and doted on hearing its favorite soprano castrato caper on high in frilly solos.[12] Evidently the spirit of Hasse still lingered at Dresden even in the early nineteenth century.

[9]Francesco Galeazzi, *Elementi teorico-pratici di musica*, 2 vols. (Rome, 1796), 2: 253.

[10]*E. T. A. Hoffmann's Musical Writings: Kreisleriana, The Poet and the Composer, Music Criticism,* ed. David Charlton, trans. Martyn Clarke (Cambridge, 1989), p. 329.

[11]Christof Bitter, *Wandlungen in den Inszenierungsformen des "Don Giovanni" von 1787 bis 1928* (Regensburg, 1961), p. 90.

[12]John Warrack, *Carl Maria von Weber,* 2nd ed. (Cambridge, 1976), pp. 188–89.

Beethoven and Rossini were not loath to call upon the galant style when it suited their purposes. It could be used, for instance, to evoke nostalgia for a golden age that had passed. Both composers grew up with the last remaining flourishes of the galant style sounding in their ears, of which Beethoven's irrepressible Minuet in G (Wo 0 10, No. 2) offers a fine specimen. With its treble melody in parallel thirds, enhanced by the delicate shadings of chromatically raised tones, this fragile minuet, practiced by generations of young pianists, could serve as an emblem of the galant style, and also as a farewell. Rossini, in his Chamber Sonata No. 2 in A (ca. 1804), managed to create two spacious and up-to-date–sounding movements as starters, then resorted to a dainty miniature, a gavotte, as his finale, a movement that could have been written long before he was born. After 1800 minuets and gavottes like these tended to sound mincingly *ancien régime.*

Haydn and Mozart stood in different relationships to the galant style. Mozart was more indebted than Haydn to French and Italian musical currents. Haydn was at his most galant in certain early works and in certain genres, such as his keyboard trios and concertos. In quartets and in symphonies he increasingly distanced himself from the style, by adopting a more obbligato way of writing parts. It was natural for him to pursue motivic development and to think in double counterpoint, whether he made use of inversion or not. Mozart was never less than genial, however he opted to compose, and so he was when he chose to imitate Haydn. Still, it seems that, at his most individual, Mozart thought first of a radiantly beautiful human voice, a high, even angelic voice. His imagination soared to sublime heights born aloft by vocal melodies. In this respect he was much closer to the galant style than Haydn. Indeed, the ultimate heir and greatest genius of the galant style, it could be argued, was Mozart.

Appendix: Boswell Visits Mannheim in 1764

THE hospitality of Carl Theodore's Palatine court described by Voltaire in 1753 contrasts markedly with that recounted by Boswell in his travel diary and letters.[1] Of course the former was the most famous writer of the age, the latter an aspiring young Scotsman of the minor nobility, doing his own Grand Tour and expecting freedom of the table wherever he went among the German courts. At Brunswick the duke had obliged him. At Berlin and Potsdam he could not even get himself presented to Frederick, in spite of some outlandish maneuvers, such as dressing up in kilts and tartan, and in spite of being protected by George Keith, tenth earl marischal of Scotland, an intimate of Frederick and one of his diplomats. Boswell arrived at Mannheim at an inauspicious time, as preparations were being made to celebrate Saint Charles Day on 4 November, the court's greatest festival. He and his servant put up at a public inn. A courtier to whom he had a letter of recommendation referred him to a Monsieur Harold, "Gentleman of the Chamber, and Irish by nation."

> I waited on Harold, and found him a hearty old fellow full of anecdotes. He has been abroad a great many years. He has been thirty years in the Elector Palatine's service.

[1] James Boswell, *Boswell on the Grand Tour: Germany and Switzerland, 1764*, ed. Frederick A. Pottle (New York, 1928; reprint 1953), pp. 165–74.

He taught his Highness to read English. He told me that I could not be presented till Monday, as the Elector was gone a-hunting this day, and as tomorrow was his *jour de fête,* when nobody was presented. I dined at the ordinary of my inn. My fever flew out upon my lips. I was a disagreeable figure. I was fretted. At three Mr. Harold's nephew waited upon me. He had long been in French service and was now a captain in the Elector Palatine's. He was a genteel young fellow, knew a good deal, and talked well, though with affectation. He carried me to hear the opera rehearsed. I was well amused for some hours, and then returned to my inn, and read English newspapers which old Harold sent me.

The rehearsal they attended on Saturday, 3 November 1764, was of Verazi's *Ifigenia in Tauride* set to music by Gian Francesco de Majo, two days before its premiere. Boswell stayed in his room all day Sunday nursing his cold. By the next day, 5 November, his condition had improved.

My cold was much better. It prevented me yesterday from hearing superb mass in the Elector's chapel. However, by keeping my room, I have shunned a fever. At eleven Harold carried me to Court. The Palace is large and elegant. There is a gallery, a passage round the whole of it, prodigiously long. There were a great many people at Court. Harold talked of not presenting me till tomorrow. After having already waited two days, this piqued me not a little, and had I not been presented this day, I should have bluntly set out the next morning. However the Grand Chambellan presented me to the Elector. His Highness asked me from whence I came. He was very swarthy, and very high and mighty. I was presented to the Electrice who was much painted, and also exceeding lofty. I saw here the Prince of Nassau-Weilburg. . . . At night I was at the opera. It was indeed superb.

But it was not sufficient to draw the young visitor out of his bad mood, as he demonstrated in his diary entry for the following day.

Why do I not talk of the beauty of Mannheim? of its streets *tirés à cordon* and lighted better than any streets that I have seen? I am in a bad humour. The Court here is insupportable after the polite reception which I have met with at others. No invitation to dine with the Elector. I told Harold his court was not hospitable, and extolled that of Brunswick. At night I was at the *comédie.*

It should be added that the entertainments were free to visitors with connections at court, like Boswell.

On Wednesday, 7 November, Boswell inspected the Jesuits' church, a large, magnificent edifice built under Carl Theodore and finished in 1756. It was connected to the opera wing of the palace via the Jesuits' college, built by the previous elector.

I went and saw the Jesuits' Church, which is a very elegant piece. The outside is of white stone, with some fine carving and one or two good statues. The inside is very fine both in painting and guilding, though a little gaudy. Some of the panels were green. The painting is either crucifixion pieces or pictures in honour of their order. . . . I asked Captain Harold today why the Court here did not ask strangers to dine. He said, "Sir, our Court preserves its grandeur by not having many strangers at its table." "Sir," said I, "if the Elector believes that, he is very much deceived; for I shall always find more grandeur at a court where there is a superb table than at a court where there is none at all." In the evening we had what is called the Académie de Musique. It was very full, and the music was excellent. I quitted this court quite discontented.

On the same day Boswell wrote a letter to his friend John Johnston summing up his experiences, with his usual petulance. Note how he puts the concert on a par with the opera and the play.

I am in a bad humour in Mannheim because I have found here a very bad court. The Elector wants, forsooth, to be a prodigious great man. He gives an opera and a French comedy and a concert, or an Academy of Music as he calls it, all which entertainments are really magnificent. But then he treats strangers with a distance which makes some of them laugh at him and others curse him, according to their temperaments. For my own part, I have had an inclination to do both. As to his table I can say nothing. Strangers are very seldom invited to dine there. I have not been asked once. What an inhospitable dog! I have been obliged to dine at an ordinary, amongst fellows of all sorts and sizes. It was one of the best tables in town, but the company disgusted me sadly. O British, take warning from me and shun the dominions of the Elector Palatine.

Thus for Boswell Mannheim was a bad court (in spite of having the best music in Germany) because his ego was bruised by a policy that limited access to the rulers for freeloading strangers.

Boswell carried his derogatory remarks further in a scurillous poem about the elector and in the sketch of a satirical letter in French to the court's *grand chambellan,* in which he mentions "his Highness's black face." In a memorandum to himself he cautioned prudence about sending the letter until he reached Stuttgart. In the event, he was prudent enough not to send it at all. He also forwent visiting Stuttgart, having been warned to avoid it by Marischal Keith, who knew all about the volcanic temper of Duke Carl Eugen.

List of Works Cited

Abel, Carl Friedrich. *Six Symphonies, opus 1,* ed. Franklin B. Zimmerman. The Symphony, 1720–1840, ed. Barry S. Brook, Series E, vol. 2. New York, 1983.

Abert, Hermann. "Die dramatische Musik." In *Herzog Karl Eugen von Württemberg und seine Zeit,* ed. Albert Pfister. 2 vols. 1: Anhang 1. Esslingen, 1907.

Abert, Hermann (ed.). *Ausgewählte ballette Stuttgarter Meister aus der 2. hälfte des 18. jahrhunderts (Florian Deller und Johann Joseph Rudolph). Denkmäler deutscher Tonkunst,* 43–44 (1913).

Ackroyd, Peter. *London: The Biography.* New York, 2001.

Alembert, Jean le Rond d'. *De la liberté de la musique.* Paris, 1759.

Alexander, R. C. (ed.). *The Diary of David Garrick Being a Record of His Memorable Trip to Paris in 1751.* New York, 1928.

Allanbrook, Wye Jamison (ed.). *The Late Eighteenth Century.* Vol. 5 of revised edition of Oliver Strunk, *Source Readings in Music History,* ed. Leo Treitler. New York, 1998.

Allegri, Luigi, and Renato di Benedetto (eds.). *Parma in Festa.* Parma, 1987.

Alpers, Svetlana, and Michael Baxandall. *Tiepolo and the Pictorial Intelligence.* New Haven, Conn., and London, 1994.

Altmann, Klaus. "Ignaz Holzbauer als Messenkomponist." In *Mannheim und Italien: Zur Vorgeschichte der Mannheimer,* ed. Roland Würtz, pp. 223–43. Mainz, 1984.

Amsterdam, Ellen Iris. "The String Quintets of Luigi Boccherini." Ph.D. diss., University of California, Berkeley, 1968.

Ancelet. *Observations sur la musique, les musiciens, les instruments.* Amsterdam, 1757; reprint 1984.

Anthony, James R. *French Baroque Music from Beaujoyeulx to Rameau.* Rev. ed. New York, 1978.

Arnason, H. H. *The Sculptures of Houdon.* New York, 1975.

Arnold, Denis. "The Corellian Cult in England." In *Nuovi Studi Corelliani,* ed. Giulia Giachin, pp. 81–88. Florence, 1978.

———."Music at the *Ospedali.*"*Journal of the Royal Musical Association* 113 (1988): 156–67.

Arnold, Denis and Elsie. "Russians in Venice: The Visit of the *Conti del Nord* in 1782." In *Slavonic and Western Music: Essays for Gerald Abraham,* ed. M. H. Brown and R. J. Wiley, pp. 123–30. Ann Arbor, Mich., and Oxford, 1985.

Arnoldson, Louise Parkinson. *Sedaine et les musiciens de son temps.* Paris, 1934.

Arnould, E. J. *La genèse du Barbier de Séville.* Dublin and Paris, 1965.

Arteaga, Stefano. *Le rivoluzioni del teatro musicale italiana dalla sua origine fino al presente.* Rev., 2nd ed. Venice, 1785.

Atlas, Allan W."On the Date of Pergolesi's Mass in F." *Studi pergolesiani* 3 (1999): 201–9.

Avison, Charles. *An Essay on Musical Expression.* London, 1752.

Bach, Carl Philipp Emanuel. *Essay on the True Art of Playing Keyboard Instruments,* trans. and ed. William J. Mitchell. New York, 1959.

———. *The Letters of C. P. E. Bach,* trans. and ed. Stephen L. Clark. Oxford, 1997.

Bailey, Colin B. "Anglo-Saxon Attitudes: Recent Writings on Chardin." In *Chardin,* ed. Pierre Rosenberg, pp. 77–97. New York, 2000.

Baillot, Pierre, Nicolas Baudiot, Charles-Simon Catel, and Jean Henri Levasseur. *Méthode de violoncelle et de basse d'accompagnement . . . adoptée par le conservatoire impérial de musique.* Paris, 1804; reprint 1974.

Balbastre, Claude-Bénigne. *C. B. Balbastre: Pièces de clavecin, d'orgue, et de forte piano,* ed. Alan Curtis. Le pupitre 52. Paris, 1974.

———. *Organ Works,* ed. Nicolas Gorenstein. 3 vols. Fleurian, 1994.

Baker, Nancy Kovaleff, and Thomas Christensen (eds.). *Aesthetics and the Art of Musical Composition in the German Enlightenment: Selected Writings of Johann Georg Sulzer and Heinrich Christoph Koch.* Cambridge, 1995.

Baker, Nicole."Italian Opera at the Court of Mannheim, 1758–1770." Ph.D. diss., University of California, Los Angeles, 1994.

Baldauf-Berdes, Jane L. *Women Musicians of Venice: Musical Foundations, 1525–1855.* Rev. ed. Oxford, 1996.

Barblan, Guglielmo."Boccheriniana." *La rassegna musicale* 29 (1959): 123–28.

Baretti, Joseph. *An Account of the Manners and Customs of Italy with Observations on the Mistakes of Some Travellers.* 2 vols. London, 1768.

———. *La frusta letteraria,* ed. L. Piccioni. 2 vols. Bari, 1932.

Barnes, Clifford R. "Instruments and Instrumental Music at the 'Théâtres de la Foire,' (1697–1762)."*Recherches sur la musique française classique* 5 (1965): 142–68.

Barnett, Dene. *The Art of Gesture: The Practices and Principles of 18th-Century Acting.* Heidelberg, 1987.

Bartha, Dénes."Haydn's Italian Opera Repertory at Esterháza Palace." In *New Looks at Ital-*

ian Opera: Essays in Honor of Donald J. Grout, ed. William W. Austin, pp. 172–219. Ithaca, N.Y., 1968.

Bartha, Dénes, and László Somfai. *Haydn als Opernkapellmeister: Die Haydn-Dokumente der Esterházy-Opernsammlung.* Budapest and Mainz, 1960.

Barthélemy, Maurice. "L'opéra-comique des origines à la Querelle des Bouffons." In *L'opéra-comique en France au xviiie siècle,* ed. Philippe Vendrix, pp. 8–78. Liège, 1992.

Batteux, Charles. *Les beaux-arts réduits à un même principe.* Paris, 1746.

Bauman, Thomas. "The Eighteenth Century: Serious Opera." In *The Oxford Illustrated History of Opera,* ed. Roger Parker, pp. 47–83. Oxford, 1994.

———. *North German Opera in the Age of Goethe.* Cambridge, 1985.

Bédarida, Henri. *Parme et la France de 1748 à 1789.* Paris, 1928.

Beechey, Gwilym. "Robert Bremner and his *Thoughts on the Performance of Concert Music.*" *Musical Quarterly* 69 (1983): 244–52.

Bellinati, Claudio. "Contributo alla biografia padovana di Giuseppe Tartini con nuovi documenti." In *Tartini: Il tempo e le opere,* ed. Andrea Bombi and Maria Nevilla Massaro, pp. 23–35. Bologna, 1994.

Bellora, Carol. "L'opera strumentale di Filippo Manfredi." *Chigiana* 20 (*Luigi Boccherini e la musica strumentale dei maestri Italiani in Europa tra sette e ottocento*) (1993): 231–45.

Benda, Franz. *Autobiography.* In Paul Nettl, *Forgotten Musicians,* pp. 204–45. New York, 1951.

Berg, Darrell M. "C. P. E. Bach's Character Pieces and His Friendship Circle." In *C. P. E. Bach Studies,* ed. Stephen L. Clark, pp. 1–32. Oxford, 1988.

———. *The Keyboard Sonatas of C. P. E. Bach: An Expression of the Mannerist Principle.* Ann Arbor, Mich., 1975.

Berlioz, Hector. *A travers chants.* Paris, 1927.

———. *The Memoirs of Hector Berlioz, Member of the French Institute. Including his travels in Italy, Germany, Russia, and England, 1803–1865,* trans. and ed. David Cairns. London, 1969.

Bettagno, Alessandro, and Giuseppe Fiocco (eds.). *Caricature di Anton Maria Zanetti.* Venice, 1969.

Betzwieser, Thomas. *Exotismus und "Türkenoper" in der französischen Musik des Ancien Régime.* Laaber, 1993.

Bitter, Christof. *Wandlungen in den Inszenierungsformen des* Don Giovanni *von 1787 bis 1928.* Regensburg, 1961.

Black, Jeremy. *The Grand Tour in the Eighteenth Century.* New York, 1992.

Blainville, Charles-Henri. *L'esprit de l'art musical ou réflexions sur la musique et ses différentes parties.* Geneva, 1754; reprint 1974.

Blanning, T. C. W. "Frederick the Great and German Culture." In *Royal and Republican Sovereignty in Early Modern Europe,* ed. Robert Oresko, G. C. Gibbs, and H. M. Scott, pp. 527–50. Cambridge, 1997.

Bleckschmidt, E. R. *Die Amalienbibliothek.* Berlin, 1965.

Blom, Friedrich (ed.). *Die Musik in Geschichte und Gegenwart.* 17 vols. Kassel, 1949–86. 2nd rev. ed., ed. Ludwig Finscher. Kassel and Stuttgart, 1994–.

Blume, Eric. "*Tom Jones* on the French Stage." In *Stepchildren of Music,* pp. 45–54. London, n.d.

Carroll, Charles Michael. "A Classical Setting for a Classical Poem: Philidor's *Carmen Saeculare." Studies in Eighteenth-Century Culture* 6 (1977): 97–111.

———. "François-André Danican-Philidor: His Life and Dramatic Art." 2 vols. Ph.D. diss., Florida State University, 1960.

Carrow, Burton Stimson. "The Relation between the Mannheim School and the Music of Franz Beck, Henri Blanchard, and Pierre Gaveaux." Ph.D. diss., New York University, 1956.

Carsten F. L. *Princes and Parliaments in Germany from the Fifteenth to the Eighteenth Century.* Oxford, 1959.

Casanova, Giacomo, Chevalier de Seingalt. *History of My Life,* trans. Willard R. Trask. 12 vols. in 6. New York, 1966–68; reprint 1997.

Cascudo, Teresa. "Iberian Symphonism, 1779–1809: Some Observations." In *Music in Spain during the Eighteenth Century*, ed. Malcolm Boyd and Juan José Carreras, pp. 144–56. Cambridge and New York, 1998.

Cavallini, Ivano. "Genio, imitazione, stile sentimentale e patetico. Gianrinaldo Carli e Tartini: Le prospettive della critica tartiniana nella seconda metà del settecento." In *Tartini: Il tempo e le opere*, ed. Andrea Bombi and Maria Nevilla Massaro, pp. 229–46. Bologna, 1994.

Charlton, David. " 'L'art dramatico-musical': An Essay." In *Music and Theatre: Essays in Honour of Winton Dean,* ed. Nigel Fortune, pp. 229–62. Cambridge, 1987.

———. *French Opera, 1730–1830: Meaning and Medium.* Aldershot, 2000.

———. *Grétry and the Growth of Opéra-Comique.* Cambridge, 1986.

———. "Orchestra and Chorus at the Comédie-Italienne (Opéra-Comique), 1755–99." In *Slavonic and Western Music: Essays for Gerald Abraham,* ed. M. H. Brown and R. J. Wiley, pp. 87–108. Ann Arbor, Mich., and Oxford, 1985.

———. "The Overture to Philidor's *Le Bûcheron* (1763)." In *D'un opéra l'autre: Hommage à Jean Mongrédien,* ed. Jean Gribenski, Marie-Claire Mussat, and Herbert Schneider, pp. 231–42. Paris, 1996.

———. "The *Romance* and Its Cognates: Narrative, Irony and *Vraisemblance* in Early Opéra Comique." In *Die Opéra comique und ihr Einfluss auf das europäische Musiktheater im 19. Jahrhundert,* ed. Herbert Schneider and Nicole Wild, pp. 43–92. Hildesheim, 1997.

Charlton, David, and Mark Ledbury (eds.). *Michel-Jean Sedaine (1719–1797): Theatre, Opera and Art.* Aldershot, 2000.

Chartier, F. L. *L'ancien chapitre de Notre-Dame de Paris et sa maîtrise d'après les documents capitulaires (1326–1790).* Paris, 1897.

Chastellux, François-Jean. *Essai sur l'union de la poésie et de la musique.* The Hague and Paris, 1765; reprint 1970.

Choron, Alexandre and François Fayolle. *Dictionnaire historique des musiciens.* Paris, 1810–11.

Christensen, Thomas. "Nichelmann contra C. Ph. E. Bach: Harmonic Theory and Musical Politics at the Court of Frederick the Great." In *Carl Philipp Emanuel Bach und die europäische Musikkultur des mittleren 18. Jahrhunderts,* ed. Hans Joachim Marx, pp. 189–220. Göttingen, 1990.

————. *Rameau and Musical Thought in the Enlightenment.* Cambridge, 1993.

Churgin, Bathia. "Alterations in Gluck's Borrowings from Sammartini." *Studi musicali* 9 (1980): 118–34.

————. "The Symphonies of G. B. Sammartini." Ph.D. diss., Harvard University, 1963.

Coli, Remigio. *Luigi Boccherini.* Lucca, 1988. 2nd ed., revised and amplified. Milan, 1992.

Cook, Elisabeth. *Duet and Ensemble in the Early Opéra-Comique.* New York and London, 1995.

Cooper, Barry. "Alberti and Jozzi: Another View." *Music Review* 39 (1978): 160–66.

Coquéau, Claude-Philibert. *Entretiens sur l'état actuel de l'Opéra de Paris.* Amsterdam, 1779.

Corneilson, Paul. "The Case of J. C. Bach's *Lucio Silla.*" *Journal of Musicology* 12 (1994): 206–18.

————. "Opera at Mannheim, 1770–1778." Ph.D. diss., University of North Carolina, 1992.

Corneilson, Paul, and Eugene K. Wolf. "Mannheim Ballet Sources, 1758–1778." In *Ballet Music from the Mannheim Court, Part I,* ed. Floyd K. Grave, pp. xxvii–xxxii. Madison, Wis., 1996.

————. "Newly Identified Manuscripts of Operas and Related Works from Mannheim." *JAMS* 47 (1994): 244–74.

————. *Piccinni: Settecento italiano.* Bari, 1928.

Cotgrave, Randle. *A Dictionairie of the French and English Tongues.* London, 1611; reprint 1950.

Cotticelli, Francesco, and Paologiovanni Maione. *Le istituzioni musicali a Napoli durante il Viceregno Austriaco (1707–1734).* Naples, 1993.

Cowart, Georgia. *Controversies over French and Italian Music, 1600–1750: The Origins of Modern Musical Criticism.* Ann Arbor, Mich., 1980.

Coyer, Abbé Gabriel-François. *Voyage en Italie.* Paris, 1776.

Crickmore, Leon. "C. P. E. Bach's Harpsichord Concertos." *Music and Letters* 39–40 (1958): 227–41.

Croix, Albert de. *L'ami des arts ou justification de plusieurs grands hommes.* Amsterdam, 1776.

Croll, Gerhard. "Gluck's Debut am Burgtheater." *Oesterreichische Musik Zeitschrift* 31 (1976): 194–202.

Cross, Eric. *Vivaldi's Late Operas.* Ann Arbor, Mich., 1981.

Cucuel, Georges. *Les créateurs de l'Opéra-Comique français.* Paris, 1914.

————. *Études sur un orchestre au xviiie siècle: L'instrumentation chez les symphonistes de La Pouplinière.* Paris, 1913.

————. *La Pouplinière et la musique de chambre au xviiie siècle.* Paris, 1913.

Cumming, Julie E. "Gluck's Iphigenia Operas: Sources and Strategies." In *Opera and the Enlightenment,* ed. Thomas Bauman and Marita Petzoldt McClymonds, pp. 217–40. Cambridge, 1995.

Cummings, Graham. "Reminiscence and Recall in Three Early Settings of Metastasio's *Alessandro nell'Indie.*" *Proceedings of the Royal Musical Association* 109 (1982–83): 80–104.

Cyr, Mary. "The Dramatic Role of the Chorus in French Opera: Evidence for the Use of Gesture, 1670–1770." In *Opera and the Enlightenment,* ed. Thomas Bauman and Marita Petzoldt McClymonds, pp. 105–18. Cambridge, 1995.

————."'Inclina Domine': A Martin Motet Wrongly Attributed to Rameau."*Music and Letters* 58 (1977): 318–25.

————."Rameau's *Les fêtes d'Hébé*." Ph.D. diss., University of California, Berkeley, 1975.

Dacier, Emile, and Albert Vuaflart. *Jean de Jullienne et les graveurs de Watteau au XVIIIᵉ siècle.* 4 vols. Paris, 1921–29.

Davenson. Henri. *Le livre des chansons ou introduction à la connaissance de la chanson populaire française.* Neuchâtel, 1962.

David, Hans. *Schobert als Sonatenkomponist.* Leipzig, 1928.

David, Tunley. *The Eighteenth-Century French Cantata.* London, 1974.

Davis, Shelley G. "C. P. E. and the Early History of the Recapitulary Tutti in North Germany." In *C. P. E. Bach Studies,* ed. Stephen L. Clark, pp. 65–82. Oxford, 1988.

Dean, Winton, and John Merrill Knapp. *Handel's Operas, 1704–1726.* Oxford, 1987.

Debrie, Christine, and Xavier Salmon. *Maurice-Quentin de la Tour: Prince des pastellistes.* Paris, 2000.

Decugis, Nicole, and Suzanne Reymond. *Le décor de théâtre en France du moyen age à 1925.* Paris, 1953.

Degrada, Francesco. "Giuseppe Sigismondo, il marchese di Villarosa e la biografio di Pergolesi." *Studi pergolesiani* 3 (1999): 251–77.

————."Pergolesi, il marchese Pianetti e il Conservatorio di S. Maria di Loreto: Su alcune relazioni tra Jesi e Napoli nel primo Settecento." *Studi pergolesiani* 2 (1988): 20–48.

Degrada, Francesco, Roberto De Simone, Dario Della Porta, and Gianni Race. *Pergolesi.* Naples, 1986.

Della Corte, Andrea. *Paisiello.* Turin, 1922.

————. *Piccinni: Settecento italiano.* Bari, 1928.

Desboulmiers, Jean-Auguste. *Histoire anecdotique et raisonné du théâtre italien, depuis son rétablissement en France jusqu'à l'année 1769.* 7 vols. Paris, 1769.

————. *Histoire du théâtre de l'opéra comique.* 2 vols. Paris, 1770.

Desnoireterres, Gustave. *Gluck et Piccinni, 1774–1800.* 2nd ed. Paris, 1875.

Deutsch, Otto Erich. *Handel: A Documentary Biography.* London, 1955.

Devriès, Anick. "Deux dynasties d'éditeurs et de musiciens: Les Leduc." *Revue belge de musicologie* 28–30 (1974–76): 195–211.

————. *Édition et commerce de la musique gravée à Paris dans la première moitié du XVIIIᵉ siècle: Les Boivin, Les Leclerc.* Geneva, 1976.

Diderot, Denis. *Correspondance,* ed. Georges Roth and Jean Varloot. 15 vols. Paris, 1955–70.

————. *Leçons de clavecin et principes d'harmonie par Mr Bemetzrieder.* Paris, 1751; reprint 1966.

————. *Les trois chapitres ou La vision de la nuit de mardi-gras au mercredi des cendres.* Paris, 1753.

Didier, Béatrice. *La musique des Lumières.* Paris, 1985.

Dietz, Hanns-Bertold. "A Chronology of Maestri and Organisti at the Cappella Reale in Naples, 1745–1800." *JAMS* 25 (1972): 379–406.

————."The Dresden-Naples Connection, 1737–1763: Charles of Bourbon, Maria Amalia of Saxony, and Johann Adolf Hasse." *International Journal of Musicology* 5 (1996): 95–130.

Dlabač, Bohumír Jan. *Allgemeine historische Künstler-Lexikon fur Böhmen.* Prague, 1815.

Dörge, Hans. *Musik in Venedig.* Wilhelmshaven, 1991.

Dounias, Minos. *Die Violinkonzerte Giuseppe Tartinis als Ausdruck einer Künstlerpersönlichkeit und einer Kulturepoche.* Wolfenbüttel and Berlin, 1935; reprint 1966.

Druilhe, Paule. *Monsigny: Sa vie et son oeuvre.* Paris, 1955.

Drummond, Pippa. *The German Concerto: Five Eighteenth-Century Studies.* Oxford, 1980.

Du Boccage, Marie Anne Le Page Fiquet. *Recueil des oeuvres.* 3 vols. Lyons, 1762.

Dubos, Jean-Baptiste. *Réflexions critiques sur la poésie, la péinture et la musique.* Paris, 1719.

Duchartre, Pierre-Louis. *La commedia dell'arte et ses enfants.* Paris, 1955.

Dunning, Albert. *Pietro Antonio Locatelli: Der Virtuose und seine Welt.* 2 vols. Buren, 1981.

Durand-Sendrail, Beatrice. *La musique de Diderot: Essai sur le hieroglyphe musicale.* Paris, 1994.

Ebersold, Günther. *Rokoko, Reform und Revolution: Ein politisches Lebensbild des Kurfürsten Karl Theodor.* Frankfurt, 1985.

Enslin, Wolfram. *Niccolò Piccinni:* Catone in Utica: *Quellenüberlieferung, Aufführungsgeschichte und Analyse.* Quellen und Studien der Mannheimer Hofkapelle 4. Frankfurt, 1996.

Escherny, Le comte d'. *Mélanges de littérature, d'histoire, de morale et de philosophie.* 2 vols. Paris, 1811.

Everett, Paul. *Vivaldi:* The Four Seasons *and Other Concertos, Op. 8.* Cambridge, 1996.

Eximeno y Pujades, Antonio. *Dell'origine e delle regole della musica.* Rome, 1774.

Fabbri, Mario. "Una nuova fonte per la conoscenza di Giovanni Platti e del suo 'Miserere.'" *Chigiana* 24 (1967): 181–202.

Farinelli, Carlo Broschi. *La solitudine amica: Lettere al conte Sicinio Pepoli.* Palermo, 2000.

Favart, Charles-Simon. *Mémoires et correspondances littéraires, dramatiques et anecdotiques,* ed. A.-P.-C. Favart. 3 vols. Paris, 1808.

Fend, Michael. "Der Fehlschlag von Glucks *Écho et Narcisse* und die Probleme einer 'musikalischen Ekloge.'" In *D'un opéra l'autre: Hommage à Jean Mongrédien,* ed. Jean Gribenski, Marie-Claire Mussat, and Herbert Schneider, pp. 31–43. Paris, 1996.

Fertonani, Cesare. *La musica strumentale di Antonio Vivaldi.* Florence, 1998.

Finscher, Ludwig. "Mozarts erstes Streichquartett: Lodi, 15. März 1770." *Analecta musicologica* 18 (1978): 246–70.

———. "Opera and Enlightenment." In *Report of the Twelfth Congress of the International Musicological Society, Berkeley, 1977,* ed. Daniel Heartz and Bonnie Wade. Kassel, 1981.

———. *Studien zur Geschichte des Streichquartetts.* Vol. 1. Kassel, 1974.

Fiske, Roger. "The Galant Style Comes to Britain." In *Music in Britain: The Eighteenth Century,* ed. H. Diack Johnstone and Roger Fiske, pp. 206–20. Oxford, 1990.

Flaherty, Gloria. *Opera in the Development of German Critical Thought.* Princeton, N.J., 1978.

Font, Auguste. *Favart, l'opéra comique et la comédie vaudeville au xviie et xviiie siècles.* Paris, 1894.

Forkel, Johann Nicolaus. *Musikalischer Almanach für Deutschland.* 3 vols. Leipzig, 1782–84.

Fornari, Giacomo. "Del declino della musica strumentale in Italia nel settecento." In *Intorno a Locatelli,* ed. Albert Dunning. 2 vols., 1: 241–74. Lucca, 1995.

Foster, Donald H. "The Oratorio in Paris in the 18th Century." *Acta musicologica* 47 (1975): 67–133.

Framery, Nicolas Étienne (ed.). *Journal de musique historique, théorique, et pratique.* 5 vols. Paris, 1770–71.

Framery, Nicolas Étienne, and Pierre Louis Ginguené (eds). *Encyclopédie methodique: Musique.* Vol. 1. Paris, 1791.

Frandson, Mary E. "Allies in the Cause of Italian Music: Schütz, Prince Johann Georg III, and Musical Politics in Dresden." *Journal of the Royal Musical Association* 125 (2000): 1–40.

Freeman, Robert S. "Farinelli and His Repertory." In *Studies in Renaissance and Baroque Music in Honor of Arthur Mendel,* ed. Robert L. Marshall, pp. 301–30. Kassel, 1974.

———. *Opera without Drama: Currents of Change in Italian Opera, 1675–1725.* Ann Arbor, Mich., 1981.

Fuller, David. "Accompanied Keyboard Music." *Musical Quarterly* 60 (1974): 222–45.

———. "Of Portraits, 'Sappho' and Couperin: Titles and Characters in French Instrumental Music of the High Baroque." *Music and Letters* 78 (1997): 149–74.

Fürstenau, Moritz. *Zur Geschichte der Musik und des Theaters am Hofe der Kurfürsten von Sachsen.* 2 vols. Leipzig, 1861–62.

Galeazzi, Francesco. *Elementi teorico-pratici di musica.* 2 vols. Rome, 1796.

Galiani, Ferdinando. *Del dialetto napoletane.* 2 vols. Naples, 1779.

———. *Correspondance inédite de l'Abbé Ferdinando Galliani.* Paris, 1818.

Gallico, Claudio. "Rinaldo da Capua: Zingara o Bohémienne." In *Venezia e il melodramma nel settecento,* ed. Teresa Muraro. 2 vols., 1: 425–36. Florence, 1978.

Garcin, Laurent. *Traité du mélo-drame, ou Réflexions sur la musique dramatique.* Paris, 1772.

Gärtner, Heinz. *John Christian Bach: Mozart's Friend and Mentor,* trans. Reinhard G. Pauly. Portland, Ore., 1994.

Gérard, Yves. *Thematic, Bibliographical and Critical Catalogue of the Works of Luigi Boccherini,* trans. Andreas Mayor. London, 1969.

Gerber, Ernst Ludwig. *Historisch-biographisches Lexikon der Tonkünstler.* 2 vols. Leipzig, 1790–92; reprint 1966.

———. *Neues historisch-biographisches Lexikon der Tonkünstler.* 4 vols. Leipzig, 1812–14; reprint 1966.

Gétreau, Florence. "Une harpiste au Concert Spirituel: Mlle Schencker en mai 1765." In *Musique—images—instruments. Revue française d'organologie et d'iconographie musicale* 1 (1995): 178–81.

Gherardi, Evaristo (ed.). *Le théâtre italien, ou le recueil de toutes les scènes françoises qui ont esté jouées sur le théâtre italien de l'Hostel de Bourgogne.* Paris, 1694.

———. *Le théâtre italien, ou le recueil général de toutes les comédies et scènes françoises jouées par les comédiens du roy, pendant tout le temps qu'ils ont été au service.* 6 vols. Paris, 1700.

Giazotto, Remo. *Vivaldi.* Milan, 1965.

Giersberg, Hans-Joachim. *Friedrich als Bauherr: Studien zur Architektur des 18. Jahrhunderts in Berlin und Potsdam.* Berlin, 1986.

Ginguené, Pierre Louis. *Notice sur la vie et les ouvrages de Nicolas Piccinni.* Paris, 1800–1801.

Giraud, Yves. "Iphigénie entre Racine et Du Roullet." In *L'opéra au xviii* siècle, ed. André Bourde, pp. 163–84. Aix and Marseilles, 1982.

Girdlestone, Cuthbert. *Jean-Philippe Rameau: His Life and Work.* New York, 1969.

Giuliani, Elizabeth. "Le public de l'Opéra de Paris de 1750 à 1760; Mesure et definition." *International Review of the Aesthetics and Sociology of Music* 8 (1977): 159–81.

Gluck, Christoph. *The Collected Correspondence and Papers of Christoph Willibald Gluck,* ed. Hedwig and E. H. Mueller Von Asow, trans. Stewart Thomson. London, 1962.

———. *Gluck. Sämtliche Werke,* ed. Gerhard Croll. Kassel, 1958–.

Goldin, Daniela. *La vera Fenice: Librettisti e libretti fra sette e ottocento.* Turin, 1985.

Goldoni, Carlo. *Tutte le opere,* ed. Giuseppe Ortolani. 14 vols. Milan, 1935–56.

Gourret, Jean. *Histoire des salles de l'Opéra de Paris.* Paris, 1985.

Grant, Kerry S. *Dr. Burney as Critic and Historian of Music.* Ann Arbor, Mich., 1983.

Grave, Floyd K., and Margaret G. *In Praise of Harmony: The Teachings of Abbé Georg Joseph Vogler.* Lincoln, Neb., 1987.

Gress, Johannes. "Händel in Dresden (1719)." *Händel-Jahrbuch 1963,* pp. 135-49.

Grétry, André-E.-M. *La correspondance générale de Grétry,* ed. Georges de Froidcourt. Brussels, 1962.

———. *Mémoires, ou essais sur la musique.* 3 vols. Paris, 1789–94; reprint 1971.

Griffin, Thomas. *Musical References in the Gazzetta di Napoli 1681–1725.* Berkeley, 1993.

Grimm, Friedrich Melchior, et al. *Correspondance littéraire, philosphique et critique par Grimm, Diderot, Raynal, Meister, etc.,* ed. Maurice Tourneux. 16 vols. Paris, 1877–82.

Grossato, Elisa. "Luigi Boccherini e Venezia." *Chigiana* 20 (*Luigi Boccherini e la musica strumentale dei maestri Italiani in Europa tra sette e ottocento*) (1993): 135–50.

Grout, Donald Jay. "The Opéra Comique and the Théâtre Italien from 1715 to 1762." In *Miscelánea en homenaje a Monseñor Higinio Anglés.* 2 vols. 1: 369–77. Barcelona, 1958–61.

———. "The Origins of the Opéra Comique." Ph.D. diss., Harvard University, 1939.

Guilcher, Jean-Michel. *La contredanse et les renouvellements de la danse française.* Paris, 1969.

Gustafson, Bruce. "Madame Brillon et son salon." *Revue de musicologie* 85 (1999): 297–332.

Gustafson, Bruce, and David Fuller. *A Catalogue of French Harpsichord Music, 1699–1780.* London, 1990.

Hansell, Kathleen Kuzmick. "Opera and Ballet at the Regio Ducal Teatro of Milan, 1771–1776: A Musical and Social History." Ph.D. diss., University of California, Berkeley, 1979.

Hansell, Sven Hostrup. "Sacred Music at the *Incurabili* in Venice at the time of J. A. Hasse." *JAMS* 23 (1970): 281–301, 505–21.

Hardie, Graham Hood. "Leonardo Leo (1694–1744) and His Comic Operas *Amor vuol sofferenza* and *Alidoro.*" Ph.D. diss., Cornell University, 1973.

Harich, Janos. "Inventare der Esterházy-Hofmusikkapelle in Eisenstadt." *Haydn Yearbook* 9 (1975): 5–125.

Harrison, Bernard. *Haydn: The "Paris" Symphonies.* Cambridge, 1998.

Hasse, Johann Adolf. *Johann Adolf Hasse e Giammaria Ortes: Lettere (1760–1783),* ed. Livia Pancino. Speculum Musicum IV. Turnhout, 1998.

Hayes, Jeremy. "*Armide,* Gluck's Most French Opera." *Musical Times* 123 (1982): 408–10.

Hayes, William. *Remarks on Mr. Avison's Essay on Musical Expression*. London, 1753.

Heartz, Daniel. "Abt Vogler on the Horn Parts in Winter's Symphony in D minor: A View from within the Mannheim Orchestra." *Historic Brass Society Journal* 12 (2000): 89–101.

———. "Approaching a History of 18th-Century Music." *Current Musicology* 4 (1969): 92–95.

———. "*The Beggar's Opera* and Opéra-Comique en Vaudevilles." *Early Music* 27 (1999): 42–53.

———. "The Beginnings of the Operatic Romance: Rousseau, Sedaine and Monsigny." *Eighteenth-Century Studies* 15 (1981–82): 149–78.

———. "Coming of Age in Bohemia: The Musical Apprenticeships of Benda and Gluck." *Journal of Musicology* 6 (1988): 510–27.

———. "The Concert Spirituel in the Tuileries palace." *Early Music* 21 (1993): 241–48.

———. "Constructing *Le Nozze di Figaro*." *Journal of the Royal Musical Association* 112 (1987): 77–98; reprinted in Daniel Heartz, *Mozart's Operas*, pp. 133–55. Berkeley, 1990.

———. "The Creation of the Buffo Finale in Italian Opera." *Proceedings of the Royal Musical Association* 104 (1977–78): 67–78.

———. "Diderot et le Théâtre-lyrique: le 'nouveau stile' proposé par *Le neveu de Rameau*." *Revue de musicologie* 64 (1978): 229–52.

———. "Farinelli and Metastasio, Rival Twins of Public Favour." *Early Music* 12 (1984): 358–66.

———. "Farinelli Revisited." *Early Music* 18 (1990): 430–43.

———. "From Garrick to Gluck: The Reform of Theatre and Opera in the Mid-18th Century." *Proceedings of the Royal Musical Association* 94 (1967–68): 111–27.

———. "Goldoni, Opera Buffa, and Mozart's Advent in Vienna." In *Opera Buffa in Mozart's Vienna*, ed. Mary Hunter and James Webster, pp. 25–49. Cambridge, 1997.

———. "Hasse at the Crossroads: *Artaserse* (Venice, 1730), Dresden, and Vienna." *Opera Quarterly* 16 (2000): 24–33.

———. "Hasse, Galuppi and Metastasio." In *Venezia e il Melodramma nel Settecento*, ed. Maria Teresa Muraro. 2 vols., 1: 309–39. Florence, 1978–81.

———. *Haydn, Mozart and the Viennese School, 1740–1780*. New York, 1995.

———. "The Hunting Chorus in Haydn's *Jahreszeiten* and the 'Airs de Chasse' in the *Encyclopédie*." *Eighteenth-Century Studies* 9 (1976): 523–39.

———. "Italian by Intention, French of Necessity: Rousseau's *Le devin du village*." In *Échos de France et d'Italie: Liber amicorum Yves Gérard*, ed. Marie-Claire Mussat, Jean Mongrédien, and Jean-Michel Nectoux, pp. 31–46. Paris, 1997.

———. "A Keyboard Concertino by Marie Antionette?" In *Essays in Musicology: A Tribute to Alvin Johnson*, ed. Lewis Lockwood and Edward Roesner, pp. 201–12. Philadelphia, 1990.

———. "*Les Lumières:* Voltaire and Metastasio; Goldoni, Favart and Diderot." In *Report of the Twelfth Congress of the International Musicological Society, Berkeley, 1977*, ed. Daniel Heartz and Bonnie Wade, pp. 233–38. Kassel, 1981.

———. "Locatelli and the Pantomime of the Violinist in *Le Neveu Rameau*." *Diderot Studies* 27 (1998): 115–27.

———."Metastasio, 'maestro dei maestri di cappella dramatici.' " In *Metastasio e il mondo musicale,* ed. Maria Teresa Muraro, pp. 315–38. Florence, 1986.

———. *Mozart's Operas,* ed. with contributing essays, by Thomas Bauman. Berkeley, 1990.

———."Opéra-Comique and the Théâtre Italien from Watteau to Fragonard." In *Music in the Classic Period: Essays in Honor of Barry S. Brook,* ed. Allan W. Atlas, pp. 69–84. New York, 1985.

———."Operatic Reform at Parma: *Ippolito ed Aricia.*" In *Atti del Convegno sul settecento Parmense nel 2º centenario della morte di C. I. Frugoni,* pp. 271–300. Parma, 1969.

———."Portrait of a Primo Uomo: Carlo Scalzi in Venice ca. 1740." In *Musikalische Ikonographie,* ed. Harald Heckmann, Monika Holl, and Hans Joachim Marx, pp. 133–45. Hamburger Jahrbuch für Musikwissenschaft 12. Laaber, 1994.

———."Terpsichore at the Fair; Old and New Dance Airs in Two Vaudeville Comedies by Lesage." In *Music and Context: Essays for John M. Ward,* ed. Anne Dhu Shapiro, pp. 278–304. Cambridge, Mass., 1985.

———."A Venetian Dancing Master Teaches the Forlana: Lambranzi's *Balli teatrali.*" *Journal of Musicology* 17 (1999): 136–51.

———. *The Verona Portrait of Mozart and the Molto Allegro in G (KV 72a).* Ala, 1995.

———."Vis Comica: Goldoni, Galuppi, and *L'Arcadia in Brenta* (Venice, 1749)." In *Venezia e il melodramma nel settecento,* ed. Maria Teresa Muraro, 2: 33–69. Florence, 1978–81.

———."Watteau's Italian Comedians." *Eighteenth-Century Studies* 22 (1988–89): 156–81.

———."The Young Boccherini: Lucca, Vienna, and the Electoral Courts." *Journal of Musicology* 13 (1995): 103–16.

Hedgcock, Frank A. *A Cosmopolitan Actor: David Garrick and His French Friends.* London, 1912.

Hell, Helmut. *Die neapolitanische Opernsinfonie in der ersten Hälfte des 18. Jahrhunderts: N. Porpora, L. Vinci, G. B. Pergolesi, L. Leo, N. Jommelli.* Tutzing, 1971.

Helm, Eugene. "The 'Hamlet' Fantasy and the Literary Element in C. P. E. Bach's Music." *Musical Quarterly* 48 (1972): 277–96.

———. *Music at the Court of Frederick the Great.* Norman, Okla., 1960.

Hennessey, Leslie Griffin. "French *conversation*—and Venetian *poesia:* Giambattista Tiepolo's *Finding of Moses.*" *Apollo* (September 1994): 33–39.

———."Friends Serving Itinerant Muses: Jacopo Amigoni and Farinelli in Europe." In *Italian Culture in Northern Europe in the Eighteenth Century,* ed. Shearer West, pp. 20–45. Cambridge, 1999.

———."Notes on the Formation of Giuseppe Wagner's Bella Maniera and His Venetian Printshop." *Ateneo Veneto* 178 (1990): 211–28.

Henseler, Thomas Anton."Musik und Theater unter Clemens August." In *Kurfürst Clemens August, Landeherr und Mäzen des 18. Jahrhunderts.* Austellung in Schloss Augustusburg zu Brühl 1961, pp. 92–98. Cologne, 1961.

Henze-Döhring, Sabine. "Orchester und Orchestersatz in Christian Cannabichs Mannheimer Sinfonien." In *Mozart und Mannheim: Kongressbericht Mannheim 1991,* ed. Ludwig Finscher, Bärbel Pelker, and Jochen Reutter, pp. 257–71. Frankfurt, 1994.

Herman, Martin M."The Turbulent Career of Jean-François Le Sueur, Maître de Chapelle." *Recherches sur la musique française classique* 9 (1969): 187–215.

Hertel, Johann Wilhelm. *Autobiographie,* ed. Erich Schenk. Graz and Cologne, 1957.

Heuvel, Jacques Van den. "Platée, opéra-bouffe de Rameau au milieu du XVIIIᵉ siècle." In *Jean-Philippe Rameau Colloque Internationale,* ed. Jérôme de La Gorce, pp. 101–7. Paris and Geneva, 1987.

Hill, John Walter. "The Anti-Galant Attitude of F. M. Veracini." In *Studies in Musicology in Honor of Otto E. Albrecht,* ed. John Walter Hill, pp. 158–96. Kassel, 1980.

———. "The Life and Works of Francesco Maria Veracini." 4 vols. Ph.D. diss., Harvard University, 1972.

———. "Vivaldi's *Griselda.*" *JAMS* 31 (1978): 53–82.

Hiller, Johann Adam. *Die Jagd,* ed. Thomas Bauman. German Opera, 1770–1800, 1. New York, 1985.

———. *Lebenbeschreibungen berühmter Musikgelehrten und Tonkünstler neuerer Zeit.* Leipzig, 1784.

——— . *Wöchentliche Nachrichten und Anmerkungen die Musik betreffend.* 5 vols. Leipzig, 1766–70; reprint 1970.

Hillsman, Walter. "Instrumental Accompaniment of Plain-chant in France from the Late 18th Century." *Galpin Society Journal* 33 (1980): 8–16.

Hochstein, Wolfgang. *Die Kirchenmusik von Niccolò Jommelli (1714–1774).* 2 vols. Hildesheim, 1984.

Hoffmann, E. T. A. *E. T. A. Hoffmann's Musical Writings: Kreisleriana, The Poet and the Composer, Music Criticism,* ed. David Charlton, trans. Martyn Clarke. Cambridge, 1989.

Hollis, George Treutt. "'El diablo vestito de fraile': Some Unpublished Correspondence of Padre Soler." In *Music in Spain during the Eighteenth Century,* ed. Malcolm Boyd and Juan José Carreras, pp. 192–206. Cambridge, 1998.

Holmes, William C. *Opera Observed: Views of a Florentine Impresario in the Early Eighteenth Century.* Chicago, 1993.

———. "Pamela Transformed." *Musical Quarterly* 38 (1952): 581–94.

Holzbauer, Ignaz. *Günther von Schwarzburg,* ed. Hermann Kretschmar. *Denkmäler deutscher Tonkunst,* 8–9 (1902).

Horn, Wolfgang. *Die Dresdner Hofkirchenmusik, 1720–1745: Studien zu ihren Voraussetzungen und ihrem Repertoire.* Kassel, 1987.

Hortschansky, Klaus. "Ignaz Holzbauers *Ippolito et Aricia* (1759): Zur Einführung der Tragédie-lyrique in Mannheim." In *Studien zur deutsch-französischen Musikgeschichte im 18. Jahrhundert,* ed. Wolfgang Birtel and Christoph-Hellmut Mahling, pp. 105–16. Heidelberg, 1986.

———. "Musiktheater in Mannheim als gestelltes Bild." In *Mozart und Mannheim: Kongressbericht Mannheim 1991,* ed. Ludwig Finscher, Bärbel Pelker, and Johann Reuter, pp. 65–80. Frankfurt, 1994.

———. "Die Rolle des Sängers im Drama Metastasios: Giovanni Carestini als Timante im *Demofoonte.*" In *Metastasio e il mondo musicale,* ed. Maria Teresa Muraro, pp. 207–34. Florence, 1986.

Howard, Patricia. *Gluck: An Eighteenth-Century Portrait in Letters and Documents.* Oxford, 1995.

Hucke, Helmuth. "Die neapolitanische Tradition in der Oper." In *Report of the Eighth Con-*

gress of the International Musicological Society, New York, 1961, ed. Jan LaRue. 2 vols., 1: 253–77. Kassel, 1961.

———. "Pergolesi's *Missa S. Eumidio.*" In *Music in the Classic Period: Essays in Honor of Barry S. Brook,* ed. Allen W. Atlas, pp. 99–116. New York, 1985.

———. "Pergolesi in der Musikgeschichte." In *Studi pergolesiani* 2 (1988): 7–19.

Hunter, Mary. *The Culture of Opera Buffa in Mozart's Vienna: A Poetics of Entertainment.* Princeton, N.J., 1998.

———. "Pamela: The Offspring of Richardson's Heroine in Eighteenth-Century Opera." *Mosaic* 18 (1985): 61–77.

Iacuzzi, Alfred. *The European Vogue of Favart: The Diffusion of the Opéra-Comique.* New York, 1932.

Irving, John. *Mozart's Piano Sonatas: Contexts, Sources, Style.* Cambridge, 1997.

Isherwood, Robert M. "The Third War of the Musical Enlightenment." *Studies in Eighteenth-Century Culture* 4 (1975): 223–45.

Istel, Edgar. *Die Entstehung des deutschen Melodramas.* Berlin and Leipzig, 1906.

Johansson, Cari. *French Music Publishers' Catalogue of the Second Half of the Eighteenth Century.* 2 vols. Stockholm, 1955.

Joli, Jacques. "Il fragore delle armi nella *Nitteti.*" In *Metastasio e il mondo musicale,* ed. Maria Teresa Muraro, pp. 99–132. Florence, 1986.

Jommelli, Niccolò. *Fetonte,* ed. Hermann Abert. *Denkmäler deutscher Tonkunst,* 32–33 (1907).

Jones, David Wyn. "Austrian Symphonies in the Royal Palace, Madrid." In *Music in Spain during the Eighteenth Century,* ed. Malcolm Boyd and Juan José Carreras, pp. 125–43. Cambridge, 1998.

Jones, William. *A Treatise on the Art of Music, in which Elements of Harmony and Air are Practically Considered.* Colchester, 1784.

Jourdain. *Seconde lettre du correcteur des Bouffons à l'écolier de Prague.* Paris, 1753.

Jullien, Adolphe. *La cour et l'opéra sous Louis XVI.* Paris, 1878; reprint 1976.

Junker, Carl Ludwig. *Musikalischer Almanach auf das Jahr 1782.* Leipzig, 1782.

———. *Zwanzig Komponisten: Eine Skizze.* Bern, 1776.

Kahl, Wili. *Selbstbiographen deutscher Musiker des 18. Jahrhunderts.* Cologne, 1948; reprint 1972.

Kavanaugh, Thomas M. *Esthetics of the Moment: Literature and Art in the French Enlightenment.* Philadelphia, 1996.

Kelly, Michael. *Reminiscences of Michael Kelly of the King's Theatre and Theatre Royal Drury Lane.* 2 vols. London, 1826; reprint 1968.

Kinsky, Georg. "Glucks Reisen nach Paris." *Zeitschrift für Musikwissenschaft* 8 (1925–26): 557–66.

Kirkpatrick, Ralph. *Domenico Scarlatti.* Princeton, N.J., 1953.

Klüppelholz, Heinz. "Die Eroberung Mexikos aus preussischer Sicht: Zum Libretto der Oper *Montezuma* von Friedrich dem Grossen." In *Oper als Text: Romantische Beiträge zur Libretto-Forschung,* ed. Albert Gier, pp. 65–94. Studia Romanica 63. Heidelberg, 1986.

Koch, Heinrich. *Musikalisches Lexikon.* Frankfurt, 1802.

———. *Versuch einer Anleitung zur Composition.* 3 vols. Leipzig, 1788–93, reprint 1969.

Kolneder, Walter. *Antonio Vivaldi,* trans. B. Hopkins. Berkeley and Los Angeles, 1970.

Kramer, Richard. "The New Modulation of the 1770s: C. P. E. Bach in Theory, Criticism, and Practice." *JAMS* 38 (1985): 551–92.

Kraus, Joseph Martin. *Etwas von und über Musik fürs Jahr 1777.* Frankfurt, 1778; reprint 1977.

Krause, Christian Gottfried. *Von der musikalischen Poesie.* 2nd ed. Berlin, 1752; reprint 1963.

Krauss, Rudolf. "Das Theater." *Herzog Karl Eugen und seine Zeit.* 2 vols. Esslingen, 1909.

Kunze, Stefan. *Die Sinfonie im 18. Jahrhundert: Von der Opernsinfonie zur Konzertsinfonie.* Laaber, 1993.

———. "Die Vertonungen der Arie 'Non so d'onde viene' von J. Chr. Bach und W. A. Mozart." *Analecta musicologica* 2 (1965): 85–111.

La Borde, Jean-Benjamin de. *Essai sur la musique ancienne et moderne.* 4 vols. Paris, 1780; reprint 1972.

La Laurencie, Lionel de. "The Chevalier de Saint-Georges: Violinist." *Musical Quarterly* 5 (1919): 74–85.

———. "Deux imitateurs des bouffons: Blavet et Dauvergne." *L'année musicale* 2 (1913): 65–125.

———. *L'école française de violon de Lully à Viotti.* 3 vols. Paris, 1922.

La Laurencie, Lionel de, and Georges de Saint-Foix. "Contribution à l'histoire de la symphonie française vers 1750." *L'année musicale* 1 (1911): 1–123.

Lagrave, Henri. *Le théâtre et le publique à Paris de 1715 à 1750.* Paris, 1972.

Lang, Alastair. "Central and Eastern Europe." In *Baroque and Rococo Architecture and Decoration,* ed. Anthony Blunt. New York, 1978.

Lang, Paul Henry. *Music in Western Civilization.* New York, 1941.

Langellier-Bellevue, Richard, and Roberte Machard. "La musique à Paris et à Versailles d'après les actes du Secrétariat de la Maison du Roi de 1765 à la Révolution." *Recherches sur la musique française classique* 19 (1979): 211–302.

Launay, Denise (ed.). *La Querelle des Bouffons.* 3 vols. Geneva, 1973.

Le Blanc, Hubert. *Défense de la basse viole contre les entreprises du violon et les prétensions du violoncel.* Amsterdam, 1740.

Le Guin, Elisabeth Covel. " 'As My Works Show Me to Be': Physicality as Compositional Technique in the Instrumental Music of Luigi Boccherini." Ph.D. diss., University of California, Berkeley, 1997.

Le Moël, Sylvie. *Le corps et le vêtement: Écrire et penser la musique au siècle des Lumières: Wilhelm Heinse.* Paris, 1996.

Lesage, René-Alain, with D'Orneval et al. *Le théâtre de la Foire ou l'opéra comique.* 10 vols. Paris, 1721–37.

Lee, Douglas A. "Christoph Nichelmann and the Early Clavier Concerto in Berlin." *Musical Quarterly* 57 (1971): 636–55.

———. "Some Embellished Versions of Sonatas by Franz Benda." *Musical Quarterly* 62 (1976): 58–71.

Le Huray, Peter, and James Day (eds.). *Music and Aesthetics in the Eighteenth and Early-Nineteenth Centuries.* Cambridge, 1981.

Leppert, Richard D. *Arcadia at Versailles: Noble Amateur Musicians and Their Musettes and*

Hurdy-gurdies at the French Court (c. 1660–1789): A Visual Study. Amsterdam and Lisse, 1978.

Lesure, François. "Mozartiana Gallica." *Revue de musicologie* 38 (1956): 115–24.

———. *L'opéra classique français, XVIIᵉ et XVIIIᵉ siècles.* Iconographie musicale 1. Geneva, 1972.

Lesure, François (ed.). *La Querelle des Gluckistes et des Piccinnistes.* 2 vols. Geneva, 1984.

Letailleur, Paulette. "Jean-Louis Laruette chanteur et compositeur: Sa vie et son oeuvre." *Recherches sur la musique française classique* 8 (1968): 161–89; 9 (1969): 145–61; 10 (1970): 57–86.

Levy, Michael. *Painting and Sculpture in France, 1700–1789.* New Haven, Conn., and London, 1992.

———. *Rococo to Revolution.* London, 1966.

Levy, Janet M. "The Quatuor Concertant in Paris in the Latter Half of the Eighteenth Century." Ph.D. diss., Stanford University, 1971.

Libby, Dennis. "The Singers of Pergolesi's *Salustia.*" *Studi Pergolesiani* 3 (1999): 173–81.

Libin, Laurence. "Keyboard Instruments." *Metropolitan Museum of Art Bulletin* (Summer 1989).

Lindgren, Lowell. "Parisian Patronage of Performers from the Royal Academy of Musick (1719–28)." *Music and Letters* 38 (1977): 4–28.

Lippmann, Friedrich. "Paisiello und Mozart in der Opera Buffa." *Analecta musicologica* 31 (1998): 117–202.

Litchfeld, R. Burr. "Naples under the Bourbons: An Historical Overview." In *The Golden Age of Naples: Art and Civilization under the Bourbons 1734–1805,* 1: 1–14. Detroit and Chicago, 1981.

Lloyd, Christopher. *The Quest for Albion: Monarchy and the Patronage of British Painting.* London, 1998.

Lonsdale, Roger. *Dr. Charles Burney.* Oxford, 1965.

Lough, John. *An Introduction to 18th-Century France.* New York, 1960.

Lühning, Helga. "Aufkündigung einer Gattungstradition: Das Metastasianische Drama, Wielands Singspielkonzept und die deutsche Oper *Günther von Schwarzburg.*" In *Mannheim und Italien: Zur Vorgeschichte der Mannheimer,* ed. Roland Würtz, pp. 162–99. Mainz, 1984.

———. "Das Theater Carl Theodors und die Idee der Nationaloper." In *Die Mannheimer Hofkapelle im Zeitalter Carl Theodors,* ed. Ludwig Finscher, pp. 88–89. Mannheim, 1992.

Macchia, Giovanni. "I fantasmi dell'opera: il mito teatrale di Watteau." In *I fantasmi dell' opera,* ed. Giovanni Macchia, pp. 1–36. Milan, 1971.

Macdonald, Robert James. "François-Joseph Gossec and French Instrumental Music in the Second Half of the Eighteenth Century." Ph.D. diss., University of Michigan, 1968.

Machard, Roberte. *Jean-Joseph Cassanéa de Mondonville: virtuose, compositeur et chef-orchestre.* Béziers, 1980.

Mackenzie, Barbara Dobbs. "The Creation of a Genre: Comic Opera's Dissemination in Italy in the 1740s." Ph.D. diss., University of Michigan, 1993.

Mamczarz, Irène. *Les intermèdes comiques italiens au XVIIIe siècle*. Paris, 1972.

Mamy, Sylvie. *Les grands castrats napolitains à Venise au XVIIIe siècle*. Liège, 1994.

Mancini, Franco. *Il Teatro di San Carlo 1737–1987*. 2 vols. Naples, 1987.

Mangani, Marco, and Remigio Coli. "Osservazioni sul catalogo autografo di Luigi Boccherini: I quintetti a due violoncelli." *Rivista italiana di musicologia* 32 (1997): 315–26.

Mann, Michael. *Heinrich Heine: Zeitungsberichte über Musik und Malerei*. Frankfurt, 1964.

Marcello, Benedetto. *Sonates pour clavecin,* ed. Luciano Sgrizzi and Lorenzo Bianconi. Le pupitre 28. Paris, 1971.

Marcuse, Sibyl. "The Instruments in the King's Library at Versailles." *Galpin Society Journal* 14 (1961): 34–36.

Markstrom, Kurt Sven. "The Operas of Leonardo Vinci Napoletano." Ph.D. diss., University of Toronto, 1993.

Marpurg, Friedrich Wilhelm. *Abhandlung von der Fuge*. Berlin, 1753; reprint 1970.

———. *Der critische Musikus an der Spree*. Berlin, 1750; reprint 1970.

———. *Historisch-Kritische Beyträge zur Aufnahme der Music*. 5 vols. Berlin, 1754–78; reprint 1970.

———. *Kritische Briefe über die Tonkunst*. 2 vols. Berlin, 1760–64; reprint 1973.

Martina, Alessandra. *Orfeo-Orphée di Gluck*. Florence, 1995.

Massip, Catherine. "La bibliothèque musicale du baron Grimm." In *D'un opéra l'autre: Hommage à Jean Mongrédien,* ed. Jean Gribenski, Marie-Claire Mussat, and Herbert Schneider, pp. 189–205. Paris, 1996.

Masson, Chantal. "Journal du Marquis de Dangeau, 1684–1720." *Recherches sur la musique française classique* 2 (1961–62): 193–223.

Masson, Paul Marie. "La Lettre sur *Omphale* (1752)." *Revue de musicologie* 27 (1945): 1–19.

———. *L'opéra de Rameau*. Paris, 1930.

Mattheson, Johann. *Das forschende Orchestre*. Hamburg, 1721; reprint 1976.

———. *Das neu-eröffnete Orchestre*. Hamburg, 1713.

———. *Der vollkommene Capellmeister*. Hamburg, 1739; reprint 1954.

Mattei, Saverio. *Memorie per servire alla vita di Metastasio ed Elogio di N. Jommelli*. Colle, 1785; reprint 1987.

Maurer, Julius. *Anton Schweitzer als dramatischer Komponist*. Leipzig, 1912.

McClymonds, Marita P. "The Evolution of Jommelli's Operatic Style." *JAMS* 33 (1980): 326–55.

———. *Niccolò Jommelli: The Last Years, 1769–1774*. Ann Arbor, Mich., 1980.

McClymonds, Marita, and Walter Rex. "Ce beau récitatif obligé de Jommelli." *Diderot Studies* 22 (1986): 63–77.

McLauchlan, Fiona. "Lotti's *Teofane* (1719) and Handel's *Ottone* (1723): A Textual and Musical Study." *Music and Letters* 78 (1997): 349–90.

McManners, John. *Church and Society in Eighteenth-Century France*. 2 vols. Oxford, 1998.

Meer, John Henry van der. "The Keyboard String Instruments at the Disposal of Domenico Scarlatti." *Galpin Society Journal* 50 (1997): 136–60.

Meikle, Robert Burns. "Leonardo Vinci's *Artaserse*: An Edition, with an Editorial and Critical Commentary." Ph.D. diss., Cornell University, 1970.

Mengelberg, Curt. *Giovanni Alberto Ristori: Ein Beitrag zur Geschichte Italienischer Kunst-herrschaft in Deutschland im 18. Jahrhunderts.* Leipzig, 1916.

Mennicke, Carl. *Hasse und die Brüder Graun als Symphoniker.* Leipzig, 1906.

Metastasio, Pietro. *Memoirs of the Life and Writings of the Abate Metastasio, in which are incorporated Translations of his Principal Letters by Charles Burney.* 3 vols. London, 1796; reprint 1971.

————. *Tutte le opere,* ed. Bruno Brunelli. 5 vols. Milan, 1943–54.

Michel, Marianne Roland. "Watteau et les *Figures de différents caractères.*" In *Antoine Watteau (1684–1721): Le peintre, son temps et sa légende,* ed. François Moureau and Margaret Morgan Graselli, pp. 117–27. Paris and Geneva, 1987.

Mies, Paul. *Das Instrumentale Rezitativ: Von seiner Geschichte und seinen Formen.* Bonn, 1968.

Miesner, Heinrich. "Aus der Umwelt Philipp Emanuel Bachs." *Bach-Jahrbuch* 34 (1937): 132–43.

————. *Philipp Emanuel Bach in Hamburg: Beiträge zu seiner Biografie und zur Musikgeschichte.* Leipzig, 1929.

Millner, Frederick. *The Operas of Johann Adolf Hasse.* Ann Arbor, Mich., 1974.

Mischiati, Oscar. "Un memoria sepolcrale di Filippo Juvarra per Arcangelo Corelli." In *Nuovi studi corelliani,* ed. Giulia Giachin, pp. 105–10. Florence, 1978.

Monnet, Jean. *Supplément au Roman comique, ou Mémoires pour servir à la vie de Jean Monnet.* 2 vols. London, 1773.

Monson, Dale E. "Galuppi, Tenducci, and *Motezuma:* A Commentary on the History and Musical Style of Opera Seria after 1750." In *Galuppiana 1985: Studi et ricerche,* ed. Maria Teresa Muraro and Franco Rossi, pp. 279–300. Florence, 1986.

Montagnier, Jean-Paul. "Le *Chant sur le Livre* au xviiie siècle: Les *Traités* de Louis-Joseph Marchand et Henry Madin." *Revue de musicologie* 81 (1995): 37–63.

Montesquieu, Charles Louis de. *Oeuvres complètes.* 2 vols. Paris, 1949.

Moore, James H. *Vespers at St. Mark's: Music of Alessandro Grandi, Giovanni Rovetta and Francesco Cavalli.* 2 vols. Ann Arbor, Mich., 1981.

Mooser, R. Aloys. *Annales de la musique et des musiciens en Russie au XVIIIe siècle.* 3 vols. Geneva, 1948–51.

————. *L'opéra-comique français en Russie au xviiie.* Geneva, 1954.

Morrow, Mary Sue. *German Music Criticism in the Late Eighteenth Century: Aesthetic Issues in Instrumental Music.* Cambridge, 1997.

Mosel, Ignaz von. *Über das Leben und Werke des Antonio Salieri.* Vienna, 1827.

Moureau, François, and Margaret Morgan Grasselli (eds.). *Antoine Watteau (1684–1721): Le peintre, son temps et sa légende.* Paris and Geneva, 1987.

Mozart, W. A. *Mozart: Briefe und Aufzeichnungen. Gesamtausgabe,* ed. Wilhelm A. Bauer, Otto Erich Deutsch, and Joseph Heinz Eibl. 7 vols. Kassel, 1962–75.

Müller, Erich H. *Angelo und Pietro Mingotti: Ein Beitrag zur Geschichte der Oper im XVIII. Jahrhundert.* Dresden, 1917.

Müller, Walther. *Johann Adolf Hasse als Kirchenkomponist: Ein Beitrag zur Geschichte der Neapolitanischen Kirchenmusik.* Leipzig, 1910.

Münster, Robert. "Die Sinfonien Toeschis: Ein Beitrag zur Geschichte der Mannheimer Sinfonie." Ph.D. diss., University of Munich, 1956.

Muraro, Maria Teresa, and Elena Povoledo. "Le scene della *Fida Ninfa:* Maffei, Vivaldi e Francesco Bibiena." In *Vivaldi Veneziano Europeo,* ed. Francesco Degrada, pp. 235–52. Florence, 1980.

Nettl, Paul. *Forgotten Musicians.* New York, 1951.

Newman, William S. "A Checklist of the Earliest Keyboard 'Sonatas' (1641–1738)." *Notes* 11 (1954): 201–12.

———. "Emanuel Bach's Autobiography." *Musical Quarterly* 51 (1965): 363–72.

———. *The Sonata in the Classic Era.* 3rd ed. New York, 1983.

Nichelmann, Christoph. *Clavier Concertos in E Major and A Major,* ed. Douglas A. Lee. Madison, Wis., 1977.

Nicolai, Friedrich. *Beschreibung der königlichen Residenzstädte Berlin und Potsdam.* 3 vols. Berlin, 1769–86.

Nicolai, Friedrich (ed.). *Allgemeine deutsche Bibliothek.* 118 vols. Berlin and Stettin, 1766–96.

Noel, Charles C. "The Crisis of 1758–1759 in Spain: Sovereignty and Power during a 'Species of Interregnum.' " In *Royal and Republican Sovereignty in Early Modern Europe,* ed. Robert Oresko, G. C. Gibbs, and H. M. Scott, pp. 580–608. Cambridge, 1997.

Noiray, Michel. "*Hippolyte* et *Castor* travestis: Rameau à l'Opéra-Comique." In *Jean-Philippe Rameau,* ed. Jérôme de La Gorce, pp. 109–25. Paris and Geneva, 1987.

Noverre, Jean-Georges. *Letters on Dancing and Ballets,* trans. Cyril W. Beaumont from the revised and enlarged edition published in Saint Petersburg, 1803. London, 1930; rev. ed. New York, 1966.

Oboussier, Philippe. "The French String Quartet, 1770–1800." In *Music and the French Revolution,* ed. Malcolm Boyd, pp. 74–92. Cambridge, 1992.

Orloff, Comte Grégoire. *Essai sur l'histoire de la musique en Italie.* Paris, 1822.

Orville, Constant D'. *Histoire de l'opéra bouffon.* 2 vols. Amsterdam and Paris, 1768.

Ottenberg, Hans-Günter. *C. P. E. Bach,* trans. Philip J. Whitmore. Oxford, 1987.

Palermo, Paola. "La musica nella Basilica di Santa Maria Maggiore a Bergamo all'epoca dell'infanzia di Locatelli." In *Intorno a Locatelli: Studi in occasione del tricentenario della nascità di Pietro Antonio Locatelli (1695–1764),* ed. Albert Dunning. 2 vols., 2: 653–748. Lucca, 1995.

Palisca, Claude. " 'Baroque' as a Music-Critical Term." In *French Musical Thought, 1600–1800,"* ed. Georgia Cowart, pp. 7–21. Ann Arbor, Mich., 1989.

Parker, Roger (ed.). *The Oxford Illustrated History of Opera.* Oxford, 1994.

Pasquali, Niccolo. *The Art of Fingering the Harpsichord.* Edinburgh, 1758.

Paymer, Marvin E. "The Pergolesi Overtures: Problems and Perplexities." *Studi pergolesiani* 2 (1988): 78–88.

Pendle, Karin. "L'opéra-comique à Paris de 1762 à 1789." In *L'opéra-comique en France au XVIIIe siècle,* ed. Philippe Vendrix, pp. 79–177. Liège, 1992.

———. "The Opéras Comiques of Grétry and Marmontel." *Musical Quarterly* 62 (1976): 409–34.

Perez, Alfonso E. Sanchez, and Eleanor A. Sayre (eds.). *Goya and the Spirit of Enlightenment.* Boston, 1989.

Pestelli, Giorgio. "Mozart et Rutini." *Analecta musicologica* 18 (1978): 291–307.

Petrobelli, Pierluigi. "Un cantante fischiate e le appoggiature di mezza battuta: Cronaca teatrale e prassi esecutiva ala meta del '700."In *Studies in Renaissance and Baroque Music in Honor of Arthur Mendel,* ed. Robert L. Marshall, pp. 363–76. Kassel, 1974.

———. *Giuseppe Tartini: Le fonti biografiche.* Venice, 1968.

———. "The Italian Years of Anton Raaff." *Mozart-Jahrbuch, 1973/74,* pp. 233–73.

———. "Pergolesi and Ghezzi Revisited." In *Music in the Classic Era: Essays in Honor of Barry S. Brook,* ed. Allan W. Atlas, pp. 213–20. New York, 1985.

———. "Tartini, Algarotti e la Corta di Dresda." *Analecta musicologica* 2 (1965): 72–90.

Pezzl, Johann. *Skizze von Wien: Ein Kultur- und Sittenbild aus der josefinischen Zeit,* ed. Gustav Gugitz and Anton Schlossar. Graz, 1923.

Pfister, Albert (ed). *Herzog Karl Eugen von Württemberg und seine Zeit.* 2 vols. Esslingen, 1907.

Philidor musicien et jouer d'échecs. Recherches sur la musique française classique 28. Paris, 1995.

Pierre, Constant. *Histoire du Concert Spirituel, 1725–1790.* Paris, 1975.

Pincherle, Marc. *Antonio Vivaldi et la musique instrumentale.* 2 vols. Paris, 1948.

Piozzi, Hester Lynch. *Observations and Reflections Made in the Course of a Journey through France, Italy, and Germany,* ed. Herbert Barrows. Ann Arbor, Mich., 1967.

Pipelet, Constance D. T. [Princesse de Salm]. *Éloge historique de Pierre Gaviniès.* Paris, 1802.

Platoff, John. "Mozart and His Rivals: Opera in Vienna." *Current Musicology* 51 (1995): 105–11.

Posner, Donald. *Antoine Watteau.* London, 1984.

Pougin, Arthur. *Monsigny et son temps.* Paris, 1908.

———. *Viotti et l'école moderne de violon.* Paris, 1888.

Preussner, Eberhard. *Die musikalischen Reisen des Herrn von Uffenbach.* Kassel and Basel, 1949.

Price, Curtis, Judith Milhous, and Robert D. Hume. *The Impresario's Ten Commandments: Continental Recruitment for Italian Opera in London, 1763–64.* London, 1992.

———. *Italian Opera in Late Eighteenth-Century London.* Vol. 1: *The King's Theatre, Haymarket, 1778–1791.* Oxford, 1995.

Prim, Abbé Jean. "Chant sur le Livre in French Churches in the 18th Century." *JAMS* 14 (1961): 37–49.

Prod'homme, J. G. "La musique à Paris, de 1753 à 1757, d'après un manuscrit de la Bibliothèque de Munich." *Sammelbände der Internationalen Musik-Gesellschaft* 6 (1904–1905): 568–87.

Prod'homme, J. G., and E. de Crauzet. *Les menus plaisirs du roi: L'École Royale et le Conservatoire de Musique.* Paris, 1929.

Prota-Giurleo, Ulisse. "Leonardo Vinci." *Convegno musicale* 2 (1965): 3–11.

———. "Notizie biografiche intorno ad alcuni musicisti d'oltralpe a Napoli nel settecento." *Analecta musicologica* 2 (1965): 112–43.

Quantz, Johann Joachim. Autobiography. In Friedrich Wilhelm Marpurg, *Historisch-Kritische Beyträge zur Aufnahme der Musik,* 5 vols. (Berlin, 1754–78): 1: 197–250; reproduced in facsimile in Willi Kahl, *Selbstbiographien deutscher Musiker des XVIII. Jahrhunderts* (Cologne, 1958).

———. *On Playing the Flute,* trans. Edward R. Reilly. New York, 1966.

Rall, Hans. *Kurfürst Karl Theodor: Regierender Herr in sieben Ländern.* Mannheim, 1993.

Ratner, Leonard. *Classic Music: Expression, Form, and Style.* New York, 1980.

Raugel, Félix. *Les grandes orgues des églises de Paris et du Département de la Seine.* Paris, 1927.

Ravenni, Gabriella Biagi. "Calzabigi e d'intorni: Boccherini, Angiolini, La Toscana e Vienna." In *La figura e l'opera di Ranieri de' Calzabigi,* ed. Federico Marri, pp. 29–71. Florence, 1989.

Rees, Abraham (ed.). *The Cyclopaedia; or Universal Dictionary of Arts, Sciences, and Literature.* 45 vols. London, 1802–19.

Reeser, Eduard. *De Klaviersonate met Vioolbegleiding in het Parisjsche Musiekleven ten Tijde van Mozart.* Rotterdam, 1939.

Reichardt, Johann Friedrich. *Briefe eines aufmerksamen Reisenden die Musik betreffend.* 2 vols. 1, Frankfurt and Leipzig; 2, Frankfurt and Breslau, 1776.

———. *Über die Deutsche comische Oper.* Hamburg, 1774. Facsimile edition with commentary and an index by Walter Salmen, Munich, 1974.

Reilly, Edward R. *Quantz and His* Versuch: *Three Studies.* New York, 1971.

Reutter, Jochen. "Franz Xaver Richters Bemerkungen über das Komponieren einer Sinfonie in Kompositionstheorie und Kompositionspraxis." In *Mozart und Mannheim: Kongressbericht Mannheim 1991,* ed. Ludwig Finscher, Bärbel Pelker, and Jochen Reutter, pp. 221–31. Frankfurt, 1994.

Rex, Walter E. "A Propos of the Figure of Music in the Frontispiece of the Encyclopédie: Theories of Musical Imitation in d'Alembert, Rousseau and Diderot." In *Report of the Twelfth Congress of the International Musicological Society, Berkeley, 1977,* ed. Daniel Heartz and Bonnie Wade, pp. 214–25. Kassel, 1981.

———. *The Attraction of the Contrary: Essays on the Literature of the French Enlightenment.* Cambridge, 1987.

———. "The 'Storm' Music of Beaumarchais' *Barbier de Séville.*" In *Opera and Enlightenment,* ed. Thomas Bauman and Marita Petzoldt McClymonds, pp. 243–59. Cambridge, 1995.

Rice, John. *Antonio Salieri and Viennese Opera.* Chicago, 1998.

Ridder-Symoens, Hilde de (ed.). *A History of the University in Europe.* Vol. 2: *Universities in Early Modern Europe, 1500–1800.* Cambridge, 1996.

Riedlbauer, Jörg. *Die Opern von Tommaso Trajetta.* Hildesheim, 1994.

Roberti, Giulio. "La musica in Italia nel secolo XVIII secondo le impressioni di viaggiatori stranieri." *Rivista musical italiana* 7 (1900): 698–729.

Robinson, Michael F. "The Governors' Minutes of the Conservatory S. Maria di Loreto, Naples." *Research Chronicle of the Royal Musical Association* 10 (1972): 1–97.

———. "Two London Versions of The Deserter." In *Report of the Twelfth Congress of the International Musicological Society, Berkeley, 1977,* ed. Daniel Heartz and Bonnie Wade, pp. 239–45. Kassel, 1981.

———. *Naples and Neapolitan Opera.* Oxford, 1972.

Robinson, Michael F., with the assistance of Ulrike Hoffmann. *Giovanni Paisiello: A Thematic Catalogue of His Works.* 2 vols. Stuyvesant, N.Y., 1991–94.

Roe, Stephen. "J. C. Bach and 'New Music, at a More Reasonable Expense.'" *Musical Times* 126 (1985): 529–31.

————. *The Keyboard Music of J. C. Bach: Source Problems and Stylistic Developments in the Solo and Ensemble Works.* New York and London, 1989.

Rogister, John. *Louis XV and the Parlement of Paris, 1737–1755.* Cambridge, 1995.

Rosa, Carlantonio de, Marquis of Villarosa. *Lettera biografica intorno alla patria ed alla vita di G. B. Pergolesi.* Naples, 1831.

Rosenberg, Pierre (ed.). *Watteau, 1684–1721.* Paris, 1984.

Rosow, Lois. "French Opera in Transition: *Sylvie* (1765) by Trial and Berton." In *Critica Musica: Essays in Honor of Paul Brainard,* ed. John Knowles, pp. 333–63. Amsterdam, 1996.

Rosselli, John. "The Castrati as a Professional Group and a Social Phenomenon, 1550–1850." *Acta musicologica* 60 (1988): 143–79.

————. *Singers of Italian Opera: The History of a Profession.* Cambridge, 1992.

Rothschild, Germaine de. *Luigi Boccherini: His Life and Works.* London, 1965.

Rousseau, Jean-Jacques. *Oeuvres complètes,* ed. Bernard Gagnebin, Marcel Raymond, and Jean-Jacques Eigeldinger. 5 vols. Paris, 1962–95.

Rushton, Julian. "*Iphigénie en Tauride:* The Operas of Gluck and Piccinni." *Music and Letters* 53 (1972): 411–30.

————. "Philidor and the Tragédie Lyrique." *Musical Times* 117 (1976): 734–37.

————. " 'Royal Agamemnon'; the two versions of Gluck's *Iphigénie en Aulide.*" In *Music and the French Revolution,* ed. Malcolm Boyd, pp. 15–36. Cambridge, 1992.

————. "Salieri's *Les Horaces:* A Study of an Operatic Failure." *Music Review* 37 (1976): 266–82.

————. "The Theory and Practice of Piccinnisme." In *Proceedings of the Royal Musical Association* 98 (1971–72): 31–46.

Russell, Raymond. *The Harpsichord and Clavichord.* London, 1959.

Russo, Luigi. *I classici italiani.* 3 vols. Florence, 1957.

Sadie, Stanley (ed.). *The New Grove Dictionary of Music and Musicians.* 20 vols. London, 1980. 2nd ed., 29 vols. London, 2001.

————. *The New Grove Dictionary of Opera.* London, 1992.

Saint-Foix, Georges de. "Les premiers pianistes parisiens: Jean Schobert, vers 1740–1767." *La revue musicale* 3 (1922): 121–36.

Saint-Non, Jean-Chrétien de. *Voyage pittoresque ou description des royaumes de Naples et de Sicile.* 5 vols. Paris, 1781–86.

Sandberger, Adolf. "Aus der Korrespondenz des pfalzbayerischen Kurfürsten Karl Theodor mit seinem römischen Ministerresidenten." In *Ausgewählte Aufsätze zur Musikwissenschaft.* 2 vols., 1: 218–23. Munich, 1921.

Sani, Bernardina. *Rosalba Carriera.* Turin, 1988.

Sartori, Claudio. "A Milano J. C. Bach in Disaccordo con il Tesoriere." *La Scala: Revista dell Opera* (15 November 1955): 29–31.

————. *I libretti italiani a stampa dalle origini al 1800.* 6 vols. Cuneo, 1993.

Savage, Roger. "A Dynastic Marriage Celebrated." *Early Music* 36 (1998): 632–35.

Scheibe, Johann Adolph. *Critischer Musikus.* Hamburg, 1745.

Scherillo, Michele. *L'opera buffa napoletana durante il settecento: Storia letteraria.* 2nd enlarged ed. Milan, 1916.

Schletterer, Hans Michael. *Joh. Friedrich Reichardt: Sein Leben und seine musikalische Thätigkeit.* Augsburg, 1865.

Schlözer, Kurt von. *General Graf Chasot: Zur Geschichte Friedrich des Grossen und seiner Zeit.* 2nd ed. Berlin, 1878.

Schmid, Anton. *Christoph Willibald Gluck: Dessen Leben und tonkünstlerishes Werken.* Leipzig, 1854.

Schmid, Ernst Fritz. *Carl Philipp Emanuel Bach und seine Kammermusik.* Kassel, 1931.

Schmitz, Hans-Bernd. *Die Klavierkonzerte Johann Christian Bachs.* Würzburg, 1981.

Schneider, Eugen. "Herzog Karls Erziehung, Jugend und Personlichkeit." In *Herzog Karl Eugen von Württemberg und seine Zeit,* ed. Albert Pfister. 2 vols., 1: 25–52. Esslingen, 1907.

Schnoebelen, Ann. *Padre Martini's Collection of Letters in the Museo Bibliografico Musicale in Bologna.* New York, 1979.

Scholes, Percy A. (ed.). *Dr. Burney's Musical Tours in Europe.* 2 vols. London, 1959.

Schönberger, Arno, and Halldor Soehner. *The Rococo Age.* London, 1960.

Schubart, Christian Friedrich Daniel. *Ideen zu einer Ästhetik der Tonkunst,* ed. Ludwig Schubart. Vienna, 1806; reprint 1969.

———. *Leben und Gesinnungen von ihm selbst im Kerker aufgesetzt.* 2 vols. Stuttgart, 1791–93; reprint 1980.

Schulenberg, David. *The Instrumental Music of Carl Philipp Emmanuel Bach.* Ann Arbor, Mich., 1984.

Schulze, Hans-Joachim. "Wann begann die 'italienische Reise' der jüngsten Bach-Sohnes." *Bach Jahrbuch* 69 (1983): 119–22; 74 (1988): 235–36.

Schwarte, Michael. "Musikaliserung von Zeit- und Bewegungsabläufen in Ignaz Holzbauers Oper *Günther von Schwarzburg.*" In *Mozart und Mannheim: Kongressbericht Mannheim 1991,* ed. Ludwig Finscher, Bärbel Pelker, and Jochen Reutter, pp. 101–17. Frankfurt, 1994.

Schwartze, Penny. "Styles of Composition and Performance in Leclair's Concertos." Ph.D. diss., University of North Carolina, 1983.

Schweitzer, Anton. *Rosamunde,* ed. Jutta Stüber. 2 vols. Bonn, 1997.

Scott, H. M. "Prussia's Royal Foreign Minister: Frederick the Great and the Administration of Prussian Diplomacy." In *Royal and Republican Sovereignty in Early Modern Europe,* ed. Robert Oresko, G. C. Gibbs, and H. M. Scott, pp. 500–26. Cambridge, 1997.

Scott, Katie. *The Rococo Interior: Decoration and Social Spaces in Early Eighteenth-Century Paris.* New Haven, Conn., and London, 1995.

Scott, Virginia. *The Commedia dell'Arte in Paris, 1644–1697.* Charlottesville, Va., 1990.

Selfridge-Field, Eleanor. "Marcello, Sant'Angelo, and *Il teatro alla moda.*" In *Antonio Vivaldi: Teatro musicale, cultura e società,* ed. Lorenzo Bianconi and Giovanni Morelli, pp. 533–46. Florence, 1982.

———. *Venetian Instrumental Music from Gabrielli to Vivaldi.* Oxford, 1975.

Shackleton, Robert. "Travel and the Enlightenment: Naples as a Specimen." In *Essays on the Age of Enlightenment in Honor of Ira O. Wade,* ed. Jean Macary, pp. 281–91. Geneva, 1977.

Sharp, Samuel. *Letters from Italy, Describing the Customs and Manners of That Country.* London, 1766.

Sheldon, David A. "The concept *galant* in the 18th century." *Journal of Musicological Research* 9 (1989): 89–108.

———. "Exchange, Anticipation, and Ellipsis: Analytical Definitions of the *Galant* Style." In *Music East and West: Essays in Honor of Walter Kaufmann,* ed. Thomas Noblitt, pp. 225–41. New York, 1981.

———. "The Galant Style Revisited and Re-evaluated." *Acta musicologica* 47 (1975): 240–70.

Sheveloff, Joel. "Domenico Scarlatti: Tercentenary Frustrations (Part 2)." *Musical Quarterly* 72 (1986): 90–118.

Sittard, Josef. *Zur Geschichte der Musik und das Theaters am Württembergischen Hofe.* 2 vols. Stuttgart, 1890–91.

Small, John. "J. C. Bach goes to Law." *Musical Times* 126 (1985): 526–29.

Smith, Kent Maynard. "Egidio Duni and the Development of the *Opéra-Comique* from 1753 to 1770." Ph.D. diss., Cornell University, 1980.

Smither, Howard E. *A History of the Oratorio.* Vol. 3: *The Oratorio in the Classical Era.* Chapel Hill, N.C., 1987.

Smollett, Tobias. *Travels through France and Italy,* ed. Frank Felsenstein. Oxford, 1979.

Sonneck, O. G. "Ciampi's *Bertoldo, Bertoldino e Cacasenno* and Favart's *Ninette à la Cour.*" *Sammelbände der Internationalen Musik-Gesellschaft* 12 (1911): 524–64.

———. "Il Giocatore." *Musical Antiquary* 4 (1912–13): 160–74.

Souchal, François. *Les Slodtz, sculpteurs et décorateurs du roi (1685–1764).* Paris, 1967.

Speck, Christian. *Boccherinis Streichquartette: Studien zur Kompositionweise und zur gattungsgeschichtlichen Stellung.* Munich, 1987.

Stählin, Jacob von. *Nachrichten von der Musik in Russland.* Published in J. J. Haigold, *Beylagen zum neuveränderten Russland.* 2 vols. Riga and Leipzig, 1769–70.

Sterne, Laurence. *A Sentimental Journey through France and Italy.* London, 1768.

Stevens, Jane R. "The Keyboard Concertos of Carl Philipp Emanuel Bach." Ph.D. diss., Yale University, 1965.

Stockigt, Janice B. *Jan Dismas Zelenka: A Bohemian Musician at the Court of Dresden.* Oxford, 2000.

Strohm, Reinhard. *Dramma per Musica: Italian Opera Seria in the Eighteenth Century.* New Haven, Conn., and London, 1997.

———. *Essays on Handel and Italian Opera.* Cambridge, 1985.

———. "Francesco Corselli's Operas for Madrid." In *Teatro y musica en España (siglo XVIII),* ed. Rainer Kleinertz, pp. 79–106. Kassel and Berlin, 1996; reprinted in Reinhard Strohm, *Dramma per Musica: Italian Opera Seria in the Eighteenth Century.*

———. "Hasse, Scarlatti, Rolli." *Analecta musicologica* 15 (1975): 220–57.

———. *Die italienische Oper im 18. Jahrhundert.* Wilhelmshaven, 1979.

———. *Italienische Opernarien des frühen Settecento (1720–1730).* 2 vols. Analecta musicologica 16. Cologne, 1976.

———. "Vivaldi's Career as an Opera Composer." In *Antonio Vivaldi: Teatro musicale, cultura e società,* ed. Lorenzo Bianconi and Giovanni Morelli. 2 vols., 2: 11–63. Florence, 1982.

Suchalla, Ernst (ed.). *Carl Philipp Emanuel Bach: Briefe und Dokumenten.* Kritische Gesamtausgabe. Göttingen, 1994.

Sulzer, Johann Georg. *Allgemeine Theorie der schönen Künste.* 4 vols. Leipzig, 1771–74.

Sutherland, David. "Domenico Scarlatti and the Florentine piano." *Early Music* 23 (1995): 243–56.

Svoboda, Karl J. *Galerien und Gala im kurfälzischen Hof zu Mannheim.* Heidelberg, 1979.

Swinburne, Henry. *Travels through Spain in the Years 1775 and 1776.* London, 1779.

Tagliavini, Luigi Ferdinando. "Le sonate per organo e cembalo di Martini." In *Padre Martini: Musica e cultura nel settecento Europeo,* ed. Angelo Pompilo, pp. 295–303. Florence, 1987.

Talbot, Michael. *Benedetto Vinaccesi: A Musician in Brescia and Venice in the Age of Corelli.* Oxford, 1994.

———. *Tomaso Albinoni: The Venetian Composer and His World.* Oxford, 1990.

———. *The Sacred Music of Antonio Vivaldi.* Florence, 1995.

———. *Vivaldi.* New York, 1993.

———. "Vivaldi and the Empire." *Informazioni e studi vivaldiani* 8 (1987): 31–50.

Tartak, Marvin. "The Two 'Barbieri.'" *Music and Letters* 50 (1969): 453–69.

Tartini, Giuseppe. *Traité des agréments de la musique,* ed. Erwin R. Jacobi. Celle, 1961.

Terry, Charles Sanford. *John Christian Bach.* 2nd ed. London, 1967.

Thomson, George W. "I primi concerti di Giuseppe Tartini: Fonti, abbozzi e revisioni." In *Tartini: Il tempo e l'opera,* pp. 347–62. Bologna, 1994.

Tiersot, Julian (ed.). *Lettres de musiciens écrites en français du xve au xxe siècle.* Turin, 1924.

Tolkoff, Audrey Lynn. "The Stuttgart Operas of Niccolò Jommelli." Ph.D. diss., Yale University, 1974.

Tomlinson, Robert. *La fête galante: Watteau et Marivaux.* Geneva, 1981.

Trimpert, Dieter Lutz. *Die Quatuors Concertants von Giuseppe Cambini.* Tutzing, 1967.

Türk, Daniel Gottlob. *Clavierschule, oder Anweisung zum Clavierspielen für Lehrer und Lernende.* Leipzig and Halle, 1789.

———. *Ksurze Anweisung zum Generalbassspielen.* Leipzig and Halle, 1791.

Turrentine, Herbert C. "The Prince de Conti: A Royal Patron of Music." *Musical Quarterly* 54 (1968): 309–15.

Tutenberg, Fritz. *Die Sinfonik Johann Christian Bachs.* Wolfenbüttel, 1928.

Twiss, Richard. "Anecdotes of Mr. Philidor, Communicated by Himself." In *Chess* 1 (1787): 149–71; 2 (1789): 215–18. Reprinted in *Pour Philidor,* ed. Jean François Dupont-Danican, pp. 51–58. Coblenz, 1994.

Uldall, Hans. *Das Klavierkonzert des Berliner Schule.* Leipzig, 1928.

Unverricht, Hubert. *Geschichte des Streichtrio.* Tutzing, 1969.

———. "Johann Anton Fils (1733–1760): Zur Herkunft und Bedeuting des Komponisten." In *Johann Anton Fils (1733–1760): Ein Eichstätter Komponist der Mannheimer Klassik,* ed. Hermann Holzbauer, pp. 11–32. Tützing, 1983.

Uriot, Joseph. *Descriptions des fêtes données pendant quatorze jours à l'occasion du jour de naissance de son altesse Serenissime Monseigneur le Duc Regnant de Württemberg et Teck.* Stuttgart, 1763.

Vann, James Allen. *The Making of a State: Württemberg, 1593–1793.* Ithaca, N.Y., and London, 1984.

Vendrix, Philippe. "La reine, le roi et sa maîtresse: Essai sur la représentation de la différence durant la Querelle des Bouffons." *Il saggiatore musicale* 5 (1998): 219–44.

Verba, Cynthia. *Music and the French Enlightenment: Reconstruction of a Dialogue, 1750–1764.* New York, 1993.

Vidal, Mary. *Watteau's Painted Conversations.* New Haven, Conn., and London, 1992.

Vio, Gastone. "I maestri di coro dei Mendicanti e la Capella Marciana." In *Galuppiana,* ed. Maria Teresa Muraro and Franco Rossi, pp. 95–111. Florence, 1986.

Vogler, Georg Joseph. *Betrachtungen der Mannheimer Tonschule.* 4 vols. Mannheim, 1778–81; reprint 1974.

———. *Le rendez-vous de chasse, ou Les vendanges interrompues par les chasseurs.* In *Ballet Music from the Mannheim Court, Part I,* ed. Floyd K. Grave. Madison, Wis., 1996.

Voltaire (François Marie Arouet). *Voltaire's Correspondence,* ed. Theodore Besterman. 150 vols. Geneva, 1953–65.

Wade, Rachel W. *The Keyboard Concertos of Carl Philip Emanuel Bach.* Ann Arbor, Mich., 1981.

Wagner, Günther. "Die Entwicklung der Klaviersonate bei C. Ph. E. Bach." In *Carl Philipp Emanuel Bach und die europäische Musikkultur des mittleren 18. Jahrhunderts,* ed. Hans Joachim Marx, pp. 231–43. Göttingen, 1990.

———. *Die Sinfonien Carl Philipp Emanuel Bachs: Werdende Gattung und Originalgenie.* Stuttgart and Weimar, 1994.

Wagner, Hans. "Die Reise Josephs II nach Frankreich 1777 und die Reformen in Oesterreich." In *Salzburg und Oesterreich,* pp. 335–60. Salzburg, 1982.

Walpole, Horace. *Correspondence.* 48 vols. New Haven, Conn., 1937–83.

Walter, Friedrich. *Geschichte des Theater und der Musik am kurpfälzischen Hofe.* Leipzig, 1898.

Walthall, Charles. "Portraits of Johann Joachim Quantz." *Early Music* 14 (1986): 500–18.

Warrack, John. *Carl Maria von Weber.* 2nd ed. Cambridge, 1976.

Wates, Roye E. "Karl Ludwig Junker, 1748–1797: Sentimental Music Critic." Ph.D. diss., Yale University, 1965.

Weber, Hermann. *Die Politik des Kurfürsten Karl Theodor von der Pfalz während des österreichischen Erfolgkrieges (1742–1748).* Bonn, 1956.

Weber, William. *Music and the Middle Class: The Social Structure of Concert Life in London, Paris and Vienna.* New York, 1975.

Weisgerber, Jean. "Qu'est-ce que le Rococo? Essai de définition comparatiste." In *Études sur le xviiie siècle,* vol. 18: *Rocaille. Rococo* (1991), pp. 11–23.

Weiss, Piero. "La diffusione del repertorio operistico nell'Italia del settecento: Il caso dell'opera buffa." In *Civiltà teatrale e settecento emiliano,* ed. Susi Davoli, pp. 241–56. Bologna, 1985.

———. "Pier Jacopo Martello on Opera (1715): An Annotated Translation." *Musical Quarterly* 66 (1980): 378–403.

Weisse, Christian Felix. *Selbstbiographie.* Leipzig, 1806.

Wessely, Othmar. *Ernst Ludwig Gerber: Ergänzungen—Berichtungen—Nachträge.* Graz, 1969.

White, Chappell. *From Vivaldi to Viotti: A History of the Early Classical Violin Concerto.* Philadelphia, 1992.

Wiesend, Reinhard. "Hasse und Mozart—ein ungleiches Paar?" *Hasse-Studien* 2 (1993): 5–27.

———. *Studien zur Opera Seria von Baldassare Galuppi.* 2 vols. Tutzing, 1984.

———. "Vivaldi e Galuppi: Rapporti biografici e stilistici." In *Antonio Vivaldi: Teatro musi-*

cale, cultura e società, ed. Lorenzo Bianconi and Giovanni Morelli, pp. 233–55. Florence, 1982.

Wille, Johann Georg. *Mémoires et journal de J. G. Wille, graveur du roi.* 2 vols. Paris, 1857.

Winter, Marian Hannah. *The Pre-Romantic Ballet.* London, 1974.

Wolf, Eugene K. "I Concerti Grossi dell'Opera I (1721) di Pietro Antonio Locatelli e le origini della sinfonia." In *Intorno a Locatelli: Studi in occasione del tricentenario della nascità di Pietro Antonio Locatelli (1695–1764),* ed. Albert Dunning. 2 vols., 2: 1169–93. Luca, 1995.

———. "Driving a Hard Bargain: Johann Stamitz's Correspondence with Stuttgart (1748)." In *Festschrift Christoph-Hellmut Mahling,* ed. Axel Beer, Kristina Pfarr, and Wolfgang Ruf. 2 vols., 2: 1553–70. Tutzing, 1997.

———. "The Orchestral Trios, Op. 1, of Johann Stamitz." In *Music in the Classic Period: Essays in Honor of Barry S. Brook,* ed. Allan W. Atlas, pp. 297–322. New York, 1985.

———. *The Symphonies of Johann Stamitz: A Study in the Formation of the Classic Style.* Utrecht, 1981.

Wolff, Hellmuth Christian. "Italian Opera 1700–1750." In *The New Oxford History of Music,* vol. 5: *Opera and Church Music 1630–1750,* ed. Anthony Lewis and Nigel Fortune, pp. 73–168. London, 1975.

———. *Oper Szene und Darstellung von 1600 bis 1900.* Leipzig, 1968.

Wörmann, Wilhelm. "Die Klaviersonate Domenico Albertis." *Acta musicologica* 27 (1955): 84–112.

Wright, Craig. *Music and Ceremony at Notre Dame of Paris 500–1550.* Cambridge, 1989.

Wright, Edward. *Some Observations made in travelling through France, Italy . . . in the Years 1720, 1721 and 1722.* 2 vols. London, 1730.

Würtz, Roland. "Ignaz Holzbauer and *Das Teutsche.*" *Studies in Music from the University of Western Ontario* 7 (1982): 89–98.

———. "Die Organisation der Mannheimer Hofkapelle." In *Die Mannheimer Hofkapelle im Zeitalter Carl Theodors,* ed. Ludwig Finscher, pp. 37–48. Mannheim, 1992.

Yorke-Long, Alan. *Music at Court: Four Eighteenth-Century Studies.* London, 1954.

Young, Percy. *A History of British Music.* London, 1967.

Zaslaw, Neal. "Rameau's Operatic Apprenticeship: The First Fifty Years." In *Jean-Philippe Rameau,* ed. Jérôme de La Gorce, pp. 23–50. Paris and Geneva, 1987.

Zechmeister, Gustav. *Die Wiener Theater nächst der Burg und nächst dem Kärtnerthor von 1747 bis 1776.* Theatergeschichte Oesterreichs III, 2. Vienna, 1971.

Zwiebach, Michael. "Marriage of Wits: Comic Archetypes and the Staging of Ideas in Five Comic Operas of Giovanni Paisiello." Ph.D. diss., University of California, Berkeley, 2000.

Index

Page numbers in **boldface** indicate a primary discussion of the subject. Page numbers in *italics* refer to illustrations.